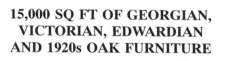

antiques

MILLER'S

PRICE GUIDE 2002

MILLER'S

antiques

LISA NORFOLK *GENERAL EDITOR*

2002
VOLUME XXIII

MILLER'S INTERNATIONAL ANTIQUES PRICE GUIDE 2002

Created and designed by
Miller's
The Cellars, High Street
Tenterden, Kent, TN30 6BN
Tel: 01580 766411
Fax: 01580 766100

This edition of Miller's International Antiques Price Guide is dedicated to Elaine Burrell

General Editor: Elizabeth Norfolk
Production Co-ordinator: Kari Reeves
Editorial Co-ordinator: Carol Gillings
Editorial Assistants: Maureen Horner, Lalage Johnstone
Production Assistants: Elaine Burrell, Gillian Charles, Ethne Tragett
Advertising Executive: Jill Jackson, Carol Woodcock, Rosemary Cooke
Advertising Assistants: Jo Hill, Melinda Williams
Designer: Philip Hannath
Advertisement Designer: Simon Cook
Jacket Design: Colin Goody
Indexer: Hilary Bird
Additional Photographers: Ian Booth, Dennis O'Reilly, Robin Saker

First published in Great Britain in 2001
by Miller's, a division of Mitchell Beazley,
imprints of Octopus Publishing Group Ltd,
2–4 Heron Quays, London E14 4JP

© 2001 Octopus Publishing Group Ltd

A CIP catalogue record for this book is
available from the British Library

ISBN 1-84000-4533

Illustrations: CK Litho, Whitstable, Kent
Lab 35, Milton Keynes, Bucks
Colour origination: Pica Colour Separation Overseas Pte Ltd, Singapore
Printed and bound: Lego SPA, Italy

A sampler, by Elizabeth Townsend, 1766, 25 x 21in (63.5 x 53.5cm) **$2,900–3,200** ⊞ WiA
A Delft plate, entitled Adam and Eve, 1730, 11½in (29cm) diam. **$4,750–5,500** ⊞ JHo
A Gothic Chippendale period mahogany armchair, c1765. **$8,300–9,000** ⊞ REI

5

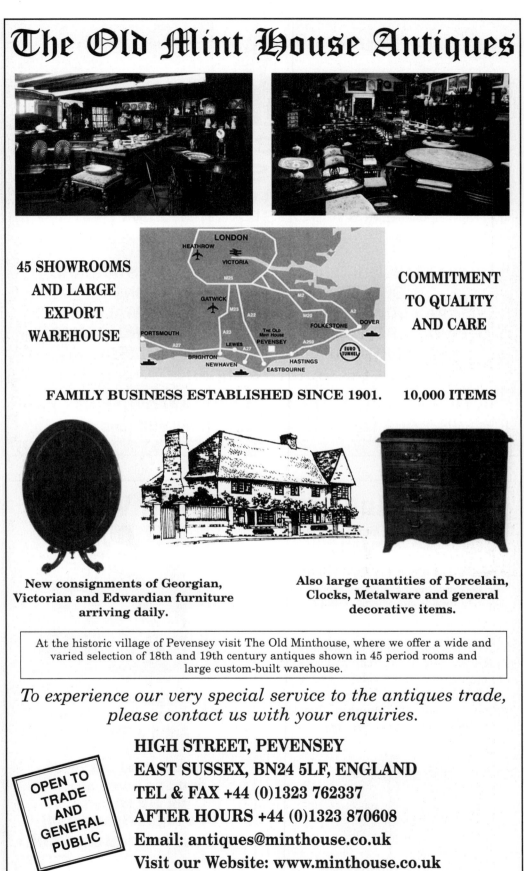

MARTIN TAYLOR
ANTIQUES
TRADE AND PUBLIC WELCOME
At Martin Taylor Antiques A warm welcome awaits
Due to recent refurbishment there is now over 8,000 sq.ft. full of beautiful antiques
Open Monday - Friday 8.30am - 5.30pm
Saturday 9:30am - 4:00pm
140B, Tettenhall Road,
Wolverhampton, WV6 0BQ.
Tel: (01902) 751166 • Fax: (01902) 746502
For more information, why not visit our website.
Web Site: http://www.mtaylor-antiques.co.uk
E-Mail:enquiries@mtaylor-antiques.co.uk
LARGEST ANTIQUES SHOWROOM IN THE MIDLANDS

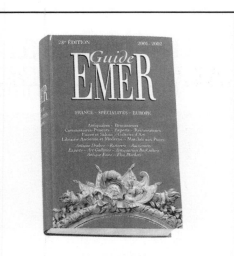

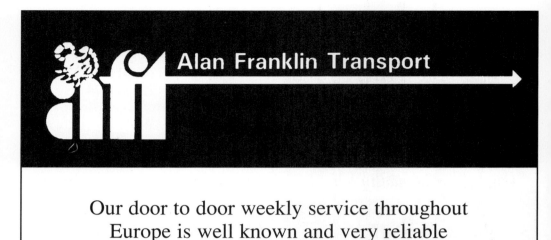

Dates	British Monarch	British Period	French Period
1558–1603	Elizabeth I	Elizabethan	Renaissance
1603–1625	James I	Jacobean	
1625–1649	Charles I	Carolean	Louis XIII (1610–1643)
1649–1660	Commonwealth	Cromwellian	Louis XIV (1643–1715)
1660–1685	Charles II	Restoration	
1685–1689	James II	Restoration	
1689–1694	William & Mary	William & Mary	
1694–1702	William III	William III	
1702–1714	Anne	Queen Anne	
1714–1727	George I	Early Georgian	Régence (1715–1723)
1727–1760	George II	Early Georgian	Louis XV (1723–1774)
1760–1811	George III	Late Georgian	Louis XVI (1774–1793) Directoire (1793–1799) Empire (1799–1815)
1812–1820	George III	Regency	Restauration Charles X (1815–1830)
1820–1830	George IV	Regency	
1830–1837	William IV	William IV	Louis Philippe (1830–1848) 2nd Empire Napoleon III (1848–1870) 3rd Republic (1871–1940)
1837–1901	Victoria	Victorian	
1901–1910	Edward VII	Edwardian	

German Period	U.S. Period	Style	Woods
Renaissance	Early Colonial	Gothic	Oak Period (to c1670)
		Baroque (c1620–1700)	Walnut period (c1670–1735)
Renaissance/ Baroque (c1650–1700)			
	William & Mary		
	Dutch Colonial	Rococo (c1695–1760)	
Baroque (c1700–1730)	Queen Anne		
			Early mahogany period (c1735–1770)
Rococo (c1730–1760)	Chippendale (from 1750)		
Neo–classicism (c1760–1800)		Neo–classical (c1755–1805)	Late mahogany period (c1770–1810)
	Early Federal (1790–1810)		
Empire (c1800–1815)	American Directoire (1798–1804)	Empire (c1799–1815)	
	American Empire (1804–1815)		
Biedermeier (c1815–1848)	Late Federal (1810–1830)	Regency (c1812–1830)	
Revivale (c1830–1880)		Eclectic (c1830–1880)	
	Victorian		
Jugendstil (c1880–1920)		Arts & Crafts (c1880–1900)	
	Art Nouveau (c1900–1920)	Art Nouveau (c1900–1920)	

Contents

MILLER'S

2002

Acknowledgements

The publishers would like to acknowledge the great assistance given by our consultants. We would also like to extend our thanks to all auction houses and their press offices, as well as dealers and collectors, who have assisted us in the production of this book.

FURNITURE:	Leslie Gillham, Gorringes, 15 The Pantiles, Tunbridge Wells, Kent TN2 5TD
	John Butterworth, Reindeer Antiques, 43 Watling Street, Potterspury, Towcester, Northamptonshire NN12 7QD
OAK & COUNTRY FURNITURE:	Denzil Grant, Drinkstone House, Drinkstone, Bury St Edmunds, Suffolk IP30 9TG
KITCHENWARE:	Skip & Janie Smithson, Hemswell Antiques Centre, Caenby Corner Estate, Gainsborough, Lincolnshire DN21 5TJ
POTTERY:	Gareth Williams, Bonhams, Montpelier Street, London SW7 1HH
PORCELAIN:	Simon Cottle, Sotheby's, 34–35 New Bond Street, London W1A 2AA
ASIAN CERAMICS & WORKS OF ART:	Peter Wain, Glynde Cottage, Longford, Market Drayton, Shropshire TF9 3PW
GLASS:	Brian Watson, Foxwarren Cottage, High Street, Marsham, Nr Norwich, NR10 5QA
SILVER:	Daniel Bexfield, 26 Burlington Arcade, London W1V 9AD
CLOCKS:	Robert Schmitt, R. O. Schmitt Fine Arts, Box 1941, Salem, NH 03079
BAROMETERS:	Derek & Tina Rayment, Orchard House, Barton, Nr Farndon, Cheshire SY14 7HT
DECORATIVE ARTS:	Mark Oliver, Phillips, 101 New Bond Street, London W1Y 9LG
RUGS & CARPETS:	Desmond North, The Orchard, Hale Street, East Peckham, Nr Tonbridge, Kent TN12 5JB
TEXTILES:	Pandora de Balthazar, Antique European Linens, P O Box 789, Gulf Breeze, Fl. 32562-0789
SAMPLERS:	Erna Hiscock & John Shepherd, Chelsea Gallery, 69 Portobello Road, London W11
TUNBRIDGE WARE:	Dianne Brick, Amherst Antiques, Monomark House, 27 Old Gloucester Street, London WC1N 3XX
PIANOS:	David Winston, Period Piano Company, Park Farm Oast, Hareplain Road, Biddenden, Kent TN27 8LJ
ANTIQUITIES:	Joanna van der Lande, Bonhams, Montpelier Street, London SW7 1HH
FOLK ART:	Robert Young, 68 Battersea Bridge Road, London SW11 3AG
POSTERS:	Paul Rennie, 13 Rugby Street, London WC1N 3QT
SCIENTIFIC INSTRUMENTS & MARINE:	Charles Tomlinson, Chester
FOOTBALL:	Norman Shiel, 4 St Leonard's Road, Exeter, Devon EX2 4L

How to use this book

It is our aim to make this book easy to use. In order to find a particular item, consult the contents list on page 19 to find the main heading – for example, Furniture. Having located your area of interest, you will find that larger sections have been sub-divided. If you are looking for a particular factory, designer or craftsman, consult the index which starts on page 804.

FURNITURE

Open Armchairs

A carved walnut armchair, the foliate- and shell-carved top rail above a caned back with punched strapwork design to the borders, with leaf-carved and scrolled arms and upholstered seat, late 17thC.
$1,300–1,600 ↗ DMC

▶ **A pair of Louis XV painted beechwood *fauteuils*,** the moulded aprons and shield-shaped backs with flower-head cresting, in need of repair, 18thC.
$2,000–2,350 ↗ HOK

A Spanish carved walnut armchair, upholstered in green and beige fabric, c1690.
$3,600–4,000 ⊞ DeG

Miller's Compares

I. A mahogany open armchair, the shaped scrolled top rail above a vase-shaped splat and drop-in seat, early 18thC.
$1,900–2,200 ↗ P

II. A mahogany open armchair, the shaped top rail above a vase-shaped splat and drop-in seat, joined by block and reel-turned stretchers, one spandrel missing, early 18thC.
$1,000–1,200 ↗ P

Although these two chairs are of a similar date and style, the superior quality of Item I can be seen in a number of its features. The grain and colour of Item I, for instance, are particularly attractive, and the top rail is far more sensuously carved, with scrolls above the splat, which is also of a more interesting shape than that of Item II. The C-scrolls and the extra shaping of the front legs of Item I are likely to have added to its appeal, and the more elegant proportions of this piece were probably regarded as more desirable than the broader, more squat appearance of Item II with its functional H-stretcher.

Chair seats

Seat rails are usually made in beech and are tenoned into the legs of the chair. Until c1840–50 corner braces were added for extra strength (*top*). These fitted into slots in the seat rails and were simply glued. After c1840–50 corner brackets were used (*bottom*). These were glued and screwed into the angle of the rails.

18thC
leg
seat rail
corner brace (simply glued)

brace

19thC
leg
seat rail
corner bracket (glued and screwed)

screws
corner bracket

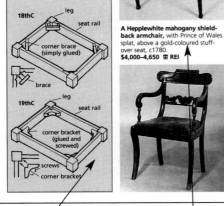

A Hepplewhite mahogany shield-back armchair, with Prince of Wales splat, above a gold-coloured stuff-over seat, c1780.
$4,000–4,650 ⊞ REI

A pair of Regency black and gilt-painted beech open armchairs, the turned and pierced triple rail backs painted with putti *en grisaille* and polychrome baskets of flowers, with caned seats, restored.
$5,000–5,800 ↗ DN

Further reading

Miller's Late Georgian to Edwardian Furniture Buyer's Guide, Miller's Publications, 1998

◀ **A George IV mahogany elbow chair,** the top rail with a gadroon crest and leaf-carved ends above an open scroll and shell horizontal bar, the drop-in seat covered in red fabric.
$500–600 ↗ WW

Miller's Compares
explains why two items which look similar have realised very different prices.

Page Tab
this appears on every page and contains the main heading under which larger sections have been sub-divided, therefore, allowing easy access to the various sections.

Price Guide
these are worked out by a team of trade and auction house experts, and are based on actual prices realised. Remember that Miller's is a price guide not a price list and prices are affected by many variables such as location, condition, desirability and so on. Don't forget that if you are selling it is quite likely you will be offered less than the price range. Price ranges for items sold at auction tend to include the buyer's premium and VAT if applicable.

Further Reading
directs the reader towards additional sources of information.

Source Code
refers to the Key to Illustrations on page 794 that lists the details of where the item was photographed.
The ↗ icon indicates the item was sold at auction.
The ⊞ icon indicates the item originated from a dealer.

Information Box
covers relevant collecting information on factories, makers, care and restoration, fakes and alterations.

Caption
provides a brief description of the item including the maker's name, medium, year it was made and in some cases condition.

BACA

BRITISH ANTIQUES AND COLLECTABLES AWARDS

presented by

MILLER'S

In association with

BBC HOMES & ANTIQUES MAGAZINE

Celebrating the Winners of BACA 2001

The Dorchester Hotel played host to the second of the British Antiques and Collectables Awards earlier this year, on Tuesday 19th June. These Awards are designed to recognise excellence across the Antiques and Collectables industry. This year saw the inclusion of eight new Awards, and it is envisaged that over the following years BACA will rotate its Awards and/or Categories to include all areas of the trade.

How to Vote for 2002

The voting process for the 2002 Awards begins now and will end in March 2002. For a voting form, please write to BACA or log on to the website:

BACA/Miller's
2-4 Heron Quays
London E14 4JP
www.baca-awards.co.uk

To date, BACA have received an overwhelming response – be it nominations, ideas, support and sponsorship. We would be very interested to hear from you on the subject of new Categories and new Awards for 2002 - but most importantly of course, we want your vote!

PROUDLY SPONSORED BY

BBC HOMES & ANTIQUES MAGAZINE   **MILLER'S CLUB**   **ANTIQUE STREET** www.antiquestreet.co.uk   **Antiques Trade GAZETTE**

CHRISTIE'S   **freeserve** www.freeserve.com   **ebaY** .co.uk

The BACA *Winners...*

CATEGORY 1
General Antiques Dealer

LONDON (INSIDE M25) sponsored by 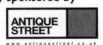.co.uk

Windsor House Antiques
28-29 Dover Street, Mayfair, London W1X 3PA

UK (OUTSIDE M25) *sponsored by*
David J. Hansord & Son
6 & 7 Castle Hill, Lincoln,
Lincolnshire LN1 3AA

CATEGORY 2
Specialist Antiques Dealers

FURNITURE
Norman Adams
8-10 Hans Road, Knightsbridge,
London SW3 1RX

CERAMICS
Roderick Jellicoe
3a Campden Street, off Kensington Church St,
London W8 7EP

CLOCKS, WATCHES & SCIENTIFIC INSTRUMENTS
Brian & Joy Loomes
Calf Haugh Farmhouse, Pateley Bridge,
Harrogate, N. Yorks HG3 5HW

SILVER & PLATE
Nicholas Shaw Antiques
Great Grooms Antiques Centre, Parbrook,
Billingshurst, West Sussex RH14 9EU

COLLECTABLES
Ropewalk Antiques
Rye, East Sussex TN31 7NA

TOYS & DOLLS
Yesterday's Child
Angel Arcade, 118 Islington High Street,
London N1 8EG

JEWELLERY
N. Bloom & Son
The New Bond St Antiques Centre,
124 New Bond Street, London W1S 1DX

ARMS & ARMOUR
Trident Arms
96-98 Derby Road, Nottingham NG1 5FB

COSTUMES & TEXTILES
Linda Wrigglesworth Ltd
34 Brook Street, London W1K 5DN

ARCHITECTURAL & GARDEN
LASSCO
The London Architectural Salvage
and Supply Co, St Michael's Church,
Mark Street, London EC2 4ER

CATEGORY 3
Auction Houses

LONDON (INSIDE M25)
Phillips
101 New Bond Street, London W1S 1SR

UK (OUTSIDE M25)
Tennants Auctioneers
The Auction Centre, Leyburn,
N. Yorkshire DL8 5SG

CATEGORY 4
Associated Awards

 **For a significant contribution to the popular appreciation of Antiques**
The BBC Antiques Roadshow

FAIR OF THE YEAR
Olympia Fine Art & Antiques Fair
June 2000, Olympia, London

BEST IN-HOUSE EXHIBITION *sponsored by*
Pelham Galleries Antiques Trade GAZETTE
"East and West:
Masterpieces of Lacquer Furniture",
24-25 Mount Street, London W1Y 5RB

AUCTIONEER OF THE YEAR
Ben Lloyd
Mallams, Bocardo House, St Michael's Street,
Oxford OX1 2DR

BEST ANTIQUES WRITER *sponsored by*
Christopher Wood
Christopher Wood Gallery, 20 Georgian
House, 10 Bury Street, London SW1Y 6AA

SERVICES AWARD: BEST FREIGHT CARRIER *sponsored by* CHRISTIE'S
Lockson
29 Broomfield Street, London E14 6BX

 **BEST ANTIQUES TOWN/VILLAGE**
Horncastle, Lincolnshire

Introduction

The antiques business remains alive and well at this time of economic downturn. While some internet companies have evaporated and stock shares have lost value, making people feel poorer than they did a year ago, business continues to be done in the antiques trade. The top of the market in every field continues strong, and dealers are singing their perennial refrain, 'There is a scarcity of masterpieces'.

When well-known collections come to market there are buyers eager for what has not been available and prices soar. The legendary Harriman-Judd collection of British art pottery from majolica to modern, bought in the 1970s and '80s by two California collectors known for their passion and extravagance, is a good example. Sotheby's sold 501 lots on 22 January for $3.2 million to American and British dealers and collectors in the saleroom with bidders from Canada, Australia and South Africa on the phones. (Another 300 lesser lots sold through Sotheby's.com.) Prices well over conservative estimates were paid for stoneware by the Martin Brothers, lustreware by William de Morgan and majolica by Minton. A Martin Brothers turtle-shaped foot warmer sold for $24,900, a rare de Morgan charger painted with fish fetched $28,350 and an 1878 Minton majolica teapot modelled as a fish with a spiny dorsal fin brought $35,250. A Minton majolica stand in the form of a life-sized African male holding a basked of fruit went for $115,750!

Victorian majolica is an American taste and so is earlier English pottery known as Mochaware. Scholars call it dipt ware because that is what the potters called it when they made it: dipt is synonymous with slip and its white body is decorated with bands of colourful slip. Much of it was exported to America in the late 18th and early 19th century for use in taverns and homes. In March at Conestoga Auction Company in Manheim, Pennsylvania, a collector paid a record $19,150 for a Mochaware mug decorated with three dipped feather-shaped 'fans' on a wide rust-coloured band and lime green bands and brown stripes on its rim and base. It eclipsed the record made twenty days earlier at Skinner's in Bolton, Massachusetts, when a pearlware eight inch baluster-form pitcher decorated in bright sky blue, rust, white and black bands with earthworm designs sold for $14,950.

Spatter ware, another English export earthenware, is as good as currency in Pennsylvania, where it was sold by the boat load in the 1820s to 1840s. At a Conestoga auction a spatter ware rainbow creamer in red, yellow, green and black sold for $10,175, a red spatter cup and saucer with red and blue fuchsias with yellow leaves sold for $8,250 and a red and black spatter handleless cup and saucer with a red thistle with green leaves fetched $7,700! The spatter ware record still stands at $18,400 paid for a rare rainbow teapot at a Sotheby's sale in 1995. A rainbow water pitcher sold at Conestoga in 1997 for $14,850. Comparable pieces have not turned up since.

'During the last year informal furniture has outsold formal,' observes Denzil Grant in his introduction to Oak & Country British furniture on page 156. The same is true of country furniture in the USA. There is keen competition for pieces with old surfaces intact and for country accessories, especially painted boxes and schoolgirl needlework. The finest quilts have brought prices not seen in a decade, while merely good quilts are more reasonably priced.

While some choose to live in the style of yeoman farmers, others prefer a more glamorous Hollywood look. 'In the last year or so good French Art Deco and Forties furniture have become part of the interior decorator's vocabulary,' said Gary Calderwood, a Philadelphia dealer.

'Forties is not a monolithic style, much of it returns to neo-classicism for inspiration so pieces work well with many other styles,' noted Bob Aibel of Modene Gallery in Philadelphia. The market for Forties furniture has been growing for the last decade but there is enough to satisfy the demand. The big names, such as Jean Michel Frank, Jean Royère and Andre Arbus are commanding big numbers; works by lesser names are more affordable.

Art Nouveau furniture, on the other hand, has lagged even though the market for Tiffany lamps and art glass vases is strong. 'Decorators don't like it,' says New York dealer Ben Macklowe. 'You will see English, French Deco and lots of Forties furniture at decorator show houses but never a room of Art Nouveau and you can get gorgeous pieces for $7,000 to $8,000, something glorious for $10,000 to $15,000, and the finest Louis Majorelle for $30,000, while a Royère piece from the 1940s will sell for $40,000 and a Jean Michel Frank can bring $60,000 to $80,000.'

A more restrained, modern style is British Arts and Crafts, which includes designs for Liberty & Co. According to John Levities, a Philadelphia dealer, interior designers and those who furnish in a wider range of periods now embrace this market, once dominated by collectors and institutions. He noted that, although there have been significant increases in prices paid for William Morris pieces because of scarcity, it is still possible to buy significant works by major designers much more reasonably than American Arts and Crafts.

'The market for American Arts and Crafts furniture has cooled a bit but it continues strong for the right pieces. Any problems with condition cuts the price in half,' said David Rago, the New Jersey auctioneer. Art pottery is so varied it is hard to generalize but there are plenty of collectors competing and, unlike furniture, there is a considerable amount of internet bidding at auction, and sales from dealers' web sites.

The Fifties is the most explosive furniture market of all. You see it pictured in all the House and Garden magazines. One of the reasons is its availability – it was mass-produced. Prices went up quickly but now the supply is exceeding the demand and they are softening. For handmade Fifties furniture designed by George Nakashima and other studio furniture makers prices remain strong. Watch the developing market for 20th-century studio furniture.

Vintage couture is the perfect accessory for vintage 20th-century design. When Renee Zellweger appeared on TV at the Academy Awards wearing a vintage John Desses yellow draped chiffon dress pictured on the cover of the catalogue for Doyle's New York 1997 Couture Sale it gave the vintage clothing market a boost. Wearable iconic clothes by well-known designers regularly bring $3,000 to $10,000, but a whopping $102,750 was paid for an 1888 Victorian court dress by Worth at Doyle's Couture and Textile sale recently.

Those who will not wear someone else's clothes have no problem wearing pre-owned costume jewellery. The landmark sales of the museum-quality collection of costume jewellery amassed by Dennis Masellis, a former payroll manager at an international law firm, now serving time in prison for embezzling $7 million, has been the focus of several sales by Doyle's, New York. Digital photographs of every lot have appeared on Doyle's website, so participation was worldwide.

Masellis had pushed costume jewellery prices to unheard of heights. He never said no and never haggled, so for seven or eight years any good costume jewellery from the 1920s to 1960s went straight to him. The sale of his collection satisfied a hungry market.

A late 1950s Christian Dior necklace made of pavé rhinestones with blue, green and pearl beaded flowers sold for $4312; a 1937 Chanel Star necklace of gilt metal with star chain pendants brought the same price. A Wiener Werkstätte choker sold for $8,050, and a Wiener Werkstätte cuff bracelet attributed to Josef Hoffman for $29,900.

A collector paid $11,500 for three matt enamel Theodor Fahrner bracelets made in Germany in the 1920s. Another collector paid $8,912 for a group of four enamel and rhinestone pins. A Versace Machine Age flower necklace, designed by Ugo Correani in Italy in 1988, of enamel, crystal and lacquer set on wire and springs sold on the phone for $10,925.

Staggering prices were paid for Bakelite, the colourful, whimsical, plastic costume jewellery. A group of three Bakelite dot and bowtie bracelets fetched $19,550, another group of six dot bracelets fetched $14,950 and another group of four dot and bowtie bracelets brought the same price. A pumpkin man brooch for which Masellis had paid $21,000 at auction in 1998 sold for $8,625. At the second sale Bakelite bracelets were offered in smaller lots. One green bracelet with cream random dots sold for $2,990, an orange one with cream dots went for $4,887, and two wide cream-colour bracelets with large red dots fetched $4,600. Celluloid sparkle bracelets encrusted with rhinestones sold for $4,025 for a lot of nine, another lot of twelve fetched $6,750!

Paul Rennie in his notes on Posters points out that film posters are the hottest corner of the long-established poster field, and that a vintage King Kong poster brought as much as a Toulouse-Lautrec at auction. 'That was the exception. Toulouse is sold as art, film posters are a separate category of collecting, title-driven, star-driven but not design-driven,' says George Theophiles, who has dealt in posters for 31 years, producing his Miscellaneous Man catalogues in New Freedom, Pennsylvania. 'The poster market got feverishly crazy, driven by the overheated economy, and French decorative posters were bringing higher and higher prices. Now the decorative market has cooled a bit but the subject-driven market for patriotic posters, circus posters, travel posters, aviation posters and particular product advertising is still hot because these posters are genuinely rare.'

As for sport, 'baseball collecting is always going to be a card hobby, but uniforms, bats, baseballs and photographs are rarer than cards, and the field is so broad it touches every type of collectable including books, autographs, advertising, games, giveaways,' said Robert Lifson, of Watchung, New Jersey, a division of Mastronet headquartered in Chicago.

The internet has proved to be a good information highway and on eBay, a big flea market on the web, there are things to be found. Dealers post their stock and auctioneers post their catalogues on their own home pages, making markets global. Buyers can find more sources on the internet but it has not made the antiques shop, antiques show, auction previews, catalogues or price guides obsolete.

Surfing the web has, in fact, brought new appreciation for the book, with its numbered pages, contents and index. When the book was invented it was a practical advance over the scroll. You don't need to scroll down endlessly to find a particular category in *Miller's Antiques Price Guide*; simply consult the table of contents on page 19. If you are looking for a particular craftsman, designer or factory consult the index, which begins on page 804.

Miller's is a price guide not a price list. The prices are worked out by a team of dealers and auction house experts based on prices paid, reflecting quality, condition, and desirability. If you are selling you may be offered less than the prices listed, and prices in one part of the country may be less than in another. If you are buying you might get a bargain if you find an American piece in an English sale. Knowledge is money in your pocket.

We are always looking to make this guide better. If we have left out what you collect, or if you have any other comments, please let us know. **Lita Solis-Cohen**

Furniture

On the face of it, quality would once again seem to be the watchword for buyers of furniture in the coming year, but only if they are blessed with deep pockets. The market has polarized to the point of schism, with the finer pieces reaching new stratospheric price heights both under the hammer and on the dealer's shop floor, while the lesser items bump along the bottom, in some cases fetching little more than they were 20 years ago. This applies as much to Continental furniture as it does to English pieces. For instance, while 19th-century French furniture with an exhibition track record, or the signature of a good maker, will usually sell very well, other examples lacking such distinction can be real problems. In particular, boulle items of that period are cheaper now than they have been for years.

So what has brought about this choppy spell in a market that, historically, has not shown itself to be subject to particularly extreme mood swings? It looked initially as though it might have been attributable to nothing more sinister than a weak Euro depressing the export trade but now it seems evident that the cause is more elemental and therefore probably more permanent. There appears to be a trend among younger buyers for more minimalist interiors featuring predominately modern design themes but often incorporating the occasional really good antique piece as a focal point. In addition to this the continued boom in the UK country house market, coupled with highly selective buying on the part of US collectors, has ensured that the demand for top quality period furniture has continued without remit while interest in pieces at the other end of the spectrum has simply faded away.

Is it all doom and gloom then for those of us who are not going to be on the receiving end of a six-figure City bonus? Definitely not has to be the answer. True, if you hanker after a piece of 18th-century Irish furniture the price will almost certainly have gone up before you have had time to arrange the second mortgage needed to purchase it, and that oak dresser which you thought about buying five years ago for $7,250 will now cost you three times that figure. But if you, like the vast majority of people, are just trying to furnish your home without antagonizing the bank's central computer any more than necessary, the downward revision of prices at the lower end of the market presents buying opportunities undreamed of for a decade or more.

So take advantage of this unusual situation and, who knows, if the US economy suffers in the way some forecasters are predicting, perhaps even that George III mahogany dining table might become a little more reasonable as well. **Leslie Gillham**

Beds

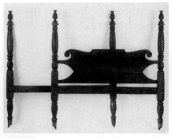

An American carved mahogany low post bed, the pineapple-carved finials on leaf-spiral and ring-carved posts ending in vase- and ring-turned legs, faults, New England, c1820, 49¼in (125cm) wide.
$3,200–3,700 ✗ SK(B)

A George III mahogany cradle, with enclosed canopy at one end, on rocker supports, 42in (106.5cm) long.
$600–725 ✗ AG

A mahogany tester double bedstead, the pair of early George III front bedposts turned and fluted, the oak back posts with a later headboard, later tester frieze with egg-and-dart mouldings and panels with scroll-carved brackets, 61in (155cm) wide.
$2,300–3,000 ✗ WW

▶ **An Irish William IV carved mahogany cradle,** by Williams & Gibton, one end with a swan-head terminal, 43¼in (110cm) long.
$4,500–5,500 ✗ P
The Dublin firm of Mack, Williams & Gibton was formed around 1912 but can be traced to the late 18th century when John Mack established a business in Abbey Street, Dublin. He was joined by Robert Gibton and moved to larger premises in Stafford Street. In 1806 they were appointed 'Upholsterers and Cabinet makers to his Majesty'. In 1812 Robert Gibton died and was succeeded by his son William. At the same time Zachariah Williams joined the partnership and the company became Mack, Williams & Gibton. John Mack died in 1829, and the firm continued to trade as Williams & Gibton until 1844, when William Gibton died and it became Williams & Sons, ceasing business in 1952.

> Items in the Furniture section have been arranged in date order within each sub-section.

A caned crib, with turned finials and stained wooden frame with brass mounts, c1840, 41in (104cm) long.
$580–720 ↗ **Mit**

A mahogany cradle, with canework panels, c1840, 42in (106.5cm) long.
$725–875 ⊞ **HON**

A Victorian mahogany half-tester bed, the serpentine-top footboard with applied carved scrolls, fitted with three recessed panels in flame veneer, 58in (147.5cm) wide.
$1,450–1,750 ↗ **DD**

A mid-Victorian double bed, the footboard with an oval panel centred with a cabochon, 64in (162.5cm) wide.
$580–720 ↗ **Bon(M)**

A cast-iron four-poster bed, c1875, 60in (152.5cm) wide.
$2,600–3,000 ⊞ **SeH**

A blue verdigris cast-iron bed, c1875, 48in (122cm) wide.
$500–600 ⊞ **SeH**

A Victorian brass double bed, the bedhead surmounted by urn finials and with stylized foliate crestings, the bed end with conforming finials and cresting, c1890, 62in (157.5cm) wide.
$1,300–1,600 ↗ **S(S)**

A French mahogany and parcel-gilt bedstead, the floral marquetry-inlaid headboard surmounted by a gilt-gesso dolphin-adorned crest panel, 19thC, 60in (152.5cm) wide.
$2,000–2,500 ↗ **DMC**

A French Empire revival mahogany bedstead, with ormolu decoration, c1890, 60in (152.5cm) wide.
$4,000–5,000 ⊞ **SeH**

FURNITURE

A pair of carved painted wood single beds, c1890, 42in (106.5cm) wide.
$2,600–3,000 ⊞ SeH

A Victorian cast-iron bedstead, with brass rings and spindle decoration, c1895, 48in (122cm) wide.
$1,100–1,300 ⊞ SeH

▶ **A black cast-iron and brass bedstead,** c1895, 48in (122cm) wide.
$800–900 ⊞ SeH

A Dutch Louis XVI-style yellow-, blue- and white-painted child's bed, the domed canopy covered with blue and white satin curtains, the sides with panels of oak leaves, 19thC, 52in (132cm) long.
$2,500–3,000 ⚒ S(Am)

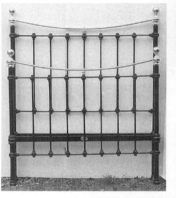

A black cast-iron and brass bedstead, c1895, 54in (137cm) wide.
$870–1,000 ⊞ SeH

A French walnut bedstead, the head surmounted by a carving depicting Bacchus, the foot carved with grape vines, c1895, 60in (152.5cm) wide.
$3,600–4,400 ⊞ SeH

Cross Reference
See Colour Review (page 98)

A Louis XV-style carved walnut bed, c1900, 60in (152.5cm) wide.
$1,800–2,200 ⊞ SWA

An inlaid mahogany bedstead, c1910, 54in (137cm) wide.
$580–650 ⊞ COLL

▶ **A beechwood four-poster bed,** with twist-turned posts, the ends with caned panels, 1920s, 36in (91.5cm) wide.
$360–440 ⚒ SWO

A George III-style mahogany bed, by Heals & Son, early 20thC, 37½in (95.5cm) wide.
$230–280 ⚒ Bon(C)

Benches

A George III upholstered mahogany bench, on tapering reeded legs headed by half flowers, one leg replaced, late 18thC, 78in (198cm) wide.
$4,750–5,500 ✕ S(NY)

A pair of Spanish hinged walnut benches, on trestle supports with iron stretchers, 17thC, 93¼in (237cm) wide.
$6,000–7,200 ✕ S(NY)

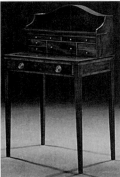

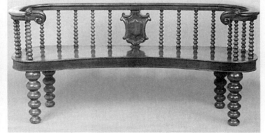

A William IV mahogany bench, now upholstered in olive leather, 44in (112cm) wide.
$2,600–3,200 ✕ NOA

A mahogany hall bench, the galleried back with central cartouche and with leaf-carved incurved arms, probably by Strahan of Dublin, 19thC, 60¼in (153cm) wide.
$1,700–2,200 ✕ HOK

A Victorian carved mahogany hall bench, by Saunders & Wooley, on reeded tapered legs, marked, 53½in (136cm) wide.
$2,900–3,200 ✕ P(EA)

A Victorian mahogany hall bench, with galleried back and solid seat, on octagonal turned tapering legs, c1850, 74in (188cm) wide.
$3,200–3,600 ✕ S(S)

A pollarded oak and ebonized hall bench, c1880, 48in (122cm) wide.
$2,600–3,000 ⊞ APO

Bonheurs du Jour

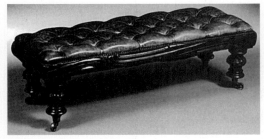

A George III mahogany and rosewood crossbanded bonheur du jour, fitted with an arrangement of seven drawers and fall front, above a fold-over writing surface and a frieze drawer, restored, c1790, 27in (68.5cm) wide.
$7,250–8,000 ✕ S(S)

A Regency mahogany and brass marquetry bonheur du jour, applied with gilt-brass mounts, the *faux* panelled doors enclosing a leather-lined fall enclosing pigeonholes and satinwood drawers, above a pair of pleated silk panelled doors, 40½in (103cm) wide.
$7,250–8,000 ✕ P

A French kingwood and porcelain-mounted bonheur du jour, the mirror recess flanked by cupboards, the fall revealing a stepped and fitted interior, c1900, 31in (78.5cm) wide.
$4,000–4,600 ✕ S(S)

A kingwood and parquetry ormolu-mounted bonheur du jour, the twin cupboard doors inlaid with floral panels above two drawers, the frieze drawer enclosing a pull-out writing section, late 19thC, 28in (71cm) wide.
$3,000–3,500 ✕ JAd

FURNITURE

A Victorian walnut bonheur du jour, the upper section with an arrangement of four drawers, and with a pull-out writing slide, slight damage, 31in (78.5cm) wide.
$2,000–2,500 ⚒ WL

An amboyna bonheur du jour, veneered with partridgewood cross-banding, with ormolu mounts and a fold-over leather-lined writing surface, 19thC, 54in (137cm) high.
$8,700–9,700 ⊞ BERA

An Edwardian inlaid rosewood bonheur du jour, the raised back with a central mirrored panel flanked by four small drawers above an inset leather writing surface, 35¾in (91cm) wide.
$1,100–1,300 ⚒ S(S)

◀ **A Sheraton-style satinwood bonheur du jour,** by W. Walker, Leeds, the double doors enclosing a mahogany-lined fitted interior of four pigeonholes above two long and three short drawers, with pull-out green baize-covered folding writing slide below, early 20thC, 19¼in (49cm) wide.
$5,000–6,000 ⚒ PFK

▶ **An Edwardian mahogany bonheur du jour,** the upper section with a hinged lid enclosing stationery compartments, above a leather-lined writing surface, 24in (61cm) wide.
$580–720 ⚒ AG

Bookcases

▶ **An American Empire mahogany cabinet book-case in two parts,** the lattice-work sliding doors enclosing adjustable shelves, the outset lower section with a pair of hinged, panelled doors enclosing shelves, early 19thC, 54in (137cm) wide.
$5,800–7,200 ⚒ SLN

A Regency flame-veneered bookcase, the upper section with astragal-glazed doors enclosing shelves, the base with cupboards, c1820, 51in (129.5cm) wide.
$9,000–10,000 ⊞ MTay

◀ **A William IV rose-wood bookcase,** carved throughout with acanthus, scrolls and stylized foliage, the base with three drawers and open central shelves flanked by panelled doors and columns, reduced in width, 59½in (151cm) wide.
$3,000–3,500 ⚒ Bea(E)

A Regency mahogany bookcase, the ebony-strung panelled doors with gilt-wood mouldings and ormolu anthemion corners, the projecting base with an ebony-strung frieze drawer and panelled cupboard doors below, flanked by turned and fluted brass-collared legs, early 19thC, 38½in (98cm) wide.
$3,000–3,700 ⚒ DMC

A late Georgian mahogany breakfront bookcase, the central double doors flanked by small doors enclosing adjustable shelves, 74in (188cm) wide.
$8,000–9,500 ⚒ DA

An early Victorian burr-oak library bookcase, the upper section with glazed doors enclosing adjustable shelves, the base with two frieze drawers above cupboards, 56in (142cm) wide.
$3,000–3,500 ➤ HYD

A Victorian mahogany bookcase, with two bar-glazed doors, and a shaped frieze drawer above two arch-panelled doors, 46in (117cm) wide.
$3,000–3,500 ➤ G(B)

► **A Gothic revival oak inverted breakfront bookcase,** c1850, 120in (305cm) wide.
$16,000–18,000 ⊞ APO

A rosewood bookcase, with brass rail gallery, the glazed double doors enclosing shelves, c1840, 48in (123cm) wide.
$1,500–1,800 ➤ WL

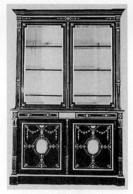

A Victorian ebonized, gilt-decorated and jasperware-mounted bookcase, the upper section fitted with adjustable shelves enclosed by a pair of glazed doors, the lower section containing two frieze drawers centred by a Wedgwood-style blue and white plaque, 57¼in (145.5cm) wide.
$2,200–2,600 ➤ P(Pr)

◄ **A Victorian oak breakfront bookcase,** by John Taylor & Son, the four glazed doors enclosing adjustable shelves, the base with two fielded panel doors flanked by plain panel doors, stamped, 102½in (260.5cm) wide.
$8,700–10,000 ➤ P(Ed)
John Taylor began trading as a wright in 1826 at 100 Rose Street, Edinburgh. After 1850 the firm became John Taylor & Son, and in 1852 they were appointed cabinet-makers and upholsterers to the Queen. By 1900 they had acquired offices and warerooms at 109 Princes Street and modern works at Gardner's Cres, Rosemount. In addition to billiard table manufacture, they were also noted for shop fittings and elaborate public house interiors.

◄ **A Victorian oak bookcase,** fitted with adjustable shelves, the base enclosed by a pair of diagonal panel doors, 48in (122cm) wide.
$1,000–1,250 ➤ TRL

A Victorian ripple-figured walnut bookcase, the three glazed doors enclosing adjustable shelves, with three conforming blind panel doors below, 77¼in (196cm) wide.
$4,000–4,500 ➤ Bri

A Victorian walnut library bookcase, the upper section with two central glazed doors flanked by open shelves, the base with four panelled doors, on a plinth, c1865, 75in (190.5cm) wide.
$8,700–10,000 ➤ E

► **A George III-style mahogany carved and blind-fret-decorated bookcase,** by Edwards & Roberts, with two astragal-glazed doors above two panelled doors, late 19thC, 36in (91.5cm) wide.
$2,300–2,500 ➤ S(S)

◄ **A mahogany bookcase,** the two glazed doors enclosing an interior fitted with leather-trimmed shelves, with a drawer below, 19thC, 42in (106.5cm) wide.
$1,800–2,400 ➤ M

A late Victorian mahogany breakfront bookcase, by Francis & James Smith of Glasgow, the four glazed panel doors enclosing adjustable shelves, the projecting base above four fielded panel doors, each door divided by a column, with enamel label, 117in (297cm) wide.
$13,500–16,500 ➤ P(Ed)
Francis & James Smith are first mentioned at Gordon and Onion Street in *The Trade Directories* of 1880. In 1893 the firm changed its name to Francis Smith, at 74–78 Gordon Street, Glasgow.

Bureau Bookcases

A Queen Anne walnut bureau bookcase, with mirrored doors above a fall-front enclosing six drawers and pigeonholes, early 18thC, 81in (205.5cm) high.
$50,000–55,000 ⊞ REI

A George I walnut bureau bookcase, with glazed inlaid doors enclosing three adjustable shelves and with two candle slides below, the fall-front enclosing a well, an arrangement of drawers, a secret drawer and pigeonholes, 41in (104cm) wide.
$30,000–35,000 ⋊ MEA

A George III mahogany bureau bookcase, with astragal-glazed doors enclosing drawers, the fall-front enclosing an interior cupboard with pull-out slides, pigeonholes and drawers, the bracket feet modified, 48in (122cm) wide.
$3,000–3,500 ⋊ DOC

A George III mahogany bureau bookcase, restored and associated, 52¼in (132.5cm) wide.
$3,600–4,400 ⋊ Bon(C)

A late Victorian mahogany, satinwood-banded and inlaid bureau bookcase, the upper section with two astragal-glazed doors, 38½in (98cm) wide.
$5,000–6,000 ⋊ P(B)

Is it original?

Check that the glazing bars match the rest of the bookcase in quality, timber and age. Breakfront wardrobes of the mid- to late 19th century are often turned into bookcases by removing the solid panels to the doors and glazing the frames.

During the late 19th century many old glazed door cabinets were removed from their bureau or cupboard bases to have feet added and the tops fitted in to make 'Georgian' display cupboards or bookcases. This was not an 18th-century form; the correct version was much taller and often had drawers to the frieze base. The low dwarf bookcases without doors became popular during the late 18th century.

A German bureau bookcase, the lower section with cylinder fall enclosing a fitted interior, 19thC, 43¼in (110cm) wide.
$2,500–3,000 ⋊ P(L)

An oak bookcase, with astragal-glazed doors above a burr-walnut veneered projecting base, with two drawers above two fielded panel doors, c1920, 49in (124.5cm) wide.
$1,250–1,400 ⊞ NAW

An Edwardian inlaid mahogany bureau bookcase, by James Shoolbred & Co, 20½in (52cm) wide.
$3,000–3,300 ⊞ MTay

An Edwardian mahogany and satinwood-cross-banded bureau bookcase, the astragal-glazed doors enclosing adjustable shelves, the fall-front concealing a fitted interior, 39in (99cm) wide.
$1,450–1,750 ⋊ CGC

An Edwardian mahogany and satinwood-banded bureau bookcase, with astragal-glazed doors, the fall-front inlaid with a fan motif, 37¾in (96cm) wide.
$2,000–2,500 ⋊ KID

Low Bookcases

A mahogany open bookcase, the variegated white and lavender marble top above two open shelves, on a plinth base, c1825, 44in (112cm) wide.
$3,000–3,500 ✗ NOA

A William IV rosewood low breakfront bookcase, with two panelled and crossbanded doors flanked by open shelves and rosette- and scroll-capped pilasters, 57¾in (146.5cm) wide.
$7,250–8,750 ✗ DN

A William IV rosewood low recessed breakfront open bookcase, the adjustable open shelves flanked by twin turned columns, with brass mounts, 48in (122cm) wide.
$1,700–2,000 ✗ P(E)

A Victorian mahogany low bookcase, the central division and uprights carved with scrolls, formerly the lower part of a library bookcase, 60¼in (153cm) wide.
$850–950 ✗ P(Ba)

A Victorian burr-walnut open bookcase, the breakfront inlaid with chevron stringing, with adjustable shelves, 72in (183cm) wide.
$2,500–3,000 ✗ L

A breakfront bookcase, with ebonized banding, with a central glazed panel door flanked by a pair of doors enclosing shelves, 19thC, 45in (114.5cm) wide.
$1,000–1,250 ✗ AG

Open Bookcases

A George III black japanned and parcel-gilt bookcase cabinet, japanning restored, late 18thC, 28¾in (73cm) wide.
$13,000–16,000 ✗ S(NY)

► A Regency mahogany graduated double-sided open bookcase, the top with bookends, the base with a drawer, flanked by brass carrying handles, one handle missing, 34in (86.5cm) wide.
$5,000–6,000 ✗ HOK

A Regency mahogany waterfall open bookcase, with two frieze drawers and three reeded graduated shelves, on later bracket feet, 41in (104cm) wide.
$5,000–6,000 ✗ S(S)

A Regency mahogany waterfall bookcase, with three graduated shelves, two drawers below, on later legs, 24in (61cm) wide.
$2,200–2,400 ✗ P(S)

► A Victorian mahogany open bookcase, the two adjustable shelves with panelled double cupboard doors below, 48in (122cm) wide.
$3,300–3,700 ✗ P(Ba)

A mahogany open bookcase on stand, the front ring-turned and spiral-ribbed tapering legs with turned feet, early 19thC, 30¼in (77cm) wide.
$1,700–2,000 ✗ WW

Revolving Bookcases

A painted satinwood revolving bookcase, the top with a candle stand above three revolving drums, late 19thC, 20½in (52cm) wide.
$5,000–6,000 ✱ HOK

▶ **An Edwardian mahogany, boxwood, satinwood and ebony-strung and banded revolving bookcase,** the two tiers each fitted with four shelves, 19in (48.5cm) wide.
$580–720 ✱ GAK

A mahogany revolving bookcase, the top inlaid to the centre in a variety of woods with a floral pattern, above a series of open shelves with foliate fretwork supports, late 19thC, 20in (51cm) wide.
$2,000–2,500 ✱ Mit

An oak revolving bookcase, early 20thC, 26¾in (68cm) wide.
$450–550 ✱ Bon(C)

An inlaid mahogany revolving bookcase on stand, c1910, 18in (45.5cm) square.
$1,200–1,400 ⊞ MTay

A French mahogany revolving bookcase and reading stand, with a ratchet-adjustable sloping square top above two folding candle stands, c1900, 22in (56cm) square.
$2,600–3,000 ✱ S(S)

> Items in the Furniture section have been arranged in date order within each sub-section.

Secretaire Bookcases

A George III Hepplewhite-style mahogany secretaire bookcase, the upper section with lancet-glazed doors and adjustable interior shelves, the lower section with a fall-front dummy drawer enclosing secretaire drawers and pigeonholes, 40in (101.5cm) wide.
$8,000–9,500 ✱ HYD

A Regency mahogany secretaire bookcase, the upper section of three adjustable shelves enclosed by two doors with Gothic glazing bars, the retractable writing surface opening to reveal a satinwood fitted interior, 46in (117cm) wide.
$2,900–3,200 ✱ DD

A William IV mahogany secretaire bookcase, the upper section enclosed by astragal-glazed doors, the base fitted with a secretaire drawer over three long drawers, 43½in (110.5cm) wide.
$2,200–2,600 ✱ L

▶ **A mahogany breakfront secretaire bookcase,** with astragal-glazed doors, c1910, 77in (195.5cm) wide.
$5,800–6,500 ⊞ CHE

A Victorian mahogany secretaire bookcase, 47in (119.4cm) wide.
$4,000–4,600 ⊞ RPh

Buckets

An Irish George III brass-bound mahogany plate bucket, with brass swing handle, 23in (58.5cm) high.
$1,150–1,450 ⚲ MEA

A George III brass-bound mahogany peat bucket, with brass bands, swing handle and liner, 13¾in (35cm) high.
$1,300–1,450 ⚲ GIL

An Irish George III brass-bound mahogany peat bucket, with brass carrying handle, 15in (38cm) high.
$5,500–6,000 ⚲ S

An Irish George III brass-bound mahogany peat bucket, with ribbed body and brass carrying handle, 17½in (44.5cm) diam.
$3,600–4,400 ⚲ Bon

A mahogany bucket, with brass lion-mask drop handles and brass-banded base, early 19thC, 15¾in (40cm) diam.
$1,800–2,200 ⚲ HOK

A Regency brass-bound mahogany bucket, with metal liner and brass carrying handle, 14in (35.5cm) wide.
$850–1,000 ⚲ P

A banded wooden bucket, fitted with brass liner and loop handle, late 19thC, 13¼in (33.5cm) high.
$1,800–2,200 ⚲ P

A William IV mahogany peat bucket, the body with leaf-carved staves, with brass liner and brass carrying handle, 19in (48.5cm) high.
$3,500–4,000 ⚲ NOA

Buffets

A William IV mahogany buffet, each tier with a three-quarter gallery below melon-carved finials, on fluted supports and turned feet, 45in (114.5cm) wide.
$1,600–1,850 ⚲ CGC

▶ **A Victorian mahogany buffet,** the ledge back carved with a vine roundel, with three shelves on pierced and scrolled brackets, the base with two drawers, 48in (122cm) wide.
$1,400–1,600 ⚲ AH

A Victorian revival walnut and part-ebonized buffet, by Gillow & Co, probably designed by Bruce Talbert, fitted with a pair of frieze drawers, over a cupboard base enclosed by a pair of doors carved with flowers and leaves, 69¼in (176cm) wide.
$2,300–2,600 ⚲ P(WM)

◀ **A Victorian mahogany buffet,** the cupboard base with two doors, with turned standards surmounted by rosette-carved finials, 39in (99cm) wide.
$725–875 ⚲ GAK

A Victorian oak and parquetry-inlaid buffet, the top inlaid with an interlocking stellar design above a frieze of embossed roundels, over a rising mechanism with folding brackets incorporating two further tiers, c1880, 42in (106.5cm) wide.
$725–875 ⚲ Hal

Bureaux

A George II mahogany bureau, the fall-front enclosing a fitted interior of drawers and pigeonholes surrounding a central cupboard door inlaid with stringing, with four long drawers below, mid-18thC, 27in (68.5cm) wide.
$4,000–4,600 ➶ S

An early George III mahogany bureau, the fall-front enclosing a fitted interior, 36¼in (92cm) wide.
$1,200–1,450 ➶ HYD

A George III mahogany bureau, the fall-front enclosing an inlaid fitted interior of cupboards, pigeonholes and drawers over a shelf and further drawers, with brass swan-neck handles and ivory escutcheons, 39in (99cm) wide.
$1,450–1,750 ➶ M

An American maple and tiger maple slant-lid bureau, possibly western Massachusetts, the lid opening to an interior of six compartments, mid-18thC, 35½in (90cm) wide.
$4,600–5,000 ➶ SK(B)

A George III flame-mahogany bureau, with inlaid decoration, the fall-front enclosing a fitted interior of drawers, pigeonholes and centre cupboard, 43¼in (110cm) wide.
$2,300–2,600 ➶ CMS

Further reading
Miller's Collecting Furniture: The Facts at Your Fingertips, Miller's Publications, 1998

A George III mahogany bureau, with rosewood crossbanding and boxwood stringing, the fall-front enclosing an interior with velvet-lined writing surface and a series of drawers, pigeonholes, cupboards and secret drawers, 36in (91.5cm) wide.
$1,200–1,450 ➶ Mit

A south German walnut bureau, the top and fall inlaid with geometric crossbanding and enclosing an interior of drawers and pigeonholes, restored, c1760, 47½in (120.5cm) wide.
$4,500–5,000 ➶ Bon

A George III mahogany and satin-wood-banded bureau, the fall-front enclosing an interior fitted with drawers and pigeonholes, 40in (101.5cm) wide.
$1,800–2,200 ➶ KID

A George III mahogany twin bureau, with two fall-fronts each enclosing a fitted interior, above five short and two long drawers, 53in (134.5cm) wide.
$1,800–2,200 ➶ L

A George III mahogany bureau, the fall-front concealing a fitted interior of pigeonholes and drawers, 39in (99cm) wide.
$870–1,000 ➶ CGC

A Dutch marquetry-inlaid oak double *bombé* **bureau,** the fall-front enclosing an arrangement of drawers and pigeonholes, over a well, 18thC, 52in (132cm) wide.
$5,800–7,200 ✗ G(B)

Buying Dutch marquetry bureaux
- beware of badly split flaps and slides
- marquetry on walnut fetches more than marquetry on mahogany, which in turn fetches more than marquetry on oak
- cylinder bureaux as a general rule fetch less than fall-front bureaux
- marquetry which includes birds and insects is slightly rarer than the usual floral marquetry

A Dutch walnut marquetry bureau, the fall-front with pull-out slide enclosing a writing surface, the drawers and pigeonholes inlaid overall with tulips and foliage, the *bombé* front with three drawers with brass rococo handles, early 19thC, 40¼in (102cm) wide.
$5,000–6,000 ✗ P(Ed)

A Flemish mahogany *bombé* **cylinder bureau,** the cylinder top enclosing a fitted interior, early 19thC, 45in (114.5cm) wide.
$1,450–1,750 ✗ JH

A Maltese banded-walnut line-inlaid bureau, the fall-front enclosing a fitted interior, late 18th/early 19thC, 44in (112cm) wide.
$5,800–7,200 ✗ G(B)

A mahogany cylinder pedestal bureau, c1860, 52in (132cm) wide.
$3,000–3,500 ⊞ HON

An oak cylinder bureau, with a satinwood-lined interior of pigeon-holes and stationery drawers, the sliding writing surface with three gilt-tooled leather insets, the central panel raising on a ratchet support, 19thC, 47½in (120.5cm) wide.
$1,000–1,250 ✗ ELR

A Louis Philippe walnut bureau, the fall-front enclosing a desk interior, over a panelled cupboard door, mid-19thC, 31¾in (80.5cm) wide.
$3,000–3,300 ✗ NOA

Prices
The price ranges quoted in this book reflect the average price a purchaser might expect to pay for a similar item. The price will vary according to the condition, rarity, size, popularity, provenance, colour and restoration of the item, and this must be taken into account when assessing values. Don't forget that if you are selling it is quite likely that you will be offered less than the price range.

◄ **An Edwardian banded mahogany bureau,** the fall-front inlaid with basket and swags, with two short and three long drawers below, 40in (101.5cm) wide.
$1,000–1,250 ✗ RPI

An Edwardian mahogany bureau, inlaid with satinwood banding and boxwood stringing, the fall-front enclosing pigeonholes, short drawers and a cupboard, 24in (61cm) wide.
$1,300–1,450 ✗ AG

FURNITURE

Cabinets

A pair of George III mahogany pedestal cabinets, each with folding hinged tops above a panelled door, enclosing adjustable shelves, one with zinc lining and slatted shelves, each with a dummy drawer below, 20in (51cm) wide.
$4,500–5,000 ⚒ S

A Victorian figured-mahogany cylinder cabinet, the top inset with marble, 14¼in (36cm) wide.
$1,100–1,250 ⊞ MTay

A north European Biedermeier fruitwood and part-ebonized pedestal cabinet, the door enclosing an interior lidded well, c1820, 17in (43cm) diam.
$5,500–6,000 ⚒ SK

A Swiss walnut wall cabinet, the door carved with a fox mask and foliage and enclosing six drawers, the base with the head of a dog, late 19thC, 38in (96.5cm) wide.
$1,750–2,000 ⚒ S(S)

A Regency rosewood medicine cabinet, with original locks, c1820, 30in (76cm) wide.
$3,200–3,600 ⊞ BERA

An Edwardian rosewood metamorphic drinks cabinet, the twin-flap top opening to reveal a removable glass-bottomed tray, the sides inlaid with ribbon-husk garlands, 24½in (62cm) wide.
$2,500–3,000 ⚒ P(NW)
In this metamorphic cabinet, the double top hinges open and the fitted interior rises up with glasses, decanters, etc.

A William IV mahogany two-tier cabinet, the upper section with four shelves, the base with two short and three long drawers, each enclosed by a pair of Gothic-style panelled doors, 58in (147.5cm) wide.
$4,500–5,000 ⚒ CAG

An Edwardian Shannon Patent mahogany circular drinks cabinet, the superstructure with a brass gallery above a pivoted panelled door inset with a fox-hunting print, rotating to reveal an interior fitted for decanters and glasses, c1910, 21½in (54.5cm) wide.
$2,200–2,600 ⚒ Bon(C)

Bedside Cabinets

A Georgian mahogany night table, c1780, 22in (56cm) wide.
$3,200–3,600 ⊞ REI

A late George III night table, the hinged top above inward-folding panelled doors, 26in (66cm) wide.
$725–875 ⚒ DN

A walnut serpentine night table, late 18thC, 19¼in (49cm) wide.
$4,000–4,600 ⚒ P(S)

A George III mahogany tray top tambour-fronted night table, c1790, 13in (33cm) wide.
$3,200–3,600 ⊞ CAT

FURNITURE

A George III mahogany night table, the two doors with ebonized stringing, enclosing a cupboard, the single drawer below with a double dummy drawer front, 20in (51cm) wide.
$725–875 ✗ GAK

A George III mahogany night table, with a tambour door and slender turned and ringed legs, 16½in (42cm) wide.
$1,100–1,350 ✗ GIL

A Regency mahogany and crossbanded bow-front night table, with a tambour door, on turned reeded legs and spool feet, 17in (43cm) wide.
$2,000–2,500 ✗ P

A pair of Biedermeier-style marble-topped mahogany bedside cabinets, with ebonized detail and variegated grey marble tops, late 19thC, 14½in (37cm) wide.
$1,000–1,250 ✗ NOA

Bureau Cabinets

A German walnut bureau cabinet, the line-inlaid doors enclosing an arrangement of drawers and pigeonholes, above a fall-front enclosing six drawers and various recesses, above three long drawers, restored, damaged, c1750, 54in (137cm) wide.
$5,500–6,500 ✗ Bon

A George III mahogany bureau cabinet, the doors with later bevelled mirror panels enclosing adjustable shelves, the fall-front enclosing a fitted interior of drawers and pigeonholes surrounding a central small cupboard, minor restoration to feet, 38½in (98cm) wide.
$11,500–14,500 ✗ S

A George III mahogany bureau cabinet, the two crossbanded and panelled cupboard doors enclosing shelves, the fall-front enclosing pigeonholes and stationery drawers, with two short and three long graduated drawers, on bracket feet, 42in (106.5cm) wide.
$3,200–3,800 ✗ ELR

A George III mahogany bureau cabinet, the doors enclosing three adjustable shelves, the ebony-strung fall-front concealing an arrangement of rosewood- and satinwood-strung drawers flanking a cupboard and a pair of *faux* books, 45¾in (116cm) wide.
$1,600–1,850 ✗ CGC

Cabinets-on-Chests

◄ **A Queen Anne walnut crossbanded and banded cabinet-on-chest,** inlaid with ebonized lines, the cushion frieze drawer over a pair of quarter-veneered doors inlaid with banded ovals enclosing four short drawers surrounded by eleven drawers, on later bracket feet, 47¼in (120cm) wide.
$22,000–26,000 ✗ P

► **A Dutch oak cabinet-on-chest,** with carved domed pediment and brass corner capitals, c1800, 82½in (209.5cm) wide.
$5,500–6,500 ⊞ MTay

A late Regency mahogany and ebony line-inlaid breakfront dining room cabinet, with four cupboard doors above four graduated drawers, flanked by cupboards, 63in (160cm) wide.
$7,250–8,500 ✗ G(B)

FURNITURE

Coal Cabinets

A Victorian inlaid rosewood fall-front coal cabinet, inlaid with motifs of musical instruments, ribbons, swags, bellflowers and boxwood stringing, 14½in (37cm) wide.
$870–1,000 ➤ JAd

A late Victorian walnut coal box with liner, the door carved with a lion's head, 15in (38cm) wide.
$400–475 ⊞ MTay

> **Cross Reference**
> See Colour Review
> (page 102)

▶ An Edwardian satin-wood, banded and inlaid display and coal cabinet, by Warings, the mirrored arcaded architectural superstructure with brass baluster galleries, a plush-lined display case below enclosed by a glazed panel door, the lower section with a drawer above a pair of panelled doors with hinged metal-lined compart-ment under, marked, 25½in (65cm) wide.
$2,300–2,600 ➤ P(E)

Corner Cabinets

A Dutch walnut corner cupboard, with mirrored doors, c1720, 42in (106.5cm) wide.
$32,000–35,000 ⊞ RGa

A mahogany bowfront corner cabinet, the two doors enclosing a fitted interior, the lower shelf fitted with three drawers, 18thC, 30in (76cm) wide.
$2,400–3,000 ➤ GAK

A George III mahogany hanging corner cupboard, the flame-veneered panelled door enclosing three shaped shelves, 42½in (108cm) wide.
$580–720 ➤ TRL

A George III mahogany corner cupboard, with double panelled doors enclosing shelves, the lower section with two single panel doors enclosing a single shelf, with later brass hinges, 38in (96.5cm) wide.
$3,000–3,500 ➤ M

A George III mahogany bowfront hanging corner cupboard, the interior fitted with three shelves enclosed by a pair of fielded panelled doors, with one small drawer below, 37½in (95.5cm) wide.
$870–1,000 ➤ LF

A George III mahogany corner cabinet, with an astragal-glazed door, c1790, 40in (101.5cm) high.
$4,400–5,000 ⊞ REI

> Miller's is a price GUIDE
> not a price LIST

A George III mahogany corner cabinet, the astragal-glazed door enclosing later painted shelves, 32in (81.5cm) wide.
$1,750–2,200 ➤ Hal

A Continental mahogany bowfront standing corner cupboard, each single panel door enclosing a shelved interior, early 19thC, 84in (213.5cm) high.
$1,000–1,250 ➤ DOC

FURNITURE

A George IV mahogany corner cupboard, with a pair of doors each with three panels and centred by an oval, the lower section also enclosed by panelled doors, 41in (104cm) wide.
$5,800–6,500 ⚲ **L**

A Victorian mahogany standing corner cupboard, the upper section with mirror-backed shelving, the canted base with a glazed door over an arched alcove, 28in (71cm) wide.
$1,000–1,300 ⚲ **AH**

▶ **An Edwardian George III-style satinwood marquetry bowfront hanging corner cupboard,** the pair of glazed panelled doors enclosing shelves, faults, 25¼in (64cm) wide.
$1,500–1,750 ⚲ **S(S)**

<table>
<tr><td>**Cross Reference**
See Colour Review
(page 102)</td></tr>
</table>

A Continental mahogany standing corner cupboard, fitted with a top drawer, 19thC, 37in (94cm) wide.
$2,300–2,500 ⊞ **MTay**

An inlaid mahogany standing corner cupboard, the astragal-glazed door enclosing a series of shaped shelves, the base with a panelled door with a central shell inlay, late 19thC, 24in (61cm) wide.
$1,500–1,750 ⚲ **Mit**

A pair of Italian gilt and gesso corner cabinets, each with a scrolling foliate-patterned top above two open shelves, flanked by carved and beaded uprights, raised on mask feet, late 19thC, 22in (56cm) wide.
$2,300–2,600 ⚲ **NOA**

A pair of Italian green-painted corner cupboards, each with an onyx top and enclosed by a panelled door set with a coat-of-arms, 28in (71cm) wide.
$1,150–1,450 ⚲ **L**

An Edwardian satinwood corner cabinet, inlaid with banding and stringing, with a single astragal-glazed door enclosing lined shelves, with a platform undertier, 22in (56cm) wide.
$1,000–1,300 ⚲ **AG**

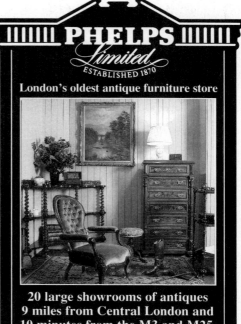

Display Cabinets

A Louis XV display cabinet, veneered in zebrawood, the glazed doors inlaid with pewter, with a red marble top, some veneers missing, glass replaced, stamped 'I. Dubois', 30¼in (77cm) wide.
$4,400–5,000 ⚑ S(Mon)
Jacques Dubois became a master cabinet-maker in France in 1742.

A George III inlaid mahogany display cabinet, the glazed doors enclosing adjustable shelves, the lower section with a pair of doors with later brass grilles enclosing shelves, c1800, 47in (119.5cm) wide.
$16,500–19,500 ⚑ S

A Dutch walnut and marquetry display cabinet, with square-paned shaped doors, the sides similarly inlaid with glazed panels, the base with two pairs of long drawers, c1800, 90½in (230cm) wide.
$9,500–11,500 ⚑ HOK

A Regency rosewood display cabinet, the superstructure with a mirrored back above a glass-topped frieze drawer, with a pair of glazed cupboard doors below and glazed sides, c1820, 38½in (98cm) wide.
$4,500–5,000 ⚑ Bon

A German Biedermeier satin birch display cabinet, with applied gilt-metal mounts, the frieze drawer above a glazed cupboard door and glazed sides enclosing glass shelves and a mirror back, above a drawer, restored, c1825, Berlin, 47¾in (121.5cm) wide.
$4,500–5,000 ⚑ S(S)

A burr-walnut side cabinet, by Gillows, with mirrored veneers and tulip-wood crossbanding, the glazed door flanked by turned, carved and gilded columns with gilt-bronze mounts, c1860, 36in (91.5cm) wide.
$6,500–7,250 ⊞ BERA

A Victorian mahogany serpentine display pier cabinet, with satinwood floral marquetry panels, the two glazed doors enclosing concave shelving, with side marquetry panels depicting classical maidens, 48in (122cm) wide.
$3,000–3,500 ⚑ AH

A Victorian Louis XIV-style boulle display cabinet, with ormolu mounts throughout and inlaid with engraved brass on a red-stained tortoiseshell ground, the upper section with a pair of glazed doors flanked by bowed glass panels and the base with a pair of oval panelled doors, 66in (167.5cm) wide.
$13,000–16,000 ⚑ HYD

A Victorian walnut display cabinet, decorated with inlaid boxwood scrolling motifs and stringing, a glazed panel door enclosing adjustable rosewood-lined shelves, flanked by applied gilt-metal motifs, 33½in (85cm) wide.
$800–950 ⚑ AG

A Victorian mahogany and marquetry display cabinet, with a pair of glazed and panelled doors with floral marquetry decoration and enclosing a series of plush-lined mahogany shelves, with plush-lined back and glazed sides, 39in (99cm) wide.
$2,300–2,900 ⚑ Mit

A Victorian walnut display cabinet, inlaid with boxwood lines and applied throughout with gilt-brass mouldings, 23¾in (60.5cm) wide.
$1,000–1,300 ⚑ Bea(E)

A Louis XV-style ormolu-mounted kingwood vitrine, with a glazed and floral-inlaid panelled door and sides, c1880, 36in (91.5cm) wide.
$3,000–3,500 ⚑ RPI

◄ A Victorian mahogany hanging display cabinet, the bevelled glazed door flanked by two tiers of bowfronted corner shelves with scroll-carved backs, 39in (99cm) wide.
$320–380 ⚲ PFK

A mahogany and marquetry display cabinet, inlaid throughout with floral sprays and applied with gilt-brass mounts, late 19thC, 39in (99cm) wide.
$2,300–2,900 ⚲ Bea(E)

An Italian neo-classical-style giltwood and polychromed vitrine, the doors with bevelled glass panels and flanked by a string of carved bell-flowers, the interior with two fabric-covered shelves with a mirrored back, c1900, 36in (91.5cm) wide.
$3,600–4,400 ⚲ NOA

An Edwardian inlaid mahogany side cabinet, the central door with a painted scene, flanked by astragal-glazed doors, 61in (155cm) wide.
$3,200–3,500 ⊞ RPh

◄ An Edwardian mahogany display cabinet, the central bowed section flanked by two doors with shaped glazing bars, with a lower panel inlaid with acanthus, C-scrolls and swags, 48in (122cm) wide.
$870–1,000 ⚲ M

An Edwardian inlaid mahogany china display cabinet, the frieze inlaid with neo-classical floral designs, the two astragal-glazed doors enclosing lined shelving, the whole inlaid throughout with boxwood stringing, 42in (106.5cm) wide.
$950–1,150 ⚲ GAK

An Edwardian mahogany display cabinet, the astragal-glazed door enclosing shelves, flanked by stiles decorated in coloured woods with ribbons and hanging baskets, with box and ebony chequered stringing, 33½in (85cm) wide.
$1,150–1,350 ⚲ ELR

An Edwardian mahogany and line-inlaid display cabinet, with a pair of glazed and part-panelled doors and sides, the interior fitted with three shelves, 42½in (108cm) wide.
$440–500 ⚲ LF

A black lacquered chinoiserie-style break-front display cabinet, with gilt decoration, the central fall-front enclosing a writing surface, drawer and pigeonholes, above a drawer and a pair of cupboard doors, flanked by glazed doors, 1930s, 52¾in (134cm) wide.
$580–720 ⚲ CGC

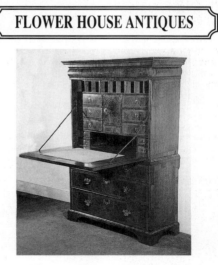

Music Cabinets

A Victorian figured and burr-walnut music cabinet, the part-glazed door enclosing shelves and drawers, flanked by spiral-turned columns, 26¾in (68cm) wide.
$1,000–1,250 ⚒ P(S)

A Victorian mahogany music cabinet, with low mirrored superstructure, the serpentine front with a relief-moulded panel door, enclosing a fitted interior, 24in (61cm) wide.
$580–720 ⚒ DOC

A Victorian mahogany music cabinet, the mirrored back with pierced fretwork frieze on turned columns, the single glazed door enclosing shaped shelves, 21in (53.5cm) wide.
$440–500 ⚒ AH

An Edwardian mahogany music cabinet, cross-banded in satinwood and line-inlaid, with mirrored superstructure over a glazed fall-front enclosing a velvet-lined compartment, with enclosed canterbury below, 48in (122cm) high.
$800–950 ⚒ G(T)

Secretaire Cabinets

A Regency pollarded oak and ebonized *escritoire*, the fall-front enclosing a fitted interior above two drawers, c1830, 60in (152.5cm) high.
$7,500–8,500 ⊞ APO

A French Empire-style figured mahogany *secrétaire à abattant*, with gilt-brass mouldings and acanthus leaf-capped capitals to the sides, with frieze drawer above a fall-front enclosing pigeonholes, small cupboard and six small drawers, with a cupboard below enclosed by a pair of panelled doors, early 19thC, 40in (101.5cm) wide.
$1,450–1,750 ⚒ CAG

A Scandinavian elm and ebonized fall-front secretaire cabinet, the frieze drawer with a fitted interior, above a fall-front flanked by female terminals, enclosing a baize-lined writing surface with a central niche surrounded by ten short drawers veneered in mulberry, above three long drawers, mid-19thC, 41in (104cm) wide.
$6,000–6,750 ⚒ S(NY)

An early Victorian mahogany secretaire cabinet, the panelled fall-front enclosing a fitted interior with drawers and pigeonholes, the sliding top enclosing a pull-out fitted writing drawer with a writing slope, flanked by lidded compartments, 44in (112cm) wide.
$4,500–5,500 ⚒ WW

A Louis Philippe *faux* bamboo fall-front *secrétaire à abattant*, with a frieze drawer above a fall-front simulating drawers, mid-19thC, 32in (81.5cm) wide.
$5,000–5,750 ⚒ SK

Writing furniture

Until the mid-17th century items of furniture used for writing were often extremely primitive. The first writing furniture specifically designed as such was derived from French and Italian furniture of the 16th century, and took the form of a fall-front cabinet on a chest or stand, with drawers, known today as a *secrétaire à abattant*. The *escritoire* was popular in Europe throughout the 18th and well into the 19th century.

An Edwardian mahogany and satinwood-banded travelling writing cabinet, by Maple & Co, the upper section enclosed by a hinged top and fall-front, the base with a frieze drawer, 33in (84cm) wide.
$4,300–5,000 ⚒ P(S)

Side Cabinets

A German marquetry side cabinet, the architectural façade inlaid with various woods and incorporating two doors fitted with engraved iron pulls and key escutcheons, the inside with engraved steel straps, locks and fitted with shelves, a long drawer below, late 16thC, 35½in (90cm) wide.
$5,500–6,500 ➤ **S(NY)**

▶ **A George IV mahogany demi-lune side cabinet,** the crossbanded top above eight drawers, one in an arched recess, flanked by curved panelled cupboard doors, 71in (180.5cm) wide.
$2,200–2,600 ➤ **CAG**

A Beromünster walnut and ebonized buffet, the upper section with two doors enclosing drawers and a single compartment and a two-door cupboard with various drawers inside, with three cupboards under, Swiss, c1745, 63in (160cm) wide.
$9,000–10,000 ➤ **S(Z)**

◀ **An American Federal mahogany commode,** with cockbeading to the single drawer and two cupboard doors, c1800, 29¾in (75.5cm) wide.
$4,600–5,000 ➤ **SK(B)**

A Dutch demi-lune commode, inlaid with boxwood and ebony, c1780, 35in (89cm) wide.
$23,000–26,500 ⊞ **REI**

An Austrian gilt-bronze-mounted mahogany *commode à portes*, with one long drawer over two doors, probably Vienna, c1800, 46in (117cm) wide.
$4,300–4,800 ➤ **S(Z)**

A Regency mahogany chiffonier, the gilt-metal galleried shelf raised on turned uprights above a cushion-fronted frieze drawer and a pair of brass grille doors flanked by split half-round columns, c1820, 36in (91.5cm) wide.
$3,200–3,800 ➤ **DMC**

A Victorian mahogany chiffonier, with shelf superstructure above drawers and cupboards, the right-hand drawer fitted for cutlery, 42in (106.5cm) wide.
$4,300–4,700 ⊞ **MTay**

Chiffoniers
A chiffonier is a low or side cabinet, with or without a drawer, with one or more shelves above. Original 18th-century pieces had solid doors which were often replaced in the 19th century with lattice or glass doors.

FURNITURE

A Dutch walnut and marquetry side cabinet, inlaid with shell medallions, floral sprays and ribbon-tied tasselled cords, with a frieze drawer above two panelled doors, early 19thC, 32¼in (82cm) wide.
$2,000–2,500 ⚒ Bea(E)

A Regency mahogany chiffonier, with later brass-inlaid galleried shelf superstructure, above a fitted frieze drawer with ebony decoration, above a pair of doors with silk panels and gilt-brass decoration, flanked by spiral columns, 39¾in (101cm) wide.
$1,300–1,450 ⚒ CMS

A William IV mahogany chiffonier, the base with two frieze drawers over two panelled cupboard doors, flanked by scrolling corbels, 38¼in (97cm) wide.
$2,600–3,200 ⚒ ELR

A William IV mahogany chiffonier, the scroll-carved back with fitted shelf, with a frieze drawer and cupboard below, flanked by foliage-carved pilasters, 32in (81.5cm) wide.
$1,200–1,450 ⚒ RBB

An early Victorian mahogany chiffonier, with carved back and shelf above a cushion-fronted drawer and two panelled doors, 38in (96.5cm) wide.
$1,200–1,450 ⚒ RPI

A Victorian serpentine burr-walnut side cabinet, inlaid with figured veneers and with ormolu mounts, c1850, 61in (155cm) wide.
$11,500–13,000 ⚒ BERA

A Victorian walnut side cabinet, the central glazed door flanked by half-round pilasters and bowed glazed ends, with gilt-metal mounts and all-over cross-banding, 46in (117cm) wide.
$3,300–4,000 ⚒ RBB

A Victorian figured walnut and marquetry-inlaid side cabinet, the half-veneered top above a glazed door enclosing lined shelves flanked by gilt-metal-mounted *faux* fluted half-columns, damaged, c1860, 33½in (85cm) wide.
$1,400–1,700 ⚒ Hal

A pair of ebonized and boulle side cabinets, applied throughout with foliate-cast gilt-brass mounts, each with a white-veined marble top and a panelled door inlaid with cut-brass and red tortoiseshell, mid-19thC, 33¾in (85.5cm) wide.
$3,600–4,300 ⚒ Bea(E)

▶ **An inverted breakfront satinwood and amboyna side cabinet,** the burr-veneered and ebony-strung top above a pair of glazed centre doors, flanked by marquetry-inlaid panelled doors, 19thC, 80in (203cm) wide.
$4,400–5,000 ⚒ DMC

A Victorian ebonized breakfront side cabinet, enclosed by three glazed doors, the whole outlined with satinwood banding and inlaid with arabesques, with gilt-metal mounts, 65in (165cm) wide.
$1,700–2,000 ⚒ DD

An American Renaissance revival rosewood side cabinet, bronze-mounted and marquetry-inlaid, the central door with bronze plaque depicting Cupid and Psyche with a satyr infant, 1860–70, 56in (142cm) wide.
$5,500–6,000 ⚒ SK

A late Victorian rosewood and marquetry side cabinet, by Collinson & Lock, the top with a pierced gilt-metal gallery above an inlaid panelled cupboard door, flanked by serpentine open shelves and reeded columns, with a drawer below, marked, c1890, 32¾in (83cm) wide.
$12,500–14,500 ◀ S
The firm of Collinson & Lock was established in London in the late 19th century, and their rapid rise to success was marked by their move in 1871 to extensive new premises in St Bride Street. In 1897 the firm was taken over by Gillows, but continued to produce furniture of this type for several years.

A Victorian mahogany serpentine chiffonier, the conforming lower section with single frieze drawer and two bead-edged panelled doors flanked by turned columns, 48in (122cm) wide.
$1,100–1,300 ⚒ LJ

A Victorian walnut and line-inlaid side cabinet, the single glazed door enclosing shelves, 30in (76cm) wide.
$1,000–1,250 ⚒ DOC

An Edwardian rosewood sideboard, the raised back with bevelled mirrors and open shelves, the base with a bowfront panelled door, decorated overall with inlaid ivory and boxwood scrolls, urns and foliate motifs, 60in (152.5cm) high.
$1,750–2,000 ⚒ AG

◀ **An Empire revival burr-walnut side cabinet,** with marble top above three drawers and four doors with foliate, figural and mask gilt-bronze mounts, late 19thC, 87in (221cm) wide.
$10,500–11,500 ⚒ SK

A Victorian mahogany parlour cabinet, the upper section with a glazed door enclosing shelving, flanked on either side by mirror-backed shelving, the base with a bowed centre with a frieze drawer over a cupboard door carved with putti, flanked on either side by a glazed cupboard door, 52½in (133.5cm) wide.
$2,400–2,900 ⚒ AH

A late Victorian ebonized and amboyna gilt-metal-mounted side cabinet, the back with jasper-ware plaque-inset pediment, above a shelf with a mirror behind, the base with a glazed cupboard flanked by reeded Corinthian pilasters, the frieze with a similar jasper-ware plaque, 32in (81.5cm) wide.
$580–720 ⚒ Bri

A Dutch mahogany and marquetry-inlaid side cabinet, with a fitted shaped frieze drawer above two doors, 19thC, 42in (106.5cm) wide.
$2,900–3,200 ⚒ G(B)

FURNITURE

Cabinets-on-Stands

A William and Mary mahogany and yew wood cabinet-on-stand, the doors inlaid with oval panels of marquetry and flowers, enclosing an oyster walnut-veneered interior fitted with an arrangement of drawers around a central cupboard door with floral marquetry-inlaid reserve, enclosing three further drawers, the George III mahogany and yew wood stand fitted with a single frieze drawer, 33½in (85cm) wide.
$1,750–2,000 ↗ **P(S)**

A Dutch Colonial hard-wood cabinet-on-stand, enclosed by a pair of panelled doors, the stand fitted with a drawer, all set with brass bosses and mounts, mid-18thC, 25in (63.5cm) wide.
$870–1,000 ↗ **L**

A George III-style ebonized and parcel-gilt chinoiserie cabinet-on-stand, the doors enclosing shelves, above a frieze drawer, c1930, 28¼in (72cm) wide.
$540–580 ↗ **P(Ba)**

> **Cross Reference**
> See Colour Review
> (page 103)

Table Cabinets

A Silesian brass-mounted and ivory-inlaid wood casket, the top engraved with a group of St Michael and the Devil above a double-headed eagle incorporating the date '1632' and enclosing ten drawers, the interior of the doors decorated with scenes of the Virgin and the Crucifixion, doors with key, losses and repair, 22½in (57cm) wide.
$20,000–23,000 ↗ **S(NY)**

A south German marquetry cabinet, the doors decorated with birds and enclosing 16 drawers, possibly Upper Rhine, c1740, 22½in (57cm) wide.
$1,450–1,600 ↗ **S(Z)**

A George III mahogany table cabinet, enclosing 12 drawers around a central cupboard, with carrying handles, 18thC, 16in (40.5cm) high.
$1,000–1,250 ↗ **RPh**

An Italian penwork table/jewellery cabinet, the hinged cover above two hinged doors enclosing two short drawers and two long drawers with compartmented tray above, all decorated in black and gilt with mythological grotesques, dated '1836', 20in (51cm) wide.
$1,350–1,600 ↗ **HAM**

A Regency gilt-metal-mounted rosewood collector's cabinet, the panelled doors enclosing 26 drawers, on later grain-painted scrolled feet, lacking two drawers, early 19thC, 21½in (54.5cm) wide.
$6,500–7,250 ↗ **S(NY)**

A Victorian parquetry-banded walnut table cabinet, the doors with geometric inlay and enclosing three drawers, 11½in (29cm) wide.
$175–200 ↗ **Bri**

▶ **An oak cigar box,** with three drawers, c1880, 12in (30.5cm) wide.
$430–470 ⊞ **MB**

Canterburies

A George III mahogany canterbury, with four divisions above a frieze drawer, 18½in (47cm) wide.
$1,750–2,000 ↗ CAG

A mahogany canterbury, with four divisions and a hinged handle, and a frieze drawer, c1810, 18in (45.5cm) wide.
$4,300–5,000 ⊞ RL

A George III mahogany canterbury, with three divisions above a frieze drawer, on original turned legs, 20in (51cm) high.
$5,000–5,600 ⊞ REI

A mahogany canterbury, the frieze drawer with lion-mask handles, c1835, 21in (53.5cm) high.
$3,000–3,300 ⊞ APO

History of canterburies

Canterburies, originally designed for storing sheet music but also used as plate holders to stand by the supper table, first appeared in England in the latter part of George III's reign and were predominantly made from mahogany and rosewood. Sheraton attributed their name to the Archbishop of Canterbury who commissioned such pieces.

Canterburies were made in other timbers from c1825 such as bird's-eye maple, and walnut during the Victorian period, when designs became more ornate. The relatively large number of 19th-century versions now on the market are a consequence of the Victorian passion for the piano.

A William IV rosewood canterbury, with shaped and carved dividers over a single drawer, c1830, 22in (56cm) wide.
$3,600–4,000 ⊞ BERA

A William IV mahogany music canterbury, the divisions with turned hand grips and centred with carved lyres, the front and back with scrolling carving and ebonized bud finials over a veneered frieze drawer, 19¾in (50cm) wide.
$3,000–3,500 ↗ WW

A William IV rosewood canterbury, the two-part hinged top opening to a well, each solid side mounted with half spindles, above a drawer and with beaded borders, mid-19thC, 25in (63.5cm) wide.
$9,800–11,800 ↗ S(NY)

A William IV rosewood canterbury, the three divisions with carved scroll motifs, above a frieze drawer, 20in (51cm) wide.
$1,800–2,200 ↗ MCA

A Victorian rosewood-veneered music canterbury, with pierced carved panels above the shaped base, and a frieze drawer, 30in (76cm) wide.
$2,200–2,600 ↗ Mit

A Victorian burr-walnut canterbury, with pierced scroll-carved supports and panels, and a frieze drawer below, 24in (61cm) wide.
$1,750–2,000 ↗ LJ

A mahogany canterbury, with three divisions and a frieze drawer, on ring-turned legs, 19thC, 19in (48.5cm) wide.
$725–875 ↗ LF

A Victorian walnut and satinwood-banded canterbury, with turned spindle divisions above an apron drawer, 23in (58.5cm) wide.
$850–1,000 ↗ P(Ba)

◀ **A late Victorian inlaid walnut canterbury whatnot,** with brass gallery, the base with a glazed door enclosing shelves, 24in (61cm) wide.
$650–800 ↗ MEA

A Victorian walnut canterbury, with pierced scroll divisions and turned fluted column supports, and bowfronted undertier fitted with a drawer, 30in (76cm) wide.
$3,200–4,000 ↗ RBB

FURNITURE

Open Armchairs

A carved walnut armchair, the foliate- and shell-carved top rail above a caned back with punched strapwork design to the borders, with leaf-carved and scrolled arms and upholstered seat, late 17thC.
$1,300–1,600 ⚲ DMC

A pair of Louis XV painted beechwood *fauteuils,* the moulded aprons and shield-shaped backs with flower-head cresting, in need of repair, 18thC.
$2,000–2,300 ⚲ HOK

A George IV mahogany elbow chair, the top rail with a gadroon crest and leaf-carved ends above an open scroll and shell horizontal bar, the drop-in seat covered in red fabric.
$500–600 ⚲ WW

A Spanish carved walnut armchair, upholstered in green and beige fabric, c1690.
$3,600–4,000 ⊞ DeG

A mahogany armchair, with downswept carved arms, upholstered in gold-coloured fabric, c1780.
$3,600–4,300 ⊞ RL

A Hepplewhite mahogany shield-back armchair, with Prince of Wales splat, above a gold-coloured stuff-over seat, c1780.
$4,000–4,600 ⊞ REI

Miller's Compares

I. A mahogany open armchair, the shaped scrolled top rail above a vase-shaped splat and drop-in seat, early 18thC.
$1,800–2,200 ⚲ P

II. A mahogany open armchair, the shaped top rail above a vase-shaped splat and drop-in seat, joined by block and reel-turned stretchers, one spandrel missing, early 18thC.
$1,000–1,150 ⚲ P

Although these two chairs are of a similar date and style, the superior quality of Item I can be seen in a number of its features. The grain and colour of Item I, for instance, are particularly attractive, and the top rail is far more sensuously carved, with scrolls above the splat, which is also of a more interesting shape than that of Item II. The C-scrolls and the extra shaping of the front legs of Item I are likely to have added to its appeal, and the more elegant proportions of this piece were probably regarded as more desirable than the broader, more squat appearance of Item II with its functional H-stretcher.

A George III mahogany lodge chair, the top rail with an adjustable headrest decorated with Masonic emblems over three reeded vertical splats, above a stuff-over serpentine seat.
$4,300–5,000 ⚲ CGC

A pair of Regency black and gilt-painted beech open armchairs, the turned and pierced triple rail backs painted with putti *en grisaille* and polychrome baskets of flowers, with caned seats, restored.
$5,000–5,800 ⚲ DN

◄ **A pair of German fruit-wood open armchairs,** each with pierced lyre-shaped splat, above a stuff-over seat, restored, early 19thC.
$2,300–2,900 ⚲ Bon

► **A George IV mahogany-framed gentleman's armchair,** with scroll arms, leather-upholstered back, seat and arms, on turned tapering front supports.
$1,800–2,300 ⚲ RBB

A William IV rosewood armchair, with stuff-over seat, on turned supports.
$400–470 ➤ **WilP**

An early Victorian rosewood armchair, with carved panel back and cabriole legs, upholstered in red and gold fabric, with buttoned back and stuff-over seat, c1850.
$2,300–2,500 ⊞ **BERA**

A pair of Victorian walnut open armchairs, carved with flowers, leaves and acanthus, c1850.
$3,600–4,000 ⊞ **NAW**

A set of six Victorian Gothic carved oak armchairs, each handrest individually carved with a fruit, the stuff-over seat upholstered in velvet fabric, c1850.
$3,600–4,000 ⊞ **MTay**

A Victorian walnut armchair, with buttoned open horseshoe back and seat, the arms and legs carved with foliage.
$360–430 ➤ **L**

A walnut open armchair, upholstered in red leather, on cabriole legs, c1860.
$1,300–1,450 ⊞ **GBr**

An American Gothic revival carved rosewood armchair, with pierced carved back and stuff-over seat, faults, possibly New York, 1850–60.
$3,600–4,000 ➤ **SK(B)**

A Victorian rosewood-framed open armchair, the buttoned back with flowerhead cresting, the padded outscrolled arms on S-supports, upholstered in gold floral fabric.
$1,200-1,450 ➤ **Bea(E)**

A Victorian button-backed walnut armchair, with foliate-carved frame, upholstered in claret-coloured fabric.
$950–1,150 ➤ **DA**

A pair of Regency-style mahogany armchairs, the drop-in seats covered in green fabric with central floral motif, c1880.
$4,000–5,000 ⊞ **CAT**

A set of six Hepplewhite-style mahogany elbow chairs, each with an oval wheel back enclosing a sinuous stylized foliate cluster, with upholstered seats, 19thC.
$5,800–7,200 ➤ **TRL**

◄ **A Victorian armchair,** the carved back panel commemorating the new century, '1900' within 'VR'.
$800–880 ⊞ **ANO**

A Louis XVI-style stained beechwood *fauteuil en cabriolet*, the ribbon-moulded top rail with floral cresting, over caned back and seat, late 19thC.
$1,400–1,600 ➤ **NOA**

A walnut and leather folding campaign chair, with buttoned brown leather back and seat, scroll arms and adjustable back, on folding supports with brass mounts, late 19thC.
$2,900–3,200 ➤ **S(NY)**

► **A George III-style satinwood and painted armchair,** with pierced splat and drapery motif cresting, above a caned seat with a trellis frieze, c1910.
$1,150–1,300 ➤ **S(S)**

FURNITURE

Upholstered Armchairs

A Scottish George III mahogany armchair, upholstered in tan leather outlined with brass studs.
$3,600–4,000 ⚒ P(Ed)

A mahogany wing armchair, with a reeded and panelled top rail and frieze, the padded arms with reptile mask terminals, upholstered in green fabric, possibly Continental, early 19thC.
$9,500–11,500 ⚒ S

A William IV rosewood-framed armchair, with upholstered back, seat and scroll arm supports, on lotus-carved front legs.
$725–875 ⚒ CGC

A Victorian mahogany desk chair, by Gillows, upholstered in burgundy red leather, c1880.
$3,000–3,500 ⚒ Bon

A Victorian mahogany-framed spoon-back armchair, with red moquette buttoned-back upholstery.
$875–1,000 ⚒ JBe

A pair of French walnut *fauteuils*, the shaped backs, scroll arms and stuff-over seats covered in pink velvet fabric, late 19thC.
$3,600–4,000 ⚒ S(S)

A pair of French Empire-style mahogany armchairs, the padded backs and loose cushion seats covered in gold wreath-patterned fabric, late 19thC.
$1,600–1,750 ⚒ S(S)

▶ **A pair of buttoned hide wing armchairs,** on mahogany cabriole legs early 20thC.
$6,500–8,000 ⚒ DMC

A Regency mahogany armchair, with upholstered back, arms and seat above a scrolled and reeded show-wood front.
$1,000–1,250 ⚒ CGC

A Victorian button-back armchair, upholstered and with a sprung seat, with turned front legs, on original brass castors.
$475–550 ⚒ WW

A late Victorian easy armchair, by Howard & Sons, Berners Street, London, with deeply upholstered back, arms and seat, on ring-turned legs, stamped mark.
$1,300–1,600 ⚒ CGC

A George III-style mahogany armchair, the stuff-over back, arms and seat upholstered in yellow embossed material, on mahogany square legs, 19thC.
$580–720 ⚒ Mit

A Victorian mahogany-framed chair, the deeply buttoned back within a moulded and scrolled frame, upholstered in grey-green dralon.
$1,000–1,250 ⚒ TEN

A pair of Edwardian mahogany club armchairs, each upholstered in brown hide, distressed, c1900.
$800–950 ⚒ Hal

A beech-legged tub armchair, with scalloped back, with later pink fabric upholstery, early 20thC.
$430–500 ⚒ PFK

Bergère Chairs

A Regency mahogany bergère, with curved caned back and scrolled arms, the seat with a squab cushion.
$3,600–4,000 ➢ P

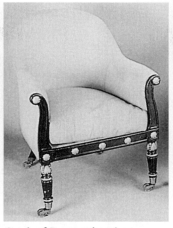

A pair of Regency bergères, later-painted in black and gilt, upholstered in yellow fabric.
$6,500–8,000 ➢ Bon(C)

A George IV carved mahogany bergère, with a caned seat and arms and lotus leaf-carved arm terminals above a drop-in seat.
$2,300–2,600 ➢ P

A George IV mahogany-framed bergère, with scroll arm terminals, now upholstered in red cloth, formerly cane panelled.
$1,000–1,300 ➢ CAG

A white-painted and parcel-gilt bergère, with caned back and sides, padded arms and squab cushion, with later decoration, mid-19thC.
$1,300–1,600 ➢ S

A Louis XV-style beech *fauteuil de bureau*, the top rail with floral cresting, the scroll arms continuing to a bowed seat frame, covered in brown leather, mid-19thC.
$2,000–2,300 ➢ NOA

A late Victorian stained satin-wood and painted bergère, by Howard & Sons, Berners Street, London, the back with an oval caned panel, the centre painted with a young girl with a puppy, with caned seat and arms, underside stamped with maker's name and number.
$2,200–2,600 ➢ CAG

A pair of late Victorian mahogany bergères, the frames inlaid and strung with satinwood, the upholstered backs, sides and seats covered in mustard fabric.
$2,300–2,900 ➢ CGC

A pair of Directoire-style beech-wood bergères, each with a caned back and seat, on turned legs headed by lozenges and anthemia, early 20thC.
$3,500–4,000 ➢ NOA

FURNITURE

Children's Chairs

A child's chair, with caned back and seat, early 19thC.
$200–230 ⊞ MLu

A child's mahogany-framed bergère-style high chair, with a caned back and sides, on a later stand, lacking restraint bar and footrest, early 19thC.
$580–720 ⚹ Bea(E)

A child's mahogany chair, on a table stand, with turned spindles, over an upholstered drop-in seat, c1810.
$870–1,000 ⊞ GBr

A child's Regency mahogany armchair, with a tapestry-covered stuff-over seat.
$430–500 ⊞ GKe

> Miller's is a price GUIDE not a price LIST

A child's early Victorian rosewood open armchair, with upholstered arms and seat.
$500–580 ⚹ WilP

▶ **A child's Louis XVI-style giltwood** *fauteuil*, with a padded back panel and stuff-over seat, the padded outcurved arms with scroll terminals, on turned, tapered and fluted legs headed with paterae, 19thC.
$900–1,000 ⚹ SLN

A child's late Victorian bentwood and embossed plywood rocking chair, faults, c1900.
$260–300 ⊞ NAW

Corner Chairs

An American Queen Anne walnut roundabout chair, the arms on vase- and ring-turned supports flanking two vasiform splats, faults, Boston, 1740–60.
$7,250–8,000 ⚹ SK(B)

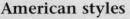

An early George III mahogany corner chair, with pierced splats and turned columns over a drop-in upholstered seat.
$1,200–1,450 ⚹ HYD

A William IV calamander corner armchair, with padded sides and seat, on lappet-carved turned legs.
$870–1,000 ⚹ DN

An Edwardian mahogany corner chair, crossbanded with satinwood and with boxwood stringing, some damage.
$450–550 ⚹ MAR

◀ **A pair of Edwardian mahogany corner chairs,** crossbanded in satinwood and with boxwood and ebony stringing, the pierced horizontal splats with inlaid paterae.
$430–500 ⚹ HAM

American styles

American furniture termed, for example, 'Queen Anne' does not necessarily date from the actual period of Queen Anne. This is because the latest fashions took about 20 years to cross the Atlantic, but the style is nevertheless of that period.

FURNITURE

Dining Chairs

A set of five George I walnut chairs, with pierced splat backs above drop-in seats, c1720.
$6,000–7,000 ⊞ APO

A pair of walnut dining chairs, with solid vase-shaped splat backs and drop-in floral needlework seats, restored, early 18thC.
$3,600–4,000 ⟋ P(S)

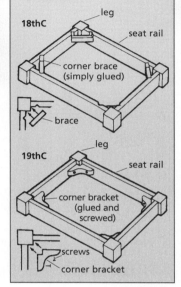

A set of four George III mahogany dining chairs, with pierced, entwined and scrolled splat backs and drop-in seats.
$1,000–1,250 ⟋ P(S)

▶ **A set of six George III mahogany dining chairs,** with pierced interlaced Gothic splats headed by carved foliate scrolls, above drop-in seats.
$4,300–5,000 ⟋ L

◀ **An early George III mahogany dining chair,** with a pierced interlaced splat above a drop-in seat.
$750–850 ⟋ P

A set of eight Irish provincial mahogany dining chairs, including two open armchairs, each with pierced interlaced splats, the seats now upholstered with close-studded imitation leather, 18thC.
$3,500–4,000 ⟋ HOK

FURNITURE

A set of eight late George III mahogany dining chairs, including two elbow chairs, with fluted and foliate-carved splats over drop-in seats.
$2,500–3,000 ⚹ **P(Ba)**

A set of five Regency mahogany dining chairs, including one armchair, with reeded X-shaped backs and close-studded leatherette stuff-over seats.
$1,800–2,200 ⚹ **S(S)**

A set of six Regency simulated rosewood dining chairs, including two open armchairs, with caned seats, one damaged, c1815.
$5,800–6,500 ⊞ **APO**

A set of six Regency mahogany dining chairs, with stuff-over seats upholstered in brown and beige fabric, c1815.
$3,600–4,400 ⊞ **MTay**

A set of four carved mahogany dining chairs, each inlaid with brass, early 19thC.
$580–720 ⚹ **WilP**

A set of four Regency rosewood dining chairs, the rosette- and acanthus-carved top rails above conforming horizontal tablet splats, the caned seats with squab cushions.
$850–1,000 ⚹ **CGC**

A set of four Regency stained beech dining chairs, with embossed brass mounts and caned seats.
$450–550 ⚹ **WilP**

A set of ten rosewood and simulated rosewood dining chairs, with brass inlay, including two armchairs, with caned seats and squab cushions upholstered with red fabric, c1820.
$18,000–21,500 ⊞ **GKe**

A set of eight Regency mahogany dining chairs, including two open armchairs, with red hide seats, c1820.
$11,500–13,000 ⊞ **APO**

A set of six Regency mahogany dining chairs, the pierced S-shaped splats centred by paterae, upholstered with red striped fabric.
$4,000–4,400 ⚹ **P**

A pair of Regency mahogany dining chairs, the pierced horizontal splats carved with lion-mask roundels above stuff-over seats.
$360–440 ⚹ **CGC**

◄ **A set of six Scottish Regency mahogany dining chairs,** including two elbow chairs, the reeded top rail carved with leaves, the pierced horizontal splats carved with thistles, above drop-in seats.
$5,800–7,200 ⚹ **P(Ed)**

A set of twelve Irish Sheraton-style inlaid-mahogany dining chairs, including two open armchairs, the bowed crest rails inlaid with lozenges, the stuff-over seats upholstered in faded hide, 19thC.
$8,000–9,500 ⚹ **HOK**

FURNITURE

A set of eight George IV mahogany
dining chairs, including two elbow
chairs, the twin mid-rails with carved
dividers above drop-in upholstered seats.
$4,400–5,000 ✗ CMS

A set of nine William IV mahogany
dining chairs, including one carver,
each with centre rail with stylized
wheatsheaf carving between scrolls,
above drop-in seats.
$4,000–4,600 ✗ TRL

A set of four Scottish early
Victorian rosewood dining chairs,
the top rails with foliate roundels
above horizontal pierced splats with
corresponding roundels, above gros-
point floral tapestry drop-in seats.
$870–1,000 ✗ P(Ed)

A set of six Victorian walnut
balloon-back dining chairs, with
scrolled bar backs and stuff-over seats.
$650–800 ✗ AH

A set of five south German Biedermeier walnut chairs, the curved top
rails decorated with palmettes, above
stuff-over seats upholstered in blue
fabric, early 19thC.
$5,000–5,500 ✗ S(Z)

A set of six William IV mahogany
dining chairs, with acanthus-carved
horizontal splats and stuff-over seats.
$1,800–2,200 ✗ CGC

A set of six Victorian mahogany
compressed balloon-back dining
chairs, with buttoned backs and
stuff-over seats.
$1,000–1,300 ✗ DMC

A set of six Victorian mahogany
balloon-back dining chairs, with
stuff-over seats.
$1,300–1,600 ✗ TRL

A set of five William IV Gothic-
style carved oak dining chairs,
the pierced tracery backs flanked by
blind tracery-moulded uprights with
crocketed spire finials, the stuff-over
seats with studded hide upholstery.
$20,000–23,000 ✗ S

A set of six early Victorian
mahogany dining chairs, including
two carvers, with foliate and ring-
moulded centre rails.
$2,200–2,600 ✗ GAK

A set of twelve Victorian
mahogany dining chairs, the
upholstered backs in a moulded
frame with central vine and grape
cartouche, above stuff-over seats.
$6,500–8,000 ✗ P(Ed)

A pair of Victorian mahogany
dining chairs, the stuff-over seats
upholstered in red fabric, c1870.
$430–500 ⊞ AnSh

A set of six Victorian mahogany balloon-back dining chairs, the buttoned red leather backs above conforming stuff-over seats.
$1,600–1,900 ➹ **Bri**

A set of six Victorian mahogany spoon-back dining chairs, each with a pierced interlaced splat back above a hide seat.
$1,750–2,000 ➹ **MEA**

◀ **A set of eight Victorian mahogany dining chairs,** with green leather-covered stuff-over seats.
$1,750–2,000 ➹ **JH**

A set of six Victorian mahogany dining chairs, each with an open scrolled bar splat over a later upholstered pink damask seat, c1850.
$1,300–1,600 ➹ **Hal**

A set of six Hepplewhite-style mahogany dining chairs, including two open armchairs, with pierced splat backs and tapestry-upholstered drop-in seats, 19thC.
$1,250–1,450 ➹ **EH**

A pair of George I-style carved giltwood dining chairs, with foliate-carved vase-shaped splats centred by painted panels depicting cherubs, the stuff-over seats covered in foliate-patterned tapestry fabric, faults, labelled G. Jetley, London, late 19thC.
$11,500–13,000 ➹ **S(S)**
G. Jetley traded from South Audley Street in Mayfair. The company handled some of the finest furniture available in England at that time.

A set of six Renaissance revival carved oak dining chairs, including two armchairs, each with a top rail centred by a cartouche flanked by carved dolphins, the backs, arms and stuff-over seats upholstered in green floral fabric, late 19thC.
$3,200–3,600 ➹ **NOA**

A set of six Victorian mahogany dining chairs, with upholstered backs and stuff-over seats, c1865.
$2,000–2,300 ⊞ **MTay**

A set of twelve George III-style mahogany dining chairs, including two armchairs, the splats shaped as four moulded vertical bars hung with festoons and trails of leaves pendant from rings, the bowfronted drop-in seats covered in oyster moiré fabric, early 20thC.
$4,350–4,700 ➹ **HAM**

A set of eight Edwardian Sheraton-style mahogany dining chairs, including two elbow chairs, inlaid with stringing, with pierced trellis splats and padded seats.
$2,000–2,300 ➹ **AH**

A set of eight barley-twist oak dining chairs, upholstered in brown and green leaf-patterned fabric, 1910.
$3,000–3,400 ⊞ **MTay**

Hall Chairs

A mahogany hall chair, with carved and pierced back panel, mid-18thC.
$1,400–1,600 ✗ TMA

A mahogany hall chair, the back in the shape of a reeded patera centred with armorials, c1790.
$1,800–2,200 ✗ HOK
The armorials are those of Anderson, Co Antrim.

A pair of Regency mahogany hall chairs, the shield-shaped backs with circular painted armorial panels, restored.
$4,000–4,600 ✗ P(Ba)

A pair of early Victorian mahogany hall chairs, with scroll-shaped pierced backs and turned front legs.
$725–875 ✗ JAd

A set of nine Victorian oak hall chairs, with cabriole legs, c1850.
$3,200–3,600 ⊞ GKe

◄ A pair of mid-Victorian mahogany hall chairs, with cartouche-shaped carved backs.
$360–430 ✗ WL

A set of six Italian walnut hall chairs, inlaid overall with trailing foliage and paterae, c1850.
$5,200–5,800 ✗ S(S)

A pair of Victorian oak hall chairs, with floral inlaid panels.
$450–550 ✗ WilP

A mid-Victorian carved mahogany hall chair, with hinged seat and castors.
$580–650 ⊞ RPh

◄ A set of five Victorian George II-style oak hall chairs, each with shaped backs painted with heraldic beasts, the dished seats on trestle end supports with painted cyphers.
$4,000–4,600 ✗ S(S)

FURNITURE

Library Chairs

A Regency mahogany metamorphic library armchair, in the style of Morgan & Sanders, the caned back and seat hinged to form a set of library steps, with inset leather treads and squab cushion.
$13,000–16,000 ⚶ S
Morgan & Sanders were specialists in the manufacture of metamorphic furniture of this kind and held the patent for what was known as the Patent Metamorphic Library Chair.

A mahogany metamorphic library chair, in the style of Morgan & Sanders, upholstered in old silk, the seat hinged to form a set of library steps with inset tooled green leather treads, early 19thC.
$8,000–9,500 ⚶ HOK

A Victorian light oak metamorphic library chair, the seat hinged to form a set of steps, c1870.
$500–550 ⊞ NAW

A Victorian mahogany metamorphic library chair, the trapezoidal seat hinged to form a set of library steps, the legs joined by a shelf, mid-19thC.
$1,800–2,200 ⚶ NOA

► **A pair of Victorian Gothic revival oak library chairs,** the castellated top rails above Gothic tracery backs and moulded open arm supports, the aprons applied with rosette motifs and with foliate-carved corner brackets.
$4,000–4,600 ⚶ CGC

An oak-framed library/ reading chair, the back, arms and seat upholstered in leather, one arm with a lacquered-brass adjustable extension with a circular dished tray, late 19thC.
$725–875 ⚶ P(Ed)

◄ **An oak library chair,** the back and stuff-over seat upholstered in imitation leather, 1880.
$550–600 ⊞ CYA

► **A Victorian mahogany library armchair,** the later-upholstered buttoned back and stuff-over bowed seat flanked by padded arms above turned spindle supports, on turned legs, restored, c1880.
$360–440 ⚶ Hal

Nursing Chairs

A mid-Victorian nursing chair, the coloured woolwork back panel and seat decorated with exotic birds and flowers.
$450–550 ⚶ Hal

A Victorian walnut-framed nursing chair, the foliate-carved top rail above an upholstered buttoned-back and serpentine stuff-over seat.
$400–460 ⚶ CGC

A Victorian mahogany nursing chair, the padded back with floral-carved cresting over a bowfronted stuff-over seat.
$180–230 ⚶ P(Ba)

A Victorian walnut nursing chair, upholstered in a floral woolwork tapestry.
$580–720 ⚶ DA

Cross Reference
See Colour Review
(page 106)

Salon Chairs

A set of five French Empire figured mahogany tub-back salon chairs, with shaped splat backs above drop-in seats, early 19thC.
$725–875 ✒ RTo

A set of four Victorian mahogany salon chairs, each with carved apron, knee and crest, with green upholstered backs and seats.
$3,200–3,500 ⊞ MTay

A set of six mid-Victorian walnut and marquetry salon chairs, the shaped pierced backs with solid burr-walnut and tulipwood crossbanded splats, each inlaid with cartouches and two parakeets on a floral spray, above a buttoned seat upholstered in green.
$6,500–8,000 ✒ P

◄ **A pair of Victorian ebonized salon chairs,** inlaid with mother-of-pearl and floral work, heightened with gilt, with caned seats.
$320–360 ✒ LJ

A set of three Victorian salon chairs, by A. Blain, Liverpool, with scroll-carved open backs, the backrests and stuff-over seats upholstered in pink fabric, marked.
$300–350 ✒ PFK

Side Chairs

An American Queen Anne maple side chair, the yoked top rail over a vase-shaped splat, above a stuff-over balloon seat, Massachusetts, 1740–60.
$4,600–5,000 ✒ SK(B)

A pair of Queen Anne walnut side chairs, with tapestry-covered seats, c1710.
$8,400–9,400 ⊞ REI

A pair of Queen Anne inlaid walnut side chairs, the central vase-shaped splat with an inlaid foliate and strapwork panel, above upholstered drop-in seats, c1710.
$8,700–10,000 ✒ S

◄ **A Louis XV green-painted *petite chaise*,** the back with a carved floral crest and stuffed panel above a sprung seat and carved apron, c1760.
$1,300–1,600 ✒ Bon

An American painted maple side chair, the carved yoke crest on a vase-shaped splat flanked by moulded raked stiles above a stuff-over seat, Portsmouth, New Hampshire, 1735–50.
$4,000–4,600 ✒ SK(B)

► **A pair of Italian rococo walnut side chairs,** with foliate-carved frames and drop-in seats, mid-18thC.
$1,400–1,600 ✒ SK

FURNITURE

A set of six Biedermeier birch and mahogany side chairs, the splats centrally decorated with a demi-lune with a neo-classical candelabra, above bowfronted drop-in seats, mid 19thC.
$6,500–8,000 ⚘ S(NY)

A pair of light golden ash side chairs, with caned backs and seats, 19thC.
$1,000–1,300 ⚘ DD

A set of six early Victorian rosewood side chairs, the open balloon backs with foliage spray scroll carving, above stuff-over sprung seats.
$2,000–2,200 ⚘ WW

A Dutch walnut and marquetry side chair, the vasiform splat inlaid with birds, flowers, shell and urn, above a serpentine stuff-over upholstered seat, 19thC.
$400–460 ⚘ HYD

A set of four Victorian oak chairs, in the style of Alfred Waterhouse, the pierced top rails with spindle-turned decoration and chip-carved roundels, above padded backs and seats, c1880.
$1,450–1,600 ⚘ S

Alfred Waterhouse (1830–1905), Gothic revivalist architect and designer, set up his practice in Manchester in 1853, moving to London some eight years later. His many designs include the Manchester Assizes, the Natural History Museum, Reading Town Hall, Balliol College, Oxford, Caius and Pembroke colleges, Cambridge, and many other educational buildings. His extensive use of red brick gave rise to the term 'red brick universities'.

A pair of French fruitwood side chairs, the stuff-over buttoned seats upholstered in green fabric, c1895.
$1,750–2,000 ⊞ RL

Miscellaneous Chairs

◀ **A mid-Victorian walnut-framed lady's chair,** the carved shaped back with a floral needlework panel above a similar stuff-over seat.
$580–720 ⚘ TMA

A George III green-painted sedan chair, with a glazed panelled door enclosing a seat and plush-lined interior, the side stencilled 'P. B. Pollington, Sedan Chair Makers and Licensee, Wadhurst', c1800, 34in (86.4cm) high.
$2,900–3,200 ⚘ S(S)

▶ **A Victorian carved walnut parlour chair,** the buttoned back and stuff-over seat upholstered in red fabric.
$800–875 ⚘ RPh

A Victorian rosewood-framed prie-dieu chair, the back and seat upholstered with tapestry, on French cabriole supports.
$230–290 ⚘ WilP

A near pair of papier mâché chairs, by Jennens & Bettridge, in black with gold and green decoration, signed and dated, 1844.
$4,400–4,800 ⊞ CRU
Papier mâché was developed and patented by Birmingham furniture maker Henry Clay from 1772 – Jennens & Bettridge obtained their Patent in 1815.

Chaises Longues & Daybeds

FURNITURE

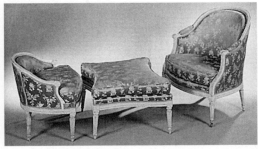

A Louis XVI white-painted *duchesse brisée*, by Chartier, each piece on tapered fluted legs headed by paterae, with loose cushions, upholstered in pink damask fabric, signed, late 18thC, 76¾in (195cm) long.
$6,500–7,000 S(Am)

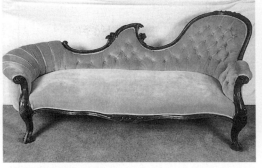

A Victorian carved walnut chaise longue, on cabriole legs, upholstered in pink velvet fabric, c1860, 76in (193cm) long.
$2,300–2,500 MTay

A Victorian walnut chaise longue, with foliate-scrolled carved frame and a buttoned back, 62in (157.5cm) long.
$700–850 L

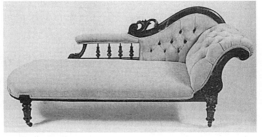

A Victorian mahogany chaise longue, the back moulded with scrolls and foliage and deeply buttoned, upholstered in beige fabric, 73in (185.5cm) long.
$650–800 GAK

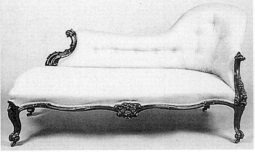

A Victorian rosewood chaise longue, the S-scroll supports and arms capped with leaves and carved with trails of flowers and foliage, the serpentine show frame centred by pairs of roses and scrolls, the back and seat covered in pink brocade fabric, 72½in (184cm) long.
$1,200–1,400 HAM

A French Charles X-style mahogany *recamier*, the overscroll backrest and foot with swan's head terminals, the rails on gilt-bronze eagle's heads, and with pierced decorative mounts, mid-19thC, 73½in (186.5cm) long.
$7,250–8,000 SLN

A Victorian carved walnut chaise longue, on cabriole legs, upholstered in red velvet, c1860, 58in (147.5cm) long.
$3,600–4,000 MTay

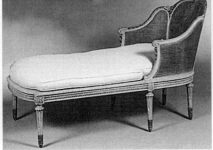

A Louis XVI-style *grisaille* and cream-painted beechwood chaise longue, with a caned back and seat, the loose cushion upholstered in beige fabric, late 19thC, 62in (157.5cm) long.
$2,200–2,600 NOA

A Colonial hardwood folding day bed, the seat with a handle lifting out three more sections, lacking screw-in legs, late 19thC, 42½in (108cm) long.
$2,500–3,000 P

FURNITURE

Chests & Coffers

A George I walnut mule chest, with a herringbone-crossbanded hinged top, the base with two drawers, 45in (114.5cm) wide.
$5,800–7,250 ⚒ HYD

A George II mahogany silver chest, with original brass carrying handles, c1740, 51in (129.5cm) wide.
$12,500–13,800 ⊞ REI

A George II mahogany mule chest, with a hinged top, the base with two drawers, 48in (122cm) wide.
$1,200–1,400 ⚒ L

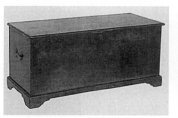

A George III mahogany blanket chest, with a hinged top, bracket feet, and locking brass side handles, 52¾in (134cm) wide.
$1,300–1,600 ⚒ Bea(E)

An Irish mahogany hall chest, the lift-up lid flanked by brass carrying handles, the stand with a shaped apron centred by a shell, reconstructed, 18thC, 51¼in (130cm) wide.
$3,000–3,500 ⚒ HOK

A mahogany silver chest, c1900, 56in (142cm) wide.
$1,200–1,300 ⊞ SWA

Chests of Drawers & Commodes

A yew wood chest of drawers, with oak sides, the figured top with sycamore crossbanding, early 18thC, 37in (94cm) wide.
$8,300–9,300 ⊞ HA

A swedish tulipwood and palisander parquetry *bombé* commode, in the style of Johan Neijber, the later shaped top above three drawers, applied with gilt-metal handles and escutcheons and angle mounts, restorations, mid-18thC, 50in (127cm) wide.
$5,000–6,000 ⚒ Bon

A walnut and feather-banded chest of drawers, with two short and three long graduated drawers, early 19thC, 40in (1101.5cm) wide.
$7,300–8,700 ⚒ KID

A George III inlaid mahogany bowfront chest of drawers, with two short and three long drawers, on splayed bracket feet, 35¾in (91cm) wide.
$1,500–1,800 ⚒ CMS

A Continental burr-walnut and marquetry chest of drawers, the top and drawer fronts profusely inlaid and crossbanded with flowers and foliage in various woods, ivory and mother-of-pearl, the sides inlaid with satinwood and ebony stringing, early 18thC, 31in (78.5cm) wide.
$4,400–5,000 ⚒ MAT

A George III mahogany bowfront chest of drawers, with crossbanded top and cockbeaded drawers, 42in (106.5cm) wide.
$750–900 ⚒ DOC

A George III mahogany chest of drawers, with a brushing slide, 30in (76cm) wide.
$4,500–5,000 ✦ E

A George III bowfront chest of drawers, 34in (86.5cm) wide.
$3,500–4,000 ⊞ CAT

A George III mahogany chest of drawers, the top inlaid with rosewood, c1790, 40in (101.5cm) wide.
$1,600–1,800 ⊞ NAW

Miller's Compares

I. A George III mahogany bowfront chest of drawers, the string-inlaid top above four long graduated drawers each with corner fan inlays, c1800, 36½in (92.5cm) wide.
$2,200–2,600 ✦ Bon(G)

II. A George III mahogany chest of drawers, the crossbanded top above four long graduated drawers, c1790, 33in (84cm) wide.
$1,000–1,300 ✦ Bon(G)

Although similar in both date and general appearance, Item I realized more at auction than Item II due to a number of factors. The bowfront is more appealing than the straight front of Item II and it is delicately inlaid, (in this case an original feature rather than a later 'improvement'), with a far more attractractively-shaped apron. The feet also appear rather more elegant than those of Item II and the overall colour of Item I is superior.

A Dutch neo-classical ormolu-mounted parquetry kingwood commode, the crossbanded top centred by a foliate marquetry panel over a pair of drawers, flanked by inlaid canted corners, on tapering square legs, late 18thC, 50in (127cm) wide.
$8,000–8,700 ✦ NOA

A north Italian walnut commode, the top inlaid with ivory with a central panel depicting a figure within an arbour flanked by chimera, with foliate scrolls and pewter-strung borders, above three graduated conforming drawers, late 18thC, 30¾in (78cm) wide.
$1,900–2,200 ✦ CGC

A George III mahogany serpentine chest of drawers, the crossbanded top and sides above the four graduated cockbeaded drawers with gilt-brass swing handles, between canted angles, raised on later ogee bracket feet, slight damage, 52½in (133.5cm) wide.
$8,700–10,200 ✦ Hal

An inlaid mahogany chest of drawers, decorated with herringbone and boxwood stringing, early 19thC, 42½in (108cm) wide.
$1,200–1,500 ✦ JAd

A mahogany bowfront chest of drawers, inlaid with stringing and satinwood crossbanding, the plum pudding mahogany top with reeded edging, with later brass drop handles, early 19thC, 40½in (103cm) wide.
$1,600–1,900 ✦ AH

◄ **An American classical mahogany chest of drawers,** the superstructure with three small drawers, with four long flame-veneered drawers below, flanked by turned spiral-reeded columns with pine cone finials, New England, early 19thC, 45in (114.5cm) wide.
$5,000–5,500 ✦ S(NY)

A Scottish Regency mahogany chest of drawers, the central deep drawer inlaid with ebonized stringing, flanked on either side by ring-turned and fluted columns, 51in (129.5cm) wide.
$1,400–1,600 ⚹ GAK

A French Charles X inlaid bird's-eye maple commode, the grey and black marble top above a frieze drawer and three long drawers, the drawers inlaid with mahogany, early 19thC, 49¾in (126.5cm) wide.
$2,600–3,200 ⚹ HAM

A north German neo-classical figured-birch commode, the pediment and superstructure raised on Ionic columns, the cabinet door fashioned as three panelled drawers and enclosing a shelved interior, early 19thC, 41in (104cm) wide.
$4,600–5,200 ⚹ NOA

Facts in brief

The chest of drawers as we recognize it today was introduced during the second half of the 17th century. It generally had two small drawers above three long drawers that varied in depth, and was mounted either on bun feet, or a stand with shaped legs and stretchers. In the 18th century, illustrations of chests of drawers frequently appeared on trade cards, and by the 1750s chests of drawers with bowed or serpentine fronts were often referred to as 'commode chests'.

An American Federal mahogany bowfront chest of drawers, the top outlined with stringing, with book inlays at the outer edges and original brass fittings, New England, faults, early 19thC, 42in (106.5cm) wide.
$3,600–4,000 ⚹ SK(B)

An American Federal cherrywood and bird's-eye maple veneer chest of drawers, attributed to Asahel Jones (1766–1822), the cherrywood top with a veneered edge over cockbeaded drawers of bird's-eye veneer, with mahogany crossbanding, brass replaced, Hubbardton, Vermont, 1810–20, 40in (101.5cm) wide.
$4,600–5,200 ⚹ SK(B)
***The Best The Country Affords,
Vermont Furniture 1765–1850,* by Kenneth J. Zogry, The Bennington Museum, 1995** states: 'In Rutland County the largest shops were located in the neighboring towns of Hubbardton and Castleton. Asahel Jones migrated from Raynham, Massachusetts, to Castleton, where he appears on the 1790 census. By 1800 he had moved to Hubbardton and remained there until his death.'

An inlaid mahogany chest of drawers, with two short and three long graduated drawers, c1820, 48in (122cm) wide.
$800–1,000 ⊞ NAW

A George IV mahogany chest of drawers, in the style of Gillows, the top with a reeded edge and protruding reeded corner pilasters, 43in (109cm) wide.
$1,800–2,200 ⚹ WW

A George IV mahogany bowfront chest of drawers, line-inlaid with boxwood, the four graduated cockbeaded drawers applied with foliate and gilt-brass ring handles, with boxwood kite-shaped escutcheons, slight damage, c1825, 38in (96.5cm) wide.
$870–1,100 ⚹ Hal

A mahogany bowfront chest of drawers, with a plain gallery, the two small and three long drawers with wooden knob handles, mid-19thC, 40½in (103cm) wide.
$580–750 ⚹ PFK

An American Classical figured mahogany chest of drawers, the corners with turned columns with spiral-twist ornament above a carved foliate panel, mid-Atlantic states, c1825, 48in (122cm) wide.
$4,400–5,100 ⚹ S(NY)

A mahogany bowfront chest of drawers, with ebony knobs, early 19thC, 46½in (118cm) wide.
$2,400–2,700 ⊞ **MTay**

A mahogany bowfront chest of drawers, the three drawers with turned brass handles, 19thC, 36in (91.5cm) wide.
$1,900–2,200 🔨 **RPI**

A Victorian fruitwood chest of drawers, with two short and three long drawers, 43¼in (110cm) wide.
$450–550 🔨 **P(Ba)**

An Italian walnut, inlaid and marquetry commode, bordered with ebonized and sycamore lines, the drawers with oval maple veneered panels decorated with birds amidst scrolling floral foliage, 19thC, 29in (73.5cm) wide.
$1,400–1,600 🔨 **P(E)**

A Scottish Victorian mahogany chest of drawers, the breakfront top above a serpentine drawer over five drawers modelled as six, and three further bowfronted graduated drawers with wooden knob handles, 51in (129.5cm) wide.
$880–1,100 🔨 **Mit**

A Victorian mahogany chest of drawers, with two short and three long drawers, on turned feet, with brass handles, 37in (94cm) wide.
$1,800–2,000 ⊞ **RPh**

A French kingwood *semainier*, with yellow-veined marble top, the drawers with chevron-veneered centre panels and conforming side panels, inlaid with boxwood stringing and with gilt-metal mounts, late 19thC, 16½in (42cm) wide.
$600–750 🔨 **CAG**
A *semainier* is so-called because it contains seven drawers – one for each day of the week. These pieces often have fall-fronts enclosing a fitted interior for writing, in which case the drawers are non-functional.

A French kingwood parquetry *bombé* commode, with serpentine outline, fitted with three drawers, with brass escutcheons and mounts, 19thC, 34¼in (87cm) wide.
$1,900–2,200 🔨 **WL**

A pair of French kingwood oval two-drawer chests, with quarter veneers and porcelain mounts, c1910, 24in (61cm) wide.
$4,000–4,400 🔨 **S(S)**

Tallboys

A George I walnut-veneered tallboy, with oak sides, the drawers flanked by fluted chamfered corners, 71in (181cm) high.
$8,400–10,200 P(S)

A George III mahogany secretaire tallboy, the drawers flanked by canted fluted corners, the fitted writing drawer above two long drawers, c1770, 40in (101.5cm) wide.
$7,300–8,000 (S)

A George III mahogany tallboy, with dentil-moulded cornice, the base with a brushing slide, the drawers all with ornate brass handles, 72in (183cm) high.
$3,650–4,400 JNic

A George III mahogany tallboy, the dentil-moulded cornice and arcaded frieze above two short and three long drawers, flanked by stop-fluted canted corners, the bottom section with a brushing slide, c1780, 44in (112cm) wide.
$8,700–10,200 Bon

A George III mahogany tallboy, the upper section with fluted canted corners, the walnut ends with cross-banding, with a brushing slide, some alterations, 40½in (103cm) wide.
$1,800–2,200 GIL

A George III mahogany tallboy, the base with a brushing slide, 41in (104cm) wide.
$2,300–3,000 CMS

A George III mahogany tallboy, the upper section with a key-pattern cornice, 44in (112cm) wide.
$2,300–2,900 L

A George I-style walnut and feather-banded tallboy, in two sections, the seven drawers flanked by fluted canted corners, faults, early 20thC, 29in (73.5cm) wide.
$2,200–2,400 S(S)

Chests-on-Stands

A William and Mary floral marquetry chest-on-stand, fitted with two short and three long graduated drawers with brass drop handles, on a later stand with period long drawer, 38in (96.5cm) wide.
$21,000–25,500 JNic

A Queen Anne burr-walnut and line-inlaid chest-on-stand, the quarter cut, crossbanded and inlaid top above drawers inlaid with boxwood and ebony lines and with later brass handles, stand adapted, 40½in (103cm) wide.
$1,000–1,300 Bri

A George I and later walnut cross-banded chest-on-stand, the cross-banded feather-strung top above feather-strung drawers with later brass pear-drop handles, on later cabriole legs, veneer losses, 39½in (100.5cm) wide.
$2,000–2,500 Hal

FURNITURE

A George I walnut chest-on-stand, with inlaid herringbone stringing and crossbanding, on later cabriole legs, 40in (101.5cm) wide.
$3,600–4,300 🔨 **Gam**

A walnut chest-on-stand, with brass swan's-neck drop handles, the cross-banded drawer fronts flanked on either side by quarter column corners, 18thC, 44in (112cm) wide.
$3,600–4,300 🔨 **Mit**

A Queen Anne-style walnut chest-on-stand, c1880, 43in (109cm) wide.
$4,000–4,700 ⊞ **CHE**

Military Chests

A George III Colonial camphorwood campaign secretaire chest-of-drawers, in two sections, the secretaire drawer enclosing drawers and pigeon-holes around a door, with two short and two long drawers below, late 18thC, 39in (99cm) wide.
$6,500–8,000 🔨 **Bon**

A mahogany brass-bound campaign chest, with an arrangement of four short and three long drawers, with brass escutcheons and drop handles, 19thC, 42in (106.5cm) wide.
$2,200–2,500 🔨 **LJ**

A Victorian teak brass-bound secretaire military chest, in two sections, the two short drawers centred by a secretaire drawer enclosing a fitted interior with an inset leather writing surface, with three long drawers below, restored, late 19thC, 39in (99cm) wide.
$2,600–2,900 🔨 **S(S)**

A camphorwood and mahogany secretaire campaign chest, with brass-mounted corners, one long drawer above a secretaire drawer enclosing drawers and pigeonholes, and three long graduated drawers with ebony lining and brass handles, 19thC, 42in (106.5cm) wide.
$2,600–3,200 🔨 **P(Ed)**

◄ **A mahogany campaign chest,** in two sections, the three short and three long drawers all with flush brass handles, 19thC, 44in (112cm) wide.
$1,500–1,800 🔨 **Bea(E)**

A brass-bound hardwood military chest, in two sections, on later bun feet, 19thC, 45in (114.5cm) wide.
$1,300–1,600 🔨 **MEA**

◄ **A camphorwood campaign chest,** in two sections, the upper secretaire drawer flanked by deep drawers, above three long drawers, mid-19thC, 39in (99cm) wide.
$3,200–3,700 🔨 **SK**

Secretaire Chests

A George III mahogany secretaire chest, the top with deep crossbanding above the secretaire drawer with applied geometric moulding to the front and enclosing a fitted interior with a series of drawers and pigeonholes, above three long graduated cock-beaded drawers, 31in (78.5cm) wide.
$4,000–4,600 ⚲ Mit

A late Georgian inlaid mahogany secretaire chest, with a crossbanded top, the top drawer with oval inlays to the fall-front enclosing a fitted interior, above three drawers, lacking leather inlay, 46¾in (119cm) wide.
$750–1,000 ⚲ PFK

▶ **A Regency mahogany library secretaire chest,** the fitted drawer with an adjustable writing surface flanked by hinged compartments with a pair of panelled doors below enclosing an interior of sliding trays, 51¼in (130cm) wide.
$3,200–3,800 ⚲ HYD

An Austrian burr-elm secretaire chest, with an arched cornice above a fall-front enclosing drawers around a cupboard, with three long drawers below inset with a beaded arched panel, flanked by turned columns, early 19thC, 42¼in (107.5cm) wide.
$1,200–1,400 ⚲ P(S)

Wellington Chests

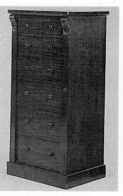

A William IV mahogany secretaire Wellington chest, the top with a pierced brass three-quarter gallery, above a frieze drawer and a secretaire drawer enclosing an inset writing surface and an arrangement of pigeon-holes and a small drawer, with three long drawers below, flanked by a side-locking mechanism and foliate-carved scroll terminals, 36¼in (92cm) wide.
$3,200–3,800 ⚲ CGC

A Victorian walnut secretaire Wellington chest, with a central secretaire drawer, five further drawers and foliate-carved uprights, 22in (56cm) wide.
$3,300–4,000 ⚲ Bea(E)

A mid-Victorian ebonized and boxwood marquetry Wellington chest, applied with gilt-metal mounts, the seven drawers flanked by uprights, one containing a locking mechanism, 23¾in (60.5cm) wide.
$1,600–1,800 ⚲ P

A Victorian mahogany Wellington chest, with six long graduated drawers, 21¼in (54cm) wide.
$3,500–4,000 ⚲ S(S)

▶ **A late Victorian oak Wellington chest,** by Edwards & Roberts, with seven drawers, 24in (61cm) wide.
$1,800–1,900 ⚲ P(Ba)
The London firm of Edwards & Roberts (established 1845) was a prolific furniture maker. It was one of the few English companies that regularly marked both the furniture it made and the items it restored, and since it dealt in antiques and modern furniture as well as reproductions, it is often difficult to tell a copy from a genuine 18th-century piece. Such confusion would not arise over typical items of the Victorian period such as the Wellington chest pictured here.

A Victorian mahogany Wellington chest, the eight graduated drawers flanked by a hinged stile, with carved terminals, 22¾in (58cm) wide.
$2,300–2,900 ⚲ P(Ba)

Clothes & Linen Presses

A burr-walnut-veneered linen press, feather-banded throughout with crossbanded and moulded doors, three false drawers and one long drawer below, altered, early 18thC, 58¼in (148cm) wide.
$4,700–5,500 ⚒ Bea(E)

A George III mahogany linen press, with panelled doors enclosing five linen trays, the base with two short and two long drawers with original brass swan-neck handles, 58in (147.5cm) wide.
$2,300–2,900 ⚒ Bri

A George III mahogany linen press, the cornice with blind fret-carved frieze over panelled doors, the base with a brushing slide and three long graduated drawers, 46¾in (119cm) wide.
$2,200–2,600 ⚒ P(L)

A George IV mahogany linen press, the pair of panelled doors flanked by spiral-twist pillars, the projecting lower part fitted with two short and two long drawers, on scroll feet, 54¼in (138cm) wide.
$2,300–2,900 ⚒ L

A George IV mahogany linen press, with panelled doors enclosing a fitted interior, the base with four graduated drawers, 51½in (131cm) wide.
$1,400–1,700 ⚒ WilP

A Regency mahogany linen press, with panelled doors enclosing slides, the base with four drawers, 49¼in (125cm) wide.
$2,200–2,600 ⚒ Bon(C)

Clothes presses
- Clothes presses were introduced c1750 and until 1780 many were made from mahogany.
- Some Victorian presses are veneered in satinwood or walnut.
- Essentially practical bedroom pieces rather than decorative drawing-room ones, they were made for all types of households.
- The quality varies: some are highly sophisticated with fine carving or, from the end of the 18th century, inlaid; others are simply-constructed and unadorned.

A William IV mahogany linen press, the panelled cupboard doors enclosing five slides, the base with two short and two long graduated drawers with turned handles, 48in (122cm) wide.
$3,300–4,000 ⚒ DA

▶ **A Sheraton revival mahogany clothes press,** inlaid with marquetry and satinwood-crossbanded, the two panelled doors inlaid with urns and enclosing sliding trays, late 19thC, 46in (117cm) wide.
$2,200–2,600 ⚒ DN

A Victorian figured mahogany clothes press, half of the top section now with hanging space, half with trays, 56¼in (143cm) wide.
$3,600–4,000 ⊞ MTay

An early Victorian mahogany linen press, the arched-panel doors inlaid with ebony banding and enclosing hanging space, the base with two short and two long drawers, brass label 'R. Garnett & Sons', 54¼in (138cm) wide.
$1,900–2,200 ⚒ S(S)

An American Federal mahogany linen press, the base with a butler's desk above full-width drawers and recessed panel doors, replaced pulls, base of different origin, labelled 'Thomas Burling', c1840, 49in (124.5cm) wide.
$2,000–2,400 ⚒ SK(B)
Thomas Burling, active 1769–97, was one of New York City's most important 18th-century cabinet-makers and produced a large number of labelled pieces.

FURNITURE

Davenports

A mahogany davenport, with fitted interior, c1820, 21in (53.5cm) wide. **$3,200–3,600** ⊞ GKe

A Victorian walnut piano-front davenport, the rising top inset with stationery compartments over a lifting lid, enclosing a sliding writing surface with a gilt-tooled inset below two drawers and pen tray, with drawers and dummy drawers below, marked 'Kerby, 545 New Oxford Street', 23in (58.5cm) wide. **$5,500–6,000** ⚒ GAK

Miller's is a price GUIDE not a price LIST

A Victorian walnut, boxwood and inlaid davenport, with a stationery compartment above a sloping fall-front enclosing four short drawers over a geometrically-strung front panel, with four drawers and four false drawers below, damaged, c1880, 21in (53.5cm) wide. **$500–600** ⚒ Hal

A George IV mahogany davenport, the swivel top with a three-quarter brass gallery and a leather-inset slope enclosing an interior with drawers and pigeon-holes, the front with four drawers and a pull-out pen and ink drawer to the side, 19in (48.5cm) wide. **$1,700–2,000** ⚒ P(S)

A Victorian walnut davenport, with a stationery cabinet with satinwood-crossbanded and boxwood-strung decoration, the slope front with a leather-inset writing surface, with four graduated drawers and four dummy drawers below, 21in (53.5cm) wide. **$1,700–2,000** ⚒ Mit

A mahogany davenport, the upper section with a stationery compartment, the gilt-tooled green leather-inset sloping front enclosing a fitted interior of two drawers, with drawers and dummy drawers below, late 19thC, 22in (56cm) wide. **$1,000–1,200** ⚒ GAK

An early Victorian rosewood davenport, with a gilt-brass scroll-pierced gallery, the slope with new gilt-tooled leather enclosing a satinwood drawer and dummy drawers, one side with a pull-out pen drawer above a slide and four graduated drawers, the other side with a dummy slide above dummy drawers, the front with leaf-petal-carved and plain-turned pillar supports, 20¾in (52.5cm) wide. **$1,800–2,200** ⚒ WW

An early Victorian walnut davenport, with pierced gallery, 19in (48.5cm) wide. **$1,900–2,400** ⚒ Bon(C)

A Victorian pollarded oak davenport, by Gillows, the sliding leather-inset writing section with a spindle-turned gallery, the side with a swivel pen drawer and lateral slides, above three drawers and opposing dummy drawers, faults, stamped, 20in (51cm) wide. **$5,000–6,000** ⚒ S(S)

◀ **A Victorian walnut davenport,** faults, c1880, 22in (56cm) wide. **$1,800–2,000** ⊞ NAW

Condition and value

The quality of these compact writing tables, introduced in the late 18th century, can vary considerably. A high quality piece, provided that it is in good condition, will achieve double the price of one of lesser quality, and three times the price of one in need of restoration.

◀ **An Edwardian rosewood and marquetry davenport,** inlaid with stringing, the hinged top with a pierced-brass gallery enclosing a compartmented interior with inkwells above a leather-inset writing surface, the pedestal inlaid with a musical trophy and with four real and four opposing dummy drawers, drawer stamped 'Thomas Turner, Manchester', faults, 22in (56cm) wide. **$1,600–1,800** ⚒ S(S)

Desks

A walnut kneehole desk, c1720, 31in (78.5cm) wide.
$23,200–26,200 ☷ REI

A George II walnut kneehole desk, with original handles, c1740, 30in (76cm) wide.
$18,800–21,000 ☷ CAT

Kneehole desk conversions

It is not uncommon for a chest of drawers to be converted into a kneehole desk. Certain checks can be made to ascertain authenticity:

- The construction of the inner sides of the small drawers should correspond with the outer sides; the dovetails should match each other and look as if they were made by the same hand.
- The runners should have caused even wear to the carcass.
- The veneers used for the sides of the kneehole, and for the recessed cupboard door, should match the rest of the piece.

▶ **A George II walnut kneehole desk,** with narrow herringbone-banding, the top quarter-veneered and with broad crossbanding, above one long drawer and six short drawers flanking a central cupboard door and with a concealed shaped frieze drawer above, the inner edges all scroll-outlined, 34¼in (87cm) wide.
$5,800–7,200 ➷ HAM

Cross Reference
See Colour Review (page 112)

A walnut kneehole desk, with feather-banding throughout, the crossbanded burr-walnut veneered top above an arrangement of eight drawers around a kneehole recess with cupboard, early 18thC, 30in (76cm) wide.
$16,000–18,800 ➷ Bea(E)

▶ **A George III mahogany and satinwood travelling writing desk,** the leather-lined hinged front enclosing a fitted interior with pigeonholes and small drawers, the whole supported on a separate later stand, c1800, 20in (51cm) wide.
$2,500–3,000 ➷ S(NY)

A Regency mahogany partner's desk, the top with a green leather insert and gadrooned rim, over a central frieze drawer flanked by two short drawers, with ebony spear-panel stringing detail to each side, 63in (160cm) wide.
$2,900–3,200 ➷ P(Ed)
The spear-panel stringing is a characteristically Scottish decorative detail that is illustrated in the *Edinburgh Cabinet Makers' Book of Prices*, 1811.

An oak combined library folio cabinet and writing desk, the sliding twin-hinged top with red leather inserts above two grille-panelled doors, early 19thC, 33½in (85cm) wide.
$11,600–13,000 ↗ S(S)

An Irish William IV rent or estate agent's desk, the later three-quarter brass gallery above a sloping hinged double top with a writing surface and money slot, above six numbered drawers, on a base with two smaller drawers, 53in (134.5cm) wide.
$1,900–2,200 ↗ MEA

A French ebonized lady's writing desk, mid-19thC, 38in (96.5cm) wide.
$2,900–3,200 ↗ JH

A Victorian mahogany pedestal desk, the superstructure containing eight drawers and a pigeonhole and a leather-inset hinged slope enclosing small drawers, late 19thC, 60½in (153.5cm) wide.
$3,200–3,600 ↗ S(S)

An American Federal mahogany and mahogany-veneered lady's desk, the upper section with two beaded and veneered doors enclosing three shaped document drawers flanked by two short drawers, above three valenced compartments, the projecting base with fold-out writing surface above three cockbeaded and veneered drawers, Massachusetts, c1810, 39½in (100.5cm) wide.
$3,500–4,000 ↗ SK(B)

An Irish Killarney-work-inlaid arbutus desk, the backboard inlaid with a crowned harp, above twin-arched panel doors inlaid with views of The Swiss Cottage and trailing shamrocks enclosing seven drawers, on a pull-out writing section flanked by column supports, inlaid overall with oval lozenges depicting views of Killarney, herringbone stringing and trailing bellflowers, mid-19thC, 30¾in (78cm) wide.
$8,700–10,200 ↗ JAd

A William IV Gothic-style carved mahogany pedestal desk, the leather-inset top above a lozenge-carved frieze drawer with scroll spandrels, flanked by panelled doors with Gothic arches flanked by clustered column uprights, one enclosing four partitions, the other a shelf on bracket scrolling-leaf feet, later top, possibly adapted, 57½in (146cm) wide.
$5,000–5,800 ↗ P(S)

A mahogany partner's pedestal desk, one pedestal with three cockbeaded graduated drawers, the other with a door simulating three drawers, with brass knob handles and Bramah locks throughout, writing inset to top missing, mid-19thC, 74in (188cm) wide.
$5,500–6,000 ↗ PF

Bramah locks
Bramah locks were introduced in the late 18th century. They are set in a characteristic circular escutcheon and have patent cylindrical keys.

A mahogany architect's desk, in the style of Gillows, the ratchet-action top above a split drop-front drawer fitted with a sliding adjustable writing surface, hinged lettered compartments below, the lower section with eight short drawers above a long drawer, locks stamped 'I. Bramah', 19thC, 39¼in (99.5cm) wide.
$3,900–4,400 ↗ P(NW)

◄ **A Victorian mahogany pedestal estate desk,** the superstructure with a writing fall enclosing pigeonholes and flanked by a pair of panelled doors, labelled 'Sopwith & Co', 58in (147.5in) wide.
$3,500–3,900 ↗ LEW

A late Victorian rosewood and marquetry writing desk, the superstructure with a mirrored back flanked by lidded compartments with false drawer fronts above two short drawers, the shaped leather-inset top above three frieze drawers, 39¾in (101cm) wide.
$2,500–2,900 ⚒ P(S)

A mahogany and crossbanded lady's desk, c1890, 42in (106.5cm) wide.
$4,000–4,700 ⊞ CHE

An Edwardian mahogany Carlton House desk, the three-quarter brass galleried superstructure with drawers and compartments above a leather-inset writing surface, over three frieze drawers, 44¾in (113.5cm) wide.
$8,000–8,700 ⚒ S(NY)

An oak pedestal desk, the top with a leather-inset writing surface and pierced-brass gallery, over five reeded drawers and two panelled cupboards, early 20thC, 48in (122cm) wide.
$400–500 ⚒ M

A late Victorian rosewood and marquetry desk, the superstructure with a three-quarter brass gallery over a gilt-tooled writing surface, the front with five drawers surrounding the central kneehole with ivorine marquetry of cornucopiae of fruit and leafy fronds, 51in (129.5cm) wide.
$3,200–3,800 ⚒ HYD

A late Victorian mahogany library desk, 48in (122cm) wide.
$1,800–2,200 ⚒ Bon(C)

An Edwardian walnut Carlton House desk, the superstructure with a central cupboard door flanked by small drawers and two hinged compartments, the serpentine top above one long and two short drawers, faults, 38½in (98cm) wide.
$1,200–1,500 ⚒ S(S)

► A walnut partner's desk, the top inset with three tooled-leather writing surfaces above brushing slides and an arrangement of drawers flanked by fluted canted sides, the opposing side fitted with drawers and cupboards, 1930s, 73½in (186.5cm) wide.
$4,400–5,000 ⚒ CGC

A mahogany pedestal desk, the top inset with a brown writing surface, over three frieze drawers, each pedestal with three graduated drawers flanked by reeded uprights, late 19thC, 35¾in (91cm) wide.
$1,600–1,900 ⚒ ELR

An Edwardian mahogany partner's desk, the indented top inset with three brown tooled-leather panels, the desk with 22 drawers and with carved acanthus-leaf and bell-husk decoration, 71¾in (182.5cm) wide.
$2,900–3,500 ⚒ P(Ba)

An Edwardian inlaid mahogany writing desk, with tooled-leather top over seven drawers, 48in (122cm) wide.
$1,600–1,900 ⚒ WilP

An oak pedestal desk, with inset green leather writing surface, above nine drawers, all drawers with mahogany linings, early 20thC, 48in (122cm) wide.
$1,900–2,200 ⊞ MTay

FURNITURE

Dumb Waiters

A George III mahogany dumb waiter, with three graduated tiers and turned columns, restored, 43¾in (111cm) high.
$2,900–3,500 ⚒ **Bon**

A George III mahogany two-tier dumb waiter, the tiers with reeded borders on a turned column and reeded tripod base, 37in (94cm) high.
$2,200–2,600 ⚒ **GH**

A George III mahogany two-tier dumb waiter, the graduated revolving reeded tiers with drop sides, some damage, 26in (66cm) diam.
$2,900–3,500 ⚒ **Bon(W)**

A Georgian-style mahogany dumb waiter, with three revolving trays, on a turned vase-shaped column, 19thC, 49in (124.5cm) high.
$1,100–1,300 ⚒ **AH**

◄ **A Grenada mahogany three-tier serving table,** with a shaped carved gallery, the middle shelf with two drawers, c1840, 36in (91.5cm) wide.
$4,300–4,700 ⚒ **S(NY)**

▶ **An oak dumb waiter,** by Globe-Wernicke, c1910, 26in (66cm) wide.
$650–750 ⊞ **GBr**

An Edwardian flame-mahogany three-tier dumb waiter, each tier crossbanded and boxwood strung, 28½in (72.5cm) wide.
$1,400–1,600 ⚒ **DA**

Frames

An Italian or Spanish gilt and painted wood frame, the upper frieze carved with two reclining putti, supported by spiral-carved Corinthian columns, the whole resting on a base fitted with a strapwork-carved drawer, some losses, 36 x 30¼in (91.5 x 77cm).
$8,000–8,700 ⚒ **S(NY)**

A Florentine carved gilt frame, mid-19thC, 18 x 21in (45.5 x 53.5cm).
$400–500 ⚒ **GAK**

A Florentine pierced, carved and gilded frame, with reverse scotia with leaf centres and corners, and reverse hollow with acanthus centres and corners, 19thC, 32¾ x 27½in (83 x 70cm).
$900–1,100 ⚒ **Bon**

▶ **A Whistler-style gilded oak frame,** with oak frieze and cluster-reeded edge, 19thC, 19 x 14½in (48.5 x 37cm).
$2,300–2,900 ⚒ **Bon**

▶ **A pair of Masonic carved boxwood frames,** the pediment with pierced foliate decoration surmounted by an eye and Masonic motifs, with columns and emblems to the sides, each contained in a glazed display case, late 19thC, 24 x 14½in (61 x 37cm).
$2,500–2,900 ⚒ **Bea(E)**

Jardinières

A German Biedermeier gilt-mounted walnut jardinière, with a tin liner, c1852, 32¼in (82cm) high.
$2,600–3,200 ⚒ S(Z)

A Dutch mahogany jardinière, with a brass swing handle and liner, the sides as open trellis work, 19thC, 23¼in (59cm) high.
$1,800–2,200 ⚒ AH

◀ **A painted toleware jardinière,** the legs and removable body painted to imitate bamboo, c1920, 23½in (59.5cm) wide.
$850–1,000 ⚒ P

An Edwardian Sheraton-style inlaid mahogany jardinière, with a brass liner, 32¼in (82cm) high.
$550–600 ⚒ Bri

▶ **A Dutch mahogany and parcel-gilt jardinière,** inlaid with brass stringing, with a brass loop handle and liner, faults, c1910, 19½in (49.5cm) high.
$1,400–1,800 ⚒ S(S)

A mahogany jardinière, inset on one side with a tiled frieze, on lyre supports, applied on either side with lion-mask ring handles, late 19thC, 37in (94cm) wide.
$320–350 ⚒ GAK

Lowboys

A walnut lowboy, inlaid with cross-banding and feather-stringing, the quarter-veneered top above three drawers, on later scroll-carved cabriole front legs, with shell- and bellflower-carved knees, restored, early 18thC, 30½in (77.5cm) wide.
$9,500–11,500 ⚒ P(S)

A walnut lowboy, with crossbanded top, inlaid canted corners and three small drawers, restored, early 18thC, 28½in (72.5cm) wide.
$2,500–2,900 ⚒ Bea(E)

A walnut lowboy, inlaid with stringing, with later restoration, early 18thC, 36in (91.5cm) wide.
$2,900–3,300 ⊞ MTay

A George I walnut lowboy, the quarter-veneered top with herringbone stringing and broad crossbanding, restored, 29in (73.5cm) wide.
$3,200–3,800 ⚒ L

A George II mahogany lowboy, with a long cockbeaded shallow drawer and two short drawers, restored, 30in (76.cm) wide.
$2,600–3,200 ⚒ Hal

▶ **A George III mahogany lowboy,** c1800, 33in (84cm) wide.
$1,500–1,700 ⊞ RPh

A George III mahogany lowboy, with a long frieze drawer and two short drawers, 30½in (78cm) wide.
$2,300–2,900 ⚒ CGC

FURNITURE

Miniature Furniture

A George III mahogany miniature chest, with two short and three long graduated drawers, 11½in (29cm) high.
$1,000–1,300 ✗ CGC

A mahogany and boxwood-lined apprentice chest, with two short and three long graduated drawers, 19thC, 9¾in (25cm) wide.
$600–750 ✗ P(Ed)

A Scottish mid-Victorian mahogany miniature chest, with a frieze drawer and three long drawers flanked by barley-twist supports, 8¼in (21cm) wide.
$750–850 ✗ P(S)

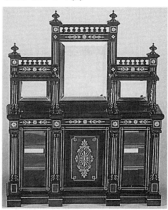

An Italian red lacquer miniature serpentine commode, decorated with comic figures, animals and floral sprays, c1770, 10¼in (26cm) wide.
$2,600–3,200 ✗ Bon

A Victorian mahogany miniature chest of drawers, with two short and three long graduated drawers, faults, c1850, 13in (33cm) wide.
$1,200–1,300 ✗ S(S)

A pair of mahogany miniature Wellington chests, the four drawers with turned wooden handles and flanking pilasters, one locking, with scroll corbals, 19thC, 16½in (42cm) wide.
$600–700 ✗ JAd

◀ **A late Victorian miniature ebony and ivory marquetry sideboard,** with a mirror back, flanked by smaller mirrors over a central panel door flanked by glazed doors, with turned uprights and scroll capitals, 15¼in (38.5cm) wide.
$2,900–3,500 ✗ P(B)

A Regency miniature chest of drawers, with two short and three long graduated drawers, 14½in (37cm) wide.
$3,600–4,000 ✗ S(S)

A Victorian mahogany miniature chest of drawers, 13¾in (35cm) wide.
$350–450 ✗ Bon(C)

A Victorian burr-walnut miniature Wellington chest, with reverse breakfront form, 15¼in (38.5cm) wide.
$300–400 ✗ L

A Victorian miniature walnut snap-top table, the top with parquetry starburst and chequerboard, with a shaped frieze, on three turned supports, with down-scroll legs, 10½in (26.5cm) wide.
$1,200–1,400 ✗ P(B)

Cheval Mirrors

A George III mahogany cheval mirror, the adjustable plate surmounted by a pierced handle, 54¼in (138cm) high.
$2,000–2,300 ⚲ P(Ba)

A Victorian mahogany cheval mirror, inlaid with marquetry panels of flowers and scroll decoration, 30¾in (78cm) wide.
$2,000–2,300 ⚲ LJ

A George III mahogany cheval mirror, the adjustable plate within reeded uprights and adjustable gilt-metal candle arms, 30in (76cm) wide.
$4,600–5,000 ⚲ S(S)

A William IV mahogany cheval mirror, the adjustable plate on tapering end supports and trestle feet, 58¼in (148cm) high.
$1,000–1,200 ⚲ CGC

◄ **A French Charles X ormolu-mounted burr-elm cheval mirror,** enclosing a modern plate, with turned columns and ormolu vase finials, together with the original arched mirror plate, c1830, 70in (178cm) high.
$3,200–3,800 ⚲ S(NY)

► **A Victorian mahogany cheval mirror,** the scrolling supports with platform base below and standing on short scrolling feet, 31in (78.5cm) wide.
$650–800 ⚲ Mit

An Austrian neo-classical walnut cheval mirror, the uprights mounted with parcel-gilt acanthus and supported on scrolled feet, the mirror plate within a rosewood grained ogee-moulded frame, mid-19thC, 34½in (87.5cm) wide.
$2,600–3,200 ⚲ NOA

Dressing Table Mirrors

A George III mahogany toilet mirror, the shield-shaped plate now bevelled, the crossbanded serpentine base with three drawers, 17½in (44.5cm) wide.
$440–500 ⚲ L

► **A mahogany line-inlaid toilet mirror,** the bowfront base with three drawers, 19thC, 20½in (52cm) wide.
$360–430 ⚲ P(Ba)

A mahogany toilet mirror, the serpentine base with three drawers, early 19thC, 18½in (47cm) wide.
$220–260 ⚲ DOC

An amboyna veneered toilet mirror, with stained turned softwood uprights, the bowfront base decorated with rosewood crossbanding and stringing centred by amboyna wood panels, 19thC, 19in (48.5cm) wide.
$580–720 ⚲ AG

► **A Victorian flame-mahogany toilet mirror,** the base with two drawers, 21in (53.5cm) wide.
$220–280 ⊞ GBr

An American Federal mahogany and mahogany-veneered dressing mirror, with string inlay, labelled 'I. Richman, New York', faults, 14in (35.5cm) wide.
$1,300–1,600 ⚲ SK(B)

Wall Mirrors

A walnut oyster-veneered cushion-framed wall mirror, late 17thC, 26in (66cm) wide.
$1,750–2,000 ⚒ PF

A giltwood wall mirror, the moulded frame surmounted by a pierced crest with flowers and scroll decoration, with later plate, c1760, 31in (78.5cm) wide.
$4,400–5,000 ⚒ Bon

A Spanish giltwood wall mirror, the leaf-carved frame flanked by pierced and scrolling leaves, surmounted by an eagle, 18thC, 33in (84cm) wide.
$4,400–5,000 ⚒ CGC

A north European carved and stained wood mirror frame, carved in high relief with figures representing the four seasons, on a background of scrolls with fruit, later mirror plate, late 18thC, 14¼in (36cm) wide.
$1,250–1,450 ⚒ Bea(E)

A George I giltwood mirror, the frame surmounted by a swan-neck pediment with flowerhead decoration, 26in (66cm) wide.
$4,500–5,500 ⚒ P(Ba)

Beware!

Be suspicious of any mirror in perfect condition. All old mirrors will have deteriorated to some extent, and will have non-reflective spots. Re-silvering reduces the value, particularly that of cheval and dressing table mirrors. Mirror glass can be replaced, but the original glass should be retained and stored carefully.

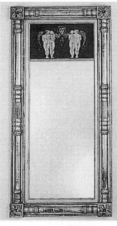

An American Classical carved giltwood pier mirror, the frame with split-turned baluster decoration, the top panel with nude figures, the *verre églomisé* panel replaced or later painted, Boston, c1810, 34in (86.5cm) wide.
$1,800–2,200 ⚒ S(NY)

◀ **A Swedish neo-classical giltwood pier mirror,** the demi-lune frieze containing a mirror plate decorated with an allegory, the mirror plate flanked by female and lion masks, early 19thC, 27¾in (70.5cm) wide.
$1,750–2,000 ⚒ NOA

A Regency convex wall mirror, the ball-studded giltwood frame surmounted by an eagle and with pierced and carved foliage, restored, 27¼in (69cm) wide.
$2,300–2,900 ⚒ Bea(E)

An Irish carved giltwood wall mirror, the cresting flanked by rosette scrolls, the sides with pendants of flowers, mid-18thC, 30¼in (77cm) wide.
$8,000–9,500 ⚒ HOK

An Anglo-Portuguese rosewood and gilt wall mirror, the plate flanked by fretwork foliate festoons, the pediment with a pierced cartouche, c1780, 17in (43cm) wide.
$2,500–3,000 ⚒ S(S)

An Irish ebonized and parcel-gilt wall mirror, the frame set with facet-cut crystal stones, 19thC, 29in (73.5cm) wide.
$1,800–2,200 ⚒ MEA

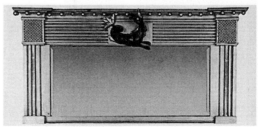

A George IV gilt-framed overmantel mirror, the plate within a cluster pilaster surround, the frieze centred by a sea horse and with trellis-panelled corners, c1825, 50in (127cm) wide.
$1,000–1,250 ⚒ S(S)

An American Federal gilt and *faux* tortoiseshell mirror, the frame with eight split balusters surrounding a gilt *verre églomisé* panel depicting an eagle below 16 stars flanked by flags, banners and cannon against a pale blue ground over mirror glass, New England, restored, c1830, 12¾in (32.5cm) wide.
$3,200–3,600 ✗ SK(B)

A late Victorian carved wood and gesso-framed overmantel mirror, with original glass, c1870, 52in (132cm) wide.
$750–850 ⊞ ASH

A giltwood frame, the frame carved with C-scrolls and acanthus, mirror plate missing, mid-19thC, 63in (160cm) wide.
$1,750–2,000 ✗ DN

A French bone and ivory mirror, applied with carved dolphins, fleur-de-lys, dragons, eagles and masks, on a ground of stylized leaves, inscribed 'SCOTORVM', Dieppe, 19thC, 20in (51cm) wide.
$1,600–1,750 ✗ F&C

A carved giltwood and gilt-gesso wall mirror, the central plate surrounded by four secondary plates, surmounted by a shell, scrolls, fruit, flowers and foliage, with scrolling foliage decoration at each corner, 19thC, 43in (109cm) wide.
$2,600–3,200 ✗ E

A French grey-painted and parcel-gilt overmantel mirror, with stucco gilded flower garlands, ribbons and bow, the backboard with a tulip cornice, late 19thC, 40in (101.5cm) wide.
$1,000–1,100 ⊞ OFM

A Victorian gilt-gesso overmantel mirror, the foliate and shell-moulded crest above shaped glass with conforming spandrels, on porcelain bun supports, 67¾in (172cm) wide.
$2,200–2,600 ✗ Bri

> Items in the Furniture section have been arranged in date order within each sub-section.

An American walnut, burr-walnut and incised Eastlake-style mirror, the frame topped by a beaded and reeded roundel flanked by fretwork, the sides of the frame with incised florals, the fluted stiles topped by ebonized cones, early 20thC, 56in (142cm) wide.
$580–650 ✗ SK

Pedestals

A pair of mahogany sideboard pedestals, with panelled doors flanked by recessed leaf-banded columns, c1825, 19in (48.5cm) square.
$6,500–8,000 ✗ HOK
Dining room pedestals were used to keep plates warm or to store bottles, plates or glasses, their interiors being fitted according to their intended use.

An American Renaissance revival marquetry-inlaid, parcel-gilt and ebonized pedestal, with an urn-shaped top, c1870, 42½in (108cm) high.
$1,450–1,750 ✗ SK

A French ormolu-mounted variegated green marble pedestal, the turned column with a baluster lower section, late 19thC, 42in (106.5cm) high.
$800–1,000 ✗ Hal

◄ **A white marble and ormolu pedestal,** with pierced scrolling foliate and leaf banding, 19thC, 44in (112cm) high.
$800–950 ✗ AH

FURNITURE

Screens

A Victorian three-fold screen, each panel with découpage decoration, 75½in (192cm) high.
$360–430 ⚒ **CGC**

A Victorian carved and gilded two-fold screen, with silk woven floral panels behind glass, c1880, 44in (112cm) high.
$750–850 ⊞ **MTay**

▶ **A Victorian walnut four-fold screen,** applied to each side with watercolours of fishing and coastal scenes, some tears, 70in (178cm) high.
$300–350 ⚒ **Hal**

A Louis XVI-style three-fold screen, the guilloche-carved frame decorated *en grisaille*, surmounted by floral wreaths, containing cloth panels painted with tropical birds and foliage, late 19thC, 45in (114.3cm) high.
$1,200–1,450 ⚒ **NOA**

A painted hide six-fold screen, one side painted with a chinoiserie scene, 19thC, 84in (213.5cm) high.
$13,700–15,200 ⚒ **S**

◀ **A Continental carved and polychromed three-fold screen,** the central panel decorated with fruit, heraldic emblems and profiles, late 19thC, 72in (183cm) high.
$2,000–2,300 ⚒ **NOA**

A late Victorian/Edwardian Sheraton revival three-fold screen, each section with a pediment inlaid with ribbons, swags and a central urn in boxwood and harewood, the surround with boxwood stringing, the lower panel with pleated foliate pattern material in green, 69in (175.5cm) high.
$1,000–1,150 ⚒ **Mit**

Fire Screens

A Victorian mahogany pole screen, on a tapering twist-turned pillar support, with a bead and woolwork floral tapestry, 58in (147.5cm) high.
$330–400 ⚒ **DA**

A Victorian rosewood pole screen, the rosewood foliate-scrolling surround enclosing a Berlin tapestrywork panel, 68ins (172.5cm) high.
$650–725 ⚒ **Mit**

A mahogany pole screen, with an earlier shield-shaped screen worked in silk satin stitch, on a turned and carved column, 19thC, 61½in (156cm) high.
$430–500 ⚒ **ELR**

A Victorian walnut and brass pole screen, the engraved brass stem with a shield-shaped tapestry and beadwork banner, 60in (152.5cm) high.
$320–380 ⚒ **EH**

▶ **A carved and moulded walnut fire screen,** with a tapestry inset, c1920, 24½in (62cm) wide.
$750–850 ⊞ **MTay**

HORNCASTLE

Two trade & retail calls
5,000 sq. ft. plus
1 hour from Newark

Seaview Antiques
Stanhope Road, Horncastle
Tel: 01507 524524
Fax: 01507 526946
Email: tracey.collins@virgin.net
Website: www.seaviewantiques.co.uk

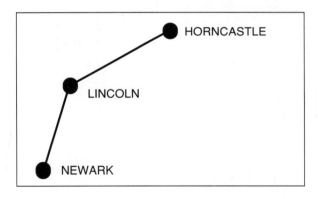

Norman Mitchell
47a East Street, Horncastle
Tel/Fax: 01507 527957
Email: norman@mitchellantique.demon.co.uk

LINCOLNSHIRE, UK

Settees & Sofas

An early Georgian walnut chair-back settee, with two shaped solid splats, the scrolled arms on shaped supports, with a drop-in upholstered seat, 51½in (131cm) wide.
$2,000–2,500 ✹ AH

A George III green-painted and parcel-gilt sofa, with a padded back and arms and loose-cushioned seat, on square tapering legs carved with bellflowers, 80in (203cm) wide.
$2,900–3,200 ✹ S(S)

▶ **A Swedish neo-classical painted and parcel-gilt settee,** with husk-carved arms and griffin supports above a foliate-carved frieze, early 19thC, 79in (200.5cm) wide.
$11,000–13,000 ✹ SK

A George III mahogany settee, upholstered in green damask fabric, restored, 76¾in (195cm) wide.
$2,500–3,000 ✹ S(S)

A Louis XVI grey-painted and carved sofa, with a padded back and arms and loose cushion seat, upholstered in apricot velvet fabric, late 18thC, 71in (180.5cm) wide.
$4,400–5,000 ✹ S

An American Federal mahogany square-back sofa, with reeded arms, arm supports and front legs, faults, Massachusetts, c1800, 76in (193cm) wide.
$2,600–3,200 ✹ SK(B)

A George IV mahogany sofa, upholstered with a patterned red flock fabric, with a squab seat and bolster cushions, restored, 78in (198cm) wide.
$1,400–1,600 ✹ WW

A George IV rosewood sofa, the padded back and stuff-over arms with gilt-brass paterae-mounted gadrooned scrolls, c1820, 85¼in (216.5cm) wide.
$21,000–23,000 ✹ S
Fresh to the market from a private source, this sofa was of high quality with carved back legs which enabled its use as a free-standing piece rather than being confined to a wall. As a result, it sold for nearly three times the mid estimate.

An American Classical revival rosewood couch, the crest with gilt-stencilled classical motifs edged in stamped metal above the scrolled arms, with ormolu mounts over the gilt-decorated arm supports and seat rail, losses, New York or Philadelphia,1820–30, 79in (200.5cm) wide.
$20,000–22,000 ✹ SK(B)

An American Classical carved mahogany sofa, with reeded scrolled arms and curving supports, repaired, 74½in (189cm) wide.
$3,200–3,600 ✹ SK(B)

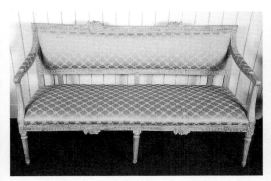

A Swedish carved and painted settee, upholstered in green brocade fabric, c1830, 61in (155cm) wide.
$2,600–2,900 ⊞ RPh

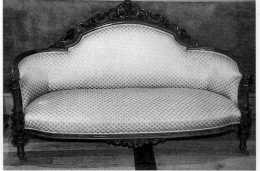

A Victorian carved walnut settee, upholstered in grey brocade fabric, 61½in (156cm) wide.
$3,200–3,600 ⊞ ChA

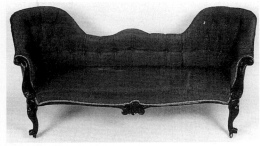

A Victorian carved walnut settee, with button-upholstered twin back panels and carved apron, 30¼in (77cm) wide.
$870–1,000 ✗ Bri

A Victorian walnut sofa, with a button-upholstered back and concave seat, on moulded cabriole legs, 53in (134.5cm) wide.
$870–1,000 ✗ L

A pair of Danish white-painted and gilded beechwood settees, with caned seats, c1870, 79in (200.5cm) wide.
$4,000–4,400 ⊞ RPh

◀ **A carved walnut settee,** upholstered in dark green velvet fabric, c1865, 57in (145cm) wide.
$1,000–1,200 ✗ LCM

▶ **A French Louis XV-style gilt-decorated settee,** with a caned back, open arms and serpentine seat with a squab cushion, 19thC, 60in (152.5cm) wide.
$440–500 ✗ CGC

▶ **A stained fruitwood settee,** the back centred by a carved flower-head medallion, with stuff-over arms and seat, with later blue plush upholstery, early 20thC, 35½in (90cm) wide.
$260–320 ✗ PFK

◀ **A mahogany cottage sofa,** with central scroll and rail-pierced splat inlaid with mother-of-pearl dots and box-wood and ebonized stringing, upholstered in beige fabric, c1900, 50in (127cm) wide.
$500–600 ✗ GAK

Definitions

Throughout the 18th century the word 'settee' was used to describe any piece of seat furniture made to accommodate two or more people, regardless of whether the back was carved or upholstered.

The term 'sofa' has Arabic origins and originally referred to a raised alcove furnished with fine rugs and cushions. Although generally interchangeable with the term 'settee', 'sofa' has tended to be used to describe larger more heavily-upholstered pieces like the ever-popular Chesterfield.

Shelves

A George III walnut hanging wall shelf, the low-galleried shelves with shaped sides above a two-drawer base, faults, restored, 36½in (92.5cm) wide.
$4,600–5,000 ➤ S(S)

A George III mahogany waterfall hanging shelf, 41in (104cm) wide.
$1,600–1,750 ➤ S(S)

A late Regency mahogany hanging shelf, the baluster-turned columns surmounted by steeple-shaped finials, 37½in (95.5cm) wide.
$580–720 ➤ HYD

A walnut hanging shelf, with turned columns, c1890, 22in (56cm) wide.
$320–360 ⊞ MLL

A George III mahogany three-tier open wall shelf, the shelves supported by turned columns interspersed with brass rods, 27in (68.5cm) wide.
$650–725 ➤ Mit

A pair of George III mahogany hanging wall shelves, each with a three-quarter gallery above three open shelves, with a pair of short drawers below, on fret-cut brackets, restored, 19¼in (49cm) wide.
$1,800–2,200 ➤ P(NW)

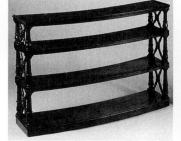

A pair of late Regency mahogany curved library shelves, with block and ring-turned supports, 40½in (103cm) wide.
$4,000–4,400 ➤ SK

A George III scarlet lacquered hanging display shelf and cabinet, the two shelves with pierced sides above a pair of serpentine doors, decorated with chinoiserie scenes, 18½in (47cm) wide.
$1,300–1,600 ➤ NOA

A pair of Irish William Moore-style bowfront satinwood-inlaid hanging shelves, each with central herringbone-banded medallions of classical figures, the aprons beneath each shelf inlaid with swags of foliage and with husk borders, late 18thC, 28¾in (73cm) wide.
$18,000–22,000 ➤ HOK
Irish antiques are currently very sought-after.

A Victorian ebonized shelf unit, the three serpentine shelves on flower-encrusted porcelain columns, with turned finials and silk-covered back board, 24½in (62cm) wide.
$1,000–1,300 ➤ AH

◀ **A pair of Regency-style patinated brass and glass wall shelves,** each in the shape of a lantern, the interior with a mirrored back and glass shelf, late 19thC, 10¾in (27.5cm) wide.
$1,300–1,600 ➤ NOA

Sideboards

A George III mahogany sideboard, crossbanded and inlaid with stringing, the central drawer flanked by two drawers, over a cellaret and a cupboard, 70¼in (178.5cm) wide.
$3,000–3,500 ➢ AH

A George III inlaid mahogany bowfront sideboard, the bowfront frieze drawer over a kneehole arch, flanked by two drawers and two dummy drawers enclosing a cellaret, 60in (152.5cm) wide.
$4,800–5,800 ➢ Mit

A Regency mahogany bowfront sideboard, in the style of Gillows, the frieze drawer with ebonized stringing, flanked by two deep drawers with brass ring-drop handles, 39in (99cm) wide.
$4,400–5,000 ➢ HYD

Facts in brief

In its earliest incarnation the sideboard was nothing more than a highly decorative table on which the host could display his best silver.

Shortly after 1770 the first designs were published for an accompanying pair of pedestals, one for use as a plate-warmer, the other as a pot cupboard. A knife urn for the top of each pedestal and a wine cistern to stand under the table completed the ensemble.

At the same time a single piece of furniture combining all the component parts of this arrangement was being developed for the less palatial dining room. The resulting creation was, at its best, a triumphant blend of practicality and style.

A George III figured-mahogany sideboard, the central drawer flanked by cellarets, all crossbanded and inlaid with quarter fans, with central sliding recessed tambour door, 60in (152.5cm) wide.
$16,000–17,500 ⊞ HA

A George III mahogany and satinwood-inlaid sideboard, 57½in (146cm) wide.
$8,700–9,700 ⊞ APO

A Danish mahogany and parcel-gilt sideboard, the upper section with a mirrored back banded in satinwood and with ebony lines, the arcaded frieze with griffin cresting, the base with a white marble top above a drawer and pierced eagle-head supports, the concave platform base with a mirror back, damaged, early 19thC, 47¼in (120cm) wide.
$2,200–2,600 ➢ P

▶ **An American Federal mahogany and mahogany-veneer sideboard,** by Reuben Swift, the bowed centre section above three cockbeaded drawers and cabinets, original drawer pulls, damaged, New Bedford, Massachusetts, 1815–20, 69½in (176.5cm) wide.
$2,000–2,300 ➢ SK(B)

A George III satinwood-crossbanded figured-mahogany sideboard, the central cutlery drawer flanked by two drawers to one side and a cellaret drawer with two dummy drawer fronts to the other, with Bramah locks, 63in (160cm) wide.
$5,000–6,000 ➢ Bri

A George III mahogany sideboard, the four drawers inlaid with stringing, with brass handles, 54in (137cm) wide.
$800–950 ➢ WilP

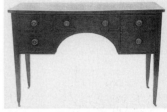

An Irish mahogany sideboard, by Gillingtons of Dublin, the concave front with ropetwist edge, the frieze with a concave drawer, flanked by two short drawers, above four cupboard doors, interspersed with reeded columns on ropetwist-turned legs, early 19thC, 85in (216cm) wide.
$3,600–4,400 ➢ HOK

An American Federal inlaid mahogany sideboard, the bowed top with crossbanded veneer edge over cockbeaded drawers and cupboard doors, faults, New England, c1810, 63¾in (162cm) wide.
$2,300–2,600 ➢ SK(B)

FURNITURE

A Regency mahogany breakfront sideboard, the central concave section with a single frieze drawer flanked by cupboards, all with geometric moulding, 72in (183cm) wide.
$4,500–5,500 ↗ RTo

A Victorian mahogany mirror-backed pedestal sideboard, the mirror frame carved with a trailing vine, the base with a white marble serpentine top, the frieze drawer flanked on either side by a cupboard door, enclosing shelving and drawers, with label inscribed 'Thomas Mills, Bradford', 84in (213.5cm) wide.
$4,000–4,600 ↗ AH

A late Victorian walnut sideboard, with three-plate mirror back and brass handles, c1890, 60in (152.5cm) wide.
$1,600–1,750 ↗ RPh

An Edwardian George III-style mahogany sideboard, with satinwood banding, the breakfront with two drawers flanked by bowfronted cupboards, 66in (167.5cm) wide.
$1,600–1,850 ↗ L

A William IV mahogany pedestal sideboard, with a carved back, the top with two drawers above a central frieze drawer flanked by tapering panel doors with drawers over, 72½in (184cm) wide.
$650–800 ↗ P(Ba)

A late Victorian rosewood and marquetry sideboard, with a mirror back, the base section with a single frieze drawer over a glazed door, flanked by open shelves with cupboards below, 55in (139.5cm) wide.
$1,300–1,600 ↗ GIL

A Victorian Renaissance-style carved oak pedestal sideboard, the upper section with a mirror surmounted by a scrolled broken pediment with a central female bust flanked by soldiers, the plate flanked by male and female caryatid supports, the base with three frieze drawers above a pair of cupboard doors flanked by caryatid pilasters, the whole carved with floral scrolls, baskets of flowers and grotesques, c1890, 91in (231cm) wide.
$5,000–5,800 ↗ Bon(C)

A Victorian Gothic-style carved oak sideboard, with three frieze drawers, over panelled cupboard doors carved with Gothic arches, leaf finials and paterae, flanked by octagonal panelled and triple-cluster columns, 68in (172.5cm) wide.
$1,200–1,450 ↗ CAG

A late Victorian pollarded oak and ebonized mirror-backed sideboard, the inverted breakfront base with a frieze drawer over a central recess, flanked by pedestal cupboards centred by heavy bosses within Greek key borders, enclosing a cutlery drawer and cellaret, damaged, c1880, 83in (211cm) wide.
$1,450–1,750 ↗ Hal

An Edwardian mahogany sideboard, the base with two central long drawers and an arched recess flanked by acanthus-carved cupboard doors, 72in (183cm) wide.
$430–500 ↗ P(Ba)

A Georgian-style mahogany-inlaid serpentine sideboard, c1910, 61in (155cm) wide.
$3,200–3,500 ⊞ MTay

Stands

A carved mahogany stand, attributed to Ince & Mayhew, with rococo-style S-scrolled legs, c1760, 28in (71cm) high.
$17,500–19,500 ⊞ REI
The partnership of William Ince and John Mayhew was established in 1759 in Broad Street (now Broadwick), Soho. As the business prospered, further premises were purchased in the area, and over 100 men were in their employ. They published *The Universal System of Household Furniture* between 1759 and 1762, and during their most influential period, from the early 1760s to the 1780s, they were associated with Robert Adam and, to a lesser extent, Thomas Chippendale. The dissolution of Mayhew and Ince's partnership was announced in 1800.

A Victorian walnut boot stand, the turned columns surmounted by finials, enclosing six shaped rests, 31¾in (80.5cm) wide.
$360–430 ♣ P(Ed)

A George III mahogany kettle stand, with a slide, turned column and tripod base, 25in (63.5cm) high.
$5,000–5,500 ⊞ GKe
Kettle or urn stands first appeared in the mid-18th century, when 'taking tea' became an important social event. Their main function was to act as a stand for a silver kettle and also possibly its heater, and they often incorporated a slide on which a teapot or cup and saucer could be placed.

A Regency wig stand, with a turned column, 14in (35.5cm) high.
$300–320 ⊞ ALA

A mahogany plant stand, with three tiers, 19thC, 29in (73.5cm) wide.
$400–450 ♣ PFK

◄ **A walnut three-shelf magazine stand,** with a quarter-veneered top and bergère sides, early 20thC, 22½in (57cm) high.
$1,000–1,250 ♣ L&E

A Portuguese red-painted and parcel-gilt corner stand, the top above a plain frieze with a carved apron on three carved cabriole legs, later painted, mid-18thC, 39½in (100.5cm) wide.
$3,200–3,500 ♣ Bon

A William IV rosewood folio stand, the slatted supports on a ratchet mechanism and with trestle ends, 36¼in (92cm) wide.
$2,100–2,300 ♣ CGC

A late Victorian three-tier jardinière stand, with a gilt-metal galleried surround, on cabriole legs, 31in (78.5cm) high.
$1,600–1,900 ⊞ BERA

A George III mahogany bookstand, the hinged top above a frieze drawer, on later base, 13½in (34.5cm) wide.
$1,000–1,150 ♣ NOA

A Victorian mahogany dressing stand, the oval adjustable mirror above a box top enclosing two spring-release compartments, 19in (48.5cm) diam.
$1,000–1,150 ♣ RBB

An Edwardian inlaid mahogany three-tier cake stand, with bevelled glass centres, 39in (99cm) high.
$450–500 ⊞ RPh

◄ **An Edwardian inlaid mahogany folding cake stand,** 35½in (90cm) high.
$240–270 ⊞ Fai

FURNITURE

Coat, Hat & Stick Stands

A Georgian mahogany hat stand, the upswept arms on a turned column with a ball finial, 62¼in (158cm) high.
$900–1,000 ⚒ P(EA)

◀ A brass and cast-iron stick stand, the top with ten divisions, with tubular end supports and a cast-iron drip tray, early 20thC, 17½in (44.5cm) wide.
$1,000–1,150 ⚒ S(S)

A George IV mahogany coat stand, the nine shaped arms finished with brass finials, a brass umbrella ring below, on a reeded tripod base with brass drip tray, some brass replaced, 74¼in (188.5cm) high.
$5,800–7,200 ⚒ Bon

A Victorian cast-iron double stick stand, with two oval apertures, foliate back and birds'-head sides, 29½in (75cm) high.
$725–875 ⚒ DMC

A late Victorian oak and brass stick stand, in the style of Shoolbred & Co, the pierced three-quarter brass gallery shelf flanked by brass urn finials, the panelled back with a brass rail above a metal drip tray, 22in (56cm) wide.
$2,000–2,300 ⚒ S(S)

An early Victorian mahogany coat stand, with eight projecting pegs surmounted by an urn finial, 74½in (189cm) high.
$2,500–3,000 ⚒ P

A late Victorian oak stick and umbrella stand, the back with a brass gallery flanked by two lower conforming galleries and a frieze drawer, with two curved tubular brass rails to either side above metal-lined drip trays and a moulded base, 39in (99cm) high.
$3,000–3,500 ⚒ MEA

Steps

A set of William IV mahogany library steps, 28in (71cm) high.
$5,000–5,500 ⊞ REI

◀ A set of mahogany library steps, the top step hinged, the second leather-lined and sliding to reveal an open compartment, 19thC, 16½in (42cm) wide.
$580–720 ⚒ P(L)

A set of mahogany library steps, with caned sides, the top step with a hinged lid, altered, 19thC, 16½in (42cm) wide.
$3,300–4,000 ⚒ S(S)

A set of Edwardian mahogany library steps, 21¼in (54cm) wide.
$3,200–3,800 ⚒ Bon(C)

A set of elm *faux* bamboo library steps, c1840, 74in (188cm) high.
$870–1,100 ⊞ GBr

Stools

A pair of walnut stools, with padded seats, on cabriole legs joined by baluster-turned stretchers, early 18thC, 26¾in (68cm) wide.
$4,500–5,500 ⚒ P

A Georgian oak commode stool, with hinged upholstered seat, shaped apron and turned legs, 18in (45.5cm) wide.
$1,000–1,300 ⊞ SWG

A pair of Swedish neo-classical painted and parcel-gilt stools, each with an upholstered seat above a leaf-tip-carved apron, late 18thC, 16in (40.5cm) wide.
$8,700–9,500 ⚒ S(NY)

A Regency mahogany footstool, the needlework cover with a central armorial device, on reeded splayed legs, 13½in (34.5cm) wide.
$360–430 ⚒ CGC

A pair of Regency mahogany and rosewood footstools, with close-studded green hide seats, c1820, 13¾in (35cm) wide.
$5,000–5,500 ⚒ S

An American classical carved mahogany footstool, the stuff-over seat with a curule base carved with leaves, C-scrolls and concentric circles, Boston, 1825–29, 22½in (57cm) wide.
$1,400–1,600 ⚒ SK(B)

A William IV rosewood stool, with tulip-carved and turned legs, the original upholstery with a pattern of stylized flowerheads and a Greek key-pattern border, 31½in (80cm) wide.
$2,200–2,400 ⚒ HYD

An early Victorian mahogany stool, with crossover supports, on bun feet, upholstered in red fabric, 24in (61cm) wide.
$725–800 ⊞ RPh

A Victorian rosewood stool, with needlework upholstery, on moulded X-frame, 18in (45.5cm) wide.
$870–1,000 ⚒ L

A Victorian mahogany serpentine stool, with cabriole legs, 36in (91.5cm) wide.
$580–720 ⚒ RPI

Items in the Furniture section have been arranged in date order within each sub-section.

A George II walnut stool, with cabriole legs, the drop-in seat upholstered in gold-coloured fabric, c1870, 20in (51cm) wide.
$2,400–2,700 ⊞ REI

A Victorian rosewood footstool, upholstered with a Berlin tapestry of multi-coloured stylized flowers, the frame with scrolling rococo decoration, 16in (40.5cm) wide.
$725–875 ⚒ Mit

FURNITURE

A late Victorian stool, with carved cabriole legs, upholstered in beige fabric, 37in (94cm) long.
$1,600–1,800 ⊞ MTay

▶ A set of three Irish Victorian mahogany stools, on baluster-turned supports, upholstered in brown buttoned hide, 58¾in (149cm) long.
$4,800–5,800 ⋏ JAd

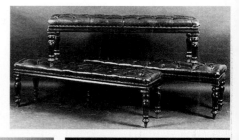

An Irish carved rosewood stool, by Strahan of Dublin, on cabriole legs with scrolling feet, upholstered in brown floral fabric, with maker's label, 19thC, 37¾in (96cm) long.
$2,900–3,200 ⋏ HOK

A pair of Eastlake giltwood footstools, on splayed legs, with needlepoint upholstery, American, c1875, 15in (38cm) diam.
$625–725 ⋏ SK

A Louis XV-style painted and parcel-gilt serpentine stool, the padded seat upholstered in striped silk, on cabriole legs, 19thC, 31in (78.5cm) long.
$950–1,150 ⋏ P

Music Stools

A Regency rosewood adjustable piano stool, on turned and reeded splayed supports, 19in (48.5cm) high.
$250–300 ⋏ ELR

A Victorian walnut piano stool, the padded hinged seat above scrolled fretwork and with silk back and sides, with a kingwood-strung drawer below, raised on melon-carved feet, 22½in (57cm) wide.
$1,300–1,600 ⋏ CGC

A William IV rosewood piano stool, the revolving later-upholstered seat stamped 'T. Norwood', the melon-fluted balustroid stem on a turned circular platform with three reeded scroll feet, 18½in (47cm) high.
$230–290 ⋏ PFK

A Regency rosewood revolving piano stool, with chair back.
$2,100–2,300 ⊞ CHE

A rosewood adjustable piano stool, by H. Brooks & Co, upholstered in red fabric, c1880, 17in (43cm) wide.
$540–620 ⊞ MTay

A Victorian walnut revolving piano stool, with carved cabriole legs, 16in (40.5cm) high.
$580–680 ⊞ RPh

A late Victorian mahogany piano stool, with a leather-covered upholstered seat and turned legs, and turned adjusting handles, 17in (43cm) wide.
$160–180 ⊞ NAW

◀ A mahogany piano stool, with upholstered seat, c1915, 20in (51cm) high.
$85–95 ⊞ NAW

An Edwardian satinwood piano stool, painted with flowers and trailing foliage, the outswept sides painted with cherubs and musical trophies, supported on ebonized ring-turned legs, the panel seat originally caned, 22½in (57cm) wide.
$800–950 ⋏ AH

Bedroom Suites

A four-piece ash bedroom suite, by Hogden of Manchester, comprising a bedside cabinet, a box commode with hinged stuff-over seat, a wardrobe with mirror plate and lacking central door, and a chest of drawers, drawers stamped with maker's name, c1880, wardrobe 91¾in (233cm) wide.
$2,300–2,900 B&L

A Victorian four-piece satinwood bedroom suite, comprising a three-door wardrobe with central mirrored door, a pedestal dressing table with a swing-frame mirror, a six-drawer chest and a five-drawer chest, most pieces stamped 'Holland & Sons'.
$4,000–4,600 MEA

A Victorian four-piece mahogany and marquetry bedroom suite, comprising a wardrobe, dressing table, marble-topped washstand and pot cupboard, wardrobe 87in (221cm) wide.
$20,000–22,500 MTay

▶ **An Edwardian mahogany part bedroom suite,** all with stringing and chequer banding, comprising a triple wardrobe, dressing table, bedside cupboard and chair, wardrobe 84in (213.5cm) wide.
$2,000–2,500 AH

An American Renaissance four-piece gilt-incised walnut bedroom suite, comprising a bedstead, tall chest of drawers, dressing table and bureau, late 19thC, bedstead 56½in (143.5cm) wide.
$25,500–29,000 S(NY)

Salon Suites

◀ **A Swiss walnut salon suite,** comprising a sofa and six chairs, with inter-laced double-oval backs, Zurich, c1790, sofa 72¾in (185cm) wide.
$4,400–5,000 S(Z)

A Victorian rosewood and simulated-rosewood salon suite, comprising a settee, two side chairs and four open armchairs, upholstered in yellow tapestry fabric.
$5,750–7,250 MEA

FURNITURE

A Victorian walnut salon suite, comprising a settee and two armchairs, the cresting rails carved with foliage above button-backed shaped stuff-over seats.
$1,450–1,600 ⚒ P(Ba)

A Renaissance revival-style ebonized and ivory marquetry salon suite, comprising a settee, two lounge chairs and two side chairs, the settee with a shaped scroll cresting inlaid with scrolling foliate marquetry, the base of the back supported by pierced foliate carving and marquetry spandrels, the side chairs with solid backs inlaid with arabesques and a monogram, upholstered in yellow fabric, possibly American, mid-19thC.
$5,800–7,200 ⚒ P
The interpretation of the Renaissance theme suggests an American manufacturer such as John Jelliff or Herter Brothers. The anthemion-shaped leaf tips are, in this period, a particularly characteristic American device. The use of chimera or classical masks is evident on pieces by both makers.

A Victorian rococo revival carved walnut salon suite, comprising a pair of elbow chairs with scrolled and leaf-carved arched crest and pierced splats above a stuff-over seat, and a matching sofa, upholstered in gold fabric.
$2,000–2,600 ⚒ AH

A mid-Victorian mahogany three-piece salon suite, comprising a chaise longue, a lady's chair and a gentleman's chair, with foliate carving and baluster turnings, upholstered in pink fabric, chaise longue 80in (203cm) long.
$725–875 ⚒ Bon(M)

A late Victorian mahogany salon suite, comprising a settee, an armchair, a low chair and a pair of upright chairs, each with foliate-carved and shaped back above an upholstered seat, upholstered in yellow fabric.
$725–875 ⚒ TRL

A French Empire-style mahogany salon suite, comprising a settee, two armchairs and four single chairs, upholstered in green fabric, c1880.
$8,700–10,200 ⊞ RPh

An Irish Georgian revival three-piece suite, comprising a sofa and a pair of open armchairs, the carved outswept arms with eagle beak terminals, upholstered in red fabric, 19thC.
$8,700–10,200 ⚒ HOK

An Edwardian inlaid rosewood salon suite, by Laverton & Co, Bristol, comprising a settee, two armchairs, four side chairs and a nursing chair, the crestings and splats inlaid with arabesque medallions in blond woods and ivory, strung throughout in ivory, the seats and backs covered in gold velour fabric.
$4,400–5,000 ⚒ HAM

A Continental neo-classical marquetry-inlaid fruit-wood salon suite, comprising a low settee and four chairs, all inlaid with scrolled foliate vines, late 19thC.
$4,500–5,000 ⚒ SK

> **Miller's is a price GUIDE not a price LIST**

▶ **A red japanned three-piece caned bergère suite,** comprising a sofa and two armchairs, 1920s.
$1,450–1,750 ⚒ Bon(C)

◀ **A black lacquered three-piece bergère suite,** with scrolled arms and caned backs, gilt-decorated with figures and foliage, 1930s.
$1,000–1,250 ⚒ CGC

Architects' Tables

A George III mahogany architect's table, with an adjustable rising top, fitted with two slides to the sides, the front dummy drawer enclosing a baize-lined sliding section over an open drawer, 36¼in (92cm) wide.
$5,500–6,500 ↗ **WL**

A George III mahogany architect's table, the top with a ratcheted centre section, with drop leaves and sliding front enclosing a fitted interior and felt-lined surface, 42in (106.5cm) wide.
$5,000–5,800 ↗ **SK**

◀ **A French mahogany architect's table,** with a hinged and ratcheted top inset with green leather, over a slide to each side flanking a frieze drawer, early 19thC, 35in (89cm) wide.
$2,500–2,900 ↗ **TEN**

▶ **A Regency mahogany secretaire architect's table,** attributed to Gillows, 42in (106.5cm) wide.
$34,000–40,000 ⊞ **RGa**
The firm of Gillows produced very high quality furniture which usually sells at a premium.

A mahogany architect's table, c1810, 33in (84cm) wide.
$2,450–2,700 ⊞ **NAW**

Breakfast Tables

A George III mahogany breakfast table, with rosewood-crossbanded tilt-top and downswept reeded legs, 53in (134.5cm) wide.
$9,000–10,000 ⊞ CAT

A George III mahogany breakfast table, the crossbanded tilt-top and quadruple splayed legs inlaid with stringing, 60¼in (153cm) wide.
$4,750–5,500 ⚒ S

A Regency mahogany breakfast table, the top with a reeded edge, on a baluster-turned column support with reeded hipped sabre legs, faults, 52¾in (134cm) wide.
$800–1,000 ⚒ S(S)

An American Classical carved mahogany breakfast table, attributed to the workshop of Duncan Phyfe, the top with one working and one dummy drawer above a carved four-pillar and platform support over four leaf-carved legs, c1820, 38in (96.5cm) wide.
$8,000–8,800 ⚒ SK(B)
Duncan Phyfe (1768–1854) worked in New York City from approximately 1790, first on Broad Street, later on Partition Street.

A Regency mahogany and rosewood-crossbanded breakfast table, lock mechanism damaged, 38½in (98cm) wide.
$1,750–2,250 ⚒ Bon(C)

A George IV mahogany breakfast table, the tilt-top raised on a ring-turned and fluted column with four fluted downswept legs, 42in (106.5cm) wide.
$580–720 ⚒ DOC

A William IV rosewood breakfast table, the tilt-top above a baluster-turned column on quadriform base, 47½in (120.5cm) diam.
$2,500–3,000 ⚒ HYD

An American Classical mahogany Pembroke breakfast table, the top supported on a central column with acanthus-leaf collars, with four acanthus-hipped downswept legs, c1825, 48in (122cm) wide.
$3,200–3,800 ⚒ S(NY)

A William IV rosewood breakfast table, the top on a turned pillar and triform plinth, 50in (127cm) diam.
$1,800–2,300 ⚒ L

A William IV mahogany tilt-top breakfast table, on a turned pedestal support, with three scrolled feet, 54in (137cm) diam.
$2,200–2,600 ⚒ WilP

A William IV rosewood breakfast table, the tilt-top on a waisted column and triform base with scroll feet, 50¾in (129cm) diam.
$1,000–1,150 ⚒ P(B)

A Victorian rosewood breakfast table, the tilt-top on a lobed baluster stem, the tripod base with leaf-carved downswept legs, 59½in (151cm) diam.
$1,700–2,200 ⚒ AH

A Victorian rosewood tilt-top breakfast table, the figured two-piece top with a turned stem and leaf-carved circular platform base on three downcurved legs with C-scroll carving to the backs, 48in (122cm) diam.
$2,200–2,600 ⚒ PFK

Colour Review

A mahogany bonheur du jour, in the Sheraton style, inlaid with ebony stringing, c1780, 39in (99cm) high.
$17,400–20,300 ⊞ REI

A Regency coromandel bonheur du jour, the secretaire drawer enclosing a velvet-lined writing surface, pigeonholes and drawers, 27½in (70cm) wide.
$7,250–8,700 ✗ P

A French boulle bonheur du jour, the serpentine upper section above a projecting lower section with a single frieze drawer fitted with a velvet-inlaid writing slide, 19thC, 33in (84cm) wide.
$2,900–3,200 ✗ LJ

A French mahogany serpentine bonheur du jour, with fretwork panel above three frieze drawers, c1860, 45¾in (116cm) wide.
$1,750–2,175 ✗ WL

A William and Mary burr-walnut and seaweed marquetry bureau, in the style of Samuel Bennett, the fall-front enclosing a sliding well, pigeonholes and drawers, on later bracket feet, the top possibly reveneered, 37½in (95.5cm) wide.
$13,000–16,000 ✗ P

A Queen Anne walnut bureau, the fall-front enclosing a shaped and stepped interior and well, 36in (91.5cm) wide.
$29,000–32,000 ⊞ REI

A George I walnut bureau, with quarter-veneered and herring-bone-banded fall-front, with original bracket feet and brass handles c1720, 36in (91.5cm) wide.
$29,000–36,000 ⊞ REI

An early Georgian burr-walnut bureau, inlaid with cross- and feather-banding, the fall-front enclosing a fitted interior, 35¼in (89.5cm) wide.
$1,000–1,100 ✗ AH

A George III black lacquered and japanned bureau, with gilt chinoiserie decoration, the fall-front enclosing pigeonholes and drawers, above a frieze drawer, 26¾in (68cm) wide.
$7,900–9,400 ✗ P

A Louis XV marquetry bureau, the fall-front enclosing a fitted interior, above two frieze drawers, restored, stamped 'A. M. Criaerd', mid-18thC, 26½in (67.5cm) wide.
$9,400–11,600 ✗ S(Mon)

▶ **A Victorian painted satinwood bureau,** with fitted interior, probably adapted from a late 18thC mahogany bureau, late 19thC, 34¾in (88.5cm) wide.
$3,600–4,300 ✗ Bon(C)

◀ **A kingwood and marquetry bureau de dame,** the fitted interior with a pull-out leather writing slide, 19thC, 35½in (90cm) wide.
$3,600–4,300 ✗ HOK

A George III mahogany bureau, the fall-front enclosing a fitted interior, with original brass fittings, c1770, 36in (91.5cm) wide.
$7,500–9,500 ⊞ BERA

A German gilt-metal-mounted rosewood bureau de dame, the fall-front enclosing a stepped interior with four drawers and a sliding compartment, 19thC, 35½in (90cm) wide.
$2,000–2,400 ✗ TEN

An Edwardian painted satinwood bureau, the fall-front enclosing a fitted interior, 37in (94cm) wide.
$5,800–6,500 ✗ P(ED)

A George IV mahogany four-poster bed, c1825, 75in (190.5cm) long. $8,000–8,800 ⊞ SeH

A French gilt-bronze-mounted mahogany *lit d'alcove,* early 19thC, 43¼in (110cm) wide. $2,400–2,700 ⚒ S(Z)

A William IV Empire-style mahogany cradle, the terminal of one support carved with an eagle's head, the other with a flowerhead and fluted spire button finial, 45in (114.5cm) long. $1,700–2,100 ⚒ HAM

A Victorian mahogany four-poster bed, with leaf-wrapped fluted columns, lion-mask carving and paw feet, with velvet drapes, 82¾in (210cm) wide. $5,100–5,800 ⚒ LJ

A mahogany four-poster bedstead, Grenada, c1840, 57in (145cm) wide. $10,000–12,300 ⚒ S(NY)

▶ **A mid-Victorian cast-iron four-poster bed,** with a blue verdigris crown and canopy, c1875, 66in (167.5cm) wide. $2,900–3,350 ⊞ SeH

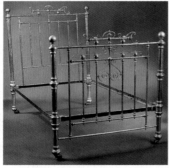

A Victorian brass double bed, the spar ends flanked by posts with ball finials and scrolling crest, 49¼in (125cm) wide. $1,000–1,200 ⚒ P(Ed)

A Victorian mahogany four-poster bed, c1880, 60in (152.5cm) wide. $11,600–13,000 ⊞ SeH

A walnut bed, with original gilding, c1890, 42in (106.5cm) wide. $850–1,000 ⊞ SWA

A Louis XV-style bed, with a carved panel to the footboard, c1900, 60in (152.5cm) wide. $2,100–2,300 ⊞ SWA

A French ash bedstead, with stringing and ormolu detail, with a matching night stand, Paris, c1890, 60in (152.5cm) wide. $2,100–2,300 ⊞ SWA

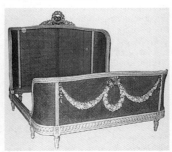

A French cane bedstead, with painted framework, decorated with carved garlands of flowers, c1890, 72in (183cm) wide. $3,600–4,600 ⊞ SeH

A late Georgian mahogany breakfront library bookcase, with astragal-glazed doors to upper section, 87½in (222.5cm) wide. $10,800–13,000 ⚷ TMA

A Queen Anne walnut bureau with later bookcase top, inlaid with herringbone banding, the fall-front opening to reveal a fitted interior with drawers, pigeonholes and well, restored, 82in (208.5cm) high. $10,100–12,300 ⚷ RTo

A Dutch walnut and banded bureau bookcase, the doors enclosing six open compartments and four short drawers above a fall-front enclosing a stepped interior of drawers, pigeonholes and a sliding well, 18thC, 40½in (103cm) high. $13,000–16,000 ⚷ P

An American Federal inlaid mahogany writing desk and bookcase, the cupboard doors enclosing an eight-compartment interior above tambour doors centring a prospect door enclosing drawers and valanced compartments, the lower case with a fold-out writing surface, southern Massachusetts, c1816, 40in (101.5cm) wide. $36,250–43,500 ⚷ SK(B)

A mahogany cabinet bookcase, by Williams & Gibton, each door with bold-cut gilt-brass grilles and carved quadrants, with white marble tops, c1830, 137¾in (350cm) wide. $10,100–12,300 ⚷ HOK

Miller's is a price GUIDE not a price LIST

A William IV mahogany bookcase, with twin glazed doors flanked by column supports with carved capitals, above twin-moulded frieze drawers on Tuscan column supports and platform base, 48in (122cm) high. $7,250–8,700 ⚷ JAd

A George IV rosewood open bookcase, c1830, 33in (84cm) wide. $1,900–2,300 ⚷ Bon

An oak breakfront five-door bookcase, with original stained glass, c1880, 114in (289.5cm) wide. $18,800–21,000 ⊞ MTay

A mahogany secretaire bookcase, the blind lozenge-trellis doors enclosing adjustable shelves, the fall-front enclosing a green leather-lined writing surface and drawers above a pair of conforming doors enclosing a shelf, restored, probably Irish, mid-19thC, 38in (96.5cm) wide. $14,500–17,500 ⚷ S

A Victorian burr-walnut library bookcase, with shaped-front frieze drawer above twin arch-panelled doors flanked by corbels, 43in (109cm) wide. $3,600–4,300 ⚷ Bri

A two-door walnut bookcase, with panelled doors, c1900, 91in (231cm) high. $2,900–3,300 ⊞ RPh

◄ **A Victorian mahogany breakfront secretaire bookcase,** the base with a central drawer fitted with bird's-eye maple-veneered drawers and pigeonholes, 92in (233.5cm) wide. $11,500–13,500 ⚷ Bea(E)

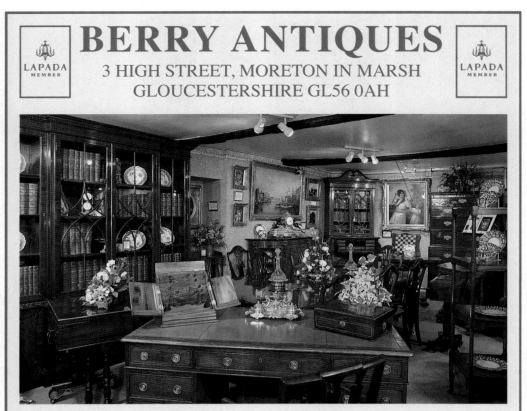

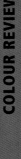

COLOUR REVIEW

A George II mahogany bureau cabinet, the panel doors enclosing adjustable shelves, the fall-front opening to reveal an arrangement of drawers and pigeonholes flanking a central cupboard door, on later shaped bracket feet, c1740, 40in (101.5cm) wide.
$27,500–30,500 ⚘ S

A Dutch figured walnut display cabinet, the interior with shaped shelves, the base with a single drawer, late 19thC, 63in (160cm) wide.
$4,300–5,000 ⚘ M

▶ **A George III inlaid mahogany secretaire bookcase,** the fitted writing drawer with small drawers and pigeonholes, c1790, 46¾in (119cm) wide.
$18,000–21,750 ⚘ HOK

A Louis Philippe-style walnut secretaire, the fossil marble top above a fall-front opening to a desk interior, the cabinet doors enclosing a single drawer, late 19thC, 40½in (103cm) wide.
$4,500–5,000 ⚘ NOA

A Queen Anne mulberry-veneered corner cabinet, the pair of doors with butterfly hinges, early 18thC, 41in (104cm) high.
$8,000–8,800 ⊞ REI

A Sheraton revival bowfront china cabinet, painted with ovals and garlands, late 19thC, 24in (61cm) wide.
$6,500–8,000 ⚘ JNic

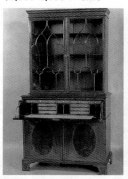

An ebony and porphyry-mounted table cabinet, the centre cupboard door veneered in Sicilian marble, previously on turned feet, 19thC, 31in (78.5cm) wide.
$6,500–8,000 ⚘ P

A solid walnut standing corner cupboard, later-carved in 17thC-style, with doors enclosing shaped shelves, with two further doors below, 18thC, 48½in (123cm) wide.
$1,400–1,700 ⚘ TEN

A William and Mary walnut-veneered escritoire, the handles and bun feet replaced, c1680, 68in (172.5cm) high.
$43,500–50,000 ⊞ REI

A Biedermeier birch, elm and satinwood inlaid display cabinet, the two glazed panelled doors over a single frieze drawer with brass drop handles, c1820, 45¼in (115cm) wide.
$2,000–2,300 ⚘ LJ

A French Transitional tulipwood, satinwood, amaranth, *bois de violette* and palissander marquetry *secrétaire à abattant*, by Jean Georges Schlichtig, with fossil marble top, the secretaire interior fitted with later mirror panels, restored, stamped 'I. G. Schlichtig', mid-18thC, 37¾in (96cm) wide.
$10,000–12,300 ⚘ Bon

◀ **A Louis Philippe palissander *secrétaire à abattant*,** the fall-front enclosing an interior fitted with an inset-leather writing slope, seven drawers and a cupboard, early 19thC, 39½in (100.5cm) wide.
$4,600–5,000 ⚘ LJ

A Scottish mahogany secretaire cabinet, c1850, 40in (101.5cm) high.
$2,600–3,000 ⊞ RPh

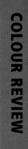

A William and Mary oyster olivewood and sycamore cabinet-on-stand, the cabinet late 17thC with a cushion frieze drawer, the fitted interior with an arrangement of drawers surrounding a central door enclosing further drawers, on later stand with knop-turned ash supports, 48in (122cm) wide.
$12,300–14,500 ✒ S

A black japanned cabinet-on-stand, the multiple hinged doors enclosing a later mirrored interior, retaining the original drawer fronts, on a later Carolean-style giltwood and composition stand, late 17thC, 41in (104cm) wide.
$4,500–5,500 ✒ P

A papier mâché and mahogany cabinet-on-stand, by Jennens & Bettridge, the panelled doors enclosing a fitted interior of five graduated drawers decorated with gilt chinoiseries, on later stand, stamped 'Jennens & Bettridge London', c1830, 44in (112cm) wide.
$17,400–20,300 ✒ Bon(C)

A Flemish tortoiseshell and ebony collector's cabinet-on-stand, with a central door enclosing tiled interior surrounded by nine small drawers, doors missing, c1680, 36¼in (92cm) wide.
$3,700–4,300 ✒ Bri

A Portuguese coromandel, ebony, ivory and tortoise-shell parquetry inlaid table cabinet-on-stand, the doors enclosing an arrangement of ten drawers around a central cupboard door, on a later stand, restored, early 18thC, 20½in (52cm) wide.
$3,200–3,600 ✒ S(S)

A Victorian thuya and walnut-veneered cigar cabinet-on-stand, applied throughout with cast-brass mounts, the door enclosing cigar trays with four small drawers, the stand with a frieze drawer, 20in (51cm) wide.
$3,400–4,000 ✒ Bea(E)

An Italian Renaissance walnut credenza, with two long drawers, interspersed with three small drawers, over two sets of double doors, Florence, early 16thC, 72¼in (183.5cm) wide.
$24,500–26,800 ♠ S(NY)

A Regency rosewood and brass marquetry side cabinet, with tilt top, 41in (104cm) wide.
$2,300–2,900 ♠ P

A pair of Victorian Louis XVI-style walnut side cabinets, by Howard & Sons, with applied gilt-metal mounts, each with a door with a brass grille enclosing shelves, c1860, 35½in (90cm) wide.
$16,000–18,800 ♠ S

A mid-Victorian burr-walnut, amboyna, thuya, rosewood and marquetry side cabinet, inlaid and crossbanded overall and applied with gilt-metal mounts and escutcheons, c1865, 74in (188cm) wide.
$8,700–10,000 ♠ Bon(C)

A parquetry and gilt-metal mounted side cabinet, by Gillow & Co, the breakfront slightly undulating, stamped, 19thC, 47¾in (121.5cm) wide.
$16,000–17,500 ♠ P(EA)

A Victorian inlaid burr-walnut bowfront side cabinet, with ormolu mounts, the central door enclosing a shelf, 61½in (156cm) wide.
$2,000–2,400 ♠ HAM

A Sheraton-style satinwood side cabinet, inlaid with rosewood-banding and parcel-gilt, painted with classical vases of flowers and vine and floral swag borders, the doors painted with 18thC ladies, late 19thC, 46¾in (119cm) wide.
$12,300–14,500 ♠ P(S)

A pair of French brass-mounted cabinets, by Jeanselme Fils Godin Cie, with matching rosewood veneers in diamond-shaped design, stamped, c1870, 37in (94cm) wide.
$11,500–12,500 ⊞ HA

A Victorian side cabinet, with burr-marquetry panels and frieze, the central doors flanked by a pair of pilasters with mirrors behind, mounted with gilt-metal classical mouldings, 74in (188cm) wide.
$3,600–4,300 ♠ RBB

A French ebonized side cabinet, with brass inlaid stringing, ormolu mounts, the door applied with coloured and stained carved ivory mounts, 19thC, 33½in (85cm) wide.
$950–1,100 ♠ DDM

A French walnut side cabinet, decorated with classical gilt-metal mounts and ornate floral marquetry, 19thC, 72in (183cm) wide.
$5,000–5,800 ♠ LJ

A German ebonized beech and Dresden porcelain cabinet, the interior veneered in walnut and the gilt-metal moulded door set with an oval porcelain plaque, 19thC, 31in (78.5cm) wide.
$5,800–7,200 ♠ DN

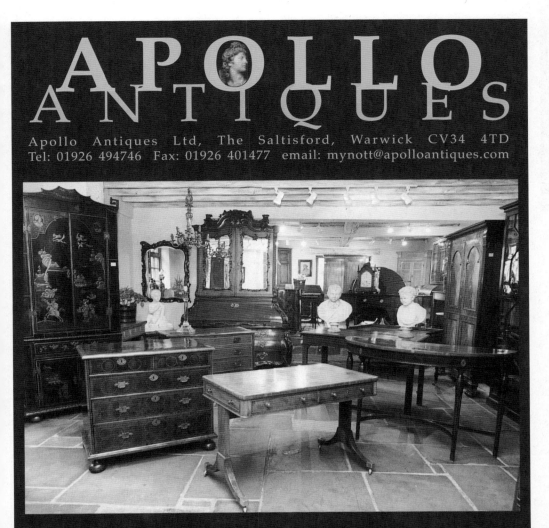

An American rococo
revival carved walnut
armchair, mid-19thC.
$5,800–6,500 ⚒ NOA

**A pair of Regency-style
armchairs,** painted with
Grecian figures, with
fluted legs and original
castors, c1880.
$16,000–18,000 ⊞ REI

**A pair of late Victorian
armchairs,** inlaid with ivory
and satinwood.
$3,000–3,300 ⊞ BERA

**A pair of Regency
mahogany bergère chairs,**
with reeded arm supports
and conforming front legs.
$16,700–20,300 ⚒ CGC

A set of eight Regency
mahogany dining chairs,
including a pair of armchairs.
$12,300–13,700 ⊞ DOA

**A set of six George IV
mahogany sabre-legged
dining chairs.**
$1,700–2,000 ⚒ DOC

**A set of eight George IV
mahogany dining chairs,**
including a pair of armchairs.
$4,500–5,500 ⚒ HAM

**A set of six Swedish
birch dining chairs,**
reupholstered, c1820.
$4,000–4,400 ⊞ RPh

A set of six Victorian
mahogany buckle-back
dining chairs.
$800–950 ⚒ RB

A set of eight George IV rosewood rail-back dining
chairs, with cane seats.
$11,500–14,500 ⚒ JAd

**A William IV pollarded oak
hall chair,** with panel seat.
$440–500 ⊞ RPh

**A Victorian mahogany
metamorphic library chair,**
with a hinged section
folding out to steps.
$1,700–2,000 ⚒ LJ

A mahogany reclining library chair,
possibly Russian, c1840.
$3,600–4,300 ⚒ S(S)

**A hardwood and parcel-gilt stool and throne
chair,** the stool with a string seat, the chair with
a carved panel back and sides, early 20thC,
stool 39in (99cm) wide.
$7,500–8,700 ⚒ P
**These items were modelled on the Bed of
the Divine Cow and a child's chair discovered
in the tomb of Tutankhamun.**

An oyster laburnum chest of drawers, the top with geometric line-inlay of holly with ash banding and cross-banding in walnut, with later drop handles, c1680, 38in (96.5cm) wide.
$29,000–32,500 ⊞ **HA**

A chest of drawers, decorated with olivewood parquetry, oyster veneers and geometric stringing, with inlaid holly border, c1715, 40in (101.5cm) wide.
$27,500–32,000 ⊞ **RGa**

A Maltese olivewood and cross-banded serpentine commode, inlaid with boxwood lines, mid-18thC, 44in (112cm) wide.
$9,500–11,500 ✦ **P**

A Dutch mahogany and floral marquetry chest of drawers, 18thC, 33½in (85cm) wide.
$3,200–3,700 ✦ **TEN**

A George III satinwood serpentine commode, crossbanded in rosewood and boxwood and inlaid with ebony stringing, the top with an inlaid oval panel, with later brass handles, 37in (94cm) wide.
$16,500–19,500 ✦ **DN**

A Regency mahogany breakfront chest of drawers, the four drawers flanked by locking cupboard doors faced with reeded decoration and with two further small drawers above, c1815, 48in (122cm) wide.
$2,300–2,900 ✦ **Bon**

A William IV mahogany chest of drawers, 50in (127cm) high.
$1,900–2,100 ⊞ **RPh**

A Victorian mahogany bowfront chest of drawers, c1850, 49in (124.5cm) wide.
$2,000–2,400 ⊞ **MTay**

A Victorian satinwood bowfront chest of drawers, inlaid with tulipwood crossbanding, c1880, 42¼in (107.5cm) wide.
$2,000–2,400 ✦ **Bon**

A mahogany estate cabinet, late 19thC, 43½in (110.5cm) wide.
$1,400–1,700 ✦ **TMA**

A north Italian burr-yew and crossbanded serpentine commode, with a marble top, late 19thC, 41¼in (105cm) wide.
$5,800–7,200 ✦ **B&L**

A mahogany serpentine chest of drawers, with a brushing slide, early 20thC, 39¼in (99.5cm) wide.
$2,900–3,200 ✦ **MTay**

A George I walnut crossbanded and feather-strung tallboy, with a brushing slide, 43¼in (110cm) wide.
$40,500–46,500 ➤ P(EA)

A walnut tallboy, the herringbone-inlaid drawers with original brass escutcheons, c1720, 41in (104cm) wide.
$19,000–21,000 ⊞ HA

A George III mahogany tallboy, with fluted canted angles, the base with a slide above three drawers, 44in (112cm) wide.
$4,300–5,000 ➤ DN

A George III mahogany tallboy, the top with a key-pattern cornice, with reeded columns flanking the upper section, with ornate brass handles, 74in (188cm) high.
$2,900–3,400 ➤ JNic

A Queen Anne figured walnut, ebony-strung and crossbanded chest-on-stand, c1705, 35in (89cm) wide.
$22,500–24,500 ⊞ RGa

◀ **A Queen Anne walnut and line-inlaid chest-on-stand,** on later cabriole legs, altered, 41in (104cm) wide.
$4,000–4,800 ➤ Bon

▶ **A Queen Anne walnut chest-on-stand,** with a cavetto frieze drawer, on a later stand with turned supports, 40¼in (102cm) wide.
$3,300–4,000 ➤ P(B)

A George III mahogany linen press, the panelled doors enclosing slides, 56in (142cm) wide.
$4,000–4,600 ✗ AH

A George III figured-mahogany linen press, the two doors enclosing slides, 49¼in (125cm) wide.
$3,000–3,500 ✗ RTo

A mahogany linen press, with original handles and escutcheons, c1780, 81in (205.5cm) high.
$9,000–10,000 ⊞ BERA

A George III mahogany linen press, with an inlaid and moulded cornice, 50¼in (127.5cm) wide.
$1,800–2,200 ✗ P(WM)

A George III mahogany and satinwood-banded linen press, 48in (122cm) wide.
$4,700–5,300 ⊞ CHE

A George III mahogany linen press, the satinwood-banded double doors enclosing a series of shelves, 50½in (127cm) wide.
$2,900–3,200 ✗ WL

A George III mahogany linen press, with later inlay, the cupboard doors enclosing a later shelved interior, restored, c1810, 51in (129.5cm) wide.
$4,600–5,000 ✗ S(S)

An Anglo-Dutch mahogany linen press, the two doors enclosing six sliding trays and three short drawers, early 19thC, 56in (142cm) wide.
$3,300–4,000 ✗ DN

A Georgian-style gentleman's mahogany linen press, the doors enclosing shelves, the lower section with a brushing slide, early 20thC, 50in (127cm) wide.
$1,000–1,200 ✗ PFK

A gilt-bronze-mounted kingwood, tulipwood and marquetry *armoire Régence,* partly remounted, the apron mount missing, c1720, 48in (122cm) wide.
$13,000–16,000 ✗ S

A George IV mahogany breakfront wardrobe, stamped 'Gillows, Lancaster', 94½in (240cm) wide.
$5,800–7,200 ✗ CGC

A Regency mahogany breakfront wardrobe, the interior with an arrangement of fixed and tray shelves, c1820, 84in (213.5cm) wide.
$7,500–9,000 ✗ S

◄ **A Victorian burr-walnut-veneered breakfront wardrobe,** the mirrored door applied with columns carved with spiralling shamrock leaves, probably Irish, 83½in (212cm) wide.
$2,100–2,600 ✗ Bea(E)

A Louis Philippe walnut armoire, the panelled doors inset with later glass panes, mid-19thC, 63in (160cm) wide.
$1,700–2,000 ✗ NOA

A Victorian flame-mahogany wardrobe, the doors flanked by carved and turned pilasters, 44in (112cm) wide.
$1,000–1,200 ✗ LJ

A mahogany davenport, with sliding top action, with a pullout hinged ink box and tray fitted above the side slide, early 19thC, 24½in (62cm) wide.
$2,900–3,200 ⊞ MTay

A Regency burr-oak and walnut davenport, with galleried top and original turned handles, c1825, 35in (89cm) high.
$11,500–13,000 ⊞ REI

A Regency rosewood davenport, with galleried top, the sloped front enclosing two opening drawers, 22¾in (58cm) wide.
$1,700–2,000 ⊞ WL

An early Victorian piano-top rosewood davenport, the rising super-structure above a hinged fall enclosing a fitted interior with a slide-out writing slope, 25¼in (64cm) wide.
$4,000–4,600 ⚒ P(S)

A burr-walnut davenport, the piano top with a later gallery above a bowed fall enclosing a fitted interior, c1860, 23¼in (59cm) wide.
$4,500–5,500 ⚒ Bon(C)

A burr-walnut harlequin davenport, with original leather writing surface, c1860, 43in (109cm) high.
$9,800–10,800 ⊞ BERA

A Victorian burr-walnut and inlaid davenport, the top raised compartment fitted for pens and stationery, the rear fitted with a hinged folio compartment, 24½in (61cm) wide.
$3,600–4,300 ⚒ WL

A Victorian burr-walnut and marquetry davenport, 23in (58.5cm) wide.
$2,000–2,400 ⚒ TMA

A walnut-veneered kneehole desk, c1720, 30in (76cm) wide.
$34,500–38,000 ⊞ REI

An Eastlake walnut and burr-walnut cylinder desk, with pull-out writing surface and rotary-action pedestal base, American, late 19thC, 59¼in (152cm) wide.
$7,200–8,700 ⚹ NOA

A Louis XV/XVI Transitional-style kingwood parquetry-inlaid and gilt-metal-mounted *bureau plat,* the two recessed drawers flanked by five drawers disguised as six, with opposing dummy drawers, c1900, 60¾in (154.5cm) wide.
$9,000–10,800 ⚹ P(S)

A pair of early Victorian Gothic revival oak display shelves, by James Barnwill of Hampshire, 1843, 50½in (128.5cm) long.
$2,900–3,400 ⚹ HAM

A mahogany dumb waiter, on turned supports, c1860, 48in (122cm) wide.
$2,300–2,500 ⊞ MTay

A coopered brassbound walnut jardinière, with lion-mask ring handles and a metal liner, restored, late 18thC, 10in (25.5cm) diam.
$1,100–1,200 ⊞ NAW

A French Empire gilt-bronze-mounted mahogany and amaranth jardinière, with a copper liner, early 19thC, 31in (78.5cm) wide.
$10,000–12,000 ⚹ S

A walnut lowboy, on cabriole legs, with pad feet, c1720, 30in (76cm) wide.
$18,500–21,000 ⊞ RGa

▶ **A mahogany and elm cross-banded lowboy,** mid-18thC, 30¼in (77cm) wide.
$1,400–1,700 ⚹ P

◀ **An Italian walnut and bone-inlaid pedestal,** 19thC, 49in (1124.5cm) high.
$1,400–1,700 ⚹ S(S)

A pair of William IV mahogany pole screens, inset with gros-point floral panels, 55in (139.5cm) high.
$1,300–1,600 ⚹ AH

A mahogany firescreen, inset with a tapestry panel, c1835, 18in (45.5cm) wide.
$700–850 ⊞ RL

A Victorian rosewood-framed screen, enclosing a needlework picture of a young girl seated by a tree, with fairies and gnomes playing among flowers, 14in (35.5cm) wide.
$2,200–2,600 ⚹ Mit

A Regency rosewood and cut-brass-inlaid chaise longue, inlaid overall with anthemia and trailing foliage, 59in (150cm) wide.
$11,600–13,600 ↗ P(S)

A Regency beech-framed and simulated rosewood chaise longue, the apron inlaid with cut-brass panels and rosette motifs, 77½in (197cm) wide.
$1,800–2,300 ↗ CGC

A George III mahogany-framed serpentine settee, with deeply-buttoned back, 42in (106.5cm) wide.
$2,100–2,600 ↗ Bea(E)

An Italian rococo walnut canapé, late 18thC, 80in (203cm) wide.
$5,800–7,200 ↗ NOA

Two George IV rosewood sofas, with scroll arms, c1825, variations in size, largest 83½in (212cm) wide.
$24,500–26,800 ↗ S

A Victorian carved rosewood twin-end settee, deeply buttoned overall, c1860, 92in (233.5cm) wide.
$8,200–9,000 ⊞ MTay

◄ **A Victorian walnut-framed boudoir couch,** with carved floral crest rail and low carved scroll arms, 49in (124.5cm) wide.
$1,000–1,200 ↗ DD

► **A George IV mahogany-framed sofa,** the crest rail carved with gadroons and scrolls, 82in (208.5cm) wide.
$4,300–5,000 ↗ DN

A Viennese satinbirch, ash and rosewood marquetry salon suite, comprising a settee, a pair of armchairs and four single chairs.
$10,000–11,500 ↗ P

A Louis XVI-style giltwood salon suite, comprising a settee, two armchairs and two single chairs, settee 79in (200.5cm) wide.
$4,600–5,000 ⊞ RPh

A giltwood-framed wall mirror, carved with a cherub swathed in flowers and foliage, damaged, late 17thC, 28in (71cm) wide.
$8,000–9,500 ⚒ Bea(E)

A Georgian wall mirror, with scroll-arched pediment and gilt-moulded and carved foliage decoration, 28in (71cm) wide.
$3,000–3,500 ⚒ RBB

A Matthias Locke-style carved gilt-wood mirror, 18thC, 35in (89cm) wide.
$43,500–50,500 ⚒ HOK

◀ **A Regency giltwood wall mirror,** with a carved rockwork cresting surmounted by an eagle with out-stretched wings, 30¾in (78cm) wide.
$5,000–5,800 ⚒ P(WM)

▶ **An American Federal giltwood mirror,** with a *verre églomisé* white tablet, Massachusetts, c1815, 21in (53.5cm) wide.
$13,500–16,000 ⚒ SK(B)

A French gilded wall mirror, with a stucco acanthus leaf crest, c1890, 32½in (82.5cm) wide.
$850–950 ⊞ OFM

A George III mahogany sideboard, the superstructure inlaid with panels of flowers and musical trophies, some later inlay and carving, 60in (152.5cm) wide.
$8,500–9,500 ⚒ S

A George III Sheraton-style boxwood-strung sideboard, the frieze with concealed central oval-panelled drawer, restored, 90½in (130cm) wide.
$10,000–11,500 ⚒ PFK

An American Federal mahogany sideboard, with bird's-eye maple and crossbanded rosewood veneer, attributed to the workshop of Thomas Seymour, Boston, 1805–15, 73in (185.5cm) wide.
$33,000–37,500 ⚒ SK(B)

A mid-Victorian oak baroque revival sideboard, carved with hunting motifs, fruit, vegetables and foliage, 85in (216cm) wide.
$4,800–5,800 ⚒ RTo

A George III mahogany bowfront sideboard, the drawers decorated with satinwood inlay, c1780, 53in (134.5cm) wide.
$16,000–18,000 ⊞ REI

A Scottish late George III inlaid mahogany bowfront sideboard, 77¼in (196cm) wide.
$7,500–9,000 ⚒ P(Ed)

A mahogany bowfront sideboard, the fitted frieze drawer with deep drawer recessed below, flanked by cellaret drawer and cupboard, c1820, 104in (264cm) wide.
$5,500–6,500 ⚒ RBB

A mahogany armorial sideboard, attributed to Strahan of Dublin, the inverted breakfront top supported by carved double-headed eagles, mid-19thC, 64½in (164cm) wide.
$10,800–12,000 ⚒ HOK

A Victorian mahogany pedestal sideboard, the frieze drawer flanked by two side drawers over two cupboard doors, with a fitted interior, c1880, 69in (175.5cm) wide.
$2,900–3,200 ⊞ RPh

A George III mahogany sideboard, c1780, 70½in (179cm) wide.
$12,000–13,500 ⊞ APO

A mahogany sideboard, with original locks and handles, c1810, 43in (109cm) wide.
$7,500–8,500 ⊞ BERA

An Irish brass-inlaid mahogany sideboard, the panelled scroll front legs with gilt-brass mounts and feet, Cork, early 19thC, 96in (244cm) wide.
$18,000–21,500 ⚒ HOK

A Victorian mahogany inverted breakfront sideboard, the mirrored back carved with an urn and fruiting vines, faults, c1860, 87in (221cm) wide.
$8,200–9,400 ⚒ S(S)

An Edwardian Georgian-style mahogany sideboard, by Warings, with satinwood and chequer banding and stringing, 72in (183cm) wide.
$1,700–2,000 ⚒ AH

*period roomset
t our showroom.*

A George III mahogany and satin-wood-banded breakfast table, 60¾in (154.5cm) wide.
$2,600–3,200 ✏ Bon(C)

A Regency mahogany and brass-inlaid breakfast table, in the style of George Oakley, c1815, 54¼in (138cm) wide.
$10,000–11,500 ✏ S

A Regency rosewood breakfast table, banded in satinwood and inlaid with cut brasswork, restored, 54¼in (138cm) wide.
$4,300–4,800 ✏ P

A George I gilded centre table, c1720, 36in (91.5cm) wide.
$16,000–18,000 ⊞ APO

A George IV pollarded oak centre table, the octagonal tilt-top with sycamore banding and inlaid thursae, top and base associated, c1825, 49in (124.5cm) wide.
$3,300–4,000 ✏ S(S)

An early Victorian rosewood tilt-top table, on faceted baluster column, 50in (127cm) diam.
$3,600–4,000 ⊞ MTay

A Victorian rosewood centre table, the frieze with scroll-carved motifs, c1840, 54¼in (138cm) wide.
$3,500–4,300 ✏ Bon

A Victorian burr-walnut centre table, by Gillow & Co, the top with amboyna, yew and tulipwood cross-banded border enclosing marquetry dolphins and shells, 42in (106.5cm) wide.
$11,500–13,500 ✏ DN

A George III carved mahogany dining table, in the style of Robert Adam, with a scrolling acanthus- and paterae-carved frieze, 108¾in (276cm) long.
$8,700–9,500 ✏ P

An early Victorian 'plum pudding' mahogany telescopic-action dining table, the circular top extending to accommodate three leaves, some damage, 147¾in (375.5cm) extended.
$24,500–29,000 ✏ P

◀ A Victorian mahogany dining table, the leaves contained in a five-tier whatnot with cupboard to rear, 54in (137cm) wide.
$6,800–8,000 ✏ HOK

▶ A Victorian satinwood drum table, by Gillow & Co, with later gilt-tooled leather insert, with frieze drawers, 42in (106.5cm) diam.
$14,500–17,500 ✏ P

◀ A George IV pollarded oak drum table, with four drawers and four dummy drawers to the frieze, 53in (134.5cm) diam.
$75,000–90,000 ✏ HAM

An American Federal mahogany card table, the frieze inlaid with swags and bellflowers, Boston, c1790, 35½in (90cm) wide.
$10,500–11,500 🔨 SK(B)

A Regency kingwood card table, with rosewood crossbanding, c1810, 35in (89cm) wide.
$4,000–4,600 ⊞ NAW

A Victorian burr-walnut card table, with satinwood crossbanding, c1860, 36in (91.5cm) diam.
$5,400–5,800 ⊞ BERA

An Irish late George III japanned pier table, heightened with gilt, 30in (76cm) wide.
$8,000–9,400 🔨 P

An Italian *faux* porphyry and parcel-gilt carved console table, with an associated marble top, late 18thC, 45¼in (115cm) wide.
$24,500–26,500 🔨 S

A mahogany games table, on cabriole legs, c1720, 26in (66cm) wide.
$32,000–35,000 ⊞ REI

A Georgian papier mâché tray table, with a central chinoiserie landscape, with mother-of-pearl inlay and heightened with gilt, and an ebonized stand with *faux* bamboo legs and stretchers, 29½in (75cm) wide.
$1,800–2,200 🔨 LJ

A specimen marble table top, in the style of Francesco Sibilio, on a later ebonized and parcel-gilt stand, early 19thC, 27¼in (69cm) diam.
$7,600–8,300 🔨 P

A Russian neo-classical brass-mounted kingwood games table, with tulipwood and fruitwood marquetry, late 18thC, 38in (96.5cm) wide.
$18,000–21,750 🔨 S(NY)

◄ **A Victorian papier mâché snap-top table,** the top painted with a family group, on a lobed baluster stem and platform base, the whole with gilt scrolling decoration, 24½in (62cm) diam.
$1,600–1,800 🔨 P(L)

A late Regency rosewood occasional table, attributed to Gillows of Lancaster, 13¾in (35cm) wide.
$4,000–4,600 🔨 P

A Victorian rosewood Sutherland table, 36in (91.5cm) wide.
$2,900–3,200 ⊞ RPh

A George III satinwood and marquetry silver table, the serpentine top fitted with a shallow gallery, c1775, 35in (89cm) wide.
$13,750–16,500 🔨 S

A Regency mahogany tea table, supported by four turned columns on a platform base and splayed feet, 36in (91.5cm) long.
$4,600–5,000 ⊞ HA

A Scottish Regency mahogany tea table, with ebonized mouldings, the hinged top with a reeded edge and swivel action, above an applied lattice-carved frieze, flanked by classical urns on a spirally-turned shaft and a platform base applied with lion-mask and leaves to the frieze, 35½in (90cm) wide.
$7,250–8,750 ➷ P(Ed)

A Regency rosewood work table, inlaid with boxwood stringing, c1810, 17in (43cm) wide.
$8,700–9,700 ⊞ REI

◀ **An Edwardian satinwood two-tier table,** with mahogany crossbanding and stringing, the removable glass tray top with parquetry edging and brass loop handles, 34¾in (88.5cm) wide.
$3,300–4,000 ➷ AH

A Regency rosewood work table, decorated with coromandel cross-banding and cut brass inlay, 30¼in (77cm) wide.
$5,800–7,200 ➷ P

A mahogany four-panel butler's tray, with drop-down sides, on later stand, c1820, 34in (86.5cm) wide.
$4,600–5,000 ⊞ RGa

A Victorian kingwood and ormolu-mounted writing table, by Gillows, with shaped tooled-leather inset top, c1870, 48¼in (122.5cm) wide.
$20,300–24,600 ➷ Bon

A George III mahogany bowfront corner wash-stand, 24in (61cm) wide.
$1,000–1,200 ➷ TMA

A George III mahogany washstand, with fitted interior and cupboard under, restored, c1800, 21in (53.5cm) wide.
$1,200–1,400 ⊞ NAW

A late Victorian pottery and mahogany wash-stand, the bowl by Browne, Westhead & Moore, with brass plug and chain, 23in (58.5cm) diam.
$1,000–1,200 ➷ HAM

A Regency mahogany whatnot, with gilt-metal galleries and handles, 17¼in (44cm) wide.
$6,500–8,000 ➷ DN

◀ **A mid-Victorian burr-walnut and inlaid whatnot cabinet,** the base fitted with a fall-front enclosing a shaped shelf, 25in (63cm) wide.
$1,300–1,600 ➷ WL

▶ **A George III mahogany cellaret,** the hinged top enclosing a partially baize-lined interior, c1770, 27½in (70cm) wide.
$11,500–13,500 ➷ S

Card Tables

A Louis XV walnut parquetry card table, enclosing a baize-lined interior, probably from the Funk workshop, Berne, c1760, 29in (73.5cm) wide.
$4,400–4,800 ⚹ S(Z)

A George I walnut and feather-banded concertina-action card table, with cabriole legs lapetted at the knee, on pad feet, 35¾in (91cm) wide.
$11,500–13,000 ⚹ P

A George II mahogany card table, the top enclosing counter wells and candleholders, with a green baize playing surface and frieze drawer, damaged, 33in (84cm) wide.
$2,600–3,200 ⚹ TRL

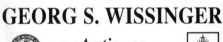

A George III satinwood card table, painted with a band of flowers within two rosewood crossbandings, 35¼in (89.5cm) wide.
$5,000–6,000 ⚹ Bon

◀ **A George III mahogany card table,** crossbanded and inlaid with boxwood with ebony stringing, 35in (89cm) wide.
$1,000–1,250 ⚹ MAT

A mahogany demi-lune card table, crossbanded and inlaid with paterae, c1770, 36in (91.5cm) wide.
$4,000–4,600 ⊞ CAT

FURNITURE

Card table construction

Several methods of construction were devised to support the folding flap. The earliest method was the same principle as the gateleg table, with both back legs swinging out on wooden hinges to 45° so that the back legs squared up with the front legs. From c1760 many card tables had a separate sliding frame, onto which the back legs were attached, and which pulled out on runners to double the width, and so support the table top.

From 1770 onwards some card tables had a single drawer, without handles, concealed in the frieze. From c1780 an innovative type with a hinged wooden concertina-action top doubled back on itself to fold neatly into the underframe.

An American Federal inlaid mahogany demi-lune card table, by William King, the string-inlaid folding top on conforming veneered base, cabinet-maker's label on fly rail, faults, restored, Salem, Massachusetts, 33¾in (85.5cm) wide.
$4,600–5,000 ⚒ SK(B)
William King (1754–1806), who worked intermittently in Salem in the late 18th century, is known to have made a Chippendale mahogany serpentine chest of drawers and a Chippendale mahogany oval tilt-top candle-stand. This is, as yet, the only documented labelled piece of King's Federal period work.

A pair of George III satin-birch tea and card tables, the serpentine hinged tops centred by an oval gonzalo alves panel with rosewood crossbanding, the tea table with a similarly inlaid interior, 33½in (85cm) wide.
$6,500–7,300 ⚒ S

A George III mahogany serpentine card table, with concertina action, c1770, 37in (94cm) wide.
$26,000–29,000 ⊞ RGa
The French styling of this table is a pointer to its exceptional quality and indicates that it was almost certainly produced by a noted maker.

An American Federal inlaid mahogany card table, the legs with inlaid fan paterae above descending foliage, faults, Boston or North Shore, Massachusetts, c1800, 36in (91.5cm) wide.
$4,300–4,700 ⚒ SK(B)

A George III inlaid mahogany folding-top card table, the hinged top in two sections inlaid with oval satinwood paterae, with a baize-lined interior and a single frieze drawer, 18in (45.5cm) wide.
$1,400–1,600 ⚒ JAd

An American Federal inlaid mahogany card table, the top veneered with a central tiger maple frieze panel outlined with crossbanded mahogany veneer and tiger maple banding, North Shore, Massachusetts, c1800, 36in (91.5cm) wide.
$10,000–11,500 ⚒ SK(B)

A matched pair of late Georgian inlaid mahogany demi-lune card tables, 36in (91.5cm) wide.
$22,000–25,000 ⚒ GME

An American Federal mahogany card table, the folding top with a long cockbeaded drawer, on five reeded tapering legs, restored, New York, c1810, 36in (91.5cm) wide.
$2,200–2,400 ⚒ SK(B)

An American mahogany swivel-top card table, the crossbanded top above a plain frieze, supported on a vasiform stem, on scrolled legs with paw feet, New York state, early 19thC, 36in (91.5cm) wide.
$2,600–3,200 ⚒ S(NY)

▶ **An American Federal Classical mahogany card table,** the fold-over shaped top on a conforming base, on turned swirled reeded legs, restored, c1815, 36in (91.5cm) wide.
$3,250–4,000 ⚒ S(NY)

A Scottish George IV mahogany card table, the hinged top with a beaded border, on a fluted and ring-turned baluster support, 37¾in (96cm) wide.
$3,000–3,500 ✦ P(Ed)

A Victorian burr-walnut kidney-shaped card table, with a fold-over top, decorated with floral marquetry and satinwood and ebony lines, 37¾in (96cm) wide.
$2,200–2,600 ✦ F&C

A Victorian walnut card table, with fold-over inlaid burr-veneered serpentine top, c1860, 36in (91.5cm) wide.
$3,200–3,600 ⊞ RPh

An Edwardian Louis XV-style king-wood fold-over card table, the parquetry top with undulating brass rim, with cast-acanthus angles and a parquetry frieze, 32¾in (83cm) wide.
$3,000–3,500 ✦ P(Ed)

▶ **An Edwardian mahogany envelope card table,** the swivel top inlaid with satinwood, rosewood and harewood scrolls, enclosing a baize-lined interior with counter wells, 44in (112cm) wide.
$1,750–2,000 ✦ DD

A George IV rosewood card table, the baize-lined folding swivel top on turned tapering twin end supports, the central stretcher with lappet carving, 21¾in (55.5cm) wide.
$1,150–1,400 ✦ DN

A Victorian inlaid burr-walnut loo table, the oval foliate-inlaid tilt-top above four turned uprights and C-scroll-carved supports, 52¼in (132.5cm) wide.
$1,800–2,200 ✦ Bri

A Victorian inlaid walnut card table, c1870, 38in (96.5cm) wide.
$3,000–3,500 ⊞ MTay

An American Classical carved-mahogany card table, the swivel top outlined with mahogany cross-banded veneer, above a mahogany and maple-veneered frieze with gilt stencilling, New York, 1840–50, 36¼in (92cm) wide.
$3,600–4,000 ✦ SK(B)

A Victorian rosewood loo table, with lobed baluster stem, scrolled base and feet, 51in (129.5cm) wide.
$1,600–1,750 ✦ AH

A late Victorian mahogany card table, by Jas. Shoolbred & Co, inlaid with rosewood veneer, boxwood and bone stringing, the flap top with marquetry inlay of mythical beasts' heads and foliage, lined with blue baize, stamped mark, 35¼in (89.5cm) wide.
$3,600–4,400 ✦ WW

An Edwardian rosewood marquetry envelope card table, with a single drawer, turned legs and shaped undertier, 21in (53.5cm) square.
$1,150–1,400 ✦ KT

Centre Tables

A George III mahogany centre table, the later green marble top above a blind Gothic fretwork-carved frieze, the legs with blind Gothic panelling headed by pierced scroll angle-brackets, 52in (132cm) wide.
$13,500–16,500 ⚑ S

A Regency rosewood centre table, the three scrolled legs on a concave platform base with carved scroll feet, 48in (122cm) diam.
$1,450–1,750 ⚑ CGC

An Italian olivewood-veneered centre table, the top inlaid with chevron stringing and crossbanded in tulipwood, above a frieze drawer, 36¾in (93.5cm) wide.
$580–720 ⚑ WW

A mid-Victorian figured walnut and inlaid centre table, the tilt-top centred by a floral marquetry medallion within eight burr-walnut-veneered segments and with rosewood banding, on a triangular canted column with three acanthus-scrolled down-curved legs, 53in (134.5cm) diam.
$5,800–6,500 ⚑ Hal

A Louis XVI mahogany centre table, by Georges Kintz, with a gilt-bronze-banded top, above a side drawer, on fluted tapering legs, stamped mark, late 18thC, 31½in (80cm) wide.
$11,500–13,500 ⚑ S
Georges Kintz, received master in 1776, produced rather simple and pure Louis XVI furniture. Most of his work is somewhat plain and has very little gilt-bronze decoration and he always selected the best mahoganies and veneers to execute his pieces. A typical feature of his work is the double fluting to the corners, as on this piece.

An American Classical mahogany centre table, with later black marble top, supported on three reeded and foliate-carved scrolled legs, c1830, 36in (91.5cm) diam.
$5,000–5,500 ⚑ S(NY)

A Victorian walnut centre table, with foliate carving, probably Irish, c1860, 57in (145cm) wide.
$7,500–8,500 ⊞ MTay

A mahogany and rosewood-parquetry centre table, the tilt-top inlaid with geometric specimen woods and with brass paterae in the centre, on an octagonal shaft and quadriform base, early 19thC, 39¾in (101cm) diam.
$1,450–1,750 ⚑ P(Ba)

A Dutch walnut and marquetry centre table, the top inlaid with a musician playing a cello, bordered by floral reserves and concentric lines, above a fluted gun-barrel stem and three floral and line-inlaid outswept legs, restored, damaged, early 19thC, 28¼in (72cm) diam.
$1,150–1,350 ⚑ Bon

A parquetry centre table, the tilt-top inlaid with a stellar motif in oak, mahogany and ebony, c1830, 40½in (103cm) wide.
$5,500–6,000 ⚑ S(S)
This piece was given to the vendor's mother in 1938 by Susie Cooper, the ceramic designer and decorator.

◄ **A Victorian oak centre table,** carved and applied with lion masks, with a side drawer, 39in (99cm) wide.
$1,800–2,200 ⚑ GAK

Console & Pier Tables

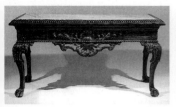

An Irish stained pine console table, the later white-veined marble top within a walnut frame, the frieze with carved shell and leaf-scroll decoration, with conforming apron, 60in (152.5cm) wide.
$21,500–24,000 ⚘ CAG
This table was reputedly purchased from the sale of the contents of Bryanstone, Blandford Forum, Dorset, the property of Viscount Portman.

A Regency gilt and gesso console table, the white marble top above an anthemion-decorated frieze and a central C-scroll cartouche, on leaf-capped scroll legs and paw feet, with a rosewood platform base and mirrored back, 38¼in (97cm) wide.
$6,500–8,000 ⚘ CGC

A Baltic neo-classical bird's-eye maple and mahogany console table, the white and grey mottled marble top above a conforming frieze fitted with three short drawers, raised on scrolled incurved supports, mid-19thC, 53¾in (136.5cm) wide.
$7,250–8,750 ⚘ S(NY)

A Swedish neo-classical ebonized and parcel-gilt console table, the grey granite top above an ebonized neo-Gothic frieze, mid-19thC, 34in (86.5cm) wide.
$5,800–7,200 ⚘ S(NY)

A Danish neo-classical giltwood and painted console table, the inset white marble top above a frieze moulded with foliage, on square trelliswork legs headed by masks, early 19thC, 35in (89cm) wide.
$3,500–4,000 ⚘ SK

A pair of Irish green-painted carved console tables, in the style of George Smith, the grey and white veined marble tops above lotus leaf-carved friezes on leopard-carved monopodiae on plinth bases, labelled under one marble 'R. Strahan & Co', 19thC, 46½in (118cm) wide.
$13,500–16,500 ⚘ P
The Dublin cabinet-maker Robert Strahan & Co was at 10–11 Chancery Lane from 1811–54, at 24–25 Henry Street from 1845–67 and at 135 St Stephen's Green from 1869–1969. The company exhibited walnut, marquetry and gilded furniture at the Dublin Great Industrial Exhibition of 1853.

An American Classical mahogany pier table, the Carrara marble top with a moulded frieze flanked by scroll supports, over a serpentine platform, faults, New York, 1840s, 42¼in (107.5cm) wide.
$2,200–2,400 ⚘ SK(B)

A pair of Italian walnut console tables, each with one drawer, on twin reeded scroll supports, faults, restored, early 19thC, 17in (43cm) wide.
$1,700–2,200 ⚘ S(S)

A giltwood console table, the green marble top with a drawer to one end, early 19thC, 66½in (169cm) wide.
$13,000–14,500 ⊞ APO

A pair of rosewood and simulated rosewood, brass-inlaid and parcel-gilt console tables, the tops with foliate rope-twist rims, the friezes with gilt-metal mounts flanked by flowerheads to either side, on leaf-capped scrolling legs with claw feet, c1830, 39¾in (101cm) wide.
$17,500–20,000 ⚘ HOK

A Napoleon III mahogany console table, the serpentine marble top with a moulded frieze, on cabriole legs and C-scroll feet, damaged, mid-19thC, 39¼in (99.5cm) wide.
$1,300–1,600 ⚘ P(Ba)

Cross Reference
See Colour Review (page 119)

FURNITURE

Dining Tables

A George II mahogany oval gateleg dining table, restored, c1740, 46in (117cm) extended.
$850–1,000 ⚒ Hal

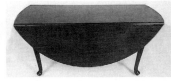

A George II mahogany oval drop-leaf dining table, on pad feet, c1750, 59½in (151cm) wide.
$8,800–9,800 ⊞ APO

▶ A George III mahogany dining table, the central drop-leaf section with demi-lune ends, c1760, 109½in (278cm) extended.
$4,500–5,000 ⚒ S(S)

A George II mahogany drop-leaf dining table, on club legs and pad feet, 51in (129.5cm) extended.
$800–950 ⚒ CGC

An Irish mahogany oval drop-leaf dining table, on cabriole gateleg supports, mid-18thC, 69in (175.5cm) extended.
$16,000–19,000 ⚒ HOK

A mahogany dining table, marked James Winter & Son, on six reeded and acanthus-carved supports with original leaf server, three full and two half leaves, early 19thC, 178½in (453.5cm) extended.
$23,000–29,000 ⚒ WilP
The price paid for this table reflects the sustained demand for large and robust dining tables and, although not to everybody's taste, the carving is of a very high quality.

◀ A George III mahogany drop-leaf dining table, on boxwood-strung square tapering legs, 45½in (115.5cm) long.
$360–440 ⚒ PFK

Facts in brief

The dining table was developed from the massive oak long tables, which later became known as 'refectory' tables, made during the late 16th and 17th centuries.

In the late 18th century Gillows produced a dining table that could be extended by the addition of loose leaves. They called it the 'Imperial Dining Table', a name that was quickly appropriated by other makers. By the beginning of the 19th century, Morgan & Sanders of Catherine Street, London, were advertising a table to seat between four and 20 people which could be 'packed in a box only ten inches deep'.

A Regency mahogany Patent extending campaign dining table, in the style of Morgan & Sanders, the band frieze opening to support leaves, with lobed reeded turned legs, with two extra leaves, c1810, 91¼in (232cm) extended.
$7,250–8,750 ⚒ Bon

A late Georgian mahogany dining table, the drop-leaf centre section with demi-lune ends, on twelve squared tapering legs, 108in (274.5cm) extended.
$2,300–2,900 ⚒ RBB

A William IV mahogany extending dining table, on turned and reeded legs, with three additional leaves, 109in (277cm) extended.
$4,000–4,500 ⚒ TEN

A late Regency mahogany extending dining table, in the style of Gillows, on ring-turned reeded legs, the top and leaves with later fixings and possibly associated, with two additional leaves, 106¼in (270cm) extended.
$9,500–11,500 ⚒ P

A French mahogany oval extending dining table, on six square tapering chamfered legs, early 19thC, 50½in (128.5cm) extended.
$5,800–7,200 ⚒ S

A William IV mahogany extending dining table, with three interchangeable leaves, on turned and melon-lobed legs, 118in (299.5cm) extended.
$4,300–5,000 ➤ WL

A William IV mahogany dining table, with three leaf insertions, on eight turned and tapering octagonal legs, with contemporary associated centre section, 176½in (448.5cm) extended.
$14,500–17,500 ➤ CGC

An early Victorian walnut dining table, on bulbous carved legs and quatrefoil platform base, extending in four sections with four extra half leaves, 139¼in (353.5cm) extended.
$3,600–4,000 ➤ P(EA)

A mid-Victorian mahogany extending dining table, with four extra leaves, 122in (310cm) extended.
$4,300–5,000 ➤ Bon(C)

A Victorian mahogany telescopic-action dining table, with a panelled frieze, on four reeded and ring-turned legs, with three additional leaves, the telescopic action stamped 'James Winter, 101 Wardour St, Soho, London', 133½in (339cm) extended.
$8,700–10,000 ➤ HAM
James Winter & Sons was a firm of furniture brokers and undertakers which traded until 1870. It is considered unlikely that any pieces stamped with their name were actually made by them.

A Victorian mahogany wind-out dining table, on turned tapered legs, with two later extra leaves, 99in (251.5cm) extended.
$2,500–2,900 ➤ Mit

A mid-Victorian walnut wind-out dining table, on leaf-carved cabriole legs and acanthus-carved feet, with two extra leaves, 88in (223.5cm) extended.
$1,000–1,250 ➤ PFK

A Victorian mahogany dining table, on ring-turned tapering legs, with two extra leaves, 104in (264cm) extended.
$2,600–3,200 ⚲ HYD

A Victorian mahogany dining table, on turned tapering legs, with one extra leaf, 94½in (240cm) extended.
$3,300–4,000 ⚲ E

A walnut extending dining table, on reeded tapering legs, with two leaves and demi-lune ends, c1890, 71in (180.5cm) extended.
$3,200–3,500 ⊞ MTay

A walnut dining or boardroom table, with two demi-lune sections on curved stretchered bases, each with two turned and fluted legs and four turned supports, with one central leg of similar form, usable as a full-length table with six extra leaves, without leaves as a circular dining table, or as a large circular dining table, the quarters radiating on grooved wooden tracks and the insertion of one long and two short leaves, c1900, 199½in (507cm) extended.
$22,000–26,000 ⚲ PFK

A French Henri II-style walnut refectory table, the plank top on turned tapering legs with stepped concave stretchers, c1900, 77¼in (196cm) extended.
$725–875 ⚲ P(Ba)

An Edwardian mahogany oval wind-out dining table, with cabriole legs and two extra leaves, c1910, 89¾in (228cm) extended.
$1,150–1,300 ⚲ S(S)

◀ **An oak refectory table,** with a shaped panelled top, c1930, 102in (259cm) long.
$2,200–2,500 ⊞ SWA

Display Tables

A Regency satinwood and tulip-wood-crossbanded display table, restored, c1815, 34¼in (87cm) wide.
$1,300–1,450 ⚲ Bon

An Edwardian walnut display table, with a velvet-lined interior and a caned shelf below, 21¼in (54cm) wide.
$575–675 ⚲ CGC

An Edwardian satinwood display table, inlaid with stylized scrolling foliage and flowers, 28in (71cm) wide.
$2,200–2,600 ⚲ Bea(E)

An Edwardian mahogany bijouterie display table, 23in (58.5cm) wide.
$360–440 ⚲ PFK

An octagonal oak display table, by Whytock & Reid, designed by and made for Sir Robert Lorimer, of Gibliston, Fife, with two hinged panels and enclosing a velvet interior, one panel with a concealed slide for the key, stamped 'Whytock & Reid' twice, 1920s, 46½in (118cm) diam.
$13,500–16,500 ⚲ P(Ed)
The glass-topped display case, or vitrine, was an essential part of the Scottish country house repertoire, and was often to be found in the lobby or library. It was a type commonly supplied by Edinburgh firms such as Scott Morton, but Lorimer commissioned them in this distinctive octagonal form by Whytock & Reid for two different houses: Gibliston, Fife; and Glencruitten, Argyll. The inspiration for the boldly-profiled leg design came from a piece of Italian furniture which Lorimer had seen on the island of Lindisfarne, and later he worked up a sketch based upon a similar detail seen in Rome.

Dressing Tables

A Louis XV amaranth-veneered *coiffeuse,* the top with a detachable panel enclosing a mirror flanked by two compartments, one containing cosmetic pots in Mennecy porcelain, over three drawers, with gilt-bronze mounts, stamped with a crowned 'C', 1745–49, 35in (89cm) wide.
$5,000–6,000 ⟋ S(Mon)

A George II burr-walnut kneehole dressing table, the quarter-veneered top with herringbone stringing and crossbanding, the lid enclosing a fitted interior with inset mirror and compartments, with a dummy drawer front and recessed cupboard flanked each side by three drawers, 30in (76cm) wide.
$8,000–9,500 ⟋ L&E

An Italian walnut, fruitwood, burr-yew and marquetry-inlaid *poudreuse,* the top with three panels centred by an oval medallion depicting a female bust, flanked by two oval reserves centred by cherubs, enclosing a central well and a dressing mirror and two flanking compartments with marquetry lids, above a slide, with a central drawer flanked by four short drawers, restored, late 18thC, 35¼in (89.5cm) wide.
$4,500–5,500 ⟋ Bon

◄ An early Victorian mahogany dressing table, the centre drawer flanked by four side drawers, on turned legs, 46in (117cm) wide.
$1,150–1,300 ⊞ RPh

◄ A Regency mahogany bow-front dressing table, with three frieze drawers, tapering reeded front legs and rectangular reeded back legs, 39in (99cm) wide.
$580–720 ⟋ GAK

► A French amboyna and ebonized dressing table, the top inlaid with a military trophy in a lozenge surrounded by acanthus foliage, enclosing a mirror and fitted interior, with gilt-metal mounts, 19thC, 23¼in (59cm) wide.
$580–720 ⟋ L

A French fruitwood *faux bamboo dressing table,* fitted with a dressing mirror, with a single frieze drawer below the marble top, c1870, 31in (78.5cm) wide.
$1,600–1,750 ⟋ SK

A harewood-veneered kidney-shaped dressing table, with triptych mirror, and matching stool, c1910, 58in (147.5cm) wide.
$1,750–2,000 ⊞ SWA

FURNITURE

Drop-Leaf Tables

A mahogany drop-leaf table, on turned legs with pad feet, 18thC, 52in (132cm) wide.
$500–600 ⚒ SWO

A George III mahogany drop-leaf table, with opposing frieze drawers, the six turned and square supports with double gateleg action, c1770, 41¼in (105cm) wide.
$5,800–7,200 ⚒ S

A walnut drop-leaf table, with ball-and-fillet turned legs and stretchers, c1670, 31in (78.5cm) wide.
$3,500–4,000 ⊞ WELL

▶ **An American Classical drop-leaf table,** with original red and yellow graining simulating mahogany to the top and tiger maple on the platform, faults, Maine, 1830–40, 37½in (95.5cm) wide.
$1,200–1,450 ⚒ SK(B)

A late George III mahogany drop-leaf table, on club legs with pad feet, 29½in (75cm) wide.
$450–550 ⚒ P(Ba)

Drum Tables

A Regency mahogany drum table, inlaid and with ebony stringing, the rotating top above four short and four dummy drawers, altered and restored, c1815, 42in (106.5cm) diam.
$12,500–14,500 ⚒ Bon(W)

A Regency mahogany drum table, the crossbanded swivel top with a replacement green leather writing surface, above an arrangement of real and dummy frieze drawers, 35½in (90cm) diam.
$12,500–14,500 ⚒ PFK

▶ **A Regency mahogany drum table,** with inset leather top, c1820, 50in (127cm) diam.
$8,500–9,500 ⊞ APO

A Regency mahogany and ebony-banded drum table, with four frieze drawers between dummy drawers, 48½in (123cm) diam.
$8,500–10,000 ⚒ P(S)

A mahogany drum table, with three real and three dummy drawers, on a baluster-turned column with four splayed legs, faults, early 19thC, 35¾in (91cm) diam.
$1,150–1,300 ⚒ S(S)

A George IV mahogany drum table, with a revolving top, and eight short drawers to the frieze, on three splayed legs, 42in (106.5cm) diam.
$6,750–7,500 ⚒ L

◀ **A Victorian mahogany drum table,** with four short and four dummy drawers to the frieze, on a leaf-carved column with scrolling tripod legs, 49in (124.5cm) diam.
$3,000–3,500 ⚒ AG

Games Tables

A late George III rosewood games/ work table, inlaid with brass and boxwood stringing, the easel-backed top inlaid for chess, flanked by compartments with hinged covers, damaged, 30in (76cm) wide.
$1,800–2,200 ✗ P(S)

A Regency mahogany Pembroke games table, the reversible centre section inlaid with a chequer board and enclosing an inlaid backgammon board, with dummy drawer fronts, including 30 turned gaming counters, c1810, 34in (86.5cm) wide.
$6,500–7,250 ✗ S

A Regency inlaid mahogany games table, the reversible top enclosing a backgammon board, the underside covered in baize with counter wells, above a satinwood frieze, one side with a small drawer, 39in (99cm) wide.
$4,400–5,000 ✗ MEA

▶ An early Victorian Killarney yew games table, the hinged top inlaid with a central panel depicting Muckross Abbey, flanked by ferns, thistles and a chequer-inlaid border, enclosing a chess, cribbage and backgammon playing surface, within shamrock borders, 31in (78.5cm) wide.
$6,500–7,250 ✗ CGC

A rosewood specimen-marble games table, the top inlaid with polychrome marbles on a yellow ground, c1830, 26in (66cm) wide.
$2,200–2,600 ✗ EH

◀ A Victorian walnut games/ sewing table, with inlaid decoration, the swivel top enclosing a chess-board, back-gammon and cribbage playing surface, with sewing box below, 28in (71cm) wide.
$1,800–2,200 ✗ RPI

A Victorian walnut and boxwood line-inlaid games/sewing table, the folding top with inlaid chess and backgammon boards, with central cribbage scorer, one drawer and sliding bag below, 22in (56cm) wide.
$1,600–1,900 ✗ E

A Victorian walnut games/reading table, the chequer-board top with a detachable book rest, enclosing a recess, on spiral-reeded end supports and flower-carved splayed legs, 35¾in (91cm) wide.
$1,300–1,450 ✗ DN

Library Tables

A rosewood library table, the frieze with two real and two dummy drawers, with beaded borders and wooden knob handles, 19thC, 52in (132cm) wide.
$3,250–4,000 ⚒ **AG**

A mahogany library table, with two carved frieze drawers, c1840, 59in (150cm) wide.
$4,000–4,500 ⊞ **GBr**

A Victorian mahogany partner's library table, with tooled-leather-inset top, three frieze drawers to each side, c1840, 59in (150cm) wide.
$7,250–8,750 ⚒ **Bon**

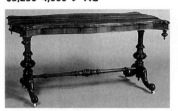

A rosewood library table, the serpentine top with lobbed pendants to the corners, the end supports with leaf-carved moulded downswept legs, mid-19thC, 61in (155cm) wide.
$3,000–3,500 ⚒ **HOK**

A Victorian pollarded oak library table, with central shallow frieze drawer, on twin octagonal vase-shaped legs, 56in (142cm) wide.
$3,600–4,400 ⚒ **CDC**

A Victorian walnut and boxwood line-inlaid library table, the top with a Morocco leather insert above three real and three dummy frieze drawers, on foliate-carved double end supports and downcurved scroll legs, damaged, c1860, 54in (137cm) wide.
$3,250–4,000 ⚒ **Hal**

Nests of Tables

A mahogany and rose-wood-banded nest of three tables, on twin rope-twist supports, early 19thC, largest 19¾in (50cm) wide.
$3,600–4,400 ⚒ **HOK**

An Edwardian mahogany nest of four tables, with satinwood stringing, the tops with raised beading, on ring-turned legs, largest 19¾in (50cm) wide.
$1,600–1,900 ⚒ **AH**

A Regency rosewood nest of four occasional tables, the tops with raised bead stringing, on turned legs and splayed feet, largest 14in (35.5cm) wide.
$7,250–8,000 ⚒ **P(S)**

An Edwardian mahogany nest of four tables, the satinwood-strung tops raised on pierced supports and trestle feet, largest 20in (51cm) wide.
$650–800 ⚒ **CGC**

An Edwardian mahogany nest of four tables, on turned legs and splayed feet, largest 21in (53.5cm) wide.
$1,600–1,750 ⊞ **NAW**

An Edwardian mahogany nest of four tables, on turned legs and splayed feet, largest 22in (56cm) wide.
$550–600 ⚒ **G(B)**

A mahogany nest of three spider-leg tables, c1925, largest 19in (48.5cm) wide.
$580–650 ⊞ **MTay**

Occasional Tables

A George III simulated-rosewood occasional table, with a frieze drawer, on turned tapered legs, 20in (51cm) wide.
$1,600–1,750 ✗ Mit

An Irish William IV mahogany occasional table, with an oak-lined frieze drawer, on a ring-turned and acanthus-carved support, 26¾in (68cm) wide.
$430–500 ✗ WW

A Victorian rosewood occasional table, on a spiral-turned column and shaped trefoil base, 21¾in (55.5cm) wide.
$500–600 ✗ CMS

A carved mahogany occasional table, c1920, 32in (81.5cm) wide.
$850–950 ⊞ MTay

A George III mahogany envelope occasional table, with fruitwood crossbanding, the double-hinged top above a frieze drawer, on square tapered legs with a shaped stretcher, c1795, 18in (45.5cm) wide.
$8,500–10,000 ✗ Bon

An early Victorian papier mâché and mother-of-pearl inlaid occasional table, the tilt-top painted with a pastoral scene, c1845, 20in (51cm) wide.
$2,200–2,900 ⊞ DOA

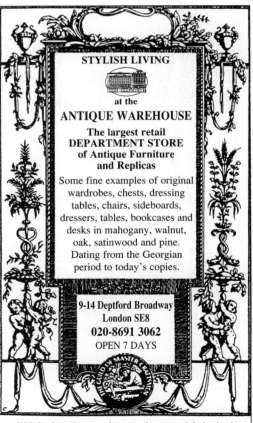

An inlaid mahogany occasional table, c1900, 15in (38cm) wide.
$750–850 ⊞ CHE

A Charles X gilt-bronze-mounted mahogany *vide-poche*, the tray top with a suspended drawer, each ring-turned column on a rectangular plinth, c1825, 25in (63.5cm) wide.
$4,000–4,400 ✗ SLN
Vide-poches are small tables with a rim around the top. Intended for use in the bedroom, a gentleman would empty his pockets into a *vide-poche* when he undressed.

▶ **An Irish Victorian walnut lace table,** by J. Byrne of Dublin, the inlaid top with a revolving candle holder, on a turned column and claw feet, c1840, 30in (76cm) high.
$3,600–4,000 ⊞ BERA

A William IV rosewood occasional table, with a parquetry top, c1830, 27in (68.5cm) high.
$6,000–6,750 ⊞ REI

Pembroke Tables

A George III sycamore and satin-wood Pembroke table, in the style of Henry Kettle, the crossbanded top with a central oval panel decorated with a floral marquetry spray, the flaps each with a plain satinwood reserve, the frieze with a real drawer enclosing a leather-lined writing slide opposed by a dummy drawer, 36in (91.5cm) extended.
$13,000–16,000 ✗ S
This table has marked stylistic affinities with a Pembroke table by Henry Kettle in the collection of The National Trust at Saltram House, Devon. Henry Kettle is recorded as partner to William Henshaw from c1770 before taking over the business and trading from premises at 18 St Paul's Chuchyard, London. In 1774 Kettle took on Philip Bell's business at 23 St Paul's Churchyard, which was to remain his main trading address.

An early George III mahogany Pembroke table, with a frieze drawer, on slender turned tapering legs with flat X-stretcher shelf, 22½in (57cm) wide.
$4,400–5,000 ✗ L

A Hepplewhite-style mahogany Pembroke table, with serpentine leaves, 18thC, 32in (81.5cm) extended.
$5,800–6,600 ⊞ CAT

A George III mahogany Pembroke table, with a drawer and adjacent dummy drawer, on square tapered legs, 30in (76cm) wide.
$2,300–2,600 ✗ MAT

A Scottish George III mahogany Pembroke table, with a frieze drawer to one end, on boxwood-lined square tapering legs, 28¼in (72cm) high.
$800–950 ✗ P(Ed)

> ## Facts in brief
>
> The first Pembroke table was probably made to the order of Henry Herbert, Earl of Pembroke (1693–1751), in the mid-18th century. Made of mahogany and with carved decoration, the tops were usually either rectangular or of butterfly/serpentine outline.
> By the last quarter of the 18th century the oval shape had become very fashionable, and styles were lighter; veneered examples replacing those made from solid wood, and decoration was inlaid or sometimes painted rather than carved. Bowfront tops were popular during this period. From the early 19th century Pembroke tables became less fashionable, and consequently were not as finely made as those of the 18th century.

An inlaid mahogany Pembroke table, early 19thC, 30in (76cm) wide.
$1,150–1,300 ⊞ RPh

A mahogany Pembroke deception table, on square tapering legs with original castors, c1800, 13in (33cm) wide.
$3,600–4,000 ⊞ RL
This is called a deception table because it incorporates a clip which, when pressed, allows one of the flaps to drop down disclosing a cupboard. The other flap lifts up as usual.

A Regency mahogany Pembroke table, with a boxwood- and ebony-strung frieze drawer, on ring-turned and tapering round legs, 42in (106.5cm) extended.
$430–500 ✗ Hal

▶ **An American Federal mahogany Pembroke table,** with a real and a dummy frieze drawer, on reeded tapering legs, early 19thC, 22½in (57cm) wide.
$1,450–1,750 ✗ SK(B)

Reading Tables

A George III mahogany reading table, the hinged top with an adjustable ratchet, the deep frieze with three shallow long drawers, damaged, 24½in (62cm) wide.
$1,600–1,900 ✗ L

A Sheraton-style octagonal West Indian satinwood reading table, with crossbanding and painted decoration, the tapered legs on barrel castors, c1790, 25in (63.5cm) wide.
$8,700–9,700 ⊞ RGa

A Regency mahogany reading table, the top with an adjustable ratchet, above three graduated drawers and opposing dummy drawers, 20in (51cm) wide.
$2,200–2,600 ✗ CGC

A Scottish Victorian yew wood writing/reading table, with a double-hinged sloping reading top enclosing a writing surface, above a single drawer with arcaded friezes to the sides, on a faceted tapered column, damaged, c1840, 20in (51cm) wide.
$2,600–3,200 ✗ Bon

Serving Tables

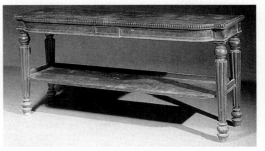

An Irish mahogany bowfront serving table, with boxwood trim, late 18thC, 74in (188cm) wide.
$13,500–16,000 ✗ HOK

A Regency mahogany carved bowfront serving table, the top with a beaded edge and panelled frieze, on reeded tapering legs joined by a shelved pot board, possibly by Gillows, 66¼in (168.5cm) wide.
$22,000–24,000 ✗ P

A Regency mahogany serving table, the frieze with two panelled drawers, on lion's paw and scrolled monopodia end supports, with panelled square-section supports to the rear, c1820, 64½in (164cm) wide.
$8,000–9,500 ✗ Bon

A William IV mahogany serving table, with a wrythen-carved centre panel, on reeded and turned legs, 72in (183cm) wide.
$2,400–2,900 ✗ MAT

An early Victorian mahogany serving table, the back with shell carving, the top with a frieze drawer to each end, on octagonal baluster legs, 54in (137cm) wide.
$2,500–3,000 ✗ P(Ba)

An Edwardian mahogany serpentine-fronted serving table, with three fluted frieze drawers, on six square-section fluted legs, incorporating 18thC timbers, 72in (183cm) wide.
$4,000–4,600 ✗ P(Ed)

A Victorian pollarded oak serving table, the top with crossbanded edge over a recessed frieze fitted with two short drawers with cushioned drawer fronts, the turned fluted front legs on a raised stepped plinth, 49in (124.5cm) wide.
$1,750–2,000 ✗ Mit

FURNITURE

Side Tables

A north European fruitwood and walnut side table, the detachable top inset with black marble flanked by a border inlaid with various woods within chequer-banded panels, with two panels dated '1714', the corners inlaid with stylized bears above a frieze drawer, early 18thC, 35¼in (89.5cm) wide.
$1,750–2,000 ⚒ CGC

A George III mahogany side table, with a frieze drawer, c1780, 35in (89cm) wide.
$3,500–4,000 ⊞ REI

An Irish mahogany demi-lune side table, the fan-inlaid top centred by a shell, the satinwood-banded panelled frieze with inlaid panels of shells, on tapering boxwood-trimmed legs inlaid with pendants of husks, late 18thC, 40¼in (102cm) wide.
$2,300–2,900 ⚒ HOK

A bowfront mahogany side table, with boxwood lining, early 19thC, 36½in (92.5cm) wide.
$1,350–1,600 ⚒ P(Ed)

A George II mahogany side table, the rouge marble top above a cavetto-moulded frieze, marble repaired, 35¾in (91cm) wide.
$8,500–10,000 ⚒ P(L)

A George III yew wood table, with tulipwood banding, c1790, 22in (56cm) wide.
$5,500–6,000 ⊞ RGa

A mahogany side table, on square legs, with a frieze drawer, c1800, 19in (48.5cm) wide.
$1,700–2,200 ⊞ RL

A Regency mahogany side table, with yew wood crossbanding, with a frieze drawer, on turned tapered supports, 36in (91.5cm) wide.
$1,000–1,300 ⚒ RBB

A pair of George III inlaid and crossbanded mahogany side tables, the three drawers with brass handles, 30¾in (78cm) wide.
$2,300–2,900 ⚒ WilP

A George III mahogany side table, the rectangular top with canted corners, c1800, 22½in (57cm) wide.
$580–720 ⚒ Bon

An American Classical figured-mahogany and parcel-gilt side table, the top with a rising lid, supported on turned column legs with gilt-scrolled capitals, New York, c1815, 35½in (90cm) wide.
$5,000–6,000 ⚒ S(NY)

An Irish George IV mahogany side table, the moulded frieze decorated with beading and centred by a single drawer, on four scroll-carved supports decorated with anthemia, leafwork and scrolls, 88¼in (224cm) wide.
$16,000–18,500 ⚒ JAd

A George IV mahogany side table, by Thomas Willson, the three moulded frieze drawers above reeded turned tapering legs, the central frieze drawer, marked, c1830, 49½in (125.5cm) wide.
$10,500–12,500 ⚹ **S**
This table is stamped T. Willson (1799–1854). He established a successful furniture-making and broking business between 1818 and 1821 at 68 Great Queen Street, London. It appears that soon after 1830 he handed over the running of the business to his wife Mary, since furniture made after that date bears her initial on the impressed stamp.

A William IV rosewood side table, with an anthemia and shell-carved frieze, the outfacing lappeted cabriole legs with anthemia tablets, with conforming back legs, 50in (127cm) wide.
$5,000–6,000 ⚹ **Hal**

A Victorian mahogany side table, c1880, 36in (91.5cm) wide.
$875–1,000 ⊞ **RPh**

Sets/pairs
Unless otherwise stated, any description which refers to 'a set' or 'a pair' includes a guide price for the entire set or the pair, even though the illustration may show only a single item.

A 17thC-style black lacquered side table, painted and gilded with chinoiserie river scenes and flowers, with a single frieze drawer, 19thC, 36¼in (92cm) wide.
$1,750–1,900 ⚹ **AH**

An amboyna, burr-walnut and ebonized drop-leaf side table, the crossbanded top inlaid with a central oval panel, above a similarly decorated frieze drawer and mounted with pierced and carved plaques, 19thC, 41¼in (105cm) wide.
$1,300–1,450 ⚹ **P(Ba)**

FURNITURE

Silver Tables

An Irish George II mahogany silver table, the later tray top above a scroll-carved outswept frieze centred by scallop shells, 32½in (82.5cm) wide.
$7,250–8,000 ✗ **P(S)**

An Irish mahogany silver table, the dish-moulded top above a shaped apron and acanthus-leaf-carved cabriole legs, mid-18thC, 29¾in (75.5cm) wide.
$20,000–23,000 ✗ **S**

A George III mahogany silver table, the top with fretwork gallery above a blind fret-carved frieze, restored, late 18thC, 30½in (77.5cm) wide.
$7,250–8,750 ✗ **S(NY)**

Sofa Tables

A George III mahogany sofa table, with ebony stringing, with two real and two dummy drawers, on splayed legs, 38in (96.5cm) wide.
$2,900–3,200 ✗ **MAT**

A Biedermeier black walnut sofa table, with a frieze drawer, on pierced trestle supports joined by a later barley-twist stretcher, mid-19thC, 40in (101.5cm) wide.
$5,000–6,000 ✗ **S(NY)**

A Regency rosewood sofa table, the top crossbanded in burr-yew with a reversible slide-out centre, enclosing backgammon and chess boards, with two frieze drawers, 68in (173cm) extended.
$8,000–9,500 ✗ **MEA**

A late Regency mahogany sofa table, with two real and two dummy frieze drawers, with inlaid ebony stringing, 37½in (95.5cm) wide.
$4,400–5,000 ✗ **WW**

A Regency rosewood sofa table, with two frieze drawers, on S-scroll end supports united by an inverted U-stretcher, with brass-inlaid legs, 61in (155cm) extended.
$3,600–4,400 ✗ **E**

A Regency rosewood and brass-inlaid sofa table, with a recessed frieze drawer, on a tapered rectangular pillar with gadrooned collar, the platform base with four hipped sabre legs, 36¼in (92cm) wide.
$3,200–4,000 ✗ **TEN**

A George IV mahogany sofa table, with two real and two dummy drawers, the baluster-turned column support on a moulded quadriform base, faults, 28¾in (73cm) wide.
$1,800–2,500 ✗ **S(S)**

A William IV rosewood-veneered and string-inlaid sofa table, the front frieze with a central drawer flanked by brass marquetry panels, 37in (94cm) wide.
$2,600–3,200 ✗ **WW**

A William IV rosewood sofa table, the drawer with a writing slope and compartments, flanked by carved flowerheads, 60¼in (153cm) extended.
$4,500–5,500 ✗ **P(Ed)**

Supper Tables

A George II mahogany supper table, with a single drop-leaf, on hipped cabriole legs and hoof feet, 40in (101.5cm) extended.
$575–725 ✗ HYD

A George III mahogany supper table, the tilt-top on a baluster-turned column and tripod downswept legs, 34½in (87.5cm) wide.
$950–1,150 ✗ HYD

A mahogany supper table, the circular top with hinged drop-leaves, on tapered club legs with pad feet, mid-18thC, 31½in (80cm) wide.
$1,000–1,250 ✗ P(S)

LOCATE THE SOURCE
The source of each illustration in Miller's can be found by checking the code letters below each caption with the Key to Illustrations, pages 794–800.

▶ **A George III mahogany tripod table,** the top later carved as a supper table with nine recesses, with spiral-twist carved column, the three downswept legs with shell-carved knees, 32in (81.5cm) diam.
$950–1,150 ✗ Mit

A George III rosewood supper table, the top with drop-leaves above a drawer fitted with a baize-lined writing slide, over concave silk-lined wire-inset doors, late 18thC, 41½in (105.5cm) wide.
$16,500–20,000 ✗ S(NY)

FURNITURE

Sutherland Tables

A Regency rosewood line-inlaid Sutherland table, the hinged top above a pair of end frieze drawers, on ring-turned legs and peg feet, c1810, 43¼in (110cm) extended.
$5,500–6,000 ⚒ Bon

A Victorian burr-walnut marquetry oval Sutherland table, on turned end supports and stretcher, 40½in (103cm) extended.
$1,000–1,150 ⚒ F&C

A burr-walnut Sutherland table, with bobbin-turned legs and original castors, c1870, 29in (73.5cm) extended.
$850–1,000 ⊞ GBr

A Victorian figured-walnut Sutherland table, with six spiral-turned tapering legs and shaped trestle feet, 41in (104cm) extended.
$850–1,000 ⚒ CGC

An Edwardian mahogany Sutherland table, with a boxwood-banded and ebony-strung border, and ring-turned spindle supports, 24in (61cm) wide.
$450–550 ⚒ GAK

An Edwardian inlaid-mahogany Sutherland table, c1910, 24in (61cm) wide.
$200–230 ⊞ NAW

Tea Tables

A George III mahogany tea table, the folding shaped oblong top with a concertina-action, the plain frieze with a drawer, 33¾in (85.5cm) wide.
$1,600–1,900 ⚒ AH

A Scottish George III mahogany and boxwood-lined tea table, the frieze enclosing a single internally-divided drawer, on square tapering legs headed with an inlaid dot motif, Edinburgh, 42in (106.5cm) wide.
$2,900–3,200 ⚒ P(Ed)
The frieze drawer which is divided for three tea 'canisters', and the 'round dot and hollow end' stringing detail, represent a typical example of Edinburgh workmanship.

A late American Federal carved mahogany fold-over card/tea table, the hinged top with a concave frieze, the column base and legs carved with acanthus foliage, 33½in (85cm) wide.
$1,400–1,600 ⚒ SLN

◄ **A Regency mahogany tea table,** the fold-over top above a frieze with figured-mahogany veneered tablets, with rosewood edge-moulding, 35in (89cm) wide.
$1,800–2,200 ⚒ Mit

A William IV flame-mahogany fold-over tea table, with a carved baluster stem above a platform base, and four paw and scroll-carved feet, 37in (94cm) wide.
$1,800–2,200 ⚒ DA

FURNITURE

An early Victorian rosewood tea table, the fold-over swivel top on an octagonal baluster column, with a foliate-carved platform and paw feet, 35¾in (91cm) wide.
$1,300–1,450 ⚲ **ELR**

An early Victorian mahogany tea table, the fold-over swivel top on a faceted tapered column, with a domed platform and paw feet, 36in (91.5cm) wide.
$1,150–1,350 ⚲ **DOC**

A Victorian walnut serpentine tea table, the swivel top on a reeded baluster column, with four carved and splayed legs, 36in (91.5cm) wide.
$850–1,000 ⚲ **TRL**

Tripod Tables

A George II mahogany wine table, on a baluster column with three scallop shell-carved cabriole legs, repaired, 17in (43cm) diam.
$500–600 ⚲ **WW**

A George III mahogany tripod table, with a bird-cage support and barrel-turned column, on scrolled pierced outswept legs, restored, possibly American, c1760, 32in (81.5cm) diam.
$5,500–6,000 ⚲ **Bon**

An early George III mahogany tripod table, the octagonal top with a crossbanded border, with a bird-cage support, on a baluster-turned column and downswept legs, 24½in (62cm) diam.
$1,450–1,750 ⚲ **HYD**

A George III mahogany tripod table, on a baluster-turned column, c1780, 31in (78.5cm) diam.
$3,600–4,000 ⊞ **APO**

A George III mahogany tripod table, the spindle-galleried top inlaid with brass stringing and centred by a brass-strung roundel, 11in (28cm) diam.
$8,500–10,000 ⚲ **S**

A George III mahogany tripod table, the snap top with a baluster-turned column and downswept legs, 28in (71cm) diam.
$725–875 ⚲ **DMC**

▶ **An early Victorian inlaid walnut tripod table,** with ebonized moulding, on a carved column, c1840, 24in (61cm) diam.
$1,450–1,600 ⊞ **RPh**

◀ **An American Classical tiger-maple candlestand,** the shaped top on a vase-and ring-turned support and tripod base, faults, New England, c1825, 28½in (72.5cm) wide.
$1,000–1,150 ⚲ **SK(B)**

A George III mahogany tripod table, the tilt-top above a gadrooned baluster and ring-turned column, on splayed legs, 32¼in (82cm) diam.
$1,000–1,200 ⚲ **GIL**

A mahogany and plum wood tripod table, with a baluster-turned column and splayed legs, early 19thC, 15in (38cm) diam.
$1,150–1,350 ⚲ **Bea(E)**

A Victorian octagonal tripod table, the inlaid crystalline top depicting dogs, on bobbin-turned supports, 22in (56cm) diam.
$580–720 ⊞ **TWr**

FURNITURE

Two-tier Tables

A George III mahogany two-tier table, c1790, 27in (68.5cm) wide.
$1,700–2,300 ⊞ RL

A mahogany satinwood-inlaid two-tier table, with a glass tray top, late 19thC, 33½in (85cm) wide.
$1,600–1,800 ⚒ WL

A late Victorian burr-walnut-veneered two-tier table, on twin turned supports, with a turned stretcher, 24in (61cm) wide.
$900–1,100 ⚒ WW

A mahogany two-tier Sutherland table, c1880, 24in (61cm) wide.
$725–800 ⊞ GBr

A beechwood two-tier table, painted with roses, c1890, 31in (78.5cm) high.
$130–145 ⊞ AL

A rosewood marquetry-inlaid two-tier table, with detachable tray top, pierced brass gallery and reeded acanthus-leaf-carved supports, 19thC, 36in (91.5cm) wide.
$850–1,000 ⚒ G(B)

◄ **An Edwardian satinwood two-tier table,** the crossbanded tray-top painted with flowers and cherubs, over a similar larger tier, on splay legs with inlaid batwing spandrels, 34¾in (88.5cm) wide.
$4,000–4,500 ⚒ P(Ed)

A Louis XVI tulipwood and stained sycamore two-tier table, by J. B. Tuart, with a three-quarter galleried top inlaid with a strapwork panel, above a frieze drawer, with a further drawer to the side, on square tapering legs joined by a shelf, stamped, late 18thC, 16in (40.5cm) wide.
$4,000–4,500 ⚒ S
Son of Jean-Baptiste I, Jean-Baptiste II Tuart worked with his father in the abbey of Saint-Germain-l'Auxerrois and subsequently set up as a *marchand mercier* in the fashionable rue Saint-Honoré. By 1775 he was considered to be one of the most important *marchands* in Paris. It has been assumed that he was a practising cabinet-maker, but this is not certain. His stamp is often found beside the stamp of another cabinet-maker who would have made the piece in question. This piece was therefore probably commissioned by Jean-Baptiste II Tuart from another cabinet-maker, but stamped by Tuart. The plain design highlighted with sycamore banding is typical of his style.

A French-style mahogany and ormolu-mounted two-tier table, by Edwards & Roberts, the kidney-shaped top surmounted by a pierced gallery with a concave frieze drawer below, stamped, 19thC, 27½in (70cm) wide.
$3,000–3,300 ⚒ P(EA)

Work Tables

A George III mahogany work table, with hinged top, 29in (73.5cm) high.
$3,200–3,600 ⊞ REI

A George III mahogany work table, with hinged top, 20in (51cm) wide.
$2,000–2,300 ⚒ Mit

An American Federal work table, the top with hinged drop-leaves flanking two fitted drawers above a sliding bag frame, replaced brass, Massachusetts, 19thC, 18½in (47cm) wide.
$3,200–3,600 ⚒ SK(B)

An American Federal cherry-inlaid work table, the square top edged with contrasting veneers, above one real and one dummy drawer, the top drawer with fittings, replaced pulls, Rhode Island, early 19thC, 17in (43cm) wide.
$3,500–4,000 ⚒ SK(B)

A Regency mahogany work table, the hinged top with a beaded rim, above demilune-shaped sides, 19¼in (49cm) wide.
$2,200–2,500 ⚒ P(B)

A George IV mahogany drop-leaf work table, c1820, 18in (45.5cm) wide.
$2,200–2,400 ⊞ CHE

A George IV rosewood Pembroke work table, the top with two hinged flaps, above a drawer with a double front and linen wells, c1825, 19in (48.5cm) wide.
$2,200–2,600 ⚒ Bon(G)

A William IV burr-elm work table, the drop-leaf top with a frieze drawer and a sliding compartment, 28¼in (72cm) wide.
$4,000–4,500 ⚒ P(Ba)

A German mahogany work table, the ebonized top inlaid with metals and mother-of-pearl, enclosing a fitted interior with a sliding workbag below, 19thC, 21¼in (54cm) wide.
$2,200–2,600 ⚒ TEN

An American Classical carved-mahogany work table, the top with stencilled patterns in black and gilt, replaced brass, New York, 1830-40, 23½in (59.5cm) wide.
$3,300–3,700 ⚒ SK(B)

An American Classical mahogany work table, the top with hinged leaves flanking two drawers above a circular shaft and shaped platform, Boston, 1835–45, 17½in (44.5cm) wide.
$950–1,100 ⚒ SK(B)

An American Classical mahogany work table, the top with hinged leaves flanking the two drawers, the top drawer with fittings, Boston, 1830s, 18in (45.5cm) wide.
$1,450–1,750 ⚒ SK(B)

▶ **A Louis Philippe ebonized boulle work table,** with ormolu mounts, fitted with an interior mirror and rosewood tray silk box, c1840, 29in (73.5cm) wide.
$1,300–1,450 ⊞ RPh

Typical features

Work tables were introduced in the late 18th century, primarily for ladies to sew at. Usually fairly small and compact, some have hinged tops with fitted interiors, others were also fitted with a silk workbag. Most of those from the late 18th century stand on four square, or turned, slender tapering legs. Pedestal supports and turned fluted legs are typical of the early 19th century, and the more desirable type has lyre-shaped supports.

As the 19th century progressed, work tables were produced in larger quantities and in a greater range of quality. Victorian work tables are characteristically made from walnut. The pull-out 'bags' of this period are often of solid form.

FURNITURE

◄ **A Napoleon III Louis XV-style ebonized boulle-inlaid work/dressing table,** by Veder of Paris, applied with gilt-metal mounts, the hinged top enclosing two lift-out trays with compartments, the reverse of the lid inset with a mirror plate, above a decorated frieze and pull-out well, 28¼in (72cm) high.
$1,450–1,750 ⚶ P(Ba)
Veder specialized in producing small unusual pieces of furniture often suitable as wedding gifts. Boulle work was a particular speciality. They were established at 3 rue du Pas-de-la-Mule in 1852, moving to 68 rue de Saint Sabin in 1870.

A Victorian mahogany and fruitwood work table, with two frieze drawers, on a ring-turned baluster fruitwood column, 23½in (59.5cm) wide.
$430–500 ⚶ WW

A Victorian mahogany work table, the hinged lid enclosing a fitted interior with work bag below, on ring-turned foliate-moulded balustered supports joined by a ring-turned stretcher, 24½in (62cm) wide.
$650–800 ⚶ GAK

A Victorian walnut lady's work table, the centre inlaid with two birds, the fitted well with a fret-work front and sides, on a turned column and four cabriole legs, 19in (48.5cm) wide.
$950–1,150 ⚶ DA

A Victorian olivewood and marquetry work table, the hinged lid enclosing a fitted interior, on spiral-turned supports joined by a stretcher, 22in (56cm) wide.
$600–700 ⚶ WilP

An Edwardian Sheraton-revival inlaid mahogany work table, with a fitted interior, lined in red fabric, c1905, 18in (45.5cm) wide.
$500–550 ⊞ NAW

◄ **A Victorian walnut work table,** with a fitted frieze drawer above a shaped apron, on spiral-twist supports joined by a turned stretcher, 20in (51cm) wide.
$430–500 ⚶ LF

An Edwardian mahogany work table, inlaid with satinwood stringing and chequered banding, the top enclosing a silk-lined interior with a spring-loaded secret drawer below, 16in (40.5cm) high.
$1,450–1,750 ⚶ DD

Writing Tables

A Regency Gothic-style oak writing table, the quatrefoil line-inlaid top above a frieze with blind fretwork carving, with one long and two short drawers, c1805, 33in (84cm) wide.
$6,500–8,000 ⚶ Bon

► **A George IV mahogany writing table,** with three drawers, c1820, 42½in (108cm) wide.
$3,500–4,000 ⊞ APO

A Regency mahogany writing table, the two drawers with lion-mask ring handles, 46¼in (117.5cm) wide.
$3,200–4,000 ⚶ DA

A George III satinwood and she-oak writing table, with an inset green tooled-leather top, the frieze with two real and two dummy drawers, c1800, 36in (91.5cm) wide.
$12,500–14,500 ⚶ S
She-oak belongs to a variety of four Australian timbers imported from New South Wales during the early 19th century, which were collectively referred to by Sheraton in his *Cabinet Dictionary*, 1803, as Botany Bay Wood. Sometimes known as casuarina, she-oak is characterized by its pronounced dappled markings (silver grain) which often lead to its mistaken identification as partridgewood.

A Regency mahogany writing table, the frieze drawer with an opposing dummy drawer, on turned tapering legs, 30in (76cm) wide.
$2,000–2,200 ✹ **CGC**

A mid-Victorian kingwood and marquetry *bureau plat*, the leather-inset top with gilt-metal edges, above three crossbanded frieze drawers, on gilt-metal-mounted cabriole legs and sabots, 48½in (123cm) wide.
$9,500–11,500 ✹ **P(L)**
Although unstamped, the quality of the construction indicates a cabinet-making firm working in the style of Edwards & Roberts or E. H. Baldock.

A French-style Victorian walnut and kingwood writing table, in the style of Donald Ross, with gilt-tooled green leather inset, gilt-metal mounts and trellis-pattern inlay, c1890, 36in (91.5cm) wide.
$7,250–8,000 ✹ **S(S)**
Donald Ross made many pieces including desks, side tables and bonheurs du jour, in the Louis XVI style with a dotted marquetry trellis in the style of the 18th-century maker J. B. Sené.

An Edwardian inlaid and grained rosewood lady's writing table, with a pierced three-quarter brass gallery, above a bowfronted frieze drawer flanked with inlaid fan angles, 30in (76cm) wide.
$950–1,100 ✹ **MEA**

A kingwood, rosewood and ormolu lady's writing table, with a leather-inset crossbanded top above two frieze drawers, 19thC, 39in (99cm) wide.
$1,400–1,600 ✹ **MAT**

A Victorian writing table, with leather-inset top above a frieze drawer, 36in (91.5cm) wide.
$1,000–1,100 ⊞ **RPh**

FURNITURE

Teapoys

A William IV rosewood teapoy, with floral marquetry and a chessboard top over a shaped and pierced apron, enclosing two caddies, on barley-sugar column end supports with stretcher, mixing bowls lacking, 24in (61cm) wide.
$1,250–1,450 ↗ **F&C**

A William IV mahogany teapoy, 17in (43cm) wide.
$2,200–2,600 ⊞ **GBr**

A pollarded elm teapoy, the sarcophagus top with a turned carved column, on a platform base with paw feet, mid 19thC, 19¼in (49cm) wide.
$2,400–3,000 ↗ **L&T**

An early Victorian mahogany teapoy, the sarcophagus top with a hinged lid enclosing lidded compartments and moulded glass bowls, with a gadrooned body on a spiral-turned column, 17¾in (45cm) wide.
$1,300–1,600 ↗ **P(Ba)**

Torchères

A Louis XIV giltwood torchère, the pierced foliate-scrolled tripartite standard decorated with flowerheads and C-scrolls, early 18thC, 67½in (171.5cm) high.
$9,500–11,500 ↗ **S(NY)**

A pair of giltwood torchères, with leaf-bound columns on three paw feet, early 19thC, 57in (145cm) high.
$3,600–4,400 ↗ **L**

◄ **A pair of George III-style tripod torchères,** c1900, 42in (106.5cm) high.
$1,000–1,150 ⊞ **NAW**

A pair of early George III mahogany tripod torchères, with baluster-knopped stems, on leaf-carved cabriole legs and claw and ball feet, 35½in (90cm) high.
$8,000–9,000 ↗ **P(S)**

► **A Victorian mahogany torchère,** the top with a pierced gallery on a fluted, turned and carved baluster column decorated with carved urns and foliage, on a quadriform support with paw feet, 59¾in (152cm) high.
$850–1,000 ↗ **JAd**

An Italian carved-walnut torchère, the top with a gadrooned edge on a tree stump column, supported by a young boy, on an ebonized platform and naturalistic base, late 19thC, 47¾in (121.5cm) high.
$4,500–5,000 ↗ **P**

Mahogany

Used in England from c1730, mahogany was imported from Jamaica, San Domingo, Cuba and Honduras. Timber from the latter two sources was frequently referred to as Spanish mahogany in recognition of Spain's colonial imprint on the area.

Despite this early use it was not until the mid-18th century that the versatility of the wood, and in particular its suitability as a raw material for the art of the carver, brought about a change in direction in English furniture design, the chief exponent being Thomas Chippendale.

Trays

A Georgian mahogany butler's tray, on a stand, c1760, 34in (86.5cm) wide.
$4,500–5,000 ⊞ REI

A mahogany butler's tray, the top with hinged sides, on an earlier ring-turned support, early 19thC, 29in (73.5cm) wide.
$2,000–2,500 ✗ GAK

A Victorian satinwood and king-wood-banded tray, the detachable top with brass carrying handles, on moulded splay legs, 23¼in (59cm) wide.
$850–1,000 ✗ P(Ba)

Wall Brackets

A pair of George III giltwood wall brackets, the shelf on a pierced C-scroll- and leaf-carved support, centred with carved flowers, c1760, 12½in (32cm) wide.
$16,500–20,000 ✗ S(NY)

A pair of carved oak brackets, each with a game bird on a rocky base, with acanthus-leaf sprays behind, 19thC, 14½in (37cm) high.
$850–1,000 ✗ WW

A pair of Italian gilt display brackets, each modelled as fruiting vine and ears of wheat issuing from an urn supporting small stands, faults, 19thC, 70in (178cm) high.
$3,000–3,500 ✗TEN

Wardrobes

▶ **An early Victorian gentleman's mahogany wardrobe,** the centre with seven drawers, flanked by ogee-moulded frame doors, 74in (188cm) wide.
$850–1,000 ✗ SWO

A George III mahogany wardrobe, the swan-neck pediment inlaid with a central foliate panel above a pair of crossbanded and satinwood-strung doors enclosing hanging space, with two long drawers below, restored, 39in (99cm) wide.
$2,000–2,500 ✗ CGC

A George IV Gothic-style mahogany break-front wardrobe, enclosed by two pairs of ogee-moulded frame doors with flame-veneered centre panels, the centre section enclosing three drawers, 86½in (219.5cm) wide.
$1,150–1,350 ✗ TRL

▶ **A French walnut armoire,** c1850, 51in (129.5cm) wide.
$2,500–3,000 ⊞ RPh

FURNITURE

A burr-walnut wardrobe, the panel doors flanked by turned columns, c1860, 55in (139.5cm) wide.
$3,200–3,600 ⊞ **GBr**

A walnut breakfront wardrobe, c1885, 108in (274.5cm) wide.
$3,500–4,000 ⊞ **SWA**

A French painted armoire, with three mirrored doors, late 19thC, 80in (203cm) wide.
$1,700–2,200 ⊞ **CF**

An Australian cedar wardrobe, by Walter Bradley & Co, the panel doors flanked by fluted half-pilasters, maker's mark in ink, c1900, 60¼in (153cm) wide.
$1,150–1,300 ➤ **P(Sy)**

◄ **An inlaid mahogany three-door wardrobe,** the central mirrored door enclosing drawers and trays, flanked by hanging cupboards with drawers below, c1900, 75½in (192cm) wide.
$5,500–6,000 ⊞ **MTay**

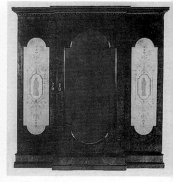

A Victorian burr-walnut and satin-birch breakfront triple wardrobe, with a shaped mirrored door enclosing four linen trays and four drawers, flanked by crossbanded and incised shaped birch-panelled doors applied with transfers of classical maidens enclosing hanging space above boot drawers, 89¾in (228cm) wide.
$1,150–1,350 ➤ **Bri**

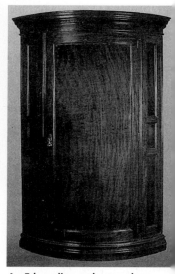

An Edwardian mahogany bow-front hall wardrobe, the panel door with applied fretwork moulding above, enclosing an interior fitted for coats and hats, 47in (119.5cm) wide.
$2,000–2,500 ➤ **Mit**

Washstands

A George III gentleman's mahogany washstand, fitted with a mirror and box compartments, c1770, 10½in (26.5cm) wide.
$1,150–1,450 ➤ **Bon(W)**

Cross Reference
See Colour Review
(page 120)

◄ **A George III gentleman's mahogany washstand,** the shaped double-hinged top enclosing three circular fittings, above a deep frieze, with a shelf below incorporating a drawer, on rope-twist-turned legs, c1770, 17½in (44.5cm) square.
$16,000–19,000 ➤ **Bon**

A George III mahogany bowfront washstand, inlaid with satinwood and ebony stringing, the lid enclosing compartments, above a pair of doors and two drawers, c1790, 34in (86.5cm) wide.
$3,000–3,500 ➤ **RBB**

A George III mahogany washstand, fitted with a soap-ball and two drawers, restored, c1790, 12¼in (31cm) diam.
$450–550 ✗ Bon(W)

A mahogany bowfront corner washstand, inlaid with boxwood stringing, c1790, 28in (71cm) wide.
$1,450–1,750 ⊞ SWA

An American Federal inlaid mahogany corner washstand, the top with openings for a chamber set above the veneered and inlaid aprons, the lower shelf with a single drawer flanked by dummy drawers, Charleston, South Carolina, 1790–1800, restored, 21½in (54.5cm) wide.
$3,200–3,600 ✗ SK(B)

A Regency mahogany corner washstand, the bowfronted top with splashback and basin well, above an under-tier fitted with a frieze drawer and two dummy drawers, early 19thC, 22½in (57cm) wide.
$725–875 ✗ Hal

A Regency mahogany washstand, with a shaped three-quarter gallery and frieze drawer, on ring-turned legs, c1810, 27in (68.5cm) wide.
$1,000–1,150 ✗ S(S)

A Dutch mahogany and marquetry washstand, the folding top inlaid with flower-filled baskets, angels and a tulip roundel, above four drawers, 19thC, 17¼in (44cm) wide.
$1,450–1,750 ✗ TEN

▶ **A Victorian mahogany washstand,** with a galleried marble top, 43in (109cm) wide.
$500–600 ⊞ RPh

An American Classical maple and bird's-eye maple veneer washstand, the marble top over a single drawer, on three vase- and ring-turned legs, New England, 1820–30, 27in (68.5cm) wide.
$1,450–1,750 ✗ SK(B)

An American Classical mahogany washstand, the bowed veneered apron flanked by small drawers, above a shelf with a drawer under, faults, probably Northshore, Massachusetts, c1825, 20½in (52cm) wide.
$1,250–1,450 ✗ SK(B)

Prices

The price ranges quoted in this book reflect the average price a purchaser might expect to pay for a similar item. The price will vary according to the condition, rarity, size, popularity, provenance, colour and restoration of the item, and this must be taken into account when assessing values. Don't forget that if you are selling it is quite likely that you will be offered less than the price range.

FURNITURE

Whatnots

A mahogany tapered four-tier whatnot, with three drawers, c1780, 64in (162.5cm) high.
$4,500–5,000 ⊞ REI

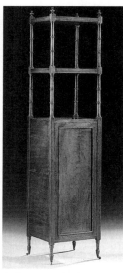

A George III mahogany whatnot, the enclosed lower section with a single panel door enclosing a shelf, c1810, 16in (40.5cm) wide.
$8,700–10,200 ♠ S

A Regency rosewood three-tier whatnot, on turned spindle supports, 13¾in (35cm) wide.
$1,300–1,600 ♠ P(Ba)

A Regency simulated rosewood four-tier whatnot, the turned supports with vase-shaped finials, with a drawer below, 18in (45.5cm) wide.
$2,600–3,000 ♠ Bea(E)

A Victorian rosewood four-tier corner whatnot, 1860–70, 50in (127cm) high.
$1,600–1,750 ⊞ RPh

A Victorian burr-walnut three-tier whatnot, with turned supports and two frieze drawers, 24in (61cm) wide.
$2,200–2,600 ♠ JD

A Victorian stained-wood four-tier whatnot, on turned supports, 18½in (47cm) wide.
$725–875 ♠ JAd

A Victorian serpentine-fronted mahogany three-tier whatnot, with barley-twist supports, 18in (45.5cm) wide.
$250–300 ♠ GAK

A Victorian rosewood corner whatnot, with three serpentine-fronted tiers, 23¼in (59cm) wide.
$600–700 ♠ L

A Victorian rosewood three-tier whatnot, the top with a pierced gallery over two lower tiers, one with a drawer, with barley-twist and C-scroll uprights, faults, 30in (76cm) wide.
$400–500 ♠ P(Ed)

A Victorian rosewood serpentine-fronted four-tier whatnot, on spiral-turned supports, 21¾in (55.5cm) wide.
$725–875 ♠ HYD

A Victorian three-tier whatnot, with a three-quarter gallery, on baluster-turned columns, with two drawers in the base fitted for cutlery, 19¼in (49cm) wide.
$650–800 ♠ CDC

Window Seats

A rosewood and brass-inlaid window seat, the drop-in seat and scroll-over sides upholstered in multi-coloured geometric needlework, the side fronts with scroll brass inlay, 27¼in (69cm) wide.
$3,600–4,400 ✗ P(NW)

A gilt-gesso and green-painted window seat, the supports with stylized lily flowers and anthemia, the legs headed with carved flowerhead paterae, with an upholstered drop-in seat and padded arms, 19thC, 41½in (105.5cm) wide.
$4,500–5,000 ✗ HAM

A Louis IV-style carved walnut and parcel-gilt window seat, with a scroll-carved frame, the padded back, seat and arms covered in peach striped fabric, late 19thC, 31in (78.5cm) wide.
$1,150–1,300 ✗ S(S)

◄ **A Hepplewhite-style mahogany window seat,** the moulded show-wood fronts terminating in florettes, the fluted serpentine frame carved with central oval paterae with bellflowers, damaged, 19thC, 36in (91.5cm) wide.
$1,800–2,200 ✗ WW

► **A scroll-end upholstered window seat,** late 19thC, 50in (127cm) wide.
$300–350 ✗ P(Ba)

Wine Coolers

Construction details

Wine coolers were lead-lined and filled with ice to keep wine bottles chilled. As the wood of which they were constructed would be constantly expanding and contracting during the course of the evening, they were bound with brass bands to prevent them from falling apart. When set on stands, these were of sturdy construction to carry the combined weight of a number of bottles, the ice and the lead liner.

A George III mahogany wine cooler on stand, with adapted interior, the fluted chamfered legs with later stretchers, 16¾in (42.5cm) high.
$1,450–1,750 ✗ P(S)

A George III mahogany brass-bound wine cooler, on a separate stand, lacking liner, 22¾in (58cm) wide.
$850–1,000 ✗ Bri

A Regency mahogany sarcophagus-shaped cellaret, c1820, 23in (58.5cm) wide.
$3,200–3,600 ⊞ REI

A mahogany cellarette, restored, altered, early 19thC, 21in (53.5cm) wide.
$1,000–1,300 ✗ Bon

A Regency mahogany cellaret, the hinged lid decorated with rosewood crossbanding and boxwood stringing, enclosing a compartmented interior, with lion mask ring handles to the sides, 15½in (39.5cm) wide.
$4,500–5,000 ✗ AG

Influence of Chippendale

Thomas Chippendale, the son of a cabinet-maker, was born in Otley, Yorkshire, in 1718 and educated at the local grammar school. After serving an apprenticeship in the family business he joined the York cabinet-making firm of Richard Wood. By 1754 he had moved to London and was established in St Martin's Lane, which gave him the opportunity to associate with other premier cabinet-makers such as William Vile, John Cobb, William Hallett and John Channon. In the same year Chippendale published *The Gentleman & Cabinet Maker's Director*, a revolutionary publication showing a wide range of furniture, lighting and fireplace designs, influenced by the Gothic, Chinese and rococo tastes.

The 'Director' was ahead of its time and highly influential, so that before long leading cabinet-makers of the period were also publishing pattern books, drawing heavily on Chippendale's ideas. At this time England was the only country where furniture was made to basic guiding rules, resulting in well-made pieces at each end of the spectrum. The furniture of the lower classes is made of solid, cheaper timbers, with pure linings, while that of the nobility had expensive veneers, carving and cabriole legs.

During the 17th and 18th centuries Europe had a fascination with the Orient and Chippendale incorporated many Chinese features into his furniture, using lacquer work, pagodas and fretwork. Great country houses, such as Nostell Priory and Harewood House, had whole rooms decorated in the Chinese taste and commissioned Chippendale to design and make the furniture.

With America's historical links with Britain, it was inevitable that the 'Director' would influence American craftsmen. Designs were seldom wholly copied, but instead would be adapted to suit individual preference, to conform with local taste or to make best use of available timbers. Due to different timbers being used, American Chippendale furniture tends to differ from its English counterpart in terms of scale and proportion. It is generally more constrained; ornamentation had to serve a purpose.

Irish Chippendale furniture is characterized by extensive use of carving. Irish cabinet-makers also tended to take liberties, or show a lack of acquaintance, with established English conventions, resulting in such differences as gadroons running in reverse direction, or carved leaf-scrolls extending downward, rather than upward, on the knees of cabriole supports. Irish furniture often has poor backboards whereas English Chippendale has panelled backs. A darker grade of mahogany was generally used, with oak or beech as secondary timbers. **John Butterworth**

Chippendale Period

A George III Chippendale period Cuban mahogany breakfront bookcase, with a pierced swan-neck pediment and step-moulded astragal-glazed doors, the base with two moulded panel doors flanked by ten graduated drawers with original swan-neck handles, c1760, 93in (236cm) wide.
$184,000–188,000 ⊞ REI
Generally breakfront bookcases are not thought to have been constructed in any notable quantity before the mid-18th century, and publication of their designs first appears in early editions of Chippendale's *The Gentleman & Cabinet Maker's Director.*

A Chippendale period mahogany cabinet, with applied blind fretwork to the cornice, the mirrored doors enclosing shelves, the base with one long drawer fitted with a writing slide above six short drawers, c1760, 56in (142cm) wide.
$120,000–135,000 ⊞ REI
There is a similarity between this piece and an illustration in *The Universal System of Household Furniture* by Ince & Mayhew, plate XXI. Ince & Mayhew were known to subscribe to Chippendale's *Director* and they, like Chippendale, favoured the use of blind fretwork decoration to the frieze and surbase.

A set of six Chippendale period oak dining chairs, with boarded seats, c1760.
$2,200–2,400 ⊞ NAW

A Chippendale period elm open armchair, with drop-in seat, c1780.
$2,300–2,600 ⊞ WELL

A pair of Chippendale period mahogany Masonic Lodge armchairs, with green hide upholstery, c1770.
$17,500–20,000 ⊞ APO

A pair of Chippendale period mahogany side chairs, with carved intertwined splats, c1770.
$3,600–4,000 ⊞ RL

A George III Chippendale period Cuban mahogany serpentine commode, the four long graduated drawers flanked by canted corners with blind fretwork decoration and carved and shaped capitals, and original swan-neck handles, c1765, 23in (58.5cm) wide.
$75,000–85,000 ⊞ REI
Examples of this type appear in a number of houses known to have been furnished by Chippendale, including Wilton House, Paxton House and Nostell Priory.

A Chippendale period mahogany double-sided desk, the crossbanded top inset with leather, the lift-up writing slope with an adjustable ratchet, one side with graduating drawers, the other side with cupboard doors decorated with flame-fielded panels and applied roundels, c1765, 49in (124.5cm) wide.
$48,000–55,000 ⊞ REI
The use of the fielded flame panel combined with a turned roundel is illustrated on a secretaire cabinet made for Paxton House, one of Chippendale's largest commissions.

A George II Chippendale period mahogany kettle stand, the turned and fluted stem with acanthus-carved knop on three downcurved legs carved with palmettes and acanthus to the knees, on claw-and-ball feet, 11in (28cm) diam.
$10,000–12,500 ⋏ PFK

A Chippendale period Cuban mahogany dressing stool, the upholstered saddle seat supported by four square legs each with inset fretwork decoration and joined by an H-stretcher, c1760, 13½in (34.5cm) wide.
$7,500–8,500 ⊞ REI
This piece has the enhancement of inset fretwork decoration as seen in *The Gentleman & Cabinet Maker's Director*, plate XXV. This illustrates a near-identical design on a chair leg that closely relates to this stool.

A Chippendale period mahogany side table, with a marble top, c1770, 35in (89cm) wide.
$3,200–3,600 ⊞ GKe

A Chippendale period mahogany open night table, with a tray top, c1770, 16in (40.5cm) wide.
$3,200–3,600 ⊞ RL

◄ **A George III Chippendale period mahogany serving tray,** with a moulded shaped edge and acanthus-carved handles, 20in (51cm) wide.
$725–825 ⋏ Mit

A pair of George III Chippendale period padouk wood sideboard pedestals with urns, the lead-lined urns with lifting lids above bases with applied beaded mouldings, one pedestal with twin cellaret drawers, the other with a cupboard and single cellaret, c1760, 15¼in (38.5cm) wide.
$58,000–65,000 ⊞ REI

Miller's Compares

I. A Chippendale period Cuban mahogany tripod table, with carved claw-and-ball feet and carved knees, c1760, 30in (76cm) diam.
$36,000–42,000 ⊞ REI

II. A Chippendale period Cuban mahogany tripod supper table, the tilt-top on a bird-cage block, on a fluted gun barrel stem and platform base, c1750, 42in (106.5cm) diam.
$24,000–27,000 ⊞ REI

The price differential between these two tripod tables is due to Item I having carved claw-and-ball feet with carving on the knees, and a wrythen-turned vase on the column. It also has an exceptional figured-mahogany top. Item II, while also a desirable piece, is of a plainer design.

Chippendale Revival

A pair of Chippendale revival mahogany Gainsborough armchairs, with carved scroll handrests, upholstered in light blue fabric, c1900.
$1,000–1,300 ↗ RTo

A Victorian Chippendale revival mahogany serpentine commode, carved throughout with trails of husks and flowerheads, 41¾in (106cm) wide.
$5,000–6,000 ↗ HAM

A pair of Chippendale revival mahogany chairs, with carved intertwined splat backs, the drop-in seats upholstered in gold fabric, 1920s.
$580–650 ⊞ RPh

A Chippendale revival carved giltwood over-mantel mirror, the rococo carved frame surmounted by a squirrel in a grotto and flanked by *ho-o* birds, with further birds and trailing oak branches to the sides and a *ho-o* bird to the base, 19thC, 47¼in (120cm) wide.
$8,700–10,200 ↗ TEN

A gilt gesso girandole, after a design by Thomas Chippendale, the plate within a framework of C-scrolls, leaves and ice-work, fitted with a pair of candle brackets, surmounted by a model of a bird, 19thC, 18½in (47cm) wide.
$1,600–1,800 ↗ P(WM)

A Chippendale revival mahogany kettle or urn stand, with a teapot slide, c1900, 27in (68.5cm) high.
$1,100–1,300 ⊞ TWr

▶ **An Edwardian Chippendale revival mahogany music cabinet,** with an astragal-glazed door, 56in (142cm) high.
$3,600–4,300 ⊞ PPC

American Chippendale

An American Chippendale figured mahogany reverse-serpentine chest of drawers, with four line-incised drawers, feet restored, Massachusetts, 1775, 37½in (95.5cm) wide.
$23,000–26,000 ↗ S(NY)

▶ **An American Chippendale mahogany pedestal partners' desk,** the top inset with crimson leather, over four graduated cockbeaded drawers and four opposing drawers to each pedestal, mid-19thC, 84in (213.5cm) wide.
$4,000–4,700 ↗ SLN

A set of five American Chippendale mahogany side chairs, the beaded serpentine crests over pierced splats flanked by scratch-beaded raked stiles, with drop-in seats, possibly mid-Atlantic states, 1760–80.
$6,500–8,000 ↗ SK(B)

An American Chippendale mahogany and parcel-gilt wall mirror, the frame surmounted by a pierced and fret-carved crest centred by a perching *ho-o* bird flanked by foliate scrollwork, the sides with flowering and fruiting trailing vine, with a fret-carved skirt, mid-18thC, 20in (51cm) wide.
$2,200–2,400 ↗ SLN

Chinese Chippendale

A set of three George III Chinese Chippendale mahogany dining chairs, with open lattice-work backs and padded seats.
$4,000–4,700 ↗ JAd

A Chinese Chippendale carved giltwood wall mirror, the frame with pagoda cresting and rococo pierced borders headed by flowers, supported on scrolls and rockwork, 18thC, 34¾in (88.5cm) wide.
$25,500–29,000 ↗ HOK

A set of Chinese Chippendale mahogany two-tier hanging shelves, with trellis openwork sides and a Vitruvian scroll-pierced section, restored, formerly the upper section of a larger item, c1760, 24½in (62cm) wide.
$2,300–2,900 ↗ S(S)

Miller's is a price GUIDE
not a price LIST

An Edwardian Chinese Chippendale mahogany dressing table, with three drawers, with blind fretwork decoration to the central drawer and the arched apron, on acanthus-carved cabriole legs with claw-and-ball feet, c1910, 45in (114.5cm) wide.
$2,500–2,800 ↗ S(S)

▶ **A George III Chinese Chippendale mahogany folding-top card table,** with a blind fretwork frieze, on four cluster column supports, 35¾in (91cm) wide.
$7,250–8,000 ↗ JAd

Irish Chippendale

◀ **A set of eight Irish Chippendale mahogany dining chairs,** including two open armchairs, with carved crest rails and inter-twined pierced splats, with close-nailed upholstered seats, on acanthus-capped cabriole legs with claw-and-ball feet, 19thC.
$18,000–22,000 ↗ HOK

A George III Irish Chinese Chippendale mahogany hall table, the marble top above a pierced fretwork frieze centred by a crest, the square supports with blind tracery panels, on pedestal feet, 52in (132cm) wide.
$110,000–130,000 ↗ JAd

Oak & Country Furniture

The last twelve months have seen a considerable rise in the value of oak, country and provincial furniture, reflecting the general shortage of good-quality items available on the market. This was demonstrated when a Welsh dresser fetched over $72,500 at auction (see page 171). Almost every corner of this market has risen in price, from farm tables to delft racks. Perhaps the only piece of furniture not to have performed quite so well is the bureau. This, I think, is because of the emergence of the computer; people now want a table/desk with a flat top surface on which to place their machine!

At most of the major fairs where I have exhibited this year, piece for piece, informal furniture has outsold formal; people tend not to dress for dinner any more, and much of their entertaining is done in the kitchen. Country furniture suits this informal environment and reflects, perhaps, the more 'dressed down' society.

Looking through this *Guide* I think one is most struck with its comprehensive approach. However, there may appear to be a huge price difference between two or more similar pieces. One should not be fooled by this into thinking that things are cheaper at one place than another; rather, as is often explained in the Miller's Compares features, the higher price reflects the huge premium in country furniture that is placed upon quality – originality, colour, patina, material and proportion. So one tripod table at $290 and another at $5,000 might initially look the same but, to a professional eye, one is badly proportioned, has an ugly stem, replaced bearers and washed out colour, while the other is in burr elm with the most gloriously drawn baluster stem the colour of speckled ripened corn, and a patina deeper than the most tempting pool on the Spey; I think you get my drift.

The other thing that affects price is practicality – hence a mule chest that looks like a dresser base is much cheaper than a dresser base because, with the former, one has to lift everything off the top to access the space inside. Another example would be sets of chairs from a similar period, where those that will only stand up to light use are generally worth less than those that will take everyday use – common sense really.

To summarize, always buy the best if you possibly can, and remember the golden rules – quality, proportion, material, patina, colour and originality.
Good hunting!

Denzil Grant

Beds

An American joined and panelled oak cradle, New England, c1700, 39in (99cm) wide.
$2,000–2,400 ✦ SK(B)

A Georgian fruitwood cradle, with a break-arch-top hood and shaped rockers, 39¾in (101cm) wide.
$360–420 ✦ Bri

A 17thC-style oak tester bed, on two turned and carved newel posts, the headboard decorated with Romanesque arches and lozenges, restored, 19thC, 65¼in (165.5cm) wide.
$2,400–2,900 ✦ Bon(W)

A beech cradle, suspended from turned uprights, with turned under-stretchers, 19thC, 41in (104cm) wide.
$360–420 ✦ AG

A Breton oak bed, with original side rails, late 19thC, 60in (152.5cm) wide.
$2,200–2,500 ⊞ SWA

A Breton oak bedstead, carved with shells and stylized flowers, c1900, 54in (137cm) wide.
$1,600–1,800 ⊞ SeH

Boxes

A carved oak bible box, 17thC, 23in (58.5cm) wide.
$800–880 ⊞ TWh

A provincial oak boarded box, with a hinged top, on a stand with panelled drawers and turned legs, restored, early 18thC, 28¾in (73cm) wide.
$2,000–2,400 ↗ Bea(E)

◀ **A Welsh oak salt box,** 19thC, 15in (38cm) wide.
$400–470 ⊞ CoA

An elm writing slope, with internal drawers, c1750, 17in (43cm) wide.
$1,100–1,300 ⊞ SEA

An inlaid oak candle box, the hinged lid crossbanded and with geometric inlay, the front crossbanded and inlaid with striated stringing lines and lozenge and quadrant motifs, late 18thC, 14in (35.5cm) wide.
$2,600–3,200 ↗ PF

Buffets

A French fruitwood buffet, with two half-drawers above two asymmetrically-panelled doors, with steel hardware, late 18thC, 55in (139.5cm) wide.
$4,300–5,000 ↗ NOA

A French fruitwood buffet, with panelled doors and original metal hardware, c1820, 53in (134.5cm) wide.
$5,000–5,500 ⊞ DeG

A French elm buffet, the two panelled doors enclosing shelves, 19thC, 48in (122cm) wide.
$900–1,100 ↗ E

Bureaux

An oak bureau, the slope enclosing pigeonholes, four small drawers and a well, early 18thC, 36in (91.5cm) wide.
$2,000–2,400 ↗ CAG

A George II oak bureau, the fall-front enclosing a stepped and fitted interior with a covered well, faults, restored, mid-18thC, 36in (91.5cm) wide.
$2,200–2,400 ↗ S(S)

A George II inlaid oak bureau, the chequer-strung mitred fall-front enclosing a serpentine-shaped cupboard door flanked by pigeonholes and drawers, above a well slide, with a later shaped apron and brass fittings, faults, restored, mid-18thC, 34in (86.5cm) wide.
$700–850 ↗ Hal

An oak bureau, the fall-front enclosing a stepped, fitted interior with secret drawers and a well, mid-18thC, 37in (94cm) wide.
$1,700–2,100 ⚷ DD

A George II oak bureau, the cleated fall-front enclosing small drawers and pigeonholes, mid-18thC, 32½in (82.5cm) wide.
$1,000–1,200 ⚷ S(S)

A George III oak bureau, the fall-front enclosing drawers and pigeon-holes, 42in (106.5cm) wide.
$1,600–1,900 ⚷ AH

A George III provincial oak bureau, the fall-front enclosing a fitted interior with a centre cupboard and column drawers, faults, 36in (91.5cm) wide.
$450–500 ⚷ DMC

LOCATE THE SOURCE
The source of each illustration in Miller's can be found by checking the code letters below each caption with the Key to Illustrations, pages 794–800.

An oak bureau, the fall-front enclosing a fitted interior with pigeonholes, drawers, secret compartments and a well, 18thC, 35½in (90cm) wide.
$700–850 ⚷ DDM

▶ **A French provincial oak bureau,** the fall-front enclosing a fitted interior with drawers and pigeonholes, early 19thC, 54in (137cm) wide.
$3,300–4,000 ⚷ P(EA)

A George III oak bureau, with four long drawers, 36in (91.5cm) wide.
$850–1,000 ⚷ L

Bureau Cabinets

◀ **A George II oak bureau cabinet,** with mahogany crossbanding, the fielded panel doors enclosing adjustable shelving, the fall-front enclosing a fitted interior with a centre cupboard initialled 'HB', with three frieze drawers below, over two short and two long drawers, dated '1754', 42½in (108cm) wide.
$4,300–5,000 ⚷ AH

Cross Reference
See Colour Review
(page 217)

▶ **An oak bureau cabinet,** with mahogany crossbanding, the later upper section with adjustable shelves, 18thC, 43½in (110.5cm) wide.
$5,500–6,200 ⊞ MTay

A Welsh George III oak bureau cabinet, the grooved and panelled cupboard doors enclosing three reeded adjustable shelves over a mitred fall-front, enclosing drawers and letter slides and a centre cupboard door, over four long graduated drawers, damaged, c1800, 37in (94cm) wide.
$2,300–2,900 ⚷ Hal

Chairs

An ash primitive turner's chair, the top rail on a ring-turned central column with turned spindle supports, above a triangular solid panel seat, inscribed 'AO 1740 MIME', 17thC.
$2,600–3,200 ➚ P(NW)

A pair of oak side chairs, the pierced scroll-top cresting rail above three moulded vertical back rails, late 17thC.
$1,400–1,700 ➚ WW

A pair of oak back stools, with a vase-shaped splat, c1720.
$1,600–1,750 ⊞ WELL

► **An American ladder-back armchair,** with ring-turned stiles and front legs, with a rush seat, probably New Jersey, mid-18thC.
$2,200–2,400 ➚ SK(B)

A carved oak wainscot chair, c1670.
$4,600–5,000 ⊞ WELL

A Yorkshire oak side chair, the back with two arcaded scroll-carved rails, late 17thC.
$1,000–1,200 ➚ P(NW)

A pair of oak side chairs, with moulded splats, 18thC.
$1,400–1,600 ⊞ SuA

A pair of oak back-stools, with bobbin-turned decoration, c1670.
$3,200–3,600 ⊞ SuA

A joined oak panelled side chair, the waved top rail with an arched panelled back, on turned baluster supports, late 17thC.
$450–550 ➚ Bon(C)

► **A George III fruitwood armchair,** with a drop-in floral needlework seat, c1760.
$1,200–1,400 ➚ S(S)

A pair of William and Mary oak side chairs, with caned seat and back panel.
$2,900–3,300 ⊞ SuA

An oak side chair, the arcaded open back above a solid seat and bobbin-turned legs, late 17thC.
$450–550 ➚ P(NW)

Country chairs

Country chairs, many of which were made in remote rural areas, developed independently from the fashionable seating featured on page 50–62.

These types of chairs are always made of solid wood from indigenous trees such as elm, yew, oak, ash and beech. The wood used can have a significant bearing on the price. Pieces made entirely or partly from yew wood are particularly sought after, while beech is more common. Dating can be difficult because designs changed little from the 18th to the early 20th century, although the patina of the wood and decorative details can help.

If the chair combines decoration typical of different periods, always date it by the latest decorative detail.

A set of six George III oak dining chairs, with pierced splats and drop-in seats.
$3,350–4,000 ⚒ Bea(E)

A ladderback armchair, with a rush seat, c1770.
$1,600–1,750 ⊞ REI

A George III oak hooded lambing chair, with a drawer beneath the seat, c1780.
$8,700–10,000 ⊞ PHA

An oak barber's chair, with pierced splats, c1780.
$2,200–2,400 ⊞ WELL
A gentleman might have sat in his bedroom in this type of chair whilst being shaved by his servant.

An American painted banister-back side chair, with a rush seat, probably from the King Family workshop, Deerfield, Massachusetts, 1780–1810.
$1,300–1,600 ⚒ SK(B)

A yew broadarm high-back Windsor chair, with an ash seat, early 19thC.
$2,200–2,400 ⊞ REI

A Thames Valley ash, elm and sycamore low stick-back Windsor armchair, legs reduced, early 19thC.
$440–500 ⚒ Bon(C)

An American bow-back Windsor rocking chair, rockers added mid-19thC, New England, early 19thC.
$720–870 ⚒ SK(B)

A pair of American black-painted chairs, with rush seats and decorated with gold foliage, and a gold and red apple centring the crests, with green, red and gold highlights, New England, early 19thC.
$900–1,100 ⚒ SK(B)

▶ **A set of four oak chairs,** with carved top rails, 1830–50.
$1,000–1,100 ⊞ NEW

A beech and elm comb-back Windsor armchair, with solid saddle seat, c1820.
$2,600–2,900 ⊞ SEA

A set of six oak country chairs, c1820.
$3,600–4,000 ⊞ DeG

A set of four George IV ash and elm ladderback chairs, with solid seats, early 19thC.
$2,200–2,400 ⚒ S(S)

A set of four Lincolnshire oak hoop-back Windsor side chairs, c1820.
$1,400–1,600 ⊞ WELL

An elm high-back Windsor chair, c1840.
$700–800 ⊞ **MIN**

A pair of American Shaker cherry and maple side chairs, with replaced tape seat, Watervliet, New York community, c1840.
$2,300–2,900 ⚒ **SK(B)**

A Dales ash nursing chair, with a rush seat, 19thC.
$160–190 ⚒ **PFK**

A Victorian beech chair.
$260–290 ⊞ **POT**

A fruitwood spindle-backed rocking chair, with a rush seat, 19thC.
$240–290 ⚒ **PFK**

A set of six Macclesfield ladderback dining chairs, including one carver, with rush seats, 19thC.
$1,300–1,600 ⚒ **CDC**

A Shaker-style rocking chair, mid-19thC.
$290–340 ⊞ **MLu**

A mixed woods provincial open armchair, with a bobbin-turned crest rail and rush seat, mid-19thC.
$200–240 ⚒ **TRL**

A Victorian elm and beech captain's chair.
$260–290 ⊞ **POT**

A set of six French provincial oak side chairs, with rush seats, the scalloped crest rail with shell carving, late 19thC.
$800–950 ⚒ **NOA**

A set of twelve 17thC-style joined oak back stools, with double waved-back stretchers with turned drop pendants, 19thC.
$4,400–5,000 ⚒ **Bon(C)**

A set of twelve Regency-style *faux* bamboo chairs, with original painted decoration and rush seats, c1870.
$7,250–8,000 ⊞ **TEMP**
These chairs were given by Earl Crawford of Balcarres in Fife to the local church for use in its meeting hall.

◄ **A harlequin set of six French fruitwood chairs,** with rush seats, c1860.
$2,900–3,200 ⊞ **DeG**

An American Shaker No. 1 Production maple rocking chair, with tape back and seat, left rocker marked 'Shaker's No 1 Trademark Mount Lebanon NY', c1900.
$620–690 ⚒ **SK(B)**

Children's Chairs

A child's oak chair, the drop-in seat upholstered with later fabric, c1780.
$950–1,100 ⊞ WELL

A George III child's ash and elm rocking chair, with a triple-spindle back and turned arms.
$340–400 🔨 Mit

A George III child's oak country-made highchair.
$360–430 🔨 L

A George III child's painted ash chair, c1790.
$1,800–2,200 ⊞ PHA

A Welsh child's primitive ash chair, c1800.
$2,200–2,900 ⊞ PHA

A Thames Valley child's beech Windsor armchair, with turned arms and a caned seat, on turned splayed legs, early 19thC.
$360–430 🔨 Bon(C)

A child's Windsor high-chair, c1820.
$850–950 ⊞ ALA

A French child's oak chair, with a shaped top rail and splat, mid-19thC.
$440–500 ⊞ NEW

◄ **An American child's painted and decorated settee,** with gold striping to the original red and brown grained surface, and with turned tapering legs, New England, 1830–40.
$1,700–2,000 🔨 SK(B)

► **A child's elm commode chair,** with stick back and original tray, mid-19thC.
$320–360 ⊞ MLu

A child's square-back Windsor chair, mid-19thC.
$320–360 ⊞ MLu

A child's spindle-back elm and beech armchair, with a rush seat, 19thC.
$220–260 🔨 SWO

A child's yew wood Windsor chair, 19thC.
$1,600–1,800 ⊞ DHA

A child's elm Windsor chair, 19thC.
$580–725 🔨 WilP

Chests of Drawers

A Charles II oak chest of drawers, with applied moulded fronts, 37in (94cm) wide.
$3,600–4,000 ⊞ WELL

An oak chest of drawers, the four long drawers decorated with geometric panelling, 38in (96.5cm) wide.
$1,000–1,200 ✗ L

An oak chest of drawers, the drawers relined, late 17thC, 43¼in (110cm) wide.
$1,400–1,600 ✗ Bon(C)

An oak chest of drawers, the two short and three long drawers outlined with ogee-mouldings, early 18thC, 38¼in (97cm) wide.
$870–1,100 ✗ P(S)

A Charles II oak and fruitwood moulded chest of drawers, the top with a dentil frieze and long shallow drawer above a central cushion and quatrefoil-moulded drawer, with two long drawers below, 38¼in (97cm) wide.
$4,000–4,600 ✗ P(EA)

An oak chest of drawers, the two short and two long drawers with re-plated pear-drop handles and original escutcheons, on replaced bun feet, c1680, 36in (91.5cm) wide.
$6,000–6,700 ⊞ REI

Further reading

Miller's Pine & Country Furniture Buyer's Guide, Miller's Publications, 2001

▶ **A Transitional chest of drawers,** the hinged top with a scroll- and vine-carved frieze above two mitred geometric cushion-moulded dummy drawers, with two further real drawers below, c1700, 34¾in (88.5cm) wide.
$3,600–4,300 ✗ P(NW)

An oak chest of drawers, c1680, 34in (86.5cm) wide.
$5,800–6,500 ⊞ REI

A stained pine and fruitwood joined blockfronted chest of drawers, the pine top above two drawers with geometric-moulded fronts, with later handles, late 17thC, 34¼in (87cm) wide.
$1,450–1,750 ✗ Bri

An oak chest of drawers, the hinged top over a long dummy drawer with moulded front, with two long fitted drawers below, late 17thC, 38¼in (97cm) wide.
$2,000–2,400 ✗ G(T)

◀ **An oak chest of drawers,** with four graduating drawers, with later handles and feet, c1700, 38in (96.5cm) wide.
$2,900–3,200 ⊞ SuA

A Queen Anne oak chest of drawers, with panelled sides, early 18thC, 33in (84cm) wide.
$2,000–2,300 ✗ S(S)

An oak and walnut-veneered chest of drawers, with two short and three long graduated crossbanded drawers, 18thC, 38in (96.5cm) wide.
$1,900–2,200 ✗ AG

A George III oak chest of drawers, with two short and three long drawers below a screw-operated linen press, 40¼in (102cm) wide.
$720–870 ✗ TMA

An American cherry chest of drawers, with four cockbeaded drawers, Connecticut, late 18thC, 39¼in (99.5cm) wide.
$4,000–4,600 ✗ SK(B)

An American painted chest of drawers, the top enclosing a till, above a case of two dummy drawers and two real drawers, with original dark brown paint, probably Connecticut, early 18thC, 37in (94cm) wide.
$19,500–21,750 ✗ SK(B)

An oak chest of drawers, with a brushing slide over two short and three long graduated drawers, 18thC, 32½in (82.5cm) wide.
$1,800–2,200 ✗ GAK

An oak chest of drawers, with four long graduated cockbeaded drawers, late 18thC, 34in (86.5cm) wide.
$580–720 ✗ DD

An elm chest of drawers, c1820, 39½in (100.5cm) wide.
$850–1,000 ⊞ AL

A Louis XV provincial oak serpentine commode, the plank top above two short and two long drawers, with figural brass handles and escutcheons, mid-18thC, 46in (117cm) wide.
$4,300–5,000 ✗ B&L

A George III oak chest of drawers, with two short and three long oak-lined, cockbeaded drawers, 36½in (92.5cm) wide.
$1,100–1,300 ✗ PFK

A Dutch oak commode, with a dentil frieze, fitted with three long drawers, the sides with fielded panels, 18thC, 36in (91.5cm) wide.
$800–950 ✗ L

An American wavy birch chest, with four thumbmoulded drawers, replaced brass, New Hampshire, late 18thC, 38¼in (97cm) wide.
$4,300–4,700 ✗ SK(B)

A George IV oak and mahogany crossbanded and inlaid chest of drawers, the two short and three long graduated cockbeaded drawers with bone escutcheons between canted feather-strung angles, with later turned handles, faults, c1825, 44in (112cm) wide.
$720–870 ⚒ Hal

An American Federal stained-maple chest of drawers, the four scratch-beaded mahogany-veneered drawers on vase- and ring-turned incised legs, with original red-stained surface, probably central Massachusetts, c1820, 42in (106.5cm) wide.
$1,100–1,300 ⚒ SK(B)

A Louis Philippe provincial elm commode, with a grey marble top above a frieze drawer over three long drawers, late 19thC, 46in (117cm) wide.
$1,400–1,600 ⚒ NOA

OAK & COUNTRY FURNITURE

Tallboys

A South Wales oak tallboy, the upper section with a secret drawer and flanked by quarter columns, over a brushing slide and three long drawers, c1760, 42in (106.5cm) wide.
$13,800–15,250 ⊞ AdA

A George III oak tallboy, with two short and three graduated long drawers, flanked by fluted canted corners, with three long drawers below, 44in (112cm) wide.
$2,900–3,500 ⚒ Bea(E)

A George III parquetry-banded oak tallboy, with three small drawers over two short and three long drawers to the upper section, and three long drawers below, with brass bat's-wing handles, 50in (127cm) wide.
$1,900–2,300 ⚒ Bri

An oak tallboy, with four short and three long graduated drawers to the upper section, and three long drawers to the lower section, 18thC, 40in (101.5cm) wide.
$1,000–1,200 ⚒ E

Chests-on-Stands

An early Georgian oak chest-on-stand, with two short and three long drawers, the stand with a central drawer flanked by two deep drawers, 38¾in (98.5cm) wide.
$2,900–3,500 ⚒ AH

A George I oak chest-on-stand, with pollarded oak crossbanding and original plate handles, c1720, 67in (170cm) high.
$18,800–21,000 ⊞ REI

A George II oak chest-on-stand, the stand with cabriole legs, with cock-beading and rococo brass handles, the drawer linings made of reclaimed timber, 66in (167.5cm) high.
$8,700–10,200 ⊞ TWh

An oak chest-on-stand, the upper section with two short and four long graduated drawers, the base with a central drawer flanked by two deep drawers, brass handles and escutcheons replaced, 18thC, 41¾in (106cm) wide.
$1,200–1,400 ⊞ WL

Cupboards

A Charles I oak livery cupboard, the fielded panel doors carved with strapwork and stylized flowerheads and a central flower pattern, the sides with carved lozenges, 40in (101.5cm) wide.
$11,000–12,000 ⚒ S(S)

A carved oak press cupboard, with two doors, 17thC, 60in (152.4cm) wide.
$3,650–4,100 ⊞ SuA

A Flemish carved oak cabinet on stand, the upper section with two panelled doors carved with lunettes, foliage and gentlemen, with similar decoration to the sides, the later stand fitted with a single long frieze drawer, 17thC, 33in (84cm) wide.
$1,400–1,700 ⚒ P(E)

▶ **An elm corner cupboard,** with reeded canted corners, c1770, 37in (94cm) high.
$1,700–2,000 ⊞ WELL

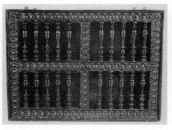

An oak mural livery cupboard, the guilloche-carved frame with four spindle-turned openings, and two doors, 17thC, 35½in (90cm) wide.
$5,800–7,250 ⚒ P(NW)

An oak press cupboard, with two carved panelled doors flanked by baluster-turned supports, restored, 17thC, 58½in (148.5cm) wide.
$1,300–1,600 ⚒ L

A William and Mary oak press cupboard, the carved frieze centred by initials and the date '1692', faults, 72in (183cm) wide.
$4,300–5,000 ⚒ S(S)

A Welsh oak mural cupboard, mid-17thC, 45in (114.5cm) wide.
$11,300–12,300 ⊞ CoA

An oak press cupboard, c1680, 56in (142cm) wide.
$5,500–6,100 ⊞ WELL

A Welsh oak cupboard, in two sections, with heart-shaped key escutcheons, c1700, 50in (127cm) wide.
$5,500–6,100 ⊞ WELL

A Louis XV French provincial elm buffet à deux corps, c1760, 48in (122cm) wide.
$5,500–6,100 ⊞ RYA

Dressers

An oak dresser, the three frieze drawers with swan-neck handles with a later plate rack and potboard, late 17thC, 81in (205.5cm) wide.
$4,000–4,600 ⚒ **CDC**

An oak dresser, the top section with open shelves, with three drawers in the shaped frieze and with a potboard below, 18thC, 60in (152.5cm) wide.
$7,250–8,700 ⚒ **LEW**

◄ **A Welsh oak dresser,** with open shelves, the base with three drawers over two cupboards flanking a small central drawer and cupboard, Merioneth-shire, c1760, 72in (183cm) wide.
$16,700–18,800 ⊞ **CoA**

An oak Welsh dresser, with a pierced canopy above three open shelves, the base fitted with four frieze drawers with later brass handles and backplates above a centre cupboard flanked by wing cupboards, with raised and fielded ogee panelled doors and blind panels, c1700, 41¾in (106cm) wide.
$72,500–87,000 ⚒ **DOD**
This magnificent oak dresser is the finest available of its type and sold for a record price due to its exceptional quality, colour and size. It was one of three dressers which had been made for three sisters in the early 18th century, and this one had remained in the family ever since. It was in original condition apart from replaced handles and dealers said they had seen nothing like it in decades. The trade bid on it to over $43,500, but it finally sold to a private collector who, although previously unaware of the fact, was related to the person who was selling it.

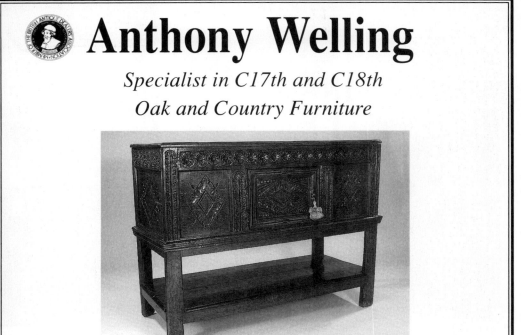

A Welsh oak dresser, with silhouette legs and shaped frieze, c1770, 108in (172.5cm) wide.
$7,250–8,000 ⊞ RYA

A George III oak dresser, with mahogany crossbanding, the three shelves and two cupboards with shell marquetry paterae, the base with three frieze drawers, 73½in (186.5cm) wide.
$3,000–3,500 ⚒ AH

▶ **A Welsh oak dresser,** with five drawers over a potboard, Cardiganshire, c1830, 72in (183cm) wide.
$10,200–11,600 ⊞ CoA

A northern France yew wood dresser, the two shelves with retaining rails above two glazed doors flanking a cupboard with arched top, the projecting base with three frieze drawers above two doors enclosing a shelf, the drawers and doors applied with a pattern in brass round-headed studs, early 19thC, 49in (124.5cm) wide.
$2,000–2,400 ⚒ HAM

A George III oak dresser, the rack with an undulating frieze above four moulded shelves, the base with three drawers above an arcaded apron, over a potboard, 67in (170cm) wide.
$5,500–6,100 ⚒ P(S)

A Georgian elm dresser, the base with three large and two small drawers, 81in (205.5cm) wide.
$5,000–6,000 ⚒ RBB

An oak dresser, inlaid with ebony, with three shelves above cupboards and drawers, c1790, 58in (147.5cm) wide.
$12,300–13,800 ⊞ REI

A French provincial Louis XVI Transitional oak *vaisselier*, the projecting lower case with two drawers and cupboard doors, late 18thC, 57in (145cm) wide.
$3,000–3,500 ⚒ NOA

A Victorian carved oak dresser, the top section with a central mirror, 61in (155cm) wide.
$580–720 ⚒ SWO

◀ **A Welsh oak dresser,** the base with an arrangement of five drawers, with later brass handles, mid-19thC, 66in (167.5cm) wide.
$3,600–4,300 ⚒ PF

Low Dressers

An oak dresser base, with three drawers, on silhouette front legs, late 17thC, 68in (172.5cm) wide.
$6,800–7,600 ⊞ WELL

An oak low dresser, with three frieze drawers and panelled ends, c1730, 62in (157.5cm) wide.
$16,700–18,200 ⊞ AdA

An oak low dresser, with two central drawers designed to look like three, flanked by two drawers and two panelled cupboard doors, 18thC, 72½in (184cm) wide.
$4,300–5,000 ⚒ DA

A North Country oak low dresser, with three frieze drawers above three drawers flanked by cupboard doors, with quarter-turned columns, c1800, 69in (175.5cm) wide.
$3,300–4,000 ⚒ Bon(C)

A Georgian fruitwood low dresser, with three cock-beaded frieze drawers and a shaped apron, on later front cabriole legs, 72½in (184cm) wide.
$1,400–1,700 ⚒ DMC

An oak dresser base, with three drawers applied with sycamore mouldings, c1720, 65in (165cm) wide.
$15,200–18,200 ⊞ PHA

An oak dresser base, with a shaped apron and pad front feet, c1740, 72in (183cm) wide.
$11,600–12,700 ⊞ DeG

An oak dresser base, inlaid with mahogany crossbanding, the plank top over three frieze drawers and a shaped apron, 18thC, 78¼in (199cm) wide.
$9,500–11,500 ⊞ WL

An oak dresser base, with three crossbanded frieze drawers and a shaped apron, 18thC, 96in (244cm) wide.
$4,300–5,000 ⚒ RBB

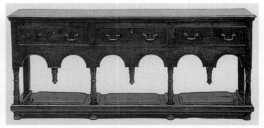

A late George III oak dresser base, with later top, with three frieze drawers above an arcaded apron with pendant finials, altered, 75½in (192cm) wide.
$3,300–4,000 ⚒ Bea(E)

Lowboys

A Georgian oak lowboy, with a fitted frieze drawer, 29in (73.5cm) wide.
$1,400–1,700 ⚹ RBB

An oak lowboy, the crossbanded top above three small drawers and an arched serpentine apron, mid-18thC, 31½in (80cm) wide.
$1,300–1,600 ⚹ P(S)

An early George III oak lowboy, the mahogany-crossbanded top above one long and three short drawers, with a shaped apron below, 32¾in (83cm) wide.
$2,500–2,900 ⚹ CGC

A Georgian oak lowboy, the three-plank top above a frieze drawer, with a shaped apron, 29in (73.5cm) wide.
$1,500–1,750 ⚹ Mit

A George III oak lowboy, with three short drawers above a scrolling apron, 31¾in (80.5cm) wide.
$650–800 ⚹ P(Ed)

An oak lowboy, the shaped frieze with three drawers with burr-elm banding and stringing, with replacement brass swan-neck handles, late 18thC, 31½in (80cm) wide.
$1,100–1,300 ⚹ WW

Racks & Shelves

A set of Charles II oak hanging shelves, with incised decoration, the three shelves with gouged motifs, restored, 30in (76cm) wide.
$3,300–4,000 ⚹ S(S)

> **Miller's is a price GUIDE not a price LIST**

▶ **An oak plate rack,** the moulded cornice above four shelves, flanked by fluted uprights, late 18thC, 50¼in (127.5cm) wide.
$720–870 ⚹ Bon(M)

A late Georgian oak plate rack, from a dresser, the sides applied with split bobbin-turned decoration, 74in (188cm) wide.
$580–720 ⚹ PFK

A George III oak delft rack, with a dentil cornice and shaped pigeonholes, c1770, 50in (127cm) wide.
$4,000–4,700 ⊞ PHA

A set of mahogany country hanging shelves, with a turned central pillar, c1770, 44½in (113cm) wide.
$1,600–1,900 ⊞ DeG

Settles & Settees

A Charles II oak settle, the lunette-carved top-rail above a panelled back and a chip-carved solid seat, faults, late 17thC, 54in (137cm) wide.
$4,300–4,800 ✗ S(S)

An oak settle, the four-panel back with a carved top rail above a hinged seat, the front with two panels, recon-structed, 17thC, 62¼in (158cm) wide.
$1,600–1,900 ✗ L&T

An oak settle, with a panelled back, mid-18thC, 72in (183cm) wide.
$2,000–2,300 ⊞ HRQ

▶ **An oak settee,** with a panelled back, 18thC, 70¾in (179.5cm) wide.
$700–820 ✗ JAd

A Welsh oak box settle, Carmarthen-shire, c1780, 36in (91.5cm) wide
$6,500–7,250 ⊞ CoA

An oak curved settle, with a panelled back, the box seat with a hinged lid, 18thC, 52in (132cm) wide.
$4,600–5,500 ✗ RBB

An American ash, pine and maple *faux* **bamboo Windsor settee,** restored, c1810, 75in (190.5cm) wide.
$5,500–6,100 ✗ SK(B)

◀ **A curved elm settle,** with a panelled back and solid seat, the base with two panelled cupboard doors, probably Welsh, late 18thC, 75¼in (191cm) wide.
$2,200–2,600 ✗ TRL

An American painted and stencilled settee, the ground paint simulating rosewood, New York, 1815–25, 76¾in (195cm) wide.
$1,000–1,200 ✗ SK(B)

OAK & COUNTRY FURNITURE

OAK & COUNTRY FURNITURE

Stands

An American Queen Anne cherrywood candle stand, the oval top above a ball-and-ring-turned column, New England, c1760, 17¾in (45cm) wide.
$900–1,000 ⚒ SK(B)

▶ **An American Federal stained-birch and butternut stand,** with a single drawer and vestiges of old red stain, New England, early 19thC, 18½in (47cm) wide.
$1,000–1,200 ⚒ SK(B)

A fruitwood candle stand, 18thC, 9in (23cm) diam.
$650–725 ⊞ DaH

A walnut and beechwood candle stand, on a turned column, c1780, 14in (35.5cm) high.
$1,100–1,300 ⊞ SuA

▶ **A yew wood candle stand,** on four ring-turned legs, c1800, 9in (23cm) long.
$600–700 ⊞ SEA

An American cherrywood candle stand, the square top with a scratch-beaded edge over a ring-turned column, impressed 'A. SHOVE', early 19thC, 15¼in (38.5cm) wide.
$1,600–1,750 ⚒ SK(B)
Abraham Shove was a Windsor chair-maker who worked in Bristol County, Massachusetts, in the early 19th century.

Stools

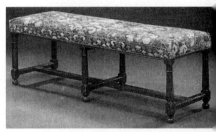

A joined oak stool, with a shaped frieze and angled turned legs, 17thC, 24in (61cm) wide.
$1,800–2,200 ⚒ Mit

An elm lace-maker's stool, c1850, 9in (23cm) wide.
$150–175 ⊞ SEA

▶ **An oak stool,** c1880, 7in (18cm) wide.
$90–110 ⊞ POT

▶ **A Charles II oak stool,** with a stuff-over studded seat upholstered in foliate tapestry, restored, late 17thC, 55in (139.5cm) wide.
$4,300–4,800 ⚒ S(S)

A pair of joined oak stools, with a shaped frieze, on turned baluster legs, 17thC, 17½in (44.5cm) wide.
$5,500–6,000 ⚒ L

Sets/pairs
Unless otherwise stated, any description which refers to 'a set' or 'a pair' includes a guide price for the entire set or the pair, even though the illustration may show only a single item.

An elm and ash stool, with a rush seat, c1900, 19in (48.5cm) wide.
$70–80 ⊞ AL

Tables

A Charles I oak refectory table, with a cleated three-plank top, on turned legs with squared stretchers, the legs extended to form an altar table, 17thC, 72½in (184cm) wide. **$4,000–4,700** ✦ HYD

A joined oak refectory table, the later mitred three-plank top above a nulled frieze, on faceted mirrored baluster legs with later stretchers, reconstructed, early 17thC, 63in (160cm) wide. **$430–500** ✦ Hal

▶ **A French oak side table,** the loose plank top above a pair of slides to the frieze enclosing a recess, on ring-turned baluster legs with stretchers, damaged, mid-17thC, 77¼in (196cm) wide. **$3,500–4,300** ✦ Bon(C)

A Charles II oak side table, on bobbin-turned legs, restored, c1670, 18in (45.5cm) wide. **$2,600–3,200** ⊞ PHA

An oak centre table, with a single drawer, c1670, 33in (84cm) wide. **$3,900–4,300** ⊞ SuA

An oak refectory table, with a carved frieze and turned legs, the top associated, c1620, 78in (198cm) wide. **$4,650–5,100** ⊞ SuA

An oak side table, with a moulded frieze drawer, on baluster-turned supports, the X-stretcher possibly later, 17thC, 29½in (75cm) wide. **$1,100–1,400** ✦ GAK

An oak table, with a single drawer and turned legs, restored, c1680, 35in (89cm) wide. **$1,900–2,200** ⊞ NAW

A cherrywood side table, late 17thC, 29in (73.5cm) wide. **$3,600–4,000** ⊞ RED

A Queen Anne oak side table, with a single drawer and turned legs, c1710, 31in (78.5cm) wide. **$4,600–5,000** ⊞ SEA

An oak side table, with a three-plank top, the frieze drawer with ovolo moulding, on turned legs with moulded square stretchers, early 18thC, 30¼in (77cm) wide. **$2,200–2,500** ✦ Bea(E)

A Georgian oak tilt-top tripod table, c1760, 25in (63.5cm) diam. **$2,600–2,900** ⊞ DBA

OAK & COUNTRY FURNITURE

OAK & COUNTRY FURNITURE

A George III oak side table, with three frieze drawers, 50in (127cm) long.
$1,900–2,200 ⚹ TMA

An oak farmhouse kitchen table, the four-plank top with cleated ends, above a recessed scratch-moulded frieze, 18thC, 86in (218.5cm) wide.
$3,200–3,800 ⚹ Mit

A French cherrywood farm table, with a bread slide and a side drawer, on tapering legs, c1840, 79in (200.5cm) long.
$4,300–5,000 ⊞ DeG

An oak snap-top occasional table, with a baluster-turned pedestal and splayed cabriole feet, 18thC, 28¼in (72cm) diam.
$1,200–1,400 ⚹ ELR

An oak and pine wine table, c1800, 17in (43cm) wide.
$580–650 ⊞ SuA

An American red-washed birch dining table, with ring-turned tapering legs and turned feet, New Hampshire, early 19thC, 43½in (110.5cm) extended.
$4,000–4,400 ⚹ SK(B)

A French fruitwood double-extending draw-leaf table, on turned legs, c1835, 59in (150cm) long.
$5,800–6,500 ⊞ DeG
In tables such as these the draw leaves pull out and the top drops down to their level. Often the leaves are in a more distressed condition than the top, as the latter would have been frequently polished, whereas the leaves were used for cutting and chopping while preparing food and were pushed away after use. This can be a good indicator of age.

Facts in brief
- **Materials:** tables of this period were made in the solid, using indigenous woods; the construction was all pegged mortise and tenon.
- **Condition:** look for areas of wear and damage on stretchers, outer edges of the legs, the top, and at the bottom of each leg – check the height of the table to see if it has been reduced as a result of damage.
- **Alterations:** a common fault is that the top will have been 'associated' with the base. Ensure that all elements concur, and that any marks on the underside of the top relate to the base; although 17th-century refectory tables should have stretchers, it is not uncommon to find them removed to allow room for chair legs.

A Spanish chestnut serving table, with three drawers, 19thC, 71in (180.5cm) long.
$1,200–1,400 ⊞ MLL

A Gothic-style oak centre table, the shaped standard ends with stretchers, 19thC, 42in (106.5cm) long.
$430–500 ⚹ RBB

A French elm round table, with turned legs, c1880, 44in (112cm) diam.
$700–770 ⊞ AL

A Victorian Elizabethan-revival carved-oak dining, hall or board-room table, by Edwards & Roberts, London, with a wind-out mechanism and four extra leaves, signed on the frame and wind-out mechanism, c1870, 157½in (400cm) extended.
$11,600–13,000 ⊞ Bns

Pine Furniture

Beds

A Georgian pine cradle, on original base, c1820, 38in (96.5cm) long.
$650–750 ⊞ DHA

An American pine Windsor day bed, the hinged fold-out bed with bamboo-turned arms, original yellow paint with brown leaf and berry stencilling and striping, seat replaced, New England, early 19thC, 84in (213.5cm) wide.
$4,500–5,000 ⚒ SK(B)

A Victorian pitch pine cradle, with a canopy and turned corner uprights, 26in (66cm) long.
$350–400 ⊞ POT

Bookcases

A painted pine waterfall bookcase, with original paint and handles, c1800, 24½in (62cm) wide.
$6,500–8,000 ⊞ DeG

A Scottish pine glazed bookcase, with barley-twist columns and three drawers, over three doors, c1830, 62in (157.5cm) wide.
$1,700–2,000 ⊞ P&T

A Regency pine bookcase, c1810, 41in (104cm) wide.
$500–650 ⊞ TPC

A pine bookcase, c1880, 34in (86.5cm) wide.
$500–600 ⊞ ByI

Cross Reference
See Colour Review
(page 229)

An American painted pine secretaire bookcase, the two doors enclosing a painted interior with three fixed shelves, above a lower case with a hinged lid enclosing a desk interior, the two cupboard doors below enclosing shelves, with dark red paint on the exterior and mustard paint on the interior, New England, early 19thC, 48in (122cm) wide.
$1,450–1,750 ⚒ SK(B)

A pine bookcase, with glazed doors enclosing shelves, 1820–40, 44in (112cm) wide.
$1,500–1,750 ⊞ HOA

A pine bookcase, c1890, 36in (91.5cm) wide.
$500–600 ⊞ AL

◄ **A pine bookcase,** converted from a wardrobe, c1890, 48in (122cm) wide.
$500–600 ⊞ P&T

Boxes

An American pine storage box, the top enclosing a well with a lidded till box, vinegar-painted with a rust-brown pattern of circles and quarter fans, New England, early 19thC, 32¾in (83cm) wide.
$430–480 ➶ SK(B)

A Dutch domed pine blanket chest, with original fittings, c1875, 39in (99cm) wide.
$320–360 ⊞ P&T

An iron-bound pine box, c1880, 34in (86.5cm) wide.
$290–330 ⊞ AL

A Victorian pine blanket box, with a deep plinth, 34in (86.5cm) wide.
$180–200 ⊞ POT

An American red-painted pine fitted storage box, with wrought-iron strap hinges and bail handles, containing 12 amber glass gin bottles, early 19thC, 18in (45.5cm) wide.
$1,800–2,200 ➶ SK(B)

An American painted pine bin, the top enclosing a canted compartment and a single drawer, with old green paint, New England, mid-19thC, 21½in (54.5cm) wide.
$780–880 ➶ SK(B)

A Victorian pine underbed box, on wooden wheels, c1880, 49in (124.5cm) wide.
$220–290 ⊞ TPC

A Romanian pine box, c1880, 53in (134.5cm) wide.
$200–250 ⊞ Byl

◀ **A pitch pine box,** c1890, 27in (68.5cm) wide.
$145–160 ⊞ P&T

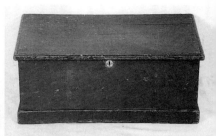

A pine box, decorated with original green paint, c1860, 28in (71cm) wide.
$200–230 ⊞ AL

A Hungarian folk art painted pine box, with later painted date '1907', c1870, 60in (152.5cm) wide.
$290–320 ⊞ Byl

A Victorian pine blanket box, on a plinth base, with original hinges and handles, 34in (86.5cm) wide.
$150–180 ⊞ POT

An Irish pine box, with original handles and a candle box, c1880, 48in (122cm) wide.
$200–250 ⊞ Byl

A pine blanket box, with original metal handles, c1890, 33in (84cm) wide
$220–250 ⊞ P&T

PINE FURNITURE

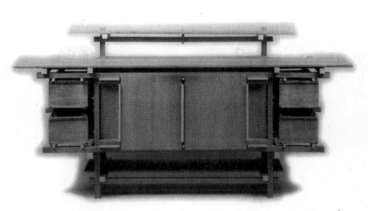

Chairs

A pine open-arm elbow chair, c1870.
$115–145 ⊞ DFA

A pine captain's chair, with saddle seat, c1875.
$180–220 ⊞ Byl

A pitch pine bishop's or priest's chair, c1880.
$580–720 ⊞ HON

A late Victorian child's pine chair.
$55–65 ⊞ HCJ

Chests & Coffers

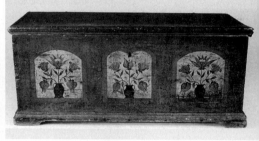

An American painted pine blanket chest, the top enclosing a till, with old green paint, Pennyslvania, late 18thC, 38¼in (97cm) wide.
$900–1,000 ⚒ SK(B)

An American painted and decorated pine dower chest, attributed to Christian Selzer (1789–1831), the front painted with white ground panels outlined in red, containing a blue vase with red, blue and yellow flowers with brown leaves, Lebanon County, Pennsylvania, late 18thC, 51½in (131cm) wide.
$6,500–8,000 ⚒ SK(B)

A German pine marriage chest, carved and painted, dated 1785, 52in (132cm) wide.
$4,600–5,000 ⊞ RYA

An Austrian Empire painted pine blanket chest, c1820, 51in (129.5cm) wide.
$2,900–3,300 ⊞ DeG

A pine blanket chest, with an internal drawer and original metal handles, c1860, 38in (96.5cm) wide.
$320–360 ⊞ P&T

> **Miller's is a price GUIDE not a price LIST**

An Austrian painted pine coffer, 19thC, 61in (155cm) wide.
$725–800 ⊞ MLL

A pine coffer, with original green paint, 19thC, 43in (109cm) wide.
$440–500 ⊞ BrH

PINE FURNITURE

Chests & Flights of Drawers

A Shaker pine chest of drawers, painted with wood-grain effect, with American locks, c1720, 32in (81.5cm) wide.
$3,000–3,500 ⊞ BrH

An American pine chest-over-drawers, the hinged top over two dummy and two real drawers, replaced brasses, probably Massachusetts, mid-18thC, 36½in (92.5cm) wide.
$1,000–1,300 ⚒ SK(B)

An American child's red-stained pine chest of drawers, early 19thC, 13in (33cm) wide.
$4,400–5,000 ⚒ SK(B)

A painted pine chest of drawers, with two short over three long drawers, decorated with a stipple finish, 19thC, 41in (104cm) wide.
$650–725 ⊞ MLL

A pine chest of drawers, with two short over three long drawers, c1840, 43in (109cm) wide.
$800–880 ⊞ P&T

A Victorian pine chest of three drawers, with a curved splashback, c1860, 40in (101.5cm) wide.
$400–440 ⊞ HRQ

A pine flight of drawers, with 48 seed drawers and original scumbled paint decoration, c1830, 50in (127cm) wide.
$4,000–4,600 ⊞ RYA

A pine chest of drawers, with three graduated drawers, c1850, 20in (51cm) wide.
$300–330 ⊞ P&T

A pine chest of drawers, with two short over three long drawers, c1860, 45in (114.5cm) wide.
$725–825 ⊞ AL

◀ **A pine collector's cabinet,** c1860, 48in (122cm) high.
$540–620 ⊞ HOA

PINE FURNITURE

An Irish pine chest of drawers, c1875, 35in (89cm) wide.
$300–350 ⊞ Byl

A Scottish pine chest of drawers, with an ogee-moulded frieze drawer over two short and three long drawers, c1880, 48in (122cm) wide.
$500–550 ⊞ HOA

A Victorian pine chest of drawers, with carved splashback and painted wood-grain effect, 38in (96.5cm) wide.
$650–800 ⊞ BrH

A pine chest of drawers, with two short over three long drawers, with original handles, c1890, 46½in (118cm) wide.
$580–650 ⊞ HRQ

A pine chest of drawers, with two short over three long drawers, with original knobs, c1890, 41in (104cm) wide.
$460–500 ⊞ POT

A pine chest of drawers, the four drawers with cast-iron handles, c1890, 16in (40.5cm) wide.
$260–290 ⊞ AL

◄ **A painted pine chest of six drawers,** with green paint, c1900, 24in (61cm) wide
$400–440 ⊞ MLL

Items in the Pine section have been arranged in date order within each sub-section.

A Hungarian pine chest of drawers, with eight drawers, c1910, 41in (104cm) wide.
$650–800 ⊞ MIN

An Edwardian pine cabinet, with three drawers and an oak-lined tilting door, c1910, 19in (48.5cm) wide.
$290–320 ⊞ P&T

Cupboards

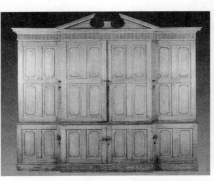

A painted pine corner cupboard, with original white paint, c1760, 48in (122cm) wide.
$16,000–17,500 ⊞ RYA

A George III pine breakfront housekeeper's cupboard, the panelled doors enclosing shelves to both the upper and lower sections, 122¾in (312cm) wide.
$20,500–24,500 ⋏ L&T

A Swedish provincial rococo green-painted cupboard, late 18thC, 74in (188cm) wide.
$17,500–20,000 ⋏ S(NY)

◀ **A north European painted pine cupboard,** each door panel painted with a flower-filled urn on a blue-green ground decorated with cream stylized foliage, the frieze initialled 'A.R.I.M.' and dated '1807', 48in (122cm) wide.
$580–720 ⋏ L

▶ **A painted pine cupboard,** with original white paint, c1820, 51in (129.5cm) wide.
$1,250–1,400 ⊞ DFA

An American painted pine cupboard, the pair of doors enclosing five shelves, with old tan over green paint, probably Rhode Island, late 18thC, 41¾in (106cm) wide.
$7,250–8,000 ⋏ SK(B)

▶ **An American painted pine cupboard,** the doors enclosing four shelves, with old blue paint, New England, early 19thC, 36½in (92.5cm) wide.
$8,000–8,750 ⋏ SK(B)

An Austrian Empire painted pine cupboard, decorated with flowers on a blue ground, c1850, 45½in (115.5cm) wide.
$5,000–5,800 ⊞ DeG

A pine cabinet, the two glazed doors enclosing shelves, with panelled sides, c1840, 36in (91.5cm) wide.
$430–500 ⊞ TPC

PINE FURNITURE

A pine corner cupboard, the four double-panelled doors flanked by reeded pilasters, 19thC, 42in (106.5cm) wide.
$580–720 ↗ MEA

▶ **A Dutch pine food cupboard,** c1870, 35in (89cm) wide.
$500–580 ⊞ P&T

A pine cupboard, the single glazed door with a key, c1880, 29in (73.5cm) wide.
$430–480 ⊞ AL

A pine linen press, c1860, 86in (218.5cm) wide.
$1,100–1,300 ⊞ HOA

◀ **A Hungarian pine display cupboard,** with a single glazed door flanked by reeded columns, c1870, 36in (91.5cm) wide.
$550–600 ⊞ MIN

A pine bedside cabinet, c1880, 18in (45.5cm) wide.
$100–120 ⊞ Byl

◀ **A pine cupboard,** with original paint, c1880, 54in (137cm) wide.
$580–650 ⊞ DFA

▶ **A pine display cabinet,** with adjustable shelves, c1880, 39in (99cm) wide.
$725–800 ⊞ HRQ

A bowfront hanging corner cupboard, c1860, 36in (91.5cm) high.
$540–620 ⊞ HOA

A Hungarian pine cupboard, with two glazed doors and a blue-stained interior, c1870, 42in (106.5cm) wide.
$870–970 ⊞ MIN

A Scottish press cupboard, the lower section with a fitted interior, 19thC, 50in (127cm) wide.
$1,000–1,250 ⊞ HOA

A pine cupboard, c1860, 48in (122cm) wide.
$850–950 ⊞ DFA

An Irish pine cupboard, with four doors, c1875, 52in (132cm) wide.
$1,000–1,250 ⊞ Byl

A pine two-piece press cupboard, cornice replaced, c1880, 47in (119.5cm) wide.
$2,300–2,600 ⊞ AL

A pine cupboard, c1880, 48½in (123cm) wide.
$1,000–1,150 ⊞ AL

An Irish pine two-door cupboard, c1880, 41in (104cm) wide.
$400–500 ⊞ Byl

A late Victorian pitch pine estate cabinet, the doors enclosing shelves fitted with red and gilt *tôle peinte* deed boxes, with stylized brass hinges and handles, 70¼in (178.5cm) wide.
$2,000–2,300 ⚒ DN

An Irish pitch pine cupboard, with turned side columns, Co Galway, c1880, 53in (134.5cm) wide.
$800–880 ⊞ HON

A pine bookcase or display cupboard, c1890, 31in (78.5cm) wide.
$680–720 ⊞ AL

A Victorian pine linen press, with a painted wood-grain effect, 41in (104cm) wide.
$1,150–1,300 ⊞ BrH

An American yellow-painted pine pie safe, possibly Georgia, 19thC, 50in (127cm) wide.
$4,000–4,600 ⚒ S(NY)

A Hungarian pine bedside cabinet, c1900, 18in (45.5cm) wide.
$230–260 ⊞ MIN

A Continental pine pot cupboard, c1920, 14in (35.5cm) wide.
$140–160 ⊞ P&T

PINE FURNITURE

Desks

A Victorian pine kneehole desk, 48in (122cm) wide.
$900–1,000 ⊞ **P&T**

An American red-painted pine desk, with a pull-out writing surface, New England, 19thC, 36in (91.5cm) wide.
$6,000–7,000 ✗ **SK(B)**

A red-stained pine desk, the lid enclosing four open compartments, New England, 19thC, 30in (76cm) wide.
$1,450–1,600 ✗ **SK(B)**

A pine clerk's desk, c1870, 72in (183cm) wide.
$600–675 ✗ **SK(B)**

An Irish pine desk, on turned legs, c1880, 33in (84cm) wide
$400–475 ⊞ **Byl**

An Irish pine desk, c1880, 21in (53.5cm) wide.
$175–200 ⊞ **Byl**

A pine clerk's desk, c1890, 23in (58.5cm) wide.
$180–200 ⊞ **POT**

A Victorian pine kneehole desk, with an inset leather top above arch-panelled doors, 48in (122cm) wide.
$1,000–1,100 ⊞ **P&T**

▶ **An Edwardian pine kneehole desk,** with drawers to one side, the other with a cupboard, c1910, 48in (122cm) wide.
$600–660 ⊞ **HRQ**

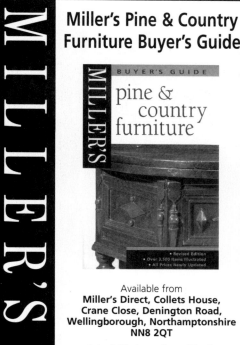
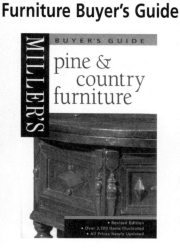

Dressers

A Georgian pine dresser, the base with three drawers above two doors, 93in (236cm) wide.
$3,600–4,000 ⊞ MIN

An American pine dresser, the glazed cupboard doors enclosing three shelves with plate grooves and a spoon rack, with later off-white paint, restored, Pennsylvania, late 18thC, 52in (132cm) wide.
$10,500–11,500 ↗ SK(B)

▶ **An Irish pine potboard dresser,** with three drawers, c1850, 72in (183cm) wide.
$2,600–2,900 ↗ P&T

An American Federal pine dresser, probably Hackensack, New Jersey, c1810, 50¾in (129cm) wide.
$11,000–13,000 ↗ SK(B)

A pine cupboard dresser, 19thC, 64in (162.5cm) wide.
$1,000–1,150 ⊞ HOA

A pine dresser, c1840, 59in (150cm) wide.
$800–900 ⊞ DFA

An Irish pine dresser, mid-19thC, 86in (218.5cm) wide.
$1,000–1,100 ⊞ HOA

An Irish pine dresser, with a single central drawer, c1860, 58in (147.5cm) wide.
$800–950 ⊞ Byl

An Irish pine dresser, c1860, 53in (134.5cm) wide.
$950–1,100 ⊞ Byl

An Irish fiddle-front pine dresser, with a potboard, c1865, 47in (119.5cm) wide.
$725–875 ⊞ Byl

A Hungarian pitch pine dresser, with original blue-painted interior, c1870, 37in (94cm) wide.
$550–600 ⊞ MIN

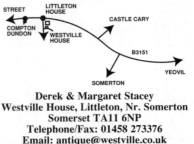
PINE FURNITURE

A Hungarian concave-fronted corner dresser, the glazed display top flanked by two cupboards, c1870, 49in (124.5cm) wide.
$950–1,100 ⊞ MIN

An Irish pine dresser, the two glazed doors above two drawers, with two cupboard doors below, c1875, 49in (124.5cm) wide.
$580–720 ⊞ Byl

An Irish pine dresser, the two glazed doors enclosing shelves above three short drawers, with two cupboard doors below, c1875, 49in (124.5cm) wide.
$680–820 ⊞ Byl

A pine pot board dresser, 19thC, 88in (223.5cm) wide.
$1,000–1,150 ⊞ HOA

An Irish pine shop drawer unit, c1875, 52in (132cm) wide.
$950–1,150 ⊞ Byl

A Hungarian pine dresser, the top with central bowfronted door, c1880, 40in (101.5cm) wide.
$800–950 ⊞ MIN

◀ **A pine dresser,** with original blue and white paint, c1880, 70in (178cm) wide.
$500–575 ⊞ DFA

An Irish pine dresser, the two glazed doors enclosing shelves above two drawers, with two doors below, c1880, 51in (129.5cm) wide.
$580–720 ⊞ Byl

▶ **An Irish pine dresser,** the two glazed doors enclosing shelves above two drawers, with two doors below, c1880, 48in (122cm) wide.
$580–720 ⊞ Byl

A French pine *buffet à deux corps,* with two glazed doors, c1890, 56in (142cm) wide.
$1,150–1,300 ⊞ MLL

Dresser Bases & Side Cabinets

A pine serpentine dresser base, with two drawers flanked by two doors, c1830, 64in (162.5cm) wide.
$800–900 ⊞ P&T

A pine sideboard, with three central drawers flanked by short drawers over cupboard doors, c1860, 55in (139.5cm) wide.
$750–850 ⊞ HOA

A Victorian pine side cabinet, c1880, 40in (101.5cm) wide.
$450–500 ⊞ HRQ

An Irish pine server, with a shaped gallery back, c1875, 50in (127cm) wide.
$360–440 ⊞ Byl

▶ **A pine dresser base,** with two drawers over two doors, c1880, 45in (114.5cm) wide.
$620–680 ⊞ P&T

◀ **An Irish pine server,** with one long drawer, c1880, 48in (122cm) wide.
$230–290 ⊞ Byl

A pine dresser base, with two drawers over two doors, c1880, 45in (114.5cm) wide.

A Dutch pine low cupboard, with three drawers, c1880, 44in (112cm) wide.
$340–380 ⊞ P&T

An Irish pine low cupboard, c1880, 52in (132cm) high.
$230–290 ⊞ Byl

An Irish pine chiffonier, c1880, 43in (109cm) wide.
$360–440 ⊞ Byl

PINE FURNITURE

A pine sideboard, with carved details, 19thC, 48in (122cm) wide.
$650–800 ⊞ HOA

A pine dresser base, with two drawers over two doors, one drawer replaced, c1885, 46in (117cm) wide.
$500–600 ⊞ AL

A pine side cabinet, with two drawers over two doors, c1890, 39in (99cm) wide.
$600–675 ⊞ AL

A pine low cupboard, with two sliding doors, c1890, 51in (129.5cm) wide.
$470–500 ⊞ P&T

A pine dresser base, with original paint, c1900, 56in (142cm) wide.
$440–500 ⊞ HOP
This piece would originally have had two further long cupboards.

A Hungarian pine dresser base, with a single drawer over two doors, c1900, 40in (101.5cm) wide.
$450–500 ⊞ MIN

Settles & Benches

A Welsh pine and elm settle, with original paint, c1770, 40in (101.5cm) wide.
$5,000–5,500 ⊞ SEA

An American painted pine settle, the seat with a hinged top, with old red varnish stain over earlier blue paint, early 19thC, 42in (106.5cm) wide.
$20,000–23,000 ⏏ SK(B)

▶ **A Continental pine bench,** c1860, 71in (180.5cm) wide.
$480–580 ⊞ Sam

◀ **A pine settle,** with a high scrolled back, c1880, 97in (246.5cm) wide.
$870–1,000 ⊞ WRe

An Irish pine settle, with pitch pine panels, c1860, 72in (183cm) wide.
$680–800 ⊞ Byl

▶ **A Hungarian painted pine box bench,** with original paint, c1900, 74in (188cm) wide.
$620–680 ⊞ MIN

A Black Forest carved pine hall seat, modelled as two standing bears supporting a bench, the back with two bears among branches, late 19thC, 62in (157.5cm) wide.
$10,000–11,500 ⏏ G(B)

Stands

An American pine stand, with old red stain and original turned knob, New England, early 19thC, 18¾in (47.5cm) wide.
$2,500–3,000 ✣ SK(B)

An American pine and maple stand, re-painted yellow, drawer knob missing, Pennsylvania, early 19thC, 18¼in (46.5cm) wide.
$725–875 ✣ SK(B)

A pine plant stand, c1870, 15in (38cm) wide.
$115–145 ⊞ P&T

A pine plant stand, with three circular shelves, c1880, 53in (134.5cm) high.
$260–290 ⊞ AL

A Hungarian pine hat stand, with original hooks, c1880, 86in (218.5cm) high.
$1,000–1,100 ⊞ MIN

A pine stick stand, with two metal drip trays, c1880, 49in (124.5cm) wide.
$220–250 ⊞ AL

A painted pine chinoiserie-style plant stand, c1900, 45in (114.5cm) wide.
$290–320 ⊞ HOP

Stools

A pine and oak stool, c1880, 28in (71cm) high.
$75–90 ⊞ Byl

A pine stool, c1890, 29in (73.5cm) high.
$85–100 ⊞ POT

A pine and elm stool, c1890, 30in (76cm) high.
$80–90 ✣ AL

A painted pine milking stool, decorated with flowers in red, green and white, c1890, 13in (33cm) diam.
$115–145 ⊞ POT

PINE FURNITURE

Tables

An American pine chair table, with early red paint, the top reshaped, New England, 18thC, 54¼in (138cm) wide.
$7,250–8,000 ✗ SK(B)

A Continental painted pine gateleg table, worm damaged, 18thC, 48½in (123cm) wide.
$2,300–2,600 ✗ SK

A Dutch provincial pine occasional table, with an octagonal slightly dished top and a frieze drawer, c1800, 32½in (82.5cm) wide.
$3,200–3,600 ✗ SK

An American pine table, the top with original white paint and green-grey painted stringing, New Hampshire, c1800, 32in (81.5cm) wide.
$6,000–7,000 ✗ SK(B)

An American painted pine table, with red-stained turned legs, New England, early 19thC, 29½in (75cm) wide.
$2,600–2,900 ✗ SK(B)

An American painted pine chair table, the yellow paint with grain-painted panels and black accents, possibly upstate New York, early 19thC, 52¼in (132.5cm) wide.
$3,600–4,000 ✗ SK(B)

◄ **An American pine and maple table,** with replaced knob, New England, early 19thC, 41in (104cm) wide.
$1,000–1,150 ✗ SK(B)

An American pine table, the red-painted base with a single drawer, the top with traces of red paint, New England, early 19thC, 46in (117cm) wide.
$3,600–4,000 ✗ SK(B)

◄ **An American pine eating board,** probably Massachusetts, early 19thC, 81¾in (207.5cm) long.
$2,200–2,500 ✗ SK(B)

A Scottish pine kitchen table, c1840, 84in (213.5cm) long.
$870–1,000 ⊞ HOA

A French pine refectory table, with six legs, c1850, 154in (391cm) long.
$5,800–6,500 ⊞ P&T

Condition

The condition is absolutely vital when assessing the value of an antique. Damaged pieces on the whole appreciate much less than perfect examples. However, a rare desirable piece may command a high price even when damaged.

PINE FURNITURE

An American painted pine dressing table, labelled 'J. G. Briggs, Charlestown, New Hampshire', the original black and gold graining simulating rosewood, 1830–33, 36½in (92.5cm) wide.
$1,000–1,150 🪙 SK(B)
The 'J. G. Briggs' label on this piece refers to a furniture warehouse opposite the Brick Meeting House in Charlestown, New Hampshire. Joseph was the son of Eliphalet Briggs, the cabinet- and chairmaker from Keene, New Hampshire.

A pine farmhouse table, c1860, 96in (244cm) wide.
$1,000–1,100 ⊞ HOA

A pine farmhouse table, 1860–70, 84in (213.5cm) wide.
$870–1,000 ⊞ HOA

> **Cross Reference**
> See Colour Review
> (page 238)

▶ **A pine farmhouse table,** c1860, 96in (244cm) long.
$1,150–1,300 ⊞ HOA

▶ **A pine farmhouse table,** c1860, 110in (279.5cm) long.
$1,000–1,100 ⊞ HOA

A Victorian lady's pine sewing table, c1860, 36in (91.5cm) wide.
$480–550 ⊞ HOA

A pine farmhouse table, c1860, 84in (213.5cm) long.
$870–1,000 ⊞ HOA

A pine table, with original brown paint on the base, c1870, 65in (165cm) long.
$400–475 ⊞ DFA

An Irish pitch pine table, c1875, 82in (208.5cm) long.
$800–950 ⊞ Byl

PINE FURNITURE

A pine drop-leaf table, c1875, 45in (114.5cm) wide.
$230–290 ⊞ Byl

A pine table, with a scrubbed top, on turned legs, c1880, 49in (124.5cm) long.
$440–500 ⊞ AL

A pine dining table, 19thC, 110in (279.5cm) wide.
$870–1,000 ⊞ HOA

A pine round drop-leaf table, c1880, 55in (139.5cm) diam
$725–850 ⊞ AL

A pine drop-leaf table, c1880, 32in (81.5cm) wide.
$350–400 ⊞ AL

A painted pine table, with turned legs and X-stretcher, c1880, 45in (114.5cm) diam.
$725–800 ⊞ MLL

A pine cricket table, one leg replaced, c1880, 29in (73.5cm) diam.
$500–600 ⊞ AL

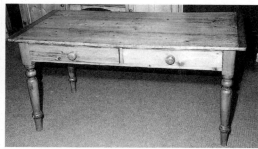

A pine table, with two side drawers and turned legs, c1890, 59in (150cm) long.
$500–600 ⊞ MIN

A pine table, with three side drawers, c1900, 80in (203cm) long.
$1,000–1,250
⊞ MIN

◀ **A pine coffee table,** 19thC, 36in (91.5cm) wide.
$350–400 ⊞ HOA

▶ **A pine work table,** with enamel top, c1950, 41in (104cm) long.
$260–290 ⊞ AL

Wardrobes

A Romanian pine wardrobe, with four doors, c1875, 87in (221cm) wide. **$650–725** ⊞ Byl

An Irish pine breakfront wardrobe, with panelled doors, Co Kerry, c1870, 65in (165cm) wide. **$800–900** ⊞ HON

◄ **A pine wardrobe,** the doors with arched panels, c1860, 48in (122cm) wide. **$900–1,150** ⊞ P&T

An Irish pine wardrobe, with mirrored door and original handles, 1875–80, 38in (96.5cm) wide. **$400–500** ⊞ Byl

A pine two-door wardrobe, c1880, 38in (96.5cm) wide. **$600–660** ⊞ AL

A Continental pine wardrobe, with two doors, c1890, 57¼in (145.5cm) wide. **$950–1,100** ⊞ HRQ

A European pine wardrobe, with carved cornice and panelled doors, 19thC, 46in (117cm) wide. **$680–780** ⊞ POT

◄ **A Hungarian pine wardrobe,** with two doors above a single drawer, c1900, 47in (119.5cm) wide. **$550–620** ⊞ MIN

A German pitch pine wardrobe, with three doors, a shaped pediment and central mirror, c1910, 64in (162.5cm) wide. **$650–725** ⊞ NOTT

◄ **A Continental pine wardrobe,** with three doors, c1910, 48½in (123cm) wide. **$870–950** ⊞ HRQ

PINE FURNITURE

Washstands

A pine corner washstand, c1820, 51in (129.5cm) high. **$400–480** ⊞ HOA

A pine washstand, c1820, 25in (63.5cm) wide. **$430–480** ⊞ AL

A pine washstand, with two drawers, c1850, 36in (91.5cm) wide. **$260–290** ⊞ P&T

A pine washstand, with two drawers above a cupboard base, c1860, 37in (94cm) wide. **$725–800** ⊞ POT

An Irish pine washstand, c1880, 35in (89cm) wide. **$175–200** ⊞ Byl

A pine washstand, painted with a wood-grain effect, c1880, 36in (91.5cm) wide. **$360–440** ⊞ BrH

A pine washstand, with a single drawer, c1890, 32in (81.5cm) wide. **$320–360** ⊞ AL

Miscellaneous

A pine overmantel mirror, flanked by relief-moulded pilasters and bracket shelves, 19thC, 60in (152.5cm) wide. **$725–875** ⚲ MEA

A pine mirror, painted with a wood-grain effect, c1880, 23in (58.5cm) high. **$260–290** ⊞ BrH

◀ **A Victorian figured pine bedroom suite,** comprising a half-tester bed, a chest of drawers, a dressing table and a washstand. **$2,500–3,000** ⚲ ELR

Miller's is a price GUIDE not a price LIST

▶ **A pine towel rail,** c1890, 36in (91.5cm) wide. **$100–120** ⊞ AL

An American blue-painted pine pantry shelf, possibly Pennsylvania, early 19thC, 60¾in (154.5cm) wide. **$3,200–3,600** ⚲ SK(B)

Kitchenware

Why collect kitchenware? There are many reasons, but most importantly, it is affordable. Although some of the items included in this section cost considerable amounts of money, many pieces such as enamel bread bins, bread boards and utensils can still be bought for under $18.

In our experience many customers seek items of quality and in good condition because they wish to use them in their modern-day kitchens. What looks more appealing than a cast-iron or gleaming copper kettle boiling on the Aga and freshly baked bread on an elaborately carved bread board? Television programmes and magazines centring attention on period dramas, and home interior design articles featuring the attractiveness of mixing old with new, have helped to generate interest in kitchenware today.

Antique kitchenware makes an eye-catching display on an old pine dresser, for instance copper and ceramic jelly moulds, tin chocolate moulds and a collection of treen butter stamps. Traditional cooking equipment can be decorative – from weighing scales to coffee grinders – so why hide them away in cupboards when the more appealing items could be on view and instantly available for use?

There is great demand for kitchenware abroad. A good example of this is enamel ware: a cream and green bread bin has increased from about $30 to around $65 because of interest shown by foreign trade. The demand for kitchenware has been so high that it has more than doubled in price in the last five years so it is now a very good investment.

A wise buy for collectors are irons. They are still comparatively cheap, fairly plentiful and will increase in value. There are many different types, from the early flat iron, which can still be bought for around $12, to the very ornate brass lace crimping iron shown on page 200.

A collection of antique treen – everyday items carved in wood, with the patina of age from years of handling – can be both attractive and useful. Butter stamps are commonly made of sycamore and offer a wide range of interesting motifs: prices for the rarer ones depicting birds or animals can range from $75 to $220. Victorian wooden carved bread boards and knives are perfectly at home in any modern-day kitchen and carry appealing mottos such as 'Welcome' or 'Our Daily Bread'; plainer examples can be found for under $75 and more elaborate ones from $145.

Decorative, useful and affordable – three excellent reasons for collecting kitchenware.

Skip and Janie Smithson

Two French baguette baskets, with original bogie wheels, c1900, largest 34in (86.5cm) long.
$1,000–1,100 ⊞ DeG

A French pottery dairy bowl, the interior with terracotta glaze decorated with a black and white geometric pattern, Savoie region, c1880, 17in (43cm) diam.
$260–290 ⊞ MLL

A creamware butter churn, mid-19thC, 15in (38cm) high.
$500–600 ⊞ SMI

An American tin sugar bowl and matching tray, painted in colours with stylized foliage and fruit, Pennsylvania, 19thC, tray 12¼in (31cm) wide.
$14,500–17,500 ➚ SK(B)
American pieces sold in the home market tend to achieve premium prices.

A sycamore butter marker, carved with a sheep, c1870, 5in (12.5cm) high.
$145–175 ⊞ WeA
Butter markers carved with an animal or bird are more unusual and therefore achieve a higher price than other types.

A copper coffee pot, 1920, 21in (30.5cm) high.
$680–780 ⊞ SEA

◄ **A sycamore butter roller,** 19thC, 5in (12.5cm) long.
$115–130 ⊞ MFB

A brass crimping machine, with tole base and drawer, with original heaters, 19thC, 12½in (32cm) wide.
$870–1,000 ⊞ SEA
Crimping machines such as this are seldom seen.

An oak cutlery box, early 19thC, 14in (35.5cm) long.
$180–220 ⊞ AnSh

An American Silver flour bin and sifter, late 19thC, 22in (56cm) high.
$290–320 ⊞ MLu

◄ **A copper fish kettle,** c1920, 17in (43cm) long.
$175–200 ⊞ AL

A Salter's cast-iron shop display egg rack, with spaces for 40 eggs, late 19thC, 10in (25.5cm) wide.
$440–500 ⊞ SMI

A Welsh copper goffering iron, 19thC, 12in (30.5cm) long.
$750–850 ⊞ SEA
Used to iron ruffs and sleeves, goffering irons are heated in boiling water. They are rarely seen and appear to be found only in Wales.

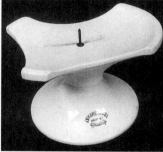

A Karvesi ham and poultry ceramic stand, marked on the base, c1910, 10in (25.5cm) wide.
$145–175 ⊞ WeA

An elm herb or cheese board, 19thC, 13in (33cm) long.
$580–650 ⊞ SEA

A shop Golden Syrup dispenser, inscribed in gold on a green ground, c1900, 15in (38cm) high.
$500–600 ⊞ SMI

Cross Reference
See Colour Review
(page 240)

A Rose Bower Dairy Co ceramic cream jar, transfer-printed in black with a view of an abbey, c1900, 3¾in (9.5cm) high.
$160–190 ➚ BBR

A Cornish Ware Cherries ceramic storage jar, with blue and white banding, black shield base mark, 1940–50, 3½in (9cm) high.
$175–225 ➚ BBR

A copper kettle, c1890, 12in (30.5cm) high.
$100–120 ⊞ TO

► **A Victorian brass twin-handled milk churn,** the front engraved with foliage and 'Watsons Farm Dairy, S H Parsons, 54 Havelock Road, Brighton', 23in (58.5cm) high.
$3,000–3,500 ➚ LAY
This type of milk churn is highly sought-after.

KITCHENWARE

A pewter marzipan or ice-cream mould, c1880, 4in (10cm) high. $85–100 ⊞ WeA

A copper and brass ten-quart milk delivery can, with plaque engraved 'G. Pobjoy, Gloucester', early 1920s, 14in (35.5cm) high. $230–290 ⊞ SMI

A ceramic mould, depicting a fox with a duck, c1830, 5½in (14cm) long. $45–50 ⊞ AL

▶ **A tin chocolate mould,** in the shape of a fish, early 20thC, 9in (23cm) long. $160–190 ⊞ MFB

A tin and copper jelly mould, impressed with acorns, c1890, 3¼in (8.5cm) long. $290–320 ⊞ MSB

A tin chocolate mould, impressed with a girl, early 20thC, 4in (10cm) high. $90–100 ⊞ B&R

A pair of steel chocolate Easter egg moulds, 1920s, largest 7in (18cm) long. $50–60 ⊞ SMI

A German ceramic jelly mould, in the shape of a rabbit, early 20thC, 10in (25.5cm) high. $90–100 ⊞ B&R

An American tin chocolate mould, impressed with a rabbit, c1920, 14¼in (36cm) high. $800–900 ⊞ MSB

◀ **A porcelain shortbread mould,** with moulded mark 'Marshall & Philip, Ironmongers, Aberdeen', c1920, 8in (20.5cm) diam. $90–100 ⊞ SMI

KITCHENWARE

A brass lace rolling pin, late 19thC, 18in (45.5cm) long.
$100–115 ⊞ SMI

A brass berry pan, c1820, 13in (33cm) diam.
$160–180 ⊞ AL

A brass bread scale, late 19thC, 11in (28cm) wide.
$175–200 ⊞ SMI

A late Victorian Salter's brass-face spring balance, weighing up to 200lb, 9in (23cm) high.
$80–90 ⊞ SMI

◄ **A fruitwood four-segment spice tower,** with original paper labels in blue on a cream ground, 19thC, 8in (20.5cm) high.
$180–220 ➢ Bon(W)
These spice towers come in various sizes – the greater the number of compartments, the higher the price.

A Salter's brass scale, c1880, 13in (33cm) high.
$90–100 ⊞ SMI

Miller's is a price GUIDE not a price LIST

A T. G. Green ceramic sugar sifter, decorated with green bands on a pink ground, 1930s, 5in (12.5cm) high.
$50–60 ⊞ UNI

A copper spoon, with a wrought-iron handle, c1780, 18in (45.5cm) long.
$290–320 ⊞ SEA

◄ **A wooden spoon,** early 19thC, 10in (25.5cm) long.
$50–55 ⊞ HCJ

A copper straining spoon, with a yew handle, c1820, 21in (53.5cm) long.
$360–420 ⊞ SEA

A Welsh oak spoon rack, c1820, 13in (33cm) wide.
$650–725 ⊞ SEA

A salt-glazed stoneware water softener, inscribed 'Lipscombe & Co, Patentees by Special Appointment to Her Majesty', and decorated with fruiting vines and the Royal coat-of-arms, c1880, 18in (45.5cm) high.
$350–380 ⊞ AL

◄ **A Hunter's Handy Hams shop advertising enamel tray,** c1920, 16in (40.5cm) long.
$115–145 ⊞ SMI

A steel rotary whisk, c1880, 12in (30.5cm) long.
$55–65 ⊞ SMI

Pottery

The factors that have influenced the pottery market in the past year are neither new nor startling. There is still a polarization in favour of quality merchandise, as the general shortage still ensures that demand far outstrips supply. Prices at this level have therefore increased disproportionately in relation to the rest of the market.

Recent majolica auctions demonstrate this widening gulf between the 'special' and the 'ordinary'. Desirability is equated with attribution and quality of decoration. Works by major factories such as Minton, George Jones and Wedgwood have proved to be the best investment, with collectors battling hard for such examples. The Harriman Judd Collection in New York witnessed four rare pieces of majolica selling for over $30,000. In comparison, the lesser documented factories in Britain, the Continent and the USA are often ignored and, therefore, their pieces are easier to acquire.

This has proved a remarkable year for British delft. Although good 18th-century blue and white plates can be purchased for as little as $145, early, rare and important dated examples can command serious prices. Recent highlights include a c1680 unrecorded model of a tabby cat, which realized $29,000, and a dated caudle cup, commemorating the 1661 coronation of Charles II, which sold for $98,000. This is interesting, as the former was restored and the latter cracked and chipped, showing that in the current market rarity takes precedence over condition for choice pieces.

This is rarely the case for Staffordshire figures, which are less susceptible to damage than delft and collectors are therefore less forgiving. Look out for political and contemporary themes and early pieces, which are more desirable as similar wares were produced throughout the 19th and 20th centuries, often reusing original moulds. The reissues sell for substantially less and can be a good way to start collecting.

It can be argued that the manipulation of technology is an important factor in market trends. Saleroom catalogues are now accessible on a universal scale, particularly through the internet. This has resulted in an increase in the number of global purchasers, especially on the higher value lots, when the shipping expenses become financially viable. There is therefore a growing uniformity of prices realized at an international level.

The pottery market, as with all fields of antiques, is governed by attribution, rarity, decorative quality and condition. Inevitably, as the most highly desirable pieces become less accessible to the average collector new and often unexplored areas will benefit, the sign of a healthy market.

Gareth Williams

Animals & Birds

A Ralph Wood model of a doe, painted in naturalistic colours, c1790, 5in (12.5cm) high.
$2,200–2,500 ⊞ JHo

A Prattware group, of a girl holding a basket of flowers and a watering can beside a sheep, a dog lying beneath, with coloured detail, the base sponged with vertical bands of blue, black and ochre, girl's head restuck, 1800–20, 6in (15cm) high.
$1,750–2,000 ⋏ P

A Staffordshire model of a parrot, decorated in green, yellow, red and buff, on a naturalistic mound, c1820, 3in (7.5cm) high.
$870–970 ⊞ JHo

A Staffordshire spill vase group, in the form of a boy and a red squirrel beside a tree flanked by two leopards, restored, early 19thC, 9in (23cm) high.
$1,300–1,450 ⋏ DN

A flatback stoneware model of a lion, with a treacle-glazed mane, early 19thC, 30in (76cm) long.
$800–950 ⊞ JBL

A Staffordshire model of a retriever, with black markings, on a green and brown rockwork base, minor glaze loss, c1820, 6¼in (16cm) wide.
$1,000–1,250 ⋏ F&C

POTTERY

Two Staffordshire pearlware models of turkeys, one with a tail and moulded feathers in pale blue and black, the other with plumage in a brighter shade of blue and yellow, their heads with red detail, on bright green hollow bases moulded and applied with flowers with iron-red detail, c1830, largest 4¼in (11cm) high.
$2,500–3,000 ⚒ P

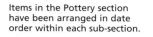

Items in the Pottery section have been arranged in date order within each sub-section.

A pair of Staffordshire models of pointers, their coats with feathered red-brown patches, wearing gilded collars, 1830–40, 5¼in (13.5cm) high.
$575–725 ⚒ P

A pair of Staffordshire brown and white retrievers, on blue bases heightened with gold, c1845, 4in (10cm) high.
$4,400–5,000 ⊞ RGa

A pair of Staffordshire models of spaniels, with iron-red markings, gilded collars and black-tipped feet, one with a nose chip, 19thC, 5½in (14cm) high.
$400–450 ⚒ GAK

A treacle-glazed model of a spaniel, possibly Derbyshire, mid-19thC, 7½in (19cm) high.
$650–725 ⚒ S(S)

A Staffordshire model of a greyhound, with sage green markings, wearing a gilt collar, the face painted in red and black enamel, fine crack to base, chip to ear, c1840, 5½in (14cm) wide.
$650–800 ⚒ P

A pair of Staffordshire models of pug dogs, the shaded orange bodies with painted black faces, with black and gilt collars, standing before red rockwork bases, 19thC, 8¾in (22cm) high.
$1,150–1,300 ⚒ Mit

A pair of Derbyshire brown salt-glazed stoneware models of spaniels, probably Brampton's, c1830, 14½in (37cm) high.
$4,000–4,500 ⚒ S

A pair of Staffordshire flatback quill holders, modelled as seated greyhounds clutching dead rabbits in their mouths, moulded and decorated with sprigs of flowers, on blue gilt-lined bases, 19thC, 6in (15cm) high.
$440–500 ⚒ GAK

A pair of Staffordshire models of spaniels, their coats and chains with gold flecks, with black paws and facial details, one paw restored, c1850, 9in (23cm) wide.
$440–500 ⚒ P

A pair of Staffordshire spaniels, with black and white coats, yellow eyes, orange muzzles and gilt chains, 19thC, 12½in (32cm) high.
$400–440 ⚒ AH

◄ **A pair of Victorian Staffordshire spaniels,** the pale brown glaze with traces of gilt, larger 12½in (32cm) high.
$115–145 ⚒ PFK

A pair of Staffordshire models of spaniels, their coats painted with red-brown patches, holding yellow baskets of flowers in their mouths, c1860, 8in (20.5cm) high.
$1,600–1,750 ✗ P(Ba)

A pair of Staffordshire models of St Bernards, each with black markings, 19thC, 10in (25.5cm) high.
$875–1,100 ✗ LAY

A Staffordshire spill vase, modelled as a dog leaning against a kennel, with gilt chains, the base with a cobalt blue band and gilt-lined rim, c1860, 8¼in (21cm) high.
$440–500 ✗ CGC

A pair of Staffordshire models of St Bernards, with gilded collars and red markings, one dog damaged and restuck, tip of one tongue lacking, 19thC, 4¾in (12cm) high.
$360–430 ✗ P(Ba)

A pair of Staffordshire models of poodles, with painted faces and gilt collars, 19thC, 8in (20.5cm) high.
$300–350 ✗ Mit

A pair of Staffordshire models of the British lion seated upon Napoleon III, the lions decorated in iron-red, Napoleon III in imperial cobalt blue uniform, cracks, chips, 1860–80, 10in (25.5cm) high.
$2,000–2,500 ✗ Hal
This model was probably produced sometime after the Anglo-French war scare of 1860.

A Staffordshire spill vase, modelled as a lioness and her cubs lying before a tree entwined by a serpent, decorated in colours on a white ground, mid-19thC, 11in (28cm) high.
$875–1,100 ✗ DN

A buff stoneware model of a lion, chips to base, 19thC, 9in (23cm) long.
$725–875 ✗ S

A Copeland majolica model of two squirrels, clambering over an oak tree, the stump forming a vase, decorated with brown and green glazes, impressed marks, restored, mid-19thC, 22in (56cm) high.
$3,600–4,400 ✗ WW

A Staffordshire model of a cat, with black markings, the base with a pale yellow border, mid-19thC, 3¾in (9.5cm) high.
$300–350 ✗ P

◄ **A spongeware cat box and cover,** the cat with sponged mustard and black markings, wearing a blue collar, on a cushion base, the cover forming part of the cat's back, chip to cover, 19thC, 4¼in (11cm) high.
$360–430 ✗ P(Ba)

A pair of Staffordshire models of rabbits, with black patches and pink noses and inner ears, eating green lettuce leaves, the eyes with yellow and black detail, c1870, 10¼in (26cm) wide.
$10,000–11,500 ✗ S(S)

POTTERY

A pair of treacle-glazed models of spaniels, with incised decoration on the coats, probably Kirkcaldy, c1880, 9½in (24cm) high.
$145–175 ➶ P(Ed)

A pottery cheese dish and cover, the cover modelled as the head of a cow, registered design No. 264998, crack to nose, late 19thC, 10in (25.5cm) long.
$115–145 ➶ PFK

A pair of Staffordshire cats, c1900, 7½in (19cm) high.
$400–450 ➶ DN

An Ewenny green-glazed cat, its features and collar incised, the base inscribed 'Hy Noath Bert', incised mark 'E. Jenkins, Ewenny Pottery 1920', chipped, restored, 15½in (39.5cm) high.
$1,600–1,750 ➶ S(S)
The Ewenny factory, near Bridgend in Wales, has been in the ownership of the Jenkins family since 1820.

A Staffordshire model of a dog, the buff body with black details, on a green base, c1880, 2½in (6.5cm) high.
$750–850 ⊞ JHo

A Staffordshire tureen and cover, modelled as a cobalt blue and white partridge on a brown and green enamelled nest, cracked, late 19thC, 8½in (21.5cm) high.
$725–800 ➶ Hal

A Gallé model of a cat, the head painted with a brown foliate head-scarf, the face inset with marbled green glass eyes, the body painted with meadow flowers and blue ribbons, signed 'E Gallé, Nancy', damaged, France, c1890, 12in (30.5cm) high.
$850–950 ➶ JBe

A Staffordshire model of a dalmatian, on a blue oval base, with gilt details, late 19thC, 5¼in (13.5cm) high.
$145–175 ➶ WW

A Staffordshire sculptured grotto group, by Fred Morris, modelled in glazed white pottery, the grotto containing two frogs among ferns and toadstools, covered with berries and fruiting brambles encircling a nest with three eggs, incised mark 'Made by Fred Morris', c1880, 9in (23cm) wide.
$650–800 ➶ P

An American chalkware seated cat, with yellow and black stripes, the ears, nose and mouth with red detail, on a yellow base, repaired, 19thC, 10in (25.5cm) high.
$5,000–5,750 ➶ SK(B)

◄ **A Wemyss Bovey Tracey black and white pig,** c1930, 16in (40.5cm) wide.
$1,450–1,750 ⊞ RdeR

Baskets

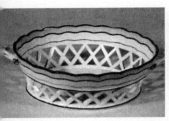

A creamware chestnut basket, possibly Leeds, with a yellow-brown banded and lobed rim, c1790, 9in (23cm) long.
$130–160 ♣ Hal

A Wemyss basket, painted with Blackberries pattern in green, black, red and yellow, 1890–1900, 8in (20.5cm) long.
$1,150–1,300 ⊞ RdeR

◀ **A pair of buff stoneware potpourri baskets,** with pierced covers, applied in white with flowers and leaves, c1820, 3½in (9cm) high.
$400–450 ♣ LFA

Bowls

A Warsaw faïence bowl, from the Royal factory Belvedere, decorated in Imari style in red, green, blue and gold, with cartouches of Arabic inscriptions, 1776–77, 9in (23cm) diam.
$6,200–6,800 ♣ S(Z)
This bowl is from the service commissioned by King Stanislaw Poniatowski of Poland for Sultan Abdul Hamid.

An English creamware punch bowl, probably Leeds, with a cartouche inscribed 'Thos & Ann Pringle', surrounded by red roses, the interior painted with a single rose beneath an iron-red loop border, 10¼in (26cm) wide.
$1,000–1,200 ♣ S(S)

A Mason's Ironstone mazarine blue bowl, decorated in gold, the interior with a peony and other flowers below a diaper rim, the exterior with insects and butterflies, impressed marks, early 19thC, 12¼in (31cm) diam.
$725–875 ♣ Bea(E)

A Mason's Ironstone footed bowl, decorated in Imari colours, the dark blue ground with gilt scrolls and ironred flowers with gilding, with floral and geometric borders and gilt rim, puce printed mark, impressed mark, mid-19thC, 13in (33cm) diam.
$580–720 ♣ Mit

A Southwick Pottery, Sunderland, washbowl, by A. Scott, the interior printed and painted with The Sailor's Return, Crimean emblems and inscriptions, the exterior with a view of the Ironbridge, and The Sailor's Departure, within purple lustre borders, impressed mark, chips, c1855, 12½in (32cm) diam.
$800–880 ♣ SAS

A Staffordshire copper lustre footed bowl, the blue ground with a motif in red, green, yellow and white, mid-19thC, 5in (12.5cm) diam.
$65–75 ⊞ SER

A Sunderland pink lustre bowl, by Moor, decorated with The Sailor's Farewell, mid-19thC, 6½in (16.5cm) diam.
$175–200 ⊞ SER

A Wemyss bowl, probably by James Sharp, painted with sprigs of white broom within a black line border, impressed 'WEMYSS', green-painted script mark, c1900, 15½in (39.5cm) diam.
$1,300–1,450 ♣ S

A Wemyss cat bowl, painted with Dog Roses pattern, with a blue-green line rim, impressed marks, c1900, 5in (12.5cm) wide.
$1,150–1,300 ♣ S(S)

POTTERY

Buildings

A Prattware money box, modelled as a brick-built cottage with a blue and ochre roof, flanked by figures of a man and a woman painted in blue, puce and green, the base sponged in black and ochre, c1800, 5in (12.5cm) high.
$1,400–1,600 ⚒ P

A Scottish Portobello cottage money box, painted in shades of blue, red, yellow and green, on ball feet, inscribed 'WILLIAM MARSHALL HEMINGLY 1844', 6¾in (17cm) high.
$1,300–1,600 ⚒ Bon(C)

A Staffordshire church, the peach glaze encrusted with foliage, with a red door and black and white windows late 19thC, 9in (23cm) high.
$100–120 ⚒ SWO

A Staffordshire double spill vase, modelled with Mr Hemming as Prince Almansor, applied with a model of an elephant extending his trunk to rescue a figure in the clocktower of a castle, enriched in colours and encrusted with foliage, c1875, 6½in (17cm) high.
$725–800 ⚒ S(S)

A Staffordshire lilac-ground pastille burner, modelled as a three-turreted castle and heightened with gilt, encrusted with coloured moss and summer blossoms, mid-19thC, 7¾in (19.5cm) high.
$950–1,000 ⚒ Bon(C)

▶ **An earthenware model of Hedingham Castle,** by E. Bingham, the detachable cover enclosing a plan of the ground floor, incised signature mark, 1864–1901, 4¾in (12cm) high.
$440–500 ⚒ CGC

A Staffordshire pastille burner, modelled as a cottage encrusted with polychrome flowers, c1880, 3in (7.5cm) high.
$145–165 ⊞ SER

Candlesticks & Chambersticks

◀ **A Whieldon type candlestick,** modelled as a tree, decorated in brown and green glaze, c1760, 12in (30.5cm) high.
$4,300–4,700 ⊞ JHo

A Mason's Ironstone miniature candlestick, with a gilt serpent loop handle, decorated in underglaze blue, iron-red and gilt with chinoiserie-style flowering branches and fences, impressed mark, minor damage, 1815–20, 3½in (9cm) diam.
$650–800 ⚒ LFA

A pair of Wemyss candlesticks, painted with Cherries pattern in pink and green, impressed 'R.H. & S.' mark, printed Goode's mark, 11½in (29cm) high.
$1,400–1,750 ⚒ P(Ed)

Centrepieces

A Mason's Cambrian Argil fruit comport, decorated in red, blue and pink with a rose and other flowers, slight damage, c1820, 15in (38cm) wide.
$1,150–1,300 ⊞ JP

A Wedgwood majolica leaf-shaped comport, in green, yellow and brown glazes, impressed mark, date code 'FNU', late 19thC, 16in (40.5cm) wide.
$440–500 ⚹ Mit

A Continental majolica centrepiece, in the form of two cherubs seated on a pair of dolphins, beside a leafy column, damaged, c1900, 14½in (37cm) high.
$1,100–1,200 ⚹ S(NY)

Cow Creamers

A Prattware cow creamer, with sponged decoration in ochre and black, the base with a mottled green glaze, horns chipped, corner of base restored, c1790, 7in (18cm) long.
$725–875 ⚹ P

A Prattware cow creamer, with sponged decoration in red-brown, on a green base, probably Yorkshire, c1800, 8in (20.5cm) long.
$2,400–2,600 ⊞ JRe

A Prattware-style cow creamer, spotted in ochre and brown, the base washed in green, early 19thC, 7in (18cm) long.
$870–1,000 ⚹ S(S)

Dishes

◄ **A Staffordshire leaf dish,** painted green, c1765, 11in (28cm) long.
$1,150–1,300 ⊞ JHo

A pair of Lakin two-handled dishes, the puce lustre border and centres bat-printed *en grisaille* with head and shoulders portraits of Captains Jones and Pike, inscribed 'Captain Jones of the Macedonian; Be Always Ready To Die For Your Country, Pike', impressed marks, 1810–17, 10in (25.5cm) long.
$1,450–1,750 ⚹ GAK
Captain Jacob Jones of the American Navy captured the vessel *Macedonian* from the British Navy in 1810. Pike was probably the captain of the vessel, although no records have been found to substantiate this. The vessel was then involved in various other actions, in Algeria and South America, finally being broken up in 1826.

POTTERY

Majolica

The word majolica is derived from 'maiolica', the term for tin-glazed earthenwares produced in Italy during the Renaissance. Majolica was introduced into England in 1847 by Joseph Arnoux, the art director for Minton. His early works were greatly influenced by Italian maiolica, but later pieces were inspired by naturalism and were decorated with the brilliant rich lustrous polychromatic glazes which we have now come to associate with majolica. These wares were a huge commercial success, allowing the factory to employ many significant modellers and artists, including Emile Lessore, Albert Carrier-Belleuse and Paul Comolera. Manufacturers such as George Jones, Wedgwood and Joseph Holdcroft, amongst others, followed suit producing a significant output of quality wares. However, majolica eventually became a victim of its own success, as a steady stream of inferior imitations were produced that undermined the commercial and artistic success of the factories and resulted in the demise of these wares around the end of the 19th century.

A George Jones majolica dish, moulded with horse chestnut leaves with twig terminal, painted in coloured glazes, raised pad mark, terminal restored, c1870, 9¾in (25cm) long.
$500–600 ⚒ DN

A Longchamp asparagus cradle, painted in green, brown and white, c1880, 15in (38cm) long.
$450–500 ⊞ MLL

A Minton majolica leaf-shaped dish, the handle in the shape of a red squirrel eating hazelnuts, date code for 1870, 10in (25.5cm) long.
$800–950 ⚒ CGC

◄ **A Wemyss dish,** painted with Bee with Hives pattern in green, yellow and brown, early 20thC, 7½in (19cm) square.
$260–320 ⚒ P(Ed)

► **A Quimper dish,** by P. Fouillon, painted in shades of blue and red on a cream ground, c1928, 12in (30.5cm) square.
$240–270 ⊞ SER

A Wedgwood dish, with bamboo-decorated border and handle, printed mark '1175', impressed mark and date code for 1888, 10in (25.5cm) diam.
$300–350 ⚒ PFK

Covered Dishes

A Mason's Ironstone sucrier and cover, painted in red, blue, green and gold on a white ground, 1830–48, 7in (18cm) long.
$320–360 ⊞ JP

A Scottish Stilton dish and cover, probably Kirkcaldy, covered with streaked brown, blue and green glazes, c1870, 12½in (32cm) high.
$580–720 ⚒ P(Ed)

A Minton majolica game pie dish and cover, with a gun dog knop and moulded panels of a hare and pheasant to the sides, decorated with coloured glazes, two small chips, impressed 'Minton' and '964', date code for 1868, 14in (35.5cm) long.
$6,800–7,800 ⚒ WW

► **A George Jones majolica sardine box and cover,** pattern No. 3549, the lid moulded with three sardines and painted in naturalistic colours, decorated in treacle and mottled green glazes, impressed marks, date cipher for 1882, 9in (23cm) long.
$875–1,000 ⚒ GAK

A George Jones majolica game dish and cover, moulded in relief with game and fern leaves in shades of green on a turquoise ground within yellow enamel rims, painted numerals, c1870, 9½in (24cm) long.
$950–1,150 ⚒ CGC

Figures

A Staffordshire salt-glazed figure of a lady, c1750, 4in (10cm) high.
$1,000–1,150 ⊞ JHo

A Staffordshire figure of a poacher, holding a cudgel and a sack, supported by a tree trunk, glazed with green and brown spots, the base and tree in green, c1780, 4¾in (12cm) high.
$200–250 ✦ P

A Staffordshire pearlware figure of Benjamin Franklin, by Frank Wood, c1785, 14in (35.5cm) high.
$4,000–4,400 ⊞ JRe

▶ **A Staffordshire figural group of the Sacrifice of Isaac,** before bocage with an altar inscribed 'He said lay not thine and upon the lad neither do thou anything unto him', restored, c1830, 8in (20.5cm) high.
$250–300 ✦ DN

A pair of pearlware figures of a gardener and his mate, painted in colours, before bocage, some damage and repair, c1790, taller 9in (23cm) high.
$1,300–1,450 ✦ P

A Wood & Caldwell pearlware figure of James Quin as Falstaff, wearing a lilac jacket and red breeches, minor damage and restoration, impressed mark, 1810–18, 9in (23cm) high.
$300–350 ✦ P(Ba)

A Staffordshire pearlware figure of Fire, wearing a black hat, before bocage, the base moulded with shell scrolls and label inscribed 'FIRE', minor losses, 1810–20, 6½in (16.5cm) high.
$230–290 ✦ P(Ba)

A Staffordshire poly-chrome group of card players, featuring Dr Syntax, c1830, 7in (18cm) high.
$5,000–5,750 ⊞ JHo
Dr Syntax is a comic character originally depicted in a series of drawings by the cartoonist Thomas Rawlinson c1800.

A Staffordshire earthen-ware pair of dandies, the man with a blue jacket and yellow trousers, the lady with a red and white dress, c1820, 7in (18cm) high.
$870–1,000 ⊞ JHo

POTTERY

A Derbyshire spirit flask, in the form of a man sitting on a barrel, inscribed 'Success to Reform' beneath, decorated in brown and buff glazes, c1835, 8in (20.5cm) high.
$500–575 ⊞ JHo

A pair of stoneware figures of Albert and Victoria, c1845, 15in (38cm) high.
$2,200–2,400 ⊞ JHo

A Staffordshire figure of William Wallace, wearing a red, yellow and green tartan cape, c1850, 15½in (39.5cm) high.
$320–350 ⊞ SER

A Staffordshire poly-chrome figure of a Scottish piper, wearing a black hat and red and black kilt, leaning against a rock, 19thC, 12¼in (31cm) high.
$180–220 ↗ AH

A Staffordshire figural group, the man wearing a blue jacket and green and red striped breeches, the lady wearing a blue jacket and a green and red plaid skirt, c1850, 8in (20.5cm) high.
$200–225 ⊞ SER

A Staffordshire figure of Napoleon, with brown hair, dressed in white, with a pink lining to his cloak and black boots, mid-19thC, 8in (20.5cm) high.
$260–290 ⊞ SER

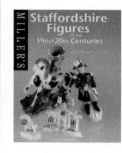

A Staffordshire figural group, by Parr entitled 'Ridley and Latimer', modelled with the two Bishops praying, tied back-to-back at the stake, c1851, 9½in (24cm) high.
$1,250–1,450 ↗ Bon(C)
Nicholas Ridley and Hugh Latimer were Protestant martyrs. Ridley was found guilty of treason after he espoused the cause of Lady Jane Grey, and Latimer was condemned as a heretic under Mary I. They were burnt at the stake opposite Balliol College, Oxford, in 1555.

A Staffordshire figure, of Rev John Elias, dressed in black, carrying a red book, c1850, 14in (35.5cm) high.
$2,000–2,300 ⊞ RGa

To find out more see *Miller's Staffordshire Figures of the 19th & 20th Centuries: A Collector's Guide* (£5.99), with over 130 colour pictures, its 64 pages are packed with invaluable information. *Order from* www.millers.uk.com *or telephone in the UK on 01933 443863*

▶ **A Staffordshire figure of Sir Charles Napier,** painted with a navy coat and white trousers, 19thC, 16in (40.5cm) high.
$870–1,000 ↗ WW

A Staffordshire figure of Napoleon, dressed in black hat and boots, green cloak with red lining, blue jacket and white breeches, c1850, 9½in (24cm) high
$450–550 ⊞ OD

▶ **A Staffordshire figural group of a rustic couple,** with a butter churn, decorated in orange, yellow, pink and black, late 19thC, 9¼in (23.5cm) high.
$250–300 ↗ SWO

A Staffordshire figural watch holder, the pink ground decorated with green and brown details, c1860, 8in (20.5cm) high.
$240–270 ⊞ SER

A Staffordshire earthenware figure of Gladstone, wearing a black frock coat, probably by Sampson Smith or Kent, 1870s, 12in (30.5cm) high.
$360–440 ✗ S(S)

A Staffordshire tobacco jar, in the form of Father Christmas, decorated in red and white, late 19thC, 7in (18cm) high.
$115–145 ✗ DD

A pair of Minton majolica figural salts, in the form of a boy and a girl, in 18thC dress, the baskets with pale blue interiors, minor cracks and restorations, 1862, 8in (20.5cm) high.
$725–875 ✗ P(S)

Slipware

Slip is a clay and water mix of a creamy consistency, which can be applied to the body of a piece of pottery of contrasting colour as a form of decoration. The slip can be trailed, dotted or combed onto the surface of an individual piece to give varying effects. Early examples were predominantly produced in the 17th century in Staffordshire, by the Toft family, William Taylor and Ralph Simpson, amongst others, and at Wrotham in Kent. These examples are usually credited as being one of the first forms of British decorative pottery. Regional variations were also produced in Devon, Yorkshire, Wales, Derbyshire and Somerset. This art form was continued well into the 19th century and was revived in the 20th century by studio potters such as Michael Cardew and Bernard Leach, who were concerned about the demise of rural traditions.

A Staffordshire model of Britannia, wearing a plumed helmet and with a lion at her side, on a green and black base, polychrome-painted in enamels and gilt, chip to helmet, late 19thC, 15in (38cm) high.
$440–500 ✗ WW

A Wedgwood black basalt figure of Venus on a rock, after the sculpture by Jean-Baptiste Pigalle, impressed mark, late 19thC, 18¾in (47.5cm) high.
$2,000–2,300 ✗ SK

◄ **A pair of Staffordshire portrait busts of John Wesley,** wearing a black enamelled cloak over a yellow and black foliate-decorated shirt, on a pedestal base sponged in green, orange and blue enamels, c1900, 10½in (26.5cm) high.
$1,000–1,100 ✗ Hal

Flatware

A Deruta armorial tazza, painted with a coat-of-arms of St George and the Dragon within foliate ornament, mid-17thC, 10½in (26.5cm) diam.
$500–600 ✗ P

A Staffordshire salt-glazed plate, entitled 'The King of Prussia', c1760, 9in (23cm) diam.
$1,250–1,400 ⊞ JHo

A Staffordshire slipware dish, decorated with a trailing meander in honey-coloured slip on a dark brown ground, minor chip to underside, short fine crack, mid-18thC, 8in (20.5cm) diam.
$1,750–1,900 ✗ P

POTTERY

A Dutch-decorated creamware plate, depicting the Baptism of Christ, decorated in red, green, cream and black, c1800, 9½in (24cm) diam.
$350–400 ⊞ JHo

A Wedgwood white jasper dish, the coiled ribbon border with a classical relief of putti, impressed mark, early 19thC, 11¼in (28.5cm) diam.
$440–480 ➢ SK

A pair of pearlware plates, painted with a butterfly hovering between two leafy branches issuing from rocks, the blue border with ochre ovals, some surface scratches, early 19thC, 9¾in (25cm) diam.
$450–500 ➢ S(S)

A set of three Whitehaven Pottery pearlware plates, with a scalloped and blue-feathered rim with leaf-moulded swags, enclosing a chinoiserie scene within a trellis border, early 19thC, 9½in (24cm) diam.
$300–350 ➢ Mit

A commemorative pearlware nursery plate, printed in black with King George III presenting a Bible to a child, above an inscription, hairline crack, c1820, 6in (15cm) diam.
$870–1,000 ➢ SAS

A Sunderland pink lustre dish, hairline crack, mid-19thC, 14½in (37cm) diam.
$160–180 ⊞ SER

A set of six English majolica green leaf-moulded plates, late 19thC, 8¼in (21cm) diam.
$180–220 ➢ WW

A George Jones majolica Christmas charger, pattern No. 11, painted with robins on a branch within a light blue border, moulded and painted with holly and mistletoe, c1870, 14in (35.5cm) diam.
$2,200–2,500 ➢ Bea(E)

A Wedgwood majolica bread tray, the centre moulded with three sickles and a sunburst on a blue ground, the rim with wheatsheaves in shades of brown, yellow and green with pink ribbon ties, raised on a circular foot, impressed marks, 1870s, 13in (33cm) diam.
$725–875 ➢ S(S)

A Mettlach charger, decorated in white and pale blue on a dark background with Roman soldiers in a boat, signed 'Stahl', German, c1885, 18in (45.5cm) diam.
$500–600 ➢ DORO

A Wemyss plate, painted with Redcurrants pattern in green and red with a green rim line, c1890, 8in (20.5cm) diam.
$500–580 ⊞ RdeR

A Sarreguemines asparagus plate, decorated in shades of yellow and green on a cream ground, France, c1890, 10in (25.5cm) diam.
$85–100 ⊞ MLL

Footbaths

▶ **A Minton Amerhurst footbath,** decorated with Japan pattern, in blue, red and green, c1830, 19in (48.5cm) wide.
$1,450–1,600 ⊞ SCO

A Mason's Ironstone footbath, decorated with Japan pattern, with flowers and leaves in blue and orange, riveted, base chip, 1820–30, 19in (48.5cm) wide.
$3,300–3,800 ⚒ WW

◀ **A Staffordshire oval footbath,** pattern No. 1991, painted with polychrome flower sprays, mid-19thC, 18¾in (47.5cm) wide.
$300–350 ⚒ WW

Garden Seats

A Minton majolica garden seat, shape No. 1116, in the shape of bamboo bound together with stiff leaves and ribbons, decorated in green, yellow and brown, one foot damaged, chips, impressed marks for 1864, 19½in (49.5cm) high.
$5,000–5,500 ⚒ SAS

A majolica garden seat, probably John Adams & Co, modelled in bold relief with ribbon-tied wheatears and corn on a brown ground, minor chips, c1870, 18½in (47cm) high.
$1,600–1,750 ⚒ SAS

A pair of Minton majolica garden seats, modelled as a cushioned seat tied with a gold ribbon, the relief-moulded flowers with details in silver and gilding, reserved on a blue ground, diamond registration mark, impressed factory marks, 1881, 18in (45.7cm) high.
$6,500–7,500 ⚒ S

A George Jones majolica garden seat, in the shape of a section of tree trunk glazed in brown and moulded with blackberry briars and leafy wild flowers, the top pierced with a central S-shaped aperture, impressed monogram over crescent mark, c1875, 20¾in (52.5cm) high.
$2,900–3,200 ⚒ S(S)

Ice Pails & Wine Coolers

An earthenware ice pail, decorated with blue glazed bands and floral motifs with gilt banding, the body decorated with arms holding an inverted fan, the interior with a liner, damaged, early 19thC, 8½in (21.5cm) high.
$115–145 ⚒ WilP

A pair of Staffordshire pottery ice pails, transfer-printed in blue with Oriental Birds pattern and decorated in coloured enamels, with a moulded leaf-capped body and moulded and twisted handles with gilt decorations, both cracked, possibly John & William Ridgway, painter's mark No. 1784, c1825, 13½in (34.5cm) high.
$1,700–2,200 ⚒ CAG

A Davenport stoneware commemorative wine cooler, decorated in relief with Nelson, the reverse with naval trophies, minor chips, impressed mark, c1850, 10¼in (26cm) high.
$950–1,150 ⚒ Bon(C)

Miller's is a price GUIDE not a price LIST

Inkstands & Inkwells

A German salt-glazed stoneware inkstand, with a lift-out well and pounce pot, decorated in cobalt blue and manganese, some damage, well replaced, 18thC, 7in (18cm) wide.
$330–380 ✗ WW

A Victorian inkwell, in the shape of a curling stone, the body mottled to simulate polished granite, with a nickel hinged cover and handle, 2½in (6.5cm) high.
$130–160 ✗ PFK

A French faïence inkstand, painted with a man chasing his wife with a broom, with a floral pink, blue, yellow and green border, slight damage, 19thC, 7¾in (19.5cm) wide.
$220–260 ✗ Bon(C)

◄ **A Wemyss inkwell and cover,** painted with Cherries pattern, painted Wemyss and Goode's mark, small chip, c1910, 4in (10cm) high.
$180–220 ✗ P(Ed)

A Quimper inkwell, in the shape of a hat, decorated in blue, orange, green and yellow on a white ground, c1920, 6in (15cm) diam.
$220–240 ⊞ MLL

Jars

A maiolica drug jar, inscribed 'VNG TO DIAPONPHOLIGOS' on a yellow band against a ground painted with scrolling foliage in blue, green and ochre, chips and hairline crack, probably South Italy, 17thC, 6¾in (17cm) high.
$850–1,000 ✗ S(S)

A pair of Savona *albarelli*, painted in blue drawn with putti in landscapes flanking a heraldic shield bearing the arms of the Franciscan Order, inscribed '*Vng. Apostolor*' and '*Eu: Suc: Ros*', marked with the lighthouse in Genoa, minor chips, early 18thC, 8in (20.5cm) high.
$2,300–2,600 ✗ P
These jars were used to contain Ointment of the Apostles (for treating wounds and ulcers) and Sweet Rosewater.

A Dorset stoneware cider jar, the pierced handles resembling owl's eyes, late 18thC, 10in (25.5cm) high.
$500–550 ⊞ SEA

A pair of Italian majolica *albarelli*, inscribed and with blue-painted floral and foliage bands and initials 'S.P.', chips, 7¼in (18.5cm) high.
$1,300–1,600 ✗ AG

◄ **A Wemyss honey pot,** painted with Bee with Hives pattern, in yellow, green, jade and black, retailed by T. Goode, early 20thC, 5½in (14cm) high.
$580–650 ⊞ SAAC

A Mason's Ironstone pot-pourri vase, decorated in Japan pattern in red, blue and gilt, repaired, 1815–20, 7in (18cm) high.
$870–1,000 ⊞ JP

An American salt-glazed Commeraws Stoneware jar, the shoulder decorated with impressed and blue-glazed swag and pendant motif, impressed maker's mark, rim chips, New York, 19thC, 11¾in (30cm) high.
$2,900–3,200 ✗ SK(B)

Colour Review

A Dutch baroque carved oak hall bench, c1800, 69in (175.5cm) wide.
$5,000–6,000 ➤ **S(Am)**

A Charles II marquetry-inlaid walnut jewel box, with sliding front panels and secret drawers, 15in (38cm) wide.
$6,500–7,250 ⊞ **SuA**

An oak box, with original lozenge carving and patina, c1675, 28¾in (73cm) wide.
$2,400–2,700 ⊞ **DeG**

An oak bible box, initialled 'FD' and dated '1803', 21in (53.5cm) wide.
$1,000–1,250 ⊞ **AdA**

◄ **A George II oak bureau,** the fall-front enclosing a stepped, fitted interior and a well, 26in (66cm) wide.
$2,000–2,400 ➤ **RBB**

An oak bureau, the fall-front enclosing a fitted interior above a well, early 18thC, 36¼in (92cm) wide.
$4,300–5,000 ➤ **Bon(C)**

► **A Welsh oak bureau,** with a fitted interior, c1780, 36in (91.5cm) wide.
$4,000–4,600 ⊞ **CoA**

An oak bureau, the fall-front enclosing a fitted interior and a well, with later handles, c1750, 31in (78.5cm) wide.
$7,600–8,400 ⊞ **SEA**

A Louis XVI French provincial fruitwood buffet, restored, late 18thC, 53in (134.5cm) wide.
$3,500–4,000 ➤ **NOA**

► **A French oak buffet,** c1830, 63½in (161.5cm) wide.
$5,800–6,500 ⊞ **DeG**

An oak bureau, the fall-front enclosing a fitted interior, c1780, 30in (76cm) wide.
$6,000–7,000 ⊞ **WELL**

Paul Hopwell Antiques

Early English Oak

Dressers, tables and chairs always in stock

A fine Queen Anne oak three drawer dresser base with shaped cockbeaded apron.
On baluster turned legs. English   c1710

A Queen Anne oak side
table on baluster turned legs
with 'H' stretcher.
English   c1710

A small Charles II laburnam,
snakewood and cedarwood
chest of three drawers.
English   c1670

Paul Hopwell Antiques

A rare 17th century oak
panelled Wainscott chair.
English   Dated 1690

A superb Geo. III
oak cupboard
dresser and rack
with six spice
drawers. Excellent
colour, condition
and patina.
North Wales   c1770

A superb Charles II
oak coffer
with drawer.
West Country c1685

COLOUR REVIEW

A James I oak wainscot chair, c1610.
$5,000–5,500 ⊞ WELL

A Charles II oak armchair, the back outlined with a border of inlaid bog oak semi-circles and with a guilloche-carved panel, the lozenge-carved seat rail fitted with a side drawer, dated '1662'.
$17,500–21,750 ⚒ S

An oak wainscot chair, with a panelled back, c1670.
$3,500–4,000 ⊞ SuA

A pair of Welsh side chairs, c1690.
$4,250–5,000 ⊞ CoA

An oak armchair, with guilloche-carved crest rail, above a panelled back, 17thC.
$2,500–3,000 ⚒ RBB

A Welsh George I oak armchair, with a panelled back, c1720.
$10,000–12,000 ⊞ PHA

A pair of joined oak backstools, with panelled seats, c1700.
$4,500–5,000 ⊞ DBA

A Welsh oak hall chair, with a panelled seat, c1720.
$2,600–2,900 ⚒ SEA

◄ A yew wood highback Windsor armchair, c1780.
$3,200–3,600 ⊞ REI

An American turned-maple and ash ladderback armchair, legs reduced, New England, early 18thC.
$5,000–6,000 ⚒ SK(B)

A set of four turned elm chairs, with rush seats, 1820.
$1,000–1,200 ⊞ ALA

◄ A set of eight North Country ladderback chairs, including two carvers, with rush seats, early 19thC.
$6,500–7,200 ⊞ DeG

A yew wood and syca-more primitive Windsor open armchair, late 18thC.
$7,200–8,000 ⊞ RYA

◄ A Welsh ash and fruitwood stickback Windsor armchair, the top rail with a waved crest above, early 19thC.
$3,600–4,300 ⚒ Bon(C)

An oak plank coffer, with scratch carving, c1595, 31in (78.5cm) wide.
$6,500–8,000 ⊞ PHA

A West Country oak coffer, dated '1618' behind the lock plate, 41in (104cm) wide.
$3,200–3,600 ⊞ SEA

An oak chest, decorated with split-baluster turning and inlaid with mother-of-pearl and bone, with a single drawer to the base, c1660, 56in (142cm) wide.
$7,200–8,000 ⊞ SuA

A Charles II oak coffer, the front carved with flower-head arches centred with an inlaid foliate pattern, restored, late 17thC, 62in (157.5cm) wide.
$2,500–3,000 ⚖ S(S)

A carved oak coffer, c1680, 44in (112cm) wide.
$1,250–1,500 ⊞ WELL

A carved oak coffer, c1680, 44in (112cm) wide.
$1,700–2,000 ⊞ WELL

An oak mule chest, the hinged top enclosing a candle box and small drawers, 18thC, 54in (137cm) wide.
$1,000–1,200 ⚖ DOC

A Welsh oak *coffor bach*, Cardiganshire, c1780, 23in (58.5cm) wide.
$4,000–4,600 ⊞ CoA

A Charles II fruitwood, oak and walnut chest of drawers, restored, 39in (99cm) wide.
$6,500–8,000 ⚖ S(S)

A George I oak bachelor's chest, c1720, 35in (89cm) wide.
$14,500–17,500 ⊞ PHA

◀ **A George II bachelor's chest,** with a slide and two short and three long graduated drawers, 29½in (75cm) wide.
$8,500–10,000 ⚖ P

▶ **An East Anglian fruitwood press chest,** with two short drawers flanking a moulded front drawer above three further drawers, late 18thC, 36in (91.5cm) wide.
$3,500–4,500 ⚖ Bon(C)

A North Country George II oak chest of drawers, crossbanded in mahogany, c1740, 35in (89cm) wide.
$7,000–8,000 ⊞ REI

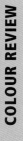

A carved oak press cupboard, the frieze initialled 'AHM' and dated '1663', 63¾in (162cm) wide.
$5,800–7,200 ⚒ **ELR**

A West Country carved oak press cupboard, c1670, 55in (139.5cm) wide.
$7,500–8,500 ⊞ **SuA**

A carved oak press cupboard, dated '1724', 54in (137cm) wide.
$12,500–14,000 ⊞ **REI**

A Flemish palissandre, oak and ebony ripplemoulded carved cupboard, the doors enclosing two shelves, 18thC, 65½in (166.5cm) wide.
$5,800–7,200 ⚒ **P**

An oak dresser, the upper section with spice doors, above three frieze drawers over a pair of panelled doors, early 18thC, 76in (193cm) wide.
$43,500–47,500 ⊞ **AdA**
This piece was formerly owned by Isambard Kingdom Brunel and is an exceptional design of outstanding colour.

A Breton ash and oak armoire, c1840, 59in (150cm) wide.
$5,000–6,000 ⊞ **DeG**

◀ **A George III breakfront oak Welsh dresser,** with seven spice drawers, c1760, 67in (170cm) wide.
$26,000–32,000 ⊞ **PHA**

A French provincial fruitwood and oak *vaisselier,* restored, early 19thC, 52in (132cm) wide.
$4,000–4,600 ⚒ **NOA**

A French walnut dresser, the cupboard doors enclosing an adjustable shelf, over a spindle-railed gallery, c1900, 55in (139.5cm) wide.
$600–750 ⚒ **Hal**

◀ **An elm, walnut and oak low dresser,** the single-plank top above a potboard, c1700, 70in (178cm) wide.
$6,500–7,250 ⊞ **WELL**

A Welsh Borders oak low dresser, crossbanded in fruit-wood, with a shaped apron under three frieze drawers, c1730, 84in (213.5cm) wide.
$39,000–43,500 ⊞ **AdA**

An oak dresser base, c1770, 55in (139.5cm) wide.
$8,500–9,500 ⊞ **DeG**

Mark Seabrook Antiques

9 West End, West Haddon, Northamptonshire NN6 7AY
Telephone: 01788 510772 Evenings: 01480 861339
Mobile: 07770 721 931

Specialising in fine country furniture,
English oak, treen, ceramics and early metalware,
with a shop at 9 West End, West Haddon,
Northants, where a warm, friendly welcome always
awaits you

ACTIVELY SEEKING GOOD QUALITY
COUNTRY FURNITURE AND EARLY
METALWARE TO PURCHASE

An oak lowboy, with four drawers, supported on cabriole legs, c1730, 33in (84cm) wide.
$4,000–4,400 ⊞ **SuA**

A George III oak lowboy, with fret-cut brackets and original swan-neck handles, c1780, 31in (78.5cm) wide.
$3,000–3,500 ⊞ **TWh**

A pair of joined oak stools, c1680, 15in (38cm) wide.
$18,000–20,000 ⊞ **AdA**

◀ **An elm high back settle,** with box seat and dentil cornice, mid-18thC, 50in (127cm) wide.
$29,000–32,000 ⊞ **AdA**

▶ **A William and Mary walnut and elm candle stand,** 15in (38cm) wide.
$5,000–5,500 ⊞ **SuA**

A Queen Anne joined beech stool, c1710, 12in (30.5cm) diam.
$4,000–4,400 ⊞ **SEA**

An oak stool, c1730, 20in (51cm) wide.
$3,600–4,000 ⊞ **REI**

An oak commode, with a single drawer, c1750, 20in (51cm) wide.
$2,000–2,400 ⊞ **SWG**

An oak box stool, on baluster-turned legs, with original butterfly hinges, c1700, 21in (53.5cm) wide.
$6,500–8,000 ⊞ **PHA**

An oak side table, with bobbin-turned legs, c1660, 33in (84cm) wide.
$4,600–5,000 ⊞ **SEA**

An oak refectory table, the triple-plank top above a frieze carved with scrolling leaves and flowerheads, mid-17thC, 116½in (296cm) long.
$30,500–36,000 ⚒ **P(NW)**

An oak close stool, c1770, 17in (43cm) wide.
$2,000–2,200 ⊞ **SEA**
A close stool is otherwise known as a commode.

▶ **An oak side table,** with a single drawer, c1680, 29in (73.5cm) wide.
$5,000–5,500 ⊞ **REI**

An oak refectory table, the cleated top with two planks, restored, 17thC, 99in (251.5cm) long.
$7,000–8,000 ⚒ **S(S)**

An oak circular tavern table, with baluster legs, c1680, 26in (66cm) diam.
$5,750–6,500 ⊞ RYA

A Charles II oak side table, with a single frieze drawer, c1680, 25in (63.5cm) wide.
$1,800–2,300 ⊞ CoHA

A Dutch inlaid oak side table, the later angled top above a panelled frieze inlaid with a geometric dogtooth pattern, 17thC, 39½in (100.5cm) wide.
$1,200–1,400 ⚒ Bon(C)

A Queen Anne oak side table, with a frieze drawer, on baluster-turned legs, c1710, 34in (86.5cm) wide.
$6,500–8,000 ⊞ PHA

A yew wood side table, on tapered and faceted pillar legs, joined by a flat X-stretcher, one section replaced, early 18thC, 30¼in (77cm) wide.
$4,600–5,500 ⚒ TEN

An oak lowboy, with a shaped frieze, c1720, 29in (73.5cm) wide.
$3,500–4,000 ⊞ WELL

A Georgian elm tavern table, with a trestle base, 54in (137cm) wide.
$1,400–1,600 ⊞ SuA

A Westmorland-type oak dining table, with a single drop leaf, c1720, 76in (193cm) long.
$8,000–9,000 ⊞ RYA

A yew wood side table, with a single drawer and original brass open-plate handles, c1730, 29in (73.5cm) wide.
$12,000–13,500 ⊞ REI

▶ **A late Victorian Elizabethan-style carved oak refectory table,** the side friezes carved with scrolling foliage, flowerheads and grape clusters, 106¾in (271cm) long.
$5,750–6,500 ⚒ P

A French provincial fruitwood side table, with a frieze drawer, early 19thC, 29¾in (75.5cm) wide.
$450–550 ⚒ NOA

A French poplar flip-top table, c1880, 118in (299.5cm) extended.
$5,000–6,000 ⊞ DeG

An oak tilt-top table, on a turned column, with a tripod base, 1860, 23in (58.5cm) diam.
$360–400 ⊞ POT

An Austrian Empire pine wedding chest, with jigsaw-style painted decoration, c1830, 37in (94cm) wide.
$4,750–5,500 ⊞ RYA

A Victorian pine traveller's chest, with original paint, inscribed 'A. J. Stanesby, London', 31in (78.5cm) wide.
$580–650 ⊞ BrH

A Swedish provincial painted pine chest of drawers, late 18thC, 51in (129.5cm) wide.
$5,000–6,000 ⚒ S(NY)

A Hungarian folk art painted pine chest, c1870, 48in (122cm) wide.
$300–350 ⊞ Byl

▶ **A Victorian wood-grain-painted chest of drawers,** the drawers painted with Tunbridge ware-style banding, 42in (106.5cm) wide.
$700–800
⊞ BrH

A Victorian painted pine chest of drawers, decorated with a wood-grain effect, c1880, 42in (106.5cm) wide.
$600–750 ⊞ BrH

A painted pine chest of drawers, with two short and three long graduated drawers, with later decoration, 19thC, 35in (89cm) wide.
$2,000–2,400 ⊞ MLL

A Swiss painted armoire, Toggenburg, dated '1752', 72in (183cm) high.
$3,000–3,500 ⚒ S(Z)

An American blue-painted pine cupboard, possibly New Hampshire, early 19thC, 36¾in (93.cm) wide.
$36,500–43,500 ⚒ SK(B)

An Austrian Empire painted pine marriage cupboard, c1820, 48in (122cm) wide.
$8,500–9,500 ⊞ RYA

A Spanish painted pine bookcase, with original *faux bois* and trompe l'oeil painted decoration, early 19thC, 67in (170cm) wide.
$16,000–18,000 ⊞ FCL

A George III pine settle, painted with wood-grain effect, 66in (167.5cm) wide. **$1,600–1,800** ⊞ BrH

A north European pine and iron-bound chest, the leather-covered hinged top with pierced straps, star motifs, initials 'H. S.' and dated '1697', with original locking mechanism, 47¼in (120cm) wide. **$2,300–2,600** ⚒ CGC

A pine blanket box, c1840, 35in (89cm) wide. **$300–350** ⊞ P&T

A pine secretaire bookcase, with two doors above three long drawers, 1870–80, 37in (94cm) wide. **$1,800–2,200** ⊞ MIN

An Irish blanket chest, Co Galway, c1870, 44in (112cm) wide. **$300–350** ⊞ HON

A pine grain bin, c1880, 32½in (82.5cm) wide. **$425–500** ⊞ AL

◀ **A Welsh pine coffer,** with eight fielded panels above two drawers, c1790, 54in (137cm) wide. **$850–1,000** ⊞ POT

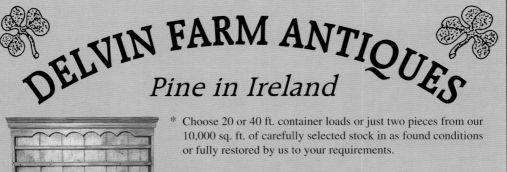

A pine chest of drawers, with three graduated drawers and a shaped apron, on bracket feet, c1810, 35in (89cm) wide.
$850–1,000 ⊞ POT

A pine chest of drawers, with two ogee drawers over two long drawers, with original ceramic knobs, c1850, 36in (91.5cm) wide.
$400–450 ⊞ P&T

A pine chest of drawers, with original turned knobs, c1850, 47in (119.5cm) wide.
$800–880 ⊞ P&T

A Hampshire pine chest of drawers, with four short and three long drawers, c1850, 42in (106.5cm) wide.
$1,000–1,200 ⊞ TPC

A set of pine and oak drawers, with original ring handles, mid-19thC, 29in (73.5cm) wide.
$250–300 ⊞ NEW

A pine chest of drawers, with two short and three long drawers, c1860, 42in (106.5cm) wide.
$450–500 ⊞ P&T

An Irish pine chest of drawers, with two short and three long drawers, c1875, 37in (94cm) wide.
$350–450 ⊞ Byl

An east European pine chest of drawers, c1875, 45in (114.5cm) wide.
$400–500 ⊞ Byl

▶ **A Victorian pine chest of drawers,** the serpentine frieze drawer and five short and three long drawers flanked by scroll-carved pilasters, 48in (122cm) wide.
$3,000–3,500 ⚒ LJ

A pine chest of drawers, with gesso mouldings and brass handles, c1890, 41in (104cm) wide.
$800–880 ⊞ AL

▶ **A pine flight of 24 drawers,** c1890, 47in (119.5cm) wide.
$850–1,000 ⊞ MLL

A pine flight of nine drawers, c1880, 28in (71cm) wide.
$250–300 ⊞ AL

A Victorian pine chest of drawers, with a frieze drawer over two short and three long drawers, c1900, 52in (132cm) wide.
$500–550 ⊞ POT

An Irish pine bath, 1850–60, 75in (190.5cm) long. $350–400 ⊞ Byl

A Louisiana vernacular cypress and pine wing-back chair, with a cane back, c1800, 23in (58.5cm) wide. $3,500–4,000 ⚒ NOA

A pair of Victorian pitch pine hall chairs. $400–450 ⊞ POT

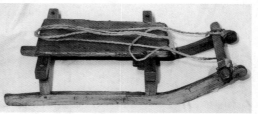

A Hungarian pine sledge, c1900, 33in (84cm) long. $100–120 ⊞ MIN

◄ **A country pine chair,** c1875. $150–175 ⊞ Byl

▶ **A Hungarian pine refrigerator,** by Andrényi Károly és Fiai, with original pine fittings, 1880, 22in (56cm) wide. $300–350 ⊞ Byl

An Irish famine or hedge chair, 1850–60. $150–175 ⊞ Byl

A south German baroque pine cupboard, with two doors, 18thC, 76¾in (195cm) wide.
$6,500–8,000 ⚒ S(Am)

A pine breakfront wardrobe, c1800, 86in (218.5cm) wide.
$4,500–5,000 ⊞ P&T

A pine two-door cupboard, c1800, 52in (132cm) wide.
$580–650 ⊞ P&T

A Hampshire pine butler's cupboard, c1800, 29in (73.5cm) wide.
$850–1,000 ⊞ TPC

A pine linen press, with fitted slide interior, c1840, 46in (117cm) wide.
$2,000–2,400 ⊞ TPC

▶ **A pine two-door cupboard,** with a shaped apron, c1840, 46in (117cm) wide.
$500–600 ⊞ P&T

◀ **A German pine two-door cupboard,** c1870, 41in (104cm) wide
$500–600 ⊞ MIN

A pitch pine corner cupboard, c1860, 41in (104cm) wide.
$1,500–1,750 ⊞ POT

A French pine bowfront corner cupboard, c1870, 78in (198cm) high.
$2,000–2,200 ⊞ HOA

An Irish pine panelled cupboard, with four original interior shelves, c1880, 44in (112cm) wide.
$850–950 ⊞ MIN

▶ **An Irish glazed pine cupboard,** Co Mayo, c1880, 48in (122cm) wide.
$800–900 ⊞ HON

An Irish pine linen press, c1875, 48in (122cm) wide.
$1,000–1,200 ⊞ Byl

A pine wardrobe, c1880, 40in (101.5cm) wide.
$700–800 ⊞ AL

▶ **An Irish pine two-door cupboard,** c1880, 45in (114.5cm) wide.
$450–550 ⊞ Byl

A pine kitchen cupboard, the two panelled doors with six drawers below, c1890, 38in (96.5cm) wide. **$450–500** ⊞ POT

A pine two-door cupboard, c1890, 54in (137cm) wide. **$1,000–1,200** ⊞ AL

A pine box cupboard, with iron bands and original handles, c1900, 41in (104cm) wide. **$350–400** ⊞ AL

A Dutch pine food cupboard, with a single door and three drawers, c1900, 36in (91.5cm) wide. **$400–450** ⊞ P&T

A Hungarian glazed pine hanging cupboard, c1900, 40in (101.5cm) wide. **$300–350** ⊞ MIN

An Austrian pine double wardrobe, with a single drawer below and carved cornice and legs, c1900, 44in (112cm) wide. **$725–800** ⊞ P&T

An Irish pine and elm dresser, early 19thC, 98in (249cm) high. **$1,500–1,750 ⊞ HOA**

An Irish pine fiddle-front dresser, c1865, 46in (117cm) wide. **$800–1,000 ⊞ Byl**

A pitch pine dresser, the base with panelled doors flanking a dog kennel, c1870, 64in (162.5cm) wide. **$1,000–1,200 ⊞ POT**

An Irish pine dresser, Connemara, Co Galway, c1870, 65in (142cm) wide. **$1,500–1,750 ⊞ HON**

An Irish pine dresser, Co Donegal, c1870, 53in (124.5cm) wide. **$650–800 ⊞ Byl**

▶ **A Cornish pine dresser,** with original glass doors and fruitwood handles, c1880, 69in (175.5cm) wide. **$6,000–7,000 ⊞ MIN**

An Irish pine dresser, c1870, 55in (139.5cm) wide. **$800–1,000 ⊞ Byl**

An Irish pine shop-drawer unit, c1875, 86in (218.5cm) wide. **$2,000–2,400 ⊞ Byl**

A pine dresser, with two drawers above two double doors, c1880, 67in (170cm) wide. **$1,500–1,750 ⊞ MIN**

◀ **A pine dresser,** with two drawers over two double doors, c1890, 77in (195.5cm) wide. **$2,000–2,400 ⊞ MIN**

▶ **A Continental pine dresser,** c1910, 51in (129.5cm) wide. **$850–1,000 ⊞ Sam**

A Scottish pine dresser base, the central door and drawers flanked by turned columns, c1850, 56in (142cm) wide.
$1,000–1,200 ⊞ P&T

A pine dresser base, with two doors and four drawers, base and back replaced, c1860, 65in (165cm) wide.
$1,000–1,200 ⊞ AL

A Lincolnshire pine chiffonier, with a carved backboard, c1870, 59in (150cm) wide.
$1,600–1,800 ⊞ MIN

A pine server, with a central recessed cupboard, c1870, 52in (132cm) wide.
$400–500 ⊞ HON

▶ **An Irish pine chiffonier,** with a carved top, c1875, 41in (104cm) wide.
$350–450 ⊞ Byl

A pine bureau, c1850, 36in (91.5cm) wide.
$1,400–1,600 ⊞ AL

A pine bureau, 19thC, 48in (122cm) wide.
$850–1,000 ⊞ HOA

A pine kneehole desk, with original turned knobs, on bun feet, 1870, 42in (106.5cm) wide.
$800–1,000 ⊞ POT

◀ **A pine knee-hole desk,** 1880, 52in (132cm) wide.
$500–600 ⊞ Byl

▶ **A pine knee-hole desk,** with an inset green leather top, c1890, 50in (127cm) wide.
$850–1,000 ⊞ TPC

A Hungarian pine kneehole desk, with five real and two dummy drawers, c1890, 55in (139.5cm) wide.
$850–1,000 ⊞ MIN

An Austrian pine desk, with fitted drawers to interior, c1900, 55in (139.5cm) wide.
$850–1,000 ⊞ POT

An Italian carved pine settle, restored, 18thC, 57in (145cm) wide. **$11,000–13,000** ⚒ S(S)

A Welsh pine box settle, c1830, 55in (139.5cm) wide. **$850–1,000** ⊞ POT

An Irish pine settle, Co Kerry, c1860, 56in (142cm) wide. **$800–950** ⊞ HON

An east European pine box settle, c1875, 77in (195.5cm) wide. **$800–950** ⊞ P&T

An Irish pine settle bed, c1875, 72in (183cm) wide. **$450–550** ⊞ Byl

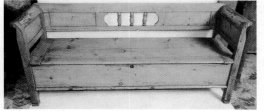

◀ **A pine church pew,** with brass fittings, c1900, 65in (165cm) wide. **$400–500** ⊞ MIN

▶ **An Irish pine settle,** c1880, 71in (180.5cm) wide. **$700–800** ⊞ Byl

◄ **A pine table,** c1810, 108in (274.5cm) long. **$1,100–1,200** ⊞ **TP**

► **A pine wash-stand,** with a central drawer, c1850, 36in (91.5cm) wide. **$220–250** ⊞ **P&T**

A pine kitchen table, with a single drawer, c1870, 47in (119.5cm) long. **$400–450** ⊞ **POT**

A pine table, with a single drawer, c1875, 41in (104cm) long. **$700–800** ⊞ **P&T**

A pine drop-leaf table, c1875, 40in (101.5cm) diam. **$250–300** ⊞ **Byl**

A pine table, with a single drawer and turned and fluted beech legs, c1880, 45in (114.5cm) wide. **$425–475** ⊞ **AL**

A pine drop-leaf table, on turned legs, c1880, 47in (119.5cm) diam. **$600–660** ⊞ **AL**

A pine cricket table, c1880, 24in (61cm) wide. **$150–175** ⊞ **Byl**

A pine gateleg table, with turned legs, the two drawers with steel handles, 19thC, 65in (165cm) extended. **$1,200–1,400** ⊞ **MLL**

A pine table, with two drawers, c1880, 59in (150cm) long. **$120–140** ⊞ **AL**

A pitch pine writing table, with a leather top and one drawer, on turned legs, c1900, 31in (78.5cm) wide. **$400–450** ⊞ **AL**

A pine work table, with a slatted under-tier, c1920, 42in (106.5cm) long. **$425–475** ⊞ **AL**

A pine table, with turned legs, c1900, 45in (114.5cm) long. **$250–275** ⊞ **POT**

► **A pine side table,** on turned legs, with a dummy drawer, c1900, 28in (71cm) wide. **$160–180** ⊞ **P&T**

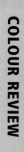

A pine washstand, with a single drawer, c1800, 30in (76cm) wide. **$320–360** ⊞ P&T

A pine dressing chest, with two short over two long drawers, c1880, 40in (101.5cm) wide. **$520–580** ⊞ P&T

A pine dressing table, with a circular mirror, c1890, 38in (96.5cm) wide. **$800–880** ⊞ AL

A Victorian pine washstand, with a single drawer, 33in (84cm) wide. **$200–230** ⊞ POT

A pine washstand, with a tiled back, c1890, 36in (91.5cm) wide. **$500–550** ⊞ AL

An Irish pine washstand/server, c1890, 34in (86.5cm) wide. **$230–280** ⊞ Byl

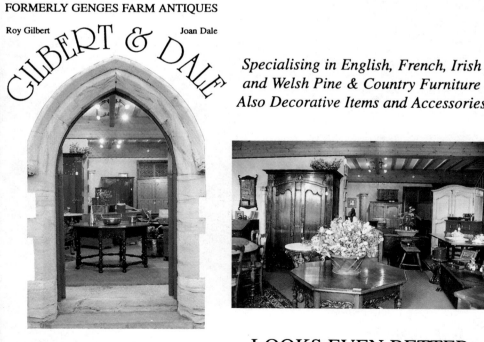

COLOUR REVIEW

A brass and iron servant's bell, c1920, 13in (33cm) high.
$175–200 ⊞ SMI

An oak dough bin, on a stand with turned legs, c1880, 38in (96.5cm) wide.
$600–660 ⊞ MLL

A copper castellated jelly mould, 1870, 3in (7.5cm) high.
$110–140 ⊞ WeA

A tin nutmeg grater, with wooden handles, c1880, 5in (12.5cm) wide.
$100–120 ⊞ WeA

A carved sycamore bread board, c1870, 12in (30.5cm) diam.
$140–160 ⊞ SMI

A brass and iron goffering iron, c1820, 10in (25.5cm) high.
$450–500 ⊞ SEA

A Georgian copper kettle, c1800, 14in (35.5cm) high.
$500–600 ⊞ SEA

A painted pine salt box, mid-19thC, 9in (23cm) wide.
$180–200 ⊞ SMI

◄ **A set of five brass scoops,** c1880, largest 8¼in (21cm) high.
$100–120 ⊞ BLA

► **A tin and brass spice container,** c1870, 6in (15cm) diam.
$110–140 ⊞ WeA

A French Savoie pottery casserole, c1900, 8in (20.5cm) high.
$60–75 ⊞ MLL

A French set of five enamel storage jars, 1920–30, 7in (18cm) high.
$120–145 ⊞ AL

A copper and tin jelly mould, in the shape of a pineapple flanked by other fruit, 1880, 8in (20.5cm) wide.
$200–240 ⊞ WeA

A bone pastry marker, c1870, 5in (12.5cm) wide
$110–140 ⊞ WeA

A set of cast-iron sweet scales, with brass pans and weights, late 19thC, 14in (35.5cm) wide.
$140–170 ⊞ SMI

Jardinières

**A pair of pearlware plant pots
and stands,** in the style of Ralph
Wood, decorated with applied masks
and festoons in shades of green
and brown on a mottled ground,
cracked and chipped, late 18thC,
5½in (14cm) high.
1,600–1,750 ⚘ **CMS**

A Minton majolica jardinière, shape
No. 1023, with six lion-mask and ring
handles on vertical strapwork terminating
in paw feet, in shades of brown and
green on a cobalt blue ground, haircrack, restoration to feet, impressed
and inscribed numerals and letters,
1866, 11in (28cm) high.
$2,600–3,200 ⚘ **S**

**A George Jones majolica plant pot
and stand,** modelled as a tree trunk,
decorated with trailing ivy and twisted
rope surround, chipped and damaged,
'GJ' monogram to base, late 19thC,
8½in (21.5cm) high.
$440–500 ⚘ **RPI**

A majolica jardinière, moulded in
relief with a continuous border of
white water lilies and green lily-pads,
and turquoise-glazed interior, restuck
section to rim, minor chips, impressed
numeral '2', possibly by Joseph
Holdcroft, c1870, 17in (43cm) wide.
2,600–3,000 ⚘ **S**

A Wedgwood majolica jardinière,
modelled in relief with a laurel garland
band, on a blue ground, beneath a
basket-moulded border, with yellow
details, rim chip, impressed marks,
1871, 15in (38cm) wide.
$900–1,100 ⚘ **LFA**

A Continental majolica jardinière,
relief-decorated with sinuous flowers
in pink, yellow and white on a brown
ground, with a blue rim, 19thC,
7in (18cm) wide.
$150–180 ⊞ **MLL**

◄ **A Continental
majolica jardinière,**
in the form of a
winged female
sphinx, a mask
between her paws,
painted in brown,
green, blue and
mustard, late
19thC, 12½in
(31.8cm) high.
$160–200 ⚘ **P(S)**

► **A Continental
majolica jardinière,**
decorated with
trailing ivy on
a green ground,
c1900, 11in
(28cm) wide.
350–400 ⊞ **MLL**

◄ **A Royal Bonn
jardinière,** the
shoulders painted
with a band
of red double
gourds, the body
with passion
flowers and
flowering vines
on a blue ground,
c1900, 16¼in
(41.5cm) wide.
$115–145 ⚘ **CGC**

POTTERY

Jugs

A medieval pottery jug, the upper section glazed in green, Humberside, 13th/14thC, 10in (25.5cm) high.
$2,300–2,600 ⊞ JHo

A coarseware drinking jug, the rim and upper body decorated with a deep olive green glaze, probably 15thC, 5in (12.5cm) high.
$750–900 ⚒ F&C

A German salt-glazed stoneware bellarmine, with orange-peel glaze, 1680–90, 9in (23cm) high.
$440–500 ⚒ RBB

A Rhenish Elector stone-ware jug, decorated with a band of figures and armorial crests in arched reserves, with a hinged pewter cover and mounts to base rim, chipped, 1602, 14½in (37cm) high.
$2,600–3,000 ⚒ P(EA)

A Westerwald salt-glazed commemorative stoneware jug, with a medallion moulded with a crowned 'GR' cypher within incised and partly-underglaze blue floral decoration, the reeded neck with manganese decoration, the body incised '3', early 18thC, 8½in (21.5cm) high.
$900–1,100 ⚒ PFK

A Staffordshire salt-glazed stoneware baluster jug and cover, with a bird-shaped knop and three lion-mask and paw feet, the body and cover decorated with an applied moulded anthemion and trellis pattern, 1750–60, 5¾in (14.5cm) high.
$600–700 ⚒ WW

▶ **A Staffordshire blue jug,** slight damage, c1765, 6½in (16.5cm) high.
$1,800–2,000 ⊞ JHo

A Staffordshire salt-glazed cream jug, each side moulded with a shell, the spout with a pair of snails above two rows of shells, decorated in blue, green, pink and brown enamels, raised on three claw feet, 1750–60, 3¾in (9.5cm) high.
$2,600–3,000 ⚒ S

A Liverpool creamware jug, transfer-printed in black with 'John Magee and the Liberty of the Press', c1790, 10in (25.5cm) high.
$6,500–7,500 ⊞ JHo
John Magee was the proprietor and printer in Dublin of *Magee's Weekly Packet* (1777) and the *Dublin Evening Post* (1779). A notable Whig and most violent critic of the government, he was arraigned in 1789 on a trumped-up libel charge brought by Francis Higgins, a journalist in the pay of the government, and by Richard Daley of the Crow Street Theatre. The trial began on 3 July 178 and Magee was found guilty on his refusal to plead. Released pending sentence, Magee continued to attack the government, and on 3 September he was re-arrested and committed to Newgate Prison, from whence he was released on bail of $580 on 29 October. Finally, in the following year on 29 February, he was sentenced to six months for contempt of court. H case provoked considerab fury in Ireland.

A Liverpool creamware jug and cover, transfer-printed in black with 'The Blessings of Peace', depicting a mother reading to her children, with revellers in the background celebrating the harvest, the reverse with a rustic scene, minor damage, c1790, 11¾in (30cm) high.
$1,100–1,300 ⚒ Bon(C)

A Liverpool creamware jug, transfer-printed in black with 'The Gipsy Fortune Teller', c1790, 5¼in (13.5cm) high.
$500–550 ⊞ JHo

A Liverpool creamware jug, transfer-printed in black with scenes of 'Summer' and 'Winter', c1790, 7¼in (18.5cm) high.
$725–800 ⊞ JHo

A Farmers' Arms jug, transfer-printed in black and polychrome painted with motto and inscriptions, a ploughing scene, a tavern scene and two drinking rhymes, damaged, c1790, 10½in (26.5cm) high.
$600–700 ⚒ Bon(C)

A Turner stoneware jug, the lower section decorated with a rustic scene, 1795–1810, 6in (15cm) high.
$800–900 ⊞ SEA

A Prattware jug, painted in typical colours with a thatched farm building flanked by haystacks, inscribed 'I W 1805', the reverse with a floral spray, chipped, 7½in (19cm) high.
$1,200–1,400 ⚒ P
Prattware is distinguished by a bold, high-temperature palette that comprises yellow-ochre, blue, green and muddy brown.

A Leeds documentary jug, with polychrome floral sprays and 'Benjamin & Martha Dean 1802' to one side, the reverse with an inscription, 6½in (16.5cm) high.
$1,000–1,100 ⚒ CDC

A stoneware jug, applied with blue sprigs, floral sprays and triumphal ornaments, possibly Spode, c1815, 9in (23cm) high.
$250–300 ⊞ RAV

▶ **A pink lustre jug,** transfer-printed in black to commemorate the death of Princess Charlotte, 1817, 6in (15cm) high.
$360–440 ⚒ SAS

An American stoneware jar, with impressed cobalt-blue swag and tassel decoration and 'Boston 1804', faults, 14¼in (36cm) high.
$2,600–3,200 ⚒ SK(B)
While not attracting much interest in the UK, the price achieved for this item demonstrates that American ceramics have a strong interest base across the Atlantic. The fact that it is impressed with a date and place of origin explains the high price for a somewhat simple object.

A Staffordshire creamware jug, transfer-printed in puce with a portrait of the Duke of Leinster, c1804, 7in (18cm) high.
$2,000–2,200 ⊞ JHo

A pair of Davenport ironstone jugs, decorated with Japan pattern in blue, orange and black on a white ground, printed anchor mark, early 19thC, 5½in (14cm) high.
$440–500 ⊞ ACO

A Spode jug, transfer-printed en grisaille with battle scenes of Sir George Brown at Alma and Sebastopol, early 19thC, 7½in (19cm) high.
$250–300 ⚒ GAK

A Staffordshire lustre jug, both sides transfer-printed in black with a man, woman and shepherd with sheep before a country house, with silver-lustre borders and a star motif beneath the spout, on a pale yellow ground, slight damage, 19thC, 5¼in (13.5cm) high.
$115–145 ⚒ WW

A Goodwin, Bridgwood & Harris jug, commemorating the death of King George IV, transfer-printed in black with a portrait, chipped, 1830, 5in (12.5cm) high.
$360–440 ⚒ SAS

POTTERY

Lustreware

Lustre is a type of decoration formed when metallic oxides are applied to pottery after an original firing then re-heated at a lower temperature to produce a metallic-type glaze. Dating back to ancient times, and subsequently used on Spanish pottery in the 15th century and in Italy during the Renaissance, lustre was not actually introduced into Britain until the early 19th century. At that time it could be categorized into three types: silver lustre, pink or purple lustre, and bronze, copper or gold lustre. Staffordshire and Sunderland were main centres of production, although many wares are inaccurately ascribed to the latter because of the views they portray.

A Sunderland lustre jug, the reserves transfer-printed with a galleon, the reverse with 'Health to the Sick, Honour to the Brave, Success to the Lover and Freedom to the Slave', 19thC, 5in (12.5cm) high.
$320–380 ➤ **DA**

A Minton wash jug, polychrome decorated with flowers and birds, c1830, 15in (38cm) high.
$1,000–1,300 ⊞ **SCO**

A Swansea pearlware jug, decorated with brightly coloured flowers and leaves, c1830, 6in (15cm) high.
$500–600 ⊞ **RdV**

A Sunderland pink lustre jug, inscribed 'The Aga-memnon in a Storm' and 'Ancient Order of Foresters', c1830, 5½in (14cm) high.
$250–300 ➤ **WW**

A pottery jug, moulded and painted with scenes of the lion tamer Van Amburgh and his lions, with a lion-shaped handle, spout restored, 1839, 8¼in (21cm) high.
$130–160 ➤ **SAS**

A brown-glazed slipware puzzle jug, 19thC, 7½in (19cm) high.
$250–300 ➤ **SWO**

A Mocha ware jug, decorated with fern-like patterns in underglaze blue and brown, on a coffee-coloured ground, mid-19thC, 8¼in (21cm) high.
$575–650 ➤ **Bea(E)**

A Sunderland pink lustre jug, decorated to one side with a west view of the Iron Bridge over the Wear, the reverse with a Masonic poem within a floral border, chipped, mid-19thC, 7in (18cm) high.
$250–300 ➤ **MCA**

A Staffordshire copper lustre jug, decorated with bands of flowers and leaves in green, yellow and pink, on a white ground, c1850, 5½in (14cm) high.
$100–120 ⊞ **SER**

A Paris Exhibition commemorative stone china jug, relief-moulded with the coats-of-arms of the exhibiting nations, decorated with gilt and coloured enamels, 1855, 14½in (37cm) high.
$1,200–1,400 ➤ **DN**
This design has been linked with the Alcock firm although there is little evidence to support such an attribution. This large coloured version appears to be very rare and may have been an exhibition piece; smaller versions in plain stone-ware, usually white and unmarked, are known but uncommon.

A Minton majolica ewer, shape No. 434, the handle and body moulded with trailing vines in green and cream on a light brown ground, the interior glazed in light blue, marked, 1860, 8¾in (22cm) high.
$440–500 ➤ **Bea(E)**

A Staffordshire jug, transfer-printed in purple with passion flowers and foliage, printed mark for Jonathan Lowe Chetham, mid-19thC, 17in (43cm) wide.
$440–500 ➤ **WW**

A stoneware puzzle jug, with sprig-moulded decoration of tavern scenes to one side, the reverse with a figure smoking a long pipe and holding keys, 19thC, 7½in (19cm) high.
$600–700 ➤ **Mit**

▶ **An Elsmore & Forster jug,** transfer-printed in black and overpainted in enamels with two jesters and various animals including cats, frogs, birds and monkeys, printed Royal Arms mark, c1860, 9¼in (23.5cm) high.
$300–350 ➤ **CGC**

A set of four Old Hall York Minster stoneware jugs, with Gothic designs of two groups of the Holy Family within columns, spires and pinnacles, embossed marks 'OHECL' Hanley', 1861–65, largest 9in (23cm) high.
$800–900 ⚒ P(Ba)
The Old Hall Earthenware Co continued Charles Meigh's works in Hanley and produced many of Meigh's earlier jug designs. The York Minster jug was one of the most successful Meigh jugs and epitomises the taste of mid-Victorian England.

A Sunderland pink lustre jug, transfer-printed in black with the Sailor's Farewell, the Cast Iron Bridge and the Mariner's Compass, within pink lustre cartouches, spout chipped, 19thC, 9in (23cm) high.
$500–600 ⚒ AG
Pieces relating to a specific place often achieve higher prices.

A majolica jug, with green, brown and yellow marbled glaze and yellow rope-shaped handle, and a pewter lid, numbered '2777' to base, late 19thC, 9¾in (25cm) high.
$150–175 ⚒ CDC

A Staffordshire advertising jug, transfer-printed in brown with 'McNish's Doctors Special Whisky' on a blue ground, the base heightened with gilt, late 19thC, 8in (20.5cm) high.
$600–700 ⚒ AH

A Mason's Ironstone jug, polychrome decorated with a flying bird among Oriental flowers, with a blue and gilt handle, c1880, 10in (25.5cm) high.
$500–550 ⚒ JP

◄ **A Scottish majolica jug,** with spiral moulding, and decorated in relief with pink flowers on a brown and yellow ground, probably Alloa, c1880, 8in (20.5cm) high.
$100–115 ⚒ P(Ed)

An Old Hall Prince Consort white stoneware jug, embossed with a portrait of Prince Albert, the reverse with his armorial bearings, reserved on a textile ground hung with his various orders, the handle modelled as further orders and insignia, restored lip, embossed mark and 'OHECL', c1862, 10¼in (26cm) high.
$300–350 ⚒ P(Ba)
This jug was made to commemorate the death of the Prince Consort in December 1861.

Cross Reference
See Colour Review
(page 292)

A pink lustre jug, commemorating the Crimean War, transfer-printed and decorated with flags and an armorial design, with inscription relating to G. A. Gardner, handle rivetted, 1867, 5½in (14cm) high.
$300–350 ⚒ SER

A Staffordshire Garibaldi jug, moulded and painted in colours with motifs of Garibaldi on horseback, the handle modelled as a flag, c1860, 10in (25.5cm) high.
$350–450 ⚒ GAK

POTTERY

A majolica jug, decorated in relief with a fan and prunus in pink and brown on a textured turquoise ground, with a brown branch handle and pink interior, c1880, 7½in (19cm) high.
$145–175 ✗ P(Ed)

An American ironstone pitcher, decorated in enamels and gilt with landscape scenes and a titled cartouche below the spout inscribed 'Senator Martin Wyckoff, of Warren County', on a wine red ground, impressed mark 'U Pottery', c1885, 10in (25.5cm) high.
$500–600 ✗ SK

An earthenware ewer, enamelled in Limoges style in white enamels with interlaced scroll and formal ornament including three masks with pendant fruit swags, on a black ground heightened with gilt, probably by Thomas John Bott for Brown-Westhead, Moore, c1889, 10½in (26.5cm) high.
$1,600–1,750 ✗ S
Thomas John Bott (1854–1932), was the son of Thomas Bott, one of the greatest exponents of the Limoges enamelling style in the second half of the 19th century. Working for the Royal Worcester porcelain factory, Bott senior (1829–70) provided some outstanding examples for the international exhibitions at this time. His son, of the same name, was also employed by the Worcester factory between 1870 and 1886, working in his father's style. He joined Brown-Westhead, Moore & Co for a short time in 1889 and later became the art director at Coalport (1890–1932).

A Dunmore amphora, the body with a dark green glaze, marked, Scotland, c1890, 13¾in (35cm) high.
$300–350 ✗ P(Ed)

A Continental jug, modelled as a pig, with a pink ham suspended from a blue band, the handle modelled as a green leaf, c1890, 8in (20.5cm) high.
$230–260 ⊞ MLL

A Brannam pottery jug, commemorating the Hungarian Millennial Exhibition, Budapest, decorated in pink, black and white on a green ground, the spout in the shape of a fish head, 1896, 5½in (14cm) high.
$125–150 ✗ SWO

◄ **A Wemyss jug,** inscribed 'The building rook'll call from the windy tall elm tree', painted in black with birds and 'Earlshall Faire A.D. 1914' within a cartouche, marked, 5¼in (13.5cm) high.
$650–750 ✗ P(Ed)

A Continental majolica jug, modelled as a fish, decorated in shades of green, white and brown, the interior glazed pink, c1900, 10in (25.5cm) high.
$360–420 ⊞ MLL

Loving Cups & Tygs

A Leeds creamware loving cup, inscribed 'I. Barns' and painted with flower sprays beneath a pink border decorated with pink and blue dots, the foot painted with brown bands, slight damage, impressed mark, c1800, 6¼in (16cm) high.
$500–600 ✗ WW

A Bristol salt-glazed stoneware loving cup, inscribed 'Joseph Holbrook' above a relief-decorated hunting scene, c1788, 8in (20.5cm) high.
$1,600–1,750 ⊞ JHo

A Nottingham brown-glazed loving cup, sgraffito-decorated with stylized flowers, 1779, 9in (23cm) high.
$2,300–2,600 ⊞ JHo

A Staffordshire copper lustre loving cup, decorated with blue bands of trailing foliage, c1840, 4½in (11.5cm) high.
$85–95 ⊞ SER

► **A Wemyss tyg,** painted with Tulips pattern in shades of orange, yellow and green, impressed mark, c1910, 5¾in (14.5cm) high.
$800–1,000 ✗ P(Ed)

◄ **A Staffordshire copper lustre tyg,** decorated with a blue band and central motif, 1840–60, 6in (15cm) high.
$180–200 ⊞ SER

Mugs & Tankards

A Bristol stoneware brown-glazed mug, moulded in relief with a figure, sheep and trees, dated '1754', 8in (20.5cm) high.
£4,500–5,500 ⊞ JHo

A Wedgwood black basalt ware mug, moulded with oak leaves and acorns, small crack, impressed mark, late 18thC, 7½in (19cm) high.
$1,100–1,300 ⋟ WW

A creamware tankard, moulded with fluted panels and decorated in shades of pink, with beaded borders, c1780, 5in (12.5cm) high.
$850–1,000 ⋟ Bon(C)

A Sunderland lustre frog mug, decorated with a commemorative print of the opening of the Iron Bridge, with bands of pink splash-lustre, the interior with a sponged brown frog to the base, minor chips, c1830, 4¾in (12cm) high.
$250–300 ⋟ P(Ba)

A creamware mug, inscribed 'Bartholamew & Eliz'h Fenwick Ryton, Let Love abide Till death divide, 1824', decorated with floral sprigs in orange, yellow, green and brown, foot chip, 5½in (14cm) high.
£450–500 ⋟ WW

A Mettlach Stein, poly-chrome decorated with Venus against a target and a town scene, 1890–1900, 7¼in (18.5cm) high.
$1,000–1,200 ⊞ PGA

A Wemyss Queen Victoria Diamond Jubilee commemorative mug, painted in red and green and inscribed 'Nae sic Queen was ever seen VR 1837–1897', between borders of leaves, painted monogram 'HEW', impressed mark 'Wemyss R. H. & S.', printed Goode's mark, 1897, 6in (15cm) high.
$180–230 ⋟ P(Ed)

A Wemyss mug, painted with Geese Feeding pattern in shades of green and puce, impressed mark 'Wemyss Ware R. H. & S.', c1900, 5½in (14cm) high.
$1,300–1,450 ⋟ S

A Wemyss mug, painted with pink Roses pattern, impressed and painted Wemyss marks, printed Goode's mark, 5¾in (14.5cm) high.
£350–450 ⋟ P(Ed)

▶ **A Wemyss mug,** painted with Cocks and Hens pattern in brown and green, c1900, 6in (15cm) high.
$600–700 ⊞ RdeR

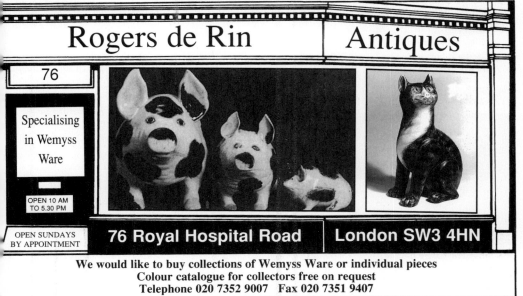

Plaques

A pair of pearlware plaques, moulded in relief with portraits of Catherine the Great and Peter III, with blue-painted details, rim chips, c1796, 6¾in (17cm) high.
$800–1,100 ⚶ S(S)

A Sunderland pearlware lustre commemorative plaque, possibly Middlesborough/North East England, the spotted purple lustre ground reserved with a portrait of Queen Caroline wearing Prince of Wales' feathers, between 'QC', hairline rim crack, incised mark, c1820, 6in (15cm) high.
$600–700 ⚶ RTo

A Sunderland lustre plaque, with puce border, inscribed 'Thou God, See'st Me' within a garland, mid-19thC, 8½in (21.5cm) wide.
$175–200 ⚶ GAK

A Sunderland lustre plaque, inscribed in black 'Prepare to Meet Thy God', within a garland and with a gold border, c1870, 8¼in (21cm) wide.
$100–120 ⊞ SER

A pair of Staffordshire portrait plaques, commemorating the marriage of Princess Charlotte and Prince Leopold, enamelled in bright colours, the moulded black and green borders simulating frames, frame chip repainted, 1816–17, 7½in (19cm) high.
$4,500–5,000 ⚶ P
Only a small number of pieces were made to commemorate the wedding of Princess Charlotte, daughter of the Prince Regent (later George IV), to Prince Leopold of Saxe Coburg, who were married on 2 May 1816. These may date from the following year when Charlotte died.

A Sunderland lustre plaque, decorated with flowers and an exotic bird in shades of pink, green, blue and yellow, mid-19thC, 8in (20.5cm) wide.
$250–300 ⊞ IS

A pair of Sèvres-style earthenware plaques, painted with rustic scenes of children at play, in pastel colours within gilt and blue bands, small chips, marked, late 19thC, 7½in (19cm) wide, in giltwood frames.
$1,000–1,200 ⚶ S(S)

A Sunderland lustre plaque, transfer-printed and decorated in colours with the Waverley design, mid-19thC, 9in (23cm) wide.
$300–350 ⚶ GAK

A Low Lights Pottery plaque, by John Carr, depicting the Revd John Knox, impressed mark 'Vedgwood', c1838, 6½in (16.5cm) high.
$350–400 ⊞ IS

A pink lustre plaque, attributed to Anthony Scott, Southwick, Sunderland, decorated with 'The Great Eastern Steam-Ship', in brown, yellow and green, c1860, 9in (23cm) wide.
$500–600 ⊞ IS
The Great Eastern was launched in 1858.

A Castle Hedingham plaque, moulded in relief with a panel depicting children and dogs within a foliate border, incised marks, 1864–1901, 8in (20.5cm) wide.
$300–330 ⚶ CGC

POTTERY

Pot Lids

The Beehive, No. 130, by F. & R. Pratt, inscribed Healey & Coys Celebrated Crystalized Honey Cream' n gold, decorated in yellow, blue and pink within gold and blue bands, c1850, 4½in (11.5cm) diam.
$2,000–2,300 ➢ SAS

Lady with Hawk, No. 106, depicting a lady with a striped bodice, c1855, 4½in (11.5cm) diam.
$250–300 ➢ SAS

Garibaldi, No. 169, by F. & R. Pratt, polychrome decorated with Garibaldi holding the Italian flag, 1864, 4in (10cm) diam.
$95–110 ⊞ SER

Children Sailing a Boat in a Tub, No. 263, by F. & R. Pratt, brown transfer-printed and painted in blue, 1880, 3in (7.5cm) diam.
$100–120 ⊞ JBL

▶ **Imperial Hotel, Russell Sq, London,** green transfer-printed with a view of the hotel, two chips repaired, late 19thC, 2½in (6.5cm) diam.
$130–160 ➢ BBR

St Paul's Cathedral with Lord Mayor's Show, No. 185, by F. & R. Pratt, late 19thC, 4¾in (12cm) diam, framed.
$100–120 ➢ DN

Napirima, Trinidad, No. 225, by F. & R. Pratt, 19thC, 4½in (11.5cm) diam.
$230–260 ➢ GAK

Master of the Hounds, No. 247, by F. & R. Pratt, 19thC, 4in (10cm) diam.
$90–115 ➢ GAK

Dr Zeimer's Alexandra Tooth Paste, with a portrait of Princess Alexandra, late 19thC, 3in (7.5cm) diam.
$110–125 ➢ BBR

Bear, Lion and Cock, No. 19, by F. & R. Pratt, depicting a lion threatening a chained and muzzled bear, c1854, 3¼in (8.5cm) diam.
$120–140 ⊞ SER

Uncle Toby, No. 328, by F. & R. Pratt, depicting a gentleman wearing a lilac coat and gold waist-coat and a girl wearing a green dress, 1860–70, 4in (10cm) diam.
$85–95 ⊞ SER

Strasburg, No. 331, by F. & R. Pratt, painted in polychrome colours with a river scene, within a marbled border, c1855, 5in (12.5cm) diam.
$100–120 ⊞ JBL

Prince of Wales and Princess Alexandra, No. 157, by F. & R. Pratt, commemorating their marriage,1863, 4¼in (11cm) diam, framed.
$75–85 ➢ DN
This lid is the early edition without the Greek key border.

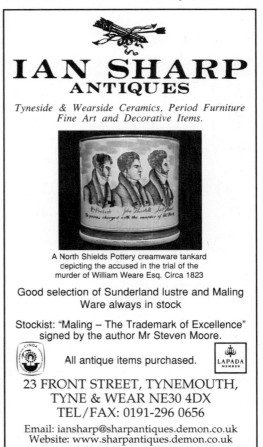

POTTERY

Sauce Boats

A Staffordshire white salt-glazed stoneware sauce boat, moulded with anthemion, flowers and diaper panels, with cobalt blue detail, some chips, mid-18thC, 6¼in (16cm) long.
$1,700–2,000 ♦ S(S)

A white salt-glazed sauce boat, moulded with relief decoration, 1765, 3½in (9cm) high.
$550–650 ⊞ JHo

A pink lustre sauce boat, decorated in pink and green on a white ground, c1840, 6in (15cm) wide.
$50–65 ⊞ AL

Services

A Wedgwood Queen's Ware part tea and coffee service, comprising 23 pieces, painted in shades of brown and blue with a band of stylized hairbells, some damage, impressed marks, associated cover to coffee pot, late 18thC.
$1,300–1,450 ♦ DN

A Copeland earthenware botanical dessert service, comprising 17 pieces, transfer-printed in puce and enamelled in colours, within a bright red border, the rims and feet moulded with gadrooning heightened in red, three plates cracked, impressed factory mark and enamelled numerals, mid-19thC.
$1,000–1,150 ♦ Bon(C)

A Pratt pottery part dessert service, comprising eight pieces, the borders transfer-printed with oak leaves within a gilt rim, enclosing polychrome prints after early 19thC artists, handles cracked and restuck, late 19thC.
$650–800 ♦ Hal

► **A Mason's dinner service,** pattern No. B4540, comprising 56 pieces, the deep blue border decorated with pink flowers and green leaves, early 20thC.
$1,600–1,800 ♦ WW

A Mason's Ironstone mazarine-blue part dinner service, comprising 23 pieces, decorated with gilt flower sprays, some pieces with impressed marks, c1820.
$1,600–1,750 ♦ WW

A Ridgway ironstone part dinner service, decorated with Simlay pattern, comprising 152 pieces, printed and painted in Imari colours with a chinoiserie vase with flowers beside Oriental flowering shrubs, damaged, printed marks, late 19thC.
$3,500–4,500 ♦ DN

A Sarreguemines majolica dessert service, comprising seven pieces, decorated with fruits, impressed marks 'V/531W', France, late 19thC.
$200–250 ♦ PFK

A Mason's Ironstone part dinner service, decorated with Japan pattern comprising ten pieces, printed and impressed marks, minor damage, c1820.
$1,200–1,400 ♦ LFA

A Wedgwood creamware dessert service, pattern No. A4933/9, comprising 17 pieces, decorated with grapevines, the bases stamped 'Wedgwood' with printed mark 'James Powell & Sons', late 19thC.
$1,000–1,200 ♦ EH

An Ashworth Ironstone dinner service, comprising 19 pieces, transfer-printed and painted with a floral pattern, 19thC.
$1,800–2,200 ♦ RBB

An Ashworth Real Ironstone China dinner service, pattern No. R/3194, comprising 80 pieces, decorated with chinoiserie flowers in iron-red, black and purple, some damage, impressed and printed marks, c1900.
$1,200–1,400 ♦ TRL

Tea Canisters

A Bovey Tracey creamware tea canister, three sides moulded in high relief with Ceres in a scrolling cartouche, the fourth side inscribed 'Sarah Bronning 1772' between flower sprays, the corners applied with flower terminals, some damage, 5½in (14cm) high.
$4,000–4,500 ↗ S

A Prattware tea canister, moulded in relief with macaroni figures, the silver cover with a bright-cut border, c1790, 5in (12.5cm) high.
$450–500 ↗ P(Ba)
It is unusual to find this canister with a silver cover.

A tea canister, transfer-printed in brown with a lady and a dog with a house in the background, late 19thC, 4½in (11.5cm) high.
$100–120 ↗ SWO

Further reading
Miller's Ceramics Buyer's Guide,
Miller's Publications, 2000

Tea & Coffee Pots

A Staffordshire agate ware Whieldon type teapot, modelled as a shell, c1755, 5in (12.5cm) high.
$5,000–5,500 ⊞ JRe
The generic term 'Whieldon type wares' is used to describe lead-glazed pottery with a cream-coloured body and underglaze colouring of green, grey, brown and slate blue. Although it is named after the Staffordshire manufacturer Thomas Whieldon he was, in fact, just one of several makers of this type of pottery, which was also produced in Yorkshire, Devon, Scotland and Belfast.

A Staffordshire white salt-glazed teapot, with relief-moulded decoration, 1745, 4½in (11.5cm) high.
$5,000–5,500 ⊞ JHo

A creamware teapot, decorated in blue, green and red with a vase of flowers to one side, the reverse with a floral spray, the reeded cross-over handle applied to the joints with flower sprays, repaired and chipped, c1770, 5¼in (13.5cm) high.
$430–470 ↗ P(Ba)

A Leeds creamware teapot, decorated with cream vertical stripes on black bands, c1770, 10in (25.5cm) high.
$5,000–5,500 ⊞ JHo

Items in the Pottery section have been arranged in date order within each sub-section.

A Leeds creamware teapot, painted in pink, red, yellow and green with floral sprays, the spout with stiff-leaf moulding, restored, c1780, 5¾in (14.5cm) high.
$600–700 ↗ Bon(C)

A pearlware teapot, moulded in relief with neo-classical urns, husks, flowers and scrolls, with enamel detail on a cream ground, inscribed 'P. D. 1795', and 'A. D. 1795' to the reverse, damaged, 6½in (16.5cm) high.
$1,000–1,200 ↗ P

▶ **A Dunmore teapot,** splashed in brown, black and green, Scotland, 1870–1900, 5in (12.5cm) high.
$230–260 ⊞ SQA

POTTERY

A Staffordshire majolica teapot, in the shape of a fish, the spout shaped as a smaller fish being swallowed, with polychrome decoration, c1900, 6in (15cm) high.
$360–440 ✗ HYD

A majolica teapot, with elephant mask spout and handle, the sides with glazed chinoiserie panels in shades of blue, brown, green and yellow, late 19thC, 4in (10cm) high.
$900–1,000 ✗ Mit

A Quimper teapot, decorated with a geometric pattern in red, blue, green and yellow, c1925, 7in (18cm) high.
$100–110 ⊞ SER

Toby & Character Jugs

A pair of Staffordshire character jugs, with covers, in the form of Punch and Judy, c1900, 11¾in (30cm) high.
$320–360 ✗ AG

A Portobello Toby jug, wearing a black hat and jacket, plum-coloured shirt and blue breeches, on a green base, Scotland, c1820, 10in (25.5cm) high.
$600–700 ⊞ JBL
The plum colour of the shirt and the black coat are both typical features of the Portobello factory.

A Toby jug, in the form of a snuff-taker, his hat forming the cover, wearing a green jacket and yellow breeches, on a green base, chips, late 19thC, 9¾in (25cm) high.
$500–600 ✗ WW

A Staffordshire Toby jug, wearing a black tricorn hat, speckled cravat, iron-red waistcoat and puce jacket, restored, late 19thC, 11in (28cm) high.
$180–220 ✗ GAK

▶ **A character jug,** in the form of Field Marshall Sir John French, designed by Sir F. Carruthers Gould for Wilkinson, holding a tricolour jug inscribed *'French pour les Francais'*, the base with initials 'FCG', hairline crack, c1918, 10in (25.5cm) high.
$600–700 ✗ DN

Tureens

▶ **A Staffordshire white salt-glazed stoneware tureen,** with tripod lion-mask and paw feet, the body decorated with cabochon punched moulding, chip, mid-18thC, 11¼in (28.5cm) high.
$250–300 ✗ Hal

A Mason's Ironstone tureen, decorated in red, blue and green on a cream ground, c1820, 7in (18cm) wide.
$650–725 ⊞ JP

A Staffordshire creamware pierced tureen, cover and stand, c1770, 9in (23cm) high.
$1,600–1,750 ⊞ JHo

◀ **A pair of Ironstone hexagonal section sauce tureens, covers and stands,** decorated with Water Lily pattern in blue, iron-red, pink, green, gilt and orange, minor damage, early 19thC, 8in (20.5cm) wide.
$600–700 ✗ WW

Vases

A Staffordshire enamelled salt-glazed vase, decorated with flowers in shades of pink and green on a cream ground, c1765, 7in (18cm) high.
$4,400–4,800 ⊞ JHo

A pair of Mason's Ironstone mazarine blue vases, the shoulders applied with gilt handles shaped as roses and buds, decorated in gold with a bird perched among flowering plants, the reverse with moths and flies among grasses, below diaper borders, covers lacking, foot chips, c1825, 7½in (19cm) high.
$450–500 ⚒ P

A pair of Portuguese faïence two-handled vases, painted in blue with stylized fruiting vines on a white ground, the necks with Greek key borders, some restoration, 19thC, 50in (127cm) high.
$5,000–5,500 ⚒ S

A creamware vase and cover, attributed to Wedgwood & Bentley, with applied Bacchus-head handles between fruiting grapevine festoons, on a black basalt plinth, damaged, c1775, 10¼in (26cm) high.
$1,000–1,100 ⚒ SK

A Wedgwood jasper dip vase, the sides sprigged in white with a frieze of classical figures, on a dark blue ground, minor firing faults, impressed mark, 19thC, 16in (40.5cm) high.
$1,800–2,200 ⚒ S(S)

A Wemyss two-handled vase, decorated with Roses pattern, with green handles, impressed mark, c1910, 11in (28cm) high.
$600–700 ⚒ P(Ed)

A pearlware flower vase, with three necks, moulded with painted swags, on twin green dolphin support, early 19thC, 7in (18cm) high.
$250–300 ⚒ WW

A Minton majolica vase, shape No. 827, moulded in relief with male and female masks and flowerhead medallions, above a stiff-leaf moulded band, some restoration to foot, impressed marks, date code for 1864, 14½in (37cm) high.
$3,000–3,500 ⚒ LFA

A Nové faïence vase, the ribbed body painted with polychrome flowers and leafy borders, rim chips, marked 'Nové' with a star, Italy, late 19thC, 9in (23cm) high.
$600–700 ⚒ WW

An amphora pottery vase, in the form of a boy dragging a vase across a rocky base, decorated in pastel colours, Austria, early 20thC, 12in (30.5cm) high.
$200–225 ⚒ CDC

POTTERY

Blue & White Transfer Ware

A Spode blue and white custard cup and cover, transfer-printed with a rural river scene, the cover with a floral border, c1810, 4in (10cm) high.
$300–330 ⊞ US

A blue and white egg cup, transfer-printed with Willow pattern, 1820–30, 2¼in (5.5cm) high.
$145–175 ⊞ AMH

A Cauldon blue and white jardinière transfer-printed with a figure in a chariot before a temple, printed mark early 20thC, 7½in (19cm) wide.
$145–175 ⋏ WW

An Elkin, Knight & Bridgwood blue and white meat plate, transfer-printed with Etruscan pattern, printed mark, early 19thC, 21½in (54.5cm) diam.
$350–450 ⋏ Mit

A blue and white meat plate, transfer-printed with Centaurs Battling Theseus pattern, the borders with Greek vases and figural medallions on a fruiting vine background, probably Spode, c1805, 16½in (42cm) wide.
$450–500 ⋏ Bon(C)

A Jones & Son blue and white dish transfer-printed with Death of Lord Nelson pattern, from the British History Series, with military trophy and floral crown repeating border, on a shaped foot, early 19thC, 11¼in (28.5cm) wide.
$9,500–10,500 ⋏ Bri

A Roger's pearlware blue and white meat plate, transfer-printed with a vase with flowers and fruit, impressed mark, c1820, 21in (53.5cm) wide.
$650–800 ⋏ WW

A blue and white platter, the rim transfer-printed with reserves of arches and architecture, the centre with fishermen and two cows before a house, early 19thC, 17in (43cm) wide.
$650–750 ⋏ CGC

A blue and white plate, attributed to Ridgway, transfer-printed with hop pickers, c1820, 10in (25.5cm) diam.
$400–475 ⊞ GN

A Spode blue and white plate, transfer-printed with Sarcophagi and Sepulchres at the Head of the Harbour at Cacamo pattern, from the Caramanian Series, with a flock of birds in the sky, printed and impressed mark, c1820, 10in (25.5cm) diam.
$220–260 ⋏ P(Ba)

A Spode meat plate, moulded with gravy channels and well, transfer-printed with Girl at the Well pattern, within a floral border, marked, early 19thC, 21in (53.5cm) long.
$450–500 ⋏ PFK

An Andrew Stevenson American view blue and white meat dish, transfer-printed with New York from Heights, Nr Brooklyn pattern, after the design by W. G. Wall, minor restoration with printed American eagle mark with title and designer's name, early 19thC, 16½in (42cm) long.
$2,500–3,000 ⋏ DN

POTTERY

A blue and white platter, transfer-printed with Albion pattern, 19thC, 14½in (37cm) long.
$145–175 ⚒ GAK

A Copeland & Garrett blue and white platter, transfer-printed with Byron's Sprays pattern, 1833–47, 21in (53.5cm) long.
$650–800 ⊞ GN

A Davenport blue and white turkey dish, transfer-printed with a landscape from the British Scenery Series, 19thC, 21in (53.5cm) long.
$320–380 ⚒ G(B)

A George Jones blue and white meat plate, decorated with Spanish Festivities pattern depicting a cock-fighting scene, impressed and printed marks, c1865, 14¼in (36cm) long.
$200–230 ⚒ Bon(C)

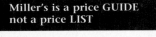

Miller's is a price GUIDE not a price LIST

A Robert Cochran & Co blue and white meat plate, transfer-printed with Syria pattern, printed mark, c1880, 13¾in (35cm) long.
$100–130 ⚒ P(Ed)

◄ A Minton blue and white footbath, transfer-printed with Trellis and Plants pattern, c1825, 20in (51cm) long.
$2,500–3,000 ⊞ GN

A Thomas Godwin blue and white footbath, transfer-printed with Scotch Scenery pattern depicting a repeated scene of a Scotsman and his lady beneath a tree, printed title cartouche with maker's initials, minor damage, early 19thC, 16¾in (42.5cm) long.
$1,000–1,200 ⚒ DN

◄ A Swansea blue and white foot-bath, transfer-printed with a lapis lazuli pattern, c1830, 17in (43cm) wide.
$1,750–2,000 ⊞ SCO

A Swansea blue and white puzzle jug, decorated with chinoiserie Long Bridge pattern, c1805, 8in (20.5cm) high.
$1,000–1,300 ⊞ SCO

► A Wedgwood Queen's Ware blue and white slop pail and cover, transfer-printed with Willow pattern, handle missing, impressed mark, c1912, 9½in (24cm) high.
$530–580 ⚒ SK

A blue and white jug, transfer-printed with birds and flowers, c1820, 8in (20.5cm) high.
$220–240 ⊞ OCH

POTTERY

Delftware

Delft is a type of blue and white tin-glazed earthenware, named after the Dutch town that was famous for the many factories specializing in its manufacture. Produced from a generally low quality clay, it was fired and then sealed by dipping it into a whitish lead glaze mixed with tin oxides. Decoration was then applied using powdered oxides.

The art of tin-glazing earthenware can be traced back to the 8th century in Europe. The Arab invasion of Spain and the ensuing cultural cross-pollination led to the manufacture of a new type of tin-glazed pottery termed Hispano-Moresque. It was not until c1440 that it was produced in Italy, flourishing as an art form in northern regions such as Urbino, Venice and Faenza and then spreading to Antwerp in Belgium. As one of the cultural capitals of Europe it was an ideal venue, the creativity and wealth attracting many artists. By the second half of the 16th century, this artistic freedom was undermined by the powerful Spanish Inquisition, whose religious persecution and violence caused many craftsmen to flee.

Attracted by the receptive attitudes and relative peace of England and the clay resources of Norfolk, many of these migrants settled in Norwich. By 1567 they were employing the skills they had learnt on the Continent and began to produce earthenwares, later to be termed English delft. It is ironic that it was produced here some thirty years before its production in Delft itself. As the potters migrated further into Britain, centres of excellence developed in Aldgate, Southwark and Lambeth in London, as well as Bristol, Liverpool, Wincanton and later Dublin and Glasgow. As the 17th century dawned, designs began to be influenced by the Chinese porcelain that the Dutch were importing into Europe in vast quantities.

Many types of wares were produced in delft, often reflecting the nature of contemporary society: pill slabs and wet and dry drug jars for pharmacies, flower bricks, plates, tiles, tankards and teapots for domestic use and posset pots for spiced liqueur-based drinks. Decorative items are rare, but tend to survive in better condition as they were not subjected to the rigours of daily use.

With the advent of creamware in Yorkshire and Staffordshire in the 1740s, the demise of delft was inevitable. Creamware was both cheap and able to withstand damage more easily. Mass-produced and aggressively marketed, particularly by Wedgwood towards the end of the 18th century, its popularity resulted in the closure of many factories in both Delft and Britain.   **Gareth Williams**

A London delft tin-glazed wine or sack bottle, losses to rim, c1650, 4¾in (12cm) high.
$3,500–4,500 ⚒ P
Usually inscribed with names and dates, a plain white bottle of this type is rarely encountered.

A Liverpool delft guglet, decorated with blue flowers on a white ground, 1765, 9½in (24cm) high.
$1,000–1,100 ⊞ JHo

A Lambeth delft blue and white bottle, painted with Oriental figures in a chinoiserie landscape, rim restored, c1770, 9¼in (23.5cm) high.
$1,000–1,300 ⚒ DN

A Dutch Delft blue and white soya bottle, inscribed 'Manderinzoya - D: Boer - Japansch Magazyn - S'Hage' rim damaged, 19thC, 7¾in (19.5cm) high.
$1,000–1,100 ⚒ S(Am)
Dirk Boer was one of the first dealers of Japanese products in Holland. An extensive assortment of Japanese, Chinese and other exotic objects was offered in his shop called 'Japansch Magazijn'.

A Dutch Delft doré chinoiserie bowl, the exterior painted in Imari colours with birds of paradise on flowering branches, beneath a lappet border, the interior with scattered floral sprigs, iron-red overglaze mark for Pieter Adriaenszoon Kocks, the factory De Grieksche A, 1701–22, 6¼in (16cm) diam.
$2,400–2,600 ⚒ S(Am)

◄ **An English delft washing bowl,** with a pie-crust edge, blue-painted with a gentleman in a landscape, II x II motifs on under-rim, blue dash mark, c1730, 10¼in (26cm) diam.
$3,200–3,600 ⚒ P

An English delft blue and white bowl, the interior inscribed 'Success to Trade', the exterior painted with sailing boats and pagodas, cracked and riveted, probably Liverpool, c1750, 9in (23cm) diam.
$1,000–1,100 ➶ WW

A Liverpool delft blue and white bowl, the interior decorated with a coat-of-arms and inscribed 'Chris Henderson of Bigland in Cumberland', c1760, 10½in (26.5cm) diam.
$7,250–8,000 ⊞ JHo

A Dutch Delft blue and white William and Mary plate, painted with a portrait of the Queen, initialled 'K.G.' and 'V.B.', late 17thC, 8½in (21.5cm) diam.
$1,100–1,300 ➶ Bea(E)

A pair of Dutch Delft herring plates, painted in blue with a fish, beneath a border of floral cartouches, one edged in yellow, the other in iron-red, 18thC, 8¾in (22cm) long.
$5,000–5,500 ➶ S(Am)

◀ **A Dutch Delft model of an infant in a high chair,** wearing a blue and white dress and green bonnet, the chair painted with floral swags above a polychrome geometric border, chipped, abrasion, 18thC, 4¾in (12cm) high.
$1,000–1,200 ➶ S(Am)

A Dutch Delft blue and white dish, in the *kraak porselein* style, painted with birds, rockwork and flowers, the border with panels of flowers and leaves, cracked, late 17thC, 15½in (39.5cm) diam.
$300–350 ➶ WW

An English delft blue and white plate, painted with 'A.R.' and dated '1719', 8½in (21.5cm) diam.
$2,500–3,000 ✗ Bea(E)

An English delft saucer dish, painted in underglaze blue with a vase of flowers flanked by the initials 'EW', the border with floral scrollwork, repaired, 1726, 9in (23cm) diam.
$1,600–1,750 ✗ PFK

A Bristol delft blue and white plate, decorated with a dog in a garden, c1740, 13in (33cm) diam.
$720–780 ⊞ JHo

A pair of Bristol delft plates, each painted in manganese with a lady beneath a tree, surrounded by foliate and trellis borders, mid-18thC, 9in (23cm) diam.
$450–500 ✗ Mit

A Bristol delft blue and white plate, decorated with a chinoiserie scene, the rim with *bianco sopra bianco* decoration, c1750, 8¾in (22cm) diam.
$200–230 ⊞ IW

An English delft commemorative plate, painted in blue with a ship sailing near a coastline, inscribed 'The Union, Ha. Klinckert, Ao 1754 6/1', restored, dated 1754, 9in (23cm) diam
$2,000–2,500 ✗ P

A London delft ballooning plate, c1785, 9in (23cm) diam.
$1,100–1,250 ⊞ JHo

A delft dish, decorated with a mother and child flanked by blue trees, with a manganese and gold border, probably English, 18thC, 14½in (37cm) diam.
$725–875 ✗ TRL

A Bristol delft blue and white plate painted with a house at the water's edge, with a fisherman and two figures in a boat to the foreground, 1730, 13in (33cm) diam.
$650–800 ✗ P(B)

An English delft polychrome Adam and Eve charger, with blue sponged decoration, the figures in blue, with a yellow band and blue dashes to the rim, probably Bristol, c1700, 13½in (34.5cm) diam.
$1,450–1,750 ✗ HYD

An English delft blue and white meat dish, painted in chinoiserie style with a pine tree in a fenced garden, haircrack, probably Liverpool, c1770, 17¼in (44cm) wide.
$850–1,000 ✗ S(S)

A Dutch Delft dish, decorated with a spray of flowers, with a floral garland border, 18thC, 13¾in (35cm) diam.
$500–600 ✗ TRL

POTTERY

An English delft charger, painted in iron-red, yellow, green and blue, with a border of swags and stylized flowers, the centre with a six-petalled flowerhead, 1720–30, 13in (33cm) diam.
$800–900 ⚒ PF

A Dutch Delft pancake plate, painted in blue, green and red with a central blossom within radiating floral motifs suspended from a foliate border, 18thC, 9in (23cm) diam.
$400–450 ⚒ S(Am)

An English delft charger, painted with a stylized chinoiserie scene and a floral border, c1760, 5¼in (13.5cm) diam.
$300–350 ⚒ DA

A Dutch Delft blue and white charger, with a shaped rim, damaged, 18thC, 12in (30.5cm) diam.
$320–380 ⚒ SWO

A Dutch Delft charger, painted in blue, centred by two Long Elizas in a chamber, the border with six cartouches enclosing pseudo *taoist* emblems, 18thC, 13¾in (35cm) diam.
$550–600 ⚒ S(Am)

◀ **An English delft flower brick,** painted in underglaze blue with chinoiserie figures, 1750–60, 5½in (14cm) wide.
$650–800 ⚒ GAK

An English delft blue and white flower brick, the sides painted with houses and trees, mid-18thC, 4½in (11.5cm) diam.
$850–1,000 ⚒ WW

A London delft blue and white drug jar, inscribed 'ROS.RUB.' surmounted by an angel's head and outstretched wings, rim section lacking, 1680–90, 7in (18cm) high.
$2,000–2,300 ⚒ P
Ros.Rub. is the abbreviated form of 'rosa rubra' or red rose. The jar would have contained a preparation made from roses and sugar.

LOCATE THE SOURCE
The source of each illustration in Miller's can be found by checking the code letters below each caption with the Key to Illustrations, pages 794–800.

A London delft blue and white pill jar, with a label inscribed 'P.HIER.CV.AGAR.' surmounted by an angel's head and outstretched wings, rim crack, c1680, 4in (10cm) high.
$3,600–4,400 ⚒ P
These pills contained a purgative made of larch agaric.

▶ **A Dutch Delft tobacco jar,** entitled 'Violette', painted in blue with a merchant and native trading, between two barrels holding tobacco leaves, a sailing ship in the background, the base marked with the *'Drye Clocken'* three bells mark in blue, c1800, 11in (28cm) high.
$650–725 ⚒ P(E)

A Dutch Delft blue and white tobacco jar, by De Porceleyne Schotel, the sides inscribed 'STRAAS BURGER' within a foliate cartouche and surmounted by a vase of flowers, haircrack to rim, blue painted mark, mid-18thC, 10½in (26.5cm) high.
$1,000–1,150 ⚒ S(S)

POTTERY

An English delft mug, painted in underglaze blue with the monogram 'F.B 1683', within a heart-shaped cartouche surmounted by a *fleur-de-lys* and flanked by beaded scrollwork, 1683, 4¾in (12cm) high.
$16,000–19,000 ⚐ S

A London delft night-light holder, cut with five arched openings, painted in blue with a floral trellis and trailing foliage, 1765–75, 4½in (11.5cm) high.
$2,200–2,400 ⚐ P
These objects were sometimes described as bird feeders.

A pair of Dutch Delft mixed-technique plaques, the centre painted with a mythological scene of Neptune rescuing Amymone from the attentions of a satyr, surrounded by polychrome crests and scrolls in high relief, pierced for hanging, restored, 18thC, 13¾in (35cm) square.
$4,000–4,500 ⚐ S(Am)

A Dutch Delft blue and white plaque, painted with a cowherd before a village, within red floral spandrels and blue sprig vignettes, 'APK' monogram in red, 19thC, 10½in (26.5cm) square.
$220–260 ⚐ CGC

A London delft ointment pot, inscribed in blue, 'Waller & Son Guilford', mid-18thC, 2¼in (5.5cm) diam.
$1,100–1,300 ⚐ P

A Dutch Delft salt, painted in blue with flower and leaf sprigs and a blue rim, rim chip, 18thC, 3½in (9cm) long
$90–100 ⚐ WW

A Dutch Delft doré chinoiserie tea canister, painted in Imari colours with chrysanthemums before rockwork and birds in flight, beneath a border of scrolling leaves and blooms, modern silver screw top, early 18thC, 5½in (14cm) high.
$3,500–4,000 ⚐ S(Am)
In order to recreate the Chinese tea ceremony, which had become so popular in the West, tea canisters decorated in the Chinese style were produced by the Dutch Delft factories, mainly in the first half of the 18th century, to contain this luxury commodity.

A London delft tile, decorated in blue with Christ and the Cross, c1760, 5in (12.5cm) square.
$145–160 ⊞ JHo

A Dutch Delft model of a slipper, the top and front painted in blue with flowers, c1700, 7½in (19cm) long.
$650–800 ⚐ Bon(C)

A Dutch Delft tile, with an octagonal scene painted in blue, depicting a couple being driven in a horse and cart, surrounded by a manganese border with *fleur-de-lys* in the spandrels, 18thC, 5in (12.5cm) square.
$145–160 ⊞ JHo

A Dutch Delft octagonal section vase and cover, with a scroll finial, painted in blue with a tulip and other flowers, the reverse with a bird in flight, mid-18thC, 16½in (42cm) high.
$200–250 ⚐ WW

A Dutch Delft blue and white vase and cover, with chinoiserie-style decoration alternating as a female figure in a courtyard setting and flowers and fence design, surmounted by a cat finial, minor damage, 18thC, 9in (23cm) high.
$875–1,000 ⚐ SK

Porcelain

Within the last year the two landmark sales of the 18th-century English porcelain collection of Dr Bernard Watney have provided a barometer for this market. Until recently in decline, the fashion for early blue and white porcelain has been revived and consequently brought renewed interest in the products of the Bow, Worcester, Limehouse and Vauxhall factories. Demand for Liverpool, with new discoveries and reattributions and Lowestoft wares, is equally passionate, the latter supported by a buoyant local market.

Alongside early polychrome Worcester examples, the coloured wares of Chelsea and Bow continue to be popular. While typical figures from Bow, or the later Chelsea Gold Anchor period, are currently less in demand, this may change with the renewed interest in this period. The stylish late 18th-century wares of the Derby factory, particularly the highly-decorated plates and teawares of the 1790s, are also attracting much interest.

Worcester porcelain of the 19th century is characterized by the achievements of the painters and modellers and the work of specific artists is pursued with as much enthusiasm as the more anonymous earlier productions. Similar in style to French porcelain, the distinctive and rare Welsh wares of Swansea and Nantgarw also have individually identifiable artists and continue to sell well. The large international fan clubs for Royal Crown Derby, Royal Worcester and Belleek ensure continued high prices, especially for decorative and rare examples in good condition.

Possibly as a result of less favourable economic conditions in Europe recently, prices for standard examples of Meissen from the 18th to the 20th centuries – especially tablewares – have remained stable. However, with the preponderance of such pieces available, it is difficult to imagine a time when Meissen generally will not continue to be popular. The same could not be said, however, for other German factories such as Fürstenberg, Ludwigsburg and Frankenthal, especially when it comes to figure collecting and items from the 19th and 20th centuries. Here, prices fluctuate widely. Neo-classical 19th-century Berlin porcelain retains its value, while the plaque market, in the doldrums for some years, shows distinct signs of improvement.

Apart from large ormolu-mounted vases, the widest disparity is that between the expensive 18th- and early 19th-century products of the Sèvres, Meissen and Vienna factories, and the much later stylized French, Dresden and Bohemian copies. Such items, however, provide a more affordable alternative for the collector with limited funds. **Simon Cottle**

Animals & Birds

A Samuel Alcock model of a Staffordshire bull terrier, painted with black markings, on a pale yellow rocky base, damaged, marked, 1830–45, 5in (12.5cm) high.
$850–1,000 ⚘ **P**
Samuel Alcock & Co (established 1826) was based at the Hill Pottery in Burslem, Staffordshire.

A Derby model of a sheep, with tan patches, the base applied with coloured flowers and green foliage, damaged, c1760, 4¼in (11cm) high.
$500–600 ⚘ **WW**

A Belleek salt, modelled as a bronzed seahorse with one front leg raised, the tail swirling round to support a shell-shaped salt, the feet and tail heightened with gilt, impressed mark, First Period, Ireland, c1880, 4in (10cm) high.
$850–1,000 ⚘ **P(Ba)**

A Longton Hall/West Pans bisque pheasant, on a tree trunk base, 1760–70, 7in (18cm) high.
$2,300–2,600 ⊞ **JUP**

A Bow group of a ewe and lamb, painted in shades of brown, black and puce, on a rockwork base, damaged, c1753, 4¾in (10cm) wide.
$850–1,000 ⚘ **DN**

Items in the Porcelain section have been arranged in factory order, with non-specific pieces appearing at the end of each sub-section.

A pair of Derby tureens and covers modelled as doves, with brown, purple and white plumage, each seated on a nest encrusted with green moss and yellow and purple flowers, restored, minor damage, puce painted '5' to each base, 1760–65, 8in (20.5cm) long.
$8,000–9,500 ⚘ **S**

A model of a swan, possibly Lowestoft, the head decorated with black and iron-red enamel, c1800, 2¾in (7cm) high.
$1,800–2,200 ⚒ P

A Paris inkstand, modelled as a brown and white spaniel with one front paw resting on a bird, the green stand fitted with an ink and pounce pot, the base moulded with gilt scrollwork, firing crack across one paw, France, mid-19thC, 8¼in (21cm) high.
$450–500 ⚒ S(S)

A Royal Worcester model of a bulldog, in Churchillian pose, by Doris Lindner, with hardwood plinth and certificate No. 480 from a limited edition of 500, this example without 'Mack' on the collar, 1968, 4½in (11.5cm) high, with cardboard box.
$450–500 ⚒ P

A Meissen model of a turkey, modelled by J. J. Kändler, the plumage painted in shades of brown and the head in blue and red, the base moulded with leaves and applied with scattered flowers, possibly later-decorated, restored, crossed swords mark in underglaze blue, Germany, late 18thC, 22¼in (56.5cm) high.
$9,500–11,500 ⚒ S

A Sèvres bisque hunting group, modelled as a deer and four hounds, on a glazed blue and gilt base, damaged, impressed interlaced 'L's, France, 19thC, 28¼in (72cm) wide.
$3,000–3,500 ⚒ WW

A Royal Worcester group of a lady on a horse, entitled 'At the Meet', by Doris Lindner, on an ebonized base, printed and impressed marks and No. '3114', 1971, 7¼in (18.5cm) wide.
$750–850 ⚒ Mit

> **Miller's is a price GUIDE not a price LIST**

◄ **A Continental bisque owl fairy light,** decorated in fawn with a brown beak and pale blue neck ribbon and bow, c1880, 4½in (11.5cm) wide.
$400–500 ⊞ ALiN

A pair of Meissen models of bustards, the plumage picked out in brown, with yellow legs, standing beside turquoise grass, both restored, crossed swords marks in blue, incised '2020' and '2021', Germany, mid-19thC, 14½in (37cm) high.
$1,800–2,200 ⚒ WW

A Victorian Royal Worcester *blanc-de-chine* elephant, with a cushioned cradle and draped back, 8in (20.5cm) long.
$800–950 ⚒ MEA

A German wild boar and hunting dog group, in the style of Meissen, modelled in a life and death struggle, repairs and losses, c1760, 10¼in (26cm) wide.
$500–600 ⚒ S(NY)

A German model of a puppy, with grey patches, wearing a silver chain collar and shield inscribed 'Won by... smooth coated fox terrier Rascal... 1885', 9¾in (25cm) high.
$180–220 ⚒ CGC

Baskets

A Belleek Henshall's Twig three-strand basket, the handle and rim applied with flowers, First Period, Ireland, 1863–90, 11in (28cm) wide.
$2,300–2,600 ⊞ **DeA**
Baskets etc with applied flowers, shamrock and other detail, made up of strands of porcelain, were introduced by the designer William Henshall. Baskets with two and three strands were made between 1865 and 1920. Four-stranded baskets were made after 1920. Early baskets are usually white with a greater variety and abundance of flowers, and a noticeably smooth and rich glaze.

A Belleek three-strand covered basket, profusely decorated with applied flowers, with hawthorn-style handles, Second Period, Ireland, 1891–1926, 12¼in (31cm) wide.
$2,500–3,000 ⚒ **JAd**

A Vienna fruit basket and stand, decorated with sprigs of flowers and gilt, Austria, c1792, 11in (28cm) wide.
$2,300–2,600 ⊞ **US**

A Worcester yellow-ground basket, the tapering lattice sides pierced with trellis, the interior painted in bright enamels with a spray of flowers on a white ground, the exterior applied with florets, with gilt line rim, damaged, restored, c1770, 7¾in (19.5cm) wide.
$1,100–1,350 ⚒ **P**

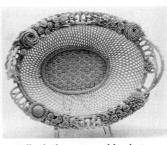

A Belleek three-strand basket, the handle terminals and rim applied with floral sprays, impressed mark 'Belleek Co Fermanagh', damaged, First Period, Ireland, 1863–90, 11¾in (30cm) wide.
$300–350 ⚒ **P(E)**

A Belleek four-strand basket, the rim applied with flowers, Second Period, Ireland, 1891–1926, 4in (10cm) diam.
$400–450 ⊞ **DeA**

A Coalport square basket, with a pierced rim, the interior painted with flowers, the exterior applied with pink flowers and green foliage, heightened with gilt, small chips, c1840, 5in (12.5cm) wide.
$725–875 ⚒ **WW**

A Worcester basket, with a reticulated rim, painted with scattered flowers, handle replaced, 1760–70, 8in (20.5cm) wide.
$175–225 ⚒ **WW**

A Belleek Sydenham Twig basket, the handle terminals applied with roses, First Period, Ireland, 1863–90, 11in (28cm) diam.
$1,250–1,400 ⊞ **DeA**

A Caughley chestnut basket and cover, the interior painted with trailing flowers in underglaze blue, the twig loop handles and loop knop applied with flowerheads and leaf terminals, rim chip and hairline firing crack, blue-painted S-mark, c1785, 8in (20.5cm) wide.
$1,300–1,600 ⚒ **LFA**

A pair of Ludwigsburg baskets, the interiors painted by Albrecht Vogelmann with sprays of flowers and scattered blooms in red, purple and green, the sides studded with gilt flowerheads, with gilt rims, crowned 'CC' monogram in underglaze blue, painter's mark 'VO', impressed 'IP2', Germany, c1785, 7½in (19cm) wide.
$5,000–6,000 ⚒ **S**
Albrecht Vogelmann was appointed in 1782 and became Senior Painter in 1787.

A porcelain basket, painted with a view of Windsor Castle, in the style of J. B. Pyne, with raised panels of flowers and green scrollwork on a pink ground, with gilt-beaded border, the handle with dolphin terminals, heightened with gilt, 1840–50, 11¾in (30cm) wide.
$725–800 ⚒ **P(Ba)**

PORCELAIN

PORCELAIN

Bough Pots

A pair of Derby bough pots and covers, painted and gilded with Oriental flowers, within scrolled borders, flanked by vertical panels of flowers, with ram's head handles, covers damaged, iron-red 'D', crown and crossed baton marks, covers damaged, c1820, 9½in (24cm) wide.
$1,150–1,350 ↗ Bon(C)

A pair of Höchst bough pots, decorated with flowers in green, purple and red, Germany, c1760, 8in (20.5cm) wide.
$2,200–2,500 ⊞ US

> Miller's is a price GUIDE not a price LIST

A Ludwigsburg bough pot, the sides moulded with a central scrolling cartouche between wide flutes, painted in polychrome enamels with flowers, with puce details and a brown line border, chipped, incised marks and painted 'KP' mark, Germany, mid-18thC, 8¼in (21cm) wide.
$600–700 ↗ WW

Bowls

A Belleek bowl, the exterior moulded with scallop shells and coral, printed black mark, First Period, Ireland, 1863–90, 11¾in (30cm) wide.
$450–500 ↗ LFA

A Coalport bowl, pattern No. V7799, the interior dusted with gilding, the exterior decorated with panels of roses on a blue ground, green factory mark, c1890, 8½in (21.5cm) wide.
$120–145 ↗ WW

◀ **A Liverpool tea bowl,** Pennington pottery, painted in underglaze blue with a chinoiserie river scene and picked out in iron-red, the interior with a pendant flowerhead band, rim chips, c1775, 3in (7.5cm) diam.
$200–230 ↗ LFA

A Derby bowl, with a pink and green floral border, and gilt rim lines, rim crack, red painted mark, c1820, 11½in (29cm) wide.
$145–175 ↗ WW

A Lowestoft bowl, decorated in the Redgrave style with flowering plants issuing from rockwork, the interior border with floral swags suspended from a shell and diaper band, restored rim chip, c1780, 9in (23cm) wide.
$450–550 ↗ P
Redgrave is a series of patterns used by Lowestoft in the 1770s and 1780s.

Four blue and white patty pans, painted with chinoiserie landscapes with figures, chipped, possibly Liverpool, c1760, 4½in (11.5cm) wide.
$1,300–1,600 ↗ RBB

▶

A Worcester potting pot, painted in blue with the Zig-Zag Fence pattern, with a diaper border at the rim reserved with floral panels, rim chip, workman's mark, c1755, 6¾in (17cm) wide.
$800–950 ↗ P

A Royal Worcester bowl, decorated by James Stinton with pheasants beneath a gilt border, printed mark, signed, 1922, 7in (18cm) diam.
$2,000–2,200 ↗ BWe

A Vauxhall patty pan, the interior painted in underglaze blue with a flowerhead and leaves, the rim with a trellis band and pendant flowers and leaves, the exterior painted with three stylized leaf sprays, 1755–58, 4¼in (11cm) wide.
$2,600–3,200 ↗ LFA
No Vauxhall example of this form appears to be recorded.

Covered Bowls & Dishes

A Belleek Fan covered sugar bowl, 1891–1926, 4½in (11.5cm) high.
$350–400 ⊞ MLa

A du Paquier bowl and cover, with a pink flower knop, decorated with moulded prunus and painted leaf and flower sprigs, restored, Vienna, Austria, c1730, 6in (15cm) wide.
$850–1,000 ⚹ WW

A Caughley sucrier and cover, printed in underglaze blue with the Three Flowers pattern, within blue bands, slight damage, blue mark, c1785, 5in (12.5cm) high.
$450–500 ⚹ SAS

A Sèvres sugar bowl and cover, by François le Vavasseur, decorated with floral sprays, with blue and gold knop and rims, marked 'W', France, c1760, 9in (23cm) wide.
$1,450–1,750 ⊞ US

A Chelsea-Derby box, the knop modelled as two billing doves with pink wings and tails, decorated with floral sprays, c1770, 4in (10cm) wide.
$4,000–4,500 ⊞ JUP
The Chelsea factory closed in 1769 and was bought the following year by the owners of the Derby factory, William Duesbury and John Heath. The two concerns operated together until the factory was closed in 1784, the wares being known today as Chelsea-Derby.

A Worcester covered butter tub and stand, decorated in underglaze blue with a rose-centred spray, c1770, stand 7in (18cm) wide.
$1,250–1,350 ⊞ JUP

Buildings

◄ **A Samuel Alcock two-piece pastille burner,** modelled as a cottage, applied with flowers in pink, green, blue and white on a lavender ground, c1830, 6in (15cm) wide.
$1,200–1,350 ⊞ WWW

► **A W. H. Goss Ann Hathaway's Cottage,** painted in naturalistic colours with a yellow thatched roof, unglazed, 1893–1929, 2½in (6.5cm) wide.
$110–125 ⊞ G&CC

◄ **A W. H. Goss Isaac Walton's Cottage, Shallow-ford,** painted in black and white with a yellow thatched roof, unglazed, 1912–29, 3¾in (9.5cm) wide.
$850–950 ⊞ G&CC

Busts

A Brown-Westhead Moore parian bust, in the style of C. Delpech, draped in a cloak, c1861, 14in (35.5cm) high.
$400–500 ⚘ SWO

A Copeland parian bust of Wellington, by Comte D'Orsey, on a socle base, slight damage, c1852, 10½in (26.5cm) high.
$180–220 ⚘ SAS

A Copeland parian bust, entitled 'Purity', by M. Noble, c1860, 13in (33cm) high.
$1,100–1,200 ⊞ JAK

A Copeland parian bust, entitled 'Autumn', by Owen Hale, wearing an off-the-shoulder blouse with a fruiting vine garland about her head, slight damage, c1881, 17½in (44.5cm) high.
$3,500–4,500 ⚘ AG

A W. H. Goss parian bust of the Earl of Derby, 1876–87, 6in (15cm) high.
$230–260 ⊞ G&CC

A W. H. Goss parian bust of Peeping Tom, 1893–1905, 4½in (11.5cm) high.
$120–145 ⊞ G&CC

A Kerr & Co, Worcester, parian bust of General Havelock, by W. B. Kirk, mid-19thC, 9in (23cm) high.
$600–650 ⊞ JAK
General Sir Henry Havelock was a prominent figure in the Indian Mutiny following the Relief of Lucknow in 1857. He died shortly afterwards.

A Royal Dux bisque bust, modelled as a fashionably dressed girl wearing a pale pink, green and yellow costume, with a pierced pink bonnet, some restoration, impressed marks and applied pink triangle mark, Bohemia, c1900, 21¾in (55.5cm) high.
$2,000–2,200 ⚘ S(NY)

A John Rose & Co Coalport parian bust of Edward Prince of Wales, commemorating the Prince's engagement to Princess Alexandra, c1863, 13½in (34.5cm) high.
$650–750 ⊞ JAK

◄ **A Sèvres bisque bust of Newton,** on a blue glazed socle base with gilt bands, impressed and incised marks, slight damage, France, c1880, 12½in (32cm) high.
$600–700 ⚘ WW

A parian bust of Captain Matthew Webb, c1875, 15½in (39.5cm) high.
$1,800–2,000 ⊞ JAK
Captain Webb was the first man to swim the English Channel.

Auction or dealer?

All the pictures in our price guides originate from auction houses and dealers. When buying at auction, prices can be lower than those of a dealer, but a buyer's premium and VAT will be added to the hammer price. Equally, when selling at auction, commission, tax and photography charges must be taken into account. Dealers will often restore pieces before putting them back on the market.

Both dealers and auctioneers will provide professional advice, so it is worth researching both sources before buying or selling your antiques.

PORCELAIN

Candlesticks & Chambersticks

A chamberstick, the moulding picked out in turquoise and gold, the pan painted with a colourful floral spray, fine crack in handle, probably Coalport, c1835, 6in (15cm) high.
$350–450 P(Ba)

A Coalport chamberstick, decorated with pink roses among green foliage, with gilt rims, Society of Arts 'Feldspar' mark, c1825, 2in (5cm) high.
$500–600 DIA

A Copeland chamberstick, decorated with roses on a yellow band, pattern 'D5944', printed mark, mid-19thC, 4¾in (12cm) high.
$100–120 WW

A Davenport chamberstick, the deep blue ground reserved with shaped panels painted with floral sprays, with gilt scrolls and foliage, fine crack in base, printed red mark, c1825, 5in (12.5cm) wide.
$200–250 P(Ba)

A pair of Herend candlesticks, with blue, red and gold relief decoration of leaves, blue marks, Hungary, early 20thC, 11¾in (30cm) high.
$220–260 DORO

A pair of Meissen candlesticks, the stems moulded with foliage and C-scrolls, decorated in colours with birds and sprigs of flowers on a white ground, one restored, crossed swords mark in underglaze blue, Germany, c1800, 10½in (26.5cm) high.
$2,500–3,000 GAK

A pair of Meissen candelabra, decorated with insects and colourful sprays of flowers and applied trailing foliage, restored, minor losses, crossed swords marks, Germany, late 19thC, 12¼in (31cm) high.
$725–875 P(Ba)

A Flight, Barr & Barr chamberstick, painted with floral sprays on a pale green ground, with gilt handle and rims, painted script marks, c1820, 1½in (4cm) high.
$1,150–1,300 DIA

A Chamberlain's Worcester chamberstick, decorated in Japan colours, c1820, 5in (12.5cm) high.
$500–600 DAN

Centrepieces

A Bow centrepiece, in the form of two putti seated on a rocky base applied with flowering branches, supporting a bowl with basketweave moulding, damaged, cover lacking, c1750, 7in (18cm) wide.
$650–800 P

A pair of Minton glazed parian table centrepieces, each modelled as a green leaf suported by two white rabbits, one leaf restored, c1864, 9½in (24cm) wide.
$1,750–2,000 JAK

An ormolu-mounted porcelain table centrepiece, the bowl decorated with putti on clouds in gilt frames and floral garlands, the base supported by a merman and with merman handles, 19thC, 14½in (37cm) wide.
$725–875 P(Ed)

Chocolate, Coffee, Punch & Teapots

PORCELAIN

A Belleek Thorn teapot, First Period, 1863–90, 4½in (11.5cm) high.
$1,300–1,450 ⊞ MLa

A Belleek Grass teapot, decorated with moulded grasses picked out in deep pink, First Period, 1863–90, 4in (10cm) high.
$1,000–1,100 ⊞ MLa

A Bow transfer-printed teapot, painted with a chinoiserie scene in overglaze enamels, c1765, 5in (12.5cm) high.
$2,000–2,200 ⊞ JUP

A Caughley coffee pot, printed in underglaze blue with scattered fruits and leaves, beneath a blue line rim, the unglazed base with 'S' mark, restored, 1780–85, 7½in (19cm) high.
$1,000–1,100 ⚹ LFA

A Caughley teapot and stand, New Oval shape, painted in coloured enamels with scattered cornflowers and gilt leaves, within gilt leaf-scroll and line borders, chips to spout, 1792–95, 5½in (14cm) high.
$450–500 ⚹ LFA

A Liverpool teapot, printed in underglaze blue with a fisherman in a boat, in a chinoiserie river landscape, the handle and spout with leaf scrolls, cover cracked and with late 18thC white metal hinge, 1760–70, 5in (12.5cm) high.
$580–650 ⚹ LFA

A Lowestoft punch pot, painted with chinoiserie figures within a fenced garden, reserved within gilt-scrolled borders on an orange ground with a raised gilt diaper design, c1775, 8¼in (21cm) high.
$5,000–6,000 ⚹ P

A Meissen chocolate pot, the ribbed sides painted with puce flowerheads, with gilt-metal mounts, turned wood handle lacking, 18thC, 6¾in (17cm) high.
$1,150–1,350 ⚹ HOK

A New Hall teapot, painted with flower sprays and pink diaper borders, 'No. 311' in red, c1800, 6in (15cm) high.
$260–320 ⚹ WW

A Philip Christian & Co, Liverpool, *famille verte* faceted teapot, decorated with Beckoning Chinaman pattern, the handle and spout picked out in purple monochrome, c1765, 5¾in (14.5cm) high.
$1,300–1,600 ⚹ LFA

A Philip Christian & Co, Liverpool teapot, painted in underglaze blue with two birds on flowering branches, with two insects in flight, beneath a trellis band, c1765, 4½in (11.5cm) high.
$1,000–1,100 ⚹ LFA

A Worcester polychrome teapot, painted in Imari colours with a building among Oriental trees and shrubbery, beneath a scalloped border enclosing trellis and peony, 1760–65, 6¼in (16cm) high.
$1,450–1,600 ⚹ Bon(C)

A Worcester teapot, painted in coloured enamels with two shaped reserves depicting Long Eliza figures within black C-scroll borders interspersed by panels of red scale work, c1770, 4¾in (12cm) high.
$725–875 ✗ CAG

A Worcester fluted teapot, painted in coloured enamels with flowers, butterflies and insects, within turquoise, blue and gilt borders, decoration later, crescent mark, c1770, 5in (12.5cm) high.
$400–500 ✗ LFA

A Worcester coffee pot, decorated in the London *atelier* of James Giles, with the Bodenham pattern of Chinese figures in coloured enamels, and in iron-red and puce with flowers and leaves, within shaped panels picked out in gilt, on a blue scale ground, cover restored, c1768, 8½in (21.5cm) high.
$2,500–3,000 ✗ LFA
This pattern takes its name from the service included in the sale of the Bodenham Collection in 1872.

Items in the Porcelain section have been arranged in factory order, with non-specific pieces appearing at the end of each sub-section.

A Worcester fluted teapot, decorated in blue and gilt with leafy wreaths and flower sprays, marked, knop re-glued, 5¼in (13.5cm) high.
$300–350 ✗ WW

◄ **A Worcester teapot,** painted in underglaze blue with Narcissus pattern, c1775, 6in (15cm) high.
$870–1,000 ⊞ JUP

A Royal Worcester hexagonal section teapot, painted with trailing flowers and with shaded blue borders, 1895, 9in (23cm) wide.
$260–320 ✗ WW

PORCELAIN

Chocolate, Coffee & Tea Services

A Capodimonte coffee service, the matching stand with gilt-metal carrying handle, Italy, c1935, 15in (38cm) wide.
$450–500 ⊞ JACK

▶ **A Coalport part tea and coffee service,** of Adelaide shape, comprising 36 pieces, pattern No. 4/456, decorated with a yellow-banded gilt-scrolled border enclosing a cobalt ground cornucopia, and centring a gilt-foliate motif, marked, c1840.
$300–350 ↗ Hal

A Caughley matched part tea and coffee service, comprising 27 pieces, printed in underglaze blue with a chinoiserie pattern of figures on a bridge, within a gilt and Fitzhugh-banded rim, painted 'S' marks, cracks and chips, c1795.
$1,000–1,300 ↗ Hal

◀ **A Derby three-piece tea set,** decorated with Imari floral pattern No. 383, 19thC, 9½in (24cm) wide.
$650–800 ↗ AH

A Coalport tea and coffee service comprising 29 pieces, painted with polychrome sprays of summer flower within gilded borders, 1815–20.
$3,500–4,000 ↗ P(E)

A cased set of six Copeland Spode coffee cups and saucers, with cerise and gold edges and floral centres, each cup with a silver holder hallmarked for Birmingham 1907, one cup with hairline crack, with six Onslow pattern silver coffee spoons, Sheffield 1913.
$400–500 ↗ GAK

A New Hall part tea and coffee service, comprising 23 pieces, pattern No. 301, each with a spirally-moulded body painted with an encircling band of gold foliage, some damage, inscribed 'Shew, Yeovill', c1800.
$500–600 ↗ Bea(E)

A Frankenthal solitaire, comprising eight pieces, each piece painted with a medallion depicting Cupid enclosed by an underglaze blue band embellished with gilt trellis, the rims with a similar border enclosing flower sprays or scattered flowers, crowned 'CT' monograms and '77, 79, 81' in underglaze blue, incised letters and numerals, cup and coffee pot cover restored, c1781, tray 11½in (29cm) wide.
$2,500–2,800 ↗ S

A Meissen *tête-à-tête*, comprising ten pieces, encrusted with forget-me-nots in blue and pink in high relief, on a white ground painted with butterflies and floral sprigs, crossed swords mark in underglaze blue, impressed '69', chips to foliage, handles to covers restored, 1860–80, tray 17½in (44.5cm) wide.
$6,500–7,500 ↗ S(Am)

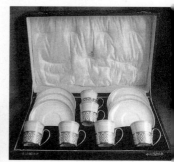

A Paragon coffee service, comprising six blue-bordered coffee cups and saucers, the cups with pierced silver holders by Adie Bros, Birmingham 1934.
$200–250 ↗ CGC

A Rockingham part tea service, comprising 18 pieces, pattern No. 1224 painted in grey with leaves and wild strawberries within a gilded scrolling foliate border, marked, damaged, c1835.
$1,150–1,350 ↗ P

A Nymphenburg faceted coffee service, comprising 13 pieces, moulded with acanthus and heightened with gilt, painted with violet and gilt-edged medallions enclosing land-scape views *en grisaille*, impressed shield mark and 'Nymphenburg' in underglaze blue and printed in green, c1900, coffee pot 8¾in (22cm) high.
$3,300–3,700 ↗ S(Am)

LOCATE THE SOURCE
The source of each illustration in Miller's can be found by checking the code letters below each caption with the Key to Illustrations, pages 794–800.

A Thuringia tea and coffee set, comprising three pieces, decorated with gilt bands of trailing foliage and forget-me-nots, inner rim of cover slightly damaged, c1800, coffee pot 5½in (14cm) high.
$300–350 ➤ DORO

A Sèvres chocolate set, comprising 14 pieces, the deep blue ground decorated in gilt and with gilt interiors, marked, c1823, 7in (18cm) high.
$3,500–4,500 ⊞ DHu

A Wedgwood bone china Liberty tea set, comprising 20 pieces, each piece printed polychrome flags, manufactured and sold for the benefit of various allied war charities, printed marks, c1917, teapot 5½in (14cm) high.
$1,400–1,600 ➤ SK

A Vienna solitaire, decorated in gilt on a white ground, restored, early 19thC.
$1,000–1,100 ➤ DORO

A Royal Worcester Shell pattern tea set, comprising five pieces, moulded with seaweed and painted in pink, green and puce on a cream glaze with gilt bands, each with an applied coral-shaped handle and three shell feet, two scallop-shaped covers, printed crown mark and '62' in green, damaged, repaired, c1862, teapot 5in (12.5cm) high.
$2,200–2,500 ➤ S

▶ **A Royal Worcester coffee service,** comprising 16 pieces, painted in coloured enamels with fruit on a shaded ground, signed, marked in puce, one saucer damaged, 1926–29.
$3,000–3,500 ➤ SAS

PORCELAIN

Clocks

A flower-encrusted clock case, attributed to Coalport, with scroll and shell moulding picked out in gold, a pierced lattice panel below the dial, the sides with turquoise panels, surmounted by a floret and applied with coloured garden flowers, movement with stamped mark for J. Le Blanc, minor losses and repair, c1835, 9¾in (25cm) high.
$725–875 ➤ P

A Dresden mantel clock, the French enamelled dial clock with Roman and Arabic numerals and a two-train movement, surrounded by cherubs holding baskets of grapes around a wine vat, on a floral-encrusted rockwork base, marked, 19thC, 15½in (39.5cm) high.
$725–875 ➤ Mit

A Dresden clock, in the style of Meissen, representing the Four Seasons, with figures of children seated amongst scrollwork and flowers, the reverse of the case painted with coloured sprigs, minor chips to flowers, c1880, 18½in (47in) high.
$1,750–2,000 ➤ P

A Dresden mantel clock, applied with blush ivory roses, surmounted by a boy flautist in rural dress, the clock face over a scallop-shaped well, flanked by a gentleman playing a mandolin and a lady in floral dress, double crossed batons mark, minor losses, late 19thC, 17in (43cm) high.
$725–875 ➤ P(Ba)

▶ **A Meissen neo-classical clock case,** flanked by two classical maidens each holding a mask for Tragedy and Comedy and a baton or a club, the whole heightened with gilt, crossed swords mark in underglaze blue, incised '818', restored, c1880, 14¼in (36cm) high.
$7,250–8,750 ➤ S

A Meissen clock case, in the style of an 18thC model, painted with scattered flower sprigs, encrusted with floral garlands and leaf swags, surmounted by a pair of love-birds and flanked by a cupid seated on a magenta robe, crossed sword marks in underglaze blue, incised 'F36', with original key, impressed and inscribed, minor restoration, c1880, 12½in (32cm) high.
$3,500–4,500 ⚒ S

▶ **A German three-piece clock garniture,** possibly Sitzendorf, the clock case mounted with a courting couple amongst polychrome flowers in front of a landscape, flanked by a pair of figural stands, damaged, late 19thC, 20in (51cm) high.
$1,600–1,800 ⚒ EH

A Moore Bros clock case, with a ribbed surround applied with pale yellow cactus flowers, flanked by a girl playing cymbals and a boy with a violin, on a base moulded with gilt-enriched bellflowers and acanthus leaves, printed and impressed marks, impressed and painted '559', damaged, 1880s, 12¼in (31cm) high.
$1,450–1,750 ⚒ S(S)

A Sèvres bisque neo-classical clock, representing Learning, the white enamel timepiece mounted on a pillar with gilt-metal embellishment, flanked by a female with an open book on her lap and a cherub studying a globe, incised mark, mid-19thC, 18in (45.5cm) high.
$870–1,000 ⚒ P(E)

A Sèvres gilt-metal-mounted mantel clock, the front and sides painted with panels of lovers in a landscape between white and gilt fluted columns against a turquoise ground, the top surmounted by an urn reserved with flower panels, minor restoration c1880, 20½in (52cm) high.
$2,500–3,000 ⚒ S(S)

Cups

A Belleek Limpet footed cup and saucer, with a lime green handle and shading to the rim, saucer restored, Second Period, 1891–1926, cup 2½in (6.5cm) high.
$400–450 ⊞ MLa

A Bloor Derby teacup and saucer, decorated in gilt with butterflies and diaper panels on a blue ground, within shaped panels and gilt scroll-moulded borders, printed marks in red, c1825.
$145–175 ⚒ SAS

▶ **A Gaudy Welsh porcellaneous cup and saucer,** decorated with a chinoiserie design in pink and green on a cobalt blue and burnt orange ground, 19thC, saucer 5¾in (14.5cm) diam.
$130–160 ⊞ CoHA

A Gaudy Welsh porcellaneous cup and saucer, decorated with Dog Tooth Violet pattern No. 100, in cobalt blue, burnt orange and turquoise on a white ground, 19thC, saucer 5½in (14cm) diam.
$115–130 ⊞ CoHA

An Italian cup and saucer, possibly Doccia, the cup painted with a lady in a landscape, the saucer with Cupid and a reclining nymph in a landscape, both vignettes within puce, gilt and iron-red foliate frames, 18thC, saucer 4in (10cm) diam.
$600–700 ⚒ CGC

Gaudy Welsh

Pottery and porcelain known as Gaudy Welsh was produced as an inexpensive form of tableware for the working classes during the 19th century by factories in north east England, the Midlands and south west England, but only to a minor extent in Wales. It was therefore never intended to be classed together under one generic term, but it became known as Gaudy Welsh in the United States and the name has become common internationally, although in the past it has also been called Swansea Cottage and Cottage Lustre. There are over 200 shapes and patterns of this distinctive ware, many of them based on early Imari ceramics, and most of them are illustrated in a book on the subject by Monica South. The colours are predominantly burnt orange, cobalt blue and shades of green.

A Lowestoft feeding cup, painted in underglaze blue with a fenced garden scene, damaged, c1768, 3in (7.5cm) high. **$1,800–2,000** ⊞ JUP

A Minton pattern teacup and saucer, pattern No. 854, Berlin, c1830, saucer 5in (12.5cm) diam. **$175–200** ⚲ WW

The Liverpool porcelain of William Reid & Co

Recent excavations of the site of the porcelain factory established by William Reid c1755 have produced considerable evidence that wares previously attributed to the other main Liverpool factories of Samuel Gilbody and Richard Chaffers were in fact made by William Reid & Co.

- Located at Brownlow Hill, the factory was the first in Liverpool to be built solely for the production of porcelain.
- It was active between 1756 and 1761, when the four partners in the firm were made bankrupt.
- Although mostly grey, the body colour of the porcelain varies from white to green or blue, sometimes achieved by deliberately tinting the glaze.
- The porcelain's translucency varies; it may be clear, yellow, buff or green.
- Barrel-shaped mugs, sauce boats and heavily-moulded milk jugs are the items most commonly seen.
- Underglaze-blue decoration is generally of Oriental inspiration, and a wide range of Chinese-style polychrome enamel patterns can be attributed to the firm, typically incorporating birds and flowers.
- Porcelain continued to be made on the site until 1767, firstly under William Ball's control and later that of James Pennington.

A William Reid, Liverpool, coffee can, painted in underglaze blue with chinoiserie flower branches, bamboo and a fence, the interior with a trellis band, slight damage, c1758, 3in (7.5cm) high. **$220–260** ⚲ LFA

A Schlaggenwald cup and saucer, decorated in purple and turquoise on a white ground, heightened with gilt, the cup interior decorated with gilt, marked, Bohemia, 1835, 2¾in (7cm) high. **$300–350** ⚲ DORO

A pair of French Sèvres-style chocolate cups, covers and stands, painted with swags and trailing foliage, late 19thC, 4¼in (11cm) high. **$300–350** ⚲ TRM

Custard Cups

An Ansbach custard cup, decorated in The Hague, with a polychrome flower spray with gilt highlights and rim, Germany, 1760–70, 3½in (9cm) high. **$500–600** ⊞ US
These pieces, known as custard cups in England, were first produced in France, probably at the St Cloud factory, from c1730. They were known as *pots à jus* and were used to contain the hot juice from the roast joint. The cover would keep the juice warm and it was drunk straight from the cup. In England these cups were only used for desserts, hence the name.

A Caughley custard cup and cover, transfer-printed in blue with Fisherman pattern, 'S' mark, c1780, 3¼in (8.5cm) high. **$350–450** ⚲ WW

A Copenhagen custard cup from the Bird Service, decorated with polychrome birds and flowers in cartouches, with a puce fruit knop and gilded bands, 1779, 3in (7.5cm) high. **$2,200–2,400** ⊞ US
The Bird Service was ordered as a present for either the Braunschweig family or, more likely, for Frederick the Great, shortly after the Copenhagen factory was taken over by King Christian VII in 1779 and renamed Royal Copenhagen Porcelain.

◄ **A Sèvres custard cup from the Fontainebleau Service,** painted in pink *camaieu* with garlands of flowers and leaves suspended from ribbon ties, beneath a gilt dentil rim, marked, 1787, 2in (5cm) high. **$320–380** ⚲ LFA

Dessert & Dinner Services

A Coalport part dessert service, comprising 17 pieces, painted with a water-scape within gilt cartouches on an ivory and cobalt blue ground, with gilt rococo and foliate decoration, printed and impressed marks, c1910.
$4,000–4,500 ⚒ Bon(C)

A botanical dessert service, comprising 24 pieces, decorated with different botanical specimens within blue borders, probably Rockingham, 19thC, plates 9in (23cm) diam.
$2,300–2,800 ⚒ MEA

A Davenport part dessert service, comprising 12 pieces, painted with summer fruits surrounded by a gilt scrolled border, 1780–86.
$1,800–2,200 ⚒ HAM

A Ridgway dessert service, comprising 28 pieces, pattern No. 4/407, with painted landscape vignettes within grey and gilt borders, c1830, comport 12½in (32cm) wide.
$1,800–2,200 ⚒ TEN

A Dresden dessert service, in the Meissen style, comprising 28 pieces, with pierced basketwork borders moulded with scrolled panels and painted with flower sprays, the centres with panels of lovers in rural landscapes within gilt borders, marked, c1860.
$4,500–5,000 ⚒ P

A Spode Feldspar dessert service, comprising 23 pieces, decorated with floral sprays within mushroom and gilt borders, some damage, c1830.
$3,500–4,000 ⊞ JAK

A Worcester Barr, Flight & Barr period dessert service, comprising 25 pieces, the spiral fluted bodies painted with brown monochrome grapes and leaves and gilt tendrils to the centres, within conforming borders, impressed marks, 1807–13, dessert plates 7¾in (19.5cm) diam.
$2,200–2,600 ⚒ P(S)

Items in the Porcelain section have been arranged in factory order, with non-specific pieces appearing at the end of each sub-section.

A Royal Worcester dessert service, comprising nine pieces, decorated in coloured enamels with orchids, flowers and leaves within a pale green and gilt *oeil-de-perdrix* border, with green and gilt gadrooned rim, some damage, marked, 1900, plates 9¼in (23.5cm) diam.
$900–1,100 ⚒ SAS

A Tressemanes & Voigt, Limoges, fish service, comprising 11 pieces, printed and painted with shell and ocean plant motifs within printed foliate-scroll borders, the rims heightened with gilt, retailed by Ovington Bros, Brooklyn, c1900, serving platter 24½in (62cm) long.
$500–600 ⚒ SK

A Victorian dessert service, comprising ten pieces, decorated with different flowers and fruit on a white ground, within a turquoise, gilt and white interlaced border, plate 9in (23cm) diam.
$850–1,000 ⚒ MEA

A dessert service, comprising 15 pieces, decorated with flower sprays, the pierced borders with floral panels, marked, late 19thC.
$800–1,000 ⚒ S(S)

Dishes

A **Belleek Shell salt dish,** with gilt-metal basket stand, First Period, 1863–90, 4in (10cm) wide.
$400–450 ⊞ MLa

A **pair of Coalport dishes,** painted in coloured enamels by Powell with *Paysanne de la Forêt Noire* and *Canton Soleure* within a gilt C-scroll roundel, the turquoise border within gilt bands, marked, c1817, 8in (20.5cm) wide.
$850–1,000 ↗ LFA
The decoration of these dishes is almost certainly taken from *Costumes des Nations Differentes, Costumes Européens*, a series of prints published by Hippolyte Leconte around 1817–19. These prints also provided inspiration for a series of figures produced by the Rockingham Factory, 1826–42.

A **Nantgarw dish,** painted in coloured enamels with a spray of flowers and leaves, the rim with baskets of flowers and leaves and scattered flowers within a broad gilt leaf-scroll band, impressed mark, minor restoration, 1814–23, 9¾in (25cm) wide.
$1,000–1,300 ↗ SAS

A **Caughley dish,** painted with scattered blue flower sprigs, marked, c1780, 8in (20.5cm) wide.
$370–440 ↗ WW

A **Dresden dish,** the centre painted in colours with a flower spray, within a border of sprays and flower sprigs, with foliate gilded rim, marked in blue, 19thC, 12in (30.5cm) wide.
$220–260 ↗ GAK

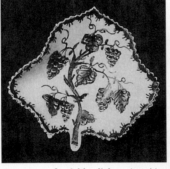

A **Lowestoft pickle dish,** painted in underglaze blue with a fruiting vine within a berry border, marked, 1765–70, 3¾in (9.5cm) wide.
$500–600 ↗ LFA

A **Vienna dish,** painted with a polychrome floral bouquet and sprigs, with moulded spiral triple reeding and basketweave border, c1765, 10in (25.5cm) wide.
$170–200 ⊞ RAV

◄ A **blue and white pickle dish,** the interior painted with a variation of the Gazebo pattern, probably Worcester, c1760, 3in (7.5cm) wide.
$220–260 ↗ RTo

A **Chelsea octagonal dish,** painted in Kakiemon style in orange, grey, black and gold with two stylized Oriental birds, one in flight and one seated on the branch of a pine tree, above a flowering hedge, restored, c1755, 8in (20.5cm) wide.
$1,100–1,450 ↗ Bon(C)

A **pair of Derby dishes,** painted in coloured enamels with sprays of flowers and leaves, the gadrooned rims with a gilt band, crowned crossed batons mark, c1820, 11in (28cm) wide.
$300–350 ↗ SAS

A **Spode botanical dish,** painted with a pink crocus, the rim decorated in gilt, c1800, 9in (23cm) diam.
$550–650 ⊞ JAK

A **Worcester dish,** decorated with the Sir Joshua Reynolds pattern, in orange, yellow, turquoise and green on a white ground within a deep blue and gilt border, First Period, c1770, 11in (28cm) wide.
$1,000–1,250 ⊞ WWW

PORCELAIN

Egg Cups

A Coalport egg cup, decorated with flowers in a cartouche on an apple-green band, c1840, 2¼in (5.5cm) high.
$110–125 ⊞ **AMH**

A Davenport egg cup, painted in iron-red, deep blue and gilt, 1870–80, 2½in (6.5cm) high.
$130–145 ⊞ **AMH**

Six Royal Crown Derby egg cups, decorated with the Imari pattern, marked, 1914, 2¼in (5.5cm) high.
$370–440 🔨 **Bon(C)**

A Royal Worcester egg cup, decorated in gilt below a light blue band, c1880, 2in (5cm) high.
$50–60 ⊞ **AMH**

Figures

An Arcadian figure of a British Soldier, with a Welsh crest, 1914–18, 5¼in (13.5cm) high.
$230–260 ⊞ **G&CC**

A pair of Emile Claus figures, emblematic of Spring and Autumn, wearing flower-decorated dresses, the bases with C-scrolls heightened with gilt, marked, c1900, 14in (35.5cm) high.
$400–450 🔨 **Mit**

A Bow *blanc-de-chine* **figure of Columbine,** c1765, 5in (12.5cm) high.
$1,800–2,200 ⊞ **DMa**

A Victorian Copeland parian figure of Narcissus, by Gibson, modelled by E. B. Stephens for the Art Union of London, 1846, 12½in (32cm) high.
$600–700 🔨 **DDM**

Cross Reference
See Colour Review
(page 296)

A Bow figure of a boy, standing beside a tree, wearing a pink jacket and green breeches, c1755, 7in (18cm) high.
$1,600–1,750 ⊞ **JUP**

A Derby bisque figural group of boys, dressed in 18thC costume and playing musical instruments, incised mark 'N333', c1780, 11¼in (28.5cm) high.
$1,300–1,600 🔨 **HAM**

A pair of Chelsea arbour groups, both the lady and the gentleman seated on balustrades in front of bocage, wearing elaborately decorated costumes, the gilt-bordered bases flanked by arms for candle nozzles, marked, both restored, 1762–69, 9¾in (25cm) high.
$3,000–3,500 🔨 **Bon(C)**

A Derby figure of a harvester, with a dog at his feet, wearing a puce jacket and hat, a decorative waistcoat and turquoise breeches, the base with three patch marks, some restoration, c1780, 7¼in (18.5cm) high.
$600–700 🔨 **Oli**

A Frankenthal figure of a street vendor, wearing a pink and blue striped dress, carrying a pink basket, on a gilt-scrolled base, damaged and repaired, marked, c1765, 7in (18cm) high.
$580–650 ⚒ P(Pr)

A Fürstenberg group of two children and a goat, modelled by Simon Feilner, one child seated on the brown and white goat feeding it a fruiting vine, the second child wearing a yellow drape, restored, incised mark 'W/o', c1770, 5in (12.5cm) high.
$1,000–1,150 ⚒ S

A W. H. Goss figure of Lady Rose, wearing a yellow and green dress with a pink shawl and bonnet, 1929–35, 6¾in (17cm) high.
$370–450 ⊞ G&CC

A W. H. Goss parian group of Lady Godiva on horseback, 1880–1905, 7in (18cm) high.
$850–950 ⊞ G&CC

A Meissen centrepiece, modelled as female figures back to back, in flowing blue and violet robes, supporting a basket painted with sprigs of flowers, c1860, 8in (20.5cm) high.
$3,500–4,000 ⊞ MAA

A Höchst figure of a gardener, modelled by Johann Peter Melchior, standing by a marbled plinth, wearing a beige hat, green coat and yellow neckerchief and breeches, restored, marked, c1770, 6¾in (17cm) high.
$1,000–1,150 ⚒ S

A Ludwigsburg figural group representing Winter, modelled as two putti beside a fire, restored, interlaced Cs mark, c1780, 7in (18cm) high.
$350–450 ⚒ P(Pr)

A Longton Hall group of two putti and a goat, the scrolled base applied with flowers and picked out in bright green, puce, iron-red and manganese, damaged, restored, c1755, 5in (12.5cm) high.
$350–450 ⚒ P

A set of four Meissen figures, emblematic of the four seasons, each classically-draped figure raised on a rococo scroll base, marked, c1860, 10in (25.5cm) high.
$2,600–3,200 ⚒ JBe

A Nymphenburg group of Diana and a dog, wearing a blue sash and holding a pink shawl, the fawn dog with brown markings, marked, restored, 19thC, 17in (43cm) high.
$1,000–1,150 ⚒ DORO

A pair of Meissen cabinet figures, wearing 18thC costume, decorated in polychrome and enriched with gilding, the man with a blue scarf over his eyes, the lady showing a look of surprise, late 19thC, taller 16½in (42cm) high.
$1,600–1,800 ⚒ HYD

A Meissen group of Bacchus and Silenus, depicting Silenus on a grey ass supported by Bacchus wearing a lilac drape, beside a maiden in a flower-patterned dress, slight losses, marked and incised '2724', c1870, 9in (23cm) high.
$1,000–1,200 ⚒ Hal

◄ **A Minton parian figure of Clorinda,** by John Bell, depicted seated with sword, shield and helmet, 19thC, 13½in (34.5cm) high.
$260–320 ⚒ DMC

PORCELAIN

A pair of Royal Dux figures, pattern Nos. 271 and 272, wearing animal skins, the man playing pan pipes, the lady with a tambourine, marked, late 19thC, 19¾in (50cm) high.
$2,200–2,600 ➧ **Bea(E)**

A Samson figural group, modelled as a nursing mother wearing a pink and white dress and green shawl, with two young children, on a scroll-moulded base, slight damage, marked, late 19thC, 10½in (26.5cm) high.
$500–600 ➧ **S**

A Schlaggenwald figure of a philosopher, wearing a puce coat, yellow waistcoat and black breeches, impressed 'S' mark, Bohemia, c1840, 7¼in (18.5cm) high.
$200–250 ➧ **DORO**

A Sèvres bisque group, in the form of a youth with two hunting dogs, one tail restored, c1860, 12in (30.5cm) high.
$2,200–2,400 ⊞ **JAK**

A Worcester figure of a baccante, modelled by Hadley, No. 1440, holding a tambourine above her head, with a tree trunk support on a rocky base, restored, 1894, 28in (71cm) high.
$1,300–1,600 ➧ **AG**

A Worcester Kerr & Binns period candle extinguisher and stand, in the form of a French cook wearing a yellow dress and ribbons, on a yellow stand, restored, slight damage, 1855–60, 3in (7.5cm) high.
$300–350 ➧ **P**
This example is the earliest version with a separate arm.

A bisque figural candle-stick, in the form of two children supporting an urn, some damage, 19thC, 15in (38cm) high.
$360–440 ➧ **SWO**

A pair of French bisque figures, the girl holding fruit in the folds of her skirt, the young man holding a flower pot and plant, painted in pastel colours of predominantly pink, blue and green, late 19thC, 15in (38cm) high.
$1,000–1,200 ➧ **DDM**

▶ **A set of four Italian figures,** modelled as two courting couples, on pedestals, damaged, mid-19thC, 5½in (14cm) high.
$250–300 ➧ **EH**

▶ **A pair of bisque figures,** in the form of a boy and a girl seated on stools and blowing bubbles, with some painted decoration, early 20thC, 12½in (32cm) high.
$725–800 ➧ **ELR**

Flasks

A Caughley flask, decorated in black with monogram 'MH', painted in *famille rose* colours with a spray of flowers and leaves surrounded by scattered flowers, c1785, 6½in (16.5cm) high.
$850–1,000 ➧ **SAS**

A pair of Minton moon flasks, decorated in raised paste gilding and silvered with grasses and insects on a blue ground, some restoration, marked, c1863, 5½in (14cm) high.
$600–700 ➧ **SAS**

A pair of Royal Worcester moon flasks, painted in Japanese style, with panels of canine scenes in the style of Landseer, in shades of brown and grey on a turquoise ground, heightened with gilding by Samuel Ranford, impressed mark, slight damage, probably by James Bradley Senior, 1860–70, 9¾in (25cm) high.
$2,300–2,500 ➧ **S(S)**

Flatware

A pair of Belleek plates, hand-painted in naturalistic colours with rural scenes, Second Period, 1891–1926, 9in (23cm) diam.
$3,200–3,600 ⊞ DeA

A pair of Davenport plates, decorated in coloured enamels with the arms of Pierce within a flower-scroll cartouche, the puce-ground border with three flower sprays within gilt cartouches, c1830, 9in (23cm) diam.
$725–875 ⋗ SAS

A Donovan plate, painted with a scene entitled 'Amor at the Hill of Difficulty' in shades of green, brown, blue, pink and red, c1820, 9in (23cm) diam.
$500–600 ⊞ STA

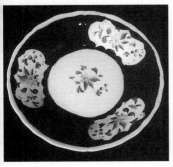

A Bow plate, decorated in *famille rose* colours with a peony and bamboo growing from rockwork, the border with three lotus sprays, chips to the rim, c1760, 8¾in (22cm) diam.
$250–300 ⋗ P(Ba)

A Derby meat plate, with gilt-enriched floral decoration in Imari colours, painted mark to base, 19¾in (50cm) long.
$260–320 ⋗ PFK

Miller's is a price GUIDE not a price LIST

A Dresden plate, decorated in pastel colours with two figures sitting beneath trees, surrounded by four moulded floral panels, a cross mark, late 19thC, 10½in (26.5cm) diam.
$145–175 ⋗ WW

◀ **A Gaudy Welsh porcellaneous bread plate,** decorated with Columbine pattern No. 45 in pink, green and yellow on a white ground, within a deep blue border, 19thC, 8½in (21.5cm) diam.
$75–95 ⊞ CoHA

A Caughley saucer dish, painted in coloured enamels with a spray of flowers and leaves and scattered flowers within a gilt line rim, 1785–90, 7¼in (18.5cm) diam.
$230–280 ⋗ LFA

A Royal Crown Derby plate, painted by Albert Gregory, with a polychrome spray of flowers on a white ground, the deep blue border with raised gilding, c1904, 9in (23cm) diam.
$3,500–4,500 ⊞ BP

PORCELAIN

PORCELAIN

Nantgarw porcelain

- Established near Cardiff in 1813 by William Billingsley, a ceramic artist from the Derby factory, with the intention of creating a rival to French porcelain.
- Due to high kiln losses the venture failed and production was moved to Swansea, where Billingsley entered into an arrangement with Lewis Weston Dillwyn of the Cambrian pottery.
- By 1817, dissatisfied with Dillwyn, Billingsley had returned to Nantgarw.
- Between 1817 and 1820 large quantities of highly translucent soft-paste porcelain with an almost glass-like white glaze were produced, much of which was sent in the white to London for decoration and sale.
- Principal output was plates, often decorated in the French manner and moulded with scroll and floral patterns.
- The body of Nantgarw porcelain is generally more thickly potted and heavier in weight than Swansea porcelain.
- Billingsley left Nantgarw in 1820 to join Coalport. William Weston Young took over the factory and employed the accomplished artist Thomas Pardoe to decorate the remaining pieces which had all been sold by 1822, leading to the factory's closure.

A Brownlow Hill, Liverpool, footed plate, attributed to William Ball or James Pennington, painted in blue with a bird perched on rockwork and a flowering plant, the border painted with Oriental flowers growing from the blue line rim, minor damage, 1760–66, 9in (23cm) diam.
$360–440 ➶ P

A Longton Hall saucer, painted in underglaze blue with two pavilions in a chinoiserie river landscape, blue-painted 'S' beside the footrim, 1755–58, 4¾in (12cm) diam.
$450–500 ➶ LFA

A set of six Minton dessert plates, painted with waterfowl within turquoise and gilt borders, marked for 1881 and 1882, 9in (23cm) diam.
$1,750–2,000 ⊞ JAK

A Nantgarw plate, painted in blue over the glaze with seven flower sprays, flower-moulded and gilt dentil rim, impressed mark, 1821–23, 9¾in (25cm) diam.
$130–145 ➶ WW

A New Hall plate, painted with a scene of Dr Syntax and the Gypsies, pattern No. 2623, with gilt foliate border, inscribed mark, c1820, 8½in (21.5cm) diam.
$500–600 ➶ DN

A pair of rue Thiroux, Paris, plates, painted in pink, yellow, red, green and blue with bouquets of flowers, iron-red marks, slight damage, French, 18thC, 9¾in (25cm) diam.
$270–320 ➶ DORO

A pair of Worcester plates, from the *atelier* of James Giles, polychrome-decorated with sprays of flowers within a brown and green border, with gilt rim, First Period, c1770, 9in (23cm) diam.
$3,000–3,500 ⊞ WWW
Giles was an outside decorator of porcelain and glass and is recorded from 1749 as a 'Chinaman' (ie vendor of porcelain) and from 1763 as an independent 'China and enamel painter'. In his Soho studio in London he decorated pieces of white porcelain made at the Worcester and Longton Hall factories, among others, from the 1760s. From 1767–71 the Worcester factory entered into an arrangement with Giles for his workshop to undertake much of their most prestigious decoration. Giles' unsigned fruit, floral and bird designs for Worcester were characterized by a looser, freer composition than was typical of the factory decoration.

A Paris cabinet plate, decorated in the Sèvres style in the manner of G. Tenier, enamelled with a lady and a boy playing a violin, the cobalt-blue border heightened with gilt, damaged, c1841, 9½in (24cm) diam.
$80–95 ➶ Hal

A Copeland Spode plate, decorated with the Chinese Rose Design No. Rd 629599, printed in black, impressed marks, 1898, 10¼in (26cm) diam.
$100–115 ⊞ ES

Ice Pails & Wine Coolers

A Caughley ice pail, printed in underglaze blue with the Pleasure Boat or Fisherman pattern, beneath spearhead and cell diaper bands, blue-painted 'X' mark, cover and liner lacking, c1785, 6½in (16.5cm) high.
$1,300–1,600 ⚒ LFA

A Coalport ice pail, decorated with gilt and deep rose bands, restored finial, stress cracks, 1815–20, 9in (23cm) high.
$1,100–1,250 ⊞ WWW

A pair of Meissen ice pails, covers and liners, the sides painted with panels of colourful birds within scroll-moulded panels picked out in gold, reserved on a ground applied all over with colourful garden flowers and fruits, the covers with painted flower sprays, crossed swords marks, handles broken and restuck, chipped, one liner with section of rim restuck, mid-19thC, 8¼in (21cm) diam.
$4,000–4,500 ⚒ P

A pair of wine coolers and covers, with gilt handles and feet, decorated with bands of foliage in shades of blue with green and iron-red, possibly Spode, early 19thC, 12in (30.5cm) high.
$1,750–2,000 ⚒ E

> ### Sets/pairs
> Unless otherwise stated, any description which refers to 'a set' or 'a pair' includes a guide price for the entire set or the pair, even though the illustration may show only a single item.

◄ **A pair of Vienna ice pails,** decorated with sprigs of flowers and gilt, c1792, 17in (43cm) high.
$7,000–8,000 ⊞ US

Inkstands & Inkwells

A Coalport inkstand, with gilt eagle-head terminals, painted in coloured enamels with flowers and leaves, within canted rectangular panels decorated in gilt with leaf scrolls and flowerheads, c1805, 6¾in (17cm) long.
$725–875 ⚒ SAS

A Coalbrookdale-style inkstand, encrusted with finely-modelled and painted flowers, probably Minton, c1830, 11½in (29cm) long.
$1,000–1,150 ⊞ DIA

A Derby inkstand, decorated in red, blue and gilt on a cream ground, 19thC, 11in (28cm) long.
$200–250 ⚒ SWO

A Sèvres-style inkstand, the *bleu celeste* ground painted with flowers and birds, the wells with hinged lids, supported on a metal mount, damaged, 19thC, 11¾in (30cm) wide.
$400–500 ⚒ WW

An inkwell, painted in coloured enamels with flowers and leaves, moulded with lion-mask roundels, the rim heightened with gilt, on three gilt feet, rim chips restored, c1820, 4in (10cm) diam.
$180–220 ⚒ LFA

A Continental turquoise-glazed inkwell, with a hinged lid, in the form of a juggling cherub balancing a drum on his knee, late 19thC, 4¾in (12cm) high.
$600–700 ⚒ WW

Jars

A Belleek Diamond biscuit barrel, decorated with green on a moulded white ground, First Period, 1863–90, 7in (18cm) high.
$1,000–1,150 ⊞ DeA

A Chantilly jar and cover, painted in Kakiemon style with children, the cover with three flower sprigs, c1735, 3¼in (8.5cm) high.
$4,000–4,500 ↗ S

A Royal Worcester biscuit jar, cover and stand, shape No. 1412, decorated with printed flowers and insects highlighted in enamels, marked, dated 1892, 7¼in (18.5cm) high.
$550–600 ↗ P(S)

A Meissen screw-top pot and cover, painted with a continuous scene with two figures in a coach being driven through a river landscape, dated at the base of a cairn, the cover with two similar vignettes, gilt-edged rims, slight damage, crossed swords mark and dot in blue, 1770, 4in (10cm) high.
$4,800–5,800 ↗ S

Jardinières

A Caughley jardinière, painted in the style of Sèvres in underglaze blue, small footrim chip, 1780–85, 4½in (11.5cm) high.
$725–875 ↗ SAS

A flower pot and stand, probably Spode, pattern No. 839, painted in coloured enamels with a rural landscape, the borders decorated with gilding, incised numeral '5', early 19thC, 6¼in (16cm) diam.
$1,250–1,450 ↗ F&C

A Belleek jardinière, white-glazed and applied with flowers and foliage, Second Period, 1891–1926, 10in (25.5cm) high.
$1,250–1,400 ⊞ DeA

Cross Reference
See Colour Review (page 300)

▶ **A Minton and Co Thorwaldsen jardinière,** the *bleu celeste* ground with raised panels of birds and musical trophies within ornate gilt borders, the corners modelled as a parian Bacchic-style figure, marked, damaged, 1862–70, 9¼in (23.5cm) high.
$500–600 ↗ Bon(C)

Jugs & Ewers

A Belleek Shell jug, marked in black, First Period, 1863–90, 9in (23cm) high.
$250–300 ⊞ DeA

◀ **A pair of Belleek flowered Aberdeen ewers,** each body encrusted with a wreath of roses, shamrocks and flowers, minor losses, marked in black, Second Period, 1891–1926, 6in (15cm) high.
$500–600 ↗ P(Ba)

A Bow milk jug, polychrome-painted with three chinoiserie figures in a garden, small rim chips, c1760, 3in (7.5cm) high.
$350–400 ↗ WW

A Bristol milk jug, painted in puce with floral sprays, lacking cover, c1775, 4in (10cm) high.
$400–450 ✗ P

A Caughley mask jug, with a cabbage-leaf-moulded body, transfer-printed in dark underglaze blue with bouquets and sprigs of flowers, titled in crescent mark, 1775–85, 9¼in (23.5cm) high.
$250–300 ✗ CGC

A Chantilly jug, hand-painted in coloured enamels with a floral spray and scattered sprigs, with five moulded rings in yellow and a brown line rim, red horn mark, spout chipped, c1730, 5¼in (13.5cm) high.
$500–600 ✗ P

A Derby jug, decorated with sprays of flowers and ears of corn in naturalistic colours and gilt, possibly by Withers, late 18thC, 7¼in (18.5cm) high.
$1,250–1,450 ✗ HYD

A pair of Bloor Derby Kedlesdon shape ewers, the side panels painted in French 18thC style, 1820–30, 11in (28cm) high.
$4,500–5,000 ⊞ RGa

A Hill Pottery parian ewer, the body decorated with a Bacchanalian scene in polychrome on a white ground, with a gilt band to the rim, neck and foot, and with a gilt handle, late 19thC, 15¼in (38.5cm) high.
$300–350 ✗ Bea(E)

A Liverpool Chaffers sparrowbeak jug, painted in underglaze blue with a pagoda and trees, c1760, 3½in (9cm) high.
$1,300–1,450 ⊞ JUP

A Lowestoft sparrowbeak jug, painted in Redgrave style with chinoiserie buildings surrounded by flowering plants, c1775, 3½in (9cm) high.
$725–875 ✗ GAK

A Meissen jug and cover, painted in *famille verte*-style with a pine tree growing in a yellow flower pot, the reverse with flowering plants, all between gilt line borders, the cover with flowering branches, crossed swords mark in underglaze blue, restored, c1735, 8in (20.5cm) high.
$5,000–6,000 ✗ S

A New Hall milk jug, pattern No. 318, painted in puce and gilt with a flower and leaf-scroll band, within gilt line borders, c1790, 4¼in (11cm) high.
$180–220 ✗ LFA

A pair of Worcester mask jugs, decorated in blue with Bouquets pattern, c1775, 8½in (21.5cm) high.
$1,150–1,300 ⊞ JUP

A pair of Worcester mask jugs, painted with clematis, passion flower, cyclamen and other flowers, the mask-head spouts possibly representing Princess Alexandra, the raised gilt bands with gilt-decorated handles and covers, green-printed marks, 1886, 7¾in (19.5cm) high.
$1,800–2,200 ✗ AG

◀ **A Royal Worcester Mephistopheles miniature character jug,** shape No. 2850, in the form of a bearded devil, wearing an orange and black costume, puce mark, 1929, 3¼in (8.5cm) high.
$500–600 ✗ P

A Royal Worcester tusk jug, shape No. 1116, painted with a colourful bird in flowering leafy grasses, with a sweetpea to the reverse, attributed to Hopewell, gilt rims and details, puce mark, c1888, 10in (25.5cm) high.
$650–800 ✗ WW

A Royal Worcester jug, with a dragon handle, decorated with pink blossom and foliage on a peach ground, 1888, 7½in (19cm) high.
$320–380 ✗ SWO

Mirrors

A Dresden wall mirror, with encrusted floral decoration and beaded blue rims, 19thC, 17¼in (44cm) high.
$350–450 ↗ Mit

A pair of Dresden-style mirrors, moulded with scrolls and shells with gold detail and applied with sprays of flowers and putti, one putto lacking arm, minor losses, late 19thC, 18in (45.5cm) high.
$1,150–1,350 ↗ P

A Sitzendorf easel mirror, with floral-encrusted border surmounted by two winged cherubs holding a garland of flowers, c1880, 13in (33cm) high.
$600–700 ↗ Mit

A German wall mirror, the rococo scroll-moulded frame fitted with three candle branches and applied with coloured flowers and figures, minor damage, late 19thC, 29¼in (74.5cm) high.
$1,800–2,200 ↗ Bea(E)

Mugs & Tankards

A Belleek Thorn mug, decorated with pink flowers, Second Period, 1891–1926, 3in (7.5cm) high.
$620–680 ⊞ MLa
This pattern, especially when coloured, is keenly sought by collectors.

A Bow mug, the body moulded with three sprays of flowering prunus and painted in *famille verte* colours with scattered flowers, some damage, 1750–55, 5in (12.5cm) high.
$500–600 ↗ WW

A Bow mug, painted in coloured enamels with exotic birds, beneath a brown line rim, broken and glued, restored, c1770, 6in (15cm) high.
$250–300 ↗ LFA

A Caughley mug, transfer-printed in underglaze blue with the Pine Cone pattern, blue-printed 'S' mark, c1785, 5½in (14cm) high.
$500–600 ↗ LFA

A Coalport mug, painted in coloured enamels with a band of flowers and leaves, on a gilt ground, some damage, probably by William Billingsley, 1800–05, 3¼in (8.5cm) high.
$600–700 ↗ LFA

A mug, painted with botanical sprigs and cherries in brown, green, yellow and puce, the base unglazed, cracked and chipped, possibly Derby, c1775, 4½in (11.5cm) high.
$2,600–3,200 ↗ P

◄ **A Lowestoft mug,** transfer-printed in blue, 1770–80, 5½in (14cm) high.
$700–800 ↗ WW

► **A Meissen tankard,** reserved with a scroll-edged panel and encrusted with coloured roses, the hinged cover with gilt-metal mounts, crossed swords mark in underglaze blue, some damage, mid-19thC, 8in (20.5cm) high.
$5,800–7,200 ↗ S(S)

A New Hall mug, transfer-printed and painted in polychrome with a continuous chinoiserie scene, minor damage, c1800, 4in (10cm) high.
$320–380 ⚒ WW

A Paris mug, decorated with figures on a yellow ground, beneath a gilt and pink border, 3¼in (8.5cm) high.
$300–320 ⚒ SWO

A Worcester tankard, transfer-printed in black with the 'King of Prussia' and military trophies, the reverse with the winged figure of Fame, signed 'Worcester', 1757, 5½in (14cm) high.
$500–600 ⚒ P

A Worcester tankard, transfer-printed in black with the Whitton Anglers pattern, from an engraving by William Wollett, the reverse with The Minuet, in the style of Francis Hayman, 1768–70, 6in (15cm) high.
$1,000–1,250 ⚒ P

A Worcester mug, decorated in blue with Plantation Print pattern, crescent mark, 1760–70, 6in (15cm) high.
$450–500 ⚒ WW

A Worcester mug, transfer-printed in underglaze blue with *La Pêche* or *La Promenade Chinoise*, hatched crescent mark, c1770, 5¾in (14.5cm) high.
$600–700 ⚒ LFA

Plaques

A Copeland plaque, by William Yale, depicting Balmoral Castle with cattle and a drover in the foreground, signed, 19thC, in an ebonized frame 12 x 16in (30.5 x 40.5cm).
$870–1,000 ⚒ AH

A Royal Worcester plaque, entitled *La Rixe,* painted by J. Stanley, after an original by Meissonier, with a tavern brawl scene, puce printed factory marks, signed, damaged, 1929, 7 x 9½in (18 x 24cm) in gilt gesso frame.
$900–1,100 ⚒ Bon(C)

A Davenport plaque, painted with a portrait of a young man, impressed and signed 'S. Chester', 1872, 10 x 8¼in (25.5 x 21cm).
$360–440 ⚒ WW

A plaque, painted in polychrome enamels with a still life of fruit, 19thC, 8in (20.5cm) wide.
$725–875 ⚒ WW

A Rozenburg plaque, polychrome painted with a farmer with sheep and cows, marked 'Rozenburg', Holland, late 19thC, in a mahogany frame 12½ x 9¾in (32 x 25cm).
$725–875 ⚒ DORO

A Meissen plaque, painted with a portrait of *La Chocolatière* carrying a tray, in tan and lilac on a blush-pink ground, 19thC, 6in (15cm) high.
$2,000–2,300 ⚒ JAd

Pot-pourri Vases

A Coalbrookdale garniture of three pot-pourri vases, with pierced covers, applied with flowers and leaves and decorated with coloured enamels, within gilt scroll borders, one vase restored, c1840, 6¼in (16cm) high.
$650–800 ⚹ SAS

A Derby pot-pourri vase and cover, decorated with the Imari pattern, with gilt handles, feet and knop, c1810, 5in (12.5cm) high.
$500–600 ⊞ RAV

A pair of St Cloud white pot-pourri vases, encrusted with flowers, c1730, 8in (20.5cm) high.
$5,000–6,000 ⊞ US

A pair of Sèvres-style pot-pourri vases, with a pompadour pink ground, with pierced covers and gilt flowerhead finials and scroll-pierced shoulders, 19thC, 8in (20.5cm) high.
$150–175 ⚹ DA

> Miller's is a price GUIDE not a price LIST

A pair of Dresden pot-pourri vases, Helena Wolfsohn factory, with pierced covers, decorated with panels of figures in garden settings, and painted floral reserves on a turquoise blue ground heightened with gilt, Augustus Rex marks, c1900, 12½in (32cm) high.
$500–600 ⚹ AG

A Royal Worcester pot-pourri jar, shape No. 301, decorated in coloured enamels and gilding, the pierced cover with a recumbent elephant and howdah finial, supported on three elephant-head feet, marked, c1872, 8¼in (21cm) high.
$1,600–1,800 ⚹ P(Sy)

A pair of French pot-pourri vases, painted with marine scenes on a navy blue ground, with gilt embellishment and green banding, the bases with painted landscape vignettes, 19thC, 12in (30.5cm) high.
$3,000–3,500 ⚹ AH

Sauce & Cream Boats

A Charles Bourne miniature London-shape cream boat, decorated in blue, iron-red and gilt, with a gilt dentil rim, marked, c1820, 3in (7.5cm) long.
$360–440 ⚹ LFA

A Bow blue and white cream boat, the ribbed body painted with buildings, trees and flowers, damaged, c1765, 4¼in (11cm) long.
$145–175 ⚹ WW

A Champion's Bristol cream boat, moulded with flowers and fruit and painted with flower sprays, damaged, c1775, 4¼in (11cm) long.
$175–200 ⚹ WW

A Caughley fluted sauce boat, transfer-printed in underglaze blue, marked, hairline crack, c1780, 6in (15cm) wide.
$400–500 ⚹ SAS

A Bristol cream boat, painted with fruit, leaves and sprays of flowers, with a rose beneath the spout, marked, c1780, 4¼in (11cm) long.
$800–950 ⚹ Bea(E)

A Caughley cream boat, painted in underglaze blue with chinoiserie Island pattern, with blue rim band, marked, c1780, 3¾in (9.5cm) long.
$650–800 ⚹ LFA

PORCELAIN

A pair of Derby blue and white sauce boats, moulded with fruits and leaves outlined in underglaze blue and with C-scroll chinoiserie landscaped cartouches, the cell border interior rim with floral sprays, mid-18thC, largest 7¾in (19.5cm) long.
$650–800 ✗ Mit

A Derby sauce boat, painted with polychrome flowers, cracked and repaired, c1760, 9¼in (23.5cm) long.
$250–300 ✗ WW

A Liverpool sauce boat, attributed to Pennington & Part, decorated with flowers in underglaze blue, c1780, 5¾in (14.5cm) long.
$500–600 ✗ SK

A Liverpool sauce boat, by Pennington & Part, transfer-printed in blue with Three Ladies pattern, c1789, 7in (18cm) long.
$450–500 ⊞ JUP

A Longton Hall sauce boat, moulded with latticework in salt-glazed style, the interior painted in *famille rose* colours, c1755, 8in (20.5cm) long.
$1,250–1,400 ⊞ JUP

A pair of Worcester sauce boats, transfer-printed in red, blue and green with sailing ships and wild flowers, c1755, 6in (15cm) long.
$6,500–7,500 ✗ JH

A Worcester sauce boat, painted in blue with a chinoiserie scene, c1757, 8in (20.5cm) long.
$800–900 ⊞ JUP

▶ A Worcester sauce boat, decorated in blue with Doughnut Tree pattern, 1770–80, 6in (15cm) long.
$725–875 ⊞ RGa

A Worcester sauce boat, the interior painted with a blue cell border and floral sprays, the exterior with a similar spray below the spout, the sides embossed with a bouquet of flowers, marked, c1765, 6¾in (17cm) long.
$725–875 ✗ P

A Worcester sauce boat, feather-moulded with embossed rococo panels, painted in blue with Man with a Bomb pattern, a striding fisherman on the reverse, a scrollwork panel and foliage inside the spout, a floral spray in the base, crescent mark in blue, c1765, 7in (18cm) long.
$1,300–1,600 ✗ P

Scent Bottles

A pair of Meissen scent bottles, encrusted with polychrome flowers, c1880, 3in (7.5cm) high.
$1,000–1,150 ⊞ DHu

◀ A St James's scent bottle, by Charles Gouyn, in the form of the Three Graces, their robes painted with flower sprays in yellow and blue with puce linings, the base with gilt-metal fitting and similar flower painting, with replacement bird-shaped metal stopper, restored, 1749–55, 4in (10cm) high.
$1,600–1,800 ✗ P
These pieces were formerly termed Girl in a Swing items, the name deriving from a figural group in the Victoria & Albert Museum. They consist principally of porcelain novelties, such as scent bottles and *bonbonnières*, and were produced in the mid-18th century by the London jeweller Charles Gouyn from his house in Bennet Street, St James's.

A scent bottle, modelled as a honeycomb, in cream with a turquoise bee, with a gilt-metal stopper, 19thC, 4in (10cm) high.
$260–320 ⊞ LBr

PORCELAIN

Spoons & Ladles

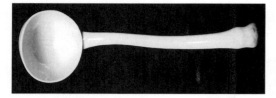

◀ **A Belleek ladle,** 1863–90, 11in (28cm) long. **$400–450** ⊞ MLa

A Caughley caddy spoon, the bowl printed in underglaze blue with a chinoiserie river landscape, within a flower, butterfly and diaper border, chip to handle, 1780–85, 4¼in (11cm) long. **$725–875** ↗ LFA

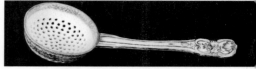

A Meissen spoon, the bowl decorated with a bouquet of flowers, heightened with gilt, c1755, 8in (20.5cm) long. **$600–700** ⊞ US

A Meissen porcelain sugar spoon, decorated with flowers to the exterior of the bowl and the handle, heightened with gilt, Germany, c1755, 8in (20.5cm) long. **$950–1,200** ⊞ US

Tea Canisters

A William Cookworthy tea canister, painted with scattered polychrome flowers and sprigs below a border of red scale and green marble panels within a gilded design, lacking cover, 1768–72, 2¾in (7cm) high. **$1,000–1,250** ↗ P

A Ludwigsburg tea canister, rib-moulded and decorated with flowers and leaves in red, blue, orange, green and pink, lacking cover, Germany, c1760, 5in (12.5cm) high. **$870–1,000** ⊞ US

A Meissen tea canister and cover, polychrome painted with sprays of flowers, c1760, 5in (12.5cm) high. **$200–250** ↗ HYD

A Worcester fluted tea canister, decorated with blue flower sprays and sprigs, lacking cover, 1770–80, 5in (12.5cm) high. **$350–450** ↗ WW

Trays

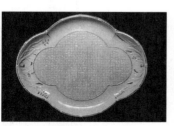

A Meissen pen tray, painted with flowers in pink and gilt, crossed swords mark, c1890, 9in (23cm) wide. **$145–175** ↗ WW

A Belleek tray, decorated in relief with grasses heightened in pink around a moulded basketweave centre, First Period, 1863–90, 15in (38cm) wide. **$1,800–2,200** ⊞ MLa

An Isleworth spoon tray, transfer-printed in blue with four vignettes, slight wear to rim, c1780, 6¾in (17cm) wide. **$3,600–4,400** ↗ P **No similar example is apparently recorded, although shards of a similar fluted shape have reputedly been excavated at Isleworth.**

◀ **A Ridgway card tray,** painted with a half-length figure of a lady dressed in pink, the blue ground border with tooled gold scrolls, printed factory Royal Warrant mark in puce, c1840,10in (25.5cm) wide. **$600–700** ↗ P

A Rockingham pin tray, the centre painted with Woton Bridge in naturalistic colours, with grey and gold shell-moulded border, puce Griffin mark, c1835, 4¼in (11cm) wide. **$1,450–1,600** ↗ P

Colour Review

A **Staffordshire Whieldon type creamware model of a parrot,** in the style of a Chinese original, restored, c1760, 6in (15cm) high.
$8,700–10,000 ↗ S

A **spill vase modelled as a pig,** beside a tree stump, possibly Staffordshire, c1820, 6in (15cm) high.
$4,650–5,250 ⊞ JHo

A **Staffordshire spill vase modelled as a horse,** beside a tree stump, c1870, 6in (15cm) high.
$360–410 ⊞ SER

A **Minton majolica spill vase modelled as a hen,** by John Henk, impressed 'Minton No. 1983', 1878, 13in (33cm) high.
$10,800–12,000 ↗ JNic

A **French majolica duck,** by Delphine Massier, Vallauris, c1880, 9in (23cm) long.
$580–650 ⊞ MLL

A **stoneware group of terriers,** by Stella R. Crofts, c1928, 7in (18cm) wide.
$480–540 ⊞ WWW

A **Staffordshire bust of Judith,** by Enoch Wood, c1790, 15¾in (40cm) high.
$650–725 ↗ HAM

A **Wemyss Plichta pig,** 1930s, 15in (38cm) long.
$1,900–2,100 ↗ AH

▶ A **Scottish Portobello figure of a fishwife,** c1790, 8¾in (22cm) high.
$1,600–1,750 ↗ P(Ed)

◀ A **pearlware figure of Hercules,** by Enoch Wood, c1800, 18in (45.5cm) high.
$1,900–2,100 ⊞ JRe

▶ A **Staffordshire model of Wellington,** 19thC, 11½in (29cm) high.
$1,200–1,400 ↗ WW

A **Staffordshire earthenware group,** entitled 'New Marriage Act', c1825, 11in (28cm) high.
$6,500–7,250 ⊞ JHo

◀ **A Nevers faïence bowl,** entitled 'Tree of Love', minor wear to rim, France, 1758, 13in (33cm) diam.
$3,200–3,600 ⚒ P

▶ **A Staffordshire leaf bowl,** c1765, 5in (12.5cm) diam.
$2,100–2,400 ⊞ JHo

A Staffordshire Whieldon type pineapple bowl, c1770, 5in (12.5cm) diam.
$650–800 ⊞ JHo

A footed bowl, painted with cornflowers, poppies and daisies, painted mark 'M.K.T.K.' and bee, c1920, 10¼in (26cm) diam.
$360–430 ⊞ P(Ed)

A Wemyss tyg, painted with Roses pattern, c1900, 8in (20.5cm) diam.
$870–1,000 ⊞ RdeR

A Scottish Portobello furniture rest, modelled as a basket of fruit, chipped, early 19thC, 4½in (11cm) high.
$290–320 ⚒ P(Ed)

A Wemyss two-handled Coronation cup and cover, impressed 'WEMYSS R.H. & S', retailers mark for T. Goode & Co, cover possibly matched, 1902, 8¾in (22cm) wide.
$2,000–2,300 ⚒ S

A W. Mason dish, transfer-printed with Linlithgow Palace, c1820, 10in (25.5cm) wide.
$700–770 ⊞ JP

> **Miller's is a price GUIDE not a price LIST**

A George Jones majolica cheese stand and cover, impressed crescent and 'GJ' monogram, marked '5251', damaged, c1875, 13in (33cm) high.
$21,750–24,000 ⚒ P

A George Jones majolica cheese dish and cover, moulded in relief with nasturtiums, painted mark '5253/80', 7½in (19cm) high.
$2,600–2,900 ⚒ AH

▶ **A Minton majolica game tureen,** with liner and cover, c1871, 13in (33cm) long.
$6,000–6,600 ⊞ RGa

A Longchamps asparagus cradle and platter, France, c1880, 14in (35.5cm) long.
$600–660 ⊞ MLL

An Italian maiolica tazza, School of Urbino, on a low foot, minor rim chips, c1540, 6¾in (17cm) diam.
$18,800–20,300 ➷ S

A Dutch decorated creamware plate, entitled 'Handel J2V7', depicting St Peter in prison, c1800, 10in (25.5cm) diam.
$400–460 ⊞ JHo

A Scottish pearlware plate, c1800, 10¼in (26cm) diam.
$110–130 ➷ P(Ed)

A Mason's plate, transfer-printed with a scene from The College Series, c1830–48, 10in (25.5cm) diam.
$200–220 ⊞ JP

A pair of pearlware plates, polychrome-decorated with exotic birds, hairline crack, 18thC, 9in (23cm) diam.
$1,100–1,300 ➷ RBB

A Minton majolica Lindsay tray, designed by Sir Coutts Lindsay, the centre painted with Venus and Neptune surrounded by putti, probably by Thomas Allen, impressed mark, 1861, 17¾in (45cm) diam.
$5,000–5,800 ➷ P

A Georges Pull earthenware Palissy plateau, centred by a raised medallion of Temperance surrounded by four cartouches of the Elements, bordered by eight muses, impressed 'PULL', France, c1869, 16¾in (42.5cm) diam.
$725–870 ➷ Bon(C)

A pair of English printed and painted plates, with lustre handles, c1880, 8in (20.5cm) diam.
$65–75 ⊞ JACK

A Wemyss plate, painted with Buttercups pattern, c1890, 8in (20.5cm) diam.
$580–720 ⊞ RdeR

A set of nine Creil creamware plates, printed with figures of Cupid dressed for months of the year, and a matching centre plate printed with St George and The Dragon, impressed mark, printed mark of Legros d'Anizy, France, c1830, largest 13in (33cm) diam.
$1,600–1,800 ➷ CAG

A Sarreguemines majolica oyster dish, France, c1900, 15in (38cm) diam.
$220–240 ⊞ MLL

A French Palissy-style platter, School of Paris, possibly by Achille or Victor Barbizet, extended crack and some minor chips, 1870–80, 19½in (49.5cm) long.
$14,500–17,500 ➷ S(NY)

A majolica garden seat, attributed to Brown-Westhead Moore, modelled as an Egyptian slave girl, section of foot and base lacking, c1875, 22in (56cm) high.
$10,000–11,500 ⚒ P

A Venice albarello, painted with a medallion, possibly St Valentine, Italy, mid-16thC, 12¼in (31cm) high.
$5,000–5,800 ⚒ S

A majolica jardinière on a stand, probably by George Jones, late 19thC, 44¼in (112.5cm) high.
$16,000–17,400 ⚒ Gam

A pair of Staffordshire jardinières and matching pedestals, late 19thC, 41in (104cm) high.
$725–875 ⚒ CAG

An Italian Castelli-style maiolica jardinière, painted on one side with a scene possibly depicting the Expulsion of Hagar and Ishmael, with the goddess Juno on the reverse, restored, late 19thC, 23in (58.5cm) wide.
$1,900–2,100 ⚒ S

A Staffordshire enamelled salt-glazed jug, c1765, 3in (7.5cm) high.
$2,100–2,300 ⊞ JHo

A German Westerwald jug, stamped 'AR', c1710, 9in (23cm) high.
$2,600–2,900 ⊞ SEA

A Prattware jug, moulded in relief with Britannia and a galleon, the reverse with a scene of the Sailor's Return, 1790–1800, 5¼in (13.cm) high.
$360–430 ⚒ Bon(C)

A Staffordshire lustre earthenware jug, moulded in relief with Bacchic figures, c1810, 5in (12.5cm) high.
$145–190 ⊞ SER

A Staffordshire lustreware jug, inscribed 'Josh & Sally Saxton 1824', inscriptions and a crest relating to Oddfellows, 1824, 7in (18cm) high.
$320–360 ⚒ DOC

A Mason's wash bowl and jug, decorated with Bandana pattern, 1840–60, jug 10in (25.5cm) high.
$650–725 ⊞ JP

A Minton majolica jug, moulded in high relief with peasants drinking and dancing, impressed mark, date code, incised '487', hairline crack to base, c1878, 10in (25.5cm) high.
$1,450–1,750 ⚒ RTo

A Gaudy Welsh jug, decorated with Cambrian Rose pattern No. 8, small restoration, 19thC, 7in (18cm) high.
$320–360 ⊞ CoHA

A Prattware scent flask, decorated with portraits of John Wesley, 18thC, 4in (10cm) high.
650–725 ⊞ LBr

A Wedgwood blue jasper silver-mounted scent bottle, c1820, 4in (10cm) high.
$1,000–1,200 ⊞ BHa

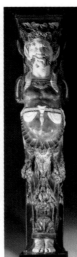

◀ **A Continental majolica pedestal,** probably French, modelled in the form of Bacchus dressed as a warrior, impressed 'MUSEES NATIONAUX...', hairline crack to base of neck, c1880, 46½in (118cm) high.
$1,900–2,100 ⚒ S

A George Jones majolica part dessert service, comprising 11 pieces, impressed marks and design registration marks, damaged, 1869.
$6,500–7,250 ⚒ LFA

A Staffordshire Toby jug, 1790, 10in (25.5cm) high.
1,400–1,600 ⊞ JHo

A Wemyss part toilet set, comprising five pieces, decorated with Cocks and Hens pattern, impressed mark, printed mark for 'T. Goode', damaged, c1900, the pail 11in (28cm) diam.
$1,400–1,600 ⚒ TEN

◀ **A pearlware Toby jug,** modelled as Hearty Goodfellow, early 19thC, 11in (28cm) high.
$725–875 ⚒ P(S)

A Mason's Francis Morley garniture, pattern No. 222, comprising three vases with covers, c1850, largest 13in (33cm) high.
$3,600–4,000 ⊞ JP

A Continental glazed majolica vase, moulded in high relief with Bacchanalian figures, with a pair of horned mask handles, one horn broken and missing, chips, slight cracks, 19thC, 23in (58.5cm) high.
$2,600–2,900 ⚒ S(NY)

◀ **A Wemyss bottle vase,** painted with hydrangeas and foliage, impressed 'WEMYSS', yellow script mark, early 20thC, 9¾in (25cm) high.
$3,900–4,300 ⚒ S

A Mason's blue and white ironstone fruit bowl, decorated with Blue Pheasant pattern, impressed mark, c1813, 10in (25.5cm) square.
$500–580 ⊞ JP

An R. Cochran & Co blue and white jug, transfer-printed with Fairy pattern, c1870, 13in (33cm) high.
$200–230 ✗ P(Ed)

A Minton blue and white jug and wash bowl, transfer-printed with Genevese pattern, printed marks, the basin with impressed mark, c1900, basin 13¾in (35cm) diam.
$290–350 ✗ PFK

A Spode blue and white plate, from the Indian Sporting Series, transfer-printed with a chase after a wolf, c1810, 9½in (24cm) diam.
$290–320 ⊞ SCO

An Adams blue and white meat plate, transfer-printed with lions, c1815, 20in (51cm) long.
$4,000–4,600 ⊞ SCO

◀ A blue and white pearlware meat plate, from the Antique Scenery Series, transfer-printed with Kirkstall Abbey, Yorkshire, 19thC, 21in (53.5cm) long.
$580–725 ✗ AH

▶ A blue and white meat platter, transfer-printed with the Stafford Gallery pattern, damaged, 19thC, 21in (53.5cm) long.
$850–1,000 ✗ HAM

A Roger's blue and white plate, from the View Series, transfer-printed with a rural scene, c1820, 10in (25.5cm) diam.
$175–200 ⊞ OCH

A Roger's blue and white plate, from the View Series, transfer-printed with a rural scene, c1820, 10in (25.5cm) diam.
$175–200 ⊞ OCH

A Hicks & Meigh blue and white dinner service, comprising 60 pieces, early 19thC, platter 19in (48.5cm) long.
$2,900–3,100 ⊞ TWr

A child's Davenport blue and white dinner service, from the British Scenery Series, comprising 33 pieces, mid-19thC, large plate 9in (23cm) wide.
$2,000–2,300 ⊞ MLu

◀ A Staffordshire blue and white soup tureen stand, from The Cities & Towns Series, probably by Charles Harvey & Sons, Longton, transfer-printed with a view of Canterbury, early 19thC, 16in (40.5cm) long.
$500–580 ✗ CAG

▶ A Roger's blue and white egg tureen, transfer-printed with Elephant pattern, c1815, 9in (23cm) high.
$1,100–1,300 ⊞ SCO

An English delft model of a tabby cat, probably London, previously unrecorded, areas of restoration to glaze, chip to one ear, c1680, 5½in (14cm) wide.
$34,800–39,000 ➤ S

An English delft blue and white punch bowl, painted with a fisherman and houses, mid-18thC, 9in (23cm) diam.
$870–1,000 ➤ WW

A Dutch Delft model of a cockerel, marked in iron-red overglaze for Jan Theunis Dijkstra, restored, 18thC, 6in (15cm) high.
$14,500–16,000 ➤ S(Am)

An English delft charger, painted with truncated oak leaves around a central leaf, rim chip, late 17thC, 13½in (34.5cm) diam.
$6,500–7,250 ➤ P

An English delft charger, painted with tulips, minor rim chips, section glued and riveted, c1720, 13¾in (35cm) diam.
$3,200–3,500 ➤ P

A pair of London delft plates, painted with flowers, Lambeth, c1760, 9in (23cm) diam.
$720–870 ⊞ SEA

A Liverpool delft plate, painted with Fazackerley floral decoration, c1760, 9½in (24cm) diam.
$800–880 ⊞ JHo

▶ A Dutch Delft doré dish, painted with a flower-filled vase, small firing crack, 18thC, 8¾in (22cm) diam.
$4,000–4,600 ➤ S(Am)

A Liverpool delft plate, polychrome-decorated with a bird on a branch, c1765, 12in (30.5cm) diam.
$2,400–2,700 ⊞ JHo

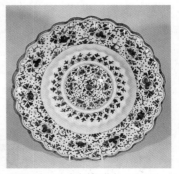

A Continental delft dish, painted with a stylized floral pattern, 18thC, 13½in (34.5cm) diam.
$430–500 ➤ AH

A Bristol delftware loving cup, polychrome-painted with a chinoiserie scene, minor chips, marked and dated '1728', 8¾in (22cm) diam.
$36,250–40,600 ➤ S

▶ A miniature English delft tankard, painted with scrolling foliage, slight damage, c1690, 2½in (6.5cm) high.
$12,300–14,500 ➤ Bea(E)

A Dutch Delft canary plaque, marked 'APK' in iron-red overglaze for the factory De Grieksche A, early 19thC, 17in (43cm) diam.
$3,900–4,300 ➤ S(Am)

A Bow group of birds, perched on a tree with a dog seated at the base, c1758, 9in (23cm) high. **$1,600–1,800** ⊞ **JUP**

A Meissen model of a parrot, perched on a tree stump, heightened with gilt, crossed swords mark in underglaze blue, incised numerals, Germany, late 19thC, 16½in (42cm) high. **$4,000–4,600** ↗ **S(Am)**

Two Meissen models of juvenile gulls, probably modelled by Max Esser, crossed swords mark in underglaze blue, incised numerals '77181' and '77180', Germany, c1920, largest 11¼in (28.5cm) high. **$2,400–2,900** ↗ **CAG**

A Schwarzburger Werkstätten group of two leopards, modelled by Etha Richter, incised and impressed marks, Germany, c1914, 17½in (44.5cm) high. **$2,300–2,600** ↗ **S**

A Bow figure of a musician, damaged, restored, c1765, 8¼in (21cm) high. **$1,700–2,000** ↗ **P**

A Chelsea figure of a Chinaman, gold anchor mark, restored, c1760, 3½in (9cm) high. **$2,600–3,200** ↗ **S(NY)**

▶ **A Derby group,** entitled The Stocking-Mender, incised mark, restored, c1780, 6¼in (16cm) high. **$1,000–1,200** ↗ **LFA**

A Meissen figure, entitled The Beggar Musician, by J. J. Kändler, from the *Cris de Paris* series, Germany, c1760, 3¾in (9.5cm) high. **$4,600–5,200** ⊞ **BELL**

A pair of Derby seated figures, c1770, 6in (15cm) high. **$1,700–2,300** ⊞ **DMa**

A pair of Meissen pagoda figures, with nodding heads, rocking hands and tongues, with crossed swords and incised marks, Germany, mid-19thC, 12½in (32cm) high. **$17,500–20,000** ↗ **WW**

A pair of Meissen figures, modelled as a gallant and his lady, crossed swords mark, incised numbers, Germany, mid-19thC, 18in (45.5cm) high. **$7,200–8,700** ↗ **HAM**

▶ **A figure of a shepherdess,** possibly Thuringia, holding a garland of flowers, Germany, late 18thC, 11½in (29cm) high. **$1,000–1,200** ↗ **DORO**

A **Belleek basket,** the cover encrusted with
~~p~~ink and yellow flowers, Second Period, Ireland,
~~1~~891–1926, 18in (45.5cm) wide.
2,000–2,300 ⊞ DeA

A **Coalport pot-pourri vase and
cover,** known as the Adelaide
basket, c1835, 9in (23cm) wide.
$3,300–3,700 ⊞ RGa

A **pair of English scent
or toilet water bottles,**
encrusted with flowers,
c1830, 10in (25.5cm) high.
$1,200–1,400 ⊞ DAN

A **Meissen purple-ground slop
bowl,** painted with *indianische Blumen,*
crossed swords mark in underglaze
blue, impressed numbers, Germany,
~~c~~1740, 6½in (16.5cm) high.
3,600–4,000 ✗ S(Z)

A **Worcester bowl,** painted with Jabberwocky
pattern, late 18thC, 8¼in (21cm) diam.
$1,100–1,300 ✗ TMA

A **Coalport chalice and
cover,** painted with a portrait
of Mrs Lowndes Stone Norton
in the style of Gainsborough,
signed by F. Sutton, c1895,
13in (33cm) high.
$3,600–4,300 ⊞ JUP

A **Samuel Alcock chamberstick and
snuffer,** c1845, 3in (7.5cm) high.
$360–400 ⊞ DIA

A **Minton comport,** painted with flowers,
c1860, 9in (23cm) high.
$400–460 ⊞ GRI

A **set of nine Vienna custard cups,** on a tray, decorated
with sprigs of flowers and bands of leaves and gilt, Austria,
c1792, cups 3in (7.5cm) high.
$5,800–6,500 ⊞ US

A **composite Sèvres desk set,** painted in coloured enamels
on a *bleu celeste* ground, with gilt-metal mounts, pen tray
damaged, France, 1860–80, candlesticks 5¾in (14.5cm) high.
$870–1,000 ✗ DN

A **pair of Derby dishes,** heightened
with gilt, one damaged, early 19thC,
13in (33cm) wide.
$290–350 ✗ CMS

A **display dish,** applied with flowers
and birds, the rim heightened with
gilt, on three feet, c1820,
10in (25.5cm) wide.
$1,600–1,800 ⊞ WWW

An **Imperial Russian porcelain egg,**
handpainted, c1880, 3in (7.5cm) long.
$1,200–1,400 ⊞ SHa

A Marcolini Meissen teapot, decorated with flowers, with a gilt-metal handle, c1800, 7in (18cm) high.
$1,400–1,700 ⊞ DHu

A Coalport teapot, cover and stand, decorated with blue and yellow borders and gilding, c1840, 10½in (26.5cm) wide.
$260–320 ⚒ WW

A French teapot and cover, painted by Phillipp Xhrowet, possibly Sèvres, c1767, 5in (12.5cm) high
$5,000–5,800 ⊞ US

▶ **A Vienna coffee set,** decorated with silhouettes of the Royal Family of Naples and Sicily, Austria, c1801, coffee pot 11in (28cm) high.
$5,800–7,200 ⊞ DHu

◀ **A Spode teapot, cover and stand,** decorated with Imari pattern No. 1495, c1810, 4¾in (12cm) high.
$1,200–1,400 ⊞ JAK

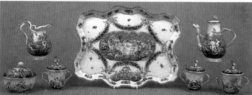

A Naples cabaret set, comprising seven pieces, moulded in relief with scenes of mythological figures, underglaze blue crown and 'N' mark, Italy, late 19thC, tray 15¼in (38.5cm) long.
$1,700–2,000 ⚒ P(S)

A pair of Brussels *écuelles*, with covers and stands, gilded and painted with a seascape view, iron-red 'N' mark, c1840, 6¼in (16cm) high.
$2,200–2,600 ⚒ S(Am)

A Coalport coffee cup and saucer, decorated with jewels, c1900, saucer 5in (12.5cm) diam.
$540–620 ⊞ JUP

A Derby coffee cup and saucer, with crowned crossed batons marks in puce, c1785, cup 2¾in (7cm) high.
$550–600 ⚒ SAS

A Gaudy Welsh porcellaneous cup and saucer, decorated with pattern No. 636, with flowers and foliage, 19thC, saucer 5¾in (14.5cm) diam.
$145–190 ⊞ CoHA

A Nymphenburg cup and saucer, painted with mythological scenes, impressed lozenge mark, Germany, c1770, cup 2¼in (5.5cm) high.
$2,900–3,500 ⚒ DORO

A Paris cup and saucer, France, 1810–20, cup 2½in (6.5cm) high.
$1,000–1,100 ⊞ US

A Worcester Chelsea-shape ewer, painted with chinoiserie scene, c1760, 3½in (9cm) high.
$2,000–2,300 ⊞ JUP

A Chamberlain cheese stand, painted with the arms of Evans and the motto 'Libertas', c1810, 10½in (26.5cm) diam. $1,100–1,300 ⚶ P

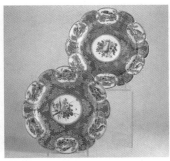

A pair of Chelsea scalloped-edge plates, decorated with reserves of birds and fruit, gold anchor marks, small chips, c1765, 8½in (21.5cm) diam. $6,500–8,000 ⚶ S(NY)

A Derby feather-edged plate, painted with botanical subjects, painter's mark for William Billingsley, late 18thC, 8½in (21.5cm) diam. $1,400–1,700 ⚶ TMA

A Royal Crown Derby plate, of Lichfield shape, painted by Edwin Trout with a view of Bakewell, 1898, 8in (20.5cm) diam. $4,300–5,000 ⊞ BP

A pair of Minton plates, painted with fruit, the reticulated borders heightened with gilt, c1856, 9in (23cm) diam. $1,600–1,900 ⊞ WWW

A six-place Minton dessert service, comprising eight pieces, each marked on base '6709A', c1870, plates 9in (23cm) diam. $290–350 ⚶ DOC

A pair of Paris Nast plates, decorated with exotic birds, France, c1800, 9in (23cm) diam. $1,500–1,700 ⊞ US

A Paris cabinet plate, from the *atelier* of Schoëlcher, marked in gold on the underside, France, early 19thC, 9¼in (23.5cm) diam. $1,900–2,200 ⚶ NOA

A Nantgarw plate, painted with flowers, impressed mark, Wales, 1814–23, 8½in (21.5cm) diam. $1,700–2,000 ⚶ SAS

A pair of Worcester Flight period dessert service saucer dishes, painted with the coat-of-arms of the Duke of Clarence within the Belt of the Garter and with the pendant Order of the Thistle Badge beneath the crown, underglaze blue crown, Flight and crescent mark, damaged, c1789, 9¾in (25cm) wide. $18,000–21,750 ⚶ Bon(C) The Duke of Clarence later became King William IV.

A French Sèvres-style platter, painted with a battle scene, the border with portrait vignettes, c1860, 16in (40.5cm) wide. $3,200–3,500 ⊞ JAK

A Vienna plate entitled 'Wellenkuss', painted with a scene of a fisherman rescuing a maiden from the sea, Austria, 19thC, 9½in (24cm) diam. $650–800 ⚶ G(B)

A Minton inkstand, attributed to Thomas Steel, painted with fruit, c1830, tray 15in (38cm) long.
$1,900–2,100 ⊞ DIA

A Coalport jardinière, decorated at Madeley by Philip Ballard, c1830, 7in (18cm) high.
$2,900–3,500 ⊞ DHu

A Lowestoft coffee can, painted with a tulip and three flower sprigs, damaged, 1765–75, 2½in (6.5cm) high
$1,400–1,600 ↗ WW

A Worcester mug, enamelled with a group of Chinese musicians playing European instruments, damaged, restored, c1756, 4¾in (12cm) high.
$8,000–9,400 ↗ P
This mug has imperfections and was therefore a 'second', sold in the white to an outside decorator. No similar mug appears to be recorded.

A Worcester green-ground mug, painted with exotic birds in gilt cartouches, c1770, 3½in (9cm) high.
$2,100–2,400 ⊞ JUP

A Chamberlain's Worcester porter mug, decorated with reserves of game, 1805–10, 7in (18cm) high.
$8,000–8,800 ⊞ RGa

A Coalport scent bottle, decorated with flowers, c1890, 5in (12.5cm) high.
$460–500 ⊞ DHu

A Lowestoft cream boat, painted with flower sprays, fine rim crack, c1775, 3in (7.5cm) long.
$725–875 ↗ WW

A sauce boat, embossed with leaves and painted with Oriental flowering plants, damaged, restored, 1765–70, 8¾in (22cm) long.
$650–800 ↗ P

◄ **A Gaudy Welsh porcellaneous tyg,** decorated with Oyster pattern No. 37, 19thC, 4in (10cm) high.
$200–220 ⊞ CoHA

A Samson Chelsea-style scent bottle, with a gilt-metal screw top, c1880, 3in (7.5cm) high.
$870–1,000 ⊞ LBr

A Meissen tureen and cover, decorated with sprays of *deutsche Blumen* and applied flowers, crossed swords in underglaze blue, impressed mark, minor damage, Germany, c1750, 11½in (29cm) wide.
$4,300–5,000 ↗ S

◄ **A Worcester blue scale sauce tureen and cover,** painted and applied with flowers, some damage, c1770, 6in (15cm) high.
$1,300–1,450 ⊞ JUP

A pair of Derby vases, painted by G. Robertson, blue mark to base, c1800, 8in (20.5cm) high.
$3,600–4,000 ⊞ DHu

A Royal Crown Derby vase, painted with a floral panel by Albert Gregory, c1910, 16in (40.5cm) high.
$3,900–4,300 ⊞ JUP

A Chelsea vase and cover, painted with a panel depicting The Toilet of Venus in the style of Boucher, c1765, 14½in (37cm) high.
$7,250–8,000 ✗ S

A Spode New Shape vase, pattern No. 1227, painted in Imari style with flowers and leaves, c1815, 5¼in (13.5cm) high.
$650–800 ✗ LFA

A pair of Minton vases, decorated with cartouches of exotic birds, probably painted by Joseph Wareham and gilded by Robins, c1850, 12in (30.5cm) high.
$3,500–3,900 ⊞ DHu

▶ A pair of Worcester Flight, Barr & Barr period vases, one painted with a view of Denbigh Castle ruins, the other with Pont Y Rhydlanfair, Caernarvonshire, impressed marks, slight damage, c1825, 11½in (29cm) high.
$8,700–10,000 ✗ Bea(E)

A Minton *pâte-sur-pâte* vase and cover, by A. Birks, shape No. 2708, decorated with panels of nymphs, marked, damaged, repaired, 1888, 20¼in (51.5cm) high.
$11,600–13,000 ✗ S

A pair of Carl Thieme Potschappel vases, painted with lovers in a rustic land-scape and applied with floral and fruit swags, marked in underglaze blue, some chips, possibly lacking covers, Germany, late 19thC, 14in (35.5cm) high.
$1,100–1,300 ✗ S(S)

A Royal Worcester Persian-style reticulated vase, by George Owen, ornamented with finely-tooled raised gilding, indistinct printed mark and shape number in gold, incised signature, cover lacking, c1900, 6¾in (17cm) high.
$14,500–17,500 ✗ P

A Worcester First Period vase, painted with Chrysanthemum pattern, c1765, 6in (15cm) high.
$1,100–1,300 ⊞ RAV

A Chamberlain's Worcester bottle vase, decorated *en grisaille* with lovers, c1835, 11in (28cm) high.
$720–870 ⊞ DAN

◀ A Royal Worcester vase, design No. 1969, the cartouche with a landscape signed by Harry Davis, 1926, 15¼in (38.5cm) high.
$8,000–9,500 ✗ L&E

A Berlin bowl, painted with a band of flowers and leaves, above a band of biscuit acanthus leaves moulded in relief on a burnished gilt ground, Germany, c1830, 10in (25.5cm) wide.
$9,400–10,800 ✦ S(NY)

A Berlin cabinet cup and saucer, with sceptre marks in underglaze blue, painter's mark 'H' and halfmoon in brown, impressed number, Germany, c1800, 3½in (9cm) high.
$1,300–1,400 ✦ S(Z)

A Berlin cup and saucer, painted with a topographical scene, Germany, c1820, 4in (10cm) high.
$1,400–1,700 ⊞ DHu

▶ **A Berlin Venetian-style jewel casket,** with fabric-lined interior, underglaze blue mark, Germany, late 19thC, 22in (56cm) wide.
$7,200–8,700 ✦ L&E

◀ **A Berlin cup and saucer,** painted with flowers, c1820, 3½in (9cm) high.
$350–400 ⊞ DeA

A pair of Berlin plates, painted with sprays of flowers, marked, Germany, c1790, 9½in (24cm) diam.
$720–870 ⊞ US

A pair of Berlin plates, with reticulated borders, c1880, Germany, 9in (23cm) diam.
$1,100–1,300 ⊞ DHu

A Berlin moulded teapot stand, painted with flowers and insects, Germany, 19thC, 5in (12.5cm) diam.
$110–125 ⊞ RAV

◀ **A Berlin teapot,** painted with flowers, Germany, c1850, 4½in (11.5cm) high.
$620–690 ⊞ DeA

A Berlin tête-à-tête, comprising 11 pieces, painted with flowers, sceptre mark in underglaze blue, impressed numerals, spouts restored, Germany, c1790, tray 14in (35.5cm) long.
$8,400–9,400 ✦ S

A Berlin vase, decorated with flowers and encircled by a band with pseudo-hieroglyphics, underglaze blue mark, incised triangle and '34', Germany, early 19thC, 7¾in (19.5cm) high.
$1,000–1,100 ✦ DORO

A Berlin topographical vase, painted with a panorama of Potsdam, the lower body painted *en grisaille* with classical decoration, sceptre mark in underglaze blue, red printed orb and KPM, restored, Germany, c1838, 30in (76cm) high.
$116,000–130,500 ✦ S(NY)
The form of this vase is one of the rarest produced by the Berlin factory – only four others are known.

A censer, modelled as a mandarin duck, the cover with five slits, Wanli period, 1573–1619, 5¾in (14.5cm) long. $7,200–8,000 ➣ S

A pair of models of *fu* lions, one with extensive kiln flaws to the glaze, 19thC, 10½in (26.5cm) high. $2,900–3,500 ➣ BB(S)

A Dutch-decorated guglet, Qianlong period, 1736–95, 9in (23cm) high. $900–1,000 ⊞ GLD

A Chinese export *famille rose* custard cup, Qianlong period, 1736–95, 3in (7.5cm) high. $360–430 ⊞ US

A numismatic powder box and cover, enamelled with the design of a Spanish trade dollar, c1805, 2½in (6.5cm) diam. $16,000–17,400 ➣ S

▶ A *sancai* figure of a lady, Tang Dynasty, AD 618–907, 15½in (39.5cm) high. $20,500–23,000 ➣ S

A *famille verte* figure of Butai, c1800, 6in (15cm) high. $650–800 ➣ RTo

A Chinese export figure of a lady, one of her removable hands holding a scroll, her back pierced with a square aperture, some damage to hands, 1775–90, 20½in (52cm) high. $8,000–8,800 ➣ S(NY)

A pair of *famille rose* candle-holders in the form of Chinese maidens, one head broken at the neck and reattached, losses at some extremities, late Qianlong period, 1736–95, 16in (40.5cm) high. $37,500–43,500 ➣ P

A provincial Ming jar, lacking cover, c1600, 12in (30.5cm) high. $4,700–5,800 ➣ RBB

A pair of Chinese export jars, painted with a phoenix among floral decoration, 1700–20, 17in (43cm) high. $5,800–6,500 ⊞ PCA

A ginger jar, Kangxi period, 1662–1722, 10in (25.5cm) high. $1,100–1,400 ⊞ GLD

◀ A pair of Canton *famille rose* jars and covers, minor damage and restoration, mid-19thC, 24½in (62cm) high. $8,000–9,500 ➣ WW

A Chinese export jelly jar and cover, c1780, 4in (10cm) high. $360–430 ⊞ US

A tortoiseshell-splashed Jizhou tea bowl, Southern Song Dynasty, 1127–1279, 4in (10cm) diam.
$16,000–18,800 ⚖ S

A Longquan celadon basin, the interior applied with a pair of biscuit fish, early Ming Dynasty, 15thC, 11¼in (28.5cm) diam.
$20,500–23,000 ⚖ S

A Chinese Imari barber's bowl, early 18thC, 11in (28cm) diam.
$1,700–2,000 ⚖ P(S)

A Canton *famille rose* bowl, 19thC, 12in (30.5cm) diam.
$1,100–1,400 ⊞ GLD

A Canton *famille rose* punch bowl, 19thC, 14½in (37cm) diam.
$500–580 ⚖ S(Am)

A *wucai* dish, for the Japanese market, Chenghua six-character mark, early 17thC, 8in (20.5cm) diam.
$3,200–3,700 ⚖ P

A pair of Chinese export plates, 1700–20, 8in (20.5cm) diam.
$1,700–1,900 ⊞ PCA

A Chinese export *famille rose* botanical plate, in the style of a European design, probably Maria Sybille Merian, hair crack to rim, c1740, 9in (23cm) diam.
$6,100–6,900 ⚖ S(NY)

A pair of *famille rose* plates, early Qianlong period, rim chips, mid-18thC, 9in (23cm) diam.
$1,200–1,400 ⚖ S(Am)

◄ **A pair of *famille verte* shallow dishes,** one with hairline crack, Kangxi period, 1662–1722, 13in (33cm) diam.
$2,900–3,200 ⚖ P(S)

A pair of Chinese export *famille rose* plates, minor chip, slight enamel damage, Qianlong period, 1736–95, 9in (23cm) diam.
$435–500 ⚖ Bea(E)

▶ **A Chinese export Tobacco Leaf pattern jardinière,** chip to foot, c1810, 10in (25.5cm) diam.
$10,000–11,600 ⚖ S(NY)

A *famille verte* lantern, on a carved wooden base, some damage, Qianlong period, 1736–95, 8in (20.5cm) high.
$3,200–3,700 ⚖ HAM

A Canton *famille rose* armorial part service, for the Scottish market, comprising seven pieces, c1810, tureen 14in (35.5cm) wide.
$8,300–10,000 ⚒ P

A Chinese export teapot, cover and stand, Qianlong period, 1736–95, 4½in (11.5cm) high.
$1,800–2,100 ⊞ GLD

A *famille rose* tureen, cover and stand, Qianlong period, 1736–95, 15¾in (40cm) wide.
$13,000–16,000 ⚒ LFA

A *kraak* vase, Wanli period, 1573–1619, 9½in (24cm) high.
$2,000–2,400 ⊞ GLD

A *sang-de-boeuf* vase, Qianlong mark and period, 1736–95, 11in (28cm) high.
$10,000–12,000 ⚒ S(NY)

A Canton vase, 19thC, 24½in (62cm) high.
$330–400 ⚒ DMC

A pair of *famille rose* vases and covers, painted with birds and flowers, 19thC, 15in (38cm) high.
$1,900–2,100 ⚒ HAM

A pair of *famille verte* vases, decorated with carp swimming among water plants, 19thC, 7¾in (19.5cm) high.
$2,000–2,400 ⚒ NOA

A pair of vases, with fitted wooden stands, both with base cracks, 19thC, 36¼in (92cm) high.
$8,000–9,500 ⚒ P

A *famille rose* vase, Early Republican period, early 20thC, 22in (56cm) high.
$9,500–10,500 ⚒ BB(S)

A pair of vases, chipped, Guangxu marks, 1875–1908, 19in (48.5cm) high.
$7,250–8,000 ⚒ BB(S)

A *famille verte* wine pot and cover, handle restored, Kangxi period, 1662–1722, 6½in (16.5cm) high.
$2,900–3,200 ⚒ S

A pair of *famille rose* water droppers, dated inscription on underside of stem, Guangxu mark and period, 1875–1908, 7½in (19cm) high.
$8,000–8,800 ⚒ S(NY)

A Satsuma bowl, the interior enamelled with sparrows flying through blooms, base damaged, Meiji period, 1868–1911, 12½in (32cm) diam.
$1,700–2,000 ⚒ RTo

An Imari ten-sided compote, the interior painted with two *shishi* enclosed by a band of flowers, 1820–40, 13½in (34.5cm) diam.
$4,000–4,800 ⚒ BB(S)

▶ **A Satsuma lidded canister,** Kinkozan impressed mark to lid and gilt signature on a black seal to the base, c1900, 4¾in (12cm) high.
$3,600–4,300 ⚒ L&E

An Imari tokkuri, the mouth with a copper rim, neck slightly reduced, minor chips, late 17thC, 10¼in (26cm) high.
$1,700–2,000 ⚒ S

▶ **An Imari figure of a geisha,** c1890, 16in (40.5cm) high.
$1,400–1,700 ⊞ GLD

A Kakiemon dish, decorated with two *ho-o* birds, chipped, Edo period, 1600–1868, 9½in (24cm) wide.
$11,500–13,500 ⚒ P

An Arita dish, with *fuku* mark, c1900, 10½in (26.5cm) diam.
$3,200–3,600 ⚒ S(NY)

An Imari charger, Meiji period, c1890, 18in (45.5cm) diam.
$450–500 ⊞ GLD

◀ **An Imari jar,** Meiji period, 1868–1911, 17¾in (45cm) high.
$3,200–3,700 ⚒ BB(S)

A Satsuma square vase, small chip, Meiji period, 1868–1911, 10½in (26.5cm) high.
$4,300–5,000 ⚒ P(Ba)

A Satsuma earthenware koro, by Kinkozan, painted with ceramic vessels, the metal cover applied with dragons, slight gilding losses, Meiji period, 1868–1911, 11in (28cm) high.
$10,200–11,500 ⚒ S
The inscription states that the vase shows all the ceramic forms of Japan, was fired ten times and took in excess of twenty weeks to produce.

A Satsuma vase, signed 'Kozan', Meiji period, 1868–1911, 9½in (24cm) high.
$3,200–3,700 ⚒ WW

◀ **A vase,** by Makuzu Kozan, signed, rim restored, 19thC, 19¼in (49cm) high.
$2,600–3,200 ⚒ S(Am)

COLOUR REVIEW

A French footed glass beaker, gilt-decorated with stylized stars and leaves, c1840, 5in (12.5cm) high.
$200–230 DORO

A set of six Moser polychrome enamel and gilded glass tumblers, Bohemia, c1860, 5in (12.5cm) high.
$13,000–16,000 ALiN

A pair of Mary Gregory-style Bohemian drinking glasses, c1880, 4in (10cm) high.
$500–650 ALiN
This type of glass was made in Bohemia in the style of pieces produced by Mary Gregory of the Sandwich Glass Co, Boston, USA, and then exported all over Europe to spa and seaside towns.

A pair of Bohemian enamelled glass cups and covers, late 19thC, 30in (76cm) high.
$2,900–3,500 P

A Bohemian drinking glass, the bowl engraved with deer, 1880–1920, 6in (15cm) high.
$500–580 BELL

A set of six hobnail-cut hock glasses, Stourbridge or Belgian, c1900, 8in (20.5cm) high.
$1,000–1,200 ALiN

◄ A glass decanter, with mother-of-pearl and cork stopper, c1840, 8in (20.5cm) high.
$290–320 GS

A Bohemian ruby-flashed glass goblet, late 19thC, 16in (40.5cm) high.
$3,200–3,700 Bea(E)

► A Nailsea glass flagon, c1810, 13¼in (33.5cm) high.
$580–650 Som

A flute-cut glass carafe, c1840, 7¼in (18.5cm) high.
$260–290 Som

A Bohemian glass decanter and beaker, c1860, 8½in (21.5cm) high.
$260–320 DORO

A cut-glass spirit bottle, with cut pear stopper, c1860, 11½in (29cm) high.
$500–580 Som

A Moser glass decanter and two liqueur glasses, applied with grapes and decorated with polychrome enamels, signed, Bohemia, c1875, decanter 9in (23cm) high.
$2,300–2,900 ALiN

► A French opaline cabaret, comprising six pieces, late 19thC, tray 11in (28cm) diam.
$850–950 NOA

A Stevens & Williams silver-mounted intaglio-cut glass biscuit barrel, 1895, 7in (18cm) diam. $2,600–3,200 ⊞ ALiN

A ruby overlay glass pedestal bowl, late 19thC, 0¾in (27.5cm) high. $1,000–1,200 ➤ Bea(E)

A Bohemian glass pedestal jar and cover, mid-19thC, 13in (33cm) high. $2,400–2,800 ➤ Bea(E)

A Victorian cranberry glass claret jug, with silver-plated mounts, c1890, 13in (33cm) high. $725–870 ⊞ CoHA

A pair of ribbed-moulded glass finger bowls, c1830, 4¾in (12cm) diam. $500–580 ⊞ Som

A Stourbridge citrus cameo glass cup and saucer, c1887, saucer 5in (12.5cm) diam. $2,200–2,600 ⊞ ALiN

▶ A Bohemian glass pedestal bowl, with alternating medallions of flowers and portraits of children, c1840, 8in (20.5cm) high. $800–950 ➤ DORO

A German *Goldrubinglas* jug, probably by Hermann Schwinger, slight damage, probably Nuremberg, c1700, 5in (12.5cm) high. $3,200–3,700 ➤ S

A Moser glass jug, applied with acorns and dragonflies and enamelled, Bohemia, c1875, 7in (18cm) high. $1,600–1,900 ⊞ ALiN

A Venetian latticino glass bowl, c1900, 4in (10cm) diam. $115–130 ⊞ GRI

A North Country wrythen-moulded glass cream jug and sugar basin, c1800, cream jug 3½in (9cm) high. $500–580 ⊞ Som

▶ A ribbed-moulded glass cream jug, c1820, 3½in (9cm) high. $360–430 ⊞ GS

A pair of Continental Persian-style glass ewers, Bohemian or Venetian, c1900, 12in (30.5cm) high. $3,900–4,300 ➤ S

A pair of Webb Queen's Burmese ware glass fairy-light shades, on clear pressed glass bases, 1870–90, 5in (12.5cm) high. $500–650 ⊞ ALiN

A set of four cameo glass salts, by Thomas Webb & Sons, Stourbridge, in a fitted case with spoons, c1885, box 6in (15cm) square.
$3,200–4,000 ⊞ ALiN

A set of three cranberry glass salts, each with a printy-cut band, c1880, 3in (7.5cm) high.
$390–430 ⊞ Som

A Bohemian double overlay gilded glass scent bottle, c1855, 10in (25.5cm) high.
$1,000–1,200 ⊞ ALiN

A Palais Royale casket with three opaline glass scent bottles, Paris, c1855, 4in (10cm) high.
$1,200–1,450 ⊞ ALiN

A Bohemian glass scent bottle and stopper, c1860, 7¼in (18.5cm) high.
$580–720 ⊞ GS

◄ **An overlay glass scent bottle,** with cut decoration and silver-gilt top, c1860, 4in (10cm) high.
$330–380 ⊞ Som

A Bohemian overlay glass scent bottle and stopper, with a second scent container within the stopper, c1870, 8in (20.5cm) high.
$1,000–1,200 ⊞ ALiN

A Victorian overlay glass scent bottle, ground rim, c1870, 6½in (16.5cm) high.
$145–180 ⊞ TWAC

A Webb Queen's Burmese ware decorated glass scent bottle, with silver top, marked, 1886, 3in (7.5cm) high.
$2,000–2,600 ⊞ ALiN

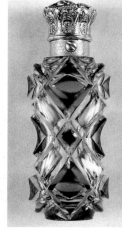

A ruby flashed glass scent bottle, 19thC, 7¼in (18.5cm) high.
$360–410 ⊞ TWAC

An overlay glass scent bottle, with silver-gilt snap top, late 19thC, 4in (10cm) high.
$725–800 ⊞ BHa

A Bohemian glass part dessert service, comprising 25 pieces, minor damage, c1840, comport 19in (48.5cm) high.
$11,500–13,000 ⚒ DORO

A Baccarat paperweight, with
initial 'B' cane and '1847', France,
in (7.5cm) diam.
2,400–2,600 ✗ Mit

▶ A Clichy paperweight, France,
855, 2¾in (7cm) diam.
3,600–4,000 ⊞ MLa

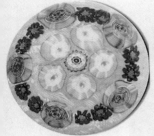

A Clichy paperweight, with a muslin
round, France, c1850, 2in (5cm) diam.
2,900–3,400 ⊞ SWB

▶ A Paul Ysart paperweight, with
'PY' cane, 1930s, 3in (7.5cm) diam.
800–900 ⊞ SWB

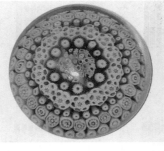

◀ A Bacchus paperweight, c1850,
3¼in (8.5cm) diam.
$2,900–3,400 ⊞ SWB

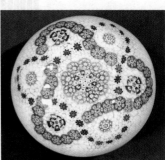

A Baccarat paperweight, with
garlands on stardust carpet ground,
France, c1848, 3in (7.5cm) diam.
$16,000–18,800 ⊞ DLP

A St Louis crown paperweight,
France, mid-19thC, 2¼in (5.5cm) diam.
$870–1,000 ✗ P

A pair of St Louis crown paperweight bud vases, c1850, 5in (12.5cm) high. $11,500–13,500 ➤ S

A pair of uranium glass vases, enamelled with birds on branches among scrolls and flowers, 1840–50, 9½in (24cm) high. $1,100–1,300 ➤ P

A St Louis crown paperweight overlay glass vase, mid-19thC, 6in (15cm) high. $6,500–7,250 ➤ P

A Victorian cranberry glass *épergne*, 22in (56cm) high. $520–620 ➤ ELR

A St Louis vase, with twisted canes, c1860, 4in (10cm) high. $320–400 ⊞ GS

A Bohemian intaglio-engraved cameo glass vase, with a portrait of Baron von Manteuffel, c1854, 9in (23cm) high. $3,300–4,300 ⊞ ALiN Baron von Manteuffel was one of the major organizers behind the unification of Germany.

A Victorian Continental glass vase, 6¼in (16cm) high. $120–145 ➤ DMC

A Venetian cameo glass vase, by Attilio Spaccarelli, 1891, 5¾in (14.5cm) high. $24,500–27,000 ➤ S

A Stevens & Williams cut-glass vase, c1875, 10in (25.5cm) high. $870–1,000 ⊞ ALiN

A French overlay glass vase, painted with gilt foliage, c1880, 12¼in (31cm) high. $650–800 ➤ DORO

A Bohemian glass vase, engraved with deer, 19thC, 12½in (32cm) high. $1,200–1,450 ➤ HOK

◄ A Bohemian cut-glass vase, with gilt-metal mounts, 19thC, 14¾in (37.5cm) high. $540–650 ➤ DORO

A Bohemian overlay glass vase and stand, with gilt scrolling foliage, vase broken from its base, some chipping, late 19thC, 19in (48.5cm) high. $3,200–3,600 ➤ S(S)

◄ A Stevens & Williams, intaglio-cut glass vase, c1895, 12in (30.5cm) high. $2,000–2,400 ⊞ ALiN

Tureens

A Caughley sauce tureen and cover, decorated in the Chamberlain's workshop with the arms of Knox of Ireland in coloured enamels, with underglaze blue and gilt flowerheads and leaves, the blue line border decorated in gilt with trailing flowers and leaves, restored, c1785, 7in (18cm) wide.
$725–875 ⚒ SAS

A Coalport tureen and cover, with gilt handles, decorated with Japan pattern with stylized foliage in underglaze blue, coloured in green, orange and red enamels and gilt, cracked, 1800–5, 7¾in (19.5cm) high.
$500–600 ⚒ Hal

A Worcester Flight, Barr & Barr period sauce tureen and cover, painted in coloured enamels with a unicorn crest and motto on a salmon ground, decorated in gilt with leaf scrolls and anthemion, restored, c1815, 6½in (16.5cm) high.
$800–1,000 ⚒ LFA

Vases

A pair of Royal Crown Derby vases, painted in the Imari style with stylized flowers in salmon, red, green and cobalt blue on a white ground, heightened with gilt, and with gilt handles and feet, c1900, 7in (18cm) high.
$800–1,000 ⚒ G(B)

A Belleek Tulip vase, highlighted in pink on an ivory ground, black stamp mark, First Period, 1863–90, 9in (23cm) high.
$1,450–1,600 ⊞ DeA

A Coalport rococo vase, the body painted with panels of birds between applied flowers, heightened with gilt, probably by Randall, c1840, 9in (23cm) high.
$600–700 ⚒ WW

A Daniels vase, painted with an Oriental figure among foliage, and exotic birds among blossom, on a green and primrose yellow ground, c1830, 8in (20.5cm) high.
$200–250 ⚒ P(E)

> Miller's is a price GUIDE not a price LIST

A Nantgarw miniature vase, probably painted by Thomas Pardoe, with chinoiserie in green monochrome and gilding, one side with a figure seated on a bench, the reverse with a bird in a tree, with gilt rims, 1817–20, 2in (5cm) high.
$3,000–3,500 ⚒ P

A Gustafsberg vase, decorated with a portrait of a girl holding a cat, within a scrolling gilt border, on a pale green ground, the scrolling gilt handles centred by paterae, Sweden, 1885, 21½in (54.5cm) high.
$600–700 ⚒ LJ

A Herend vase, decorated in polychrome with a bouquet of flowers surrounded by sprigs of flowers, on a white ground, the rim decorated in gilt with a scrolling design, slight damage, blue marks, Hungary, early 20thC, 12¼in (31cm) high.
$400–450 ⚒ DORO

◄ **A Minton** *pâte-sur-pâte* **vase and cover,** decorated by Alboin Birks with a figure of Venus and a winged cupid, the reverse with a group of trophies, on a peacock blue ground, with gilt handles and rims, gilt printed marks, damaged, c1910, 13in (33cm) high.
$1,750–2,000 ⚒ TEN

A Paris vase and cover, the hand-painted panel of lovers in a landscape signed by Poitevin, the reverse with a landscape, on a red-brown background, with gilt decoration and gilt-metal handles, fitted for electricity, repair to foot, c1870, 36in (91.5cm) high.
$725–875 ➶ DW

A Royal Worcester vase, with reticulated rim, decorated with flowers heightened with gilt, on an ivory ground, marked, 1889, 10in (25.5cm) high.
$480–580 ➶ L

A Royal Worcester vase and cover, painted by H. Davis, with a landscape with classical ruins and a river with cattle, in a tooled gilt reserve on an underglaze blue ground, the sides applied with lion-mask and ring drop handles, signed, foot cracked, early 20thC, 19¼in (49cm) high.
$7,250–8,750 ➶ L&E

A Sèvres *pâte-sur-pâte* vase and cover, by J. Gely, decorated with an exotic bird in flight on one side, a butterfly among blossom and grasses on the reverse, on a celadon ground, with gilt highlights, on a gilt-metal mount with berried leaf wreath, finial restuck, minor chips, signed, 1860–70, 16½in (42cm) high.
$4,500–5,500 ➶ S
Leopold-Jules-Joseph Gely is recorded as a sculptor and modeller at Sèvres 1850–88. He is regarded as one of the first and best of the manufactory's *pâte-sur-pâte* decorators, and his work in the 1850s was largely responsible for perfecting the technique.

A Royal Worcester vase and cover, painted by C. H. C. Baldwyn, with flying swans on a light blue ground, signed, c1897, 10½in (26.5cm) high.
$5,800–6,600 ⊞ JUP

A pair of French vases and covers, with mauve glazing and enriched with gilt, pseudo-interlaced 'L' marks to base, damaged, late 19thC, 13½in (34.5cm) high.
$1,300–1,600 ➶ DMC

A Spode vase, pattern No. 711, enamelled with groups of flowers on a gilt ground, on a pearl-banded pedestal, marked, 1815–20, 8¼in (21cm) high.
$3,000–3,300 ➶ LAY

A Worcester vase, transfer-printed in black with Rural Lovers pattern in the style of Gainsborough, the reverse with Milking Scene, surrounded by birds in flight, c1765, 7in (18cm) high.
$1,000–1,150 ➶ P

A pair of Grainger's Worcester vases, one decorated with a bird on a bough, the other with two scroll design panels of butterflies, each with a blue and gilt ground and gilt handles, damaged, early 20thC, 8in (20.5cm) high.
$300–330 ➶ DMC

A Staffordshire spill vase, pattern No. 80, painted in coloured enamels with flowers and leaves on a blue ground, with orange flowerhead medallions and gilt leaf-scrolls, within beaded bands, c1820, 6½in (16.5cm) high.
$450–550 ➶ LFA

A Royal Worcester vase and cover, decorated with gilt and painted with Stratford-on-Avon church in the moonlight, with gilt dragon handles, c1889, 20in (51cm) high.
$5,500–6,000 ⊞ BELL

A Royal Worcester Sabrina Ware vase, by Mary Eaton, shape No. H294, painted with fish among swirling weed and bubbles in pale green, blue and turquoise, marked, 1905, 10¼in (26cm) high.
$650–800 ➶ P
While the male painters at Royal Worcester were permitted to sign their work by this date, female painters like Miss Eaton were not allowed to sign until the 1920s.

Berlin

Hard-paste porcelain was first made in Berlin 250 years ago, when W. K. Wegely established a factory to produce porcelain in the Meissen style. The factory closed in 1757 due to high losses in the kilns and the outbreak of the Seven Years War. Marked with a 'W' in blue, pieces from this short-lived venture are rare. The Berlin Königliche Porzellan Manufaktur (KPM) was founded in 1761 by J. E. Gotzkowsky and was taken over by Frederick II of Prussia in 1763, under whose patronage production continued under the direction of modellers from Meissen, such as F. E. Meyer. Off-white with a yellowish, slightly grey hue, and identified by an underglaze-blue sceptre mark, 18th-century Berlin porcelain is generally extremely fine. The factory's modellers developed crisp moulded borders based on the osier or basketwork patterns of the 1760s – used especially by Meissen – and delicately painted with flowers and figures. Berlin is chiefly noted for its large decorative pieces and superb dinner services, the neo-classical designs of the late 18th century being exquisitely accomplished. With the rise of the bourgeoisie at the beginning of the 19th century, and the development of the Empire style, single, purely decorative, cabinet cups and saucers became popular in preference to complete services. From the 1820s the KPM painters collaborated with artists who were also architects and sculptors to produce 'Berliner Vedutenporzellan' – architectural and town views framed by complex tooled gilding. The manufacture of large painted vases increased dramatically, reaching a peak in the 1830s and 1840s but more affordable wares such as lithophanes and pipe bowls were also produced.

Berlin is particularly known for its plaques, which are of the highest standard. Plaques dating from 1840–60 mostly feature signed copies after the Old Masters, especially scenes from the Bible. The works of R. Dittrich, A. Lutz and the Wagner family are considered among the best. By the 1880s subjects had become more daring and stylish, depicting scantily-clad nymphs and girls wearing traditional Middle Eastern costume. Early 20th century pieces had a distinctly Art Nouveau feel.

Berlin experimented with previously unfashionable neo-Renaissance styles in the 1860s, making copies of Italian maiolica and German stoneware. Facing financial difficulties in the 1870s, Hermann Seger was appointed technical director and Louis Sussmann-Hellborn the first artistic director. A man of great talent, Seger became responsible for reviving the factory with his series of new glazes and other technical innovations. **Simon Cottle**

A Berlin white bisque lion, on a *faux* lapis lazuli plinth, restored, red printed KPM and orb mark, c1840, 6½in (16.5cm) long.
$8,000–9,000 ➤ S(NY)

> **Cross Reference**
> See Colour Review (page 302)

▶ **A Berlin coffee pot and cover,** decorated on one side with a polychrome scene of a peasant couple and musicians, the reverse with a minstrel surrounded by a young man and a mother and children, the spout and handles decorated in lilac and gilt, the cover with two vignettes and surmounted by a flower knop, restored, sceptre mark in underglaze blue, c1765, 9in (23cm) high.
$1,600–1,750 ➤ S(Z)

A Berlin cup and saucer, the cup painted with a view of the Royal Palace Herrenhausen and gilt interior, both pieces with gold borders, marked, sceptre marks in underglaze blue and brown eagle marks with KPM on both pieces, 1844–47, 5in (12.5cm) high.
$2,500–3,000 ➤ DORO

A Berlin coffee can and saucer, the can with a cartouche painted *en grisaille* with a portrait of a lady, on a deep blue ground with gilded scroll borders, the saucer with a gilded initial 'J' entwined with roses, late 19thC, sceptre marks, 2¼in (6.5cm) high.
$1,450–1,750 ➤ P

A Berlin cup and saucer, the cup painted with the arms of Wille of Silesia and Hesse, the matt blue ground with gilt borders of scrolling foliage and trailing leaves, sceptre mark in underglaze blue, c1820, 5in (12.5cm) high.
$1,750–2,000 ➤ S

PORCELAIN

A Berlin sweetmeat dish, in the form of a gallant, wearing a floral jacket, standing beside a basket supported on a scrolled stand heightened with gilt, damaged, underglaze blue sceptre mark, 18thC, 8½in (21.5cm) high.
$250–300 ✗ Bri

A Berlin group, entitled 'Dichtkunst', The Art of Poetry, in the form of a struggling writer, an angel and a putto, 19thC, 12¼in (31cm) high.
$180–240 ✗ P(Pr)

A Berlin figure of a sculptress, with a child at her feet, blue sceptre mark, base cracked, 1870–90, 12in (30.5cm) high.
$250–300 ✗ P(Pr)

A Berlin group, in the form of a mother and her two children, underglaze blue sceptre mark, 19thC, 7in (18cm) high.
$300–350 ✗ EH

A Berlin dish, polychrome painted with a spray of flowers between *feuille de choux* borders, c1780, 9in (23cm) square.
$870–1,000 ⊞ US

A Berlin dessert plate, decorated with a polychrome flower spray and three sprigs, with a Königsglatt pattern border, c1785, 9½in (24cm) diam.
$600–700 ⊞ US

A Berlin cabinet plate, decorated with a Berlin monument, within a broad gilt band, the border with puce and orange poppies with green foliage, restored, printed KPM and sceptre mark, 19thC, 9½in (24cm) diam.
$220–260 ✗ P(Ba)

A set of 24 Berlin botanical plates, each painted with a polychrome floral spray within gilt scroll borders, sceptre mark in underglaze blue, KPM stencilled in red, c1830, 9½in (24cm) diam.
$5,500–6,000 ✗ S

A set of six Berlin dessert plates, painted in enamels with an owl perched on either a branch or rockwork, surmounted by insects and floral sprigs within mint-green and gilded rims, printed marks, 1849–70, 8½in (21.5cm) diam.
$950–1,150 ✗ CGC

A Berlin plate, decorated with a lady with flowing auburn hair, within a deep blue and gilt border, c1890, 9¾in (25cm) diam.
$850–950 ⊞ DeA

A Berlin plaque, painted with a lady in a white dress and grey cloak holding a Roman lamp, on a gilt ground, KPM marks, c1840, 8in (20.5cm) wide.
$4,500–5,500 ⊞ MAA

▶ **A Berlin milk jug and cover,** the spirally-fluted body painted in coloured enamels with flowers and leaves within turquoise, puce and gilt borders, 19thC, blue mark, 5¼in (13.5cm) high.
$200–230 ✗ SAS

PORCELAIN

A Berlin plaque, painted by F. Sturm, in the style of D. Teniers, with a polychrome scene of peasants making merry outside an inn, signed, impressed No. 'II', KPM and sceptre marks, mid-19thC, 12 x 15¼in (30.5 x 38.5cm).
$7,250–8,000 ⚘ S

A Berlin plaque, painted in the Renaissance style with St Cecilia at the organ, KPM and impressed sceptre mark, c1860, 12½ x 10¼in (32 x 26cm) framed.
$2,500–3,000 ⚘ DN
St Cecilia is the patron saint of music.

A Berlin plaque, painted with a head and shoulders portrait of a gypsy girl with a shawl around her shoulders, impressed sceptre and KPM mark, 1870–80, 5¾in (14.5cm) high.
$870–1,000 ⚘ WW

A Berlin plaque, painted with a woman peeling apples, possibly in the style of the Dutch Old Master Gerrit Dou, impressed KPM mark, late 19thC, 12½ x 10in (32 x 25.5cm), in a giltwood frame.
$2,500–3,000 ⚘ SK

A Berlin plaque, painted by Müller, with a portrait of a young woman with dark hair wearing a black dress, signed, c1880, 10 x 8in (25.5 x 20.5cm).
$5,500–7,000 ⊞ MAA

A Berlin plaque, painted with a scene of a beggar wearing a white shirt and offering coins to Christ, KPM impressed factory and sceptre mark, 19thC, in a gilt gesso frame, 10¾ x 8¾in (27.5 x 22cm).
$870–1,000 ⚘ Bon(C)

A Berlin plaque, painted with a Neapolitan youth, in the style of Richter, wearing a white shirt and brown cloak, impressed mark, c1900, 10½in (26.5cm) high.
$2,500–3,000 ⚘ DORO

A Berlin shell-shaped salt, painted with birds, insects and flowers, supported by a grey and yellow dolphin, c1895, 2½in (6.5cm) high.
$250–300 ⊞ RAV

A Berlin Meissen-style dinner, coffee and tea service, pattern No. 36, comprising 167 pieces, polychrome decorated with bouquets and sprigs of flowers and butterflies on a white ground, the tureens with putto knops, sceptre marks in underglaze blue, red painter's marks, early 20thC.
$12,500–14,500 ⚘ DORO

◄ **A Berlin dinner service,** probably in the style of Friedrich Elias Meyer in 1765, comprising 75 pieces, decorated with bouquets of flowers surrounded by borders of rocaille cartouches enclosing yellow trelliswork with gilt flower stems, sceptre mark in underglaze blue, KPM and orb in iron-red, impressed numerals and painted numbers, early 20thC.
$34,000–38,000 ⚘ S(Am)

A Selection of Chinese Dynasties & Marks
Early Dynasties

Neolithic	10th – early 1st millennium BC	Tang Dynasty	618–907
Shang Dynasty	16th century–c1050 BC	Five Dynasties	907–960
Zhou Dynasty	c1050–221 BC	Liao Dynasty	907–1125
Warring States 480–221 BC		Song Dynasty	960–1279
Qin Dynasty	221–206 BC	*Northern Song*	960–1127
Han Dynasty	206 BC–AD 220	*Southern Song*	1127–1279
Six Dynasties	222–589	Xixia Dynasty	1038–1227
Wei Dynasty 386–557		Jin Dynasty	1115–1234
Sui Dynasty	581–618	Yuan Dynasty	1279–1368

Ming Dynasty Marks

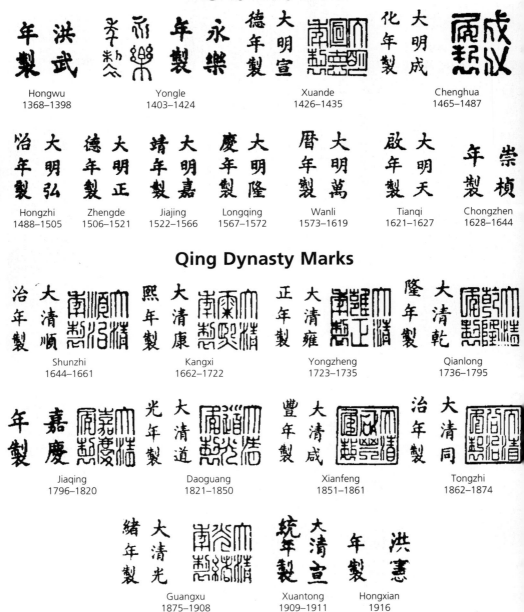

Hongwu
1368–1398

Yongle
1403–1424

Xuande
1426–1435

Chenghua
1465–1487

Hongzhi
1488–1505

Zhengde
1506–1521

Jiajing
1522–1566

Longqing
1567–1572

Wanli
1573–1619

Tianqi
1621–1627

Chongzhen
1628–1644

Qing Dynasty Marks

Shunzhi
1644–1661

Kangxi
1662–1722

Yongzheng
1723–1735

Qianlong
1736–1795

Jiaqing
1796–1820

Daoguang
1821–1850

Xianfeng
1851–1861

Tongzhi
1862–1874

Guangxu
1875–1908

Xuantong
1909–1911

Hongxian
1916

Chinese Ceramics
Animals & Birds

A pottery equestrian group, painted with red and black details to the face, clothing and tack, Western Han Dynasty, 206 BC–AD 220, 24in (61cm) high.
$10,000–12,500 ✤ S

A green-glazed pottery model of two sheep in a pen, Han Dynasty, 206 BC–AD 220, 8in (20.5cm) diam.
$450–500 ⊞ TeW

A green-glazed duck, with incised details, Tang Dynasty, 618–907, 2½in (6.5cm) high.
$400–500 ⊞ GLD

◀ A pair of porcelain pug dogs, the eyes with black and white detail, with pink spotted tongues and gilt bells on red painted collars, the bodies painted in grey and salmon simulating fur, Qianlong period, 1736–95, 10¼in (26cm) high.
$30,000–35,000 ✤ MEA
Export pug dogs are very rare – particularly a matching pair.

◀ A pair of Chinese export famille rose elephant candle holders, each with a pink saddle on an iron-red and gilt-edged green saddle blanket with beaded salmon fringes, candle sconces missing, minor damage and restoration, mid-19thC, 10¾in (27.5cm) high.
$5,000–6,000 ✤ S(NY)

◀ A Chinese export glazed biscuit model of a quail, with aubergine, green, yellow and black plumage, beak restored, 19thC, 7½in (19cm) high.
$2,600–3,200 ✤ S(NY)

▶ A pair of turquoise-glazed models of parrots, standing on pierced aubergine glazed rocks, beaks restored, 19thC, 7½in (19cm) high.
$360–440 ✤ P

A famille rose model of a cockerel, decorated in pink, green, yellow and white, with orange crest, comb and details, crest restored, early 19thC, 8in (20.5cm) high.
$300–350 ✤ WW

CHINESE CERAMICS

Bowls

A bowl, marbled with brown and white clay and partly glazed in yellow, late Tang Dynasty, c900, 4¼in (11cm) diam.
$850–1,000 ✤ S(Am)

A Yaozhou celadon bowl, moulded with peony and lotus, Song Dynasty, 12thC, 5in (12.5cm) diam.
$1,600–2,000 ⊞ GLD

A famille verte bowl, painted in enamels with a frieze of flowerheads in alternating colours, the rim with panels of flowers on a cell ground, the interior with leafy spearheads issuing from a central medallion, rim chipped, Kangxi period, 1662–1722, 6in (15cm) diam.
$800–1,000 ✤ P

A blue and white bowl, decorated with the Eight Daoist Immortals in a rocky landscape, rim chipped, Chenghua mark but Kangxi period, 1662–1722, 9in (23cm) diam.
$500–600 ↗ WW

A bowl and cover, painted with panels of flowers and symbols in blue, turquoise, jade and orange on a white ground, top damaged and finial replaced, Kangxi period, 1662–1722, 9¼in (23.5cm) wide.
$320–380 ↗ CMS

An octagonal blue and white tea bowl and saucer, from the *Vung Tau* cargo, c1690, bowl 3in (7.5cm) wide.
$580–650 ⊞ RBA
The Chinese ship the *Vung Tau* was on its way to the Dutch trading post of Jakarta, loaded with Chinese items for the great houses of Europe, when it was wrecked off the coast of Vietnam c1696. The cargo was salvaged c1990.

A pair of f*amille rose* **bowls,** painted with magnolia, peony and apple blossoms on a white ground, minor damage, six-character mark, Yongzheng mark and period, 1723–35, 7in (18cm) diam, on later carved wood stands.
$12,500–14,500 ↗ HAM

A Chinese export *famille rose* guglet and basin, painted with a flower-filled urn reserved on a cod's roe ground, interspersed with blue and white and *famille rose* floral sprays, Qianlong period, 1736–95, guglet 9½in (24cm) high.
$2,200–2,600 ↗ L

A Cantonese bowl, painted in enamel and gilt with figural and floral panels beneath a band decorated with birds, butterflies and flowers, on a gilded ground, late 18thC, 14¾in (37.5cm) diam.
$725–875 ↗ CGC

◄ **A *famille rose* punch bowl,** the exterior painted with flower sprays, butterflies and insects, the foot with gilded flowers and leaves, the interior with a central flower spray and gilded leaf and flower border, riveted, rim crack, Qianlong period, 1736–95, 15¾in (40cm) diam, with a hardwood stand.
$2,000–2,300 ↗ P(Ba)

A Batavian blue and white tea bowl and saucer, from the Nanking cargo, decorated with a peony and bamboo, c1750, 4½in (11.5cm) diam.
$350–400 ⊞ RBA
The Dutch East India Company's ship *Geldermalsen* sank near Java in 1751 while on its way from Canton to Amsterdam with a cargo of 126 gold bars and a particular type of blue and white porcelain known as Nanking, hence the name. It was discovered and brought to the surface in 1985 and auctioned the following year in the city which had been the ship's intended destination over 200 years previously. Destined for the upper and emerging middle classes in Europe, there was little in the cargo to excite the purist collector of Asian ceramics, but the romantic story of the salvage attracted intense media coverage and therefore public interest, which was reflected in the prices achieved. Now, some 15 years later, items from the Nanking cargo still command a premium over a comparable piece of Chinese export porcelain.

◄ **A Cantonese *famille rose* basin,** decorated with a maiden in an interior, surrounded by figures in a landscape, within a floral border, late 18thC, 13¾in (35cm) diam.
$350–450 ↗ TRM

◄ **A Lang yao bowl,** with a ripe cherry-coloured glaze, 19thC, 14in (35.5cm) diam.
$5,800–7,400 ↗ SK

Boxes

A Canton *famille rose* box and cover, decorated with panels of figures, flowers and birds, 19thC, 7½in (19cm) long.
$250–300 ↗ WW

> **Cross Reference**
> See Colour Review (page 303)

An underglaze blue and white box and cover, painted in outline and wash with two five-clawed dragons chasing flaming pearls above breaking waves, the cover with similar pattern around a medallion enclosing an image of a beast, Chenghua mark but Qianlong period, 1736–95, 2¾in (7cm) diam.
$1,150–1,350 ↗ P

A Chinese export porcelain snuff box, painted in *famille rose* enamels with a European lady holding a dish of flowers, the inside of the cover painted with two birds squabbling over a frog, with contemporary European gilt-metal mounts, damaged, Qianlong period, 1736–95, 2¾in (7cm) diam.
$650–800 ↗ P(EA)

Censers

A green-glazed pottery Hill censer and cover, damaged, Han Dynasty, 206 BC–AD 220, 9in (23cm) high.
$200–250 ↗ WW
The cover is moulded to represent a hill.

A Longquan tripod censer, applied overall with a bluish-green glaze, large gilded repair to rim, Southern Song Dynasty, 1127–1279, 5in (12.5cm) high.
$2,200–2,500 ↗ S

A pale olive-green celadon censer, with taotie-mask feet, hairline crack, Yuan Dynasty, 1279–1368, 10in (25.5cm) diam.
$1,600–1,800 ⊞ PCA

> **Miller's is a price GUIDE not a price LIST**

► A celadon censer, with incised leaf-scroll decoration, 16thC, 11in (28cm) diam, with later pierced domed hardwood cover and stand.
$650–750 ↗ P

A celadon censer, the sides carved with bands and raised flower motifs, the centre of the exterior unglazed, impressed with a foliate medallion and burnt red-brown in the firing, 16thC, 11½in (29cm) diam, on later stand.
$850–1,000 ↗ HAM

Cups

A set of five Chinese Imari cups, decorated with a stylized lotus flower and leaf scroll, Kangxi period, 1662–1722, 3in (7.5cm) high.
$725–875 ↗ WW

A Chinese export coffee cup, painted in pastel colours with a scene from the Italian *Commedia dell'Arte*, the diaper border painted *en grisaille*, minor rim chips, c1740, 2½in (6.5cm) high.
$2,300–2,600 ↗ S(NY)

An enamelled stem cup, painted by Jin Pinqing in the Qianjiang palette with a golden pheasant on rocks, signed and dated 1891, 4¾in (12cm) diam.
$2,500–3,000 ↗ S(Am)
Jin Pinqing was employed as a decorator at the Imperial kiln in Jingdezhen in the Tongzhi and Guangxu periods. The Qianjiang palette is a pale umber colour.

CHINESE CERAMICS

Dishes

A **Longquan saucer,** the exterior incised with fluted decoration, decorated overall with a rich green-grey glaze, Song Dynasty, 960–1279, 6½in (16.5cm) diam.
$950–1,150 ⚘ P
Longquan wares usually have a pale grey body covered by a thick, opaque, bluish-green, slightly bubbly glaze. Typical pieces are bowls, vases, archaic forms and items for the scholar's desk.

▶ A *kraak porselein* **blue and white dish,** decorated with birds, rockwork and flowering plants, the rim painted with reserves of flowers and precious objects, Wanli period, 1573–1619, 20in (51cm) diam.
$10,000–11,500 ⊞ PCA

LOCATE THE SOURCE
The source of each illustration in Miller's can be found by checking the code letters below each caption with the Key to Illustrations, pages 794–800.

A *kraak porselein* **blue and white dish,** Wanli period, 1573–1619, 8in (20.5cm) diam.
$650–800 ⊞ GLD

A **celadon dish,** the interior incised with a peony branch in bloom, with upright flowering branches in the paired ribs of the interior and exterior walls, a scroll pattern on the rim flange, 16thC, 17in (43cm) diam.
$4,300–4,800 ⚘ BB(S)

A *famille verte* **dish,** painted with exotic birds among flowers, Kangxi period, 1662–1722, 10½in (26.5cm) long.
$800–950 ⚘ P

▶ A **blue and white soup dish,** from the *Nanking* cargo, decorated with Three Pavilion pattern, c1750, 9in (23cm) diam.
$500–600 ⊞ RBA

A **Chinese export** *famille rose* **dish,** decorated with Mandarin pattern, c1790, 9½in (24cm) wide.
$600–700 ⊞ Wai

A **Chinese export** *famille rose* **triple-shell sweetmeat dish,** after a Bow porcelain original, modelled with an iron-red and gilt dolphin handle, c1765, 7½in (19cm) wide.
$8,000–9,000 ⚘ S(NY)
Dishes such as this are seldom seen.

◀ A **blue and white deep dish,** from the *Diana* cargo, painted with the Chinese *Shou* character for longevity, c1817, 11in (28cm) diam.
$350–400 ⊞ RBA
The *Diana* was sailing for Madras loaded with tea, spices and 11 tons of Chinese blue and white porcelain made at the imperial kilns of the Emperor Chia Ching, much of it decorated with the Fitzhugh pattern, when she sank off Malacca in March 1817. The cargo was recovered in 1985 and sold the following year in Amsterdam.

A **blue and white deep dish,** from the *Tek Sing* cargo, painted with a chrysanthemum surrounded by flowe sprigs, c1820, 8in (20.5cm) diam.
$330–380 ⊞ RBA
The *Tek Sing* (True Star) was bound for Batavia (Jakarta) with a cargo of tea, silk, vermilion, glass beads, Indian inks and Chinese ceramics for the wealthy Chinese community in Java, when she sank in the Gaspar Straits in 1822. Retrieved cargoes from wrecks invariably appeal to the public imagination and fetch higher prices than similar pieces that have survived in a more mundane way.

Ewers & Jugs

A green-glazed proto-porcelain ewer and cover, decorated with an allover impressed whorl design, the exterior with a pale olive glaze, Warring States period, 480–221 BC, 8½in (21.5cm) high.
$7,250–8,750 ⚒ S(NY)

A *sancai*-glazed phoenix-head ewer, moulded on both sides with peacocks flanking floral decoration, and applied overall with a dark green glaze splashed with amber and cream, Tang Dynasty, 618–907, 9¼in (23.5cm) high.
$18,000–22,000 ⚒ S(NY)

◄ **A blue and white ewer and cover,** decorated with a pagoda and houses in a mountain landscape, cover reglued, Transitional period, 1640–50, 6in (15cm) high.
$1,250–1,450 ⚒ WW

A green-glazed pottery ewer and cover, applied with incised concentric ring-bordered leaf and geometric decoration imitating metalware, Liao Dynasty, 907–1125, 7in (18cm) high.
$1,150–1,350 ⚒ S(NY)

A blue and white ewer, Transitional period, c1650, 9in (23cm) high.
$3,200–4,000 ⊞ GLD

A faceted Qingbai ewer and cover, the cover with two tiers of projecting peaks simulating a pagoda roof, decorated with a thin greenish glaze, Northern Song Dynasty, 960–1127, 8½in (21.5cm) high.
$13,500–16,000 ⚒ S

An underglaze blue and white ewer, for the Islamic market, painted in outline and wash with insects and butterflies hovering by shrubs, within panels reserved on diaper-work grounds, slight damage, Kangxi period, 1662–1722, 10¼in (26cm) high.
$43,500–50,500 ⚒ P
Certain Chinese porcelain vessels made in this period for the Islamic market are well-known, although scarce, and ewers are relatively uncommon.

► **A blue and white sparrow's beak ewer,** decorated with a floral design, 1680–90, 6½in (16.5cm) high.
$1,600–1,800 ⊞ PCA

A blue and white ewer and cover, decorated with the Eight Buddhist Emblems, handle cracked, rim chipped, Kangxi period, 1662–1722, 7in (18cm) high.
$470–570 ⚒ WW

A famille rose ewer, enamelled with ladies, a deer and cranes in a fenced garden, in brown, grey and shades of green on a white ground, slight damage, Qianlong period, 1735–96, 9in (23cm) high.
$580–650 ⚒ S(Am)

◄ **A porcelain jug,** decorated in blue and white with a bird and flowering plants, with orange detail, late 18thC, 9in (23cm) high.
$300–350 ⚒ SWO

A Chinese export porcelain jug, the spout moulded as a human bearded mask, above an enamelled griffin coat-of-arms, the sides painted *en grisaille* with an urn, with gilt detail, handle rebuilt, spout and neck glued, c1800, 10in (25.5cm) high.
$550–650 ⚒ S(NY)

CHINESE CERAMICS

Figures

A figure of a seated boy from the *Tek Sing* cargo, c1720, 3in (7.5cm) high.
$1,250–1,350 ⊞ RBA

A Cizhou painted figure of Guanyin, wearing robes outlined in brown slip and bordered by a scroll design, on a cream ground covered in a transparent glaze, Yuan Dynasty, 1279–1368, 14¾in (37.5cm) high.
$650–800 ↗ S(NY)

A straw-glazed pottery figure of a foreign merchant, holding a ewer in his right hand, with overall crackled greenish-yellow glaze, early Tang Dynasty, 7thC, 12in (30.5cm) high.
$725–800 ↗ S(NY)

A *wucai* figure of a smiling boy, standing on a base painted with peonies, clutching a vase of lotus, wearing a diaperwork apron and a lappet collar, with precious objects painted on his thighs, minor chip, c1650, 11¼in (28.5cm) high.
$1,400–1,700 ↗ P

▶ **A *famille rose* taper holder,** in the form of a kneeling boy, dressed in a floral jacket and with iron-red trousers, proffering a bowl with an aperture in the base, Jiaqing period, 1796–1820, 6¼in (16cm) high.
$600–700 ↗ P

▶ **A Chinese export *blanc de chine* group of the Madonna and Child,** adapted from a version of Guanyin, the base modelled with a grotesque lion mask, early 18thC, 13½in (34.5cm) high.
$5,500–6,000 ↗ S(NY)

Flatware

A Jun saucer dish, Song Dynasty, 12thC/13thC, 7in (18cm) diam.
$1,000–1,250 ⊞ GLD
Jun wares are glazed in an opaque, lavender-blue colour, usually splashed with purple derived from copper oxide.

Items in the Chinese Ceramics section have been arranged in date order within each sub-section.

A Chinese export armorial charger, painted with the arms of Percival for the first Earl of Egmont, surrounded by a cell diaper border with four shaped landscape reserves, the wide border painted with flowerheads on leafy vines, three stylized flowerheads and a thistle crest, minor crack, riveted repair, c1730, 15¼in (38.5cm) diam.
$5,500–6,000 ↗ S(NY)
The first Earl of Egmont was President of the State of Georgia in 1733.

A blue and white charger, painted with a pavilion on a distant cliff in a rocky landscape with leafy trees in the foreground, minor chips, Kangxi period, 1622–1722, 13in (33cm) diam.
$2,600–3,200 ↗ P

▶ **A pair of blue and white porcelain plates,** painted with birds on a flowering tree within a border of fruiting foliage, 18thC, 10¼in (26cm) diam.
$1,000–1,150 ↗ AH

CHINESE CERAMICS

A Chinese export *famille rose* plate, painted in enamels with peonies and other flowers, with a bamboo border, heightened with gilt, mid-18thC, 9in (23cm) diam.
$145–175 PFK

A religious subject plate, after a European print, painted *en grisaille* with The Adoration of the Shepherds, within a foliate du Paquier-style scroll-work border, with gilt detail, Qianlong period, c1750, 9in (23cm) diam.
$2,200–2,600 S
Du Paquier was Europe's second porcelain factory, founded in Vienna in 1718.

A blue and white charger, decorated with two figures beneath a tree, Qianlong period, 1736–95, 16½in (42cm) diam.
$600–700 WW

An octagonal charger, painted with a brown duck among peonies and other garden flowers, within a pink and blue diaper border decorated with flowers and scrolls, Qianlong period, 1736–95, 17in (43cm) diam.
$2,500–3,000 Bea(E)

A pair of Chinese Imari porcelain plates, decorated with flowers and a screen in iron-red, blue, green and gilt, the reverse painted with prunus blossom, mid-18thC, 9¾in (25cm) diam.
$450–500 CDC

◄ **A blue and white saucer,** from the *Tek Sing* cargo, painted with a basket of flowers, c1820, 4½in (11.5cm) diam.
$130–145 RBA

► **A *famille rose* soup plate,** decorated with a landscape scene, early 19thC, 8½in (21.5cm) diam.
$65–80 SWO

A pair of *famille rose* chargers, painted with Mongolians on horseback, the rims with three trailing flower sprays, minor damage and repair, Qianlong period, 1736–95, 13¾in (35cm) diam.
$1,800–2,200 LFA

Garden Seats

A Longquan celadon garden seat, the reticulated mid-section decorated with a pair of playful lions among flowering lotus and peony blossoms, c1600, 17in (43cm) high.
$8,000–9,000 BB(S)

A pair of Canton *famille rose* garden seats, painted with scenes of dignitaries, warriors and attendants within lappet, fruit and butterfly borders, the sides and tops pierced with cash motifs, one cracked, Qing Dynasty, c1900, 18in (45.5cm) diam.
$2,600–3,200 S(S)

A pair of blue and white garden seats, decorated with continuous lotus scrolls between bands of studs and scholar's objects, the tops with lotus scrolls, the bodies and tops with pierced cash motifs, one cracked, 18thC, 19¼in (49cm) high.
$10,000–11,500 WW

CHINESE CERAMICS

Jars

A green-glazed jar, Tang Dynasty, 618–907, 9in (23cm) high.
$950–1,150 ⊞ GLD

A Henan wine jar, decorated with bow string marks around the base and tan-specked black glaze, with wave-patterned interior, 15thC, 15in (38cm) high.
$1,450–1,750 ⚒ SK

A pair of *famille rose* **porcelain baluster jars,** with reserves from the Story of the Stone, and leaf-shaped reserves on a green ground painted with flowers, 18thC, 22in (56cm) high.
$4,500–5,000 ⚒ SK
The Story of the Stone is usually referred to as *The Dream of the Red Chamber,* a famous Chinese novel written by Cao Xueqin c1760.

Sets/pairs
Unless otherwise stated, any description which refers to 'a set' or 'a pair' includes a guide price for the entire set or the pair, even though the illustration may show only a single item.

A pale green celadon jar, moulded with Buddhist emblems around the body, Yuan Dynasty, 1279–1368, 8¾in (22cm) high.
$1,000–1,250 ⊞ PCA

A pair of blue and white jars, the vertically ribbed bodies painted with roundels of precious objects between borders of cracked ice, one with rim chips, Kangxi period, 1662–1722, 8¾in (22cm) high, with carved wooden covers and stands.
$1,000–1,150 ⚒ P

▶ **A blue and white waterpot,** decorated with a bird in flight above sprays of flowers issuing from rocky outcrops, the rim with a lattice design border, c1670, 2¾in (7cm) high.
$800–950 ⚒ P

A blue and white jar, painted with three panels, each depicting two boys holding the stems of lotus flowers, reserved on a wave-patterned ground, the panels divided by flower sprays, 18thC, 8¾in (22cm) high, with a pierced wood cover.
$430–480 ⚒ P

A jar, decorated in underglaze blue with a band of floral sprays below a band of scrolling designs and flowers, neck reduced, Ming Dynasty, 15thC, 9in (23cm) high.
$1,450–1,750 ⚒ S(Am)

A covered jar, painted in blue with ladies at leisure, 1700–20, 4in (10cm) high.
$600–700 ⊞ PCA

A Cantonese *famille rose* **jar and cover,** the top with floral designs, and bands of foliate ornament on a *café au lait* ground, the body decorated with flowers, butterflies, leaves and other ornament, early 19thC, 10¼in (26cm) high, with a carved hardwood stand.
$320–380 ⚒ TRM

CHINESE CERAMICS

Jardinières

A Chinese export *famille rose* jardinière, the body painted with vases of chrysanthemums, prunus blossoms, peacock feathers and coral among flowers and rockwork, damaged, c1760, 15in (38cm) high.
$3,000–3,500 S(NY)

A Chinese export hexagonal jardinière, painted in underglaze blue with birds and flowers issuing from rocks, the rim with *ruyi*, geometric and floral pattern, cracked, rim chip, 18thC, 9½in (24cm) high.
$2,300–2,600 P

A *famille rose* jardinière, painted in enamels with stylized pheasants, birds and flowering plants within a rocky fenced garden, between red key and foliate blue-ground borders, with red-glazed *taotie*-mask handles, c1900, 12½in (32cm) high.
$450–500 P

Mugs & Tankards

A Chinese export *famille rose* mug, decorated with a classical urn and floral sprigs within a shaped raised border and underglaze blue floral sprigs, chipped, Qianlong period, 1736–95, 6in (15cm) high.
$320–380 Hal

A *famille rose* beaker, decorated with panels of figures playing with dogs, 18thC, 6in (15cm) high.
$360–440 MEA

▶ **A Chinese export tankard,** painted with panels of figures in *famille verte* enamels, with blue and white gilded borders, 19thC, 5¼in (13.5cm) high.
$400–500 HOK

A blue and white mug, the body painted with pagodas and figures on a barge, the seahorse-moulded handle with scale detail, 18thC, 5½in (14cm) high.
$220–260 GAK

A Chinese export mug, painted in black and green with scaly dragons and flaming pearls, heightened with gilt, 1800–30, 4¾in (12cm) high.
$250–300 LFA

Services

◀ **A Chinese export European subject part tea service,** comprising six pieces, painted *en grisaille* and brown with a young lady seated at a table threading gold beads, assisted by an old lady wearing spectacles, rim chips, cover to milk jug lacking, c1740, jug 3½in (9cm) high.
$4,500–5,000 S(NY)

A part dinner service, comprising seven pieces, the centre enamelled in blue with the crest of a lion within four triangular panels characteristic of the Fitzhugh pattern, tureen handle restuck, c1785, tureen 13½in (34.5cm) wide.
$4,000–4,500 P
The Fitzhugh pattern is characterized by a border of four split pomegranates and butterflies and was made for the American market, being named after the person who first ordered it.

▶ **A *famille rose* part tea service,** comprising 20 pieces, the matched pieces painted with panels of figures, birds, blossom and insects within foliate borders, 19thC.
$725–875 P(E)

Tea & Coffee Pots

A Dutch-decorated teapot, painted in red, blue and gilt, Qianlong period, 1736–95, 4in (10cm) high.
$725–875 ⊞ GLD

A Yixing red stoneware foliate form teapot, the body moulded with petal-shaped lappets, Qing Dynasty, mid-19thC, 5½in (14cm) wide.
$1,750–2,000 ⚒ P

A Chinese export coffee pot, for the American market, painted in brown monochrome with a displayed eagle bearing a shield monogrammed 'JMC' in gilt between blue and gilt borders, repaired, c1795, 9½in (24cm) high.
$1,600–1,850 ⚒ S(NY)

A Yixing export teapot, moulded in low relief with two scholars crossing a bridge in a garden with pavilions, cover restored, 18thC, 4¼in (11cm) high.
$1,250–1,450 ⚒ S(Am)

Yixing

Yixing county in eastern China contains some of the country's most beautiful scenery and has, therefore, traditionally attracted poets and artists. The Yixing pottery culture is very old, originating in the 11th century and reaching maturity in the 16th century. The area became particularly famous for Zisha (purple clay) teapots and scholars' table-ware. Yixing teapots are constructed of three basic clays, the high kaolin content meaning that they can be fired to a high temperature to give a strong stone-like quality whilst retaining some porosity. Although the ceramics bear the county name, they were actually produced in the town of Dingshuzhen, which still supports a thriving ceramics industry today.

A Yixing stoneware teapot, with robin's-egg glazing, the base moulded with an illegible potter's seal, 18thC, 9½in (24cm) high.
$11,500–13,000 ⚒ S

Tureens

A Chinese export *famille rose* tureen and cover, painted with sprays and sprigs of flowers, the cover applied with leaves, Qianlong period, 1736–95, 9½in (24cm) high.
$4,500–5,000 ⚒ P

A blue and white tureen and cover, the base decorated with two birds perched on rockwork beneath peony branches, Qianlong period, 1736–95, extensive damage, 14¼in (36cm) wide.
$725–875 ⚒ WW

A pair of sauce tureens and covers, painted in the Rockefeller pattern, with figural and landscape panels on a floral gilt ground, c1790, 7in (18cm) diam.
$8,000–9,500 ⚒ S

◀ **A Chinese export vegetable tureen and cover,** painted in iron-red and turquoise enamels with the badge of the 2nd Warwickshire Regiment within an inscribed oval garter enclosing the Sphinx and the number '24', the rim with band borders, c1812, 11½in (29cm) long.
$850–1,000 ⚒ S(NY)

A blue and white tureen and cover, decorated with a landscape scene, 19thC, 15in (38cm) wide.
$2,000–2,500 ⚒ DD

CHINESE CERAMICS

Vases

A **celadon vase,** incised with a bird, Song Dynasty, 12thC, 7½in (19cm) high.
$950–1,150 ⊞ GLD

A *famille rose* **vase and cover,** moulded with tendrils and squirrels and reserved with panels of figures, the cover with iron-red monochrome landscape panels, Qianlong period, 1736–95, 19¾in (50cm) high.
$3,500–4,000 ⚡ DN

A pair of Canton *famille rose* **vases,** painted with panels of figures, birds and flowers, reserved on a ground decorated with butterflies and flowers and heightened with gilt, 19thC, 17¾in (45cm) high.
$2,000–2,500 ⚡ HAM

A **Cizhou bottle,** the buff body covered with white slip carved away to form bands of angled key frets, leaf scrolls separating flowerheads and two narrower leaf-scroll bands, minor chips, Jin/Yuan Dynasty, 12th–14thC, 10¼in (26cm) high.
$8,000–9,000 ⚡ BB(S)
Cizhou wares came from many different kilns in northern China, although Cixian (Cizhou) itself was the most important site. It is characterized by bold shapes and decoration on a slip-covered body.

A **bottle vase,** painted in underglaze blue with a river landscape, beneath diaper, spearhead and cell diaper bands, c1800, 10in (25.5cm) high.
$300–350 ⚡ SAS

A **bottle vase,** painted in enamels with bats and peach boughs with foliage, six-character Qianlong mark in red, 1736–95, 21in (53.5cm) high.
$650–800 ⚡ SK

A **blue and white vase,** from the *Vung Tau* cargo, c1690, 4½in (11.5cm) high.
$650–725 ⊞ RBA

A **Chinese export** *famille rose* **vase and cover,** decorated with a landscape, lid restored, c1800, 8¼in (21cm) high.
$450–500 ⚡ WW

A **square vase,** decorated with figures before a building and trees, damaged, late 19thC, 20½in (52cm) high.
$360–440 ⚡ SWO

A **blue and white vase,** decorated with a river landscape scene, Kangxi period, c1700, 10in (25.5cm) high.
$1,750–2,000 ⊞ Wai

A **pair of Chinese export urns and pierced covers,** for the American market, the bodies moulded with drapery swags, painted in blue with floral sprigs above a band of stylized acanthus leaves, c1800, 17in (43cm) high.
$10,000–12,500 ⚡ S

A *famille noir* **vase,** painted with prunus on a black ground, *faux* Chenghua six-character mark in underglaze blue to base, 19thC, 28¾in (73cm) high.
$1,300–1,600 ⚡ RTo

The Hoi An Cargo

This huge cargo of late 15th-century Vietnamese ceramics was found in the early 1990s by fishermen off Hoi An (previously known in the West as Faifo) in central Vietnam. The pieces are from kilns in the northern province of Hai Duong, which at the time was the country's largest area of ceramic production and an expanding industry, due to a ban by the Chinese on maritime exports. They were being transported to markets in South East Asia when the ship sank possibly in a raging typhoon. It is a particularly exciting discovery as it gives us an extensive overview of the glazes, forms and patterns of Vietnamese ceramics of that period, much of it unknown until now. The excavation was sponsored by the Vietnamese government and a proportion of the finds given to the country's museums, the remainder being sold at auction in the United States.

A Vietnamese blue and white double gourd bottle, decorated with three *chich choe* separated by lotus scrolls, between a band of jewelled lotus petals on the shoulder and plain lotus petals above the foot, with ribboned gourds and crossed rhinoceros horns and pearls on the upper lobe, chip to foot pad, c1500, 7in (18cm) high.
$5,800–6,500 ✦ BB(S)

A Vietnamese blue and white covered box, with lion finial, the cover painted with three spotted animals, the sides with panels of alternating bamboo or flowering plants and diaper trellis patterns, the interior tray with a single water plant, tray chipped, c1500, 6½in (16.5cm) diam.
$10,500–11,500 ✦ BB(S)

A Vietnamese blue and white stem cup, the interior with a chrysanthemum sprig in bloom, the inside of the rim banded with a diamond diaper pattern, the exterior with a lotus flower and leaf-scroll band above jewelled lappets, the stem encircled by a coin diaper band, cracked, c1500, 4¾in (12cm) high.
$12,500–14,500 ✦ BB(S)
This is the only blue and white stem cup of lotus decoration in the cargo. Elegantly painted, it combines the best of form and function in Vietnamese ceramics.

A Vietnamese blue-glazed ewer, decorated with unglazed panels bearing traces of red pigment and gilt and reticulated as parrots among foliage, hairline crack, c1500, 9¼in (23.5cm) high.
$3,600–4,400 ✦ BB(S)

A Vietnamese blue and white dish, painted with a flowering lotus plant beneath a border of scalloped petals surrounded by a trailing lotus meander, the exterior decorated with a jewelled lappet band, c1500, 13½in (34.5cm) diam.
$2,200–2,600 ✦ BB(S)

A Vietnamese barbed rim dish, decorated in underglaze blue and enamelled with a pair of birds perched on a flowering tree, with red and green enamel details, enclosed by alternating cloud and diaper-filled lappets, the exterior painted with a stiff lappet band, c1500, 11½in (29cm) diam.
$4,000–4,500 ✦ BB(S)

A Vietnamese blue and white double-headed bird-form ewer, chip to rim, c1500, 4¾in (12cm) high.
$3,200–3,800 ✦ BB(S)

◄ **A Vietnamese blue and white jar,** the central band with three mongoose-style animals among bamboo and rocks, the cover with a band of lotus flowerheads, the bud-form finial with cloud whorls, chipped, cracked, c1500, 11½in (29cm) high.
$3,500–4,000 ✦ BB(S)

A Vietnamese blue and white kneeling figure of a court official, dressed in a long robe decorated with *ruyi*-formed clouds, sacred pearls and flowerheads, holding on his knee a vase decorated with clouds and pearls, chipped, neck restored, c1500, 11in (28cm) high.
$8,700–9,500 ✦ BB(S)

A Vietnamese blue and white *kendi*, decorated with two birds among cloud whorls, a double cloud collar ringing the neck above a lotus petal band on the shoulder, with stopper, chipped, c1500, 6½in (16.5cm) high.
$3,200–3,600 ✦ BB(S)

Japanese Ceramics

Japanese Chronology Chart

Jomon period (Neolithic)	circa 10,000–100 BC	Muromachi (Ashikaga) period	1333–1568
Yayoi period	circa 200 BC–AD 200	Momoyama period	1568–1600
Tumulus (Kofun) period	200–552	Edo (Tokugawa) period	1600–1868
Asuka period	552–710	*Genroku period*	*1688–1703*
Nara period	710–794	Meiji period	1868–1911
Heian perio	794–1185	Taisho period	1912–1926
Kamakura period	1185–1333	Showa period	1926–1989

Animals

An Arita ewer and cover, modelled as a *minogame*, the shell panels painted in iron-red and gilt, 17thC/18thC, 7¾in (19.5cm) long.
$2,000–2,300 ➤ S(Am)

A Hirado group, in the form of a young boy playing a pipe and seated on a buffalo, Meiji period, 1868–1911, 7½in (19cm) long.
$360–440 ➤ RTo

A Bizen *koro* and cover, in the shape of a stylized lion, with incised detail, Meiji period, 1868–1911, 3½in (9cm) high.
$115–145 ➤ P
Bizen has been known for its dark red-brown stoneware since the 12th century. It has an ash glaze which is deposited on it from the pine-wood burning in the kiln. Bizen is famous for its tea-ceremony wares and also sculptures and finely executed export wares.

▶ **A pair of porcelain models of elephants,** wearing saddle-cloths enamelled in colours with roundels of exotic cranes, on geometric and leaf-scroll grounds in red and turquoise, with black and floral borders and gold detail, damaged, repaired, Meiji period, 1868–1911, 6in (15cm) high.
$1,000–1,150 ➤ P(Ba)

▶ **A Hirado white-glazed water dropper,** in the shape of a puppy, Meiji period, c1900, 3¼in (8.5cm) high.
$850–1,000 ⊞ GLD

◀ **A Hirado white-glazed ox censer and cover,** its back with an aperture, the saddle as a cover, cover chipped, mid-19thC, 9½in (24cm) high.
$2,600–3,200 ➤ S(Am)

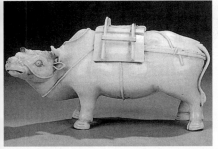

A Hirado white-glazed group of two playful puppies, Meiji period, c1900, 6in (15cm) long.
$2,200–2,700 ⊞ GLD

A Hirado white-glazed porcelain group of frolicking *shishi*, with underglaze blue detail and bisque eyes, 19thC, 10in (25.5cm) long.
$13,500–16,000 ➤ SK

A Satsuma model of a *shishi*, painted with stylized floral designs in gilt enamel on a cream ground, ear repaired, Meiji period, 1868–1911, 11½in (29cm) high.
$3,000–3,500 ➤ BB(S)

JAPANESE CERAMICS

Bowls

An Imari bowl and cover, the cover painted with phoenix, maple tree and flowers, the sides in iron-red and gilt with plants flowering between blue lines, c1700, 5in (12.5cm) diam.
$350–400 ↗ CGC

A European-subject Imari bowl and cover, decorated with panels of Dutchmen, camels and symbols on a geometric patterned ground in underglaze blue, iron-red, gilt and enamels, 19thC, 4¼in (11cm) diam.
$400–450 ↗ S(Am)

An Imari faceted bowl, the interior decorated with stylized flowers, the exterior with flowers within diaper and washed blue borders, rim chip, late 19thC, 8in (20.5cm) diam.
$80–95 ↗ Hal

▶ **A Satsuma earthenware bowl,** decorated with flowers, a duck and birds, 19thC, 5in (12.5cm) diam.
$2,500–3,000 ↗ FBG

An Imari bowl, decorated with peony among foliage, 19thC, 6in (15cm) diam.
$360–440 ↗ SWO

▶ **An Imari peach-shaped bowl,** the interior painted with a maiden seated beside rocks beneath a tree, with a commemorative Chenghua mark, Meiji period, 1868–1911, 10¼in (26cm) diam.
$580–650 ↗ P

A pair of Imari bowls, decorated with panels of flowers and foliage, rim chips, 19thC, 6¼in (16cm) diam.
$320–380 ↗ WW

Dishes

An Imari dish, the underside decorated with flower sprays, c1700, 13½in (34.5cm) diam.
$6,500–8,000 ↗ S(NY)

An Arita dish, decorated in blue and white with a river landscape, c1690, 13in (33cm) diam.
$1,450–1,750 ⊞ Wai

A Kakiemon dish, on three feet, the rim with eight notches, decorated in iron-red, yellow, green, blue and black with a bird perched on bamboo above blossoming prunus, 18thC, 5½in (14cm) diam.
$1,800–2,200 ↗ WW

◀ **A set of eight Imari fish dishes,** the centres painted with birds among flowers, the tail, face and fins in underglaze blue with gilt detail, one damaged, Meiji period, 1868–1911, 8¼in (21cm) diam.
$2,200–2,500 ↗ S(S)

A Hirado porcelain oyster dish, decorated with applied shellfish and crabs in brown, blue and white, 1880–1900, 9in (23cm) wide.
$500–600 ⊞ MCN

Figures

A polychrome figure, wearing a floral robe decorated with flowers and bird roundels, late 19thC, 20½in (52cm) high.
$600–700 ⚲ WW

A Satsuma figure of Daikoku, wearing a gold kimono, c1900, 9in (23cm) high.
$900–1,000 ⊞ TWr
Daikoku is a God of Wealth.

Miller's is a price GUIDE not a price LIST

A Satsuma figure of Buddha, wearing a floral robe in red, blue, green and gold on a white ground, holding a scroll, impressed mark, early 20thC, 4in (10cm) high.
$360–440 ⚲ WW

◀ **A Satsuma figure of a *bijin*,** wearing a kimono decorated with fans among stylized motifs, slight cracks to base, Meiji period, 1868–1911, 21½in (54.5cm) high.
$5,800–6,500 ⚲ S

Flatware

An Arita blue and white charger, the centre painted with a vase of peony and pomegranates, the well with lobed panels of flowers, rim crack, late 17thC, 18in (45.5cm) diam.
$1,250–1,450 ⚲ S(Am)

▶ **An Imari charger,** with twin panels, depicting a phoenix in flight and a dragon, between foliate and diaper-patterned panels, 19thC, 18in (45.5cm) diam.
$360–440 ⚲ TRM

An Imari charger, decorated in red and blue, 19thC, 18in (45.5cm) diam, on a hardwood stand.
$230–280 ⚲ SWO

An Imari charger, painted with alternate panels of fabulous birds, shrubs and flowers, 19thC, 18¼in (46.5cm) diam.
$350–400 ⚲ AG

A Satsuma saucer dish, painted with a screen panel depicting deities among clouds, in red, green, brown and gilt on a cream ground, signed 'Matsumoto Hozan', six-character marks, Meiji period, 1868–1911, 12¼in (31cm) diam.
$500–600 ⚲ CMS

A red Kutani charger, decorated in polychrome and gilt with a procession of figures beside a lake, with a border of scrolls, phoenixes and blossom, Meiji period, 1868–1911, 15¼in (38.5cm) diam.
$300–350 ⚲ HYD

◀ **A porcelain charger,** painted in underglaze blue with two doves on a branch, with Mount Fuji in the distance, early 20thC, 18in (45.5cm) diam.
$145–175 ⚲ PFK

JAPANESE CERAMICS

Jars

▶ A pair of blue and white porcelain lidded jars, with interior covers, decorated with blossoming shrubs including chrysanthemum and prunus, with a band of prunus and cracked ice, c1900, 13¾in (35cm) high.
$725–875 ➶ **M**

A Tamba ware *sake* jar, decorated with the Seven Gods of Luck, signed 'Kenzan', 19thC, 16in (40.5cm) high.
$600–700 ➶ **SK**
Tamba ware is named after a type of ancient pottery from Tamba Province.

A Satsuma jar and cover, decorated with two swirling nymphs below a frieze of birds of paradise and flowers on a lozenge design green ground, with raised gilded collars to centre and base, Meiji period, 1868–1911, 5in (12.5cm) high.
$500–600 ➶ **P**

◀ A lidded ginger jar, with interior cover, decorated in the Imari palette with trees and blossom on a brocaded ground c1900, 11½in (29cm) high.
$470–570 ➶ **PF**

Censers & Koro

Cross Reference
See Colour Review (page 307)

A Satsuma *koro* and cover, the body with an enamel and gilt spiral pattern on brocade panels and dense flowerheads, restored finial and handle, inscribed mark on base, Meiji period, 1868–1911, 4½in (11.5cm) wide.
$1,750–2,000 ➶ **P**

◀ A Satsuma *koro* and cover, painted in colours with game birds in a landscape, the cover applied with a seated warrior clutching a pastille burner, late 19thC, 24in (61cm) high.
$1,000–1,150 ➶ **GAK**

A Satsuma *koro* and cover painted in gilt and coloured enamels with chrysanthemum and peonies by pierced rocks and a *ho-o* bird in a similar setting, the cover pierced with three apertures, signed 'Satsuma yaki Tomanobu', 19thC, 10in (25.5cm) high.
$2,600–3,200 ➶ **P**

Teapots

A pair of silver-mounted Arita teapots, painted with European four-masted ships and smaller craft, in the style of the Dutch 17thC marine painters, between borders of sea creatures, floral panels and lappets around the foot, one handle restuck, 18thC, 8in (20.5cm) wide.
$16,500–19,000 ➶ **P**
These teapots are particularly desirable because they feature European ships – a rare subject – and are a pair.

An Arita teapot, painted in underglaze blue with a European landscape, lid missing, Chinese Ming mark, 18thC, 4¾in (12cm) high.
$2,500–3,000 ➶ **S(Am)**
Because of the European subject, this teapot would have sold for much more if the lid had not been missing.

A Satsuma teapot, decorated with a band of warriors, with gold detail, handle repaired, Meiji period, 1868–1911, 4in (10cm) high.
$450–500 ➶ **P**

Items in the Japanese Ceramics section have been arranged in date order within each sub-section.

Vases

A pair of Imari lidded vases, late 17thC, 5in (12.5cm) high.
$650–800 ⊞ **GLD**

An Imari gourd vase, decorated with flowers in iron-red, blue and gilt, 19thC, 12½in (32cm) high.
$300–350 ⚒ **SWO**

A Hirado blue and white porcelain vase, the central basket body with two handles between tiers of moulded chrysanthemum petals, the neck with two handles and painted with a lappet collar, with a cutwork base, base inscribed 'ko-Hirado' in underglaze blue, chips, Meiji period, 1868–1911, 9in (23cm) high.
$3,000–3,300 ⚒ **BB(S)**

Imari

The term 'Imari' describes the underglaze blue with on-glaze iron-red and gold decoration found on Japanese Arita porcelain, and on Chinese ceramics made in imitation of Arita from the early 18th century. Although the Japanese wares were made in and around Arita in the province of Hizen, they were shipped from the nearby port of Imari, hence the name. Items produced were typically large display pieces designed to complement the grand interiors of European houses. Apart from tablewares and room ornaments, such as vases and bottles, figures were also popular as they exemplified the exoticism of Japan to the western market.

A *meiping*, decorated in underglaze white, green and grey with a crane beside lotus leaves and a pod, on a pink ground, the reverse ground graduating to white, signed 'Kanzan' (Denshichi), late 19thC, 9½in (24cm) high.
$2,600–3,200 ⚒ **S(NY)**
After being invited to the Kotô kilns during 1857–62, the artist moved to Kyoto and began calling himself Kanzan, using western-style pigment and kilns.

A pair of Kutani vases, applied to both sides with fan and knot mounts and painted with birds among foliage, within iron-red and gilt borders, six-character mark, late 19thC, 12in (30.5cm) high.
$450–500 ⚒ **GAK**

A Satsuma vase, with portraits of Oriental sages to the sides and with one female figure, on a gilt ground with raised scrollwork above a red matt ground, seal mark to underside and impressed mark, Meiji period, 1868–1911, 22in (56cm) high.
$850–1,000 ⚒ **Mit**

A pair of Satsuma vases, modelled in high relief with kingfishers and terrapins by a weed-edged pond, between parcel-gilt lattice bands, impressed two-character mark within double gourd reserve, Meiji period, 1868–1911, 12in (30.5cm) high.
$1,600–2,000 ⚒ **EH**

A pair of Imari pottery vases, painted in iron-red and blue with flowers and birds among scrolling foliage, over a blue stiff-leaf band, with gilt detail, 19thC, 24¼in (61.5cm) high.
$2,500–3,000 ⚒ **AH**

An earthenware vase, decorated with panels of *samurai* and other figures, on a brocade ground, cracked, 19thC, 24¼in (61.5cm) high.
$600–700 ⚒ **DN**

A spherical earthenware vase, with four flat faces, painted with a vegetable vendor, a *samurai*, a woman and child, and a man combing the mane of a *shishi*, within gilt frames, on a midnight blue ground with butterflies, florets and shading, two-character mark in gilt, late Meiji period, c1900, 5in (12.5cm) high.
$2,600–3,200 ⚒ **TEN**

Korean Ceramics

KOREAN CERAMICS

A celadon bowl, the interior moulded with a peony bloom encircled by peonies and leafy meanders, below a band of scrolling leaves, the exterior inlaid with four chrysanthemum roundels reserved on a reverse-inlaid leafy ground, restored body crack, Koryo Dynasty, 12thC, 7¾in (19.5cm) diam.
$5,800–7,200 ✔ **S(NY)**

A blue and white fish bowl, the sides painted with four stylized auspicious characters, the interior decorated with a fish, Choson Dynasty, 19thC, 8in (20.5cm) diam.
$4,500–5,500 ✔ **S(NY)**

A celadon cosmetic box and cover, the cover incised with a phoenix with wings spread in flight, encircled by scrolling foliage, the box decorated with cloud clusters, Koryo Dynasty, 12thC, 3¾in (9.5cm) diam.
$17,500–20,000 ✔ **S(NY)**

A celadon bowl, the sides carved with twelve double-fluted petal-shaped panels, covered in pale green crackled glaze, Koryo Dynasty, 12thC/13thC, 5⅜in (14.5cm) high.
$2,600–3,200 ✔ **P**

A blue and white bowl and cover, the cover painted with auspicious roundels alternating with beribboned auspicious emblems, the box decorated with chrysanthemums on leafy stalks, Choson Dynasty, 19thC, 10¼in (26cm) diam.
$4,500–5,500 ✔ **S(NY)**

A celadon cosmetic box and cover, the cover inlaid with a floret encircled by smaller flowerheads on a scrolling vine, the shoulder decorated with lunettes and key fret, box rim chipped, Koryo Dynasty, 12thC, 3¼in (8.5cm) diam.
$13,000–14,500 ✔ **S(NY)**

◀ **A** *punch'ong* **ware stem cup,** the celadon-glazed body inlaid in white slip with a grass-patterned band above a band of flowerheads, the foot with stylized tendril patterns, Choson Dynasty, 15thC, 3¾in (9.5cm) high.
$5,000–6,000 ✔ **BB(S)**

▶ **A cup stand,** the collar lobed in five petals, each incised with a leafy chrysanthemum spray, the cup decorated with a key fret at the inturned rim, repaired, Koryo Dynasty, 12thC, 5in (12.5cm) diam.
$5,000–6,000 ✔ **S(NY)**

A stoneware bowl, the interior inlaid in white slip with bands of grass, circles lotus petals and a central flowerhead the exterior with the same pattern, chips to foot, Choson Dynasty, 15thC/16thC, 7in (18cm) diam.
$2,500–3,000 ✔ **BB(S)**

A porcelain bowl, decorated overall with a milky-white glaze with a blue cast, hairline cracks, Choson Dynasty, 19thC, 9in (23cm) diam.
$2,500–3,000 ✔ **BB(S)**

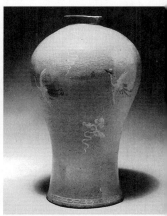

A celadon vase, the sides inlaid with four cranes in flight among stylized cloud wisps, the base decorated with a key fret band, Koryo Dynasty, 13thC/14thC, 11½in (29cm) high.
$20,000–22,500 ✔ **S(NY)**

Glass

The current impression is that there has been a dramatic increase in glass prices during the last year or so, which is interesting at a time when inflation is at its lowest for many years. If this is true, one might ask why it has happened.

Generally prices start with the auction houses, which serve as an open market insofar as such a thing can exist. Incidentally, it is important to note that, while many types of collectable glass are offered on internet auction sites, 17th- and 18th-century glass is usually to be found only in a live auction, where the goods can be viewed.

In January 2001 a sale took place which gave one an opportunity to explore how far increases in costs are real or just apparent. The Maynard Collection of 70 or so glasses ranged over most style groups: balusters, plain stems, air-twists, opaque-twists and so on – the sort to be found in any serious collection. None of these glasses had been on the market since 1945, when they were given as a 21st birthday present in the belief that they would one day prove a good investment.

Over a 55-year period this was undoubtedly true. Certainly the combined hammer price of approximately $23,000 was considerably more than the original cost. Of course no-one knows what that was, but a little research suggests that it was probably less than $275.

To arrive at this figure I analyzed the results of the sale of the Henry Brown Collection in 1947. This was a major collection which contained many important glasses unlikely to appear in sales today, but it was possible to extract the prices of 70 pieces similar to those in the Maynard Collection. The total cost came to approximately $235. This seems astounding, but it is important to remember that, at the time, $8 a week was a common wage.

Taking the Brown Collection as a baseline I compared the prices realized at other collection sales. Taking a similar selection of 70 glasses I examined the Smith Collection (1967–68) and the Cranch Collection (1997). The results were as follows: Smith – $3,600, Cranch – $8,750. If these figures are plotted on a graph, the result is interesting. Between 1947 and 1997 the rise in value was consistent at approximately $1,750 over each ten-year period. During the last four years, however, the increase has been almost ten times the rise of the previous ten years.

The evidence seems to support the idea that the price of antique glass *has* increased much more during the last few years than in the past, particularly pieces of the finest quality. Collecting glass must therefore surely be a good investment both in the long term and, recently, in the short term. **Brian Watson**

GLASS

Ale & Wine Glasses

A *façon de Venise* goblet, the flared bowl above three hollow ovoid knops divided by mereses and short sections, on a folded conical foot, possibly Liège, mid-17thC, 9½in (24cm) high.
$5,000–5,500 ⚒ S

A glass, with a trumpet-shaped deceptive bowl, the ball-knopped stem enclosing a tear, on a folded foot, c1700, 4½in (11.5cm) high.
$1,300–1,600 ⚒ LFA

A heavy baluster wine glass, with a conical deceptive bowl, the stem with baluster and single knop enclosing tears, on a conical folded foot, early 18thC, 5¾in (14.5cm) high.
$1,450–1,750 ⚒ PFK

A heavy baluster wine glass, the rounded funnel-shaped bowl with a solid base, the stem with a wide angular and basal knop enclosing tears, on a folded conical foot, c1710, 7in (18cm) high.
$2,300–2,900 ⚒ P

Early 18th century drinking glasses

The development of lead crystal glass at the end of the 17th century meant that the British glass industry began to flourish in its own right, and was no longer dependent on imported items and materials. It also marked the end of Venetian influence on the style of British glassware. Drinking glasses took on the baluster form that was already familiar on silverware and furniture, and there was an emphasis on strength and simplicity.

GLASS

A baluster wine glass, with a drawn stem and annulated true baluster knop, on a domed and folded foot, c1720, 6½in (16.5cm) high.
$1,000–1,200 ⊞ Som

A gin glass, with a bell bowl, the stem with an inverted baluster knop and basal ball knop, on a folded conical foot, c1740, 5in (12.5cm) high.
$350–400 ⊞ Som

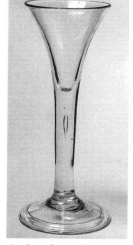

A wine glass, with a drawn trumpet bowl, the plain stem enclosing a tear, on a folded foot, c1740, 7¼in (18.5cm) high.
$300–350 ⊞ TWAC

A soda glass baluster wine glass, the bell bowl with a solid base over a cushion knop, with double annulated knop and inverted baluster, on a domed and folded foot, c1725, 5¼in (13.5cm) high.
$650–750 ⊞ BrW

A balustroid wine glass, with a drawn trumpet bowl, the stem with a ball knop enclosing a tear, on a domed plain foot, c1740, 6¾in (17cm) high.
$800–900 ⊞ BrW

A wine glass, the trumpet bowl engraved with fruiting vine, the long drawn stem with base inverted baluster and basal ball knop, on a plain conical foot, c1740, 6½in (16.5cm) high.
$900–1,000 ⊞ Som
Glasses similar to this can be seen in Sir Godfrey Kneller's early 18th-century paintings of London's Kit-Kat Club.

◄ **A goblet,** with a honey-comb-moulded conical bowl, the plain stem with shoulder and base knops, on a conical foot, c1745, 7½in (19cm) high.
$900–1,000 ⊞ GS

A German engraved goblet, the funnel bowl cut with three panels, the first with owls perched on a rocky outcrop, the second with a cornucopia spilling fruit, the third monogrammed 'DC' surmounted by a coronet, the stem with fluted ball knop above a fluted inverted baluster, on a folded conical foot, lacking cover, dated 1734, 11½in (29cm) high.
$1,900–2,200 ⋔ Bon(C)

A balustroid wine glass, with a flared bell bowl, the stem enclosing a tear from base of bowl to central knop, with a basal knop above a conical folded foot, 1700–40, 5½in (14cm) high.
$350–400 ⋔ PFK

A light baluster wine glass, with a rounded funnel bowl, the stem with two knops and inverted baluster, on a domed foot, c1740, 7¼in (18.5cm) high.
$1,300–1,500 ⋔ S(S)

A wine glass, the ogee bowl engraved with a band of hatching and floral sprays, on a plain stem and plain conical foot, c1750, 5in (12.5cm) high.
$200–300 ⊞ Som

A wine glass, the bell-shaped bowl engraved with a fruiting vine band, the plain stem with two ball knops, on a domed foot, c1750, 6½in (16.5cm) high.
$650–800 ✗ CAG

A wine glass, the round funnel bowl engraved with a band of fruiting vine, on a plain stem and folded conical foot, c1750, 6in (15cm) high.
$320–360 ⊞ GS

A wine glass, with a cup bowl, the stem with an indistinct incised twist, on a plain conical foot, c1750, 5in (12.5cm) high.
$450–500 ⊞ Som

A wine glass, with a bell bowl, the multiple-spiral air-twist stem applied with a central three-ring annular collar, on a domed foot, c1750, 6¼in (16cm) high.
$750–850 ✗ P

◀ **An ale glass,** the rounded funnel bowl with half-panel moulded base, on a double-series air-twist stem and conical foot, c1760, 8in (20.5cm) high.
$600–750 ✗ P(Ba)

◀ **A Silesian stemmed goblet,** with an ogee bowl, the stem with worked diamonds on the shoulder, on a folded foot, c1750, 6½in (16.5cm) high.
$725–800 ⊞ BrW

A wine flute, with a long bell bowl, on a multiple-series air-twist double-knopped stem, c1750, 9in (23cm) high.
$1,400–1,500 ⊞ BrW

A Hessen goblet and cover, the funnel bowl engraved with a continuous view of men working in a mine, the stem with a flattened knop and teared inverted baluster, on a folded domed foot, Altmünden or Lauenstein, 1750, 11¾in (30cm) high.
$26,000–32,000 ✗ S
While mining scenes are rare on glass, several examples are recorded in reference books.

A wine glass, with an engraved octagonal ogee bowl, the stem with a double-series opaque twist, on a plain conical foot, c1760, 6in (15cm) high.
$1,600–1,800 ⊞ Som

An ale glass, the round bowl engraved with hops and barley, on a double-series opaque-twist stem and a conical foot, c1765, 6¾in (17cm) high.
$450–600 ⊞ GS

A cordial glass, the bowl with moulded flutes engraved with floral sprays, the opaque-twist stem with a pair of spiral tapes within a multi-ply spiral band, c1765, 6½in (16.5cm) high.
$700–900 ⚲ P

A composite-stemmed wine glass, the rounded funnel bowl engraved with a band of flowers above an annulated knop, over a double-series opaque-twis stem, on a plain foot, c1765, 7½in (19cm) high.
$1,900–2,200 ⚲ S(S)
A composite stem is one that has two or more different sections.

▶ **A wine glass,** the ogee bowl painted in white enamel with a fruiting vine branch with tendrils and a bee in flight, the veins of the vine leaves scratched through the enamel, on a double-series opaque-twist stem with a spiral gauze within two spiral threads, 1765–75, 6in (15cm) high.
$1,600–1,900 ⚲ P
The painting of the vines, and the use of a very thin white enamel, differs from enamelled glasses attributed to the Beilby workshop. The treatment of the vine leaves in particular resembles the gilded decoration associated with the atelier of James Giles in Soho.

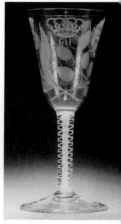

A floral-engraved wine glass, with a knopped facet-cut stem, on a conical foot, c1765, 6in (15cm) high.
$600–750 ⊞ JHa

A wine glass, with a waisted bucket bowl, on a mixed-twist stem, c1765, 6½in (16.5cm) high.
$750–850 ⊞ BrW

Foot shapes

Flanged | Plain conical | Firing

Domed folded | Conical folded | Domed Square

A Lynn wine glass, the funnel bowl moulded with three horizontal ribs, on a double-series opaque-twist stem with a multi-threaded spiral band surrounding a central column of two thicker spiralling threads, c1770, 5¾in (14.5cm) high.
$1,450–1,750 ⚲ LFA

A Jacobite goblet, known as The Hay Goblet, the pointed round funnel bow engraved with the crowned initials 'I*H' between a thistle and a seven-petalled rose and bud, on a double series opaque-twist stem, on a conical foot, small chips to footrim, c1768, 9in (23cm) high.
$9,500–11,500 ⚲ S
An applied paper label on the foot of this glass written in ink states: 'One of a pair, stated to have been the gift of Prince Charles to his treasurer and secretary JOHN HAY, who served throughout the 1745 campaign, was major-domo of the Household & went with Charles to Rome in 1766, created a baronet & left Charles' service in 1768 Dec. 8th. Both glasses capd.'

A wine glass, the round funnel bowl engraved with an Italianate scene, on a hexagonally-cut facet stem, 1770, 6in (15cm) high.
$950–1,100 ⊞ BrW

A wine glass, the bell bowl engraved around the rim with floral sprays, the hexagonal-cut stem with three vertical rows of lozenge-shaped facets, on a foot with a rosebud and two leaves, minor chips to stem, c1785, 6in (15cm) high.
$450–550 ⚒ P

A Dutch goblet, the funnel bowl engraved with a seated figure above the armorials of the seven provinces flanked by galleons at sea, above a Latin inscription, the stem with diamond-shaped knops at the shoulder, on a folded conical foot, 18thC, 7¾in (19.5cm) high.
$1,200–1,400 ⚒ S(Am)

A pair of Dutch roemers, the ogee bowls on stems applied with three raspberry prunts and with flared folded feet, 18thC, 7in (18cm) high.
$1,200–1,400 ⚒ S(Am)

LOCATE THE SOURCE
The source of each illustration in Miller's can be found by checking the code letters below each caption with the Key to Illustrations, pages 794–800.

A Bohemian goblet, the bowl engraved with flowers, on a red colour-twist stem, the foot engraved with leaves, 18thC, 9in (23cm) high.
$320–400 ⚒ DORO

A rummer, the ovoid bowl engraved with a Greek key band and hops, barley and a shield with the monogram 'JAR', on a plain stem, with a conical foot, dated 1807, 8½in (21.5cm) high.
$600–660 ⚒ DN

A goblet, the ovoid bowl engraved with star-looped decoration and an eight-pointed star in each loop, on a domed lemon squeezer foot, c1810, 7¼in (18.5cm) high.
$200–240 ⊞ Som

A rummer, the ovoid bowl on a lemon squeezer foot, c1810, 5½in (14cm) high.
$145–160 ⊞ TWAC

A rummer, the cup bowl engraved with a two-masted sailing ship, the reverse with an anchor, with a plain stem and a plain conical foot, c1820, 4¼in (11cm) high.
$400–440 ⊞ Som

A green wine glass, with a cup bowl, the hollow stem with a milled collar and raspberry prunts, on a trailed conical foot, c1820, 4½in (11.5cm) high.
$130–150 ⊞ Som

A set of 12 rummers, the bucket-shaped bowls with diagonal and facet-cut bands, on blade-knopped stems, c1820, 6½in (16.5cm) high.
$1,500–1,750 ⚒ LFA

A pair of wine or sherry glasses, on knopped stems, c1830, 5½in (14cm) high.
$100–150 ⊞ TWAC

GLASS

A set of 12 green wine glasses, with conical bowls, on knopped stems and plain feet, c1830, 5in (12.5cm) high.
$1,200–1,400 ⊞ Som

A goblet, the bell-shaped bowl engraved with a profile of an officer, possibly Napoleon, within a laurel garland, flanked by buildings and a hunting scene in a river landscape, above a facet-cut band, on a knopped stem, c1840, 5½in (14cm) high.
$360–430 ⚹ LFA

A glass goblet, possibly Richardson's, the tapering bowl engraved with African animals, birds and insects among foliage, wit a hunter aiming a shotgu the facet-cut baluster ster on a star-cut spreading circular foot, mid-19thC, 9¼in (23.5cm) high.
$2,200–2,500 ⚹ S(S)

Collecting Bohemian glass

- The quality of the colour and overall condition are the main determinants of the value of 19th century Bohemian glassware.
- Feel the item carefully to detect any damage; often chips are less obvious on coloured glass.
- Look for damage to feet; ornate feet can easily be re-cut, but they will be smaller and may look out of proportion.
- Blue-stained Bohemian glass often fades; this can seriously affect value.
- Goblets were often made with covers; those with covers are worth 25 per cent more than those without.

A set of nine Bohemian Alsatian-style amber glasses, the bowls engraved with fruiting vines, c1860, 5in (12.5cm) high.
$1,500–1,700 ⊞ ALiN

A set of six Baccarat hock glasses, with cranberry bowls on clear stems and feet, France, 1885, 8in (20.5cm) high.
$1,000–1,300 ⊞ ALiN

A Bohemian crystal drinking goblet, the bowl engraved with a dragoon, dated '1863', 7in (18cm) high.
$2,300–2,900 ⊞ ALiN

A straw opal champagne glass, designed by T. G. Jackson for James Powell, Whitefriars, c1877 5in (12.5cm) high.
$950–1,150 ⊞ ALiN

A Bohemian dark green goblet, engraved with an inscription in white enamel between bands of yellow scrolls, minor damage to rim, late 19thC, 5½in (14cm) high.
$320–400 ⚹ DORO

A set of four wine goblets, with diamond-cut bowls, on circular cut feet, c1900, 6in (15cm) high.
$250–300 ⚹ WW

A Bohemian amber-tinted goblet, engraved with a clear band depicting a hunting scene, on a facet-cut stem, minor damage to foot, mid-19thC, 8¼in (21cm) high.
$850–1,000 ⚹ DORO

A Dutch wine flute, the bowl engraved with a medallion with the initials 'Br.R.S.', the reverse with Masonic implements within a double-headed snake medallion, heightened wit gilt, on a conical foot, 1910, 9¾in (25cm) high.
$1,000–1,200 ⚹ S(Am)

Beakers & Tumblers

A **façon de Venise** latticino beaker, inset with spiral translucent blue and white threads, possibly Liège, 17thC, 3½in (9cm) high.
$1,750–2,000 ➤ **S**

A **Bohemian engraved beaker,** inscribed '*Herbst*' above a female figure emblematic of Autumn, the reverse with flowers, early 18thC, 5in (12.5cm) high.
$850–1,000 ➤ **Bon(C)**

A **Dutch glass beaker,** decorated in coloured enamels with a heart, birds, flowers and leaves, 18thC, 3¼in (8.5cm) high.
$150–175 ➤ **LFA**

A **Russian goblet,** engraved with a bust of Catherine the Great, her monogram surmounted by a coronet and the Russian double-headed eagle with the Order of St George, bordered with flowers and fruit, mid-18thC, 6½in (16.5cm) high.
$750–850 ➤ **Bon(C)**

◀ A **tumbler,** engraved with the insignia of the Order of Oddfellows, c1850, 5in (12.5cm) high.
$150–180 ⊞ **TWAC**

A **Vienna beaker,** decorated by Anton Kothgasser, with two hands issuing from clouds exchanging a wedding ring over two doves by two burning hearts, the reverse with an inscription in French, c1830, 4¼in (11cm) high.
$5,000–5,800 ➤ **DORO**

A **tumbler,** engraved with hops and barley, fruiting vine motifs, crossed hay fork and pitchfork and initials 'TB', c1800, 3¾in (9.5cm) high.
$250–300 ⊞ **Som**

▶ A **Bohemian green beaker,** by Harrach, carved with reeds and bullrushes, c1880, 4½in (11.5cm) high.
$450–550 ⊞ **ALiN**

A **pair of stipple-engraved shooting glasses,** probably on Stourbridge blanks, signed 'A.P. Haag, Kenilworth', c1880, 4in (10cm) high.
$650–800 ⊞ **ALiN**

Bottles & Decanters

◀ A **serving bottle,** applied with a scroll handle and thumbpiece, on a kick-in base, c1715, 5½in (14cm) high.
$4,600–5,000 ➤ **S**

▶ A **Jacobite decanter,** engraved with an eight-petalled rose and two buds, the reverse inscribed 'Fiat', with associated faceted spire stopper, tip of stopper chipped, c1750, 11½in (29cm) high.
$16,000–19,000 ➤ **S**
It is thought that there is only one other example of this piece known.

A **cruciform decanter,** c1760, 8½in (21.5cm) high.
$750–850 ⊞ **GS**

A **Bohemian *milchglas* bottle,** polychrome decorated with a portrait of a lady within a cartouche, surrounded by flower sprigs, damaged rim, lacking stopper, c1780, 8in (20.5cm) high.
$200–240 ➤ **DORO**

GLASS

GLASS

A decanter, with three annulated neck rings and flute-cut base, with a target stopper, c1800, 9½in (24cm) high.
$300–350 ⊞ Som

A decanter, with triple ring neck and moulded basal flutes, engraved with a band of loops and diaper around the body, the base lightly moulded with 'CORK GLASS CO', with cut bulls-eye stopper, stopper with minor chips, possibly married, c1800, 10¾in (27.5cm) high.
$700–850 ⚒ P

A pear-shaped green carafe, with an everted rim, c1810, 6¾in (17cm) high.
$200–220 ⊞ Som

An onion-shaped turquoise green carafe, c1840, 7¾in (19.5cm) high.
$300–330 ⊞ Som

A Bohemian yellow uranium glass decanter, with a facet-cut body and stopper, c1850, 7in (18cm) high.
$300–350 ⚒ DORO

An amethyst shaft-and-globe flask and stopper, c1860, 9in (23cm) high.
$300–350 ⊞ GS

▶ **An alabaster glass decanter,** by H. G. Richardson, with gilt decoration, c1865, 10in (25.5cm) high.
$850–1,000 ⊞ ALiN

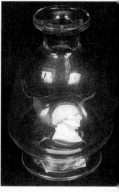

A glass carafe, decorated with a sulphide portrait of Gladstone, lacking stopper, probably by John Ford & Co, Edinburgh, c1880, 5¾in (14.5cm) high.
$360–440 ⚒ P(Ed)

Bowls

A rib-moulded bowl, on a flared rib-moulded foot with a folded rim, c1700, 7in (18cm) diam.
$2,500–3,000 ⚒ S

An Irish bowl, with a band of flat-cut facets and geometrically arranged splits, above a band of stylized foliage, on a square lemon squeezer foot, Cork, c1790, 14in (35.5cm) wide.
$2,500–3,000 ⚒ HOK

A bowl and cover, cut with flutes and shallow diamonds on a square lemon squeezer foot, c1800, 7½in (19cm) high.
$1,000–1,200 ⊞ Som

A blue tea caddy bowl, on an applied foot, c1800, 4¼in (11cm) high.
$200–220 ⊞ Som

An Irish fruit bowl, the facet-cut bowl with turn-over rim, on a centre-knopped stem and square lemon squeezer foot, early 19thC, 7¼in (18.5cm) high.
$750–850 ⚒ S(S)

A bowl and stand, by Perrin & Geddes, Liverpool, with turn-over rim, detachable stand and overall prismatic cutting, the foot with a star-cut base, minor chips, c1815, 11½in (29cm) high.
$950–1,200 ⚒ S

An Irish turn-over lip-cut pedestal bowl, with deep hobnail cut rim, with separate stand with spreading step cuts, c1835, 11¼in (28.5cm) diam.
$2,900–3,500 ⚒ HOK

A French frosted opaline glass lidded *compotier* and stand, attributed to the St Louis Glassworks, decorated overall with tiny gilt domes, the lid with gilt stem finial, the stand with gilt rim, mid-19thC, 11½in (29cm) diam.
$650–800 ⚒ NOA

An Osiris yellow and red bowl, by Stevens & Williams, c1880, 4in (10cm) high.
$1,300–1,600 ⊞ ALiN

◄ A cut-glass rose bowl, on a silver stand, marked for Chester 1924, 12½in (32cm) diam, with wirework flower rose.
$500–600 ⚒ AG

A pair of Scottish glass bowls, decorated with fish in polychrome enamel, marked 'HW' for Hannah Walton, c1895, 5in (12.5cm) diam.
$900–1,100 ⊞ ALiN

GLASS

Dumps

◄ A green dump, with a fish inclusion, late 19thC, 3¾in (9.5cm) high.
$230–260 ⊞ RWA

► A green dump, with a clay pipe bowl inclusion, late 19thC, 4¼in (11cm) high.
$200–220 ⊞ RWA

A Victorian Stourbridge dump, with a flower inclusion, 7in (18cm) high.
$320–380 ⚒ DA

► A green dump, in the shape of an inkwell with a stopper, c1860, 5in (12.5cm) high.
$150–200 ⊞ JBL

Inclusions

Dumps were usually made out of waste green bottle glass by apprentice glass-makers in centres such as Sunderland, Stourbridge and Wakefield. Because of their weight, those with the rain pattern of bubbles were most commonly used as paperweights or doorstops, whereas those with inclusions, and the elaborate fountain weights, were meant for viewing above ground level on chimneypieces or as table decorations. Examples with inclusions used clay pipe bowls, sulphides or terracotta to form representations such as politicians, military heroes and animals, these materials being capable of withstanding the high temperatures needed for making such pieces.

GLASS

Epergnes

A Victorian cranberry and clear glass four-branch *épergne,* with a cranberry petal-shaped base, 18½in (47cm) high.
$580–650 ⚒ **Mit**

A Victorian cranberry glass *épergne,* on a spreading foot base with a wavy-edged everted rim, 21½in (54.5cm) high.
$870–1,100 ⚒ **Bri**

A glass and silver-plated *épergne,* on an oak tree stem, the base with a stag, late 19thC, 20in (51cm) high.
$350–430 ⚒ **ELR**

A Victorian cranberry glass *épergne,* the trumpets decorated with clear glass trails, the two clear glass scrolling arms supporting two baskets, 22in (56cm) high.
$870–1,000 ⚒ **M**

Jars

◀ **A George III jar and cover,** the body with slice, lozenge and spiral-fluted cuttings, with altered silver-mounted rim, probably by Matthew Boulton, the cover now cut with a slot for a spoon, Birmingham 1803, 7in (18cm) high.
$250–300 ⚒ **CAG**

▶ **A blue-tinted jar and cover,** the sides flat-cut with diamond and petal pattern, 19thC, 11¾in (30cm) high.
$2,500–3,000 ⚒ **S(S)**

A turquoise overlay jar and cover, the roundels bordered in white and cut to reveal clear glass, the domed cover with gilt-metal pine-cone finial, mid 19thC, 7in (18cm) high.
$300–350 ⚒ **P(Ba)**

Jelly & Sweetmeat Glasses

An Irish cut-glass custard cup and cover, c1820, 4in (10cm) high.
$580–650 ⊞ **US**

A jelly glass, on a flattened knop with a series of double beads, with a domed and folded foot, c1740, 4½in (11.5cm) high.
$750–850 ⚒ **P**

A pair of custard cups, with flute-cut bases, on plain conical feet, c1820, 3½in (9cm) high.
$80–90 ⊞ **Som**

A Silesian stem sweet-meat glass, with cut bowl and lobe-cut conical foot, c1760, 6in (15cm) high.
$600–700 ⊞ **BrW**

▶ **A pair of American Pairpoint-style comports,** cut and etched with flowers and swags, the lids with air bubble spire finials, the baluster stems on air bubble knops, with loaded Watson & Sons sterling silver feet, c1900, 14¼in (36cm) high.
$2,500–3,000 ⚒ **SK**

ugs

◄ **A water jug,** cut with arcades of diamonds and fine flutes, c1815, 7in (18cm) high.
$450–500 ⊞ Del

▲ **An Amberina jug and stopper,** with a clear glass handle, c1880, 10½in (26.5cm) high.
$400–450 ⊞ GS
Amberina is a clear amber glass containing a small amount of gold in solution. When sections of a vessel are reheated they change to a rich ruby red.

A pair of Victorian lobed jugs, the pink and white tinted satin glass painted with flowers and butterflies, 13in (33cm) high.
$130–150 ⚒ AG

A frosted glass ewer, with a gilt twist frieze to the lower body and a gilt lozenge band to the neck, the base with blue overlay foliate panels decorated in gilt, the handle in the shape of a blue serpent with gilt scales coiling around the body, foot replaced, late 19thC, 11¾in (30cm) high.
$300–350 ⚒ P(Ba)

Mugs & Tankards

A Continental *milchglas* mug, painted with a man drinking, inscribed 'Fuego', 18thC, 4in (10cm) high.
$170–220 ⚒ WW

A mug, with trailed bands to the rim and gadrooning to the base, raised on a knopped pedestal stem containing a groat, 1836, 4½in (11.5cm) high.
$500–650 ⊞ GS

A German light green glass tankard, decorated in coloured enamels with a coat-of-arms, the reverse with an ox's head above a castle and a forest, late 19thC, 13¼in (33.5cm) high.
$650–800 ⚒ DORO

Lamps & Lighting

A pair of table lustres, the step-cut sconces with fold-over rims, on ovoid columns above faceted knops, on star-cut bases, c1830, 10½in (26.5cm) high.
$1,250–1,500 ⚒ LFA

A pair of Sowerby Ivory Queen's Ware pressed glass candlesticks, on square stepped bases moulded with foliate swags, minor damage, moulded mark, c1880, 10¼in (26cm) high.
$230–290 ⚒ S(S)

A pair of cut-glass table lustres, with bulbous turned and faceted columns, and cut and scalloped bases, damaged, c1900, 14¼in (36cm) high.
$870–970 ⚒ P(Ba)

Miller's is a price GUIDE not a price LIST

GLASS

Paperweights

A Baccarat mushroom paperweight, the millefiori canes surrounded by a torsade of white gauze entwined by cobalt blue threads, on a star-cut base, bruise to base, mid-19thC, 3¼in (8.5cm) diam.
$1,000–1,300 ↗ Bon(C)

An American clear glass paperweight, enclosing a sulphide portrait of Lajos Kossuth of Hungary, c1845, 2¼in (5.5cm) diam.
$320–360 ⊞ SWB
Lajos Kossuth was a Hungarian statesman and leader of the 1848 Hungarian Revolution. After its failure he fled to Turkey, and then toured around Europe and America in an unsuccessful attempt to enlist support.

◄ **A Baccarat faceted snake paperweight,** the green reptile with dark green markings, a red mouth and eyes, on an upset muslin ground, cut with a ten-sided window and diamond facets to the sides, chipped, c1850, 3in (7.5cm) diam.
$4,000–4,500 ↗ S

A St Louis paperweight, with yellow, orange, red and green fruit on latticino, c1850, 2½in (6.5cm) diam.
$1,000–1,300 ↗ JNic

A Baccarat paperweight, enclosing a yellow and puce pansy with green foliage, on a star-cut base, 19thC, 2¼in (5.5cm) diam.
$700–850 ↗ SWO

A Clichy closepack millefiori paperweight, with brightly coloured canes and green and pink roses, mid-19thC, 3¼in (8.5cm) diam.
$1,800–2,200 ↗ DN

◄ **An Old English-style paperweight,** with red, blue and mauve canes on a white ground, c1850, 3in (7.5cm) diam.
$450–500 ⊞ SWB

LOCATE THE SOURCE
The source of each illustration in Miller's can be found by checking the code letters below each caption with the Key to Illustrations, pages 794–800.

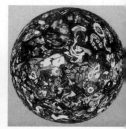

A scrambled paperweight with animal and flower canes, 19thC, 3½in (9cm) diam.
$580–700 ↗ Mit

Salts

A pair of Lobmeyr Renaissance-style cut and engraved salts, Vienna, Austria, c1880, 3½in (9cm) high.
$870–1,000 ⊞ ALiN

◀ **A blue wrythen-moulded salt,** with a plain stem and plain conical foot, c1800, 3in (7.5cm) high.
$120–130 ⊞ Som

A panel-moulded salt, on a round foot, c1760, 2¾in (7cm) diam.
$130–150 ⋏ LFA

Scent Bottles

◀ **A cut-glass scent bottle,** with a silver top, London 1893, 4½in (11.5cm) high.
$220–240 ⊞ TWAC

An Amberina scent bottle, in the shape of a fish, shaded from a deep amber head to a paler tail, with gold foil inclusions, the fins and scales with raised gilding, the silver tail by William Graeme, marked 1884, 6in (15cm) long, the external glass neck filled with plaster.
$1,300–1,600 ⋏ P

A white opaline scent bottle, the gold mount with a hinged cover with initials in ruby and white *faux* jewels, 19thC, 3¾in (9.5cm) high, in a fitted case.
$750–850 ⋏ Bon(C)

To find out more see *Miller's Perfume Bottles: A Collector's Guide* (£5.99), with over 130 colour pictures, its 64 pages are packed with invaluable information. *Order from* www.millers.uk.com *or telephone in the UK on 01933 443863*

◀ **A cut-glass scent bottle,** with ten sides, the gilt-metal top mounted with blue cabochon stones, possibly American, 19thC, 4¾in (12cm) high.
$180–230 ⋏ SK

Vases & Urns

◀ **A pair of Victorian celadon-tinted opaque vases,** painted in yellow, mauve, brown, white and green with pansies, the rims heightened with gilt, 12in (30.5cm) high.
$220–260 ⋏ PFK

▶ **A Continental enamelled glass vase and stand,** made in sections, decorated overall in enamels and gilt with flowers, foliage and scrolls, rim damaged, 19thC, 30¼in (77cm) high.
$3,500–4,500 ⋏ WW

An Empire-style vase, with gilt-metal twist and leaf handles, the rim and base cast with a laurel leaf, probably French, c1830, 6¾in (17cm) high.
$260–320 ⋏ P

GLASS

A pair of Victorian Jack-in-the-Pulpit vases, with purple-tinted white bodies on citrine feet, 6½in (16.5cm) high.
$150–180 ⚒ LF

A Stourbridge cameo vase, the yellow ground overlaid with opaque white and carved with flowering shrubs, minor chip, possibly Richardson, c1880, 10¾in (27.5cm) high.
$1,500–1,750 ⚒ Bon(C)

◄ **A French opaque white floor vase,** the top and foot painted pink with gilt detail, the body painted with four birds perched on floral branches, c1900, 31½in (80cm) high.
$850–1,000 ⚒ SK

A Bohemian ruby-flashed vase, the ten sides engraved with deer and landscape vignettes and rocaille C-scrolls, late 19thC, 21¼in (54cm) high.
$500–600 ⚒ DN

► **A Stourbridge rock crystal-style vase,** decorated with floral swags, shell and foliate scrolls, c1910, 7¼in (18.5cm) high.
$450–500 ⚒ HAM

A pair of Bohemian cranberry glass urns, each with white overlay and painted with a classical scene, the reverse with a floral panel reserved on a gilt scrolling foliate ground, on cylindric plinths with floral panels and leaf-moulded bases, 19thC, 13½in (34.5cm) high
$3,000–3,300 ⚒ AH

Miscellaneous

► **A glass linen smoother,** with bobbin-knopped handle, c1780, 4in (10cm) high
$130–150 ⊞ Som

An opaque white glass tea canister, painted with a bullfinch in a branch, below a puce cartouche with 'Green' in black, the reverse with bouquets and sprigs of flowers in coloured enamels, rim damaged, 18thC, 5¼in (13.5cm) high.
$1,500–1,650 ⚒ P(EA)

A Victorian silver-mounted glass bell, with an amber-tinted spirally-fluted bowl, the handle embossed with flowers and C-scrolls, with a silver clanger, 7½in (19cm) high.
$300–330 ⚒ LFA

A miniature salver, the gadrooned dish on a bobbin-knopped stem, c1700, 2½in (6.5cm) high.
$750–850 ⊞ BrW

A pair of cranberry glass baskets, with crimped rims and dimpled borders, applied with clear glass handles, 19thC, 6½in (16.5cm) high.
$250–300 ⚒ GAK

► **A Victorian witch ball,** with a royal blue mirrored interior and lacquered brass suspender, 12in (30.5cm) diam.
$250–300 ⚒ PFK
Witch balls are large coloured glass spheres, often silvered inside giving a metallic effect. They were hung in windows to repel the evil eye and bring good luck. They have fittings for hanging similar to those found on Christmas tree decorations and are very fragile. Colours include dark blue, green and cranberry. Some witch balls were made with Nailsea-style decoration. Similar items are found in eastern Europe, but these are used as garden decorations and often have necks.

Silver

The past year has been an interesting one, as I have seen quite a change in the values of some areas of silver and in attitudes towards collecting. The simplicity, weight and quality of silver manufactured in the reign of George II makes it highly desirable and it is becoming ever more difficult to find, which is pushing up prices. Collectors are preferring to have one very good piece rather than several mediocre ones, and this approach will stand them in good stead as although most collectors do not buy in order to resell, perfect examples, even if initially expensive, represents an excellent long-term investment.

Early and provincial Scottish silver has been steadily moving up the scale for a number of years now and I really do not see this changing in the foreseeable future. There are now dedicated auction sales for Scottish antiques, and dealers are finding this a fertile marketplace.

The most visible area of change is Irish silver of all periods. It has been amazing to watch the snowballing effect in this field; anything from a salt spoon to an early 18th-century dishing is enthusiastically fought for and prices

are increasing dramatically. My shop, those of other dealers, and the auction houses are besieged by collectors and dealers asking for Irish silver. Supply is scarce due to low output, Ireland's current buoyant economy, and Americans with Irish ancestry being keen to buy some of their history. Furthermore, many more people are collecting silver and would like to have at least one Irish piece in their collection, so the supply and demand theory comes into play, increasing values. As Irish silver has always been sought-after by dedicated collectors I do not expect items to decrease in value, but I am sure prices will slow down in time, although when is hard to predict.

Another area to watch is small collectables; anything that can be placed in a cabinet is acquired by the avid antiques hunter. As the population grows and homes become smaller, space and finance can become an issue, so collecting these little pieces will suit any pocket and home and it can be as much fun learning about makers and dates of small items as the larger and more expensive articles of silver. **Daniel Bexfield**

Baskets

A George III silver basket, by William Plummer, engraved with rococo armorials, the sides pierced with leaf-scrolls, latticework and flowerheads, London 1760, 15in (38cm) long, 39oz.
$17,500–20,500 ↗ S
William Plummer was highly regarded for his pierced silverware. His work is highly sought-after and this is reflected in the price.

A silver cake basket, by R. Morton & Co, pierced and embossed with quatrefoils, ovals, paterae and swags, Sheffield 1775, 13in (33cm) diam, 35oz.
$3,200–3,750 ↗ TEN

A George III silver table basket, by Richard Morton, pierced with bright-cut bands of pales, urns and swags, Sheffield 1777–78, 13in (33cm) diam, 24.77oz.
$8,700–9,500 ⊞ NS

A George III silver cake basket, by Robert Hennell I, the interior engraved with two bright-cut bands, the foot with a similar band, London 1785, 13¾in (35cm) long, 28oz.
$2,300–2,900 ↗ DN

A George III silver sugar/sweetmeat basket, with a pierced and beaded rim, probably by Hester Bateman, London c1783, 6in (15cm) long.
$1,000–1,300 ↗ GAK

A George III silver sugar basket, by William Turton, with alternate raised and matt fluting, gilt lined, London 1783, 7¾in (19.5cm) high, 7.75oz.
$700–770 ↗ CGC

SILVER

An Irish Georgian silver basket, by Thomas Jones, Dublin 1785, 14in (35.5cm) long.
$8,700–9,500 ⊞ **WELD**

A George III silver sugar basket, by John Hutson, the bright-cut body with a swing handle, London 1787, 7in (18cm) long, 8oz.
$900–1,000 ⚒ **MEA**

A George III silver sugar basket, by John Denziloe, bright-cut engraved wit swags and festoons and the letter 'L within a cartouche, London 1787–8 6½in (16.5cm) high, 8.16oz.
$1,900–2,200 ⊞ **NS**

An Irish George III silver helmet sugar basin, by G. P. & W., Dublin 1799–1800, 9in (23cm) long.
$3,600–3,900 ⊞ **WELD**

A Victorian silver sugar basket, pierced with stylized scroll patterns, with a clear glass liner, Birmingham 1858, 5¼in (13.5cm) high, 8oz.
$400–450 ⚒ **P(E)**

Piercing

Piercing is created by cutting and punching out pieces of silver to produce an ornate, decorative and delicate design. When looking at pierced silver, always spend a little extra time studying the work as often splits and damage can occur through careless handling and cleaning. Also look for silver solder joins that may have been repaired by a silversmith – these will be little raised lumps of solder and can be slightly different in colour. If an item has been split or repaired take this seriously into consideration when pricing a piece.

A Victorian silver sugar basket, by Joseph & Edward Bradbury, the wirework sides overlaid with vine leaf motif, with a blue glass liner, London 1871, 5¼in (13.5cm) high, 5.5oz.
$250–300 ⚒ **FHF**

A pair of Victorian pierced silver sweetmeat baskets, by Mappin Brothers, Birmingham 1899, 4¼in (11cm) long, 5oz.
$220–250 ⚒ **CGC**

An Edwardian silver sweetmeat basket, by Walker & Hall, embossed with masks and scrolls and pierced with stars, Sheffield 1903, 8in (20.5cm) wide, 6.5oz.
$220–260 ⚒ **F&C**

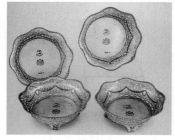

A set of four silver fruit baskets, by Charles Clement Pilling, the pierced sides with bead and reel borders, engraved with crests and armorials, London 1912–14, 8¼in (21cm) diam, 44oz.
$2,500–2,900 ⚒ **DN**
The crest and motto are of St Aubyn (family of the Barons St Levan of St Michael's Mount) above the arms of the Corporation of the City of Plymouth.

A silver basket, by The Goldsmiths & Silversmiths Co, with a blue glass liner, London 1904, 4½in (11.5cm) high.
$440–500 ⚒ **SWO**

A pierced silver basket, Sheffield 1927, 11in (28cm) long.
$500–600 ⚒ **SWO**

SILVER

Bowls

A George II silver porringer, with George Andrews' mark struck over William Cripps, London 1763, 4in (10cm) high.
$870–1,000 ⊞ CoHA
George Andrews was doubtless the retailer of this piece and struck his mark over that of the maker, William Cripps.

A George III silver sugar bowl, by James MacKay, with a chased band of flowers and foliage around the rim and engraved with a crest, motto and 'F', Edinburgh 1809–10, 5½in (14cm) diam, 11.5oz.
$3,000–3,600 ⊞ NS

An Irish George III silver sugar bowl and cream jug, by J. Fray, 1814, 5in (12.5cm) diam.
$1,600–1,750 ⊞ WELD

An American silver bowl, by Gorham Manufacturing Co, with chased reeded body, the rim with embossed gadrooned edge, with repoussé foliate pattern on a textured background, Providence 1886, 10½in (26.5cm) diam, 23oz.
$500–600 ⋏ SK

An Irish fluted silver bowl, by C. Lamb, with a coin inset base, Dublin 1902, 3½in (9cm) diam.
$600–660 ⊞ SIL

► An American silver bowl, by Bailey, Banks & Biddle Co, the sides with C-scroll and foliate chasing, the interior with a monogram, early 20thC, 10¾in (27.5cm) diam, 19oz.
$600–725 ⋏ SK

A Victorian silver punch bowl, the body with repoussé decoration of foliate scrolls and flowerheads, with a shield to each side, London 1892, 10in (25.5cm) diam, 30oz.
$1,200–1,400 ⋏ Mit

An American silver trophy bowl, by Howard & Co, engraved with a presentation inscription, c1900, 8½in (21.5cm) diam, 22oz.
$1,000–1,250 ⋏ S(NY)

A Victorian silver sugar bowl, the panelled sides with repoussé decoration, retailed by Messrs Thomas, 1865, 4¾in (12cm) diam, 2.75oz.
$230–300 ⋏ L

A Victorian silver-gilt bowl, by J. D. & S., decorated in relief with fruit among foliage, with beaded edge, inscribed, Sheffield 1883, 10¼in (26cm) long, 13.4oz, in a fitted case.
$450–500 ⋏ Bea(E)

A silver bowl, London 1890, 4in (10cm) high.
$200–230 ⋏ SWO

A silver porringer and spoon, by Moss Morris, the body with rustic twig handles terminating in flower sprays, the spoon with ivy design stem, 1911, porringer 6in (15cm) wide overall, 9.5oz.
$300–350 ⋏ L

A pierced silver fruit bowl, by Mappin & Webb, Sheffield 1932, 9½in (24cm) diam, 23.5oz.
$450–500 ⋏ CGC

SILVER

Boxes

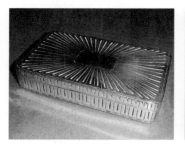

A Dutch silver tobacco box, the top with a radiating linear decoration, marked, Utrecht 1810, 4½in (11.5cm) long.
$320–380 ⚒ PFK

A French silver box, the lid decorated with chased scroll and floral design, with engine-turned decoration to the base, c1840, 3¼in (8.5cm) long.
$250–300 ⚒ LJ

An embossed silver jewel box, Birmingham 1880, 9in (23cm) long.
$1,500–1,750 ⊞ TWr

◄ **A Victorian silver trinket box,** by James and William Deakin, Chester 1898, 3½in (9cm) long.
$450–500 ⊞ BEX

A German silver soap box, by C. Becker, c1890, 3½in (9cm) long.
$300–330 ⊞ BEX

An Edwardian silver cigar casket, by William Comyns, the double compartments divided by a mounted cigar lighter, the hinged covers engraved with a crest and monogram, with cedarwood lining, London 1901, 13in (33cm) long.
$1,250–1,400 ⚒ P(E)

An Edwardian silver tobacco box, engraved with ivy leaf designs, with a gilt interior, Birmingham 1905, 3½in (9cm) long.
$150–175 ⚒ GAK

A George V silver presentation casket, by D. & C. Edwards, decorated with bands of Celtic designs, surmounted by a crest of a rampant lion and a shield, the lid engraved with initials, Glasgow 1916–17, 11in (28cm) long, 48.78oz.
$2,400–2,600 ⊞ NS

Candlesticks & Chambersticks

A pair of Danish loaded silver candlesticks, by Ditlev Brasenhauer, with later detachable nozzles, Copenhagen 1699, 4¼in (11cm) high.
$7,250–8,000 ⚒ S
These candlesticks are marked with the Zodiac signs of Pisces and Aries indicating that one was hallmarked between 18 February and 20 March, the other between 20 March and 20 April, 1699.

A pair of Irish early George II cast silver candlesticks, by Thomas Bolton, with octagonal Silesian stems, Dublin 1728, 6in (15cm) high, 20oz.
$11,600–13,800 ⚒ WW

A pair of Irish George II silver candlesticks, by G. Cartwright, Dublin 1736, 9in (23cm) high.
$18,000–20,000 ⊞ WELD

◄ **A George III silver chamberstick** by James Gould, with a Victorian replacement extinguisher, London 1742, 5¼in (13.5cm) diam, 10.5oz.
$400–470 ⚒ CGC

George III silver taper-stick, by E.C., with a knopped [st]em on a hexagonal [rib]bed base, London 1769, [..]n (15cm) high, 6oz.
[..]950–1,200 ✗ E

A pair of silver candlesticks, by John Carter, with octafoil cluster columns and foliate sconces, the bases embossed with masks, swags, sprays and beading, York 1770, 12¼in (31cm) high.
$4,000–4,500 ✗ TEN

► **A pair of George III silver chambersticks,** with detachable nozzles (not hallmarked), maker's mark possibly for R. Gainsford, Sheffield 1810, 21.5oz.
$900–1,100 ✗ AG

[A] **pair of Victorian loaded [s]ilver candlesticks,** by [E]dward Hutton, in the [s]hape of Ionic columns with [fl]uted stems, the bases [w]ith scale pattern borders, [1]888, 11in (28cm) high.
[..]1,200–1,400 ✗ L

A pair of loaded silver candlesticks, by H. H., modelled as classical Corinthian reeded columns with detachable sconces, marked, Sheffield 1891, 6in (15cm) high.
$500–600 ✗ Hal

A pair of Portuguese cast silver candlesticks, by J. P. V. D., decorated with raised bands of flowers, Lisbon town and maker's marks, early 19thC, 8½in (21.5cm) high, 22.5oz.
$1,200–1,400 ✗ F&C

A Victorian silver taperstick, by George Hewett, decorated with masks and asymmetrical designs, the stem formed as three young boys, London 1844–45, 6in (15cm) high, 7.90oz.
$3,600–4,000 ⊞ NS

◄ **A pair of Victorian loaded silver candlesticks,** decorated with rams' masks, festoons and fronds, London 1892, 6in (15cm) high.
$870–1,000 ✗ Bea(E)

A pair of French fluted silver candlesticks, 19thC, 12½in (32cm) high.
$580–750 ✗ RBB

◄ **A pair of Adam-style loaded silver candlesticks,** with repoussé decoration of acanthus leaves, festoons and rams' heads, Sheffield 1919, 11½in (29m) high.
$500–600 ✗ CDC

SILVER

Card Cases

A Victorian silver card case, by Nathaniel Mills, the front with a view of a cathedral in relief, the reverse chased overall with scrolls and textured foliage, damaged, Birmingham 1844, 4in (10cm) high, 2oz.
$2,500–2,900 ⚒ S(S)

A silver castle-top card case, by Cronin & Wheeler, the front embossed with a raised image of St Paul's Cathedral, the front and reverse embossed with floral and foliate scrolls, the reverse with an initialled cartouche, Birmingham 1847, 4in (10cm) high.
$1,000–1,200 ⚒ Bon

▶ **A silver card case,** engraved with clover and a monogram 'E.M.C', the reverse with a harp, Birmingham 1901, 3¾in (9.5cm) high.
$320–360 ⚒ SWO

◀ **A Victorian silver card case,** by George Unite, embossed with flowers and sea shells, Birmingham 1882, 4in (10cm) long.
$470–500 ⊞ BEX

A Victorian silver calling card case, with engine-turned and acanthus scroll engraving, damaged, Birmingham 1856, 4in (10cm) high.
$100–130 ⚒ EH

A silver card case, by F. K. Marson, Birmingham 1876, 4in (10cm) high.
$300–350 ⊞ CoHA

A Victorian silver card case, by George Unite, engraved with wading bird in a swamp, the reverse with finches, foliage and a fan, Birmingham 1879, 3½in (9cm) high, 2oz.
$360–450 ⚒ WW

Casters

A pair of Irish George III silver sugar casters, by Edward Workman, Dublin 1715, 6in (15cm) high.
$11,600–13,000 ⊞ WELD

▶ **A George III silver muffineer,** by Samuel Wheat, the stem decorated with flowers and a vacant cartouche, London 1760, 5½in (14cm) high.
$580–720 ⚒ FHF

▶ **A George II-style silver-gilt Britannia standard sugar caster,** by William Comyns, the lid with a scrolled finial, the body with a gadrooned band and repoussé spiral foliate and bead decoration, with three scroll handles, London 1896, 6in (15cm) high, 7oz.
$400–470 ⚒ B&L

An Irish silver sugar caste Dublin 1913, 7in (18cm) hig
$950–1,000 ⊞ SIL

◀ **A pair of Victorian 18thC-style silver muffineers,** 1897, 5in (12.5cm) high.
$250–300 ⚒ SWO

SILVER

Centrepieces

silver comport, by Horace
Woodward & Co, decorated with
chased sprays and pendants, 1897,
10½in (26.5cm) diam, 25.5oz.
1,900–2,200 ✗ TEN

A loaded silver tazza, by F. & S.,
Birmingham 1918, 5¼in (13.5cm) diam.
$90–110 ✗ CGC

A Victorian silver pedestal stand,
with stag's head and snake ornament,
the base with engraved foliate
decoration and winged paw feet,
glass bowl missing, London 1873,
6in (15cm) high, 11.5oz.
$300–350 ✗ F&C

Christening Sets

A French silver-gilt christening set, by L.B.,
comprising a knife, fork and spoon, with shell-
scrolled handles, maker's mark, late 19thC,
in a fitted case.
$120–150 ✗ CGC

an 18thC-style silver
christening set, by
Higgins, comprising a two-
handled bowl and spoon,
London 1886, 8in (20.5cm)
wide, in a fitted case.
$470–500 ⊞ HEB

Further reading
*Miller's Collecting Silver: The Facts at Your
Fingertips*, Miller's Publications, 1999

A silver christening set, by Charles
Clement Pilling, comprising a cup,
spoon and napkin ring, London
1904, cup 2½in (6.5cm) high, 3.5oz,
in a fitted case.
$230–290 ✗ SWO

Cheroot & Cigarette Cases

A Victorian silver cheroot case, by William Summers,
London 1878, 3½in (9cm) long.
$450–500 ⊞ BEX

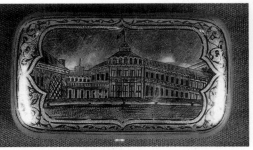

A Russian silver niello-decorated cheroot case,
Moscow 1881, 3¾in (9.5cm) long.
$1,200–1,400
⊞ SHa

A Russian silver niello-decorated cheroot case,
Moscow 1890, 3in (7.5cm) long.
$880–1,000 ⊞ BEX

► A silver letter
cigarette case,
London 1893,
4in (10cm) long.
$1,900–2,000
⊞ SHa

SILVER

Coffee Pots & Teapots

A Scottish George III silver teapot, by James Hewitt, engraved with neo-classical ribbon-tied floral garlands suspending a cartouche engraved with a crest, motto and initials, Edinburgh 1782–83, 10¾in (27.5cm) long, 21.75oz.
$2,600–2,900 ⊞ NS

► **A George I Britannia standard silver teapot,** by Samuel Margas, with a wooden handle and finial, London 1721, 5¼in (13.5cm) high, 14oz.
$3,300–4,000 ⚒ LJ

Britannia standard silver

In 1696 the standard of silver was raised from 92.5 per cent to 95.8 per cent and was known as Britannia standard. The increase was due to the amount of sterling silver coinage being melted down for manufacturing purposes, which caused a shortage of minted coins in circulation. After 24 years of Britannia silver the Sterling 92.5 per cent standard was reintroduced in 1720. However, the Britannia standard has remained available to silversmiths.

A George III silver teapot, with bright-cut decoration, with treen handle and finial, London 1796, 6in (15cm) high, 16oz.
$440–500 ⚒ GAK

An Irish silver teapot, by James Breading, the bright-cut body with a pricked laurel leaf cartouche, Dublin 1807, 11½in (29cm) long.
$1,400–1,600 ⚒ HOK

A George IV faceted silver coffee pot, on anthemion scroll feet, with wooden scroll handle, maker's mark rubbed, 1829, 9¾in (25cm) high, 28oz
$550–600 ⚒ P(S)

A William IV silver teapot, by E. E. J. & W. Barnard, crested, decorated with flowers and acanthus and with a flower finial, London 1834, 6¾in (17cm) high, 29.8oz.
$500–600 ⚒ Bea(E)

An Irish embossed silver coffee pot, by R. Sawyer, Dublin 1849, 11in (28cm) high.
$2,600–2,900 ⊞ SIL

A Victorian silver teapot, by F. B. McCrea, the body embossed with floral swags, 1888, 5¼in (13.5cm) high, 13oz.
$200–250 ⚒ L

A silver coffee pot, by Alfred Ernest Skinner & Co, the body engraved with foliate scrolls, Birmingham 1861, 11in (28cm) high, 30oz.
$470–500 ⚒ B&L

A silver coffee pot, by James Dixon & Sons, Sheffield 1918, 9in (23cm) high, 21.25oz.
$230–290 ⚒ CGC

A Victorian silver coffee pot, by William John Sears, Sheffield 1889, 10in (25.5cm) high.
$1,750–1,850 ⊞ BEX

Coffee & Tea Services

three-piece parcel-gilt tea set, the gadrooned bodies
ith shell corners and fluted bases, Edinburgh 1814,
0¼in (26cm) long.
1,400–1,600 ✗ HOK

An American four-piece silver tea service, with foliate-
engraved and bright-cut bodies, New York, early 19thC,
teapot 10½in (26.5cm) high, 102oz.
$2,200–2,500 ✗ SK

William IV four-piece silver
ea and coffee service, by the
arnards, London 1832, coffee pot
½in (24cm) high, 76oz.
1,750–2,000 ✗ CGC

An American neo-classical silver
tea service, by Eoff & Connor,
comprising four pieces, with shell
and leaf milled decoration, all with
presentation inscription, c1840,
11¼in (28.5cm) high.
$1,900–2,200 ✗ SK(B)

A Victorian three-piece silver coffee
service and salver, by Aldwinckle
& Slater, the basin by Slater, Slater &
Holland, 1987, chased and engraved
with diagonal straps and foliage, vacant
and monogrammed cartouches, London
1880–81, 16¼in (41.5cm) diam, 110oz.
$2,300–3,300 ✗ S(S)

five-piece silver tea and coffee service, decorated
vith pierced and beaded tops, with ball feet, armorial
ngraving, London 1901, 70oz.
1,200–1,300 ✗ E

A Victorian four-piece silver tea and coffee service,
by John Johnson and Alfred Springthorpe, engraved with
anthemia and scrolls and key borders, London 1882, 68oz.
$1,900–2,200 ✗ DN

four-piece Regency-style silver tea service, by
Barracloughs, in the style of Paul Storr, with gadrooned
bands and feet, the handles modelled as serpents,
London 1917.
1,750–2,000 ✗ TEN

A four-piece silver tea/coffee service, by E. V., with
gadrooned borders, marker's mark, Sheffield 1936, 71.25oz.
$870–1,000 ✗ DD

► A George V
three-piece silver
tea service, by
Mappin & Webb,
with gadrooned
rim and double
serpent scrolled
handles, bearing
engraved armorial
crest, London 1919.
$800–950 ✗ HAM

SILVER

Condiment Pots

An Irish George I silver salt cellar, by Thomas Jones, Dublin c1725, 5in (12.5cm) long.
$650–750 ⊞ WELD

A George III silver mustard pot, by William Burwash, with lobed decoration and gadrooned border, 1817, 3¼in (8.5cm) diam, 6oz.
$500–600 ⚒ L

► **A Victorian silver mustard pot,** London 1892, 3in (7.5cm) high.
$320–400 ⊞ CoHA

► **A pair of early George II silver salts,** by Charles Kandler I, with mask, shell and baroque cartouche appliqués to the cast scroll legs, the interiors later gilded, London 1731, 3in (7.5cm) high, 12oz.
$1,500–1,600 ⚒ WW

◄ **A pair of Victorian silver salts,** by Hamilton & Inches, embossed with thistle sprays, the handles formed as thistle heads and foliage set with faceted Cairngorm quartz, and a pair of salt spoons with thistle finials, maker's mark, Edinburgh 1871, 4in (10cm) diam, 6oz.
$1,800–2,200 ⚒ P(Ed)

An Edwardian silver mustard, with bright-cut decoration, pierced with flowerhead and scrolled design, with a blue glass liner, Chester 1901 3½in (9cm) wide.
$150–175 ⚒ GAK

Cups & Goblets

A Charles II silver caudle cup, by Thomas Sutton, the body embossed with full-blown flowers, with serpent scroll handles, engraved initials, London 1674–75, 2½in (6.5cm) high, 3.39oz.
$5,800–6,500 ⊞ NS

A William IV silver goblet, by the Barnards, engraved with name, London 1837, 5in (12.5cm) high.
$350–400 ⚒ GAK

◄ **A late Victorian silver pedestal cup,** by Mappin & Webb, with repoussé decoration of trailing leaves and berries, 1900, 5½in (14cm) high, 5oz.
$200–250 ⚒ P(EA)

► **An American three-handled silver trophy cup,** by Tiffany & Co, the lower body chased with scrolling fruiting vine, beneath an engraved inscription, with a gilt interior, 1891–1902, 9in (23cm) high, 65oz.
$4,350–4,650 ⚒ S(NY)

A pair of Victorian silver goblets, by Messrs Josiah Williams & Co, engraved with a cart horse, a horse-drawn brougham and sprays of ferns below a frieze of ivy leaves and berries, with gilded interiors, Exeter 1878, 7½in (19cm) high.
$1,000–1,300 ⚒ WW

SILVER

Cutlery

A set of six Irish silver Dog nose forks, by David King, Dublin 1706–07, 7½in (19cm) long.
$7,250–8,000 ⊞ SIL

A Victorian Fiddle pattern silver part table service, by Thomas Wallis, comprising 29 pieces, London 1851, 58.2oz.
$750–850 ↗ Bea(E)

Two silver seal top spoons, York hallmarks, maker's mark indistinct, late 16th/early 17thC, 6in (15cm) long.
$2,200–2,600 ↗ RBB

A Russian silver-gilt dessert service, by Sazikov, comprising 46 pieces, the handles engraved with a coat-of-arms, St Petersburg 1873, knives 8¼in (21cm) long.
$4,000–4,400 ↗ S

▶ **A King's pattern silver cutlery set,** by FH, comprising 23 pieces, 1892–93, 58oz.
$870–1,000 ↗ SWO

A set of 12 Irish George III Old English pattern silver dessert forks, by Michael Keeting, engraved with armorials, Dublin 1774, 11oz.
$2,000–2,500 ↗ DN

A set of six Dutch silver apostle spoons, the cast handles with figures, twist shafts and different saint terminals, London import mark, 1890, 6¾in (17cm), 9.5oz, in a fitted case.
$150–175 ↗ Bri

An American Colonial pattern silver flatware service, comprising 167 pieces, some monogrammed, Newburyport, Massachusetts, early 20thC, 165oz excluding knives.
$3,300–3,800 ↗ SK

Four silver knives, by Omar Ramsden, London 1931.
$870–950 ⊞ SHa

SILVER

Dishes

A German parcel-gilt silver sweetmeat dish, maker's mark worn, Augsburg, 17thC, 4¾in (12cm) diam, 4.3oz.
$4,000–4,600 ⚒ **S(Z)**

A pair of George IV silver shell-shaped butter dishes, by William Eaton, the handles with monograms, each on three whelk feet, London 1824, 5½in (14cm) long, 10oz.
$1,300–1,600 ⚒ **DN**

A silver warming pan or entrée dish, by William Pitts, London 1789, 12in (30.5cm) long.
$4,500–5,000 ⊞ **BEX**

A pair of William IV silver meat dishes, by Paul Storr, with gadroon borders and engraved with a contemporary coat-of-arms and crest, 1834, 17½in (44.5cm) long.
$5,000–6,000 ⚒ **L**

▶ **An American footed silver serving dish,** by Tiffany & Co, the interior reeded with repoussé and engraved foliate decoration, the pierced handle shaped as a fleur-de-lys, monogrammed, New York 1891–1902, 15½in (39.5cm) long.
$3,000–3,300 ⚒ **SK**

◀ **An American silver platter and drip tray,** by Ferdinand Fuchs & Bros, embossed and pierced with twigs and cherries, New York 1884–91, 14in (35.5cm) long, 32oz.
$1,000–1,200 ⚒ **SK**

A George III silver pap boat, probably by Stephen Adams, London 1771, 4in (10cm) long.
$175–225 ⚒ **GAK**

Four George II silver salad dishes, by George Methuen, with central armorials engraved c1790, London 1759, 9½in (24cm) diam, 69oz.
$11,500–13,000 ⚒ **S**
Dishes of this type were known as sallet or salad dishes and were used to serve cooked vegetables or fresh salads.

Covered Dishes

A William IV silver tureen, by Richard Sibley, on four scroll acanthus leaf terminal feet, the lid with a gourd, flower and vine finial, the body engraved 'PEH', London 1835, 8¾in (22cm) high, 33.5oz.
$1,000–1,300 ⚒ **LJ**

▶ **A silver entrée dish and cover,** by John Round, with gadrooned handle, Sheffield 1913, 11in (28cm) long.
$1,600–1,800 ⊞ **HEB**

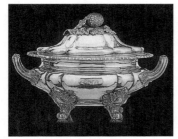

◀ **A set of four silver entrée dishes, covers and handles,** by Thomas Bradbury & Sons, engraved with armorials, London 1913–14, 10¼in (26cm) long, 178oz.
$4,000–4,600 ⚒ **DN**

Dish Rings

A Victorian silver dish ring, the pierced sides chased with exotic birds, scrolls, flowers and rustic scenes, with vacant oval cartouche on one side, maker's mark slightly obscured, with blue glass liner, London 1895–96, 7in (18cm) wide, 11.26oz.
$2,800–3,200 ⊞ NS

A Continental Irish-style silver dish ring, embossed, pierced and engraved with birds among flowers and scrolls within beaded borders, with a glass liner, import marks, London 1900, 7½in (19cm) diam.
$800–950 ⋋ RTo

An Irish Edwardian silver dish ring, by Charles Lamb, Dublin 1902, 8¼in (21cm) diam.
$1,000–1,200 ⋋ CGC

Facts in brief

Originating in Ireland from the mid-18th century, the dish ring was used to keep hot plates off the table. They are mostly pierced and repousséd with rural scenes of people, animals and castles. They were reproduced from the 1890s to 1920 in Ireland as well as London. Occasionally they can be found with blue glass liners that were made at a later date so the ring could be used as a bowl. Irish dish rings are most sought after, as is all Irish silver, so examine pieces carefully, especially around the hallmark, as a number of Edwardian examples have had their marks removed and replaced with 'Georgian' marks in an attempt to increase their value.

An Irish silver dish ring, by William Egan, Cork, with pierced repoussé chased and engraved bird and foliage decoration, Dublin 1919, 5½in (14cm) diam.
$1,300–1,600 ⋋ JAd

Dressing Table Sets

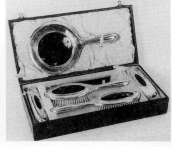

A pair of James II silver hairbrushes, London c1685, 3in (7.5cm) wide.
$4,300–4,800 ⊞ BEX

A silver embossed manicure set, Birmingham 1904–08, in a fitted case, case 10½in (26.5cm) long.
$650–725 ⊞ PSA

A silver and tortoiseshell-backed dressing table set, with non-matching comb, Birmingham 1924, in a fitted case.
$175–225 ⋋ GAK

Ewers & Jugs

An Irish silver cream jug, with leaf-capped flying C-scroll handle, on three lion-mask and paw feet, the underside engraved with a crest, struck sterling and maker's mark DK, c1740, 6in (15cm) high.
$4,300–5,000 ⋋ HOK

A George III silver jug, with a leaf-capped S-scroll handle, engraved with a later crest, probably by William Cripps, London 1764, 9¾in (25cm) high, 35oz.
$5,000–6,000 ⋋ WW

A George III neo-classical-style silver milk jug, with a central band of foliate engraving, maker's mark S.H., London 1771, 3½in (9cm) high.
$250–300 ⋋ SWO

Cross Reference
See Colour Review
(page 409)

A George III silver cream jug, with beaded edging and bright-cut with festoons and an oval panel, marked 'W.D.', possibly William Dorrell, London 1787, 5in (12.5cm) high, 3.6oz.
$500–600 ⋋ Bea(E)

SILVER

A George III silver cream jug, by GB, with beaded rim and bright-cut engraved decoration, London 1793, 5in (12.5cm) high.
$250–300 ⚒ GAK

A Victorian silver claret jug, with monk finial to the lid, the body engraved with peacock feathers, London 1882, 14in (35.5cm) high, 28oz.
$575–725 ⚒ Mit

A silver jug, by Joseph & Joseph Angell, with repoussé decoration, London 1831, 8in (20.5cm) high.
$725–800 ⊞ HEB

A late Victorian silver mulled ale jug, by Henry Archer, the body engraved with an initial beneath a Royal Prince's coronet, Sheffield 1898, 7½in (19cm) high, 22oz.
$650–800 ⚒ WW

A Victorian silver-mounted claret jug, by E. Marshall, decorated with panels showing signs of the Zodiac, Edinburgh 1869–70, 13½in (34.5cm) high, 24.7oz.
$2,500–3,000 ⊞ NS

A Victorian silver-gilt Armada-pattern claret jug, by Martin & Hall, with repoussé floral decoration and embossed cherubs around cartouches, 12¼in (31cm) high, 29.5oz.
$1,700–2,000 ⚒ L

◀ **A silver hot milk jug,** by Thomas Bradbury & Sons, with an ebony handle, London 1925, 9¼in (23.5cm) high, 17oz.
$150–175 ⚒ WW

An American silver covered jug, by Bigelow Bros & Kennard, the lid with cast swan finial, monogrammed and dated to centre, Boston c1860, 8¾in (22cm) high, 16oz.
$550–600 ⚒ SK

An Edward VII silver hot water jug, embossed with flowers and scroll-work, Chester 1905, 9½in (24cm) high, 13.9oz.
$150–175 ⚒ Bea(E)

Frames

A late Victorian silver photograph frame, surmounted by a scrolled wirework crest, London 1900, 8¼in (21cm) wide.
$400–480 ⚒ DMC

An Edwardian silver photograph frame, pierced and embossed with foliate and scroll patterns, with green velvet easel back, London 1901, 6in (15cm) wide.
$430–500 ⚒ GAK

▶ **A silver hanging photograph frame,** by William Comyns, London 1907, 5in (12.5cm) wide.
$430–500 ⊞ CoHA

A pair of Edwardian silver photograph frames, the fronts gadrooned to bead edges, the arched tops with vacant oval cartouches, with leather easel backs, maker's mark overstamped by Marion & Co, Birmingham 1903, 6in (15cm) wide inside measurement.
$875–1,000 ⚒ WW

A silver double photograph frame, with ribbon crest, c1906, 4in (10cm) wide.
$680–750 ⊞ THOM

SILVER

nkstands & Wells

A late Victorian silver inkstand, by Herbert Charles Lambert, fitted with two glass wells with pounce pot and taperstick covers, between two pen trays with hinged covers, backing glass well, London 1894, 10¾in (27.5cm) wide.
$725–875 ⚒ RTo

A Victorian silver inkwell, the flattened capstan shape with gadroon border, Sheffield 1897, 5in (12.5cm) diam, 8oz.
$300–350 ⚒ L

A late Victorian silver inkwell, by Gibson & Langman, the fluted body with a cover engraved with an armorial, glass liner damaged, London 1898, 4¼in (11cm) diam, 8.25oz.
$300–350 ⚒ CGC

A Victorian silver inkstand, by John Grinsell & Sons, with gadrooned border and two pen rests, the hinged lid with engraved presentation inscription, with fixed centre compartment and two glass inkwells with silver mounts, London 1899, 11½in (29cm) wide, 35oz.
$725–875 ⚒ HOLL

A silver inkwell, by Mappin & Webb, London 1899, 5in (12.5cm) diam.
$360–430 ⚒ SWO

A silver inkstand, by Synyer & Beddoes, with a square glass bottle with silver mount, inscribed, Birmingham 1914, 18¼in (46.5cm) diam.
$150–175 ⚒ CGC

Inscriptions

Generally inscriptions on silver will reduce the value and desirability of an item, so do take care when collecting and pricing any such pieces. However, the absolute opposite applies if the inscription is of historic interest or is connected to a famous family or person.

Kettles

◀ **A William IV silver tea kettle, stand and lamp,** by James MacKay, the kettle chased with a band of flowers and foliate scrolls, Edinburgh 1835–36, 14in (35.5cm) high, 61.82oz.
$5,800–6,500 ⊞ NS

A Victorian silver tea kettle and cover, by T.B. & S, the cover with a recumbent greyhound finial, Birmingham 1893, 8¾in (22cm) high, 29.5oz.
$500–600 ⚒ P(E)

A late Victorian silver spirit kettle, stand and lamp, by The Goldsmiths & Silversmiths Co, with turned wood handle, London 1898, 11in (28cm) high, 29.5oz.
$725–875 ⚒ P(E)

Menu Holders

A pair of silver crystal menu holders, by G. Bercheman & Sons, London 1913, in fitted case, case 5in (12.5cm) wide.
$1,300–1,500 ⚒ BEX

A set of Irish silver menu holders, Dublin 1913, 1¼in (3cm) wide, in fitted case.
$800–900 ⊞ SIL

A pair of silver menu holders, by C&N, applied with paste-set thistle sprays, Edinburgh 1922, 2½in (6.5cm) wide.
$430–500 ⚒ P(Ed)

SILVER

Mugs & Tankards

◄ **An American silver tankard,** by Samuel Minott and William Simpkins, the body engraved 'The Gift of Mrs. Sarah Adams: (Relict of mr. Edward Adams late of Milton) to the first Church in Braintree', marked 'Minott' in italics and 'W.S.', Boston c1760, 8¾in (22cm) high, 28oz.
$101,000–116,000 🔨 S(NY)
This tankard was one of 11 pieces of 17th- and 18th-century silver put up for sale by the First Congregational Society of Quincy, originally known as the Braintree Church. The collection encompasses the entire history of the craft of silver-smithing in colonial Boston, as it includes examples from all the major workshops. The pieces were donated to the church by the eminent families of the time, including the Adams and Quincy families, of which the American presidents John Adams and John Quincy Adams were members and for whom this church is the final resting place. Silver objects acquired by religious institutions are of particular importance to historians because the circumstances of their creation are usually better documented than pieces commissioned for private use.

A Victorian silver mug, the panelled body with engraved strapwork decoration and a scrolled handle, London 1856, 3¼in (8.5cm) high, 4oz.
$300–350 🔨 SWO

A Victorian silver christening mug, by the Barnards, with fluted lower body, London 1888, 3½in (9cm) high, 5.25oz.
$220–260 🔨 CGC

A silver mug commemorating the coronation of King George V, 1911, 6in (15cm) high.
$725–800 ⊞ SHa

Napkin Rings

A set of six Victorian silver napkin rings, by William Evans, with engine-turned decoration and initials, London 1866, 1¾in (4.5cm) wide, 4.25oz, in a fitted case.
$360–430 🔨 CGC

A set of four silver napkin rings, with engine-turned decoration, 1924 1½in (4cm) wide, in a fitted case.
$190–230 🔨 SWO

◄ **A Russian silver napkin ring,** Moscow 1888, 1½in (4cm) wide.
$190–230 ⊞ SHa

Salvers & Trays

A pair of Irish George III silver salvers, by Joseph Jackson, with gadroon borders, the reserve with later engraving, Dublin 1782, 9in (23cm) diam, 29oz.
$1,400–1,600 🔨 JAd

A George III silver card waiter, by W.B., with a reeded border, on four panel feet, London 1783, 9¾in (25cm) wide, 15oz.
$1,100–1,400 🔨 P(S)

A George II silver salver, by Gabriel Sleath, with a piecrust border, on scroll and hoof feet, the centre later-engraved with a coat-of-arms, 1735, 13½in (34.5cm) diam.
$2,200–2,600 🔨 L

A George IV silver salver, by James Hobbs, with a floral-decorated and panelled border, on foliate scroll feet, London 1824, 9½in (24cm) diam, 21oz.
$300–350 ✗ F&C

An American silver salver, by Tiffany & Co, the centre with engraved ivy leaf and berry pattern surrounding a circle with swags of fruit, on three pierced feet with embossed beading, New York 1854–70, 10in (25.5cm) diam, 20oz.
$875–950 ✗ SK

An Edwardian silver tray, by William Hutton & Sons, the cast gadrooned border with mask and shell-scroll motifs, London 1908, 26¾in (68cm) long, 132oz.
$1,300–1,600 ✗ Bri

> Items in the Silver section have been arranged in date order within each sub-section.

Sauce Boats

A pair of George II silver sauce boats, by John Jacobs, on three hoof feet, engraved with a crest, one repaired, London 1752, 7in (18cm) long.
$1,100–1,400 ✗ RBB

A Sottish George III silver sauce boat, by Lothian & Robertson, with acanthus-capped scroll handle, engraved with a monogram, Edinburgh 1761–62, 7¼in (18.5cm) long, 7.32oz.
$2,300–2,600 ⊞ NS

An Irish George III silver sauce boat, by Matthew West, Dublin c1775, 7in (18cm) long.
$1,900–2,100 ⊞ WELD

A Georgian-style silver sauce boat, with leaf-capped flying scroll handle, Birmingham 1911, 8in (20.5cm) long, 11.5oz.
$300–350 ✗ GAK

A pair of silver sauce boats, by JBC & S, with flying scroll leaf-moulded handle, on three stepped paw feet, London 1931, 8in (20.5cm) long.
$580–720 ✗ Hal

A silver sauce boat, by William Hutton & Sons, with scroll and gadrooned border, and leaf-capped scroll handle, on a raised shaped shell and oval foot, London 1895, 5½in (14cm) high, 14oz.
$430–500 ✗ Bon

Scent Bottles

A Victorian silver-mounted glass scent bottle, by Sampson Mordan & Co, with a suspensory ring and chains, with a hinged cover and glass stopper, London 1879, 2¾in (7cm) long.
$300–350 ✗ WW

A Victorian spiral-fluted silver scent bottle, by Sampson Mordan & Co, London 1889, 3¼in (8.5cm) long, in a fitted case.
$300–350 ✗ CGC

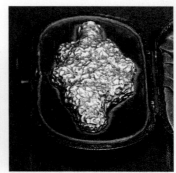

An Edwardian silver-gilt scent bottle, in the shape of a nugget, with a glass liner, Chester 1908, 3in (7.5cm) long, in a fitted case.
$950–1,100 ⊞ ALiN

SILVER

Serving Implements

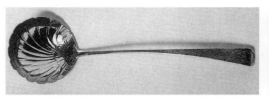

An Irish silver shell bowl soup ladle, by J. Craig, Dublin c1765, 13in (33cm) long.
$1,300–1,500 ⊞ SIL

► **A set of four Irish silver rattail Fiddle pattern sauce ladles,** by W. Cummins, crested, Dublin 1823, 8oz.
$1,000–1,200 ⚒ MEA

A pair of Victorian silver grape scissors, by J. G., with engraved decoration, Birmingham 1862, 6in (15cm) long, in a fitted case.
$500–580 ⚒ L

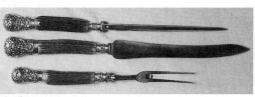

A Victorian silver and horn carving set, by Allen & Darwin, Sheffield 1895–96, 15in (38cm) long.
$400–470 ⊞ BEX

A George IV silver fish slice, by WK, with pierced blade and moulded handle, maker's mark, London 1823, 12½in (32cm) long, 5oz.
$175–225 ⚒ WilP

A Victorian silver Fiddle pattern soup ladle, by William Eaton, London 1840, 13in (33cm) long.
$350–400 ⊞ ASAA

A silver Stilton scoop, by A. Taylor, with an ivory handle, Birmingham 1865, 9in (23cm) long.
$500–580 ⊞ SHa

A Victorian silver bread fork, by Harrison Bros & Howson, the wrythen ivory handle with floral and foliate embossed ferrule and finial, Sheffield 1897, 8¾in (22cm) long.
$220–260 ⚒ CGC

Snuff Boxes

Silver Piqué

Piqué is the term used for a decorative inlay of silver, usually into tortoiseshell and occasionally ivory. The tortoiseshell is carved with a design into which the silver is applied. The silver in the form of wire, minute dots and stars makes up the pattern of slightly larger pieces of silver in the shape of figures, birds, cherubs, swags and flowers etc. These larger pieces of inlay are often engraved to give further definition. Silver piqué decoration was used from the 1670s; mother-of-pearl and gold were also sometimes used with the silver.

A French silver-gilt snuff box, by Antoine Daroux, the hinged cover embossed with figures in a town square, the sides with bucolic scenes and the base with figures picnicking, Paris 1760, 3in (7.5cm) long.
$1,300–1,600 ⚒ S(S)

► **An Irish George III silver and cowrie-shell snuff box,** by Bartholomew Stokes, Dublin c1770, 3in (7.5cm) long.
$1,800–2,000 ⊞ WELD

A William and Mary silver piqué snuff box, c1690, 3½in (9cm) diam.
$2,300–2,600 ⊞ BEX

A George III silver snuff box, with cast basketweave body and cover and engraved inscription, London 1808, 2½in (6.5cm) long.
$550–600 ⚲ SWO

A Georgian silver snuff box, by Nathaniel Mills, Birmingham 1826, 3in (7.5cm) long.
$360–430 ⊞ CoHA

An Imperial Russian silver niello snuff box, Moscow 1892, 2½in (6.5cm) long.
$1,000–1,100 ⊞ SHa

A Victorian silver snuff box, by Charles Rawlings and William Summers, with engraved inscription to inside of lid, London 1843–44, 3½in (9cm) long, 4.25oz.
$1,900–2,100 ⊞ NS

◄ **A Victorian silver table snuff box,** by Thomas Edwards, the cover with presentation inscription within a chased foliate border, with engine-turned sides and base, London 1840, 4¾in (12cm) long, 8.3oz.
$450–550 ⚲ Bea(E)

Strainers

A George II silver orange/lemon strainer, by David Hennell, London 1751, 8in (20.5cm) long.
$430–500 ⊞ BEX

A Scottish silver lemon strainer, by Robert Gray of Glasgow, with a reeded border and scroll handle, hallmarked Edinburgh, c1780, 4in (10cm) diam.
$540–620 ⚲ P(Ed)

◄ **A Scottish George II silver lemon strainer,** by Dougal Ged, Edinburgh 1740–41, 6½in (16.5cm) long, 2.99oz.
$2,200–2,400 ⊞ NS

Tea Canisters

A George III chinoiserie-style silver tea canister, by Parker & Wakelin, the body with borders of engraved scrolls framing four Chinese characters, the cover with a flower spray finial, 1762, 4¼in (11cm) diam, 15.5oz.
$5,000–6,000 ⚲ L

A pair of George III silver tea canisters, repoussé-decorated with alternating strips of swirl fluting and floral sprays, with vacant rocaille cartouches, London 1768, 5in (12.5cm) high, 17.5oz.
$4,000–4,600 ⚲ WW

A Continental silver tea canister, the body repoussé-decorated and engraved with foliage and scrolls surrounding cartouches of cherubs and a family playing music, late 19thC, 5in (12.5cm) high, 8oz.
$500–600 ⚲ SK

A George III-style tea canister, by Walker & Hall, with lion-mask handles and gadrooned borders, Sheffield 1911, 5in (12.5cm) high, 12oz.
$500–600 ⚲ L

Items in the Silver section have been arranged in date order within each sub-section.

SILVER

Toast Racks

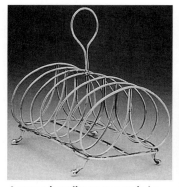

A seven-bar silver toast rack, by Hampston, Prince & Cattles, York 1800–01, 6½in (16.5cm) long, 6.08oz.
$1,200–1,400 ⊞ NS

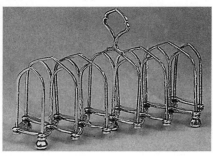

▶ **A pair of Edward VII five-bar silver toast racks,** Chester 1904, 3¼in (8.5cm) long.
$180–230 ⚒ Bea(E)

◀ **A Victorian seven-bar silver toast rack,** by Edward Gilbert, the concertina action with Gothic arched divisions, 1883, 4½in (11.5cm) long, 7.5oz.
$725–800 ⊞ P(S)

Vesta Cases

▶ **A silver and enamel novelty vesta case,** by Sampson Mordan & Co, the front enamelled with a horse-drawn carriage, London 1886, 2¼in (5.5cm) long.
$1,200–1,400 ⚒ Bon

A sterling silver vesta case, Birmingham 1903, 1½in (4cm) wide.
$220–240 ⊞ BWA

◀ **A silver and enamel novelty vesta case,** by George Heath, the front enamelled with a pointer dog in a hilly landscape, London 1887, 2in (5cm) high.
$1,000–1,300 ⚒ Bon

▶ **A sterling silver vesta case,** Birmingham 1910, 2in (5cm) high.
$100–120 ⊞ BWA

Vinaigrettes

▶ **A George III silver vinaigrette,** by William Ellerby, London 1826, 1½in (4cm) long.
$1,100–1,200 ⊞ BEX

A George IV silver vinaigrette, by John Bettridge, Birmingham 1820, 1in (2.5cm) long.
$540–620 ⊞ BEX

A Victorian silver and gilt vinaigrette, by Aston & Son, Birmingham 1858, 1in (2.5cm) high.
$340–370 ⊞ CoHA

◀ **A silver vinaigrette,** maker's mark L&C, 19thC, ¾in (2cm) long.
$300–330 ⊞ LBr

SILVER

Silver Plate

A Victorian silver-plated biscuit box, decorated with neo-classical bright-cut engraving, supported within a rustic bower, crested, registration mark, 1876, 7½in (19cm) wide.
$360–430 ✦ F&C

A Victorian silver-plated biscuit barrel, 8in (20.5cm) high.
$100–120 ✦ SWO

A late Victorian silver-plated double biscuit box, the shell-moulded hinged body with two compartments, decorated with rococo chasing, sprays and scrolls, 11½in (29cm) long.
$360–430 ✦ WW

A Sheffield plate wirework cake basket, with gadrooned rim and swing handle, 19thC, 11in (28cm) long.
$145–175 ✦ GAK

A pair of Sheffield plate candlesticks, c1770, 12in (30.5cm) high.
$900–1,000 ⊞ DIC

A pair of Old Sheffield plate candlesticks, c1840, 10in (25.5cm) high.
$400–440 ⊞ ASAA

A pair of silver-plated candlesticks, with gadrooned detail, on loaded bases, 19thC, 12in (30.5cm) high.
$175–200 ✦ GAK

A Georgian-style silver-plated coffee pot, by Harrison Bros & Howson, c1920, 9in (23cm) high.
$120–130 ⊞ ASAA

An Edwardian silver-plated fruit comport, embossed and pierced with shells and fruit, 10½in (26.5cm) diam.
$100–120 ✦ GAK

A late Victorian silver-plated bacon dish, with three-quarter fluted decoration, with presentation inscription, 12in (30.5cm) long.
$175–225 ✦ GAK

A Victorian silver-plated dish cover, c1880, 11in (28cm) long.
$320–360 ⊞ ASAA

A silver-plated rollover breakfast dish, with engraved decoration, c1880, 13in (33cm) long.
$580–720 ⊞ DIC

371

SILVER PLATE

A silver-plated and cut-glass entrée dish, by Mappin & Webb, c1900, 14in (35.5cm) long.
$100–120 ⊞ ASAA

An Old Sheffield plate meat dish, by C. F. Younge, the rim with repoussé decoration and rococo scrolls and foliage, stamped, 19thC, 27½in (70cm) long.
$1,400–1,700 ➚ ELR

An Old Sheffield plate serving dish, with winged cherub finials, the lid decorated with fruiting vine motifs, the body decorated with bacchanalian fawns, goats and dogs, with acanthus-decorated base, early 19thC, 10in (25.5cm) high.
$300–350 ➚ Mit

A set of four silver-plated egg cups and stand, by Walker & Hall, c1910, 7½in (19cm) wide.
$75–85 ⊞ TO

► An Edwardian silver-plated *épergne*, the loaded base with a rope-twist stem and scroll branches, holding three glass posy holders, 13in (33cm) high.
$175–225 ➚ GAK

An Old Sheffield plate samovar, the reverse stamped 'Best, London', c1820, 18in (45.5cm) high.
$430–500 ➚ Mit

◄ An Elkington Mason silver-plated copy of an ivory German Stein, c1850, 12in (30.5cm) high.
$1,100–1,300 ⊞ DIC

A silver-plated Elkington-style figure of a Native American warrior, now mounted as a lamp, c1855, 25in (63.5cm) high.
$1,900–2,200 ➚ NOA

A late Georgian Sheffield plate tea urn, with reeded handles, the cover with a flower finial, 14in (35.5cm) high.
$220–260 ➚ RBB

◄ A Victorian silver-plated tray, engraved with foliage, within a pierced and beaded border, 28¾in (73cm) wide.
$360–430 ➚ F&C

A Victorian silver-plated kettle and stand, embossed with C-scroll cartouches, foliage and flowers, with burner, 17in (43cm) high.
$430–500 ➚ P(S)

A pair of George III Sheffield plate boat-shaped sauce tureens and covers, with reeded borders and lion-mask handles, re-plated, 10in (25.5cm) long.
$725–875 ➚ DN

An Irish silver-plated and cut-glass vase, with foliate decoration, the stem with a Royal Dublin Society silver medallion, mid-19thC, 10¼in (26cm) high.
$175–200 ➚ F&C

Wine Antiques

**set of four Victorian stoneware spirit
barrels,** with brass taps, decorated in relief
with royal coat-of-arms, lions and knights on
orseback, labelled Brandy, Whisky, Rum and
in, 10½in (26.5cm) high.
500–600 ➚ DDM

A mahogany bottle carrier,
18thC, 17¼in (44cm) wide,
on a modern stand.
$3,200–3,600 ➚ S

A creamware bottle coaster, with
lion-mask and ring handles, printed
with amusing poetic texts, rim chip,
late 18thC, 4¼in (11cm) diam.
$550–600 ➚ Bea(E)

◄ **A late Victorian silver-
plate mounted glass
claret jug,** by Walker &
Hall, with hobnail-cut
body, 12½in (32cm) high.
$550–650 ➚ P(S)

► **A silver-gilt mounted
glass novelty decanter,**
modelled as a champagne
bottle, maker's mark of
John Grinsell & Sons,
London 1893,
12½in (32cm) high.
$1,700–2,200 ➚ Bon

A silver decanter label, by Gervais
Wheeler, with shell and foliage
decoration, 1831, 2in (5cm) wide.
$200–230 ⊞ CoHA

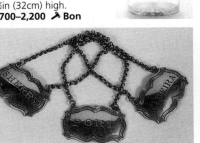

A set of three silver decanter labels, Sherry,
Port and Madeira, London 1837, 2½in (6.5cm) wide.
$430–500 ⊞ PSA

◄ **A late Victorian silver-plated three-
bottle decanter and stand,** with cut and
engraved glass bottles, 16in (40.5cm) high.
$160–200 ➚ CGC

**A campaign officer's mahogany
decanter box,** c1850, 15in (38cm) long.
$750–825 ⊞ MB

**A coromandel and brass-banded decanter
box,** with three decanters and six glasses,
c1880, 12in (30.5cm) long.
$4,000–4,600 ⊞ RGa

◄ **A George III silver wine funnel,** with
detachable rim, 5in (12.5cm) high.
$1,000–1,200 ⊞ HEB

**A mahogany cylinder top travelling
decanter box,** with six spirit bottles
and two glasses, all gilt-painted
with vine decoration, 19thC,
10¼in (26cm) long.
$900–1,100 ➚ JH

A silver folding corkscrew, with a steel worm, probably Irish Provincial by R. P., 18thC, open 4in (10cm) long.
$1,800–2,200 ✗ MEA

A corkscrew, maker's mark of Samuel Pemberton, the mother-of-pearl handle mounted with vertical silver bands, with a steel worm, c1800, 3in (7.5cm) long.
$460–550 ✗ Bon

▶ **A Thomason Variant corkscrew,** with bronze top handle and turned walnut raising handle, royal coat-of-arms applied to the outer bronze barrel, c1810, 7in (18cm) long.
$360–430 ⊞ CS

A four-pillar open-frame double-action corkscrew, with turned bone top handle and steel side-raising handle, c1820, 8in (20.5cm) long
$220–250 ⊞ CS

A London Rack corkscrew, with bone handle and brush, 19thC, 7in (18cm) long.
$650–725 ⊞ JOL

◀ **A double-action corkscrew,** with bone handle, the bronze barrel decorated with autumn fruits, early 19thC, 7in (18cm) long.
$1,100–1,300 ✗ LW

A silver pocket corkscrew, maker's mark of I. R. crowned, the wooden handle with ribbed decoration, early 19thC, 2¾in (7cm) long.
$580–720 ✗ Bon

A double-action corkscrew, with bone handle, royal coat-of-arms applied to a tablet on the brass barrel, c1820, 7in (18cm) long.
$200–220 ⊞ CS

A Thomason-type double-action corkscrew, with bone handle, the bronze barrel with royal coat-of-arms, 19thC, 7in (18cm) long.
$300–350 ✗ LW

A Victorian double-pillar rack corkscrew, the wooden handle with a brush, 8in (20.5cm) long.
$160–175 ⊞ JOL

A corkscrew, the boxwood handle with a foil cutter and Codd bottle pusher, 19thC, 5in (12.5cm) long.
$140–170 ⊞ JOL

◀ **A King's Screw narrow rack corkscrew,** with wire helix, shaped bone handle, turned steel side handle, the brass barrel with royal coat-of-arms, 19thC, 7½in (19cm) long.
$500–580 ✗ DN

▶ **An American novelty silver-plated combination corkscrew,** by Alfred Flander, comprising screw, bottle opener, measure and spoon, 1932, 9in (23cm) long.
$250–300 ✗ S(S)

Clocks

The market for longcase clocks in original condition continues to flourish, with demand reflecting the buoyant mood of the previous two years. Prices for good quality specimens, particularly those made with thirty-four and eight-day movements, have risen by around fourteen per cent per annum over the same period. The sector of most significant increase over the last year has been for enamelled faces, especially for clocks with fine, slim cases boasting eight-day movements, which have become harder to find as a consequence. Demand too has continued to increase for brass dial longcases in good original condition.

In general, market values for carriage clocks has been steady over the past eighteen months, although English clocks with painted panels have seen the best returns, followed closely by enamelled clocks. As always, the rarest clocks are those with chronometer escapements, and values for these have risen dramatically over the past year.

The market in French and German table clocks has been steady, though not spectacular over the past twelve months, with prices barely holding their own against last year. There are always exceptions to this rule, and early French clocks continue to generate customary interest.

In horological terms the movements of English bracket clocks (also known as table clocks) are historically regarded as the best in the world. Those which have been properly maintained from new have shown increases in value in line with those of the finest eight-day longcase clocks.

As in past years, the value of, and the demand for, original clocks far outstrips that for composite clocks (those which have been reconstructed from parts culled from various damaged originals). Though many composites are especially handsome, they have no definable pedigree, and as such are worth only what the buyer would give for their apparent beauty.

As in any year, to be attractive to a buyer, a clock in original condition will also have to appeal to the heart, the eye and the mind. And for many buyers, practicality is also an issue, as a longcase is not only a clock but a piece of furniture too. Over the past twelve months a number of fine original clocks have made poor prices simply because they are too tall to fit into today's homes. By contrast, demand for simple, smaller clocks in original condition has risen well above the average of preceding years, a trend likely to continue.

Samuel Orr

British Bracket, Mantel & Table Clocks

A mantel clock, by Jonathan Lowndes, London, the verge movement pull quarter repeat on one bell, the dial with cherub spandrels, in an ebonized oak case, late 17thC, 13¾in (35cm) high.
$8,000–9,500 ➤ TEN

► A black lacquer bracket clock, by Thomas Gardner, London, the twin fusee five-pillar movement with a verge escapement and bob pendulum striking on a bell, the dial with mock pendulum aperture and calendar, c1750, 20½in (52cm) high.
$5,800–7,200 ➤ Bon

◄ A George I walnut eight-day bracket clock, by John Taylor, London, the two-train fusee movement striking on a bell, the case with brass flaming urn finials, 18¼in (46.5cm) high.
$7,000–8,000 ➤ L&T

An ebonized table clock, by Charles Blanchard, London, the eight-day five-pillar movement with verge escapement striking and repeating the hours on a bell, the brass dial with date aperture and strike/silent feature to the arch, c1750, 18in (45.5cm) high.
$9,500–10,500 ⊞ PAO

CLOCKS

Cases

Clocks can often be dated from the wood of which the case is constructed:
- If the veneer is walnut or ebony, it will probably date from c1660–1860
- If the veneer is lacquered or inlaid with marquetry, the date is likely to be c1700–45
- If the veneer is mahogany, it will date from c1730 onwards

A George III ebonized bracket clock, inscribed Philip Lloyd, Bristol, the two-train movement striking on a bell with pull repeat, the dial with strike/silent adjuster, date aperture, Roman and Arabic numerals, 21¼in (54cm) high.
$3,200–3,600 ⚒ P(S)

A George III mahogany bracket clock, inscribed W. M, Newington, Surrey, the movement engraved with floral decoration, 18¼in (46.5cm) high, with a modern wall bracket.
$4,700–5,700 ⚒ JAd

▶ **A George III ebonized bracket clock,** by W. Drury, London, with single chain movement, 9½in (24cm) high.
$1,300–1,600 ⚒ Bea(E)

A George III mahogany mantle clock, by Allan & Caithness, with single fusee movement, 8in (20.5cm) high.
$5,800–7,200 ⚒ HYD
Allan & Caithness are recorded at 119 New Bond Street, London between 1800 and 1804.

A Regency mahogany and brass-inlaid bracket clock, by Jas Daniels, London, the eight-day two-train fusee movement with five pillars, anchor escapement, rack strike on a bell and pendulum hold fast, 16in (40.5cm) high.
$800–950 ⚒ DN

A George III mahogany table clock, by Roberts, Ashford, the five-pillar two-train bell striking and trip repeating, the fusee movement with anchor escapement, the silvered dial with calendar dial, strike/silent dial in the arch 20½in (52cm) high.
$4,000–4,800 ⚒ S

A mahogany table/bracket clock, inscribed Isaac Rogers London, the eight-day two-train fusee movement with anchor escapement striking the hour on a bell with repea c1810, 16in (40.5cm) high.
$7,500–8,500 ⊞ PAO
Isaac Rogers was made Master Clockmaker in 181.

A Regency figured mahogany and brass-inlaid bracket clock, inscribed Earnshaw, London, the two-train fusee movement striking on a single bell, 16in (40.5cm) high.
$3,300–4,000 ⚒ DD

◀ **A mahogany bracket clock,** by James Condliff, Liverpool, the two-train gut fusee movement with anchor escapement, 21½in (54.5cm) high, with a later conforming bracket.
$2,900–3,200 ⚒ P

◄ **A Regency carved mahogany bracket clock,** inscribed Francis Walker, Maryport, with two-train fusee movement, 16in (40.5cm) high.
$2,200–2,600 ✗ **Mit**

An English four-glass mahogany bracket clock, inscribed W. Webster, with eight-day chain driven fusee timepiece movement and platform escapement, c1820, 7in (18cm) high.
$6,000–6,800 ⊞ **SO**

A late Regency rosewood and brass-inlaid repeater mantel clock, by W. T. Ferrier, Hull, the later fusee movement striking on a bell, 20½in (52cm) high.
$2,000–2,400 ✗ **M**

> When sold at auction, clocks have sometimes had alterations to their movements, or are in unrestored condition, which may be reflected in the prices realized.

A George IV inlaid mahogany mantel clock, the painted metal dial inscribed Barraud, London, the case decorated with ebony stringing and applied brass Greek key banding, 17in (43cm) high.
$1,400–1,600 ✗ **JAd**

▶ **A George IV mahogany bracket clock,** the steel dial inscribed Elliot, London, 30in (76cm) high.
$9,800–11,500 ✗ **JAd**

CLOCKS

Dials

Clocks can usually be dated from the type of dial:
- Square dials date from c1660
- Broken arch dials date from c1720
- Silvered or painted dials date from c1760

◀ **A burr walnut four-glass bracket clock,** by Dent, London, c1830, 10in (25.5cm) high.
$4,700–5,100 ⊞ SO

A pollarded oak mantel clock, the gilt dial inscribed Phillips Brothers, London, the two-train fusee movement with anchor escapement and trip repeat striking on a coiled gong, with strike/silent lever at XII, the case with applied foliate carving and scrolls, faults, c1850, 22in (56cm) high.
$1,400–1,700 ↗ S(S)

A rosewood bracket clock, by William Martin, London, the eight-day double fusee movement with anchor escapement, striking the hours on a bell with repeat, c1835, 17in (43cm) high excluding finial.
$6,500–7,250 ⊞ PAO

An early Victorian rosewood bracket clock, with silvered dial and single fusee movement, in a Gothic case, 14½in (37cm) high.
$870–1,000 ↗ SWO

A mahogany mantel clock, by James McCabe, London, the two-train bell striking fusee and chain movement with anchor escapement and rise and fall regulation, c1835, 9½in (24cm) high.
$3,600–4,300 ↗ S

▶ **A Scottish brass-inlaid mahogany table clock,** inscribed William Pringle, Edinburgh, the eight-day movement with anchor recoil escapement striking the hours on a bell, c1840, 17¼in (44cm) high.
$4,300–4,700 ⊞ PAO

◀ **A Victorian mantel time-piece,** by Marshall, London, the balance wheel visible in the arch of the dial, the fusee and chain movement with ratchet-tooth lever escapement, c1850, 6¾in (17cm) high.
$1,200–1,400 ↗ S

▶ **A green tortoiseshell and gilt-metal portico clock,** the exposed movement with white enamel dial and blue numerals, with sunburst pendulum, mid-19thC, 14in (35.5cm) high.
$1,200–1,400 ↗ AH

CLOCKS

An inlaid mahogany bracket clock, inscribed Walshaw, Liverpool, the twin fusee movement with anchor escapement striking on a bell, 19thC, 18¼in (46.5cm) high.
$1,100–1,300 ⚹ **P(Ba)**

An oak chiming bracket clock, by Penlington & Hutton, Liverpool, the triple fusee movement chiming on eight bells and a single wire hour gong, c1870, 29in (73.5cm) high, with a matching bracket.
$1,400–1,700 ⚹ **Bon**

A carved oak quarter chiming bracket clock, by Barraud & Lunds, London, the triple-chain fusee movement with anchor escapement striking on eight bells and a gong, mid-19thC, 26½in (67.5cm) high.
$2,300–3,000 ⚹ **P**

An ebonized and gilt-metal bracket clock, by W. R. Cave, Deal, with triple fusee chiming movement, decorated with putto and dragon surmounts, 19thC, 21½in (54.5cm) high.
$2,000–2,400 ⚹ **AH**

◄ **An ebonized mantel clock,** the dial and backplate inscribed J. H. Allis, with twin fusee movement and anchor escapement striking on a gong, 19thC, 18½in (47cm) high.
$650–800 ⚹ **Bea(E)**

► **A Victorian ebonized bracket clock,** the eight-day triple fusee movement chiming on Cambridge chimes and eight bells, 18½in (47cm) high.
$2,200–2,600 ⚹ **RBB**

A Victorian mahogany bracket clock, the eight-day fusee movement with Westminster and Whittington chimes, chiming on eight bells and five gongs, 22¾in (58cm) high.
$3,600–4,300 ⚹ **AH**

A mahogany and box-wood-inlaid bracket clock, by E. Dent & Co, London, the eight-day double fusee movement with anchor escapement striking the hour and half hour on a gong, c1890, 16in (40.5cm) high.
$5,800–6,800 ⊞ **PAO**

Miller's is a price GUIDE not a price LIST

◄ **A late Victorian carved walnut bracket clock,** the gilt-brass dial with slow-fast regulation disc, with German Lenzkirch movement, chiming on two gongs, 15½in (39.5cm) high.
$1,000–1,200 ⚹ **CGC**

An ebonized bracket clock, with three-train fusee movement striking on eight bells and a gong, c1900, 18in (45.5cm) high
$1,100–1,300 ⚒ Mit

A mahogany four-glass mantel timepiece, by C. Lupton, London, with single fusee movement, late 19thC, 9¼in (23.5cm) high.
$2,900–3,200 ⚒ Bon

A mahogany bracket clock, by I. & T. Farr, Bristol, the twin fusee movement with anchor escapement, the silvered dial with strike/silent switch, late 19thC, 19in (48.5cm) high.
$5,400–6,000 ⚒ P

A mahogany quarter chiming bracket clock, the triple fusee chain movement striking on a gong and chiming on eight bells, or Westminster chimes on four gongs, with brass dial and subsidiary dials in the arch for strike/silent, late 19thC, 25½in (65cm) high.
$3,500–3,800 ⚒ P

Miller's is a price GUIDE not a price LIST

◀ **A mahogany world time mantel timepiece,** the eight-day movement with club-tooth lever escapement, the painted dial inscribed 'The Willis World Clock, Africa House, Kingsway, London', with concentric revolving 2 x 12 hour dial with minutes dial below, the outer dial divided into continental segments indicating the time in a number of worldwide locations, c1930, 13½in (34.5cm) high.
$870–1,000 ⚒ S

An Edwardian silver-mounted marble clock, with four columns flanking a base metal timepiece, Sheffield 1907, 5in (12.5cm) high.
$450–550 ⚒ FHF

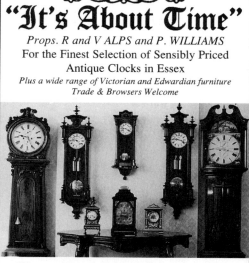

An oak drum clock, inscribed GWR, c1920, 6in (15cm) high
$400–440 ⊞ TIC

Cross Reference
See Colour Review (page 411)

A rosewood and boxwood-strung mantel clock, the French eight-day spring-driven movement striking the half hour on a gong, stamped Paris, early 20thC, 10in (25.5cm) high.
$300–350 ⚒ PFK

A gold clock, inscribed 'Congratulations to the Schneider Trophy Cup winner from a few of his comrades at Butts School', 1931, 2in (5cm) high.
$360–430 ⊞ COB

Continental Bracket, Mantel & Table Clocks

A German Gothic chamber clock, the iron posted movement with brass wheel trains, with verge and foliot escapement, painted chapter ring replaced, probably south German, mid-17thC, 13¾in (35cm) high.
$4,000–4,600 ✗ S

A Danish brass-mounted ebonized musical and chiming table clock, by David Caillatte, the three-train bell striking fusee movement with verge escapement, chiming the quarters on six bells and playing one of four tunes hourly on nine bells with 17 hammers, the dial with calendar aperture and subsidiary dials in the arch for strike/silent music selection, c1770, 19½in (49.5cm) high.
$17,500–20,500 ✗ S
David Caillatte was a Master Clockmaker in Copenhagen in 1771.

A French Louis XVI ormolu mantel clock, by Viger, Paris, the movement with tic-tac escapement and countwheel for bell strike, c1775, 12in (30.5cm) high.
$8,000–8,800 ⊞ JIL

▶ **A French Empire gilt and patinated bronze mantel clock,** the dial surmounted by a figure of Diana the huntress, attributed to Jacques Auguste d'Etour, c1800, 20in (51cm) high.
$9,400–10,200 ⊞ JIL
Jacques Auguste d'Etour is recorded as working in Paris from 1776.

A south Netherlandish ormolu-mounted black and white marble portico clock, the enamel dial inscribed F. Ovijn à Courtraij, striking on a bell, the drum case surmounted by Minerva, 1780, 24in (61cm) high.
$4,600–5,000 ✗ S(Am)

A French bronze mantel clock, with a two-train French movement, the case surmounted by a female figure with a lyre, 19thC, 17½in (44.5cm) high.
$500–600 ✗ DMC

A French ormolu mantel timepiece, inscribed Ferdinand Berthoud, Paris, the movement with lever platform escapement, on a white marble base, early 19thC, 13½in (34.5cm) high.
$1,400–1,700 ✗ Bea(E)

A French Charles X ormolu-mounted patinated bronze mantel clock, the chapter ring with Roman numerals centring a shield flanked by crossed flags, raised on a rectangular base fitted with helmets and palmettes, above paw feet cast with plumed helmets, mid-19thC, 14½in (37cm) high.
$2,000–2,300 ✗ S(NY)

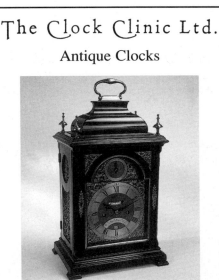
CLOCKS

CLOCKS

A French ormolu clock, by Pons, Paris, the dial inscribed Mugnier, the silk-suspended pendulum striking on a bell, c1830, 13in (33cm) high.
$3,300–4,000 ⊞ JIL

A French ormolu clock, the eight-day movement with silk suspension, the countwheel striking the half hour and hour on a bell, c1850, 14in (35.5cm) high.
$1,100–1,300 ⊞ K&D

► **A French ormolu mantel clock,** by Japy Frères, the case surmounted by a cherub, the eight-day movement striking on a bell, 19thC, 17¼in (44cm) high.
$870–1,000 ↗ WW

A French gilt-lacquered brass mantel clock, inscribed Le Roy & Fils, Paris, the suspended eight-day movement striking on a bell, with a mercury compensated pendulum, 19thC, 14¼in (36cm) high, with original key.
$1,100–1,300 ↗ WW
Le Roy & Son traded in London from 1857 to 1881.

A French rosewood and marquetry mantel clock, the eight-day striking movement by Henri Marc, Paris, c1840, 8in (20.5cm) high.
$2,000–2,200 ⊞ SO

A French boulle mantel clock, the movement striking on a gong, applied with gilt-scrolled mounts to the edges and door, 17¼in (44cm) high.
$720–870 ↗ Bea(E)

A French red boulle mantel clock, the eight-day movement by Le Roy, Paris, 19thC, 12in (30.5cm) high.
$500–600 ↗ GAK

A French ormolu and bronze mantel clock, with a silvered dial, the eight-day movement striking the half hour and hour on a bell, c1850, 15in (38cm) high.
$1,200–1,400 ↗ K&D

A French rosewood and stained portico clock, inscribed Laine A Paris, inlaid with scrolling box-wood motifs, the two-train movement striking on a bell, 19thC, 20½in (52cm) high.
$580–720 ↗ P(L)

◄ **A French porcelain striking clock,** the eight-day movement by Henri Marc, Paris, striking on a bell, c1840, 14in (35.5cm) high, with stand.
$1,900–2,200 ⊞ SO

A French Louis XVI-style gilt-bronze and marble mantel clock, the backplate stamped with the Vincenti trademark, the countwheel striking on a bell, c1860, 17in (43cm) high.
$4,000–4,600 ⊞ JIL

A French walnut parquetry table clock, the eight-day movement striking on a bell, c1870, 15in (38cm) high.
$2,600–3,000 ⊞ SO

A French black and gilt clock, the eight-day movement with platform escapement striking on a bell, c1870, 15in (38cm) high.
$4,000–4,400 ⊞ SO

A French green onyx and ormolu four-glass mantel clock, with drum gong striking movement, 1880s, 15½in (39.5cm) high.
$800–950 ↗ Bon

A German mantel clock, with three chain movement chiming and striking on five rod gongs, the dial with chime/silent regulation dials in arch, Gustave Becker trademark, c1880, 8in (20.5cm) high.
$580–650 ⊞ KB
Gustav Becker is noted as being in business in Freiburg, Germany, from 1819 to 1885.

A French bronze and ormolu mantel timepiece, modelled as a putto playing a trumpet with a drum over its shoulder, on a naturalistic base and a marble plinth, the single train movement with replaced lever platform escapement, 19thC, 8½in (21.5cm) high.
$1,100–1,300 ↗ P(EA)

▶ **An Austrian porcelain-mounted mantel clock,** the panels of dark blue gilded ground painted with classically draped maidens, signed J. Traub, the underside marked for Franz Dorfl, Vienna, late 19thC, 13½in (34.5cm) high.
$1,400–1,700 ↗ CGC

A French Napoleon III gilt-bronze and marble mantel clock, in the Louis XVI style, the dial surmounted by an eagle, late 19thC, 19¾in (50cm) high.
$4,000–4,500 ↗ NOA

CLOCKS

A French boulle marquetry ormolu-mounted mantel clock, with two-train striking movement, Paris, late 19thC, 12in (30.5cm) high.
$360–430 ↗ Mit

Items in the Clock section have been arranged in date order.

A French gilt-brass-mounted mantel clock, the eight-day striking movement in a case inset with pink glazed porcelain, the panels decorated with exotic birds and cherubs, late 19thC, 14¼in (36cm) high.
$1,100–1,400 ↗ CAG

A French Louis XIV-style ormolu striking mantel clock, the porcelain dial and panels painted with lovers and landscapes, with pink borders, with a glass dome, late 19thC, 13½in (34.5cm) high.
$1,000–1,200 ↗ L

CLOCKS

A French gilt spelter mantel clock, modelled as an Arab seated on a camel, the eight-day brass movement with outside count-wheel striking on a bell, the backplate stamped 'Vincenti', damaged, late 19thC, 18½in (47cm) high.
$1,700–2,000 ➶ **P(Ba)**

A French porcelain and ormolu mantel clock, with five inset pink porcelain panels with floral and cherub decoration, the dial with strike/silent regulation dials in arch, late 19thC, 13¼in (33.5cm) high.
$1,400–1,700 ➶ **P**

A German walnut Westminster chime bracket clock, the eight-day triple-barrel brass movement striking on a gong, the brass dial with twin subsidiary dials for slow/fast and strike/silent, backplate stamped 'Lenzkirch Agu', late 19thC, 24¾in (63cm) high.
$1,600–1,750 ➶ **P(Ba)**

A French ormolu and *champlevé* enamel mantel clock, the eight-day two-train movement striking the hour, with half hour passing strike on a bell, the case, dial and pendulum decorated in enamel with foliate designs in blue and gilt, late 19thC, 16½in (42cm) high.
$1,600–1,900 ➶ **DN**

A French boulle mantel clock, in red and black tortoiseshell with ormolu mounts, with eight-day movement, on a matching plinth base, c1895, 14in (35.5cm) high.
$1,000–1,100 ⊞ **K&D**

A German Black Forest carved wood mantel clock, the case surmounted by an eagle with outstretched wings, a fallen goat below, with French bell-striking movement, 19thC, 23¼in (59cm) high.
$1,100–1,400 ➶ **CGC**

A French ormolu and gilt-metal mantel clock, surmounted by a cherub beside a fountain, the striking cylinder movement stamped Raingot Frères, Paris, late 19thC, 14in (35.5cm) high.
$290–320 ➶ **TRM**

A French mahogany timepiece, with eight-day movement, c1900, 9in (23cm) high.
$600–660 ⊞ **SO**

◀ **A German oak mantel clock,** by Winterhalder & Hofmeier, with gong striking movement, early 20thC, 16in (40.5cm) high.
$220–260 ➶ **Bon**

A French brass mantel clock, modelled as an antique-style bell, cast in high-relief with bands of scrolling foliage, fleurs-de-lys, and figures within quatrefoil panels, interspersed with Latin inscriptions, the eight-day brass movement striking on a bell, stamped 'E. P. Depose', c1900, 12¼in (31cm) high.
$290–320 ➶ **P(Ba)**

A French mahogany and marquetry clock, with eight-day striking movement, c1900, 12in (30.5cm) high.
$1,200–1,400 ⊞ **SO**

▶ **A German gilt-mounted ebonized chiming bracket clock,** the triple-going barrel movement chiming on eight bells and a coil hour gong, the silvered dial with a strike/silent lever in the arch, early 20thC, 25in (63.5cm) high.
$1,000–1,200 ➶ **Bon**

A French tortoiseshell and gilt timepiece, with eight-day movement, c1900, 8in (20.5cm) high.
$950–1,050 ⊞ **SO**

Carriage Clocks

A French brass carriage clock, with eight-day striking movement, c1880, 5in (12.5cm) high.
$1,000–1,200 ⊞ SO

A French brass gorge-cased carriage timepiece, by Henri Jacot, Paris, the movement with platform lever escapement, c1880, 5¾in (14.5cm) high.
$580–720 ⋏ CGC

A French gorge-cased carriage clock, by Guy Lemaille, Paris, c1880, 6½in (16.5cm) high.
$2,900–3,200 ⊞ BELL

A French gilt-brass *petit sonnerie* carriage clock with alarm, by Le Roy & Fils, London, the silvered lever platform escapement with push repeat striking on two gongs, with signed enamel dial, alarm dial and subsidiary arabic alarm dial, late 19thC, 7½in (19cm) high.
$3,600–4,000 ⋏ P

A French gilt-brass and painted porcelain carriage clock, the dial inscribed I. Langelaan, Southsea, and painted with a rural scene, the repeating gong striking movement with lever platform escapement, the side panels painted with romantic scenes, c1890, 7in (18cm) high, with travelling case.
$3,600–4,000 ⋏ S(S)

A French five minute repeating carriage clock, the eight-day movement striking the half hour and hour on a gong, c1895, 7in (18cm) high.
$2,000–2,200 ⊞ K&D

A gilt-brass repeating carriage clock, the platform lever escapement and drum movement striking on a gong, the five panel case engraved with foliate scrolls, c1900, 4½in (11.5cm) high.
$720–870 ⋏ Hal

A French carriage time-piece, by Henri Jacot, Paris, c1900, 4in (10cm) high.
$2,200–2,400 ⊞ JeF

◀ An Edwardian silver carriage clock, by H. C. D., Birmingham, with enamel dial, 1908, 3in (7.5cm) high.
$1,700–2,000 ⊞ NS

A French brass carriage clock, with a porcelain dial, with eight-day movement, c1900, 4½in (11.5cm) high.
$500–600 ⊞ K&D

A gilt-brass carriage clock, with diamanté border, the eight-day movement with cylinder platform escapement, c1900, 6in (15cm) high.
$1,200–1,400 ⊞ JIL

▶ A brass carriage clock, the eight-day striking and repeating movement with alarm, early 20thC, 7½in (19cm) high.
$500–600 ⋏ E

A French gilt-brass carriage clock, the enamel dial with regulation at XII, the drum gong striking movement with a replaced lever escapement, early 20thC, 9¼in (23.5cm) high.
$580–720 ⋏ Bon

CLOCKS

Cartel Clocks

A French gilt ormolu cartel wall clock, the case surmounted by a putto and trailing vine leaves, the 12-piece enamel dial with a decorated centre, with silk-suspended movement striking on a bell, mid-19thC, 21in (53.5cm) high.
$1,100–1,300 ⚒ Bon

A French Louis XVI-style ormolu cartel clock, by Marti & Cie, the dial inscribed Mesnard, Boulogne, the eight-day movement with silvered lever platform escapement and rack striking on a bell, c1890, 8in (20.5cm) high.
$3,500–4,000 ⊞ JIL

Miller's is a price GUIDE not a price LIST

A French ormolu cartel clock, the two-train movement with rack striking on a bell, with a cherub mask pendulum, late 19thC, 27½in (70cm) high.
$1,400–1,600 ⚒ P

A French Louis XV-style ormolu cartel clock, the restored enamel dial signed 'Le Faucheur Hger du Roi Paris', the case surmounted by a figure of Minerva, the movement of long duration Brocot anchor escapement, with half hour rack striking on a bell, c1860, 36¾in (93.5cm) high.
$5,500–6,500 ⚒ S(Am)

Electric Clocks

A black electric automata mantel timepiece, by Vitascope Industries, the case inset with a glazed aperture with the model of a three-masted ship on a simulated choppy sea cutting the waves in synchronization with the movement, early 20thC, 12½in (32cm) high.
$580–720 ⚒ P

A French battery-driven clock, by Bulle, on a wooden base with a glass dome, c1930, 11in (28cm) high.
$260–300 ⊞ BWA

A French electric time-piece, by Bulle, the exposed movement with coil pendulum oscillating over a fixed U-shaped magnet, on a giltwood base covered by a cut-glass dome, c1925, 11in (28cm) high.
$1,200–1,400 ⚒ S

Garnitures

A French rouge marble and ormolu-mounted brass clock garniture, the eight-day movement with hand-painted enamel dial and striking on a bell, with matching side urns, late 19thC, clock 16¼in (41.5cm) high.
$800–950 ⚒ DA

A French ormolu and marble clock garniture, the white marble case flanked by a classical maiden and a cherub, with two candelabra each shaped as Pan supporting two candle sconces, c1890, clock 9¾in (25cm) wide.
$870–1,000 ⚒ Bri

A French three-piece gilt-metal and porcelain clock garniture, with two-train striking movement, the porcelain dial decorated with birds, surmounted by an urn, the base with panel decorated with a courting couple, with a pair of royal blue and enamel decorated candlesticks, late 19thC, clock 14¼in (36cm) high.
$720–870 ⚒ P(Ed)

A French three-piece marble and ormolu clock garniture, with two-train striking movement, with two marble urns with ormolu mounts, c1900, clock 18½in (47cm) high.
$1,200–1,400 ⋏ SK

A French gilt-bronze and marble mantel clock, by Samuel Marti, the case flanked by Venus and Cupid, with a pair of matched gilt-bronze twin-light candelabra, c1900, clock 13½in (34.5cm) high.
$2,100–2,300 ⋏ P(Ba)

A cast-brass clock garniture, the bell striking movement in a cast gilt case, with a pair of matching three-light candelabra, early 20thC, clock 15in (38cm) high.
$580–720 ⋏ Bon

Lantern Clocks

A lantern clock, by Thomas Kalston, London, the 30-hour striking movement with foliot balance verge, c1670.
$8,700–9,500 ⊞ SO

A brass lantern clock, by John Cotsworth, London, with alarm mechanism, set in an oak wall shelf, restored, c1670, 15in (38cm) high.
$5,500–6,000 ⋏ SK(B)
John Cotsworth was a freeman of The Worshipful Company of Clockmakers, a City of London craft guild founded by Royal Charter in 1631. The company's purpose was to regulate and encourage 'the art and mystery' of watch and clockmaking, with particular emphasis on quality control, training and welfare.

Miller's Compares

I. A lantern clock, by Richard Savage, Shrewsbury, with original verge escapement, dated 1692, 15in (38cm) high.
$8,000–9,500 ⊞ BL

II. A lantern clock, by Abraham Weston, Lewes, the movement replaced c1900 with a single fusee movement, unrestored, c1700, 15in (38cm) high.
$1,400–1,700 ⊞ BL

These two lantern clocks look superficially similar. Item I, however, survives entirely as made in the 1690s with the original verge escape-ment and today any original verge lantern clock is a rare item. Like all genuine lantern clocks it has a single hand and is wound daily. Item II was made about the same time but was converted in the late 19th century by having its move-ment completely replaced with a new spring clock movement of the day, making it two-handed and of eight-day duration. This is known as a 'conversion' lantern clock and is therefore of much lesser value.

A hybrid lantern clock, by George Clarke, London, the 30-hour posted frame movement with verge escapement and count-wheel strike, mid-18thC, 6in (15cm) high.
$7,200–8,700 ⋏ DN
George Clarke of Leadenhall Street, first recorded in 1725, livery of the Clockmakers Company 1787.

A brass lantern clock, signed William Rose of Ailesbury, 18thC, with 19thC single fusee movement with passing strike, 14½in (37cm) high.
$580–720 ⋏ Bon

A brass reproduction ting-tang quarter striking lantern clock, by James Walker, London, the two-train fusee movement striking on two bells mounted above, c1880, 17½in (44.5cm) high.
$1,800–2,200 ⋏ Bon

A brass lantern clock, with two-train fusee movement striking on two gongs and overhead bell strike, with an ebonized plinth, late 19thC, 17in (43cm) high.
$1,300–1,600 ⋏ DMC

CLOCKS

Longcase Clocks

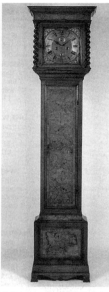

An oak longcase clock, by John Martin, Bristol, with two-train five-pillar movement striking on a bell, the dial with subsidiary seconds dial and date aperture, the door inlaid with star motif, early 18thC, 86in (218.5cm) high.
$3,600–4,400 ➶ HYD

An oak longcase clock, inscribed George Horsnaile Warfield, with 30–hour birdcage movement, single hand and brass dial, c1740, 78½in (199.5cm) high.
$5,500–6,000 ⊞ ALS

A chinoiserie-decorated oak eight-day longcase clock, by Sam Harris, London, the dial with seconds and date in the arch, early 18thC, 93¼in (237cm) high.
$3,600–4,400 ➶ TEN

A burr-walnut longcase clock, by Fromanteel & Clarke, with two-train five-pillar movement striking on a bell, c1700, 88in (223.5cm) high, in associated case.
$8,700–10,000 ➶ HYD
Christopher Clarke was married to Fromanteel's youngest daughter, Ahasuerus. The partnership of the two clockmakers was formed in Amsterdam and they are recorded as working c1700.

A mahogany longcase clock, inscribed James Evill, Bath, the silvered dial with subsidiary seconds and date dial, the arch engraved with an eagle, decorated in neo-classical style, c1750, 95in (241.5cm) high.
$10,800–13,000 ➶ MEA
The decoration is reputed to have been executed later by Angelica Kauffmann.

A red lacquer longcase clock, by Francis De La Balle, London, with five-pillar rack and bell striking movement, the dial with subsidiary seconds and a calendar aperture, the case with gilt chinoiserie and concave-sided pediment with a central mirror, c1750, 88in (223.5cm) high.
$2,600–3,200 ➶ Bon

◄ **A mahogany eight-day longcase clock,** the movement striking the hours on a bell, the engraved brass dial with second hand and date aperture, c1760, 82in (208.5cm) high.
$10,000–11,300 ⊞ SO

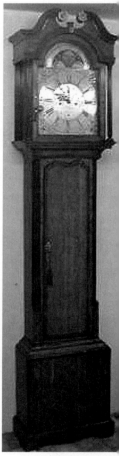

A crossbanded-oak and mahogany eight-day longcase clock, by William Thompson, Chester, striking the hours on a bell, the brass dial with cherub-head spandrels, the arch with moonphase, c1757, 90in (228.5cm) high.
$9,800–10,500 ⊞ NCL
In 1757 Haley's comet was visible from earth. The event has been depicted on the moon dial of this clock.

A mahogany eight-day longcase clock, by Charles Edward Gillitt, Manchester, mid-18thC, 96in (244cm) high.
$9,500–11,500 NSF

► **A country oak longcase clock,** the 30-hour movement striking the hours on a bell, with a brass dial, c1770, 81in (205.5cm) high.
$2,300–2,600 K&D

An oak eight-day longcase clock, inscribed John Pack, Harleston, the five-pillar movement striking the hours on a bell, the brass dial with seconds and date aperture, the arch with strike/silent feature and serpent spandrels, the broken arch top with Norfolk cresting and three brass finials, c1765, 87in (221cm) high.
$10,800–12,000 PAO

An oak longcase clock, inscribed Henry Baker, Malling, the 30-hour striking movement with an engraved brass dial and single hand, 18thC, 81½in (207cm) high.
$1,900–2,200 MCA

An oak longcase clock, by Harris, Wellington, the 30-hour movement striking on a bell, the associated brass dial with cast mask spandrels, the centre engraved with trailing vines, the case inlaid with boxwood, harewood and mahogany, pediment reduced, 18thC, 78in (198cm) high.
$1,750–2,000 P(L)
A Richard Harris is known to have worked as a clockmaker at Wellington in Shropshire c1770.

CLOCKS

CLOCKS

A mahogany eight-day longcase clock, by Francis Perigal, London, the five-pillar movement with strike/silent ring to the arch, flanked by chased rococo mounts incorporating exotic birds, the centre with seconds dial and calendar aperture, 18thC, 89in (226cm) high.
$13,000–16,000 ⚡ LAY

An oak longcase clock, inscribed C. Lowther, Westerdale, with 30-hour chiming movement, the dial arch painted with a study of a native, with date aperture, 18thC, 81in (205.5cm) high.
$1,600–1,900 ⚡ DD

An oak longcase clock, with 30-hour striking movement, the painted dial with flowers in the spandrels, 18thC, 78in (198cm) high.
$725–850 ⚡ E

◀ **A black lacquer longcase clock,** by John Massingham, Fakenham, with four-pillar rack and bell striking movement, the painted dial with a subsidiary seconds and calendar sector, in an associated case with gilt chinoiserie and foliate-decorated sides, c1770, 84in (213.5cm) high.
$1,000–1,200 ⚡ Bon

A lacquered eight-day longcase clock, by Marm. Storr, London, 18thC, 84in (213.5cm) high.
$4,650–5,500 ⚡ SWO

A mahogany and oak eight-day longcase clock, by George Lumly, Bury, the movement striking on a bell, the silvered dial with date and seconds, c1780, 92in (233.5cm) high.
$1,750–2,000 ⚡ DA

An oak longcase clock, by George Hewitt, Marlborough, with 30-hour movement, brass dial and with Father Time automaton to the arch, c1780, 83½in (212cm) high.
$5,500–6,000 ⊞ ALS

An oak and mahogany longcase clock, by Wilkinson, Wigton, the 30-hour movement striking on a bell, with painted dial and moonphase to the arch, c1775, 88in (223.5cm) high.
$4,000–4,500 ⊞ NCL

A George III figured mahogany longcase clock, by James Scholefield, London, with five-pillar movement, the brass dial with strike/silent feature to the arch, with subsidiary seconds dial and calendar aperture and gilt castle-gateway spandrels, c1780, 92½in (235cm) high.
$10,250–12,250 ⚡ Bri

Miller's Compares

I. An oak longcase clock, by Jackson of Thirsk, with 30-hour movement, the First Period white dial by James Wilson, the case with mahogany trim, c1790, 84in (213.5cm) high.
$4,400–4,700 ⊞ **BL**

II. An oak longcase clock, by Mills of Gloucester, with 30-hour movement, and white dial, the case with mahogany trim and inlays, 1820s, 78in (198cm) high.
$3,200–3,600 ⊞ **BL**

Both clocks pictured here are genuine 30-hour painted dial clocks in their original oak cases and in good condition. However, there is a subtle difference in their prices because although Item II is small, a good commercial point, Item I has the advantage of having a First Period high quality dial. It also has an unusually slender case with desirable additional features of mahogany crossbanding, dentil mouldings and blind fretwork.

◄ **A George III figured mahogany eight-day longcase clock,** inscribed Harvey, Weymouth, the four-pillar movement with pull hour trip repeat, the painted dial with blue-ground Roman numerals and subsidiary seconds dial, calendar aperture and cottage scene to the arch, in a London-made case with original ball and spire finials, c1780, 101½in (258cm) high.
$6,500–7,250 ↗ **Bri**

Movements

Longcase clocks come with one of three distinct movements: 30-hour, eight-day or one-month. Most clocks come with the eight-day or 30-hour movement: the cost of one-month movements was originally so prohibitive that such clocks are very rare.

A mahogany longcase clock, by William Vale, London, the dial with subsidiary seconds, with associated four-pillar rack and bell striking movement, c1785, 96in (244cm) high.
$3,000–3,500 ↗ **Bon**

A George III oak longcase clock, by Bennett Edwards, Dereham, with 30–hour bell-striking posted frame movement, the enamel dial with floral spandrels and calendar aperture, plinth reduced, 74½in (189cm) high.
$725–875 ↗ **CGC**

CLOCKS

CLOCKS

A George III mahogany eight-day longcase clock, inscribed Fielders, Atherstone, the movement striking on a bell, the painted dial with subsidiary seconds dial and date aperture, 85¾in (218cm) high.
$1,600–1,750 ➤ WL

A George III walnut eight-day longcase clock, by David Lockwood, Swaffham, with striking movement and brass dial, 94in (239cm) high.
$3,700–4,400 ➤ NSF

A Scottish George III oak eight-day longcase clock, by John Fortune, Lauder, with striking movement, the dial with seconds dial, 81in (205.5cm) high.
$1,200–1,300 ➤ EH

A Scottish George III mahogany eight-day long case clock, by J. Graham, Elie, the two-train movement with anchor escapement, the silvered dial with subsidiary seconds and date dials, 86¾in (220.5cm) high.
$7,250–8,750 ➤ L&T

A Scottish George III mahogany longcase clock, by John Hamilton, Glasgow, the brass dial with calendar apertures to the centre inscribed strike and quarter and silent hours, with associated three-train six-pillar movement, the hood with pierced fretwork side panels, 88in (223.5cm) high.
$1,400–1,600 ➤ HYD

An Irish George III mahogany eight-day long case clock, by John Houston, Dublin, the brass dial and arch painted with hunting scene, the trunk and base later carved, 92in (233.5cm) high.
$3,200–3,600 ➤ EH

◄ **A George III mahogany longcase clock,** by William Nash, Bridge, the two-train movement with anchor escapement striking on a bell, the brass dial with subsidiary seconds dial and date aperture, surmounted by a moonphase, 85½in (217cm) high.
$4,000–4,600 ➤ P(EA)

A George III oak eight-day longcase clock, inscribed ?. Pyke, Bridgwater, the brass dial decorated with floral engraving, with floral spandrels, calendar ring acking, 77in (195.5cm) high. $2,200–2,600 ≯ TAM

Thomas Pyke (1771–1824) brass founder and clock-maker of Bridgwater, Somerset, is recorded as having worked on the church clocks at Fitzhead, Cossington, Goathurst, Curry Rivel, Lydeard St Lawrence and North and South Petherton, and supplied new clocks at Queen Camel and Chard.

A George III elm eight-day longcase clock, by Rich Webb, Hook Norton, the brass dial engraved with a flowering urn and scrolls, with urn spandrels, later restorations to dial and plinth, 76in (193cm) high. $1,500–1,750 ≯ F&C

► A George III eight-day mahogany and boxwood-strung longcase clock, by Wainwright, Nottingham, the bell striking movement with Walker falseplate, the brass dial with moonphase, seconds dial and calendar aperture, with cherub-head spandrels and rococo engraved centre, 89¼in (226.5cm) high. $4,350–5,000 ≯ CGC

A George III mahogany eight-day longcase clock, by Scotchmer, Islington, with striking movement, the painted dial with strike/silent to the arch, with subsidiary date and second hand, the hood and trunk flanked by fluted columns with brass inlay, 91in (231cm) high. $10,875–13,000 ≯ Mit

An Irish George III eight-day long-case clock, by St Martin, Dublin, 85in (216cm) high. $1,900–2,200 ≯ SWO

A George III oak long-case clock, by Jabez Stock, London, the two-train movement with anchor escapement striking on a bell, with nameplate to the arch, 84¼in (214cm) high. $1,600–1,900 ≯ P(EA)

A mahogany longcase clock, by Thomas Atherton, London, the two-train movement with anchor escapement, the brass dial with subsidiary seconds and date aperture, 18thC, 85in (216cm) high. $4,000–4,700 ≯ P

CLOCKS

A George III oak and mahogany-crossbanded longcase clock, inscribed John Sidery, Hampstead Norris, with 30-hour bell strike movement, the painted dial with calendar aperture, 77½in (197cm) high.
$650–800 ⚒ RTo

A mahogany longcase clock, by James Wilsdon, Kingston, the two-train five-pillar movement with anchor escapement, the brass dial with recessed subsidiary seconds and date aperture, the hood decorated in the corners with stylized painted flowers, the trunk and base in the form of a stepped half column, 18thC, 89in (226cm) high.
$5,000–6,000 ⚒ P

A Scottish George III mahogany eight-day longcase clock, inscribed Robert Clidsdale, Edinburgh, the three-train striking movement chiming on eight bells, with silvered brass dial, the trunk door with mahogany crossbanding and boxwood stringing, 86in (218.4cm) high.
$7,000–8,000 ⚒ Mit

An oak eight-day longcase clock, inscribed John Adams, Cakemore, with painted early Wilson dial, mahogany hood columns and trunk quarter-columns, c1795, 84in (213.5cm) high.
$8,000–9,000 ⊞ ALS

A George III mahogany longcase clock, with two-train anchor escapement, the dial with two subsidiary dials, the base with later-inlaid urn, 82¼in (209cm) high.
$2,200–2,600 ⚒ P(Ed)

An oak eight-day longcase clock, by Thomas Lister Snr, Luddenden, the movement striking on a bell, the brass dial engraved to the centre with leafy sprays and signature, with moonphase and calendar aperture, c1760, 80½in (204.5cm) high
$2,500–3,000 ⚒ M

◄ **An oak and mahogany eight-day longcase clock,** inscribed Wainwright, Nottingham, with striking movement, the floral painted dial with date aperture, late 18thC, 79in (200.5cm) high.
$725–875 ⚒ FHF

An Irish mahogany long-case clock, the painted dial with subsidiary seconds dial flanked by fluted pilasters, the carved pediment with grotesque mask, damaged, late 18thC, 84in (213.5cm) high.
$2,500–3,000 ⚘ MEA

An oak eight-day longcase clock, by B. Willoughby, Bristol, with striking movement, the case carved with trailing floral decoration and an armorial to the base, with brass dial, late 18thC, 90in (228.5cm) high.
$1,300–1,600 ⚘ FHF

A George III oak and mahogany-crossbanded longcase clock, inscribed John Webster, Salop, the 30-hour movement striking on a bell, the date aperture painted with a central bird and fan motifs to the spandrels, c1800, on a later plinth, distressed, 81in (205.5cm) high.
$950–1,200 ⚘ Hal

◄ **An oak and mahogany-crossbanded eight-day longcase clock,** by James Baker, Montacute, the movement striking on a bell, the painted dial with date and seconds, c1800, 79in (200.5cm) high.
$3,500–4,000 ⊞ K&D

A mahogany eight-day longcase clock, inscribed John Walker, London, the movement striking on a bell, with date work and strike/silent mechanism in the arch, c1800, 87in (221cm) high.
$20,300–22,500 ⊞ SO

An oak and mahogany Gillows-style longcase clock, by John Lawrence, with 30-hour movement and painted dial, c1800, 87in (221cm) high.
$2,600–2,900 ⚘ NCL

An oak eight-day longcase clock, with striking movement, the painted dial with date aperture, c1800, 84in (213.5cm) high.
$1,500–1,750 ⚘ CAG

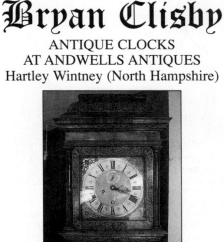

A Scottish mahogany and box-wood-inlaid eight-day longcase clock, inscribed Alexander Miller, Perth, the movement striking the hours on a bell, the dial with seconds and date, with crown painted in the arch with inscription '*Honoris Justicus Merces*', c1800, 84in (213.5cm) high.
$11,600–12,600 ⊞ PAO

A mahogany chequer-banded and line-inlaid longcase clock, by W. Heath, Newcastle, the two-train movement with anchor escapement striking on a bell, the painted dial with moonphase to the arch, with subsidiary seconds dial and date aperture, early 19thC, 90¼in (229cm) high.
$2,900–3,500 ➶ P(S)

An oak eight-day longcase clock, inscribed Abraham Shaw, Billingborough, with painted dial, c1800, 84½in (214.5cm) high.
$6,000–7,000 ⊞ ALS

An inlaid mahogany eight-day longcase clock, by George Hunt, Bristol, the white enamel dial and moonphase decorated with a landscape and seascape, with squirrel spandrels, early 19thC, 85½in (217cm) high.
$3,600–4,400 ➶ F&C

◄ **A Scottish mahogany and boxwood-lined eight-day longcase clock,** by A. Paterson, Edinburgh, the movement with anchor escapement striking on a bell, the white-painted dial with date dial, early 19thC, 81in (205.5cm) high.
$1,900–2,200 ➶ P(Ed)

A Georgian mahogany eight-day longcase clock, inscribed John Parr, Liverpool, the movement with moonphase, with painted dial, 78in (198cm) high.
$5,000–6,000 ➶ RBB

A brass-inlaid mahogany-veneered eight-day longcase clock, inscribed J. Leach, Romsey, the movement striking on a bell, the painted dial with subsidiary seconds and calendar dials, early 19thC, 77in (195.5cm) high.
$2,200–2,600 ➶ WW

A mahogany eight-day longcase clock, by George Forster, Sittingbourne, the five-pillar movement striking on a bell, with date work and painted enamelled dial, the London-style case with fretwork to the hood, c1801, 87in (221cm) high.
$11,600–12,600 ⊞ SO

A mahogany and cross-banded longcase clock, by Moorhouse, Liverpool, the two-train movement with anchor escapement and bell strike, with enamel dial, 93¼in (237cm) high.
$1,750–2,250 ➶ P(E)

An oak longcase clock, with 30-hour chiming movement, the case inlaid with mahogany and rosewood bands, the doors inlaid with a satinwood shell, with enamel dial, early 19thC, 87in (221cm) high. **$1,000–1,200** ⚒ DD

A George III inlaid mahogany longcase clock, by B. E. Coates & Sons, Wakefield, with four-pillar rack and bell striking movement, the painted dial with subsidiary seconds and calendar, with floral painted spandrels and a painting of a cottage to the arch, c1810, 91in (231cm) high. **$2,000–2,400** ⚒ Bon(M)

A Scottish mahogany eight-day longcase clock, inscribed David Murray, Edinburgh, the movement with dead-beat escapement striking the hours on a bell, the centre with seconds and centre date, the case inlaid with boxwood stringing, c1810, 80in (203cm) high. **$10,200–11,400** ▦ PAO

An Irish late George III mahogany eight-day longcase clock, by O'Shaughnessy, Cork, the four-pillar movement with anchor escapement striking on a bell, the painted dial with subsidiary seconds dial, 82in (208.5cm) high. **$1,000–1,200** ⚒ HOLL

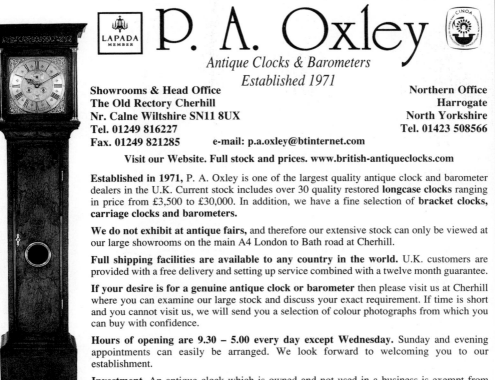

A late George III mahogany eight-day longcase clock, inscribed Dolly Rollison, Halton, with striking movement, the case inlaid with stringing, the earlier brass dial with seconds dial and date aperture, 85in (216cm) high.
$1,400–1,600 ⚹ **AG**

A Scottish Regency mahogany eight-day longcase clock, by Thomas Pomphrey, Lochgilphead, the painted dial with subsidiary seconds and date dials, 81in (205.5cm) high.
$3,200–3,600 ⚹ **Mit**

A Scottish late Regency mahogany eight-day longcase clock, inscribed J. R. & W. Laing, Glasgow, the movement striking on a gong, the painted dial with subsidiary second and date dials, 76¾in (195cm) high.
$4,500–5,500 ⚹ **ELR**

A Scottish mahogany eight-day longcase clock, by John Law, Beith, the movement striking on a bell, the brass dial with seconds hand and date aperture, c1820, 80in (203cm) high.
$7,600–8,300 ⊞ **SO**

An oak and mahogany-crossbanded eight-day longcase clock, inscribed William Preddy, Langport, the movement striking on a bell, the dial with seconds dial and date aperture, c1815, 82in (208.5cm) high
$4,350–5,000 ⊞ **PAO**

An oak and mahogany eight-day longcase clock, inscribed Saml Newnes, Whitchurch, the movement striking on a bell, the dial with subsidiary seconds dial and date aperture, faults, c1820, 91in (231cm) high.
$2,500–3,000 ⚹ **S(S)**

A George IV oak eight-day longcase clock, by Edward Elliott, Lenham, the four-pillar movement with rack strike on a bell, the painted dial with subsidiary seconds dial, an automaton man-of-war in the arch, bell lacking, plinth restored, 85in (216cm) high.
$2,700–3,200 ⚹ **DN**

A mahogany longcase clock, by Grimalde & Johnson, London, the two-train movement with anchor escapement striking on a bell, the silvered dial with subsidiary seconds, with silent/strike lever, early 19thC, 77½in (197cm) high.
$8,400–10,200 ⚒ P Grimalde & Johnson are listed as working from 1809 to 1825.

A flame mahogany eight-day longcase clock, inscribed Roberts, Bath, with Adam and Eve automaton to the arch, c1830, 92½in (235cm) high.
$13,000–14,500 ⊞ ALS

A George IV mahogany eight-day longcase clock, by Coates, Wigan, with two-train movement striking on a bell, the painted dial with subsidiary dials, the Sheraton-style case with flame-veneered door, 92in (233.5cm) high.
$2,900–3,200 ⚒ HYD

An oak and mahogany-crossbanded longcase clock, inscribed Simms, Witney, the 30-hour movement striking the hours on a bell, the painted dial with a date aperture, the case with inlay and stringing, c1830, 80in (203cm) high.
$2,200–2,400 ⊞ K&D

An Austrian Louis Philippe ebony and boulle longcase clock, by Gebb Rodeck, Vienna, in the Louis XIV style, the 30-day movement with chime on the half hour, the fitted music box with a mechanical device to play different tunes each hour, with gilt-mounted Old Father Time finial, 19thC, 78in (198cm) high.
$16,000–19,000 ⚒ G(B)

A French Philippe provincial longcase clock, painted with mythological figures and flowering vines, the enamel dial marked 'Serre à Dax', within a repoussé brass bezel depicting cherubs among flowers, mid-19thC, 93in (236cm).
$2,500–3,000 ⚒ NOA

An inlaid oak and mahogany-crossbanded eight-day longcase clock, inscribed T. Andrews, New Buckenham, c1840, 82¾in (210cm) high.
$5,800–6,500 ⊞ **ALS**

A flame-mahogany eight-day longcase clock, inscribed Ballard, Cranbrook, the movement striking the hours on a bell, the dial with seconds and date dials, the spandrels painted with flowers, c1840, 81in (205.5cm) high.
$7,500–8,500 ⊞ **PAO**

An Irish Victorian mahogany eight-day longcase clock, inscribed C. & C. Sivel, Dublin, the movement striking on a gong, with subsidiary seconds dial, 79in (200.5cm) high.
$1,000–1,250 ⚲ **WW**

An oak longcase clock, by Calver, Eye, the posted 30-hour movement with outside countwheel strike, the cream-painted dial with subsidiary seconds and date aperture, mid-19thC, 72¾in (185cm) high.
$1,300–1,500 ⚲ **P**
Mrs Susan Calver, Eye, is listed as working from 1830 to 1853.

A mahogany drumhead longcase clock, inscribed G. Kistler, Penzance, with four-pillar rack and bell striking movement, the lower case carved with foliage, c1850, 79in (200.5cm) high.
$2,300–2,900 ⚲ **Bon**

An oak, mahogany and rosewood-crossbanded eight-day longcase clock, by Davy, Tavistock, the movement striking on a bell, the dial painted with country scenes incorporating seconds and date indicators, the door with marquetry inlay, mid-19thC, 81½in (207cm) high.
$3,500–3,800 ⊞ **K&D**

▶ **An oak longcase clock,** inscribed P. Carless, Tewkesbury, with four-pillar rack and bell striking movement, the painted dial with subsidiary seconds dial and calendar aperture, with gilt-foliage painted spandrels, 19thC, 77in (195.5cm) high.
$1,000–1,200 ⚲ **Bon**

A Victorian crossbanded mahogany eight-day longcase clock, by J. Barron, Leeds, the movement striking on a bell, the painted dial with a classical charioteer to the arch and personifications of the continents to the spandrels, with two subsidiary dials, 92½in (235cm) high.
$1,750–2,250 ⚲ **P(L)**

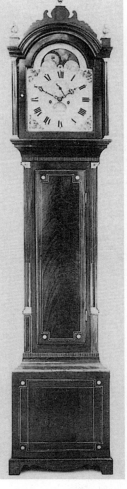

CLOCKS

A Scottish Victorian mahogany drumhead eight-day longcase clock, inscribed R. Brand, Banchory, the movement with anchor escapement striking on a bell, the painted dial with subsidiary seconds dial and date, 82in (208.5cm) high.
$2,900–3,200 ⚒ P(Ed)

An inlaid mahogany longcase clock, the two-train movement with anchor escapement, the repainted dial with subsidiary seconds dial, with classically dressed female figures to the spandrels and the arch, 19thC, 94in (239cm) high.
$3,600–4,300 ⚒ P

A carved oak longcase clock, by Samuel Burgess, London, the two-train movement with anchor escapement and bell strike, the brass dial with subsidiary seconds dial and date aperture, with a silvered plate to the arch bearing an eagle and inscribed 'Tempus Fugit', the trunk door and base carved with a maskhead, 19thC, 96¾in (246cm) high.
$1,750–2,250 ⚒ P(E)

A Scottish inlaid mahogany longcase clock, by James Hardie & Co, Aberdeen, 19thC, 72¾in (185cm) high.
$4,000–4,500 ⚒ TRL

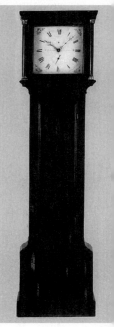

A Scottish Victorian mahogany eight-day longcase clock, by Robert Keith, Edinburgh, the anchor escapement striking on a bell, the painted dial with reclining figure to the arch and floral sprigs to the spandrels, with subsidiary seconds and date dials, 84in (213.5cm) high.
$2,500–3,000 ⚒ P(Ed)

A Scottish Victorian mahogany eight-day longcase clock, by W. Ellis, Ardrossan, the anchor escapement striking on a gong, the painted dial decorated with the four seasons, with subsidiary seconds and date dial, 87in (221cm) high.
$3,000–3,300 ⚒ P(Ed)

A Irish mahogany eight-day longcase clock, inscribed R. Meeson, Omagh, the enamelled dial with subsidiary second hand, 19thC, 80in (203cm) high.
$1,600–1,900 ⚒ Mit

An oak longcase clock, inscribed W. Tanner, Hailsham, the 30-hour four-pillar movement with outside locking plate striking on a bell, the painted dial with subsidiary seconds and calendar, the spandrels decorated with gilt foliage, 19thC, 76in (193cm) high.
$600–700 ⚒ Bon

A mahogany and cross-banded longcase clock, the 30-hour movement with secondary dials, 19thC, 83½in (212cm) high.
$3,350–4,000 ↗ AH

A late Victorian oak longcase clock, by Arnold & Lewis, Manchester, with moonphase mechanism to the hood, with subsidiary Whittington/Westminster chimes with strike/silent dial, and a seconds dial within the chapter ring, 82½in (209.5cm) high.
$4,350–5,000 ↗ WL

A mahogany eight-day longcase clock, by Russells Ltd, Liverpool, the movement striking on a coiled gong, the brass dial with subsidiary seconds ring, late 19thC, 84in (213.5cm) high.
$2,600–3,200 ↗ P(NW)

A oak and walnut eight-day longcase clock, the weight-driven movement striking the hours on a gong, with a brass dial, c1900, 56in (142cm) high.
$5,000–5,500 ⊞ PAO
This type of weight-driven small longcase clock has become very sought after.

A French spelter eight-day clock, after Louis Hottot, in the shape of an Arabic tower, the enamel dial with embossed brass centre, the Japy Frères movement striking on a coil, the base with an applied figure of a Moorish girl indicating the time, 19thC, 42in (106.5cm) high.
$3,200–3,600 ↗ HOLL

A German mahogany longcase clock, the chain pull-winding movement sounding on four wire gongs at the hour and half hour, with brass dial, early 20thC, 78in (198cm) high.
$500–600 ↗ Bon

◀ A mahogany longcase clock, the three-train four-pillar movement chiming the quarters on eight tubular gongs and striking on a further gong, the dial with subsidiary dials for seconds, chime/silent and Westminster, Whittington and St Michael chimes, early 20thC, 94in (239cm) high.
$7,250–8,750 ↗ DN

Novelty Clocks

An Austrian alabaster night timepiece, the movement with verge and balance escapement connected to an ormolu drum revolving against a serpent pointer, the drum enclosing an oil and taper lamp, c1820, 13in (33cm) high.
$8,700–10,000 ⚒ S

An Austrian picture clock, by Johann Putmann, with musical automaton, dated 1857, 37½in (95.5cm) wide.
$4,300–5,000 ⚒ S(Z)

▶ **A French polished bronze mystery swinging timepiece,** the eight-day movement with Brocot escapement, in a black-painted globe forming the upper part of a gridiron pendulum, the plinth inscribed 'Moreau. Mattu.', c1885, 49½in (125.5cm) high.
$13,700–16,000 ⚒ S

A French lighthouse timepiece, the eight-day movement with duplex escapement, the tall balance mounted with vertical glass rods simulating the revolving light, with enamel dial, c1890, 9¾in (25cm) high.
$2,200–2,500 ⚒ S

A silvered brass lighthouse clock, the door centred by a gilt watch-type Roman dial, the two-train movement with anchor escapement and inverted pendulum linked to the coloured filters in the head, minute and inoperative second hands lacking, movement stamped 'Vincenti 1756', late 19thC, 22in (56cm) high.
$2,900–3,200 ⚒ P

A German lighthouse timepiece, with single train movement, the main dial and eight subsidiary dials showing times in various cities on single drive train, in tinplate case, early 20thC, 22½in (57cm) high.
$950–1,150 ⚒ SK(B)

A late Victorian novelty mantel clock, in the form of a drop-forge press, with hammered and brass-effect finish, damaged, 18in (45.5cm) high.
$2,300–2,900 ⚒ FHF

Miller's is a price GUIDE not a price LIST

Skeleton Clocks

A brass skeleton clock, with passing strike, the single fusee movement with pierced brass Gothic-style frame, beneath a glass dome, mid-19thC, 16in (40.5cm) high.
$1,300–1,600 ⚒ Bon

A Victorian skeleton clock, by Kettlewell, Leeds, the chain fusee movement with anchor escapement, with pierced brass Gothic-style frame, on a rosewood base, 9¾in (25cm) high.
$720–870 ⚒ L

A brass skeleton clock, the two-train fusee movement with anchor escapement striking on a bell, on brass-strung mahogany base, with cracked glass dome, 19thC, 15in (38cm) high.
$1,100–1,300 ⚒ P(Ba)

A Victorian brass skeleton mantel clock, in the shape of a cathedral, the two-train fusee movement with anchor escapement and four spoke wheelwork striking the half hour on a bell, on a grey-veined white marble base, with glass dome and key, striker lacking, 13½in (34.5cm) high.
$800–950 ⚒ PFK

Wall Clocks

A wooden wall clock, by Lautier, Bath, with eight-day A-plated fusee movement, with convex glass, c1795, 12in (30.5cm) diam.
$4,600–5,000 ⊞ SO

A brass 30-hour wall marriage clock, the dial inscribed 'Richard Savage de Much Wenlock Fecit, 1696', the lantern-style movement with verge escapement and external locking plate striking on a bell, engraved with tulips and thistles, the surround with later-reduced corners, on later carved oak bracket, faults, 13½in (34.5cm) high.
$6,500–8,000 ⚹ S(S)

A mahogany drop-dial wall timepiece, the enamel dial inscribed Mann, Norwich, the single fusee movement with anchor escapement, the case with boxwood stringing, early 19thC, 37in (94cm) high.
$2,500–3,000 ⚹ P(E)

◀ **An Austrian Biedermeier mahogany five light wall clock,** by Anton Carl Greil, Vienna, with maplewood stringing and enamel dial, c1840, 42in (106.5cm) high.
$5,800–6,500 ⊞ C&A

A mahogany weight-driven wall longcase clock, with four-pillar rack and gong striking movement, the painted dial with subsidiary seconds inscribed John Brown, Manchester, the trunk with inlaid barley-twist stringing, early 19thC, 65in (165cm) high.
$2,200–2,600 ⚹ Bon

A Welsh early Victorian mahogany drop-dial wall clock, the dial inscribed D. Goodman, Pontypridd, the two-train fusee movement striking on a bell, c1845, 12in (30.5cm) diam.
$1,000–1,300 ⚹ Hal

A mahogany drop-dial wall clock, the enamel dial inscribed Webster, London, with single fusee movement, 19thC, 7in (18cm) diam.
$800–950 ⚹ SWO

A German Vienna-style walnut wall clock, the eight-day movement striking the half hour and hour on a gong, c1895, 42in (106.5cm) high.
$620–700 ⊞ K&D

American Clocks

Collecting clocks by early American makers is a game for the advanced collector, but there are still many factory-produced clocks that are very affordable for the beginner. Indeed, it is often a factory-made 'OG', produced after the Civil War, or a spring-wound banjo from the early 20th century that are the first acquisitions of someone newly bitten by an interest in this field.

And it is the area where there is much to choose from and compare with, that provides the greatest opportunity for investment growth. Accordingly, factory-produced American clocks (1850–1920) have experienced the greatest increase in demand over the last decade. The five most popular brands have been Ansonia, Seth Thomas, Kroeber, Waterbury and Welch, all companies that produced clocks of high quality and are easily identifiable from the catalogues that they produced containing line drawings of their models. Reprints of these catalogues may be found on the internet or at any good bookstore.

If asked to predict which clocks would prove the best investment over the next decade, we would say American factory-produced weight-driven wall regulators of all sizes. Since 1950, when serious clock collecting began, these models have in general increased ten-fold in value, with certain examples doing even better. For instance, at a recent sale in New Hampshire an E. Howard Regulator No. 60 sold for $34,000 (plus twelve per cent premium), a new record for this model. A good eye and careful research can help you pick those 'better' examples. Some models we would recommend at present are a Seth Thomas No. 2 Regulator, a clean Welch Regulator No. 3, or a Waterbury Willard series weight-driven banjo. As always, originality and condition are prime considerations. For example, a poorly finished and distressed Seth Thomas No. 2 might sell for $600, while a pristine example would easily fetch three times as much.

The internet has had a tremendous effect on collecting in all areas, with thousands of sites available to browse through in search of that special clock. On-line auctions have produced some amazingly high prices for many clocks, but especially for American weight-driven wall regulators. People who would otherwise not have such easy access to old clocks, or information on them, are now able to bid and acquire rare items. As with any medium, it is important that the 'buyer beware' and is satisfied with the integrity of the seller and what rights there are (if any) to return an item that is not as described. **Robert Schmitt**

An American cherrywood eight-day longcase clock, with striking movement, the brass dial inscribed Benjamin Willard, Lexington, with a boss inscribed 'Tempus fugit', with second hand and calendar aperture, bonnet restored, c1771, 82in (208.5cm) high.
$13,700–16,000 ⚴ SK(B)

An American Federal mahogany banjo clock, attributed to Simon Williard, Boston, Massachusetts, the later box door panel decorated with a bucolic scene, c1810, 40in (101.5cm) high.
$3,200–3,600 ⚴ S(NY)

An American inlaid mahogany mantel clock, inscribed Daniel Balch, Newburyport, Massachusetts, c1790, 28¾in (73cm) high.
$50,750–56,000 ⚴ S(NY)

An American Federal mahogany *églomisé* clock with paper label inscribed 'Eli Terry and Sons', Plymouth Connecticut, the painted wooden dial with gilt spandrels enclosing the wooden 30-hour movement, restored, 1810–15, 31¼in (79.5cm) high.
$2,200–2,400 ⚴ SK(B)

▶ **An American Empire shelf clock,** inscribed J. C. Brown, Forrestville, with eight-day brass weight-driven movement, 1840s, 31½in (80cm) high.
$870–1,000 ⊞ AC

An American ginger-read clock, by Ansonia lock Co, c1870, 2in (56cm) high.
220–240 ⊞ **CoD**

A New Haven mahogany dial wall clock, c1880, 23in (58.5cm) high.
$150–180 ⚒ **ROSc**

An American perpetual calendar walnut mantel clock, by Seth Thomas Clock Company, with an enamel dial above a calendar dial, 19thC, 20in (51cm) high.
$400–460 ⚒ **Hal**

An American black wood mantel clock, by Sessions Clock Co, the brass eight-day movement striking the half hour on a bell and the hour on a gong, 1890s, 11¼in (28.5cm) high.
$350–400 ⊞ **AC**

An American clock, by Ansonia Clock Co, entitled Swing No. 1, c1894, 1in (28cm) high.
2,600–3,200 ⚒ **ROSc**

An Ansonia oak ginger-bread clock, restored, c1895, 22in (56cm) high.
$220–240 ⚒ **ROSc**

An E. Ingraham & Co rosewood-veneered poplar Dew Drop timepiece, dial re-papered, c1900, 23in (58.5cm) high.
$250–300 ⚒ **ROSc**

An American gilt and patinated bronze and marble clock, the dial fitted with a gilt-bronze face decorated with putti, flowers, urns, dragons and masks, attributed to Caldwell & Co, New York, early 20thC, 25in (63.5cm) high.
$16,600–18,800 ⚒ **S(NY)**
From its establishment in 1895, Edward F. Caldwell & Co, New York, ranked among the leading American designers of lighting fixtures and objects of vertu. They began to diversify from 1910, producing desk sets, clocks, andirons and furniture.

CLOCKS

A Waterbury Clock Co eight-day porcelain Parlor No. 6 mantel clock, striking the hours on a gong, pendulum missing, c1905, 10in (25.5cm) high.
$300–360 ⚒ **ROSc**

▶ **A Seth Thomas Chime Clock No. 95,** with three-rain movement and silvered dial with bronze numerals, c1922, 11in (28cm) high.
$220–260 ⚒ **ROSc**

A New Haven eight-day golden oak Duchess shelf clock, c1900, 18in (45.5cm) high.
$145–175 ⚒ **ROSc**

A New Haven eight-day Whitney spring banjo clock, striking the hours on a single straight steel rod, with silvered dial, c1925, 30in (76cm) high.
$275–325 ⚒ **ROSc**

A Seth Thomas oak Regulator No. 2, c1920, 36in (91.5cm) high.
$1,750–2,250 ⚒ **ROSc**

British Regulators

A George III table regulator, by Robert Newman, Peckham, with eight-day T-shaped weight-driven movement with Thiout's deadbeat escapement, the dial with outer 2 x 12 hours ring enclosing subsidiary dials for minutes and seconds, baluster dial pillars, bolt and shutter maintaining power, in brass-mounted ebonized case, c1800, 19¾in (50cm) high. **$10,000–12,000** ⚒ S

A Cuban mahogany longcase regulator, by Edward Jones, Bristol, the eight-day striking movement with Harrison's Maintaining Power, c1820, 83in (211cm) high. **$13,000–14,500** ⊞ ALS

A mahogany longcase regulator, by R. Hull, Newmarket, the single train shaped movement with six shaped pillars, six spoke wheels, maintaining power and deadbeat escapement, the dial with outer minute dial and seconds and hour subsidiary dials, 19thC, 72¾in (185cm) high. **$10,000–12,000** ⚒ P

A mahogany regulator wall clock, inscribed Hans Jonathan, Bishop Auckland with four-pillar movement and anchor escapement, the brass dial with single train movement, with subsidiary hour and seconds hand, 19thC, 57½in (146cm) high. **$2,600–3,200** ⚒ Mit

Continental Regulators

A French mahogany four-glass table regulator, by Le Sieur, Paris, the two-train movement with outside pinwheel escapement and countwheel strike on a bell, with heavy nine rod gridiron pendulum, early 19thC, 19¾in (50cm) high.0 **$8,300–10,000** ⚒ P

A walnut Vienna regulato the eight-day spring-driver movement striking on a gor c1870, 32in (81.5cm) high **$2,300–2,600** ⊞ SO

A German Biedermeier mahogany and ormolu-mounted longcase regulator, the brass posted movement with pinwheel escapement, c1820, 93in (236cm) high. **$2,600–3,200** ⚒ S(Am)

▶ **A Black Forest wall regulator,** the going barrel movement with deadbeat escapement, the gridiron pendulum suspended from the backboard, with applied ebonized mouldings, Germany, late 19thC, 13¾in (35cm) high. **$1,800–2,200** ⚒ P

A Biedermeier mahogany and boxwood-strung regulator, with 30-day movement and enamel dial, c1850, 46in (117cm) high. **$9,700–10,700** ⊞ C&A

▶ **A Vienna-style regulator wall clock,** by Gustav Becker, the eight-day striking movement with adjustable pendulum and ivorine level, late 19thC, 42in (106.5cm) high. **$260–320** ⚒ Mit

Colour Review

silver basket, by Elkington & Co,
rmingham 1898, 13¾in (35cm) long.
1,000–1,200 ➹ RTo

A George III silver punch bowl,
by Philip Rundell, London 1819,
13½in (34.5cm) diam, 64oz.
$2,300–2,900 ➹ Mit

An Irish embossed silver bowl,
by J. Morton, Dublin 1929,
5in (12.5cm) diam.
$580–640 ⊞ SIL

silver and steel owl button hook, by Crisford & Norris,
rmingham 1910, 8in (20.5cm) long.
500–580 ⊞ BEX

A pair of Queen Anne
silver tapersticks, by
Edward Yorke, London
1713, restored,
4in (10cm) high, 7oz.
$17,500–20,000 ➹ KT

A pair of silver candle-
sticks, London 1887,
6in (15cm) high.
$900–1,000 ⊞ HEB

An embossed silver
coffee pot, by Benjamin
Godfrey, London 1763,
12in (30.5cm) high.
$3,600–4,300 ➹ HOK

▶ A Norwegian frosted
silver-gilt coffee set, by
David Andersen Christiana,
with bands of champlevé
enamel, Oslo 1897, 25¾oz.
$2,300–2,900 ➹ TEN

George I silver caster, by
erre Platel, London 1714,
n (23cm) high, 18oz.
8,700–10,000 ➹ WW

George III silver-gilt dessert
ervice, by George Smith & William
earn, comprising 73 pieces, the
nives by Moses Brent, London 1793,
e dessert knives with later blades
y John Harris 1825.
3,900–4,300 ➹ S

A Victorian silver cruet,
by J. & N. Creswick, fitted
with eight bottles, Sheffield
1847–48, 10½in (26.5cm)
high, 23oz.
$3,900–4,300 ⊞ NS

▶ A Victorian silver dog
collar, by John Linegar,
Birmingham 1871–72,
6¾in (17cm) diam, 5½oz.
$1,700–2,000 ⊞ NS

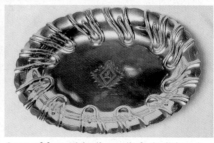

A set of four Irish silver-gilt fruit dishes, by
R. Williams, Dublin c1765, 12in (30.5cm) long.
$29,000–32,000 ⊞ WELD

A George III silver nutmeg grater, in the shape of an acorn, by Robert Sallam, London c1765, 1½in (4cm) high, ½oz.
$2,000–2,200 ⊞ NS

A French silver posy holder, c1870, 4¼in (11cm) long.
$600–700 ⊞ SHa

A Victorian silver baby's rattle, by William Summers, London 1887, 4½in (11.5cm) long, in fitted case.
$1,600–2,000 ⊞ BEX

► **A Victorian silver salver,** by J. B. & E. B., London 1866, 12in (30.5cm) diam.
$600–660 ↗ RBB

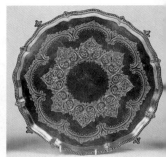

An Irish embossed silver sauce boat, by C. Lamb, Dublin 1910, 6in (15cm) long.
$1,100–1,300 ⊞ SIL

A George III silver tea caddy, by John Hampston and John Prince, York 1779–80, 4¼in (11cm) high, 10oz.
$14,500–16,500 ⊞ NS

◄ **An Irish silver teapot,** by J. M. & E. M., Dublin 1838, 12in (30.5cm) long.
$1,400–1,600 ⊞ HEB

An Irish silver tea caddy, by Hopkins & Hopkins, Dublin 1899, 3in (7.5cm) high.
$870–1,000 ⊞ SIL

A Victorian silver four-piece tea set, by Barnard Brothers, London 1878, 10in (25.5cm) high.
$3,200–4,000 ⊞ CoHA

A Scottish silver four-piece tea service, by Lawson & Co, embossed and chased with various scenes from the works of Robert Burns, Glasgow 1912, hot water pot 8in (20.5cm) high, 60oz.
$2,700–3,000 ↗ P(Ed)

An Irish silver soup tureen, bearing the armorials of the Earls of Shannon, by John Lloyd, Dublin 1782, 15in (38cm) long.
$23,000–26,000 ⊞ WELD

A Scottish silver and agate vinaigrette, by W. Crouch & Son, Edinburgh 1866, 1¾in (4.5cm) long.
$1,900–2,100 ⊞ BEX

A set of six George III silver-gilt teaspoons, by Paul Storr, London 1819–20, 5½in (14cm) long, 10½oz.
$3,200–3,600 ⊞ NS

A red-lacquered eight-day bracket clock, by George Howlett, Marlborough, the fusee movement striking on a bell, with verge escapement, c1770, 21in (53.5cm) high.
$12,300–13,500 ⊞ SO

A George III painted and cut-glass musical table clock, by Markwick, Markham, Perigal, London, for the Turkish market, with six-pillar, three-train fusee movement with later anchor escapement, case redecorated, 27¼in (69cm) high.
$16,000–18,500 ⋏ S

A George III mahogany table clock, by Rogers & Clarke, London, with two-train fusee movement and anchor escapement, 19½in (49.5cm) high.
$2,600–3,200 ⋏ AH

A Scottish satinwood bracket clock, by William Cooper, Hamilton, embellished with ebony, early 19thC, 15¾in (40cm) high.
$5,500–6,500 ⋏ HOK

▶ A Regency brass-inlaid mahogany bracket clock, by Bentley & Beck, London, the five-pillar twin-fusee bell-striking movement with trip hour repeat, 1823, 19½in (49.5cm) high.
$4,000–4,600 ⋏ Bri

◀ A calamander eight-day bracket/table clock, by John Roger Arnold, London, the movement striking and repeating the hours on a bell, c1810, 16½in (42cm) high.
$9,400–10,000 ⊞ PAO

A Chippendale-style astronomical/astrological eight-day bracket clock, by Thomas Berry, Ormskirk, the later triple fusee movement chiming on nine bells, late 18thC, 31in (78.5cm) high.
$72,500–87,000 ⋏ RBB
This clock had stood untouched in the hall of a country residence for years. It is an exceptional piece as the astronomical and astrological features are extremely rare and the case, dated 1787, bears a label for the cabinet-maker James Moorcroft of Ormskirk who was associated with Thomas Chippendale. Although some people thought the piece was crudely constructed in places, others were of the opinion that they would never see another like it, and one person was prepared to do battle to $72,500 to secure it.

▶ A Regency brass-inlaid mahogany eight-day clock, by S. Gremels Schwar & Co, Greenwich, the movement striking on bell, 22in (56cm) high.
$2,300–2,900 ⋏ AG

An ormolu eight-day portico clock, by Paul Garnier, with gilded mounts, the movement striking the half hour and hour on a bell, c1865, 17in (43cm) high.
$4,600–5,000 ⊞ K&D

◄ A French Empire ormolu
eight-day clock, by
Gentilhomme, Paris, with
original fire gilding, the
movement striking on a bell,
c1810, 17in (43cm) high.
$8,000–8,800 ⊞ JIL

A French inlaid-mahogany
and gilt-bronze portico
clock, the movement
striking on a bell, mid-
19thC, 32in (81.5cm) high.
$725–800 ⊞ KB

A French ormolu-
mounted boulle-cased
bracket clock, inscribed
'French City Observatory,
London', the two-train
movement striking on a gong,
19thC, 14in (35.5cm) high.
$2,600–3,200 ⚒ G(B)

A Black Forest wooden
chamber clock, attributed to
Michael or Joseph Laserer,
with painted wooden dial,
countwheel lacking, 18thC,
12in (30.5cm) high.
$5,500–6,000 ⚒ S

A French ormolu eight-
day mantel clock, by
Marti, Paris, the movement
striking on a bell, c1870,
12in (30.5cm) high.
$3,200–3,600 ⊞ SO

► A French tortoiseshell
boulle eight-day mantel
clock, by Marti, Paris, the
movement striking the half
hour and hour on a gong,
c1890, 18in (45.5cm) high.
$1,900–2,100 ⊞ K&D

A French brass-inlaid
mahogany eight-day
mantel clock, by
Martin, Paris, c1900,
15in (38cm) high.
$1,300–1,400 ⊞ PTh

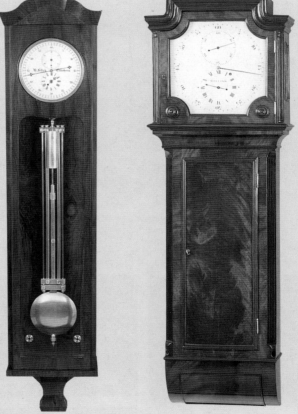

A Cromwellian lantern clock, by Thomas Loomes, London, the posted movement with conversion to verge and pendulum escapement, alarm disc and train missing, c1655, 13¼in (33.5cm) high.
$10,000–12,300 ✒ S

A French lantern clock, by Le Franc, Vire, the original verge escapement with silk suspension, striking the half hour and hour, restored, dated '1746', 13in (33cm) high.
$3,600–4,300 ⊞ BL

A gilt-brass and silvered carriage clock, by Le Roy et Fils, Paris, the brass lever escapement with a plain brass balance wheel, c1840, 6¼in (16cm) high.
$8,700–9,500 ✒ Bon
The back is engraved 'This Clock formerly belonged to Thomas Carlyle 1795–1881 and was given to him by Lord Ashburton. Sold at Sotheby's with other Carlyle relics June 14th 1932'.

An eight-day carriage clock, by P. & A. Drocourt, the lever movement striking the half hour and hour on a gong, with repeat and alarm, 19thC, 5½in (14cm) high, with red leather carrying case.
$2,300–2,900 ✒ HAM

A gilt gorge-cased carriage clock, by Henri Lepine, retailed by Dent, repeating on a bell, the white enamel dial with Roman numerals, c1855, 5in (12.5cm) high.
$5,500–6,000 ⊞ JIL

A gorge-cased champlevé-panelled carriage clock, by Drocourt, c1890, 6½in (16.5cm) high.
$4,600–5,200 ⊞ BELL

A brass-cased carriage clock, with hand-painted side panels and a repeater movement, late 19thC, 7in (18cm) high.
$2,600–3,200 ✒ JAd

An early George III gilt-wood cartel clock, the dial inscribed Joshua Hewlett, Bristol, the two-train fusee movement with verge escapement striking on a bell, lacking bell stand, c1760, 24in (61cm) high.
$10,800–12,000 ✒ S

◄ **A Louis XVI-style ormolu-mounted marble garniture,** by Japy Frères, the clock with eight-day movement striking on a bell, c1890, 14in (35.5cm) high.
$4,000–4,600 ⊞ JIL

A French gilt-bronze and painted-porcelain mantel clock garniture, the bell-striking Japy movement with Brocot suspension, faults, c1880, candelabra 23¼in (59cm) high.
$10,000–11,500 ✒ S(S)

A silver-gilt clock, by Cartier, the enamel surround set with diamonds, c1910, 3¼in (8.5cm) diam.
$7,600–8,300 ⊞ SHa

◄ **A French marble and patinated-bronze clock garniture,** the clock case and obelisks incised with hieroglyphs, late 19thC, clock 17¼in (44cm) wide.
$6,500–7,250 ✒ P

A French gilt-metal eight-day steeple mantel clock, late 19thC, 23in (58.5cm) high.
$1,300–1,600 ✒ RBB

A walnut-inlaid longcase clock, by Simon de Charmes, London, the five-pillar trip-repeating rack and bell striking movement with five wheels in each train, c1715, 77¾in (197.5cm) high.
$16,000–18,500 ✗ S

A walnut longcase clock, by Thomas Kefford, Royston, with a brass dial, early 18thC, 72in (183cm) high.
$5,000–6,000 ✗ MEA

A burr walnut eight-day longcase clock, by Brownless, Staindrop, with three-train quarter chiming movement on six bells by countwheel, c1725, 92in (233.5cm) high.
$36,250–43,500 ⊞ ALS

A walnut longcase clock, by Simon de Charmes, London, decorated overall in floral marquetry, early 18thC, 104¾in (266cm) high.
$4,700–5,700 ✗ HOK

◀ **A burr walnut longcase clock,** by Windmills, London, the movement with ringed pillars, anchor escapement and inside countwheel strike, early 18thC, 92in (233.5cm) high.
$8,300–10,000 ✗ P

An eight-day longcase clock, by John Meredith, London, the five-pillar movement striking the hours on a bell, with strike/silent facility to the arch, the green lacquer case with gilt chinoiseries, c1750, 98in (249cm) high.
$10,800–12,000 ⊞ PAO

An oak eight-day longcase clock, by William Miller, Southampton, the five-pillar movement striking the hours on a bell, c1755, 86in (218.5cm) high.
$8,700–9,700 ⊞ PAO

▶ **A mahogany longcase clock,** by James Tregent, London, with five-pillar rack and bell striking movement, c1770, 99in (251.5cm) high.
$6,500–8,000 ✗ Bon

A Welsh fruitwood longcase clock, by Richard Watkins, Merthyr Tydfil, with a brass dial and 30-hour movement, c1750, 79in (200.5cm) high.
$5,000–5,500 ⊞ CoA

An oak and mahogany eight-day longcase clock, by James Kelsey, Hull, the movement striking on the hour, c1770, 91½in (232.5cm) high. **$2,600–3,200** ✗ M

An American walnut longcase clock, by Benjamin Morris, New Britain, Pennsylvania, with four-pillar rack and bell striking movement, 1777, 103½in (263cm) high. **$50,750–58,000** ✗ Bon

A Welsh oak longcase clock, by James Harvey, Abergavenny, the 30-hour movement with anchor escapement, striking on a bell, bell lacking, 18thC, 78in (198cm) high. **$1,400–1,700** ✗ P(EA)

A George III mahogany eight-day longcase clock, by Richard Stimson, Ely, the movement rack striking on a bell, c1780, 99in (251.5cm) high. **$18,000–20,000** ⊞ JIL

◀ **An oak longcase clock,** by Thomas Gregory, Odiham, the four-pillar movement with Dutch twin-bell striking movement, c1780, 80½in (204.5cm) high. **$3,600–4,300** ✗ Bon

An inlaid oak eight-day longcase clock, by Samuel Davy, Norwich, the five-pillar movement striking the hours on a bell, the dial with strike/silent feature to the arch, c1775, 83in (211cm) high. **$9,800–10,800** ⊞ PAO

A George III mahogany and banded eight-day longcase clock, by Harriman, Workington, 90in (228.5cm) high. **$3,300–4,000** ✗ E

A George III oak and mahogany longcase clock, now with 13in arched white dial inscribed 'E W Bank, Elland', the 30-hour four-pillar count-wheel movement striking on a bell, 89in (226cm) high. **$800–900** ✗ DOC

A George III oak and mahogany eight-day longcase clock, the arch painted with a figure on a horse by a stable, with a striking movement, 89in (226cm) high. **$1,400–1,700** ✗ E

◀ **A George III stained softwood eight-day longcase clock,** the break-arch dial painted with a lakeland scene, inscribed 'Jackson & Son, Tavistock', the movement striking on a bell, 85in (216cm) high. **$1,600–1,900** ✗ RTo

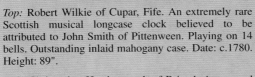

An oak and mahogany-crossbanded eight-day longcase clock, by Heaton, Bierley, c1780, 89¼in (226.5cm) high.
$2,400–2,900 ⚒ **AH**

An oak and mahogany-crossbanded eight-day longcase clock, by Shaw, Newcastle, the painted dial with moonphases, the movement striking the hours on a bell, c1785, 91in (231cm) high.
$5,500–6,000 ⊞ **K&D**

A mahogany longcase clock, with painted dial, the moonphase stamped to the reverse with 'Wilson, Birm', the four-pillar movement striking the hours on a bell, possibly by H. Lees, Middleton, c1790, 86¾in (220.5cm) high.
$5,000–6,000 ⚒ **B&L**

A walnut longcase clock, by John Ellicott, London, the twin-train movement with five ringed pillars and anchor escapement, 18thC, 100½in (255.5cm) high.
$13,000–16,000 ⚒ **P**

An oak eight-day longcase clock, by Samuel Collett, Illminster, with early 'Wilson' painted dial, c1790, 80in (203cm) high.
$7,000–7,700 ⊞ **ALS**

◀ **A mahogany eight-day longcase clock,** by Clare, Manchester, the silvered and brass dial with rolling moon and engraved armillary sphere and globe, c1790, 101¼in (257cm) high.
$8,700–10,000 ⚒ **TEN**

An oak eight-day longcase clock, by Willliam Giscard, Ely, the movement striking the hours on a bell, the corners of the dial painted with roses and foliage, the arch with an oval rural scene with a lady, c1795, 81in (205.5cm) high.
$6,500–7,250 ⊞ **PAO**

A George III mahogany eight-day longcase clock, by Joseph Denton, Hull, the arch painted with a miniature of a lady, the movement striking on a bell, c1790, 91in (231cm) high.
$11,500–13,000 ⊞ **JIL**

▶ **A Scottish flame-mahogany eight-day longcase clock,** by Francis Henderson, Musselburgh, with a painted dial, c1795, 85in (216cm) high.
$10,800–11,800 ⊞ **ALS**

An oak eight-day longcase clock, by Richard Wright, Chelmsford, with five-pillar striking movement, late 18thC, 87in (221cm) high.
$3,300–4,000 ⚒ **CAG**

Edward Jones, Bristol, 1818-30. Classic late Regency Cuban mahogany striking regulator with high count wheel trains, dead beat escapement, and Harrison's maintaining power. 83in (211cm).

Allan Smith

LONGCASE CLOCKS

'Amity Cottage' 162 Beechcroft Road
Upper Stratton, Swindon, Wiltshire SN2 7QE
PHONE/FAX: (01793) 822977 · MOBILE: 07778 834342
Email: allansmithclocks@lineone.net
INTERNET (ON-LINE CATALOGUE): www.allan-smith-antique-clocks.co.uk

Open any day or evening by appointment

I try to maintain stocks which are decorative, unusual, of good quality, proportions and originality. I can usually offer automata, moonphase, painted dial, brass dial, 30-hour, 8-day, London and provincial examples in oak, mahogany, lacquer, walnut and marquetry. From circa 1700 to circa 1840. All properly and sympathetically restored to very high standards. 40-50 good examples usually in stock.

Colour brochure available on request

Worldwide shipping

Clockfinder service

Insurance valuations

Fine clocks always wanted

12 Months Written Guarantee

FREE UK DELIVERY & SETTING UP
(Less than 10 minutes from M4 junction 15)

John Ebsworth, London. Circa 1685. Fine and rare olivewood and marquetry longcase clock with 10in brass dial, bolt and shutter maintaining power and five latched pillars. Original rising hood. 78in (198cm).

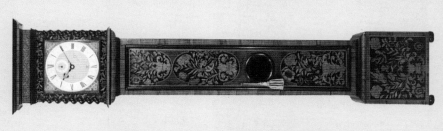

An inlaid mahogany eight-day longcase clock, by Abraham, Frome, the arch with automata depiction of Adam and Eve, the movement striking on a bell, c1800, 90in (228.5cm) high. **$12,300–13,500 ⊞ PAO**

A George III oak and mahogany-crossbanded eight-day longcase clock, the painted enamel dial with moonphase and castle and with painted spandrels, 91¾in (233cm) high. **$2,900–3,500 ⚒ L&E**

▶ **An oak and mahogany eight-day longcase clock,** by Peter Booth, Dukinfield, with a painted dial, the four-pillar false plate movement with anchor escapement, early 19thC, 90in (228.5cm) high. **$850–1,000 ⚒ DOC**

A mahogany eight-day longcase clock, by William Hall, North Shields, with moonphase in the arch, the movement striking on a bell, formerly with sweep date hand, faults, c1800, 93in (236cm) high. **$5,400–6,000 ⚒ S(S)**

A mahogany eight-day longcase clock, by F. Harrison, Hexham, the arch painted with a fisherman mending his net, pediment depleted, early 19thC, 89in (226cm) high. **$1,600–1,900 ⚒ PFK**

A George III mahogany eight-day longcase clock, by William Collett, Uxbridge, the arch painted with a farmyard scene, with rocking see-saw to the striking five-pillar movement, 90in (228.5cm) high. **$12,300–14,500 ⚒ CAG**

An oak and mahogany-crossbanded longcase clock, by Edward Thompson, Ellesmere, the painted dial with rolling moonphase, the spandrels painted with figures emblematic of the seasons, with twin-train movement, early 19thC, 87in (221cm) high. **$1,800–2,200 ⚒ DMC**

A mahogany eight-day longcase clock, by Lamplough, Bridlington, the arch depicting the Judgement of Solomon, the spandrels painted with figures emblematic of the seasons, early 19thC, 85¾in (218cm) high. **$2,900–3,200 ⚒ TEN**

◀ **An inlaid oak eight-day longcase clock,** by Newall, Cleobury, the white dial with moonphase to the arch, with painted figures to the spandrels, the door inlaid with a country scene and eagle roundel, c1810, 87¾in (223cm) high. **$4,500–5,500 ⚒ Bri**

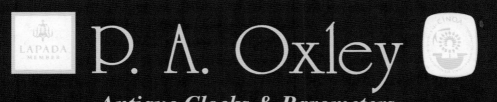

An oak eight-day long-case clock, by David Bell, Stirling, the movement striking the hours on a bell, the arch and corners of the dial painted with flowers, c1825, 85in (216cm) high.
$5,000–5,800 ⊞ PAO

An oak and mahogany-crossbanded eight-day longcase clock, by Edward Bell, Uttoxeter, the arch dial painted with rural scenes, 19thC, 86¼in (219cm) high.
$2,100–2,600 ✗ WL

► A mahogany eight-day longcase clock, by John Bullock, Melksham, the arch painted with a family and a horse and carriage passing through a toll, the movement striking the hours on a bell, c1830, 87in (221cm) high.
$9,500–10,500 ⊞ PAO

An oak eight-day longcase clock, by Edward Crow, Faversham, the spandrels painted with roses and with a country house scene to the arch, the movement striking the hours on a bell, c1820, 86in (218.5cm) high.
$7,250–8,000 ⊞ PAO
The cresting on the hood is a typical feature of Kentish clocks.

A mahogany longcase clock, by Thomas Whitford, London, with five-pillar rack and bell striking movement, c1820, 91in (231cm) high.
$6,800–8,000 ✗ Bon

A Welsh pine longcase clock, by Phillips, Narberth, Pembrokeshire, the spandrels and arch painted with rural scenes, early 19thC, 85in (216cm) high.
$2,100–2,300 ⊞ POT

A flame-mahogany eight-day longcase clock, by A. Guanella, Bristol, with a painted dial and moonphase, c1830, 84in (213.5cm) high.
$10,800–12,000 ⊞ ALS

A mahogany eight-day longcase clock, by Samuel Collings, Thornbury, with moonphase to the arch inscribed 'High Water at Bristol Quay', the brass dial formerly silvered, with a striking movement, 19thC, 89in (226cm) high.
$4,300–5,000 ✗ CAG

A Scottish mahogany and boxwood-lined eight-day longcase clock, by Edward Brown, Edinburgh, the anchor escapement striking on a bell, 19thC, 84½in (214.5cm) high.
$4,300–5,000 ✗ P(Ed)

◄ An oak longcase clock, by S. Shortman, Newnham with 30-hour movement, c1830, 84½in (214.5cm) high.
$3,600–4,000 ⊞ MTay

A flame mahogany and string-inlaid eight-day longcase clock, with moonphase to the arch, the movement striking the hours on a bell, c1840, 90in (228.5cm) high.
$10,000–11,500 ⊞ PAO

A Scottish early Victorian mahogany eight-day drumhead longcase clock, by D. Saunders, Dumbarton, the twin-train movement with anchor escapement, 80¾in (205cm) high.
$2,200–2,600 ⚒ P(Ed)

An early Victorian figured mahogany eight-day longcase clock, by H. Yeomans, Nottingham, the dial painted with groups of saints, with striking movement, feet lacking, 87¾in (223cm) high.
$2,300–2,900 ⚒ P(WM)

A mahogany eight-day longcase clock, by Thomas Knight, Bristol, with moonphase, the spandrels painted with flowers and foliage, the movement striking the hours on a bell, c1845, 89in (226cm) high.
$9,300–10,300 ⊞ PAO

A Scottish oak and mahogany eight-day longcase clock, by Walter Leighton, Montrose, with chiming movement, mid-19thC, 90in (228.5cm) high.
$1,300–1,600 ⚒ DD

A mahogany eight-day longcase clock, with satinwood line inlay, the movement striking on a bell, 19thC, 77½in (197cm) high.
$1,300–1,600 ⚒ RTo

◄ **A Welsh oak and mahogany eight-day longcase clock,** by S. Furtwengler, Llanelli, c1860, 89in (226cm) high.
$4,000–4,600 ⊞ CoA

► **A late Victorian carved mahogany longcase clock,** by Gaydon & Sons, Kingston-on-Thames, the three-train movement with anchor escapement striking the quarters on eight bells and four gongs, 94½in (240cm) high.
$5,000–5,800 ⚒ P(EA)

A Jersey inlaid mahogany eight-day longcase clock, by Thomas De Gruchy, the case with boxwood stringing and ivory inlays, the painted dial with moonphase to the arch, c1850, 79½in (202cm) high.
$4,600–5,500 ⚒ B&L

A Jersey mahogany eight-day longcase clock, with striking movement, 19thC, 92in (233.5cm) high.
$3,300–4,000 ⚒ SWO

A late Victorian oak longcase clock, by Arnold & Lewis, Manchester, with moonphase mechanism, the case with foliate, scrolled and gadrooned details, 82½in (209.5cm) high.
$4,300–5,000 ⚒ WL

A Frisian polychrome-painted quarter-striking alarm *stoelklok*, the movement with verge escapement, 18thC, 29in (73.5cm) high.
$1,900–2,200 ➶ **S(Am)**

◄ **An American Federal time and strike *églomisé* shelf clock,** by Aaron Willard, Boston, Massachusetts, restored, c1817, 35in (89cm) high.
$8,000–8,800 ➶ **SK(B)**

A German walnut wall clock, the spring-driven movement striking on a gong, late 19thC, 32in (81.5cm) high.
$580–650 ⊞ **KB**

A mother-of-pearl inlaid rosewood eight-day wall clock, by Ebenezer Rossiter, Clevedon, the fusee movement with shaped plates and anchor escapement, with drop dial, c1875, 28in (71cm) high.
$3,200–3,600 ⊞ **PAO**

◄ **An American cast-iron clock,** by Ansonia, c1880, 17¾in (45cm) high.
$360–430 ⊞ **BLA**

A German walnut and fruitwood wall clock, with single-train timepiece spring-driven movement, the trunk door inset with mercury thermometer, the base with an aneroid barometer, late 19thC, 28in (71cm) high.
$500–600 ➶ **PFK**

A Laterndluhr mahogany wall regulator, by Alexander Reschnovan in Zombar, with maplewood stringing, the enamel dial signed, c1825, 62in (157.5cm) high.
$98,000–108,000 ⊞ **C&A**

A Victorian mahogany skeletonized longcase regulator, attributed to John Smith & Son, London, the movement with deadbeat escapement, c1860, 81¼in (206.5cm) high.
$50,000–70,000 ⚒ **S**

▶ **A French gilt and marble four-glass table regulator,** by Cro Garnier & Cia, the twin-train movement with deadbeat escapement, mid-19thC, 20½in (52cm) high.
$9,000–10,000 ⚒ **P**

A rosewood _grande sonnerie_ eight-day Vienna regulator, striking the hours and quarters, c1840, 42in (106.5cm) high.
$7,250–8,000 ⊞ **SO**

A walnut eight-day Vienna regulator, with maintaining power mechanism and deadbeat escapement, c1840, 40in (101.5cm) high.
$3,300–3,800 ⊞ **SO**

A silver pair-cased verge watch with alarm, by Soret, London, late 17thC, 60mm diam.
$2,500–2,900 ⚒ P

A Swiss gold and enamel cylinder watch, by Achard, Geneva, c1780, 51mm diam.
$4,300–4,700 ⊞ PT

A French gold and enamel verge watch, c1810, 42mm diam.
$3,600–4,000 ⊞ PT

A Swiss gold and enamel watch, by Tannen, Kufstein, in the shape of a lute, set with seed pearls, with a later Swiss keyless watch movement, 19thC, 64mm long.
$1,400–1,700 ⚒ P

◄ **An 18ct gold hunter cased watch,** by James McCabe, London, with duplex escapement, 1820, 55mm diam.
$1,900–2,200 ⚒ S

A Swiss gold, enamel, ruby and diamond form watch, modelled as a beetle, c1870, 50mm long.
$8,700–10,000 ⊞ SHa

A Swiss gold and enamel form watch, by Stauffer, Geneva, in the shape of a stylized leaf, set to one side with diamonds, late 19thC, 32mm wide.
$2,200–2,600 ⚒ P

A French enamel fob watch, mounted on silver and decorated with seed pearls, c1880, 25mm wide.
$1,400–1,600 ⊞ BeE

A lady's gold and enamel hunter cased lapel watch, by Girard Perregaux, c1900, 24mm diam.
$2,200–2,400 ⚒ S(NY)

A gold hunter pocket watch, by Edward F. Ashley, with associated 9ct white and yellow gold fob chain, c1900, 50mm diam, with original box.
$580–720 ⚒ LJ

A Swiss silver-gilt and turquoise fob watch, on a matching fob, early 20thC, 28mm diam.
$290–320 ⚒ Bon

A Swiss gold and enamel cylinder fob watch, with a bow, early 20thC, 31mm diam.
$290–340 ⚒ Bon

A Baume & Mercier Continental gold mystery watch, the dial with 12 diamond numerals around a rotating centre set with two further diamonds, one larger than the other to indicate hours and minutes, c1960, 34mm diam.
$1,000–1,200 ⚷ P

A Jaeger LeCoultre platinum and diamond bracelet watch, dial inscribed 'Cartier', 1950s, 6in (15cm) long.
$14,500–16,000 ⚷ RM

◄ A Glycine Watch Co platinum, diamond and emerald bracelet watch, retailed by Tiffany, c1930, 6in (15cm) long.
$2,600–3,200 ⚷ S

An 18ct gold Omega Constellation watch and bracelet, 1966, with original box and paperwork.
$2,100–2,300 ⊞ JoV

A Rolex Bubbleback bi-colour automatic watch, with non-factory-made bracelet, 1940s, 32mm diam.
$1,700–2,000 ⚷ Bon

A Rolex 10ct gold watch, with an associated bracelet, c1950, 35mm diam.
$500–600 ⚷ LJ

A Vacheron & Constantin 18ct gold and diamond bracelet watch, with integrated mesh bracelet, Geneva, c1950, 30mm long, with fitted case.
$2,600–3,200 ⚷ S(NY)

A mahogany wheel barometer, by Luiseti, London, c1780, 41in (104cm) high. **$5,000–5,800** ⊞ RAY

A George III mahogany wheel barometer, by Pioti, Lincoln, 37in (94cm) high. **$900–1,100** ✗ DOC

▶ **A mahogany wheel barometer,** by J. Gironimo, Bristol, inlaid with boxwood and ebony stringing, c1840, 10in (25.5cm) diam. **$1,700–2,000** ⊞ PAO

◀ **A French painted wood stick barometer,** by A. Goubeaux, Paris, c1820, 38in (96.5cm) high. **$1,700–2,200** ⊞ RAY

A satinwood wheel barometer, by Lione & Somalvico & Co, London, crossbanded with tulipwood, c1800, 43in (109cm) high. **$5,000–6,500** ⊞ RAY

A French giltwood-framed *églomisé* and foil wall barometer, the gilt dial signed 'Gohin Père et Fils/rue Neuve S. Eustache 24', Paris, early 19thC, 34in (86.5cm) high. **$3,600–4,300** ✗ NOA

A mother-of-pearl-inlaid rosewood wheel barometer and timepiece, by J. & C. Corbetta, London, c1840, 49in (124.5cm) high. **$5,000–6,000** ✗ S

A flame-mahogany bow-front stick barometer, by Troughton, London, c1830, 37in (94cm) high. **$10,000–11,000** ⊞ AW

◀ **A Victorian rosewood clock barometer,** by G. Rossi, Norwich, the case inlaid with mother-of-pearl, c1850, 53in (134.5cm) high. **$5,800–7,200** ⊞ RAY

A Scottish early Victorian mahogany wheel barometer, by Favone, Dundee, level bezel missing, 43¼in (110cm) high. **$1,400–1,700** ✗ P(Ed)

A French-style carved giltwood wheel barometer, by Silo, London, c1860, 44in (112cm) high. **$2,100–2,300** ⊞ PAO

Watches

Pocket Watches

A Dutch silver pair-cased verge watch, by J. van der Cloesen, Leiden, mid-18thC, 56mm diam.
1,500–1,700 ✗ S(Am)

A silver pair-cased verge watch, by G. Greenfield, London 1770, 50mm diam.
$900–1,000 ⊞ PT

An Irish 22ct gold pair-cased cylinder watch, by George Walker, Dublin 1744, 49mm diam.
$3,000–3,300 ⊞ PT

A sterling silver pair-cased verge pocket watch, painted with farm scenes, 1800, 55mm diam.
470–550 ✗ LJ

A Swiss engraved gold quarter-repeating cylinder watch, by Vacheron & Constantin, the rear cover with distressed enamel scene, mid-19thC, 34mm diam.
$870–1,000 ✗ P

A George III silver pair-cased pocket watch, by G. Peekey, London, the outer case with floral and foliate chased surround, the back embossed with classical figures among ruins, 40mm diam.
$400–470 ✗ GAK

◀ An American gold full hunter watch, by Waltham Watch Co, Massachusetts, c1870, 54mm diam.
$870–1,000 ⊞ PT

Miller's is a price GUIDE not a price LIST

A silver open-faced verge watch, by William Brownsword, Nottingham, the enamel dial decorated with Masonic symbols, in a later case, marked for London 1882, 52mm diam.
440–500 ✗ Bon

A silver-cased chrono-graph, by J. Harris & Son, Manchester, marked Chester 1884, 65mm diam.
$470–540 ⊞ GLa

WATCHES

A 14ct gold hunter minute watch, by Henry Moser, with repeating keyless lever movement, c1890, 51mm diam.
$3,000–3,300 ⚲ S

A silver open-faced pocket watch, with a later-painted scene of countryside, Chester 1891.
$360–400 ⊞ HARP

A late Victorian 18ct gold half hunter pocket watch, 50mm diam.
$580–720 ⚲ GAK

An 18ct gold open-faced pocket watch, by Arthur Brewer, 1895, dial 35mm diam.
$320–370 ⊞ HARP

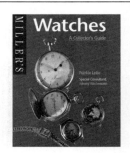

To find out more see *Miller's Watches: A Collector's Guide* (£5.99), with over 130 colour pictures, its 64 pages are packed with invaluable information. *Order from* www.millers.uk.com *or telephone in the UK on* 01933 443863

A 14ct gold lady's open-faced pocket watch, c1897, 30mm diam.
$370–440 ⊞ DQ

A Swiss gold and enamel open-faced fob watch, by Patek Philippe, the case with a purple *guilloche* enamelled back set with a central gemstone, c1900, 32mm diam.
$1,500–1,750 ⚲ Bon

A GWR guard's pocket watch, by Northwood & Sons, Bedford, c1920.
$300–360 ⊞ TIC

A Swiss 18ct gold engine-turned hunter pocket watch, stamped, c1910, 40mm diam.
$550–600 ⊞ GLa

An American 14ct gold open-faced pocket watch, by Illinois, signed by A. Lincoln, c1926, 50mm diam.
$1,000–1,100 ⊞ GLa

A 9ct gold half hunter pocket watch, by J. W. Benson, London 1927, with a gold triangular link watch chain, cased.
$500–600 ⚲ KID

An nickel open-faced railway watch, by English Watch Co, for Iraq State Railways, c1920, 55mm diam.
$170–200 ⚲ Bon

Wristwatches

An Eterna 18ct gold calendar wristwatch, with automatic centre seconds, with gilt dial, 1970s, 33mm diam, on a 14ct gold bracelet.
$440–500 ✗ Bon

A Swiss Side-of-the-Wrist Driver's watch, inscribed Craftsman, manual wind, 1930s.
$580–650 ⊞ HARP

An Arisco silver wrist-watch, with hinged front and back and enamelled dial, 1920s.
$5–110 ⊞ JoV

A Bulova stainless steel Spaceview Tuning Fork wristwatch, 1964, 35mm diam.
$500–580 ⊞ Bns

◀ **A Longines 9ct gold lady's demi-hunter wristwatch,** with 16 jewel lever movement, c1908, 30mm diam.
$650–850 ⊞ GLa

▶ **An Omega silver wrist-watch,** with white porcelain dial, c1918, 35mm diam.
$500–600 ⊞ Bns

An Omega 14ct gold moonphase wristwatch, c1950, 38mm diam.
$3,000–3,300 ⊞ TWD

A Record Watch Co military wristwatch, manual wind, with luminous markers and hands, c1950.
$190–220 ⊞ HARP

◄ **A Swiss 18ct gold and diamond set wristwatch,** for Rado, with 17 jewel movement, c1930, 20mm diam.
$1,450–1,700 ⊞ GLa

A Swiss Rolex silver lever wristwatch, with luminous hands, London 1916, 34mm diam.
$1,100–1,250 ⊞ PT

A Rolex Oyster Perpetua Chronometer Bubble-back pink-gold and stainless steel wrist-watch, self-winding, water-resistant, 1940s.
$3,000–3,300 ⊞ Bns

A Rolex stainless steel wristwatch, with 15 jewel movement, numbered case, 1940s.
$1,600–1,900 ⚲ FHF

A Rolex Precision lady's cocktail wristwatch, early 1950s, 17mm diam.
$2,300–2,500 ⚲ P

A Rolex 18ct gold lady's wristwatch, 1960s, 18mm diam.
$360–430 ⚲ Bon

A Smiths Astral 9ct gold wristwatch, 1970, 75mm diam, in original box
$160–180 ⊞ AOH

A Universal rose-gold-plated moonphase calendar wristwatch, with manual wind movement, original dial, c1945.
$1,600–1,800 ⊞ HARP

A Stowa pilot's aluminium wristwatch, with luminous hour and minute numerals, with centre seconds, mid-20thC, 55mm diam.
$870–1,000 ⚲ P

A Van Cleef & Arpels 18c gold bracelet watch, c1960, 13mm wide.
$2,000–2,300 ⚲ S(G)

◄ **A Vertex British army issue wristwatch,** 1950s
$230–250 ⊞ JoV

WATCHES

Barometers

Barometers continue to be a popular item in the antiques market and, as with every other speciality, there have been varying grees of growth in prices over recent years. ailability, quality and fashion are the factors at influence both dealer and auction prices. Perhaps for most buyers barometers come at e end of their list of requirements when rnishing a home with antiques. But, with the ntinuing preoccupation in the media with e vagaries of our weather, and the peculiar ends that seem to be occurring at present, it not surprising that many people would like be able to forecast changes in the weather r themselves.

The standard banjo or wheel barometer is still eat value, despite slightly increasing in price between about $725 and $1,450, depending whether it has been bought unrestored at action, or in restored condition from a dealer. ick barometers have seen a bigger increase in ice, and it is almost impossible to find a od example for less than $1,450.

As with every field of antiques, the rare and fine amples fetch higher prices, so the most desirable heel barometers now sell for over $2,625 and e best stick barometers in excess of $7,250. The more decorative barometers, for instance e wonderfully ornate French examples (*see* page 432), are being seen as complementary to other wall-hung items such as mirrors and paintings and this trend will no doubt escalate as interior designers become involved and appreciate their value.

The demise of the mercury barometer dates from the mid-19th century, when production began of aneroid barometers and barographs that were both cheaper to manufacture and easier to transport. Victorian aneroid barometers can be purchased for as little as a few hundred dollars, and travelling barometers with two or three inch dials are also becoming popular. Admiral Fitzroy barometers of this period now fetch between $580 and $1,300 and are being bought as decorative objects as well as working instruments.

Barographs are now sought-after, but due to limited supply, particularly of instruments with mahogany cases and bevelled glasses, the price range is currently between $870 and $1,750.

At the top end of the market it is not unusual to see prices of over $72,500 being paid for the rarest of instruments dating from the beginning of the 18th century and made by the finest English clockmakers. However, even if your disposable income limits you to less exalted pieces, barometers remain a fascinating collecting area with good investment potential.

Derek and Tina Rayment

Stick Barometers

mahogany stick arometer, by Abraham haw, Billingborough, ith silvered scales, 780, 35½in (90cm) long.
,600–4,300 ⊞ RAY

A Cuban mahogany stick barometer, by G. Adams, London, with silvered brass register plate and exposed tube, c1790, 38½in (98cm) long.
$3,300–3,900 ⊞ AW

A Dutch inlaid mahogany barometer, by Gebr. Bazerga, Rotterdam, with engraved pewter dial, restored, 18thC and later, 47¾in (121.5cm) high.
$3,600–4,300 ➴ S(Am)

◄ **A mahogany stick barometer,** by James Long, London, c1780, 36in (91.5cm) long.
$6,500–7,250 ⊞ RAY

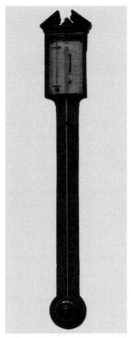

A late George III boxwood and ebony line-inlaid mahogany stick barometer, the silvered plate with thermometer and vernier scale, 40in (101.5cm) high.
$720–870 ⚒ **E**

When sold at auction, barometers have sometimes undergone alterations to their mechanisms, or are in unrestored condition, which may affect the prices realized.

A mahogany stick barometer, by G. B. Ronchetti, Manchester, the silvered brass register plate with exposed tube, c1810, 38in (96.5cm) high.
$2,600–2,900 ⊞ **AW**

A French Louis Philippe rosewood stick barometer, by Chevallier, Paris, mid-19thC, 41½in (105.5cm) high.
$1,500–1,700 ⚒ **NOA**

A Scottish oak stick barometer, by Hay & Lyall, Aberdeen, with bone aslant scale, 38in (96.5cm) long.
$2,000–2,200 ⚒ **PAO**

◄ **An oak carved stick barometer,** by Markham Gainsborough, c1875, 40in (101.5cm) high.
$2,300–2,600 ⊞ **AB**

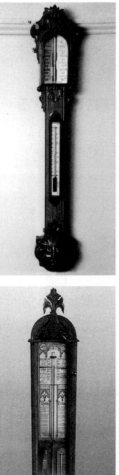

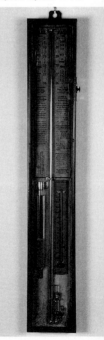

A walnut stick barometer, by Chamberlain, London, with ivory register plates, c1870, 39in (99cm) long.
$2,200–2,600 ⊞ **AW**

A French fruitwood stick barometer, by Pardi & G. Corti, Strasbourg & Luneville, c1850, 38in (96.5cm) long.
$950–1,200 ⊞ **RAY**

▶ **An oak Admiral Fitzroy's barometer,** the glazed case with paper label, with design registration mark 8th August 1881, 47in (119.5cm) high.
$880–1,100 ⚒ **Mit**

A miniature mahogany Admiral Fitzroy's barometer, with original charts, c1880, 34½in (87.5cm) high.
$800–1,000 ⊞ **RAY**

Wheel Barometers

A George III mahogany barometer, by B. Biola, Cambridge, with boxwood stringing and shell medallion inlay, 37¾in (96cm) high.
$1,000–1,200 ➔ P(EA)

A Louis Philippe mahogany wheel barometer, with an ormolu profile bust of a gentleman, with a perpetual calender inset under the glass, mid-19thC, 36¾in (93.5cm) high.
$1,500–1,700 ➔ NOA

A Scottish shell-inlaid mahogany wheel barometer, by G. Papina, Glasgow, c1840, 38in (96.5cm) high.
$1,700–2,000 ⊞ AB

A flame-mahogany wheel barometer, by Joseph James Dallaway, London, c1802, 37in (94cm) high.
$1,600–1,800 ⊞ AB

A mahogany and box-wood-strung wheel barometer, by Monli & Moiana, Leeds, early 19thC, 39in (99cm) high.
$1,300–1,450 ➔ P

A rosewood barometer, by Joseph Long, London, with inset timepiece, the case outlined with mother-of-pearl foliage, c1820, 51in (129.5cm) high.
$5,000–6,000 ➔ Bon

◄ **A mahogany and tulipwood-crossbanded barometer,** by A. Pastorelli, for Cross St, Hatton Garden, London, c1820, 51in (129.5cm) high.
$4,000–5,000 ⊞ RAY

BAROMETERS

A mahogany wheel barometer, by A. Riva, Marlborough, with silvered brass scale, hygrometer and level, c1840, 10in (25.5cm) diam.
$2,200–2,400 ↗ **PAO**

A Scottish rosewood and mother-of-pearl inlay barometer, by I. & A. McNab, Perth, with bowed thermometer box, c1850, 40in (101.5cm) high.
$2,200–2,600 ⊞ **RAY**

◄ **An Irish Victorian rosewood wheel barometer,** by Spears & Co, Dublin, the outside edges with raised decoration, 37in (94cm) high.
$320–380 ↗ **FHF**

A carved mahogany wheel barometer, with two recording hands engraved '10AM Today' and '10AM Yesterday', c1850, 55in (139.5cm) high.
$2,500–2,700 ↗ **S(S)**

A mahogany wheel barometer, by Joseph Aprile, Sudbury, with thermometer, hydrometer and level, the case with inlaid decoration, 19thC, 37¾in (96cm) high.
$650–800 ↗ **CMS**

◄ **A rosewood wheel barometer,** with silvered dial, hygrometer, boxed spirit thermometer, convex mirror and spirit level, c1870, dial 8in (20.5cm) diam.
$720–800 ⊞ **KB**

A Victorian walnut wheel barometer, decorated with C-scrolls, 39¾in (101cm) high.
$580–730 ↗ **ELR**

◄ **A papier mâché and mother-of-pearl-inlaid wheel barometer,** with thermometer, hygrometer and level, late 19thC, 39in (99cm) high.
$580–730 ↗ **DN**

A Dutch mahogany wheel barometer, by Kleman, Amsterdam, with thermometer and hygrometer, c1870, 42¼in (107.5cm) high.
$1,200–1,400 ↗ **S(Am)**

◄ **A mahogany wheel barometer,** with thermometer, the case inlaid with stringing, 19thC, 39in (99cm) high.
$730–870 ↗ **AH**

Aneroid Barometers

A French brass-cased aneroid barometer, by E. J. Dent, Paris, with silvered dial and mercury crescent thermometer, in mahogany box, c1852.
$1,300–1,500 ⊞ KB
Edward John Dent, 1790–1853, was the first to import Vidie barometers into England. This example was probably made by Lucien Vidie in Paris, who engraved Dent's name on it as the retailer.

A Victorian oak-framed aneroid barometer, 13in (33cm) diam.
$170–220 ⚲ SWO

A Victorian mahogany aneroid barometer, with hand-carved rope-twist frame, c1870, 11in (28cm) diam.
$580–680 ⊞ JIL

A brass aneroid barometer, by M. Pillischer, London, with curved mercury thermometer, c1880, dial 4¼in (11cm) diam.
$320–360 ⊞ KB

A Victorian brass aneroid barometer, by J. Hicks, London, 5in (12.5cm) diam.
$450–550 ⊞ JIL

A mahogany aneroid barometer, by Anthony Casartelli, Liverpool, with boxwood inlay, c1876, 34in (86.5cm) high.
$800–900 ⊞ AB

A Victorian pocket aneroid barometer and altimeter, by Negretti & Zambra, London, the reverse with presentation date 1891, 2in (5cm) diam, in original case.
$550–600 ⊞ JIL

An oak aneroid barometer, by H. Hughes & Son, with curved thermometer, c1880, 6in (15cm) diam.
$290–340 ⊞ AB

BAROMETERS

An Irish oak aneroid barometer, by Yeates & Son, Dublin, the enamel dial with mercury thermometer below, carved with fruiting vine above C-scrolls, late 19thC, 11in (28cm) wide.
$250–300 ⚒ Mit

A Continental silver aneroid barometer, on a marble stand, c1890, 9in (23cm) high.
$1,700–2,200 ⊞ RAY

A gilt-brass pocket aneroid barometer, c1900, 3in (7.5cm) diam, in original case.
$230–260 ⊞ DHo

◄ **A miniature aneroid barometer,** the engraved silver-plated case on a green marble base, c1890, 8in (20.5cm) high.
$800–1,000 ⊞ RAY

Cross Reference
See Colour Review
(page 432)

► **An Edwardian marquetry-inlaid mahogany aneroid baro-meter and thermometer,** by Gaunt & Arnsley, 33in (84cm) high.
$360–430 ⚒ G(B)

An Edwardian inlaid ros[e] wood aneroid baromet[er], 30in (76cm) high.
$500–600 ⚒ SWO

A dark oak aneroid barometer, with barley-twist pillars, c1920, 28in (71cm) high.
$350–400 ⊞ AB

A German aneroid baro[me]ter, by G. P. Goerz, Berlin, early 20thC, 9in (23cm) high.
$150–180 ⊞ ET

► **A brass-cased aneroid barometer,** by Short & Mason, distributed by Tycos, New York, with altitude adjustment, c1930, 6in (15cm) diam.
$120–130 ⊞ RTW

arographs

◀ **A late Victorian oak-cased weather station,** by Negretti & Zambra, with a quarter striking clock, the barometer flanking the brass barrels, the base with a chart drawer, 25in (63.5cm) wide.
$2,000–2,200 🔨 **WW**

A French barograph, with lift-up lid, stamped 'R.F., Paris, No. 26830', late 19thC, 12in (30.5cm) long.
$800–950 🔨 **P(NW)**

◀ **An oak-cased barograph,** by Negretti & Zambra, early 20thC, 13in (33cm) wide.
$650–750 ⊞ **RTW**

French brass-cased barograph, Richards & Co, c1900, in (35.5cm) wide.
,200–1,400 ⊞ **OCS**

An oak-cased barograph, by ort & Mason, with a chart drawer, 920, 14½in (37cm) wide.
00–$1,000 ⊞ **OCS**

A walnut-cased barograph, with concealed movement, c1910, 13in (33cm) wide.
$880–1,100 ⊞ **RTW**

◀ **An ebonized-cased barograph,** with silver-plated movement, mercury thermometer and chart drawer, 1920s, 15in (38cm) wide.
$1,200–1,300
⊞ **RTW**

A light oak-ased barograph, Negretti & ambra, with ercury thermo-eter and chart awer, c1925, in (35.5cm) wide.
,200–1,300
RTW

◀ **An American single diaphragm barograph,** by Taylor Instrument Co, with perspex lid and mahogany base, 1930s, 13in (33cm) wide.
$440–500 ⊞ **RTW**

Decorative Arts
Aesthetic Movement Furniture

A Victorian satinwood centre table, by Marsh & Jones, in the style of Charles Bevan, the inlaid border with mahogany stringing, c1880, 42in (106.5cm) diam.
$7,200–8,700 ⚘ **CGC**

An ebonized davenport, with amboyna panels, crossbanding and stringing, the interior of the upper section fitted with drawers and pigeonholes, over a hinged slope with a frieze drawer, the door below enclosing inscribed leather-trimmed shelves, c1875, 23¾in (60.5cm) wide.
$1,200–1,400 ⚘ **AH**

A fruitwood and mother-of-pearl-inlaid mahogany washstand, with inset marble to with two side chairs with foliate inlay, c1875, washstand 45in (114.5cm) wide.
$2,000–2,400 ⚘ **SK**

◀ **An ebonized occasional table,** in the sty of E. W. Godwin, the frieze with fretwork decoration, c1880, 25in (63.5cm) high.
$2,200–2,600 ⚘ **LAY**

Arts & Crafts Ceramics

An Ault pottery wall pocket, designed by Dr Christopher Dresser, decorated in blue, green and brown, c1890, 6in (15cm) diam.
$800–880 ⊞ **HUN**

A Brannam pottery pitcher, decorated in sgraffito with a peacock and abstract foliage in blue and green, incised mark and date, 1898, 12½in (32cm) high.
$175–200 ⚘ **P(E)**

A Bretby pottery amphora-shaped floor vase, the amber ground with a band of stylized flowers to the base and a Vitruvian scroll band to the neck, c1889, 31½in (80cm) high, on a brass stand marked S. H. for Samuel Heath & Sons, Birmingham.
$725–875 ⚘ **Bri**

A Burmantofts faïence vase, moulded and painted with stylized flowers and foliage in shades of blue, turquoise green, brown and yellow all tube-lined in white, impressed mark and number, c1890, 18in (45.5cm) high.
$725–875 ⚘ **P(L)**

A William de Morgan dish, decorated in red and yellow lustre with Winged Lions Fishing pattern, the reverse decorated with anthemia and concentric rings, minute hair crack, impressed mark, c1890, 14¼in (36cm) diam.
$4,300–5,000 ⚘ **WW**

A William de Morgan bottle vase, decorated in Persian style with flowers and leaves in shades of blue and green, c1880, 15¾in (40cm) high.
$5,800–7,200 ⚘ **P**

William de Morgan pottery
William Frend de Morgan (1839–1917) was the most significant potter to be connected with the English Arts & Crafts Movement. He worked with many different artists throughout his life and many of his designs were executed by others. He is best known for his decorative tiles, but also created numerous chargers, plates, dishes and vases, hand-painted with all-over decoration.

William de Morgan Ilham-period dish, painted in Persian colours by Charles Passenger, the centre with two birds squabbling over a snake, within a lappet border painted with mice, the reverse decorated with coloured bands, signed, c1880, ¼in (28.5cm) diam.
£10,000–12,000 ✦ KID

Linthorpe Pottery jug, 1885–90, 8in (20.5cm) high.
£230–280 ⊞ DSG

Minton charger, by D. Rochfort, depicting Cleopatra holding a snake surrounded by a border of peacock feathers, impressed mark and with presentation inscription by the artist to the underside, 1877, 15½in (39.5cm) diam.
£1,400–1,700 ✦ P

A William de Morgan ruby lustre vase, decorated with dragons in a frieze between foliate borders, 1880s, 10in (25.5cm) high.
$2,500–3,000 ✦ S(NY)
Ex-Harriman Judd Collection.
Allen Harriman and Edward Judd were American coin dealers who had a passion for British Art Pottery and amassed an extensive collection, which was sold in New York in January 2001.
Due to the size of the collection and fears of flooding the market, the sale was heavily publicized, with the result that the awareness of this type of pottery has greatly increased in the United States.

An earthenware charger, on a Pinder, Bourne & Co blank, painted with flowers surrounded by a floral border, in blue, green and rust-red on a cream ground, impressed marks and monogram, c1880, 20½in (52cm) diam.
$450–550 ✦ P
Pinder, Bourne & Co was taken over by Henry Doulton in 1877. A number of blanks would have remained in circulation, some of which are sure to have been taken by the factory's decorators. This charger has been painted overglaze and is of a more simple design and may have been made as a painter's own decorative piece or as an apprentice piece.

◄ A Dagobert Pêche box and cover, for Vereinigte Wiener und Gmunder Keramik, decorated with a lattice design enclosing stylized motifs, in black on white, impressed marks, Austria, 1912, 8in (20.5cm) high.
$900–1,100 ✦ P

A set of three Victorian graduated jugs, decorated with a design in the style of Dr Christopher Dresser, largest 10in (25.5cm) high.
$1,300–1,500 ✦ RPI

► A Linthorpe Pottery dish, by Dr Christopher Dresser, in a streaky green, brown and white glaze, 1879–82, 8in (20.5cm) wide.
$500–550 ⊞ NCA

A Linthorpe Pottery moulded vase, by Dr Christopher Dresser, decorated with a yellow and green flower on a green-glazed body, 1879–82, 5in (12.5cm) high.
$580–650 ⊞ NCA

A Ruskin Pottery high-fired stoneware vase, covered with a speckled deep red and mauve glaze, impressed mark, 1906, 6in (15cm) high.
$1,300–1,600 ✦ S(NY)
Ex-Harriman Judd Collection.

A Linthorpe Pottery earthenware vase, by Dr Christopher Dresser, the central pierced globular section held with four tubular curving supports, decorated with a streaky brown and green glaze, c1880, 16in (40.5cm) high.
$6,500–7,250 ✦ P

A pair of Ruskin Pottery orange lustreware candlesticks, c1915, 7in (18cm) high.
$360–400 ⊞ GAA

◄ An L. Wessel charger, incised and painted in bright enamels with a Persian-style floral pattern resembling mosaic, stamped and painted marks, Germany, c1900, 22¾in (58cm) diam.
$1,100–1,400 ✦ P

Arts & Crafts Furniture

◀ **A Gustav Stickley oak double bedstead,** America, 1905–09, 58in (147.5cm) wide.
$10,500–11,500
⚒ **BB(L)**

An oak revolving bookcase, c1880, 58in (147.5cm) high.
$2,500–3,000 ⚒ **S(S)**

Items in this section have been arranged in subject order.

An E. W. Godwin Austri oak bookcase, probably executed by Reuben Burk designed for Dromore Castle, Ireland, 1869, 48in (122cm) wide.
$30,500–33,500 ⚒ **S**
Dromore Castle was Godwin's largest domestic commission, executed between 186 and 1870. This is one o a set of six original boo cases which lined the corridor of the castle.

An oak bookcase, c1900, 18in (45.5cm) wide.
$450–550 ⊞ **PVD**

▶ **An oak bureau bookcase,** the glazed doors enclosing adjustable shelves, the fall-front enclosing a fitted interior, c1900, 28in (71cm) wide.
$650–800 ⚒ **Mit**

A Liberty & Co stained beechwood and upholstered open armchair, with foliate figured fabric padded back and seat, fabric attributed to C. F. A. Voysey, faults, c1890.
$950–1,150 ⚒ **S(S)**

A set of six oak dining chairs, with upholstered backs and seats, c1900.
$650–800 ⚒ **GAK**

A William Birch child's inlaid oak rocking chair, with a rush-seat, c1900.
$500–600 ⊞ **PVD**

A set of six oak dining chairs, attributed to a design by Ernest Archibald Taylor, probably made by Wylie & Lockhead, c1905.
$1,300–1,600 ⚒ **Bon(W)**

◀ **A Gustav Stickley oak desk,** the superstructure with two short drawers flanked by cubbyholes, America, 1905–09, 38in (96.5cm) wide.
$2,300–3,000
⚒ **BB(L)**

A Liberty & Co oak rush-seated chair, the toprail with a heart-shaped aperture, c1900.
$2,300–3,000 ⊞ **PVD**

A set of eight Ernest Gimson stained-ash Clissett chairs, with rush seats, c1910.
$3,200–3,600 ⚒ **S**

n oak desk, the hinged top nclosing a sliding frieze drawer ted with stationery compartments d hinged leather-covered writing irface, c1910, 39in (99cm) wide.
,700–2,000 ⚒ AH

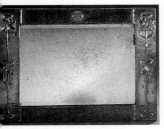

n embossed copper mirror, the des with stylized embossed plants d surmounted by a small Ruskin- yle roundel, c1900, 21½ x 29½in 4.5 x 75cm).
2,200–2,500 ⚒ S(S)

Liberty & Co copper mirror, the ammered frame set with a sea- reen Ruskin plaque to each corner , 1910, 28 x 22in (71 x 56cm).
2,600–3,000 ⚒ P

Liberty & Co oak stick stand, he sides with heart-shaped cutouts, 1900, 31in (78.5cm) wide.
500–600 ⚒ PVD

► A Cotswold School oak drop- eaf Sutherland table, the panelled rieze decorated with wooden studs, arly 20thC, 25in (63.5cm) high.
500–600 ⚒ S(S)

A Scottish Wylie & Lockhead glazed-top oak dresser, designed by E. A. Taylor, c1900, 38in (96.5) wide.
$7,200–8,700 ⚒ PVD
Ernest Archibald Taylor was a Scottish painter and furniture designer who was influential in bringing the designs of the Glasgow School to a wider public. His furniture was mostly made by the Glasgow firm of Wylie & Lockhead. In 1908 he moved to Manchester to work for George Wragge Ltd.

A William Birch oak twin-seat settee, c1890, 40½in (103cm) wide.
$2,500–3,000 ⚒ S(S)

A Victorian mahogany wardrobe, the mirror door enclosing four slides and two drawers, flanked by cupboard doors enclosing hanging rails, slides and a shoe drawer, some sections of plinth renewed, c1880, 85½in (217cm) wide.
$1,500–1,700 ⚒ Hal

An oak dresser, the superstructure with a pair of astragal-glazed doors above a pair of frieze drawers and a central door enclosing a slide and lead-lined divided slides flanked by smaller cupboard doors, all applied with ornamental metal strapwork, hinges and handles, c1900, 63in (160cm) wide.
$3,000–3,300 ⚒ P

An oak settle, with a painted panel depicting maidens gathering flowers, 1890–1900, 38in (96.5cm) wide.
$1,100–1,300 ⚒ WM

An oak games table, designed by Charles Annesley Voysey for J. S. Henry, with the suits inlaid in copper on each side, with a green baize top, c1900, 35in (89cm) high.
$10,000–12,000 ⚒ Bon

A Limbert oak lamp table, America, early 20thC, 45in (114.5cm) long.
$2,300–3,000 ⚒ BB(L)

DECORATIVE ARTS

Arts & Crafts Lighting

A silver-plated *electrolie*
with vaseline glass shades
c1900, 26in (66cm) high.
$1,400–1,700 ⊞ TLG

**A copper and opaque
glass hanging lantern,**
c1880, 8in (20.5cm) square.
$500–550 ⊞ PVD

A copper lantern, with
original Webb or Whitefriars
glass shade, c1900,
10in (25.5cm) high.
$600–680 ⊞ PVD

◄ **A pair of
brass wall
lights with
period glass
shades,** c1900,
11in (28cm) wide.
**$900–1,100
⊞ CHA**

**A W. A. S. Benson
copper and brass oil
lamp,** with Victorian-style
etched-glass globe shade,
c1900, 32in (81.5cm) high.
$1,400–1,500 ⊞ HUN

A hammered copper an
mica table lamp, early
20thC, 15½in (39.5cm) high
$2,300–2,700 ⚒ BB(L)

Miller's is a price GUIDE
not a price LIST

Arts & Crafts Metalware

► **A William Connell pewter box,**
designed by A. E. Jones, mounted
with a Ruskin roundel and a heart,
c1900, 8in (20.5cm) wide.
$1,600–1,800 ⊞ SHa

**A Wiener Werkstätte silver
basket,** designed by Josef Hoffmann,
Vienna, the sides pierced and
embossed with a repeating pattern
of stylized flowerheads in a grid,
marked with monograms and
signature and stamp, Austria, c1910,
8½in (21.5cm) long, 18oz.
$16,000–18,500 ⚒ S(NY)

**An Omar Ramsden silver sugar
bowl,** with hammered sides and
frieze of flowerheads separated by
Tudor rose motifs on a wavy ground,
with inscription below the frieze, 1919,
5½in (14cm) diam, with a matching
spoon by Ramsden & Carr, 1918.
$1,100–1,400 ⚒ P

**An A. E. Jones hammered silver-
plated casket,** the hinged cover applied
with a heart-shaped Ruskin plaque
surrounded by four rosettes,
with cedarwood interior, stamped
marks, c1910, 5in (12.5cm) wide.
$650–725 ⊞ DAD

A copper charger, in the style of John
Pearson, with embossed and hammered
decoration, c1890, 24in (61cm) diam.
$725–875 ⚒ Bon(W)

A wrought iron candelabra, stampe
'Artificer's Guild, 9 Maddox St, London
early 20thC, 10¾in (27.5cm) high.
$650–800 ⚒ BLH
**The Artificer's Guild was founded
by Nelson Dawson in 1901, passing
to the control of Montague
E. Fordham in 1903, and being
registered at the Maddox Street
address between 1903 and 1906.
The work of the Guild extended
to stained glass, wrought iron,
silver and jewellery; much of the
design was by Edward Spencer.**

Collectors' note:
Arts & Crafts brass and copper should not be polished. A dark, rich patina is preferred and therefore shiny pieces sell for less.

An embossed copper charger, in the style of John Pearson, the well embossed with a snake roundel within a border of fruit and foliage, 1900, 16in (40.5cm) diam.
$900–1,000 S(S)
John Pearson was one of the major artist-craftsmen of the Newlyn School of copperwork. His skill led to his appointment as Chief Metal Craftsman at the School and Guild of Handicraft, founded in 1888 by C. R. Ashbee.

A silver-plated inkstand, decorated with a botanical design, with a cut-glass inkwell, c1880, 8in (20.5cm) long.
$450–500 SHa

A copper jardinière, on three paw feet, c1900, 12in (30.5cm) high.
$210–230 WAC

A slant-front coal box and matching brass fender, the coal box decorated with peacocks and heart-shaped foliage, one foot missing, the fender reverse-embossed with a flower flanked by peacocks, the sides with fruiting vines, early 20thC, 18in (45.5cm) long.
$2,600–3,200 P(WM)

A Keswick School of Industrial Art silver salt and spoon, the salt with a pointed arch frieze beneath beads, hallmarked Chester 1908, 1½in (4cm) diam., the spoon Chester 1907.
$400–460 Mit

Dr Christopher Dresser
Dresser's motto was 'Truth, Beauty and Power' and he applied this to his pioneering designs from the 1860s through to the start of the 20th century. A simplicity of form, often deeply involved with Japanese aesthetic imagery, characterized much of his work. The aficionado can choose from fabric designs, ceramics for Ault and Linthorpe and, of course, his highly prized metalwork designs – Dresser teapots have on occasions passed the $140,000 mark at auction. The collector of more limited means can still find Dresser designs for Hukin & Heath or Heath & Middleton at under $750, because some of these metalwares were produced in large numbers. Dresser-style claret jugs with his characteristic ebonized wood handles are also affordable at around $450–700. An impressed facsimile signature is to be found on his pottery designs, and much of his metalwares need to be checked against original pattern books unless stamped 'Designed by Dr C. Dresser'.

A Victorian Walker & Hall silver-mounted glass claret jug, in the style of Dr Christopher Dresser, with an engraved cover and ebonized handle, Sheffield 1898, 9½in (24cm) high.
$400–460 RBB

► **A Scottish silver sugar caster,** by R. Stewart, Glasgow, hallmarked London 1905, 6½in (16.5cm) high, 4¾oz.
$230–290 F&C

A patinated copper stick stand, repoussé-decorated with stylized flowers, c1900, 26in (66cm) high.
$580–720 MoS

A Benham & Froud black patinated iron teapot, designed by Dr Christopher Dresser, with studded decoration, on an integral base cut with stylized cloud motifs, c1882, 8¼in (21cm) high.
$8,000–9,500 S

► **A Newlyn copper tray,** with a raised pierced gallery, the centre with an inscription, c1925, 13¾in (35cm) wide.
$110–130 P(B)

◄ **A John Pearson beaten copper tray,** 'JP' in a beaded oval mark to the reverse, c1890, 25in (63.5cm) long.
$145–170 P(B)

Doulton

A Doulton faïence wall plaque, painted in coloured enamels in the Turkish Iznik style, with radiating flowers and leaves on a pale yellow ground, within a blue ground flowerhead and leaf-scroll band, monogram, impressed marks for 1878, 19½in (49.5cm) diam.
$1,100–1,400 ✗ LFA

A pair of Doulton Lambeth stoneware vases, the bodies with relief-moulded undulating decoration on a mottled sea-green and ochre ground, impressed marks, dated 1883, one with initials AS, 7in (18cm) high.
$450–550 ✗ PFK

A Doulton Lambeth bird vase, by Mark V. Marshall, decorated in shades of brown, blue and olive, c1888, 5in (12.5cm) high.
$1,100–1,300 ⊞ JE

A Doulton Lambeth faïence moon flask, painted by Ada Dennis with two girls picking primroses, the reverse with Mannerist cherub and foliate scrolls, initials, number, c1890, 9½in (24cm) high.
$3,000–3,500 ✗ Bri

A pair of Doulton Lambeth majolica jardinières and pedestals, decorated with scrolls, fluting and swags in shades of brown, yellow, green and blue, impressed mark, late 19thC, 47½in (120.5cm) high.
$2,200–2,600 ✗ Mit

A Doulton Burslem porcelain plate, commemorating Queen Victoria's Diamond Jubilee in 1897, transfer-printed with a portrait in colours, 9¼in (23.5cm) diam.
$145–175 ✗ SAS

Doulton & Co (1815–present)

Between 1826 and 1956, Doulton & Co occupied premises in Lambeth, London, producing commercial and industrial stoneware and porcelain figures. In 1883, a second factory opened at Burslem, Staffordshire, which concentrated on the manufacture of earthenware and bone china, notably earthenware dinner services and bone china tea sets. The firm became Royal Doulton in 1901, under warrant from King Edward VII.

A Royal Doulton jug, commemorating Queen Victoria's Diamond Jubilee in 1897, 7½in (19cm) high.
$130–160 ✗ SWO

◄ **A pair of Royal Doulton stoneware ewers,** decorated in marbled glaze with roundels and oval pendant drops in shades of green, yellow, brown and blue, impressed mark and initials, early 20thC, 10¼in (26cm) high.
$430–500 ✗ DMC

A Doulton Lambeth Natural Foliage ware jug, by Eliza Simmance, with designs of impressed leaves in brown and green glazes, impressed marks, 1880–91, 7¾in (19.5cm) high.
$300–350 ✗ L

A Royal Doulton stoneware documentary tyg, commemorating the marriage of Humbert N. Ussher, 1906, the body with a blue-glazed rim bearing signatures of fellow workers at the Doulton factory, impressed mark, 7¼in (18.5cm) high.
$725–875 ✗ CAG

▶ **A Royal Doulton cabinet plate,** by P. Curnock, decorated with enamelled floral cartouches, on a cobalt blue and gilt ground, printed mark and number, early 20thC, 10in (25.5cm) diam.
$200–240 ✗ Hal

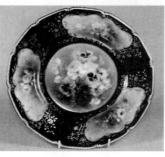

A Royal Doulton stoneware jug, commemorating the Coronation of Their Majesties King Edward VII and Queen Alexandra, 1901, 7½in (19cm) high.
$160–180 ✗ EH

DECORATIVE ARTS

◄ **A Royal Doulton soap dish,** in the shape of a dragonfly at the edge of a pond, c1910, 6in (15cm) diam.
$145–175 ⊞ DSG

A pair of Royal Doulton vases, with overpainted incised floral pattern, impressed mark, c1910, 14½in (37cm) high.
$260–320 ➤ JBe

A matched pair of Royal Doulton vases, decorated in blue and green, one signed Maud Bowden, c1912, 15¾in (40cm) high.
$580–720 ➤ WilP

Doulton Lambeth stoneware vase, by Frank . Pope, decorated in nades of green and blue n a deep pink ground, 1895, 10in (25.5cm) high.
900–1,100 ⊞ GAA

A pair of Royal Doulton vases, with a geometric panel on a washed-blue and silicon ground, impressed marks, c1900, 10in (25.5cm) high.
$300–350 ➤ GAK

Royal Doulton porcelain figure, Crinoline Lady, wearing a blue gown, 924–38, 3in (7.5cm) high.
725–875 ➤ Bea(E)

A Royal Doulton figural group, London Cry, designed by L. Harradine, model No. HM749, decorated in shades of red, blue and mauve, on a green oval base, haircracks, 1925–38, 6½in (16.5cm) high.
$580–650 ➤ PFK

A Royal Doulton figure, Pauline, designed by L. Harradine, wearing a blue and lilac gown and a green bonnet, marked, 1931–40, 6in (15cm) high.
$230–300 ➤ BBR

A Royal Doulton figural group, Scotties, designed by L. Harradine, model No. HN1281, painted in red and black enamels, printed marks, 1928–38, 5½in (14cm) high.
$1,600–1,900 ➤ BLH

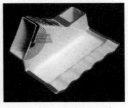

Royal Doulton character ug, Mephistopheles, designed by Charles J. Noke and H. Fenton, decorated n brown and beige on a ed and brown ground, 937–48, 6in (15cm) high.
$1,000–1,200 ➤ P(L)

A Royal Doulton loving cup, commemorating the Silver Jubilee of King George V and Queen Mary, 1935, moulded with a portraits medallion, the reverse with a knight in armour on his horse before Windsor Castle, numbered 377 from a limited edition of 1,000, 10¼in (26cm) high.
$360–430 ➤ SAS

A Royal Doulton match striker, Tango, decorated in red and black on a white ground, 1930s, 4½in (11.5cm) long.
$220–240 ⊞ BEV

► **A Royal Doulton Sung vase,** signed A. Eaton, decorated with a continuous sepia-coloured scene of an English manor garden with statuary and a woman, on a vermilion-red ground under a flambé glaze, painted and impressed marks, c1930, 17in (43cm) high.
$9,400–11,500 ➤ P(M)

► **A Royal Doulton Lambeth stoneware vase,** by Vera Huggins, decorated with a bird of paradise in brown and shades of blue on a mottled cream ground, 1930, 12in (30.5cm) high.
$1,800–2,000 ⊞ GAA

DECORATIVE ARTS

Martin Brothers

◀ **A Martin Brothers stoneware egg cup,** with reservoirs for salt and pepper picked out in blue, incised mark, rim chips, 1909, 4¾in (12cm) long.
$300–350 ⚹ **LFA**

A Martin Brothers ston ware bird jar, on a blac painted wooden socle, head restored, marked, c1885, 12½in (32cm) hig
$9,500–11,500 ⚹ **S(NY)**
Ex-Harriman Judd Collection.

A Martin Brothers stoneware square tobacco jar, modelled with stylized leaves, on a shaded blue ground, the cover with a coiled dragon in relief, hairline cracks, incised marks, dated 1901, 7in (18cm) high.
$3,200–3,600 ⚹ **LFA**

A pair of Martin Brothers stoneware tall vases, decorated with lappets and foliage above fantastic birds, incised marks, c1875, 25in (63.5cm) high.
$6,500–8,000 ⚹ **S(NY)**
Ex-Harriman Judd Collection.

◀ **A Martin Brothers stoneware vase,** incised with scaly monsters among scrolling foliage, inscribed marks, dated 1894, 7¾in (19.5cm) high.
$3,600–4,300 ⚹ **S(NY)**
Ex-Harriman Judd Collection.

A Martin Brothers Wally Bird stoneware jar and cover, partially glazed in blue, green-brown and white, on an ebonized wooden plinth, minor losses, incised marks, dated 1911, 12in (30.5cm) high.
$7,250–8,750 ⚹ **Bon**

A Martin Brothers stoneware vase, incised with amusing birds conversing among tall grasses, inscribed marks, dated 1903, 7in (18cm) high.
$3,000–3,500 ⚹ **S(NY)**
Ex-Harriman Judd Collection.

A Martin Brothers ston ware vase, decorated wit fish and seaweed in brow blue and green, small rim chip, incised signature an date, 1888, 9in (23cm) hig
$2,000–2,500 ⚹ **HAM**

LOCATE THE SOURCE
The source of each illustration in Miller's can be found by checking the code letters below each caption with the Key to Illustrations, pages 794–800.

Moorcroft

A Moorcroft Macintyre Aurelian ware teapot, designed by William Moorcroft, 1890s, 6in (15cm) high.
$580–720 ⊞ **GAA**

Cross Reference
See Colour Review (page 487)

◀ **A Moorcroft Macintyre Florian ware jug,** tubelined with a peacock pattern on a dark blue ground, printed and painted marks, c1900, 7¾in (19.5cm) high.
$3,600–4,300 ⚹ **BWe**

A Moorcroft Macintyre Aurelian ware two-handled vase, decorated in blue, iron-red and gold with stylized poppies and panels, printed marks, c1900, 12¼in (31cm) high
$800–950 ⚹ **WW**
Ex-Harriman Judd Collection.

▶ A Moorcroft pedestal bowl, decorated with Cornflower pattern in pink, ochre and green on a mottled ground, cracks and chips, signature mark, dated 1914, 5½in (14cm) high.
$725–875 ✗ AG

A Moorcroft Macintyre chocolate pot, decorated in green, blue and buff, 1903, 5¾in (14.5cm) high.
1,100–1,300 ⊞ DSG

A Moorcroft two-handled vase, decorated with Claremont toadstools pattern on a shaded green ground, restored rim, impressed and painted marks, dated 1914, 7½in (19cm) high.
1,500–1,700 ✗ LFA

A Moorcroft vase, decorated with Pomegranate pattern on a dark blue ground, impressed mark and signature, 1920s, 10¼in (26cm) high.
$900–1,100 ✗ Mit

A Moorcroft vase, decorated with Pomegranate pattern in shades of red and orange, on a Tudric pewter base, c1920, 9¼in (23.5cm) high.
$480–580 ✗ BWe

A Moorcroft Macintyre Florian ware vase, decorated with a butterfly pattern in various shades of blue, rim chips, printed and painted marks, 1898–1905, 9½in (24cm) high.
$725–875 ✗ RTo

▶ A Moorcroft pottery preserve jar, decorated with Pansy pattern, in mauve, pink and green on a pale green ground, impressed marks, with Tudric beaten pewter cover, c1925, 4in (10cm) high.
$500–600 ✗ Bea(E)

A Moorcroft vase, decorated with Peacock Wisteria pattern in bands of blue and cream, enclosing panels of stylized flowers in tones of red and blue, painted initials, impressed marks, c1925, 6in (15cm) high.
$1,300–1,600 ✗ LJ

A Moorcroft vase, decorated with Moonlit Blue pattern in powder blue and green on a dark blue ground, with a hammered Tudric pewter base, impressed marks, c1925, 9¾in (25cm) high.
$2,600–3,200 ✗ PF

A Moorcroft vase, tube-lined and decorated with a leaf and berry pattern in red, green and purple on a blue ground, impressed mark and painted initials, 1930s, 12¼in (31cm) high.
$900–1,100 ✗ TEN

A Moorcroft covered jar, decorated with Pomegranate pattern in shades of red and blue, impressed mark, 1929, 16in (40.5cm) high.
$3,600–4,300 ✗ TREA

Art Nouveau

Just as Darwin's theory of evolution challenged the 19th-century intellectual world with new ideas, so the world of art took its own stance against the Classical and Renaissance images of the past. Throughout Europe and Japan Art Nouveau symbolized a new beginning where old styles were replaced with an original art form based on the Gothic and rococo, but with a fresh interpretation derived from the observation of nature and natural forms. The poppy in full bloom with long trailing tendrils was to become a potent symbol, expressing female sexuality and emancipation, and was often seen in association with a liberated female image, depicted with long flowing hair or emerging nymph-like from water.

At the 1900 Paris Exhibition, manufacturers and great artists of the era gathered to display how far this new style had evolved. But by 1920 the sensuous curves and sensual charm of Art Nouveau had waned in favour of the clean-cut lines of Art Deco. The style faded from view except in the architecture of the period such as the Paris Metro façades by Hector Guimard, and it wasn't until the early 1960s that art enthusiasts began to turn their attention to its charms again.

Dealers began to trade in Gallé, Lalique and Tiffany glass, Mucha posters, and the bronzes of Raoul Larche. These were first seen in street markets such as London's Portobello Road but, by the early 1970s, galleries in both London and New York were showcasing Art Nouveau to a receptive and eager public. Before long auction houses on both sides of the Atlantic began to include specialist sales in their calendars and soc a price structure began to evolve as furniture, objects and posters were traded across the world. In the US, Tiffany glass became widely admired and documented and in particular leaded glass table lamps, so that by the 1990s, some top examples had exceeded $1m at auction. In Japar during the 1980s, a seemingly insatiable appetite for Lalique, Daum and Gallé glass evolved where by vast quantities were stockpiled like so many stocks and shares, only to crash in value in the late 1980s as the art world plunged into recessior

Over the last year or so, the market has seen collectors focus on names with a good track reco at auction, such as Knox, WMF and Majorelle. Th criteria for selecting pieces are a respected maker designer and good condition without restoratior as collectors now seem to desire one excellent example rather than several more affordable item Currently, there is little competition in the sale room for merely decorative Art Nouveau so it is good time to focus on this area. **Mark Olive**

Art Nouveau Ceramics

An Amphora two-handled vase, enamelled with storks among grasses on a matt mottled brown ground, impressed marks and numerals, Bohemia, late 19thC, 17½in (44.5cm) high.
$330–400 ➤ S(S)

▶ **An Elton ware vase,** with blue and maroon glaze and moulded with alpine flowers, c1900, 6in (15cm) high.
$350–380 ⊞ HUN

A Clifton vase, decorated with a green and khaki crystalline glaze, incised mark, signed, America, dated 1906, 11in (28cm) high.
$1,300–1,600 ➤ TREA

A pair of bronze-mounted Bretby vases, in the Japanese style, c1905, 10in (25.5cm) high.
$260–300 ⊞ HUN

A Howell & James plate, hand-painted with a portrait of a woman on a mottled blue ground, c1890, 9in (23cm) diam.
$220–240 ⊞ DSG

A Della Robbia earthen-ware two-handled vase decorated by Cassandra Annie Walker, polychrome painted with a maiden an flowers, incised marks, date 1903, 13¼in (33.5cm) high
$3,600–4,300 ➤ Bon(C)

A French three-piece solitaire, by A. de Feure, made by GDA, in shades o pink, green and cream, marked, Limoges, c1900, pitcher 7½in (19cm) high.
$1,000–1,200 ➤ P(Z)

◄ **A Grueby vase,** with sculpted and applied water lilies beneath a green matt glaze, restored, impressed mark, America, dated 1907, 10in (25.5cm) high.
$3,600–4,300
⚒ **TREA**

A Minton Secessionist pottery vase, decorated with splashed coloured enamels and outlined in black, with applied scroll-type handles, printed mark and number, c1907, 6¾in (17cm) high.
$230–300 ⚒ **Hal**

A Bernard Moore flambé vase, c1910, 7¼in (18.5cm) high.
$320–380 ⊞ **DSG**

A Minton orange lustre-glazed vase, c1873, 9in (23cm) high.
$220–260 ⊞ **DSG**

A Minton vase, with floral decoration on a pale blue ground, 1900–08, 9in (23cm) high.
$260–320 ⚒ **MAR**

Cross Reference
See Colour Review
(page 483)

A pair of stoneware tile panels depicting Aurore and Crepuscule, after Alphonse Mucha, each painted with a scantily-clad woman, one panel with two restored tiles, c1900, each panel 19½ x 46¼in (49.5 x 117.5cm).
$8,000–9,500 ⚒ **S**

Bernard Moore, 1853–1935

Bernard Moore and his brother, Samuel, succeeded their father in his porcelain factory at St Mary's Works, Longton, and began trading as Moore Brothers. From 1905, at Wolfe Street, Stoke-on-Trent, Moore specialized in producing art pottery which made strong use of flambé glazes in deep red, decorated in black or grey. His work used strong, good shapes often of Oriental inspiration. The quality of his draughtsmanship was always high. Common motifs include fish, nocturnal animals and birds – bats and owls often appear silhouetted against a moonlit yet blood-red sky.

A Pilkington's Royal Lancastrian indigo blue vase, c1915, 10in (25.5cm) high.
$260–300 ⊞ **HUN**

A Continental green and white jasper ware plaque, depicting a nymph reaching up to bend down a flower, late 19thC, 12¼ x 6in (31x 15cm).
$145–175 ⚒ **CDC**

A Pilkington's Royal Lancastrian art pottery vase, by Gordon Forsyth, decorated with silver lustre bacchanalian figures of a maiden and a goat flanked by trees, with branches to the rim and base against a mottled shaded red lustre ground, impressed and gilt marks, c1913, 8¾in (22cm) high.
$950–1,150 ⚒ **Mit**

A Van Briggle vase, with moulded floral design beneath a green and dark purple matt glaze, incised mark, America, dated 1905, 10in (25.5cm) high.
$3,000–3,500 ⚒ **TREA**

◄ **A dark red ceramic umbrella stand,** with pierced metal mount, the interior glazed in light turquoise, probably Austria, after 1910, 24¾in (63cm) high.
$300–350 ⚒ **DORO**

Art Nouveau & Art Pottery Clocks

A Martin Brothers stoneware mantel clock, the housing surmounted by a leashed bear, the base with a titled banner 'Bear and Forbear', firing cracks, inscribed marks, 1881, 8¾in (22cm) long.
$5,000–6,000 ↗ S(NY)
Ex-Harriman Judd Collection.

A bronze mantel clock, late 19thC, 10in (25.5cm) high.
$850–1,000 ↗ TMA

A beaten brass and enamel mantel clock, attributed to George Walton, the copper dial heightened with blue-green enamel encircled by stylized plant motifs and tendrils, c1900, 9½in (24cm) high.
$2,500–3,000 ↗ P

A French inlaid mahogany table clock, by F. Martin, c1900, 11in (28cm) high.
$1,600–1,600 ⊞ MI

A Wileman & Co Foley Intarsio ware clock, by Frederick A. Rhead, painted with panels of maidens inscribed 'DIES' and 'NOX', the central panel depicting two sailing boats with lilies in the foreground inscribed 'CARPE DIEM', foot chipped, printed and painted marks, c1900, 11½in (29cm) high.
$2,200–2,600 ↗ S(NY)

A Liberty & Co Tudric pewter clock, with enamel dial, c1915, 6in (15cm) high.
$3,000–3,300 ⊞ OND

Art Nouveau Figures & Busts

An Austrian cold-painted bronze figure of a dancing girl, by Franz Bergman, stamped mark, c1900, 5in (12.5cm) high.
$1,900–2,200 ⊞ MI

A Belgian carved ivory and gilt-bronze figure, entitled The Sower, by E. Bernoud, early 20thC, 15¾in (40cm) high.
$5,500–6,000 ↗ S(NY)

◄ **A gilt-bronze inkwell,** in the form of a maiden seated on a naturalistic base, signed A. Clerget, France, c1905, 8in (20.5cm) high.
$2,600–3,000 ⊞ MI

A Goldscheider pottery figure of a water carrier, modelled as a maiden holding an urn, with bronze-style glaze, restored, impressed mark, Austria, c1900, 41½in (105.5cm) high.
$1,500–1,700 ↗ P

An Austrian bronze figure entitled Little Windy Day, by Franz Bergman, modelled as a female figure, the moveable skirt lifting to reveal the lower torso, on a bronze base, signed 'Nam Greb' to skirt and 'Greb' to base, c1900, 5½in (14cm) high.
$725–875 ↗ LJ
Pieces by Franz Bergman are often stamped NAMGREB – that is, Bergman spelt backwards.

A Goldscheider bronze and ivory figure of a girl, by Georges Van der Straeten, seated on a naturalistic rocky outcrop with a book at her feet, incised mark, Austria, early 20thC, 11½in (29cm) high.
$1,900–2,100 ⚒ LJ

A French bronze model of a boy, Mime Antique, marked Lou de Rome, c1895, 7½in (19cm) high.
$2,900–3,200 ⊞ MI

A Continental terracotta bust of Auriela, her black hair and green dress applied with flowerheads, stamped Cologne, 19thC, 22¾in (58cm) high.
$320–380 ⚒ AH

◄ A bronze figure of a reclining female nude, with flowing hair, lying on a bed of flowers, on a naturalistic base, c1900, 24in (61cm) long.
$725–875 ⚒ Mit

An Austrian carved ivory and bronze figure, entitled Dancer, by Peter Tereszczuk, early 20thC, 22½in (57cm) high.
$8,000–8,800 ⚒ S(NY)

Art Nouveau Furniture

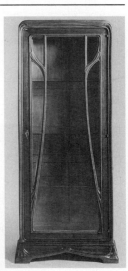

◄ A Belgian Secessionist inlaid oak side cabinet, c1900, 29in (73.5cm) wide.
$500–600 ⚒ S(S)

A French carved walnut, marquetry and marble buffet, by Louis Majorelle, c1909, 64in (162.5cm) wide.
$18,000–21,500 ⚒ S(NY)

A French carved mahogany cabinet, by Louis Majorelle, c1900, 23½in (59.5cm) wide.
$11,500–13,500 ⚒ S(NY)

A French carved mahogany poppy cabinet, ormolu-mounted and with burr-walnut and mirrored doors, by Louis Majorelle, c1900, 81in (205.5cm) wide.
$8,000–9,500 ⚒ S(NY)

◄ A French fruitwood marquetry poppy cabinet, by Louis Majorelle, c1900, 25½in (65cm) wide.
$6,500–8,000 ⚒ S(NY)

An Edwardian mahogany cabinet, by Liberty & Co, the central section with boxwood stringing and abalone inlay, above a bowed lower section flanked by four glazed doors, 54in (137cm) wide.
$2,200–2,600 ⚒ TRL

A pair of Austrian beechwood chairs, by J. J. Kohn, c1900.
$1,400–1,700 ⊞ OND

DECORATIVE ARTS

A French carved mahogany upholstered armchair, by Louis Majorelle, c1900.
$13,000–14,500 ⚄ S(NY)

An Austrian beech open armchair, with upholstered back and seat, produced by Thonet, Vienna, needing restoration, designed before 1904.
$500–600 ⚄ DORO

An Austrian bentwood caned day bed, by Kohn, c1910, 74in (188cm) long.
$3,000–3,400 ⊞ APO

A French gessoed and gilt-wood mirror, by Hector Guimard, modelled with stylized organic motifs, 52½in (133.5cm) high.
$13,500–16,500 ⚄ S

A set of four side chairs, inlaid with fruitwoods and pewter, c1910.
$3,000–3,600 ⊞ MI

An Austrian wrought iron jardinière, with original removable liner, Vienna, 1910–15, 37¾in (96cm) high.
$800–950 ⚄ DORO

An Italian vellum, ebonized wood, repoussé hammered copper and pewter-inlaid plant stand, by Carlo Bugatti, c1900, 45in (114.5cm) high.
$10,000–11,000 ⚄ S(NY)

> **Miller's is a price GUIDE not a price LIST**

An Italian vellum, wood and repoussé hammered copper settee, by Carlo Bugatti, c1900, 96in (244cm) long.
$11,000–13,000 ⚄ S(NY)

An Austrian three-piece bent beechwood salon suite, by Marcel Kammerer, comprising a settee and two armchairs, produced by Thonet, Vienna, c1906, settee 48in (122cm) long.
$10,000–12,000 ⚄ S(NY)

A French walnut and marquetry-inlaid occasional table, by Emile Gallé, the top inlaid with a butterfly above foliage and ferns, faults, marquetry signature, c1895, 35¾in (91cm) wide.
$3,000–3,500 ⚄ S(S)

A French walnut two-tier table, by Emile Gallé, both tiers inlaid with stylized flowers and leaves, marquetry mark, c1900, 29¼in (74.5cm) high.
$1,700–2,000 ⚄ S(S)

A French walnut and burr elm-inlaid side table, the crossbanded top above a stylized frieze with shaped panels, indistinct signature, c1900, 33½in (85cm) wide.
$580–720 ⚄ P(B)

An Austrian beech *Fledermaus* table, by Josef Hoffmann, for J. & J. Kohn, repainted in white lacquer, maker's mark, Vienna, 1906–07, 26in (66cm) high.
$1,000–1,200 ⚄ DORO

Art Nouveau Glass

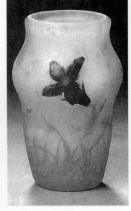

A Daum vase, acid-etched with sailing ships in a lakeside scene, with an orange ground, France, c1900, 3½in (9cm) high.
$1,100–1,300 ⊞ OND

◄ **A French Croismare cameo glass vase,** grey mottled with blue and overlaid with shades of pink and green, acid-etched with floral motifs, signed, c1900, 14½in (37cm) high.
$4,300–5,000 ⚒ P(Z)

A Daum etched and enamelled square glass vase, the interior of the clear glass decorated in white and blue with fuchsias, cameo mark, France, c1900, 4¾in (12cm) high.
$2,300–2,500 ⚒ S(S)

A Daum cameo glass vase, the frosted glass mottled with pale blue, blue and yellow at the base, overlaid in green and carved with blue gentian flowers, signed, France, c1910, 4in (10cm) high.
$3,600–4,300 ⚒ P(Z)

A set of six Emile Gallé enamel-decorated glasses, France, c1900, 2in (5cm) high.
$2,300–2,600 ⊞ OND

An Emile Gallé cameo glass scent bottle and stopper, the clear glass overlaid in pink and purple, acid-etched with myosotis flowers and leaves, signed, France, c1900, 5¼in (13.5cm) high.
$2,900–3,200 ⚒ P(Z)

An Emile Gallé cameo glass vase, decorated in shades of pink and brown, France, c1900, 6in (15cm) high.
$1,000–1,100 ⊞ OND

An Emile Gallé marqueterie-de-verre, verrerie parlante glass vase, the grey glass interior decorated with bubbles, amber rim and purple base, inlaid with purple, yellow and white engraved butterflies, two internal cracks to base, engraved inscription, signed, c1900, 6¾in (17cm) high.
$6,500–8,000 ⚒ P(Z)

A Russian Gus Crystal Works cameo glass vase, decorated with trees by a mountain lake in shades of purple, inscribed 'YU.S.N.M. N-k Gus-Krust' (Yuri Stepanovich Nechayev-Maltsov, heir of Gus'Khrustal'nyy), c1900, 16in (40.5cm) high.
$4,000–4,400 ⚒ S(NY)
With the death of I. S. Maltsov in 1880, the family's control of the Gus Crystal works was interrupted. From 1884 to 1894 the factory was operated by the government. In 1894 it became part of the joint-stock company of the Maltsov glassworks. Yu. S. Nechayev-Maltsov, a descendant of I. S. Maltsov, was the last owner of the glassworks.

Early Daum designs

The Daum glassworks in Nancy, France, was established as a family business during the 1870s and was soon producing designs that won medals for the firm in Chicago, Brussels and finally the Paris 1900 International Exhibition. Their characteristic cameo glass designs from this period were floral subjects in the Art Nouveau style, cut with hydrofluoric acid and then fire-polished. Wheel-carving was also a favoured technique in order to achieve a fire-textured finish of great quality. Unlike the Gallé glassworks, we tend to associate Daum with the use of polychrome enamels and gilt-colour in the presentation of their Art Nouveau period glass. These pieces are much favoured by modern collectors, in particular the winter landscape designs heightened with enamelled 'snow'. Pieces are signed 'Daum Nancy', often with the cross of Lorraine.

An Emile Gallé cameo glass vase, the triple overlay streaked with a band of pink at the neck and base, overlaid in yellow and brown, etched with primroses among foliage, signed, France, c1900, 6in (15cm) high.
$580–720 ⚒ Hal

A Loetz iridescent glass vase, with Diaspora pattern, Austria, c1900, 5in (12.5cm) high.
$500–550 ⊞ OND

A Loetz-style glass vase, the green glass with iridescent blue trailed decoration, early 20thC, 5½in (14cm) high.
$190–220 ⚒ PFK

A Loetz-style glass vase, decorated with trails and oil lustre, early 20thC, 11¼in (28.5cm) high.
$650–800 ⚒ WW

A pair of leaded glass windows, attributed to John Lafarge, America, c1900, 42in (106.5cm) high.
$18,000–22,000 ⚒ S(NY)

An iridescent glass vase, the elongated twisted square section covered in a vibrant peacock blue oil-spot design on a clear green ground, probably by Loetz, c1900, 11¾in (30cm) high.
$650–800 ⚒ RTo

A Muller Frères cameo glass two-handled vase, decorated with brambles on a frosted ground, signed, France, c1900, 11in (28cm) high.
$4,600–5,000 ⚒ S(NY)

An Auguste Jean enamelled glass vase, signed, France, c1900, 12in (30.5cm) high.
$800–900 ⊞ OND

A Legras glass vase, Montjoye, enamelled with flowers, France, c1900, 11in (28cm) high.
$550–650 ⊞ OND

A fan top vaseline glass vase, c1900, 7in (18cm) high.
$200–250 ⊞ GRI

▶ **A Tiffany Favrile glass bottle vase,** the gold iridescent body resembling a sea urchin, signed, early 20thC, 8in (20.5cm) high.
$800–950 ⚒ S(S)

A René Lalique glass vase *Lézards et Bluets,* moulded with cornflowers, tendrils and climbing lizards in deep purple/black, signed, France, 1913, 13¼in (33.5cm) high.
$23,000–25,500 ⚒ P

A glass vase, attributed to Loetz, the clear glass washed with blue-gold iridescence, c1900, 6in (15cm) high.
$260–300 ⚒ S(S)

A Byzantine glass, designed by Carl George Von Reichenbach for Poschmeyer Oberwieslau, Munich, 1906, 6in (15cm) high.
$2,000–2,400 ⊞ ALiN

Art Nouveau Jewellery

A silver and cabochon opal brooch, c1890, 1¼in (3cm) diam.
$1,000–1,200 S(S)

A Liberty & Co silver and enamel Cymric buckle, with stylized honesty with seed pods hanging beneath, on a blue-green enamel ground, Birmingham 1906, 3½in (9cm) wide.
$600–660 P(B)

A silver and enamel belt buckle, by W. H. Haseler, each half applied with triangles lightly spot-hammered, with white and blue-green enamel decoration, the two halves soldered together, Birmingham 1910, 2½in (6.5cm) wide.
$360–430 Bon

A set of six Liberty & Co silver Cymric buttons, designed as flowerheads with a central turquoise boss, 1901, 1in (2.5cm) diam, with Liberty fitted leather-covered case.
$400–480 S(S)

Further reading
Miller's Art Nouveau & Art Deco Buyer's Guide, Miller's Publications, 2001

◄ **A silver and blue-green enamel pendant,** by Charles Horner, Chester 1907.
$300–350 DD

Art Nouveau Lighting

Three copper two-branch wall lights, with heart-shaped motifs, the top inset with Ruskin-style cabochons, c1890, 15in (38cm) high.
$1,700–2,000 Mit

An Emile Gallé cameo glass and bronze hibiscus lamp, signed, France, c1900, 8½in (21.5cm) high.
$13,000–14,500 S(NY)

A gilt-bronze five-light chandelier, the five curving candle arms ending in iris blossoms, fitted for electricity, c1900, 45in (114.5cm) high.
$3,500–4,000 BB(L)

A Doulton Lambeth stoneware metal-mounted oil lamp, by Francis E. Lee and Edith Lupton, incised with stylized foliage, upper section probably matched, impressed and incised marks, 1883, 26in (66cm) high.
$1,900–2,100 S(NY) Ex-Harriman Judd Collection.

► **An Austro-Hungarian four-light patinated-metal ceiling light,** with glass shades, c1900, 52½in (133.5cm) high.
$450–550 DORO

An Austrian patinated-metal and slag glass table lamp, the shade set with irregular green glass jewels, the border with striated green and white tiles, early 20thC, 21½in (54.5cm) high.
$2,200–2,400 BB(L)

A pair of Continental silver-plated desk lamps, with red glass insets, possibly Austrian, c1900, 14in (35.5cm) high.
$1,400–1,700 TLG

A Tiffany Favrile glass, shell and bronze nautilus lamp, impressed mark, America, 1899–1920, 13in (33cm) high.
$7,200–8,700 ⚲ **S(NY)**

A Tiffany patinated-bronze floor lamp, with an American iridescent gold and yellow glass shade, impressed mark, America, early 20thC, 55¾in (141.5cm) high.
$4,000–4,600 ⚲ **BB(L)**

A Tiffany Favrile yellow glass and bronze vine border lamp, impressed marks, America, 1899–1918, 22½in (57cm) high.
$14,500–17,500 ⚲ **S(NY)**

A Tiffany Favrile amber and green glass and patinated-bronze geometric lamp, impressed marks, America, 1898–1928, 22in (56cm) high.
$12,500–14,500 ⚲ **BB(L)**

A Tiffany Favrile golden yellow damascene glass and bronze lamp, impressed mark, America, 1899–1918, 17¾in (45cm) high.
$8,700–10,000 ⚲ **S(NY)**

▶ **A Tiffany Favrile glass and patinated-bronze hanging hall lamp,** the shade in light amber shaded with violet iridescence and decorated with green and white striped feathers, signed, America, early 20thC, 41in (104cm) high.
$6,900–7,600 ⚲ **BB(L)**

A French bronze oil lamp, by George Ledru, c1904, 26in (66cm) high.
$1,600–1,800 ⊞ **MI**

Art Nouveau Metalware

A Liberty & Co silver and mixed metal bowl, on four rivetted copper legs, the border with 16 green hard-stone cabochons, on scroll feet, Birmingham 1900, 8in (20.5cm) diam, 26.45oz.
$4,000–4,600 ⚲ **Bon**

A Liberty & Co pewter box and cover, after a design by Archibald Knox, embossed with a stylized foliate and chequered pattern, slight dents, impressed marks, c1905, 4½in (11.5cm) high.
$580–650 ⚲ **Hal**

◀ **A William Hutton & Sons silver casket,** the hinged cover with a heart-shaped recess with relief figure of Pan emerging from a seashell, the corners applied with mother-of-pearl panels in fronds of seaweed, the body applied with yachts, the interior lined in green velvet, London 1902, 8in (20.5cm) diam.
$4,600–5,500 ⚲ **CGC**

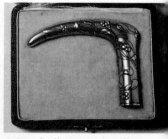

A French silver cane handle, c1900, 5in (12.5cm) long, in original fitted case.
$750–825 ⊞ **SHa**

A Liberty & Co pewter chamberstick, by Archibald Knox, the border entwined with stylized budding foliage, c1900, 7¼in (18.5cm) wide.
$500–600 ⊞ **DAD**

A Gorham martelé silver charger, with shaped and waved rim, each lobe with embossed leaf and buds, embossed monogram, Providence, America, c1900, 13in (33cm) diam.
$5,800–6,500 ⚒ SK

A WMF pewter charger, the centre cast with a maiden, surrounded by flowers on sinuous tendrils, stamped marks, Germany, c1905, 19¾in (50cm) diam.
$1,800–2,200 ⚒ P

A set of Tiffany & Co silver-coloured metal cutlery, comprising 36 pieces, each decorated with various Japanese-style motifs, stamped marks, America, designed 1880.
$18,000–20,000 ⚒ S

A Liberty & Co silver cigarette case, with spot-hammered decoration, the lid inlaid with blue, green and red enamel borders, Birmingham 1929, 3¼in (8.5cm) square.
$230–290 ⚒ Bon

A William Hutton & Sons silver twin photograph frame, the embossed decoration with green and purple enamel details, worn, Birmingham 1902, 4½in (11.5cm) wide.
$900–1,000 ⚒ SWO

A gilt-bronze dish, by Alexandre Vibert, with figure of a reclining lady, France, 1900–10, 5in (12.5cm) wide.
$1,600–1,750 ⊞ MI

An Edwardian silver photograph frame, by William Nathan, decorated with stylized birds and flowers, Chester 1903–04, 12¼in (31cm) high.
$1,900–2,100 ⊞ NS

A silver photograph frame, cast with a bird to one side and with flowering branches, maker's mark J.A.&S., Birmingham 1907, 9½in (24cm) high.
$650–800 ⚒ P

A French bronze jardinière, by Joseph Chéret, modelled in high relief with nymphs swimming and dancing in the water, signed, c1890, 22in (56cm) diam.
$13,500–16,000 ⚒ S

Cross Reference
See Colour Review
(page 490)

A Tiffany & Co chrysan-themum pitcher, the body and handle with repoussé and engraved flowers and scroll motifs, America, c1880, 9¼in (23.5cm) high, 33oz.
$4,300–4,700 ⚒ SK

A WMF silver-plated and glass claret jug, the body with scroll-cut decoration, Germany, c1900, 12in (30.5cm) high.
$450–550 ⚒ Bon(G)

A Liberty & Co Tudric pewter jug, by Archibald Knox, with rattan handle, c1900, 7¼in (18.5cm) high.
$900–1,000 ⊞ PVD

► **A Tiffany & Co silver and horn ladle,** America, c1860, 15in (38cm) long.
$1,600–1,800 ⊞ SHa

A William Hutton & Son silver mug, the sides chased with stylized flowers between cut-out panels, 1902, 3½in (9cm) high, 4.5oz.
$550–650 ⚒ P

A Tiffany & Co tea and coffee set, comprising six pieces, the lids with cast flower finials, with applied monograms to the bodies, America, 1891–1902, coffee pot 12in (30.5cm) high, 128oz.
$3,200–3,800 ⚒ SK

A Gorham martelé vase, the hammered body with flared and waved rim embossed with leaves, the body embossed with daffodils, the foot with buds and leaves, embossed monogram, Providence, America, c1900, 8in (20.5cm) high, 33oz.
$5,800–6,500 ⚒ SK

◄ **A Liberty & Co silver three-piece tea set,** chased with vine leaves and grapes, with hammered finish below applied plait band, with composition handle and finial, Birmingham 1914, 26.3oz.
$1,100–1,300 ⚒ S(S)

A French bronze vase, by Maurice Bouval, applied with a weeping girl, the body applied with leaves, signed, c1900, 8in (20.5cm) high.
$2,900–3,200 ⊞ MI
Bouval was a pupil of the French realist sculptor Jean Alexander Joseph Falurre, 1831–1900.

An American bronze vase, by Heintz Art Metal Shop, Buffalo, New York, the body applied with a silver rose, impressed marks, c1912, 12½in (32cm) high.
$300–350 ⚒ RTo

A pair of silver trumpet-shaped vases, by William Comyns, with raised floral decoration and loaded bases, London 1902, 5¼in (13.5cm) high.
$230–290 ⚒ FHF

A matched pair of Edwardian two-handled vases, embossed with Tudor rose medallions, 1907 and 1909, 8in (20.5cm) high, 14.5oz.
$720–800 ⚒ P(S)

A silver vase, Birmingham 1910, 7in (18cm) high.
$220–280 ⊞ CoHA

► **A Liberty & Co silver Cymric wine flask mount and collar,** the handle and collar with tied ribbon decoration and oval enamel insets, Birmingham 1902, 7in (18cm) high, 6oz.
$4,000–4,600 ⚒ KID

Art Deco Ceramics

A Burleigh Ware jug, decorated with Kingfisher pattern in shades of yellow, orange, green and brown, 1931, 8in (20.5cm) high.
$220–260 ⊞ ERC

A Burleigh Ware hot water jug, decorated with Dawn pattern in black, green and yellow on a cream ground, 1930s, 6in (15cm) high.
$145–165 ⊞ BUR

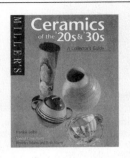

A Carlton Ware jug, decorated with a stylized red tulip on a cream ground, 1930–32, 4¼in (11cm) high.
$145–175 ⊞ StC

A pair of George Clews & Co Chameleon ware vases, decorated in orange and green drip glaze on a blue ground, c1930, 7½in (19cm) high.
$220–260 ⊞ AOT

A Susie Cooper milk/cream jug, decorated with flowers and foliage in pink, yellow and green, 1930s, 3in (7.5cm) high.
$30–35 ⊞ WAC

◄ **A Crown Ducal coffee set,** comprising 17 pieces, decorated with borders of orange trees, printed marks, c1920.
$300–350 ↗ WW

A Goldscheider pottery wall mask, modelled as a young lady with green curled hair and orange lips, chip to underside, printed mark, impressed numbers, Austria, c1930, 10¼in (26cm) high.
$450–550 ↗ Bea(E)

A set of ten German painted tiles, by Friedrich Hudler, decorated with figural and animal scenes in muted colours on a crackled cream ground, painted monogram, c1920, 5in (12.5cm) square.
$580–650 ↗ P
Friedrich Hudler won a gold medal at the 1937 Paris Exhibition.

A Limoges part dinner service, comprising 88 pieces, decorated with Sprig pattern in gold on a white ground, France, early 20thC.
$870–1,000 ↗ **NOA**

▶ **A Rookwood Pottery vase,** relief-decorated with petals in a light red matt glaze, impressed mark, America, dated 1922, 12½in (32cm) high.
$1,000–1,100 ↗ **FBG**

A Poole Pottery octagonal faceted vase, decorated with a stylized foliate pattern in brown and grey enamels, cracks to rim, impressed marks, incised number, c1930, 8in (20.5cm) high.
$115–175 ↗ **Hal**

A Rosenthal figure of a boy on a dragonfly, designed by Ferdinand Liebermann, painted in pastel colours, marked, Germany, 1920s, 5¾in (14.5cm) wide.
$300–350 ↗ **P(B)**

A Royal Copenhagen stoneware vase with a copper lid, by Patrick Nordström, the speckled green-blue glaze with blue crystalline glaze to the shoulders, the lid with stylized flower finial, marked with cypher and number, Danish, c1925, 10in (25.5cm) high.
$3,600–4,300 ↗ **P**

A Hancock & Sons Rubens ware spill vase, hand-painted by F. X. Abraham with Pomegranate pattern in polychrome on a black ground, c1930, 6½in (16.5cm) high.
$145–175 ⊞ **PIC**

A pair of Ruskin Pottery triangular section lamp bases, on stepped feet, in streaked orange, blue and green matt and crystalline glazes, impressed marks, c1930, 12½in (32cm) high.
$580–720 ↗ **FHF**

▶ **A Shelley Pottery bowl,** by Walter Slater, with enamel decoration on a green and mauve lustre ground, signed, c1930, 8in (20.5cm) diam.
$650–720 ⊞ **TWr**

A pair of Shelley Harmony ware vases, decorated in orange, white and grey, the interior with an apple green glaze, 1930s, 7½in (19cm) high.
$290–320 ⊞ **DEC**

A ceramic jug, with trailed blue and green decoration, c1920, 7¼in (18.5cm) high.
$145–165 ⊞ **Mit**

A Van Briggle pottery vase, entitled Lorelei, in burgundy and deep blue matt glaze, incised marks, America, c1925, 10½in (26.5cm) high.
$1,100–1,300 ↗ **TREA**

Shelley pottery

Based in Longton, Staffordshire, the Shelley potteries flourished under Percy Shelley who employed both Frederick Rhead and later Walter Slater as art directors in the early part of the 20th century. In the Art Deco period it was their teaware that exuded a distinctive style much favoured by collectors today. Both shape and pattern are important in determining price, with strong Art Deco shapes such as Mode and Vogue in the Sun-Ray pattern at the top of the collector's list. Walter Slater's own designs, often with fish painted on a lustre ground, have a strong collectors' market, as do the rather bizarre Boo-Boos and child studies designed by Mabel Lucie Attwell for Shelley in the 1930s.

Clarice Cliff

A Clarice Cliff conical sugar bowl, decorated with Honolulu pattern, in orange, green, black and yellow on a cream ground, 1930s, 2¾in (7cm) high.
$580–720 ⚘ Bon(C)

A Clarice Cliff Wilkinson Fantasque charger, decorated with Broth pattern, the slightly ribbed body painted in green, blue and orange, 1929–30, 17¾in (45cm) diam.
$2,300–2,900 ⚘ CDC

A Clarice Cliff Bizarre cake plate, decorated with Idyll pattern, with a yellow, green and pink border, handle lacking, 1930s, 8¾in (22cm) diam.
$230–290 ⚘ RTo

A Clarice Cliff fruit bowl, decorated with Aurea pattern, with green and yellow interior rim, 1930s, 8in (20.5cm) diam.
$330–400 ⚘ Mit

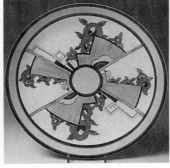

A Clarice Cliff charger, decorated with Newport pattern, in green, yellow and orange, the rim with yellow and black bands, 1934, 13½in (34.5cm) diam.
$725–800 ⚘ P

A Clarice Cliff Inspiration dish, the centre painted with a stylized four-leaf flower within a border of stylized wave motifs, painted marks for Newport Pottery, 1930s, 18in (45.5cm) diam.
$2,200–2,600 ⚘ KID

LOCATE THE SOURCE

The source of each illustration in Miller's can be found by checking the code letters below each caption with the Key to Illustrations, pages 794–800.

◀ **A Clarice Cliff Apple preserve pot,** decorated with Taormina Orange pattern, with an orange tree, minor firing crack, 1930s, 3½in (9cm) high.
$300–350 ⚘ RTo

A Clarice Cliff Stage Coach cigarette box, decorated in black, yellow and red, restored, 1931, 8in (20.5cm) long.
$1,300–1,450 ⊞ MI
Most examples of this piece date from 1926.

A Clarice Cliff octagonal plate, decorated with Nasturtium pattern, in orange, green and yellow on a cream and *café-au-lait* ground, 1930s, 9in (23cm) diam.
$290–320 ⚘ Bon(C)

A Clarice Cliff Dover jardinière, decorated in colours with Rhodanthe pattern, 1930s, 7½in (19cm) diam.
$580–720 ⚘ F&C

A Clarice Cliff Fantasque octagonal jardinière, decorated in coloured enamels with a stylized leaf band, 1930s, 3½in (9cm) high.
$360–430 ⚘ LFA

DECORATIVE ARTS

A Clarice Cliff Newport Bizarre pot, decorated with Lightning pattern, late 1920s, 2½in (6.5cm) high.
$870–1,000 ✦ GAK

A Clarice Cliff Harvest teapot, decorated in green, orange, yellow and red on a cream ground, c1940, 9in (23cm) long.
$300–350 ✦ WW

Cross Reference
See Colour Review (page 499)

A Clarice Cliff Bonjour coffee set, comprising 13 pieces, decorated with Pine Grove pattern, with orange bands, 1935, pot 7½in (19cm) high.
$1,300–1,450 ✦ P

A Clarice Cliff vase, the light green glazed ribbed body moulded with two parrots perched on a leafy branch, minor chip, 1935, 8¼in (21cm) high.
$260–320 ✦ RTo

A Clarice Cliff Bizarre tea and coffee service, comprising 36 pieces, decorated with Secrets pattern, enamelled in green, brown, orange and yellow, depicting red-roofed cottages, with flowering tree to the reverse, one cup damaged, c1935, large plate 9in (23cm) diam.
$2,600–3,200 ✦ CAG

Charlotte Rhead

A Charlotte Rhead bowl, decorated in green and orange on a cream ground, 1930s, 9½in (24cm) diam.
$210–240 ⊞ PrB

A Charlotte Rhead twin-handled dish, for Bursley Ware, centred with a circular lattice surrounded by a floral border, in yellow, orange, brown and green, heightened with gilt, 1930s, 11in (28cm) long.
$100–125 ✦ P(B)

A Charlotte Rhead plaque, for Wood & Sons Bursley Ware, decorated with poppies in red, orange, blue and buff, heightened with gilt, late 1920s, 16in (40.5cm) diam.
$1,700–2,000 ✦ LT

A pair of Charlotte Rhead vases, for Crown Ducal, decorated with the Manchu pattern in green and gilt, 1930s, 10½in (26.5cm) high.
$450–550 ✦ Mit

▶ **A Charlotte Rhead vase,** for Crown Ducal, polychrome decorated with Persian Rose pattern, with yellow rims, c1938, 5½in (14cm) high.
$320–380 ⊞ AOT

A pair of Charlotte Rhead vases, for Crown Ducal, decorated with Byzantine pattern, in brown, blue and orange lustre on a speckled orange ground, 1930s, 8½in (21.5cm) high.
$360–430 ✦ PFK

Art Deco Carpets

A Paul Haesaerts tufted wool carpet, by de Sadeleer, decorated with abstract naturalistic motifs with repeating diamond pattern and geometric border, in shades of brown, black, grey and cream, designer and manufacturer's monograms, Holland, 1925, 165¼ x 85¾in (419.5 x 218cm).
$12,300–14,500 🔨 S

▶ **An Edouard Bénédictus wool carpet,** woven in shades of orange, pink, brown, green, mauve, white, black and blue, with stylized flowers and leaves within mauve and black border, France, c1925, 95¼ x 145in (242 x 368.5cm).
$9,500–11,500 🔨 S

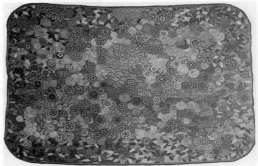

◀ **An Edward McKnight-Kauffer modernist rug,** woven with a geometric pattern, in deep and pale blue, brown and beige, artist's woven monogram, America, c1930, 82¾ x 47¾in (210 x 121.5cm).
$10,000–12,000 🔨 P

▶ **A Savonnerie carpet,** woven in beige, brown and khaki on a black ground, France, c1930, 136 x 89in (345.5 x 226cm).
$7,250–8,000 🔨 S

Art Deco Clocks & Watches

A bronze mantel clock, cast from a model by P. Follot, signed, French, 1925, 10in (25.5cm) wide.
$7,250–8,000 ⊞ MI

A René Lalique opalescent glass Inseparables clock, the panel moulded with pairs of budgerigars on blossoming branches flanking a gilt-metal dial with eight-day movement, minor chips to edge, signed, France, c1930, 4¼in (11cm) high.
$1,000–1,200 🔨 RTo

An Atmos black hardstone and red- and beige-veined marble timepiece, with chromium plating, J. L. Reutter patent, signed, France, c1935, 9in (23cm) high.
$3,600–4,000 🔨 S(G)

A Jaz Bakelite clock, with glass inserts, France, 1930, 9in (23cm) high.
$290–320 ⊞ JEZ

▶ **A Rolex 18ct white gold and diamond wristwatch,** with 9ct white gold bracelet, Swiss, c1920, ½in (1.5cm) wide.
$1,450–1,600 🔨 LJ

A diamond wristwatch, c1925, 6½in (16.5cm) long.
$3,200–3,600 🔨 S

Art Deco Figures

A bronze figure of a nude female dancer, by Alzner, on a marble base, dated 1932, 15½in (39.5cm) high.
$1,400–1,600 ⚘ JAd

An Austrian bronze figure of a snake charmer, by Franz Bergman, c1930, 17in (43cm) high.
$4,600–6,000 ⊞ OND

An ivory figure, by L. Bidarf, on a marble base, signed, 1920, 7in (18cm) high.
$3,200–4,000 ⊞ ASA

A Rosenthal porcelain figure of a ballet dancer, by D. Charol, incised and printed marks, Germany, 1920s, 13in (33cm) high.
$230–290 ⚘ P(B)

A Frenh bronze and ivory figure of a young lady, by Demêtre H. Chiparus, Paris, on a white onyx base, signed, early 20thC, 8in (20.5cm) high.
$2,000–2,300 ⚘ S(S)
Demêtre Chiparus was born in Romania.
He lived in Paris and studied under A. Mercier and J. Boucher and exhibited at the Salon from 1914 to 1928.

Hagenauer (Austrian, established 1898)

The Hagenauer Werkstätte (workshops) were founded in Vienna in 1898 by Carl Hagenauer (1872–1928). Initially the firm specialized in practical and ornamental artefacts – such as metal tablewares, lamps, mirrors and vases, but from 1910–30 it became famous for the metal figurines and groups, which were exhibited throughout Europe.

Carl Hagenauer's eldest son Karl joined the firm in 1919 and, with his brother Franz, took over in 1928. In the 1930s their designs were at the forefront of the New Realism.

A bronze figure of a nude female, by Harriet Frishmuth, on a marble base, signed and copyrighted 1918, 20in (51cm) high.
$11,000–13,000 ⚘ TREA

A Hagenauer bronze figure of a boy under a palm tree, Austria, 1920s, 9in (23cm) high.
$1,600–1,800 ⊞ ANO

◄ **A bronze figure of a hunter,** by Maurice Guiraud-Rivière, signed, c1925, 21¾in (55.5cm) high.
$950–1,150 ⚘ P

A Hagenauer patinated-bronze figure, Austria, 1930s, 9½in (24cm) high.
$4,000–4,400 ⊞ MI

A bronze and ivory figure of a young lady with enamelled fan, by Alexander Kélèty, her dress bronze-inlaid with copper alloy scroll designs, on a brown-veined onyx base with later inscriptional plate, signed, 1930s, 25½in (32cm) high.
$6,500–8,000 ⚘ PFK

An Austrian black patinated-bronze and ivory group of a woman and her horse, by Bruno Zach, on an onyx base, signed, early 20thC, 7¾in (19.5cm) long.
$2,300–2,900 ✗ S(S)

A bronze and ivory figure, cast and carved from a model by Martel, on a green and black onyx base, France, c1925, 12in (30.5cm) high.
$6,400–7,000 ⊞ ART

A green patinated-bronze figure, Leda and the Swan, by Charles Sykes, modelled as a naked figure and swan in close embrace, signed, 1920, 12in (30.5cm) high.
$3,200–3,700 ✗ P

◀ An Austrian bronze figure, Kicking Girl, by Bruno Zach, on an onyx base, c1925, 17¼in (44cm) high.
$2,500–3,000 ✗ P
Zach is famous for his erotic, slightly prurient portraits of the Berlin demi-monde. His subjects are nearly always female – multiple figures being rare – but pairs exist, usually of dancers or lovers.

A bronze and ivory figure of a dancer, on a green onyx base, hands repaired, c1930, 11¼in (28.5cm) high.
$1,700–2,000 ✗ BB(L)

An Austrian bronze and ivory figure, on a stepped green onyx base, c1920, 9½in (24cm) high.
$870–1,000 ✗ LJ

Art Deco Furniture

A French rosewood and mahogany bed, the head and footboard modelled as stylized shells and upholstered in caramel leather, with conforming side rails and base, with original drawing, dated 1939, 62½in (159cm) wide.
$6,500–8,000 ⚲ **S**

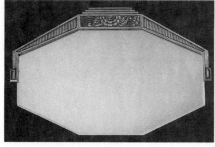

A silvered wood wall mirror, in the style of Paul Follot, the plate with a half surround of a stylized floral-carved tablet, shuttered tapering panels and stylized scrolls, c1930, 37¾in (96cm) wide.
$580–720 ⚲ **P**

▶ **A pair of walnut-veneered open armchairs,** with new upholstery, 1925–30.
$1,000–1,200 ⚲ **DORO**

A walnut-veneered drawing room suite, comprising nine pieces, 1930s.
$3,000–3,400 ⚲ **Bea(E)**

A satin birch dining table, the top inlaid with brass stringing and centred by a removable well, 1930s, 74¾in (190cm) long, with a matching console table.
$1,300–1,600 ⚲ **S(S)**

A burr elm and walnut cocktail cabinet, the upper section with a pair of doors enclosing a mirrored and fitted interior, with doors below, 1930s, 31½in (80cm) wide.
$650–800 ⚲ **CGC**

A pair of demi-lune console tables, with frieze drawers and gilt-metal scroll bracket supports, 1930s, 24in (61cm) wide.
$900–1,000 ⚲ **S(S)**

Miller's is a price GUIDE not a price LIST

▶ **A Heal & Sons walnut coffee table,** c1935, 20in (51cm) diam.
$450–550 ⚲ **M**

An oak-veneered display cabinet, with leaded glass door panels, labelled 'Superlative', Leeds, 1930s, 40in (101.5cm) diam.
$725–800 ⊞ **BDA**

A Paul Frankl desk, by Frankl Studios, with black top and drawer fronts with red accents and silver trim, and a book-shelf at one end, original drawer pulls, Austria, 1930s, 44in (112cm) wide.
$2,200–2,600 ⚲ **TREA**

A walnut-veneered wardrobe and matching dressing table, the ward-robe with a central hanging rail and hooks, a drawer to the base, enclosed by a bowfronted door, flanked by two cupboards with ivory handles, the table with etched stylized motifs in gilt, 1930, 67in (170cm) wide.
$870–1,000 ⚲ **WW**

Art Deco Glass

A Charder cameo glass vase, acid-etched in relief with scarabs, France, 1925, 15½in (39.5cm) high. **$2,300–2,900 ⚒ BWe**

A Daum straw-coloured acid-etched glass vase, cut with sunflowers, France, c1930, 7in (18cm) high. **$1,200–1,400 ⊞ ART**

A René Lalique glass scent bottle, La Belle Saison, for Houbigant, signed, France, 1925, bottle 5½in (14cm) high, in a fitted green and gold box simulating shagreen. **$3,000–3,500 ⚒ P**

A Louis Majorelle and Daum glass vase, the pale turquoise glass with purple splashes and gold foil inclusions blown into a wrought iron armature with applied hammered flower-heads, signed, France, c1925, 12½in (32cm) high. **$5,000–6,000 ⚒ BB(L)**

To find out more see *Miller's Glass of the '20s & '30s: A Collector's Guide* (£5.99), with over 130 colour pictures, its 64 pages are packed with invaluable information. *Order from* www.millers.uk.com *or telephone in the UK on* 01933 443863

A René Lalique blue-stained opalescent bowl, Coupe Muguet, signed, France, c1930, 9½in (24cm) diam. **$1,300–1,600 ⊞ RUSK**

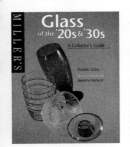

A Monart glass vase, with a milk white body, the interior decorated with filigree canes on a rich brown ground, Scotland, c1920, 9½in (24cm) high. **$1,100–1,300 ⚒ P(Ed)**

A Schneider wrought iron-mounted mottled orange and purple glass vase, Epines, signed, France, c1922, 17¾in (45cm) high. **$2,200–2,400 ⚒ P(Z)**

A long-stemmed glass vase, with white and blue stripes, probably Thüringia, Germany, 1925–35, 9in (23cm) high. **$230–290 ⚒ DORO**

A James Powell Whitefriars ruby threaded glass vase, c1930, 6in (15cm) high. **$230–260 ⊞ RUSK**

A WMF Myra Kristal iridescent glass vase, Germany, 1925, 5in (13cm) high. **$260–290 ⊞ OND**

◄ **A D'Avesn glass vase,** the smoked glass heightened with blue staining and moulded with a band of stylized fish and geometric decoration, indistinct painted mark to base, France, 1930s, 10¾in (27.5cm) high. **$1,100–1,300 ⚒ S(S)**

An enamelled glass scent bottle, 1920s, 6in (15cm) high. **$110–125 ⊞ TWAC**

DECORATIVE ARTS

Art Deco Jewellery

A diamond bar brooch, depicting two birds flying towards the sun, portrayed by a diamond, c1930, 3in (7.5cm) wide.
$4,500–5,000 ⚒ RPI

A French silver bracelet, by Jean Desprès and Etienne Cournault, signed, c1928, 7½in (19cm) long.
$35,000–39,000 ⚒ S(NY)

A Mexican silver bracelet, inlaid with lapis lazuli stone, 1930s, 7½in (19cm) long.
$290–360 ⊞ ASA

An old-cut diamond ring, c1930.
$2,900–3,200 ⚒ GAK

► **A French pâte-de-verre pendant,** by Gabriel Argy-Rousseau, the grey glass moulded with a thistle flower in purple and red, signed, c1925, 2½in (6.5cm) diam.
$870–1,000 ⚒ P

A pair of diamond earrings, c1925.
$4,000–4,600 ⚒ WW

► **A René Lalique opal-escent glass pendant,** moulded with the head of a girl holding a bird in one hand, flanked by another bird with outstretched wings, original silk cord and tassel, signed, France, pendant 1½in (4cm) long.
$1,400–1,700 ⚒ LAY

A diamond and platinum plaque ring, c1930.
$1,300–1,600 ⚒ LJ

Art Deco Lighting

◄ **A Desny nickelled-bronze desk lamp,** signed, France, c1930, 11¾in (30cm) high.
$15,000–17,500 ⚒ S(NY)

A René Lalique Ronceaux clear and frosted glass *plafonnier*, moulded in high relief with curved motifs, minor damage, signed, France, after 1926, 14¾in (37.5cm) diam.
$3,000–3,500 ⚒ Bon

◄ **A Paul Follot carved, ebonized and gilt-wood standard lamp,** France, c1925, 58in (147.5cm) high.
$6,500–8,000 ⊞ MI

A Martinuzzi glass chandelier, by Venini, the shades bordered with green thread, the stem with *pulegoso* glass elements, Italy, c1935, 23¾in (60.5cm) high.
$3,200–3,600 ⚒ P(Z)

A Francis Paul chromium-plated and frosted glass light fixture, produced by René Pottier, France, c1937, 14½in (37cm) high.
$3,600–4,300 ⚒ BB(L)

Art Deco Metalware

An A. R. Horder & Co silver beaker, set with three ivory cabochons, Birmingham 1937, 3in (7.5cm) high, 2oz.
$300–350 ⚖ Bon

A hand-beaten silver fruit bowl, by Hugh Wallis, Altrincham, chased around the rim with a band of cherries and foliage, with applied corded border, Chester 1939, 13in (33cm) diam.
$1,100–1,300 ⊞ DAD

Georg Jensen

Georg Jensen was born in Denmark in 1866. After working as a potter and sculptor he became a silversmith, winning first prize at the San Francisco World's Fair in 1915. As the popularity of his work increased he took on key designers such as Harald Nielsen, Henning Koppel and Johan Rohde to design for his retail outlets. His Art Nouveau jewellery incorporates images from nature such as birds perched amid foliage, often highlighted with opal or green agate. His flatware designs are of particular interest to collectors, with an early design such as Magnolia Blossom selling at a premium price against more commonly seen designs such as the Acanthus or Acorn patterns. Collectors generally prefer his designs with pre-war import marks.

A Danish silver flatware service, by Georg Jensen, comprising 30 pieces, decorated with Dahlia pattern, designed 1912, Copenhagen, c1920, 28oz.
$9,000–10,000 ⚖ S(NY)

A Camille Fauré enamel-on-copper vase and cover, incised and enamelled with stylized motifs in shades of blue, violet, pale blue and black, signed, France, c1925, 13¼in (33.5cm) high.
$5,500–6,500 ⚖ P(Z)

A four-piece silver-coloured metal tea and coffee service, by Jean E. Puiforcat, with ebony finials and handles, France, c1925, teapot 4¾in (12cm) high.
$12,300–14,500 ⚖ S

A four-piece silver tea service, London 1938, 49.5oz.
$580–720 ⚖ GAK

▶ **A three-piece silver tea service,** the teapot with an ivory finial, possibly by Emile Viners, London 1934, teapot 6¼in (16cm) high, 17oz.
$720–870 ⚖ Bon

A Mappin & Webb silver condiment set, Birmingham 1933, tray 5¼in (13.5cm) diam, 8.75oz.
$430–500 ⚖ CGC

A George VI silver mug, by A. E. Jones, Birmingham 1942–43, 2in (5cm) high, 3.4oz.
$500–550 ⊞ NS

A four-piece silver tea service and tray, by S.B. & S., the teapot and jug with simulated ebonized handles and finials, Chester 1932, the tray Chester 1931, 13in (33cm) wide, 89oz.
$1,800–2,200 ⚖ P(E)

A Johan Rohde four-piece silver tea and coffee service, by Georg Jensen, designed 1933–36, stamped with a post-war mark, coffee pot 7in (18cm) high.
$8,000–8,800 ⚖ P(Z)

Twentieth-Century Design
Ceramics

◀ **A Ruskin Pottery ginger jar on a stand,** decorated with blue and orange matt glazes, impressed and raised marks, c1930, 10½in (26.5cm) high.
$720–870 ⚒ FHF

Two Wedgwood Coronation mugs, designed by Eric Ravilious, 4in (10cm) high.
l. 1953, decorated in pink, yellow and black.
r. 1937, decorated in blue, yellow and black, slight damage.
$290–350 ⚒ SWO

A Wedgwood vase, with cream glaze, designed by Keith Murray, 1930–40, 6½in (16.5cm) high.
$360–430 ⊞ BEV

An earthenware vase, by Alan Caiger-Smith, with a lustrous yellow foliate design on a white ground, painted mark ACS, c1950, 11½in (29cm) high.
$360–430 ⚒ P(B)

A Katherine Pleydell-Bouverie stoneware bowl, covered in a thick dark green dripping glaze with white splashes, impressed mark, c1955, 7¼in (18.5cm) diam.
$360–430 ⚒ F&C

A Hans Coper pottery vase, decorated with a mottled brown glaze, crazed and minor chip, impressed seal mark, early 1950s, 5¼in (13.5cm) high.
$870–1,000 ⚒ RTo

A Gustavsberg faïence vase, by Stig Lindberg, decorated with painted tear-shaped motifs in pale yellow, black and blue glazes on a white ground, Sweden, designed c1953, 13¾in (35cm) high.
$400–460 ⚒ P(Ba)

A Michael Anderson pineapple stoneware ewer, glazed in shades of brown, c1960, 6¼in (16cm) high.
$145–180 ⊞ DSG

◀ **A Rörstrand pottery jug,** by Gunnar Nylund, Sweden, 1950s, 10¼in (26cm) high.
$170–220 ⊞ MARK

A Royal Worcester cake tray, by Scottie Wilson, transfer-printed with an exotic bird and a castle in black and grey on a white ground, c1960, 13½in (34.5cm) long.
$115–145 ⊞ DAD
Scottie Wilson, who claimed to be illiterate, was 'discovered' working in a clockmaker's workshop in Toronto. He came to London and was at his most prolific in the 1960s, associating with Picasso and Miró. Apart from his work for Royal Worcester, he also made items in terracotta and produced silk scarves for Liberty's.

A stoneware vase, by William Ruscoe, with a painted black design on a speckled grey ground, incised 'William Ruscoe 1965', 10in (25.5cm) diam.
$430–480 ⚒ P

◀ **A pair of Pilkington's Royal Lancastrian pottery vases,** with a mottled lavender glaze, c1975, 11in (28cm) high.
$600–700 ⊞ HUN

Furniture

A pair of Thonet chromium-plated club chairs, by Mart Stam, with cantilever frame, the seat and back upholstered in green dog-tooth check Rexene, Austria, 1929.
$1,450–1,750 ➤ P(Ba)
Made for the staff recreation club of the BATA factory, the two chairs were part of a shipment brought to Britain when BATA, a Czechoslovakian company, relocated to escape the Nazis in 1938 and settled in Tilbury, Essex. This design is the first formal armchair of Stam's using the cantilever principle.

A Ole Wanscher rosewood easy chair, by P. Jeppesen, No. 149, with a woven cane seat and leather-covered cushions, Denmark, 1949.
$1,100–1,300 ➤ TREA

A Norwegian teak sewing table, the half-hinged top with a rotating shelf, with leather-lined material store, 1962, 23in (58.5cm) diam.
$290–350 ➤ TRL
This piece won first prize in a Norwegian design competition in 1962.

A Thonet tubular metal framed stool, designed by Le Corbusier, Pierre Jeanneret and Charlotte Perriand, with original metal label, Austria, c1930, 18½in (47cm) high.
$5,000–5,800 ➤ S

A Stanley W. Davies walnut hanging bookshelf, the sides with exposed dovetails and ebony wedged-through tendons, carved 'SWD 1933' to interior corner, 36in (91.5cm) wide.
$1,450–1,750 ➤ M

A pair of Nanna and Jorgen Ditzel rattan chairs, on turned teak uprights joined by stretchers, Denmark, 1950.
$430–500 ➤ P(Ed)

▶ An Artek birch cabinet, by Alvar Aalto, Finland, designed 1935–40, 36in (91.5cm) wide.
$1,900–2,300 ⊞ PLB

A Ludwig Mies van der Rohe mahogany sofa, produced by Jerry Griffith, upholstered in a pale green suede, America, c1940, 91in (231cm) long.
$4,600–5,000 ➤ BB(L)
This piece was owned by the noted architect James DeForrest Ferris, who studied at the Illinois Institute of Technology under the personal tutelage of Ludwig Mies van der Rohe. While a student, he obtained a suite of 13 pieces of furniture from the Mies van der Rohe workshop in Chicago. This is a rare pre-production sofa from this suite, which retains its original suede upholstery.

A DKR chromium-plated chair, designed by Charles Eames in 1951, with white vinyl bikini pads, America, 1980s to present day.
$360–430 ⊞ MARK

A Herman Miller set of four aluminium Group armchairs and table, by Charles and Ray Eames, the chairs covered with ribbed black fabric with aluminium arms and base, the table with laminated top with vinyl edging on an aluminium pedestal base, America, c1958, table 60¼in (153cm) diam.
$2,300–2,900 ➤ Bri

A Hille sideboard, by Robin Day, on a birch carcass with two rosewood veneered doors, flanking an ebonized sliding door, enclosing a shelved interior, on blackened tubular steel uprights joined by blackened steel stretchers, c1960, 84in (213.5cm) wide.
$1,000–1,300 ➤ P(Ba)

A French fibreglass chair, with cream leather upholstery, probably by Airborne Industries, France, late 1960s.
$500–650 ⊞ MARK

Glass

An Iittala Lichen glass vase, by Tapio Wirkkala, the mould-blown clear glass with acid frosted surface, Finland, designed 1949, 8¾in (22cm) high.
$950–1,150 ✦ P(Ba)

An Aureliano Toso Oriente glass vase, by Dino Martens, entitled Nabucco, with original paper label, Italy, c1952, 9½in (24cm) high.
$8,000–8,800 ✦ S(NY)

► **A Skruf glass bowl,** by Bengt Edenfalk, Sweden, 1970s, 5in (12.5cm) high.
$230–260 ⊞ MARK

A Cenedese glass bottle, designed by Fulvio Bianconi, applied with blue, black and grey pattern, Italy, c1950, 13½in (34.5cm) high.
$4,000–4,600 ✦ S(NY)

► **An Orrefors glass vase,** etched with a young girl looking at the moon and stars, Sweden, c1950, 6in (15cm) wide.
$400–440 ⊞ MI

Three Orrefors Graal glass vases, by Edvard Hald, internally-decorated in green with fish swimming among seaweed, signed, Sweden, 1952, largest 6in (15cm) high.
$2,200–2,500 ✦ BB(L)

► **A Vasart green and pink glass bowl,** decorated with blue swirls, signed, Scotland, 1950s, 8in (20.5cm) diam.
$95–110 ⊞ SAN

Two Holmegaard cased glass bottle vases, in yellow and red, Denmark, 1970s, 8in (20.5cm) high
$160–190 each ⊞ PLB

Jewellery

A Georg Jensen brown enamel and sterling silver abstract brooch, designed by Henning Koppel, Denmark, c1947, 1¼in (3cm) wide.
$870–1,000 ⊞ DID

A diamanté and cabochon necklace, designed by Kenneth Lane, 1960s.
$290–320 ⊞ FMa

A Torun Vivianna Bülow-Hübe silver-coloured metal choker, hung with pendant drops with lapis lazuli beads, stamped mark, Denmark, 1950s, 4in (10cm) diam.
$4,500–5,000 ✦ S

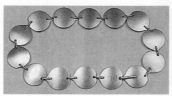

A Continental silver necklace, by Hans Hansen, with 15 stylized tulip panel links, Denmark, c1970, 15in (38cm) long.
$580–720 ✦ P(L)

A Georg Jensen silver bangle, No. 117, Denmark, c1960.
$300–350 ✦ WilP

A sterling silver pendant and chain, by Tony White, with suspended oval agate, hallmarked, Australia, c1960.
$230–260 ✦ LJ

Lighting

Polaroid Corporation bakelite and aluminium executive desk lamp, by Walter Dorwin Teague, Model No. 114, with paper label to base, America, 1939–41, 12in (30.5cm) high. **$2,100–2,400** ➤ **TREA**

A spiral-twisted aluminium appliqué, entitled Flamme, by Serge Mouille, with mottled black finish, France, 1958, 15in (38cm) high. **$4,600–5,500** ➤ **S**

A steel and perspex lamp, the stylized cylindrical steel body set with nine radiating clear perspex fans, c1960, 30¾in (78cm) high. **$145–175** ➤ **LJ**

A Luber three-section purple plastic twist light, by Verner Panton, Switzerland, 1970, 107in (272cm) high. **$3,400–3,700** ⊞ **MARK**

plastic and chrome hanging lamp, by Harvey Guzzini, c1970, 17in (43cm) high. **$650–725** ⊞ **ZOOM**

An Italian chrome Sputnik hanging lamp, 1970s, 24in (61cm) high. **$650–800** ⊞ **PLB**

A Vistosi white cased-glass lamp, Italy, late 1960s, 18in (45.5cm) high. **$475–525** ⊞ **PAB**

▶ **A O-Luce white enamelled aluminium Atollo lamp,** designed by Vico Magistretti, Italy, 1977, 27½in (70cm) high. **$260–320** ➤ **P(Ba)**

Metalware

hammered silver porringer, by Henry George Murphy, the handle pierced and chased with the Tree of Life motif, London 1938, in (12.5cm) long. **$1,700–2,000** ⊞ **DAD**

A Georg Jensen silver powder compact, No. 231N, the cover applied with a stylized dolphin, Denmark, import marks for 1952, 2½in (6.5cm) diam. **$250–290** ➤ **P(L)**

A silver and silver-gilt serving dish and cover, by Stuart Devlin, with silver-gilt filigree-work handles, the cover forming a second serving tray when removed, stamped marks, 1976, 10½in (26.5cm) wide. **$1,700–2,000** ➤ **P(Ba)**

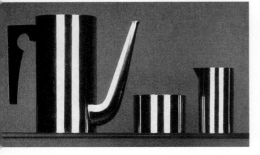

◀ **A Stelton stainless steel Cylinda-Line tea service,** by Arne Jacobsen, comprising four pieces, with dark brown wooden handles, Danish, 1967, 6¾in (17cm) high. **$360–430** ➤ **DORO**

A Collet-Texture coffee service, by Stuart Devlin, comprising four pieces, with all-over chased, horizontal textured decoration, with mahogany handles, stamped, 1977, coffee pot 9¾in (25cm) high. **$2,900–3,200** ➤ **P(Ba)**

Rugs & Textiles

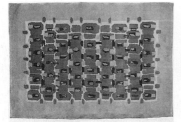

A Leleu wool carpet, designed by Paul Leleu, with woven LELEU tag, France, c1950, 68 x 100¾in (172.5 x 254.5cm). **$8,300–10,000** ↗ **S(NY)**

A woollen rug, with a cubist pattern in yellow, orange, blue, black and cream on a brown ground, 1950s, 50in (127cm) square. **$220–260** ↗ **TREA**

Miller's is a price GUIDE not a price LIST

A pair of Fidelis curtains by Anthony Sharp, decorate with Nucleus pattern in red and brown on an orange ground, late 1950s 93 x 48in (236 x 122cm). **$115–145** ↗ **P(Ed)**

Sculpture

A German pewter sculpture, by Brigitte Matschinsky-Denninghoff, 1955, 13½in (35cm) high. **$3,300–3,700** ↗ **S(Am)**

A Danish wooden sculpture of two lovers, by Simone, 1960s, 15½in (39.5cm) high. **$550–600** ⊞ **ZOOM**

A pair of painted wooden sculptures, by Viktor IV, entitled Viktoren Ans, Holland, dated A'dam 19 VI. 1966, 30in (76cm) high. **$1,900–2,200** ↗ **S(Am)**

◀ **A bronze sculpture,** by Charlotte van Pallandt, entitled De Zicke, signed, 1961, probably Holland, edition of ten, 4in (10cm) high. **$2,400–2,600** ↗ **S(Am)**

A welded steel sculpture, by Jack Denst, the biomorphic flowerlike shape on a walnut base, signed, probably America, 1962, 66in (167.5cm) high. **$950–1,150** ↗ **TREA**

◀ A pair of Multi Art plastic cube wall sculptures, by Flemming Hvidt, Denmark, early 1970s, each cube 3in (7.5cm) square. **$145–175** ⊞ **PAB**

A wooden sculpture, by Brian Willsher, signed and dated 1978, 8¾in (22cm) high. **$500–600** ↗ **Bon(C)**

A marble sculpture of a small tortoise on socle, by Max Ernst, signed and numbered 128/150, German, executed in 1975 12½in (32cm) high. **$8,700–9,500** ↗ **S(Am)**

essential guides
for the collector

Someone somewhere buys a Miller's book every
two minutes! Whether your passion is for antiques
or collectables, our impressive range of guides will
meet your needs. From porcelain to paperweights,
from furniture to fashion, a Miller's guide will help you
identify, authenticate and value your favorite pieces.
Compiled with the help of an international team of
experts, our books provide thousands of photographs,
independently assessed price ranges, insider collecting
tips, as well as all the essential background information
you need on antiques and collectables of every type.

MILLER'S

Miller's Price Guides

Miller's best-selling price guides are the ultimate reference books, ideal for both the experienced dealer and the first time collector. Completely new each year, Miller's price guides offer expert advice, thousands of new photographs, independently assessed price ranges, insider collecting tips and essential background information.

Antiques Price Guide 2002
US $35.00　　**CA $50.00**

Collectables Price Guide 2001
US $29.95　　**CA $39.95**

Classic Motorcycles Yearbook and Price Guide 2002
US $19.95　　**CA $ 29.95**

Collector's Cars Yearbook and Price Guide 2002
US $35.00　　**CA $49.95**

isbn 1 84000 453 3

isbn 1 84000 386 3

isbn 1 84000 440 1　isbn 1 84000 441 X

Miller's Buyer's Guides

The Miller's Buyer's Guide series provides invaluable reference material for the enthusiast as well as the experienced collector. Each guide concentrates on a popular area of collecting and features thousands of examples, which are illustrated, authenticated and given an up-to-date price range by a team of top dealers and auction house specialists.

Art Nouveau & Art Deco

Ceramics

Chinese & Japanese Antiques

Clocks & Barometers

Glass

Late Georgian to Edwardian Furniture

Pine & Country Furniture

US $29.95　　　　**CA $39.95**

isbn 1 84000 361 8

isbn 1 84000 375 8

isbn 1 84000 374 X

Miller's Collector's Guides

Miller's Collector's Guides provide an essential introduction to popular subjects for the budding collector. Reflecting the growing trend in the antiques market towards 'collectibles' – small, often affordable items – these practical guides are filled with ideas on how to form a collection, what to specialize in and how to identify objects.

Advertising Tins

Blue & White Pottery

Ceramics of the '20s & '30s

Ceramics of the '50s & '60s

Costume Jewellery

Glass of the '20s & '30s

Goss & Crested China

Handbags

Paperweights

Pens & Writing Equipment

Perfume Bo

Popular Gla

Postcards

Powder Compacts

Sewing Accessories

Smoking Accessories

Soft Toys

Staffordshir Figures

Watches

Corkscrews Wine Antiq

US $9.99　　　　**CA $14.95**

isbn 1 84000 373 1

isbn 1 840000 430 4

isbn 1 84000 439 8

Miller's Collecting....

Fascinating and informative guides on specific areas of collecting. These guides cover a wide range of topics on a particular subject, providing a price guide, and information on items worth thousands of pounds to pieces that can be picked up for less than £10. These guides have something for all collectors with an excellent range of interesting and affordable items from across the field.

Collecting the 1960s
US $26.95   **CA $39.95**

Collecting the 1950s
US $26.95   **CA $39.95**

Collecting Books
US $29.95   **CA $45.00**

Collecting Fashion & Accessories
US $26.95   **CA $36.95**

Collecting Prints & Posters
US $29.95   **CA $45.00**

Collecting Textiles
US $29.95   **CA $39.95**

isbn 1 84000 390 1

isbn 1 84000 079 1

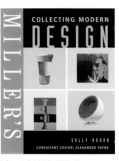
isbn 1 84000 405 3

Miller's The Facts At Your Fingertips

These best-selling guides to popular collecting subjects combine historical background with practical advice for the collector by focusing on items that are available and affordable. They also look at identifying and dating pieces, assessing condition and recognizing maker's marks. Each item is given a realistic price range while Fact Boxes highlight key collecting areas.

Collecting Glass

Collecting Furniture

Collecting Silver

Collecting Teddy Bears & Dolls

Collecting Antiques & Collectables

Collecting Pottery & Porcelain
US $19.95   **CA $29.95**

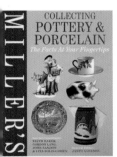
isbn 1 85732 898 1

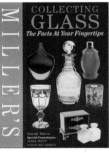
isbn 1 84000 191 7

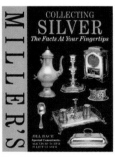
isbn 1 84000 143 7

Two new series from Miller's

Introducing two brand new series from Miller's with a decidedly American accent. The Insider's Guides concentrate more on hints and techniques for assessing condition, avoiding fakes, spotting bargains and estimating fair value. The Treasure or Not? series helps the collector to develop an appraiser's eye and a connoisseur's knowledge by comparing 60 pairs of similar items and looking at what makes one more valuable than the other.

Miller's Insider's Guide to

Toys & Games

Furniture
US $24.95   **CA $39.95**

Miller's Treasure or Not?

How to Compare & Value

American Art Pottery

American Quilts
US $24.95   **CA $37.95**

isbn 1 84000 379 0

isbn 1 84000 380 4

isbn 1 84000 382 0

isbn 1 84000 381 2

Miller's Checklists & Fact Files

Two invaluable pocket size series. Miller's Pocket Fact Files are compact reference guides for the specialist collector and enthusiast providing excellent identification and dating information. Miller's Antiques Checklists provide simple question-and-answer lists, advising what to look for and how to distinguish between the genuine article and a fake, an original and a copy.

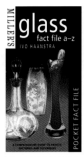

isbn 1 84000 280 8   isbn 1 85732 273 8   isbn 1 84000 429 0   isbn 0 85533 689 7

Other Miller's Titles

No antiques lover should be without the classic Miller's Antiques Encyclopedia. Two new titles that are also proving invaluable for the collector are *Miller's Antiques Shops, Fairs & Auctions*, an essential guide to fairs, dealers, auction houses, insurance valuers, repairers, restorers, packers and shippers, and *Miller's Antiques Art & Collectables on the Web*, featuring over 1000 websites from around the world. And for all those teddy bear enthusiasts, we are delighted to present our irresistible new title, *Miller's Teddy Bears: A Complete Collector's Guide*. These titles are just a selection from our complete Miller's list. To see the complete range of titles available, visit our website **www.millers.uk.com**

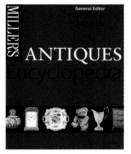
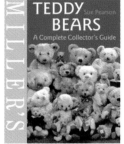

isbn 1 85732 747 0   isbn 1 84000 391 X   isbn 1 84000 360 X   isbn 1 84000 459 2

How to Order

To see the complete range of titles and to buy online, visit our website www.millers.uk.com

To order in the USA, please contact: *Customer Services and Distribution Center, Phaidon Press Inc, 7195 Grayson Road, Harrisburg, PA 7111. tel: 1877 Phaidon (toll-free)*

To order in Canada , please contact : *McArthur & Company Publishing Ltd, 322 King Street West, Suite 402, Toronto, Ontario, M5V 1J2. tel: 416 408 4007.*

www.millers.uk.com

Colour Review

An Arts and Crafts mahogany and oak suite, of hall stand and two chairs, the tiles by John Moyr-Smith for Minton, c1880, 43¼in (110cm) wide.
$2,000–2,200 ✎ HOK

A late Victorian Aesthetic Movement walnut sideboard, 74¾in (190cm) wide.
$1,500–1,750 ⊞ WL

An Arts and Crafts copper-mounted oak cupboard bookcase, c1890, 55½in (141cm) wid
$5,000–5,500 ✎ S(S)

An American oak bookcase, by L. & J. G. Stickley, 1906–12, 30in (76cm) wide.
$11,000–13,000 ✎ BB(L)

An Arts and Crafts oak bureau, designed by J. S. Henry, c1890, 33¾in (85.5cm) wide.
$2,200–2,500 ⊞ APO

A set of four oak side chairs, designed by Richard Norman Shaw, 1876.
$580–650 ✎ Bri
Originally designed for the Tabard Inn, Bedford Park.

A set of ten Arts and Cra oak chairs, by J. Shoolbred Co, with leather-covered se including two carvers, c189
$7,250–8,750 ⊞ PVD

An Arts and Crafts mahogany hall stand, with coppered metalware, c1890, 44in (112cm) wide.
$800–950 ⊞ MTay

A Victorian Arts and Crafts oak dresser, with mirror shelf back, 54in (137cm) wide.
$500–600 ✎ RTo

An Arts and Crafts mahogany occasional table, by George Jack for Morris & Co, London, c1888, 30in (76cm) wide.
$20,000–23,000 ✎ P
This model was exhibited at the Arts and Crafts Exhibition Society in 1889.

An Arts and Crafts oak sideboard, the design registered for 1901, 64in (162.5cm) wide.
$1,200–1,450 ✎ RBB

◄ **An Arts and Crafts two-seater settee,** c1905, 35in (89cm) long.
$600–700 ✎ P(B)

► **An Arts and Crafts oak sideboard,** by Shapland & Petter, the doors inset with copper panels, stamped mark, c1905, 72½in (184cm) wide.
$2,000–2,500 ✎ Bon(W)

A **cameo crystal sherry decanter,** the panels cut in the Aesthetic style, late 19thC, 10½in (26.5cm) high. $2,900–3,500 ⚖ L&E

A pair of William de Morgan snake tiles, impressed mark, c1885, 8in (20.5cm) high. $7,200–8,700 ⚖ P

◄ **A Burmantofts faïence jardinière and stand,** impressed marks, jardinière 11in (28cm) high. $1,000–1,100 ⚖ P(L)

A Della Robbia pottery _albarello_, by Cassandia Annie Walker, incised mark, 1904, 14¾in (37.5cm) high. $5,800–6,500 ⚖ S(NY)

Linthorpe jardinière, designed by Dr Christopher Dresser, c1884, 13in (33cm) wide. $1,300–1,500 ⊞ HUN

◄ **A Minton Art Pottery hand-painted dish,** 1872, 9in (23cm) diam. $190–230 ⊞ DSG

An Arts and Crafts silver bowl, by Mappin & Webb, 1905, 8in (20.5cm) diam, 26.5oz. $1,200–1,400 ⚖ P

An American Newcomb College Pottery _solitaire_, comprising seven pieces, by Joseph Fortune Meyer, decorated by Désiré Roman, signed and numbered, c1912. $3,600–4,300 ⚖ NOA

► **A gold pendant,** by Murrle, Bennett & Co, set with two matrix cabochons and five seed pearls, maker's monogram, c1905, 2½in (6.5cm) high. $1,100–1,300 ⊞ DAD

A John Ruskin vase, with flambé-effect soufflé glaze, c1906, 6¾in (17cm) high. $900–1,000 ⊞ GAA

pair of A. E. Jones silver and copper candlesticks, c1900, 10in (25.5cm) high. $720–800 ⊞ SHa

A John Pearson copper casket, the lid cast with a bird of prey, 1900, 9½in (24cm) long. $800–900 ⚖ Bon

► **An Arts and Crafts silver and enamel box,** by Child & Child, London 1888, 4in (10cm) diam. $540–620 ⊞ ANO

A Louis Majorelle carved walnut marquetry buffet, France, c1908, 39in (99cm) wide.
$17,500–22,000 ⚒ S(NY)

An Art Nouveau mahogany display cabinet, c1905, 54½in (138.5cm) wide.
$3,000–3,500 ⚒ AH

An Art Nouveau inlaid mahogany armchair, by J. S. Henry, c1900.
$4,000–4,500 ⊞ MI

A Louis Majorelle carved mahogany five-piece salon suite, with original yellow velvet upholstery, France, c1900, settee 62in (157.5cm) long.
$30,000–35,000 ⚒ S(NY)

A French Art Nouveau walnut display cabinet, attributed to Majorelle, c1900, 41in (104cm) wide.
$6,000–7,000 ⚒ BB(L)

A mahogany and marquetry display cabinet, inlaid with harewood, sycamore and abalone, retailed by Liberty & Co, possibly by J. S. Henry, c1905, 48in (122cm) wide.
$3,500–4,500 ⚒ P

An Austrian oak armchair, the seat upholstered with new fabric, Vienna, 1901–02.
$800–950 ⚒ DORO

An Art Nouveau mahogany and marquetry display cabinet, inlaid with sycamore, harewood and fruitwood, possibly retailed by Liberty & Co, c1905, 50in (127cm) wide.
$3,500–4,000 ⚒ P

A Louis Majorelle rosewood and marquetry music cabinet, France, c1900, 66in (167.5cm) high.
$6,800–7,800 ⊞ APO

An Art Nouveau oak-framed fire screen, the brass wire outlines filled in with coloured glass beads, c1900, 17¼in (44cm) square.
$600–700 ⚒ P(B)

An Art Nouveau mahogany and inlaid display cabinet, c1900, 23in (58.5cm) wide.
$4,000–4,500 ⊞ MI

A Louis Majorelle walnut and fruitwood music cabinet, France, c1900, 28½in (72.5cm) wide.
$7,250–8,750 ⚒ S

An Art Nouveau carved mahogany hall rack, gilt-bronze mounted with ormo— poppy and dragonfly, possib— by Maison Albert Darras, c1900, 55in (139.5cm) wid—
$13,000–14,500 ⚒ S(NY

◄ **An Emile Gallé inlaid marquetry fruitwood table,** France, c1900, 22in (56cm) long.
$2,300–2,600 ⊞ OND

An Ault primula leaf-shaped vase, c1895, 4in (10cm) high.
$220–240 ⊞ HUN

An Amphora vase, Bohemia, c1910, 13in (33cm) high.
$300–330 ⊞ DSG

An Adrian Dalpayrat glazed stoneware vase, moulded with two handles, impressed mark, c1900, 32½in (82.5cm) high.
$13,000–16,000 ↗ S(NY)

A Bretby dripped-glaze lamp base, c1910, 12in (30.5cm) high.
$400–450 ⊞ HUN

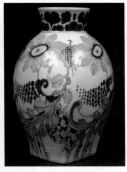

A Della Robbia pottery vase and cover, incised 'D.R.' and monograms for C.A. Walker and Ruth Bate, 1898, 12¼in (31cm) high.
$1,000–1,250 ↗ P(WM)

A Della Robbia pottery vase, c1897, 9in (23cm) high.
$1,300–1,450 ⊞ DSG

▶ **A Gouda Zuid-Holland earthenware vase,** Holland, c1910, 8in (20.5cm) high.
$1,000–1,150 ⊞ MI

A Gouda Ivora factory vase, Holland, c1925, 8½in (21.5cm) high.
$350–450 ⊞ OO

A Belgian Guerin vase, c1900, 16in (40.5cm) high. $180–230 ⊞ DSG

A Bavarian Art Nouveau Kronach porcelain vase, factory mark, c1900, 10in (25.5cm) high. $3,200–3,600 ⊞ MI

A Jean Massier bottle vase, France, c1910, 10in (25.5cm) high. $200–250 ⊞ DSG

A Minton Seccessionist garden seat, tube-lined with flowers, c1900, 20½in (52cm) high. $1,300–1,450 ➢ BWe

▶ **A Minton Seccessionist vase,** 1900–10, 11½in (29cm) high. $470–550 ⊞ DSG

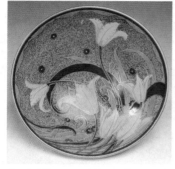

An Art Nouveau Minton lustre pottery bowl, 'Tulipa', 19thC, 9in (23cm) diam. $350–450 ➢ TMA

A Pilkington's lustre bowl, by Richard Joyce, c1900, 9½in (24cm) diam. $1,300–1,600 ⊞ ASA

A pair of Bernard Moore drip-glaze vases, c1910, 7½in (19cm) high. $500–650 ⊞ DSG

A Eugène Grasset stone-ware plaque, for Emile Muller, from the Les Heures series, restored, France, 1894, 18 x 7in (45.5 x 18cm). $5,000–6,000 ➢ S

◀ **A Rozenburg ceramic vase,** decorated with Birds of Paradise pattern, Holland, 1909, 22½in (57cm) high. $4,500–5,000 ⊞ OO

A Pilkington's Royal Lancastrian lustre vase, by William S. Mycock, decorated with irises, impressed mark and number, lustre year cypher, c1914, 10¾in (27.5cm) high. $3,500–4,500 ➢ S(NY) Ex-Harriman Judd Collection.

▶ **A Wood & Sons tube-lined double gourd vase,** decorated with Elers pattern by Frederick Rhead, 1920s, 10in (25.5cm) high. $350–400 ⊞ BDA

A Rookwood vase, with an incised design, America, 1904, 14in (35.5cm) high. $1,150–1,350 ➢ TREA

A Doulton Lambeth faïence pottery jug, monogram, printed mark, c1880, 8¾in (22cm) high. $260–280 ⚲ WW

A Doulton stoneware ewer, decorated by George Tinworth, incised initials, impressed marks, dated 1874, 10in (25.5cm) high. $500–600 ⚲ Bea(E)

A Doulton Lambeth stoneware jardinière and stand, by Mark V. Marshall, c1895, 25½in (65cm) high. $5,000–6,000 ⊞ JE

A Royal Doulton Chang vase, by Charles J. Noke, 1920–30, 10in (25.5cm) high. $3,500–4,500 ⊞ DSG

A pair of Moorcroft Macintyre Florian Ware bottle vases, each with printed factory mark, painted signature, c1903, 8¾in (22cm) high. $2,200–2,600 ⚲ DD

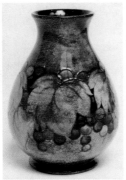

◄ **A Moorcroft flambé vase,** decorated with Leaf and Berry pattern, signed, c1925, 7in (18cm) high. $1,300–1,450 ⊞ GAA

A Moorcroft Macintyre footed vase, decorated with Pomegranate pattern, c1910, 10in (25.5cm) high. $10,000–11,500 ⊞ Lan

A pair of Daum cameo glass vases, silver-mounted around the base, gilt signature, France, c1895, 5in (12.5cm) high.
$2,700–3,000 ⊞ MI

A Daum glass vase, acid-etched and enamelled with internal splashes of colour, France, c1900, 5in (12.5cm) high.
$1,000–1,150 ⊞ OND

An iridescent glass vase, attributed to Loetz, c1900, 6½in (16.5cm) high.
$3,000–3,300 ⊞ MI

◄ **A Gallé cameo glass vase,** signed, France, c1900, 13in (33cm) high.
$3,200–3,700 ➶ BB(L)

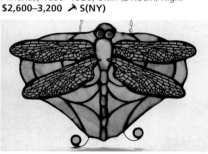

An iridescent lava pattern glass vase, attributed to Loetz, Bohemia, c1900, 3½in (9cm) high.
$1,150–1,300 ⊞ OND

An Orivit Art Nouveau pewter-mounted glass jardinière, impressed mark and number, Germany, c1900, 9½in (24cm) diam.
$1,600–1,850 ➶ RTo

A Palme & König glass bowl, Bohemia, c1900, 7¼in (18.5cm) diam.
$350–450 ⊞ DSG

▶ **A Tiffany favrile glass experimental vase,** America, 1899–1920, 8½in (21.5cm) high.
$2,600–3,200 ➶ S(NY)

A pair of Theresienthal liqueur glasses, Austria, c1900, 5in (12.5cm) high.
$800–950 ⊞ OND

A Tiffany Favrile glass and bronze filigree hanging ornament, in the shape of a dragon-fly, 1899–1918, 10in (25.5cm) high.
$5,500–6,500 ➶ S(NY)

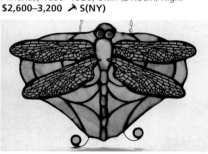

An Art Nouveau iridescent glass vase, probably by Loetz, Bohemia, c1900, 7½in (19cm) high.
$725–875 ➶ RTo

A set of six Art Nouveau glass finger bowls and under dishes, probably Theresienthal, Austria, c1900, 7in (18cm) diam.
$4,500–5,500 ⊞ ALiN

▶ **A Bohemian amethyst flashed glass vase,** probably by Moser, late 19thC, 10in (25.5cm) high.
$600–700 ➶ RTo

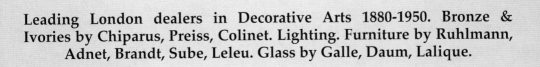

A WMF pewter basket, with glass liner, Germany, c1906, 5in (12.5cm) high.
$450–550 ⊞ OND

A pair of Deakin & Francis sweetmeat baskets, Birmingham 1910–11, 5in (12.5cm) diam.
$500–550 ⊞ NS

A Liberty & Co Tudric pewter box, with enamel inset top, marked and numbered, c1915, 4in (10cm) long.
$1,000–1,150 ⊞ OND

A William Hutton & Sons three-piece silver and abalone coffee set, London 1902, coffee can 6¾in (17cm) high.
$3,500–4,000 ⚒ P

A Liberty & Co enamelled pewter dish, c1902, 11in (28cm) wide.
$1,250–1,400 ⊞ SHa

A French Art Nouveau gilt-bronze dish, signed J. Ofner, c1910, 7in (18cm) diam.
$1,450–1,600 ⊞ MI

An Art Nouveau silver and enamel photograph frame, by Omar Ramsden and Alwyn Carr, Birmingham 1907, 6in (15cm) high.
$2,200–2,600 ⊞ DAD

A Liberty & Co silver dressing table set, with turquoise stones, Birmingham 1906.
$1,800–2,200 ⊞ SHa

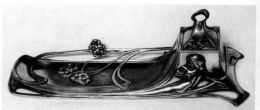

A WMF pewter inkwell, Germany, c1904, 12in (30.5cm) wide.
$800–950 ⊞ SHa

◄ An Orivit Art Nouveau pewter-mounted glass claret jug, Germany, c1910, 12½in (32cm) high
$1,000–1,150 ⊞ DAD

A pair of Liberty & Co silver napkin rings, Birmingham 1903, minor damage, 1¾in (4.5cm) high.
$870–1,000 ⚒ RTo

A William Hutton & Sons silver tray, London 1902, 12in (30.5cm) long.
$870–1,000 ⊞ SHa

A Susse Frères gilt-bronze tray, designed by Albert Cheuret, France, c1910, 15in (38cm) diam.
$2,500–3,000 ⊞ MI

A set of five Arts and Crafts copper and bronze wall lights, c1895, 14in (35.5cm) high.
$1,600–1,750 ⊞ TLG

An American Arts and Crafts hammered copper and mica desk lamp, early 20thC, 19in (48.5cm) high.
$5,000–5,500 ✗ BB(L)

A Gallé pomegranate *plafonnier,* the shade with cameo mark, France, 1900, 20½in (52cm) diam.
$11,000–13,000 ✗ S

A Gallé cameo glass and bronze flower-shaped lamp, signed in intaglio, France, c1900, 22in (56cm) high.
$20,000–22,000 ✗ S(NY)

An Art Nouveau brass table lamp, with vase-line glass shade, c1900, 18in (45.5cm) high.
$550–600 ⊞ TLG

A Pairpoint glass and silvered-metal lamp, interior-painted with a scene of two peacocks, marked, America, early 20thC, 22½in (57cm) high.
$8,500–10,000 ✗ BB(L)

A Pairpoint 'puffy' reverse-painted glass and parcel-gilt lamp, the base with impressed mark, minor chip to rim, America, 21½in (54.5cm) diam.
$11,000–13,000 ✗ S(NY)

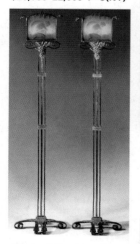

A pair of Steuben glass and wrought iron floor lamps, with Oscar Bach bronze mounts, America, c1910, 68in (172.5cm) high.
$7,250–8,750 ✗ S(NY)

► **A Tiffany-style leaded glass and bronze table lamp,** minor faults, early 20thC, 23in (58.5cm) high.
$4,000–4,500 ✗ S(NY)

A Tiffany favrile opalescent glass and silvered twisted-wire ceiling light, some damage, America, 1894–1918, 36in (91.5cm) high.
$40,000–45,000 ✗ S(NY)

A Tiffany favrile glass and patinated-bronze acorn floor lamp, stamped 'Tiffany Studios', America, 1898–1928, 57¾in (146.5cm) high.
$10,500–12,500 ✗ BB(L)

► **A Tiffany favrile glass and bronze prism lamp,** impressed marks, America, 1899–1920, 21in (53.5cm) high.
$11,500–13,500 ✗ S(NY)

A Tiffany favrile glass and bronze swirling leaf lamp, impressed marks, America, 1899–1920, 22½in (57cm) high.
$18,000–22,000 ✗ S(NY)

A pair of Art Nouveau bronze triple wall lights, with frosted glass shades, 1910, 30in (76cm) high.
$2,000–2,300 ⊞ TLG

A pair of Leleu gilt-bronze table lamps, with Muller Frères glass shades, stamped mark, France, c1915, 15in (38cm) high.
$2,400–2,800 ⊞ TLG

A Duffner & Kimberly leaded glass and gilt-bronze Wisteria chandelier, impressed mark, America, c1910, 24in (61cm) diam.
$72,500–80,000 ⚒ S(NY)

A Duffner & Kimberly leaded glass and bronze Iris lamp, America, c1915, 22½in (57cm) high.
$11,500–13,500 ⚒ S(NY)

A Duffner & Kimberly leaded glass and patinated-bronze Water Lily lamp, America, early 20thC, 26¾in (68cm) high.
$14,500–17,500 ⚒ BB(L)

A Gabriel Argy-Rousseau pâte-de-verre and wrought iron veilleuse, France, 1928, 9in (23cm) high.
$18,000–22,000 ⚒ S(NY)

A pair of Quezal bronze and glass three-light sconces, inscribed mark, America, c1915, 10in (25.5cm) high.
$8,700–10,200 ⚒ S(NY)

A Fix Masseau gilt-bronze figure, entitled Le Secret, base stamped, foundry mark, c1900, 11in (28cm) high.
$5,800–6,500 ✗ S

A Watrin bronze and ivory figure, signed, France, c1900, 13½in (34.5cm) high.
$4,800–5,400 ✗ LJ

A gilt and patinated-bronze sculpture, entitled Eté, cast from a model by D. H. Chiparus, c1920, 29in (73.5cm) wide
$12,800–14,000 ⊞ MI

▶ **An Art Deco bronze and ivory figure of a dancer,** by L. Sosson, on an onyx pedestal, inscribed signature, early 20thC, 14¼in (36cm) high.
$4,000–4,400 ✗ S(S)

A Demêtre H. Chiparus cold-painted bronze and ivory figure, entitled Hindu Dancer, on a marble base, France, c1925, 42½in (108cm) high.
$21,750–24,000 ✗ P

A Demêtre H. Chiparus bronze and ivory figure, entitled The Little Sad One, on a marble base, signed, France, c1925, 6¾in (17cm) high.
$5,800–7,200 ✗ LJ

A Demêtre H. Chiparus bronze figure, entitled Favourite Unveiled, c1925, 8in (20.5cm) high.
$3,500–4,000 ⊞ OND

A Goldscheider figural group of two chorus girls, by Dakon, marked, with incised signature, Austria, c1928, 14½in (37cm) high.
$3,600–4,300 ✗ P

A Goldscheider ceramic figure of a butterfly dancer, by Josef Lorenzl, minor restoration, Austria, 1923–24, 15in (38cm) high.
$870–1,000 ✗ DORO

A Paul Phillippe bronze and ivory figure of a pierrot, Germany, c1920, 15in (38cm) high.
$4,300–5,800 ⊞ ASA

A Lorenzl bronze figure of a naked lady, holding aloft two laurel garlands, on an onyx base, Austria, 1930s, 12in (30.5cm) high.
$2,200–2,900 ⊞ ASA

▶ **An Austrian bronze and bone model of a dancer,** on an onyx socle, one finger missing, Vienna, 1930–50, 7¾in (19.5cm) high.
$900–1,000 ✗ DORO

An Art Deco satinbirch cocktail cabinet, attributed to Ray Hille, c1935, 46½in (118cm) wide.
$2,600–3,200 ⚒ P

An Art Deco walnut open book-shelf unit, c1935, 36in (91.5cm) wide.
$500–550 ⊞ MTay

An Art Deco leather-upholstered club chair, France, early 20thC.
$870–1,000 ⚒ NOA

An Art Deco mahogany sideboard, c1940, 94½in (240cm) long.
$2,400–2,900 ⚒ BB(L)

An Art Deco walnut dining suite, comprising nine pieces, quarter-veneered and crossbanded, c1930, table 73½in (186.5cm) long.
$5,500–6,000 ⚒ AH

An Art Deco burr-walnut dining suite, comprising 11 pieces, c1930, table 80in (203cm) long.
$6,500–8,000 ⚒ S(NY)

An Art Deco sycamore and walnut dining suite, comprising eight pieces, c1935, table 71¼in (181cm) long.
$3,600–4,300 ⚒ P

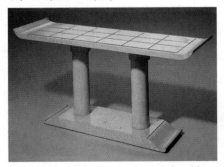

► An Art Deco pair of calamander and satinwood occasional tables, stamped 'M.A', France, c1928, 24in (61cm) wide.
$1,400–1,600 ⚒ P

An Art Deco bird's-eye maple console table, the top inset with pink mirror tiles, attributed to Ray Hille, c1935, 21in (53.5cm) wide.
$720–870 ⚒ P

An Art Deco nest of three walnut tables, Austria, c1935, largest 28in (71cm) high.
$1,200–1,300 ⊞ MTay

◄ A Gustave Gautier stained beech nest of tables, the tops with removable glass plates, France, largest 44in (112cm) wide.
$5,000–5,800 ⚒ S

An Art Deco sycamore and walnut two-tier occasional table, c1935, 26¾in (68cm) diam.
$1,400–1,700 ⚒ P

bough vase, c1920,
⅛in (8.5cm) high.
125–145 ➚ P(Ed)

A Burleigh Ware coffee set, by Charlotte
Rhead, comprising 12 pieces, decorated with
Orchard pattern, c1930.
$800–950 ⊞ BUR

A Burleigh Ware
Kingfisher jug, 1930s,
10in (25.5cm) high.
$260–320 ⊞ CoCo

Carlton Ware Handcraft bowl,
930s, 7½in (19cm) diam.
220–260 ⊞ BDA

A pair of Carlton Ware candlesticks, decorated
with Hollyhocks pattern, 1930s, 3½in (9cm) high.
$260–290 ⊞ BEV

A Carlton Ware ginger
jar and cover, decorated
with Humming Bird
pattern, blue printed
factory mark, 1920s,
12½in (32cm) high.
$2,900–3,500 ➚ S(NY)

A Carlton Ware Buttercup sugar
asin, 1936–37, 3in (7.5cm) high.
115–130 ⊞ StC

Carlton Ware vase, decorated with
rd on Waterlily pattern No. 3530,
id-1930s, 4¾in (12cm) high.
720–800 ⊞ StC

A Crown Devon Art Deco fish
et, comprising 13 pieces, plates
in (23cm) long.
360–400 ⊞ JACK

A Carlton Ware Handcraft
vase, decorated with
Honesty pattern, printed
and painted marks, c1929,
10in (25.5cm) high.
$1,000–1,100 ⊞ MI

Hancock & Sons Corona
vare vase, decorated
vith Daffodil pattern,
924, 6in (15cm) high.
220–260 ⊞ PIC

A Crown Devon gilded
lustre vase, by C. Howe,
decorated with Sylvan
Butterflies pattern, signed,
c1930, 5in (12.5cm) high.
$145–175 ⊞ AOT

A Crown Devon vase,
decorated with a stylized
chinoiserie dragon, 1930s,
9½in (24cm) high.
$650–725 ⊞ MD

A Crown Devon vase,
decorated with a stylized
floral pattern, 1930s,
9in (23cm) high.
$290–320 ⊞ StC

A Crown Devon vase, decorated with flowers, 1930s, 9½in (24cm) high.
$260–290 ⊞ MD

A Hancock & Sons vase, by Molly Hancock, decorated with Cremorne pattern, 1924, 7in (18cm) high.
$320–360 ⊞ PIC

▶ **A Gouda Zuid-Holland hand-painted earthenware vase,** c1920, 4in (10cm) high.
$200–220 ⊞ MI

A Gouda Zuid-Holland miniature vase, decorated with Crocus pattern, c1928, 3in (7.5cm) high.
$95–115 ⊞ OO

A Grimwades Byzanta Ware dish, 1930s, 9½in (24cm) wide.
$230–290 ⊞ DSG

A set of Maling lustreware sundae dishes, c1935, 4in (10cm) wide.
$290–320 ⊞ JACK

A Poole Picotee Ware vase, c1920, 6¼in (16cm) high.
$115–130 ⊞ DSG

An American Newcomb College Pottery vellum-glazed pitcher, potted by Joseph Fortune Meyer, decorated by Anna Frances Simpson, signed, 1924, 8in (20.5cm) high.
$2,400–2,900 ⚒ NOA

◀ **A Shelley Queen Anne shape part tea service,** comprising 22 pieces, minor damage, c1935.
$650–720 ⚒ Bea(E)

A Royal Lancastrian vase, by Gladys Rogers, c1935, 11½in (29cm) high.
$470–540 ⊞ DSG

A Hancock & Sons Rubens Ware bowl, by F. X. Abraham, decorated with Pomegranate pattern, signed, 1928, 9in (23cm) diam.
$200–230 ⊞ PIC

▶ **A Wedgwood Fairyland Lustre bowl,** by Daisy Makeig-Jones, the exterior decorated with Castle on a Road pattern, the interior with Bird in a Hoop pattern, numbered, c1920, 7¼in (18.5cm) wide.
$3,200–3,600 ⚒ WW

A pair of German Art Deco bookends, in the form of a pierrot and pierrette, 1920s, 6in (15cm) wide.
$300–350 ⊞ BAO

A Clarice Cliff Fantasque Bizarre Gaiety flower basket, decorated with Berries pattern, printed marks, 1930s, 14in (35.5cm) high.
$2,000–2,200 ⊞ MI

A Clarice Cliff Wilkinson's jug, decorated with Passion Fruit pattern, late 1920s, 8in (20.5cm) high.
$160–190 ↗ DMC

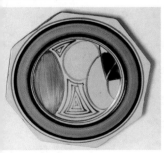

A Clarice Cliff octagonal plate, decorated with Orange Melons pattern, c1930, 6in (15cm) wide.
$450–550 ⊞ MD

A Clarice Cliff Fantasque octagonal plate, decorated with Orange Flower pattern, 1930s, 8½in (21.5cm) wide.
$360–430 ↗ DD

A Clarice Cliff ribbed bowl, decorated with Aurea pattern, c1936, 9¼in (23.5cm) diam.
$450–550 ↗ Bea(E)

A Clarice Cliff beehive honeypot and cover, decorated with Taormina pattern, 1930s, 4in (10cm) high.
$580–720 ↗ RTo

A Clarice Cliff jug, shape No. 36, decorated with Melons pattern, c1930, 6in (15cm) high.
$230–290 ↗ SWO

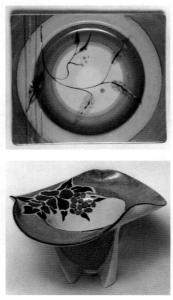

A Clarice Cliff Bizarre egg cruet set, decorated with Original Crocus pattern, c1930, 5in (12.5cm) high.
$1,700–2,200 ⊞ MI

A Clarice Cliff Bizarre double inkwell, decorated with Berries pattern, c1930, 4in (10cm) high.
$1,900–2,200 ⊞ MI

A Clarice Cliff Bizarre jug, decorated with My Garden Flame pattern, 1930s, 9in (23cm) high.
$650–$720 ⊞ MD

◄ A Clarice Cliff Bizarre plate, decorated with blue Kelverne pattern, 1936, 9in (23cm) wide.
$360–400 ⊞ MD

A Clarice Cliff Bizarre watercress strainer, 1920s, 9in (23cm) diam.
$300–350 ⊞ MD

◄ A Clarice Cliff vase, decorated with Nuage pattern, lip restored, printed marks, 1930s, 11in (28cm) high.
$1,100–1,300 ⊞ MI

A Gabriel Argy-Rousseau *pâte-de-verre* **glass vase,** signed in intaglio, France, c1926, 6¼in (16cm) high.
$8,000–9,500 ⚒ **Bon**

A Gabriel Argy-Rousseau *pâte-de-verre* **glass bowl,** entitled Etoiles, France, 1924, 3¾in (9.5cm) diam.
$4,300–5,000 ⚒ **S**

▶ **A Daum cameo glass vase,** signed, France, c1920, 26¼in (66.5cm) high.
$5,000–5,800 ⚒ **BB(L)**

A Daum acid-etched and enamelled glass vase, France, c1920, 12in (30.5cm) high.
$3,900–4,300 ⊞ **ART**

A Lalique opalescent glass box and cover, entitled Deux Sirènes, moulded mark, France, design 1921, 10in (25.5cm) diam.
$2,200–2,400 ⚒ **P**

A Lalique glass vase, entitled Gros Scarabées, engraved mark, France, after 1923, 11½in (29cm) diam.
$9,500–11,500 ⚒ **S**

An André DeLatte cameo glass vase, decorated with Egyptian dancing girls, signed, France, c1925, 6¼in (16cm) high.
$1,700–2,000 ⚒ **TREA**

▶ **A Le Verre Français cameo glass vase,** France, signed, c1925, 15in (38cm) high.
$3,600–4,000 ⚒ **BB(L)**

A Schneider glass vase, signed, France, c1925, 13in (33cm) high.
$5,000–5,800 ⚒ **TREA**

An Almeric V. Walter *pâte-de-verre* **glass vase,** modelled by Henri Bergé, moulded marks, France, c1925, 8¾in (22cm) high.
$3,900–4,600 ⚒ **S(NY)**

A Le Verre Français etched glass vase, signed, France, c1925, 9in (23cm) high.
$2,900–3,200 ⊞ **MI**

▶ **An Art Deco flashed glass scent bottle,** c1930, 6in (15cm) high.
$190–220 ⊞ **TWAC**

A Steuben glass bowl with twisting-ring handles, designed by Frederick Carder, America, c1917, 10in (25.5cm) diam.
$14,000–16,000 ⚒ **S(NY)**

An Art Deco emerald and diamond necklace, c1930. $16,000–18,500 ✛ LJ

A Cartier enamel, coral, diamond, silver-gilt and platinum compact, France, c1925, 1½in (4cm) wide. $2,900–3,500 ✛ S(G)

A Georg Jensen silver-coloured metal rose bowl, by Johan Rohde, designer and factory marks, Denmark, c1925, 8in (20.5cm) wide. $5,800–7,200 ✛ S

A Georg Jensen Acorn pattern silver soup ladle, with ebonized wooden shaft, maker's mark, Danish hallmarks and London import marks, Danish, c1920, 13½in (34.5cm) long. $1,600–1,900 ✛ P

A Georg Jensen silver christening mug, inscribed and dated, Danish, 1930, 4in (10cm) high. $1,900–2,100 ✛ DAD

An Art Deco silver cocktail shaker, Sheffield 1935, 11in (28cm) high. $1,700–2,200 ✛ WELD

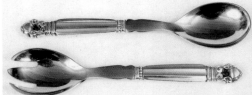

A pair of Georg Jensen Acorn pattern silver servers, Danish, c1930, 6in (15cm) long. $220–360 ✛ ASA

A French wrought iron and glass vase, by Chapelle, Nancy, c1920, 21in (53.5cm) high. $6,000–6,800 ✛ MI

A David Andersen Art Deco silver and enamel tea caddy, Norway, c1930, 5in (12.5cm) high. $1,100–1,300 ✛ DAD

An Art Deco three-piece silver tea set, by A. E. Jones, Birmingham 1934–35, teapot 4in (10cm) high, 27oz. $1,900–2,200 ✛ NS

An Asprey & Co silver dinner service, comprising 17 pieces, London 1939, 329oz. $12,300–14,500 ✛ S

A Bauhaus set of three painted wooden dolls, by Oskar Schlemmer, each with detachable upper part enclosing a hollow interior, Germany, c1925, largest 6¼in (16cm) high. $18,000–21,500 ✛ S

A Limoges enamel-on-copper vase, by Camille Fauré, inscribed mark, France, mid-20thC, 12in (30.5cm) high. $4,300–5,000 ✛ S(NY)

A set of six cantilever chairs, by Ludwig Mies van der Rohe, the tubular chrome-plated frames with leather sling seats, including two armchairs, designed Germany 1926.
$720–870 ⚷ P(Ed)

An enamelled tubular steel and fabric chair, by Marcel Breuer, model No. B3 Wassily, manufactured by Thonet, c1928.
$18,000–21,500 ⚷ S(NY)

A set of six beech dining chairs, by Sir Basil Spence, manufactured by Thonet, designed c1934.
$2,400–2,900 ⚷ P(Ed)

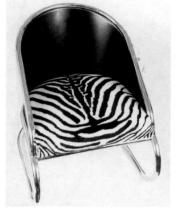

A chromed tubular steel and bent plywood upholstered chair, by Jean Royère, c1936.
$8,000–9,000 ⊞ MI

A laminated birch high-backed cantilever framed armchair, by Alvar Aalto, model No. 400, Finland, designed 1935–36.
$4,600–5,500 ⚷ S

A black webbed lounge chair, by Alvar Aalto, model No. 406, Finland, 1946.
$580–650 ⊞ PLB

◀ **A black enamelled and chrome framed marshmallow sofa,** by George Nelson for Herman Miller, with Alexander Girard's Mogul stripe upholstery, 1950s, 51in (129.5cm) wide.
$16,000–18,000 ✗ **TREA**

▶ **A moulded sheet-metal and foam orange-slice chair,** designed by Pierre Paulin in 1959, for Artifort, 1980s.
$870–$1,000 ⊞ **MARK**

A painted oak oil rig desk and chair, by Stephen Owen, 1980s, table 52in (132cm) long.
$2,200–2,600 ✗ **P(Ed)**

An epoxy and metal nest of tables, by Gaetano Peche, for Fish Studios, 1990s, largest 16in (40.5cm) wide.
$1,000–1,300 ✗ **TREA**

A Danish teak dining suite, by Frem Røjle, comprising an extending table and four chairs, marked 1960s, table 41¼in (105cm) diam.
$870–1,000 ⊞ **ZOOM**

▶ **A cast-aluminium and wool fabric sofa,** designed by Morrison & Hannah, for Knoll International, mid-1970s, 70in (178cm) long.
$430–500 ⊞ **MARK**

A Ruskin blue crysta-line vase, c1928, 12in (30.5cm) high.
$650–725 ⊞ GAA

A David Leach stoneware pot, impressed DL and St Ives seals, c1950, 10in (25.5cm) diam.
$800–880 ✗ P

A Venini glass figural decanter, by Gio Ponti, model No. 3878, Italy, c1948, 11in (28cm) high.
$5,000–6,000 ✗ S(NY)

A John Piper earthenware charger, artist's monogram and dated 1972, 21¼in (54cm) diam.
$1,400–1,700 ✗ Bon

◄ **An Upchurch Pottery jug,** c1935, 7in (18cm) high.
$230–250 ⊞ HUN

A John de Burgh Perceval earthenware bowl, the exterior moulded with striated gum leaves and with two stylized lizard handles, signed, dated 1957, 19in (48.5cm) diam.
$2,400–2,900 ✗ P(Sy)

A Poole Delphis vase, 1970s, 8in (20.5cm) diam.
$115–130 ⊞ DSG

A Dame Lucie Rie porcelain bowl, impressed LR seal, c1983, 10in (25.5cm) diam.
$14,500–17,500 ✗ P

► **An Ercole Barovier glass vase,** Italy, c1951, 9¾in (25cm) high.
$2,900–3,200 ✗ P(Z)

◄ **An Orrefors Ariel glass vase,** by Ingeborg Lundin, Sweden, c1960, 7in (18cm) high.
$3,600–4,300 ✗ S(NY)

A Murano glass vase, Italy, 1950s, 19½in (50cm) high.
$300–350 ⊞ DSG

A set of three Riihimaen glass vases, Finland, 1970s, 6in (15cm) high.
$200–225 ⊞ PAB

A Murano glass sculpture, by A. Dona, signed, Italy, 1980s, 21in (53.5cm) high.
$2,300–2,600 ⊞ FMa

Lamps & Lighting
Ceiling & Wall Lights

LAMPS & LIGHTING

A pair of embossed steel wall appliqués, the oval backplates decorated with stylized flower motifs, c1800, 15in (38cm) high.
$1,400–1,600 ✗ P

A gilt-bronze rococo-style hall lantern, cast with C-scrolls and with seated putti at each corner, fitted for electricity, mid-19thC, 29in (73.5cm) high.
$3,200–3,600 ✗ S(S)

A pair of Italian gilt-iron and tin ten-branch chandeliers, applied overall with glass lustre drops and gilt-tin leaves, 19thC, 30in (76cm) high.
$1,700–2,000 ✗ S(S)

Always check that electric lighting conforms to the current safety regulations.

◄ An American gilt-lacquered brass and patinated-antimony two-light gasolier, attributed to Starr, Fellows & Co, New York, the bowl ornamented with ivy and anthemia, with cut-and-etched blown-glass shades, fitted for electricity, mid-19thC, 30in (76cm) high.
$1,400–1,600 ✗ NOA

A Georgian brass lantern, with glazed panelled sides and scrolling mounts, 24in (61cm) high.
$2,200–2,600 ✗ AG

A five-branch frosted-glass chandelier, hung throughout with lustres, 19thC, 60in (152.5cm) high.
$1,600–1,900 ✗ HOK

A French Empire patinated-bronze three-branch chandelier, the bowl ornamented with bearded masks and centred by a pineapple pendant, early 19thC, 27½in (70cm) high.
$5,800–7,200 ✗ NOA

A gilt-metal hall lantern, 19thC, 45in (114.5cm) high.
$1,700–2,000 ✗ AH

A German brass chandelier, the central stem with a figure of the crowned Virgin Mary with child, 17thC, 29in (73.5cm) high excluding later hanging mount.
$2,600–3,200 ✗ P(WM)

► A brass lantern, with hinged door and scroll mounts, 19thC, 33in (84cm) high.
$720–870 ✗ Mit

A Swedish neo-classical gilt-bronze and crystal six-branch chandelier, early 19thC, 32in (81.5cm) wide.
$4,600–5,500 ✗ NOA

A gilt-bronze gasolier, 1860–70, 36in (91.5cm) high.
$720–870 ⊞ JW

A crystal chandelier, one branch damaged, 19thC, 51¼in (130cm) high.
$720–870 ✗ WilP

An American gilt-lacquered patinated-bronze and antimony three-light gasolier, attributed to Starr, Fellows & Co, New York, the corona surmounted by festooned rams' heads, mid-19thC, 28in (71cm) high.
$4,000–4,600 ⚒ **NOA**

A pair of French patinated and gilt-bronze wall lights, with leaf-cast nozzles on shaped leafy branches, 19thC, 10¾in (27.5cm) high.
$2,200–2,400 ⚒ **S(S)**

An Edwardian opaline glass bowl light, with brass surround and chains, c1900, 18in (45.5cm) diam.
$950–1,050 ⊞ **CHA**

A brass wall light, c1910, 7in (18cm) high.
$130–145 ⊞ **RUL**

A gilt-brass hall lantern, applied with foliate mounts and pierced lotus leaf finials, on scroll feet, lacking one leaf and two feet, 19thC, 34in (86.5cm) high.
$5,000–5,800 ⚒ **S(S)**

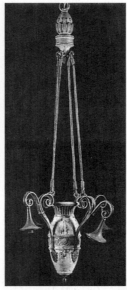

A Continental poly-chromed-bronze and wood four-branch chandelier, the corona with a pineapple finial supporting silk cords, the urn ornamented in the Etruscan style, fitted for electricity, late 19thC, 36in (91.5cm) high.
$2,500–3,000 ⚒ **NOA**

A copper-oxidized and vaseline glass lantern, c1900, 15in (38cm) high.
$750–850 ⊞ **TLG**

Two pairs of silvered and gilt-brass chandelier wall lights, in the Elizabethan revival-style, the chandelier branches cast with satyr masks and foliage, c1880, 14in (35.5cm) high.
$2,500–3,000 ⚒ **S(S)**

A French gilt-brass and diamond-cut glass centre light, late 19thC, 17¼in (44cm) diam.
$1,100–1,400 ⚒ **RTo**

An Austrian yellow metal and glass chandelier, in the French Empire-style, Vienna, c1900, 37in (94cm) high.
$1,400–1,700 ⚒ **DORO**

A cast gilt-brass electrolie the six torch lights supporte on a frame of entwined branches, late 19thC, 56¾in (144cm) high.
$3,600–4,300 ⚒ **JAd**

A Tiffany brass three-branch wall sconce, mounted with a Longwy tile decorated with an enamel bird and landscap pattern on a blue ground, impressed marks, America, late 19thC, 19¾in (50cm) high.
$850–950 ⚒ **SK**

A pair of French bronze metal and bronze putti wall lamps, with glass rose-petal shades, c1900, 16in (40.5cm) high.
$2,300–2,600 ⊞ **TLG**

◄ **An American gilt-bron five-branch chandelier,** decorated with roundels, bellflowers and swags, possibly by E. F. Caldwell & Co, New York, early 20thC, 23in (58.5cm) hig
$2,600–3,200 ⚒ **S(NY)**

able & Standard Lamps

pair of American bronze mps, hung with faceted lass prisms, the base cast ith lion mask and scrolls, cking glass shades, the ase drilled for electricity, 825, 24in (16cm) high. 3,000–3,400 ≯ S(NY)

n opaque glass and ilt-brass oil lamp, ainted with flowers and lt trellis, fitted for ectricity, mid-19thC, 1in (53.5cm) high. 500–600 ≯ S(S)

Bradley & Hubbard gilt-etal oil lamp, with six etal-shaped green and blue ass panels on a foliage-ierced font, the base applied ith putti masks, American, 9thC, 25in (63.5cm) high. 450–550 ≯ DuM

A Bohemian ruby cased-glass lamp, the standard engraved with grape leaves and a deer in a woodland setting, fitted for electricity, mid-19thC, 20in (51cm) high. **$650–800** ≯ **NOA**

An ormolu oil lamp, engraved with continuous bands of mythological figures, on an ebony base, 19thC, 5in (12.5cm) high. **$200–240** ≯ **TMA**

An American gilt-lacquered bronze lamp, with later cut and etched blown glass shade, fitted for electricity, mid-19thC, 21in (53.5cm) high. **$900–1,000** ≯ **NOA**

A pair of gilt-bronze oil table lamps, mounted with Coalport-Derby porcelain painted with flowers on a white ground, some damage, fitted for electricity, mid-19thC, 33in (84cm) high. **$2,600–3,000** ≯ **S(S)**

◄ **A pair of bronze oil lamps,** cast as urns and covers with bacchanalian friezes of satyrs and cherubs, 19thC, 19in (48.5cm) high. **$1,400–1,700** ≯ **L&T**

A pair of bronze lamp bases, the fluted stems with baluster cast acanthus, c1830, 15in (38cm) high. **$1,000–1,200** ≯ **HOK**

A silver-plated column oil lamp, the amber glass shade etched with scrolling foliage above a cut-glass reservoir, 19thC, 38in (96.5cm) high. **$1,100–1,300** ≯ **Mit**

A Moore Brothers porcelain oil lamp, c1870, 24in (61cm) high. **$1,700–1,900** ⊞ **TWr**

LAMPS & LIGHTING

A brass gas table lamp, with peach-coloured acid-etched moulded glass shade, fitted for electricity, c1870, 26¼in (66.5cm) high.
$870–1,000 ⊞ CHA

A brass electric table lamp, the engraved clear glass shade a with a ruby thread decoration, c1890, 20¾in (52.5cm) high.
$720–870 ⊞ CHA

A Mappin & Webb regimental silver double-burner oil lamp, with a cut-glass reservoir, the loaded base with presentation inscription to the Officers 3rd Battalion Royal Fusiliers, with moulded opaque white and clear-glass shade, c1898, 26in (66cm) high.
$3,300–3,600 ⚒ PF

A Victorian gilt-brass oil lamp, with a blue glass shade, the base applied with dolphins, 19¾in (50cm) high.
$580–720 ⚒ WilP

A brass oil lamp, with a Burmese glass font, on a Corinthian column, 19thC, 18in (45.5cm) high.
$140–170 ⚒ GAK

An American patinated-bronze lamp, the cut-and etched-glass shade decorated with grapevines, suspending faceted crystal pendants, the standard on a marble pedestal, lacking font, fitted for electricity, late 19thC, 26in (66cm) high.
$1,700–2,200 ⚒ NOA

A cast-metal oil lamp, with a dark blue glass font, c1900, 22in (56cm) high.
$125–145 ⚒ GAK

A Victorian double-burner paraffin lamp, the pink spirally-fluted satin glass cistern enamelled with flowers, on a brass reeded and knopped stem, with a black glazed stoneware base, 14in (35.5cm) high.
$260–320 ⚒ PFK

An American cut-glass lamp, lacking some prisms, c1900, 26½in (67.5cm) high.
$4,000–4,600 ⚒ S(NY)

▶ **An Edwardian silver oil lamp,** by The Goldsmiths & Silversmiths Co, the stem decorated with twisted bands of rose and foliate decoration, surmounted by a cut-glass reservoir with a silver-plated burner and lamp support, 19¾in (50cm) high.
$720–870 ⚒ Bon

A brass gas table lamp, with a green etched glass shade, fitted for electricity, early 20thC, 17¾in (45cm) high.
$720–870 ⊞ CHA

A brass table lamp, with a mottled pink, green and cream glass shade, 1920s, 19in (48.5cm) high.
$230–260 ⊞ LIB

Rugs & Carpets

An Axminster carpet, Wilton Factory, the Aubusson design with a medallion in red and ivory on an indigo field, the borders with flowers and leaves on an ivory and gold ground, worn, with holes, c1850, 229 x 180in (581 x 457cm).
$36,000–43,500 ➤ **WW**
This carpet was made for the vendor's family home and had remained *in situ* until it was put up for sale early in 2001. It was extensively damaged to the centre by countless decades of scraping by dining chairs and the vendors had considered consigning it to the scrapheap, but luckily they decided to take advice from their local auctioneers first and, to their complete amazement, it sold to the trade for over six times the bottom estimate.

An Ushak rug, with hooked and angled centre medallion and spandrels in blues, greens and gold on a red field, enclosed by a floral border, some wear, Turkey, c1890, 48in (122cm) square.
$290–320 ⊞ **DNo**

A yastik, with two concentric diamond medallions flanked by half-medallions in navy blue, ivory, red, gold and aubergine on the blue-green field, east Anatolia, c1900, 31 x 18in (78.5 x 45.5cm).
$800–880 ➤ **SK(B)**

A needlepoint rug, with a red trellis design in blue and ivory on a dark blue ground, enclosed by a floral and dark green border and two guard stripes, 1920s, 52 x 63in (132 x 160cm).
$430–500 ➤ **WW**

An Aubusson carpet, with a central medallion in rose, ivory, violet, brown and green on a red field, with an aubergine outer border, areas of restoration and wear, France, 19thC, 156 x 116in (396 x 294.5cm).
$10,000–11,500 ➤ **SK(B)**

A Ladik prayer rug, the central red-purple panel with archaic device below the stepped prayer arch, with pale green top panel, the bottom panel with three tulips on a dark blue ground, some wear, central Anatolia, c1900, 66 x 45in (167.5 x 114.5cm).
$650–720 ⊞ **DNo**
Ladik prayer rugs are distinguished by the stylized floral panel that appears above the *mihrab*, or at the base of the field. The flowers, known as *lale* in Turkish, are thought to be tulips, although no tulip has the multiple leaves seen on Ladik rugs.

A European carpet, with an allover design of flowerheads and leaves on a plum field, enclosed by a floral main border, probably Dutch, early 20thC, 127 x 89in (322.5 x 226cm).
$160–190 ➤ **WW**

A Spanish carpet, with an allover design of leaves, tendrils and flower-heads in gold and brown on an ivory field, mid-20thC, 156 x 115in (396 x 292cm).
$16,600–20,300 ➤ **S(NY)**

> The rugs in this section have been arranged in geographical sequence from west to east, in the following order: Europe, Turkey, Anatolia, Caucasus, Persia, Turkestan, India and China.

A Ladik prayer rug, the plain madder field surmounted by a double arched indigo *mihrab* panel supported by a stylized tulip panel, central Anatolia, c1850, 69 x 41in (175.5 x 104).
$1,100–1,300 ➤ **P**

RUGS & CARPETS

A Gendje rug, with three hooked and serrated medallions in red, blue, green, ivory and gold on a mid-blue field, decorated with stylized animals and flowerheads, with part date in top main border, some end fraying, west Caucasus, c1880, 61 x 46in (155 x 117cm).
$2,300–2,500 ⊞ **DNo**

A salt bag, with five stars in sky blue, ivory, gold and blue-green on a red field, with sky blue hook motif border, slight moth damage, southwest Caucasus, late 19thC, 18 x 18in (45.5 x 45.5cm).
$800–900 ⋌ **SK(B)**

A Kuba Konakend rug, the dark blue field decorated with large flowerheads, an *Afshan* design of forked tendrils in ivory and small ivory flowers, enclosed by a reciprocal latchhook ivory main border and floral subsidiary borders, northeast Caucasus, late 19thC, 65 x 43in (165 x 109cm).
$1,000–1,200 ⋌ **SLN**

▶ **A Seichur rug,** the white field with two red, blue and black star medallions, within an abrashed green main border, with rose and yellow linked flowerhead motifs, east Caucasus, 60 x 42½in (152.5 x 108cm).
$3,300–4,000 ⋌ **DN**

A tree Kazak rug, the madder field with octagonal medallions flanked by stylized trees, geometric motifs and camels, framed by an abrashed blue-green border, southwest Caucasus, dated 1310 AH (AD1892), 106 x 83in (269 x 211cm).
$8,000–8,800 ⋌ **P**
This tree-shrub design derives from 16th- and 17th-century Safavid Garden carpets, which were stylized and adapted by Kurdish weavers in northwest Persia during the 18th century, and then further adapted by the southwest Caucasian weavers of the 19th century. This particular example is unusual because of the wealth of minor design motifs which surround the trees and octagonal medallions. In particular the large variety of engaging zoomorphic motifs give this rug much of its charm.

A soumakh rug, with triple medallion design in red, blue and brown on a madder ground, some wear, east Caucasus, 71 x 50in (180.5 x 127cm).
$950–1,100 ⊞ **DNo**

A Fachralo Kazak prayer rug, the madder field centred by a stellar medallion flanked by rosettes and geometric motifs beneath the *mihrab* with an ivory arrow-head border, southwest Caucasus, dated 1327 AH (AD1909), 74 x 57in (188 x 145cm).
$2,400–2,700 ⋌ **P**

A Chi Chi carpet, the mid-indigo field with an allover serrated leaf lattice design, framed by a sky blue *Kufic* inner border, with a charcoal rosette and slant leaf outer border, northeast Caucasus, c1870, 124 x 77in (315 x 1195.5cm).
$10,800–11,800 ⋌ **P**
This rug is a rare example of Chi Chi weaving because of the presence of two principal borders. In addition to the traditional rosette and slant-leaf border associated with this design group, there is also a well-drawn stylized Kufic motif border, of a type more commonly associated with Kuba rugs.

A Shirvan rug, with three petal medallions interspersed with stylized birds, animals and flowerheads, in pale caramel, olive and ivory on a black field, enclosed by an ivory main border, some wear, east Caucasus, c1880, 72 x 49in (183 x 124.5cm).
$870–950 ⊞ **DNo**

Mosul rug, the black field ⌐corated with caramel and red ⌐teh, enclosed by a caramel, black ⌐d red hooked main border and ⌐o minor floral borders, ends ⌐ayed, Kurdistan, c1900, ⌐ x 38in (150 x 96.5cm).
⌐50–500 ⊞ **DNo**

Karaja rug, the field with shrubs ⌐ pale gold, blue, brown and red on ⌐rust field, enclosed by triple floral ⌐rders, northwest Persia, c1900, ⌐ x 33in (137 x 84cm).
⌐20–700 ⊞ **DNo**

Shahsavan *kilim,* decorated with ⌐rizontal saw-tooth bands with rows ⌐ stepped cruciform stars in pale ⌐een, yellow, red, blue and ivory, ⌐nclosed by reciprocating squares to ⌐rm a border, some repairs, slight ⌐sses, northwest Persia, late 19thC, ⌐4 x 63in (366 x 160cm).
⌐,000–8,800 ☭ **S(NY)**

A Heriz carpet, the terracotta field decorated with a large leaf design in blue, gold, ivory and red, enclosed by a dark blue palmette main border and floral and gold subsidiary borders, northwest Persia, c1910, 132 x 96in (335.5 x 244cm).
$5,200–6,600 ⊞ **GY**

A Kurd rug, the diamond medallion inset with leaf motifs in navy blue, red, rust, gold and light blue-green on an ivory field, with ivory border, some wear, guard stripes partially missing, northwest Persia, early 20thC, 68 x 43in (173 x 109cm).
$580–650 ☭ **SK(B)**

A Tabriz carpet, the ivory ground decorated with a concentric medallion in red and blue, with allover flower sprays, enclosed by a main and two subsidiary floral borders, northwest Persia, c1920, 114 x 79in (289.5 x 200.5cm).
$4,300–5,000 ⊞ **LIN**

◄ **A Tabriz carpet,** with an allover floral design in red, blue, green and gold on an ivory field, enclosed by a conforming main border and twin guard stripes, northwest Persia, c1930, 120 x 84in (305 x 213.5cm).
$4,000–4,800 ⊞ **GY**

A Bidjar runner, with five chequer-edged medallions in different colours on a camel field broken by diagonal and vertical bands of flowerheads on dark brown, enclosed by triple floral borders, northwest Persia, late 19thC, 156 x 44in (396 x 109cm).
$5,000–5,800 ☭ **BB(S)**

Identifying rugs

A useful way to identify rugs is by a process of elimination. By examining the front, the back, the edges and the ends, you can decide what kind of rug it isn't, before eventually deciding what kind of rug it is.

Recognizing the patterns used in the field and in the borders, determining whether a Persian or Turkish knot is used, whether cotton is used in the foundation or pile, whether silk or metal plays a part, looking at the colours used and their clarity, seeing how the ends and edges are finished, will all play a part in the process of identification.

A useful reference book is *How to Identify Persian rugs and Other Oriental Rugs* by C. J. Delabere May (London 1920, later reprint 1964).

A Shahsavan bag, the ivory field centred by an aubergine cruciform medallion flanked by angular chestnut-brown motifs, framed by an indigo rosette border, northwest Persia, c1880, 22 x 12in (56 x 30.5cm).
$3,600–4,000 ☭ **P**

A Sarouk Feraghan carpet, the deep blue field decorated with large floral sprays in four quarters, interspersed with similar floral arrangements in red, blue and gold, enclosed by a red floral main border and twin subsidiary borders, west Persia, c1920, 139 x 114in (353 x 289.5cm).
$5,800–6,500 ⚒ S(S)

A Sarouk Mahal rug, the light red field decorated with a profusion of roses and other shrubs in light colours, enclosed by floral borders in similar colours, west Persia, c1900, 82 x 54in (208.5 x 137cm).
$800–900 ⚒ DNo
This rug is woven with a European-influenced design and was made for the American market.

A Hamadan rug, decorated with two linked diamond medallions in turquoise on a dark blue field strewn with poly-chrome flowerheads, enclosed by red spandrels, with a flowerhead and dark blue main border and two floral and red subsidiary borders, west Persia, c1900, 88 x 60in (223.5 x 152.5cm).
$1,700–2,200 ⊞ LIN

A Ziegler Mahal rug, with diamonds containing lilies in red, blue and ivory on a midnight blue field, enclosed by triple narrow borders, worn, west Persia, c1890, 82 x 55in (208.5 x 139.5cm).
$500–550 ⊞ DNo

A Sarouk Feraghan rug, decorated with a petal medallion with pendants on a plant-strewn field, enclosed by segmented spandrels, a floral main border and two subsidiary borders, west Persia, c1900, 82 x 51in (208.5 x 129.5cm).
$3,200–3,600 ⚒ SLN

A Malayer rug, the dark blue field with central pink and mustard medallion, the mid-blue main border with pink floral guards, slight wear and losses, outer guards missing, west Persia, c1900, 72 x 50in (183 x 127cm).
$160–190 ⚒ WW

A Khamseh bagface, with a horse and rider surrounded by stars in navy blue, gold, ivory, red-brown, light and dark blue-green on a rust-red field, with ivory border, some wear and end fraying, southwest Persia, early 20thC, 36 x 33in (91.5 x 84cm).
$1,000–1,300 ⚒ SK(B)

A Kurdistan bagface, the main panel of diagonal squares containin hooked symbols in red, blue, green and brown, enclosed by red and blu floral borders and guard stripes, the skirt with zig-zag pattern in red, blu ivory and browns, some fraying, repair in the skirt, west Persia, c192 42 x 34in (106.5 x 86.5cm).
$400–450 ⊞ DNo

A Senneh *kilim,* the midnight blue ground decorated with a dense Herati design in light reds, blues, ivory and gold, enclosed by a narrov gold floral main border and multiple guard stripes, west Persia, c1900, 216 x 101in (548.5 x 256.5cm).
$3,200–3,700 ⚒ Bon(C)

A Ziegler carpet, the tomato-red fiel with central dark blue medallion, the dark blue main border with palmett and leaf-bracket repeat between flo and geometric guards, pieces missir patches of wear, corner patched, Sultanabad, northwest Persia, 1885–9 206 x 168in (523 x 426.5cm).
$10,800–13,000 ⚒ WW

A **Mamassani Lors carpet,** the red field with diamond poles of red diamonds with ivory latchhook outlines, the central diamond field in chocolate brown with a Memling *gül* surrounded by animals, Fars, southwest Persia, c1920, 114 x 87in (289.5 x 221cm).
1,400–1,700 ✗ WW

An **Isfahan rug,** with a concentric petal medallion in blue, pale red and gold on a light red field densely decorated with flowerheads and leaves, with a floral blue main border, worn, central Persia, c1880, 74 x 55in (188 x 139.5cm).
720–800 ⊞ DNo

A **Maslaghan rug,** with lobed diamond medallion in brown, blue and ivory on midnight blue on an abrashed pale red field, enclosed by spandrels decorated with multi-coloured flowerheads, with a main blue border, central Persia, c1920, 60 x 40in (152.5 x 101.5cm).
850–950 ⊞ DNo

Understanding rugs

Rugs are works of art, the result of technical skill and creative inspiration. Many were made by the weavers for their own satisfaction and use.

It is important to find out why the rug was made, and how and where it was used. For example, sometimes rugs were commissioned by rulers for their own use or to be given as a present to another ruler.

Other areas of study which will contribute to the understanding of rugs are:

- The history of each country and the main areas where rugs were produced.
- The customs, way of life, family patterns, division of labour and religion of the people concerned.
- Geography and climate explain the location and movement of the tribes and their flocks of sheep from which the wool comes.
- A knowledge of plants and flowers and other dye sources such as cochineal, cobalt and iron will help both to identify the rug and to understand the production process.
- Above all, constant handling and visual examination of rugs is essential to the learning process.

A **Lori bag,** with hooked diamond medallion flanked by octagons in red, blue, ivory, gold, aubergine and blue-green on the midnight blue field, with ivory hooked triangle border, slight moth damage, some wear, southwest Persia, early 20thC, 22 x 19in (56 x 48.5cm).
$870–1,000 ✗ SK(B)

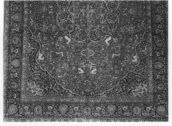

A *kurk* **Kashan carpet,** the shaped pale red field with a pale green and navy central medallion and large navy spandrels, decorated closely throughout with a floral design in light colours and deer and unicorns in ivory, enclosed by a palmette and navy main border, central Persia, 1910–20, 174 x 125in (442 x 317.5cm).
$16,500–18,000 ⊞ LIN
Kurk refers to the soft quality of the wool used in the pile of this type of carpet.

◄ A **Qum carpet,** the ivory ground decorated with an allover *boteh* design with associated floral devices in light blue, green, gold and red, enclosed by a main border and two floral and light blue subsidiary borders, central Persia, c1930, 122 x 88in (310 x 223.5cm).
$9,000–10,000 ⊞ GY

A **Shiraz rug,** the light red field with lobed medallion in light red, blue and ivory, enclosed by triple multi-coloured floral borders and outer guard stripe, part missing at one end and one corner frayed, southwest Persia, c1920, 40 x 33in (101.5 x 84cm).
$400–440 ⊞ DNo

A **Veramin carpet,** the ivory ground decorated with a formal flowerhead and wild lily design in pale red, blue and gold, enclosed by multiple floral borders, central Persia, c1910, 195 x 132in (495.5 x 335.5cm).
$10,000–12,000 ✗ S

A pair of Belouch bagfaces, with star of Islam in octagon in light red and with animal tree design in brown and vibrant blue, on a blue field filled with shrubs, enclosed by an ivory and flower stem border, with original backs, one hole, northeast Persia, c1900, 72 x 34in (183 x 86.5cm).
$470–520 ⊞ DNo

A rug, by the Basseri tribe of the Khamseh Confederacy, the dark blue field with three conjoined hexagons in mid-blue and pistachio green, the surrounding field with stylized leaf, pomegranate and chicken motifs with small animals, with ivory corners, red border with pomegranate and chicken pattern between ivory guards, slight wear and loss, south Persia, late 19thC, 79 x 48in (200.5 x 122cm).
$800–950 ⚒ WW

A Mashad Sabir carpet, the ivory field decorated all over with sprays of flowers in light red, blue and brown, enclosed by a floral and gold main border and various subsidiary borders, northeast Persia, c1930, 156 x 117in (396 x 297cm).
$5,800–7,200 ⚒ S

A Dorush rug, with petal medallion and spandrels in red, brown, navy and pistachio green on a cochineal field, enclosed by hatched and flowerhead borders in similar colours, worn, Khorasan, northeast Persia, c1880, 65 x 46in (165 x 117cm).
$430–480 ⊞ DNo

An Afshar rug, the ivory field with an allover floral design, framed by a indigo alternating rosette and palmette border, southeast Persia, dated 1311 AH (AD1893), 67 x 51in (170 x 129.5cm).
$2,400–2,700 ⚒ P

Prices

The price ranges quoted in this book reflect the average price a purchaser might expect to pay for a similar item. The price will vary according to the condition, rarity, size, popularity, provenance, colour and restoration of the item, and this must be taken into account when assessing values. Don't forget that if you are selling it is quite likely that you will be offered less than the price range.

A lattice Afshar rug, with a design of in-facing tulips in red within a green lattice pattern on a caramel coloured ground, enclosed by triple floral borders, southeast Persia, late 19thC, 71 x 57in (180.5 x 145cm).
$2,000–2,400 ⚒ SLN
Lattice Afshars are much sought after.

An Afshar rug, with reciprocal *boteh* and scattered flowerheads in pale red, green, blue, ivory and gold on a midnight blue field, enclosed by a flowerhead and leaf ivory main border, a red flowerhead inner border and outer guard stripes, some wear, southeast Persia, c1920, 71 x 49in (180.5 x 124.5cm).
$1,100–1,300 ⊞ DNo

An Ersari *torba*, the red ground decorated with an eight-pointed star in a flattened *kejebe gül*, enclosed by a floral border, southwest Turkestan, c1875, 20 x 64in (51 x 162.5cm).
$4,300–4,700 ⚒ S(NY)
A *torba* is a small bag originally made with a *kilim* back. Usually only the piled bagface remains. They are also used as animal trappings.

Kirghiz reed screen, missing [u]pper embroidered panel, minor [lo]sses, north Turkestan, early 20thC, [1]9 x 120in (175.5 x 305cm).
[$]4,500–5,000 ⚒ S(NY)
[C]hirmagan ashkana chiy (kitchen [sc]reens) are traditionally used in [th]e *yurt* as freestanding space [d]ividers. Such screens are [e]laborately decorated with designs [th]at are closely related to the [m]otifs and format of Turkoman [k]notted pile and felt weavings.

Tekke *ensi*, the quartered garden [p]lan with rust field of plant motifs in [n]avy blue, red, ivory and blue-green, [w]ith dark brown *elem*, west Turkestan, [la]te 19thC, 55 x 46in (139.5 x 117cm).
[$]500–580 ⚒ SK(B)

Khotan rug, the central medallion [in] light red containing a red and gold [fl]owerhead, on an ivory field decorated [w]ith pots with plants and other symbols [i]n red, green and navy, enclosed by [a] diagonal and flowerhead light red [b]order and a plain outer margin, [m]issing at one end, east Turkestan, [1]880, 57 x 31in (145 x 78.5cm).
[$]500–580 ⊞ DNo

A Yomut Turkoman prayer rug, in light red, blue, yellow, purple, brown and ivory, decorated with a totem crown on central vertical pillar repeated in the panel below the quartered field, the top panel of rosettes, enclosed by ivory *syrga* inner and outer frames, the bottom panel with Yomut tree design, northwest Turkestan, c1890, 68 x 49in (172.5 x 124.5cm).
$850–950 ⊞ DNo

A *khelleh*, the ivory field decorated with three medallions and stylized floral symbols, enclosed by a swastika field, flowerhead and wave borders, east Turkestan, late 19thC, 168 x 87in (426.5 x 221cm).
$8,700–10,000 ⚒ S
Khelleh are long narrow carpets which are nevertheless wider than runners.

A Salor *chuval*, with six *güls* in three rows in red, ivory and indigo on a crimson field, enclosed by a *chamtos* border and with a flowerhead crimson skirt, west Turkestan, 64 x 35in (162.5 x 89cm).
$580–650 ⊞ DNo

A Kizil Ayak prayer rug, the field composed of serrated panels in pink, gold, brown and indigo, each containing a star of Islam beneath a multiple hooked prayer arch, in ivory, navy and light red, enclosed by triple floral borders, some wear, Afghanistan, 47 x 37in (119.5 x 94cm).
$580–650 ⊞ DNo

A Saryk main carpet, the deep brown-red field with four rows of ten *güls* flanked by secondary *güls* with four *kochak* extensions, small re-weaves, original ends and sides missing, middle Amu Darya region, east Turkestan, c1800, 97 x 92in (246.5 x 233.5cm).
$21,750–26,000 ⚒ WW
The secondary *gül* on this carpet with four ram's head hooks (*kochak* extensions) is a feature usually found on Salor main carpets, and is unique to this Saryk weaving.

An Indo-Persian silk carpet, the gold flower-filled field centred with a sprigged medallion with pendants in red, gold, ivory and charcoal, enclosed by complementary spandrels and wide floral borders, c1880, 136 x 105in (345.5 x 266.5cm). **$5,800–7,200 ➤ S**

An Amritsar carpet, with an insignia and inscription 'Fortune Favours The Brave', surrounded by an allover floral design on a red field and with similar patterned border, north India, c1890, 213 x 156in (541 x 396cm). **$13,700–16,700 ➤ S**

An Amritsar carpet, the ivory field with an allover design of palmettes and leafy vines, framed by an olive-green border of further palmettes, north India, c1890, 142 x 110in (360.5 x 279.5cm). **$7,250–8,000 ➤ P**

A Bikaner bed *dhurrie*, the slit-tapestry woven cotton with pinkish-red field with two rows of rosettes surrounded by floral motifs, the main blue border between yellow repeat guards, inner yellow guard and outer red repeat guard, Bikaner Jail, north India, early 20thC, 83 x 74in (211 x 188cm). **$2,300–2,900 ➤ WW** **This *dhurrie* is one of four known examples of this design. The design was probably inspired by a Senneh *kilim*; it is known that old Persian carpets were imported to be used as models in the rug-making industries of Bikaner Jail.**

▶ **A Chinese rug,** the blue field decorated with blue, gold and ivory dogs of Fo and objects from the *Hundred Antiquities*, enclosed by two flower sprig borders, early 19thC, 68 x 37in (172.5 x 94cm). **$1,100–1,300 ➤ SLN**

A Peking rug, with mythological symbols in dark and light blue on an ivory field and main border, the inner and outer frame in blue, part of borders missing, China, c1900, 49 x 27in (124.5 x 68.5cm). **$180–200 ⊞ DNo**

▶ **A Chinese rug,** the gold field covered with lotus flowers and tendrils overlaid with a blue fret, enclosed by a floral and blue border, c1920, 312 x 39in (792.5 x 99cm). **$5,500–6,000 ➤ BB(S)**

> **Cross Reference**
> See Colour Review (page 603)

A Chinese carpet, the gold field decorated with peony sprigs and a tree peony medallion and matching spandrels in red, ivory and blue-black, enclosed by pearl, swastika fret and peony sprig borders, late 19thC, 143 x 111in (363 x 282cm). **$2,600–3,200 ➤ SLN**

A Chinese rug, the burnt-orange field and outer margin with a mid-blue main border, superimposed with pots with plants in blue, ivory and red, ends damaged, c1920, 47 x 25in (119.5 x 63.5cm). **$260–290 ⊞ DNo**

RUGS & CARPETS

Textiles

America is the source of a large number of today's magnificent textiles – primitives, needlelaces, sheets, pillow shams, blanket covers, bedcovers, quilts, table linen, hand towels etc – some of which were bought by 'Grand Tourists' in Europe many years ago. Until fairly recently, these textiles often languished in dark dank places, frequently overlooked in favour of more highly prized family heirlooms such as furniture, silver, paintings and porcelain. However, scarcity drives up prices, raises the level of interest, and today America is enjoying a textile renaissance, with the market rapidly expanding and with price increases of some ten to three thousand percent in the past five years. The textile collecting area falls into certain major areas: trousseau collections, for those who want to preserve the past and use it in everyday life; resource buying by collectors who appreciate beautiful textiles but also want investment quality antique linens, lace etc; volume buying, often by other dealers, who have a rapid turnover in specific areas such as pillow shams, hand towels etc; and interior design, where the strategic use of antique textiles can provide the final exquisite touch. For a younger generation, a revival of interest in the home and in entertaining has also fuelled a demand for fine antique table and bed linen,

and many collectors want to rebuild the traditional family linen supplies or re-create a trousseau for themselves or their descendents.

Whatever your reasons for collecting, search out a reputable dealer who will be willing to educate you and with whom you can build up a mutually beneficial buying relationship that may include a 'trade-back' facility. Also check out potential buying venues – shops, flea markets, estate sales, family linen closets, thrift stores. But, as ever, it is always a case of 'buyer beware', and an apparent bargain from an unknown source may turn out to be worthless as it falls to pieces in your hands because of damage from dry rot, fold burns or climate extremes.

As for price, quality always retains its value, even in a down market, so always buy the very best you can afford. The factors that determine price are: condition, quality, age, design, market climate, availability (the law of supply and demand applies to textiles also), buyer and placement possibilities (for the speculator or dealer), and category or type of textile. Proper storage and care is an essential part of maintaining textiles, and it may be worthwhile to seek out a firm that provides a full maintenance laundry and repair and restoration service. **Pandora de Balthazar**

Covers & Quilts

French *Toile de Jouy* quilted printed cotton bedspread, 19thC, 76 x 53in (193 x 134.5cm).
£3,000–3,500 ⊞ MGa

An American double-sided coverlet fragment, the ivory ground with blue roundels within a border of American eagles, inscribed 'Liberty,' each corner inscribed 'H. Farmerville. 1833. Beaty', missing border at one end, 85 x 72in (216 x 183cm).
$650–800 ✗ S(NY)

▶ **An Irish patchwork coverlet,** with plain cream and printed cottons, with a blue and brown border, the whole quilted with a chevron design, faults, c1840, 75½ x 84¼in (192 x 214cm).
$2,000–2,300 ✗ P

A George III silkwork picture, depicting a young girl in a bonnet carrying a basket of grapes, 6½in (16.5cm) wide, in period oval gilt frame.
$500–600 ✗ DA

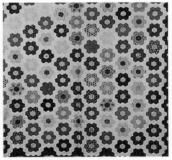

A Flower Garden coverlet, inscribed 'Septimus H. Ward's Grandmother, Hannah Kendrew' on the ivory cotton reverse, hand-sewn and pieced together from hexagonal printed and plain polychrome cottons, dated 1794, 105 x 92½in (266.5 x 235cm).
$850–1,000 ✗ S(S)

An early Victorian glazed cotton patchwork double bedcover, with a pattern of triangles and floral hexagons, with predominantly green and red printed cottons, 86 x 97in (218.5 x 246.5cm).
$870–1,000 ➢ DN

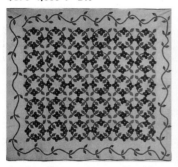

An American cotton appliquéd quilt, the pattern of red and green rose wreaths with a meandering vine border on a white ground, with red binding, mid-19thC, 79 x 68in (200.5 x 172.5cm).
$500–600 ➢ SK(B)

Condition

The condition is absolutely vital when assessing the value of an antique. Damaged pieces on the whole appreciate much less than perfect examples. However a rare desirable piece may command a high price even when damaged.

A white ground *susani,* embroidered with two columns of trailing flowers and foliage in pink, brown, yellow and green, bordered by flowerheads and leafy tendrils, probably Shakrhizabaz, mid-19thC, 69 x 46in (175.5 x 117cm).
$720–870 ➢ WW

A Victorian silk patchwork hand-embroidered and quilted bed cover, in shades of red, blue, green and yellow on a gold ground, 56 x 42in (142 x 106.5cm).
$190–230 ⊞ DE

A Leek red velvet cover, with a printed blue cotton border embroidered in yellow, blue and red silks with hook-tipped cones and tendrils, late 19thC, 38¼ x 37in (97 x 94cm).
$330–400 ➢ P

◀ **A Durham floral quilt,** with elaborate quilting, in green and white on a red ground, with plain rose reverse, c1900, 97 x 93in (246.5 x 236cm).
$430–500 ⊞ JJ

A cotton chintz coverlet, in shade of brown and red on a natural groun hand-quilted and decorated with panels of urns, birds and flowering vines, mid-19thC, 90¾ x 79in (230.5 x 200.5cm).
$2,200–2,400 ➢ SK(B)

A Welsh Victorian patchwork quilt, 91 x 56in (231 x 142cm).
$580–720 ⊞ JJ

A Welsh patchwork flannel quilt Severn Valley, 19thC, 85 x 77in (216 x 195.5cm).
$720–800 ⊞ COA

A Nurata *susani,* embroidered in coloured silks with a central design flowers surrounded by floral sprays, enclosed by borders of flowerheads, sprays and leaves, Turkistan, late 19thC, 90 x 64in (228.5 x 162.5cm).
$3,000–3,500 ➢ DN

Embroidery & Needlework

An Italian silk altar frontal, embroidered with polychrome silks and silver thread, 17thC, 39 x 108in (99 x 274.5cm).
$5,000–6,000 ⊞ MGa

A feltwork picture, depicting Summer, worked in polychrome colours on a cream ground, c1800, 15 x 14in (38 x 35.5cm), framed.
$580–650 ⊞ PSC

An American needlework memorial, in silk and watercolour depicting a woman kneeling by two memorials in memory of Paul Mandell 1809 and his wife Susannah, Massachusetts, c1812, 16½ x 20½in (42 x 52cm), framed.
$1,100–1,300 ≯ SK(B)

A chenille silkwork picture, in shades of cream, red, green and brown, framed, c1820, 16 x 12in (40.5 x 30.5cm).
$320–360 ⊞ PSC

A needlepoint picture, depicting a country scene with castles in the distance, mid-17thC, 7 x 8in (18 x 20.5cm), framed.
$2,200–2,600 ⊞ WWo

A Georgian silkwork picture, entitled Anthony & Cleopatra, depicting figures within a landscape with stumpwork detail, 18½ x 29in (47 x 73.5cm), in a rosewood frame with gilt slip.
$330–400 ≯ RBB

A pair of silkwork pictures, worked in satin and moss stitches with painted features, damaged, early 19thC, 19 x 16½in (48.5 x 42cm), with later *verre églomisé* and giltwood frames.
$1,900–2,200 ≯ P(Ba)

A silkwork picture, worked in tan and russet shades with a child with a dog and puppy, with painted faces and hands, late 18thC, 10 x 8in (25.5 x 20.5cm), framed.
$1,200–1,400 ⊞ WWo

A silkwork picture, depicting a young lady and gentleman in a garden setting, early 19thC, 9 x 7in (23 x 18cm), framed and glazed.
$360–430 ≯ TMA

A plushwork and bead picture, the foliage in tent stitch with the leaves and stems in beadwork, 19thC, 18¾ x 14in (47.5 x 35.5cm), in a gilt painted frame.
$430–500 ≯ WW

◄ **A needlework picture,** by Ann Bright, with a verse beneath a goldfinch and its nest of eggs, surrounded by a foliate meander border, some damage, 1829, 16½ x 12½in (42 x 32cm).
$580–720 ≯ L

TEXTILES

A pair of woolwork pictures, depicting a lady with a dog in a parkland, and a gentleman playing a lute, 19thC, 9¼ x 8½in (23.5 x 21.5cm), in rosewood frames.
$400–460 ✗ **AH**

A Victorian needlework picture, depicting a seated musketeer, 27½ x 27in (70 x 68.5cm), in a maple frame.
$260–320 ✗ **WL**

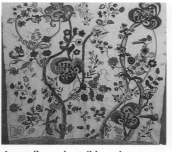

A needlework wall hanging, embroidered with flowers and birds, 19thC, 49½ x 52in (125.5 x 132cm).
$400–460 ✗ **MEA**

A petit-point panel, depicting the Madonna and Child, 19thC, 9½ x 8¾in (24 x 22cm), in a moulded gilt frame.
$160–190 ✗ **WilP**

▶ **A length of French ivory-coloured batiste,** the borders embroidered in beige silk thread, c1910, 48 x 11in (122 x 28cm).
$1,100–1,300 ⊞ **AE**

A Berlin woolwork picture, depicting Greek rustics in a rural landscape, 19thC, 27 x 17½in (68.5 x 44.5cm), in a gilt frame.
$360–430 ✗ **Mit**

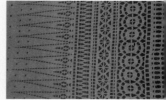

A length of French white lawn, with pale blue embroidery, c1910, 53 x 48in (134.5 x 122cm).
$1,400–1,600 ⊞ **AE**

Lace

A Bedfordshire white linen Maltese bobbin lace flounce, with an undulating semi-circular pattern and flowerheads, mid-19thC, 17¾ x 340in (45 x 864cm).
$260–320 ✗ **P**

▶ **A linen tablecloth,** with machine lace insertion, c1920, 90 x 106in (228.5 x 269cm).
$260–290 ⊞ **JuC**

◀ **A Burano needlelace border,** designed with trailing blossom and isolated sprigs, with *oeil de perdrix* fillings to the undulating border, Italy, late 18thC, 4¾ x 78¾in (12 x 200cm).
$170–200 ✗ **P**

A Spanish blonde silk bobbin lace shawl, c1840, 15 x 86in (38 x 218.5cm)
$130–150 ⊞ **JuC**

◀ **A French ivory-embroidered lawn panel,** for the upper bodice of a gown, edged with lace, c1910, 60in (152.5cm) long.
$2,000–2,300 ⊞ **AE**

A Chemical lace jacket, c1910.
$100–120 ⊞ **JuC**
The silk ground is machine-embroidered and the silk is then disolved away with chemicals.

Samplers

English samplers are known from the 16th century but as these have rarely come onto the open market, their value is mostly a matter for speculation. The 17th-century sampler can be categorized in two groups: spot samplers, which have randomly spaced designs – probably the work of mature needlewomen and, as such, seldom named or dated; and, more commonly, band samplers. These are long bands of design, either worked in coloured silks or white work, occasionally a combination of both. Band samplers are very similar and the price has remained static, in the low thousands. However, known provenance, the addition of figures, or boxers as they are often referred to, or the use of exceptional colour and design, greatly increases their desirability and price.

With the introduction of needlework in newly formed schools in the early 18th century, as well as the influence of private governesses, the bands of patterns were replaced by lines of text, religious teaching and virtues. By the mid-18th century, the sampler had become shorter and squarer and incorporated border patterns, for they were intended to be displayed as well as to instruct. The greatest diversity of sampler design was from the late 18th to the mid-19th century, when needlewomen incorporated into their work motifs drawn from their personal surroundings such as cottages and great houses, birds and animals. By the end of the 19th century there was a downturn in quality with samplers generally being worked in wool resulting in coarser styles and design.

With the quality of work and their decorative appeal, the market in samplers has become increasingly academic with considerable interest in the production of school samplers. The National School Society (Church of England) and British School Society (Methodist) founded in 1797 have their following, but there is more interest in a few key schools, in particular the Quaker School at Ackworth in Yorkshire (founded 1779) and the subsequent schools at Nailsea, York and Westtown in North America. The privately funded orphanages, such as Cheltenham (1806) and later Ashley Down in Bristol (1836) are also important. These all have their own unique style and are a must for any serious collector.

With enthusiasts looking to fill gaps in their collections, it is rare examples such as miniature, watch and needlework pocket samplers or school-work samplers showing additional instruction, such as mathematical work, for instance, that are unpredictable in value and make the headlines.

Erna Hiscock and John Shepherd

A linen whitework sampler, the upper section designed with bands of drawn thread with an undulating ribbon and plant pattern, the middle section with needlepoint lace in geometric patterns, the lower with a mermaid and merman, probably English, mid-17thC, 11¾ x 5¼in (30 x 13.5cm), framed.
$2,900–3,200 ⚒ P

A band sampler, with a band of whitework, worked in coloured silks, possibly Irish, dated 1717, 11½ x 20in (29 x 51cm).
$6,500–7,250 ⊞ WiA

LOCATE THE SOURCE

The source of each illustration in Miller's can be found by checking the code letters below each caption with the Key to Illustrations, pages 794–800.

A needlework sampler, by Mary Fowler, worked in coloured silks on a linen ground with a verse and stag-hunting scene, 1744, 15¾ x 10¾in (40 x 27.5cm), on an oak panel in a contemporary ebonized and parcel-gilt frame.
$1,000–1,200 ⚒ F&C

◄ A sampler, by Mary King, 1771, 9 x 6in (23 x 15cm), in an ebonized frame.
$500–580 ⊞ HIS

A tablet sampler, by Susannah Platt, embroidered with Adam and Eve, the Lord's Prayer and the Nicene Creed, some moth damage, dated 1776, 17¾ x 12in (45 x 30.5cm), in an ebonized and gilt glazed frame.
$11,300–12,300 ⚒ S(S)
Samplers inscribed with a Creed or the Ten Commandments became increasingly popular in England from the 1720s. Their format was similar to the painted boards displayed in churches of the day, with the appropriate religious tract set out for the education of the congregation.

A Spanish sampler, the linen ground embroidered with yellow, green and blue silks, the centre with a double-headed eagle, some wear, 1785, 42 x 13½in (106.5 x 34.5cm).
$1,300–1,600 ⚒ P

A needlework sampler, by Mary Lee, depicting a motto, alphabet and stylized trees, flowers and birds, 1786, 21¾ x 12¾in (55.5 x 32.5cm), framed.
$450–550 ⚒ WilP

▶ **A Scottish sampler,** the wool ground embroidered in mainly blue, cream and red silks, with alphabets above birds, trees, spot motifs and flowers, late 18thC, 12½ x 9¾in (32 x 25cm), mounted.
$1,600–1,800 ⚒ P

A tablet sampler, by Elizabeth Eastes, embroidered with the Ten Commandments, 1788, 23 x 19in (58.5 x 48.5cm), framed.
$3,000–3,400 ⊞ HIS

A sampler, by Martha Mann, the linen ground worked in silks with an alphabet and numerical bands, above a verse, winged cherubs flanked b caged birds, dated 1789, 15¼ x 8in (38.5 x 20.5cm
$850–1,000 ⚒ S(S)

A sampler, by Elizabeth Allen, embroidered with a verse 'To my ever Honoured Parents', 1801, 11 x 19in (28 x 48.5cm), framed.
$3,600–4,000 ⊞ HIS

▶ **An American Quaker school marking sampler,** worked by Abigail Woolley, Philadelphia, dated 1805, 12 x 9in (30.5 x 23cm).
$4,300–5,000 ⚒ FIN

A needlework sampler, inscribed 'Map of England and Wales by Betsey Scot 1793', worked in silk threads on a linen groun 24½ x 20½in (62 x 52cm).
$1,900–2,200 ⚒ SK(B)
Samplers such as this are particularly popular in the United States where this example wa sold, hence the high price realized.

A sampler, by Catherine Monro, the wool ground embroidered in red silk with a multiplication table, faults, probably Scottish, 1815, 5 x 5½in (12.5 x 14cm).
$5,800–6,500 ⚒ P
Samplers such as this are seldom seen.

A needlework sampler, by Hannah Pring, 1818, 19½ x 13in (49.5 x 33cm).
$250–300 ⚒ SWO
This piece needed cleaning, hence the lower price.

A sampler, by Rachel Pries depicting a red house surrounded by various moti 1818, 17 x 12¼in (43 x 31c in a rosewood frame.
$430–500 ⚒ TRL

A Continental sampler, worked in coloured silks with various spot motifs, early 19thC, 15 x 12in (38 x 30.5cm).
$1,300–1,600 ⊞ WiA

A sampler, by Sarah Sargant, worked in green, blue, brown and yellow with various spot motifs including flowers, trees and animals around alphabets and verses, stained and discoloured, 1818, 16¼ x 17¼in (41.5 x 44cm), in an oak frame.
$220–260 ⋏ LF

A sampler, by Elizabeth Wedd, the linen ground embroidered in green silk, with an alphabet with crowns and geometric motifs to each side, 1818, 10½ x 12¾in (26.5 x 32.5cm), framed.
$260–320 ⋏ WW

An American sampler, by Hannah Challenor, Pennsylvania, worked in green, yellow, red and blue silks on a linen ground, with Adam and Eve beneath the apple tree, above Solomon's Temple flanked by two ladies, dated 1818, 22¼ x 23in (56.5 x 58.5cm).
$10,800–13,000 ⋏ S(NY)

A needlework sampler, by Eliza Sanders, embroidered with the alphabet, biblical quotes, trees and birds, 1819, 17 x 13in (43 x 33cm).
$360–430 ⋏ Bon(G)

A needlework sampler, by Mary Demain, decorated with the alphabet, verse, potted plants and birds, 1822, 18½ x 16in (47 x 40.5cm), framed.
$430–500 ⋏ EH

A Welsh sampler, worked in coloured silks on a wool ground, 19thC, 16 x 12in (40.5 x 30.5cm).
$2,100–2,300 ⊞ WiA

A needlework sampler, by Ann Burton, decorated with a country cottage, verse, flowers and animals within a foliate border, 1823, 17 x 12½in (43 x 32cm).
$2,100–2,300 ⋏ Bea(E)

An American needlework sampler, by Martha Mary Miller, Newport, with alphabet panels above a verse and the maker's identification, surrounded by a stylized floral border, 1823, 17¼in (44cm) square, framed.
$2,200–2,400 ⋏ SK(B)

A sampler, by Mary Davis, worked in cotton on a linen ground, with religious verse, Newton Cottage, angels, dogs, birds, flowers and trees, some damage, 1825, 19 x 20in (48.5 x 51cm).
$170–200 ⋏ WL

▶ **A needlework sampler,** by Jane Park, embroidered on linen with the alphabet and numbers with text below and with a house flanked by plants in jardinières above animals and trees, 1823, 16½ x 12½in (42 x 32cm), in a gilt frame.
$1,300–1,600 ⋏ Mit

TEXTILES

A memorial sampler, with text 'Sarah Duxbury To The Memory of her Dear Brother who died Aug 3 1823', worked with verses, trees, vases of flowers, a church and a figure with staff, dated 1829, 9¾ x 12in (25 x 30.5cm), framed.
$580–720 ➤ P(WM)
This sampler is very attractive, but the memorial theme and the staining kept the price down.

An American sampler, worked by Louisa Martha Vanlaw, Ohio, dated 1834, 17½ x 16¾in (44.5 x 42.5cm).
$19,500–21,750 ➤ FIN

A sampler, by Catherine Rosser, worked in silks and gilt thread with a castle and house over a verse and with flowers, butterflies and other motifs, 1841, 18½ x 12¼in (47 x 31cm).
$720–870 ➤ GH

▶ **A sampler,** by Ruth Hainsworth, worked in coloured thread with a verse, squirrel, bird in a branch, butterflies and bouquets of flowers, 1846, 20 x 24in (51 x 61cm).
$720–870 ➤ HYD

A needlework sampler, by Harriet Haynes, depicting stylized flowers, birds, the alphabet and numbers, 1831, 11 x 7½in (28 x 19cm), in a rosewood frame.
$500–600 ➤ WilP

A sampler, by Ann Alsope, embroidered with alphabets and numbers, dated 1837, 11½ x 9½in (29 x 24cm), framed.
$350–400 ⊞ PSC

A needlework sampler, by Mary Hannah Lister, embroidered in brightly-coloured wool on a linen ground, depicting a dovecot, animals, flowering plants and a verse, 1845, 15½in (39.5cm) square.
$720–870 ➤ F&C

A sampler, by Alice Holt, embroidered with a house and a tree and with alphabets, numbers and a verse over various spot motifs, 1834, 11 x 8in (28 x 20.5cm), framed.
$800–880 ⊞ HIS

A silk sampler, by Hannah Griffiths embroidered with a verse surrounded by various spot motifs, 1840, 17 x 13in (43 x 33cm).
$2,400–2,700 ⊞ HIS

Items in the Samplers section have been arranged in date order.

A sampler, by Mary Smith, the wool ground embroidered in coloured silk with Adam and Eve, a verse, flowers and birds, faults, 1842, 16¾ x 12¾in (42.5 x 32.5cm), mounted.
$450–500 ➤ P

A sampler, by Emma Woodburn, embroidered with silk on gauze with alphabets, verse and various spot motifs, 1847, 17½ x 17in (44.5 x 43cm).
$430–500 ✣ GAK

A pair of samplers, by sisters Mary and Margaret Vergette, embroidered with alphabets and numbers, the earlier one with a verse, 1849 and 1852, 7in (18cm) square.
$480–520 ⊞ PSC

A sampler, by Elizabeth Matthews, embroidered in brown silks with butterflies, a verse, trees, dogs, birds and flowers, dated 1850, 21 x 17in (53.5 x 43cm), in a rosewood frame.
$580–720 ⊞ JPr

A miniature French school sampler, by Adèle Lagazy, dated 1850, 5 x 6in (12.5 x 15cm), framed.
$540–580 ⊞ HIS

A sampler, by Emma Wright, worked in green and shades of brown and beige, with a verse within trees, flowering jardinières, windmills and birds, 1851, 19 x 18¼in (48.5 x 46.5cm), framed.
$580–720 ✣ P(WM)

A sampler, by Fanny Barber, embroidered with a verse, birds, urns and a house within a geometric floral border, dated 1863 on the reverse, 12in (30.5cm) square.
$430–500 ✣ DA

Cross Reference
See Colour Review (page 606)

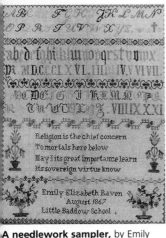

A needlework sampler, by Emily Elizabeth Raven, worked in coloured silks depicting alphabets, a religious verse, vases of flowers and flowering trees, 1867, 16 x 12¼in (40.5 x 31cm).
$650–720 ✣ CAG

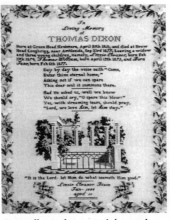

A needlework memorial sampler, inscribed 'In Loving Memory of Thomas Dixon', worked by his daughter Lizzie Eleanor Dixon, detailing the names and dates of birth of Thomas Dixon's three surviving children, above a mourning verse and a monument, dated 1888, 24 x 18½in (61 x 47cm), in a gilt slip and mahogany frame.
$320–380 ✣ PFK

◄ **A French woolwork sampler,** signed with a monogram 'MA', embroidered with the alphabet in pink and green over various polychrome spot motifs including a female figure, a flaming heart and a bouquet of flowers, 19thC, 18½in (47cm) square.
$160–200 ✣ TMA

A needlework sampler, by Sarah Bounds, embroidered with silks and cotton on a cream ground, with religious verse, a mansion, birds, Dalmatians, fruiting vine and rosebuds within a strawberry leaf border, 19thC, 16¾ x 12¼in (42.5 x 31cm).
$1,700–1,900 ✣ WL

TEXTILES

Tapestries

A Brussels tapestry cushion,
16thC, 18 x 17in (45.5 x 43cm).
$2,300–2,900 ⊞ MGa

A Louis XIV mythological tapestry, depicting a scene from Ovid's *Metamorphoses* with Narcissus and Echo, probably from the atelier of Raphael de la Planche, Paris, c1660, 124 x 88½in (315 x 225cm).
$5,000–6,000 ➢ S(Z)

An Aubusson tapestry runner, designed with a garland of flowers at each end with a vase of roses woven in green, blue and pink wool on a cream ground, backed, France, mid-19thC, 23¾ x 470in (60.5 x 185cm).
$230–290 ➢ P

A Flemish tapestry fragment, depicting a parkland scene, late 17thC, 71¼ x 45¼in (181 x 115cm).
$3,200–3,600 ➢ S(Z)

◄ **A Flemish Biblical tapestry,** early 18thC, 124 x 101in (315 x 256.6cm).
$7,200–8,000 ➢ Bon

An Aubusson tapestry, depicting a courting shepherd and shepherdess lying beside a mountainous riverside landscape, France, 18thC, 90½ x 69in (230 x 175.5cm).
$4,000–4,600 ➢ S(Am)

An Aubusson verdure tapestry, depicting a courting couple beside a river in a forest, within a floral garland border, France, 17thC, 113 x 144in (287 x 366cm).
$8,500–9,500 ➢ P

◄ **A Brussels tapestry fragment,** depicting group of travellers with donkeys in a wooded landscape, within a brown velvet border, 17thC, 119 x 31¼in (302.5 x 79.5cm).
$3,200–4,000 ➢ SK

► **A Flemish hunting tapestry,** depicting huntsmen and their dogs in pursuit of a hare and woodland birds, within a border of fruiting branches, reduced in size, one border missing, 17thC, 97 x 84in (246.5 x 213.5cm).
$7,000–8,000 ➢ P

A Brussels tapestry, depicting the triumph of Julius Caesar, within a border of fruiting garlands and masks, early 17thC, 137 x 165in (348 x 419cm).
$7,200–8,000 ➢ S(NY)

An Aubusson *portière*, France, 19thC, 150 x 80in (381 x 203cm).
$2,300–2,900 ➢ Bon(C)

Costume

A cream leather and silk drawstring purse, embroidered with coloured beads, with a bird either side of a plant sprouting acorns, the upper section with 'The gift of a frend 637', 5¼in (13.5cm) high.
$3,300–4,000 ➶ **P**

A set of four steel and jasper buttons, each depicting a classical scene, with a border of cut steel pellets, late 18thC, 1½in (4cm) diam.
$1,700–2,000 ➶ **S(S)**

A copper alloy buckle, engraved with stylized flowers, inscribed 'Henry Platt', dated 1708, 5¾in (14.5cm) long.
$1,300–1,600 ➶ **PFK**

A pair of cream satin shoes, c1820.
$140–170 ⊞ **JuC**

▶ **A child's knitted and beaded bonnet,** in blue, green and red on a cream ground, Swiss or German, c1820, 5in (12.5cm) diam.
$230–260 ⊞ **JuC**

A French embroidered silk purse, 18thC, 7in (18cm) wide.
$330–430 ⊞ **MGa**

A pair of lady's embroidered muslin elbow cuffs, c1760, 14in (35.5cm) diam.
$80–90 ⊞ **JuC**

A white satin beaded bag, c1835, 7in (18cm) wide.
$130–160 ⊞ **TT**

A lady's hand-embroidered cotton bonnet, c1860.
$60–75 ⊞ **JuC**

◀ **A wool and silk Paisley shawl,** in shades of orange, green and black, c1860, 78¾ x 59in (197.5 x 150cm).
$650–800 ⊞ **JPr**

▶ **A Victorian pink silk petticoat,** with machine lace detail.
$100–120 ⊞ **DE**

A child's yellow satin dress, mid-19thC.
$230–290 ➶ **WW**

A broderie anglaise christening robe, c1870, 42in (106.5cm) long.
$140–160 ⊞ **JuC**

A Victorian cotton sun bonnet,
c1870, 14in (35.5cm) long.
$60–75 ⊞ JuC

► **A hand-woven and embroidered cashmere shawl,** with a black and turquoise pattern on a red and orange ground, c1880, 69in (175.5cm) square.
$850–1,000 ⊞ JPr

A Victorian Paisley wool shawl, in shades of red, blue and yellow, 60 x 120in (152.5 x 305cm).
$290–320 ⊞ L&L

A pale blue two-piece day suit, with built-in bustle, c1880.
$430–500 ⊞ DE

◄ **A pair of French child's wooden clogs,** the shaped heel highlighted in red, the instep with a carved flower motif, 19thC.
$170–200 ⋏ P

An Edwardian afternoo[n] dress, in light pink cotton with lace trim.
$125–145 ⊞ DE

A Turkish pale green silk bag, embroidered with coloured silks and designed with a vase of flowers to one side, a butterfly and an inscribed pedestal between two trees to the other, late 19thC.
$360–430 ⋏ P

An Edwardian hand-worked cotton blouse.
$75–100 ⊞ DE

◄ **A silk georgette flapper dress,** in shades of blue and grey, c1920.
$140–170 ⊞ DE

A mauve crêpe and beadwork cocktail dress[,] the skirt stitched with whit[e] and clear glass beads and blue silk embroidery depicting stylized flowerheads, 1920s.
$115–145 ⋏ ELR

An Edwardian hat, with ostrich feathers, labelled 'Affleck and Brown Manchester'.
$140–190 ⊞ TT

A gentleman's top hat, by J. Wippell & Co, Exeter, in a wine plush-lined hide case, early 20thC.
$115–145 ⋏ PFK

Fans

An Italian fan leaf, painted with mythological figures in a landscape, c1720, 25in (63.5cm) wide, in an antique carved frame on a stand.
$2,200–2,600 ⊞ LDC

A fan, painted with mythological figures on clouds, the guard sticks with silver piqué decoration, c1740, 10in (25.5cm) wide.
$580–720 ⊞ LDC

A fan, the leaf painted with a classical scene depicting The Triumph of Galatea, the reverse with flowers and foliage on a brown ground, the ivory sticks and guards with piqué decoration, c1740, 10in (25.5cm) wide.
$1,200–1,400 ⚒ WW

A fan, the leaf painted with a rural a rock, the pierced and carved ivory sticks and guards coloured and gilded with figures, animals, birds and buildings, 18thC, 11¾in (30cm) wide.
$1,600–1,900 ⚒ WW

A French lacquered ivory brisé fan, painted with figures enjoying a *fête champêtre*, the reverse with figures watching boats by a river, with chinoiserie decoration, c1750, 8½in (21.5cm) wide.
$2,200–2,600 ⊞ LDC

A fan, the leaf painted with a landscape of towers and ruins by a river with fishing boats, with pierced ivory sticks, the guard sticks carved with storks, c1760, 11in (28cm) wide.
$1,000–1,200 ⊞ LDC

A fan, the paper leaf painted with figures accompanied by a drummer, with pierced and gilded sticks, c1770, 10in (25.5cm) wide.
$250–300 ⚒ P

A fan, the paper leaf painted with nymphs and *amoretti* resting on clouds strewn with flowers, with carved ivory sticks, possibly Italian, c1770, 10½in (26.5cm) wide.
$580–720 ⚒ P

A fan, the painted leaf with silvered and gilded ivory sticks and pierced guards, the reverse stamped, Russian warrant mark, dated 1773, 11in (28cm) wide.
$430–500 ⚒ WW

A fan, the lithographed leaf painted and gilded with flowers and foliage, the centre depicting a family in medieval dress with châteaux in the background, the reverse with figures in a landscape, the pierced and carved ivory sticks and guards gilded and silvered with flowers and foliage, 18thC, 10½in (26.5cm) wide.
$1,000–1,200 ⚒ WW

An Italian fan, the chicken-skin leaf painted with St Peter's Basilica, flanked by roundels of the Doves of Pliny, the ivory sticks pierced, gilded and silvered and applied with steel roundels, the guards applied with cut-steel beads, late 18thC, 11in (28cm) wide, together with original card case.
$850–1,000 ⚒ S(S)

◀ **An Italian Grand Tour fan,** the chicken-skin leaf painted with nymphs and putti by a stream, the reserves decorated with vignettes of Roman ruins, doves and Pompeiian motifs, c1780, 21¾in (55.5cm) wide, in an antique gilt frame.
$1,200–1,400 ⊞ LDC

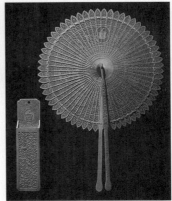

A Chinese export ivory cockade fan, the sticks carved and pierced with a coat of arms, medallions of trees, pagodas and dwellings and roundels of flowerheads among trailing blossom, c1790, 15in (38cm) long, with a carved ivory wall case designed with phoenix and blossom.
$11,500–14,500 ⚒ P

A fan, decorated with a lady standing under a tree, her face of painted ivory on a silk leaf embroidered with sequins, c1810, 8½in (21.5cm) wide.
$100–120 ⊞ LDC

A fan, the hand-tinted lithographed leaf with a mirror on the guard, with pierced ivory sticks and guards, mid-19thC, 9in (23cm) wide, in original box.
$220–260 ↗ WW

An Italian fan, in the form of a flag, with a leaf of plaited straw bound to the wooden spine, with a turned ivory ferule, probably 18thC, 15½in (39.5cm) wide.
$460–550 ↗ P

◀ **A Chinese export brisé fan,** the goose feathers painted in a speckled design, with carved and pierced tortoiseshell sticks, with marabou feather tips, c1840, 13½in (34.5cm) wide.
$230–290 ↗ P

An ivory brisé fan, carved and pierced with flowers and foliage around a central shield with a carved monogram, the guards carved with flowers and birds, 19thC, 8½in (21.5cm) wide, mounted on a display board.
$300–350 ↗ WW

A fan, the hand-painted leaf with flowers on the reverse, with silvered and gilded mother-of-pearl sticks and guards, mid-19thC, 10¾in (27.5cm) wide.
$430–500 ↗ WW

A Belgian fan, the Brussels *point de gaze* lace leaf with a central flower and trailing blossom, flowers and leaves, the mother-of-pearl sticks with gilt flowers and birds, c1850, 9¾in (25cm) wide.
$540–580 ↗ P

A carved ivory brisé fan, the central medallion depicting a river scene with trees, a pagoda and other buildings, flanked by elaborate fruit bowls, among floral sprigs and birds in flight, 19thC, 10½in (26.5cm) wide.
$1,700–2,000 ↗ S

A fan, with a hand-painted leaf and pierced ivory sticks and guards, mid-18thC, 11¼in (28.5cm) wide.
$360–430 ↗ WW

A Belgian fan, the ivory silk leaf applied with Brussels bobbin lace designed with a flowering leafy stem, with pierced bone sticks, c1870, 11¾in (30cm) wide, in a satin-covered box stamped 'Tiffany & Co Union Square'.
$360–400 ↗ P

▶ **A Canton fan,** the paper leaf painted with figures on terraces, with ivory faces and silk clothes, the sticks lacquered in black and gold, framed, c1870, 21¾in (55.5cm) wide.
$650–800 ⊞ LDC

◀ **A French fan,** the black Chantilly bobbin lace leaf designed with pillars and arches over flowers and blossom behind a slatted fence, backed with white gauze and with a white marabou feather edge, with tortoiseshell sticks, faults, Paris, c1870, 14¼in (36cm) wide, with a white satin-covered box stamped 'Tiffany & Co'.
$540–580 ↗ P

A Belgian fan, the Brussels *point de gaze* lace leaf designed with a bouquet of roses and forget-me-nots, with mother-of-pearl sticks, c1880, 13in (33cm) wide, with a satin-covered box with label marked 'Telesphore Des Marés'.
$1,000–1,200 ↗ P

A Japanese export fan, the paper leaf painted with a hillside and bridges, figures and thatched cottages, the reverse with prunus and wistaria blossom, the *Shibayama*-decorated guards designed with bamboo shoots surmounted by a crane, c1880, 15in (38cm) wide.
$650–725 ⚒ P

A Belgian fan, the Brussels *point de gaze* lace leaf designed with flowers, leaves and blossom, with gilt-decorated mother-of-pearl sticks, faults, c1890, 14in (35.5cm) wide, with a red satin box labelled 'J. Duvelleroy'.
$290–320 ⚒ P

An Irish fan, the Carrickmacross lace leaf designed with ribbon bows and flower sprays, with mother-of-pearl sticks, c1890, 9¾in (25cm) wide, with a card box labelled 'Fredk Penberthy, London'.
$330–400 ⚒ P

A miniature fan, the silk leaf decorated with gold sequins, with painted bone sticks, c1900, 6in (15cm) wide.
$110–125 ⊞ FAN

A Cantonese fan, painted in watercolour and bodycolour with chinoiserie figures in pavilions, their faces painted on ivory, the blades pierced and carved with similar scenes, the sticks carved in deep relief with figures in garden settings, 19thC, 11¾in (30cm) wide, in original fitted black lacquered case with gilt figural decoration.
$330–400 ⚒ PFK

A Chinese export fan, the paper leaf painted with an interior scene with ivory and silk appliqué, the reverse with a pheasant, with pierced sandalwood sticks, late 19thC, 11in (28cm) wide, with a black and gilt lacquer box.
$200–240 ⚒ P

A Spanish fan, the Tenerife black lace leaf designed with wheels, the scalloped edge backed with white gauze, with tortoiseshell sticks, c1890, 9½in (24cm) wide, with a card box labelled 'J. Duvelleroy, London'.
$720–800 ⚒ P

A Belgian fan, the Brussels needle-point appliqué lace leaf with a chrysanthemum, other flowers and leaves, with gilt-decorated mother-of-pearl sticks, faults, c1900, 9¾in (25cm) wide.
$230–290 ⚒ P

◄ **A black ostrich feather fan,** with tortoiseshell sticks and guards, early 20thC, 8¼in (21cm) wide.
$90–100 ⚒ WW

A fan, the Maltese bobbin lace leaf of cream silk designed with a central peony, the surround with tulips, flowers and leaves, with pierced bone sticks, faults, c1890, 13½in (34.5cm) wide, with a card box labelled 'Marcot'.
$300–350 ⚒ P

A Chinese export fan, the asymmetrical silk and paper leaf embroidered with cranes, ducks, other birds, a grasshopper and blossoming tree, the ivory guards carved with dragons, birds and blossom, mice, fruit and vines, c1890, 13¼in (33.5cm) wide, with a black and gilt lacquer box.
$1,200–1,400 ⚒ P

A fan, the north Italian bobbin lace leaf with a vignette of an angel on a pedestal, a flower bloom to either side, the surround with scrolling tendrils and leaves and reserves with an angel and cherub, with late 18thC carved and gilded ivory sticks, late 19thC, 11½in (29cm) wide, with a card box labelled 'E. Dreyfous'.
$430–500 ⚒ P

A fan, the Buckinghamshire bobbin lace leaf designed with an inverted tulip and poppies, with shaped mother-of-pearl sticks, early 20thC, 10¼in (26cm) wide, with card box labelled 'J. Duvelleroy'.
$1,300–1,450 ⚒ P

FANS

Jewellery
Bangles & Bracelets

A coral cameo bracelet, set in gold, c1830, clasp 1in (2.5cm) diam.
$320–370 ⊞ Ma

A portrait miniature woven hair bracelet, the plaque depicting a lady, c1840, cased.
$500–600 ⚒ HAM

A pearl and diamond cluster bangle, incorporating a locket, c1860.
$3,200–3,600 ⊞ RES

◀ **A Victorian gold, half-pearl an blue-enamelled hinged bangle,** th front opening to reveal three oval glaze locket compartments, the front with two starburst motifs, on a snap clasp
$800–950 ⚒ RTo

▶ **A gold and micro-mosaic bracelet,** set with five plaques depicting Roman architectural vistas, maker's marks, c1860, 7in (18cm) long.
$2,600–3,200 ⚒ S

▶ **A Victorian hinged bangle,** the front formed as a turquoise-set bud between foliate sides, on a snap clasp.
$400–460 ⚒ JBe

A Victorian 15ct gold hollow hinged bangle, set with a ruby, split pearl and single old-cut diamond in a decorative panel.
$430–500 ⚒ FHF

A Victorian gold meshwork bracelet, the engraved scrolled panel with a centre diamond surrounded by small turquoise stones.
$160–190 ⚒ GAK

A pair of late Victorian 9ct gold bangles, each hinged and with a suspended knotted ball set with turquoises, Birmingham 1897.
$300–350 ⚒ Bri

A late Victorian hinged bangle, with overlaid decorative borders to the front and an engraved section to the reverse, 2¾in (7cm) diam.
$500–600 ⚒ Bon

A diamond and sapphire flexible bracelet, with 49 brilliant-cut diamonds and 40 square-cut sapphires, c1920.
$950–1,150 ⚒ F&C

◀ **An Edwardian 9ct gold bangle,** set with a cushion-cut aquamarine flanked by two seed-pearl-set flowers, hallmarked Aronson & Co.
$500–600 ⚒ LJ

JEWELLERY

Brooches

A diamond brooch, set with cushion-shaped and rose-cut diamonds, with a later brooch fitting, c1800.
$800–950 ⚒ S

A Victorian cruciform brooch, set with citrines.
$430–500 ⚒ L

An early Victorian 9ct gold mourning brooch, the central flower carved from agate and surrounded by pearls, the black background inscribed 'In memory of', with a hinged glass locket to the reverse, 1½in (4cm) long.
$180–220 ⊞ ReJ

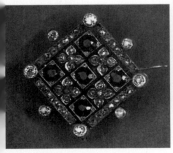

A French diamond and sapphire lapel brooch, c1860.
$1,900–2,200 ⊞ RES

A seed pearl brooch, with a central glazed locket section, c1800.
$110–130 ⚒ LJ

A yellow metal and blue enamel brooch, the centre and edge set with pearls, 19thC, 1in (2.5cm) wide.
$130–160 ⚒ SWO

An early Victorian black onyx and pearl mourning brooch, with a locket to the reverse, inscribed 'In memory of', 2½in (6.5cm) wide.
$470–580 ⊞ Ma

Cross Reference
See Colour Review (page 609)

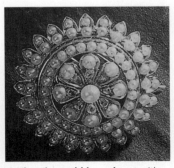

A Victorian gold brooch, set with half-pearls surrounding a pearl and rose-cut diamond floral centre, with a seed-pearl-mounted fine link chain for a pendant mount.
$580–720 ⚒ L&T

A micro-mosaic gold brooch, inlaid with a brightly-coloured butterfly, c1820, ¾in (2cm) wide.
$720–870 ⚒ F&C

A Victorian mourning brooch, depicting two doves on a tomb underneath a tree, with a garnet border over black enamel and a double row of seed pearls, inscribed 'In Memory of William Cozens who died 14 Jan 1842 Aged 31 Years'.
$400–460 ⚒ FHF

A Scottish silver and brown agate brooch, the central thistles set with amethysts and citrines, c1860, 2½in (6.5cm) high.
$580–720 ⊞ BWA

A French 18ct gold and amethyst brooch, c1880, 1¼in (3cm) diam.
$950–1,100 ⊞ GLa

JEWELLERY

An 15ct gold miner's brooch, the miner's pan applied with nuggets and overlaid with a pick and shovel, surrounded by a grape, leaf and tendril border, c1880.
$290–320 ⚒ LJ

A Victorian pearl and diamond-set crescent brooch.
$460–550 ⚒ L&T

A Scottish silver and agate brooch with imitation stone mounts, c1890, 1½in (4cm) diam.
$75–85 ⊞ BWA

A diamond, pearl and ruby bird brooch, with rose-cut diamonds in a pavé setting, 19thC.
$580–720 ⚒ Bea(E)

19th century insect brooches

Jewellery in the shape of dragonflies, bees, butterflies, moths and even flies became popular from the mid-19th century onwards, in accordance with the general public's rising interest in natural history. The most colourful examples were made in the later part of the century, when the use of coloured enamels and semi-precious stones became prevalent.

The quality of such jewellery varies enormously owing to the demand from all levels of 19th-century society, and consequently many pieces are relatively inexpensive.

◄ **A pearl and diamond brooch,** in the shape of a bee with cabochon ruby eyes, resting on a spray of wheat, decorated with rose-cut diamonds interspersed with pearls, c1890.
$1,600–1,750 ⚒ S

► **An Australian 15ct gold seed pearl brooch,** in the shape of a dagger set with a butterfly, hallmarked Levinson, c1900.
$180–220 ⚒ LJ

A 15ct gold brooch, set with a green sapphire surmounted by a natural yellow zircon, the arms set with graduated seed pearls, possibly Australian, c1900.
$140–170 ⚒ LJ

◄ **A Victorian black opal and cut diamond bar brooch,** c190_ 2¼in (5.5cm) long
$1,100–1,300 ⊞ GLa

A diamond brooch, in the shape of an openwork stylized pair of wings and set with circular-cut diamonds, c1900.
$1,400–1,700 ⚒ HAM

An Edwardian guilloche enamel, rose-cut diamond and blonde tortoiseshell brooch, 1½in (4cm) diam
$400–500 ⚒ Bon

A Russian silver niello memorial locket brooch, the design worked with human hair, 1916, 1in (2.5cm) wide.
$170–220 ⊞ Ma

An Austrian jade, coral and diamond brooch, Salzburg, c1940, 2½in (6.5cm) wide.
$5,000–6,000 ⚒ S(G)

LOCATE THE SOURCE
The source of each illustration in Miller's can be found by checking the code letters below each caption with the Key to Illustrations, pages 794–800.

JEWELLERY

Cameos

An Italian onyx cameo demi-parure, comprising a gold pendant brooch mounted with a black and white onyx cameo, the gold frame decorated with scrolls and beads, with a matching pair of earrings suspended from chains, c1865.
$3,200–3,700 ↗ **WW**

A shell cameo, depicting Zeus in the form of an eagle and Hebe in a landscape, in a gold frame, 19thC, 1½in (4cm) wide.
$140–170 ↗ **DN(H)**

▶ **A Victorian carved shell cameo brooch,** depicting a profile of a bearded man, in a gold frame, late 19thC, 1¾in (4.5cm) long.
$380–430 ↗ **DuM**

A Victorian cameo brooch, depicting a classical scene of a lady driving a chariot through clouds, in a pinchbeck frame.
$300–350 ↗ **Bri**

A Victorian carved lava cameo brooch, 2¼in (5.5cm) wide.
$430–500 ↗ **CGC**

A Victorian shell cameo brooch, with a revolving bezel, depicting a classical bust of a young woman, in a pinchbeck frame applied with acorns and oak leaves, inscribed 'J. H. Steward', 1½in (4cm) high, with original velvet-lined case.
$580–720 ↗ **F&C**

A cameo brooch, carved with mythological figures, a throne and a tree, c1870, 1½in (4cm) wide.
$430–500 ↗ **JBe**

A stamped pink shell cameo brooch, suspended from a 15ct gold bar, c1875, 1in (2.5cm) diam.
$500–580 ⊞ **GLa**

Collecting cameos

• Cameos depicting men are not as popular with collectors as those depicting women. Cameos with male faces can therefore be more affordable.
• The fact that a cameo is not in its original frame will not necessarily affect value, as long as the frame is contemporary. An old cameo in a modern frame is much less desirable.
• Shell cameos, because they are carved along the grain, often have stress lines. With age, dryness and general wear and tear these stress lines can develop into visible cracks, which will drastically reduce the value.
• Some cameos can be found in their original leather cases, which often give the name of the jeweller and add considerably to the value of the piece.

◀ **A cameo bracelet,** the five shell plaques carved with classical maidens in profile, each set in a silver-gilt collet with a rope border, with a 9ct yellow gold clasp, c1900.
$240–290 ↗ **LJ**

A Victorian shell cameo parure, the filigree mounts set with seed pearls, brooch 2in (5cm) diam.
$3,200–3,600 ⊞ **BeE**

JEWELLERY

Cufflinks

A pair of silver cufflinks, 18thC.
$200–230 ⊞ JBB

A pair of American 10ct gold cufflinks, c1950.
$130–145 ⊞ JBB

▶ A pair of gold cufflinks, each with a mother-of-pearl disc centred with a gold bead and bordered by white and gold dot enamel, stamped 18, early 20thC, in an Asprey case.
$300–350 ⋌ DN

A pair of gold cufflinks, each set with blue *plique-à-jour* enamel with a foliate motif of a square-shaped ruby and a diamond flowerhead, flanking a central band of diamonds, late 19thC.
$1,200–1,400 ⋌ HAM

A pair of Edwardian gold cufflinks, each with a blue enamel border enclosing a mother-of-pearl panel with a central opal.
$500–600 ⋌ Bon

A pair of Edwardian cufflinks, the oval mother-of-pearl panels with white enamel borders and turquoise centres.
$500–600 ⋌ Bon

Cross Reference
See Colour Review
(page 610)

Earrings

A pair of gold, emerald and diamond pendant earrings, c1830, faults.
$3,200–3,600 ⋌ DN

A pair of 15ct gold earrings, in the shape of three interwoven circles applied with fine Etruscan wirework, each set with six faceted garnets, c1880.
$430–480 ⋌ LJ

▶ A pair of Georgian rose-cut diamond cluster earrings, in gold and silver mounts, c1800.
$500–600 ⋌ LJ

A pair of Victorian gold-mounted coral earrings, 1in (2.5cm) long.
$180–220 ⊞ Ma

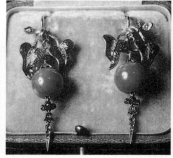

A pair of late Victorian gold, coral and enamel drop earrings, 1½in (4cm) long, in a fitted case.
$4,700–5,400 ⊞ BeE

▶ A pair of onyx and diamond earrings, set in platinum, c1910, 2¾in (7cm) long.
$4,700–5,400 ⋌ S(G)

A pair of gold-mounted aquamarine drop earrings, c1875.
$1,900–2,100 ⊞ RES

Necklaces

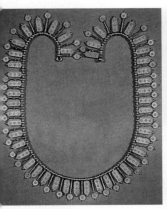

A gold necklace, by John Brogden, in the shape of small panels with twisted wirework and granulation decoration, threaded on a fine foxtail chain, one link missing, mid-19thC.
$5,800–7,200 ✗ Mal(O)

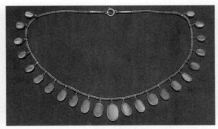

A Victorian moonstone fringe necklace, suspended from a woven gold necklet, cased.
$1,000–1,200 ✗ P(L)

A French Victorian 18ct gold bead necklace, c1900, 16in (40.5cm) long.
$2,600–2,900 ⊞ WIM

A Victorian jet locket and chain.
$100–120 ✗ SWO

A 15ct gold, pearl and sapphire pendant necklet, c1870.
$1,200–1,400 ⊞ GLa

A Victorian gold locket, with split pearl and turquoise stylized motif, on a collar with alternating burnished and gilded shaped panels.
$2,300–2,900 ✗ FHF

A Victorian gold-framed pale blue stone leaf necklace, in a fitted case.
$870–1,000 ✗ GAK

A seed pearl necklace, with a white gold filigree clasp set with diamonds and sapphires, c1900, 11½in (29cm) long.
$140–170 ✗ LJ

A late Victorian pendant, set with half-pearls, on an associated torpedo link gold chain with pearl spacers.
$870–1,000 ✗ KID

A platinum, seed pearl and diamond three-row necklace, on a Victorian peridot and cultured pearl clasp, c1905.
$7,200–8,000 ✗ HAM

An Edwardian necklet, with centre heart-shaped garnet and pearl cluster, flanked by pearl-set sprays, stamped 15.
$1,100–1,400 ✗ WL

◄ A French diamond necklace, decorated with a profusion of marquise, pear-shaped and brilliant- and step-cut diamonds, French assay marks, 1960s, 17in (43cm) long.
$522,000+ ✗ S(G)
This magnificent diamond necklace is from the collection of the late Begum Sultan Mohamed Shah, the fourth and last wife of the late Aga Khan III. It contains a brilliant-cut diamond weighing 4.20 carats.

► A natural opaque Baltic amber necklace, c1920, 44in (112cm) long.
$320–370 ⊞ Ma

JEWELLERY

Pendants

A pendant, the enamelled panel set with old-cut diamonds, the silver setting backed with gold, early 19thC.
$800–950 ✗ WL

A Victorian turquoise and pearl star pendant, c1865, cased.
$1,900–2,100 ⊞ RES

An enamel and half-pearl cross, by Robert Philips, late 19thC, 3in (7.5cm) long, on a chain.
$580–720 ✗ Bon

A black onyx commem-orative locket, set in gold, with a silver and pearl flower, c1860, 1½in (4cm) long.
$470–570 ⊞ Ma

A Victorian gold brooch/pendant, set to the centre with a diamond and mounted on a yellow metal chain.
$360–430 ✗ GAK

◀ **A late Victorian St Espirit brooch/pendant,** in the shape of a dove with ruby eyes and set thoughout with diamonds, with a leaf and diamond drop, lacking three stones.
$1,100–1,300 ✗ DN

An Edwardian diamond and seed pearl pendant, c1900, on a modern 14ct gold chain set with five modern diamonds.
$950–1,150 ✗ LJ

A Victorian 18ct gold pendant, the interlinked pendant surmounted by a blue-enamelled pearl-set leaf, with a further leaf drop, c1860, on an 18ct gold chain.
$500–600 ✗ LJ

A Victorian gold locket, set with a Brazilian cut diamond within a raised star, 2¼in (5.5cm) long.
$580–720 ✗ F&C

A 15ct gold aquamarine and pearl pendant, c1900, 9in (23cm) long.
$650–720 ⊞ GLa

▶ **A diamond and sapphire entwined hearts pendant,** set in platinum, 1920s, 1½in (4cm) long.
$5,000–5,500 ⊞ BeE

A Victorian 15ct gold pendant, decorated with a rose-cut diamond and enamel star, the glazed back enclosing a lock of hair, on a 9ct gold chain.
$720–800 ⊞ GLa

A Victorian gold strapwo... **pendant,** with royal blue enamel studded with diamonds and suspended with pearl drops.
$1,000–1,200 ✗ WW

A sapphire and diamond brooch/pendant, c1920, 1¾in (4.5cm) diam.
$6,500–8,000 ✗ S(G)

Rings

A William and Mary gold memorial ring, with a panel of plaited hair behind faceted glass, the reverse inscribed 'Dyed Novem 6: 1698', with traces of black and white enamel on the leaf-chased shoulders, the back with a hairwork panel.
$1,400–1,700 ➤ HYD

A gold buckle ring, enamelled in blue and white, with a rose-cut diamond-mounted buckle, 19thC.
$580–720 ➤ Bea(E)

A late Victorian sapphire and diamond cluster ring, with a gold mount.
$1,400–1,700 ➤ WW

► A black opal, diamond and gold ring, c1900.
$2,000–2,300 ➤ LJ

A George III memorial ring, with a sepia miniature depicting a woman seated beneath a willow tree next to a tomb with an urn, with inscription to reverse 'John Lancashire ob 9 December 1784 ae 76'.
$500–600 ➤ FHF

A Victorian ruby and diamond four-row ring, c1875.
$2,600–2,900 ⊞ RES

A gold and ivory miniature ring, depicting a putto with a swan, within a blue-enamelled border applied with gold foliage, with a later inscription, late 18thC.
$1,200–1,400 ➤ S(S)

A diamond five-stone ring, set in 18ct gold, Birmingham 1896.
$300–350 ➤ L

A five-stone opal and diamond chip dress ring, in a white metal setting, chip to one opal, early 20thC.
$160–190 ➤ PFK

A 14ct gold ring, set with amethysts and seed pearls, several pearls missing, early 19thC.
$160–190 ➤ SWO

A Victorian garnet and half-pearl ring, engraved to the reverse 'J. L. to M. W. 1848'.
$430–500 ➤ Bon

A 15ct gold ring set with five graduated opals, late 19thC.
$320–380 ➤ WilP

A gentleman's diamond ring, by Benson, in a ribbed 18ct gold mount, 1938.
$3,600–4,000 ➤ TEN

Stickpins

A garnet and diamond stick pin, set in silver and gold, in the shape of a flower, 19thC.
$500–600 ➤ DN

► A gem-set gold horseshoe stick pin, c1900, 1½in (4cm) long.
$650–800 ⊞ ANTH

A turquoise and coral hat pin, 19thC, 4in (10cm) long.
$580–720 ➤ S(G)

A gold skull stick pin, with rose-cut diamond eyes, and sprung hinged jaw, 19thC.
$950–1,150 ➤ Bon

A late Victorian Etruscan revival gold stick pin, the hinged cover with applied fine wire ropetwist and bead border, enclosing a locket interior.
$260–320 ➤ Bon

JEWELLERY

Enamel

A Russian silver-gilt and cloisonné enamel beaker, by Gustav Klingert, Moscow, with gilt interior, 1893, 2¼ n (5.5cm) high.
$1,200–1,400 ⊞ NS

A Swiss 18ct gold and enamel table snuff box, maker's mark crowned GRG, Geneva, c1790, 4in (10cm) wide.
$13,000–14,500 ⊞ BEX

An enamel patch box, the cover inscribed 'A Present from Salisbury' within a blue painted border, the interior with a mirror, 18thC, 1¾in (4.5cm) diam.
$300–350 ⚒ HYD

An enamelled patch box, with gilt-metal mounts, the cover painted with a figure in a landscape, the interior with a mirror, c1800, 1¾in (4.5cm) diam.
$190–220 ⚒ AH

A French silver and enamel pill box, 1860s, 1½in (4cm) diam.
$360–430 ⊞ BAO

An Austrian silver and purple enamel box, by R. S., c1910, 1¾in (4.5cm) diam.
$720–800 ⊞ BEX

◀ **A French enamel cup,** painted with polychrome birds and flowers on white reserves on a translucent blue ground, the stem decorated in turquoise within bead borders, the base signed and dated Durand 1861, Paris, 4½in (11.5cm) high.
$4,600–5,000 ⚒ S
This is possibly an experimental piece since, unusually for this type of French enamel work, it is signed and dated on the base. Also one small panel on the bowl has been left undecorated.

A hand-painted mother-of-pearl *carnet de bal* card case, with enamel plaques to both sides, with silver mounts, c1770, 3½in (9cm) high.
$680–750 ⊞ LBr

▶ **An Imperial Russian silver and enamelled *kovsh*,** by Pavel Ovchinikov, Moscow 1876, 2in (5cm) wide.
$1,200–1,400 ⊞ SHa

An enamel-on-copper plaque of St Martin, by W. B. Simpson & Sons, the face flesh tinted, the mitre set with rubies *en cabochon*, surmounted by green and white striped bands, late 19thC, 20in (51cm) diam.
$2,200–2,600 ⚒ Mit

A Limoges enamel portrait plaque, France, c1900, 7in (18cm) high, framed.
$540–600 ⊞ WAC

◀ **A Limoges enamel portrait plaque,** France, c1900, 4in (10cm) diam, in a giltwood frame
$430–480 ⚒ SK

Fabergé

A pair of Fabergé silver asparagus tongs, the handles decorated with shells and engraved with armorials, Moscow, Russia, c1890, 10¾in (27.5cm) long.
$2,600–3,200 ⚲ S(NY)

▶ **A Fabergé chalcedony, rose-cut diamond and gold brooch,** workmaster A. Holmström, St Petersburg, Russia, before 1896, 1½in (4cm) wide.
$5,800–7,200 ⚲ S

▶ **A Fabergé heart brooch,** the Siberian moss agate within a border of diamonds, Russia, c1900, 1¼in (3cm) wide.
$9,400–10,800 ⊞ SHa

A Fabergé Imperial Russian *samorodok* cigarette case, Moscow, 1896–1907, 3in (7.5cm) wide.
$3,500–4,000 ⊞ SHa
***Samorodok* is a form of stipple decoration with the appearance of bark.**

▶ **A Fabergé silver dish,** the handle decorated with Slavic motifs, Moscow, Russia, 1908–17, 4in (10cm) diam.
$2,900–3,200 ⊞ Wa

A Fabergé silver cigarette case, workmaster Julius Rappoport, with a separate vesta compartment at one end and a winder at the top to wind the cord match, the cover applied with a foliate panel beside a gold monogram, marked IP, Russia, 1896–1908, 2¾in (7cm) wide.
$1,400–1,700 ⚲ P

A Fabergé novelty menu holder, workmaster Henrik Wigström, modelled as the collar of an officer's full dress uniform of the Semenovski Guard Regiment, enamelled in light blue with red piping and chased wheatsheaf silver lace embroidery, Russia, 1908–17, enamel damaged, 5¼in (13.5cm) long.
$8,000–8,800 ⚲ P

A Fabergé pencil holder, workmaster V. Soloviev, with two-colour gold mounts, enamelled in bright daffodil yellow over wavy engine-turning, applied with a jewelled trefoil, with lemon gold laurel border, St Petersburg, Russia, 1908–17, minor restoration, 3in (7.5cm) long.
$4,700–5,400 ⚲ S

▶ **A Fabergé silver salt,** the top with pink guilloche enamel bordered by gold bands above a silver base, Russia, c1900, 3¼in (8.5cm) long.
$4,300–4,700 ⚲ Mit

Gold

A French gold-mounted snuff box, the lid inset with a miniature within a gold ropetwist frame, the sides and base striped in gold, red and cream enamel, with a tortoiseshell lining, Paris, c1780, 2¾in (7cm) diam.
$3,200–3,600 ⚒ S

A Swiss engraved gold snuff box, c1820, 3in (7.5cm) long.
$4,800–5,400 ⊞ SHa

An Imperial Russian gold cigarette case, by G Lundell, St Petersburg, c1900, 4in (10cm) long.
$4,800–5,400 ⊞ SHa

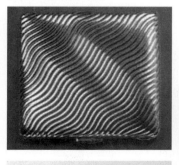

A French gold vinaigrette, c1800, 1¼in (3cm) diam.
$1,600–1,800 ⊞ BEX

A French three-colour gold snuff box, by Barthélemy Pillieux, the lid inset with a central rosette, the reeded ground dotted with pellets within entwined lemon gold borders, maker's mark of Paris, 1782, 2½in (6.5cm) diam.
$2,400–2,900 ⚒ S

A gold and agate snuff box, c1820, 1¾in (4.5cm) long.
$1,600–1,800 ⊞ BEX

A French gold pill box, all-over chased with swags of foliage and flowers, 19thC, 2¼in (5.5cm) diam.
$1,000–1,200 ⚒ LT

◄ **A French 18ct gold powder compact,** c1930, 2½in (6.5cm) square.
$1,600–1,800 ⊞ RES

An Irish gold snuff box, by John Ebbs, Dublin 1808, 2in (5cm) long.
$5,800–6,500 ⊞ WELD

A Swiss gold and enamel snuff box, the lid with a polychrome enamel cutout painted with a falconry scene against an engraved landscape, bordered with flower garlands on a black ground with book spine sides, the base engraved with further flowers, Geneva mid-19thC, 2½in (6.5cm) long.
$3,300–3,700 ⚒ S

A 9ct gold cigarette case, by Walker & Hall, decorated in enamel with a shire horse, Chester 1921, 3½in (9cm) long.
$3,600–4,000 ⊞ THOM

A 9ct gold treasury ink stand, the interior with two gold-mounted glass inkwells and presentation inscription dated 1929, 9in (23cm) wide, 49.5oz.
$5,800–6,500 ⚒ L

◄ **A French wooden nécessaire with gold implements,** the case lined in silk and plush, the gold fittings worked where appropriate with foliate motifs on a *sablé* ground, maker's mark rubbed, probably Antoine Beauvisage, Paris, 1819–1932, 5in (12.5cm) long.
$1,400–1,700 ⚒ S

Asian Works of Art

Cloisonné & Enamel

A Chinese cloisonné enamel incense burner, standing on three elephant feet, decorated with lotus scrolls, the reticulated lid with a dog finial, early 19thC, 7½in (19cm) high.
$290–350 ⚒ WW

A pair of Chinese Canton enamel hand warmers, painted with panels of Buddhistic lions, pups and cranes on a pink ground reserved with a floral meander, with pierced covers, damaged, restored, Qianlong period, 1736–95, 4¼in (11cm) high.
$1,750–2,000 ⚒ S(S)

A pair of Chinese cloisonné enamel stirrups, the rims enamelled with flowers, vases, books and other domestic items, on rich blue grounds, 19thC, 6in (15cm) high.
$330–400 ⚒ P

A Chinese cloisonné enamel clasp, c1900, 5in (12.5cm) wide.
$340–380 ⊞ JBB

A pair of Chinese cloisonné enamel *lingzhi*, each applied with bats and the Eight Buddhist Emblems and rising from a jardinière with *shou* medallions encircled by bats, *wufu* and stylized lotus, 18thC, 14¾in (37.5cm) high.
$12,300–14,300 ⚒ S
Wufu means literally 'the five happinesses' which are long life, riches, tranquillity, love of virtue and a good end to one's life, and is symbolized by the character *fu* repeated five times, or by five bats.

A Japanese cloisonné enamel vase, with a basketweave design in bamboo colour, signed Hayashi Hachizaemon, c1900, 6in (15cm) high.
$3,300–4,000 ⚒ SK
The time-consuming work that went into making this piece is reflected in the elevated price realized.

A Japanese cloisonné enamel vase, by Ota Tame-siro, painted in shades of blue on a pale green ground, with silver rim and base, maker's intaglio flowerhead mark, c1900, 11in (28cm) high.
$870–1,000 ⚒ PFK

▶ **A Japanese cloisonné enamel vase,** the blue ground decorated with white egrets, with circle and twin duck mark to base, early 20thC, 15½in (39.5cm) high.
$580–720 ⚒ DMC

A pair of Chinese ormolu-mounted enamel cups, with bamboo patterned handles, the interiors painted with sprays of coloured flowers on a white ground, with ruby exterior, Qianlong period, 1736–95, 1½in (4cm) high.
$440–500 ⚒ F&C

A Chinese cloisonné enamel hors d'oeuvres set, the central stand decorated with dragons, surrounded by six fan-shaped dishes decorated with flowering branches and baskets of flowers on a sky blue ground, late 19thC, 24in (61cm) diam overall.
$650–800 ⚒ P(Ba)

A pair of Japanese cloisonné enamel vases, decorated with seated monkeys, Meiji period, 1858–1911, 4¾in (12cm) high.
$4,000–4,600 ⚒ BLH

Glass

A Beijing turquoise blue glass bowl, carved on the exterior with a long-tailed bird confronting a butterfly among large peonies, incised mark and period of Qianlong, 1736–95, 6½in (16.5cm) wide.
$8,700–10,200 ➤ S

A Chinese rock crystal censer and cover, carved in light relief with archaistic designs, applied on either side with *taotie* masks and pendant ring handles, lacking one ring handle, 19thC, 6¼in (16cm) high.
$730–870 ➤ P

A group of three reverse glass paintings, variously painted with a shepherdess, a woman nursing her child, and a woman seated at a garden table, 18thC, 2 x 2¾in (5 x 7cm), in giltwood frames.
$2,600–2,900 ➤ S(S)

A pair of Chinese reverse glass paintings, each depicting riverscape in shades of green, brown and blue, 19thC, 22in (56cm) wide, framed.
$3,600–4,300 ➤ P

◀ **Two Peking yellow glass bottle vases,** carved in high relief with stylized lotus scrolls, Qianlong mark to bases, 1736–95, 8¾in (22cm) high
$9,700–10,700 ➤ S(NY)

A Chinese export reverse glass painting, depicting Christ on the cross and Mary Magdalene weeping below, 1780–1800, 8 x 6in (20.5 x 15cm), in a later silvered frame.
$3,600–4,000 ➤ S(NY)

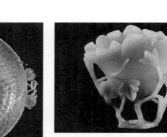

Jade

A Chinese Moghul-style spinach jade bowl, carved with tiers of chrysanthemum petals, flanked by lotus handles, 19thC, 13in (33cm) wide.
$2,300–2,600 ➤ S

A Chinese green nephrite water coupe, with five *qilin* crawling across its rim, the interior carved with scrolling clouds, 18thC, 9½in (24cm) diam.
$4,600–5,500 ➤ BB(S)

A Chinese celadon jade brushwasher, in the shape of a lotus pod supported on stems, 19thC, 5in (12.5cm) high.
$1,400–1,600 ➤ S

A Chinese spinach jade tripod incense burner and cover, with shallow relief phoenix divided by six vertical flanges, one handle restuck, 18thC, 6¼in (16cm) wide, with a carved wood stand.
$2,500–2,900 ➤ P

A Chinese celadon jade brush rest, carved in relief with boughs of peaches beside mountains, the reverse with ducks, 19thC, 6in (15cm) long.
$850–1,000 ➤ P

A Chinese Moghul-style celadon jade cup, the two handles formed as lotus, 19thC, 5in (12.5cm) wide.
$1,400–1,700 ➤ S

Gifts of Jade

According to Chinese tradition, a family was thought fortunate to bear a son, and in celebration often presented male progeny with a piece of jade. It was therefore common to be congratulated by friends on 'a fine piece of jade', meaning a male child.

Lacquer

A Chinese cinnabar lacquer box, the top carved with a garden scene, the exterior walls of the cover and base carved with lotus flower and scrolling leaf cartouches, the remaining surfaces finished in a coat of black lacquer, chips, repairs, 18thC, 12¼in (31cm) square.
$1,900–2,300 ⚡ BB(S)

A Chinese red and black lacquer cosmetic box, Han Dynasty, 206 BC–AD 220, 4½in (11.5cm) high.
$3,600–4,400 ⊞ TeW

A Japanese gilt lacquer box, with a three-clawed dragon on the cover, the interior tray decorated in gold *takamaki-e* with Jurojin and a crane, signed Hokyo Kanko, Meiji period, 1866–1911, 4¼in (11cm) diam.
$5,000–5,800 ⚡ BB(S)
Jurojin was one of the Japanese Immortals.

A Japanese black and gold lacquer picnic set, the top decorated with a carp leaping from the water, the four-tiered food storage box, tray and box with flower sprays, 18thC, 7½in (19cm) wide.
$1,500–1,800 ⚡ S(Am)

A Japanese lacquered tray, decorated with a scene of birds in a tree on a basketweave ground, inlaid with ivory, horn and mother-of-pearl, Meiji period, 1868–1911, 30in (76cm) long.
$2,600–2,900 ⚡ SK

◀ **A Japanese wooden pipe case and fabric tobacco pouch,** the case simulating bamboo, attached with a cord and carved agate *ojime* to a floral decorated silk pipe case, Meiji period, 1868–1911, 8¾in (22cm) long.
$650–800 ⚡ P

A Chinese lacquer box, in five sections with a lid, early 20thC, 14in (35.5cm) high.
$450–550 ⚡ SWO

Metalware

A Japanese carved gilded-copper box, with two ring handles, 16thC, 13in (33cm) long.
$4,300–5,000 ⚡ S(NY)

▶ **A Chinese silver snuff box,** the hinged cover with a figural scene, the sides and base chased with foliate decoration, gilded interior, 19thC, 3¼in (8.5cm) long, 4oz.
$580–730 ⚡ Bon

A Chinese bronze temple bell, 18thC or earlier, 50in (127cm) high.
$8,000–8,800 ⚡ SK

A Japanese silver bowl, Japanese character marks on base, c1900, 7in (18cm) diam, 12oz.
$360–430 ⚡ CGC

ASIAN WORKS OF ART

A Chinese metal alloy snuff box, embossed with bamboo, late 19thC, 3in (7.5cm) long.
$290–360 ⊞ ES

A Chinese silver pill box, modelled as a book, by MK, c1900, 1¼in (3cm) long.
$430–470 ⊞ BEX

A Chinese bronze brush pot, the sides decorated in relief with three-clawed dragons, one clasping a flaming pearl, among cloud scrolls in a granulated sky, probably 19thC, 4in (10cm) high.
$720–870 ⚒ P

▶ **A Chinese bronze censer,** cast with dragons, animals' heads and stylistic decoration over a base of six elephants' heads, late 19thC, 29in (73.5cm) high, on a stained wood table stand.
$1,300–1,600 ⚒ P(WM)

A Chinese archaic bronze censer, the pierced lid depicting mountains, animals and people, the foot with openwork representing coiled dragons, Han Dynasty, 206 BC–AD 220, 7in (18cm) high.
$3,600–4,300 ⚒ S(Am)

A Chinese bronze censer, with mask knees to the three supports, and pierced wood cover and stand, 16thC, 4½in (11.5cm) diam.
$220–260 ⚒ RBB

Items in the Asian Works of Art section have been arranged in subject order within each sub-section.

A Chinese gilded-copper incense burner, the sides cast with a band of emblems and precious objects beneath a border of stylized scrolls, flanked by *chilong* handles, 17thC, 6½in (16.5cm) wide.
$5,500–6,000 ⚒ S

A bronze censer, the handles cast as stylized dragons' heads, the sides with broad *taotie* masks below zoomorphic bands, the pierced wood cover with a white jade finial carved as a boy with a gourd, c1700, 9in (23cm) diam, on a pierced wood stand.
$580–720 ⚒ P

A Japanese bronze ikebana stand, cast with a dragon emerging from a ball of fire beneath a detachable drip pan, on three scroll legs in the shape of stylized elephant trunks, Meiji period, 1868–1911, 11¾in (30cm) diam.
$220–260 ⚒ KID

A Chinese silver egg cup stand, marked with pseudo English marks, maker's mark of Sunshing, crested, 19thC, 8in (20.5cm) high, 18oz.
$800–950 ⚒ Bon

A Japanese white metal incense ball, pierced and engraved with *ho-o* birds among foliage, Meiji period, 1868–1911, 6¼in (16cm) diam.
$580–720 ⚒ RTo

A Chinese cast-bronze hand-warmer, with a movable strap handle, the cover reticulated in a basketweave pattern, signed Zhang Mingqi, c1600, 5½in (14cm) long.
$5,800–7,200 ⚒ BB(S)

An archaic bronze oil lamp and stand, the stand supported on four kneeling figures, showing turquoise patination, Han Dynasty, 206 BC–AD 220, 10in (25.5cm) long.
$3,600–4,300 ⚒ S

A Chinese bronze libation vessel, c1100 BC, 7in (18cm) high.
$9,500–11,500 ⊞ GLD

► An Indian silver teapot, c1900, 5in (12.5cm) high.
$650–800 ⊞ BEX

A Chinese silver three-piece tea service, by Luen Wo, Shanghai, cast in relief with blossoming prunus sprigs, the handles in the shape of branches, late 19thC, teapot 9in (23cm) high.
$2,200–2,600 ➤ S
Luen Wo was one of the most prolific silversmiths working in Shanghai during the 19th century, producing items of high quality workmanship.

◄ A Chinese bronze vase, decorated with pendant shield-shaped panels, 19thC, 9½in (24cm) high.
$170–220 ➤ WW

A Japanese silver vase, incised with foliate decoration, the body inset with eight *Shibayama* panels depicting birds perched on branches and baskets of flowers in mother-of-pearl, coral and abalone, slight damage, Meiji period, c1900, 10½in (26.5cm) high.
$950–1,150 ➤ HAM

◄ A Korean bronze ceremonial water vessel, applied to one side with a spout with cupped mouth fitted with a hinged cap, extensive corrosion, c12thC, 17in (43cm) high.
$2,000–2,500 ➤ BB(S)

Wood

A Chinese or Indian camphorwood tambour writing box, made for the Western market, c1860, 19in (48.5cm) long.
$1,200–1,400 ⊞ TWh

A Japanese wooden fireplace crane, 19thC, 12in (30.5cm) high, with a fitted iron stand.
$1,000–1,200 ➤ SK

A Japanese wood Noh mask of Sanko-jo, painted on gesso ground, with red and black stained details, the hair, moustache and beard of horse hair, worm eaten, chipped, late 18thC, 4in (15cm) high.
$1,900–2,200 ➤ S
Sanko-jo is a humble old man in Japanese traditional plays.

Three Japanese carved wood and lacquered Noh masks, with hideous expressions, glass eyes, real hair facial details and tasselled cords, mounted on a shield-shaped framed panel, central plaque insert missing, Meiji period, 1868–1911, 25¼in (64cm) high.
$870–1,000 ➤ TEN

A Chinese boxwood *ruyi* sceptre, in the form of a *lingzhi* spray, carved with a bat on the cloud head, 19thC, 13¾in (35cm) high.
$2,200–2,400 ➤ S
The *ruyi* sceptre had its origin in the humble back-scratcher, a stick about 18in (45.5cm) long with a bent hand at one end. As the Imperial scratchers became more fancy, the shape developed into the form we know today. On court celebration days, *ruyi* sceptres would be presented to the Emperor who would then give them to favoured ministers or subjects. The sceptres were made in many materials and invariably carry auspicious symbols such as 'pine and crane' (longevity) or 'phoenix and peony' (prosperity).

ASIAN WORKS OF ART

Arms & Armour

A Japanese *okegawa go mai do*, the front plate illustrating the monk Endo Morito by a waterfall, with later carving and gold and silver overlay, the sides decorated with waves and foliate tendrils, c1600.
$3,600–4,300 ▲ BB(S)

▶ **A pair of Indian arm defences,** decorated with shaped panels filled with flowers and foliage in gold *koftgari*, with early padded fabric lining embroidered with flowers and foliage, c1800, 11½in (29cm) long.
$2,000–2,300 ▲ S(S)

A Japanese 62-plate *sujibachi-kabuto*, black lacquered with gilded-copper *igaki* and *fukurin*, the gilt-lacquered wood crest modelled as a boar with iron tusks, glass eyes and a moving tongue, c1700.
$10,800–13,000 ▲ S

An Indian Mughal dagger, the blade with a gold damascened mount, the scabbard with copper-gilt mounts, the jade hilt in the shape of a parrot, c1700, 13½in (34.5cm) long.
$7,300–8,700 ▲ Bon

An Indian dagger, the steel hilt with a ram's horn head in relief, 18thC, blade 6¾in (17cm) long, in a later leather-covered sheath.
$220–260 ▲ WAL

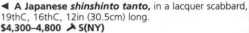

An Indian sword, the blade decorated with gold scrollwork, the silver-encrusted iron hilt punched and decorated with gold, blade 26½in (67.5cm) long, in a fabric-covered wooden sheath.
$1,500–1,800 ▲ S(S)

◀ **A Japanese *shinshinto tanto*,** in a lacquer scabbard, 19thC, 16thC, 12in (30.5cm) long.
$4,300–4,800 ▲ S(NY)

A Japanese ivory *tanto*, carved in relief with sages in thatched buildings among pine trees in a rocky garden, Meiji period, 1868–1911, 13¾in (35cm) long.
$950–1,150 ▲ P

A Nepalese silver-mounted *kukri*, in a black water buffalo horn sheath with silver mounts, the locket embossed with twin gilt lions and cabochon-cut turquoise, the sides embossed with dragons among clouds, chape with gilt peacock and foliage, 19thC, blade 11½in (29cm) long, and two horn-hilted companion knives.
$360–430 ▲ WAL

Tsuba

A Japanese *tsuba*, pierced with *monsukashi* among inlaid brass *karakusa*, signed Hirata Doden (?), Edo period, 17thC, 3in (7.5cm) long.
$2,200–2,400 ▲ S

A Japanese iron *tsuba*, with brass-inlaid decoration of leaves, c1700, 2½in (6.5cm) wide.
$290–320 ▲ Herm

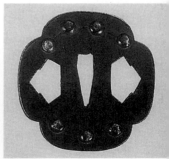

A Japanese iron *tsuba*, probably later restored, signed Nakamura Muneyoshi Saku, dated 1865, 3in (7.5cm) wide.
$230–290 ▲ Herm

Miller's is a price GUIDE not a price LIST

ASIAN WORKS OF ART

Clocks & Watches

A Dutch watch, for the Japanese market, the interior with a grotesque mask, the outer case pierced with dolphins, a bouquet of flowers and a classical bust, signed Madelaine a Middlebour, in a leather cover with silver mounts, with a Japanese silver chain inlaid with gold and a bronze *netsuke* of a cymbal with zodiac symbols, c1700.
£13,700–16,700 ♣ SK

A gilt-brass and polychrome cloisonné enamel carriage clock, by Vrard & Co, Shanghai, with subsidiary alarm dial, the quarter-repeating gong-striking movement with platform lever escapement, 1885, 6½in (16.5cm) high.
£8,700–9,400 ♣ S(NY)

A Japanese coromandel pillar clock, mid-19thC, 18in (45.5cm) high.
£1,500–1,800 ♣ EH

A Japanese brass lantern clock, with an iron mechanism and brass dial, the painted chapter ring now with Roman numerals, the engraved brass hour hand in the form of a prunus leaf on a red lacquered centre, verge escapement, striking the hours on a bell, c1740, 11in (28cm) high.
£2,900–3,200 ♣ S(Am)

A Chinese gilt-brass quarter-striking automaton clock, with enamel dial, the two-train chain fusee movement with verge escapement, 18thC, 16in (40.5cm) high.
£7,300–8,000 ♣ S(NY)

A Japanese bedside clock, decorated with dense foliage, signature to base, Meiji period, 1868–1911, 3½in (9cm) high.
£580–720 ♣ RTo

◄ **A Japanese rosewood bracket clock,** the verge movement with fusee, the base with a key drawer, 19thC, 5½in (14cm) high.
£5,000–5,800 ♣ S(NY)

Figures & Models

◄ **A Chinese carved wood articulated doctor's figure,** with traces of lacquer and original paint and with human hair attachments, bearing an inscription in ink dating the figure to 1478, restored, 48in (122cm) high.
£3,200–3,600 ♣ GH
This figure would be have been used by patients to indicate to their doctor where they felt pain.

A Sino-Tibetan bronze Buddha, seated on a plinth, with traces of gilt, 16thC, 6½in (16.5cm) high.
£290–350 ♣ RBB

◄ **A pair of Chinese carved limestone Buddhist guardian lions,** 19thC, 30in (76cm) high.
£1,000–1,200 ♣ SK

A Chinese carved ivory figure of an Immortal, with a leashed dragon on his knee and one foot resting on a demon, 19thC, 13½in (34.5cm) high.
£900–1,100 ♣

Cross Reference
See Colour Review
(page 615)

A Japanese carved ivory group of two kneeling figures, playing Go, one smoking an opium pipe, Meiji period, 1868–1911, 5½in (14cm) high.
$1,900–2,200 ⚒ **TRL**

◄ **A Chinese carved ivory figure of a bearded Shoulao,** holding a peach in one hand and a staff in the other, 19thC, 12in (30.5cm) high.
$360–430 ⚒ **AH**
Shoulao is the star god of longevity.

A Japanese ivory okimono of two theatrical figures, 19thC, 6in (15cm) high.
$650–800 ⚒ **DA**

Okimono

Japanese *okimono* (literally meaning 'put things') are small, well-carved and often mixed-media figures, made during the Meiji and Taisho periods (1868–1926) for display in cabinets and on shelves and for export to Europe and the USA. Many *okimono* are signed, but only a few of their makers are considered important.

◄ **A Japanese carved ivory okimono,** depicting a figure of an old man with a child on his arm and a rake in his hand, late 19thC, 8½in (21.5cm) high.
$720–870 ⚒ **PFK**

A Japanese ivory carving of a man with a boy on his back, Meiji period, 1868–1911, 10½in (26.5cm) high.
$3,200–3,700 ⊞ **BeE**

A Japanese ivory carving of a man with his child, and holding a cricket cage, Meiji period, 1868–1911, 7½in (19cm) high.
$2,400–2,700 ⊞ **LBO**

A pair of Japanese bronze figures, the boy reading a book with a bundle of sticks on his back, his companion walking with a basket on her back and carrying a kettle and an axe, 19thC, 19in (48.5cm) high.
$1,700–2,000 ⚒ **HAM**

A set of three carved ivory models of badgers, each playing a musical instrument, Meiji period, 1868–1911, 3¾in (9.5cm) high.
$2,900–3,500 ⚒ **P**

A Japanese bronze group of three wolves, male, female and infant, late 19thC, largest 12¼in (31cm) long.
$580–720 ⚒ **Mit**

A carved okimono, depicting a peasant with drum and gourd, early 20thC, 8¾in (22cm) high.
$230–290 ⚒ **L&E**

A Japanese bronze model of a puppy, signed Eirako, c1900, 4in (10cm) long.
$900–1,100 ⊞ **PCA**

A pair of Japanese root-wood crabs, 19thC, 8in (20.5cm) long.
$1,800–2,200 ⊞ **KJ**

ASIAN WORKS OF ART

Furniture

A Chinese export black japanned miniature cabinet, decorated in gilt with figures in garden settings beside temples and pavilions within floral borders, enclosing five interior drawers, 1800, 17½in (44.5cm) high.
500–600 ⚘ HYD

A Japanese black lacquered table cabinet, gilt-decorated with birds within trees and landscapes, with two small sliding doors above a pair of cupboard doors enclosing open shelves and small drawers, above two further drawers, Meiji period, 1868–1911, 12½in (32cm) high.
$800–900 ⚘ P(S)

Chinese chairs

Chinese round-back or horseshoe-back armchairs are considered to be more important than the traditional upright style of chair. These chairs would be reserved for important guests and are often featured in ancestral portraits. Horseshoe-back chairs are usually slightly oversized, again indicating their importance.

The majority of Chinese domestic chairs were made in pairs. They would usually be placed against a wall, each side of a small table upon which tea would be served.

A Japanese two-part cabinet, with iron mounts, 19thC, 41in (104cm) wide.
$1,200–1,400 ⚘ SK

A pair of Chinese rosewood horseshoe-back chairs, c1780.
$12,800–14,000 ⊞ REI

A pair of Chinese lacquered wood armchairs, c1820.
$2,600–2,900 ⊞ APO

◄ A pair of Chinese hardwood armchairs, the splats carved with a vase of flowers, deer, a bat and foliage, late 19thC.
$320–380 ⚘ WW

A Japanese carved hardwood corner cupboard, with *Shibayama* panels, 19thC, 34¼in (87cm) wide.
950–1,200 ⚘ DN

A Chinese painted wood four-tiered chest, with metal banding, 19thC, 33in (84cm) wide.
$1,300–1,500 ⊞ MLL

► An Indian Vizagapatam davenport, inlaid with ivory birds and flower scrolls within chequered and feathered ebony and ivory banding, the recess enclosed by folding doors opening to reveal five drawers and pigeonholes, both sides fitted with drawers, 19thC, 34in (86.5cm) wide.
$4,600–5,000 ⚘ EH
Vizagapatam is the generic name for Indian ivory-inlaid furniture from the region of Vizagapatam, a port on the east coat of India. In its day it was an important trading port for South East Asia, serving Japan and Korea and was also India's largest shipbuilding centre.

ASIAN WORKS OF ART

A padoukwood desk, moulded with dragons and smoke clouds and fitted with a frieze drawer, probably Burmese, early 20thC, 46in (117cm) wide.
$650–750 ➹ GAK

A pair of Chinese elm stands, Henan Province, early 19thC, 34in (86.5cm) high.
$650–800 ⊞ K

A Chinese rosewood mirror, c1900, 27¼in (69cm) wide.
$140–170 ➹ Bon(C)

◄ **An Anglo-Indian carved ebonized convex wall mirror,** surmounted by an eagle, 19thC, 47¾in (121.5cm) high.
$1,600–1,900 ➹ TRL

◄ **A pair of Indian carved ebony jardinière stands,** each with a well carved as a basket issuing flowers and fruit, late 19thC, later painted, 33in (84cm) high.
$3,200–3,600 ➹ Bon

► **A southern Chinese elm stool,** with traces of lacquer, early 19thC, 20in (51cm) wide.
$360–430 ⊞ OE

An Anglo-Indian hardwood tilt-top centre table, pierced and carved throughout with fruiting vines, acanthus and lotus, mid-19thC, 47½in (121cm) diam.
$2,900–3,400 ➹ Bea(E)

A nest of four Chinese lacquered tables, decorated with flowers, lotus blossoms and birds in tones of gold, c1860, largest 18in (45.5cm) wide.
$2,900–3,500 ➹ S(NY)

A Chinese export black lacquer sewing table, the hinged top decorated with landscapes and various motifs, the divided interior containing ivory implements and lidded compartments, early 19thC, 18¾in (47.5cm) wide.
$2,200–2,400 ➹ NOA

◄ **A Chinese elm altar table,** with original paint, central China, 19thC, 66in (167.5cm) long.
$1,100–1,300 ⊞ K

A Japanese lacquer trunk-on-stand, painted with landscape scenes, 18thC, 35½in (90cm) wide.
$2,200–2,400 ➹ SK

A Chinese elm table, c1870, 40in (101.5cm) diam.
$320–350 ⊞ MIN

A Chinese rosewood and marquetry centre table, inlaid in ivory with animals and scrolling foliage, faults, restored, 49½in (125.5cm) wide.
$1,900–2,200 ➹ S(S)

nro

Japanese four-case lacquer inro, with inlaid decoration of a cart surrounded by autumn grasses, the reverse with ants and a praying mantis, fitted with an ivory manjua netsuke with a carved metal disc of quail, and an ojime decorated with silver and gold, 19thC, 3½in (9cm) high.
5,000–7,000 ✦ S(NY)

A Japanese four-case lacquer inro, decorated in gold takamakie with red and silver details with a cockerel on a drum on one side, a hen and chicks on the other, chip, signed Toyu saku, 19thC, 4in (8.5cm) high.
3,200–3,600 ✦ S

A four-case lacquer inro, by Shunsho, decorated with maple leaves on a swirly ground simulating a river, slight chips, signed, 19thC, 2¾in (7cm) high.
$2,600–3,200 ✦ S
The natural scenery depicted is probably an allusion to the legend of Narihira who composed a famous poem while admiring the Yamashiro Tama river or the Tatsu gawa covered with autumnal maple leaves.

A four-case gold-ground lacquer inro, decorated on both sides with a hawk tied to a perch, minor damage, signed Kajikawa, 3½in (9cm) high.
$1,000–1,200 ✦ P

Cleaning
Inro and other lacquer wares should only be cleaned by an expert. Netsuke are generally made of wood or ivory, and can be cleaned first with a soft toothbrush. Ivory can then be cleaned with natural lanolin, although this must be wiped off after a short while to avoid the material becoming sticky.

A Japanese five-case lacquer inro, decorated in gold, silver, red and green lacquer with an elephant carrying on his back four children dressed for a festival, and on the reverse a fifth child left behind waving to get the attention of the others, with ivory ojime and manju, signed Kansai, 19thC, 4in (10cm) high.
$4,500–5,500 ✦ BB(S)

A Japanese three-case lacquer inro, decorated in gilt with flowers among foliage on a black ground, signed Kajikawa, Meiji period, 1868–1911, 2½in (6.5cm) high.
$360–430 ✦ P

Netsuke

Japanese carved wood netsuke, in the form of a foreigner holding two cymbals, 18thC, 4in (10cm) high.
950–1,100 ⊞ JaG

A Japanese netsuke, depicting a sage carved from ivory within a cave formed from a dried natural fruit, probably early 19thC, 2in (5cm) high.
$1,900–2,200 ✦ S

▶ **A Japanese ivory netsuke of a dragon fish,** with inlaid amber-toned eyes, cracks, signed Toyokazu, 19thC, 2¾in (7cm) long.
$2,200–2,600 ✦ BB(S)

A Japanese ivory netsuke of a mask of Okame, Meiji period, 1868–1911, 1¾in (4.5cm) high.
$330–390 ✦ P(B)

A carved wood netsuke of a monkey, cleaning with its paws the hair on its left leg, its eyes inlaid with horn, the details incised and contrasted in greyish brown stain, 19thC, 1¾in (4.5cm) high.
$850–1,000 ✦ P

Robes & Costume

A Japanese Satsuma ceramic belt buckle, c1890, 2in (5cm) diam.
$90–100 ⊞ **JBB**

A Chinese summer court hat, in ivory silk over a woven bamboo frame overlaid with twisted red silk fringe, bearing flower-decorated gilt insignia and pearl bead to brim, with blue cotton-covered shaped box, late 19thC.
$700–800 ⚒ **P**

A Chinese court headdress, the silk-covered wire frame with silvered and gilded dragons, phoenix, characters and flowers embellished with kingfisher feathers, coiled metal thread and beads, 19thC.
$1,200–1,400 ⚒ **P**

◄ **A Chinese court vest,** with rank badges of a three grade official and embroidered with egrets, peacocks and a gold dragon-in-cloud motif, 19thC.
$2,500–3,000 ⚒ **SK**

> Items in the Asian Works of Art section have been arranged in subject order within each sub-section.

▶ **A Chinese sleeveless gown,** the deep purple ground embroidered with birds, butterflies and flowers, with borders of phoenix, butterflies, birds and flowers, c1900.
$2,200–2,600 ⚒ **SK**

Snuff Bottles

A Chinese coral bottle, carved as a vase set with a cat raising a paw from rockwork towards three butterflies, early 20thC, 2¼in (5.5cm) high.
$1,300–1,600 ⚒ **S**
The subject of cat, peony and butterflies form the rebus *fugui maodie*, 'Live long and prosper', the characters for cat and butterfly being homonyms for living to 70 and 80 years.

A Chinese jade snuff bottle, carved with a sage seated in a grotto under a pine tree, with a coral stopper, 1750–1850, 3in (7.5cm) high.
$1,800–2,200 ⚒ **BB(S)**

A Chinese snuff bottle, carved from a section of richly patinated rootwood, gnarled around a small russet pebble, the wood variegated from a dark brown through to a light caramel, 19thC, 3½in (9cm) high.
$430–500 ⚒ **P**

A Chinese cinnabar lacquer snuff bottle, carved in deep relief on both sides with a phoenix among clouds, 19thC, 2¾in (7cm) high.
$360–430 ⚒ **P**

▶ **A Chinese Suzhou black and white nephrite snuff bottle,** carved with the figure of Li Bo sleeping beneath a pine tree, the reverse with a poetic inscription heightened with gold pigment, with a rose quartz and jadeite stopper, 19thC, 2½in (6.5cm) high.
$6,000–7,500 ⚒ **BB(S)**
Suzhou is a town in eastern China, which was famous for its snuff bottle carving.

Textiles

A Chinese export semi-circular ivory silk cover, embroidered in satin, coloured silks and gold thread, with two pheasants and peonies, the surround with phoenix, birds, deer, rabbits, a cat, flowers and leaves, damaged, 19thC, 79in (200.5cm) long.
430–500 ⚲ P

A Chinese silk embroidery, depicting a two-clawed dragon, 19thC, 11in (28cm) diam, framed and glazed.
$450–500 ⚲ SK

A Chinese ivory silk panel, embroidered with pheasants, ducks, a parrot and other birds among pebbles, and a tree and blossom, in mainly cream, brown and grey silks, late 19thC, 14in (35.5cm) diam, in a hardwood frame.
$1,600–1,800 ⚲ P

A set of four Japanese *kesi* woven silk panels, designed in pink, grey and cream silks and gold thread with two ladies and children at leisure in garden scenes, each displaying one of the four seasons, late 19thC, 11in (28cm) wide.
800–1,000 ⚲ P

A pair of Chinese paradise flycatcher rank badges, for a 9th rank civil official, some damage, 19thC, 11¾in (30cm) wide.
$150–180 ⚲ WW

A Chinese throne back, the camel field with three blue dragons and two flaming pearls, holy mountain with water and wave base, scrolling lotus border on three sides, original borders or edges missing, Ningxia, central China, 19thC, 29in (73.5cm) wide.
$360–430 ⚲ WW

Miscellaneous

A set of four Chinese prints, depicting dignitaries and attendants, warriors and scenes of punishment, 19thC, 17in (43cm) square, framed and glazed.
$1,400–1,600 ⚲ S(S)

◀ A Japanese wood-cut print of a young woman, kneeling in front of a young samurai in a suit of armour, signed Koryusaiga, 1764–88, 26½ x 5in (67.5 x 12.5cm).
$2,600–2,900 ⊞ JaG

Japanese rattan writing box and cover, the cover inset with three bronze panels, each with incised and gilt-laid decoration, the black lacquered interior fitted with an ink slab and silver water dropper, Meiji period, 1868–1911, 6¼in (16cm) long.
1,000–1,300 ⚲ P

▶ A Tibetan painted thanka, depicting a seated Yellow Cap sect monk, gouache-decorated with a Buddha surrounded by deities, damaged, c1800 or earlier, 26 x 16in (66 x 40.5cm), in a brocade silk mount, framed and glazed.
$300–350 ⚲ WW
A thanka is a Tibetan painting of divinities, used on the walls of temples and shrines as a subject for meditation, and on banners.

Further reading
Miller's Chinese & Japanese Antiques Buyer's Guide, Miller's Publications, 1999

ASIAN WORKS OF ART

Islamic Works of Art

Arms & Armour

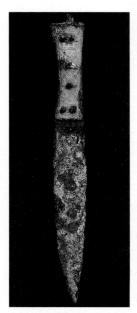

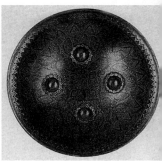

▶ **An Indo-Persian shield,** decorated overall with concentric arrangements of flowers and foliage within shaped cartouches all in gold *koftgari*, early 19thC, 14in (35.5cm) diam.
$1,000–1,200
➤ **S(S)**

◀ **A Persian dagger,** with carved ivory hilt, the double-edged blade of hollow diamond section, the ivory grip carved in low relief on each side with a courting couple, repaired, 19thC, blade 10½in (26.5cm) long
$1,300–1,600 ➤ **S(S)**

A Persian dagger, the ivory hilt incised with triangular panels with dot and circle motifs, all within a cross-hatched border, 10th/11thC, 12¼in (31cm) long.
$2,200–2,600 ➤ **Bon**
Surviving Islamic daggers from before the 15th/16th century are rare. The decoration on the hilt was used on ivory from Egypt and Persia from the 9th century onwards.

An Islamic double-edged Damascus blade dagger, the silver-mounted grip with filigree decoration, the silver scabbard with floral engraving and chasing, Ottoman, 18th/19thC, 13¾in (35cm) long.
$5,800–6,500 ➤ **Herm**

A Persian silver and black enamel standard, 19thC, 18in (45.5cm) high.
$1,800–2,100 ⊞ **SAMI**

▶ **A Qajar gold damascened steel helmet, shield and armguard,** each with openwork panels of either arabesques or inscription, Persia, 19thC, shield 18½in (47cm) diam.
$4,000–4,600 ➤ **Bon**

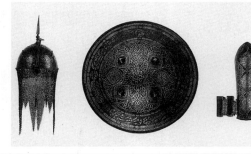

Ceramics

A Nishapur bowl, decorated with a bird in olive green and red, Persia, c10thC, 5¾in (14.5cm) diam.
$650–750 ⊞ **CrF**

An Afghan pottery dish, decorated in green on a yellow ground, 12thC, 10in (25.5cm) diam.
$2,600–2,900 ⊞ **SAMI**

A Bamiyan unglazed pottery bowl, decorated with a frieze of palmette medallions with bands of inscription above, Persia, 11th/12thC, 5½in (14cm) diam.
$1,500–1,800 ➤ **Bon**
This unglazed bowl would have been the prototype from which a mould was made, in order to make further bowls of the same type.

Kashan tile, decorated in blue
nd yellow, 13thC, 9in (23cm) high.
1,900–2,200 ⊞ SAMI

An Isnik pottery dish, decorated in
raised red, cobalt blue, green and black
with a band of interlocking circles on
a scroll ground centred on a rosette,
the rim with wave and rock pattern,
the exterior with stylized flowerheads,
17thC, 10in (25.5cm) diam.
$1,500–1,800 ⚒ Bon

A Qajar polychrome faïence tile,
depicting a seated ruler with phoenix
and serpent, Persia, c1800,
21in (53.5cm) square.
$2,200–2,400 ⚒ SLN

**Qajar polychrome-glazed fritware
le,** depicting a seated lady in a
alace garden listening to musicians,
ersia, 19thC, 13 x 17in (33 x 43cm).
3,600–4,000 ⊞ ArM

▶ **A Persian polychrome-glazed tile,**
decorated with a sultan surrounded
by warriors, the floor decorated with
leaf-scrolls on a turquoise ground,
with a leaf-scroll border, one corner
cracked and broken, 19thC,
20 x 23¼in (51 x 59cm).
$400–440 ⚒ P

urniture

▶ **A Syrian pewter and mother-of-pearl-inlaid
all-front chest,** 19thC, 58in (147.5cm) wide.
3,200–3,600 ⚒ SK

**Middle Eastern brass-inlaid blanket
hest,** with three base drawers, late 19thC,
4in (137cm) wide.
1,900–2,200 ⚒ SK

▶ **A Damascus hall stand,** inlaid
with mother-of-pearl and ebony,
carved in relief with an inscription,
with a central polychrome-enamelled
copper panel with figures, minarets,
crescents and inscriptions, c1900,
74in (188cm) high.
$2,200–2,500 ⚒ Bon

ewellery

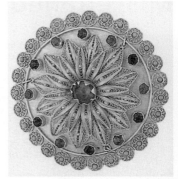

pair of Persian gold bracelets,
ach hinged on one side, the shank
erminals of stylized rams' heads with
pplied gold wire elements, each clasp
ecorated with an interlacing strapwork
esign, 11th/12thC, 2½in (6.5cm) diam.
7,300–8,000 ⚒ S

A Qajar gold pendant, set with
synthetic rubies, green beryl and
pearls, the reverse with spiral wire
decoration, Persia, 19thC,
1½in (4cm) diam.
$870–1,000 ⚒ Bon

**A Qajar turquoise-set gold filigree
pendant,** the centre set with
coloured pastes, surrounded by a
band of circles set with turquoises,
Persia, c1900, 3¼in (8.5cm) diam.
$1,200–1,400 ⚒ Bon

Metalware

▶ **An Afghan bronze oil lamp,** 13thC, 8in (20.5cm) long. $4,000–4,400 ⊞ SAMI

A Khorasan bronze incense bowl, with an openwork frieze of roundels containing palmettes, with a band of *Kufic* inscription and a band of depressed circles, Persia, 11th/12thC, 8in (20.5cm) diam. $870–1,100 ✚ Bon

▶ **A Persian bronze ewer,** the lid with a bird finial, the handle cast with palmette-shaped thumb-rest, 12th/13thC, 9½in (24cm) high. $650–750 ✚ P

A silver plate and cover, decorated with pink, green and blue enamel, dated 1864, 9in (23cm) diam. $1,300–1,500 ⊞ SAMI

Wood

▶ **An Afghan wood panel,** carved in deep relief with a fruiting vine, 8th/9thC, 8 x 13½in (20.5 x 34.5cm). $4,600–5,000 ✚ Bon

A Fatamid wood panel, carved in relief with a bird with an outstretched wing against a scrolling vine, Egypt, 11th/12thC, 2½in (6.5cm) square. $3,500–4,000 ✚ Bon

▶ **An Ottoman wood Koran stand,** overlaid with horn and mother-of-pearl, Turkey, 18thC, 24½in (62cm) high. $2,300–2,600 ⊞ ArM

An Indo-Persian holy man's mendicant's bowl, made from half a *coco-de-mer* nut and carved in relief with panels of floral scrollwork and Islamic inscriptions, dated 1876, 11½in (29cm) long, with brass carrying chains. $290–350 ✚ PFK

Miscellaneous

◀ **A Beykoz glass pitcher with cover,** with wheel-cut and gilt decoration of arches and diamond-shaped medallions, each enclosing floral and foliate motifs, with bands of floral sprays above and below, Turkey, early 19thC, 16in (40.5cm) high. $10,200–11,600 ✚ S

▶ **An Ottoman marble wall fountain,** the back carved with floral sprays surmounting a shell, Egypt, 19thC, 33½in (85cm) high. $1,000–1,200 ✚ Bon

A Turkish textile panel, the black cloth heavily embroidered with couched metallic thread, with a design of a vase and flowers within a portico, late 19th/early 20thC, 41½ x 32in (105.5 x 81.5cm). $1,000–1,200 ✚ SK

Architectural Antiques

Iron

... cast-iron ogee balcony, ...9thC, 294in (747cm) long.
...1,100–1,300 ✗ SWO

A wrought-iron candle sconce, c1890, 55in (139.5cm) high, now used as a plant holder.
$260–290 ✗ HOP

French cast-iron figure f a putto, supporting an ...rn on his head, mid-19thC, ...5in (114.5cm) high.
...1,700–2,000 ✗ S(S)

A Victorian painted cast-iron font or jardinière, with a panel frieze above Gothic-style pilasters, 40in (101.5cm) high.
$1,100–1,300 ✗ ME

A pair of cast-iron folly cannon, painted and weathered, late 19thC, 26in (66cm) long, housed in oak four-wheeled carriages.
$1,000–1,200 ✗ TAM

A painted cast-iron royal coat-of-arms, the central shield flanked by lion and unicorn supporters, 19thC, 32in (81.5cm) wide.
$1,900–2,200 ✗ S(S)

A set of cast-iron railway stanchions, with fleur-de-lys-decorated capitals, 1870s, 144in (366cm) high.
$1,400–1,700 each ⊞ A&H

... Fiske cast-iron fountain, the bowl with egg-...nd-dart moulded everted rim, on a leaf-cast ...ctagonal base, surmounted by a zinc figure ...f a putto holding a fish, America, c1900, ...8in (122cm) high.
...5,000–6,000 ✗ S(S)

...oseph Winn Fiske established an ornamental ...onworks in 1858 and enjoyed a prosperous ...xistence making all varieties of ornamental ...on. His sons, John W. and Joseph W. Fiske, ...oined the firm in about 1899. The foundry ...vas one of the first to popularize the use of ...lloys and zinc for the figures in fountains ...vhich, unlike cast iron, were not susceptible ...o rust. Not all Fiske's wares were marked.

A pair of Irish Georgian cast-iron gates, signed G. M. Murphy, Belfast, 120in (305cm) wide.
$1,400–1,700 ⊞ HON

A Veritas cast-iron heater, with original electrical wiring and red glass lining, the removable domed top with brass handle, the two doors with brass knobs, carrying handles to each side, c1903, 21in (53.5cm) high.
$360–400 ⊞ HOP

◀ **A pair of Irish Regency iron gates,** the uprights terminating in spear finials, 112in (284.5cm) wide.
$5,800–7,200 ✗ NOA

ARCHITECTURAL ANTIQUES

An American cast-iron hall tree, with seven hooks and a central mirror, with later black paint, c1858, 72in (183cm) high.
$1,000–1,200 ↗ SK(B)

A George V red-painted iron wall-mounted post box, 30in (76cm) high.
$430–500 ↗ SWO

Miller's is a price GUIDE
not a price LIST

A Coalbrookdale-style cast-iron plant stand, the two tiers, four central trays and four base trays pierced with anthemia and foliage, early 20thC, 40in (101.5cm) high.
$650–800 ↗ S(S)

A pair of French wrough[t] iron plant stands, with scrolling floral shafts, late 19thC, 55in (139.5cm) hig[h]
$2,500–3,000 ↗ NOA

A Victorian Parkinson & Co cast-iron and copper street lamp, the reeded column with stylized leaf decoration, lacking light fitting, 162¼in (412cm) high.
$720–800 ↗ WL

A Regency-style wrought-iron armchair, the back pierced with three interlaced arches decorated with a diamond pattern, 19thC.
$3,300–3,700 ↗ S(S)

▶ **A set of four wrought-iron garden chairs,** with mesh seats, now painted green, early 20thC.
$430–500 ↗ PFK

A set of four painted iron and wood folding garden chairs, c1920, and a round iron table.
$650–725 ⊞ MLL

A pair of green-painted wrought-iron garden elbow chairs, late 19thC
$300–350 ↗ GAK

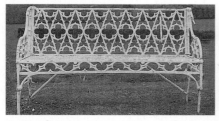

A pair of Gothic-style cast-iron garden benches, with pierced backs and honeycomb seats, 19thC, 56in (142cm) wide.
$2,200–2,400 ↗ MEA

A cast-iron mangle table, with the mangle removed and a pitch-pine top bolted to the base, c1900, 30in (76cm) long.
$200–220 ⊞ HOP

◀ **A pair of Victorian cast-iron garden urns,** with applied swags, rams' heads and putto lifts, painted white, 25in (63.5cm) high.
$3,500–4,000 ↗ WW

A cast-iron umbrella stand, in the form of a boy and serpent, c1890, 34in (86.5cm) high.
$1,200–1,400 ⊞ SEA

Bronze

A bronze church bell, by Newcome, 1614, 38in (96.5cm) high.
$3,000–3,600 ⊞ WEL

A bronze horizontal sundial, by Whitehurst & Son, Derby, with Arabic outer minutes scale and Roman hours, the months scale divided by acanthus scrolls, dated 1812, 12¼in (31cm) diam, on a gritstone plinth.
$1,400–1,600 ⋏ TEN

◄ **A Regency bronze hall lantern,** with a suspension chain, early 19thC, 35in (89cm) high.
$5,800–7,200 ⋏ S(S)

Lead

◄ **A lead figure of Mercury,** late 19thC, 29in (73.5cm) high.
$11,200–12,300 ⊞ RECL

► **A lead garden figure of a nude bathing girl,** seated on a rocky plinth moulded with leafy plants, c1925, 28in (71cm) high.
$3,200–3,600 ⋏ RBB

A lead cistern, initialled and dated T C 1699, 40in (101.5cm) long.
$3,000–3,500 ⋏ SWO

Insurance values

Always insure your valuable antiques for the cost of replacing them with similar items, regardless of the original price paid. Both dealers and auctioneers will provide a valuation service for a fee.

Marble

► **A marble sundial top,** marked H. C. 1716, 18in (45.5cm) square.
$350–400 ⋏ TRM

◄ **A French marble planter,** the sides carved with swags of summer flowers, 19thC, 29in (73.5cm) wide.
$2,200–2,400 ⋏ S(S)

An Italian white marble figure of Flora, after Canova, holding a garland of flowers, 19thC, 44in (112cm) high.
$2,500–3,000 ⋏ S(S)

An Italian marble fountain, in five sections, 19thC, 56in (142cm) high.
$2,000–2,200 ⊞ HOP

Stone

A carved sandstone model of a Labrador, 19thC, 32in (81.5cm) high. **$3,300–3,900** ⚒ S(S)

A pair of reconstituted stone finials, 1930s, 53in (134.5cm) high. **$3,500–4,000** ⊞ WRe

A Scottish carved sandstone multi-dial sundial, the sides with shaped lead gnomon and calibrated with hours, c1800, 24in (61cm) high. **$2,000–2,400** ⚒ S(S)

A stone head, probably King Richard II, 15thC, 9in (23cm) high. **$1,000–1,200** ⊞ OCH

A pair of Bath stone obelisks, c1845, 81in (205.5cm) high. **$1,700–2,000** ⊞ WEL

A Portland stone sundial stand, c1830, 40in (101.5cm) high. **$2,900–3,200** ⊞ DOR

◄ **A pair of limestone urns,** with gadroon banding, mid-19thC, 25in (63.5cm) high. **$2,300–2,600** ⊞ RECL

A weathered composition figure of a child and birds, early 20thC, 28in (71cm) high. **$1,300–1,450** ⊞ RECL

A carved sandstone plaque, mid-1800s, 43in (109cm) high. **$1,000–1,200** ⊞ DOR

▶ **A granite pillar,** 17thC, 83in (211cm) high. **$1,200–1,400** ⊞ RECL

A stone urn, the foliage-bordered top above a band of masks and convolvulus, with fluted oak leaf and foliage decoration below, 19thC, 26in (66cm) diam, on a composition base. **$1,200–1,400** ⚒ E

> **Cross Reference**
> See Colour Review
> (page 619-620)

▶ **A pair of limestone urns,** 1920–30, 44in (112cm) high. **$1,900–2,200** ⊞ RECL

A carved Portland stone finial, 19thC, 45in (114.5cm) high. **$1,400–1,700** ⚒ S(S)

A granite urn, carvings missing, 19thC, 66in (167.5cm) high. **$200–220** ⊞ HOP

Terracotta

A quantity of blue terracotta ropetwist edging tiles, c1900, 9in (23cm) wide.
$6–7 each ⊞ HOP

A pair of terracotta chimney pots, c1890, 36in (91.5cm) high.
$190–210 ⊞ HOP

▶ A quantity of Victorian terracotta red and blue quarry tiles, 6in (15cm) square.
95c–$1.25c each ⊞ HOP

◀ terracotta seat, the back centred with a bearded mask, the terminals in the shape of seated winged lions, early 20thC, 24in (61cm) wide.
1,300–1,450 ⊀ S(S)

Wirework

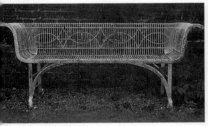

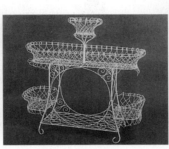

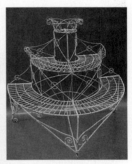

A Victorian wirework conservatory plant stand, 47in (119.5cm) wide.
$220–260 ⊀ SWO

A wirework plant stand, 19thC, 40½in (103cm) wide.
$400–450 ⊀ L&E

◀ wirework seat, the back decorated with intertwined arches, early 20thC, 1in (180.5cm) wide.
2,600–2,900 ⊀ S(S)

Wood

A limewood cresting, carved with flowering and budding foliage and wheatsheafs on tasselled swags, 19thC, 59½in (151cm) long.
$1,700–2,000 ⊀ P(S)

Items in the Architectural Antiques section have been arranged in subject order within each sub-section.

A Boulton & Paul wooden summerhouse, on a revolving base, c1930, 126in (320cm) square.
$13,000–14,500 ⊀ S(S)
Boulton & Paul, based in Norwich, Norfolk, made a wide range of garden furniture and summerhouses from the late 19th to the late 20th century. This summerhouse is one of a type called Sunshine Rooms.

◀ pair of American painted pine capitals, carved with floral devices, scrolls and acanthus leaves, with old grey paint, early 19thC, 6in (40.5cm) wide.
2,300–2,900 ⊀ SK(B)

▶ An oak floral carving, 9thC, 16in (40.5cm) long.
260–290 ⊞ MLL

Bathroom Fittings

A Beaven & Sons basin, with original nickel taps, c1895, 28in (71cm) wide.
$1,300–1,600 ⊞ WRe

▶ **A French Louis XV beechwood and caned** *baignoire*, mid-18thC, 56in (142cm) long.
$7,200–8,700 ➶ S(Z)

A Shanks & Co cast-iron bath, on lion's paw feet, with original brass fittings, reconditioned with vitreous enamel, c1895, 73in (185.5cm) long.
$5,000–5,800 ⊞ WRe

A Doulton & Co mahogany lavatory seat, c1897.
$350–430 ⊞ WRe

A Thomas Twyford Deluge white embossed lavatory pan, c1890, 17in (43cm) high.
$1,800–2,200 ⊞ WRe

A Shanks & Co cast-iron lavatory cistern, late 19thC.
$260–320 ⊞ DOR

A set of Victorian polished brass roll-top bath taps, with collars, reconditioned, 6in (15cm) high.
$400–470 ⊞ WRe

▶ **A Young & Marten Palatine washstand,** with white marble top, c1895, 26in (66cm) high.
$2,600–2,900 ⊞ WRe

An Art Deco nickel-plated bath tap mixer set, 5in (12.5cm) high.
$580–720 ⊞ WRe

▶ **A brass soap dish,** c1920, 10¾in (27.5cm) wide.
$95–110 ⊞ LIB

A tin hip bath, with original paint, c1860, 37in (94cm) long.
$220–250 ⊞ DOR

A George Jennings Deep Seal lavatory pan, c1890, 16in (40.5cm) high.
$650–800 ⊞ DOR

An I. Finch stoneware boat bath, c1875, 65in (165cm) long.
$5,800–6,500 ⊞ WRe

Doors & Door Furniture

A mid-Victorian oak chapel door, with a York stone surround, 80in (203cm) high.
$3,300–3,700 ⊞ RECL

◄ **A Victorian pine front door,** 30in (76cm) wide.
$320–360 ⊞ DOR

George III mahogany door, the six bead-moulded and fluted panels with foliate-carved borders, locking door furniture, 1775, 48in (122cm) wide.
8,000–8,800 ⋌ S

A Victorian Gothic pine door, with glazed panels, 34in (86.5cm) wide.
$360–430 ⊞ DOR

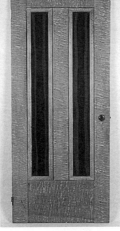

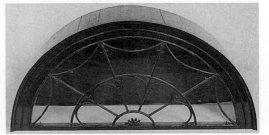

A Georgian mahogany fanlight, with lunette and hexagonal astragal-glazed front panel, 39¾in (101cm) high.
$1,100–1,300 ⋌ P(EA)

pair of carved oak and fruitwood door jambs, each carved with the mask of a mythical beast, late 19thC, 74in (188cm) high.
2,000–2,300 ⋌ S(S)

An American panelled door, painted to resemble exotic wood, possibly Maine, 19thC, 31½in (80cm) wide.
$1,000–1,150 ⋌ SK(B)

pair of rosewood and brass door handles, 1880, 2½in (6.5cm) diam.
100–115 OIA

A Hobbs Hart & Co door lock, 1930–40, 6in (15cm) wide.
190–220 ⊞ OIA

Fireplaces

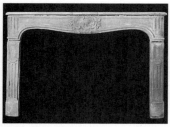

A French carved limestone fire surround, late 18thC, 64in (162.5cm) wide.
$1,600–1,900 ✗ S(S)

An American Federal blue-painted fire surround, the mantel shelf with incised and fluted decoration and panels, early 19thC, 70in (178cm) wide.
$1,300–1,600 ✗ S(NY)

A Belgian black marble fire surround, with freestanding turned marble columns and cast-iron insert, c1820, 74in (188cm) wide.
Surround **$8,700–9,500**
Insert **$870–950** ⊞ ASH

A Victorian polished cast-iron fire surround, with mirrored overmantel, 76in (193cm) high.
$330–400 ✗ SWO

A white marble fire surround, with original cast-iron insert, c1870, 73in (185.5cm) wide.
$23,000–26,000 ⊞ DOR

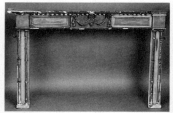

A Regency carved pine and gilt gesso fire surround, the central projecting plaque with carved ribbon and tassel swags, contemporary painted decoration, 61in (155cm) wide.
$1,300–1,600 ✗ RTo

A white marble fire surround, with serpentine mantel shelf and fluted keystone, the cast-iron register grate with bronze mount, c1860, 84in (213.5cm) wide.
Surround **$5,100–5,500**
Insert **$2,000–2,200** ⊞ NOST

A marble fire surround, with carved corbel and lipped mantel shelf, c1870, 64in (162.5cm) wide.
$1,900–2,100 ⊞ ASH

▶ **A Georgian-style carved pine fire surround,** the tablet carved in high relief with a pierced basket of fruit flanked by scrolling foliage and lions' heads, the jambs carved with acanthus volutes above festoons of foliage, 19thC, 79in (200.5cm) wide.
$7,000–8,000 ✗ S(S)

A George III marble fire surround, with turned roundels, fluted jambs and cast-iron insert, c1800, 50in (127cm) wide.
Surround **$3,000–3,500**
Insert **$870–950** ⊞ ASH

A late Regency carved and panelled white marble fire surround, 72in (183cm) wide.
$9,800–10,800 ⊞ WRe

A Victorian white marble fire surround, with serpentine shelf, the corbel keystone flanked by bullrushes within bellflower-carved moulding, c1870, 88in (223.5cm) wide.
$8,500–10,000 ✗ S(S)

A Continental fire surround, in carved statuary marble, 19thC, 64in (162.5cm) wide.
$11,500–12,300 ⊞ NOST

An Art Nouveau cast-iron combination grate, c1905, 0in (101.5cm) wide. **900–1,000** ⊞ **NOST**

An Edwardian cast-iron combination grate, 0in (76cm) wide. **230–250** ⊞ **BYG**

A Regency barley-twist cast-iron fireplace, 6in (91.5cm) wide. **1,000–1,100** ⊞ **WEL**

◀ **An American Colonial revival carved and celadon-green-painted pine fire surround,** with projecting bowed and dentil-moulded mantel on demi-lune turned bracket over fielded panelled fire surround, New England, late 19thC, 65in (165cm) wide. **$4,750–5,400** ➷ **SK(B)**

A white marble fire surround, the serpentine top on a moulded façade with gadrooned opening, centred with a cabochon-carved keystone, late 19thC, 62in (157.5cm) wide. **$4,500–5,000** ➷ **NOA**

A Continental rococo-style white marble fire surround, with alabaster mounts, the grate with brass canopy and matching brass side panels, late 19thC, 65in (165cm) wide. **Surround $5,000–5,800** **Interior $900–1,000** ⊞ **NOST**

◀ **A Coalbrookdale cast-iron fire basket,** c1840, 36in (91.5cm) wide. **$3,000–3,500** ⊞ **ASH**

A polished iron and brass register grate, 1840, 47in (119.5cm) wide. **3,600–4,300** ⊞ **WRe**

An anodized steel and brass fire grate, c1920, 36in (91.5cm) wide. **850–950** ⊞ **ASH**

Fireplace Accessories

A pair of elm bellows, c1770, 26in (66cm) long.
$700–770 ⊞ SEA

A pair of brass and oak mechanical fire bellows, the wheel on pierced scrollwork support, dated 1862, 25½in (67.5cm) long.
$300–350 ↗ PFK

A Georgian brass coal scuttle, 19in (48.5cm) long.
$140–180 ⊞ HCJ

A cast-iron lion chimney ornament, 19thC, 6in (15cm) long.
$115–130 ⊞ MFB

An embossed brass log bin, c1910, 30in (76cm) wide.
$580–650 ⊞ ASH

A George III polished steel fender, the frieze pierced with fluting, 44in (112cm) wide.
$450–550 ↗ AH

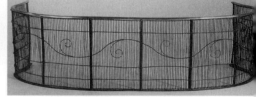

A wirework fender, with brass rim and horizontal scroll decoration, possibly American, c1800, 40½in (103cm) long
$2,200–2,400 ↗ SK(B)

A Coalbrookdale cast-iron serpentine-shaped fender, c1840, 60in (152.5cm) wide.
$2,200–2,400 ⊞ ASH

A George IV brass kerb fender, decorated with rope moulding and pierced anthemia panels, 52¾in (134cm) wide.
$2,000–2,300 ↗ JAd

A cast-iron fender, with cast brass bosses in the shape of sunflowers, c1870, 54in (137cm) wide.
$870–950 ⊞ ASH

A French patinated and gilt-bronze kerb fender, the central extendable rail flanked by twin mastifs reclining on pedestals with applied acanthus mounts, 19thC, 33½in (85cm) wide.
$1,100–1,300
↗ P(Ba)

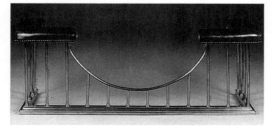

A brass and leather-upholstered club fender, late 19thC, 59in (150cm) wide.
$3,000–3,500 ↗ Bon

▶ An Edwardian brass kerb, of classic architectural form, 60in (152.5cm) wide.
$1,400–1,600
⊞ ASH

pair of American Chippendale
ngraved metal and iron bell
ndirons, the urn-on-urn finials
ith engraved tassel bows and
wags, possibly Philadelphia,
te 18thC, 26¾in (68cm) high.
7,200–8,700 ⚒ SK(B)

A pair of American brass andirons,
each with a flame finial above a
faceted ball, New York, repaired billet
bars, late 18thC, 21½in (54.5cm) high.
$3,200–3,600 ⚒ SK(B)

A pair of American Federal
brass ball-top andirons, probably
New England, early 19thC,
12in (30.5cm) high.
$1,000–1,150 ⚒ S(NY)

A pair of wrought-iron fire tongs, c1770,
19in (48.5cm) long.
$230–250 ⊞ SEA

pair of brass mesh spark guards,
ach surmounted by a wreath and
bbons, centred with a quiver of
rrows, pipes and foliage, on acanthus
nd cloven feet, early 20thC,
4in (188cm) wide.
1,400–1,600 ⚒ Bea(E)

A set of three polished steel fire irons, with
faceted mushroom knops, 19thC,
30in (76cm) long.
$1,100–1,200 ⚒ P

A pair of Regency cast-
iron fire dogs, in the form
of female figures,
18in (45.5cm) high.
$870–950 ⊞ ASH

pair of American brass
earth hooks, early
9thC, 5in (12.5cm) high.
900–1,000 ⚒ S(NY)

A wrought-iron trammel,
1750, 41in (104cm) long.
1,000–1,100 ⊞ SEA

wrought-iron brazier, c1680, 21in (53.5cm) long.
650–725 ⊞ SEA

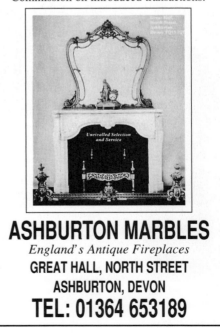

Sculpture

A German gilt-bronze lion, probably a support for a candlestick, 15thC, 2¼in (5.5cm) high.
$500–600 ⚒ S(S)

A south German or Austrian ivory figure of Christ crucified, the reverse inscribed with a monogram and 1515 apparently changed from 1615, some losses, 12½in (32cm) high.
$6,000–6,600 ⚒ S(NY)

A German carved wood figure of a mermaid, probably 17thC, 35½in (90cm) long.
$7,250–8,000 ⚒ S(Z)

A South American Colonial carved wood figure, 17thC, 26in (66cm) high.
$1,900–2,100 ⚒ SLN

A pair of south German carved ivory plaques, with representations of Wealth and Poverty, c1680, each 3 x 4in (7.5 x 10cm), framed.
$3,500–4,000 ⊞ AEF

A lead bust of Charles I, after a model by Le Sueur, on a white marble plinth applied with a cherub maskhead, 18thC, 15¾in (40cm) high.
$950–1,150 ⚒ P

A carved dark oak female figure, 19thC, 20in (51cm) high.
$750–850 ⊞ AMR

An Italian Grand Tour, Naples bronze statue, depicting a young Bacchus being carried aloft, c1820, 27in (68.5cm) high.
$6,500–7,250 ⊞ CAT
Items such as these are replicas of excavated Roman artefacts, purchased as Grand Tour souvenirs in the 19th century.

▶ **A bronze group of a donkey with an eastern boy,** by Alfred Dubucand, inscribed, France, mid-19thC, 10¼in (26cm) wide.
$2,500–3,000 ⚒ P(Ed)

A pair of north Italian ivory putti, one holding a seashell and the other a fish, early 19thC, 9in (23cm) high.
$5,000–5,500 ⊞ LBO

A carved wood figure of a saint, his green and red robes heightened with gilt, 19thC or possibly earlier, 19¼in (49cm) high.
$360–430 ⚒ AH

A German Gothic-style polychrome wood figure of St George and the Dragon, 19thC, 37¾in (96cm) high.
$1,400–1,700 ⚒ S(S)

A bronze figure of a cherub, seated on a tree stump, with a gilt-brass basket surmount for a lamp, on a dark grey mottled base, probably French, 19thC, 10½in (26.5cm) high.
$360–430 ⚒ PFK

A marble bust of Homer, after the Antique, in excavated condition, 19thC, 19¾in (50cm) high.
$850–1,000 ⚒ P(G)

A bronze group of a fighting greyhound and leopard, after G. Grootaers, the base inscribed 'Groupe du Monument Commemoratif de la Victoire de St Cast, 1758 Bretagne', dated 1858, 17in (43cm) high.
$1,900–2,200 ⚒ HYD

A white marble portrait bust of a young woman, by William Brodie, on an ebonized cylindrical pedestal, signed, 1861, 42in (106.5cm) high.
$1,900–2,200 ⚒ L

A carved white marble figure of a putto, holding a shell to his ear, his right foot on a tortoise, by Carl Steinhauser, signed and dated Roma 1865, 28in (71cm) high, on a contemporary white marble pedestal.
$6,500–8,000 ⚒ CAG

A Victorian bronze model of a stag, on a carved walnut stand with fruiting vine decoration, 20in (51cm) wide.
$430–500 ⚒ Mit

◀ **An Italian carved alabaster bust of Mary,** on a turned socle and cylindrical pedestal with revolving top, damaged, 19thC, 45½in (115.5cm) high.
$1,000–1,200 ⚒ CAG

A French bronze figure of a girl, Inspiration, by Mathurin Moreau, signed and bearing the stamp of the Société des Bronzes de Paris, on a brass revolving stand, 19thC, 27in (68.5cm) high.
$2,600–3,200 ⚒ DW

A terracotta bust of an African man, 19thC, 22in (56cm) high.
$650–800 ⚒ Mit

A marble model of a bull terrier, 19thC, 28¾in (73cm) long.
$11,000–12,300 ⚒ L&T

▶ **A Dieppe carved ivory figure of Christ,** a bearded figure behind him holding up a cloak or shroud, France, 19thC, 5 x 3½in (12.5 x 9cm), in an engine-turned ebony frame.
$4,000–4,600 ⚒ DN

An alabaster bust of a young girl, wearing a gilt-metal crown, 19thC, 13½in (34.5cm) high.
$720–870 ⚹ AH

An Italian ivory group of cupids embracing Psyche, after Antonio Canova, on an ivory base, c1880, 5in (12.5cm) high.
$2,300–2,700 ⊞ LBO

A French plaster bust of Eros, after the Antique, late 19thC, 25in (63.5cm) high.
$1,400–1,600 ⚹ NOA

A Russian carved schist bear, with glass eyes, base slightly damaged, late 19thC, 6in (15cm) wide.
$500–600 ⚹ Bon(W)

A pair of French bronze Marly horses, after Cousteau, on ebonized and brass-inlaid bases, 19thC, 28in (71cm) high.
$3,200–3,600 ⚹ BWe
The originals of these horses were modelled in stone by Guillaume Cousteau for Louis XIV's Chateau Marly and now stand at the entrance to the Champs Elysées. Most reproductions date from c1850–1920.

A pair of cast-iron fox head door stops, 19thC, 6in (15cm) long.
$600–700 ⊞ SEA

An Italian bronze figure of a youth playing a tambourine, by J. Sanson, Rome, late 19thC, 28in (71cm) high.
$4,000–4,600 ⚹ LAY

A French bronze model Hound at Rest, by P. J. Mêne, 19thC, 12in (30.5cm) long.
$4,000–4,600 ⊞ RGa

A French bronze figure of Ariadne after the Antique, foundry mark F. Barbedienne, 19thC, 14½in (37cm) wide.
$1,300–1,600 ⚹ P
The original marble was first recorded in the Vatican collection in 1512 and then moved to the Museo Pio Clementino. The first bronze cast appears to have been that made for François I which can be found in the Louvre.

A French group of a ram, ewe and lamb, by Isidore Jules Bonheur, signed, late 19thC, 18½in (47cm) wide.
$5,000–6,000 ⚹ JNic

A patinated bronze group of a young doe startled by a toad crossing its path, by Ary Bitter, early 20thC, 22½in (57cm) wide.
$1,200–1,400 ⚹ Bri

A French terracotta group of a mother and child, 1910–20, 17in (43cm) high.
$300–360 ⊞ DSG

Metalware

Brass

A Dutch brass and copper tobacco box, one side engraved with a portrait of William IV of Orange above his crest, the reverse with Princess Anne of Orange with her child, c1748, 6¼in (16cm) long.
$650–800 ⚘ S(S)
William of Orange married Anne, daughter of George II of England, in 1734 and their child was born in 1748. It seems likely, therefore, that this box was engraved to commemorate the birth of the baby.

▶ **A Regency brass tea urn,** the swivel spigot with an ivory finial, 17¼in (44cm) high.
$115–145 ⚘ PFK

A pair of brass candlesticks, c1670, 8in (20.5cm) high.
$2,200–2,400 ⚘ Bon(W)

A Russian cross, with panels depicting festivals and seraphim in brass and enamel, 19thC, 15in (38cm) high.
$900–1,100 ⊞ ICO

A Dutch brass extending reading lantern, c1770, 7in (18cm) high.
$850–950 ⊞ SEA

A brass platter, with Masonic engraving, early 19thC, 17½in (44.5cm) diam.
$400–450 ⊞ AnSh

Bronze

A pair of Victorian gilt-bronze and bronze candlesticks, each foliate-decorated nozzle supported by a crane wearing a coronet collar and standing on a rocky base, 15¾in (40cm) high.
$5,000–6,000 ⚘ P

▶ **A set of American gilt-bronze and glass candlesticks,** cast as baskets of flowers supporting the candle branches, on marble bases, 19thC, largest 16½in (42cm) high.
$1,600–1,900 ⚘ S(NY)

◀ **A bronze centrepiece,** the plinth embellished with a gilt representation of the eternal flame, supported on swan form monopodiae with lions' paw feet, 19thC, 18½in (47cm) high.
$1,700–2,000 ⚘ BLH

Miller's is a price GUIDE not a price LIST

▶ **A Russian bronze crucifix,** with panels depicting festival scenes, 18thC, 9in (23cm) high.
$400–440 ⊞ ICO

Copper

A Victorian copper samovar, with acanthus-cast scrolling handles and a brass tap, 18½in (47cm) high.
$650–720 ⚲ P(Ed)

▶ A pair of copper fire extinguishers, each mounted with brass plaques and an eagle with outstretched wings, marked 'Waterloo Fire Extincteur, 75 Victoria St, London SW1, Year 1937', 29in (73.5cm) high, each with original steel spanner.
$300–350 ⚲ MCA

◀ An Edwardian engrave copper drinks tray, c191 22in (56cm) long.
$65–75 ⊞ WAC

Iron

A Victorian iron and wood bird cage, with pull-out trays to base, 42in (106.5cm) wide.
$360–430 ⚲ WL

A south German painted iron casket, the underside holding the lock mechanism with two bolts, the front painted with noble figures, set on a pierced, floral and foliate painted base, early 17thC, 5in (12.5cm) high.
$3,200–3,600 ⚲ S(S)

A south German wrought-iron miniature casket, with blind fretwor ornament and original painted green and white floral decoration, wrough iron carrying handles, interior locking mechanism, with replacement key, 17thC, 7¾in (19.5cm) wide.
$2,400–2,600 ⚲ F&C

◀ An iron cellar candleholder, late 18thC, 11in (28cm) long.
$500–560 ⊞ SEA

A wrought-iron rushlight, on a turned wood base, probably sycamore, 18thC, 11¼in (28.5cm) high.
$650–720 ⚲ S(S)

A Victorian cast-iron tobacco jar, by Crawley of Manchester and Sheffield, with internal presser, 5in (12.5cm) high.
$75–85 ⚲ PFK

◀ A wrought-iron press, the bar with a slot for a die, the front with engraved crest, c1600, 15in (38cm) high.
$500–600 ⚲ SK(B)

An iron rushligh holder, c1750, 37in (94cm) hig
$850–950 ⊞ SE/

Pewter

A pewter charger, by I. P., London, the rim engraved with the crest of a stag within mantled feathers and a row of unidentified hallmarks, the reverse with touchmark and ownership inititals A W, c1680, 25½in (65cm) diam.
4,400–4,800 ✗ S(S)

A pewter quart ale jug, by . McPherson, Deptford, c1860, in (15cm) high.
85–95 ⊞ HEB

A Dutch pewter plaque, with a border of alternate lobes and points, the centre engraved with a vase of flowers flanked by initials EB, touchmark HW, dated 1643, 12½in (32cm) diam, later-mounted on a wooden board.
300–350 ✗ PFK

A single-reeded pewter charger, 1730, 17in (43cm) diam.
$600–660 ⊞ SEA

▶ **A York pewter flagon,** with plume thumb piece, the base with touchmark initital ..H, possibly John Harrison, restored, later cover, c1720, 10½in (26.5cm) high.
$720–870 ✗ S(S)

◀ **A set of four Irish pewter haystack measures,** stamped Austin Cork, 19thC, largest 7½in (19cm) high.
$600–660 ✗ AH

A Scottish Victorian pewter tankard, by McKellar, Glasgow, touch-mark of Glasgow, 7in (18cm) high.
$45–55 ✗ P(Ed)

A pewter dish, by Stynt Duncumb, Bewdley, 18thC, 15in (38cm) diam.
$320–380 ⊞ AnSh

◀ **A pewter pint measure,** by Joseph Morgan, early 19thC, 5in (12.5cm) high.
$115–145 ⊞ AnSh

A Glasgow pewter gill measure, c1830, 5in (12.5cm) high.
$145–175 ⊞ TWr

A pewter pot and cover, c1860, 11½in (29cm) high.
$75–85 ⊞ TO

METALWARE

Folk Art

olk Art – the unpretentious decorative arts of academically untrained artists and artisans – is an increasingly buoyant collecting area. Trade and shop signs, ships' figureheads, samplers, needlework pictures, woven rag rugs, quirky sculpture, love tokens, lighting devices, have all continued to command attention and increasingly high prices.

Collectors consistently cherish originality; intimate, quirky, idiosyncratic features; untouched, as found, weathered and patinated surface; rarity; scale; and provenance. An original provenance, for example a named and dated love token, a particular regional variety or known maker of a marriage chest or weather-vane, evidence of previous owners, where a shop sign originally stood or hung, can add multiples to value, as can even the relatively recent history of which collection a piece was a part.

Scale can also be important, with items of exceptionally large size and decorative appeal being more sought-after than less significant examples, particularly in the case of weather-vanes and trade signs. Decoy birds, particularly from pioneer collections, known makers and in untouched condition, and paint-decorated games boards with interesting colours and bold graphic qualities have increased significantly in value recently and can now achieve spectacular prices.

Strong colours and condition are paramount and again anything with a direct provenance, names or dates, animal motifs, particularly bold naive images, houses and family histories childrens' names and ages, charming images of toys, heart and soul motifs will command a premium.

However, as always with a growing market, the faker is inevitably drawn in. Look for genuine signs of use, weathering and wear. Early metalwork should be joined with rivets not solder. Wood shrinks with time and breaks up an original paint surface, showing cracks and fractures. Original paint will not be found in scratches, blemishes or worm tracks. Genuine pieces should be dry and bear their scars and bruises proudly as evidence of a long life.

Many of these items were historically ignored and overlooked as valid artworks and much has been lost to us. Recent discoveries fresh to the market inevitably excite particular interest and enthusiasm. The great secret is to preserve pieces in their original condition and to trace and retain any information concerning their history and origins.

Robert Young

A Continental gilt-metal birdcage, on a wooden base, late 19thC, 24in (61cm) wide.
$1,100–1,300 ⚒ SK

An American pine birdcage, the slats decorated with green, blue, red and turquoise paint, 19thC, 21in (53.5cm) high.
$1,500–1,800 ⚒ S(NY)

An American paint-decorated box, the tops, sides and front covered with geometric compass-drawn snowflake flowers in red and white on a grey-green ground, probably Lancaster, Pennsylvania, hinges replaced, c1800, 15½in (39.5cm) wide.
$22,000–25,000 ⚒ S(NY)

An American Federal walnut and yellow pine box, the hinged top outlined in stringing and centred with an inlaid star, the case with applied mouldings, stringing and fan inlays, repaired, early 19thC, 10¼in (26cm) wide.
$5,000–5,500 ⚒ SK(B)

An American wooden trinket box, with a sliding lid, two carved hearts extending from one end, various inlay decoration including contrasting wood, heart and diamond motifs in abalone, initials FLM, ivory-inlaid initials MWM and 1850, polychrome-decorated with a vine, pinwheel and potted plant, inlay losses, 1850, 8in (20.5cm) long.
$3,200–3,500 ⚒ SK(B)

A wrought-iron rushlight nip, with original paint-decorated base, c1760, 10in (25.5cm) long.
$1,500–1,700 ⚒ RYA

An American chalkware whippet, the black and white dog seated on a grey base, Livingston, New York tag, c1850, 18in (45.5cm) high.
$1,800–2,200 ✖ SK(B)
Ex-Peter Brams Collection.

▶ **A George III painted dummy board figure of a seated lady,** in a long striped dress peeling apples, 46¾in (119cm) high.
$11,000–13,000 ✖ Bea(E)

A French Sarreguemines advertising model of a goose, on a painted landscape base, c1900, 17¾in (45cm) high.
$1,100–1,300 ✖ P(S)

A hand-carved and paint-decorated shop sign, c1780, 18in (45.5cm) high.
$3,500–3,800 ✖ RYA

A cast-zinc carousel horse, by Parker Brothers, painted cream with a beige saddle and blue saddlecloth, 1930s, 64in (162.5cm) long.
$900–1,000 ⊞ DRG

An American carved yellow pine figure of George Washington, his clothing painted brown with traces of gilt, mounted on a carved cruciform poplar base, inscribed 'Pope Norris' under right arm, possibly South Carolina, c1840, 26¼in (66.5cm) high.
$14,000–16,000 ✖ SK(B)
Ex-Brenda and Ken Fritz Collection.

A carved wood figure of a lady, painted with a red dress and white apron with painted lace detail, on a stand, 19thC, 20¼in (51.5cm) high.
$17,000–20,000 ✖ SK(B)
Ex-Brenda and Ken Fritz Collection.

Folk Art is a very broad term, encompassing many collecting areas. For other examples refer to the sections on Kitchenware, Marine, Metalware, Treen, Boxes, Textiles and toys.

A papier mâché shop display pig, early 20thC, 26in (66cm) high.
$700–800 ⊞ SMI

An American carved and painted pine Native American Chief cigar-store figure, by John L. Cromwell, New York, mounted on a rolling wood and concrete base, nose and chin broken and repaired, c1850, 70in (178cm) high.
$70,000–80,000 ✖ S(NY)

A painted wood trade or shop figure, carved in the form of a Scotsman taking snuff, wearing a plumed hat, red jacket, kilt and green sash, some damage, 19thC, 36in (91.5cm) high.
$3,000–3,500 ✖ CAG

A carved oak tobacc-onist figure, in the form of a Scotsman, polychrome-painted and gilded, wearing a plumed headdress and costume, his right arm carved to hold cigars, America or British, 19thC, 34½in (87.5cm) high.
$6,500–7,000 ✖ SK(B)

A papier-mâché display figure of a highlander, seated on a rock, playing bagpipes, 19thC, 9¾in (25cm) high.
$400–500 ✖ P(Ed)

FOLK ART

A painted wood dummy board, the reverse with a hinged back leg, 19thC, 37in (94cm) high.
$800–1,000 S(S)

An American hooked rug, with multi-coloured circles scallops, and sunburst, with a black and grey braided border, probably Amish, Ohio, c1900, 39 x 37in (99 x 94cm).
$2,200–2,500 SK(B)
Ex-Brenda and Ken Fritz Collection.

An American pine spoon and candle wall shelf, the crest fitted with a slotted spoon rack above a case with three shelves with scalloped front edge, the whole painted with stars, flowers and leaves in dark green on a mustard yellow ground, New England, c1820, 26in (66cm) high.
$17,000–20,000 S(NY)

A wooden campaign flag holder, painted red, white and blue, c1863, 30 x 24in (76 x 61cm).
$320–350 DRG
This flag holder would have been used on a train or wagon that was travelling with a political campaign.

A carved and polychrome painted wooden frame, 1929, 36 x 24in (91.5 x 61cm).
$1,600–1,750 DRG
This frame was made by an out-of-work New Hampshire artist during the Great Depression in 1929 and 1930.

A French and Indian War rum horn, by Michael Byrne, engraved with renderings of General Hooker's Armey at Niagara, General Woollf Armey, Lake George, Crown Point, Loubeck, Lake Ontario, centring the British coat-of-arms, aperture with sun rays, a gentleman and a lady, dated 1761, 5in (12.5cm) high.
$9,500–11,000 S(NY)

▶ **A hand-carved and painted butcher's shop model,** c1870, 27in (68.6cm) wide.
$15,000–17,000 RYA

An American hooked rug, worked in red, blue, green and beige fabric with two blue cornucopiae filled with rose, lily and pansy blossoms, mounted on a stretcher, c1850, 42 x 70in (106.5 x 178cm).
$15,000–17,000 S(NY)

An American hooked rug, depicting a recumbent lion among jungle flowers and trees, hooked fabric in shades of brown, green, red, pink and yellow with a red and multi-colour diagonal striped border, late 19thC, 30½ x 61in (77.5 x 155cm).
$700–800 SK(B)

A wool on linen hooked rug, depicting a sheep and a fox, worked in cream, beige, pink, red and shades of green, 1930–40, 24 x 36in (61 x 91.5cm).
$600–675 DRG

◀ **Two American pine stools,** by Ralph and Martha Cahoon, the black ground with a border painted yellow and brown to simulate rope, one decorated with a sailor holding a bouquet of flowers dancing the hornpipe, the other with a mermaid holding a similar bouquet, Cotuit, Massachusetts, 1930–40, largest 25½in (65cm) diam.
$1,800–2,000 SK(B)

FOLK ART

An American trade sign, the wrought-iron bracket suspending a cast zinc boot painted in golden brown, 19thC, 22½in (57cm) high.
$1,400–1,600 SK(B)

An American wood and iron watchmaker's trade sign, the white dial with black Roman numerals within a mustard-painted frame, 19thC, 22in (56cm) diam.
$1,500–1,700 SK(B)

◄ **An American double-sided wooden trade sign,** depicting three graduated stacked barrels painted in yellow, green and red, with gilt bands and black lettering, late 19thC, 49½in (125.5cm) high.
$2,700–3,000 SK(B)

A copper soda trade sign, c1920, 15½in (39.5cm) high.
$500–550 MSB

An American woven wool tapestry, worked with the North Eastern Seaboard of America depicting various provinces, dated 'MDCXXVI', early 20thC, 57in (145cm) high.
$400–500 RFA

A verdigris copper weather vane, modelled as a cockerel, on a stone base, 18thC, 20in (51cm) high.
$3,000–3,400 RYA

An American copper weather vane, modelled as an eagle on a sphere, on a carved oak base, 19thC, 72in (183cm) high.
$800–1,000 DuM

An American moulded copper weather vane, modelled as a cow, with weathered ochre, yellow and verdigris surface and traces of gilt, late 19thC, 33in (84cm) long, with a stand.
$9,000–11,000 SK(B)

A copper weathervane, modelled as a rooster, 19thC, 11½in (29cm) high.
$500–600 PFK

An American gilt-copper and iron weather vane, in the shape of a sailing ship, no west directional, some gilt loss, Gloucester, Massachusetts, late 19thC, 25in (63.5cm) long.
$2,300–2,500 SK(B)

An Alpine sheet-iron weathervane, modelled as a crowing rooster, 19thC, 17in (43cm) high.
$180–220 Herm

A patinated copper weathervane, in the shape of a sailing boat, early 20thC, 29in (73.5cm) high.
$1,000–1,200 DD

A sheet-metal weathervane, in the form of a man and lady riding a tandem bicycle with moving rear wheel, c1930, 28½in (72.5cm) high, on a stand.
$1,800–2,200 S(NY)

FOLK ART

Papier Mâché

A pair of Regency papier mâché decanter coasters, with gilt bands of trailing stiff leaves above vertical orange striations, 5in (12.5cm) diam.
$700–800 ⚒ CGC

A papier mâché counter box, hand-painted with an armorial, c1810, 5in (12.5cm) long.
$60–70 ⊞ MB

A Regency papier mâché tray, 32in (81.5cm) long, on a later stand.
$2,600–2,900 ⊞ WELL

A papier mâché tray, painted overall with gilt leaves and blue and red flowers on a black ground, some damage, stamped Clay, Pall Mall, London, early 19thC, 31in (78.5cm) wide.
$720–870 ⚒ DN

A black-painted papier mâché tray, with gilt-decorated border and rim, the field painted with three-masted sailing ships involved in a skirmish, one flying the ensign of St George, another flying the French Tricolour, 19thC, 17in (43cm) wide.
$300–350 ⚒ PFK

A pair of George IV aubergine lacquer papier mâché vases, by Jennens & Bettridge, with gilt and painted chinoiserie decoration depicting pavilions, figures and blossoming trees, stamped mark beneath a crown, c1830, 20in (51cm) high.
$5,000–6,000 ⚒ S
These vases were made using a special technique whereby paper sheets were applied over a core of the desired shape. When half the final thickness had been built, a clean cut was made through the core with a sharp tool; the two sections were pulled apart and the core removed. Both halves were then brought together and the remainder of the sheet was pasted over and stoved.

Jennens & Bettridge

Jennens & Bettridge (1816–64) are the better known of the many Birmingham papier mâché manufacturers with showrooms in Belgrave Square, London. By 1825 they had attracted the patronage of King George IV being appointed 'japanners in ordinary to His Majesty'. In later years they also received commissions from King William IV and Queen Victoria. The firm exhibited a large range of stock at the 1851 Great Exhibition including a pianoforte and a child's cot decorated by the sculptor John Bell.

A Victorian papier mâché wine tray, with two decanter wells, the border decorated with scrolling foliage with shades of red, blue and ivory detail, the underside impressed 'Jennens & Bettridge makers to the Queen', with retail label inscribed R. Redgrave, 1847, 15in (38cm) wide.
$1,900–2,200 ⚒ NOA

◀ **A papier mâché letter box,** the cover inlaid in *Shibayama* style with mother-of-pearl, 19thC, 8in (20.5cm) wide.
$145–175 ⚒ GAK

▶ **A German papier mâché snuff box,** painted with a family scene, the lid interior also painted, painted mark Stobwassers Fabrik in Braunschweig, c1900, 4in (10cm) wide.
$500–600 ⚒ SK

A papier mâché rack, with chinoiserie decoration in gilt and colours, c1880, 8in (20.5cm) high.
$115–130 ⊞ MLL

Treen

A Scottish sycamore and alder bicker, 19thC, 3in (7.5cm) diam.
$290–320 ⊞ AEF
A bicker is used to contain liquor or porridge.

A Regency rosewood table book stand, with brass bun feet, damaged and restored, 15¼in (38.5cm) wide.
$580–720 ⚒ Bon

A turned sycamore bowl and chopper, 19thC, 10in (25.5cm) wide.
$430–480 ⊞ MFB

A Scottish staved wooden bowl, the twin handles pierced with hearts, the base stamped Glasgow, 19thC, 8¾in (22cm) diam.
$290–340 ⚒ P(Ed)

A carved and turned oak fruit bowl, carved with a mouse, by Robert (Mouseman) Thompson, Yorkshire, c1930, 9½in (24cm) diam.
$110–130 ⊞ CoCo

A William IV mahogany cotton bobbin holder, the octagonal stem carved with tulip heads, with eight bobbin spindles, 12½in (32cm) high.
$290–320 ⚒ DA

▶ **A Victorian walnut and brass book slide,** c1860, 13in (33cm) long.
$220–250 ⊞ MB

A Victorian oak bootjack, 34in (86.5cm) long.
$170–190 ⚒ SWO

A pair of Italian carved wood altar candlesticks, early 17thC, 32in (81.5cm) high.
$4,300–5,000 ⊞ DBA

A George III mahogany book carrier, inlaid with tulipwood banding and boxwood stringing, c1790, 20in (51cm) wide.
$4,000–4,600 ⚒ S

A Georgian mahogany snuff box, c1820, 3in (7.5cm) diam.
$230–260 ⊞ SEA

A Victorian stained beech novelty box, in the shape of a lady's shoe, the hinged oval brass cover engraved and stamped with maker's mark, 8¼in (21cm) long.
$1,100–1,300 ⚒ TEN

Sets/pairs

Unless otherwise stated, any description which refers to 'a set' or 'a pair' includes a guide price for the entire set or the pair, even though the illustration may show only a single item.

A pair of Portuguese Colonial turned hardwood candlesticks, 18thC, 17½in (44.5cm) high.
$2,300–2,600 ⚒ P(E)

A mahogany cat, c1840, 15in (38cm) wide.
$145–160 ⊞ AnSh

A mahogany cheese coaster, moulded at either end with roundels, 18thC, 15in (38cm) wide.
$360–430 ⚒ GAK

A carved wood chocolate mill, c1850, 11in (28cm) long.
$60–75 ⊞ WAB
This item was used to stir chocolate.

An Irish carved bog oak mead cup, c1860, 5½in (14cm) high.
$3,200–3,600 ⊞ WELD

A fruitwood dog kennel, 19thC, 19in (48.5cm) long.
$2,300–2,900 ⊞ DOA

A cedarwood footed cup, the bucket bowl with reeded bands, late 17thC, 8in (20.5cm) high.
$1,600–1,900 ⚒ S(S)

▶ **A walnut drinking set,** c1840, bottle 10in (25.5cm) high.
$870–1,000 ⊞ AEF

A French coquilla nut snuff flask, carved with a classical scene, c1820, 3in (7.5cm) long.
$650–750 ⊞ AEF

A Colonial coconut wine goblet, inscribed, named and dated 1743, 8½in (21.5cm) high.
$6,000–7,000 ⚒ RYA

A Friesland carved oak foot warmer, the top and side panels pierced with rosettes, 18thC, 8in (20.5cm) high.
$720–800 ⚒ S(S)

A carved wood glove stretcher, c1890, 7in (18cm) long.
$180–210 ⊞ MLa

▶ **A mahogany and fruitwood knitting sheath,** chip-carved with geometric patterns and hearts, lacking inlay to one side, early 19thC, 8in (20.5cm) long.
$115–145 ⚒ P(WM)

A Welsh wooden knitting sheath, dated 1813, 7in (18cm) long.
$650–730 ⊞ SEA

A wooden hookback ladle, with stylized animal head handle, early 19thC, 11in (28cm) long.
$180–220 ⊞ NEW

◀ **A carved sycamore ladle,** with double spiral-twist stem, 19thC, 15¼in (38.5cm) long.
$650–720 ⚒ S(S)

A William IV walnut Lazy Susan, the revolving table with a simulated carved bamboo border, 20in (51cm) diam.
$620–720 ⚒ TMA

A carved oak Lazy Susan, c1840, 24in (61cm) diam.
$2,900–3,200 ⊞ CAT

◀ **A pierced sycamore love spoon,** 19thC, 9in (23cm) long.
$1,450–1,750 ⚒ S(S)

A Welsh carved pine love token, c1840, 25in (63.5cm) long.
$500–550 ⊞ MFB

A carved wood nut cracker, in the shape of a crocodile, c1800, 6in (15cm) long.
$115–130 ⊞ FA

▶ **A carved wood nut-cracker,** in the shape of a ram's head, with glass eyes, c1900, 9in (23cm) long.
$260–290 ⊞ MLa

A Friesland carved mahogany and red walnut mangling board, inscribed with names, dated 1636, 34in (86.5cm) long.
$1,400–1,700 ⚒ DMC

Miller's is a price GUIDE not a price LIST

A rosewood pestle and mortar, c1800, pestle 14in (35.5cm) long.
$950–1,100 ⚒ E

An Edwardian mahogany money box, 8in (20.5cm) long.
$115–130 ⊞ MB

A carved wood tobacco tamper, decorated with a coursing greyhound, 18thC, 3in (7.5cm) high.
$650–720 ⊞ AEF

▶ **A Victorian carved wood photograph frame,** 18in (45.5cm) wide.
$400–470 ⊞ AMR

A Continental carved wood powder flask, 17thC, 6in (15cm) diam.
$1,600–1,800 ⊞ AEF

A mahogany reading stand, c1800, 18in (45.5cm) wide.
$1,150–1,300 ⊞ REI

A turned yew wood salt, c1800, 4in (10cm) wide.
$230–260 ⊞ SEA

A mahogany miniature spiral staircase, with dark rosewood-grained finish, late 19thC, 22in (56cm) high.
$1,600–1,750 ⚒ SK

A French carved wood spoon, c1820, 10in (25.5cm) long.
$650–720 ⊞ AEF

A turned oak tobacco jar, by James Marshall of Beverley, the underside with printed trademark, mid-19thC, 8in (20.5cm) high.
$800–1,100 ⚒ S(S)

A Continental carved wood tobacco jar, in the shape of an owl, with glass eyes, some damage, early 20thC, 11in (28cm) high.
$1,750–2,200 ⚒ Bon(W)

A French fruitwood tobacco rasp, carved with the figure of Louis IX, the reverse with busts of a couple and a rasp, 18thC, 7¾in (19.5cm) long.
$2,200–2,400 ⚒ S(Z)

A pair of Edwardian mahogany urns and covers, with boxwood and chequer stringing, inlaid with shield-shaped panels enclosing floral inlaid paterae, 22¾in (58cm) high.
$2,600–3,200 ⚒ L&T

▶ **A Flemish oak washboard,** carved in high relief with figures and a lion within foliate borders, dated 1702, later-pierced with a keyhole, 26in (66cm) long.
$730–800 ⚒ F&C

A mahogany pocket watch case, with cruciform crest, oak lozenge-shaped inlay, notch-carved border and mirrored stars, 19thC, 7¾in (19.5cm) wide.
$200–240 ⚒ DN

A mahogany and fruitwood skein winder, with side-mounted yarn counter dial and turned ivory spindle and handle, damaged, c1790, wheel 11¾in (30cm) diam.
$720–870 ⚒ Bon(W)

A decorated mulberry, boxwood and *lignum vitae* wool winder, late 18thC, 14in (35.5cm) wide.
$800–880 ⊞ CoHA

Tunbridge Ware

Tunbridge ware is a type of wood mosaic made largely in the Tonbridge and Tunbridge Wells areas of Kent. It originated in the 17th century, but blossomed in the 18th and 19th centuries when Tunbridge Wells developed as a fashionable spa and visitors expected to purchase souvenirs produced by local craftsmen.

The original Tunbridge ware consisted of simple turned wooden wares, often painted, or decorated with printed paper labels. In the 19th century techniques known as stickware and half-square mosaic were developed, together with the tessellated mosaic, which resulted in the elaborate designs that were produced in the second half of the century. By the 20th century the industry was in decline. Competition from cheap imports and the onset of WWI were contributing factors, with production finally ceasing in the 1930s.

It was not until the 1980s, when Sotheby's organized an exhibition and auction, that interest in Tunbridge ware began to develop again. Today, collectors have a wide range of items to choose from, such as sewing and writing accessories, toys, jewellery, pictures and furniture, not to mention the ubiquitous box. Boxes were made for a variety of uses such as storing gloves, handkerchieves, tea, snuff or stamps. A fine example of a small piece is the stamp box inlaid with mosaic depicting Queen Victoria's head, on page 589.

Tunbridge ware incorporated a whole range of designs from geometric to floral, made from local woods such as oak, holly, yew, sycamore and maple, which were combined with various foreign timbers. The glove box illustrated on page 587 is veneered in bird's-eye maple with a floral mosaic and achieves a very pleasing effect. Topographical pieces involved the craftsmen in many hours of work: the Pantiles picture on page 622 is said to contain some 25,000 pieces and took around three months to make.

There were a number of important makers of Tunbridge ware in the 19th century, and labelled examples, usually denoting items of good quality, are now keenly sought. The Wise, Burrows and Fenner families were producing Tunbridge ware over a long period. Edmund Nye, Thomas Barton and Henry Hollamby were all well-known makers in the second half of the 19th century and produced exceptionally fine work.

For those beginning a collection, quality and condition are all-important. Badly damaged pieces should be avoided if possible, and 19th-century examples are likely to be of a higher standard than those made in the 20th century. **Dianne Brick**

A Tunbridge ware book stand, inlaid with sprays of fuchsias and roses, c1860, 13in (33cm) long.
$580–650 ⊞ AMH

► **A Tunbridge ware glove box,** inlaid with a view of Eridge Castle, c1860, 9½in (24cm) long.
$620–690 ⊞ TUN

A Tunbridge ware box, the top with a print of Bonchurch Church, Isle of Wight, c1860, 4¼in (11cm) long.
$260–290 ⊞ VB

A Tunbridge ware box, inlaid with a moth, c1835, 5¾in (14.5cm) long.
$360–430 ⊞ AMH

A Tunbridge ware box, inlaid with a view of Eridge Castle, c1860, 5½in (14cm) long.
$620–690 ⊞ TUN

A Tunbridge ware sewing box, with pin-cushion top, c1870, 7in (18cm) long.
$450–500 ⊞ TUN

◄ **A Tunbridge ware writing box,** inlaid with a view of Eridge Castle, some damage, c1850, 10in (25.5cm) long.
$450–550 ⚶ GAK

A Tunbridge ware handkerchief box, 1860–70, 6in (15cm) square.
$520–580 ⊞ TUN

A Tunbridge ware clothes brush, c1880, 7in (18cm) long.
$95–110 ⊞ VBo

A Tunbridge ware button hook, c1920, 4in (10cm) long.
$260–290 ⊞ VB

A Tunbridge ware box, inlaid with a lion design, c1870, 3½in (9cm) long.
$400–450 ⊞ AMH

A Tunbridge ware chamberstick, c1870, 3in (7.5cm) diam.
$200–220 ⊞ AMH

Miller's is a price GUIDE
not a price LIST

A Tunbridge ware cotton-reel box, painted with a ruin in a landscape, c1820, 9in (23cm) long.
$460–500 ⊞ AMH

A Tunbridge ware cotton-reel box, 1880–90, 5in (12.5cm) long.
$180–200 ⊞ VBo

► **A Tunbridge ware counter box,** c1845, 1¼in (3cm) diam.
$140–160 ⊞ AMH

A Tunbridge ware cribbage board, c1880, 9in (23cm) long.
$110–120 ⊞ VBo

A Tunbridge ware travelling draughts set, c1890, 5in (12.5cm) square.
$580–650 ⊞ VB

A Tunbridge ware easel and frame, c1880, 16in (40.5cm) high.
$730–800 ⊞ AMH

A Tunbridge ware Oxford-style frame, c1880, 4½in (11.5cm) wide.
$190–220 ⊞ PSA

Condition

The condition is absolutely vital when assessing the value of an antique. Damaged pieces on the whole appreciate much less than perfect examples. However a rare desirable piece may command a high price even when damaged.

◄ **A Tunbridge ware Chalybeate Spring-stained bird's-eye maple glove box,** with Vandyke cross-banding and beaded moulded edges, c1860, 10in (25.5cm) long.
$650–720 ⊞ PSA

In order to change the colour of veneers such as maple or ash from yellow/brown to grey, they were immersed in the Chalybeate Spring water taken from the well at the Pantiles, Tunbridge Wells. Time and repolishing usually removes the grey effect and it is therefore unusual today to find a piece that still appears grey.

A Tunbridge ware glove box, 1870–80, 9in (23cm) long.
$390–430 ⊞ VBo

Two Tunbridge ware glove boxes, c1845, 9½in (24cm) long.
l. with a view of Penshurst Place, damaged, **$400–470**
r. $145–175 ⊞ GAK

A Tunbridge ware turned rosewood inkstand, with cut-glass ink bottle, c1860, 3½in (9cm) diam.
$580–650 ⊞ TUN

► **A Tunbridge ware and rosewood inkstand,** decorated with a dog and foliage, glass ink bottles missing, faults, c1860, 9¾in (25cm) wide.
$500–580 ⚒ Bon(W)

◄ **A Tunbridge ware inkstand,** with cut-glass ink bottle, c1870, 4in (10cm) diam.
$360–430 ⊞ AMH

A pair of Tunbridge ware knitting needle ends, c1870, 1½in (4cm) long.
$260–290 ⊞ AMH

A Tunbridge ware letter rack, with Vandyke veneers, carrying handle missing, early 19thC, 8in (20.5cm) long.
$520–580 ⊞ PSA

A Tunbridge ware necklace, comprising 25 turned beads, c1870, 23in (58.5cm) long.
$870–950 ⊞ VB

TUNBRIDGE WARE

A Tunbridge ware needles box, 19thC, 2½in (6.5cm) wide.
$390–430 ⊞ **AMH**

▶ **A Tunbridge ware pen,** c1880, 7in (18cm) long.
$180–210 ⊞ **PSA**

A Tunbridge ware notebook cover, inscribed 'A Present from Hastings', c1890, 3½in (9cm) long.
$260–300 ⊞ **VB**

A Tunbridge ware nutmeg grater, c1860, 1¾in (4.5cm) high.
$160–180 ⊞ **VB**

A Tunbridge ware pin wheel, c1860, 1½in (4cm) diam.
$110–125 ⊞ **PSA**

A Tunbridge ware pin wheel, c1870, 2¼in (45.5cm) diam.
$150–165 ⊞ **AMH**

A Tunbridge ware rouge pot, with a glass liner, c1880, 1in (2.5cm) diam.
$180–200 ⊞ **VB**

A Tunbridge ware thread waxer and pincushion, by Thomas Barton, c1870, 1½in (4cm) high.
$130–145 ⊞ **AMH**

A Tunbridge ware puzzle box, by Edmund Nye, with printed instructions, c1850, 1¾in (4.5cm) square.
$190–220 ⊞ **VB**

A Tunbridge ware scent bottle box, with two bottles with silver-plated tops, c1870, 5in (12.5cm) long.
$320–360 ⊞ **VBo**

◀ **A Tunbridge ware sewing weight,** c1850, 1½in (4cm) diam.
$430–500 ⊞ **AMH**

A Tunbridge ware double-ended pin holder, c1870, 1½in (4cm) long.
$110–125 ⊞ **PSA**

A Tunbridge ware ring stand, c1850, 3in (7.5cm) high.
$110–125 ⊞ **VBo**

A Tunbridge ware simulated rosewood sewing box, the hinged lid with a hand-coloured print, enclosing original tape measure, pincushion and threads, on four brass ball feet, c1820, 6¾in (17cm) wide.
$540–610 ⚒ **CGC**

A Tunbridge ware sovereign holder, c1860, 1½in (4cm) high.
$130–145 ⊞ PSA

▶ **A Tunbridge ware stamp box,** by Green of Rye, commemorating the reign of three kings in 1936, 5¼in (13.5cm) long.
$260–290 ⊞ VB

A Tunbridge ware stamp box, inlaid with Penny Black design, c1850, 1½in (4cm) long.
$230–250 ⊞ VB

A Tunbridge ware stamp box, c1870, 1½in (4cm) long.
$260–290 ⊞ AMH

A Victorian Tunbridge ware teapoy, enclosing four lidded compartments with bird and butterfly designs, the whole decorated with geometric and floral designs, 19in (48.5cm) wide.
$5,000–5,800 ⋏ RBB

A Tunbridge ware trinket box, c1890, 4in (10cm) long.
$190–210 ⊞ VBo

A Tunbridge ware rosewood tea caddy, some damage, 1845–50, 8½in (21.5cm) long.
$320–380 ⋏ SWO

Cross Reference
See Colour Review (page 622)

▶ **A Tunbridge ware thread waxer,** 19thC, ¾in (2cm) high.
$90–110 ⊞ PSA

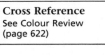

Two Tunbridge ware thread winders, c1870, 1½in (4cm) diam.
$145–165 each ⊞ AMH

◀ **A Tunbridge ware yo-yo,** c1850, 2¾in (7cm) diam.
$620–690 ⊞ AMH

Boxes

A north Italian octagonal wood casket, the lid inlaid with interlacing stars on a horn ground centred by a gilt-iron handle, the panels inset with glass painted in imitation tortoiseshell and marble panels above a geometric frieze and a border of alternating bone and wood, the sides with painted scenes of towns and seascapes, damaged, restored, c1500 and later, 8½in (21.5cm) high.
$5,800–7,200 ⚒ S(NY)

An oyster-veneered walnut lace box, 18thC, 19in (48.5cm) wide.
$580–720 ⚒ Mit

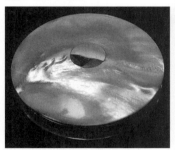

A French mother-of-pearl box, with gold inlay, c1780, 2½in (6.5cm) diam.
$290–320 ⊞ MB

A tortoiseshell tea caddy, with an ivory ball finial and plush-lined interior, early 19thC, 8in (20.5cm) wide.
$2,000–2,300 ⚒ Mit

▶ **A William IV mahogany writing box,** with two secret drawers and black leather interior, 16in (40.5cm) long.
$360–430 ⊞ OTT

An ivory and gold piqué snuff box, c1680, 3½in (9cm) wide.
$2,900–3,500 ⊞ BEX

A French carved ivory pomander, c1760, 3in (7.5cm) diam.
$1,900–2,100 ⊞ BEX

A mahogany voting box, painted with 'Yes' and 'No', early 19thC, 17in (43cm) high.
$1,150–1,300 ⚒ SWO

An ivory patch box, with a portrait bust of Queen Anne, c1710, 3¾in (9.5cm) long.
$500–580 ⊞ LBr

A George III ivory and tortoiseshell-banded canister, the front panel with silver escutcheon above a shield-shaped cartouche, later relined, lid damaged, 5½in (14cm) high.
$2,100–2,400 ⚒ P(BA)

A north European burr-ash box, with a divided interior, the side fitted with a secret compartment, mid-19thC, 13in (33cm) wide.
$800–950 ⚒ NOA

◀ **A penwork workbox,** decorated throughout with flowers, leaves and geometric borders, with gilt-brass ring handles and paw feet, early 19thC, 9in (23cm) wide.
$1,000–1,200 ⚒ S

A Mauchline ware snuff box, decorated with a dog and a rodent, inscribed 'A Minute too late', c1830, 3½in (9cm) wide.
$180–220 ⊞ OD

A mahogany cutlery box, with two lidded compartments, early 19thC, 16in (40.5cm) wide.
$300–350 ⚷ GAK

An Anglo-Indian ivory box, c1840, 4in (10cm) wide.
$230–260 ⊞ MB

An early Victorian coromandel sewing box, inlaid with scrolling foliage in mother-of-pearl and pewter, the pink silk-lined interior with a lift-out tray containing six mother-of-pearl winders and other sewing accessories, 12¼in (31cm) wide.
$1,000–1,200 ⚷ CGC

A rosewood workbox, brass-inlaid with foliate decoration, with interior compartments, 19thC, 11½in (29cm) wide.
$450–550 ⚷ AG

A Victorian coromandel desk *aide-mémoire*, decorated with gilt-brass Gothic strapwork, a hinged clasp to the top releasing five spring-loaded ledgers bearing the titles Memoranda, Visits & Addresses, House Expenses, Daily Journal and Cash Account, the clasp engraved Halstaff and Hannaford, 228 Regent Street, 8¾in (22cm) wide.
$1,000–1,200 ⚷ P(S)

A workbox in the shape of a grand piano, with inlaid keyboard and sealed music box, the interior fitted with mother-of-pearl tools, damaged, 19thC, 12in (30.5cm) wide.
$720–870 ⚷ GH

◀ **A Victorian coromandel casket,** the hinged cover and front with engraved and shaped brass strapwork, 9in (23cm) wide.
$130–160 ⚷ WW

A silver-mounted tortoiseshell casket, with applied floral pierced centre, corner panels and escutcheon, 19thC, 8in (20.5cm) wide.
$1,700–2,000 ⚷ DMC

◀ **A coromandel cigar box,** with a cedar wood lining, c1860, 12in (30.5cm) wide.
$430–500 ⊞ MB

A malachite box, with a wood-lined interior, 19thC, 4in (10cm) wide.
$430–500 ➤ AH

A Victorian mother-of-pearl-veneered tea caddy, engraved and inlaid with flowers, enclosing two lidded compartments, 6¾in (17cm) wide.
$1,600–1,900 ➤ Bri

A brass-inlaid walnut writing slope, with secret drawers, c1860, 9in (23cm) wide.
$460–580 ⊞ MB

A French palm and burr-palm glove box, Paris, c1860, 13in (33cm) wide.
$900–1,000 ⊞ OTT

► **An oak cigar box,** in the shape of a sentry box, c1870, 15in (38cm) high.
$290–320 ⊞ MB

A Victorian boulle stationery box, with cut-brass inlay on a tortoiseshell ground, 9in (23cm) wide.
$650–720 ➤ CDC

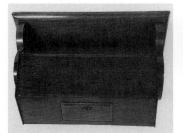

A Victorian mahogany tombola box, c1890, 19in (48.5cm) wide.
$360–430 ⊞ WAB

A Victorian ebonized and cross-banded tea caddy, with three sections and rising top, marked 'Sorrento', with dancing figure and inlaid decoration, 12½in (32cm) wide.
$580–650 ➤ DLC

Miller's is a price GUIDE not a price LIST

A French gilt-metal jewellery box, applied with painted ovals of Parisian landmarks among engraved and applied foliate scrolls, late 19thC, 6¼in (16cm) wide.
$650–720 ➤ P(Ed)

◄ **A Continental walnut, ebonized and inlaid hexagonal musical cigar box,** the white bead knob turns to open the six mother-of-pearl and brass-inlaid doors, the musical box playing four tunes, late 19thC, 78½in (199.5cm) diam.
$800–880 ➤ NOA

An Imperial Russian lacquer box, by Lukitin, with original interior, c1890, 3½in (9cm) diam.
$870–950 ⊞ SHa

◄ **An American tiger maple box,** with a brass handle and ivory escutcheon, 19thC, 31½in (80cm) long.
$800–880 ➤ SK(B)

An ivory-bound coromandel cigar/cigarette box, with twin birch-lined compartments, c1900, 9in (23cm) wide.
$870–1,000 ⊞ CORO

BOXES

Music
Cylinder Musical Boxes

A Czechoslovakian musical box, by Rzebitshek, the 12¼in (31cm) cylinder playing six airs, contained in a mahogany case with stringing to lid and front, Prague, 1860s, 18½in (47cm) wide.
$3,600–4,400 ✧ P(WM)
This box is unusual in having the base teeth of the comb to the right.

A Swiss musical box, by Jacot & Son, with three cylinders, contained in an oak case, c1890, 34in (86.5cm) wide.
$5,500–6,500 ✧ SLN

A Swiss cylinder musical box, the 6in (15cm) cylinder playing eight airs, in a wooden case, c1890, 16in (41cm) wide.
$900–1,100 ✧ DuM

A Swiss musical box, the 13¾in (35cm) cylinder playing eight airs, with six bells struck by three gilt-metal Chinamen with a clapper in each hand and nodding heads, contained in a rosewood, tulipwood-banded and floral marquetry case, late 19thC, 24in (61cm) wide.
$3,600–4,300 ✧ DN

A Swiss musical box, by Nicole Frères, the 13¼in (33.5cm) cylinder playing six airs, contained in a stained wood case with a trophy-inlaid lid, 19thC, 20in (51cm) wide.
$1,900–2,200 ✧ CGC

A musical box, by Mermod Frères, the 13½in (34.5cm) cylinder playing 12 airs, contained in a grained wood case with veneered and inlaid front and lid, inner lid and divisions replaced, c1890, 30in (76cm) wide.
$1,600–1,750 ✧ SK(B)

A Swiss PVF musical box, playing ten airs, contained in a rosewood and marquetry-inlaid case decorated with birds and a snake in wheat and rushes, 19thC, 22¾in (58cm) wide.
$580–720 ✧ CMS

A Swiss musical box, by B. H. Abrahams, the 6¼in (16cm) cylinder playing ten airs, with three bells in sight, in a wooden case with lift-off lid, c1900, 14½in (37cm) wide.
$800–880 ✧ Bon

A Swiss musical box, the cylinder playing eight popular airs, contained in a marquetry-inlaid case, c1880, 13¾in (35cm) wide.
$580–650 ✧ F&C

A Swiss cylinder musical box, accompanied by drums and bells, contained in an inlaid wooden case, c1890, 16in (40.5cm) wide.
$2,600–3,200 ⊞ GWe

A musical box, the 8in (20.5cm) cylinder playing six airs, contained in a wooden case stained to simulate coromandel, with brass carrying handles, late 19thC, 16¼in (41cm) wide.
$720–870 ✧ PFK

A Swiss cylinder musical box, in an inlaid wooden case, c1900, 14in (35.5cm) wide.
$1,000–1,150 ⊞ GWe

MUSIC

Disc Musical Boxes

A Victorian Polyphon disc musical box, with 12 discs, contained in an inlaid walnut case, 21¼in (54cm) wide.
$2,300–2,900 ↗ WilP

A Symphonion disc musical box, with a collection of discs, contained in a walnut case, c1900, 17¼in (44cm) wide.
$2,300–2,600 ↗ SWO

A Brittania Polyphon disc musical box, with seven discs, contained in a walnut case with fretwork, painted decoration and crossbanded surround, c1900, 20in (51cm) high.
$1,250–1,450 ↗ Mal(O)

An Olympia upright disc musical box, No. 6566, with approximately 32 discs, with twin-comb mechanism and coin-slide, contained in a two-piece mahogany cabinet with disc storage to side, sounding boards replaced, c1900, 70in (178cm) high.
$7,200–8,700 ↗ SK(B)

A Swiss disc musical box, by B. H. Abrahams, contained in a walnut-veneered cabinet surmounted by a clock, c1900, 27in (68.5cm) high.
$2,900–3,200 ⊞ GWe

◀ **A German Polyphon coin-operated disc musical box,** with 39 discs, contained in a walnut-veneered case with glazed door, the pediment surmounted by a clock, c1900, 26¼in (66.5cm) wide.
$8,000–8,800
↗ AG

A Criterion disc musical box, with 14 discs, single comb mechanism, contained in an oak case, c1908, 21¼in (54cm) long.
$2,300–2,900 ↗ SLN

Mechanical Music

A George III silver-gilt engine-turned musical box, by Joseph Biggs or John Booth, with chased floral border, complete with key, 1818, 3¼in (8.5cm) long.
$2,000–2,300 ↗ P

◀ **A late Victorian Penny in the Slot barrel piano,** the 36in (91.5cm) barrel playing nine tunes, with crank-driven mechanism, contained in a walnut case with incised, carved and gilded floral decoration, inset with two bevelled mirrors and a decorated window, 44in (112cm) wide.
$1,300–1,600 ↗ DD

An American rosewood melodion, c1850, 31in (78.5cm) wide.
$850–950 ↗ DuM

▶ **A boudoir grand pianola,** by John Broadwood & Sons, London, with one pianola roll playing 'Sonata Apassionata in F Minor' by Beethoven, the satinwood case with mahogany line-inlaid decoration, early 20thC, 78in (198cm) wide.
$500–600 ↗ RTo

A singing bird in a cage automaton, the bird with coloured feathers, his head and tail moving as he sings, late 19thC, 21¼in (54cm) wide.
$3,600–4,300 ↗ TEN

Phonographs

An American Edison spring motor phonograph, with Bettini reproducer and silver Bettini horn, with spare arm and shaving attachment for Edison reproducer, c1897, 16½in (42cm) wide.
$3,200–3,600 ⊞ ET
This is an exceptional item, as this model is seldom seen with a Bettini attachment and reproducer and original Bettini horn.

An Edison Model A concert phonograph, with 5in (12.5cm) mandrel, early recorder, shaver, Triton motor, in an oak case with accessories and drawer, c1900.
$3,200–3,600 ⋌ SK(B)

▶ **An Edison Model D Red Gem phonograph,** in an oak case, with original 19in (48.5cm) eight-petal horn, c1910, 10in (25.5cm) wide.
$950–1,200 ⊞ HHO

An Edison home phonograph, in a mahogany case, c1905, 15in (38cm) wide.
$950–1,100 ⊞ HHO
Examples of this phonograph in a mahogany case are seldom seen, and would have cost more than other models when new.

Gramophones

An HMV Junior Monarch gramophone, in an oak case, with an oak horn, c1912, 14in (35.5cm) square.
$1,800–2,200 ⊞ HHO

A German gramophone, in an oak case with record storage drawers, early 20thC, 16½in (42cm) wide.
$200–250 ⋌ Herm

A Columbia Table Grand gramophone, c1930, 12in (30.5cm) wide.
$230–260 ⊞ HHO

A Peter Pan miniature portable gramophone, 1920s, 6½in (16.5cm) square.
$220–260 ⊞ HHO

◀ **An Academy mahogany cabinet gramophone,** decorated with urns, ribbons, bellflower swags and pendants above double doors, early 20thC, 22in (56cm) wide.
$430–500 ⋌ PFK

A HMV internal horn travelling table gramophone, Model 113, in a mahogany case, 1930s, 17in (43cm) wide.
$290–350 ⋌ P(WM)

MUSIC

Musical Instruments

A German cello, by Albin Wilfer, Leipzig, 1913, length of back 30in (76cm).
$8,700–10,200 ↗ **Bon**

A cello, probably Italian, labelled Vincenzo Sannino Fece in Napoli anno 1914, length of back 30in (76cm).
$10,200–12,200 ↗ **GH**

A cello, by Arthur Richardson, Crediton, 1919, length of back 30in (76cm).
$13,000–16,000 ↗ **P**

An American Model Tubaphone No. 9 five-string banjo, by the Vega Company, Boston, the peg head and ebony fingerboard with mother-of-pearl inlay, 1926, head 11in (28cm) diam, with case.
$5,000–5,500 ↗ **SK**

An American guitar, by C. F. Martin & Co, Nazareth, with mahogany back and sides and spruce top, the mahogany neck with ebony fingerboard inlaid with mother-of-pearl, 1926, length of back 20½in (52cm), with case.
$3,600–4,000 ↗ **SK**

A giltwood harp, by Erard, the fluted column terminating in female terms and cherub capital, the plinth ornamented by angels playing lyres, early 19thC, 67in (170cm) high.
$6,500–7,250 ↗ **NOA**

A Regency satinwood and parcel-gilt harp, by J. Schwieso & S. Erard, London, the fluted column with classical winged figure capital and anthemion frieze to the base, the soundboard and bow decorated with Renaissance-style arabesque borders of black penwork, some strings lacking, 67in (170cm) high.
$3,600–4,300 ↗ **PFK**

A French guitar, with rose-wood back and ribs, c1820.
$500–600 ↗ **Bon**

▶ **A late Regency harp,** the head of the gilt and ebonized fluted stem with Graeco-Egyptian gilt gesso decoration, the brass adjustment plate inscribed Barry, London, the soundboard with neo-classical gilt figures and bands of scrolling foliage with putti to an ebony-veneered soundbox, the base with winged seahorses, 68in (172.5cm) high.
$3,200–3,600 ↗ **WW**

A manual harpsichord, by Jacobus & Abraham Kirkham, converted to a two-manual harpsichord, late 18thC, with later alterations, 92in (233.5cm) wide, in a mahogany case.
$16,000–17,500 ↗ **BLH**

Pianos

Henry Ford used to say 'you can have any colour, so long as it is black'. There is much more choice available to the aficionado of period pianos, as the best examples are not only exceptional pieces of furniture, but also fine musical instruments that can be worthwhile investments. With the increased interest in period performance, the ruling troika of Steinway, Bechstein and Blüthner has loosened its grip on the market.

In years past prospective purchasers were advised to find an 'overstrung' piano, a term that describes a layout in which the bass strings cross over the plain steel strings of the higher notes. Although patented by Steinway in 1859, overstringing did not come into general use until the last quarter of the 19th century. Many wonderful antique pianos were therefore made without overstringing, and some makers such as Erard built superb 'straight-strung' instruments well into the early 20th century. Full cast-iron frames were not used in most pianos until the latter part of the 19th century, and while essential for the high tension of modern instruments, they are not necessary in earlier period pianos.

Until recently, 18th-century Viennese instruments were the most sought-after, but that has changed as musicians' interests have widened. The market for grand pianos of the 1840s has expanded considerably – particularly for examples by Erard and Pleyel.

The early square pianos, often mistakenly called 'spinets', have gradually become more valuable, but only the best examples with superb casework and in entirely original condition, or expertly restored, have risen in price. Many were later converted into desks by having the keyboards removed. They can be beautiful pieces of furniture, but now their value as musical instruments is once again recognized and they are more valuable as pianos than desks.

For more modern instruments, the period just before WWI is often considered the best. The craftsmanship and materials for high-quality instruments were still available to piano manufacturers, and so the highly decorative pianos of this time have started to fetch much higher prices.

It is important, when looking for an antique piano, to consider what the instrument will be used for and choose one from an appropriate period. A square piano, for example, can be a wonderful domestic instrument, but is not suitable for playing Rachmaninoff, while a large black concert piano may be totally inappropriate for most domestic settings. If you buy an unrestored instrument, it is important to seek expert advice as restoration of antique pianos is a highly specialized art. A poorly-restored piece will have its value compromised and will be a frustrating musical instrument as well. **David Winston**

◄ **A French square piano,** by Swanen, Paris, the mahogany case with boxwood and ebony inlay banding, restored, 1792, 45¾in (116cm) wide.
$11,500–13,500
⊞ **PPC**

A George III mahogany square piano, the satinwood-crossbanded and kingwood-strung case by Joshua Done, London, 65¾in (167cm) wide.
$500–600 ⋋ **CGC**

◄ **A George III mahogany and rosewood-crossbanded box piano,** by Clementi & Co, London, with brass and ebony stringing, 68in (173cm) wide.
$1,300–1,600
⋋ **TRM**

A Compensator grand piano, by William Stodart, London, in a rosewood case, restored, c1835, 81in (205.5cm) long.
$27,500–30,500 ⊞ PPC

A grand piano, by Erard, in a Sheraton-style rosewood case inlaid with swags and cartouches, c1880, 84in (213.5cm) long, with stool.
$5,800–7,200 ↗ P(Ba)

An American rosewood grand piano, by Steinway & Sons, New York, Model O, c1905, 70in (178cm) long.
$8,000–9,500 ⊞ PEx

An American ebony grand piano, by Steinway & Sons, New York, Model A, c1908, 74in (188cm) long.
$8,000–9,500 ⊞ PEx

▶ **A mahogany grand piano,** by Mason & Hamlin, with a black leather-covered adjustable stool, restored, c1924, 69in (175.5cm) wide.
$9,500–10,200 ↗ DuM

A French ebonized and boulle upright piano, by Pape et fils, Paris, with gilt-metal mounts, inlaid throughout with scrolling brass foliate decoration, the serpentine supports flanked by female terms, faults, c1860, 57in (145cm) wide.
$2,600–3,200 ↗ S(S)

A rosewood grand piano, by John Broadwood & Sons, late 19thC, 78in (198cm) long.
$1,900–2,200 ↗ NOA

A German rosewood grand piano, by Blüthner, Leipzig, on simulated rosewood legs, 1906, 58in (147.5cm) wide.
$1,300–1,600 ↗ P(Ed)

An American rosewood boudoir grand piano, by Steinway & Sons, New York, signed, c1872, 79in (200.5cm) long.
$10,200–12,300 ↗ DOC

A grand piano, by John Broadwood & Sons, late 19thC, 60in (152.5cm) long
$2,000–2,400 ↗ MAR

A French flame-walnut grand piano, by Gaveau, Paris, restored, 1905, 56¼in (143cm) wide.
$18,500–21,500 ⊞ PPC

A French flame-walnut grand piano, by Gaveau, Paris, in Sunburst veneer pattern, restored, c1929, 58in (147.5cm) wide.
$30,500–35,000 ⊞ PPC

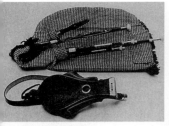

A set of Northumbrian small pipes, by Robert Reid, North Shields, the blackwood chanter with six brass keys, three blackwood drones with ivory and brass mounts, blackwood blowpipe to leather bag with cover, and mahogany bellows, early 19thC, in 21in (53.5cm) wooden pipe case. **$1,800–2,200** ⚹ **AG**

► **A pochette,** the bone tailpiece and fingerboard incised with primitive masks, the back inlaid with geometric patterns of flowerheads, the head inlaid with mother-of-pearl borders terminating in a mask-head finial, probably early 20thC, 17¼in (44cm) long. **$2,000–2,400** ⚹ **GH**

A viola, the back decorated with purfling set in a geometric pattern, c1740, length of back 15¼in (38.5cm). **$2,600–3,200** ⚹ **Bon**

A viola, c1840, 16in (40.5cm) long, with a silver and nickel-mounted bow. **$4,500–5,500** ⚹ **GH**

◄ **An Italian violin,** by Antonio Mariani, Pasaro, 1660s, length of back 14in (35.5cm), with case. **$10,500–11,500** ⚹ **SK**

A French silver-mounted viola bow, by J. B. Vuillaume, with original ebony frog and silver and ebony adjuster, converted from self-rehairing style, stamped, c1845, 69grams. **$19,500–27,750** ⚹ **SK**

A Bohemian violin, by Joannes Helmer, Prague, labelled, 1755, length of back 14¼in (36cm). **$4,000–4,600** ⚹ **Bon**

LOCATE THE SOURCE

The source of each illustration in Miller's can be found by checking the code letters below each caption with the Key to Illustrations, pages 794–800.

◄ **A violin,** by Charles Maucotel, London, labelled, dated 1858, length of back 14in (35.5cm). **$8,700–10,200** ⚹ **GH**

A French violin, by Ch. J. B. Collin-Mezin, Paris, labelled, 1889, length of back 14¼in (36cm).
$4,600–5,000 ✕ **Bon**

A French violin, labelled Lutherie Antique Jean-Baptiste Colin, annee 1887, length of back 14in (35.5cm), with case, with two bows, one silver-mounted.
$1,300–1,600 ✕ **E**

A composite violin, possibly Italian, 19thC, length of back 14in (35.5cm), with case.
$3,600–4,300 ✕ **GH**

A Belgian violin, by Auguste & Georges Falisse, Brussels, labelled, 1907, length of back 14¼in (36cm)
$2,900–3,500 ✕ **Bon**

An Italian violin, by Michelangelo Puglisi, Catania, labelled, 1919, length of back, 14in (35.5cm), with case and two nickel-mounted bows.
$4,000–4,600 ✕ **P**

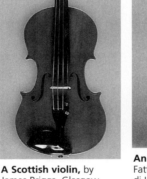

A Scottish violin, by James Briggs, Glasgow, labelled, 1921, length of back 14in (35.5cm).
$5,800–7,200 ✕ **Bon**

An Italian violin, labelled Fatto da Contavalli Primo di Luigi nel 1930 in Imola, signed, length of back 14in (35.5cm).
$7,250–8,750 ✕ **GH**

An American violin, by E. W. Beebe, Philadelphia, labelled, 1937, length of bac 14in (35.5cm), with case.
$4,000–4,600 ✕ **SK**

A silver-mounted violin bow, by Samuel Allen, London, stamped mark, c1900, 61grams.
$4,600–5,000 ✕ **P**

A gold and tortoiseshell violin bow, by A. R. Prager, early 20thC.
$2,300–2,900 ✕ **RFA**

A silver and ebony violin bow, by Hill & Sons, dated 1929.
$2,600–3,200 ✕ **RFA**

A French silver-mounted violin bow, by Eugène Sartory, Paris, stamped mark, c1930, 63grams.
$7,300–8,700 ✕ **SK**

Colour Review

A gilt-bronze and glass chandelier, Sweden or Russia, early 19thC, 36½in (92.5cm) high. $2,500–2,700 ✗ S(Z)

A pair of Louis Philippe gilt-bronze-mounted Paris porcelain table lamps, fitted for electricity, France, mid-19thC, 24in (61cm) high. $4,000–4,400 ✗ NOA

A moulded and cut-glass chandelier, probably Baccarat, minor damage, restored, mid-19thC, 48in (122cm) high. $7,600–9,000 ✗ S(S)

A gilt-bronze six light plafonnier, 19thC, 9in (23cm) high. $800–1,000 ✗ P

A Meissen porcelain chandelier, minor damage, crossed swords mark, 1860–70, 27½in (70cm) high. $5,800–7,400 ✗ DORO

A Victorian brass pendant gas light, with etched cranberry glass shade, fitted for electricity, c1880, 26½in (67.5cm) high. $450–550 ⊞ CHA

A pair of French brass oil wall lights, signed 'Déposé J. N. Paris', c1880, 16in (40.5cm) high. $3,500–3,800 ⊞ MI

A brass portable gas table lamp, with period acid-etched shade, fitted for electricity, c1880, 23in (58.5cm) high. $700–900 ⊞ CHA

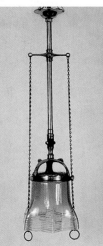

A Victorian brass gas lamp, with original shade, c1890, 24in (61cm) high. $200–300 ⊞ JW

A cast-brass and cut-glass ceiling lamp, c1895, 7in (18cm) diam. $450–550 ⊞ TLG

A Moore Bros pottery oil lamp, minor damage, printed marks, 1880s, 14½in (37cm) high. $750–900 ✗ S(S)

A brass table lamp, with cranberry glass shade, fitted for electricity, c1900, 22¾in (58cm) high. $650–750 ⊞ CHA

An Edwardian brass centre light, with cut-glass shades, c1910, 26in (66cm) high. $1,500–1,600 ⊞ CHA

An American Venetian glass lamp base, fitted for electricity, 1920, 40in (101.5cm) high. $650–750 ⊞ RUL

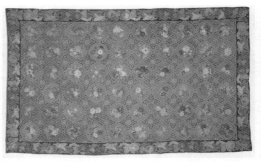

A French needlework carpet, restored, size possibly reduced, 19thC, 224 x 145in (569 x 368.5cm).
$19,500–21,500 ⚒ **Bon**

An Aubusson carpet,
France, 19thC, 177 x 111in (450 x 282cm).
$4,650–5,500 ⚒ **Bon(C)**

▶ **An Alcaraz carpet,** restored, Spain, mid-16thC, 124 x 61in (315 x 155cm).
$9,800–11,600 ⚒ **S(NY)**

A European Savonnerie-style carpet, damaged, early 20thC, 325 x 177in (826 x 449.5cm).
$13,000–16,000 ⚒ **S(NY)**

A Bessarabian rug, Balkans, c1850, 96 x 72in (244 x 183cm).
$10,200–11,600 ⚒ **S**

A Gendje rug, west Caucasus, slight damage, c1880, 82 x 51in (208.5 x 129.5cm).
$2,900–3,200 ⊞ **DNo**

A Bordjalou Kazak prayer rug, Caucasus, c1880, 72 x 50in (183 x 127cm).
$3,200–3,600 ⊞ **DNo**

◀ **A Karachov Kazak rug,** Caucasus, damaged, late 19thC, 96 x 52in (244 x 132cm).
$6,000–7,500 ⚒ **SK(B)**

A Konya prayer rug, central Anatolia, damaged, repaired, 18thC, 65 x 46in (165 x 117cm).
$16,000–19,000 ⚒ **SK(B)**

A Marasali Shirvan prayer rug, Caucasus, damaged, c1890, 65 x 49in (165 x 124.5cm).
$5,800–6,500 ⊞ **DNo**

◀ **A Baku** *boteh-khila* **carpet,** east Caucasus, damaged, late 19thC, 148 x 62in (376 x 157.5cm).
$5,500–5,800 ⚒ **SK(B)**

A *Soumakh* **carpet,** east Caucasus, c1885, 108 x 84in (274.5 x 213.5cm).
$7,500–9,000 ⊞ **GY**

A Heriz carpet, north-west Persia,
c1900, 161 x 111in (409 x 282cm).
$9,000–10,000 ➶ SLN

A Karaja carpet, north-west Persia,
c1920, 162 x 111in (411.5 x 282cm).
$1,750–2,000 ➶ Bon(C)

A Bakhtiyari carpet, west Persia,
c1910, 163 x 127in (414 x 322.5cm).
$10,900–12,000 ➶ S(S)

A Senneh pictorial rug, west Persia,
light damage, c1900, 72 x 56in
(183 x 142cm).
$1,300–1,500 ⊞ DNo

A Ziegler Sultanabad carpet, west Persia,
c1910, 165 x 172in (419 x 437cm).
$14,500–17,500 ⊞ GY

A Feraghan Sarouk carpet,
north Persia, c1900,
105 x 142in (266 x 360cm).
$16,000–17,400 ➶ BB(S)

A Shiraz rug, south-west Persia, outer guard
strips missing, c1910, 50 x 35in (127 x 89cm).
$350–400 ⊞ DNo

◀ A Yezd pushti, south Persia, c1920,
29 x 23in (73.5 x 58.5cm).
$750–950 ⊞ LIN

A pair of Kashan rugs,
central Persia, c1900,
83 x 53in (211 x 134.5cm).
$6,400–7,300 ⊞ DNo

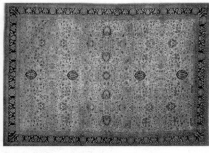

An Indian carpet, c1920, 237 x 172in
(602 x 437cm).
$8,700–9,500 ➶ BB(S)

A Chinese carpet, late 19thC,
208 x 143in (528.5 x 363cm).
$4,600–5,000 ➶ SLN

▶ An Agra rug, north India, early 20thC,
80 x 59in (203 x 150cm).
$1,750–1,850 ➶ WW

A silk patchwork quilt, dated 1718, 65 x 74in (165 x 188cm). **$4,600–5,000** ✗ DN

An American pieced and appliquéd *broderie perse* **quilt,** by Mrs Freeland, on a linen ground, c1830, 99 x 114in (251.5 x 289.5cm). **$5,500–6,000** ✗ S(NY)

A Bochara silk *susani,* Uzbekistan, 1840–60, 88 x 58in (223.5 x 147.5cm). **$8,000–9,000** ⊞ LIN

An American embroidered wool coverlet, by Rebecca C. Hayward, the back with original 19thC paisley material, Winchendon, Massachusetts, c1849, 99¼ x 86½in (252 x 219.5cm). **$18,800–22,500** ✗ SK(B)

A Bochara *susani,* the cotton ground embroidered with silks, Uzbekistan, mid-19thC, 99 x 64in (251.5 x 162.5cm). **$5,500–5,800** ✗ P

A Victorian strip-work hand-stitched quilt, 84 x 70in (213.5 x 178cm). **$120–150** ⊞ DE

A Welsh red paisley quilt, slight damage, Carmarthenshire, c1880, 84 x 68in (213.5 x 172.5cm). **$400–450** ⊞ JJ

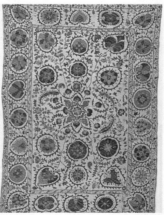

A Bochara *susani,* Uzbekistan, late 19thC, 96 x 66in (244 x 167.5cm). **$2,300–2,900** ✗ S

An American wool flannel and cotton Amish bar quilt, probably Lancaster County, Pennsylvania, late 19thC, 84 x 76in (213.5 x 193cm). **$4,300–5,000** ✗ S(NY)

A hand-stitched patchwork quilt, c1930, 88 x 84in (223.5 x 213.5cm). **$150–180** ⊞ DE

▶ **An American pieced calico school house quilt,** c1930, 74 x 75in (188 x 190.5cm). **$4,000–4,500** ✗ S(NY) It appears that these log cabin school houses were made in the 1930s; the bright blue sashings and the quilting was done more recently.

An American embroidered cotton and wool quilt top, Kentucky, dated 1922, 83 x 74in (211 x 188cm). **$2,200–2,600** ✗ SK(B)

A needlework pillow cover, early 18thC, 23 x 33in (58.5 x 84cm).
$10,200–11,500 ⊞ MGa

A George II needlepoint panel, damaged, 37¼ x 41in (94.5 x 104cm), within an 18thC Continental walnut fire screen.
$1,500–1,900 ⚒ Bon

A silver-wire and coloured silk embroidered wallet-style pouch, with ink label attached inscribed 'Embroidered case the work of Lady Jane Grey - Miss Skipworth', 17thC, 4¼ x 2¾in (11 x 7cm) closed.
$1,200–1,500 ⚒ P(WM)

A silk needlework picture of flowers, c1810, 12in (30.5cm) wide, framed.
$650–750 ⊞ PSC

A Brussels tapestry cushion, 16thC, 17 x 18in (43 x 45.5cm).
$2,600–3,000 ⊞ MGa

A wool and silk picture, depicting a rustic scene, possibly Continental, late 18thC, 12 x 14in (30.5 x 35.5cm), framed.
$1,600–1,900 ⊞ WWo

A Flemish tapestry, depicting a woodland clearing, 17thC, 113½ x 100in (288.5 x 254cm), enclosed by a later border of exotic birds, vases issuing flowers and trailing vines.
$8,700–10,000 ⚒ P(Ed)

A fragment of Flanders tapestry, depicting a scene from The Iliad, late 17thC, 96 x 85in (244 x 216cm).
$8,700–9,500 ⚒ S(Mon)

A Bruges tapestry, depicting the discovery of the infant Oedipus, early 17thC, 137 x 98in (348 x 249cm).
$13,000–16,000 ⚒ S(NY)

An Aubusson garden tapestry, left border restored, early 18thC, 78 x 92½in (198 x 235cm).
$8,700–9,700 ⚒ S(Z)

◄ A Brussels genre tapestry panel, depicting a rustic scene, early 18thC, 110 x 124in (279.5 x 315cm).
$13,000–16,000 ⚒ S(NY)

► A pastoral tapestry, with swags of flowers and hunting trophies around a panel depicting a maiden with horse and sheep, probably Berlin, 108¼ x 104¼in (275 x 265cm).
$8,700–10,000 ⚒ P(Z)

An Aubusson chinoiserie tapestry panel, 18thC, 79 x 100in (200.5 x 254cm).
$15,200–17,200 ⚒ S(NY)

COLOUR REVIEW

A George III sampler, worked with 'The Garden of Eden', by Martha Twine, 17 x 12¾in (43 x 32.5cm), framed.
$1,900–2,300 ⚡ CAG

A sampler, by Esther Baldwin, dated 1833, 17 x 13in (43 x 33cm).
$2,000–2,200 ⊞ SEA

An asylum school darning sampler, by Esther Walker, 1841, 17 x 15in (43 x 38cm), framed.
$6,500–7,300 ⊞ HIS

A Victorian woolwork sampler, by Mary Porter, dated 1857, 24in (61cm) square, in a rosewood frame.
$800–950 ⚡ Hal(C)

An American sampler, by Ann Borton, New Jersey, embroidered in silk on a gauze ground, dated 1820, 20½ x 21in (52 x 53.5cm).
$50,000–60,000 ⚡ S(NY)

A sampler, by Jane Davis, 1836, 10¾ x 12in (27.5 x 30.5cm), mounted on a cushion.
$750–900 ⚡ CAG

A sampler, embroidered with spot motifs including Jim Crow, c1850, 17 x 15in (43 x 38cm), framed.
$700–750 ⊞ PSC
Jim Crow was a character in a popular 19th century plantation song. The name was later used to describe the practise of racial segregation in the United States.

A woolwork sampler, by Mary Simpson, c1860, 17in (43cm) square.
$370–450 ⊞ JPr

▶ **A Victorian sampler,** by Alice Sarah Farrer, 1887, 26 x 20in (66 x 51cm), in a gilt slip and oak frame.
$750–900 ⚡ PFK

A sampler, by Sarah Lewin, worked in silks on linen, 1827, 15½ x 12¼in (39.5 x 31cm), in a bird's-eye maple frame.
$1,200–1,400 ⚡ HAM

A sampler, by Jane Harry, the centre worked with cross-stitch, the border of raised-work embroidery, 1836, 17¾ x 12¼in (45 x 31cm), framed.
$6,500–8,000 ⚡ Bea(E)

A sampler, by Ann Snow, 1836, 20¾ x 24¾in (52.5 x 63cm), framed.
$1,900–2,300 ⚡ Bri

A fan, the leaf with a scene of the Return of the Prodigal Son, with oiled and gilded mother-of-pearl guard sticks, c1740, 10in (25.5cm) wide, in a glazed case.
$950–1,200 ✗ DN

A Cantonese ivory brisé fan, the leaf painted with a coat-of-arms, flanked by lilies and magnolia panels, c1790, 10¼in (26cm) wide, with original card case, lacking cover.
$1,500–1,650 ✗ S(S)

A fan, the leaf painted with the Finding of Moses, with pierced mother-of-pearl sticks, c1740, 10in (25.5cm) wide.
$1,200–1,500 ⊞ LDC

A fan, the leaf painted on the front with a classical scene of Venus, Mars and other figures, the sticks and guards with silver piqué decoration, 18thC, 10½in (26.5cm) wide.
$1,750–2,000 ✗ WW

A fan, the leaf painted with a woodland scene, with ivory sticks, faults, late 18thC, 10in (25.5cm) wide.
$500–600 ✗ P

A fan, the paper leaf painted with a figural scene, with mother-of-pearl sticks, c1860, 10¾in (27.5cm) wide.
$500–600 ✗ P

▶ A Spanish lithographic fan, depicting a courtly scene, with ivory sticks and mother-of-pearl guard sticks, c1850, 10½in (26.5cm) wide.
$450–580 ⊞ LDC

A fan, the leaf depicting a woodland scene, late 19thC, 10in (25.5cm) wide, with white silk-covered box labelled 'J. Duvelleroy, London'.
$400–450 ✗ TMA

A gold and coral bracelet, terminating in turquoise set hands, c1820, 6½in (16.5cm) long.
$1,400–1,600 ↗ S(S)

A gold, citrine and hardstone bracelet, c1860, 7½in (19cm) long.
$500–600 ↗ S

A Victorian gold bangle, set with diamond and enamel star motifs, c1860.
$1,600–1,800 ⊞ RES

An enamelled gold, coral and diamond hinged bangle, 19thC.
$750–900 ↗ DN

◄ **A Victorian turquoise and gold flexible bracelet,** c1865.
$1,500–1,600 ⊞ RES

A Victorian gold hinged bangle, set with half-pearl trefoils.
$600–700 ↗ RTo

A Victorian enamel-decorated gold hinged bangle, set with emeralds, diamonds and cultured pearls.
$700–900 ↗ FHF

◄ **A 15ct gold and turquoise bracelet,** c1880.
$230–290 ↗ LJ

A Bohemian silver-gilt and garnet bangle, c1880.
$230–290 ↗ LJ

► **A 15ct gold, opal and diamond bangle,** c1900.
$400–480 ↗ LJ

A gold bracelet, mounted with turquoise-studded gold spheres and a matching locket, c1880.
$1,700–2,000 ↗ WW

An Italian *pietra dura* bracelet, set in gold, c1840, 1¼in (3cm) wide, in original box.
$1,200–1,300 ⊞ Ma

A Victorian pearl and diamond gold bangle, c1860.
$2,900–3,300 ⊞ RES

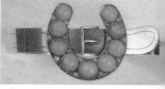

A Victorian coral and gold bangle, c1875.
$2,500–2,800 ⊞ RES

A Victorian gold, natural pearls and enamel bangle, 2½in (6.5cm) wide, in original box.
$3,600–4,000 ⊞ WIM

A Victorian half-pearl hinged bangle, 2¼in (5.5cm) diam.
$1,000–1,300 ↗ Bon

◄ **A Bohemian silver-gilt and garnet bracelet,** c1930, 1in (2.5cm) wide.
$750–850 ⊞ Ma

An enamelled gold, rose diamond and seed-pearl brooch, mid-19thC. $1,000–1,200 ➶ Bea(E)

A Victorian 15ct gold and natural-pearl brooch, 1in (2.5cm) wide. $2,000–2,250 ⊞ WIM

A Victorian citrine brooch, in engraved silver mount. $550–650 ➶ P(Ed)

An aquamarine, white enamel and ruby brooch, 1880–1900, 1½in (4cm) wide. $4,000–4,700 ⊞ ANTH

► A late Victorian tourmaline and diamond brooch. $3,000–3,500 ➶ P(Sy)

A Scottish silver and citrine brooch, c1860, 2½in (6.5cm) diam. $900–1,100 ⊞ BWA

A butterfly brooch, set with diamond chips, sapphires, rubies and half-pearls, c1880. $600–750 ➶ P(L)

► A Victorian Etruscan-style gold and lapis lazuli brooch, 2½in (6.5cm) long. $1,600–1,750 ➶ L

A Victorian sapphire and diamond horseshoe brooch. $3,000–3,500 ➶ HYD

An emerald and diamond-mounted dragonfly brooch, with ruby eyes, 19thC. $2,300–2,900 ➶ Bea(E)

A 15ct gold and amethyst brooch, c1860. $400–450 ➶ LJ

A Victorian gold brooch and pendant, set with amethysts. $800–950 ➶ L&T

A Victorian bee brooch, set with diamonds, rubies and a synthetic citrine, c1880, 1¼in (3cm) wide. $330–370 ⊞ GLa

A late Victorian amethyst and diamond shamrock brooch, 1¼in (3cm) wide. $1,700–2,000 ➶ Bon

A gold, enamel and diamond butterfly brooch, with ruby eyes, c1900. $1,800–$2,200 ➶ S(S)

A cameo brooch, with 15ct gold mount, c1830, 3in (7.5cm) wide.
$600–750 ⊞ Ma

An Italian hardstone cameo brooch and earrings set, the gold mounts set with seed pearls, c1880.
$3,600–4,000 ⊞ BeE

A Victorian shell cameo, in a modern 9ct gold brooch mount.
$600–800 ✎ P(L)

A cameo brooch, mounted in pinchbeck, c1880, 2in (5cm) diam.
$330–360 ⊞ GLa

A cameo brooch, in an 18ct gold frame, mounted in a rotating panel with locket section to reverse, c1880, with original fitted leather case.
$430–500 ✎ LJ

A pair of Russian chalcedony cufflinks, by A. Gorianov, St Petersburg, with enamelled gold mounts, 1896–1908, ¾in (2cm) diam.
$6,500–7,250 ✎ S

A pair of 15ct gold tassel earrings, set with seed pearls, c1860.
$750–800 ✎ LJ

A pair of Victorian gold earrings, set with a blue enamel star and single half-pearl.
$700–850 ✎ B&L

A pair of late Victorian Etruscan-style 15ct gold earrings, 2in (5cm) long.
$2,600–2,900 ⊞ BeE

A gold and enamel ring, with a portrait of King William III, late 18thC.
$750–900 ⊞ JSM

A George III memorial ring, with woven hair panel and black and white enamel decoration to the underside.
$370–450 ✎ FHF

A Victorian diamond and enamel ring.
$2,300–2,600 ⊞ WIM

A Victorian 18ct gold and emerald ring.
$4,600–5,000 ⊞ WIM

A sapphire, emerald and diamond ring, 19thC.
$500–600 ✎ Bea(E)

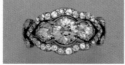

A diamond ring, 19thC.
$5,000–5,800 ✎ S

A cultured pearl and diamond ring, c1900.
$1,600–1,900 ✎ S(G)

An opal and diamond ring, c1925.
$5,000–6,000 ✎ S

◀ **A pink topaz parure,** early 19thC, in fitted case. $4,300–5,000 ⚒ WW

A Georgian gold and garnet necklace, with detachable quatrefoil brooch, bar brooch, stickpin and flowerhead ear studs, with two hair pins, cased. $2,900–3,500 ⚒ HAM

A gold cannetille necklace, set with a foiled topaz, emeralds, rubies and diamonds, c1820, 15½in (39.5cm) long, in fitted case. $4,000–4,600 ⚒ S

A gold, enamel, pearl and diamond demi-parure, 1865–70, in original fitted case. $6,500–8,000 ⚒ P(L)

An aquamarine and 9ct gold necklace, c1900. $580–750 ⚒ LJ

A diamond-set enamel and gold locket pendant, c1800, 2½in (6.5cm) long. $4,300–5,000 ⚒ L

A Victorian turquoise enamel, gold and half-pearl pendant locket, on an 18ct gold chain. $600–700 ⚒ B&L

A Victorian sapphire and diamond brooch pendant, in gold fronted with silver. $1,400–1,800 ⚒ TEN

An Australian tourmaline, seed pearl and 15ct gold necklace and earring suite, hallmarked by Willis & Sons, c1900. $600–750 ⚒ LJ

An Edwardian opal and diamond pendant, c1905. $4,000–4,600 ⚒ HAM

A diamond, turquoise and white gold pendant, c1890, 2in (5cm) long. $5,000–4,800 ⊞ BeE

An 18ct gold, almandine, garnet and diamond teardrop and bow pendant, c1900, 20in (51cm) long. $1,000–1,200 ⊞ GLa

▶ **An Edwardian aquamarine, ruby and seed pearl pendant.** $550–650 ⚒ P(L)

An Edwardian 15ct gold, citrine and half-pearl pendant. $600–750 ⚒ B&L

A Swiss pearl, gold and enamel snuff box, some damage to enamel of lid, Geneva, c1790, 3½in (9cm) wide.
$5,000–6,000 ⚒ S

A silver and pink enamel compact/ pill case, import mark for London 1926, 2½in (6.5cm) long.
$580–650 ⊞ BEX

A pair of Russian silver-gilt *champlevé* **enamel salt cellars,** maker's mark BK, St Petersburg, c1890, 2½in (6.5cm) diam.
$2,350–2,600 ⊞ NS

A Fabergé silver-gilt and enamel miniature frame, workmaster M. Perchin, St Petersburg, with ivory back, Russia, before 1896, 4½in (11.5cm) high, in original fitted wooden case.
$40,500–46,500 ⚒ S

A Bilston enamel patch box, c1840, 2in (5cm) long.
$600–650 ⊞ BAO

An enamel nutmeg grater, with gilt-metal mounts, early 19thC, 2in (5cm) high.
$750–900 ⚒ Bon

A Bilston enamel snuff box, with metal rim and hinge, early 19thC, 1¾in (4.5cm) long.
$1,200–1,400 ⚒ L&E

A Fabergé silver and enamel photograph frame, workmaster A. Nevalainen, St Petersburg, Russia, 1896–1908, 7½in (19cm) high.
$58,000–65,000 ⚒ S

◀ **A Swiss gold, mother-of-pearl and enamel** *aide-mémoire,* c1850, 2½in (6.5cm) wide.
$9,800–10,800 ⊞ SHa

A Limoges enamel box, France, c1880, 3in (7.5cm) wide.
$1,600–1,800 ⊞ SHa

A Limoges enamel plaque, France, c1900, 5in (12.5cm) diam.
$1,200–1,300 ⊞ OND

A pair of Russian silver-gilt cloisonné enamel serving spoons, by Alexander Lyubavin, St Petersburg, 1896–1908, 7¾in (19.5cm) long.
$2,300–2,500 ⊞ NS

A gold and enamel snuff box, the lid applied with an earlier enamel miniature of King George I, probably Geneva, c1770, 3¼in (8.5cm) wide.
$9,500–11,500 ⚒ S

A French gold and turquoise pill box, in the shape of a lady's fob watch, c1800, 1½in (4cm) diam.
$2,600–2,900 ⊞ BEX

A Canton enamel *famille rose* clock face, early 19thC, 10¼in (26cm) wide.
$800–950 ➶ S(NY)

A Chinese cloisonné enamel dish, slight wear, 16th/17thC, 12¼in (31cm) diam.
$880–1,200 ➶ P

A Chinese cloisonné enamel censer and cover, 19thC, 3½in (9cm) high.
$320–360 ➶ LJ

A Japanese brass and copper cloisonné vase, slight damage, Meiji period, 1868–1911, 19¾in (50cm) high.
$1,000–1,200 ➶ P(Sy)

A Japanese cloisonné vase, Ando Jubei mark, Meiji period, 1868–1911, 9¾in (25cm) high.
$600–750 ➶ WW

A pair of Chinese cloisonné ducks, c1900, 10in (25.5cm) long.
$2,600–2,900 ⊞ BeE

▶ A Chinese jadeite vase and cover, carved with a dragon coiled round the shoulder chasing a flaming pearl, above incised waves, c1800, 4½in (11.5cm) high.
$7,250–8,700 ➶ S

A Chinese aventurine-splashed blue Beijing glass censer, incised mark and period of Qianlong, 1736–95, 4¾in (12cm) wide.
$43,500–47,500 ➶ S

A Japanese blue lacquered fan-shaped box, with four graduating stacking storage compartments, c1860, 15in (38cm) high.
$1,750–2,200 ➶ P(Sy)

◀ A Japanese relief-carved lacquer 'flower basket' wall vase, the back decorated with a peacock on a prunus branch in gilt lacquer, slight wear, Meiji period, 1868–1911, 35½in (90cm) high.
$1,300–1,600 ➶ P

A Chinese parcel-gilt-bronze tripod incense burner, Qing Dynasty, 9½in (24cm) high, with carved *huanghuali* stand and cover.
$2,200–2,600 ➶ RTo

◀ An Indian parquetry wooden box, with hinged fall-front, decorated in ivory, the interior with six drawers, 17thC, 12in (30.5cm) wide.
$5,000–6,000 ➶ Bon

A Japanese red lacquered *tatami hikone gusoku*, Edo period, 1600–1868.
$24,600–29,000 ✗ BB(S)

A Japanese lacquered-metal *ryubu men*, the metal throat guard laced with silk, Edo period, 1600–1868.
$2,200–2,350 ✗ BB(S)

◄ **A Japanese *ken*,** in cloisonné enamel mounts, 19thC, 15in (38cm) long.
$8,700–10,000 ✗ S

An Indian painted papier mâché powder flask, Mughal or Deccan, c1700, 7¼in (18.5cm) diam.
$2,300–2,900 ✗ Bon

A Japanese red lacquer four-case *inro*, the lower case with inner divisions, 18thC, 3¾in (9.5cm) high.
$1,600–1,900 ✗ S

◄ **A Japanese gilt and red lacquered four-case *inro*,** signed Bunryusai (Kajikawa Bunryusai), slight wear, 19thC, 3¼in (8.5cm) high.
$2,900–3,500 ✗ P

An Indian gem-set and enamel gold necklace and earrings, each set with diamonds, rubies and emeralds, early 20thC, necklace 7in (18cm) diam.
$4,300–5,000 ✗ Bon

A *Shibayama* ivory *manjua netsuke*, signed, Meiji period, 1868–1911, 2in (5cm) diam.
$1,600–1,800 ✗ P

A Chinese turquoise glass overlay snuff bottle, 19thC, 3½in (9cm) high.
$4,000–4,600 ✗ BB(S)

A Chinese formal silk court robe, with woven chocolate brown and coloured silks and gold thread, late 19thC.
$5,000–6,000 ✗ P

A Chinese tourmaline bottle, carved with a bat with outstretched wings, 1820–1900, 2in (5cm) high.
$3,500–4,300 ✗ S

A Chinese Imperial Yellow silk throne cushion cover, with yellow silk lining, mid-19thC, 40½ x 50½in (103 x 128.5cm).
$5,800–6,500 ✗ P

◄ **A Chinese silk and wool embroidered wall hanging,** late 19thC, 78¾ x 62¼in (200 x 158cm).
$1,300–1,600 ✗ RTo

▶ A Chinese lacquered wood figure of an official, with tufts of hair attached for the beard and moustache, c1600, 34¼in (87cm) high.
$5,000–5,800 ✗ S(Am)

A Chinese bronze mythical beast, modelled with a paw in his mouth, 17thC, 2in (5cm) long.
$950–1,200 ⊞ GLD

A Chinese gilt-bronze seated Buddha, lacking base, late Ming Dynasty, 17thC, 13¼in (33.5cm) high.
$8,000–8,700 ✗ BB(S)

A Sino-Tibetan giltwood figure of Garuda, 18thC, 20½in (52cm) high.
$5,800–7,250 ✗ S(NY)

◀ A Japanese Tokyo School ivory figure of a fisherman, signed Hozan, Meiji period, 1868–1911, 13in (33cm) high.
$8,700–9,500 ⊞ LBO

A Chinese carved nephrite group of an elephant and boy, c1800, 5½in (14cm) high.
$11,300–13,000 ✗ BB(S)

A Japanese gilt-bronze koro, in the shape of a crouching shishi, c1860, 9in (23cm) high.
$1,900–2,200 ⊞ PCA

▶ A Japanese ivory okimono of a fisherman, signed Tomomine, rod replaced, Meiji period, 1858–1911, 9in (23cm) high.
$1,400–1,600 ✗ S(S)

A Japanese ivory figural group, Meiji period, 1868–1911, 16½in (42cm) high.
$9,500–11,500 ✗ L&E

A Japanese bronze model of a hawk, with gilt eyes, minor damage, Meiji period, 1868–1911, 9½in (24cm) long.
$580–750 ✗ WW

A Japanese wood okimono of a rat catcher, 19thC, 3in (7.5cm) high.
$4,000–4,500 ✗ P(B)

A Japanese bronze group, modelled as an elephant being attacked by two tigers, on a hardwood base, c1900, 21¼in (54cm) long.
$2,200–2,400 ✗ P(S)

A **Chinese red lacquer and gilt marriage bed,** the interior panel painting depicting mythical scenes and characters, c1830, 96in (244cm) square.
$7,250–8,700 ⊞ SeH

A **Chinese export child's bamboo chair,** late 19thC.
$180–220 ⊞ MLu

An **Indian carved hardwood cabinet,** c1850, 49in (124.5cm) wide.
$5,000–5,800 ⊞ APO

◀ A **polychrome painted cabinet,** possibly Tibetan, late 19thC, 39in (99cm) wide.
$2,600–3,200 ↗ NOA

An **Anglo-Japanese parquetry cylinder-top bureau cabinet,** late 19thC, 55in (139.5cm) wide.
$8,700–10,000 ↗ P(Ed)

◀ A **pair of Chinese walnut official's chairs,** Shanxi Province, c1820.
$1,750–1,900 ⊞ OE

A **pair of northern China elm scholar's cap chairs,** early 19thC.
$1,500–1,900 ⊞ K

▶ A **Japanese lacquer chest on legs,** decorated in gold *takamakie* and *kirigane* over a *nashiji* ground, c1800, 31¼in (79.5cm) long.
$7,600–8,400 ↗ S

A **Singhalese Dutch colonial-style carved ebony cabinet,** 19thC, 51½in (131cm) high.
$4,000–4,600 ↗ TEN

A **pair of Chinese *huanghuali* chairs,** the seats formerly caned, restored, 18thC.
$4,350–5,000 ↗ BB(S)

An **Indian silver throne,** c1860.
$11,600–13,000 ⊞ Q&C
This throne belonged to the Maharaja of Balrampur.

◄ A Chinese export nailed-hide and poly-chrome painted chest, 19thC, 44in (112cm) long.
$5,500–6,000 ➚ S

► A Korean brass-mounted elm marriage chest, 19thC, 35½in (90cm) wide.
$880–1,200 ➚ HAM

A Chinese export lacquer fall-front writing desk, inlaid with mother-of-pearl, shell and gilding, minor damage, 19thC, 23¼in (59cm) wide.
$3,900–4,400 ➚ S(Am)

A Chinese 11-fold coromandel screen, 18thC, 112in (284.5cm) high.
$19,500–21,500 ➚ S(NY)

► A Chinese *huanghuali* wood table screen, late 19thC, 25¼in (64cm) high.
$600–750 ➚ SAS

A southern China bamboo altar table, with black lacquer top, 19thC, 87in (221cm) long.
$3,600–4,300 ⊞ K

A Japanese gilt-copper-mounted black and gilt lacquer *hioke*, containing a copper basin, some damage, 19thC, 22in (56cm) long.
$3,200–3,600 ➚ BB(S)

A southern China elm altar table, late 19thC, 43½in (110.5cm) long.
$800–900 ⊞ GHC

A pair of Chinese hard-wood stands, c1860, 20in (51cm) high.
$2,350–2,650 ⊞ REI

A Chinese fruitwood altar table, 19thC, 41in (104cm) long.
$1,000–1,200 ⊞ OE

◄ A Tibetan elm scripture table, early 20thC, 29in (73.5cm) long.
$1,500–1,600 ⊞ OE

► A Colonial padouk wood sewing table, c1890, 30in (76cm) long.
$800–900 ➚ Bon(W)

An Ayyubid pottery bowl, Raqqa, Syria, 13thC, 9in (23cm) diam.
$18,850–22,500 ✗ S

An Iznik pottery jug, Turkey, late 16thC, handle restored, 8¼in (21cm) high.
$11,600–13,600 ✗ Bon

A Kubachi polychrome dish, north-west Persia, c1600, 13¼in (33.5cm) diam.
$7,250–8,000 ✗ S

An Iznik pottery dish, depicting a piebald horse, minor damage, 17thC, 10½in (26.5cm) diam.
$6,400–7,250 ✗ P

A Safavid green-glazed pottery bottle, Persia, early 17thC, 4¾in (12cm) high.
$4,350–5,000 ✗ Bon

A Safavid underglaze and slip-painted pottery dish, Persia, 1673, 10¼in (26cm) diam.
$20,300–23,200 ✗ Bon

A fragment of a celestial sphere, depicting the signs of the Zodiac, in gouache on paper laid down on canvas, with later textile backing, probably retouched at a later date, Timurid, Persia, late 15thC, 15¾in (40cm) diam.
$5,500–6,500 ✗ Bon

An Ottoman diamond-set and enamel gold bracelet, Turkey, 19thC, 6½in (16.5cm) long.
$5,800–6,500 ✗ Bon

◄ **An illustration from a manuscript of Persian poetry,** depicting a prince taking refreshments while seated in a landscape, in gouache with gold on paper, attributable to Muhammad Qasim, Isfahan, Persia, early 17thC, re-margined miniature 8 x 5in (20.5 x 12.5cm).
$13,750–16,000 ✗ S

An Ottoman parquetry wood scribe's pen box, with sliding lid, decorated in mother-of-pearl, tortoiseshell, bone, various woods and metal strips, c1800, 12¼in (31cm) long.
$1,300–1,600 ✗ Bon

An Ottoman jade-hilted diamond and emerald-set presentation dagger, Ottoman Empire and India, the blade 1664–65 and later, 18in (45.5cm) long.
$9,500–11,600 ✗ S

A pair of Süleymaniye covered dishes, enamelled and gilded on a copper body, with later wood-gilt finials, Turkey, c1800, 8½in (21.5cm) diam.
$12,300–14,500 ✗ S

▶ **An Ottoman painted wood panel,** with integral frame, Turkey, 19thC, 26¾ x 36¾in (68 x 93.5cm).
$2,200–2,600 ✗ Bon

A pair of cast-iron garden seats, c1820, 38in (96.5cm) wide. $2,000–2,300 ⊞ HON

◀ A pair of cast-iron garden urns, early 19thC, 27¼in (69cm) high. $1,250–1,500 ⚹ P(E)

A brass polychrome enamelled sundial plate, early 20thC, 13 x 12in (33 x 30.5cm). $1,500–1,750 ⚹ S(S)

A rouge marble door surround, applied with ormolu mounts, early 20thC, 67in (170cm) wide. $3,350–3,750 ⚹ S(S)

A stoneware finial, in the shape of a crown, some cracks, probably Coadstone, c1830, 17in (43cm) high. $2,600–2,900 ⚹ S(S)

A rose marble font, 1860, 46in (117cm) high. $5,000–5,500 ⊞ APO

A lead garden figure of a putto, on a concrete plinth, damaged, early 20thC, 49in (124.5cm) high. $2,200–2,600 ⚹ RBB

A composite stone eagle, 1920s, 33in (84cm) high. $1,200–1,350 ⊞ Recl

A pair of Victorian fireclay garden lions, by R. Brown & Son, Paisley, 41¾in (106cm) long. $5,800–7,250 ⚹ P(Ed)

▶ A Royal Doulton stoneware wash-down closet, Improved Pedestal Simplicitas, with raised acanthus-leaf decoration, late 19thC, 16in (40.5cm) high. $870–950 ⊞ DOR

A wooden well bucket, with iron banding, 19thC, 19in (48.5cm) high, on later stand. $450–500 ⊞ MLL

A wooden summer house, with thatched roof and stained-glass windows, early 20thC, 83¾in (213cm) wide. $2,200–2,600 ⚹ P(L)

▶ A floral-painted lavatory pan, inscribed 'The Rivolite', c1880, 18in (45.5cm) high. $1,000–1,200 ⊞ WEL

Miller's is a price GUIDE not a price LIST

A Scottish George III pine and gesso fire surround, Edinburgh, 71½in (181.5cm) wide.
$2,300–2,900 ➶ P(Ed)

A George III-style cast-iron and steel grate, c1840, 34in (86.5cm) wide.
$2,400–2,700 ⊞ ASH

A cast-iron register grate, with original tiles, c1870, 40in (101.5cm) wide.
$1,750–1,900 ⊞ WRe

A cast-iron fireplace, with original tiles and brass trim, c1880, 40in (101.5cm) wide.
$1,300–1,450 ⊞ DOR

A carved pine fire surround, with added volutes, c1890, 107in (272cm) wide.
$10,000–11,500 ⊞ WRe

An Art Nouveau cast-iron fire surround, by G. A. Booth, Preston, with a marble mantel shelf and original tiles, shelf damaged, c1903, 45¾in (116cm) wide.
$1,450–1,750 ➶ TEN

An Edwardian copy of an earlier style oak fireplace surround, 73in (185.5cm) wide.
$2,900–3,200 ⊞ MIN

A late Victorian Adam-style brass and steel fire grate, 35in (89cm) wide.
$4,500–5,000 ➶ P

◀ **A French Louis-XVI-style cast-brass** *chenet* **fender,** c1870, 50in (127cm) wide.
$1,000–1,150 ⊞ ASH

A Louis XVI-style burnished cast-iron and brass fire basket, c1920, 30in (76cm) wide.
$870–950 ⊞ ASH

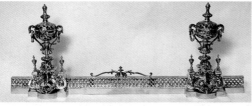

A brass fender, on lion's paw feet, 19thC, 45¼in (115cm) wide.
$1,150–1,300 ➶ P

A brass fender, with cut and engraved tooling, c1890, 54in (137cm) wide.
$2,200–2,400 ⊞ ASH

◀ **A pair of brass and iron decorative fire dogs,** 19thC, 21in (53.5cm) long.
$870–1,000 ⊞ SEA

▶ **A brass coal scuttle,** c1870, 28in (71cm) long.
$350–380 ⊞ ASH

An Edwardian brass folding fireguard, 37¾in (96cm) wide.
$440–500 ➶ Bea(E)

A Burgundian carved marble group of the Adoration, c1480, 6in (15cm) wide.
$18,000–20,000 ⊞ AEF

A French ivory portrait plaque of King Louis XIV, c1670, 4in (10cm) wide.
$5,000–5,500 ⊞ AEF

A pair of south German ivory figures of musicians, c1820, 12in (30.5cm) high, on carved wooden plinths.
$6,000–7,000 ⊞ LBO

A late Romanesque polychrome pinewood Madonna and Child, Roussillon, 13thC, 35¼in (89.5cm) high.
$22,000–26,000 ⚒ S(Z)

A pair of French bronze models of bulls, entitled Un Taureau Cadre, and Un Taureau se Défendant, by Antoine-Louis Barye, c1880, 11in (28cm) high.
$37,500–43,500 ⊞ RGa
These models were of the highest quality and therefore stamped with a gold seal by the foundry.

A jewelled carved ivory figure of Kunigunde of Bavaria, Austrian or south German, late 19thC, 11½in (29cm) high.
$10,000–11,500 ⚒ S

An Italian carved Carrara marble figure of Cupid, by Pio Fedi, 1875, 31in (78.5cm) high.
$8,000–8,800 ⚒ P(S)

A gilt-bronze and patinated-bronze model of Joan of Arc, by Raoul François Larche, signed, 32¼in (82cm) high.
$4,300–5,000 ⚒ P

A French bronze figure of David, signed A. Mercie, with one foot resting on the head of Goliath, 19thC, 28¼in (72cm) high.
$6,000–7,000 ⚒ LJ

An ivory figure of Titania, with Puck and Bottom at her feet, 19thC, 21in (53.5cm) high.
$8,700–9,500 ⊞ LBO

A pair of bronze models of Marly horses, on ebonized boulle work plinths, 19thC, 23¼in (59cm) high.
$3,300–4,000 ⚒ HAM

An Austrian bronze group of a tiger hunt, on a marble plinth, damaged, c1900, 10½in (26.5cm) high.
$1,000–1,300 ⚒ Bon(M)

◄ **An Italian alabaster figure,** after a model by Pugi, c1900, 20½in (52cm) high.
$2,900–3,200 ⚒ TEN

A Tunbridge ware box, inlaid with cubes and Van Dyke borders, c1830, 11in (28cm) wide.
$1,450–1,750 ⊞ AMH

A Tunbridge ware box, inlaid with starburst motif and leaf mosaic borders, c1850, 7in (18cm) square.
$1,000–1,100 ⊞ VB

A Tunbridge ware glove box, 1860–70, 10in (25.5cm) long.
$400–450 ⊞ VBo

A Tunbridge ware stationery box, inlaid with floral mosaic, c1870, 8¼in (21cm) wide.
$1,000–1,150 ⊞ AMH

▶ **A Tunbridge ware caddy spoon,** mid-19thC, 4in (10cm) long.
$500–600 ⊞ PSA

A Tunbridge ware dressing table box, with pin cushion and perfume bottles, c1860, 9in (23cm) long.
$900–1,000 ⊞ TUN

A Tunbridge ware travelling inkwell, c1860, 3in (7.5cm) high.
$320–360 ⊞ VB

A Tunbridge ware photograph frame, late 19thC, 6in (15cm) wide.
$400–450 ⊞ TUN

A Tunbridge ware framed picture, inlaid with a picture of The Pantiles, Tunbridge Wells, mid-19thC, 9½in (24cm) wide.
$870–1,000 ⚒ S(S)

A Tunbridge ware sewing cabinet, the top inlaid with a picture of Bayham Abbey ruins, with three drawers, and sewing compartments in the lid, c1870, 9½in (24cm) wide.
$2,000–2,300 ⊞ AMH

A Tunbridge ware obelisk thermometer, c1880, 7in (18cm) high.
$230–250 ⊞ VBo

A Tunbridge ware humming top, c1850, 4in (10cm) long.
$580–650 ⊞ AMH

A Tunbridge ware rosewood tea caddy, inlaid with a picture of Tonbridge Castle, the interior with two lidded divisions, mid-19thC, 9¾in (25cm) wide.
$1,200–1,450 ⚒ S(S)

◀ **A Tunbridge ware rosewood tray,** with geometric veneers, repaired, damaged, c1830, 12in (30.5cm) long.
$725–800 ⊞ PSA

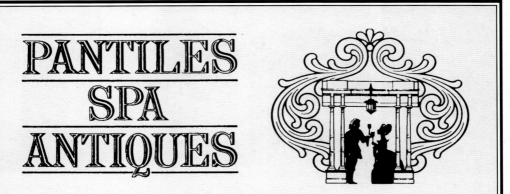

A Tudor brass candle-stick, mid-16thC, 13¼in (33.5cm) high.
$20,000–23,000 ➷ S(S)

A William IV copper samovar, surmounted with a hunting dog finial, c1835, 16½in (42cm) high.
$300–350 ➷ Hal(C)

A Louis XV ormolu *brûle-parfum*, attributed to the workshop of Jean Jacques Caffieri, mounted with Nevers glass figures and Vincennes flowers, France, c1750, 8in (20.5cm) high.
$12,500–14,000 ⊞ US

A pair of French ormolu and *griotte* marble tazzas, c1840, 15in (38cm) high.
$4,500–5,000 ➷ S(NY)

A Regency toleware tray, 25¾in (65.5cm) long.
$2,000–2,500 ➷ AH

A pair of black and gilt japanned toleware chestnut urns and coffee urn, early 19thC, chestnut urns 12¼in (31cm) high.
$8,500–9,500 ➷ S

A black lacquered papier mâché tea tray, early 19thC, 31in (78.5cm) wide.
$1,450–1,600 ➷ TMA

A Victorian lacquered papier mâché tray, 30in (76cm) wide.
$1,000–1,150 ⊞ TWr

A French boxwood and bone comb, losses, 4in (10cm) wide.
$7,250–8,000 ➷ S(NY)

A lignum vitae wassail bowl, 17thC, 11in (28cm) diam.
$5,000–6,000 ➷ RYA

◀ **A Dutch wooden snuff box,** in the form of a monk, 18thC, 5in (12.5cm) high.
$2,200–2,400 ⊞ AEF

A pair of Scottish carved wooden snuff boxes, depicting scenes from Robert Burns' poems, c1800, 6in (15cm) long.
$1,750–2,000 ⊞ BWA

A carved squirrel nut cracker, possibly sycamore, c1870, 6in (15cm) high.
$290–320 ⊞ MLa

A Scottish carved sycamore snuff box, depicting a Robert Burns scene, c1830, 6in (15cm) long.
$725–875 ⊞ TWr

An engine-turned fruitwood snuff or pill box, c1850, 3½in (9cm) diam.
$350–400 ⊞ SEA

Icons

A Russian icon of an Old Testament Prophet holding a scroll, the background stripped and the icon mounted in a later panel, 16thC, 14 x 12in (35.5 x 30.5cm).
$6,100–6,800 ⊞ ICO

A Russian icon of Christ Pantocrator, Karelian School, surrounded by miniature scenes of the orthodox festivals, c1650, 20 x 17in (51 x 43cm).
$7,200–8,000 ⊞ ICO

A Russian pierced bronze icon of St George slaying the Dragon, c1650, 3 x 2½in (7.5 x 6.5cm).
$500–600 ⊞ ICO

A Creto-Venetian icon of St George slaying the Dragon, the warrior saint on a grey charger, his red lance piercing the dragon's throat, 17thC, 10½ x 8½in (27 x 21.5cm).
$2,600–3,200 ⋟ P

> Items in the Icon section have been arranged in date order.

A Greek icon of the Deisis, depicting the enthroned Christ flanked by the Mother of God and John the Baptist, edges worn, c1700, 9¾ x 8¾in (25 x 22cm).
$2,000–2,300 ⋟ P

▶ **A Russian icon of the Fiery Ascension of the Prophet Elijah,** Palekh School, c1800, 12½ x 10½in (32 x 26.5cm).
$6,600–7,600 ⋟ JAA

A Russian icon of a young Prophet Saint, 17thC, 15 x 14in (38 x 35.5cm).
$4,000–4,700 ⊞ ICO

A Russian icon of Saints Zossima and Savaati, holding an image of their monastery, standing beneath the Mother of God of the Sign in nimbus, some repainting, c1800, 21 x 17¼in (53.5 x 44cm).
$1,300–1,600 ⋟ P

A Russian pierced bronze icon of St Nicholas of Mojuish, c1700, 3 x 2½in (7.5 x 6.5cm).
$580–650 ⊞ ICO

▶ **A Russian brass icon of Saints Zossima and Savaati,** surrounded by Saints and Prophets, c1820, 6 x 5in (15 x 12.5cm).
$290–320 ⊞ ICO

A Russian icon of St George slaying the Dragon, Princess Elisaba stands nearby, the border painted with four saints, 28 x 22½in (71 x 57cm).
$3,600–4,000 ↗ P

A Russian icon of the Resurrection, surrounded by festival scenes in miniature with the four Evangelists in the corners, mid-19thC, 14 x 12in (35.5 x 30.5cm).
$950–1,100 ⊞ ICO

A Russian icon of the Tikhvin Mother of God, with a multiple-piece silver-gilt riza with applied enamel halo and garments overlaid in silver filigree, hallmarked Moscow, 1908–17, 9½ x 8½in (24 x 21.5cm).
$5,800–7,200 ↗ JAA

Insurance values

Always insure your valuable antiques for the cost of replacing them with similar items, regardless of the original price paid. Both dealers and auctioneers will provide a valuation service for a fee.

▶ **A Russian brass quadratych,** decorated with festival scenes and four Venerations of the Virgin and Child, 19thC, each panel 7 x 4in (18 x 10cm).
$290–320 ⊞ ICO

A Russian icon of St George and the Dragon, 19thC, 7 x 5¾in (18 x 14.5cm).
$4,000–4,400 ⊞ RKa

An Imperial Russian icon, with silver mount, hallmarked, 1858, 4 x 3in (10 x 7.5cm).
$1,600–1,800 ⊞ SHa

A Russian brass and enamel icon of The Pokrov, 19thC, 6¾ x 3¾in (17 x 9.5cm).
$640–700 ⊞ RKa

A Russian icon of a crowned patriarch holding a Bible, oil on panel with a repoussé and engraved brass riza, 19thC, 6¼ x 5½in (16 x 14cm), in a gold-painted wooden frame within a glazed and hinged outer case.
$430–500 ↗ DW

A Russian miniature icon of St Nicholas, covered by a silver riza, Moscow marks, c1900, 2in (5cm) square.
$400–440 ⊞ ICO

A Russian icon of the Madonna and Child, Moscow School, oil on panel, the engraved silver oklad applied with blue enamel name plaques, hallmarked Moscow, maker's mark 'AE', early 20thC, 8 x 6¼in (20.5 x 16cm), in a black wooden frame.
$580–720 ↗ DW

Portrait Miniatures

A portrait miniature of Lady Beechey, a self-portrait, Miss Anne Phyllis Jessop, in white robes, hairline crack, the reverse signed and dated 1799, 2¾in (7cm) high, in a gilded wood frame.
$330–400 ⚒ P

An American portrait miniature of Julia Clarke Brewster, attributed to John Brewster Jr, Connecticut area, in original gilded copper locket case and original red leather case, c1820, 2¼in (5.5cm) high.
$5,000–6,000 ⚒ SK(B)
John Brewster Jr advertised in newspapers that he painted portraits for $15 and miniatures for $5.

A portrait miniature of a lady in a white dress, by J. Brown, signed with a monogram, the reverse with date, c1806, 2¾in (7cm) high.
$580–720 ⚒ CGC

A portrait miniature of the Hon Caroline Barrington, wearing a white dress, by Adam Buck, painted on card, signed and dated, 1820, 1½in (11.5cm) high, in a red leather travelling case.
$1,000–1,200 ⚒ Bon

A portrait miniature of a member of the Luard family, wearing a white dress decorated with bows, and leaning on a chair draped with a fur stole, pencil and watercolour on card, signed and dated 1835, 11½in (29cm) high.
$850–950 ⚒ P

An American portrait miniature of a young boy, by John Carlin, c1850, in original gold and blue enamel brooch frame, 1½in (4cm) high.
$5,600–7,000 ⊞ AUG
John Carlin (1813–91), who studied in Philadelphia with John Neagle, graduated from the Pennsylvania Institute for the Deaf and Dumb before moving to Paris to study with Paul Delaroche. In 1841, Carlin set up a studio in New York, exhibiting at the National Academy of Design from 1845–86. His account book lists over 2,000 miniatures.

A portrait miniature of a young lady, wearing a white dress, by Richard Cosway, on card, in a gold frame, the reverse glazed to reveal locks of hair in the form of a fleur-de-lys, c1800, 2¾in (7cm) high.
4,000–4,600 ⚒ Bon

A portrait miniature of Alderman Peter J. Nevins of New York City, by Thomas Seir Cummings, in original gold engine-turned locket frame, c1850, 2½in (6.5cm) high.
3,200–4,000 ⊞ AUG

A portrait miniature of a gentleman, by Mr Thomas Cox, watercolour on ivory, early 19thC, 3in (7.5cm) high.
$450–500 ⊞ PSC

A portrait miniature of Mrs Spencer Smith, in a white dress, by Mrs Edwin Dalton, née Magdalena Ross, painted on porcelain, the reverse inscribed with sitter's and artist's details, in a papier mâché frame, dated 1836, 4in (10cm) diam.
$3,200–3,600 ⚺ P

A portrait miniature of a young girl, wearing a rust-coloured dress with a white collar, attributed to Cornelius Durham, c1845, 4½in (11.4cm) high, in a gilt-metal mount and giltwood frame.
$1,300–1,600 ⚺ S

A French portrait miniature of a gentleman, wearing a blue drape, a lace cravat tied with a red ribbon, and a gold-embroidered doublet, attributed to Jacques Philippe Ferrand, oil on copper, in a carved wood frame, the reverse inscribed 'abbaye de fontevrault', c1680, 4in (10cm) high.
$2,200–2,400 ⚺ S
Although renowned in his lifetime, the work of Jacques Philippe Ferrand is now shaded in obscurity. A pupil of Mignard, who in turn had studied under Poussin in Rome, Ferrand was appointed a painter to the Regent, as well as a valet to King Louis XIV. He was accepted at the Academy in 1687 and became a member three years later.

An American portrait miniature of a young lady, by Anson Dickinson, in a gilt-metal pendant frame with chased foliate border, c1830, 3in (7.5cm) high.
$5,300–6,500 ⊞ AUG
Anson Dickinson was a native of Milton, Connecticut. He moved to New York City in 1804 and there received instruction from Edward Greene Malbone. His sitters included Sam Houston, General Jacob Brown, Washington Irving and Gilbert Stuart.

A portrait miniature of a young girl, with auburn curls, by William Egley, in a gilt frame with brooch pin fitting, c1830, 1¾in (4.5cm) high.
$2,400–2,700 ⊞ BHa

A pair of portrait miniatures of the Reverend James Kevill and his wife, he wearing a black coat and white stock, she wearing a white dress and pink shawl, by John Cox Dillman Engleheart, signed and dated 1815, 3in (7.5cm) high, in ormolu frames with oak leaf and acorn motifs.
$7,200–8,700 ⚺ Bon

A portrait miniature of Master Greville J. M. B. Chester, by Annie Dixon, in a gilt frame, signed, dated 1870, 3½in (9cm) high.
$4,300–4,700 ⊞ BHa

An American portrait miniature of Mrs Elvira Warriner, wearing a blue dress, signed Ellsworth, in a mahogany frame, mid-19thC, 3½in (9cm) high.
$12,300–14,500 ⚺ SK(B)
James Sanford Ellsworth (1802–74) was an itinerant artist who worked primarily in the Connecticut River Valley and the Berkshires from the 1840s to the 1850s painting miniature water-colours on paper This portrait displays a typical Ellsworth convention - the grey, clover-shaped cloud over the sitter's head.

A portrait miniature of Hannah Withers, wearing a dress with a lace fichu, a sprig of foliage in her corsage, by James Ferguson, c1750, 2½in (6.5cm) high, in a turned wood frame.
$430–500 ⚺ Bon

A half length portrait miniature of a lady, wearing a lace shawl, by J. H. F., British School, watercolour on ivory, signed with monogram, dated 1865, 4½in (11.5cm) high, in an ormolu frame.
$1,000–1,200 ↗ RTo

A portrait miniature of an elderly lady, wearing a bonnet, by Alexander Gallaway, in a gold frame, c1810, 2¼in (5.5cm) high.
$580–720 ↗ CGC

A portrait miniature of a young lady, in white lace, reclining on a chaise longue, by James Holmes, in a gilt-metal frame, c1830, 4¼in (11.5cm) high.
$2,300–2,600 ⊞ BHa

A portrait miniature of a gentleman, probably by Nathaniel Hone, signed with monogram 'NH', gold-backed, in interlaced paste-set frame, dated 1764, 1½in (4cm) high.
$1,400–1,700 ↗ MEA

A portrait miniature of George II, painted in the manner of Charles Jarvis, in original shagreen case, early 19thC, case 2in (5cm) wide.
$1,600–1,900 ↗ WW

A portrait miniature of a young girl, wearing a white turban, dress and a blue shawl, by Patrick McMoreland, in a gold bracelet-clasp frame with a brooch pin, c1775, 1¾in (4.5cm) high.
$1,400–1,600 ⊞ BHa

A portrait miniature of a gentleman, wearing a black coat and cream waistcoat, by Miss S. Newell, in an ormolu slip, signed and dated 1838, 3¾in (9.5cm) high, in a leather travelling case.
$580–720 ↗ Bon

A portrait miniature of Mrs F. Rhodes, wearing a white dress and fur stole, by Sir William John Newton, in an ormolu slip, the reverse signed and dated 1834, 4½in (11.5cm) high, in a damaged red leather travelling case.
$430–500 ↗ Bon

A portrait miniature of a gentleman, wearing a dark coat, white cravat and stock, by Andrew Robertson, in a wooden frame, c1800, 2¾in (7cm) high.
$1,600–1,900 ↗ CGC

A portrait miniature of a gentleman, by Samuel Shelley, in original gold bracelet clasp, c1770, 1¼in (3cm) high.
$1,600–2,000 ⊞ AUG

A portrait miniature of a gentleman, wearing a turquoise coat, by John Smart, initialled and dated 1771, 1¼in (3cm) high.
$5,800–7,200 ↗ GH

A portrait miniature of a gentleman, wearing a blue coat with a black collar and white stock, by William Wood, in a gold frame, the reverse with plaited hair and seed pearls, c1800, 3in (7.5cm) high.
$4,300–5,000 ↗ CGC

A portrait miniature of Captain Joseph Adlam, painted on ivory, the reverse with a lock of hair mounted with half pearls, on an engine-turned opalescent ground, 18thC, 2½in (6.5cm) high.
$360–430 ↗ F&C

A portrait miniature of a gentleman, painted on ivory, American School, in original gilded-copper case, c1800, 3in (7.5cm) high.
$3,200–3,600 ↗ SK(B)

A portrait miniature of a gentleman, painted on ivory, in a copper frame, the reverse with monogram in seed pearls on a blue enamel ground with a plaited hair border, early 19thC, 2½in (6.5cm) high, with a red leather carrying case.
$1,700–2,000 ↗ AH

A pair of portrait miniatures, designed with coloured beads, glass fragments and gilt wires, 19thC, 11in (28cm) high.
$400–460 ↗ TMA

A portrait miniature of an elderly lady, wearing a brown dress and green checked shawl, watercolour on card, c1830, 3in (7.5cm) high.
$290–320 ⊞ PSC

A portrait miniature of a lady, painted on ivory, 19thC, 4¼in (11cm) high.
$170–220 ↗ SWO

An Australian portrait miniature of a lady, wearing a lace bonnet, painted on ivory, the reverse with a curled lock of hair, in a 15ct gold mount, 19thC, 3in (7.5cm) high.
$4,000–4,600 ↗ LJ

◀ **A portrait miniature of a young lady,** hand-painted on ivory, c1910, 3¾in (9.5cm) high, in a 14ct gold frame, the original leather box doubling as an easel.
$430–500 ↗ DuM

Silhouettes

A silhouette of a gentleman, wearing a frilled cravat and bow, by Mrs Isabella Beetham, cut-out on card, c1785, 3½in (9cm) high, in a turned pearwood frame with gilded inner border.
£430–500 ⚓ Bon

A pair of silhouettes of William and Mary Ewart, he wearing a coat, white stock and frilled cravat, she wearing a décolleté dress with fichu tied at her corsage, by John Butterworth, painted on ivory in shades of grey, c1795, 2½in (6.5cm) high, ormolu-mounted in black wood frames.
$1,200–1,400 ⚓ Bon
These profiles show two particular characteristics of Butterworth's work – the 'nick' separating the arm from the rest of the truncation; and the painting of the sitter's hair in a mass of strokes and thinned pigment.

A silhouette of the Reverend James Annesley Burrowes, holding a top hat, lithographic interior background, view of Oxford in the distance, by Augustin Edouart, cut-out on card, signed, dated 1833, 10¾in (27.5cm) high, in a maple wood frame.
$360–430 ⚓ P

A silhouette of an officer of a grenadier company, probably from a Foot Guards regiment, in uniform with gold epaulette, by William Hamlet the Elder, reverse-painted on glass in black and gold, plaster background, early 19thC, 2¾in (7cm) high, in a papier mâché frame.
£580–720 ⚓ P

A silhouette of a gentleman, on plaster, by Miers, labelled, 1790, 5in (12.5cm) high.
$430–500 ⊞ PSC

A silhouette of Mrs Meredith Darby, wearing ribbon and feathers in her hair, a fichu and ribbon bow at her corsage, by C. H. Sandhegan, painted on convex glass backed with silk, dated 1794, 2¼in (5.5cm) high, in a hammered gilded-brass frame.
$950–1,150 ⚓ Bon

A silhouette of a lady, set in pearl and gold frame, 1830, ¼in (3cm) high.
£170–220 ⊞ Ma

A silhouette of a family group, with painted drapes and floor, the background in pencil and crayon on paper giving a three-dimensional effect, early 19thC, 8½ x 10in (21.5 x 25.5cm) wide, in a gilt frame.
$1,200–1,400 ⚓ AH

▶ A silhouette of a gentleman, cut-out, c1830, 3in (7.5cm) high.
$160–180 ⊞ PSC

Antiquities

A pair of Egyptian alabaster cosmetic vessels with lids, Middle Kingdom, 21st–18thC BC, 2in (5cm) high.
$1,300–1,600 ⊞ HEL

The items in this section have been arranged chronologically in sequence of civilizations, namely Egyptian, Near Eastern, Greek, Roman, Byzantine, western European, British and Anglo-Saxon.

An Egyptian rock crystal model situla, with two pierced loops on the rim for fitting the handle, New Kingdom, c14th–13thC BC, 1½in (4cm) high.
$4,000–4,600 ⚒ Bon
A situla is a ritual liquid container. An example of this size would probably have been a model or a votive object.

An Egyptian wooden sarcophagus mask, the face with traces of gesso and blue pigment, 14th–13thC BC or later, 10½in (26.5cm) high.
$1,200–1,400 ⚒ P

An Egyptian limestone fragment depicting two figures carrying a duck, Late Period, c6th–4thC BC, 7in (18cm) wide.
$720–870 ⊞ HEL

An Egyptian bronze figure of seated Harpocrates, hand and part of crown missing, Late Period, c7th–2ndC BC, 8in (20.5cm) high.
$1,000–1,300 ⚒ Herm

An Egyptian wooden model of the Horus Falcon, with traces of polychrome and gilding, lower legs missing, Late Period, 716–30 BC, 12in (30.5cm) long.
$3,600–4,300 ⚒ S(NY)

An Egyptian bronze figure of Osiris, holding the crook and flail, wearing the *atef*-crown with striated plumes and tassel behind, 26th–30th Dynasty, 664–342 BC, 8in (20.5cm) high.
$3,600–4,300 ⚒ S(NY)

An Egyptian bronze model of a cat, one ear repaired, Late Period, after 600 BC, 3in (7.5cm) high.
$2,300–2,600 ⚒ P

An Anatolian neolithic grey ware idol, with pin prick and incised decoration, headdress damaged, c5th–4th millennium BC, 3½in (9cm) high.
$870–1,000 ⚒ Bon

► A terracotta foundation cone, cuneiform inscribed for Gudea, ruler of Lagash, c2100 BC, 5in (12.5cm) high.
$600–660 ⊞ OTT

An Egyptian wood pane from a sarcophagus, painted in red, yellow and white on a black ground with the figure of the sky goddess Nut, with wings outstretched, kneeling ove four columns of hieroglyph cracked and repaired, Ptolemaic Period, c300–30 B 36¾ x 12½in (93.5 x 32cm
$2,300–2,500 ⚒ P

A cuneiform clay tablet, listing domestic accounts for successive days, Middle Babylonian, c1600 BC, 4½ x 4in (11 x 10cm).
$330–400 ✗ P

An Assyrian steatite head, possibly of a eunuch or a female, with finely detailed hair falling to the shoulders in wavy locks, a hole in the base of the neck for attachment, 7th–6thC BC, 1in (2.5cm) high.
$7,200–8,000 ✗ Bon

A Near Eastern bronze bowl, the body decorated with two rows of lobes, incised with hatching, with ray-shaped petals moulded around the base, some cracks, 5th–4thC BC, 6½in (16.5cm) diam.
$3,600–4,300 ✗ Bon

A Parthian calcite head of a man, with inlaid eyes, the neck drilled underneath for attachment, 1st–2ndC AD, 2½in (6.5cm) high.
$6,200–7,600 ✗ S(NY)

A Greek geometric pottery cup, with painted decoration, 8th–7thC BC, 2½in (6.5cm) high.
$400–460 ⊞ HEL

A Syrian grey basalt panel, carved in relief with laurel wreaths and rosettes within stepped square panels, Hauran region, 3rd–6thC AD, 37¾ x 24¾in (96 x 63cm).
$1,100–1,300 ✗ P(Z)

◀ **A late Minoan pottery cup,** with stylized decoration, c12thC BC, 3½in (9cm) diam.
$720–870 ⊞ HEL

A Corinthian pottery alabastron, painted with a seated winged lion, and rosettes in the field, the details added in red and white, circa early 6thC BC, 9¼in (23.5cm) high.
$8,000–8,800 ✗ S(NY)

A Greek core-formed translucent cobalt blue glass aryballos, decorated with opaque yellow and turquoise glass trails combed into a zig-zag pattern around the body, with yellow spirals above and a line of yellow and turquoise glass below, with applied turquoise glass handles, late 6th–5thC BC, 2½in (6.5cm) high.
$2,400–2,900 ✗ Bon

A terracotta figure of a woman, with traces of blue pigment, Magna Graecia, mid-4thC BC, 12½in (32cm) high.
$8,000–9,000 ✗ S(NY)

An Apulian Red Figure bell krater, with added cream and white slip, depicting a running woman carrying a beribboned wreath or tambourine in one hand and casket in the other, and Eros carrying a patera in his left hand and a ribbon in his right, Greek South Italy, mid-4thC BC, 9¼in (23.5cm) high.
$2,500–2,900 ✗ Bon

▶ **An Apulian black glazed pottery cup,** Greek South Italy, c4thC BC, 3in (7.5cm) high.
$190–210 ⊞ Sama

A Greek pottery plaque, relief-decorated with a hunting scene, c4thC BC, 5 x 6in (12.5 x 15cm).
$500–600 ⊞ HEL

A Greek gold wreath, the pairs of laurel or olive leaves attached with gold wire, 4th–3rdC BC, 10in (25.5cm) diam.
$6,500–8,000 ↗ S(NY)

A Daunian buff pottery storage vessel, decorated in dark brown and orange slip with a geometric motif and four fish on the rim interior, Greek South Italy, rim repaired, c3rdC BC, 9in (23cm) high.
$1,100–1,300 ↗ Bon

An Etruscan bronze figure of a standing bearded male, holding the remains of a cornucopia, c6th–5thC BC, 2¼in (5.5cm) high.
$800–880 ⊞ ANG

An Etruscan bronze flat-backed figure of a draped priest, wearing a headdress and holding a patera in his left hand, right arm missing, c3rdC BC, 3¾in (9.5cm) high.
$650–725 ⊞ ANG

A Roman bronze oinochoe, with trefoil lip, handle missing, c5thC AD, 5in (12.5cm) high.
$360–430 ↗ Herm

A Roman green glass sprinkler flask, the base pinched out to form the feet, extended below the rim to form a collar, c3rd–4thC AD, 4in (10cm) high.
$400–440 ⊞ LBr

◀ **A Roman bronze mouse,** clutching a ball of food between its front paws, tail missing, 1st–2ndC AD, 2in (5cm) long.
$2,000–2,400 ↗ Bon

A pair of Roman buff ware jugs, Tunisia, 2ndC AD, 3in (7.5cm) high.
$140–170 ⊞ OTT

A Roman green glass jug, with tubular neck and applied handle, surface iridescence, c2nd–4thC AD, 5in (12.5cm) high.
$230–250 ⊞ Sama

A pair of Roman gold earrings, set with teardrop-shaped cabochons, possibly amber, the tubular pendants with triple globular terminals decorated with granules, c1st–2ndC AD, 2in (5cm) long.
$800–880 ↗ P

A Roman glass cameo, carved with a bust of a woman of fashion in opaque white over transparent glass, in a beaded gold mount with suspension loop, 1st–2ndC AD, 1¼in (3cm) high.
$2,200–2,400 ↗ P

A Roman marble head, with a curly beard and a garland in his hair, the back unmodelled, 2nd–3rdC AD, 5¼in (13.5cm) high.
$2,300–2,900 ↗ Bon

▶ **A Roman Janus-headed mould-blown amber glass vase,** with a face of Janus to each side, c3rdC AD, 4in (10cm) high.
$1,300–1,600 ⊞ LBr

A Roman pottery redware beaker, with reeded loop handle, North Africa, 3rd–4thC AD, 4¾in (12cm) high.
$190–220 ⚘ **F&C**

A Byzantine hollow bronze steelyard weight, in the form of a draped figure wearing an elaborate headdress with moulded and chased decoration, a suspension loop surmounting the head, 6th–7thC AD, 5½in (14cm) high.
$1,200–1,400 ⚘ **Bon**

A Roman iridescent glass vessel, the body covered with fine trailing, surface worn and damaged in places, c1stC AD, 6in (15cm) high.
$140–160 ⊞ **OTT**

An early Christian iconographic silver finger ring, with chi-rho monogram engraved on the bezel, the Balkans, 4thC AD or later, 22mm diam.
$160–180 ⊞ **ANG**

► **A Roman redware terracotta oil lamp,** the discus decorated with an amphora, c4th–5thC AD, 6in (15cm) long.
$130–160 ⊞ **OTT**

A Roman bronze grazing horse brooch, with engraved eye, pin missing, 1stC AD, 1½in (4cm) long.
$120–140 ⊞ **ANG**

A Roman bronze double lion bow brooch, the lions standing back to back, pin missing, 1stC AD, 1in (2.5cm) long.
$260–290 ⊞ **ANG**

► **An Anglo-Saxon disc brooch,** engraved with an animal, with a notched border, Lincolnshire, 9thC AD, 1in (2.5cm) diam.
$180–220 ⊞ **ANG**

A socketed celt, with a single loop for attachment, the blade curved and sharpened for use, Bronze Age, c900 BC, 4½in (11.5cm) long.
$220–260 ⚘ **F&C**

Pre-Columbian Art

A Nayarit seated female figure, San Sebastian-style, with legs to one side, holding a cup on her right knee, wearing a nose ring and multiple ear ornaments, arm and top of head restored, West Mexico, Protoclassic period, c100 BC–AD 250, 12½in (32cm) high.
$1,450–1,750 ✗ Bon(C)

A Mayan mould-made bottle, moulded on obverse and reverse with the profile head of a deity, the sides moulded with a double band of glyphs, the recessed areas marked by red pigment, Late Classsic period, 550–950 AD, 3¼in (8.5cm) high.
$4,000–4,600 ✗ S(NY)

A Mayan jade ornament, carved with three prongs and circular hole for thumb, with incised triangular and geometric forms, in bright apple green, Late Classic period, c550–950 AD, 3¼in (8.5cm) high.
$5,000–6,000 ✗ S(NY)

A pottery human effigy vessel, the seated figure with one arm resting on a raised knee and extending to his shoulder, painted with a reddish-brown slip, Jalisco, c100 BC–AD 250, 10in (25.5cm) high.
$870–1,000 ✗ SK(B)

A Mayan standing figure, wearing a loincloth with beaded fringe, necklace and beaded turban with projecting plumes, areas painted with blue, cream and red pigment, Jaina, Late Classic period, c550–950 AD, 8in (20.5cm) high.
$8,700–9,500 ✗ S(NY)

A Chancay standing female figure, painted in cream with black details, c1100–1400 AD, 25¾in (65.5cm) high.
$5,000–6,000 ✗ S(NY)

A Nazca culture poly-chrome pottery effigy vessel, the head and connected spout painted with the image of a fisher-man and his nets, minor damage, Peru, c100–300 AD, 6¾in (17cm) high.
$1,000–1,200 ✗ SK(B)

A Mayan polychrome plate, decorated with a seated dignitary wearing an elaborate headdress, in dark orange and black on a light orange ground, surrounded by two large bands with pseudo-glyphs, slight damage, c550–950 AD, 12¾in (32.5cm) diam.
$4,500–5,000 ✗ SK(B)

▶ **A feline pottery vessel,** with vestigial limbs and tail forming loops for suspension, probably Chimu, c1000 AD, 7½in (19cm) long.
$220–260 ✗ F&C

A pair of Carchi/Nariño gold ornaments, each hammered and repoussé decorated with a human face, surrounded by fine bead-work, pierced at the top, Capuli phase c500–1000 AD, 3in (7.5cm) diam.
$5,000–6,000 ✗ S(NY)

A Mayan polychrome three-legged pottery vessel, decorated with panels of warrior heads in profile, with chequered geometric and stylized feather devices in shades of orange and red on a cream ground, Honduras, c550–95? AD, 8¼in (21cm) high.
$1,100–1,300 ✗ SK(B)

A Muisca gold ornament, with a medallion placed within three rows of openwork diamond pattern forming the stylized body of an avian, with parrot heads terminating at the top row, and flattened tails on the other rows, with five suspension loops for possible ornamentation, c1300–1500 AD, 7¼in (18.5cm) long.
$4,600–5,500 ✗ S(NY)

Tribal Art

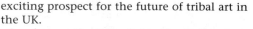

The decision by leading UK auction houses to move their tribal art sales to the USA is unfortunate and possibly ill-timed. Whilst the commercial rationale in searching for the most lucrative market for their activities can be understood, it does seem to have happened at an inappropriate time, for unfortunately it seems to have coincided with a sudden awakening amongst a large group of younger, globe-trotting and aesthetically aware people, of the place and value of non-European sculpture and tribal arts within the fine arts and antiques world.

This upsurge in interest may well have had its seeds in the Royal Academy's exhibition on Africa or be propelled by the interior driven minimalist look which seems to have entered the market. Whatever the catalyst, the reality is unquestionable. We have a long way to go before we reach the large clientele which haunts the Sablon in Brussels or the artist/collectors who ferret through the back streets of the Left Bank in Paris, each in search of the piece that will fill the gap in their respective collections. But at long last the tribal art scene in London is becoming exciting and, interestingly, driven by demand from a new clientele, which is young, well-travelled and inquisitive – an exciting prospect for the future of tribal art in the UK.

So what are the new aficionados in London and New York buying? Bold dynamic textiles such as the Kuba dance skirts and Shoowa textiles of Zaire – abstract creations in appliqué, patchwork and embroidery which have an immediate rapport (they were collected by Klee and appear in Cartier-Bresson's photographs of Matisse's studio, so it's not a new phenomenon). The textiles have an immediacy, like the simple bold iron currency pieces from Africa which appeal because of their obvious sculptural qualities. Prices for them are low in comparison to other areas of tribal art, and the work is honest and above board and purchasers are not hide bound by the constraints of forming a definitive collection of some well-documented tribal group or concerns about pedigree. In the more conventional areas of mask and figure collecting, good pieces are still to be found, while tribal art from non-African societies remains an exciting field of exploration. The African market is now even more overloaded with a frightening number of pseudo masks, airport art, copies and downright forgeries, so proceed with care, and go to dealers you can trust.

Gordon Reece

An Apache pictorial coiled tray, woven in willow and devil's claw, with a floret medallion in the basin enclosed by a series of human and animal figures, Native American, 14¾in (35.5cm) diam.
$5,800–6,500 ⚘ **S(NY)**

◄ **A Northwest Coast twined polychrome basket,** decorated with butterflies in yellow and dark brown, Native American, early 20thC, 6½in (16.5cm) diam.
$800–900 ⚘ **SK(B)**

A Blackfoot elk skin pouch, the hide flap with a geometric beadwork border, the base applied with a hide panel ornamented with bands of beadwork and metal cones, Native American, 13in (33cm) wide.
$870–1,000 ⚘ **P**

A Navajo regional rug, woven in handspun wool in natural ivory and black, aniline red, green and maroon, enclosing a pair of concentric stepped diamonds, flanked above and below with a cross containing an hourglass, Native American, 83½ x 46½in (212 x 118cm).
$4,300–4,700 ⚘ **S(NY)**

A Blackfoot tobacco pouch, decorated on both sides with a floral polychrome beaded panel on a white ground, the fringes ornamented with tubular orange beads, Native American, 17in (43cm) long excluding fringes.
$1,600–1,800 ⚘ **P**

A Navajo rug, with an open red field within a black border, Native American, c1930, 80 x 52in (203 x 132cm).
$3,600–4,000 ⚘ **TREA**

An elkhorn club, with natural striations, probably southern North American Plains, Native American, late 19thC, 20in (51cm) long.
$580–720 ⚒ Bon(C)

A Tlingit carved horn spoon, the handle carved in the form of two totemic figures surmounted by a raven, Northwest Coast, Native American, late 19thC, 9in (23cm) long.
$2,200–2,400 ⚒ SK(B)

A Plateau beaded hide panel, contour-beaded in white, pink, yellow, sienna, blue and green glass beadwork, with a deer flanked by birds perched on leafy stalks, 6¼in (16cm) square.
$1,100–1,300 ⚒ S(NY)

A bison's head headdress, worn by a medicine man, probably Cheyenne, decorated with bands of glass beads in turquoise, red and white, a knife attached to the headband with an identical decorated scabbard, North American Plains, Native American, 1900–20, 42½in (108cm) long.
$1,600–1,800 ⚒ Herm

A pair of hide fringed gauntlets, the cuffs decorated with motifs in metal and blue beads on a white bead ground, the hands with three beadwork strips with diagonal stripes, North American Plains, 15¾in (40cm) long.
$580–650 ⚒ P
This item was collected in Calgary, c1920.

A pottery jar, decorated with brown and black geometric motifs on a buff ground, Native American, possibly Zuni, early 20thC, 5½in (14cm) diam.
$320–360 ⚒ DuM

An Arapaho beaded commercial hide dispatch bag, the beaded panel with green, red and navy blue hour glass and cross devices on a white ground, Central Plains, Native American, 18in (45.5cm) long.
$1,600–1,800 ⚒ SK(B)

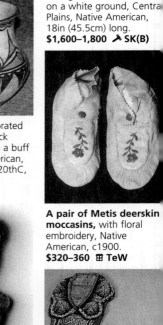

A pair of Metis deerskin moccasins, with floral embroidery, Native American, c1900.
$320–360 ⊞ TeW

A woven plate, with a zig-zag pattern, Native American, mid-20thC, 12in (30.5cm) diam.
$320–360 ⚒ DuM

A Salish wood totem pole, carved with a whale surmounted by an eagle, above a bird perching on a beaver, painted in cream, black and brown, 32¾in (83cm) high.
$290–320 ⚒ P

A child's pair of mouse skin and beadwork moccasins, 1930s, 4in (10cm) long.
$110–125 ⊞ PSC

▶ **An Inuit ivory female figure,** with a disc hat, dot eyes and slit mouth, 4in (10cm) long.
$2,600–3,200 ⚒ P

A pair of suede moccasins, the tops and cuffs decorated with floral motifs in red, white, blue and grey beads, Native American.
$580–650 ⚒ DN

► **A Guro carved wood mask,** with hair combed high, Ivory Coast, 21in (53.5cm) high.
$140–170 ⚷ DuM

A Ghanaian terracotta vessel, the body decorated with alternating incised linear crescent and dot motifs, with red ochre patina, probably Ashanti, 15in (38cm) diam.
$3,200–3,600 ⚷ S(NY)

A Dogon wrought-iron equestrian figure, the figure with arms outstretched and holding a sceptre, Mali, 6¼in (16cm) high.
$4,000–4,600 ⚷ S(NY)
Equestrian figures in metal are found in many cultures across West Africa. Iron smelting and forging in most societies falls under the purview of blacksmiths, who have traditionally produced farm implements and weapons as well as important ritual objects made of iron. It has been said that 'Among the Dogon and the Bamana, the blacksmith is an intermediary between man and God, in both a symbolic and practical sense'.

A pair of Chiwara male and female antelope headdresses, Mali, early 20thC, 27in (68.5cm) long.
$2,900–3,200 ⊞ ELM

A Fon wooden stool, supported on a coopered barrel, the base carved either end with a rifle, with whitish patina, Ghana, late 19thC, 19½in (49.5cm) wide.
$320–360 ⚷ F&C

► **A Kirdi iron item of status currency,** northern Nigeria, 19thC, 32in (81.5cm) high.
$400–460 ⊞ ELM

An Egagham skin-covered headdress, the wood base carved in two halves, each side in the form of a human face with details such as lips and scarifications stained dark brown, Nigeria, 13¾in (35cm) high.
$4,000–4,400 ⚷ P

A Yoruba culture polychrome wood equestrian figure, his right hand holding a fly whisk, with overall traces of pigment, printed on the back of the base 'Lagos Bt. of Webster, May 1897 p.1498', Nigeria, 12¼in (31cm) high.
$1,200–1,400 ⚷ SK(B)

A Sidamo embossed elephant leather shield, south west Ethiopia, late 19thC, 18½in (47cm) wide.
$220–260 ⚷ Herm
The shape of these shields is achieved by putting the leather over a form, then drying or sun-baking.

◄ **A Congolese beaten iron throwing knife,** the convex surface with raised line decoration, flat on the reverse, evidence of delamination, 19thC, 26in (66cm) long.
$450–500 ⊞ GV
Throwing knife had a range of up to 100 yards and were deadly accurate at 20–30 yards.

► **A Punu mask,** the face painted with creamy white pigment, with red-painted lips, the temples and forehead with square and lozenge cicatrized scars and similarly coloured, beneath a domed coiffure with side chignons, Gabon, mid-20thC, 12¼in (31cm) high.
$3,600–4,300 ⚷ Bon(C)
This item was acquired in Gabon, 1948–53.

A Punu mask, with a blackened lip framing the oval face, with red and black highlights, Gabon, 11½in (29cm) high.
$4,000–4,500 ⚷ S(NY)

An Oromo rhinoceros skin hand shield, partially decorated in red and white, mounted with two brass stars, 19thC, 9½in (24cm) wide.
$360–430 ⚷ Herm

TRIBAL ART

A **Luba ceremonial iron axe,** with a wooden shaft, the pommel in the form of a female head wearing a bead and cowrie shell necklace, Democratic Republic of Congo, 19thC, 21in (53.5cm) high, mounted on a wooden base.
$1,700–2,000 ➶ **Herm**

Two **Zulu spears and a cowhide shield,** c1920, South Africa, shield 21in (53.5cm) wide.
$115–145 ⊞ **CYA**

A **Kuba wooden royal guardian figure,** the post with incised geometric panels surmounted by a Janus head, Democratic Republic of Congo, early 20thC, 79½in (202cm) high.
$5,800–7,200 ➶ **Bon(C)**

◀ A **Kuba chief's carved wood stool,** raised on two tiers of convex struts incised with geometric designs, with old ironwork repair, Zaire, 19thC, 12in (30.5cm) diam.
$2,200–2,400 ➶ **F&C**

An **African carved wood bowl,** possibly a drum, with incised banding, 19thC, 10in (25.5cm) diam.
$140–170 ➶ **DuM**

◀ An **African wood mask,** c1900, 17in (43cm) high.
$260–290 ⊞ **GV**

▶ A **Himalchal Pradesh carved wood mask,** depicting the Hindu monkey god Hanuman, painted in natural coloured pigment, India, 19thC, 12in (30.5cm) high.
$1,300–1,450 ⊞ **GRG**

A **Vili carved wood statue,** the standing nude pregnant female figure with body scarification, Democratic Republic of Congo, 19thC, 18in (45.5cm) high.
$140–170 ➶ **DuM**

A **Congolese carved ivory tusk,** with five panels depicting figures dressed in European garb and carrying weapons, 19thC, 13¾in (35cm) high.
$1,000–1,200 ➶ **SK(B)**

A **Zulu hardwood headrest,** with carved splayed end supports, South Africa, 19thC, 12in (30.5cm) long.
$460–550 ➶ **F&C**

A **Zulu knobkerry,** with deeply incised carved decoration, South Africa, 24in 961cm) long.
$95–115 ➶ **WAL**

◀ A **Tsonga headrest,** the central column support flanked by two arcs with circular protrusions, South Africa, 6¼in (16cm) high.
$3,300–3,700 ➶ **P**

A **Khond two-piece wooden tribal door,** carved with relief panels of humans, animals and sun motifs, India, mid-19thC, 71in (180cm) high.
$3,000–3,500 ⊞ **GRG**

A Sarawak pig mask, used in planting ceremonies, Bahay or Modang Dayak tribe, 1910–20, 28in (71cm) high.
$4,000–4,400 ⊞ **GRG**

A hardwood food bowl, carved in relief with stylized fish, Huon Gulf, New Guinea, 35in (89cm) long, on a mid-19thC colonial-style turned hardwood stand.
$1,200–1,400 ↗ **PFK**

A Sumba woman's black cotton sarong, embroidered with nassa shells and stone beads with an ancestral figure with tail surrounded by two centipedes, two scorpions and a beetle, Lesser Sunda Islands, Indonesia, 47in (119.5cm) long.
$360–430 ↗ **Bon**

A wooden fetish stick, the top carved in the form of a tribal chief and the bottom with swirling patterns, accentuated with white and ochre pigment, New Guinea, 19thC, 23in (58.5cm) long.
$460–500 ↗ **ASB**

An Aborigine pineapple-head club, incised with parallel grooves, the striking surface deeply cut into four registers of hobnails, northern Queensland, Australia, 26¾in (68cm) long.
$140–170 ↗ **Bon**

An Aboriginal hardwood spear thrower, with geometrical incised decoration to one side, peg lacking, Australia, 33in (84cm) long.
$130–160 ↗ **PFK**

A carved Kauri gum portrait bust of Hokianga chief Tamati Whaka Nene, New Zealand, early 20thC, 13¼in (33.5cm) high.
$5,000–6,000 ↗ **P(Sy)**
In 1840, Hokianga chief Tamati Whaka Nene was a pivotal figure in the signing of the famous treaty of Waitangi, considered a founding document in the history of New Zealand. This sculpture was probably carved by Mr Robert Couch senior, c1905, and is one of between six and eight heads carved for a private collector around that time. The left ear of each was deliberately broken on completion to break the 'Tapu' or mystical power of a life-like carving, making it safe by no longer representing the individual too accurately. It is believed that five heads from the group are in museum collections.

A Maori wooden canoe baler, the scoop-shaped bowl with projecting looped handle terminating in a tiki head, bowl cracked, with old rivets, New Zealand, 17in (43cm) long.
$1,300–1,600 ↗ **P**

A Fijian hand club, the rootwood head inset with a circular marine ivory plug, with a bound shaft, the grip carved with bands of zig-zag ornament, with red-brown glossy patina, early 19thC, 16½in (42cm) long.
$870–1,000 ↗ **F&C**

A Maori nephrite pendant of Hei-Tiki, the stylized form pierced at the top for a suspension, late 19thC, New Zealand, 4in (10cm) long.
$950–1,150 ↗ **Bea(E)**

◄ **A hardwood club or bat,** with two reeded sides and waisted handle, Oceania, 15½in (39.5cm) long.
$400–440 ↗ **CGC**

► **A Duala or ceremonial paddle,** the blade decorated with old pigments in geometric motif of mustard, red ochre and black on one side and a figure on the other, Oceania, 58¼in (148cm) long.
$2,000–2,400 ↗ **S(NY)**

Books & Book Illustrations

Eric Ambler, *The Dark Frontier*, published by Hodder & Stoughton, first edition, 1936, 8°, original blue cloth lettered in black, dust-jacket.
$4,300–4,700 ⚲ S

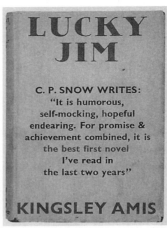

Kingsley Amis, *Lucky Jim*, published by Gollancz, first edition, 1953, 8°, original green cloth in yellow dust-jacket with red and black lettering.
$3,000–3,500 ⊞ B&J

Hugo Arnot, *The History of Edinburgh*, published by Creech, Edinburgh, first edition, 1779, 4°, with frontispiece and folding map, in original calf.
$300–350 ⚲ WilP

Jane Austin, *Sense and Sensibility*, first edition with Chris Hammond illustrations, rebound in green leather, 1899, 7 x 5in (18 x 12.5cm).
$580–640 ⊞ BAY

William Atkinson, *Views of Picturesque Cottages with Plans, Selected from a Collection of Drawings taken in different parts of England, and intended as Hints for the improvement of Village Scenery*, 1805, 4°, 20 black and white aqua plates, original printed wrappers.
$450–500 ⚲ DW

W. H. Auden, *Sonnet, On the Provincial Lawn*, published by Cambridge University Press, 1935, 24°, No. V of five copies on Brussels vellum, of an edition of 22, slipcase.
$1,000–1,100 ⚲ BBA
This is an example of Fredric Prokosch's privately printed editions of single poems, mainly the work of his friends or contemporaries. They span the years 1933–69 and all were issued in a small, or very small, number of copies, 8° or 24° in format. Each was printed on a variety of papers, bound in a wide range of marbled or decorated paper, with a printed label on the upper cover, with a watercolour frontispiece by Prokosch and inserted in a calf-backed marbled board slip case.

▶ **Charlotte Brontë,** *Villette*, by Currer Bell, published by Smith, Elder & Co, three volumes, first edition, 1853, 8°, original greyish-olive morocco cloth, covers blind-stamped with three line borders enclosing floral designs, spines lettered with gilt, each volume preserved in collector's lined half blue morocco.
$11,500–13,000 ⚲ S

John C. Bourne, *The History and Description of the Great Western Railway, including its Geology*, 1846, 2°, 47 views on 33 tinted lithographed plates, two hand-coloured maps, hand-coloured geological chart, two lithographed vignettes, by David Bogue, later half morocco.
$3,000–3,500 ⚲ Bon

Enid Blyton, *It's Mr Plod!*, original Noddy artwork by Robert Tyndall, 1960, depicts Mr Plod with notebook outside Noddy's house, Noddy is coming around the corner in his car, watercolour illustration used in Noddy book No. 21, mounted and framed, 4¾in (12cm) square.
$870–950 ⊞ B&J

◀ **Frances Hodgson Burnett,** *The Secret Garden*, published by Heinemann, first edition, 1911, 8°, eight full-page colour plates and pictorial endpapers by Charles Robinson, original green cloth with gilt vignettes and titles.
$1,200–1,300 ⊞ **B&J**

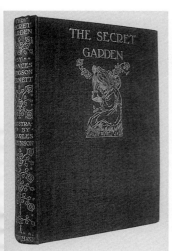

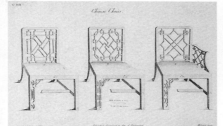

Thomas Chippendale, *Cabinet Making*, 1754–55, 2°, library cloth, illustrated with engravings, title pages missing.
$2,200–2,600 🔨 **AG**

G. K. Chesterton, *The Secret of Father Brown*, published by Cassell & Co, first edition, 1927, 8°, original black grained cloth, blind-stamped ruled border on upper cover, spine stamped in gilt.
$1,300–1,600 🔨 **S**

◀ **J. P. Donleavy,** *The Ginger Man*, published by the Olympia Press, Paris, first edition of author's first book, 1955, 8°, original light-green paper covers printed in white and black.
$2,400–2,600 🔨 **S**

▶ **Charles Dickens,** *David Copperfield*, illustrated by H. K. Browne, published by Bradbury & Evans, London, first edition, 1850, 9 x 6in (23 x 15cm).
$650–725 ⊞ **BAY**

Agatha Christie, *Death on the Nile*, published by Collins for The Crime Club, first edition, 1937, 8°, original red cloth lettered in black, dust-jacket.
$8,000–8,800 🔨 **S**

The Diverting History of John Gilpin, c1890, 4°, a volume of watercolour drawings, each with verse captions in manuscript, window mounted on card, 14 pages of typed text, 4¾ x 3¾in (12 x 9.5cm).
$430–500 🔨 **P**
These drawings were published as a Christmas greeting, to advertise Colman's mustard.

Isak Dinesen, *Out of Africa*, Karen Blixen, first edition, 1937, 8°, original cloth gilt, with dust-jacket.
$1,300–1,600 🔨 **DW**

▶ **Benjamin Franklin,** *Political, Miscellaneous, and Philosophical Pieces*, first edition, for J. Johnson, 1779, 8°, portrait frontispiece, three plates, folding table, contemporary tree calf, rebacked.
$1,400–1,600 🔨 **BBA**

BOOKS & BOOK ILLUSTRATIONS

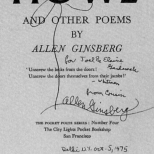

Allen Ginsberg, *Howl and other poems*, introduction by William Carlos Williams, published by City Lights, San Francisco, first edition, 1956, small 4°, presentation copy to his cousin with typed note, signed on the title and with sunflower drawing 'For Joel & Elaine Gaidemak from cousin Allen Ginsberg Delhi N.Y. Oct. 5, 1975, publisher's black paper wrappers with silver letterpress, title on wrap-around strip laid down.
$7,200–8,000 ↗ **S(NY)**

Miller's is a price GUIDE not a price LIST

Evert Ysbrants Ides, *Three Years Land Travels... from Mosco to China*, first English edition, 1706, 4°, folding map, 30 plates, bound in contemporary sprinked calf, spine gilt.
$2,000–2,300 ↗ **BBA**
The author (c1660–1700) went, at an early age, to Russia where he opened a flourishing trading station. As one of Peter the Great's counsellors he was sent to China in 1692 to conclude a commercial treaty with the Emperor Kangxi and to fix the boundary between the two empires. He left Moscow in March and reached the Great Wall of China in October. The mission was entirely successful and Ides returned, via Tartary and Siberia, in January 1694. He was next sent, as Imperial Commercial Counsellor, to explore the regions around Archangel and the White Sea. Ides died soon after his return, probably as a result of the rigours of the journey.

Oliver Goldsmith, *The Deserted Village*, published by Essex House Press, No. 128 of 150 copies printed on vellum, 1904, 8°, with hand-coloured frontispiece by C. R. Ashbee, heightened in gilt, hand-painted initials and tailpiece in red, green and blue, with the first initial illuminated, original blind-stamped vellum, gilt-lettered spine.
$650–800 ↗ **P**

Jessie M. King, *The High History of the Holy Graal*, translated from Old French by Sebastian Evans, No. 5 of 225 copies, published by Dent, deluxe edition, 1903, small 4°, illustrated title page and 22 other illustrations, white vellum with decoration in blue and gilt.
$6,500–7,250 ⊞ **B&J**

Henry Wadsworth Longfellow, *The Song of Hiawatha*, first English edition, 1855, 8°, bound in contemporary blind-stamped cloth gilt.
$330–400 ↗ **DW**

Histoire Naturelle en Miniature de 48 Oiseaux, Avec des Descriptions, miniature book published by Guyot et de Pelafol, Paris, 1816, 48 hand-coloured plates, bound in contemporary half calf with label, marbled boards, 2¾ x 2½in (7 x 6.5cm).
$360–430 ↗ **F&C**

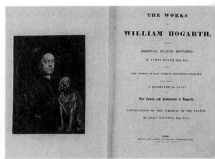

The Works of William Hogarth, edited by John Nichols, after 1821, engraved portrait and 115 plates, bound in half leather.
$1,600–1,900 ↗ **WL**

Carl Krackhart, *Neues illustriertes Konditoreibuch*, published by Heinrich Killinger, Leipzig, c1912, 4°, 52 double-page plates.
$500–600 ↗ **Bon**

Robert Ladbrooke, *Views of the Churches of Norfolk*, in five volumes, first edition, Norwich, 1843, 4°, c682 lithographed plates bound in alphabetical order, in later calf-backed cloth, gilt spines.
$2,600–3,200 ↗ **P**
Complete sets of Ladbrooke's work are scarce.

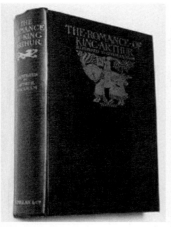

The Romance of King Arthur, abridged by Alfred W. Pollard from Malory's *Morte d'Arthur*, published by Macmillan, illustrated by Arthur Rackham, first Rackham edition, 1917, 8½ x 7in (21.5 x 18cm).
$350–380 ⊞ BAY

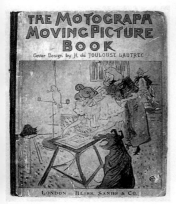

The Motograph Moving Picture Book, illustrated by F. J. Vernay, Yorick etc, cover design specially drawn for the book by H. de Toulouse Lautrec, 1898, 4°, 23 coloured plates and with the transparency needed to make the pictures 'move' contained in a pocket at the front, original cloth-backed coloured pictorial boards.
$130–160 ⚒ F&C

R. Padre Fra Noe, *Viaggio da Venezia al S. Sepolcro,* published by Gio Antonio Remondini, Bassano, 1742, 8°, a travel guide from Venice to the Church of the Holy Sepulchre, Jerusalem, via Corfu, Tunis, Cairo, Babilonia etc, illustrated with woodcuts, in later cloth binding.
$330–400 ⚒ PFK

MOBY-DICK

OR,

THE WHALE.

BY

HERMAN MELVILLE,

NEW YORK:
HARPER & BROTHERS, PUBLISHERS.
LONDON: RICHARD BENTLEY.
1851.

William Morris, *A Dream of John Ball and a King's Lesson,* 1892, 4°, limited to 311 copies of which this is one of 300 on paper, printed in red and black, wood-engraved frontispiece by W. H. Hooper after Edward Burne-Jones, original vellum gilt, slipcase.
$1,900–2,200 ⚒ S
This was the first of the Kelmscott Press books to contain a full-page illustration.

Cross Reference
See Colour Review (page 731)

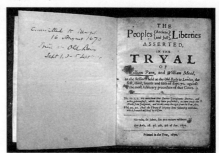

Philpott's Kent, collected by John Philpott, printed by William Godbid, 1659, 11 x 7in (28 x 18cm).
$1,600–1,750 ⊞ CBO

► **William Penn,** *The People's Ancient and Just Liberties Asserted, in the Tryal of William Penn, and William Mead, at the Sessions held at the Old-Baily in London, the first, third, fourth and fifth of Sept. 70,* London, first edition, 1670, 4°, later marbled boards and endpapers.
$720–870 ⚒ SLN

◄ **Herman Melville,** *Moby Dick; or The Whale,* first American edition, New York, 1851, 12°, bound in later half morocco.
$2,000–2,300 ⚒ SK(B)

Beverley Robinson Morris, *British Game Birds and Wildfowl,* 1855, large 4°, with 60 hand-coloured plates, bound in library cloth.
$1,300–1,600 ⚒ AG

Jersey & Guernsey Views, published by M. Moss, a collection of 34 lithographs by Gauci, Westall, Harding and Haghe from drawings by Shepherd, De Garis, Neel, Compton and Young, Guernsey, 1829–33, oblong 2°, some on India paper, bound with a hand-coloured lithographed map of Guernsey, inset plan of St Peter's Port, bound in contemporary half roan, upper cover almost detached, 10½ x 14¼in (26.5 x 36cm).
$2,600–3,200 ⚒ BBA

Florence Nightingale, *Observations on the Evidence Contained in the Stational Reports Submitted to her by the Royal Commission on the Sanitary State of the Army in India,* first edition, 1863, slim 8°, wood engravings, original cloth.
$1,000–1,200 ⚒ DW

Arthur Rackham, an ink and watercolour illustration entitled 'There was an old woman who lived in a village', signed and dated 1904, 9 x 6in (23 x 15cm).
$9,400–10,000 🔨 **S**
This was reproduced in *The Fairy Tales of the Brothers Grimm,* **published by Constable in 1909.**

Humphry Repton, *Designs for the Pavillon at Brighton,* first edition, 1808, 2°, aquatint frontispiece, hand-coloured plan and 18 plates and vignettes, nine hand-coloured, original boards, rebacked and recornered in calf.
$7,250–8,000 🔨 **BBA**

Charles Ricketts, *Beyond the Threshold,* published by Curwen Press, 1929, 4°, privately printed, one of 150 copies, written and illustrated by Ricketts, under the pseudonym 'Jean Paul Raymond', five full page black and white illustrations, bound in full burgundy morocco with cover design in gilt by Ricketts.
$1,200–1,400 ⊞ **B&J**

Rubaiyat of Omar Khayyam, translated by Edward Fitzgerald, published by Vale Press, 1901, small 4°, woodcut frontispiece and illustrations by Charles Ricketts, limited to 310 copies on paper, original cloth-backed boards.
$220–260 🔨 **DW**

Egon Schiele, *Das Egon Schiele Buch,* published by Wiener Graphischen Werkstätte, Vienna, 1921, 8°, 62 black and white illustrations, limited edition No. 248 of 1000, original decorated boards with leather backstrip.
$180–210 🔨 **DW**

Walter Scott, *The Poetical Works of Sir Walter Scott,* published by A. & C. Black, Edinburgh, 1868, the Mauchline ware cover depicting scenic views of Scotland.
$240–300 🔨 **P(Ed)**

Sir Walter Scott, *Provincial Antiquities and Picturesque Scenery of Scotland,* two volumes in one, 1826, large 4°, illustrated with engravings, gilt-cloth.
$400–480 🔨 **AG**

Maurice Sendak, a full colour art print entitled 'Max Howling at the Moon', New York, 1971, signed by the artist, 9¼ x 20¼in, (23.5 x 51.5cm).
$580–720 🔨 **BBA**

William Shakespeare, *A Midsummer Night's Dream,* published by Constable & Co, London, first edition, 1914, with Heath Robinson illustrations, 11 x 9in (28 x 23cm).
$430–500 ⊞ **BAY**

Charles Hamilton Smith, *Costume of the Army of the British Empire, according to the last regulations, 1814, Designed by an Officer on the Staff,* published by Colnaghi, 1815, 2°, 54 hand-coloured aquatint costume plates by J. C. Stadler after Smith, six hand-coloured plates of regimental colour, bound in contemporary maroon morocco gilt.
$3,600–4,300 🔨 **Bon**

William Stukeley, *Itinerarium Curiosum: or Antiquities in Great Britain,* 1776, 2°, illustrated with engravings, bound in gilt-calf.
$1,300–1,600 🔨 **AG**

Jonathan Swift, *Gulliver's Travels,* published by J. M. Dent, illustrated by Arthur Rackham, first Rackham edition, 1909, 9 x 7in (23 x 18cm).
$200–220 ⊞ BAY

Alfred Lord Tennyson, *Maud, A Monodrama,* published by Kelmscott Press, Hammersmith, 1893, 8°, one of 500 copies on paper, with the errors uncorrected, original limp vellum, gilt-lettered spine.
$1,100–1,300 ⚒ P

William Makepeace Thackeray, *Vanity Fair,* published by Bradbury & Evans, London, 1849, 9 x 6in (23 x 15cm).
$400–440 ⊞ BAY

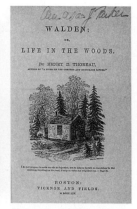

Henry David Thoreau, *Walden, or Life in the Woods,* first edition, Boston, 1854, 8°, original cloth with map.
$5,000–6,000 ⚒ SK(B)

John Ronald Reuel Tolkien, *The Lord of the Rings,* in three volumes, first edition, London, 1954–55, 8°, folding map to each volume.
$16,000–17,500 ⊞ HAM

William A. Toplis and John Oxenham, *The Book of Sark,* published by Hodder & Stoughton, London, 1908, 2°, limited edition No. 305 of 500, signed by the author and artist.
$1,900–2,200 ⚒ B&L

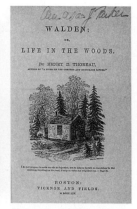

Louis Wain and Charles Morley, *Peter; a Cat o'One Tail. His Life and Adventures,* published by Pall Mall Gazette, first edition, 1892, slim 4°, black and white illustrations to text by Louis Wain, original printed wrappers.
$330–380 ⚒ DW

◄ **The Works of Oscar Wilde,** in 15 volumes, first collected limited edition, 1908–22, 8°, one of 1000 copies on handmade paper, modern red morocco-backed cloth, leather labels with gilt title on spines, top edge gilt, other sides uncut.
$2,900–3,200 ⚒ BBA

P. G. Wodehouse, *The Pothunters,* published by A. & C. Black, London, first edition, second issue, 1902, 8°, ten plates by R. Noel Pocock, publisher's grey-blue pictorial cloth, gold and light blue lettering.
$1,000–1,200 ⚒ Bon

Virginia Woolf, *The Waves,* published by Hogarth Press, first edition, 1931, 8°, original purple cloth in dust-jacket designed by Vanessa Bell.
$4,000–4,400 ⊞ B&J

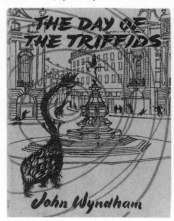

John Wyndham, *The Day of the Triffids,* published by Michael Joseph, first English edition, 1951, 8°, original green cloth lettered in silver, with dust-jacket.
$1,000–1,100 ⚒ S

BOOKS & BOOK ILLUSTRATIONS

Maps & Atlases
World

Willem & Jan Blaeu, *Nova totius terrarum orbis geographica ac hydrographica tabula*, full sheet engraved map, geographic regions partially hand-coloured in outline, decorative elements hand-coloured in full, Dutch text verso, Amsterdam, c1646, 19½ x 24in (49.5 x 61cm).
$8,700–10,000 ↗ S(NY)

Pieter Van der Aa, *Nova Orbus Terraquei Tabula Accuratissime Delineata*, hand-coloured double-page engraved double-hemisphere world map, decorated with figures and creatures, Leyden, c1714, 19¾ x 26in (50 x 66cm).
$5,500–6,000 ↗ P

Philippus Cluverius, *Intruductionis in Universam Geographiam*, double-page engraved plate and 45 double-page maps, contemporary calf, Amsterdam 1676 or later, 4°.
$2,000–2,300 ↗ BBA

H. Moll, *Atlas Minor*, including California depicted as an island, 62 maps, calf, 1732, 4°.
$8,700–9,400 ↗ Gam

Edward Wells, *A New Sett of Maps both of Antient and Present Geography*, second impression, 41 double-page engraved maps, including two double-hemisphere world maps and maps of North America, South America and English Plantations in America, contents loosely contained in old boards, 1706, 2°.
$7,250–8,000 ↗ DW

Guillaume de L'Isle, *Mappemonde à l'usage du Roy, augmenté en 1755 des Nouvelles Découvertes*, later colour, some restoration, Philippe Buache, Paris, c1755, 17½ x 26¾in (44.5 x 68cm).
$1,600–1,750 ⊞ AMP

Africa

▶ **Sebastian Munster,** *Africa XXV Nova Tabula*, Latin text edition, woodcut, printed by Henri Petri, Basle, c1560, printed area 11½ x 14¾in (29 x 37.5cm).
$1,000–1,150 ⊞ Alte

J. N. Bellin, *Carte de la Coste Orientale d'Afrique*, coloured map of the eastern coast of Africa from the Cape of Good Hope to Cape Delgado, copperplate, Paris, c1750, 9 x 9½in (22 x 24cm).
$210–230 ⊞ JOP

John Speed, *Africae, described, the manners of their Habits, and buildinge. newlt done into English by I.S.*, with ten costume vignettes to the sides, eight city prospects, including Tangiers, Alexandria and Grand Canary along the top, verso with English text 'The Description of Africa' containing a mixture of fact and amusing myth, later colouring, some restoration, printed by Bassett & Chiswell, London, 1676, 15¼ x 20in (39 x 51cm).
$4,000–4,600 ⊞ Alte

◀ **J. N. Bellin,** *Carte de la Baye de Sainte Hélène*, coloured chart of St Helena Bay, on the Atlantic coast of Africa, copperplate, Paris, c1750, 6¼ x 8¼in (16 x 21cm).
$115–145 ⊞ JOP

Americas

Theodore de Bry, *Occidentalis Americae partis, vel earum vel Regionum quas Christophorus Columbus,* engraved map sheet showing the Carribean Islands, Florida, and portions of Latin and South America, a few repairs, printed by Bry, Frankfurt, 1594, 14½ x 18¼in (37 x 46.5cm).
$8,300–10,000 ✗ S(NY)
The map accompanied the account of Benzoni's travels in these waters between 1541 and 1556. It is one of the very few maps of the era to concentrate on the West Indies, Florida, Venezuela, Columbia and Central America.

Matthias Seutter, *Novus Orbus Sive America Meridionalis et Septentrionalis,* hand-coloured, framed, Augsberg, 1730 or later, 21 x 24in (53.5 x 61cm).
$1,700–1,900 ✗ SK(B)

LOCATE THE SOURCE
The source of each illustration in Miller's can be found by checking the code letters below each caption with the Key to Illustrations, pages 794–800.

Joseph Scott, *The United States Gazetteer,* 19 folding engraved maps, uncoloured as issued, contemporary tree calf, rebacked preserving original title label, Philadelphia, 1795, 12°.
$4,600–5,000 ✗ P
This was the first gazetteer of the United States.

John Speed, *A Map of Americas,* hand-coloured, engraved, text on verso, dated 1626, 11½ x 15in (29 x 38cm).
$580–650 ⊞ ES

Guillaume de L'Isle, *L'Amerique Septentrionale,* later colour, Paris, c1700, 18¼ x 24in (46.5 x 61cm).
$1,800–2,000 ⊞ AMP
L'Isle has discarded the guesswork of earlier cartographers and left blank the unknown areas to the north.

Tobias Conrad Lotter, *Pensylvania Nova Jersey et Nova York cum Regionibus ad Fluvium Delaware in America sitis, Nova Delineatione,* double-page engraved map extending from the Potomac to New Hampshire, original body colour, professionally remargined, Augsburg, c1745, 22½ x 19½in (57 x 49.5cm).
$1,100–1,300 ✗ Bon
This map presents the Middle Colonies and New England in such a manner that the Pennsylvania region is shown on an enlarged, over-emphasized scale at the expense of the remainder of the map detail. The map is also of considerable interest in that it shows Long Island as a peninsula of New York province.

▶ **C. Smith,** steel engraving of America, published 1833, 15 x 11in (38 x 28cm).
$115–145 ⊞ MAG

Pierre du Val, *Canada,* The Eastern Seaboard, from Hudson's Bay down to Chesapeak Bay, with the western Great Lakes open-ended, New York is marked 'N. Amsterdam al=Manhate', original outline colour, Paris, 1672, 4 x 4¾in (10 x 12cm).
$360–400 ⊞ Alte

John Senex, *A Map of Louisiana and of the River Mississippi,* engraved map from *A New General Atlas, Containing a Geographical and Historical Account of All the Empires, Kingdoms, and Other Dominions of the World,* original outline colour, London, 1719, 20½ x 23½in (52 x 59.5cm).
$3,200–3,600 ✗ NOA
The British mapmaker Senex stole the design for this map from his French competitor de L'Isle's 1718 *Carte de la Louisiane et du Cours du Mississippi.* An 18th-century Parisian critic called the Senex production 'a most impudent plagiarism'. Greatly readable, useful and entertaining in English translation, the map delineates the ranges of 'Wandering Indians and Maneaters' in present-day Louisiana and Texas, as well as Indian nations 'promiscuous and destroyed'. Not remarkably, Senex edits down the sphere of French influence in North America (influence exaggerated in de L'Isle's map).

Asia, Indonesia & Oceania

Jodocus Hondius, *Japan,* a reduced version of his folio map of 1606, published in the *Atlas Minor* 1606–21, later colour, Amsterdam, 1607, 6 x 7¼in (15 x 18.5cm).
$460–500 ⊞ Alte

Victor Levasseur, *Océanie,* steel-engraved map from the *Atlas Universel Illustré,* with a decorative engraved border including vignettes of costumes and portraits, original outline colour with additions on the vignettes, Paris, c1850, 12½ x 17¾in (32 x 45cm).
$140–180 ⊞ Alte

P. Goos, *Pascaerte Vande Zuyd-Zee Tussche California En Ilhas De Ladrones,* chart showing the island of California, Japan and Carpentaria, with north to the right, lower border trimmed and reinstated, Amsterdam, 1666, 17 x 21¼in (43 x 54cm).
$2,300–2,600 ⊞ JOP
This chart is one of the earliest examples recording the observations of Tasman's voyages.

Carolus Allard, *Nova Tabula Indiae Orientalis,* engraving with later coloured outlines and details, late 17thC, 17¾ x 22in (45 x 56cm).
$800–950 ⚲ RTo

Giovanni Antonio Magini, *India Orientalis,* the Far East, after Ortelius, showing northwest America, set in a page of text, Galignani, Venice, c1597, 5¼ x 7in (13.5 x 18cm).
$450–500 ⊞ Alte

India, original watercolour map of the River Ganges on eight sheets, executed in blue, red and brown inks, delineating its towns, forts and tributaries, British Military, India, c1820, 8 x 12½in (20.5 x 32cm).
$1,100–1,300 ⚲ Bon

Europe & the Middle East

John Speed, *Newe Mape of Germany,* hand-coloured, engraved, text on verso, printed by George Humble, dated 1626, 15¼ x 20in (38.5 x 51cm).
$650–725 ⊞ ES

John Speed, *Greece,* hand-coloured, engraved, English text on verso, printed by Bassett & Chiswell, 1676, 15½ x 20in (39.5 x 51cm).
$580–650 ⚲ DW

Mercator/Hondius, copper engraving of Crete and Greek Islands, published 1636, 15 x 20in (38 x 51cm).
$450–500 ⊞ MAG

P. Cluverius, copper engraving of Switzerland, 1711, 11 x 15in (28 x 38cm).
$110–125 ⊞ MAG

Pierre du Val, *La France en toute son estendue sous le Roy Louis XIV l'an 1668,* engraved map, inscribed by Louis XIV, declaring his love for France, 'To me my heart, to me the blood & the life of my joy, Louis', signed above the cartouche, Paris 1668, 16¾ x 21in (42.5 x 53.5cm).
$10,000–11,500 ⚲ S(NY)
Du Val (1618–83) was geographer to the king. His cartographic work is known for its accuracy and clarity, with his maps sought-after not only for their aesthetic value but also for their usefulness as historical documents. Du Val learned his geographic expertise from his uncle, Nicolas Sanson, the distinguished cartographer.

Great Britain & Ireland

Christopher Saxton, *Herefordshire,* with cartouche, two armorials, coloured, early edition, 1577–79, 16 x 21in (40.5 x 53.5cm).
$3,000–3,500 ➤ RBB

John Speed, *Hantshire described and divided,* engraved by Jodocus Hondius, including a plan of Winchester and crests of local noble families, later colour, printed by George Humble, London, 1627, 14¾ x 20in (37.5 x 51cm).
$1,300–1,450 ⊞ Alte

J. Blaeu, copper engraving of the North Riding of Yorkshire, 1646, 21 x 16in (53.5 x 40.5cm).
$650–725 ⊞ MAG

Alain Manesson Mallet, *Escosse,* map of Scotland, showing the Orkneys, Shetlands and Faroes, published in a German edition of *Description de l'Univers,* later colour, Frankfurt, 1684, 6 x 4in (15 x 10cm).
$140–180 ⊞ Alte

William Kip, *A Map of Cornwall,* hand-coloured engraving, c1600, 12 x 15¾in (30.5 x 40cm), framed.
$430–480 ➤ P(EA)

Henrik Hondius, *Magnae Britanniae et Hiberniae Tabula,* British Isles, double-page engraved map with an inset map of the Orkneys, Latin text, original hand-colouring, 1631 or later, 15 x 20in (38 x 51cm).
$720–800 ➤ Bon

Willem Blaeu, *Hibernia Regnum Vulgo Ireland,* original colour, French text edition, Amsterdam, c1650, 15½ x 19¾in (39.5 x 50cm).
$870–1,000 ⊞ AMP

Robert Morden, *Westmorland,* an engraved county map, framed, late 17thC, 14¼ x 16½in (36 x 42cm).
$230–290 ➤ PFK

▶ ***The New Description and State of England,*** first edition, 55 double-page engraved maps, half of one map detached but present, contemporary calf, for Robert Morden etc, 1701, 8°.
$2,000–2,300 ➤ BBA

John Speed, *The Countie Pallantine of Lancaster Described and Divided into Hundreds, 1610,* hand-coloured with inset plan, eight Royal portraits, with text to verso, printed by Bassett & Chiswell, 1676 or later, 17½ x 22½in (44.5 x 57cm), framed and glazed.
$580–650 ➤ HAM

John Speed, *The Kingdome of England,* hand-coloured, engraved, text on verso, printed by George Humble, dated 1632, 15¼ x 19¾in (38.5 x 50cm).
$650–720 ⊞ ES

John Speed, *Gloucestershire,* hand-coloured engraved map with plans of Gloucester and Bristol, 1670, 15¾ x 20½in (40 x 52cm).
$620–680 ➤ HOLL

John Overton, *Surriae,* hand-coloured, late 17thC, 15 x 19in (38 x 48.5cm).
$1,000–1,200 ➤ Gam

◀ **Herman Moll,** *A New Description of England and Wales, with the Adjacent Islands, with a particular account of the Products, Trade, and Manufactures of the respective places in every County,* two folding general maps, 48 single-page engraved maps, mostly of counties, contemporary half-calf, rear cover deficient, first edition, 1724, 2°.
$4,300–5,000 ↗ **DW**

▶ **Sir William Petty,** *The County of Cork,* engraved map, c1740, 27 x 38½in (68.5 x 98cm).
$800–900 ↗ **MEA**

▶ **A Map of the Hundreds of Stowting Street & Heane and of Bircholt Barony and Franchise,** 1779, 24 x 21½in (61 x 54.5cm).
$260–290 ⊞ **CBO**

J. **Rocque,** *The Small British Atlas,* 54 maps, contemporary red morocco 1762, 4°.
$4,600–5,500 ↗ **GAM**

Bowles or Kitchin, *A new and complete map of Scotland, and Islands thereto belonging,* some outline colouring, framed and glazed, four sheets, c1780, 45¾ x 39½in (116 x 100.5cm).
$1,300–1,600 ↗ **P(Ed)**

Samuel Clark, *Reuben Ramble's Travel through the Counties of England,* 40 lithographed maps, surrounded b illustrations depicting scenes in that county, original cloth, 1845, 8°.
$2,000–2,300 ↗ **S**

◀ **T. Moule,** *Surrey,* steel engraving c1845, 8 x 10in (20.5 x 25.5cm).
$100–120 ⊞ **MAG**

Town & City Plans

▶ **J. Andrews,** *A Collection of Plans of the Most Capital Cities of Every Empire...in Europe and some Remarkable Cities in the other three parts of the World...from Actual Surveys,* 42 engraved plans, disbound, 1772, 4°.
$1,800–2,200 ↗ **BBA**

A View of London about the Year 1560, a reduced facsimile of one of the first plans of London, incorrectly attributed to Agas, showing St Paul's Cathedral, London Bridge with buildings on it, the Globe and the Bull-Baiting Ring, later colouring, London, c1738, 12¼ x 18¾in (31 x 47.5cm).
$800–880 ⊞ **Alte**

Miller's is a price GUIDE not a price LIST

John Rocque, *A Survey of the City of Kilkenny,* Ireland, double-page town map engraved by G. Byrne, 1758, 19¾ x 27¾in (50 x 70.5cm).
$2,900–3,200 ↗ **Bon**

Cole and Roper, a plan of Oxford, copper engraving, 1808, 10 x 8in (25.5 x 20.5cm).
$95–110 ⊞ **MAG**

Dolls
Selected Makers

A Georgene Averill Bonnie *bébé* bisque-headed character doll, with cloth body and composition arms and legs, America, 1920s, 15in (38cm) high.
$1,400–1,600 ⊞ DOL

A Chad Valley Princess Elizabeth doll, the felt face with painted features, blue glass eyes and brown hair, velvet jointed body, wearing a pink cotton dress and felt overcoat, 1930s, 21in (53.5cm) high.
$580–720 ⚒ Bon(C)

An EFFanBEE composition character doll, 'Bubbles', America, c1930, 24in (61cm) high.
$580–650 ⊞ DOL

A Carl Bergner three-faced bisque-headed doll, with cloth body and composition hands and lower legs, Germany, 1890s, 12in (30.5cm) high.
$2,200–2,600 ⊞ DOL

A Chad Valley Snow White and the Seven Dwarfs, all with labels, Snow White with inoperative key-wind musical mechanism, 1930s, Snow White 15½in (39.5cm) high.
$720–800 ⚒ S(S)

A DEP bisque-headed doll, with weighted brown glass eyes and ball-jointed wood and composition body, impressed 'DEP 15', Germany, c1900, 31in (78.5cm) high.
$1,250–1,450 ⚒ S(S)

▶ **A EFFanBEE Grumpikins doll,** with composition head and breast-plate, soft body and composition arms and legs, wearing original dress and bonnet, America, 1927, 12in (30.5cm) high.
$140–180 ⊞ DOL

A Cameo Doll Co composition Scootles doll, by Rose O'Neill, with sleep eyes, wearing an original cream dress with red, blue and yellow detail, 1920–30, 15½in (39.5cm) high.
$870–1,000 ⊞ DOL
Scootles were created by Rose O'Neill in 1925 and made from bisque and fabric composition. They were produced in a large number of sizes and in both black and white. Rose O'Neill was also the inspiration behind the Kewpie dolls shown on page 658.

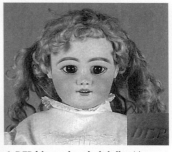

A DEP bisque-headed doll, with paper-weight eyes and composition jointed body, the head inscribed 'DEP 10', Germany, c1905, 21¾in (55.5cm) high.
$720–870 ⚒ B&L

DOLLS

A Heinrich Handwerk bisque-headed doll, mould No. 99, with paperweight eyes and eight ball-jointed wood and composition body, Germany, c1890, 27in (68.5cm) high.
$1,600–1,900 ⊞ **DOL**

A Hertel, Schwab & Co bisque-headed baby doll, with fixed blue eyes, painted hair and moulded fore-lock, five-piece composition body, Germany, c1910, 11in (28cm) high.
$430–500 ⊞ **BaN**

A Gebrüder Heubach bisque-headed doll, No. 320, with composition five-piece body, Germany, c1915, 20in (51cm) high.
$260–290 ⊞ **PSA**

A Gebrüder Heubach Revalo doll, for Gebrüder Olaver, with bisque head and body, c1920, 10in (25.5cm) high.
$500–580 ⊞ **PSA**

A Heubach Koppelsdorf bisque-headed baby doll, mould No. 300, with five-piece body, Germany, c1920, 14in (35.5cm) high.
$300–440 ⊞ **PSA**
Armand Marseille's son, also called Armand, married the daughter of Ernst Heubach of Koppelsdorf, and in 1919 the two companies merged to form the Koppelsdorf Porcelain Factory, producing bisque character and baby dolls. Ernst Heubach should not be confused with Gebrüder Heubach, an unconnected company.

A Ideal Novelty & Toy Co composition Shirley Temple doll, with original wig and red and white dress, America, c1934, 21in (53.5cm) high.
$900–1,000 ⊞ **DOL**

A Jumeau pressed bisque-headed portrait *bébé* doll, with extreme almond-shaped blue spiral paperweight eyes and eight ball-jointed wood and composition body, wearing a cream dress with red detail, head marked '3', France, c1883, 13½in (34.5cm) high.
$12,300–13,700 ⊞ **DAn**

▶ **A Tête Jumeau bisque-headed doll,** with wood and composition body, France, 1890s, 29in (73.5cm) high.
$2,500–2,800 ⊞ **DOL**

A Helen Jenson Gladdie doll, with bisqueline head, cloth body and composition arms and legs, wearing original red and green tartan clothes and bonnet, c1929, 19½in (49.5cm) high.
$2,500–2,800 ⊞ **DOL**

A Jumeau bisque-headed child doll, with brown paperweight eyes, jointed wood and composition body, wearing original cream dress with fawn pinafore, incised mark '13', France, c1890, 26in (66cm) high.
$3,200–3,600 ⊞ BaN

A Tête Jumeau bisque-headed doll, with wood and composition jointed body, wearing a navy and white sailor dress, France, c1907, 16in (40.5cm) high.
$2,200–2,400 ⊞ DOL

A Jumeau bisque-headed doll, with paperweight eyes and wood and composition jointed body, France, c1907, 23in (58.5cm) high.
$2,200–2,400 ⊞ DOL

► **A Kämmer & Reinhardt Simon & Halbig bisque-headed doll,** with weighted brown glass eyes and ball-jointed wood and composition body, impressed '85' and 'W' on forehead, Germany, c1890, 33½in (85cm) high.
$1,200–1,400 ⋏ S(S)
Simon & Halbig also made heads for other doll manufacturers, including Kämmer & Reinhardt, Schmidt & Dressel, Jumeau and Roullet & Decamps. They usually carry the marks of both firms.

A French bisque-headed doll, with fixed blue glass eyes, on a repainted ball-jointed composition body, possibly Jumeau, head restored, marked 'VW', 1910–20, 26in (66cm) high.
$1,600–1,900 ⋏ P(WM)

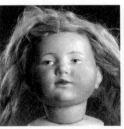

A Kämmer & Reinhardt Simon & Halbig bisque-headed walking doll, with weighted blue glass eyes and wood and composition body, impressed '62' and 'W' on forehead, Germany, c1890, 24½in (62cm) high.
$650–720 ⋏ S(S)

A Kämmer & Reinhardt bisque-headed character doll, 'Marie', with painted blue eyes and ball-jointed turned wood and composition body, some damage, impressed 'K&R10139', Germany, 15½in (39.5cm) high.
$2,200–2,600 ⋏ S(S)

► **A Kämmer & Reinhardt mulatto bisque-headed doll,** with weighted brown glass eyes and a fully jointed composition body, damage to base of neck, Germany, c1910, 25in (63.5cm) high.
$500–600 ⋏ Bon(C)

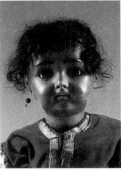

Bodies

The body of a doll is a crucial factor in the assessment of its origin, history and worth. Bisque dolls' bodies vary enormously in style, materials, construction and quality, and a working knowledge of the various body types available is therefore invaluable to the collector. Illustrated here are examples of commonly-found body types.

The gusseted kid body, with wide shoulders and hips, was used on bisque shoulder-headed fashion dolls.

In French-jointed bodies, used on early French bébés, each pair of limbs is connected by means of a ball fixed to one of the limbs.

This wood and composition body is jointed, with fixed wrists, and was made in Germany in c1890.

In eight ball- (or floating-ball) jointed bodies, each pair of limbs slides over a shared but unconnected 'floating' ball joint.

This German jointed toddler body has the pronounced side hip joints and distinctive fat tummy used on character dolls produced after c1910. This type of toddler body was made in both wood and composition.

This type of five-piece, bent-limb composition baby body was used on a number of baby and character dolls after 1910 until the outbreak of WWII.

A Kämmer & Reinhardt bisque-headed tiny child doll, with five-piece composition body, original wig and clothes, Germany, c1910, 7½in (19cm) high.
$400–460 ⊞ BaN

l. A Kämmer & Reinhardt bisque-headed doll, with weighted brown glass eyes and fully jointed composition body, Germany, c1910, 13in (33cm) high.
$320–360
r. A Cuno & Otto Dressel bisque-headed doll, with weighted blue glass eyes and fully jointed composition body, Germany, c1910, 24in (61cm) high.
$650–720 ⊞ Bon(C)

◀ **A Kämmer & Reinhardt Simon & Halbig bisque-headed character doll,** mould No. 122, with wood and composition ball-jointed toddler body, wearing a cream dress with blue banding, Germany, c1920, 19in (48.5cm) high.
$1,100–1,300 ⊞ DOL

▶ **A German bisque-headed doll,** with weighted blue glass eyes and ball-jointed composition body, probably Kämmer & Reinhardt, lacking one tooth, impressed '192', 1920s, 34in (86.5cm) high.
$800–950 ⚲ P(WM)

A Kämmer & Reinhardt bisque-headed character toddler doll, with blue flirty sleep eyes and a fully articulated wood and composition body, wearing a white and red-dotted dress, impressed mark 'K*R Simon Halbig 126 46', Germany, early 20thC, 20in (51cm) high.
$680–720 ⚲ SK(B)

DOLLS

A Kämmer & Reinhardt bisque-headed character doll, with weighted blue glass eyes and ball-jointed composition body, impressed 'K*R Simon & Halbig, 117/A, 42', Germany, 1920s, 23in (58.5cm) high.
$3,600–4,300 ⚲ P(WM)

A German bisque shoulder-headed doll, with fixed blue glass eyes and gusseted kid body with bisque lower arms, impressed '10', probably Kestner, c1870, 22¾in (58cm) high.
$500–600 ⚲ S(S)

A Kestner child doll, No. 146, with fixed brown eyes and jointed wood and composition body, Germany, 1890s, 26in (66cm) high.
$1,450–1,750 ⊞ BaN

A J. D. Kestner bisque-headed character baby doll, No. 211, with weighted blue glass eyes and composition body, Germany, c1910, 15in (38cm) high.
$720–870 ⚲ Bon(C)

A Kestner bisque-headed character baby doll, with brown sleep eyes, cloth body with side-swivel cloth legs, composition hands, the squeaker mechanism in the body not working, Germany, c1920, 17in (43cm) high.
$580–720 ⚲ SK(B)

A Käthe Kruse *Schlenkerchen* doll, with painted features, pressed and oil-painted double-seam head and separately stitched thumbs, stamped, Germany, c1922, 13in (33cm) high.
$5,800–6,500 ⚲ SK(B)

A set of Madame Alexander quintuplet dolls, with composition bodies, painted features and moulded hair, all wearing original romper suits and bonnets in pink, blue, yellow and mauve, seated in a yellow and green wooden garden swing-chair, America, c1930, dolls 7in (18cm) high.
$720–870 ⚲ Bon(C)

A Limoges bisque-headed doll, with five-piece composition body, France, c1910, 8in (20.5cm) high.
$130–145 ⊞ PSA

◀ **An Armand Marseille bisque-headed doll,** with weighted blue glass eyes, blonde mohair wig and ball-jointed wood and composition body, impressed 'AM13 DEP', Germany, c1910, 29in (73.5cm) high.
$500–580 ⚲ S(S)

▶ **An Armand Marseille bisque-headed composition doll,** with ball-jointed body and original cream lace dress and hat, Germany, 1890s, 40in (101.5cm) high.
$2,900–3,200 ⊞ DOL

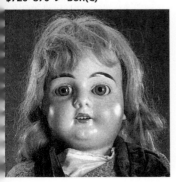

An Armand Marseille bisque-headed doll, with jointed composition body, wearing a cream dress and apple-green cloak, marked 'AM 1894', Germany, c1900, 9in (23cm) high.
$500–580 ⊞ PSA

An Armand Marseille bisque-headed Dream Baby doll, mould No. 341, with blue sleep eyes and original cream lace clothes, Germany, c1920, 14in (35.5cm) high.
$330–370 ⊞ BaN

A poured wax shoulder-headed doll, with fixed blue glass eyes and cloth body, with poured wax lower limbs, probably by Montanari, shoulder-plate restored, mid-19thC, 21in (53.5cm) high.
$500–600 ↗ S(S)

An Armand Marseille bisque-headed doll, with blue sleep eyes, stamped 'A II M.D.R.G.M.', Germany, early 20thC, 25½in (65cm) high.
$130–145 ↗ DMC

An Armand Marseille bisque-headed Oriental doll, with a composition body, Germany, 10in (25.5cm) high.
$720–870 ⊞ BaN

A Mattel Barbie doll, wearing a black and white swimming costume, America, 1960s, 11½in (29cm) high, in original box.
$260–290 ↗ Bon(C)

◄ **A Reliable Toy Co doll,** the composition head with blue sleep eyes, with a fabric body and composition limbs, dressed in original clothes, Canada, 1940s, 17in (43cm) long, in original box.
$100–120 ↗ PFK

An Armand Marseille bisque-headed character baby doll, No. 990, with five-piece composition body, wearing a pale blue suit and bonnet, Germany, c1920, 12in (30.5cm) high.
$400–440 ⊞ PSA

An Armand Marseille bisque-headed character doll, with intaglio blue eyes and curved-limb over-painted composition body, impressed mark '700/70', Germany, c1920, 9in (23cm) high.
$1,000–1,300 ↗ S(S)

A Kewpie composition doll, with original pink, white and blue clothing, 1930s, 11in (28cm) high.
$400–440 ⊞ DOL
The first Kewpies were made in 1913 at the Kestner factory in Germany, but soon were being manufactured at other factories in Germany and America.

Miller's Compares

I. A Grace Storey Putnam bisque-headed Bye-Lo baby doll, with cloth body, wearing original cream lace dress and bonnet, made in Germany for the American market, 1925–26, 18in (45.5cm) high.
$1,150–1,300 ⊞ DOL

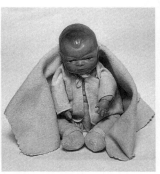

II. A Grace Storey Putnam composition Bye-Lo baby doll, wearing original clothes, 1930s, 13in (33cm) high.
$350–400 ⊞ DOL

Grace Storey Putnam (active c1922–30) was an art teacher at Mills College, Oakland, California. She designed various dolls' heads and in particular the popular Bye-Lo baby, made in Germany for the American market. As can be seen here, the value of these dolls can vary: Item I is an example of the largest size made by the company and dates to early in the production period. It is also made of bisque. Item II, being smaller, later and made from the less desirable composition, sold for considerably less than Item I.

A Schoenau & Hoffmeister bisque-headed doll, with weighted blue glass eyes and a fully jointed composition body, Germany, c1910, 24in (61cm) high.
$340–400 ⚲ Bon(C)

A Simon & Halbig bisque-headed character doll, with blue sleep eyes and ball-jointed composition body, original clothes, impressed mark with star, Germany, c1910, 18in (45.5cm) high.
$430–500 ⚲ F&C

An S.F.B.J. bisque-headed doll, mould No. 60, with fixed glass eyes and jointed composition body, 1900–10, 22in (56cm) high.
$500–600 ⚲ CGC

A Jumeau bisque-headed doll, for S.F.B.J., with blue paperweight eyes, jointed wood and composition body, with original *café au lait* clothes, stamped, France, c1907, 13in (33cm) high.
$2,000–2,300 ⊞ EW

A set of five Norah Wellings Jollyboy sailor dolls, c1930, 5in (12.5cm) high.
$180–220 ⚲ RPI
Norah Wellings, a former Chad Valley designer, set up her own company with her brother Leonard in Wellington, Shropshire. They produced a wide variety of character dolls, including sailors, South Sea Islanders and pixies, which typically have well-modelled velvet or felt heads with zig-zag stitched seams on the back of the head and body. Norah Wellings' dolls are not uncommon, but to be of value they must be in good condition and with original clothing, as cloth is hard to restore.

A Kämmer & Reinhardt Simon & Halbig bisque-headed character doll, mould No. 121, with composition bent-limb baby body, cream clothes, yellow hair and green bonnet, c1920, 14in (35.5cm) high.
$720–800 ⊞ DOL

◄ **A Jules Steiner bisque-headed *bébé* doll,** with fully jointed composition body and original clothes, head and body signed, France, c1890, 18½in (47cm) high.
$4,350–4,750 ⊞ EW

DOLS

Unknown Makers

l. A German papier-mâché shoulder-headed doll, with painted features, moulded hair and bun, on a kid body with wooden lower limbs, in original costume and later blue jacket, c1835, 9in (23cm) high.
$650–720
r. A papier-mâché shoulder-headed doll, with black glass eyes and kid body, in original costume, probably French, c1835, 9in (23cm) high.
$500–580 ✗ S(S)

A wax-over-composition slit-head doll, with cloth body and leather arms, in original *café au lait* dress, c1837, 25in (63.5cm) high, in a wooden case.
$1,300–1,600 ⊞ DOL

A German wooden doll, with carved head, mortise and tenon peg-jointed wooden body and original silk clothes, early 19thC, 9in (23cm) high.
$1,000–1,200 ✗ SK(B)

A poured wax doll, with blue glass eyes and painted features, cloth body, wax lower arms and legs, original clothes, c1860, 17in (43cm) high, with a small leather trunk of clothes and accessories.
$800–880 ✗ Bon(C)

A German china-headed pedlar doll, with jointed wooden body and limbs, c1840, 6in (15cm) high, on a wooden base.
$1,300–1,500 ⊞ DAn

A German papier-mâché shoulder-headed doll, with painted eyes, kid body and wooden lower limbs, c1840, 15in (38cm) high.
$500–600 ✗ SK(B)

▶ **A wax-over-composition pedlar doll,** with blue glass eyes, the cloth body with leather arms, c1860, 19in (48.5cm) high, on a wooden base with glass dome.
$800–950 ✗ Bon(C)

A French swivel-headed fashion doll, with fixed blue glass eyes, cloth-over-wood body and original costume, one leg missing, minor damage, c1860, 13in (33cm) high.
$500–600 ✗ S(S)

DOLLS

A Victorian wax-headed doll, with inset blue eyes, rag body and composition limbs, 24in (61cm) high.
$220–260 ✣ PFK

A French bisque swivel shoulder-headed fashion doll, with fixed blue glass eyes and kid leather body, wearing original turquoise costume, some damage, c1870, 10in (25.5cm) high.
$950–1,100 ✣ Bon(C)

A German shoulder-headed doll, with key-wind walking mechanism, wearing a pink silk dress, c1870, 10in (25.5cm) high.
$300–350 ✣ SWO

A German parian doll, with blue glass eyes and moulded hair, a cloth body and bisque lower arms and legs, wearing a pale blue silk and lace dress, odd lower legs, c1880, 14in (35.5cm) high.
$300–350 ✣ Bon(C)

A pedlar doll and wares, 1880–1910, 15in (38cm) high, on a wooden base with glass dome.
$5,800–6,500 ⊞ EW

A wax-over-composition doll, Queen Victoria as an old lady, with remains of grey wig, the lower arms jointed to move simultaneously, damaged, c1890, 10½in (26.5cm) high.
$580–720 ✣ S(S)

A German bisque-headed doll, with blue glass eyes and fully jointed body, wearing original white dress, c1910, 23in (58.5cm) high.
$580–720 ✣ Bon(C)

A French bisque miniature doll, c1900, 5½in (14cm) high, with a trunk of accessories.
$1,800–2,200 ⊞ EW

▶ **An American composition Shirley Temple doll,** with sleep eyes and jointed arms and legs, c1930, 18in (45.5cm) high.
$530–580 ✣ DuM

A German bisque-headed doll, with weighted brown glass eyes and fully jointed composition body, c1910, 23in (58.5cm) high.
$460–540 ✣ Bon(C)

Dolls' Houses & Accessories

A wooden dolls' house, the exterior repainted black and white, the front opening in two sections to reveal six rooms, bathroom and hall, wired for light, with wooden base and carrying handles, c1880, 52½in (133.5cm) wide, with a quantity of 1960s furniture and effects.
$1,000–1,200 ✣ S(S)

A Continental oak dolls' house, the roof with carved details of apples, pears and foliage, engraved to front, the windows and doors opening to reveal four rooms, hallway and landing, with central door to each floor, engraved date, 1887, 38in (96.5cm) wide.
$1,200–1,400 ✣ Bon(C)

A Lines Brothers furnished dolls' house, with lithographed and painted wooden exterior in green, orange and ochre, the sides opening to reveal two ground floor rooms with original wallpapers and an attic, early 20thC, 15in (38cm) wide.
$1,000–1,200 ✣ Bon(C)

◄ **A Dutch dolls' kitchen room set and contents,** with painted green and cream walls and red plank flooring, 1890s, 27in (68.5cm) wide.
$800–1,000 ✣ Bon(C)

A wooden dolls' house, with an opening front, back and roof, with some period wallpaper and furniture, early 20thC, 50in (127cm) high.
$580–650 ✣ SWO

A Tri-ang mock-Tudor wooden dolls' house, the exterior painted cream with flowers to the walls, the front opening in two hinged sections to reveal four rooms and staircase, all with original flooring, wallpapers and curtains, c1930, 33¾in (85.5cm) wide.
$500–600 ✣ S(S)

An Amersham dolls' bungalow, the exterior painted cream and with painted and applied trees and flowers, the hinged front opening to reveal two rooms with light fittings, some losses, c1940, 14½in (37cm) high.
$250–300 ✣ S(S)

A Tri-ang Welsh *Y Bwthyn Bach* thatched cottage, with painted yellow thatch roof, 1930s, 28in (71cm) wide.
$390–430 ⊞ DOL
This is a copy of the child-sized play house made for the young Princess Elizabeth by the Principality of Wales.

An ivory dolls' house dolls' stand, c1880, 3in (7.5cm) high.
$115–145 ⊞ PSA

A dolls' house wax doll, with cream blouse and red skirt, c1880, 8in (20.5cm) high.
$220–240 ⊞ PSA

A gilt dolls' house candlestick, c1880, 2½in (6.5cm) high.
$180–210 ⊞ PSA

► **A glass dolls' house water jug set,** c1880, jug 1½in (4cm) high.
$65–75 ⊞ PSA

Teddy Bears

A Bing mechanical teddy bear, in good working order, Germany, c1910, 12in (30.5cm) high.
$4,600–5,000 ⚒ CalT
A key to activate the wind-up mechanism which moves the bear's head from side to side is located under the right arm.

A Chiltern Hygenic Toys blonde plush teddy bear, late 1930s, 24¾in (63cm) high.
$340–400 ⚒ CGC

An American teddy bear, replaced shoe-button eyes, retains one glass eye which may be original, possibly Ideal, c1915, 18in (45.5cm) high.
$190–220 ⚒ SK(B)
Included with the bear are several of the original owner's childhood books, her school diplomas and a photocopy of a photograph of her as a child.

◄ **A Merrythought golden mohair teddy bear,** with orange glass eyes, fully jointed, 1930s, 21in (53.5cm) high.
$500–600 ⚒ Bon(C)

A Farnell brown mohair teddy bear, with black boot-button eyes, swivel head, jointed arms and hips, c1912, 11in (28cm) high.
$720–870 ⚒ Bon(C)

An American Yes/No mohair mechanical teddy bear, with mohair foot and paw pads and glass eyes, mechanism in good working order, probably Ideal, c1915, 14½in (37cm) high.
$2,500–2,800 ⊞ CalT

A Farnell gold plush teddy bear, 1920s, 19¾in (50cm) high.
$1,250–1,450 ⚒ CGC

A Steiff cinnamon mohair teddy bear, Germany, 1904–05, 13in (33cm) high.
$2,300–2,600 ⊞ BaN

◄ **A Steiff light brown mohair teddy bear,** with black boot-button eyes, swivel head and movable arms and legs, nose and mouth restitched, Germany, c1909, 19in (48.5cm) high.
$2,900–3,200 ⚒ Bon(C)

A Merrythought teddy bear, replaced left glass eye, c1930, 20in (51cm) high.
$240–300 ⊞ TED

TEDDY BEARS

A Steiff brown mohair teddy bear, with original boot-button eyes, hand pads replaced, Germany, c1908, 11in (28cm) high.
$1,300–1,600 ⊞ TED

A Steiff blonde plush teddy bear, with black boot-button eyes and jointed limbs, growl inoperative, some damage to pads, Germany, c1910, 16½in (42cm) high.
$2,900–3,200 ↗ TEN

A Steiff mohair teddy bear, with black button eyes and swivel-jointed body, stitched snout, mouth stitching missing, c1910, Germany, 12½in (32cm) high.
$2,300–2,500 ↗ S(S)

A Steiff gold-blonde mohair teddy bear, with glass eyes and deep growl, Germany, 1920s, 17in (43cm) high.
$1,500–1,800 ⊞ TED

▶ **An Edwardian hump-backed teddy bear,** with glass eyes and jointed head, arms and legs, 23in (58.5cm) high.
$80–95 ↗ DA

A Steiff off-white mohair teddy bear, with original glass eyes and new felt pads, Germany, c1930, 16in (40.5cm) high.
$1,450–1,750 ⊞ TED

A Steiff/Hermann brown mohair teddy bear, with pink glass eyes, swivel head, jointed arms and hips and in-turning wrists, Germany, 1942, 20in (51cm) high.
$730–870 ↗ Bon(C)
This bear comes with an original letter, in German with English translation, relating how it had been made for a German couple who lived in the mountains and made a pet of a real bear, which had broken wrists and bloodshot eyes and visited their home every day. When it died the couple asked the Steiff factory to make them a bear in its memory, but they refused. However, on hearing the story, the factory-workers secretly made a bear. It had broken wrists like the real bear, but the employers found out and it was sent to the Sussenguth factory, in 1942, to be finished there. As they didn't have red, they gave it pink eyes to resemble the bloodshot eyes of the original bear.

A Steiff brown mohair teddy bear, with orange glass eyes, Germany, 1950s, 16in (40.5cm) high.
$800–950 ↗ Bon(C)

▶ **A golden mohair teddy bear,** with black boot-button eyes, old repairs, pads replaced, Germany, 1900–10, 30in (76cm) high.
$3,000–3,500 ↗ TAM

Toys
Mechanical Toys

A bisque-headed pierrot musical automaton, wearing a silk costume, standing on a box enclosing the movement, 19thC, 16in (40.5cm) high.
$230–290 ↗ DA

A seated fur monkey automaton, with painted face, hands and feet, on composition frame, the movement of the tail working the glass eyes, mouth and left front paw, late 19thC, 11½in (29cm) high.
$220–260 ↗ AH

► A tinplate Arnold Mac 700 clockwork motorcycle and rider, Germany, c1955, 5in (12.5cm) long.
$360–400 ⊞ ET

◄ A Marx Merrymakers tinplate mouse band, the lithographed piano with mechanism to side and stop/start handle, 1930s, piano 6½in 16.5cm) wide.
$870–1,000 ↗ Bon(C)

A Rosco Toys Charley Weaver Bartender, battery-powered with cocktail shaker and glass, c1950, 7in (18cm) high, with original box.
$65–80 ↗ AH

◄ A Durham Industries Cyclops plastic battery-powered robot, America, 1960s, 10in (25.5cm) high.
$115–145 ⊞ PLB

Money Banks

A cast-iron Paddy and the Pig money bank, by J. & E. Stevens, patent date 1882, 7in (18cm) high.
$1,200–1,400 ↗ S(S)
Paddy eats the coin from the pig's snout when the trotter is depressed.

► A cast-iron mechanical lighthouse money bank, with green house and red lighthouse, c1880, 10½in (26.5cm) high.
$7,300–8,000 ↗ S(NY)
When 20 nickels were deposited, the plunger on top of the lighthouse could be depressed and a trap door at the bottom could be withdrawn to extract the coins.

An American cast-iron mechanical money bank, late 19thC, 6in (15cm) high.
$260–290 ↗ DuM

TOYS

A cast-iron Jonah and the Whale mechanical money bank, by Shepherd Hardware, boat replaced, c1890, 10¼in (26cm) high.
$2,000–2,300 ⚒ S(NY)
When the lever is depressed, the whale opens his mouth, Jonah thrusts his son into the mouth, depositing a coin. When the lever is released Jonah returns to the back of the boat and the whale flaps his jaw in appreciation.

A cast-iron money bank, with articulated arm and open mouth, late 19thC, 5½in (14cm) high.
$75–90 ⚒ DA

A cast-iron Punch and Judy mechanical money bank, c1900, 6¼in (16cm) wide.
$440–500 ⚒ DuM

Noah's Arks

A brown-painted Noah's Ark, with removable roof, on wheels, containing Noah and his wife and a quantity of animals, c1900, 20in (51cm) long.
$870–1,100 ⚒ P(S)

A German wooden Noah's Ark, with brown painted base, the painted and stencilled sides in blue, grey and orange, with side sliding panel and over 100 pairs of colourfully painted animals, late 19thC, 23in (58.5cm) long.
$5,800–7,200 ⚒ Bon(C)

▶ **A German wooden Noah's Ark,** with removable sides revealing the hull, with a large collection of carved and painted wooden animals, part of hull missing, late 19thC, 22½in (57cm) long.
$720–870 ⚒ P(WM)

◀ **A late Victorian painted Noah's Ark,** with an assortment of composition animals, 26in (66cm) long.
$650–800 ⚒ Mal(O)

Rocking Horses

▶ **An American wooden rocking horse,** by J. A. Yost, with red-brown painted body, on a black-painted platform with the American flag and red pinstripes and stars, Philadelphia, 1860–90, 73in (185.5cm) long.
$1,900–2,200 ⚒ SK(B)

A Swedish wooden prancing rocking horse, some later painting, Dalarna, early 19thC, 49in (124.5cm) long.
$2,600–3,200 ⊞ FCL

▶ **A Victorian rocking horse,** c1860, 56in (142cm) long.
$1,400–1,600 ⊞ GKe

A Victorian wooden rocking horse, painted dapple grey, on a red painted stand, 71in (180.5cm) long.
$2,900–3,200 ⚒ HYD

A wooden rocking horse, painted dapple grey, fully restored, c1900, 48in (122cm) high.
$6,000–6,600 ⊞ RGa

A wooden rocking horse, painted cream, early 20thC, 32in (81.5cm) high.
$320–360 ✗ SWO

A wooden rocking horse, by G. & L. Lines, painted dapple grey, with a red saddle blanket, restored, c1910, 43in (109cm) long.
$2,600–2,900 ⊞ CRU

A wooden rocking horse, by J. Collinson, with original dapple grey finish, on a wooden trestle base, early 20thC, 52½in (133.5cm) high.
$650–720 ✗ S(S)

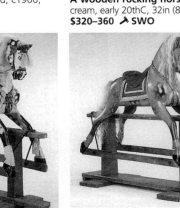

A wooden rocking horse, with original dapple grey finish and stirrups, replaced leathers, mane and tail, on a stained wooden stand, c1930, 52¾in (134cm) high.
$5,000–5,800 ✗ S(S)

A wooden rocking horse, painted dapple grey, retailed by Harrods, poor condition, 1950s, 45in (114.5cm) high.
$870–930 ✗ SWO

Soldiers

A Britains set of 10th Hussars (Prince of Wales's Own Royal), set No. 315, with five pieces, 1920–40, in original box.
$340–400 ✗ P(WM)

A Britains Types of the Colonial Army, Australian Infantry, set No. 1545, with eight pieces, some damage, 1930s, in original box.
$500–600 ✗ P(WM)

► A CBG set of Mignot Lancers of the Vistula, with six pieces, Germany, 1920s, in original box.
$320–350 ✗ Bon(C)

Trains

A Bing O gauge spirit-fired 4–4–0 LNWR tank locomotive, paintwork missing from black tank side, slight damage to boiler, c1904.
$440–500 ✗ AH

An Elettren O gauge electric 4–4–4–4 pantograph locomotive, FS CA 0428, 1950s.
$500–600 ✗ P(WM)

A Hornby O gauge clockwork Metropolitan electric locomotive, with printed maroon Metropolitan livery, with two coaches, early 1930s.
$360–430 ✗ WAL

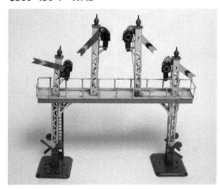

A Hornby electric signal gantry, c1932, 14in (35.5cm) wide.
$1,200–1,500 ⊞ HOB

A Hornby O gauge 4–6–2 LMS Princess Elizabeth locomotive and tender, 1937–39, in original red display box.
$1,500–1,800 ✗ P(WM)

An Exley O gauge restaurant carriage, c1938.
$440–500 ⊞ HOB

A cast-iron floor train, with black 2–2–0 steam locomotive attributed to Carpenter, black four-wheeled tender, burnt-orange New York Central and Hudson baggage car and passenger car by Harris, c1910, 43in (109cm) long.
$2,000–2,300 ✗ S(NY)

A Hornby O gauge Colman's Mustard wagon, c1923.
$2,600–2,900 ⊞ HOB

A Hornby O gauge clockwork goods train set, c1923, in original box.
$390–430 ⊞ HOB

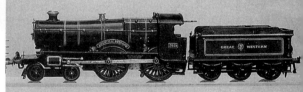

A Hornby O gauge clockwork 4–4–0 County of Bedford locomotive, and six-wheeler Great Western tender, finished in GWR livery, early 1930s.
$580–720 ✗ WAL

A Hornby Series E320 O gauge Flying Scotsman locomotive, No. 4472, with smoke deflectors and green LNER livery, a No. 2 Special tender, four wheels replaced, a No. 2 Special Pullman coach 'Loraine' and composite 'Arcadia', c1936, in E320 Flying Scotsman set box.
$580–650 ✗ S(S)

A Hornby E220 O gauge The Bramham Moor locomotive, No. 201, in LNER green livery and in base of original box, with No. 2 Special tender in original red box, c1936, 16in (40.5cm) long.
$3,200–3,600 ✗ S(S)

. **A Hornby clockwork 4–4–4 GWR locomotive,** finished in GWR green, 1940–50, 10in (25.5cm) long.
$230–290

. **A Hornby electric 4–4–2 locomotive,** finished in LMS red, 1940–50, 10in (25.5cm) long.
$290–350 ⚲ AH

A Hornby Dublo goods brake, finished in grey with black detail, c1952, with original blue and white box.
$65–75 ⊞ CWO

A Hornby Dublo N2 electric BR tank engine, finished in BR black and red livery, 1950s, 6in (15cm) long, with original blue box.
$75–90 ⊞ HAL

A Hornby Dublo set No. 2023 Caledonian electric passenger train, with a City of London locomotive, tender and two coaches finished in maroon livery, 1959–64, in original box.
$220–260 ⚲ Bon(C)

A Leeds Model Co Great Western locomotive, c1937, 7in (18cm) long.
$260–290 ⊞ HOB

A Märklin O gauge live steam locomotive, with tender, finished in green, red and black livery, Germany, c1912, 11in (28cm) long.
$480–530 ⊞ DQ

A Lionel Hell Gate Bridge, No. 300, repainted in grey, with brick-effect arches, America, c1930, 28¾in (73cm) long.
$870–950 S(S)

◀ **A Meccano red goods van,** with a grey roof, 1949–54, 3in (7.5cm) long, with original blue box.
$80–90 ⊞ CWO

Miller's Compares

I. A Wrenn Bodmin OO gauge 4–6–2 locomotive, No. W2236a, with green BR livery, c1970, in box stamped 'Packer No. 2'.
$400–450 ⚲ P(WM)

II. A Wrenn OO gauge Lyme Regis locomotive, No. W2237, c1970.
$180–220 P(WM)

As with all areas of collectables, it is the rarity factor that usually determines an appreciable difference in price between two apparently similar pieces. In the case of the trains pictured here, Item I, the Bodmin, was produced in far fewer numbers than Item II and was decorated in dark green, which is a less common colour than the standard light green of Item II.

TOYS

Vehicles

A Karl Bub lithographed tinplate limousine, finished in deep red, with original driver, the windshield and frame replaced, c1920, 12in (30.5cm) long.
$2,600–2,900 ✦ S(NY)

A Corgi Toys Ecurie Ecosse blue racing car transporter, early 1960s, 8in (20.5cm) long, with original blue and yellow box.
$115–145 ⊞ HAL

A Corgi Toys Central Park Garage, in bright blue, yellow, red and white, battery-powered garage sign to the front, 1962–64, 24in (61cm) long, vehicles not included in price.
$650–800 ✦ WAL

A Corgi Toys Chipperfields Circus, Gift Set No. 23, second issue with giraffe carrier, c1965.
$360–430 ✦ P(WM)

A Dinky Toys Sharp's Toffee Maidstone commercial vehicle, with black and red body, 1930s, 7¼in (18.5cm) long.
$500–600 ✦ CGC

A Crescent Toys Scamell Scarab with Shell BP Tanker, No. 1276, 6½in (16.5cm) long, with original box.
$145–175 ✦ RAR

▶ **A Dinky Toys Petrol Station,** No. 48, 1935–40, 5in (12.5cm) long, with original box.
$430–500 ✦ P(WM)

A Dinky Toys Foden 14 Ton Tanker, first type, with dark blue cab, light blue tank and hubs, late 1940s, 7in (18cm) long.
$40–50 ⊞ HAL

A Dinky Supertoys Mighty Antar Low Loader with Propeller, No. 986, with red cab and grey low-loader, 1951–61, 11½in (29cm) long.
$125–145 ✦ AH

TOYS

A Distler tinplate limousine, lithographed in red, yellow and black with orange roof and wings, with liveried chauffeur, clockwork mechanism faulty and incomplete, one rear door missing, 1920s, 12in (31cm) long.
$650–720 ↗ S(S)

A Kanto tinplate battery-powered Space Patrol vehicle, finished in blue, red, yellow and silver, Japan, c1955, 13in (33cm) long, with original box.
$3,600–4,000 ↗ S(NY)

A Foden Shackleton Toy FG Platform Lorry, grey with red mudguards, clockwork mechanism within cab, with key, 1948–52, 9in (23cm) long, with original box.
$430–480 ↗ S(S)

A Tri-ang Spot-On E.R.F. 68G Flatbed Lorry, c1960, 8¼in (21cm) long, with original box.
$115–145 ↗ AH

A Strauss clockwork Leaping Lena jalopy, lithographed in black and decorated with graffiti, America, 1930s, 8in (20.5cm) long.
$340–400 ↗ P(WM)
When operated, the car moves forward while the bonnet and front wheels tilt up and down.

A Günthermann General tinplate clockwork double-decker bus, with open cab, staircase and covered upper deck, Germany, c1930, 9¼in (23.5cm) long.
$2,600–2,900 ⊞ HOB

▶ **A Lesney Models of Yesteryear 1899 Horse-drawn Bus,** No. Y-12, with red body and chassis and brown horses, c1959, 3in (7.5cm) long.
$160–180 ⊞ WI

A Mamod model steam-powered car, 1948, 16in (40.5cm) long.
$180–220 ⊞ HOB

A Continental diecast Tour de France Red Cross ambulance, with cream and red livery, c1960.
$100–120 ↗ WAL

A Tri-ang red double-decker London bus, 1950–60s, 22½in (57cm) long.
$100–120 ↗ PFK

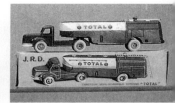

A JRD diecast Total articulated petrol tanker, with red cab and red and white trailer, late 1950s, with original yellow, red and white box.
$145–175 ↗ WAL

A Lesney Matchbox Transporter set, with six cars, German export example, 1959, in original box.
$340–380 ↗ WAL

A Schuco (US-Zone) Elektro 5311 MK De Luxe Ingenico set, late 1940s, cars 10½in (26.5cm) long, in original red box.
$430–500 ↗ P(WM)

A Tri-ang milk lorry, with red cab and blue body, and a complete set of eight Tri-ang Dairies milk churns, 1950–60s, 16in (40.5cm) long.
$100–120 ↗ PFK

Miscellaneous Toys & Games

A pair of carved wooden horses, by F. H. Ayres, painted in cream and dapple, with original leather tack, c1890, 12in (30.5cm) long, on a wooden base with wheels.
$300–350 ✗ Bon(C)

A felt-covered brown cow on wheels, with glass eyes, early 20thC, 11½in (29cm) long.
$250–300 ✗ SK(B)

A Britains Farm Waggon, No. 5F, with green body, red wheels and a cream horse, c1950, 9in (23cm) long.
$130–145 ✗ RAR

► **A Britains Zoo set,** No. 24Z, 1950s, in original box.
$1,200–1,400 ✗ WAL

A Regence ivory chess set, one set stained red, c1840, king 3½in (9cm) high.
$1,300–1,600 ⊞ TMi

A Jaques Staunton ivory chess set, one set stained red, 19thC, king 4½in (11cm) high, in a Carton Pierre box.
$2,900–3,200 ✗ CMS

An early Victorian mahogany folding bagatelle board, with baize lining and inlaid interior, 22in (56cm) wide.
$180–220 ✗ MCA

A glass chessboard, with mahogany frame, 19thC, 20in (51cm) square.
$180–220 ⊞ TWr

◄ **An American maple doll's cradle,** 19thC, 18in (45.5cm) long.
$260–290 ✗ DuM

► **A mahogany and yew cribbage board,** c1800, 9¼in (23.5cm) long.
$500–600 ⊞ SEA

A set of 28 bone dominoes, the wooden box with a sliding cover centred by a navette-shaped bone medallion, the sides inlaid, lacking dice and cover to the dice compartment, possibly Napoleonic prisoner-of-war work, early 19thC, box 6in (15cm) long.
$115–145 ✗ PFK

An American Columbia or the Land of the West gameboard, with coloured lithographic images of American states, and cities and events in American history, c1850, 23 x 28in (58.5 x 71cm), framed and glazed.
$1,450–1,750 ✗ SK(B)

An Edwardian doll's pram, c1910, 33in (84cm) long.
$800–900 ⊞ DOL

Ephemera
Annuals, Books & Comics

More Rupert Adventures, Daily Express, 1943.
$180–210 ⚒ CBP

The Adventures of Mickey Mouse, Walt Disney, published by George G. Harrap & Co, colour illustrations throughout, original colour-printed picture boards with matching dust-jacket, 1931, 8°.
$1,200–1,300 ⚒ DW
This is probably one of the finest surviving copies of this very early and scarce English edition Mickey Mouse book in its original dust-jacket.

Amazing Stories Annual, first publication of *The Master Mind of Mars* by E. Rich Burroughs, and *Under The Knife* by H. G. Wells, 1927.
$320–360 ⚒ CBP
This was the only annual published under this title.

Captain Marvel Adventures, issue No. 4, 1941.
$320–360 ⚒ CBP

Blue Bolt Weird Tales, issue No. 113, 1952.
$60–75 ⚒ CBP

> **Cross Reference**
> See Colour Review
> (page 740)

▶ **Action Comics,** issue No. 73, Superman propaganda war story, 1944.
$80–95 ⚒ CBP

The Dandy's Desperate Dan Annual, 1953.
$145–175 ⚒ CBP

Hawkman, issue No. 1, 1964.
$50–60 ⚒ CBP

Peanuts, Charles Schulz, pen and ink with brushwork and white highlights, on paper, signed and with an additional presentation signature at the top, 1959, framed and glazed, 7 x 29in (18 x 73.5cm).
$6,500–7,300 ⚒ S(NY)

▶ **The Adventures of Tintin and the Picaros,** by Hergé (George Rémi), coloured strip cartoons, inscribed and dated 1977 by the author below an original sketch of the heads of Tintin and Snowy, in original pictorial wrappers, 1976, large 8°.
$580–720 ⚒ P

Autographs

Henry Wadsworth Longfellow, a signed stanza with a note presenting his compliments, dated 11th July 1865, framed with photograph.
$1,000–1,250 ⚲ SK(B)

Charles II, an autographed letter, signed 'Charles P' as Prince of Wales to his cousin Prince Rupert, dated Bristol, May 4th 1645.
$2,000–2,200 ⚲ DW
This was written at the height of the Civil War, when the Prince was only 14 years old, two months after he had made his final parting with his father, Charles I.

Prince John, youngest son of George V, a collection of Royal memorabilia deriving from his nanny, Mrs 'Lalla' Bill, including a pair of Queen Victoria's silk gloves, a photograph of Prince John as a young man with his dog, signed 'Johnny 1918', with accompanying letter on crown-embossed card 'My Dear Lottie – I am sending you and Rob a photograph of me. Lala and I give you our Love [drawing] this is your friend Lala crying. Best love to Mrs May with love from Johnny'.
$2,300–2,600 ⚲ P
Prince John was a severe epileptic, whom the Royal Family kept hidden from the world at Wood Farm near Sandringham from 1916. The photograph shows him in the last year of his life, aged 12 or 13, when his fits had grown worse and more frequent, and Queen Mary is said to have visited him often at Wood Farm. His death in 1918 greatly distressed her.

► **Robert E. Lee and Mary Custis Lee,** a pair of signed albumen prints, c1869, 3½ x 2in (9 x 5cm), both mounted on cards and framed.
$4,650–5,000 ⚲ S(NY)

Princess Alexandra, a handwritten letter to the Countess of Shannon, 1888, 4 x 3in (10 x 7.5cm).
$360–440 ⊞ AEL

Gloria Swanson, a signed and inscribed sepia photograph, 1941, 13 x 10in (33 x 25.5cm).
$1,300–1,450 ⚲ VS

Richard and Robert Gillow, of the Lancastrian firm of cabinet-makers and upholsterers, an autographed letter to Charles Udale, Agent to John Christian Esquire of Workington Hall, concerning the shipping of 'three painted floor cloths' via the port of Whitehaven, for delivery to Workington Hall, 5th April, 1789.
$580–720 ⚲ PFK
John Christian was the first cousin of Fletcher Christian who became famous as the leader of the mutiny on the Bounty.

◄ **Sir John Gielgud,** a handwritten quotation from Hamlet, signed and dated 1936.
$170–200 ⚲ F&C

EPHEMERA

Cigarette Cards

John Player & Sons, Charles Dickens Characters, set of 50, 1923.
$85–100 ⊞ **WI**

Taddy, Famous Actors/Actresses, set of 25, 1903.
$290–320 🔨 **P**

Ogdens, Modern British Pottery, set of 50, 1925.
$60–70 ⊞ **MAr**

John Player & Sons, Old England's Defenders, set of 50, 1898.
$650–720 🔨 **P**

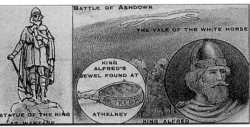

Smiths, Battlefields of Great Britain, set of 50, 1913.
$500–600 🔨 **P**

W. D. & H. O. Wills, Riders of the World, Australian edition, set of 50, 1913.
$115–130 ⊞ **WI**

W. D. & H. O. Wills, Old Inns, set of 40, 1939.
$85–95 ⊞ **MAr**

Postcards

A suffragettes postcard, depicting Mrs Despard and Mrs Cobham Sanderson waiting for Mr Asquith, c1909.
$200–240 🔨 **VS**

An Edwardian postcard, showing a London bus.
$30–40 ⊞ **WI**

▶ **A set of six postcards,** by Raphael Kirchner, depicting portraits of Viennese ladies, 1901.
$220–260 🔨 **P**

A commemorative postcard, for the first flight of the Zeppelin from Germany to Brazil, posted from Brazil on the day it landed, 24 May 1930.
$115–130 🔨 **VS**

An Edwardian postcard, depicting passengers in a horse-drawn trap.
$25–30 ⊞ **WI**

Postcards
A Collector's Guide

To find out more see *Miller's Postcards: A Collector's Guide* (£5.99), with over 130 colour pictures, its 64 pages are packed with invaluable information. *Order from* www.millers.uk.com *or telephone in the UK on* 01933 443863

EPHEMERA

Posters

The last ten years has been a period of dynamic and exciting change in the market for vintage posters. These changes are the result of a more widespread perception of their quality and cultural significance, due to an increase in auction house, publishing and curatorial activity.

The internet revolution has created an interest in the visual qualities of graphic design and focussed attention on things that can easily be transported – worldwide! The internet has also helped bring together an international community of poster collectors and enthusiasts.

Posters have been collected since they first appeared in the 1860s, following the development of colour lithography. It is partly because of the poster mania that first sprang up in the 1890s that museum collections exist and that interesting images by the early masters of poster art – Cheret, Mucha and Toulouse-Lautrec – are still to be found. During the 20th century, poster design has embraced various styles and developed in association with particular political or cultural phenomena, which gives the potential collector a wide variety of entry points into the market.

The most significant groups collected are film and advertising posters. For film posters anything before 1960 is rare, and value is dictated by film title, star quality and cultural significance. It's not surprising, then, to see Audrey Hepburn, Marilyn Monroe and James Bond regularly reported among the top prices in this field. Advertising images are generally presented in thematic groups – travel, shipping, aviation. Recently, Swiss and mountain resort posters have been successfully sold to skiing enthusiasts. The idea of collecting design as an identifiable characteristic in poster art is also gaining a following. So, the range of possibilities is huge.

The valuation systems for posters is not straight-forward – vintage King Kong can be worth more than Toulouse-Lautrec! However, in general the better it looks the more valuable it will be. Many poster images are very rare, but some great examples, which have been collected and traded since they first appeared, can still be found – at a price. Condition should be considered, but posters are, in the end, just bits of old paper – it's a miracle that they've survived at all. The standard conservation technique is to mount the poster onto a paper or linen support.

Prices for posters are generally under the $2,900 mark. A budget of about $1,450 per year is certainly enough to get started and, as in any collecting field, it is best to do a little research before buying.   **Paul Rennie**

An American poster, advertising N. E. Rum from the Crystal Spring Distillery, Boston, Massachusetts, c1880, 18 x 24in (45.5 x 61cm), possibly in original frame.
$3,200–3,600 ↗ SK(B)

An Aubrey Beardsley poster, advertising children's books, lithographed and printed in light purple and black, on linen, overall restoration, 1894, 30 x 20in (76 x 51cm).
$2,600–3,200 ↗ S

A Dutch poster, by Theodorus M. A. A. A. Molkenboer, advertising Elias P. van Bommel, Boekbinder, linocut on japan, 1897, 33¾ x 24½in (85.5 x 62cm).
$1,450–1,600 ↗ VSP

A Highland Railway poster, published June 1905, 40¼ x 30in (102 x 76cm).
$190–220 ↗ ONS

◄ **A Cunard Line Lusitania poster,** 1910, 12 x 10in (30.5 x 25.5cm).
$1,450–1,750 ↗ HAld

Cross Reference
See Colour Review
(page 740)

► **A Cunard Line travel poster,** by E. Sanderson & Co, 'Europe – America', chromolithograph, early 20thC, 39 x 24½in (99 x 62cm).
$580–650 ↗ ELR

A French poster of Mistinguett, by Daniel de Losques (David Thoroude), linen backed, 1911, 63¼ x 40¼in (160.5 x 102cm). **$1,050–1,350** ⚒ BB(L) Some artists used a name or mark to distinguish commercial work from other types of work.

A French poster, by Leonetto Cappiello, advertising Cognac Monnet, linen backed, 1927, 79 x 51in (200.5 x 129.5cm). **$5,500–6,000** ⚒ BB(L)

A poster, by E. J. Kealey, advertising The Aberdeen Line To England & South Africa, colour lithograph, c1930, 40 x 24¾in (101.5 x 63cm). **$500–600** ⚒ P(Sy)

A French poster, by Jules Chéret, advertising the Exposition Internationale de Lyon, on japan paper, 1913, 29¼ x 41in (74.5 x 104cm). **$870–1,000** ⚒ VSP

A Swedish poster, advertising *Glödande Kol*, paper backed, 1920, 39 x 27in (99 x 68.5cm). **$550–620** ⊞ REEL

An American 'work ethic' poster, Ready to Spring, coloured, Chicago, minor damage, 1929, 43¾ x 36¼in (111 x 92cm). **$360–430** ⚒ RTo

A poster for LMS Railway, by Norman Wilkinson, c1930, 40 x 50in (101.5 x 127cm). **$9,500–11,500** ⊞ REN

A William Fox poster, advertising *A Fool There Was*, linen backed, 1915, 22 x 14 in (56 x 35.5cm). **$4,000–4,700** ⊞ REEL

A Belgian poster, advertising Paume d'Or, 1924, 38¼ x 24¾in (97 x 63cm). **$175–200** ⚒ VSP

A poster, advertising St Albans Route 84 from Golders Green, after Edward McKnight Kauffer, colour lithograph, dated 1929, 39¼ x 25in (99.5 x 63.5cm). **$580–720** ⚒ S(S)

A WWI poster, advertising British Army Wounded Horses Day, 24 x 20in (61 x 51cm). **$190–220** ⚒ ONS

A Paramount poster, advertising *Rolled Stockings*, paper backed, 1927, 36 x 14in (91.5 x 35.5cm). **$1,900–2,200** ⊞ REEL

◀ **A poster,** advertising St Albans Route 84 from Golders Green, after Edward McKnight Kauffer, colour lithograph, dated 1929, 39¼ x 25in (99.5 x 63.5cm). **$580–720** ⚒ S(S)

A London Underground poster, by Aubrey Hammond, Jack & Jill An Underground Fairytale, with original Underground envelope, 1932, 40¼ x 50in (102 x 127cm). **$360–430** ⚒ ONS

A poster, advertising Grande Casino Peninsular, some damage, 1933, 40½ x 29in (103 x 73.5cm).
$160–190 ➚ ONS

A Belgian poster, advertising *The Last of the Mohicans/Le Dernier Des Mohicans*, paper backed, 1936, 20 x 14in (51 x 35.5cm).
$320–360 ⊞ REEL

Richmond Station for the River

A poster, Richmond Station for the River, after Jean Dupas, lithograph, 1930s, 39¾ x 25in (101 x 63.5cm).
$2,200–2,400 ➚ S(S)

A Hamburg-Amerika Linie poster, c1935, 38½ x 26¾in (98 x 68cm).
$180–220 ➚ VSP

A French poster, advertising *Hotel Du Nord*, linen backed, 1938, 31 x 24in (78.5 x 61cm).
$4,000–4,700 ⊞ REEL

▶ **An American WWII poster,** by John McCrady, Cigarette Drive, A Smoke for Victory Tag Day October Third, silkscreen print, 1942, 23 x 17in (58.5 x 43cm).
$1,100–1,300 ➚ NOA
In March 1942, the Federal Art Project was reorganized as the Graphic Section of the War Service Program, and McCrady found himself designing posters that could further the World War II effort. Because the posters were designed as functional tools of the American offensive, they were used and discarded, not treated as works of art. These posters are quite different from anything else that McCrady produced.

▶ **A recruiting poster,** for the ATS, by Abram Games, 1941, 30 x 20in (76 x 51cm).
$5,800–7,200 ⊞ REN
Games designed three posters for this campaign. This, the first, was banned by Churchill, and very few survive.

ÉÉN DOEL - ÉÉN WIL !
De bevrijding van onze Rijksgenooten in Indie · Meldt U als Oorlogsvrijwilliger

A poster, for the Allied Liberation of Holland, by F. H. K. Henrion, 1945, 20 x 30in (51 x 76cm).
$1,750–2,200 ⊞ REN
F. H. K. Henrion was born in Nuremberg, Germany, emigrated to England in 1939 and adopted British nationality in 1946. He studied in Paris with Paul Colin and in the late 1930s worked in Paris and London designing posters, packaging and exhibitions. His work for the Ministry of Information and the US Office of War Information in London established his reputation. His work often uses elements of photomontage and collage and has a surrealist quality.

A poster, advertising *The Fast Lady*, 1962, 29½ x 39½in (75 x 100cm).
$200–220 ⊞ **Dri**

An Ealing Films poster, by John Piper, c1946, 30 x 40in (76 x 101.6cm).
$2,900–3,600 ⊞ **REN**
John Piper (1903–92) was born in Epsom, Surrey. He began by studying law in his father's firm and writing poetry and went on to study at Richmond School of Art and the RCA. During the 1930s he abandoned abstract art for a more romantic portrayal of buildings and places. It is for this British romanticism that Piper has become renowned. He painted the after-effects of war on England's architectural heritage as part of Recording Britain. Piper's diverse talent is shown in his painting, book illustration and design, textiles, ceramics and, of course, the stained glass of Coventry Cathedral. In 1983 the Tate Gallery showed a retrospective of his work.

A poster for *The Financial Times,* by Abram Games, 1951, 30 x 20in (76 x 51cm).
$3,650–4,350 ⊞ **REN**
Abram Games RDI OBE (1914–96) was one of Britain's most important poster designers. He started work as a lettering artist in a London studio and during WWII designed posters for the War Office. From 1946–53 he was tutor in graphic design at the Royal College of Art. His work has achieved international acclaim and has been awarded many prizes.

A poster, advertising a Gene Pitney concert at the Gaumont, Wolverhampton, black, white, yellow and red lettering on same colour background, damaged, 17 November 1965, 29½ x 39¾in (75 x 101cm).
$180–220 ⚒ **Bon(C)**

A poster, advertising a Yardbirds concert in Bishop's Stortford, red and black lettering on a white background, damaged, 9 April 1966, 29¼ x 19¾in (74.5 x 50cm).
$500–600 ⚒ **Bon(C)**

A poster, advertising a Hendrix and the Move concert at the Royal Albert Hall, sellotape on borders, 14 November 1967, 20 x 15in (51 x 38cm).
$1,250–1,450 ⚒ **Bon(C)**

A German poster, advertising The Beatles in *Yellow Submarine*, 1968, 32¾ x 23½in (83 x 59.5cm).
$220–260 ⚒ **VSP**

A Czechoslovakian poster, advertising *100 Rifles/100 Pusek*, 1969, 33 x 23in (84 x 58.5cm).
$145–185 ⊞ **REEL**

▶ **A poster,** advertising *Le Mans,* with Steve McQueen, linen backed, light spotting, 1971, 31½ x 39½in (80 x 100.5cm).
$500–580 ⊞ **Dri**

A record shop promotional poster, 'Strawberry Fields Forever', featuring John Lennon with straw hair, 1970s, 32 x 22¾in (81.5 x 58cm).
$250–300 ⚒ **Bon(C)**

A British Lion poster, advertising *The Man who fell to Earth,* 1977, 11¾ x 15¾in (30 x 40cm).
$115–145 ⊞ **CTO**

A Ladd Company poster, advertising *Blade Runner*, 1982, 40 x 30in (101.5 x 76cm).
$200–220 ⊞ **SEY**

Rock & Pop

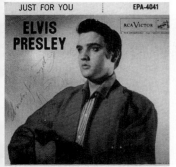

An Elvis Presley EP record, 'Just For You', autographed by Elvis Presley, c1957.
$720–870 ♪ Bon(C)

A leather pouch, containing a manicure set, signed by Elvis Presley on the outside in ballpoint pen, late 1950s.
$580–720 ♪ DW
This was obtained when the original owner was visiting a friend in Germany and was taken to see the house where Elvis was living and, on that day, he was signing autographs. Apparently Elvis was sitting by a window in the house and held up each item for the public to see it before signing. Autographic material from Elvis' service period in Germany is rare.

◄ The Beatles Monthly Book, 23 copies, illustrated, 1963–67, 8°.
$30–40 ♪ WilP

A Buddy Holly and The Crickets UK tour programme, signed, 1958, 11¾ x 8¼in (30 x 21cm).
$1,600–1,800 ♪ S

A complete set of Beatles Fan Club Christmas flexi discs, by Parlophone, with sleeves, mounted, 1963–69.
$580–720 ♪ Bon(C)
The disc for 1963 has a reproduction sleeve.

◄ A Jan & Dean LP record, original soundtrack from *Ride the Wild Surf*, Liberty Records, 1964.
$35–45 ⊞ TOT

Further reading
Miller's Collecting the 1960s, Miller's Publications, 1999

A hand bill with booking form, for a concert featuring The Animals, Carl Perkins, etc, Colston Hall, Bristol, 1964, 9 x 6in (23 x 15cm).
$60–75 ⊞ CTO

A set of Beatles autographs, 1964, framed, 20in (21cm) square.
$1,000–1,200 ⊞ BTC

Miller's is a price GUIDE not a price LIST

► A set of The Who autographs, the reverse with Spencer Davis Group autographs, 1964–65.
$360–430 ♪ Bon(C)

A Rolling Stones UK tour programme, 1965, 8 x 10in (20.5 x 25.5cm).
$45–55 ⊞ CTO

The Deviants Disposable LP record, Stable Records, 1968.
$80–90 ⊞ TOT

Autographs of all the members of the Jimi Hendrix Experience, late 1960s.
$320–360 ✗ DW

A Beatles Gala Première ticket, for *Let It Be*, 1970, 6 x 4in (15 x 10cm).
$145–175 ⊞ BTC

An autographed ABBA LP record, 1970s.
$730–800 ✗ Bon(C)

A Pink Floyd demonstration single record, Arnold Layne, 1967.
$430–500 ✗ Bon(C)

A Motown Memories LP record, Tamla Motown, 1968.
$35–45 ⊞ TOT

An Elvis Presley signed colour photograph, in a gilt frame, c1970, 14¼ x 11in (36 x 28cm).
$720–870 ✗ DW

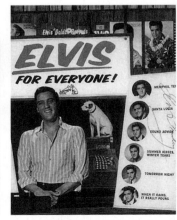

An autographed 'Elvis for Everyone' LP record, 1970s.
$360–430 ✗ Bon(C)

The Beatles, individual autographs by Paul McCartney, George Harrison and Ringo Starr, under a typed statement confirming that the signatures were obtained at a Basingstoke hotel, with a newspaper photograph and article about McCartney, 11 September 1967.
$580–720 ✗ VS

The Beatles White Album, Apple Records, No. 0000006, 1968.
$4,000–4,600 ✗ Bon(C)
Having commissioned several artists of the period to come up with ideas for the first album cover after Sergeant Pepper, Richard Hamilton's idea of a plain cover was used with the addition of a serial number, proposed by Paul McCartney, for use in a bingo-type competition, which never happened. The individual number on each album has since become a status symbol, and a way of ascertaining its rarity. Some sources claim that there may have been more than one copy of each number printed, but although it has often been assumed that John, Paul, George and Ringo, as well as chosen employees, were given lower numbers, no specific documentation or official records confirm who was given which numbered record. It is known, however, that a No. 6 belongs to Neil Aspinall.

A Queen autographed single record, 'Kind of Magic', 1980s.
$360–430 ✗ Bon(C)

Scientific Instruments
Calculating Instruments

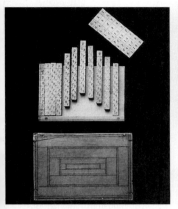

A brass arithmometer, by Thomas de Colmar, with 12 digit display windows, seven smaller digit displays and six sliding indices, missing hinged writing screen, France, c1860, 18in (45.5cm) wide, in an oak case.
$3,600–4,300 ⚹ S

A Midget Brunsviga Type Calculator, by the Muldivo Calculating Machine Co, with a bentwood top, c1900, 12in (30.5cm) wide.
$95–115 ⊞ TOM

A set of boxwood Napiers Bones, with ten single rods, fixed single rod and three rod tablet, all with stamped numerals, damaged, early 18thC, in a fitted boxwood case, 3¾in (9.5cm) wide.
$3,500–4,000 ⚹ S

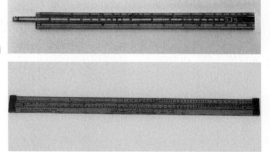

▶ **A Soho ivory slide rule,** c1820, 11in (28cm) long.
$360–430 ⊞ TOM

▶ **A Dring & Fage boxwood slide rule,** for sarking, lining and flooring, designed by James Liddell, Falkirk, c1880, 24in (61cm) long.
$140–170 ⊞ TOM
Sarking, lining and flooring are terms used in the building trade. Sarking refers to boards used in the construction of slate roofs.

Compasses & Dials

A universal equinoctial dial, by Gilbert Wright & Hooke, London, with silvered compass rose inset with two bubble levels, hinged hour ring, gnomon and latitude arc, signed, c1800, 4¾in (12cm) diam, in a fitted wooden case.
$1,200–1,400 ⚹ S

A brass ring dial, with incised scales to the outside for months, days and zodiac signs, and similar incised scales to the inside, c1700, 6½in (16.5cm) diam.
$2,500–2,900 ⚹ Bea(E)

A German brass and silvered-brass universal equinoctial pocket dial, by Johann Willebrand, Augsberg, the hinged hour ring with gnomon, four-pointed magnetic compass, shaped latitude arc, base engraved with latitudes for various European cities, signed, early 18thC, 2in (5cm) diam, in a fitted leather case.
$1,100–1,300 ⚹ S

◀ **A brass planispheric astrolabe,** with four plates and decorative rete and alidade, c1900, 3½in (9cm) diam.
$580–720 ⚹ Bon
Astrolabes were used for the study and measurement of heavenly bodies. Using them, time could be found by day or night, latitude could be found, elementary surveying operations could be performed by angular measurement and the position of the stars for any moment of time could be determined or demonstrated.

An Austrian glazed brass compass, by Voigtlander Brothers, Vienna, with engraved dial, c1800, 6in (15cm) wide, in a wooden case.
$160–190 ⚹ Herm

Globes & Armillary Spheres

A 12in terrestrial globe, by J. & W. Cary, with Cook's voyages and dates recorded, on four mahogany quadrant arc supports with horizontal ring, dated 1816.
$4,000–4,600 ⚶ S

▶ **An American Loring's 10in celestial globe,** with brass meridian circle, on a walnut stand, some damage, Boston, 1854, 17½in (44.5cm) high.
$3,200–3,600 ⚶ SK(B)

A German globe, Berlin, 19thC, 11in (28cm) high, on an ebonized baluster column and base.
$320–380 ⚶ RBB

Two American Federal globes, by J. Wilson & Sons, Albany, NY, one a terrestrial globe dated 1828 and the other a celestial globe dated 1826, on wooden bases, 18¼in (46.5cm) high.
$9,000–10,500 ⚶ FBG

A terrestrial table globe, by Newton & Son, London, on a turned mahogany tripod stand, 19thC, 9¾in (25cm) high.
$2,300–3,000 ⚶ L&T

A French miniature terrestrial globe, by J. Lebègue & Cie, Paris, mounted on an inclined axis on a cast-metal stand, the geographical indications on the globe based for longitude on the meridian of Paris, c1880, 2¼in (5.5cm) diam.
$1,400–1,700 ⚶ S
The Lebègue company of Paris specialized in the production of globes until the early 20th century. Miniature globes mounted on cast stands and with an inclined axis are very uncommon.

A 12in terrestrial globe, by Cox, London, with brass meridian scale and printed horizon bearing the months of the year and zodiac signs, on a mahogany tripod stand, early 19thC, 26in (66cm) high.
$6,000–7,000 ⚶ P(G)

A French armillary sphere, supported by a cast-spelter figure of Atlas, on a marble base, c1880, 29in (73.5cm) high.
$5,800–6,500 ⊞ RGa

A Continental Copernican armillary sphere, paper on paste board and wood, composed of five standard circles edged in red with planetary information to one side and with eliptic band edged in red with zodiacal illustrations, with sun ball and a 1in terrestrial globe, on a turned, ebonized support, restored, all paper coverings are later facsimiles, globes replaced, late 19thC, 17in (43cm) high.
$720–870 ⚶ Bon

An American 11in terrestrial globe, by Gilman & Joslin, Boston, mounted within a brass meridian engraved with four quadrant degree scales, the stand with horizontal ring applied with printed zodiac calendar scale, on three brass-mounted turned supports decorated in gilt, horizontal scale damaged, 19thC, 39in (99cm) high.
$3,200–3,600 ⚶ CAG

An American Rand McNally 12in lunar globe, the surface of the moon including 'Dark Side' named, with results of Russian interplanetary exploration of 1959 and American Apollo flights, signed, 1960s, on a plastic base, 14½in (37cm) high.
$140–170 ⚶ Bon

Medical & Dental

A chemist's mahogany flight of 20 drawers, c1880, 48in (122cm) wide.
$1,100–1,400 ⊞ AL

A Hungarian chemist's pine flight of 62 drawers, c1890, 138in (350.5cm) wide.
$4,000–4,400 ⊞ MIN

A Victorian apothecary's mahogany display cabinet, 19in (48.5cm) wide.
$900–1,000 ⊞ RPh

Three boxwood medicinal containers, with screw tops, one by S. Mawson & Sons containing a 1oz stoppered bottle, one by S. Mawson & Thompson, and one tumbler shape with calibrated glass measure, late 19thC, largest 3in (7.5cm) high.
$65–80 ✹ PFK

▶ A dentist's portable oak chair, with adjustable height, back and headrest, leather seat replaced, probably late 19thC.
$1,200–1,400 ✹ SK(B)

An Edwardian rosewood or padouk wood dentist's cabinet, with ceramic top, 52in (132cm) wide.
$650–800 ✹ MEA

A set of maple apothecary jars, each inscribed in black, early 20thC, 5¾in (14.5cm) high.
$250–300 ✹ DORO

Sets/pairs

Unless otherwise stated, any description which refers to 'a set' or 'a pair' includes a guide price for the entire set or the pair, even though the illustration may show only a single item.

A figured-mahogany travelling medicine chest, with velvet lining, fitted for 14 bottles, one missing, early 19thC, 6¾in (17cm) wide.
$850–950 ✹ DA

An apothecary's mahogany box, early 19thC, 7½in (19cm) square.
$800–900 ⊞ LBr

SCIENTIFIC INSTRUMENTS

A mahogany homeopathic medicine chest, retailed by Leith & Boss, St Paul's Churchyard, with 30 small green glass bottles, two fitted drawers below, 19thC, 9¼in (23.5cm) wide.
$1,200–1,400 ↗ DMC

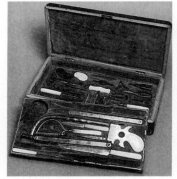

A German amputation and trepanning set, by C. Appelius, Mainz, with a fitted velvet interior, two lift-out trays each containing various instruments, some with ivory handles, some items missing, in a pine case with mahogany veneer, damaged, c1800, box 11in (28cm) wide.
$1,400–1,700 ↗ P

A surgeon's hand-operated amputating chain saw, by Mayer & Meltzer, with ebony handles and length of chain, 19thC, with original leather case, 12in (30.5cm) wide.
$1,100–1,300 ↗ RBB

A set of surgeon's instruments, by Brady & Martin, Newcastle, including a tray of 11 ivory-handled scalpels, possibly incomplete, late 19thC, in a mahogany brass-bound box, 14in (35.5cm) wide.
$480–540 ↗ LAY

A set of chemist's cut-glass bottles, with enamel labels, c1880, 6in (15cm) high.
$100–110 ⊞ NN

An American field surgeon's set, by Lentz & Sons, Philadelphia, with all-metal instruments, early 20thC, 10½in (26.5cm) long, in metal case with canvas outer case.
$360–430 ↗ SK(B)

A pottery apothecary's leech jar and cover, by Samuel Alcock & Co, painted in shades of green, ochre and gilt, inscribed in gilt on a green ribbon panel, cover cracked, c1840, 13½in (34.5cm) high.
$5,000–6,000 ↗ DN

A Victorian silver medicine spoon, by George Unite & Sons, Birmingham 1895, 6½in (16.5cm) long.
$460–500 ⊞ BEX

A pair of Georgian silver spectacles, with telescopic arms and a leather-covered case, Birmingham hallmarks, 5in (12.5cm) wide.
$125–145 ↗ SWO

An American tooth extractor, by W. R. Goulding, New York, marked Baker & Riley patented 1845, 6¾in (17cm) long.
$1,400–1,700 ↗ SK(B)

A pair of silver spectacles, by William Jamieson, Aberdeen, the arms double hinged, maker's mark, c1810, 5in (12.5cm) wide.
$720–870 ↗ Bon

An ivory and yew wood stethoscope, c1840, 7in (18cm) long.
$950–1,150 ⊞ TOM

SCIENTIFIC INSTRUMENTS

Marine

Barometers

◀ **A William IV rosewood ship's barometer,** with an ivory register scale inscribed G. Gowland, Liverpool, above a silvered sympiesometer scale, 38½in (98cm) high.
$3,400–4,000 ⚲ P(Ed)

A silver barometer, by J. Hicks, the reverse engraved 'Admiralty Prize Compulsor Mathematics H.M.S. Britannia December 1903', in a fitted leather case with a compass and an ivory thermometer, London 1901–02, 3½in (9cm) high.
$800–900 ⚲ SWO

▶ **A gilded-metal hanging treble-faced barometer, thermometer and eight-day clock,** with a compass, 19thC, 10in (25.5cm) high.
$1,600–1,900 ⊞ CoHA

> **Cross Reference**
> See Colour Review (page 739)

Cannons

A composite iron and copper cannon, with brass lifting handles in the form of dolphins, probably Dutch, mid-17thC, 42¼in (107.5cm).
$9,600–11,600 ⚲ S
This gun is similar in construction to two guns recovered from the wreck of the *Batavia* which sank in 1628 off the coast of Western Australia.

A pair of ship's signalling cannon, with ring-turned cast-iron barrels, early 19thC, 26in (66cm) long, on associated oak carriages.
$1,600–1,900 ⚲ DN

▶ **A Victorian brass-barrelled miniature naval cannon,** the chase engraved 'Relic of Royal George sunk 1782 raised 1840', 7½in (19cm) long, on a wheeled wooden carriage.
$720–870 ⚲ Bon

Chronometers & Timekeepers

◀ **A two-day marine chronometer,** by D. McGregor & Co, London and Glasgow, with single fusee anchor escapement, in a mahogany and brass-bound box, 19thC, box 7in (18cm) wide.
$2,200–2,600 ⚲ WilP

▶ **A German two-day marine chronometer,** by Chronometerwerke, Wempe, Hamburg, with spring detent escapement, in mahogany deck box, damaged, mid-20thC, box 7¼in (18.5cm) wide.
$870–1,000 ⚲ Bri

An American silver keyless lever deck watch, by Elgin National Watch Co, Illinois, with up-and-down, c1900, 2¼in (6.5cm) diam, in original mahogany box.
$3,000–3,500 ⚲ S(G)

MARINE

Model Ships

A gaff-rigged pond yacht, with wooden hull and applied lead keel, early 19thC, hull 56in (142cm) long.
$1,600–1,900 ✦ G(B)

An American marine shadow box, depicting a carved and painted three-masted ship on the water, imperfections, 19thC, 18½in (47cm) long.
$1,500–1,750 ✦ SK(B)

A model of an unnamed, three-deck, first rate ship, with a solid timber hull and painted decoration, pierced hammock netting and contemporary rigging, in a bronze frame showcase, early 19thC, 32in (81.5cm) long.
$4,700–5,500 ✦ P

A half-hull model of a ship, painted and varnished in black, brown and ochre, c1870, 14in (35.5cm) high.
$360–430 ⊞ TWr

An American carved and painted wood half-hull of a model sailing vessel, painted white above and green below the waterline, mounted in a frame with ochre ground, late 19thC, 29in (73.5cm) wide.
$3,200–3,700 ✦ SK(B)

An American carved and painted model of a three-masted ship, the *Aurora*, painted black with gilt trim, on a wooden base beneath a glass case, minor imperfections, late 19thC, 23in (58.5cm) long.
$1,400–1,600 ✦ SK(B)

A wooden model of a three-masted ship, with string rigging and canvas sails, late 19thC, 34in (86.5cm) long.
$480–580 ✦ DuM

A ship diorama, the three-masted vessel the *Phyche* with a smaller boat against a painted background, late 19thC, 31in (78.5cm) wide.
$830–1,000 ✦ S(S)

A Scottish model of a rowing boat, c1920, 34in (86.5cm) long.
$460–550 ⊞ TWr

An Edwardian pond yacht, the hollowed timber hull painted red to the waterline and black below, with original cotton mainsail, 54¾in (139cm) long.
$2,900–3,200 ✦ P

► **A wooden racing pond yacht,** designed and built by Daniels, c1930, 54in (137cm) high.
$2,000–2,400 ⊞ RGa

A wooden pond yacht, 1930, 35in (89cm) long.
$720–870 ⊞ CYA

A pond yacht, with black-finished hull and white *faux* strip decking, automatic rudder, 1950s, 54in (137cm) long, with a stand.
$850–1,000 ✦ BKS

MARINE

Nautical Handicrafts

A carved ivory box, the hinged lid with an incised panel depicting a whale attacking boats, on a basketweave ground, 19thC, 3½in (9cm) wide.
$580–720 ↗ AH

A scrimshaw pan bone panel, depicting a whaling ship and four open boats with the hunt in progress, surrounded by an engraved foliate border, the lower corners marked 'W & E', incomplete, early 19thC, 12¼in (13cm) long.
$720–800 ↗ LAY

▶ **An American whalebone busk,** engraved with various motifs including a romantic couple, an eagle and a flag and a mermaid, with red and blue polychrome highlights, 19thC, 13¼in (33.5cm) long.
$3,600–4,000 ↗ SK(B)
Scrimshaw with a known American provenance is keenly collected in the United States.

A sailor's woolwork picture of a clipper, on a calm green sea, worked in split and straight stitch wool thread, in glazed gilt-wood frame, c1850, 17½ x 25in (44.5 x 63.5cm).
$580–720 ↗ S(S)

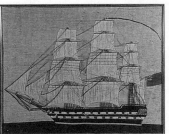

A sailor's workwool picture of a three-masted ship, 19thC, 19 x 26in (48.5 x 66cm).
$1,500–2,000 ↗ Bea(E)

A nautilus shell, decorated and engraved by C. H. Wood, commemorating the 'Glorious Victories achieved by the immortal Nelson', and the whole being executed with no other instrument than a penknife, a similar specimen of which was accepted by Her Most Gracious Majesty the Queen, The Right Hon The Lord Mayors of London & York 1850 & 1851', mid-19thC, 9½in (24cm) high.
$840–1,000 ↗ P

Navigational Instruments

▶ **A Georgian ebony and ivory octant,** Hadley's Quadrant, by D. Primavesi, Cardiff, 10in (25.5cm) radius, in contemporary mahogany box.
$1,000–1,300 ↗ F&C

◀ **A fruitwood nocturnal,** stamped with months and hours, the volvelle with indicators for Great Bear and Lesser Bear, and divided date scale and hours, the reverse with compass rose, lunar age scale for tides, and Pole Star correction for latitude, the centre with brass-framed sight, stamped with the owner's name and date, 'C. Cook 1719', 8in (20.5cm) high.
$6,500–7,200 ↗ SK(B)

▶ **A silver Henry Wynne technical *aide-mémoire* volvelle,** the obverse designed for trigonometrical calculations used in navigation, the reverse with rotatable disc engraved with a spherical triangle with named parts which may be set against sine and tangent divisions on the fixed rim, signed, c1680, 1¾in (4.5cm) diam.
$13,700–16,000 ↗ S
Henry Wynne (1640–1709) was apprenticed in the Clockmaker's Company to Ralph Gretorex in 1654. Free in 1662 and Master of the Company in 1692, Wynne worked at various locations in Chancery Lane and was a notable craftsman. The device pictured here is of importance to the history of scientific vulgarization for providing the name of the maker of such pieces. Only two similar examples have been recorded, both in brass, and unsigned.

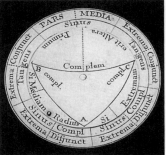

MARINE

A rosewood, brass and ivory octant, by Molteni, Paris, 19thC, 12in (30.5cm) radius, in a fitted oak case.
$530–580 ↗ DuM

A brass quadrant, applied with a paper label inscribed '1658 H. Sutton fecit', 11½in (29cm) radius, with a leather pouch.
$5,800–6,500 ↗ L

An ebony and brass sextant, with bone scale and vernier, inset with a plaque inscribed 'G. H. C. Cowland, Sunderland', in a mahogany box bearing a label for Frodsham & Keen, Liverpool, 19thC, 11½in (29cm) radius.
$500–580 ↗ GAK

Ships' Fittings

◀ **A brass bell,** from HMS *Whitehall*, 1924, 12¼in (31cm) diam.
$4,000–4,700 ↗ P
HMS *Whitehall* was an Admiralty modified W Class destroyer built in the mid-1920s by Messrs Swan Hunter Ltd of Wallsend-on-Tyne. In May 1940, she took part in Operation Dynamo making evacuation trips to Dunkirk bringing back a total of 3,453 soldiers. In 1944, she was allocated to the Bristol Channel to act as escort for the Normany Landings, Operation Neptune, escorting the supply convoys from Milford Haven to the beaches and back. In June 1945, she was paid off into reserve at Barrow and scrapped on 27 October of that year.

An American ash and cedar sail-maker's bench, with tacked canvas seat, and a variety of sail-maker's tools, possibly New England, early 19thC, 78½in (199.5cm) long.
$1,900–2,200 ↗ SK(B)

▶ **A brass ship's companionway lamp,** made by Bulpit, Birmingham, c1890, 20in (51cm) high.
$330–390 ⊞ CRN

A wooden ship's carving, depicting a mermaid, some remnants of polychrome decoration, 19thC, 28in (71cm) high.
$4,600–5,000 ↗ FBG

Miscellaneous

A White Star Line silver-plated fruit bowl, 1890–1930, 20in (51cm) diam.
$1,100–1,300 ↗ HAld

A souvenir album from HM armed merchant cruiser *Teutonic*, White Star Royal Mail Line, at the Jubilee Naval Review, Spithead 26 June 1897, photographed and engraved by Stas. Waley & Co, London, printed for private circulations only, covers missing, 1898, 14½ x 19¾in (37 x 50cm).
$650–800 ↗ P

A framed and glazed model anchor, made from reclaimed materials recovered in 1840 from the *Royal George*, sunk at Spithead in 1782, 4½in (11.5cm) long.
$320–360 ↗ Bon

LOCATE THE SOURCE
The source of each illustration in Miller's can be found by checking the code letters below each caption with the Key to Illustrations, pages 794–800.

A Battersea enamel box, decorated for the American market, depicting The Constitution in polychrome enamel, the interior with a mirror, the box decorated in pink, late 18thC, 2in (5cm) wide.
$2,600–2,900 ⚘ SK(B)

British Antarctic Expedition 1901 silver-plated cutlery, comprising nine pieces, all engraved 'Discovery 1901' on the handle, the reverse with maker's stamp for Joseph Rogers, Sheffield.
$5,800–6,500 ⚘ P
The National Antarctic Expedition of 1901–04 set sail on board *Discovery* on 31 July, loaded with enough food for 47 men: 150 tons of roast pheasant, 500 of roast turkey, whole roast partridges, jugged hare, duck and green peas, rump steak, cheese, 27 gallons of brandy and whiskey, 60 cases of port, 36 cases of sherry, 28 cases of champagne and 1,800 pounds of tobacco.

An RMS *Titanic* silk postcard, not postally used, 1912, 3 x 5in (7.5 x 12.5cm).
$2,000–2,400 ⚘ HAld

RMS *Titanic* and *Olympic* second class brochure, 1911–12, 4 x 5in (10 x 12.5cm).
$1,400–1,600 ⚘ HAld

An Admiralty pattern diving helmet, by Siebe, Gorman & Co, with Siebe Gorman canvas diving suit, front and back weights, brass diving boots, belt with brass diving knife and frog, mid-20thC.
$3,600–4,400 ⚘ P

A fold-out plan of first class passenger accommodation, on the White Star Line *Olympic* and *Titanic*, 1911.
$5,000–6,000 ⚘ HAld

▶ **A silver toast rack,** with the house flag of the White Star Line engraved on the handle, stamped Elkington & Co, possibly 1870, 7in (18cm) long.
$400–470 ⚘ P

◀ **A Walker's Cherub ship's log,** c1900, box 20in (51cm) wide.
$320–360 ⊞ TWr
This instrument is for logging the ship's speed and distance travelled.

An oak open armchair, by Goodall, Lamb and Heighway, Manchester, made from reclaimed timber from Nelson's flagship *Foudroyant*, c1899.
$500–600 ⚘ HAM
HMS *Foudroyant* was used in several of Nelson's most famous actions. Commissioned in 1789, she was scrapped in 1897 and this firm, continuing the old tradition of making amusing artefacts from reclaimed timber of old ships of the line, sold this chair for £10.3s.6d, noting that it cost 25 percent more to work this timber because it had been immersed in salt water.

A postcard from the Titanic, sent on 10th April 1912, saying that it is a very fine ship and that the writer will be disembarking at Queenstown in a few hours' time.
$8,000–8,800 ⚘ HAld

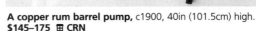

A copper rum barrel pump, c1900, 40in (101.5cm) high.
$145–175 ⊞ CRN

Cameras

A George Hare half-plate mahogany and brass tailboard camera, with Ross lens, for single and stereo photographs, maroon leather bellows, c1885.
$360–430 ⊞ APC

A Leica III chrome camera, with a Summar lens and maker's case and lens cap, Germany, 1937, with a Leitz red Leica III box.
$400–460 ✗ P(WM)

A French Lubo 41 press camera, by Lucien Beaugers, Paris, leather-covered wood body, with a Berthiot Flor f/4.5 120mm, lens No. 464940, with two plate magazines, in a leather carrying case, c1941.
$1,000–1,200 ✗ S

A Rouch's Eureka detective camera, with built-in quarter-plate changing box, sliding box focussing, c1887.
$430–500 ✗ P(WM)

A Leica IIIc camera, No. 390197K, 5cm f/2 lens, No. 584591, Germany, 1936–46, in ever-ready case.
$1,900–2,200 ✗ SK(B)

A Leica M3 (SS) camera, with a fitted Leica-meter MC and Summaron 35mm f2.8 lens and spectacle view-finder, Germany, 1958, with maker's ER case and lens cap.
$850–950 ✗ P(WM)

A Nikon SP camera, No. 6208979, with Nikkor 5cm f/1.4 lens, No. 404317, in ever-ready case, c1957.
$3,200–3,600 ✗ SK(B)

A Rolliflex Original camera, with a 75mm f3.8 Zeiss Tesar lens in a Compur shutter, Germany, 1931, with a later variant serial number 104861.
$60–75 ✗ P(WM)

▶ **A Rolleiflex 3.5F Model 5 camera,** with a Xenotar 75mm/f3.5 lens, with case and lens caps, Germany, c1979.
$320–360 ✗ P(WM)

A Leica IIIa camera, No. 235073, various accessories, not Leica, c1937.
$250–300 ✗ SWO

A London Stereoscopic Co King's Own tropical camera, with folding front panel, teak body with brass fittings, c1905, 9¾in (25cm) closed.
$1,700–2,200 ⊞ APC

A Praktiflex camera, by KW, Dresden, rewind knob missing, mirror clouded, with carrying case, Germany, 1939.
$800–900 ✗ KOLN

CAMERAS

A Voigtländer folding camera,
shutter speed to 1/1000 second, 1908.
$360–400 ✗ **KOLN**

A Voigtländer Virtus folding camera, shutter speed to 1/250 second, Germany, from 1933.
$330–370 ✗ **KOLN**

A Voigtlander Vitessa L camera,
with a Color-Skopar 50mm f2.8 lens in a Synchro-Compur shutter, Germany, 1960, with maker's ER case and with a Weston Master V and Viceroy 80 exposure meter.
$160–190 ✗ **P(WM)**

A Russian engraved silver-coloured gentleman's ring camera, with a lion's face in relief, the hinged front plate revealing the camera lens and shutter mechanism, designed and manufactured by the KGB Second Directorate, which dealt with Soviet internal security, c1960.
$8,700–9,400 ✗ **RM**

A Zeiss Ikon Contarex camera, with Bullseye exposure meter window and 50mm f2 Planar lens, Germany, 1960, with maker's case and cap.
$320–360 ✗ **P(WM)**

A quarter-plate mahogany sliding box wet plate camera, marked 'H Square & Co, Makers, King William St., London Bridge', with Darlot lens and two photographic plates, c1855.
$2,300–2,900 ⊞ **APC**

Optical Devices & Viewers

A No. 1 diascope viewer, red leather, with 7 x 5in (18 x 12.5cm) coloured glass plate in hinged upper section enclosed by doors, over mirror base, patent date 1908.
$250–300 ↗ SK(B)

A Busch-type kaleidoscope, the leather-covered cardboard body mounted on an ebonized turned wooden stand, c1870, 11¾in (30cm) high.
$450–550 ⊞ APC

A kaleidoscope, on an ebonized stand, 19thC, 17¼in (44cm) high.
$870–1,000 ↗ P(WM)

◄ **A Kinora,** by the British Mutoscope and Biograph Co, London, the three lenses and mechanism set in a mahogany box mounted on a steel and mahogany column, mechanism modified and replaced, early 20thC.
$3,600–4,000 ↗ P(WM).
This was intended for three people to view a moving picture flicker reel at one time. The reel is driven by clockwork wound by a large knob on the side.

A teak and nickel-plated Miniature Pullman collapsible magic lantern, by JLS & Co, c1910, 13¾in (35cm) long.
$720–870 ⊞ APC

A walnut table stereo viewer, 1860–70, 8in (20.5cm) wide.
$1,100–1,400 ↗ P(WM)

An American Holmes-style stereo viewer, on a polished wooden base, c1900.
$130–150 ⊞ APC

A French folding stereographoscope in a walnut box with ebony stringing and inset brass escutcheon, c1870, box 9½in (24cm) wide, closed.
$720–870 ↗ Bon

A rosewood stereoscope viewer, 19thC, 8in (20.5cm) high, with a collection of stereoscope cards.
$125–145 ↗ TRL

A Chase's folding stereoscope, the rosewood body with chinoiserie-decorated tin hood and divider, inset folding handle, old repairs, patent dated 16 July 1872, 14½in (37cm) long.
$180–220 ↗ SK(B)

A walnut stereoscope, the hinged brass cover opening to reveal a two-division sliding box between twin-arched lens viewing, late 19thC, 11½in (29cm) high, with 18 monochrome stereoscopic paper view slides, in a box.
$950–1,250 ↗ Hal

Arms & Armour

Armour

A composite blackened steel pikeman's armour, partly early 17thC.
$3,600–4,300 ⚒ Bon

A composite full armour, the breast and backplate German, mainly c1635.
$21,750–24,000 ⚒ S(S)

A south German iron morion, late 16thC, 10½in (26.5cm) high.
$2,300–2,700 ⚒ Herm

A Continental 16thC-style black and white part suit of armour, lacking helmet and left arm guard, 19thC.
$4,800–5,400 ⚒ SK

A Civil War pikeman's part armour, mid-17thC.
$4,300–4,700 ⚒ Gle

A French Napoleonic steel breastplate, with brass rivets and original musket ball dent, c1840.
$1,100–1,300 ⊞ ARB

▶ **A German steel Maximilian helmet,** restored, c1540.
$10,500–11,600 ⊞ ARB

A German iron breastplate, c1700.
$400–460 ⚒ Herm

An Italian breastplate, late 16thC.
$2,900–3,500 ⚒ S(NY)

◀ **A pikeman's pot,** some rivets missing, early 17thC, 9½in (24cm) high.
$1,000–1,200 ⚒ Bon

A steel cabasset morion, late 16thC.
$3,300–3,700 ⚒ Gle

A trooper's bridle gauntlet, mid-17thC.
$1,300–1,600 ⊞ ASB
Bridle gauntlets were worn by cavalry men to provide protection for the arm which held the reins and was normally stationary during a melee.

A Victorian copy of a 16thC-style burgonet, late 19thC.
$720–800 ⊞ ASB

◀ **A pair of German tassets,** c1550, 18½in (47cm) long.
$4,000–4,400 ⚒ S(NY)

Crossbows

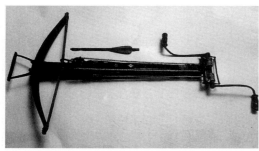

A Flemish crossbow, with windlass, 17thC, 49in (124.5cm) long.
$4,300–4,700 ⊞ **ARB**

▶ **A German steel stonebow,** with fruitwood butt, mid-17thC, tiller 24¾in (63cm) long.
$2,200–2,400 ⚒ **S(NY)**

LOCATE THE SOURCE

The source of each illustration in Miller's can be found by checking the code letters below each caption with the Key to Illustrations, pages 794–800.

◀ **A stonebow,** by Garron, Preston, c1790, 32in (81.5cm) long.
$1,400–1,700 ⊞ **ARB**

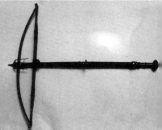

A stonebow, by J. Johnson, Manchester, c1790, 30in (76cm) long.
$2,900–3,500 ⊞ **ARB**

Edged Weapons

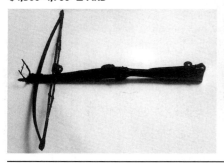

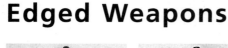

A medieval sword, in excavated condition, early 12thC, blade 23in (58.5cm) long.
$3,600–4,300 ⚒ **S(NY)**

A fluted steel composite rapier, stamped both sides with crowned G at forte, with wire-bound grip, c1600, blade 34½in (87.5cm) long.
$2,400–2,600 ⚒ **WAL**

A cup-hilted rapier, with roped steel wire-bound grip, early 17thC, blade 32in (81.5cm) long.
$1,900–2,200 ⊞ **ASB**

A Cromwellian mortuary sword, with double-edged blade, the hilt chiselled with naïve decoration, 17thC, 39½in (100.5cm) long.
$2,400–2,700 ⊞ **GV**

An Irish small sword, Dublin, c1750, 41in (104cm) long.
$8,000–8,800 ⊞ **WELD**

◀ **A north European small sword,** with single knuckle bow and pierced shell guards, c1660, 36in (91.5cm) long.
$2,600–3,200 ⊞ **ARB**

A Spanish bilboe hilted broadsword, with double-edged blade and sharkskin-covered grip, 18thC, blade 35in (89cm) long.
$1,100–1,300 ⊞ **ASB**

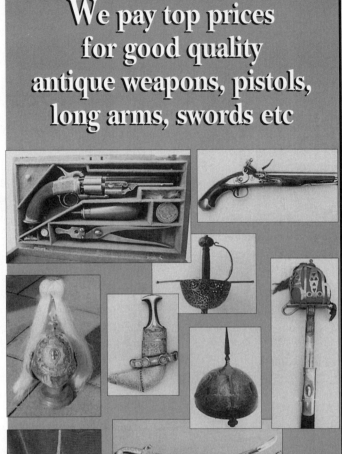

A hunting hangar, the single-edged blade with brass hilt and brass shell guard, stag horn grip, mid-18thC, 21in (53cm) long.
$240–270 ⊞ GV

An Venetian schiavona, with original scabbard, c1700, 39in (99cm) long.
$2,200–2,600 ⊞ ARB

A naval cutlass, with single-edged blade and turned dark wood grip, possibly American, early 19thC, blade 27in (68.5cm) long.
$650–725 ⊞ ASB
This type of cutlass was issued to American seamen during the war of 1812.

▶ **An American naval sword handle and guard,** decorated on either side with an American eagle, early 19thC, 5in (12.5cm) long.
$720–800 ⋊ S

A Royal Navy Admiral's sword, by John Prosser, Maker to the King & Royal Family, London, with single-edged blade, double-edged towards the point, gilt-brass half basket guard, gilt-brass lion's-head pommel and wire bound shagreen covered grip, in original black leather scabbard with gilt-brass mounts decorated with stylized foliage and bands of oak leaves, c1825, blade 30in (76cm) long.
$1,300–1,600 ⋊ Bon

An early Victorian 1822 pattern infantry field officer's sword, by Fisher & Co, etched with crowned VR cyphers and foliate sprays within panels, the brass hilt with fishskin-covered grip, in its brass scabbard, blade 32in (81.5cm) long.
$250–300 ⋊ WAL

An American sabre, the single-edged blade of European origin, with horn grip, in original black leather scabbard, 1770–90, blade 30in (76cm) long.
$950–1,100 ⊞ ASB

A French Ecole de Mars sword, with double-edged blade, the brass grip cast with a design of over-lapping feathers, in original brass scabbard lined in wood covered in brown velvet, c1790, blade 21in (53.5cm) long.
$500–600 ⋊ Bon

A French cuirassier's model AN XI broad sword, with brass hilt and wire-bound grip, the double fullered blade engraved 'The sword of a French cuirassier engaged at Waterloo, brought from the fields at battle and presented to John Barnado Es by W. Wickens', early 19thC, blade 38in (96.5cm) long.
$2,600–3,200 ⋊ WD

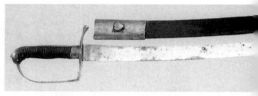

A south German or Austrian infantry sabre, the blade with double-edged point, with iron-mounted leather scabbard, early 19thC, 29in (73.5cm) long.
$140–170 ⋊ Herm

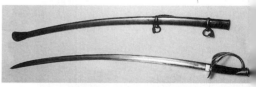

An American Civil War cavalry sword, with brass hilt, stamped US, with original scabbard, dated 1848, 43in (109cm) long.
$580–720 ⊞ ARB

A police hangar, the blade etched Parker Field, with brass hilt and fishskin grip, with brass-mounted leather scabbard, c1850, blade 29in (73.5cm) long.
$400–470 ⊞ WSA

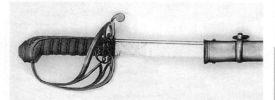

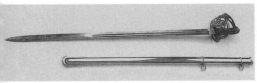

An Irish Victorian regimental officer's sword, by Henry Wilkinson, London, the blade etched with Queen's crown over Irish mermaid harp, with shagreen and wire grip, in original polished steel scabbard, blade 33in (84cm) long.
$430–500 ↗ **WA**

An American Bowie knife, the pewter handle with black composition grips, inlaid with mother-of-pearl circles, the single-edged blade etched on one side with the inscription, 'The Americans Pride, Equal Rights, Equal Laws And Justice to All', c1860, blade 7in (18cm) long.
$1,000–1,200 ⊞ **ASB**

A Victorian silver-mounted dirk, the mounts decorated with thistle borders and sprays, the grip carved with knotwork, c1870, 18in (45.5cm) long.
$2,200–2,400 ⊞ **NS**

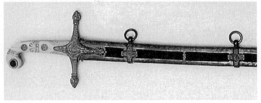

A 15th Hussars officer's levee sword, by Hawkes & Co, London, the blade etched with crowned King's 15th Hussars, with regulation brass mounts and two-piece ivory grips, in its copper gilt-mounted scabbard engraved with foliate fenestrated panels filled with black fishskin, c1870, blade 32in (81.5cm) long.
$1,000–1,200 ↗ **WAL**

A knife, by Unwin & Rogers, with carved bone hilt, 19thC, 10in (25.5cm) long.
$290–320 ⊞ **GV**

A Gordon Highlanders silver-mounted officer's dirk, Scotland, 19thC, 17½in (44.5cm) long.
$2,900–3,200 ⊞ **CCB**

A Spanish folding lock-knife, with single-edged clipped-back blade stamped with maker's name and mark, brass-mounted handle set on each side with four cowhorn grip-scales, blade repaired, 19thC, closed 19¾in (50cm) long.
$470–540 ↗ **Bon**

A German bayonet, by R. Stock & Co, Berlin, 1898/05 pattern saw-backed blade, with scabbard, c1900, 19in (48.5cm) long.
$85–100 ⊞ **AnS**

An Artillery Officer's sword, the blade etched on both sides with trophies and floral decoration on a gilt ground, with brass lion's head pommel and wire-bound fishskin grip, Prussia, Germany, 1900, 37¼in (94.5cm) long.
$400–460 ↗ **Herm**

Firearms

An Irish flintlock blunderbuss, with London proofs, walnut full stock with brass furniture, wooden ramrod, c1790, barrel 15¾in (40cm) long.
$870–1,000 🔨 **WD**

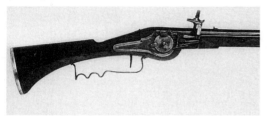

A German 14 bore military wheel lock carbine, the breech struck with the mark of Georg Zellner of Zell am Wallersee, with figured hardwood full stock and wooden ramrod, c1630, barrel 29½in (75cm) long.
$2,900–3,500 🔨 **S(NY)**

An Enfield two-band rifled carbine, with regulation lock bearing Crown over VR and stamped 1856 Tower, barrel 24¾in (63cm) long.
$650–725 ⊞ **GV**

An Irish Dublin Castle Brown Bess musket, the ramrod an old replacement, 1740s, 58in (147.5cm) long.
$2,600–2,900 ⊞ **GV**
This gun was apparently one of around 300 made and would have been used to protect the occupants of the Castle during events such as potato famines.

A Bank of Ireland Brown Bess flintlock musket, the lock plate with crown over GR and Tower, the stock stamped Bank of Ireland around a harp, storekeeper's mark of 1788, with socket bayonet and ramrod, 1780–90, barrel 38in (96.5cm) long.
$4,600–5,500 🔨 **WA**
This musket would have been issued to the Bank's own corps of guards.

Condition

The condition is absolutely vital when assessing the value of an antique. Damaged pieces on the whole appreciate much less than perfect examples. However a rare desirable piece may command a high price even when damaged.

A brass-mounted flintlock blunderbuss, c1800, 29in (73.5cm) long.
$430–500 🔨 **Mit**

A brass-barrelled flintlock blunderbuss, with London proof marks, late 17thC barrel, the breech punched with flowering foliage, trophies of arms and grotesque masks, with walnut full stock and foliate-engraved brass mounts, one ramrod pipe missing, early 19thC, 27¼in (69cm) long.
$870–1,000 🔨 **Bon**

An Irish 16 bore flintlock carbine, by W. & J. Rigby, Dublin, with walnut stock and brass furniture, c1823, barrel 22in (56cm) long.
$900–1,100 🔨 **WD**
Carbines of this type were made for Post Office, Police and Customs officers.

A flintlock blunderbuss, by Tipping, with full stocked two stage barrel and wooden ramrod, c1780, barrel 14½in (37cm) long.
$1,300–1,600 ⊞ **EP**

A land pattern flintlock musket, the barrel signed H. Nock, London, full stocked with brass mounts, with steel ramrod, the butt plate dated 1796, 42in (106.5cm) long.
$2,900–3,200 🔨 **Gle**

An India pattern Brown Bess musket, with ordnance proofs, the lock plate marked 'Tower, Crown, CR', the walnut full stock with regulation brass furniture, with iron ramrod, c1805, barrel 39in (99cm) long.
$1,800–2,000 ⊞ **WSA**

A German 65 bore wheel lock holster pistol, the full pearwood stock decorated overall with brass wire and mother-of-pearl, some restoration, c1630, 29½in (75cm) long.
$8,000–9,500 ➶ **WAL**

A pair of flintlock holster pistols, by Buckmaster, the three-stage brass barrels with London proofs and maker's mark, with walnut full stocks and ramrods with brass button tips, c1735, barrel 8¾in (22cm) long.
$6,500–7,250 ⊞ **WSA**

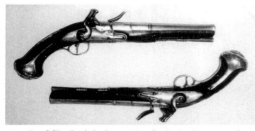

A pair of German flintlock pistols, smooth bore, calibre 13mm, the gilt-brass mounts relief-decorated with baroque shells and scrolls, mid-18thC, 12½in (32cm) long.
$1,700–2,200 ➶ **Herm**

A cannon-barrelled flintlock pistol, by Griffin, London, the walnut handle with shaped silver escutcheon surmounted by a helmet, further mount to side depicting flags and trophies, the silver butt cap cast with the arms of the East India Company, c1770, 12in (30.5cm) long.
$1,100–1,400 ➶ **CAG**

A pair of silver-mounted flintlock pistols, by Jover, converted to percussion by Hollis, with horn-tipped ramrods, in a fitted velvet-lined mahogany case with Hollis trade label and some accessories, the silver hallmarked for John King, London 1777, 15½in (39.5cm) long.
$6,800–8,000 ➶ **CGC**

▶ **A pair of double-barrelled flintlock holster pistols,** by J. Manton, c1785, restocked 1810, 17in (43cm) long.
$11,500–13,000 ⊞ **WSA**

A Silesian 80 bore combined axe and flintlock pistol, the barrel incised with foliage and scrolls, the haft inlaid with horn and mother-of-pearl, with a later steel-tipped wooden ramrod, late 17thC, 24¾in (63cm) long.
$4,000–4,600 ➶ **S(NY)**

A heavy Dragoon flintlock pistol, the walnut full stock with brass trim, marked with GRII Crown and dated 1745, 19in (48.5cm) long.
$3,200–3,600 ⊞ **SPA**

A pair of Dragoon-type 16 bore flintlock officer's pistols, by John Probin, with private Birmingham proofs, walnut full stocks with brass regulation furniture and wooden ramrods, c1760, barrels 9in (23cm) long.
$2,200–2,600 ➶ **WD**

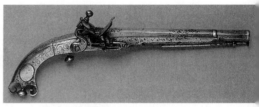

A Scottish steel flintlock belt pistol, the barrel engraved and inlaid with silver scrolls, the lock with horizontal sear signed Murdoch, the full stock engraved with scrolls and inlaid with silver brass, turned steel ramrod, c1770, barrel 8½in (21.5cm) long.
$4,000–4,600 ➶ **P(Ed)**

A cannon-barrelled flintlock boxlock pistol, by Griffin & Tow, London, the figured-walnut handle inset with a silver oval cartouche of helmet, sword and cannon, the butt cap embossed with a grotesque mask, c1780, 12in (30.5cm) long.
$1,000–1,200 ➶ **CAG**

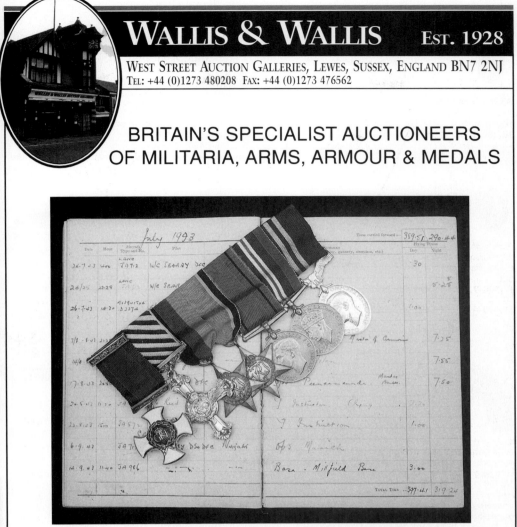
ARMS & ARMOUR

A converted duelling pistol, by John Manton, with walnut full stock and engraved iron furniture, brass-tipped ramrod, 1790, barrel 11in (28cm) long.
$2,300–2,600 ⊞ WSA

A pair of flintlock duelling pistols, by Wogdon & Barton, London, c1795, 15in (38cm) long.
$4,300–4,700 ⚒ CGC

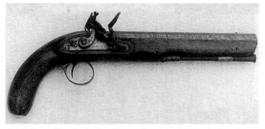

A 23 bore flintlock duelling pistol, by H. Nock, London, with octagonal damascus twist barrel, the walnut stock with steel furniture, c1800, barrel 9½in (24cm) long.
$1,200–1,400 ⊞ ASB
Henry Nock was gunsmith to George III from 1789 onwards and was one of the most important English gunmakers of the 18th century. He is best remembered by firearms historians for his patent breech of 1787, for his screwless lock of 1786 and for the seven-barrelled volley guns made for the Navy.

A short sea service flintlock pistol, with ordnance proofs, walnut full stock with regulation brass furniture and iron ramrod, c1810, barrel 9in (23cm) long.
$1,600–1,750 ⊞ WSA
This type of pistol was converted from a long sea service pistol, c1818, and is now rarely seen.

A travelling pistol, with a drum and nipple conversion to percussion, early 19thC, barrel 4¾in (12cm) long.
$230–250 ⊞ GV

A brass-mounted 16 bore officer's flintlock pistol, by Joshua Shore, c1790.
$1,300–1,450 ⊞ SPA
Joshua Shore emigrated to America in 1815 where he invented the percussion cap.

A flintlock gunmetal blunderbuss pistol, by Ryan & Watson, London, with under lever bayonet, c1800, 14in (35.5cm) long.
$2,100–2,300 ⊞ ARB

An American model 1808 Navy flintlock pistol, by Simeon North, Berlin, Connecticut, with an early hickory ramrod, perhaps the original, 1808–10, barrel 10in (25.5cm) long.
$8,700–10,000 ⚒ S(NY)

A 36 bore flintlock duelling pistol, by Prosser, London, with walnut full stock, silver barrel wedge plates and engraved silver butt, with horn-tipped ramrod and worm, c1820, 13½in (34.5cm) long.
$1,600–1,900 ⚒ WAL

A double-barrelled percussion cap pistol, by Dawson, Grantham, with top-mounted sprung bayonet, walnut stock, early 19thC, 8in (20.5cm) long, in fitted mahogany case with accessories.
$1,100–1,300 ⚒ DD

A flintlock pistol, by Theophilus Richards, London, with iron barrel, the butt cap, escutcheon and side plate in silver, area behind barrel tang inlaid with silver wire, 1790–1830, barrel 6½in (16.5cm) long.
$2,200–2,400 ⊞ GV

A walnut pocket pistol, by Askey, Bedale, early 19thC, 7in (18cm) long.
$290–330 ⊞ MB

A Spanish 19 bore miquelet flintlock belt pistol, with part-round, part octagonal steel barrel, walnut stock and brass furniture, c1820, barrel 10in (25.5cm) long.
$1,000–1,200 ⊞ ASB

A pair of American 20 bore flintlock pistols, with figured walnut full stocks and brass mounts, a pair of faceted ramrod pipes each with a wooden ramrod, early 19thC, barrels 8in (20.5cm) long.
$2,000–2,300 ⚒ S(NY)

A six-shot .38 hand rotated pepperbox percussion pistol, by H. Meredith, 1830–35, 8½in (21.5cm) long.
$1,100–1,300 ⊞ SPA

A 28 bore full stock percussion holster pistol, signed Richardson, London, the walnut stock with steel furniture, c1840, barrel 9in (23cm) long.
$900–1,000 ⊞ ASB

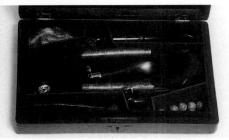

A pair of gentleman's pocket pistols, by Smith, London, with concealed triggers and rifle barrels, the walnut handles decorated with silver grotesque masks, in mahogany case with all the original accessories, c1840, box 10in (25.5cm) wide.
$4,300–4,700 ⊞ ARB

An Irish 20 bore percussion pistol, by W. & I. Rigby, Dublin, with figured-walnut full stock and stirrup ramrod, 1848, 9¼in (23.5cm) long.
$1,000–1,200 ⚒ Bon

An American 31 calibre percussion pepperbox pistol, by Blunt & Syms, the case-hardened frame engraved with foliage, with plain walnut grips, c1850, barrel 4in (10cm) long.
$360–430 ⚒ WD

A pair of percussion duelling pistols, by William London, with walnut half stock, octagonal barrels, the locks engraved with scrolling foliage, mid-19thC, 12in (30.5cm) long, with a mahogany brass-bound case.
$2,200–2,600 ⚒ AH

A 90 bore self-cocking Webley Bentley-type open frame percussion revolver, the octagonal barrel with dovetailed foresight and six-shot cylinder, chequered walnut grip, the top flat engraved R. Brooke, with Birmingham proofs, c1850, barrel 4¾in (12cm) long.
$260–320 ⚒ WD

► **A 60 bore self-cocking hammerless six-shot percussion pepperbox revolver,** by Henry Tatham, London, with fluted barrels engraved with a band of foliage around the muzzles, chequered figured-walnut grip scales, London proof marks, c1850, 9½in (24cm) long, in original brass-mounted fitted mahogany case, with full accessories.
$5,800–7,200 ⚒ Bon

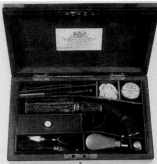

A .44 Tranter percussion five shot revolver, with side hammer and safety retainer, c1850, 11in (28cm) long.
$1,600–1,750 ⊞ SPA

A pepperbox revolver, stamped Martin, London, with bar hammer, six barrels, and chequered grip, mid-19thC, 8½in (21.5cm) long.
$400–440 ⚒ Bea(E)

An American Model Army cap and ball six-shot Colt .44 revolver, the steel barrel inscribed Col Samuel Colt, New York US America, the stock with brass mounts, c1860, 14½in (37cm) long.
$870–1,000 ⚒ ELR

> **Miller's is a price GUIDE not a price LIST**

► **A transitional revolver,** by Samuel Harper, Birmingham, 1861, 12in (30.5cm) long, in original mahogany case with accessories and original bill of sale.
$3,600–4,000 ⊞ ARB

An American Government Starr model .44 calibre model 1863 Army six-shot single action percussion revolver, with plain one-piece walnut grooved grip stamped with US Ordnance Inspector's cartouche, 1863–65, barrel 8in (20.5cm) long.
$2,900–3,200 ⊞ ASB
The American Government bought approximately 25,000 Starr revolvers during the Civil War, making it the major model of revolver bought by the Union, after Colt and Remington.

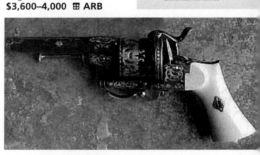

A 9mm six-shot pinfire revolver, by Larranga Y Ga Eibar, the blued frame cylinder and barrel with applied gold decoration, with steel ejector rod, trigger and sight, ivory grips, late 19thC, 9in (23cm) long.
$4,700–5,000 ⊞ GV

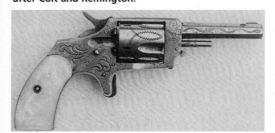

An American .32 five-shot single action revolver, the barrel and frame with scroll engraving, with mother-of-pearl grips, action defective, c1875, barrel 2¾in (7cm) long.
$460–500 ⊞ ASB

A 54 bore six-shot double action pin fire revolver, with chequered walnut grips and Birmingham proof marks, late 19thC, 11¼in (28.5cm) long.
$320–380 ⚒ Bon

A German 19.5mm calibre wheel lock rifle, with engraved iron mounts and bone-inlaid walnut full stock, c1800, 49¼in (125.5cm) long.
$4,000–4,600 ⚔ **Herm**

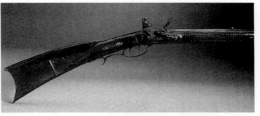

An American brass-mounted tiger maple flintlock rifle, by Joseph Golcher, Philadelphia, Pennsylvania, with 54 calibre barrel and brass and silver inlays on the stock, c1800, 54in (137cm) long.
$5,000–5,800 ⚔ **SK(B)**

An American 100 bore percussion Kentucky rifle, with octagonal sighted barrel and striped maple half stock with brass mounts, later incomplete wooden ramrod, mid-19thC, 35¾in (91cm) long.
$950–1,100 ⚔ **Bon**

An American .31 calibre Pennsylvania rifle, the breech section inscribed Carter, the tiger-striped maple stock with brass furniture, c1840, barrel 46in (117cm) long.
$950–1,100 ⊞ **ASB**

A Volunteer two-band Enfield rifle, the lock signed Thomas Turner beneath a crown, the lock and furniture engraved with trophies of arms, dated 1860, 49in (124.5cm) long.
$1,400–1,600 ⊞ **GV**

A 577 three-band Enfield-type percussion rifle, by John Aston, Hythe, with walnut full stock, chequered at waist, iron furniture and original iron ramrod, c1860, barrel 39in (99cm) long.
$800–950 ⚔ **WD**

► **An American Allen's patent .44 breech loading rim-fire rifle,** with walnut fore end and butt, minor split, 1860–71, barrel 26in (61cm) long.
$460–550 ⚔ **Bon**

Polearms

The head of a late medieval polearm, 16thC, 19in (48.5cm) long.
$720–800 ⊞ **ASB**

A French spontoon head, mid-18thC, 14in (35.5cm) long.
$500–580 ⊞ **ASB**
This item is of the type carried by French officers and NCOs in America during the French and Native American wars of the 1750s.

A German or Swiss halberd, with later wooden staff, possibly early 16thC, 20½in (52cm) long.
$580–720 ⚔ **Bon**

A halberd, the head with etched decoration, on its original reeded oak haft, 17thC, 84in (213.5cm) long.
$1,100–1,400 ⚔ **WAL**

◄ **A Continental 17thC-style steel partizan,** the blade etched with a shield flanked by foliate scrolls and the date 1620, 90½in (230cm) long.
$500–580 ⚔ **SK**

ARMS & ARMOUR

Militaria

Badges

A silver Highland Borderers Militia officer's glengarry badge, 1853–81.
$430–500 ➤ DNW

A Victorian other ranks' glengarry badge, of the 3rd Volunteers Battalion, South Staffordshire Regiments, minor wear.
$100–120 ➤ WAL

A 91st Argyllshire Highlanders other ranks' brass glengarry badge, 1864–81.
$340–380 ➤ DNW

◄ A WWII cap badge, of the Long Range Desert Group.
$300–350 ➤ WAL

► A Royal Irish Regiment other ranks' brass glengarry cap badge, pre-1902.
$300–350 ➤ WA

Costume

◄ A 24th, (2nd Warwickshire) Regiment other ranks' 1857 pattern full dress red tunic, with the owner's canvas hold-all containing account book, monthly settlements, clothing account and savings bank account and parchment certificate for No. 1834 Private John Martin, 2/24th Foot.
$580–720 ➤ WAL
The parchment certificate shows that Private Martin enlisted 10th December 1866, aged 18, and was discharged after 75 days' service on 18 February 1867 'in consequence of payment of the regulated Compensation of £20' (a large sum in those days – evidently life in the army was not at all to his liking).

A Lancashire Regiment Boer War tunic, c1900.
$85–100 ➤ SWO

Items in the Militaria section have been arranged in date order within each sub-section.

◄ A naval uniform belonging to Prince Adalbert von Preussen, as Lieutenant Commander, comprising cap, jacket and trousers, c1915.
$4,600–5,000 ➤ Herm

► A Life Guard's complete ceremonial uniform, 1950–60.
$5,000–6,500 ⊞ Q&C

A Royal Engineers Lieutenant Colonel's complete wardrobe, 1942.
$900–1,000 ⊞ CYA

Helmets & Headdresses

A Lübeck Light Infantry Battalion enlisted man's shako, Germany, c1865. $950–1,100 ✎ Herm

A Georgian army officer's cocked hat. $260–320 ✎ WA

A Victorian 9th Queen's Royal Lancers officer's lance cap, with gilt ornaments. $5,000–6,000 ✎ WAL

A German WWI *Pickelhaube*, 9in (23cm) high. $290–320 ⊞ AnS

◄ **A Victorian Fife and Forfar Yeomanry 1871 pattern white metal helmet,** with bi-metal helmet plate, white metal fittings and red horsehair plume. $900–1,100 ✎ S(S)

A 14th Hussars officer's sable busby, with ostrich feather plume, pre-1922. $1,000–1,300 ⊞ Q&C

A Grenadiers officer's bearskin, with carrying tin, c1930. $870–950 ⊞ Q&C

Helmet Plates

A 3rd Royal Surrey Militia officer's shako plate, 1855 pattern. $400–480 ✎ Gle

A Capetown Highlanders other ranks' white metal helmet plate, 1885–89. $150–200 ✎ DNW

A Victoria Rifles officer's metal helmet plate, 1887–96. $180–220 ✎ DNW

A 3rd Lanarkshire Rifles Volunteers other ranks' bronzed shako plate, 1902–08. $100–120 ✎ WAL

Orders & Medals

A Waterloo medal,
awarded to Lieutenant
James Robinson, 32nd
Regiment, Foot, fitted with
replacement steel clip and
ring suspension, 1815.
$1,800–2,200 ✦ **Gle**

**A Military Order of the
Tower and Sword medal,**
Commander's gold neck
badge, 1810–20.
$3,600–4,000 ✦ **DNW**

A group of five medals, awarded to Capt. C. McM.
Laing, Royal Scots Fusiliers and Royal Air Force, Military
Cross, GVR, the reverse inscribed 'Gallipoli 1915', Air
Force Cross, GVR, the reverse inscribed 'Mediterranean
1919, 1914–15 star, British War and Victory medals.
$2,300–2,900 ✦ **DNW**

A group of five medals, awarded to W. E. Holloway,
DSM George V, 1914–15 Star, BWM, Victory, Naval LS & GC.
$1,000–1,300 ✦ **WAL**

A group of three Victorian medals, Crimean War,
'Sebastopol', Indian Mutiny 'Relief in Lucknow' awarded
to Wickens, and a Turkish Crimea Medal, Sardinia issue.
$650–750 ✦ **WL**

Miller's Compares

I. An MGS medal,
awarded to Lieut. W.
Fendall, 4th Dragoons,
with Talavera, Albuhera,
Vittoria and Toulouse
clasps, 1793.
$1,900–2,200 ✦ **WAL**

II. An MGS medal,
awarded to Sgt Charles
Hay, Royal Sappers and
Miners, with Vittoria and
St Sebastian clasps, 1793.
$720–870 ✦ **WAL**

The price for which a military medal will sell is
governed by a number of factors, such as the
campaign for which it was awarded or the
particular act of bravery it represents. In the
case of the two Military General Service medals
pictured above, Item I has four clasps (these
increase a medal's desirability) and was awarded
to the commanding officer of a cavalry
regiment, whereas Item II has two clasps and
was awarded to a Sergeant in the infantry.
Medals awarded to members of the Cavalry
often sell for a higher price and Item I has the
added advantage of its recipient fighting in
more campaigns than that of Item II.

A WWII group of six medals, awarded to LSgt. G. L.
Saunders, 1st Medium Regiment, Royal Artillery,
Distinguished Conduct Medal Geo VI, 1939–45 Star,
Africa Star, Burma Star, Defence Medal and War Medal.
$3,000–3,500 ⊞ **RMC**

A WWII group of five medals, awarded to J. Shelton,
5/2nd Searchlight Regiment Royal Artillery, Distinguished
Conduct Medal Geo VI, 1939–45 Star, Defence Medal,
War Medal, Long Service and Good Conduct Medal and
Geo VI (Ind Imp).
$2,600–2,900 ⊞ **RMC**

Powder Flasks

A German engraved stag horn powder flask, 16thC, 9in (23cm) long.
$2,900–3,300 ⊞ AEF

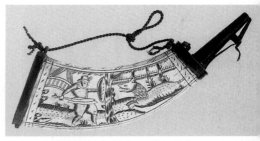

A German horn powder horn, with iron mounts, engraved on one side with a huntsman and a wild animal, the other with circular decoration, early 17thC, 13¾in (35cm) long.
$700–800 ⋏ Herm

An American Navy brass powder flask, decorated on both sides with an anchor, inscribed 'U.S.N.', early 18thC, 7½in (19cm) long.
$1,600–1,800 ⋏ S

A German brass powder flask, the body decorated with elaborate tracery, with two lobed lug handles, 18thC, 4¾in (12cm) wide.
$250–300 ⋏ P

An American engraved powder horn, signed 'By J. Gay', attributed to Jacob Gay (working 1758–87), inscribed 'Gideon Booth his horn made at Winter Hill Decm: 1775', flanked on the right by the British coat-of-arms with banners inscribed 'success to America' on the left with floral scrolls, decorated with a scene of duelling soldiers, a mermaid, deer, and other decorative devices, mounted with later sterling silver fittings marked 'Tiffany and Co', some damage, late 18thC, 15in (38cm) long.
$36,500–43,500 ⋏ SK(B)
Pieces attributable to specific makers are of particular interest to collectors.

A powder horn, c1800, 17in (43cm) long.
$95–110 ⊞ GV

A leather and brass powder flask, made for Lord Percy, Duke of Northumberland, c1800, 7in (18cm) long.
$260–300 ⊞ SPA

Miscellaneous

A gunner's linstock, the Victorian haft covered in red velvet with brass studs, c1600, 80in (203cm) long.
$1,500–1,600 ⊞ WSA

A gunner's brass rule, marked with details of charges for brass guns and howitzers, mortars iron and brass, iron guns and howitzers, the reverse graduated to 1/20in and scaled for calculations, 18thC, 12in (30.5cm) long.
$1,600–1,800 ⋏ S(S)

▶ **A mahogany campaign writing slope,** late 18thC, 18in (45.5cm) wide.
$870–1,000 ⊞ CoHA

◀ **A silver two-handled vase-shaped cup and cover,** engraved with armorials and presentation inscription from the Eagle Troop of Berwickshire Yeoman Cavalry to Capt. Tom Spottiswoode, maker's mark M & F, Edinburgh, dated 1802, 18in (45.5cm) high, 82½oz.
$2,600–3,200 ⋏ Bea(E)

MILITARIA

A pair of 87th Regiment Royal Irish Fusiliers epaulettes, in gold bullion decorated with shamrocks, the silver bullion grenade with gilt eagle, gilded brass surround, c1830.
$950–1,100 ✦ WA

A Continental steel bullet mould, made for a high grade pistol set, c1840, 8in (20.5cm) long.
$190–210 ⊞ ARB

A patchwork cover, made from soldiers' uniforms by prisoners of the Crimean War, 48 x 47in (122 x 119.5cm).
$500–550 ⊞ DNo

A Royal Aberdeenshire Highlanders Militia officer's shoulder belt plate, silver-plate with gilt mounts, c1858–81.
$550–650 ✦ Gle

An American Civil War broadside, printed in Gloucester, Massachusetts, 1861–62, 18½ x 23¼in (47 x 59cm).
$800–870 ✦ SK(B)

A Victorian Methodist Guards Brigade (Newfoundland) white metal waist belt clasp.
$80–95 ✦ WAL
This was one of the Church Brigades and quasi-military units, volunteers from which made up over half the 1st Newfoundland Regiment raised in 1914.

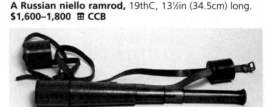

A Russian niello ramrod, 19thC, 13½in (34.5cm) long.
$1,600–1,800 ⊞ CCB

A photograph frame, with regimental standards and arms commemorating the Boer War, Birmingham 1900, 1in (2.5cm) high.
$500–600 ✦ Bea(E)

A Victorian silver-plated model cheese drum, by Potter, Aldershot, 5in (12.5cm) diam.
$800–1,000 ⊞ Q&C

A leather-covered three-draw army telescope, with lens caps, 1900–20, 11in (28cm) long.
$400–500 ⊞ SPA

A Spanish Civil War commemorative card, of General Sanjurjo, with three Spanish overprint stamps, Pro Malaga, 1937.
$130–160 ✦ VS

A black bakelite identification model aeroplane, Ilyussian IL2, used in WWII to identify aircraft, 1940s, 8in (20.5cm) wide.
$115–145 ⊞ APC

A piece of ship's plating, ripped and bent from a German shell, with a photograph of HMS *Fearless*, signed by the officers, with an inscription 'Part of Plate from HMS *Fearless* Showing the Hole made by The First German Shell That Struck an English Warship 20th August 1914', mounted on a wooden plinth with four pairs of wooden artillery shells as feet,
$1,700–2,000 ✦ P

◄ A WWII cased brass marching compass, with mother-of-pearl dial, dated 1942, 2¼in (5.5cm) diam.
$180–210 ⊞ SPA

Sport
Baseball

A Walter Johnson wool baseball blanket, 1914. $400–440 ↗ HALL

◄ A Stenzel's Rooter button, featuring 'C. O'Neil', c1904, 1½in (4cm) diam. $1,200–1,400 ⊞ HUNT This is believed to be Peaches O'Neil who played for Cincinnati in 1904. Jake Stenzel played from 1890–99 with several teams including Baltimore and Cincinnati.

A Babe Ruth souvenir pin, 1920–30, ¾in (2cm) diam. $2,100–2,300 ⊞ HUNT

A Goudy Sport Kings Gum baseball card, depicting Babe Ruth, 1934. $1,000–1,100 ↗ HALL

◄ A baseball cigarette card, depicting C. Y. Young, 1910. $480–540 ↗ HALL

A Hutch leather baseball glove, 1960s, 11in (28cm) wide. $35–45 ⊞ TRA

► A baseball trophy, presented by Rawlings Co to local team champion, 1922, 10in (25.5cm) high. $580–650 ⊞ HUNT

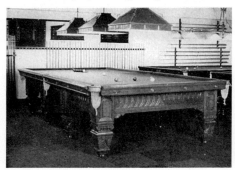
Billiards

A Burroughs & Watts billiard ball box, with ivory balls, c1865, 19in (48.5cm) wide. $650–720 ⊞ WBB

A Victorian mahogany cue stand, the triform top with spring cue fittings, some replaced, the base revolving and fitted to receive the cue ends, 47in (119.5cm) high. $580–720 ↗ Mit

► An oak marker scoreboard cabinet, with four revolving panels for cue racks, score markers and slate, c1885, 72in (183cm) high. $10,800–12,300 ⊞ WBB

A Gillows mahogany billiards table, with wooden base, c1820, 144 x 72in (366 x 183cm).
$29,000–36,500 ⊞ WBB

A George Wright burr-mahogany billiards table, c1860, 144 x 72in (366 x 183cm).
$10,800–12,300 ⊞ WBB

◄ **A Thurston walnut billiards/dining table,** c1870, 120 x 60in (305 x 152.5cm).
$23,200–26,200 ⊞ WBB

A Riley walnut billiards/dining table, c1900, 79 x 41in (200.5 x 104cm).
$3,000–3,400 ⊞ MTay

◄ **A Riley billiards/dining table,** with mahogany lift-up mechanism, c1920, 84 x 36in (213.5 x 91.5cm).
$3,600–4,000 ⊞ WBB

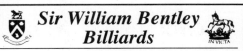

A Burroughs & Watts mahogany billiards table, with an oak scoreboard, rests, cues, sets of balls, an iron, a brush and a cover, late 1930s, 151 x 80¼in (383.5 x 204cm), and snooker light.
$2,300–2,900 ⚒ HAM

► **A Victorian tile,** depicting two men in 16thC costume playing billiards, c1890, 6in (15cm) square.
$75–85 ⊞ WAB

Boxing

A silver-gilt and enamelled Lonsdale Belt, by Mappin & Webb for the British Boxing Board of Control Welterweight Championship of Great Britain, won by Brian Curvis, 1964, the central panel with enamelled bust of Lord Lonsdale, hallmarked Sheffield 1961, 34½in (87.5cm) long.
$7,300–8,000 ⚒ S

A pugilist horse brass, 1880, 3in (7.5cm) wide.
$50–60 ⊞ PJo

A Staffordshire group of two pugilists, Heenan and Sayers, 19thC, 9¼in (23.5cm) high.
$720–800 ⚒ RTo

A pair of leather boxing training mitts, 1920s, 10in (25.5cm) long.
$50–60 ⊞ SPT

A pair of child's fabric boxing gloves, 1930s, 8in (20.5cm) long.
$65–75 ⊞ SPT

A red satin boxing jacket, the front embroidered in gold with 'Las Vegas Hilton', the reverse with full details of the Mike Tyson v Frank Bruno fight, 25 February 1989.
$60–70 ⚒ MUL

A silver lustreware pugilist jug, with sepia vignettes of Molineux and Cribb, 19thC, 6¾in (17cm) high.
$500–600 ⚒ HYD

A Wincarnis Boxing Club gold medal, the front with enamelled yellow and brown crest, the reverse engraved 'F. Joyce winner "London Cup" Nov 24th 1927', in original Fattorini Birmingham box.
$90–100 ⚒ MUL

► A photograph of Muhammad Ali, taken by Liefer c1970, signed and authenticated by Ali in March 2000, 58/100, 20 x 16in (51 x 40.5cm).
$800–870 ⊞ SMW

A ticket for the Willard v Dempsey twelve round fight, Toledo Athletic Club, 4 July 1919, mounted as a plaque, 8 x 10in (20.5 x 25.5cm).
$300–350 ⚒ Bon(C)

A black and white photograph, depicting Muhammad Ali pushing back The Beatles in the ring, Miami Beach, 18 February 1964, signed by Ali, framed and glazed, 22 x 25in (56 x 63.5cm).
$720–870 ⚒ Bon(C)

◄ An unused ticket for the Muhammad Ali v Brian London fight, Earl's Court, August 1966, mounted as a plaque, 7 x 10in (18 x 25.5cm).
$160–190 ⚒ Bon(C)

Colour Review

A George III mahogany knife box, with fitted interior, 9in (23cm) wide.
$500–600 ⚘ RBB

A Russian walrus ivory coffer, late 18thC, 10¾in (27.5cm) wide.
$1,400–1,600 ⚘ NOA

A Georgian inlaid mahogany jewel box, with a drawer, 13in (33cm) wide.
$580–650 ⊞ MB

A Georgian gilt-metal-mounted mahogany writing box, with coromandel wood veneered interior and original bottles, 20in (51cm) wide.
$600–700 ⚘ TMA

A Regency gilt-metal-mounted tooled leather sewing box, with fitted interior, 9in (23cm) wide.
$1,000–1,150 ⚘ P

A Regency tortoiseshell tea caddy, with ivory line and edging and silver mounts, 4in (10cm) high.
$6,000–7,000 ⚘ TMA

◀ **An inlaid mahogany tea caddy,** c1815, 7in (18cm) wide.
$350–400 ⊞ MB

A Regency dome-topped tortoiseshell tea caddy, with silver ball feet, c1820, 7in (18cm) wide.
$3,600–4,400 ⊞ BBo

A George IV mahogany dressing case, with cut-brass inlay, containing silver-topped accessories, with drawer to base, London 1821–22, 12½in (32cm) wide.
$1,150–1,350 ⊁ RBB

A Louis Philippe ormolu-mounted ebonized rosewood and boulle writing box, the interior with a fall-front writing surface and four tiered compartments, above a drawer, mid-19thC, 12in (30.5cm) wide.
$1,150–1,350 ⊁ NOA

▶ **A boulle scent casket,** inlaid with brass and mother-of-pearl, containing four bottles with gilt-metal tops, c1840, 5in (12.5cm) wide.
$1,750–2,000 ⊞ BAO

A tortoiseshell tea caddy, with pewter stringing, the interior with two compartments, 19thC, 8in (20.5cm) wide.
$3,000–3,500 ⊁ AH

▶ **A William IV pollarded oak and rosewood banded jewel box,** with mother-of-pearl dot inlay, enclosing a tray with various compartments, 13in (33cm) wide.
$600–700 ⊁ P(Ed)

◀ **A satinwood, bird's-eye maple and rosewood parquetry tea caddy,** 19thC, 12in (30.5cm) wide.
$1,100–1,250 ⊞ CRU

▶ **An early Victorian lady's rosewood sewing box,** with inlaid brass decoration and original Bramah lock, 9in (23cm) wide.
$320–370 ⊞ OTT

A Victorian amboyna-veneered tea caddy, c1860, 15in (38cm) wide.
$850–1,000 ⊞ NAW

A rosewood box, inlaid with mother-of-pearl, c1860, 12in (30.5cm) wide.
$145–160 ⊞ BWA

A Victorian burr-walnut sewing box, with brass fittings, 10in (25.5cm) wide.
$250–300 ⊞ OTT

An Imperial Russian hand-painted lacquer box, by Vichnaichov, c1870, 8in (20.5cm) wide.
$1,600–1,800 ⊞ SHa

An inlaid mahogany box, with partitioned internal shelf, c1870, 11½in (30cm) wide.
$350–400 ⊞ BWA

A tortoiseshell jewellery box, with silver mounts, Chester 1893, 8in (20.5cm) wide.
$1,800–2,300 ⊞ BBo

◀ **A malachite-inlaid brass jewel box,** by Howell James & Co, London, slight damage, late 19thC, 9¾in (25cm) wide.
$360–440 ↗ Hal

▶ **A French burr yew wood sewing box,** with tulipwood and kingwood stringing, 19thC, 11in (28cm) wide.
$360–440 ⊞ OTT

A Russian icon of St Nicholas, with scenes from his life and miracles, Moscow, 16thC, 12½ x 10½in (32 x 26.5cm).
$8,500–10,000 ⊞ RKa

A Greek icon of the Raising of Lazarus, Epirus, dated 1611, 15½ x 12in (39.5 x 30.5cm).
$7,250–8,000 ⊞ RKa

A Veneto-Cretan icon of St Catherine, Greece, 17thC, 17½ x 14½in (44.5 x 37cm).
$12,500–14,500 ⚒ S

A Russian inset icon of the head of Christ, covered by a late 19thC silver-gilt riza, 17thC, 11 x 12½in (28 x 32cm).
$3,500–3,800 ⊞ ICO

A Russian provincial icon of St John the Baptist, 17thC, 13 x 11in (33 x 28cm).
$3,000–3,300 ⊞ ICO

A Russian icon of St Procupius and St Joanna, with a metal riza, c1740, 13 x 11in (33 x 28cm).
$2,400–2,700 ⊞ ICO

◀ **A Russian icon of the four Evangelists,** with an inset bronze cross, 18thC, 19 x 17in (48.5 x 43cm).
$4,000–4,500 ⊞ ICO

A Greek icon of the Dormition of the Virgin, painted on a gold ground, early 18thC, 18½ x 15in (47 x 38cm).
$5,000–6,000 ⚒ S

◀ **A Russian icon of St Nicholas,** with a silver-gilt riza, Moscow, 1884, 4 x 3in (10 x 7.5cm).
$650–725 ⊞ ICO

▶ **A Russian icon of the Tikhvin Mother of God,** painted on gold, in a silver-gilt oklad, marked I.G., St Petersburg, 1769, 12½ x 10¾in (32 x 27.5cm).
$7,250–8,000 ⚒ S

A Greek icon of the Mother of God Hodegetria, 18thC, 7¾ x 5¾in (19.5 x 14.5cm).
$2,200–2,500 ⊞ RKa

A Swiss cylinder musical box, by Nicole Frères, contained in a rosewood-veneered box inlaid with coloured woods and enamel, c1870, 22in (56cm) wide.
$5,000–6,000 ⊞ GWe

A French silver-gilt singing bird box, 19thC, 4¼in (11cm) wide.
$2,500–3,000 ↗ LJ

A Swiss pair of singing birds, with intermittent song, in a brass cage on a giltwood base, late 19thC, 21in (53.5cm) high.
$10,000–11,500 ⊞ RGa

A mahogany and satin-wood single manual harpsichord, by Abraham & Joseph Kirkman, London, with stained fruitwood and holly inlay, 1793, 37¼in (94.5cm) high.
$35,000–40,000 ↗ P

◄ A Dital harp, by Edward Light, London, c1810, 24in (61cm) high.
$4,000–4,500 ↗ P

A French Erard giltwood and bird's-eye maple harp, mid-19thC, 70in (178cm) high.
$13,000–14,500 ↗ NOA

A cello, by Charles Harris, 1820, length of back 29½in (75cm).
$17,500–22,000 ↗ GH

A Regency Brazilian rosewood square piano, by J. D. R. & J. C. Scott, London, with ormolu foliate mounts, 71¼in (181cm) wide.
$5,000–6,000 🔨 P(Sy)

An American Classical ebonized and stencil-decorated mahogany piano, by Joseph Hiskey, Baltimore, Maryland, c1820, 73in (185.5cm) wide.
$8,000–9,000 🔨 S(NY)

A French Cuban mahogany grand piano, by Pleyel, Paris, c1837, 76in (193cm) long.
$39,000–43,500 ⊞ PPC

A burr-walnut grand piano, by Collard & Collard, London, late 19thC, 82in (208.5cm) wide.
$4,500–5,500 🔨 NOA

A French mahogany and gilt-bronze mounted piano, by Erard, 19thC, 55in (139.5cm) wide.
$16,000–17,500 🔨 S(Z)

A French Sheraton Revival-style grand piano, by Erard, with marquetry inlay, 1896, 82¾in (210cm) long.
$58,000–65,000 ⊞ PPC

A French figured-mahogany grand piano, by Erard, Modèle Trianon, inlaid with boxwood and ebony banding, the legs with brass-inlaid flutes and ormolu mounts, c1914, 82¾in (210cm) long.
$65,000–73,000 ⊞ PPC

A rosewood grand piano, by F. W. C. Bechstein, c1900, 78¼in (199cm) wide.
$3,500–4,500 🔨 LJ

A rosewood, ebony-strung and walnut-banded grand piano, by Grotrian Steinweg Nacht, the top and sides inlaid with bird's-eye maple, c1906, 68in (172.5cm) wide.
$11,600–13,000 🔨 P(Ba)

A viola, by James & Henry Banks, Salisbury, stamped marks, dated 1803, length of back 15¼in (38.5cm).
$9,500–11,500 🔨 Bon

An Italian violin, by Julius Caesar Gigli, Rome, old restorations to back, c1760, length of back 14in (35.5cm), in fitted case.
$12,300–14,500 🔨 S

An Italian violin, by Giulio Degani, Venice, 1893, length of back 14½in (37cm).
$11,500–13,500 🔨 P

An Italian violin, by Giulio Degani, Venice, 1898, length of back 13in (33cm), cased.
$24,500–29,000 🔨 GH

A portrait miniature of a young lady, by Frederick Buck, c1820, 2¾in (7cm) high, in a red leather travelling case.
$950–1,200 ⚒ Bon

A portrait miniature of Princess Maria Casimire Clementina Sobieski, attributed to Rosalba Carriera, c1720, 3¼in (8.5cm) high, in a brass frame.
$7,250–8,700 ⚒ Bon

A portrait miniature of a lady, by Pierre Adolphe Hall, painted on ivory, c1785, 2in (5cm) high, in a gold frame with plaited hair border overlaid with gold openwork inscription, with glazed hair reverse.
$16,000–19,000 ⚒ S

An enamel portrait miniature of a lady, by Gaspard Lamuniere, with a gold-plated brooch clasp frame, signed, mid-19thC, 2in (5cm) high.
$1,000–1,250 ⚒ P

A portrait miniature of a gentleman, by Thomas Hazlehurst, in a gold frame, the reverse with a spray of hair held with gold wire and seed pearls, signed with initials, 1740–1821, 3in (7.5cm) high.
$4,300–4,800 ⚒ P

A portrait miniature of a gentleman, by Walter Stephens Lethbridge, signed and dated 1806, 3in (7.5cm) high, in a gold frame.
$750–900 ⚒ P

A portrait miniature of an officer, by Andrew Plimer, in a gold locket, face missing, c1790, 2¼in (5.5cm) high.
$3,600–4,300 ⚒ CGC

A pair of portrait miniatures of a gentleman and his wife, by William Wood, in gold frames, 1800, 3½in (9cm) high.
$8,000–9,000 ⊞ BeE

A watercolour portrait miniature of a gentleman, painted on ivory, c1800, 4in (10cm) high.
$320–400 ⊞ PSC

A portrait miniature of a gentleman, by J. Tourmeau, in a gold frame, c1800, 3½in (9cm) high.
$2,300–2,600 ⊞ SHa

A watercolour portrait miniature of a lady, painted on ivory, 1820, 4in (10cm) high, framed.
$400–480 ⊞ PSC

◄ **A watercolour portrait miniature of a lady,** painted on ivory, c1890, 3½in (9cm) high, framed.
$260–320 ⊞ PSC

Four Egyptian polychrome limestone canopic jars, the lids each in the form of the head of one of the Four Sons of Horus, 26th Dynasty, 664–525 BC, largest 7½in (19cm) high.
$14,500–17,500 🔨 S(NY)

An Egyptian carnelian amulet of a couchant bull, c5thC BC, 1in (2.5cm) long.
$5,800–7,250 🔨 Bon

A Mycenaean pottery jug, with banded decoration, 12thC BC, 7in (18cm) high.
$450–550 ⊞ HEL

An Attic Black Figure olpe, some restoration, 550–530 BC, 10in (25.5cm) high.
$7,250–8,000 🔨 Bon

A Greek bronze strainer, c5th–3rdC BC, 11in (28cm) long.
$11,500–13,500 🔨 S(NY)

A Greek core-formed glass oinochoe, c4thC BC, 4½in (11.5cm) high.
$23,000–25,500 🔨 S(NY)

An Apulian black-glazed pelike, Greek colonies of Southern Italy, c4thC BC, 8in (20.5cm) high.
$400–500 ⊞ OTT

A Greek hollow gold gnostic amulet, each facet incised with a line of Greek letters inlaid in niello, 2nd–1stC BC, 1¼in (3cm) long.
$5,500–6,000 🔨 Bon

A Roman bronze bowl, c1stC, 8¾in (22cm) wide.
$6,500–8,000 🔨 S(NY)

◄ **A Campanian Red-Figure fish plate,** with added white slip, Greek colonies of Southern Italy, 4thC BC, 7in (18cm) diam.
$3,600–4,400 🔨 Bon

An Anglo-Saxon gold pendant cross, c700, 1in (2.5cm) diam.
$5,500–6,500 🔨 Bon

► **A Byzantine mosaic panel,** c4th–5thC, 47 x 38in (119.5 x 96.5cm).
$7,250–8,700 🔨 S(NY)

A Roman purple glass bowl, 4thC, 6½in (16.5cm) diam.
$4,000–4,600 🔨 Bon

A pair of leather and beaded moccasins, Native American, c1850, 10in (25.5cm) long.
$500–600 ⊞ PSC

A Central Plains beaded hide bag, Native American, c1870, 21in (53.5cm) long.
$6,500–7,500 ↗ SK(B)

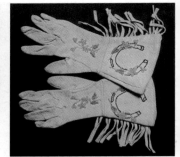

A pair of Cree deerskin gauntlets, with beaded decoration, Native American, 1930s, 13in (33cm) long.
$130–145 ⊞ TeW

◀ **A Dogon mask,** surmounted by Yasioine, Mali, early 20thC, 38in (96.5cm) high, on a stand.
$3,600–4,000 ⊞ ELM
Yasioine is the only female admitted into the Awa male society.

A Navajo Germantown pictorial weaving, woven in commercially dyed wool, minor damage, Native American, c1890, 58 x 37in (147.5 x 94cm).
$3,600–4,300 ↗ SK(B)

A beadwork bag, Native American, late 19thC, 4in (10cm) square.
$175–200 ⊞ PSC

An Mmadwa stool, the top decorated with brass studding, Ashanti, Ghana, c1900, 20in (51cm) long.
$950–1,100 ⊞ ELM
This stool is for an unmarried female of high rank.

A Lwalwa mask, border of the Democratic Republic of Congo and Angola, early 20thC, 9in (23cm) high.
$2,300–2,600 ⊞ ELM

A Mossi mask, in the shape of a bird's head, West Africa, 22¼in (56.6cm) long.
$4,300–5,000 ↗ S(NY)

A Luba memory board, decorated with beads and cowrie shells, central Africa, 10in (25.5cm) high.
$5,800–7,250 ↗ S(NY)

A Sepik River, Biwat, shield, Papua New Guinea, 69in (175.5cm) high.
$3,600–4,300 ↗ S(NY)

A South African headrest, probably Tsonga, Mozambique, early/mid-20thC, 5½in (14cm) high.
$13,000–16,000 ↗ Bon(C)

◀ **A Maori tinder box,** the eye inlaid with *haliotis* shell, New Zealand, 4½in (11.5cm) wide.
$3,200–3,600 ↗ S(NY)

Allerneuestes Theaterbilderbuch, 'Very latest theatre picture book', published by J. F. Schreiber, Eklingen, with four chromolithographed pop-up plates of stage sets, original cloth-backed chromolithographed pictorial boards, Germany, c1870, 4to.
$450–480 ⚒ **BBA**

William Curtis, *Flora Londinensis, or Plates and Descriptions of Such Plants As Grow Wild in the Environs of London,* six parts in two volumes, contemporary calf gilt, 1775/77/98, folio.
$8,700–10,000 ⚒ **L**

Lord George Byron, *The Prisoner of Chillon,* illuminated by W. & G. Audsley, chromolithographed by W. R. Tymms, published by Day & Son, 1865, folio.
$250–300 ⚒ **DW**

The Illuminated Calendar For 1845 and Home Diary, chromolithograph illustrations by Owen Jones and hand-colouring, decorated vellum, 8vo.
$190–220 ⚒ **HAM**

◀ **Alexander McDonald,** *A Complete Dictionary of Gardening,* two volumes, London 1807, 11 x 9in (28 x 23cm).
$5,000–5,500 ⊞ **AHa**

Jean Baptiste Balthazar Sauvan, *Picturesque Tour of the Seine, from Paris to the Sea: With Particulars Historical and Descriptive,* published by Ackerman, contemporary half maroon morocco gilt, 1821, large 4to.
$2,300–2,900 ⚒ **DW**

◀ **Robert Warner,** *Select Orchidaceous Plants,* First Series, original green cloth gilt, 1862–65, large folio.
$5,000–6,000 ⚒ **DW**

The Lithographs of Chagall, Monte Carlo: André Sauret, New York: George Braziller, 1960, folio.
$1,300–1,600 ⚒ **SLN**

Lord Thomas Littleton Powys Lilford, *Coloured Figures of the Birds of the British Islands,* second edition, seven volumes, contemporary half red morocco gilt, 1891–97, 8vo.
$1,300–1,600 ⚒ **L**

James Ralfe, *The Naval Chronology of Great Britain... from ..1803, to... 1816,* three volumes, contemporary diced green calf, 1820, 8vo.
$5,000–6,000 ⚒ **BBA**

Francis Henry Salvin and William Brodrick, *Falconry in the British Isles,* second edition, John Van Voorst, 1783, 8vo.
$2,900–3,200 ⚒ **S**

A German papier mâché shoulder-headed doll, with kid leather body and carved wooden lower arms and legs, c1820, 13¾in (35cm) high.
$3,200–3,600 ⚲ Bon(C)

A DEP bisque-headed doll, with a composition body, Germany, c1890, 27in (68.5cm) high.
$1,200–1,300 ⊞ PSA

A Jumeau bisque-headed fashion doll, France, c1875, 18in (45.5cm) high.
$5,000–5,800 ⊞ DAn

A Jumeau bisque-headed bébé doll, France, c1880, 19in (48.5cm) high.
$9,800–10,800 ⊞ EW

A Tête Jumeau bisque-headed doll, with lever mechanism to the eyes, on a fully jointed wood and composition body, France, c1890, 26in (66cm) high.
$4,400–4,700 ⚲ Bon(C)

A J. D. Kestner bisque-headed doll, with composition ball-jointed body, mould No. 214, Germany, 1920s, 33in (84cm) high.
$1,600–1,800 ⊞ DOL

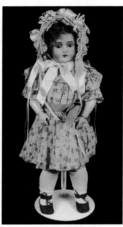

A J. D. Kestner bisque-headed doll, with a composition body, Germany, c1910, 23in (58.5cm) high.
$750–850 ⊞ PSA

A Simon & Halbig bisque-headed doll, with composition ball-jointed body, mould No. 1079, with sleep eyes, made for the French market, Germany, late 19thC, 36in (91.5cm) high.
$2,900–3,200 ⊞ DOL

A Schoenhut & Hoffmeister bisque-headed doll, with articulated wooden body, Germany, early 20thC, 25in (63.5cm) high.
$230–300 ⚲ PFK

▶ **An Armand Marseille bisque-headed doll,** with a jointed composition body, mould No. AM 390, with re-made clothing, Germany, c1915, 18in (45.5cm) high.
$400–450 ⊞ PSA

An Armand Marseille bisque shoulder-headed doll, with a kid body, Germany, c1890, 21in (53.5cm) high.
$450–500 ⊞ BaN

◀ **An SFBJ bisque-headed doll,** mould No. 301, with a jointed composition body, France, c1918, 18in (45.5cm) high.
$320–380 ⚲ B&L

▶ **A French bisque swivel-shoulder-headed doll,** retailed by Simonne, with bisque lower arms, and kid body, late 19thC, 17½in (44.5cm) high.
$4,400–4,700 ⚲ SK(B)

A plush teddy bear, early 20thC, 24in (61cm) high.
$500–600 ⌕ PAC

A Bing plush teddy bear, c1910, 20in (51cm) high.
$7,000–8,500 ⊞ BaN

A Farnell mohair teddy bear, paw pads re-covered, c1920, 20in (51cm) high.
$2,000–2,250 ⌕ Bon(C)

A Merrythought mohair teddy bear, with a small bald patch, right eye missing, c1930, 25in (63.5cm) high.
$900–1,200 ⌕ Bon(C)

A Steiff mohair teddy bear, c1907, 13½in (34.5cm) high.
$2,500–3,000 ⊞ TED

A Steiff mohair teddy bear, c1920, 24in (61cm) high.
$3,600–4,500 ⌕ Bon(C)

◄ **A Lefray mohair teddy bear,** with plush pads, 1955–60, 30in (76cm) high.
$230–300 ⊞ TED

A Bandai battery-powered Ferrari Gear Shift car, Japan, c1960, 11in (28cm) long, with original box.
$220–280 ⊞ HAL

A Britains Fordson Super Major Diesel Tractor, No. 9525, 1960s, 4in (10cm) long, with original box.
$300–350 ✗ RAR

A Dinky Toys trade pack of six caravans, various colours, 1930s, box 7 x 4in (18 x10cm).
$1,300–1,600 ✗ WAL

An Exley Third Class restaurant car, with Great Western crest, c1935, 17in (43cm) long.
$450–580 ⊞ HOB

A Günthermann tinplate clockwork model of a General double decker bus, c1910, 10in (25.5cm) long.
$1,600–1,900 ✗ BWe

A Günthermann Kaye Don's Silver Bullet, the tail-fin re-soldered, Germany, c1930, 22in (56cm) long, with original box.
$1,000–1,200 ✗ S(S)

A Hornby O gauge clockwork Southern locomotive, c1930, 11in (28cm) long.
$500–600 ⊞ HOB

◄ A Hornby Dublo LMS electric locomotive, c1939, 5in (12.5cm) long.
$200–250 ⊞ HAL

► A Hubley cast-iron floor train, America, c1920, 34in (86.5cm) long.
$1,600–1,900 ✗ S(NY)

A Matchbox Models of Yester-Year London Transport tram, early 1960s, 3in (7.5cm) long.
$70–90 ✗ HAL

A Welker & Crosby cast-iron and wood floor train, America, c1885, 35in (89cm) long.
$3,600–4,300 ✗ S(NY)

► A German painted tin train set, comprising buildings, track and figures, c1900.
$10,000–11,500 ✗ RBB

A wooden dolls' house on a stand, the facade and sides with painted brick effect, balustrade added at a later date, early 19thC, 26in (66cm) wide.
$4,000–4,600 ↗ Bon

A wooden dolls' house, painted with a stone effect, late 19thC, 23½in (59.5cm) wide.
$2,900–3,400 ↗ Bon

A bisque, papier mâché and composition advertising automaton of Santa Claus riding a mule, one hand missing, some damage and restoration, c1900, 18in (45.5cm) high.
$2,600–2,900 ↗ P(WM)

A J. & E. Stevens monkey and coconut money bank, trap door to base missing, America, late 19thC, 8½in (21.5cm) high.
$1,200–1,400 ↗ Bon(C)

A wooden rocking horse, on bow rockers, 1850–60, 84in (213.5cm) long.
$9,800–10,800 ⊞ RGa

▶ **A German clockwork hand-painted trapeze artiste,** c1900, 7in (18cm) high.
$1,200–1,400 ↗ P(WM)

An Ives cast-iron horse-drawn caisson, with a bronze cannon, c1895, 22in (56cm) long.
$9,800–10,800 ↗ S(NY)

A Dent cast-iron oversized Fire Pumper, c1911, 25in (63.5cm) long.
$7,300–8,000 ↗ S(NY)

◀ **A German marquetry games board,** inlaid with bone and brass, the interior marked with two panels for backgammon, 19thC, 21¾ x 19in (55.5 x 48.5cm).
$2,900–3,400 ↗ P

An Irish arbutus games box, with marquetry-inlaid banding, the interior fitted for backgammon, probably West Cork, Kilarney, 19thC, 18in (45.5cm) square.
$750–850 ↗ WW

▶ **A tin Mechanical Mighty Robot,** 1960s, 5in (12.5cm) high, with original box.
$150–170 ⊞ PLB

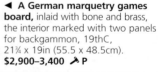

An American painted Parcheesi gameboard, New England, 1870–80, 27½in (70cm) square.
$6,000–7,250 ↗ SK(B)

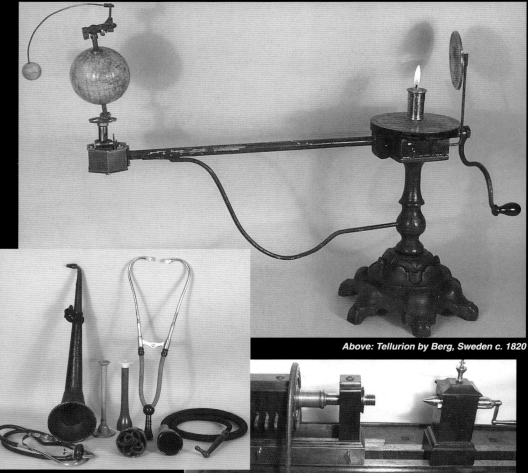

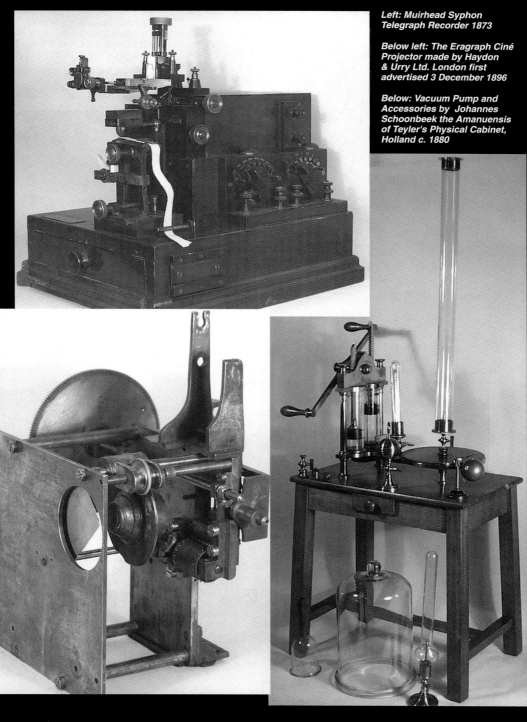

COLOUR REVIEW

A Thomas de Colmar arithmometer, the ebony veneered fitted case inlaid with brass, France, c1858, 23in (58.5cm) long.
$3,300–3,900 ⊞ TOM

A Lords Patent Calculator, by W. Wilson, c1890, 13in (33cm) diam, in a mahogany case.
$3,300–3,900 ⊞ TOM

A Bartholomew Koch brass horizontal inclinable table dial, mid-18thC, 6¾in (17cm) wide.
$30,500–33,500 ⚒ S

> **Miller's is a price GUIDE not a price LIST**

A Powell & Lealand No. 3 compound mono-cular microscope, dated 1845, 16in (40.5cm) high, in a mahogany case, with a separate case of accessories.
$10,200–11,600 ⚒ S

An early Victorian Newton's terrestrial globe, 20in (51cm) wide, on a mahogany stand.
$10,800–13,000 ⚒ DN

◄ **A Smith & Beck microscope,** c1850, 20in (51cm) high, with a mahogany case.
$3,500–4,000 ⊞ BWA

A Merzback & Falk table globe, Brussels, early 20thC, 19in (48.5cm) diam, on a mahogany stand.
$2,200–2,300 ⚒ NOA

An Elliot Brothers station pointer, c1870, 21in (53.5cm) long, in original mahogany case.
$650–750 ⊞ ETO

A Swift binocular microscope, 1860–70, 20in (51cm) high, with accessories, with a mahogany case.
$1,750–2,200 ⊞ SPA

A French brass instrument for taking measurements in three dimensions, by Michallon, signed, c1790, 3½in (9cm) long, with original oak case.
$5,800–6,500 ⚒ S

An American Keufel & Esser brass surveyor's compass and clinometer, New York, c1890, 4in (10cm) wide, in a mahogany case.
$320–360 ⊞ WAC

A Passemant 4in reflecting tele-scope, with leather-bound brass tube, France, mid-18thC, tube 30¼in (76cm) long, in a fitted mahogany case.
$17,500–20,000 ⚒ S

A Buss of London excise officer's gauger's leather bag, fitted with various rules, c1870, 13in (33cm) long.
$1,600–1,900 ⊞ TOM

A Victorian wood and composition diorama of a schooner, in a rosewood frame, 15½in (39.5cm) wide. $1,750–2,200 ⚲ HAM

A Josh Penlington, Liverpool, two-day marine chronometer, in a rosewood case, mid-19thC, 7in (18cm) wide. $2,900–3,200 ⚲ P

A Charles Frodsham marine chronometer, with eight-day movement, in a brass-bound rosewood case, c1875, 8in (20.5cm) wide. $9,800–10,800 ⚲ Mit

A scrimshaw whale's tooth, inscribed 'Free Trade and Sailors Rights', 19thC, 7½in (19cm) long. $5,500–6,000 ⚲ P

A miniature ebony and brass octant, by Parnell, London, c1790, 8in (20.5cm) long, in original mahogany box. $2,300–2,900 ⊞ TOM

▶ **An American carved and painted pine ship's figurehead of a young lady,** probably New England, c1850, 24in (61cm) high. $7,900–8,700 ⚲ S(NY)

A pair of Regency mezzotints laid under glass, of the barge and car which conveyed Lord Nelson's body from Greenwich to St Paul's, published February 1806, 10 x 14in (25.5 x 35.5cm). $1,200–1,300 ⚲ Mit

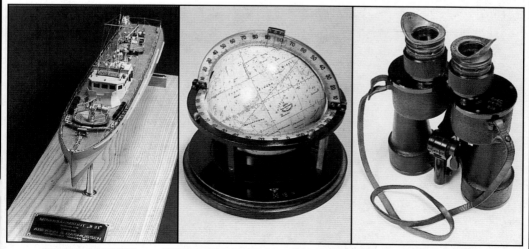

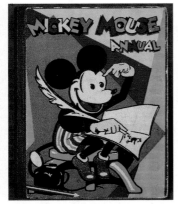

Mickey Mouse Annual, Walt Disney Studios, published by Dean & Son, rebacked, 1930, 4to.
$120–150 ⚒ **DW**

The Dandy Comic, No. 3, 1937.
$800–950 ⚒ **CBP**

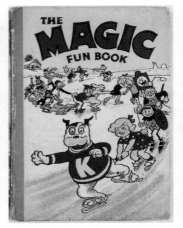

The Magic Fun Book, No. 1, published by D. C. Thomson & Co, 1941, small folio.
$700–800 ⚒ **DW**

W. A. & A. C. Churchman, Prominent Golfers, set of 12 cigarette cards, 1931.
$330–400 ⚒ **P**

John Player & Sons, Types of Horses, set of 25 cigarette cards, 1939.
$100–120 ⊞ **MAr**

A French poster, by Alphonse Mucha, printed by F. Champenois, two creases, tiny tear, signed, 1898, 25½ x 19in (65 x 48.5cm).
$13,000–14,500 ⚒ **S(NY)**

A Belgian Red Star Line Dover to New York poster, by Henri Cassiers, 1909, 45 x 61in (114.5 x 155cm).
$3,600–4,000 ⚒ **VSP**

A Swiss Ste Croix les Rasses poster, with monogram RH, 1922, 40¼ x 25in (102 x 63.5cm).
$2,300–2,600 ⚒ **VSP**

A French Veuve Amiot poster, by Leonetto Cappiello, 1922, 64 x 47½in (162.5 x 120.5cm).
$1,750–2,000 ⚒ **BB(L)**

An Australian National Travel Association Poster No. 1, The Landing of Captain Cook at Botany Bay 1770, by Percy Trompf, c1930, 40 x 50in (101.5 x 127cm).
$1,200–1,400 ⚒ **P(Sy)**

◄ **A Jimi Hendrix Experience Fillmore Auditorium poster,** by Hapshash & The Coloured Cat, printed by Osiris Visions, June 1967, 29½ x 19½in (75 x 49.5cm).
$300–350 ⚒ **Bon(C)**

A German composite half-armour, minor repairs, comprehensively 16thC, with a pair of later full arm defences.
$17,500–21,000 ✗ S(NY)

A cuirass suit of armour, c1620.
$21,750–24,750 ⊞ ARB

A south German hunting knife, with carved bone grip and companion knife and fork, 18thC, 26in (66cm) long, with a leather-covered wooden scabbard.
$1,800–2,200 ✗ Herm

A Victorian Scottish officer's gilt-mounted dress dirk, the wooden hilt set with gilt studs, the pommel set with a stone, blade 12½in (32cm) long, in a leather scabbard, with companion knife and fork en suite.
$3,600–4,400 ✗ P(Ed)

An American officer's sabre, the forte engraved with a martial trophy incorporating a Cap of Liberty and the American stars and stripes shield and other motifs, with carved bone grip and original brass scabbard, c1780, blade 30in (76cm) long.
$2,200–2,400 ✗ ASB

A German general's gilt-mounted sabre, with wooden grip, c1810, 39¾in (101cm) long.
$8,000–9,500 ✗ Herm
This item belonged to Field Marshall Carl Philipp Joseph, Count von Wrede.

A Silesian 11 bore Miquelet-lock gun, the fruitwood stock inlaid with white horn and mother-of-pearl, mid-17thC, barrel 32¾in (83cm) long.
$6,500–8,000 ✗ Bon

A cannon-barrelled flintlock pistol, by Griffin & Tow, with a silver-mounted walnut stock, London, c1780, 12in (30.5cm) long.
$1,750–1,900 ⊞ WSA

A Dutch brass-barrelled flintlock blunderbuss pistol, by Mouchin A. Rotterdam, with walnut fullstock and brass mounts, action requires attention, c1750, 12½in (32cm) long.
$2,900–3,400 ✗ WAL

A pair of double-barrelled tap action over-and-under 70 bore cannon-barrelled flintlock boxlock pocket pistols, by Verncomb, Bristol, the frames and barrels of German silver, with walnut butts inlaid with silver wire scrolls and flowers, c1785, 6¼in (16cm) long.
$4,750–5,750 ✗ WAL

A brass-barrelled flintlock coaching blunderbuss pistol, by Barwick, Norwich, c1800, 14in (35.5cm) long.
$1,500–1,600 ⊞ SPA

▶ **A 76 bore six-shot Cooper's Patent ring trigger underhammer percussion pepperbox revolver,** with nickel-mounted walnut stock, c1850, 8½in (21.5cm) long.
$1,300–1,500 ⊞ SPA

A Lt Colonel's 13th Rajputs, The Shekhawati Regiment, full dress tunic, early 20thC.
$950–1,200 ✦ WAL

A Lithuanian Tartar Squadron fur hat, 1812–14.
$14,500–17,500 ✦ Herm

▶ **A Victorian 4th Royal Irish Dragoon Guards Cavalry trooper's helmet.**
$1,100–1,300 ⊞ ASB

A German WWI Pickelhaube, 1914, 9in (23cm) high.
$400–500 ⊞ Q&C

An Imperial German trooper's helmet, with parade eagle of the Garde du Corps, c1915.
$4,400–5,000 ✦ WAL

◀ **A group of four medals awarded to Colonel William Bennett, the Yorkshire Regiment (Green Howards),** Ginnis' gold D.S.O., V.R., with Garrard & Co case of issue; India General Service 1854–95 one clasp, North West Frontier; Egypt & Sudan 1882–89, one clasp, The Nile; Khedive's Star 1884–86.
$6,500–8,000 ✦ DNW

▶ **A WWII group of five medals to Sergeant Air Observer R. J. Ellis, 75 New Zealand Squadron, R.A.F.,** DFM; Campaign Stars for 1939–45 and Air Crew Europe; Defence and War Medals.
$1,200–1,500 ✦ DN

A group of eight decorations and medals awarded to Captain R. A. Hermon, The Royals, D.S.O., O.B.E., General Service Medal with Palestine bar; Star 1939–45; Africa Star with 8th Army bar; Italy Star; Defence Medal 1939–45; War Medal 1939–45 with oak leaf spray.
$4,400–5,000 ✦ RTo

A copper and brass powder flask, c1850, 8¼in (21cm) long.
$220–240 ⊞ SPA

A silver vesta case, by Samson Mordan & Co, the front enamelled in colours with a Hussar on horseback, London 1901, 1¼in (3cm) wide.
$1,300–1,500 ✦ CAG

An embroidered corded silk guidon of the St Thomas-in-the-Vale Light Horse, presented to the Troop by H.R.H. Prince William Henry, Duke of Clarence, later King William IV, dated March 1783, 44in (112cm) long.
$13,000–16,000 ✦ Bon

An embroidered silk banner of the County Carlow Legion, depicting Hibernica, c1780, 28 x 26in (71 x 66cm).
$3,500–4,000 ✦ MEA

A Topps Gum baseball card, depicting Mickey Mantle, 1961.
$470–540 ⊞ HALL

A Fleer Gum Rookie baseball card, depicting Wilt Chamberlain, 1961.
$1,000–1,100 ⊞ HALL

A Victorian marquetry-inlaid full-size billiard table, with six-shade light fitting.
$100,000–110,000 ⊞ WBB

A London Palladium Sullivan v Papke boxing match single sheet handbill, 1911, 4 x 10in (10 x 25.5cm).
$150–180 ⚒ Bon

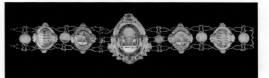

A 9ct gold and enamel Lonsdale Belt for the National Sporting Club Light Weight Boxing Championship 1919–30, by Mappin & Webb, hallmarked London 1919, 32in (81.5cm) long.
$16,000–17,500 ⚒ S

▶ **A cricket bat,** made by S. A. Spires, Kingston-on-Thames, signed by the members of the Hampshire and Yorkshire teams and the umpires, stamped 'Special Selected Hants XI England XI The John Arnold autograph', c1930.
$400–500 ⚒ WW

A hand-coloured engraving, *The Game of Cricket as playd in the Artillary Ground, London,* after Francis Hayman RA (1708–76), 7 x 10¾in (18 x 27.5cm), in contemporary gilt slip and ebonized frame.
$300–400 ⚒ PFK

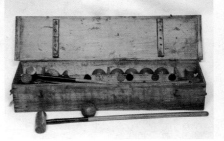

A wooden croquet set, c1920, box 37in (94cm) long.
$350–400 ⊞ MLL

A George III Irish Racing Trophy silver salver, by Thomas Walker, the reverse with inscription, Dublin 1739, 12in (30.5cm) diam.
$18,000–20,500 ⊞ WELD

An oak and brass jockey scales, by Thornhill & Co, London, with a leather-covered seat, c1900, 38in (96.5cm) wide.
$2,900–3,200 ⚒ HOLL

◀ **A wooden table box,** fitted with five compartments, the hinged cover painted with a jockey on horseback, 19thC, 5¼in (13.5cm) wide.
$620–720 ⚒ TMA

A silver trophy cup and cover, by Edmond Johnson, inscribed 'Bray Harriers, Point to Point Races, Calary Challenge Cup', with names of recipients, Dublin 1903, 29½in (75cm) high.
$2,300–2,500 ⚒ HOK

A G. Little & Co 3¼in plate wind trout fly reel, with horn handle, 1880.
$170–190 ⊞ PSA

A Hardy 3¾in brass-faced wide drum reel, with Turk's head tension lock and patent line guide, c1905, 4in (10cm) diam.
$750–800 ⊞ SPA

A cased Golden Roach, by J. Cooper & Sons, inscribed 'Golden Roach, Taken from the River Frays. Oct 8th 1911', case 11½ x 19in (29 x 48.5cm).
$1,750–2,200 ➤ P(Ba)

An Olympic Games 18ct gold medal and participant's cap for football, the medal rim engraved 'Winner, Association Football, Clyde H. Purnell', 1908.
$3,600–4,300 ➤ Bon

► A 12ct gold Aston Villa double winner's medal, the obverse inscribed 'League Champions, English Cup Winners, 1897', the rim inscribed 'T. Wilkes'.
$3,600–4,400 ➤ S
This medal depicts both the League championship trophy and the FA Cup, the latter a replica of the one stolen and never recovered when Villa previously held the Cup.

A Chelsea v Glasgow Rangers programme, Varsity Stadium, Toronto, 5 June, 1954.
$500–600 ➤ Bon

A Jules Rimet Cup official Wembley Stadium flag, 1966, 140 x 73in (355.5 x 185.5cm).
$2,900–3,200 ➤ S

A Sir Stanley Matthews CBE illumination, presented by the Football Association to mark the Occasion of his 70th birthday, January 1985, 14 x 10in (35.5 x 25.5cm), in glazed frame.
$1,900–2,200 ➤ LT

A Tom Morris, St Andrews, golden beech long-nosed driver, with hickory shaft, c1875.
$5,800–7,200 ➤ S

An American Boston Bruins at Boston Gardens hockey programme, 1932.
$90–120 ⊞ HALL

A silver-plated kettle on stand, by Philip Ashberry & Sons, Sheffield, the lid surmounted by a lady tennis player, the stand modelled as two pairs of crossed racquets, c1900, 11½in (29cm) high.
$2,600–3,200 ➤ S

A Prattware ceramic jug, decorated with a shooting scene, c1820, 8in (20.5cm) high.
$870–1,000 ⊞ SEA

Cricket

John Wisden, *The Cricketers' Almanac*, 1866, 8°.
$4,400–5,000 ⚒ **ANA**

◀ **Frederick Lillywhite,**
The English Cricketers' Trip to Canada and the United States, first edition, 1860, 23 full-page wood-engraved plates, folding map, original cloth-backed boards, small 8°.
$290–350 ⚒ **DW**

John Wisden, *The Cricketers' Almanac for 1925*, edited by Sydney H. Pardon, with 'Cricketers of the Year', original hard cover.
$290–350 ⚒ **MUL**

▶ **A fully signed England v Australia cricket bat,** Duncan Fearnley Supreme 1989, 33in (84cm) long.
$230–260 ⊞ **SMW**

A Grainger presentation cricketing loving cup, one side painted in colours with cricket stumps, a bat and a ball in front of a tent within a cartouche, the other side inscribed 'Presented To Mr. John Clarke by the Members of the W.V.C.C. Feby 1858', printed mark in grey, 5in (12.5cm) wide.
$2,200–2,500 ⚒ **P**
According to Berrow's Worcester Journal of 6 March 1858, this mug was presented to Mr John Clarke, the Treasurer of the Victoria Cricket Club, Worcester, during a supper at the Beauchamp Arms Hotel to mark his departure from the club.

◀ **A photograph of the England Cricket Team on the South African tour,** with original autographs, 1930, 11 x 12in (28 x 30.5cm).
$115–145 ⊞ **WAB**

A black and white postcard photograph of SS *Maloja*, the face signed in ink by 16 of the MCC touring team to Australia 1924–25.
$540–620 ⚒ **ANA**

A postcard of Donald Duck, Mickey Mouse and Goofy playing cricket, postmarked 1938.
$45–50 ⚒ **WW**

A cricketing trophy, comprising a cricket bat resting against a set of silver cricket stumps alongside a cricket ball, with inscribed plaque, on a wooden base, plaque dated 1909, 6¾in (17cm) high.
$580–720 ⚒ **P(Ba)**

SPORT

Equestrian

SPORT

A pair of silver-plated nickel candlesticks, with a socket formed as an upturned jockey's cap, the stem comprising three crossed riding crops, on stirrup-form bases, c1900, 8½in (21.5cm) high.
$250–300 ⚹ PFK

A French bronze group of a mounted polo player, by Isidore Bonheur, signed with Peyrol foundry stamp, c1875, 14in (35.5cm) high.
$34,800–43,500 ⊞ RGa

The official race card for the Bridgwater Races meeting, Saturday 23 July 1927, 4pp, 8°.
$65–80 ⚹ TAM

A signed photograph, of the jockey Gordon Richards, c1940, 14 x 12in (35.5 x 30.5cm).
$90–100 ⚹ DW

A Caucasian black leather-over-wood saddle, late 19thC, 14¼in (36cm) high.
$5,000–5,800 ⚹ Herm

A Western embossed leather saddle, by Keystone Bros, San Francisco, the sterling silver engraved corner plates depicting bucking bronco riders, America, 1930s, 27in (68.5cm) wide.
$1,000–1,200 ⚹ SK(B)

A pair of Spanish carved walnut stirrups, with embossed leather straps, stamped 'Ernesto Caedehas', 19thC, 10¼in (26cm) wide.
$400–470 ⚹ DN

◀ **An Irish silver-gilt two-handled trophy cup,** by Waterhouse & Co, Dublin, the cover decorated with flowers and foliage, the sides cast with grotesque masks and pendant swags, commemorating Bryan owned and ridden by Alexander Gilroy, giving a list of races run from 1887–90, including 2nd in the Irish Grand National 1889, 15in (38cm) high, 78oz, in a fitted oak case.
$2,900–3,200 ⚹ E

▶ **An Anglesey Hunt Cup,** by Henry Holland, silver and parcel-gilt, the cover modelled as a running horse, the twin handles in the form of dragon supporters, decorated with chased and embossed flowers and foliage, with ebonized socle, 1870, 15¾in (40cm) high, 63oz.
$6,500–8,000 ⚹ P(S)

A silver and enamel vesta case, by S. Mordan & Co, the front enamelled with an image of three steeple chase riders, the jockeys dressed in blue, yellow and red with white jodhpurs, maker's mark, London 1892, 2¼in (5.5cm) wide.
$1,700–2,000 ⚹ Bon

◀ **An 18ct gold cup,** the pull-off cover embossed with a border of grapes and vine leaves round a pine cone finial, the sides embossed with swags of grapes and vine leaves between two rams' masks, the turned wood plinth with the inscription 'The King's Gold Vase, The Gift of His Majesty, Ascot 1927', sponsor's mark of Garrard & Co, sculptor's signature of Charles Sykes, London 1927, 13in (33cm) high, in a fitted wooden case.
$8,700–9,500 ⚹ RFA
The cup was presented by King George V to F. W. Horlock Esq, when his horse, Adieu, won the Gold Cup Vase at Ascot in 1927. The race is now known as the Queen's Vase.

Fishing

James Chetham, *The Anglers Vade Mecum*, third edition, 1700, one engraved plate depicting fish, bound in 20thC half leather.
$650–800 ✗ MUL

Colonel Robert Venables, *The Experienced Angler*, reprint of 1662 original, published by T. Goshen, London, 1827, 8 x 5in (20.5 x 12.5cm).
$430–480 ⊞ OPB

A bronze bust of Izaak Walton, rim stamped by Gorham Co, registration mark and number 25, signed by the artist F. Ziegler, late 19thC, 5in (12.5cm) high.
$500–580 ✗ MUL

Catalogue of High Class Fishing Tackle, 91st edition, published by C. Farlow & Co, with colour plates, c1931.
$100–120 ✗ MUL

> **Cross Reference**
> See Colour Review
> (page 743-744)

A leather pot-bellied fishing creel, late 18thC, 12½in (32cm) wide.
$4,000–4,600 ✗ TEN

◄ **A stuffed and mounted trout,** by J. Cooper & Sons, in a bowfronted case with gilt lettering to front 'Taken at Overstaunch, by C. Wadsworth, Sept 16th 1891, Weight 5½lbs', case 27½in (70cm) wide.
$800–950 ✗ BLH

A stuffed and mounted barbel, by J. Cooper & Sons, in a gilt-lined bowfronted case with card to interior inscribed 'Barbel. Caught by Charles Hardy, Fox & Grapes Angling Society from the canal at Alrewas, August 1904. Weight 4¼lbs.', case 29in (73.5cm) wide.
$2,900–3,500 ✗ P(Ba)

A stuffed and mounted carp, in a bowfronted case, gilt inscription to front 'Carp 10lbs, taken at Ilford by A. Mason 1947', fish loose on mount, case 29in (73.5cm) wide.
$580–720 ✗ WilP

SPORT

A stuffed and mounted pike, in a bowfronted case, with gilt inscription 'Pike 19lbs caught by A. W. Brooks, Sonning, March 1965, 3lbs. Line No. 6 Hook', case 40in (101.5cm) wide.
$430–500 ➹ AH

A stainless steel gut gauge and salmon fly scale, engraved with maker's name, Chesterman, Sheffield, and 'Sold by Hardy Bros. Ltd.', 1930s, 4in (10cm) long.
$115–145 ⊞ OTB

A hand-held brass gut twist engine, fitted with wooden handle grips and all-brass crank handle, c1860, 8in (20.5cm) long.
$480–580 ➹ MUL

A brass finish line dryer, by Haynes, Cork, c1910, 10in (25.5cm) long.
$100–120 ⊞ WAB

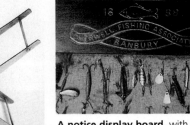

A notice display board, with carved banner heading 'Cherwell Fishing Association Banbury, with hinged glazed door enclosing baits/lures and mounts, late 19thC, 21 x 27in (53.5 x 68.5cm).
$250–300 ➹ MUL

▶ **A nickel-silver jointed Cleopatra lure,** by Gregory, Birmingham, with non-flexible segmented body, fins engraved with maker's name, c1890, 4in (10cm) long.
$1,000–1,200 ⊞ OTB

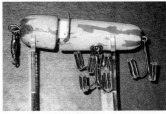

An American wooden Decker bass lure, Lake Hopatcong, New Jersey, 1900–15, 3in (7.5cm) long.
$170–220 ⊞ JVM

▶ **A Hardy the White-Wickham Dummy bait,** dark wood variety, advertised as being for kahawai and kingfish, c1935, 5in (12.5cm) long.
$1,900–2,300 ➹ P(Ba)

◀ **An ash-headed landing net,** on a bamboo pole, c1930, head 14in (35.5cm) diam.
$75–85 ⊞ OTB

An Allcock Aerial 3¾inch fishing reel, 1930s.
$240–270 ⊞ SPA

An Allcock Easicast 4inch casting reel, with grey enamelled alloy finish and moveable dual function U-shaped line guide/casting brake, 1930s.
$60–75 ⊞ OTB

An Eaton & Deller platewind salmon fishing reel, with horn handle, c1870.
$115–145 ⊞ PSA

A Chas Farlow & Co 4inch Patent Lever salmon winch, with knurled and slotted iron drag regulator to backplate, with tapered dark horn handle, quadruple pillared cage, c1885.
$190–230 ↗ P(Ba)

A Hardy Hercules 2¾inch Special Pattern fly reel, with raised constant check housing to frontplate, waisted brass foot pierced twice, triple pollared cage and stained ivorine handle, c1890.
$400–470 ↗ P(Ba)

A Hardy Perfect Houghton 2⅝inch brass-faced trout fly reel, with strapped tension screw, early check, ivorine handle and brass foot, early 1900s.
$1,100–1,300 ⊞ EP

SPORT

A Hardy 3¾inch Ex-Wide Silex Major fly reel, with across the drum ivorine brake lever, ribbed brass foot, twin ivorine handles and rim tension regulator, c1928.
$290–350 ↗ MUL

Items in the Fishing reels section have been arranged in maker order.

A Hardy St George 3⅜inch fly reel, with ribbed brass foot, two-screw drum latch and grey agate-lined nickel-silver line guide, 1930s.
$170–220 ↗ OTB

A Hardy Uniqua 4inch Spitfire model salmon fly reel, with ribbed brass foot, telephone drum latch and plain alloy finish, 1940s.
$200–260 ⊞ OTB

◄ **A Hardy Altex 4inch No. 3 reel,** c1935.
$145–175 ⊞ SPA

A Hardy Fortuna 7inch Big Game reel, with non-reversing handles, and capstan-style drag, 1950s.
$950–1,150 ⊞ OTB

A G. Little & Co 4inch brass Hercules-style reel, with raised constant check housing to faceplate, quadruple pillared cage, pierced and waisted brass foot and dark horn handle, c1890.
$230–260 ⋏ P(Ba)

A P. D. Malloch 4¼inch brass and ebonite platewind salmon reel, with constant check and ivorine handle, late 19thC.
$145–175 ⋏ P(Ed)

A P. D. Malloch 2⅝inch brass sidecaster reel, with rim-mounted check button, bolted turn mechanism and brass line guide and foot, c1920.
$260–290 ⊞ EP

A 3inch walnut and brass star-back Nottingham reel, with Bickerdyke line guard, c1930.
$45–55 ⊞ WAB

A Hugh Snowie 3¼inch bronze and brass trout fly reel, with horn handle, Inverness, Scotland, c1880.
$115–145 ⊞ PSA

◄ **A Turnbull 4inch brass and ebonite salmon fly reel,** with nickel-silver rims, fixed check, ivorine handle and brass foot, Edinburgh, Scotland, c1910.
$145–175 ⊞ EP

► **An American nickel-silver 2½inch multiplying reel,** with triple-pillared cage, ivory handle to counterbalanced and offset serpentine winding arm, c1880.
$800–1,000 ⋏ P(Ba)
This reel is typical of New York makers and may have been made by either Bates or Conroy.

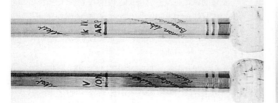

◄ **A 2¼inch brass spike fitting crankwind reel,** with curved crank bone handle and fixed check, c1880.
$500–600 ⊞ EP

A pair of Norman Woodward MK IV cane coarse fishing rods, signed by Richard Walker, comprising a 10ft MK IV carp and a 10ft MK IV Avon rod, c1960.
$1,700–2,000 ⋏ P(Ba)
Norman Woodward and Richard Walker were both members of The Tenchfishers, a club founded in 1954 whose membership was limited to ten members and included some of the country's top coarse fishermen. The rods were made by Norman Woodward, who had an engineering background as well as angling expertise, and they were designed, inspected and approved by Richard Walker, a founding member of the club.

A Gregory Colorado spoon, the nickel silver retaining original red paint to spindle lead and underside, original scarlet wool bound treble trace and gimp, c1890, 2¾in (7cm) long.
$360–430 ⋏ P(Ba)

Football

I nterest in football memorabilia continues to grow and new sources are springing up all the time. The first specialist football auction was in 1989; now, hardly a month passes without one taking place somewhere, and there is an increasing number of items selling through the internet.

Pieces with special connections will always do well. Two obvious examples are any items connected with the 1966 World Cup, and anything to do with Manchester United, arguably the most popular club in the world. A ceramic whisky decanter commemorating the 25th anniversary of United's European Cup victory in 1968 made significantly more than a porcelain figure contemporary with and commemorating Arsenal's first game in Paris in 1930.

In recent years hitherto minor areas in football memorabilia have done particularly well, as collectors seek out still-affordable targets. Match tickets, particularly from FA Cup Finals, have risen sharply in value, and badges, especially FA stewards' badges and the like, look set to follow.

Jerseys have always been popular but, with the enormous proliferation of replicas and players being given a plurality of 'real' jerseys for each major game, it is difficult to ensure authenticity. Replica jerseys signed by players are often sold at auction, but these are really the stuff of charity dinners and are not proper memorabilia.

Another currently fashionable area – and one of which to be wary – is the montage. Gathering a hotchpotch of more or less related items and framing them up to sell as a single item at a premium may produce nice wall displays but not sound investments. Many of these 'montages' will be dismembered for their individual contents in years to come.

Bound volumes of programmes are also often dismembered. If the programmes have been stripped of their covers before binding, then there is no point in breaking the volume. If not, then a significant profit can be made by selling the programmes individually, especially if the volume contains a single great rarity that may be worth more than all the rest put together. Early programmes are generally much sought-after, with FA Cup Finals, especially pre-Wembley ones and Internationals, the most desirable.

An item will always be much more sought-after if it has clear links with a famous and popular player, such as Sir Stanley Matthews or Bobby Moore, the latter commanding an even higher premium if specifically linked with the 1966 World Cup. In brief, rare items in good condition will continue to rise steadily in value. There is much on offer and no sign of any falling off in popularity. **Norman Shiel**

A pair of West Ham United autograph pages, dated 26–30 March 1962, signed in ink by 16 players and officials including Bobby Moore, Geoff Hurst and John Bond, with an informal team group photograph stuck to the reverse of one page.
$160–190 ☞ MUL
The value of this piece is significantly enhanced by including the signatures of two World Cup '66 stars, especially the late Bobby Moore.

A World Cup 1966 autographed montage, the signatures including Moore, R. Charlton, J. Charlton, Hurst and Sir Alf Ramsey, with photographs and the words 'Some people are on the pitch, they think it's all over. It is now!' scripted and signed by Kenneth Wolstenholme, glazed and framed, 30 x 29in (76 x 73.5cm).
$3,600–4,300 ☞ P(NW)

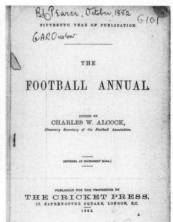

Charles W. Alcock, *The Football Annual*, 15th year, with original stiff printed wrappers, 1882, slim 8vo.
$200–250 ☞ DW
This is one of the very earliest regular football publications in the world. First produced in 1868 as John Lilywhite's Football Annual, it derives its inspiration from the established cricketing guides. From 1869–1908 it was under the sole editorship of Charles Alcock.

A leather football, by J. Salter & Son, Aldershot, 1950s.
$75–80 ⊞ PSA

◀ **A pair of brown leather child's football boots,** c1920.
$140–160 ☞ SPT
Adult football boots have survived in reasonable numbers for most of the 20th century, but children's are far more scarce.

A set of Wills Association Footballers cigarette cards, set of 50, 1939.
$80–90 ⊞ MAr

► **A Doulton Lambeth jug,** depicting football and rugby players, in blue and brown, c1893, 7½in (19cm) high.
$1,000–1,200 ↗ P(NW)
The scenes depict the transitional period from early football to rugby football. Doulton wares depicting football are far less common than other sports.

An ink cartoon, 'Finney Testimonial Match', depicting Stanley Matthews, Tommy Finney, Wilf Mannion and others, from Preston Newspaper, March 1960, 13¾ x 10in (35 x 25.5cm).
$690–750 ↗ LT

► **A Continental spelter figure of a footballer,** on a marble base, c1940, 12in (30.5cm).
$250–300 ↗ Bon(C)

A French white porcelain figure, by Sarreguemines, commemorating the first match between R. C. Paris and Arsenal F. C. at Colombes Stadium, Paris, 11 November 1930, mounted on a naturalistic base with French dedication.
$360–430 ↗ MUL

Miller's Compares

I. A menu card, for the Celebration Dinner & Dance following the Cup Final 1957 between Manchester United and Aston Villa, held at the Savoy Hotel on 4 May 1957, with red and white ribbons to the spine.
$870–1,000 ↗ ANA

II. A menu card, for the Civic Banquet held in honour of Wolverhampton Wanderers winning the F. A. Cup, held on 25 May 1960, with the seating arrangements, with gold ribbon to spine.
$125–145 ↗ ANA

There is little difference in date between these two menu cards, and in fact they were expected to realize similar prices. However, Item I sold for many times in excess of its estimate, because of the magnetism of Manchester United, and possibly also because this particular menu dates from the year before the plane crash in Munich, when eight members of the team as well as staff and journalists were killed.

An England v Ireland International match card, played at The Dell, 9 March 1901, old sellotape repairs, one fold detached.
$5,500–6,000 ↗ S
This is the only England match ever to have been played at The Dell. The game also marked the international debut of C. B. Fry. A significant number of these very early Southampton match cards has come onto the market recently of which this is by far the rarest and most valuable. This was the only full international appearance of of C. B. Fry, the greatest all round sportsman of his day. He played for Southampton in the 1902 F. A. Cup Final.

An 18ct gold and enamel Football Association medal, inscribed 'Angleterre v Continent, FIFA 26 Octobre 1938', 1in (2.5cm) high, in original box.
$1,700–2,000 ↗ LT
Matthews had an outstanding game against the Rest of Europe in this fixture to commemorate the 75th anniversary of the Football Association. England had never lost at home to any overseas country and won this game 2–1.

◄ **A Continental .750 gold U.E.F.A. Cup winner's medal season 1971–72,** the obverse inscribed 'Coupe UEFA 1972', the reverse cast with a goalkeeper in front of a goal net.
$8,000–8,800 ↗ S
Quite a number of European medals have come onto the market in recent years. Those awarded to foreign players will fetch less in Britain than those awarded to British players. This specimen represents an early British success in Europe.

SPORT

An Everton Football Club 1878–1928 black and white photograph, for the Jubilee Banquet, Philharmonic Hall, Liverpool, 24 April 1929, 9½ x 11½in (24 x 29cm), mounted on board.
$200–250 ✗ P(NW)

A signed photograph of Sir Geoff Hurst, scoring a hat-trick in the World Cup England v Germany1966, 5 x 8in (12.5 x 20.5cm).
$170–220 ⊞ SMW
One of the most abiding images of modern sport is Hurst's hat-trick goal at the end of extra time in the 1966 World Cup Final.

A black and white portrait photograph of Bobby Moore, signed in ink.
$220–260 ✗ ANA

A white metal and enamel plaque to Stanley Matthews, for his appearance in Great Britain v Rest of Europe, Glasgow 10 May 1947, 6 x 5¼in (15 x 13.5cm).
$1,100–1,300 ✗ LT

A silver plate and enamel plaque commemorating the Football Association Charity Shield Match, England World Cup Team v F. A. Canada Tour Team, 20 September 1950, F. Phillips Medallist Aldershot to back, 4¾ x 4¼in (12 x 11cm).
$1,100–1,300 ✗ LT
The F. A. Charity Shield was first contested in 1908 and participants in pre-war games were awarded superb gold medals based on the design of the shield itself. Post war austerity led to the issue of plaques such as this. Usually the game was between the league champions and F. A. Cup finalists but on this occasion the England World Cup Team (that had been humiliated by the USA) defeated the F. A. Canada touring team.

A bronze plaque, inscribed 'Stanley Matthews 1915 presented by the Royal Mint to Sir Stanley Matthews on the Occasion of his 80th Birthday, 1st Feb 1995', 6¾in (17cm) diam.
$870–1,000 ✗ LT

A collection of 19 Arsenal F. C. 1936–38 autographed black and white Real Photographic Postcards, by Lambert Jackson, 18 members of the 1937–38 League Championship side and eight members of the 1936 F. A. Cup winning team, all signed in ink, players include Drake, Bastin, Hapgood, Male, Compton, Nelson and Swindin.
$1,600–1,900 ✗ MUL
Arsenal were the dominant English club side of the 1930s. Sets of signed real photo postcards of leading teams of the 1930s now regularly fetch over $1,450.

▶ **A Spanish poster,** by Pietro Psaier, published by Invictor, Madrid, World Championship Jules Rimet Cup Winners 1966, featuring Bobby Moore, 53 x 35in (134.5 x 89cm), framed and glazed.
$2,600–3,200 ✗ S

Cross Reference
See Colour Review (page 744)

◀ **A Birmingham City v West Bromwich Albion F. A. Cup Final match programme,** 1931.
$360–430 ✗ ANA

▶ **An F. A. Cup Final programme,** Arsenal v Huddersfield, 26 April 1930.
$580–720 ✗ MUL
This is Arsenal's finest F. A. Cup triumph made even more interesting because it was in Herbert Chapmans new club (Arsenal) defeating his former club (Huddersfield). Unusually both clubs shared the post match banquet because of the Chapman link.

▶ **An England v Germany match programme,** 1 December 1954, signed in ink on the team pages by 31 players and officials.
$360–430 ⚲ ANA

An Everton v Manchester City F. A. Cup Final official programme, 29 April 1933.
$500–600 ⚲ Bon(C)
This was the first Cup Final in which players' shirts were numbered.

An Arsenal v Charlton War Cup Final, 1 May 1943.
$430–500 ⚲ MUL
Wartime austerity reduced the Cup Final programmes to very simple four-page items but the price remained at 6d. Fans were invited to put these programmes into bins for salvage after the game, thus increasing the rarity.

◀ **A Workington v Manchester United Association Football official souvenir programme,** Saturday 4 January 1958, printed in red and black on a white ground.
$65–80 ⚲ PFK
This programme is particularly desirable because it concerns an ex-league club and Manchester United, and there was also a record crowd at this game.

◀ **A Manchester United v Wolverhampton Wanderers programme,** 8 February 1958, numbered '20'.
$5,000–6,000 ⚲ P(NW)
The match did not take place on this day due to the Munich air disaster on the 6 February 1958. All programmes for this match were printed on the day the team's plane crashed, in readiness to be delivered to the ground on the 7 February. Once it had been relayed that the team plane had crashed, the printers C. Nicholls ordered all the programmes to be destroyed. Over the years a very small number have appeared from time to time, any such copies were no doubt removed as souvenirs by the printer's staff. It is known that a 30,000–40,000 print run would have been ordered initially but no more than a handful have ever surfaced.

A wooden football rattle, 1938, 11in (28cm) long.
$75–85 ⊞ WAC

◀ **A Scottish No. 9 shirt,** Umbro Tangeru light weight label, probably belonging to the forward Laurie Reilly, 1950s.
$580–720 ⚲ LT

An England No. 6 Airtex white shirt, worn by Bobby Moore during the pre-1970 World Cup tour to Central and South America in 1969.
$1,600–1,900 ⚲ Bon(C)
In the summer of 1969 England played Mexico (0–0), Mexico City; Uruguay (2–1), Montevideo and Rio de Janeiro, Brazil (1–2).

An 18ct gold pocket watch, the reverse inscribed 'Presented to Harold P. Hardman on his 21st birthday 1903 by the Blackpool Football Club Committee', 2in (5cm) diam.
$870–1,000 ⚲ P(NW)
Watches were a popular gift to footballers for all sorts of occasions. Monetary rewards were very strictly controlled and in Hardman's case, as an amateur he could accept no money at all.

An England 1966 World Cup No. 6 international white jersey, worn by Bobby Moore.
$9,500–11,500 ⚲ S
It is impossible to indicate to which game this jersey relates, as Bobby Moore played in all five games when England wore the customary white shirts. These matches comprised the three Group One games against Uruguay, Mexico and France; and the quarter-final and semi-final against Argentina and Portugal respectively. The value of this jersey is directly related to the World Cup connection.

SPORT

Golf

A feather ball, 18thC, 2in (5cm) diam.
$3,600–4,300 ➤ SLM

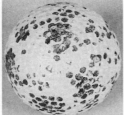

A gutta percha golf ball, The Colonel, white painted, worn, c1890.
$90–100 ➤ GTH

The Funny Side of Golf, from the pages of Punch, with numerous black and white golf cartoons and humourous illustrations, with original green linen-backed picture boards, c1909, 4to.
$175–200 ➤ DW

A gentleman's mahogany golf cabinet, by Hindley & Wilkinson, London, the two doors carved with crossed golf clubs embellished with ribbons and trailing flowers, impressed maker's stamp, late 19thC, 32¼in (82cm) wide.
$17,400–21,750 ➤ LAY

A set of six Continental sterling silver golfing buttons, c1920, 1in (2.5cm) diam, boxed.
$145–175 ⊞ JBB

◀ **A longnose scared head putter,** stamped D. Lowe to head, slight damage, c1900.
$300–350 ➤ Bon(C)

London & the Home Counties Duplex Map, Golf Edition, printed by John Bartholomew & Son, Edinburgh, 1930s.
$80–95 ➤ MUL

An R. Ferguson beech head longnose long spoon, with a replacement horn insert, c1880.
$2,300–2,500 ➤ P(NW)
Robert 'Bob' Ferguson won the Open in three successive years in 1880, 1881 and 1882. He was a gifted club maker but did not spend much time in the trade, preferring to spend his time coaching after his best playing days were over. Consequently, few examples of his work remain.

A Whistler perforated steel-shafted mashie, the Wright & Ditson iron head stamped with the patent dates for the shaft, 1914 and 1916.
$2,900–3,200 ➤ S
This shaft was patented by Allan Lard and produced only in 1918 and 1919. A shortage of steel following WWI caused manufacturing to cease.

◀ **A Scottish silver hallmarked medal,** Clarenden Golf Club 1895, 4in (10cm) high.
$1,600–1,750 ➤ MUL

A silver trophy in the shape of an ink well, for Royal St David's Golf Club, with an emblem of an owl and crossed swords decorating the hinged lid, 1930, 8in (20.5cm) diam.
$320–360 ➤ P(NW)

A black and white photograph, by Francis Caird Inglis, depicting The Grand National Tournament at St Andrews, c1858, 8½ x 11¼in (21.5 x 28.6cm).
$625–725 ➤ SLM

A Woodbury gravure, entitled 'Grand Golf Tournament by Players on Leigh Links 17th May 1867', depicting Tom Morris and others.
$4,300–5,000 ➤ BLH

A black and white photograph, entitled 'Professionals at Morton Hall, 8th June 1901', depicting J. H. Taylor, Harry Vardon and others.
$1,300–1,600 ↗ BLH
This was one of the many Scotland v England touring matches held 1901–02.

An American Augusta National Golf Club First Annual Invitation Tournament programme, bound green card, 22–25 March, 1934.
$12,300–14,500 ↗ SLM

An Edwardian brass-mounted oak golfer's stand, with divisions for golf clubs, rack for balls and hooks for cap and shoes, 32in(81.5cm) high.
$650–800 ↗ Bon(C)

Hockey

A wooden hockey stick, 1930s, 36in (91.5cm) long.
$35–40 ⊞ SPT

◀ **An HMS Vanguard hockey trophy shield,** 1950–60, 12 x 10in (30.5 x 25.5cm).
$90–100 ⊞ COB

▶ **A silver hockey trophy,** 1926, 8in (20.5cm) high, on a wooden base.
$80–100 ⊞ WAB

Ice Hockey

▶ **An American Suffield High School hockey team jacket,** blue and white, Connecticut State Champions, by Deerfoot, 1950s.
$110–125 ⊞ TRA

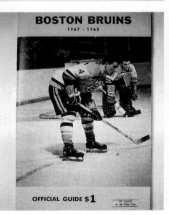

An American Cheshire County hockey team college jacket, red and white, by Hatcher, Connecticut, 1960s.
$110–125 ⊞ TRA

A pair of Boston Bruins Hockey Player photo metal pins, from Boston Garden, depicting John 'Pie' McKenzie and Gerry 'Cheese' Cheevers, 1972, 3in (7.5cm) diam.
$50–55 ⊞ HALL

◀ **A pair of ice hockey leather goal keepers pads,** 1960s, 29in (73.5cm) high.
$110–125 ⊞ TRA

A Boston Bruins Hockey Media Guide, depicting Bobby Orr on the cover, 1968.
$70–80 ⊞ HALL

Rowing

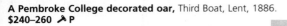

A Pembroke College decorated oar, Third Boat, Lent, 1886.
$240–260 ✗ P

► A Radley College Eight decorated oar, Henley
Royal Regatta, 1902.
$320–360 ✗ P

A wooden scale model of a coxless four
rowing boat, c1920, 46in (117cm) long.
$500–650 ⊞ WAB

◄ A pair of oars,
c1950, 72in
(183cm) long.
$50–60 ⊞ AL

► An Olympic/Leander Rowing club plaque, with cut-down rudder with
gilt inscription 'XVth Olympiad, Helsinki' awarded to the Leander Club to
commemorate winning The Grand Challenge Cup 1952, Henley Royal Regatta,
with gilt inscription with details of crew and defeated teams.
$190–220 ✗ MUL
The same team went on to represent Great Britain at the Helsinki
Olympics in 1952, finishing fourth.

Rugby

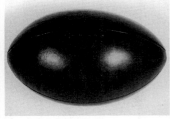

A leather rugby ball, by Mark Cross
& Co, 1950s.
$85–95 ⊞ PSA

Miller's is a price GUIDE
not a price LIST

A Northern Rugby Football Union
Challenge Cup gold medal, awarded
to J. Owen, with three county crests
and a rose to the centre, together
with a programme for the final
versus Hunslet at Fartown,
Huddersfield, and two pictorial
postcards of the Hull team, 1908.
$1,300–1,600 ✗ Bon(C)

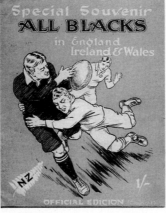

A Special Souvenir All Blacks in
England Ireland & Wales
brochure, with coloured pictorial
wrappers, 1924, 8vo.
$120–140 ✗ ANA

A Rugby International Wales XV
black and white photograph, with
hand-written legend on the back,
1933, 10 x 12in (25.5 x 30.5cm).
$90–100 ✗ MUL

A St John's Rugby Football Club
velvet cap, 1910–11.
$65–80 ⊞ WAB

A Victorian Football League
luncheon menu, in honour of the
English Rugby Football team, held at
Melbourne on 13 June 1899, with
coloured pictorial covers, signed in
pencil by 21 players and guests.
$750–850 ✗ ANA
Signatures include Gwyn Nicholls,
Bucher, Hickey, Harrison, Melville,
Nicholson and Atkinson.

SPORT

Shooting

A Victorian leg-of-mutton leather gun case, c1880, 28in (71cm) long.
$145–175 ⊞ STS

◀ *American Wild Fowl Shooting,* by Joseph W. Long, first edition, New York, 1874, 7½ x 5in (19 x 12.5cm).
$240–270 ⊞ OPB

A drinking glass, engraved with a grouse shooting scene, early 20thC, 7in (18cm) high.
$1,000–1,200 ⊞ ALiN

A 14 bore single barrelled flintlock sporting gun, by Wogdon, with walnut half stock with chequered wrist, engraved steel mounts and silver side plate engraved with hunting scenes, with brass-tipped ramrod, c1775, 52in (132cm) long.
$2,000–2,200 ✗ WAL

A royal sporting gun, by Twigg, with 38.75 inch re-browned twist barrel, walnut half stock with engraved iron furniture, the silver escutcheon with the Royal Arms surmounting the Prince of Wales' feathers and 'Ich Dien', with horn-tipped ramrod, c1778.
$10,200–11,600 ⊞ WSA
Made for King George IV when he was Prince of Wales.

An 18 bore flintlock sporting gun, by H. Nock, the barrel with Birmingham proofs, with walnut full stock and brass furniture, wooden ramrod, c1800, barrel 38in (96.5cm) long.
$300–350 ✗ WD

A flintlock single barrelled fowling piece, by Ward, with octagonal-to-round barrel, half stock, with steel mounts, the cock an old replacement, c1810, barrel 33in (84cm) long.
$870–950 ⊞ GV

A 15 bore double-barrelled percussion sporting gun, by Westley Richards, London, with re-browned twist sighted barrels, figured walnut half stock, foliate scroll engraved steel mounts and brass-mounted ramrod, in brass-mounted mahogany case with accessories, mid-19thC, barrel 30in (76cm) long.
$1,600–1,900 ✗ Bon

A German 9mm half stock percussion target rifle, by Gebrüder Rempt in Suhl, with walnut stock, the barrel breech chiselled with flowers and foliage, the steel furniture, breech tang and lock plate engraved with leaves and foliage, all the major furniture components decorated with gold hightlighted deer and chamois in a naturalistic setting, one ramrod pipe missing, c1865, barrel 31½in (80cm) long.
$3,600–4,200 ⊞ ASB

A hunting powder horn, by James Dickson & Sons, Sheffield, c1840, 13in (33cm) long.
$260–320 ⊞ ARB

An Elite chrome telescopic shooting stick, 1930s, 334in (86.5cm) long.
$85–95 ⊞ SPT

◀ **A copper and pewter shooting trophy,** 1908, 10½in (26.5cm) high.
$115–145 ⊞ WAB

Tennis

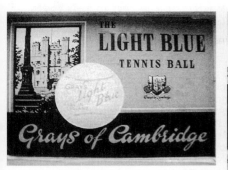

A Grays of Cambridge The Light Blue tennis ball box with six used balls, dated 1949.
$190–220 ✗ MUL

The Annals of Tennis, by Julian Marshall, first edition, 1878.
$3,000–3,500 ✗ MUL

A Roy Ullyett original cartoon, used 5 July 1968, depicting Billie Jean King on her way to another final, 20 x 16in (51 x 40.5cm).
$180–230 ✗ Bon(C)

A bronze figure of a tennis player, fixed to a marble ashtray, early 20thC, 6in (15cm) high.
$145–175 ✗ MUL

▶ A pair of Continental bisque tennis figures, c1890, 12in (30.5cm) high.
$260–320 ⊞ WAB

A tilted long handled Real Tennis racket, with convex wedge, inlaid head, neck and shoulders, the handle with original leather butt, c1870.
$2,300–3,000 ✗ MUL

◀ A tilted tennis racket, by Henry Mallings, Woolwich, with convex wedge, with oval grip handle and leather butt cap, c1880.
$2,000–2,300 ✗ MUL

A pine lawn tennis box, with tennis rackets and balls, box 38in (96.5cm) long.
$1,500–1,800 ✗ MUL

LOCATE THE SOURCE

The source of each illustration in Miller's can be found by checking the code letters below each caption with the Key to Illustrations, pages 794–800.

A Hawcridge's Patent 1887 Triangular Racket Press.
$75–85 ✗ MUL

▶ A ceramic tennis shoe, display model, c1890, 5in (12.5cm) long.
$100–115 ⊞ WAB

A Real Tennis racket, by Grays, Cambridge, c1950, 27in (68.5cm) long.
$180–220 ⊞ SMW

Glossary

We have defined here some of the terms that you will come across in this book. If there are any terms or technicalities you would like explained or you feel should be included in future, please let us know.

acid engraving: Technique of decorating glass by coating it in resin, incising a design and exposing the revealed areas to hydrochloric acid fumes.

Afshan: Design classification of a Caucasian rug from the Baku area.

agate ware: 18thC pottery, veined or marbled to resemble the mineral agate.

albarello: Pottery vessel used for storing pharmaceutical ingredients.

amboyna: Yellowish-brown burred wood imported from the West Indies and used as a veneer.

anchor escapement: Said to have been invented c1670 by Robert Hooke or William Clement. A type of escape mechanism shaped like an anchor, which engages at precise intervals with the toothed escape wheel. The anchor permits the use of a pendulum (either long or short), and gives greater accuracy than was possible with the verge escapement.

arabesque: Scrolling foliate decoration.

armoire: Large French cupboard or wardrobe, usually of monumental character.

associated: Term used in antiques, in which one part of an item is of the same design but not originally made for it. See **marriage**.

automaton: Any moving toy or decorative object, usually powered by a clockwork mechanism.

barley-twist: Form of turning, popular in the late 17thC, which resembles a spiral of traditional barley sugar.

bezel: Ring, usually brass, surrounding the dial of a clock, and securing the glass dial cover.

bisque: French term for biscuit ware, or unglazed porcelain.

blanc-de-chine: Translucent white Chinese porcelain, unpainted and with a thick glaze, made at kilns in Dehua in the Fujian province from the Song Dynasty and copied in Europe.

bombé: Outswelling, curving or bulging. Term used to describe a chest with a bulging front. In fashion during Louis XV period.

bonheur du jour: Small French writing table with a raised back comprising a cabinet or shelves.

boteh: Stylized design of afloral bush found on rugs, similar to a Paisley design.

bracket clock: Originally a 17thC clock which had to be set high up on a bracket because of the length of the weights; now sometimes applied to any mantel or table clock.

bureau de dame: Writing desk of delicate appearance and designed for use by ladies. Usually raised above slender cabriole legs and with one or two external drawers.

bureau plat: French writing table with a flat top and drawers in the frieze.

cabaret set: Tea set on a tray for three or more people.

calamander: Hardwood, imported from Sri Lanka (of the same family as ebony), used in the Regency period for making small articles of furniture, as a veneer and for crossbanding.

camaieu: Porcelain decoration using different tones of a single colour.

cameo glass: Two or more layers of coloured glass in which the top layer/s are then cut or etched away to create a multi-coloured design in relief. An ancient technique popular with Art Nouveau glassmakers in the early 20thC.

candle slide: Wooden slide to hold a candlestick.

cartouche: Ornate tablet or shield surrounded by scrollwork and foliage, often bearing an inscription, monogram or coat-of-arms.

cased glass: One layer of glass, often coloured, sandwiched between two plain glass layers or vice versa, the outer layer engraved to create a decorative effect. An ancient technique revived in the 19thC. See **cameo glass** and **overlay**.

celadon: Chinese stonewares with an opaque grey-green glaze, first made in the Song Dynasty and still made today, principally in Korea.

cellaret: Lidded container on legs designed to hold wine. The interior is often divided into sections for individual bottles.

champlevé: Enamelling on copper or bronze, similar to cloisonné, in which a glass paste is applied to the hollowed-out design, fired and ground smooth.

chapter ring: Circular ring on a clock dial on which the hours and minutes are engraved, attached or painted.

character doll: One with a naturalistic face, especially laughing, crying, pouting, etc.

chilong: Chinese mythical dragon-type lizard.

Chinese Imari: Chinese imitations of Japanese blue, red and gold painted Imari wares, made from the early 18thC.

chinoiserie: The fashion, prevailing in the late 18thC, for Chinese-style ornamentation on porcelain, wall-papers, fabrics, furniture and garden architecture.

chuval: Turkic word meaning bag.

cistern tube: Mercury tube fitted into stick barometers, the lower end of which is sealed into a boxwood cistern.

clock garniture: Matching group of clock and vases or candelabra made for the mantel shelf. Often highly ornate.

cloisonné: Enamelling on metal with divisions in the design separated by lines of fine metal wire. A speciality of the Limoges region of France in the Middle Ages, and of Chinese craftsmen to the present day.

coin silver: Silver of the standard used for coinage, ie .925 or sterling.

coromandel: Imported wood from the Coromandel coast of India, of similar blackish appearance to calamander and used from c1780 for banding, and for small pieces of furniture.

countwheel: Wheel with segments cut out of the edge or with pins fitted to one face, which controls the striking of a clock. Also known as a locking plate.

cuerda seca: Tile-making technique, developed in Iran in the 15thC, whereby the colours of the design were separated by an oily substance which leaves a brownish outline.

cut-glass: Glass carved with revolving wheels and abrasive to create sharp-edged facets that reflect and refract light so as to sparkle and achieve a prismatic (rainbow) effect. Revived in Bohemia in the 17thC, and common until superseded by pressed glass for utilitarian objects.

cyma: Double-curved moulding. Cyma recta is concave above and convex below; cyma reversa the other way round. Also known as ogee and reverse ogee moulding. Popular with 18thC cabinet-makers.

Cymric: Trade-name used by Liberty & Co for a mass-produced range of silverware inspired by Celtic art, introduced in 1899 and often incorporating enamelled pictorial plaques.

deadbeat escapement: Type of anchor escapement, possibly invented by George Graham and used in precision pendulum clocks.

Delft: Dutch tin-glazed earthenwares named after the town of Delft, the principal production centre, from the 16thC onwards. Similar pottery made in England from the late 16thC is also termed 'delft' or 'delftware'.

deutsche Blumen: Naturalistically painted flowers, either single or tied into bunches, used as a popular decorative motif on 18thC pottery and porcelain.

dhurrie: Cotton flatweave rug or carpet from India.

diaper: Surface decoration composed of repeated diamonds or squares, often carved in low relief.

ding: Chinese three-legged vessel.

diorama: Miniature three-dimensional scene.

dog of Fo: Buddhist guardian lion.

doucai: Decoration on Chinese porcelain using five colours.

écuelle: 17th and 18thC vessel, usually of silver, but also of ceramic, for serving soup. Has a shallow, circular bowl, two handles and a domed cover. It often comes complete with a stand.

églomisé: Painting on glass. Often the reverse side of the glass is covered in gold or silver leaf through which a pattern is engraved and then painted black.

elem: End panels or skirts of Turkoman carpets.

ensi: Rug used as a tent door by Turkoman tribes.

escapement: Means or device which regulates the release of the power of a timepiece to its pendulum or balance.

faïence: Tin-glazed earthenwares named after the town of Faenza in Italy, but actually used to describe products made anywhere but Italy, where they are called maiolica.

famille jaune/noire/rose/verte: Chinese porcelain in which yellow, black, pink or green respectively are the predominant ground colours.

fauteuil: French open-armed drawing room chair.

fielded panel: Panel with bevelled or chamfered edges.

filigree: Lacy openwork of silver or gold thread, produced in large quantities since end 19thC.

flatware (1): Collective name for flat pottery and porcelain, such as plates, dishes and saucers.

flatware (2): Cutlery.

fluted: Border that resembles a scalloped edge, used as a decoration on furniture, glass, silver and porcelain items.

fusee: 18thC clockwork invention; a cone-shaped drum, linked to the spring barrel by a length of gut or chain. The shape compensates for the declining strength of the mainspring thus ensuring constant timekeeping.

gadroon: Border or ornament comprising radiating lobes of either curbed or straight form. Used from the late Elizabethan period.

gilding: Process of applying thin gold foil to a surface. There are two methods. Oil gilding involves the use of linseed oil and is applied directly onto the woodwork. Water gilding requires the wood to be painted with gesso. The term is also used in ceramics, glass etc.

girandole: Carved and gilt candle sconce incorporating a mirror.

goncalo alves: Brazilian timber sometimes mistaken for rosewood.

grisaille: Monochrome decoration, usually grey, used on ceramics and furniture during the 18th and 19thC.

guéridon: Small circular table designed to carry some form of lighting.

guilloche: Pattern of twisting bands, spirals, double spirals or linked chains.

gül: From the Persian word for flower – usually used to describe a geometric flowerhead on a rug.

halberd: Spear fitted with a double axe.

hard paste: True porcelain made of china stone (petuntse) and kaolin; the formula was long known to, and kept secret by, Chinese potters but only discovered in the 1720s at Meissen, Germany, from where it spread to the rest of Europe and the Americas. Recognized by its hard, glossy feel.

harewood: Sycamore which has been stained a greenish colour. It is used mainly as an inlay and was known as silverwood in the 18thC.

herati: Overall repeating design of a flowerhead within a lozenge issuing small leaves. Used in descriptions of rugs.

hiramakie: Japanese term for sponged gold applied level with the surface.

hirame: Japanese lacquer decorated with gold and silver leaf.

hongmu: Type of wood used in the manufacture of Chinese furniture.

ho-o: Mythical Chinese bird, similar to a phoenix, symbolizing wisdom and energy.

huanghuali: Type of Oriental wood, much admired for its colour.

Imari: Export Japanese porcelain of predominantly red, blue and gold decoration which, although made in Arita, is called Imari after the port from which it was shipped.

inro: Japanese multi-compartmental medicine or seal container, carried suspended from the sash of a kimono.

intaglio: Incised gemstone, often set in a ring, used in antiquity and during the Renaissance as a seal. Any incised decoration; the opposite of carving in relief.

ironstone: Stoneware, patented 1813 by Charles James Mason, containing ground glassy slag, a by-product of iron smelting, for extra strength.

jadeite: Type of jade, normally the best and most desirable.

Jugendstil: German Art Nouveau style.

Kakiemon: Family of 17thC Japanese porcelain decorators who produced wares decorated with flowers and figures on a white ground in distinctive colours: azure, yellow, turquoise and soft red. Widely imitated in Europe.

kejebe gül: Cruciform medallion based on the eight-pointed star, usually in navy or ivory, most commonly found in Salor Turkoman rugs.

kiku mon: Japanese stylized chrysanthemum.

kilim: Flat woven rug lacking a pile.

kilin: Chinese mythical beast with a lion's tail, cloven hooves and the scales of a dragon.

kinrande: Japanese brocade decoration.

kiri: Japanese name for the Paulownia flower.

kirin: Japanese mythical beast.

knop: Knob, protuberance or swelling in the stem of a wine glass, of various forms which can be used as an aid to dating and provenance.

kochak: Ram's horn motif mainly found on Turkoman rugs.

koro: Japanese incense burner.

kovsh: Russian vessel used for measuring drink, often highly decorated for ornamental purposes from the late 18thC.

kraak porselein: Dutch term for porcelain raided from Portuguese ships, used to describe the earliest Chinese export porcelain.

krater: Ancient Greek vessel for mixing water and wine in which the mouth is always the widest part.

kufic: Arabic angular script – used in rugs to refer to stylized geometric calligraphy.

lingzhi: Type of fungus or mushroom, used as a motif on Chinese works of art.

Lithyalin: Polished opaque glass resembling hardstones, patented by Friedrich Egermann in 1829 at his factory in Haida, northern Bohemia.

loaded: In silverware, a hollow part of a vessel, usually a candlestick, filled with pitch or sand for weight and stability.

Long Eliza: Elongated female figure found on Kangxi blue and white export porcelain. The name derives from the Dutch 'lange lijsen'.

lunette: Semi-circular decorative motif popular for carved friezes in the Jacobean and Victorian periods.

made up: Piece of furniture that has been put together from parts of other pieces of furniture. See **marriage**.

maiolica: Tin-glazed earthenware produced in Italy from the 15thC to the present day.

majolica: Heavily-potted, moulded ware covered in transparent glazes in distinctive, often sombre colours, developed by the Minton factory in the mid-19thC.

manjua: Japanese bun filled with sweet bean paste, now applied to the shape of a *netsuke*.

marriage: Joining together of two unrelated parts to form one piece of furniture. See **associated** and **made up**.

merese: Flat disc of glass which links the bowl and stem, and sometimes the stem and foot, of a drinking glass.

mihrab: Prayer niche with a pointed arch; the motif which distinguishes a prayer rug from other types.

millefiori: Multi-coloured, or mosaic, glass, made since antiquity by fusing a number of coloured glass rods into a cane, and cutting off thin sections; much used to ornament paperweights.

nashiji: Multitude of gold flakes in Japanese lacquer.

netsuke: Japanese carved toggles made to secure *sagemono* (hanging things) to the *obi* (waist belt) from a cord; usually of ivory, lacquer, silver or wood, from the 16thC.

niello: Black metal alloy or enamel used for filling in engraved designs on silverware.

oinochoe: Small ancient Greek jug with handles.

ojime: Japanese word meaning bead.

okimono: Small, finely carved Japanese ornament.

olpe: Type of ancient Greek jug.

ormolu: Strictly, gilded bronze but used loosely for any yellow metal. Originally used for furniture handles and mounts but, from the 18thC, for inkstands, candlesticks etc.

overlay: In cased glass, the top layer, usually engraved to reveal a different coloured layer beneath.

overstuffed: Descriptive of upholstered furniture where the covering extends over the frame of the seat.

palmette: In rugs, a cross-section through a stylized flowerhead or fruit.

pâte-de-cristal: Glass that is crushed into fine crystals and and then bound together so that it can be moulded rather than having to be worked in its molten state.

pâte-de-verre: Translucent glass created by melting and applying powdered glass in layers or by casting it in a mould.

pâte-sur-pâte: 19thC Sèvres porcelain technique, much copied, of applying coloured clay decoration to the body before firing.

penwork: Type of decoration applied to japanned furniture, principally in England in the late 18th/early 19thC. Patterns in white japan were applied to a piece which had already been japanned black, and then the details and shading were added using black Indian ink with a fine quill pen.

pier glass: Mirror designed to be fixed to the pier, or wall, between two tall window openings, often partnered by a matching pier table. Made from mid-17thC.

pietra dura: Italian term for hardstone, applied to a mosaic pattern of semi-precious stones and marble.

plate: Old fashioned term, still occasionally used, to describe gold and silver vessels; not to be confused with Sheffield plate, or plated vessels generally, in which silver is fused to a base metal alloy.

plique-à-jour: Enamelling technique in which a structure of metal strips is laid on a metal background to form enclosed areas which are then filled with transparent enamels. When the backing is removed, a transparent 'stained glass' effect is achieved.

plum pudding: Type of figuring in some veneers, produced by dark oval spots in the wood. Found particularly in mahogany.

pole screen: Small adjustable screen mounted on a pole and designed to stand in front of an open fire to shield a lady's face from the heat.

poudreuse: French dressing table.

powder flask: Device for measuring out a precise quantity of priming powder, suspended from a musketeer's belt or bandolier and often ornately decorated. Sporting flasks are often made of antler and carved with hunting scenes.

powder horn: Cow horn hollowed out, blocked at the wide end with a wooden plug and fitted with a measuring device at the narrow end, used by musketeers for dispensing a precise quantity of priming powder.

pressed glass: Early 19thC invention, exploited rapidly in America, whereby mechanical pressure was used to form glassware in a mould.

printie: Circular or oval scoop out of glass, sometimes called a lens.

prunt: Blob of glass applied to the stem of a drinking vessel both as decoration and to stop the glass from slipping in the hand.

Puritan spoon: Transitional style of silver spoon, linking early English to modern types. Similar to a slip top but with a broader stem, its name derives from its plain form.

pushti: Rug measuring approximately 3ft x 2ft.

qilin: Alternative spelling of **kilin** - a Chinese mythical beast.

quarter-veneered: Four consecutively cut, and therefore identical, pieces of veneer laid at opposite ends to each other to give a mirrored effect.

register plate: Scale of a barometer against which the mercury level is read.

regulator: Clock of great accuracy, thus sometimes used for controlling or checking other timepieces.

rocaille: Shell and rock motifs found in rococo work.

rummer: 19thC English low drinking goblet.

ruyi: Chinese presentation sceptre.

sancai: Three-colour decoration on Chinese porcelain.

sang-de-boeuf: (lit. ox-blood) A bright red glaze used extensively on Chinese ceramics during the Qing Dynasty.

S.F.B.J.: Société de Fabrication de Bébés et Jouets; association of doll makers founded 1899 by the merger of Jumeau, Bru and others.

Shibayama: Lacquer applied with semi-precious stones and ivory.

shinshinto: Japanese term meaning 'new new', referring to edged weapons produced between 1800 and 1868.

shishi: Japanese mythical beast, a lion-dog.

shou **symbol:** Formal, artistic version of the Chinese character *shou*, meaning long-life.

shoulder-head: Term for a doll's head and shoulders below the neck.

shoulderplate: Area of a doll's shoulder-head below the neck.

siphon tube: U-shaped tube fitted into wheel barometers where the level of mercury in the short arm is used to record air pressure.

soft paste: Artificial porcelain made with the addition of ground glass, bone-ash or soap-stone. Used by most European porcelain manufacturers during the 18thC. Recognized by its soft, soapy feel.

spadroon: Cut-and-thrust sword.

spandrel: Element of design, closing off a corner.

spelter: Zinc treated to look like bronze and much used as an inexpensive substitute in Art Nouveau appliqué ornament and Art Deco figures.

spontoon: Type of halberd often carried by junior infantry officers and senior non-commissioned officers.

standish: Silver inkstand.

strapwork: Repeated carved decoration suggesting plaited straps.

stumpwork: Embroidery which incorporates distinctive areas of raised decoration, formed by padding certain areas of the design.

susani: Central Asian hand-embroidered bridal bed-cover.

sympiesometer: Instrument that uses a gas and coloured oil to record air pressure.

syrga **frame:** Continuous fork or bird-like motif on a white ground, mainly found on Turkoman rugs.

takamakie: Technique used in Japanese lacquerware in which the design is built up and modelled in a mixture of lacquer and charcoal or clay dust, and then often gilded.

tanto: Japanese dagger.

Taotie: Chinese mythical animal which devours wrong-doers.

tassets: Overlapping plates in armour for the groin and thighs.

tazza: Wide but shallow bowl on a stem with a foot; ceramic and metal tazzas were made in antiquity and the form was revived by Venetian glassmakers in 15thC. Also made in silver from 16thC.

teapoy: Piece of furniture in the form of a tea caddy on legs, with a hinged lid opening to reveal caddies, mixing bowl and other tea drinking accessories.

tear: Tear-drop shaped air bubble in the stem of an early 18thC wine glass, from which the air-twist evolved.

tester: Wooden canopy over a bedstead supported on either two or four posts. It may extend fully over the bed, known as a full tester, or only over the bedhead half, known as a half tester.

tête-à-tête: Tea set for two people.

thuyawood: Reddish-brown wood with distinctive small 'bird's-eye' markings, imported from Africa and used as a veneer.

timepiece: Clock that does not strike or chime.

tin glaze: Glassy opaque white glaze of tin oxide; re-introduced to Europe in 14thC by Moorish potters; the characteristic glaze of delftware, **faïence** and **maiolica**.

tombak: Alloy of copper and zinc.

touch: Maker's mark stamped on much, but not all, early English pewter. Their use was strictly controlled by the Pewterer's Company of London: early examples consist of initials, later ones are more elaborate and pictorial, sometimes including the maker's address.

transfer-printed: Ceramic decoration technique perfected mid-18thC and used widely thereafter for mass-produced wares. An engraved design is transferred onto a slab of glue or gelatin (a bat), which was then laid over the body of the vessel, leaving an outline. This was sometimes coloured in by hand.

trumeau: Section of wall between two openings; a pier mirror.

tsuba: Guard of a Japanese sword, usually consisting of an ornamented plate.

Tudric: Range of Celtic-inspired Art Nouveau pewter of high quality, designed for mass-production by Archibald Knox and others, and retailed through Liberty & Co.

tulipwood: Yellow-brown wood with reddish stripe, imported from Central and South America and used as a veneer and for inlay and crossbanding.

tyg: Mug with three or more handles.

verge escapement: Oldest form of escapement, found on clocks as early as 1300 and still in use in 1900. Consisting of a bar (the verge) with two flag-shaped pallets that rock in and out of the teeth of the crown or escape wheel to regulate the movement.

vernier scale: Short scale added to the traditional 3in (7.5cm) scale on stick barometers to give more precise readings than had previously been possible.

verre églomisé: Painting on glass. Often the reverse side of the glass is covered in gold or silver leaf through which a pattern is engraved and then painted black.

vesta case: Ornate flat case of silver or other metal for carrying vestas, an early form of match. Used from mid-19thC.

vitrine: French display cabinet which is often of bombé or serpentine outline and ornately decorated with marquetry and ormolu.

Vitruvian scroll: Repeated border ornament of scrolls that resemble waves.

WMF: Short for Württembergische Metallwarenfabrik, a German foundry that was one of the principal producers of Art Nouveau metalware.

wucai: Type of five-colour Chinese porcelain decoration.

yastik: Anatolian word for small weavings made for cushion covers or to sit on.

yen yen: Chinese term for a long-necked vase with a trumpet mouth.

yurt: Tent with felt-covered walls and a framework of poles, lived in by nomadic and semi-nomadic herds people.

Directory of Specialists

If you wish to be included in next year's directory, or if you have a change of address or telephone number, please contact Miller's Advertising Department by April 2002. We advise readers to make contact by telephone before visiting a dealer, therefore avoiding a wasted journey.

20thC Design
London
Zoom, Arch 65,
Cambridge Grove W6
Tel: 07000 9666 2002
Mobile: 07958 372 9753
eddiesandham@hotmail.com
www.retrozoom.com

Americana
USA
Allan Katz Americana,
25 Old Still Road, Woodbridge,
Connecticut 06525
Tel: 001 203 393 9356

Antiques Dealers' Assn
Oxfordshire
Thames Valley Antique Dealers'
Association (TVADA), The Old
College, Queen Street,
Dorchester-on-Thames OX10 7HL
Tel: 01865 341639
antiques@tvada.co.uk
www.tvada.co.uk

Antiquities
Dorset
Ancient & Gothic,
Bournemouth BH7 6JT
Tel: 01202 431721

Architectural Antiques
Cheshire
Nostalgia, Hollands Mill, 61 Shaw
Heath, Stockport SK3 8BH
Tel: 0161 477 7706
www.nostalgiafireplaces.co.uk

Devon
Ashburton Marbles,
Great Hall, North Street,
Ashburton TQ13 7DU
Tel: 01364 653189
*Antique fireplaces, surrounds &
accessories.*

Gloucestershire
Minchampton Architectural
Salvage Co, Cirencester Road,
Stroud GL6 8PE
Tel: 01285 760886
masco@catbrain.com
www.catbrain.com

Somerset
Wells Reclamation & Co,
Coxley, Nr Wells BA5 1RQ
Tel: 01749 677087

Surrey
Drummond's Architectural
Antiques Ltd, The Kirkpatrick
Buildings, 25 London Road
(A3), Hindhead GU26 6AB
Tel: 01428 609444
Open 7 days.

Arms & Militaria
Cheshire
Armourer–The Militaria
Magazine, Published by
Beaumont Publishing Ltd,
1st floor Adelphi Mill,
Bollington SK10 5JB
Tel: 01625 575700
editor@armourer.co.uk
www.armourer.co.uk
*A bi-monthly magazine for
military antique collectors &
military history enthusiasts*

*offering hundreds of contacts for
buying & selling, articles on all
aspects of militaria collecting plus
the dates of UK militaria fairs &
auctions. Available on subscription*
Gloucestershire
Q&C Militaria, 22 Suffolk Road,
Cheltenham GL50 2AQ
Tel: 01242 519815
Mobile: 07778 613977
john@qc-militaria.
freeserve.co.uk
www.qcmilitaria.com

Kent
Sporting Antiques,
10 Union Square, The Pantiles,
Tunbridge Wells TN4 8HE
Tel: 01892 522661
*Specialist dealers in antique
arms, armour, pistols –
sporting & military inclusive of
all accessories & tools. Books &
prints. We buy & sell.*

Lincolnshire
Garth Vincent, The Old Manor
House, Allington,
Nr Grantham NG32 2DH
Tel: 01400 281358
garthvincent@cs.com
www.guns.uk.com

Surrey
West Street Antiques, 63 West
Street, Dorking RH4 1BS
Tel: 01306 883487
weststant@aol.com
www.antiquearmsandarmour.
com

Sussex
Wallis & Wallis,
West St Auction Galleries,
Lewes BN7 2NJ
Tel: 01273 480208
auctions@wallisandwallis.co.uk
www.wallisandwallis.co.uk

Yorkshire
Andrew Spencer Bottomley,
The Coach House, Thongs
Bridge, Holmfirth HD7 2TT
Tel: 01484 685234
andrewbottomley@
compuserve.com

Barographs
Somerset
Richard Twort
Tel: 01934 641900
Mobile: 077 11 939789

Barometers
Berkshire
Alan Walker,
Halfway Manor, Halfway,
Nr Newbury RG20 8NR
Tel: 01488 657670
Mobile: 07770 728397
www.alanwalker-
barometers.com

Somerset
Knole Barometers,
Bingham House,
West Street,
Somerton TA11 7PS
Tel: 01458 241015
Mobile: 07785 364567
dccops@btconnect.com

West Yorkshire
Weather House Antiques,
Kym S. Walker, Foster Clough,
Hebden Bridge HX7 5QZ
Tel: 01422 882808/886961
Mobile: 07889 750711
kymwalker@btinternet.com

Beds
Wales
Seventh Heaven,
Chirk Mill, Chirk, Wrexham,
County Borough LL14 5BU
Tel: 01691 777622
www.seventh-heaven.co.uk

Worcestershire
S. W. Antiques, Abbey
Showrooms, Newlands,
Pershore WR10 1BP
Tel: 01386 555580
sw-antiques@talk21.com
www.sw-antiques.co.uk

Billiard Tables
Berkshire
William Bentley Billiards,
Standen Manor Farm,
Hungerford RG17 0RB
Tel: 01488 681711

Surrey
Academy Billiard Co,
5 Camp Hill Industrial Estate,
Camphill Road,
West Byfleet KT14 6EW
Tel: 01932 352067

Books
Surrey
David Aldous-Cook,
PO Box 413, Sutton SM3 8SZ
Tel: 020 8642 4842
*Reference books on antiques &
collectables*

USA
Lamps: By The Book, Inc, 514
14th Street, West Palm Beach,
Florida 33401
Tel: 001 561 659 1723
booklamps@msn.com
www.lampsbythebook.com
Also buy leather-bound books

Wiltshire
Dominic Winter Book Auctions,
The Old School, Maxwell
Street, Swindon SN1 5DR
Tel: 01793 611340
info@dominicwinter.co.uk
www.dominicwinter.co.uk

Boxes & Treen
Berkshire
Mostly Boxes, 93 High Street,
Eton, Windsor SL4 6AF
Tel: 01753 858470
Open Mon–Sat 9.45am–6.30pm

Hertfordshire
Bazaar Boxes
Tel: 01992 504 454
Mobile: 07970 909 206
bazaarboxes@hotmail.com
*Specialists in tortoiseshell,
ivory, mother-of-pearl, tea
caddies, period furniture &
objects of vertu. On show at
The Woburn Abbey Antiques
Centre or by appt*

London
Coromandel
Tel: 020 8543 9115
Mobile: 07932102756

Gerald Mathias, Antiquarius, 135
King's Road, Chelsea SW3 4PW
Tel: 020 7351 0484
fineantiqueboxes@
geraldmathias.com
www.geraldmathias.com

Somerset
Alan & Kathy Stacey
Tel: 01963 441333
antiqueboxes@cwcom.net
*By appt only. Cabinet-making,
polishing, carving & specialists in
tortoiseshell, ivory & mother-
of-pearl on boxes, caddies &
furniture. See main advert in
Boxes section.*

British Antique Furniture Restorers' Association
BAFRA Head Office,
The Old Rectory, Warmwell,
Dorchester DT2 8HQ
Tel: 01305 854822
headoffice@bafra.org.uk

Bedfordshire
Duncan Michael Everitt, DME
Restorations Ltd, 11 Church
Street, Ampthill MK45 2PL
Tel: 01525 405819
duncan@dmerestorations.com
www.dmerestorations.com
Full furniture restoration service

Berkshire
Ben Norris & Co, Knowl Hill
Farm, Knowl Hill, Kingsclere,
Newbury RG20 4NY
Tel: 01635 297950
*Gilding, carving & architectural
woodwork*

Cambridgeshire
Ludovic Potts, Unit 1 & 1A,
Haddenham Business Park,
Station Road, Ely CB6 3XD
Tel: 01353 741537
mail@restorers.co.uk
*Traditional repairs, boulle,
walnut, oak, veneering, up-
holstery, cane, rush & gilding*

Devon
Tony Vernon, 15 Follett Road,
Topsham, Exeter EX3 0JP
Tel: 01392 874635
*All aspects of conservation &
restoration including gilding,
carving, upholstery, veneering &
polishing. Accredited member
of BAFRA; the British Antique
Furniture Restorers' Association*

Dorset
Michael Barrington,
The Old Rectory, Warmwell,
Dorchester DT2 8HQ
Tel: 01305 854822
*The conservation & restoration of
antique & fine furniture & clocks.
Clock dials & movements,
barometers, upholstery,
mechanical music, automata &
toys, antique metalwork ferrous
& non-ferrous.*

Philip Hawkins,
Glebe Workshop, Semley,
Shaftesbury SP7 9AP
Tel: 01747 830830
hawkinssemley@hotmail.com
Early oak restoration specialist

Essex

Clive Beardall, 104B High
Street, Maldon CM9 5ET
Tel: 01621 857890
www.clivebeardall.co.uk
*Open Mon–Fri 8am–5.30pm
Sat 8am–4pm*

Gloucestershire

Alan Hessel,
The Old Town Workshop,
St George's Close, Moreton-in-
Marsh GL56 0LP
Tel: 01608 650026

Stephen Hill, Brewery Antiques,
2 Cirencester Workshops,
Brewery Court,
Cirencester GL7 1JH
Tel: 01285 658817
Mobile: 07976 722028

Hampshire

John Hartley, Johnson's Barns,
Waterworks Road, Sheet,
Petersfield GU32 2BY
Tel: 01730 233792
*Comprehensive furniture
restoration. Large workshops.*

David C. E. Lewry, Wychelms,
66 Gorran Avenue, Rowner,
Gosport PO13 0NF
Tel: 01329 286901
Furniture

Hertfordshire

John B Carr, Charles Perry
Restorations Ltd, Praewood
Farm, Hemel Hempstead Road,
St Albans AL3 6AA
Tel: 01727 853487
*Specialists in restoration &
conservation.*

Clifford J. Tracy Ltd,
Unit 3 Shaftesbury Industrial
Centre, Icknield Way,
Letchworth SG6 1HE
Tel: 01462 684855
*Restoration of antique
furniture, marquetry, inlaid
ivory, brass & tortoiseshell,
woodturning, polishing,
gilding, general cabinet-
making & complete re-
upholstery service. Worm-
infested furniture is guaranteed
clear by non-toxic methods. Free
estimates. Our own transport
for collections & delivery*

Kent

Timothy Akers,
The Forge, 39 Chancery Lane,
Beckenham BR3 6NR
Tel: 020 8650 9179
www.akersofantiques.com
*Longcase & bracket clocks,
cabinet-making, French
polishing*

Benedict Clegg,
Rear of 20 Camden Road,
Tunbridge Wells TN1 2PT
Tel: 01892 548095

Bruce Luckhurst,
Little Surrenden Workshops,
Ashford Road, Bethersden,
Ashford TN26 3BG
Tel: 01233 820589
restoration@woodwise.
newnet.co.uk
www.bruceluckhurst.co.uk
*One year course available, also
weekend & five day courses.*

Lancashire

Eric Smith Antique Restorations,
The Old Church, Park Road,
Darwen BB3 2LD
Tel: 01254 776222
*Furniture, vernacular furniture,
longcase clocks. Registered
with Museums & Galleries
Commission, London*

London

Oliver Clarke,
Heritage Restorations,
96 Webber Street SE1 0QN
Tel: 020 7928 3624
18th & 19thC furniture

Robert H. Crawley, Aberdeen
House, 75 St Mary's Road,
Ealing W5 5RH
Tel: 020 8566 5074

Sebastian Giles,
Sebastian Giles Furniture,
11 Junction Mews W2 1PN
Tel: 020 7258 3721
Comprehensive

Rodrigo Titian, Titian Studio,
318 Kensal Road W10 5BN
Tel: 020 8960 6247
enquiries@titianstudios.co.uk
www.titianstudios.co.uk
*Carving, gilding, lacquer,
painted furniture & French
polishing. Caning & rushing.*

Norfolk

Michael Dolling, Church Farm
Barns, Glandford, Holt NR25 7JR
Tel: 01263 741115

Roderick Nigel Larwood,
The Oaks, Station Road,
Larling, Norwich NR16 2QS
Tel: 01953 717937
*Restorers of fine antiques &
traditional finishers*

Scotland

William Trist, 135 St Leonard's
Street, Edinburgh EH8 9RB
Tel: 0131 667 7775
*Antique furniture restoration.
Cabinet & chairmakers, cane &
rush seating, upholstery.*

Shropshire

Richard A Higgins,
The Old School, Longnor,
Nr Shrewsbury SY5 7PP
Tel: 01743 718162
*All fine furniture, clocks, move-
ments, dials & cases, casting,
plating, boulle, gilding, lacquer-
work, carving, period upholstery.*

Somerset

Stuart Bradbury, M. & S.
Bradbury, The Barn, Hanham
Lane, Paulton, Bristol BS39 7PF
Tel: 01761 418910
*Antique furniture conservation
& restoration.*

Alan & Kathy Stacey
Tel: 01963 441333
antiqueboxes@cwcom.net
*By appt only. Cabinet-making,
polishing, carving & special-ists
in tortoiseshell, ivory & mother-
of-pearl on boxes, caddies &
furniture. See main advert in
Boxes section.*

Robert P. Tandy, Unit 5, Manor
Workshops, West End, Nailsea,
Bristol BS48 4DD
Tel: 01275 856378
*Traditional antique furniture
restoration & repairs.*

Surrey

David J. Booth, 9 High Street,
Ewell, Epsom KT17 1SG

Tel: 020 8393 5245
Restoration & large showrooms

Michael Hedgecoe,
21 Burrow Hill Green,
Chobham, Woking GU24 8QS
Tel: 01276 858206
Mobile: 07771 953870

Gavin Hussey, 4 Brook Farm,
Clayhill Road, Leigh RH2 8PA
Tel: 01306 611634
Mobile: 07711 281661
www.restoreantiques.com
Antiques restoration

Timothy Naylor, 24 Bridge
Road, Chertsey KT16 8JN
Tel: 01932 567129

Sussex

Simon Paterson,
Whitelands, West Dean,
Chichester PO18 0RL
Tel: 01243 811900
sp@hotglue.fsnet.co.uk
*Boulle work, marquetry, clock
case & general restoration &
repair*

Albert Plumb,
Albert Plumb Furniture Co,
Briarfield, Itchenor Green,
Chichester PO20 7DA
Tel: 01243 513700
Cabinet-making, upholstery

West Midlands

Phillip Slater, 93 Hewell Road,
Barnt Green,
Birmingham B45 8NL
Tel: 0121 445 4942
Inlay work, marquetry

Wiltshire

William Cook, High Trees
House, Savernake Forest,
Nr Marlborough SN8 4NE
Tel: 01672 513017
william.cook@virgin.net

Yorkshire

Rodney F Kemble, 16 Crag
Vale Terrace, Glusburn,
Nr Keighley BD20 8QU
Tel: 01535 636954/633702
*Furniture & small decorative
items*

Cameras

Lincolnshire

Antique Photographic Co Ltd
Tel: 01949 842192
alpaco@lineone.net
www.thesaurus.co.uk/cook

Ceramics

Surrey

Julian Eade
Tel: 020 8394 1515
Mobile: 07973 542971
*Doulton Lambeth stoneware &
Burslem wares. Royal
Worcester, Minton & Derby*

Clocks

Cheshire

Coppelia Antiques, Holford
Lodge, Plumley Moor Road,
Plumley WA16 9RS
Tel: 01565 722197
Open 7 days by appt

Devon

Musgrave Bickford Antiques,
15 East Street,
Crediton EX17 3AT
Tel: 01363 775042

Essex

It's About Time, 863 London
Road, Westcliff on Sea SS0 9SZ
Tel: 01702 472574
IAT@clocking-in.demon.co.uk
www.clocking-in.demon.co.uk

Gloucestershire

Jeffrey Formby,
Orchard Cottage, East Street,
Moreton-in-Marsh GL56 0LQ
Tel: 01608 650558
www.formby-clocks.co.uk
Visitors by appt

The Grandfather Clock Shop,
Styles of Stow, The Little
House, Sheep Street,
Stow-on-the-Wold GL54 1JS
Tel: 01451 830455
info@stylesofstow.co.uk
www.stylesofstow.co.uk
Open Mon–Sat or by appt

Jillings Antique Clocks,
Croft House, 17 Church Street,
Newent GL18 1PU
Tel: 01531 822100
Mobile: 07973 830110
clocks@jillings.com
www.jillings.com
Open Fri & Sat or by appt

Greater Manchester

Northern Clocks, Boothsbank
Farm, Worsley M28 1LL
Tel: 0161 790 8414
info@northernclocks.co.uk
www.northernclocks.co.uk
*Open Thurs, Fri, Sat
10am–5pm or by appt*

Hampshire

Bryan Clisby Antique Clocks at
Andwells Antiques, High Street,
Hartley Wintney RG27 8NY
Tel: 01252 842305

The Clock-Work-Shop
(Winchester), 6A Parchment
Street, Winchester SO23 8AT
Tel: 01962 842331

Kent

Campbell & Archard Ltd,
Lychgate House, Church Street,
Seal TN15 0AR
Tel: 01732 761153
pnarchard@aol.com
www.campbellandarchard.co.uk
Open by appt

Gem Antiques, 28 London
Road, Sevenoaks TN13 1AP
Tel: 01732 743540
www.gemantiques.com

Gaby Gunst, 140 High Street,
Tenterden TN30 6HT
Tel: 01580 765818
Closed Sun

The Old Clock Shop, 63 High St,
West Malling ME19 6NA
Tel: 01732 843246
www.theoldclockshop.co.uk
Open Mon–Sat 9am–5pm

Derek Roberts, 25 Shipbourne
Road, Tonbridge TN10 3DN
Tel: 01732 358986
drclocks@clara.net
www.qualityantiqueclocks.com

London

The Clock Clinic Ltd, 85 Lower
Richmond Road SW15 1EU
Tel: 020 8788 1407
clockclinic@btconnect.com
www.clockclinic.co.uk
*Open Tues–Fri 9am–6pm Sat
9am–1pm closed Mon*

Pendulum, King House,
51 Maddox Street W1R 9LA
Tel: 020 7629 6606

Roderick Antiques Clocks, 23
Vicarage Gate W8 4AA
Tel: 020 7937 8517

W. F. Turk, 355 Kingston Road,
Wimbledon Chase SW20 8JX
Tel: 020 8543 3231

Norfolk
Keith Lawson L.B.H.I.,
Scratby Garden Centre,
Beach Road, Scratby,
Great Yarmouth NR29 3AJ
Tel: 01493 730950
www.antiqueclocks.co.uk
Open 7 days

Oxfordshire
Craig Barfoot Antique Clocks,
Tudor House,
East Hagbourne OX11 9LR
Tel: 01235 818968
Mobile: 07710 858158
craig@tinyworld.co.uk

Republic of Ireland
Jonathan Beech,
Westport, Co. Mayo
Tel: 00 353 98 28688
www.antiqueclocks-
ireland.com
*Member of the Irish Antique
Dealers' Association*

Scotland
John Mann Antique Clocks,
The Clock Showroom,
Canonbie, Near Carlisle,
Galloway DG14 0SY
Tel: 013873 71337/71827
Mobile: 07850 606 147
jmannclock@aol.com
www.johnmannantiqueclocks.
co.uk

Somerset
Kembery Antique Clocks,
Bartlett Street Antiques Centre,
5 Bartlett Street, Bath BA1 2QZ
Tel: 0117 956 5281
Mobile: 07850 623237
kembery@kdclocks.co.uk
www.kdclocks.co.uk

Staffordshire
The Essence of Time Antique
Clocks, Unit 2 Curborough
Farm Antiques & Crafts Centre,
Curborough Hall Farm, Watery
Lane, Off Eastern Avenue
Bypass, Lichfield WS13 8ES
Mobile: 07944 245064
*Open Wed, Thurs, Fri, Sat &
Sun 10.30am–5pm*

Surrey
The Clock House, 75 Pound
Street, Carshalton SM5 3PG
Tel: 020 8773 4844
Mobile: 07850 363 317
markcocklin@theclockhouse.
co.uk
www.theclockhouse.co.uk
*Open Tues–Fri 9.30am–4.30pm
Sat 9am–6pm or by appt*

The Clock Shop, 64 Church
Street, Weybridge KT13 8DL
Tel: 01932 840407/855503
*Open Mon–Sat 10am–6pm
closed Wed*

E. Hollander, 1 Bennetts Castle,
89 The Street, Capel,
Dorking RH5 5JX
Tel: 01306 713377
Clock restoration

Horological Workshops,
204 Worplesdon Road,
Guildford GU2 9UY
Tel: 01483 576496
enquiries@horologicalworksho
ps.com

Sussex
Sam Orr Antique Clocks, 36
High Street, Hurstpierpoint,
Nr Brighton BN6 9RG
Tel: 01273 832081
Mobile: 07860 230888
www.samorr.co.uk

USA
R. O. Schmitt Fine Art,
Box 1941, Salem,
New Hampshire 03079
Tel: 603 893 5915
bob@roschmittfinearts.com
www.antiqueclockauction.com
*Specialist antique clock
auctions*

Warwickshire
Summersons, 172 Emscote
Road, Warwick CV34 5QN
Tel: 01926 400630
www.summersons.com
*We offer a complete restoration
service for antique clocks &
barometers. We also under-take
dial restoration, cabinet-work &
French polishing, wheel-
cutting, one-off parts made,
clock hands cut, fret-work,
silvering/gilding, polishing/
laquering, restor-ation parts &
materials, insurance valuations,
free estimates & advice.
WANTED: Clocks & barometers
in any condition.*

Woodward Antique Clocks,
14 High Street, Tettenhall,
Wolverhampton WV6 8QT
Tel: 01902 745608
www.antiqnet.co.uk/woodward

Wiltshire
P. A. Oxley Antique Clocks,
The Old Rectory, Cherhill,
Nr Calne SN11 8UX
Tel: 01249 816227
p.a.oxley@btinternet.com
www.british-antiqueclocks.com
*Open Mon–Sat 9.30am–5pm
closed Wed or by appt*

Allan Smith Clocks, Amity
Cottage, 162 Beechcroft Road,
Upper Stratton,
Swindon SN2 7QE
Tel: 01793 822977
Mobile: 07778 834342
allansmithclocks@lineone.net
www.allan-smith-antique-
clocks.co.uk

Yorkshire
Time & Motion, 1 Beckside,
Beverley HU17 0PB
Tel: 01482 881574

North Yorkshire
Brian Loomes, Calf Haugh
Farm, Pateley Bridge HG3 5HW
Tel: 01423 711163
www.brianloomes.com

Comics
London
Comic Book
Postal Auctions Ltd, 40–42
Osnaburgh Street NW1 3ND
Tel: 020 7424 0007
comicbook@compuserve.com
www.compalcomics.com

Courses
Scotland
The Thomas Chippendale
School of Furniture, Gifford,
East Lothian EH41 4JA
Tel: 01620 810680
www.chippendale.co.uk
*Furniture design, making &
restoration courses*

Decorative Arts
Gloucestershire
Ruskin Decorative Arts,
5 Talbot Court,
Stow-on-the-Wold,
Cheltenham GL54 1DP
Tel: 01451 832254

*Specializing in the Decorative
Arts 1860–1930. Arts & Crafts,
Art Nouveau & Art Deco items.
Cotswold School Movement incl.
Guild of Handicraft, Gordon
Russell & Gimson, The Barnsleys*

Greater Manchester
A. S. Antiques, 26 Broad Street,
Pendleton, Salford M6 5BY
Tel: 0161 737 5938
Mobile: 07836 368230
as@sternshine.demon.co.uk
Open Thurs, Fri, Sat or by appt

Lincolnshire
Art Nouveau Originals, Stamford
Antiques, Stamford PE9 1PX
Tel: 01780 762605
anoc@compuserve.com

London
20th Century Glass,
Kensington Church Street
Antique Centre,
58–60 Kensington Church
Street W8 4DB
Tel: 020 7938 1137
Mobile: 07971 859848
*Open Thurs, Fri & Sat 12–6pm
or by appt*

Art Nouveau Originals,
4/5 Camden Passage,
Islington N1 8EA
Tel: 020 7359 4127
Mobile: 0777 4718096
anoc@compuserve.com
Open Wed & Sat or by appt

Artemis Decorative Arts Ltd,
36 Kensington Church
Street W8 4BX
Tel: 020 7376 0377/7937 9900
Artemis.w8@btinternet.com

Rumours, 4 The Mall,
Upper Street, Camden Passage,
Islington N1 0PD
Tel: 020 7704 6549
Mobiles: 078 36 277274
/07831 103746
Rumdec@aol.com
Moorcroft

Shapiro & Co, Stand 380,
Gray's Antique Market,
58 Davies Street W1Y 5LP
Tel: 020 7491 2710
Fabergé

Republic of Ireland
Mitofsky, 101 Terenure Road
East, Dublin 6
Tel: 00 353 1 492 0033
info@mitofskyartdeco.com
www.mitofskyartdeco.com

Suffolk
Puritan Values at the Dome, St
Edmunds Business Pk, St Edmunds
Road, Southwold IP18 6BZ
Tel: 01502 722211
Mobile: 07966 371676
sales@puritanvalues.com
www.puritanvalues.com
*10,000 sq ft of space. Open 7
days 10am–6pm. Specializing
in Arts & Crafts movement &
Decorative Arts 1850–1915*

Surrey
Gooday Gallery, 14 Richmond
Hill, Richmond TW10 6QX
Tel: 020 8940 8652
Mobile 077101 24540
Decorative antiques 1880–1980

Sussex
Art Deco Etc,
73 Upper Gloucester Road,
Brighton BN1 3LQ
Tel: 01273 329268
poolepottery@artdeco.co.uk
Decorative Arts ceramics

USA
JMW Gallery, 144 Lincoln
Street, Boston MA02111
Tel: 001 617 338 9097
www.jmwgallery.com
*American Arts & Crafts,
Decorative Arts, American Art
Pottery, Mission furniture,
lighting, colour block prints,
metalwork*

Dolls
Cheshire
Dollectable, 53 Lower Bridge
Street, Chester CH1 1RS
Tel: 01244 344888/679195

Ephemera
Nottinghamshire
T. Vennett-Smith, 11 Nottingham
Road, Gotham NG11 0HE
Tel: 0115 983 0541
info@vennett-smith.com
www.vennett-smith.com
Ephemera auctions

Republic of Ireland
Whyte's Auctioneers, 30
Marlborough Street, Dublin 1
Tel: 00 353 1 874 6161
info@whytes.ie
www.whytes.ie

Exhibition & Fair
Organizers
Surrey
Cultural Exhibitions Ltd, 8
Meadrow, Godalming GU7 3HN
Tel: 01483 422562

USA
Forbes & Turner, 45
Larchwood Road, South
Portland, Maine 04106
Tel: 001 207 767 3967
LindaT@aol.com
www.ForbesandTurner.com

Exporters
Devon
Pugh's Farm Antiques, Monkton,
Nr Honiton EX14 9QH
Tel: 01404 42860
sales@pughs-antiques-export.com
www.pughs-antiques-
export.co.uk
Open Mon–Sat

Nottinghamshire
Antiques Across the World,
James Alexander Buildings,
London Road/Manvers Street,
Nottingham NG2 3AE
Tel: 0115 979 9199
tonyrimes@btinternet.com

Suffolk
Wrentham Antiques,
40–44 High Street, Wrentham,
Nr Beccles NR34 7HB
Tel: 01502 675583

East Sussex
International Furniture Exporters,
The Old Cement Works, South
Heighton, Newhaven BN9 0HS
Tel: 01273 611251

The Old Mint House, High
Street, Pevensey BN24 5LF
Tel: 01323 762337
antiques@minthouse.co.uk
www.minthouse.co.uk
*Open Mon–Fri 9am–5.30pm
Sat 10.30am–4.30pm or by appt*

Fishing
Hampshire
Evans & Partridge, Agriculture
House, High Street,
Stockbridge SO20 6HF
Tel: 01264 810702
Sporting auctions

London

Angling Auctions,
PO Box 2095 W12 8RU
Tel: 020 8749 4175
neil@anglingauctions.demon.co.uk

Shropshire

Mullock & Madeley, The Old
Shippon, Wall-under-Heywood,
Church Stretton SY6 7DS
Tel: 01694 771771
auctions@mullockmadeley.co.uk
www.mullockmadeley.co.uk
Sporting auctions

Furniture

Bedfordshire

Transatlantic Antiques Ltd,
101 Dunstable Street,
Ampthill MK45 2JT
Tel: 01525 403346

Berkshire

Hill Farm Antiques, Hill Farm,
Shop Lane, Leckhampstead,
Nr Newbury RG20 8QG
Tel: 01488 638541
*Specialists in antique dining
tables*

The Old Malthouse, 15 Bridge
Street, Hungerford RG17 0EG
Tel: 01488 682209
hunwick@oldmalthouse30.free
serve.co.uk

Cumbria

Anthemion, Cartmel, Grange-
Over-Sands LA11 6QD
Tel: 015395 36295
Mobile: 07768 443757

Derbyshire

Spurrier-Smith Antiques,
28, 30, 39 Church Street,
Ashbourne DE6 1AJ
Tel: 01335 343669
/342198/344377

Essex

F. G. Bruschweiler (Antiques)
Ltd, 41–67 Lower Lambricks,
Rayleigh SS6 7EN
Tel: 01268 773 761
fred@fbruschweiler.demon.
co.uk
www.business.virgin.net
/f.bruschweiler

Lancaster House Antiques,
359a Holland Road,
Holland-on-Sea CO15 6PD
Tel: UK 01255 813135
FRANCE 0033(0)299344075
lloyd @englishantiques.co.uk
www.englishantiques.co.uk
*18th & 19thC furniture,
investment pieces, objet d'art,
boxes, clocks, services*

Gloucestershire

Berry Antiques, 3 High Street,
Moreton-in-Marsh GL56 0AH
Tel: 01608 652929
chris@berryantiques.com
berryantiques.com
berryantiques.co.uk
*Open Mon–Sat 10am–5.30pm
Sun 11am–5pm closed Tues*

Hertfordshire

Collins Antiques, Corner House,
Wheathampstead AL4 8AP
Tel: 01582 833111
www.antique-finder.co.uk

Kent

Lennox Cato,
1 The Square, Church Street,
Edenbridge TN8 5BD
Tel: 01732 865988
Mobile: 07836 233473
cato@lennoxcato.com
www.lennoxcato.com
Member of BADA

Flower House Antiques, 90 High
Street, Tenterden TN30 6HT
Tel: 01580 763764

Pantiles Spa Antiques,
4, 5, 6 Union House,
The Pantiles,
Tunbridge Wells TN4 8HE
Tel: 01892 541377
Mobile: 07711 283655
psa.wells@btinternet.com
www.antiques-tun-wells-
kent.co.uk

Gillian Shepherd,
Old Corner House Antiques,
6 Poplar Road, Wittersham,
Tenterden TN30 7PG
Tel: 01797 270236
Open Weds–Sat 10am–5pm

Sutton Valence Antiques,
North Street, Sutton Valence,
Nr Maidstone ME17 3AP
Tel: 01622 843333
svantiques@aol.com
www.svantiques.co.uk

Lincolnshire

Norman Mitchell,
47a East Street, Horncastle
Tel: 01507 527957
Mobile: 07850 802219
norman@mitchellantique.
demon.co.uk

Seaview Antiques, Stanhope
Road, Horncastle LN9 5DG
Tel: 01507 524524
tracey.collins@virgin.net
www.seaviewantiques.co.uk

London

Adams Rooms Antiques &
Interiors, 18–20 The Ridgeway,
Wimbledon Village SW19 4QN
Tel: 020 8946 7047
info@antiques-index.com
www.antiques-index.com
*Open Mon–Fri 9am–5pm Sat
10am–5pm*

Antique Warehouse, 9–14
Deptford Broadway SE8 4PA
Tel: 020 8691 3062
antiquewarehouse@surfnet.co.uk
www.antique-warehouse.
co.uk/index.html

Oola Boola,
139–147 Kirkdale SE26 4QJ
Tel: 0208 291 9999
Mobile: 07956 261252
oola.boola@teleco4u.net

Reindeer Antiques Ltd,
81 Kensington Church
Street W8 4BG
Tel: 020 7937 3754
www.reindeerantiques.co.uk

Georg S. Wissinger,
166 Bermondsey Street SE1
Tel: 020 7407 5795

Middlesex

Robert Phelps Ltd,
133–135 St Margaret's Road,
East Twickenham TW1 1RG
Tel: 020 8892 1778/7129
antiques@phelps.co.uk
www.phelps.co.uk
*Mon–Fri 9am–5.30pm Sat
9.30am–5.30pm Sun 12am–4pm*

Northamptonshire

Reindeer Antiques Ltd,
43 Watling Street, Pottersbury,
Nr Towcester NN12 7QD
Tel: 01908 542407
www.reindeerantiques.co.uk

Nottinghamshire

Newark Antiques Warehouse,
Old Kelham Road,
Newark NG24 1BX

Tel: 01636 674869
enquiries@newarkantiques.co.uk

Oxfordshire

The Chair Set, 18 Market
Place, Woodstock OX20 1TA
Tel: 01993 811818
Mobile: 07711 625 477
*Sets of chairs, furniture &
accessories for the dining room*

Georg S. Wissinger Antiques,
Georgian House Antiques,
21 & 44 West Street,
Chipping Norton,
Tel: 01608 641369

Surrey

Dorking Desk Shop, 41 West
Street, Dorking RH4 1BU
Tel: 01306 883327
www.desk.uk.com
Antique desks

J. Hartley Antiques Ltd, 186
High Street, Ripley GU23 6BB
Tel: 01483 224318

Ripley Antiques, 67 High
Street, Ripley GU23 6AN
Tel: 01483 224981

Sussex

British Antique Replicas,
School Close, Queen Elizabeth
Avenue, Burgess Hill RH15 9RX
Tel: 01444 245577
Mon–Sat 9am–5.30pm

Dycheling Antiques,
34 High Street, Ditchling,
Hassocks BN6 8TA
Tel: 01273 842929
www.antiquesweb.co.uk

Jeroen Markies Antiques Ltd,
16 Hartfield Road,
Forest Row RH18 5HE
Tel: 01342 824980

sales@markies.co.uk
www.markies.co.uk
www.jeroenmarkies.com

Stable Antiques, Adrian Hoyle,
98a High Street,
Lindfield RH16 2HP
Tel: 01444 483662
a.hoyle@cwcom.net
Regency furniture

USA

Antique Associates at West
Townsend, PO Box 129W,
473 Main Street,
West Townsend,
Massachusetts 01474
Tel: 001 978 597 8084
drh@aaawt.com

Axe Antiques,
275 Alt. A1A (SR811),
Jupiter, Florida 33477
Tel: 001 561 743 7888
www.axeantiques.com
*Also fine art, vintage pillows,
seals, militaria & architectural
elements*

Dragonflies,
24 Center Street, Wolfeboro,
New Hampshire 03894
Tel: 001 603 569 0000
cathy@antiquefest.com
www.antiquefest.com
*Folk Art, mahogany speed boat
models, maps, antiquarian
books*

Douglas Hamel Antiques,
56 Staniels Road, Chichester,
New Hampshire 03234
Tel: 001 603 798 5912
doughamel@shakerantiques.com
www.shakerantiques.com
*We buy, sell & locate Shaker
antiques*

Frank & Barbara Pollack,
1214 Green Bay Road,
Highland Park, Illinois 60035
Tel: 001 847 433 2213
fpollock@compuserve.com
American antiques & art,
American primitive paintings,
furniture, toleware, Folk Art &
accessories of 18th, 19th &
20thC

Warwickshire

Apollo Antiques Ltd,
The Saltisford,
Birmingham Road,
Warwick CV34 4TD
Tel: 01926 494746/494666
www.apolloantiques.com

Coleshill Antiques & Interiors,
12–14 High Street,
Coleshill B46 1AZ
Tel: 01675 467416

West Midlands

Martin Taylor Antiques,
140B Tettenhall Road,
Wolverhampton WV6 0BQ
Tel: 01902 751166
Mobile: 07836 636524
enquiries@mtaylor-antiques.co.uk
www.mtaylor-antiques.co.uk

Wiltshire

Cross Hayes Antiques,
Unit 6 Westbrook Farm,
Draycot Cerne,
Chippenham SN15 5LH
Tel: 01249 720033
www.crosshayes.co.uk
Shipping furniture

Glass
Somerset

Somervale Antiques,
6 Radstock Road,
Midsomer Norton,
Bath BA3 2AJ
Tel: 01761 412686
Mobile: 07885 088022
ronthomas@somervaleantiques
glass.co.uk
www.somervaleantiques
glass.co.uk

Ivory & Tortoiseshell
Somerset

Alan & Kathy Stacey
Tel: 01963 441333
antiqueboxes@cwcom.net
By appt only. Cabinet-making,
polishing, carving & specialists
in tortoiseshell, ivory & mother-
of-pearl on boxes, caddies &
furniture. See main advert in
Boxes section.

Jewellery
London

Wimpole Antiques, Stand 349,
Grays Antique Market,
58 Davies Street W1Y 2LP
Tel/Fax: 020 7499 2889

Kitchenware
Lincolnshire

Skip & Janie Smithson
Tel: 01754 810265
Mobile: 07831 399180
Dairy bygones, enamel wares,
laundry items & advertising

Lighting
Canada

Andrew W. Zegers Antiques,
25 Rodman Street, St
Catherines, Ontario L2R 5C9
Tel: 001 905 685 4643
Art & accessories, antique
formal upholstered & country
furniture

Marine
Hampshire

Mariner's Antiques, Dolphin
Quay Antiques Centre, Queen
Street, Emsworth PO10 7BU
Tel: 01420 476718
Mobile: 07710 330700
www.mariner's-antiques.com
Specialists in marine paintings &
prints, Royal Navy & shipping
line memorabilia, nautical books,
ship models & nautical antiques

Shropshire

Mark Jarrold
Tel: 01584 841210
Mobile: 07776 193193
markjarrold@btinternet.com
Marine instruments

Markets & Centres
Derbyshire

Chappells Antiques Centre, King
Street, Bakewell DE45 1DZ
Tel: 01629 812496
www.chappellsantiquescentre.com
30 established dealers (incl. BADA
& LAPADA members) of quality
antiques decorative & collectors
items 17th–20thC. Tea & coffee
house. Mon–Sat 10am–5pm.
Sun 11am–5pm. Closed Christ-
mas Day, Boxing Day & New
Year's Day. Ring or view web-
site for brochure, parking info.

Matlock Antiques, Collectables
& Riverside Café, 7 Dale Road,
Matlock DE4 3LT
Tel: 01629 760808
Prop W. Shirley. Over 70
dealers. Open 7 days
10am–5pm incl Bank Hol

Devon

Colyton Antiques Centre, Dolphin
Street, Colyton EX24 6LU.
Tel: 01297 552339

Essex

Debden Antiques, Elder Street,
Saffron Walden CB11 3JY
Tel: 01799 543007
Mon–Sat 10am–5.30pm Bank
Hols 11am–4pm. 30 quality
dealers in a 17thC Essex barn.
Large selection of 16th–20thC
oak, mahogany & pine
furniture, watercolours & oil
paintings, rugs, ceramics, silver
& jewellery. Garden furniture &
ornaments.

Gloucestershire

The Antiques Emporium,
The Old Chapel, Long Street,
Tetbury GL8 8AA
Tel: 01666 505281
Open Mon–Sat 10am–5pm,
Sun 1–5pm. 38 dealers.
jewellery, clocks, Art Deco,
books, furniture, treen, flat-
ware, glass, china, porcelain &
decorative accessories

Jubilee Hall Antique Centre,
Oak Street, Lechlade GL7 3AY
Tel: 01367 253777

Humberside

Hull Antique Centre, Anderson
Wharf, Wincolmlee, Hull HU2 8AH
Tel: 01482 609958
www.@thehullantiquecentre.com
Open Mon–Fri 9am–5pm Sat &
Sun 10am–4pm

Kent

Malthouse Arcade, High Street,
Hythe CT21 5BW
Tel: 01303 260103

Tunbridge Wells Antiques,
12 Union Square, The Pantiles,
Tunbridge Wells TN4 8HE
Tel: 01892 533708

Lancashire

The Antique Centre,
56 Garstang Road,
Preston PR1 1NA
Tel: 01772 882078
Open 7 days a week

Kingsmill Antique Centre,
Queen Street, Harle Syke,
Burnley BB10 2HX
Tel: 01282 431953
Open 7 days 10–5pm, 8pm
Thurs. Trade welcome

Lincolnshire

Hemswell Antique Centre,
Caenby Corner Estate,
Hemswell Cliff,
Gainsborough DN21 5TJ
Tel: 01427 668389
info@hemswell-antiques.com
www.hemswell-antiques.com
Open 7 days 10am–5pm

London

Antiquarius Antiques, 131/141
King's Road, Chelsea SW3 5ST
Tel: 020 7351 5353
antique@dial.pipex.com
Open Mon–Sat 10am–6pm

Bond Street Antiques Centre,
124 New Bond Street W1Y 9AE
Tel: 020 7351 5353
antique@dial.pipex.com
Open Mon–Sat 10am–5.30pm

Kensington Antique Centre,
58–60 Kensington Church
Street W8 4DB
Tel: 020 7376 0425

The Mall Antiques Arcade,
Camden Passage N1 0PD
Tel: 020 7351 5353
antique@dial.pipex.cpm
Tues, Thurs, Fri 10am–5pm Wed
7.30am–5pm Sat 9am–6pm

Nottinghamshire

Newark Antiques Centre,
Regent House, Lombard Street,
Newark NG24 1XP
Tel: 01636 605504

Oxfordshire

Antiques on High,
85 High Street,
Oxford OX1 4BG
Tel: 01865 251075
Open 7 days 10am–5pm. Sun &
Bank Hols 11am–5pm. 35 dealers
with a wide range of quality
stock.

Chipping Norton Antiques
Centre, Ivy House,
Middle Row, Market Place,
Chipping Norton
Tel: 01608 641369

Deddington Antiques Centre,
Market Place, Bull Ring,
Deddington,
Nr Banbury OX15 0TW
Tel: 01869 338968
Four floors of antiques incl
period furniture, silver,
porcelain, oils & water-colours,
jewellery & much more. Ample
free parking. Open 7 days
Mon–Sat 10am–5pm, Sun
11am–5pm. On A4260
Oxford–Banbury, minutes from
junct 10, M40.

Somerset

Bartlett Street Antiques, 5–10
Bartlett Street, Bath BA1 2QZ
Tel: 01225 466689

Surrey

Kingston Antiques Market,
29–31 London Road, Kingston-
upon-Thames KT2 6ND
Tel: 020 8549 2004/3839
www.antiquesmarket.co.uk
Open 7 days

Sussex

Churchill Antiques Centre,
6 Station Road, Lewes BN7 2DA
Tel: 01273 474842

Wales

Afonwen Craft & Antique
Centre, Afonwen, Nr Caerwys,
Nr Mold, Flintshire CH7 5UB
Tel: 01352 720965
Tues–Sun 9.30am–5.30pm,
closed Mon, open Bank Hols.
Largest centre in North Wales
& the borders. 40 dealers.
Fabulous selection of antiques,
china, silver, crystal, quality
collectables, fine furniture,
oak, walnut, mahogany, pine
from around the world.
Excellent restaurant, large
car park

Offa's Dyke Antique Centre,
4 High Street, Knighton,
Powys LD7 1AT
Tel: 01547 528635/528940

Warwickshire

Barn Antiques Centre, Station
Road, Long Marston, Nr
Stratford-upon-Avon CV37 8RB
Tel: 01789 721399
Over 13,500 sq ft. Open 7 days
10am–5pm. Antique furniture,
antique pine, linen & lace, old
fireplaces & surrounds,
collectables, pictures & prints,
silver, china, ceramics & objet
d'art. Licensed Bistro

Yorkshire

Cavendish Antique &
Collectors Centre,
44 Stonegate, York YO1 8AS
Tel: 01904 621666
Open 7 days 9am–6pm. Over
50 dealers.

Headrow Antiques, Headrow
Shopping Centre, The
Headrow, Leeds LS1 6JE
Tel: 0113 2455 344
25 dealers in ceramics,
furniture, jewellery, silver,
buttons & collectables. NCP car
park on Albion Street.

Sheffield Antiques Emporium &
The Chapel, 15–19 Clyde
Road, (off Broadfield Road),
Heeley, Sheffield S8 0YD
Tel: 0114 258 4863
Open 7 days. Over 70 dealers
incl specialists in clocks, Art
Deco, French furniture, books,
pine, fabrics, porcelain & much
more. Upholstery, furniture
restoration, re-caning, pottery
restoration, French polishing,
delivery, refreshments. Suitable
for trade & retail

Stonegate Antiques Centre,
41 Stonegate, York YO1 8AW
Tel: 01904 613888
Open 7 days 9am–6pm. Over
110 dealers on 2 floors.

Medals
Hampshire

Romsey Medal Centre, 5 Bell
Street, Romsey SO51 8GY
Tel: 01794 324488
post@romseymedals.co.uk
www.romseymedals.co.uk

Miniatures
Gloucestershire
Judy & Brian Harden Antiques, PO Box 14, Bourton on the Water, Cheltenham GL54 2YR
Tel: 01451 810684
Portrait miniatures

Money Boxes
Yorkshire
John & Simon Haley, 89 Northgate, Halifax HX1 1XF
Tel: 01422 822148

Musical Instruments
Gloucestershire
Piano-Export, Bridge Road, Kingswood, Bristol BS15 4FW
Tel: 0117 956 8300
Open Mon–Fri

Kent
Period Piano Company, Park Farm Oast, Hareplain Road, Biddenden, Nr Ashford TN27 8LJ
Tel: 01580 291393
www.periodpiano.com
Specialist dealer & restorer of period pianos

Nottinghamshire
Turner Violins, 1–5 Lily Grove, Beeston NG9 1QL
Tel: 0115 943 0333
turnerviolins@compuserve.com

Oak & Country
Kent
Douglas Bryan Antiques, The Old Bakery, St Davids Bridge, Cranbrook TN17 3HN
Tel: 01580 713103

London
Robert Young Antiques, 68 Battersea Bridge Road, SW11 3AG
Tel: 020 7228 7847
Country furniture & Folk Art

Northamptonshire
Paul Hopwell, 30 High Street, West Haddon NN6 7AP
Tel: 01788 510636
hopwellp@aol.com
www.antiqueoak.co.uk

Mark Seabrook Antiques, 9 West End, West Haddon NN6 7AY
Tel: 01788 510772
Mobile: 07770 721931

Surrey
The Refectory, 38 West Street, Dorking RH4 1BU
Tel: 01306 742111
www.therefectory.co.uk
Refectory table specialist

Anthony Welling, Broadway Barn, High Street, Ripley GU23 6AQ
Tel: 01483 225384

Oriental
Buckinghamshire
Glade Antiques, PO Box 939, Marlow SL7 1SR
Tel: 01628 487255
Mobile: 07771 552 328
sonia@gladeantiques.com
www.gladeantiques.com

USA
Mimi's Antiques, 8763 Carriage Hills Drive, Columbia MD 21046
Tel: 001 410 381 6862
mimis1@erols.com
www.mimisantiques.com

18th & 19thC Chinese Export porcelain, American & English furniture, Continental porcelain, paintings, sterling, Oriental rugs

Packers & Shippers
Dorset
Alan Franklin Transport, 26 Blackmoor Road, Ebblake Ind Est, Verwood BH31 6BB
Tel: 01202 826539

Paperweights
Cheshire
Sweetbriar Gallery, Robin Hood Lane, Helsby WA6 9NH
Tel: 01928 723851
sweetbr@globalnet.co.uk
www.sweetbriar.co.uk

London
Marion Langham
Tel: 020 7730 1002
ladymarion@btinternet.com
www.ladymarion.co.uk

USA
The Dunlop Collection, PO Box 6269, Statesville NC 28687
Tel: (704) 871 2626 or Toll Free (800) 227 1996

Pine
Cumbria
Ben Eggleston Antiques, The Dovecote, Long Marton, Appleby CA16 6BJ
Tel: 01768 361849
Trade only

Essex
English Rose Antiques, 7 Church Street, Coggeshall CO6 1TU
Tel: 01376 562683
Mobile: 07770 880790
englishroseantiques@hotmail.com
Large selection of English & Continental pine furniture. Open Mon–Sun 10am–5.30pm closed Wed

Hampshire
Pine Cellars, 39 Jewry Street, Winchester SO23 8RY
Tel: 01962 777546/867014

Kent
Old English Pine, 100 Sandgate High Street, Sandgate, Folkestone CT20 3BY
Tel: 01303 248560

Up Country, The Old Corn Stores, 68 St John's Road, Tunbridge Wells TN4 9PE
Tel: 01892 523341
www.upcountryantiques.co.uk

Lancashire
Ben Eggleston Antiques, 1st Floor Preston Antique Centre, The Mill, Newhall Lane, Preston
Tel: 01772 794498
Retail & trade

Netherlands
Jacques Van Der Tol, Antiek & Curiosa, Antennestraat 34, 1322 A E Almere-Stad
Tel: 00 313 653 62050
www.jacquesvandertol.nl

Nottinghamshire
A. B. Period Pine, The Barn, 38 Main Street, Farnsfield, Newark NG22 8EA
Tel: 01623 882288
www.abperiodpine.co.uk
Open Mon, Tues, Thurs, Fri 10am–3pm Sat 10am–5pm

Oxfordshire
Julie Strachey, Southfield Farm, North Lane, Weston-on-the-Green OX6 8RG
Tel: 01869 350833
Antique farm & country furniture in pine, oak, etc. Ironwork & interesting pieces for the garden (no repro). By appt. Junct 9 M40 2 miles. Established 27 years.

Republic of Ireland
Delvin Farm Antiques, Gormonston, Co Meath
Tel: 00 353 1 841 2285
info@delvinfarmpine.com
john@delvinfarmpine.com
www.delvinfarmpine.com

Honan's Antiques, Crowe Street, Gort, County Galway
Tel: 00 353 91 631407
www.honansantiques.com

Somerset
Gilbert & Dale Antiques, The Old Chapel, Church Street, Ilchester, Nr Yeovil BA22 8ZA
Tel: 01935 840464
Painted pine & country

Westville House Antiques, Littleton, Nr Somerton TA11 6NP
Tel: 01458 273376
antique@westville.co.uk
www.westville.co.uk

Sussex
Bob Hoare Antiques, Unit Q, Phoenix Place, North Street, Lewes BN7 2DQ
Tel: 01273 480557
bob@antiquebob.demon.co.uk
www.antiquebob.demon.co.uk

Ann Lingard, Ropewalk Antiques, Ropewalk, Rye TN31 7NA
Tel: 01797 223486

Graham Price, Apple Store, Chaucer Industrial Estate, Dittons Road, Polegate BN26 6JF
Tel: 01323 487167
www.grahampriceantiques.co.uk

Warwickshire
Pine & Things, Portobello Farm, Campden Road, Nr Shipston-on-Stour CV36 4PY
Tel: 01608 663849

Wiltshire
North Wilts Exporters, Farm Hill House, Brinkworth SN15 5AJ
Tel: 01666 510876
Mobile: 07836 260730
Mon–Sat 8am–6pm or by appt

Sambourne House Antiques, Minety, Malmesbury SN16 9RQ
Tel: 01666 860288

Porcelain
Bedfordshire
Transatlantic Antiques Ltd, 101 Dunstable Street, Ampthill MK45 2JT
Tel: 01525 403346

Essex
Barling Porcelain
Tel: 01621 890058
stuart@barling.uk.com
www.barling.uk.com

Hampshire
Goss & Crested China Centre & Museum, incorporating Milestone Publications, 62 Murray Road, Horndean PO8 9JL

Tel: (023) 9259 7440
info@gosschinaclub.demon.co.uk
www.gosscrestedchina.co.uk
Goss & Crested china

London
Diana Huntley Antiques, 8 Camden Passage, Islington N1 8ED
Tel: 020 7226 4605
diana@dianhuntleyantiques.co.uk
www.dianehuntleyantiques.co.uk

Marion Langham
Tel: 020 7730 1002
ladymarion@btinternet.com
www.ladymarion.co.uk
Belleek

Shropshire
Teme Valley Antiques, 1 The Bull Ring, Ludlow SY8 1AD
Tel: 01584 874686

Somerset
Andrew Dando, 4 Wood Street, Queen Square, Bath BA1 2JQ
Tel: 01225 422702
www.andrewdando.co.uk
English, Oriental & Continental porcelain

Pottery
Berkshire
Special Auction Services, The Coach House, Midgham Park, Reading RG7 5UG
Tel: 0118 971 2949
www.invaluable.com/sas/
Commemoratives, pot lids & Prattware, fairings, Goss & Crested, Baxter & Le Blond Prints

Buckinghamshire
Gillian Neale Antiques, PO Box 247, Aylesbury HP20 1JZ
Tel: 01296 423754
Mobile: 07860 638700
Blue & white transfer-printed pottery 1780–1860

Hampshire
Millers Antiques Ltd, Netherbrook House, 86 Christchurch Road, Ringwood BH24 1DR
Tel: 01425 472062
mail@millers-antiques.co.uk
www.millers-antiques.co.uk

Kent
Serendipity, 125 High Street, Deal CT14 6BQ
Tel: 01304 369165/366536
dipityantiques@aol.com
Staffordshire pottery

Gillian Shepherd, Old Corner House Antiques, 6 Poplar Road, Wittersham, Tenterden TN30 7PG
Tel: 01797 270236
Open Weds–Sat 10am–5pm

London
Jonathan Horne, 66 Kensington Church Street W8 4BY
Tel: 020 7221 5658
H@jonathanhorne.co.uk
www.jonathanhorne.co.uk
Early English pottery

Rogers de Rin, 76 Royal Hospital Road SW3 4HN
Tel: 020 7352 9007
Wemyss

Monmouthshire
Nicholas Frost, 8 Priory Street,
Monmouth NP25 3BR
Tel: 01600 716687
nick@frostantiques.com
www.frostantiques.com
Staffordshire figures

Somerset
Andrew Dando, 4 Wood Street,
Queen Square, Bath BA1 2JQ
Tel: 01225 422702
www.andrewdando.co.uk
*English, Oriental & Continental
pottery*

Tyne & Wear
Ian Sharp Antiques,
23 Front Street,
Tynemouth NE30 4DX
Tel: 0191 296 0656
iansharp@sharpantiques.
demon.co.uk
www.sharpantiques.demon.co.uk
Tyneside & Wearside ceramics

Wales
Islwyn Watkins,
Offa's Dyke Antique Centre,
4 High Street, Knighton,
Powys LD7 1AT
Tel: 01547 520145
*18th & 19thC pottery, 20thC
country & studio pottery*

Warwickshire
Paull's of Kenilworth, Beehive
House, 125 Warwick Road,
Old Kenilworth CV8 1HY
Tel: 01926 855253
Mobile: 07831 691254
janicepaull@btinternet.com
www.janicepaull-ironstone.com
Masons Ironstone

Publications
London
Antiques Trade Gazette,
115 Shaftesbury Avenue
WC2H 8AD
Tel: 0207 420 6646

France
Guide Emer, Paris
Tel: (1) 427 42715
*Guide of French & European
antiques*

West Midlands
Antiques Magazine,
H.P. Publishing, 2 Hampton
Court Road, Harborne,
Birmingham B17 9AE
Tel: 0121 681 8000
subscriptions@
antiquesbulletin.com
www.antiquesbulletin.com

Restoration
London
Oliver Clarke,
Heritage Restorations,
96 Webber Street SE1 0QN
Tel: 020 7928 3624
18th/19thC furniture specialist

Northamptonshire
Leather Conservation,
The University College
Campus, Boughton Green
Road, Moulton Park,
Northampton NN2 7AN
Tel: 01604 719766
*Conservation & restoration of
leather screens, wall hangings,
car, carriage & furniture
upholstery, saddlery, luggage,
firemens' helmets & much,
much more. On the register
maintained by Conservation
Unit of the Museum &
Galleries Commission.*

Rock & Pop
Cheshire
Collector's Corner,
PO Box 8,
Congleton CW12 4GD
Tel: 01260 270429
dave.popcorner@ukonline.co.uk

Rocking Horses
Essex
Haddon Rocking Horses Ltd,
5 Telford Road, Clacton-on-Sea
CO15 4LP
Tel: 01255 424745
millers@rockinghorses.uk.com
www.rockinghorses.uk.com

Rugs & Carpets
Gloucestershire
Samarkand Galleries,
7–8 Brewery Yard,
Sheep Street, Stow-on-the-
Wold GL54 1AA
Tel: 01451 832322
mac@samarkand.co.uk
www.samarkand.co.uk
*Antique rugs from Near East &
Central Asia. Antique Nomadic
weavings. Decorative carpets.
Tribal artefacts. Contact: Brian
MacDonald FRGS.*

Kent
Desmond & Amanda North,
The Orchard,
186 Hale Street,
East Peckham TN12 5JB
Tel: 01622 871353
*Unusual, decorative & beautiful
old & antique Tribal & Nomadic
rugs, carpets, runners from
Persia, The Caucasus, Anatolia,
& Central Asia. Rugs, runners
mostly £100–£2000; carpets
mostly £400–£4000. Not a
shop, just a shed so telephone
first*

Scientific Instruments
Cheshire
Charles Tomlinson,
Chester
Tel: 01244 318395
Charles.Tomlinson@lineone.net
charles.tomlinson@btinternet.com
www.lineone.net/-
charles.tomlinson

Kent
Sporting Antiques,
10 Union Square,
The Pantiles,
Tunbridge Wells TN4 8HE
Tel: 01892 522661
*Theodolites, sextants, levels,
marine & military compasses,
microscopes, telescopes &
drawing instruments. We buy
& sell*

Scotland
Early Technology,
Monkton House,
Old Craighall, Musselburgh,
Midlothian EH21 8SF
Tel: 0131 665 5753
michael.bennett-
levy@virgin.net
www.earlytech.com
Open any time by appt

Services
Canada
AntiqueCanada.com,
PO Box 23068,
St Catherines,
Ontario L2R 7P6
brad@antiquecanada.com
AntiqueCanada.com
Antiques website

London
Antique Street, 14th floor,
20 Eastbourne Terrace W2 6LE
Tel: 0870 742 0540
jane.brown@antiquestreet.co.uk
www.antiquestreet.co.uk

Invaluable, Catherine House,
76 Gloucester Place W1H 4DQ
Tel: 020 7487 3401
www.invaluable.com

Silver
Bedfordshire
Transatlantic Antiques Ltd,
101 Dunstable Street,
Ampthill MK45 2JT
Tel: 01525 403346

Gloucestershire
Corner House Antiques &
Ffoxe Antiques, High Street,
Lechlade GL7 3AE
Tel: 01367 252007
Tues–Sat 10am–5pm or by appt

London
Daniel Bexfield, 26 Burlington
Arcade W1V 9AD
Tel: 020 7491 1720
antiques@bexfield.co.uk
www.bexfield.co.uk

The Silver Fund Ltd, 40 Bury
Street, St James's SW1Y 6AU
Tel: 020 7839 7664
dealers@thesilverfund.com
www.thesilverfund.com

Shropshire
Teme Valley Antiques, 1 The
Bull Ring, Ludlow SY8 1AD
Tel: 01584 874686

USA
Antique Elegance
Tel: 001 617 484 7556
gloriab415@aol.com
*Also jewellery, pottery,
porcelain, orientalia, cut-glass,
paintings, rugs & furniture*

Imperial Half Bushel,
831 North Howard Street,
Baltimore, Maryland 21201
Tel: 001 410 462 1192
patrick.duggan@worldnet.att.net
www.imperialhalfbushel.com

Sports & Games
Kent
Sporting Antiques, 10 Union
Square, The Pantiles,
Tunbridge Wells TN4 8HE
Tel: 01892 522661
*Fishing rods, reels, trophies,
books & prints. Golf & general
antique sporting goods.*

Nottinghamshire
T. Vennett-Smith,
11 Nottingham Road,
Gotham NG11 0HE
Tel: 0115 983 0541
info@vennett-smith.com
www.vennett-smith.com
Sporting auctions

USA
Triple 'L' Sports, PO Box 281,
Winthorp, Maine 04364
Tel: 001 207 377 5787
lllsport@ctel.com
*Winchester collectables,
fishing, hunting, trapping,
knives, primitives, baseball,
football, golf, tennis,
memorabilia & advertising*

Teddy Bears
Oxfordshire
Teddy Bears of Witney, 99
High Street, Witney OX8 6LY
Tel: 01993 702616/706616

Textiles
Lancashire
Decades, 20 Lord Street West,
Blackburn BB2 1JX
Tel: 01254 693320
*Victorian to 1970s classic
clothing, accessories, jewellery,
textiles, lace, linen & much more*

London
Erna Hiscock & John Shepherd,
Chelsea Galleries,
69 Portobello Road W11
Tel: 01233 661407
Mobile: 0771 562 7273
erna@ernahiscockantiques.com
www.ernahiscockantiques.com
Antique samplers. Sat only 7–3pm

USA
Antique European linens,
PO Box 789, Gulf Breeze,
Florida 32562–0789
Tel: 001 850 432 4777
pandora@antiqueeuropeanline
ns.com

M. Finkel & Daughter,
936 Pine Street, Philadelphia,
Pennsylvania 19107-6128
Tel: 001 215 627 7797
mailbox@finkelantiques.com
www.finkelantiques.com
*America's leading antique
sampler & needlework dealer*

Toys
Middlesex
Hobday Toys
Tel: 01895 636737
wendyhobday@freenet.co.uk

Sussex
Wallis & Wallis, West Street
Auction Galleries, Lewes BN7 2NJ
Tel: 01273 480208
grb@wallisandwallis.co.uk
www.wallisandwallis.co.uk

Yorkshire
John & Simon Haley,
89 Northgate, Halifax HX1 1XF
Tel: 01422 822148

Tunbridge Ware
Kent
Bracketts, Auction Hall, The
Pantiles, Tunbridge Wells TN1 1UU
Tel: 01892 544500
www.bfaa.co.uk
Tunbridge ware auctioneers

London
Amherst Antiques, Monomark
House, 27 Old Gloucester
Street WC1N 3XX
Mobile: 07850 350212
amherstantiques@monomark.
co.uk

Watches
Lancashire
Brittons Jewellers, 34 Scotland
Road, Nelson BB9 7UU
Tel: 01282 697659
info@brittons-watches.co.uk
www.brittons-watches.co.uk
www.antique-jewelry.co.uk

London
Pieces of Time, (1–7 Davies
Mews), 26 South Molton
Lane W1Y 2LP
Tel: 020 7629 2422
info@antique-watch.com
www.antique-watch.com

Yorkshire
Harpers Jewellers Ltd, 2/6
Minster Gates, York YO1 7HL
Tel: 01904 632634
harpers@talk21.com
www.vintage-watches.co.uk

Directory of Auctioneers

Auctioneers who hold frequent sales should contact us by April 2002 for inclusion in the next edition.

London
Angling Auctions,
PO Box 2095 W12 8RU
Tel: 020 8749 4175
neil@anglingauctions.
demon.co.uk

Bloomsbury Book Auctions,
3/4 Hardwick Street,
Off Rosebery Avenue EC1R 4RY
Tel: 020 7636 1945

Bonhams & Brooks,
65–69 Lots Road, Chelsea SW10 0RN
Tel: 020 7393 3900

Bonhams & Brooks, Montpelier Street,
Knightsbridge SW7 1HH
Tel: 020 7393 3900
www.bonhams.com

Christie's South Kensington Ltd,
85 Old Brompton Road SW7 3LD
Tel: 020 7581 7611

Comic Book Postal Auctions Ltd,
40–42 Osnaburgh Street NW1 3ND
Tel: 020 7424 0007
comicbook@compuserve.com
www.compalcomics.com

Dix-Noonan-Webb,
1 Old Bond Street W1X 3TD
Tel: 020 7499 5022

Glendinings & Co,
101 New Bond Street W1Y 9LG
Tel: 020 7493 2445

Lloyds International Auction Galleries,
118 Putney Bridge Road SW15 2NQ
Tel: 020 8788 7777
www.lloyds-auction.co.uk

Lots Road Galleries,
71–73 Lots Road,
Chelsea SW10 0RN
Tel: 020 7351 7771

Onslow's, The Depot,
2 Michael Road SW6 2AD
Tel: 020 7371 0505

Phillips, de Pury & Luxembourg,
101 New Bond Street W1Y 0AS
Tel: 020 7629 6602
www.phillips-auctions.com

Phillips Bayswater,
10 Salem Road W2 4DL
Tel: 020 7229 9090

Sotheby's,
34–35 New Bond Street W1A 2AA
Tel: 020 7293 5000

Spink & Son Ltd,
69 Southampton Road,
Bloomsbury WC1B 4ET
Tel: 020 7563 4000

Berkshire
Dreweatt Neate,
Donnington Priory, Donnington,
Newbury RG13 2JE
Tel: 01635 553553
fineart@dreweatt-neate.co.uk

Law Fine Art, Fir Tree Cottage,
Church Lane, Brimpton RG7 4TJ
Tel: 0118 971 0353
info@lawfineart.co.uk
www.lawfineart.co.uk

Buckinghamshire
Amersham Auction Rooms,
125 Station Road, Amersham HP7 0AH
Tel: 01494 729292
www.thesaurus.co.uk/amersham

Bourne End Auction Rooms,
Station Approach, Bourne End SL8 5QH
Tel: 01628 531500

Cambridgeshire
Cheffins Grain & Comins,
2 Clifton Road, Cambridge CB2 4BW
Tel: 01223 213343

Cheshire
Dockree's, Landmark House,
1st Floor, Station Road,
Cheadle Hulme SK8 7BS
Tel: 0161 485 1258
www.invaluable.com/dockrees

Halls Fine Art Auctions,
Booth Mansion, 30 Watergate Street,
Chester CH1 2LA
Tel: 01244 312300/312112

Maxwells of Wilmslow,
133A Woodford Road,
Woodford SK7 1QD
Tel: 0161 439 5182

Phillips North West, New House,
150 Christleton Road,
Chester CH3 5TD
Tel: 01244 313936

Wright Manley, Beeston Castle
Salerooms, Tarporley CW6 9NZ
Tel: 01829 262150

Cornwall
Martyn Rowe,
Truro Auction Centre, City Wharf,
Malpas Road, Truro TR1 1QH
Tel: 01872 260020

Cumbria
Penrith Farmers' & Kidd's plc,
Skirsgill Salerooms,
Penrith CA11 0DN
Tel: 01768 890781
penrith.farmers@virgin.net

Phillips Carlisle, 48 Cecil Street,
Carlisle CA1 1NT
Tel: 01228 42422

Thomson, Roddick & Medcalf,
Coleridge House, Shaddongate,
Carlisle CA2 5TU
Tel: 01228 528939

Devon
Bearnes, St Edmund's Court,
Okehampton Street,
Exeter EX4 1DU
Tel: 01392 422800

Bonhams & Brooks West Country,
Devon Fine Art Auction House,
Dowell Street, Honiton EX14 8LX
Tel: 01404 41872

Phillips, 38–39 Southernhay East,
Exeter EX1 1PE
Tel: 01392 439025

The Plymouth Auction Rooms,
Edwin House, St John's Road,
Cattedown, Plymouth PL4 0NZ
Tel: 01752 254740

Rendells, Stonepark,
Ashburton TQ13 7RH
Tel: 01364 653017
stonepark@rendells.co.uk
www.rendells.co.uk

Martin Spencer-Thomas,
Bicton Street, Exmouth EX8 2SN
Tel: 01395 267403

Taylors, Honiton Galleries,
205 High Street, Honiton EX14 8LF
Tel: 01404 42404

Dorset
Cottees of Wareham, The Market,
East Street, Wareham BH20 4NR
Tel: 01929 552826

Hy Duke & Son,
Dorchester Fine Art Salerooms,
Dorchester DT1 1QS
Tel: 01305 265080

Phillips Sherborne,
Long Street Salerooms,
Sherborne DT9 3BS
Tel: 01935 815271

Riddetts of Bournemouth,
177 Holden Hurst Road,
Bournemouth BH8 8DQ
Tel: 01202 555686

Essex
Ambrose, Ambrose House,
Old Station Road,
Loughton IG10 4PE
Tel: 020 8502 3951

Cooper Hirst Auctions,
The Granary Saleroom,
Victoria Road, Chelmsford CM2 6LH
Tel: 01245 260535

Leigh Auction Rooms,
John Stacey & Sons,
88–90 Pall Mall,
Leigh-on-Sea SS9 1RG
Tel: 01702 77051

G. E. Sworder & Sons,
14 Cambridge Road,
Stansted Mountfitchet CM24 8BZ
Tel: 01279 817778
www.sworder.co.uk

Flintshire
Dodds Property World,
Victoria Auction Galleries,
9 Chester Street,
Mold CH7 1EB
Tel: 01352 752552

Gloucestershire
Bristol Auction Rooms,
St John's Place, Apsley Road,
Clifton, Bristol BS8 2ST
Tel: 0117 973 7201
www.bristolauctionrooms.co.uk

The Cotswold Auction Company Ltd,
The Coach House, Swan Yard,
9–13 Market Place,
Cirencester GL7 2NH
Tel: 01285 642420
info@cotswoldauction.co.uk
www.cotswoldauction.co.uk

Mallams, 26 Grosvenor Street,
Cheltenham GL52 2SG
Tel: 01242 235712

Moore, Allen & Innocent,
The Salerooms, Norcote,
Cirencester GL7 5RH
Tel: 01285 646050
fineart@mooreallen.co.uk
www.mooreallen.co.uk

Specialised Postcard Auctions,
25 Gloucester Street,
Cirencester GL7 2DJ
Tel: 01285 659057

Tayler & Fletcher, London House,
High Street, Bourton-on-the-Water,
Cheltenham GL54 2AP
Tel: 01451 821666
bourton-tf@lineone.net
www.tayler-and-fletcher.co.uk

Wotton Auction Rooms,
Tabernacle Road,
Wotton-under-Edge GL12 7EB
Tel: 01453 844733
www.wottonauctionrooms.co.uk

Greater Manchester
Bonhams & Brooks, St Thomas's
Place, Hillgate, Stockport SK1 3TZ
Tel: 0161 429 8283

Capes Dunn & Co, The Auction
Galleries, 38 Charles Street,
Off Princess Street M1 7DB
Tel: 0161 273 6060/1911

Hampshire
Evans & Partridge, Agriculture House,
High Street, Stockbridge SO20 6HF
Tel: 01264 810702

Jacobs & Hunt, 26 Lavant Street,
Petersfield GU32 3EF
Tel: 01730 233933
www.jacobsandhunt.co.uk

George Kidner, The Old School,
The Square, Pennington,
Lymington SO41 8GN
Tel: 01590 670070
www.georgekidner.co.uk

May & Son, 18 Bridge Street,
Andover SP10 1BH
Tel: 01264 323417
mayandson@enterprise.net

D. M. Nesbit & Co,
Fine Art and Auction Department,
Southsea Salerooms,
7 Clarendon Road, Southsea PO5 2ED
Tel: 023 9286 4321
auctions@nesbits.co.uk
www.nesbits.co.uk

Phillips Fine Art Auctioneers,
54 Southampton Road,
Ringwood BH24 1JD
Tel: 01425 473333

Phillips of Winchester,
The Red House, Hyde Street,
Winchester SO23 7DX
Tel: 01962 862515

Herefordshire
Brightwells Ltd, Ryelands Road,
Leominster HR6 8NZ
Tel: 01568 611122
fineart@brightwells.com
www.brightwells.com

Morris Bricknell, Stuart House,
18 Gloucester Road,
Ross-on-Wye HR9 5BU
Tel: 01989 768320

Nigel Ward & Co, The Border
Property Centre, Pontrilas HR2 0EH
Tel: 01981 240140

Hertfordshire
Brown & Merry, Tring Market
Auctions, The Market Premises,
Brook Street, Tring HP23 5EF
Tel: 01442 826446
sales@tringmarketauctions.co.uk
www.tringmarketauctions.co.uk

G. E. Sworder incorporating
Andrew Pickford,
The Hertford Saleroom,
42 St Andrew Street,
Hertford SG14 1JA
Tel: 01992 583508

Humberside
Dickinson Davy & Markham,
Wrawby Street, Brigg DN20 8JJ
Tel: 01652 653666

Kent
Bracketts, Auction Hall,
Pantiles, Tunbridge Wells TN1 1UU
Tel: 01892 544500
www.bfaa.co.uk

Calcutt Maclean Standen,
The Estate Office, Stone Street,
Cranbrook TN17 3HD
Tel: 01580 713828

The Canterbury Auction Galleries,
40 Station Road West,
Canterbury CT2 8AN
Tel: 01227 763337

Mervyn Carey, Twysden Cottage,
Benenden, Cranbrook TN17 4LD
Tel: 01580 240283

Gorringes, 15 The Pantiles,
Tunbridge Wells TN2 5TD
Tel: 01892 619670
www.gorringes.co.uk

Ibbett Mosely, 125 High Street,
Sevenoaks TN13 1UT
Tel: 01732 452246/456731

Lambert & Foster, 102 High Street,
Tenterden TN30 6HT
Tel: 01580 762083

B. J. Norris, The Quest, West Street,
Harrietsham, Maidstone ME17 1JD
Tel: 01622 859515

Phillips Fine Art Auctioneers,
49 London Road, Sevenoaks TN13 1AR
Tel: 01732 740310

Lancashire
Smythe's, 174 Victoria Road West,
Cleveleys FY5 3NE
Tel: 01253 852184

Leicestershire
Gildings, 64 Roman Way,
Market Harborough LE16 7PQ
Tel: 01858 410414
Email: sales@gildings.co.uk
www.gildings.co.uk

Heathcote Ball & Co, Castle Auction
Rooms, 78 St Nicholas Circle,
Leicester LE1 5NW
Tel: 0116 253 6789
www.heathcote-ball.clara.co.uk

Lincolnshire
Marilyn Swain Auctions,
The Old Barracks, Sandon Road,
Grantham NG31 9AS
Tel: 01476 568861

Merseyside
Cato Crane & Co, Liverpool Auction
Rooms, 6 Stanhope Street, Liverpool
L8 5RF Tel: 0151 709 5559
www.cato-crane.co.uk

Outhwaite & Litherland,
Kingsway Galleries, Fontenoy Street,
Liverpool L3 2BE
Tel: 0151 236 6561

Norfolk
Keys, Aylsham Salerooms,
Off Palmers Lane, Aylsham NR11 6JA
Tel: 01263 733195
www.aylshamsalerooms.co.uk

Garry M. Emms & Co Ltd,
Great Yarmouth Salerooms,
Beevor Road (off South Beach Parade),
Great Yarmouth NR30 3PS
Tel: 01493 332668
www.gt-yarmouth-auctions.com

Thomas Wm Gaze & Son,
Diss Auction Rooms, Roydon Road,
Diss IP22 3LN
Tel: 01379 650306
www.twgaze.com

Knight's, Cuckoo Cottage,
Town Green, Alby, Norwich NR11 7HE
Tel: 01263 768488

Northamptonshire
Merry's Auctioneers,
Northampton Auction & Sales Centre,
Liliput Road, Brackmills,
Northampton NN4 7BY
Tel: 01604 769990

Northern Ireland
Anderson's Auction Rooms Ltd,
Unit 7 Prince Regent Business Park,
Prince Regent Road,
Castereagh BT5 6QR
Tel: 028 9040 1888

Nottinghamshire
Bonhams & Brooks, 57 Mansfield
Road, Nottingham NG1 3PL
Tel: 0115 947 4414

Arthur Johnson & Sons Ltd,
The Nottingham Auction Centre,
Meadow Lane, Nottingham NG2 3GY
Tel: 0115 986 9128

Mellors & Kirk, The Auction House,
Gregory Street, Lenton Lane,
Nottingham NG7 2NL
Tel: 0115 979 0000

Neales, 192 Mansfield Road,
Nottingham NG1 3HU
Tel: 0115 962 4141

Phillips, 20 The Square,
Retford DN22 6XE
Tel: 01777 708633

T. Vennett-Smith,
11 Nottingham Road,
Gotham NG11 0HE
Tel: 0115 983 0541
info@vennett-smith.com
www.vennett-smith.com

Oxfordshire
Holloways (RICS), 49 Parsons Street,
Banbury OX16 5PF
Tel: 01295 817777
enquiries@
hollowaysauctioneers.co.uk
www.hollowaysauctioneers.co.uk

Mallams, Bocardo House,
24 St Michael's Street,
Oxford OX1 2EB
Tel: 01865 241358
oxford@mallams.co.uk

Phillips, 39 Park End Street,
Oxford OX1 1JD
Tel: 01865 723524

Simmons & Sons, 32 Bell Street,
Henley-on-Thames RG9 2BH
Tel: 01491 571111
www.simmonsandsons.com

Soames County Auctioneers,
Pinnocks Farm Estates,
Northmoor OX8 1AY
Tel: 01865 300626

Republic of Ireland
James Adam & Sons,
26 St Stephen's Green, Dublin 2
Tel: 00 3531 676 0261

Christie's Dublin,
52 Waterloo Road, Dublin 4
Tel: 00 353 1 6680 585

Hamilton Osborne King,
4 Main Street, Blackrock, Co. Dublin
Tel: 353 1 288 5011
blackrock@hok.ie
www.hok.ie

Mealy's, Chatsworth Street,
Castle Comer, Co Kilkenny
Tel: 00 353 56 41229
info@mealys.com www.mealys.com

Whyte's Auctioneers,
30 Marlborough Street, Dublin 1
Tel: 00 353 1 874 6161
Email: info@whytes.ie
www.whytes.ie

Scotland
Christie's Scotland Ltd,
64–166 Bath Street, Glasgow G2 4TG
Tel: 0141 332 8134

Lyon & Turnbull, 33 Broughton
Place, Edinburgh EH1 3RR
Tel: 0131 557 8844

Macgregor Auctions,
56 Largo Road, St Andrews,
Fife KY16 8RP
Tel: 01334 472431

Phillips Scotland, 65 George Street,
Edinburgh EH2 2JL
Tel: 0131 225 2266

Phillips Scotland, The Beacon,
176 St Vincent Street,
Glasgow G2 5SG
Tel: 0141 223 8866

Sotheby's, 112 George Street,
Edinburgh EH2 4LH
Tel: 0131 226 7201

Thomson, Roddick & Medcalf,
60 Whitesands, Dumfries DG1 2RS
Tel: 01387 255366

Thomson Roddick & Medcalf,
20 Murray Street, Annan DG12 6EG
Tel: 01461 202575

Thomson Roddick & Medcalf,
44/3 Hardengreen Business Park,
Eskbank, Edinburgh EH22 3NX
Tel: 0131 454 9090

Shropshire
Hall & Lloyd Ltd, Cosford Auction
Rooms, Long Lane, Cosford TF11 8PJ
Tel: 01902 375555

Halls Fine Art Auctions,
Welsh Bridge, Shrewsbury SY3 8LA
Tel: 01743 231212

Mullock & Madeley, The Old Shippon,
Wall-under-Heywood,
Church Stretton SY6 7DS
Tel: 01694 771771
info@mullockmadeley.co.uk
www.mullockmadeley.co.uk

Walker, Barnett & Hill,
Cosford Auction Rooms
Long Lane, Cosford TF11 8PJ
Tel: 01902 375555

Somerset
Aldridges, Newark House,
26–45 Cheltenham Street,
Bath BA2 3EX
Tel: 01225 462830

Clevedon Salerooms,
Herbert Road, Clevedon BS21 7ND
Tel: 01275 876699

Gardiner Houlgate,
The Bath Auction Rooms,
9 Leafield Way, Corsham,
Nr Bath SN13 9SW
Tel: 01225 812912
gardiner-houlgate.co.uk
www.invaluable.com/gardiner-houlgate

Greenslade Taylor Hunt Fine Art,
Magdelene House, Church Square,
Taunton TA1 1SB
Tel: 01823 332525

Lawrence Fine Art Auctioneers,
South Street, Crewkerne TA18 8AB
Tel: 01460 73041

Phillips, 1 Old King Street,
Bath BA1 2JT
Tel: 01225 310609

Staffordshire
Louis Taylor Auctioneers & Valuers,
Britannia House, 10 Town Road,
Hanley, Stoke on Trent ST1 2QG
Tel: 01782 214111

Wintertons Ltd,
Lichfield Auction Centre,
Fradley Park, Lichfield WS13 8NF
Tel: 01543 263256
www.wintertons.co.uk

Suffolk
Dyson & Son, The Auction Room,
Church Street, Clare CO10 8PD
Tel: 01787 277993
Email: info@dyson-auctioneers.co.uk
www.dyson-auctioneers.co.uk

Lacy Scott & Knight, Fine Art
Department, The Auction Centre,
10 Risbygate Street,
Bury St Edmunds IP33 3AA
Tel: 01284 763531

Olivers, Olivers Rooms,
Burkitts Lane, Sudbury CO10 1HB
Tel: 01787 880305

Phillips, 32 Boss Hall Road,
Ipswich IP1 59J
Tel: 01473 74049

Surrey
Ewbank,
Burnt Common Auction Room,
London Road, Send,
Woking GU23 7LN
Tel: 01483 223101
www.ewbankauctions.co.uk

Hamptons International,
Baverstock House, 93 High Street,
Godalming GU7 1AL
Tel: 01483 423567
fineart@hamptons-int.com
www.hamptons.co.uk

Lawrences Auctioneers,
Norfolk House, 80 High Street,
Bletchingley RH1 4PA
Tel: 01883 743323
www.lawrencesbletchingley.co.uk

John Nicholson,
The Auction Rooms, Longfield,
Midhurst Road, Fernhurst GU27 3HA
Tel: 01428 653727

Phillips Fine Art Auctioneers,
Millmead, Guildford GU2 5BE
Tel: 01483 504030

Richmond & Surrey Auctions Ltd,
Richmond Station, Kew Road,
Old Railways Parcels Depot
Richmond TW9 2NA
Tel: 020 8948 6677

P. F. Windibank, The Dorking Halls,
Reigate Road, Dorking RH4 1SG
Tel: 01306 884556/876280
sjw@windibank.co.uk
www.windibank.co.uk

East Sussex
Burstow & Hewett, Abbey Auction
Galleries and Granary Salerooms,
Lower Lake, Battle TN33 0AT
Tel: 01424 772374

Gorringes Auction Galleries,
Terminus Road,
Bexhill-on-Sea TN39 3LR
Tel: 01424 212994
bexhill@gorringes.co.uk
www.gorringes.co.uk

Graves, Son & Pilcher,
Hove Auction Rooms,
Hove Street, Hove BN3 2GL
Tel: 01273 735266

Edgar Horn's Fine Art Auctioneers,
46–50 South Street,
Eastbourne BN21 4XB
Tel: 01323 410419
www.edgarhorns.com

Raymond P. Inman,
The Auction Galleries,
35 & 40 Temple Street,
Brighton BN1 3BH
Tel: 01273 774777
www.raymondinman.co.uk

Rye Auction Galleries, Rock Channel,
Rye TN31 7HL
Tel: 01797 222124

Wallis & Wallis, West Street Auction
Galleries, Lewes BN7 2NJ
Tel: 01273 480208
auctions@wallisandwallis.co.uk
www.wallisandwallis.co.uk

West Sussex
John Bellman Auctioneers,
New Pound Business Park,
Wisborough Green,
Billingshurst RH14 0AZ
Tel: 01403 700858
jbellman@compuserve.com

Peter Cheney, Western Road
Auction Rooms, Western Road,
Littlehampton BN17 5NP
Tel: 01903 722264/713418

Denham's, The Auction Galleries,
Warnham, Horsham RH12 3RZ
Tel: 01403 255699/253837
denhams@lineone.net

Sotheby's Sussex, Summers Place,
Billingshurst RH14 9AD
Tel: 01403 833500

Rupert Toovey & Co Ltd, Star Road,
Partridge Green RH13 8RA
Tel: 01403 711744
auctions@rupert-toovey.com
www.rupert-toovey.com

Worthing Auction Galleries Ltd,
Fleet House, Teville Gate,
Worthing BN11 1UA
Tel: 01903 205565
worthing-auctions.co.uk
www.worthing-auctions.co.uk

Tyne & Wear
Phillips North East,
30/32 Grey Street,
Newcastle-upon-Tyne NE1 6AE
Tel: 0191 233 9930

Wales
Peter Francis, Curiosity Sale Room,
19 King Street, Carmarthen SA31 1BH
Tel: 01267 233456
Peterfrancis@valuers.fsnet.co.uk
www.peterfrancis.co.uk

Morgan Evans & Co Ltd,
30 Church Street, Llangefni,
Anglesey, Gwynedd LL77 7DU
Tel: 01248 723303/421582
llangefni@morganevans.
demon.co.uk
www.morganevans.com

Rogers Jones & Co,
33 Abergele Road,
Colwyn Bay LL29 7RU
Tel: 01492 532176
www.rogersjones.ukauctioneers.com

J. Straker Chadwick & Sons,
Market Street Chambers,
Abergavenny,
Monmouthshire NP7 5SD
Tel: 01873 852624

Wingetts Auction Gallery,
29 Holt Street, Wrexham,
Clwyd LL13 8DH
Tel: 01978 353553
auctions@wingetts.co.uk
www.wingetts.co.uk

Warwickshire
Locke & England, 18 Guy Street,
Leamington Spa CV32 4RT
Tel: 01926 889100
www.auctions-online.com/locke

West Midlands
Biddle & Webb Ltd, Ladywood,
Middleway, Birmingham B16 0PP
Tel: 0121 455 8042
antiques@biddleandwebb.
freeserve.co.uk

Frank H Fellows & Sons,
Augusta House, 19 Augusta Street,
Hockley, Birmingham B18 6JA
Tel: 0121 212 2131

Phillips, The Old House, Station Road,
Knowle, Solihull B93 0HT
Tel: 01564 776151

Weller & Dufty Ltd,
141 Bromsgrove Street,
Birmingham B5 6RQ
Tel: 0121 692 1414
wellerdufty@freewire.co.uk
www.welleranddufty.co.uk

Wiltshire
Henry Aldridge & Son,
Unit 1 Bath Road Business Centre,
Devizes SN10 1XA
Tel: 01380 729199

Dominic Winter Book Auctions,
The Old School, Maxwell Street,
Swindon SN1 5DR
Tel: 01793 611340
info@dominicwinter.co.uk
www.dominicwinter.co.uk

Woolley & Wallis, Salisbury
Salerooms, 51–61 Castle Street,
Salisbury SP1 3SU
Tel: 01722 424500

Worcestershire
Philip Laney, The Malvern Auction
Centre, Portland Road, off Victoria
Road, Malvern WR14 2TA
Tel: 01684 893933

Philip Serrell, The Malvern Saleroom,
Barnards Green Road,
Malvern WR14 3LW
Tel: 01684 892314

Yorkshire
Boulton & Cooper,
St Michael's House, Market Place,
Malton YO17 0LR
Tel: 01653 696151

H. C. Chapman & Son,
The Auction Mart, North Street,
Scarborough YO11 1DL
Tel: 01723 372424

Cundalls, 15 Market Place,
Malton YO17 7LP
Tel: 01653 697820

Dee, Atkinson & Harrison,
The Exchange Saleroom,
Driffield YO25 7LJ
Tel: 01377 253151
exchange@dee-atkinson-
harrison.co.uk
www.dee-atkinson-harrison.co.uk

David Duggleby, The Vine Street
Salerooms, Scarborough YO11 1XN
Tel: 01723 507111
auctions@davidduggleby.
freeserve.co.uk
www.davidduggleby.com

Andrew Hartley,
Victoria Hall Salerooms,
Little Lane, Ilkley LS29 8EA
Tel: 01943 816363
ahartley.finearts@talk21.com

Lithgow Sons & Partners,
Antique House, Station Road,
Stokesley, Middlesbrough TS9 7AB
Tel: 01642 710158/710326

Morphets of Harrogate,
6 Albert Street, Harrogate HG1 1JL
Tel: 01423 530030

Phillips Leeds, 17a East Parade,
Leeds LS1 2BH
Tel: 0113 2448011

Tennants, The Auction Centre,
Harmby Road, Leyburn DL8 5SG
Tel: 01969 623780

Tennants, 34 Montpellier Parade,
Harrogate HG1 2TG
Tel: 01423 531661

Wilkinson & Beighton Auctioneers,
Woodhouse Green, Thurcroft,
Rotherham SY3 8LA
Tel: 01709 700005

Austria
Dorotheum, Palais Dorotheum,
A-1010 Wien, Dorotheergasse 17
Tel: 0043 1 515 600

Australia
Leonard Joel Auctioneers,
333 Malvern Road, South Yarra,
Victoria 3141 Tel: 03 9826 4333
decarts@ljoel.com.au
jewellery@ljoel.com.au
www.ljoel.com.au

Phillips, Level 1, 1111 High Street,
Armadale 3143, Melbourne,
Victoria NSW 2025
Tel: (613) 9823 1949

Phillips Sydney, 162 Queen Street,
Woollahra, Sydney NSW 2025
Tel: 00 612 9326 1588

Brussels
Horta, Hotel de Ventes,
16 Avenue Ducpetiaux 1060
Tel: 02 533 11 11

Canada
A Touch of Class,
92 College Crescent, Barrie,
Ontario L4M 5C8
Tel: 001 705 456 1901
auctions@barbr.ichards.com
www.barbrichards.com

Bailey's Auctions, 467 Elmira Road,
North Guelph, Ontario N1H 6J4
Tel: 001 519 823 1107
auctioneer@baileyauctions.com
www.baileyauctions.com

Deveau Galleries,
Robert Fine Art Auctioneers,
297–299 Queen Street, Toronto,
Ontario M5A 1S7
Tel: 00 416 364 6271

D. & J. Ritchie Inc., Auctioneers &
Appraisers of Antiques & Fine Arts,
288 King Street East, Toronto,
Ontario M5A 1K4
Tel: (416) 364 1864

Waddington's Auctioneers,
111 Bathurst Street,
Toronto M5V 2RI
Tel: 001 416 504 9100
vb@waddingtonsauctions.com
www.waddingtonsauctions.com

When the Hammer Goes Down,
440 Douglas Avenue,
Toronto, Ontario M5M 1H4
Tel: 001 416 787 1700
bidcalr@home.com www.bidcalr.com

Channel Islands
Bonhams and Langlois,
Westaway Chambers, 39 Don Street,
St Helier, Jersey JE2 4TR
Tel: 01534 22441

Bonhams & Martel Maides Ltd,
Allez St Auction Rooms,
29 High Street,
St Peter Port, Guernsey GY1 4NY
Tel: 01481 713463/722700

China
Sotheby's, Li Po Chun Chambers,
18th Floor, 189 Des Vouex Road,
Hong Kong Tel: 852 524 8121

Denmark
Bruun Rasmussen-Havnen,
Pakhusvej 12, DK–2100, Copenhagen
Tel: +45 70 27 60 80
havnen@bruun-rasmussen.dk
www.bruun-rasmussen.dk

Finland
Hagelstam, Bulevardi 9 A, II kerros,
00120 Helsinki
Tel: 358 (0)9 680 2300
www.hagelstam.fi

Germany
Auction Team Koln,
Postfach 50 11 19, 50971 Koln
Tel: 00 49 0221 38 70 49
auction@breker.com

Hermann Historica OHG,
Postfach 201009, 80010 Munchen
Tel: 00 49 89 5237296

Sotheby's Berlin,
Palais anmFestungsgraben,
Unter den Linden,
Neue Wache D-10117
Tel: 49 (30) 201 0521

Sotheby's Munich, Odeonsplatz 16,
D–80539 Munchen
Tel: 49 (89) 291 31 51

Hong Kong
Christie's Hong Kong,
2203–5 Alexandra House,
16–20 Chater Road
Tel: 00 852 2521 5396

Israel
Sotheby's Israel, Gordon 38,
Tel Aviv 63414
Tel: 972(3)522 3822

Italy
Christie's Rome,
Palazzo Massimo, Lancellotti,
Piazza Navona 114, Rome 00186
Tel: 00 396 687 2787

Sotheby's, Palazzo Broggi,
Via Broggi, 19, 20129 Milano
Tel: 02 295001
www.sothebys.com

Sotheby's Rome, Piazza d'Espana 90,
00187 Rome
Tel: 39(6) 69941791/6781798

Mexico
Galeria Louis C. Morton,
GLC A7073L IYS, Monte Athos 179,
Col Lomas de Chapultepec CP11000
Tel: 52 5520 5005
Email: glmorton@prodigy.net.mx
www.lmorton.com

Monaco
Sotheby's Monaco, Le Sporting d'Hiver,
Place du Casino, 98001 Cedex
Tel: 00 377 93 30 8880

Christie's (Monaco), S.A.M.,
Park Palace, Monte Carlo 98000
Tel: 00 337 9325 1933

Netherlands
Christie's Amsterdam,
Cornelis Schuystraat 57 107150,
Amsterdam
Tel: (3120) 57 55 255

Sotheby's Amsterdam,
De Boelelaan 30, 1083 HJ,
Amsterdam
Tel: 00 31 20 550 22 00

Van Sabben Poster Auctions,
PO Box 2065, 1620 EB Hoorn
Tel: 31 229 268203
uboersma@
sabbenposterauctions.nl
www.vsabbenposterauctions.nl

Singapore
Christie's, Unit 3 Park Lane,
Goodwood Park Hotel, 22 Scotts Road
Tel: (65) 235 3828

Sotheby's (Singapore) Pte Ltd,
1 Cuscaden Road, 01–01 The Regent
Tel: (65) 732 8239

Sweden
Bukowskis, Arsenalsgatan 4,
Stockholm–SE111 47
Tel: 08 614 08 00
info@bukowskis.se
www.bukowskis.se

Switzerland
Christie's (International) S.A,
8 Place de la Taconnerie,
1204 Geneva
Tel: 00 4122 319 1766

Phillips, Kreuzstrasse 54,
8008 Zurich
Tel: 00 41 1 254 2400

Phillips Geneva, 9 rue Ami-Levrier,
CH–1201 Geneva
Tel: 00 41 22 738 0707

Sotheby's, 13 Quai du Mont Blanc,
Geneva CH–1201
Tel: 00 41 22 908 4800

Sotheby's Zurich, Gessneralee 1,
CH–8021 Zurich
Tel: 00 41 1 226 2200

Taiwan
Sotheby's Taipei, 1st Floor,
No 79 Secl, An Ho Road, Taipei
Tel: 00 886 2 755 2906

USA
Frank H. Boos Gallery,
420 Enterprise Court,
Bloomfield Hills, Michigan 48302
Tel: 001 248 332 1500

Butterfields, 220 San Bruno Avenue,
San Francisco CA 94103
Tel: 00 1 415 861 7500

Butterfields, 7601 Sunset Boulevard,
Los Angeles CA 90046
Tel: 00 1 323 850 7500

Butterfields, 441 W. Huron Street,
Chicago IL 60610
Tel: 00 1 312 377 7500

Christie, Manson & Woods
International Inc, 502 Park Avenue,
New York 10022
Tel: 001 212 636 2000

Christie's East,
219 East 67th Street,
New York NY10021
Tel: 001 212 606 0400

William Doyle Galleries,
175 East 87th Street, New York 10128
Tel: 212 427 2730

Du Mouchelles,
409 East Jefferson, Detroit,
Michigan 48226
Tel: 001 313 963 6255

Eldred's, Robert C. Eldred Co Inc,
1475 Route 6A, East Dennis,
Massachusetts 0796 02641
Tel: 00 1 508 385 3116

Freeman Fine Art of Philadelphia Inc,
1808 Chestnut Street,
Philadelphia PA 19103
Tel: 001 215 563 9275

Gene Harris Antiques,
203 S 18th Avenue,
Marshalltown IA 50158
Tel: 641 752 0600

The Great Atlantic Auction Company,
2 Harris & Main Street,
Putnam CT06260
Tel: 001 860 963 2234
www.thegreatatlanticauction.com

Hunt Auctions,
75 E. Uwchlan Avenue Suite,
130 Exton, Pennsylvania 19341
Tel: 001 610 524 0822
info@huntauctions.com
www.huntauctions.com

Randy Inman Auctions Inc,
PO Box 726, Waterville,
Maine 04903–0726
Tel: 001 207 872 6900
inman@inmanauctions.com
www.inmanauctions.com

Jackson's Auctioneers & Appraisers,
2229 Lincoln Street,
Cedar Falls IA 50613
Tel: 00 1 319 277 2256

Paul McInnis Inc Auction Gallery,
21 Rockrimmon Road, Northampton,
New Hampshire 03862–2336
Tel: 001 603 964 1301

New Orleans Auction Galleries Inc,
801 Magazine Street, AT 510 Julia,
New Orleans, Louisiana 70130
Tel: 00 1 504 566 1849

Northeast Auctions, 93 Pleasant
Street, Portsmouth NH 03810-4504
Tel: 001 603 433 8400
neacat@ttlc.net

Phillips New York,
406 East 79th Street,
New York NY10021
Tel: 00 1 212 570 4830

R. O. Schmitt Fine Arts, Box 1941,
Salem, New Hampshire 03079
Tel: 603 893 5915
bob@roschmittfinearts.com
www.roschmittfinearts.com

Skinner Inc, 57 Main Street,
Bolton MA 01740
Tel: 00 1 978 779 6241

Skinner Inc, The Heritage On The
Garden, 63 Park Plaza,
Boston MA 02116
Tel: 001 617 350 5400

Sloan's, C. G. Sloan & Company Inc,
4920 Wyaconda Road, North
Bethesda MD 20852
Tel: 00 1 301 468 4911/669 5066
www.sloansauction.com

Sloan's Auctioneers & Appraisers,
Miami Gallery,
8861 NW 18th Terrace, Suite 100,
Miami, Florida 33172
Tel: 00 1 305 592 2575/800 660 4524

Sotheby's, 1334 York Avenue,
New York NY 10021
Tel: 00 1 212 606 7000

Sotheby's, 9665 Wilshire Boulevard,
Beverly Hills, California 90212
Tel: (310) 274 0340

Sotheby's, 215 West Ohio Street,
Chicago, Illinois 60610
Tel: 00 1 312 670 0010

Treadway Gallery Inc and John
Toomey Gallery, 2029 Madison Road,
Cincinnati, Ohio 45208
Tel: 001 513 321 6742
www.treadwaygallery.com

Wolfs Gallery,
1239 W 6th Street,
Cleveland OH 44113
Tel: 216 575 9653

Braswell Galleries,
125 West Ave, Norwalk CT06854
Tel: 001 203 899 7420

Swann Galleries Inc,
104 East 25th Street,
New York 10010
Tel: 00 1 212 2544710

For unique antiques

Vintage Pillows by Belle Designs®
Highly Carved Furniture
Swords & Canes
Arms & Armor
Fine Art

AXE ANTIQUES

275 Alt. A1A • Jupiter, Florida, 33477
Palm Beach County
561-743-7888 • 1-877-689-1730
www.axeantiques.com

ALWAYS ACTIVE BUYERS

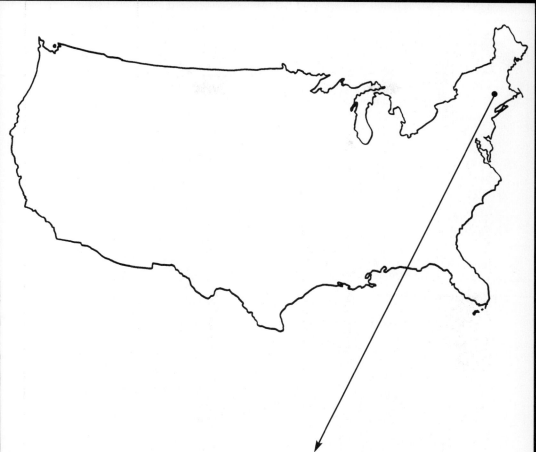

Antique Associates at West Townsend

Take advantage of our dealer and consignor collections that have been assembled for YOU, the serious antiquer …

Our merchandise is the result of our quest to offer you what is, quite simply, unobtainable at many shops. Here at Antique Associates, you can choose from one of the largest selections of quality American, period, country and formal furniture in the country. Or, you may want to personalize your collection by selecting from among one of New England's finest sources of decorative arts and accessories.

We pride ourselves on offering the finest in service as well. All items sold are unconditionally guaranteed … for without you, the customer, there is no business.

Please contact us with your wanted items. We welcome both trade and personal buyers and sellers. We communicate via email, snail mail, telephone, fax, and, of course, more than welcome your personal visit to our store. Let us work for you. We'll show you why we have earned the reputation as "America's Finest Multiple Dealer Shop".

P.O. Box 129W, 473 Main Street
West Townsend, MA 01474
(978) 597-8084 fax 597-6704
drh@aaawt.com

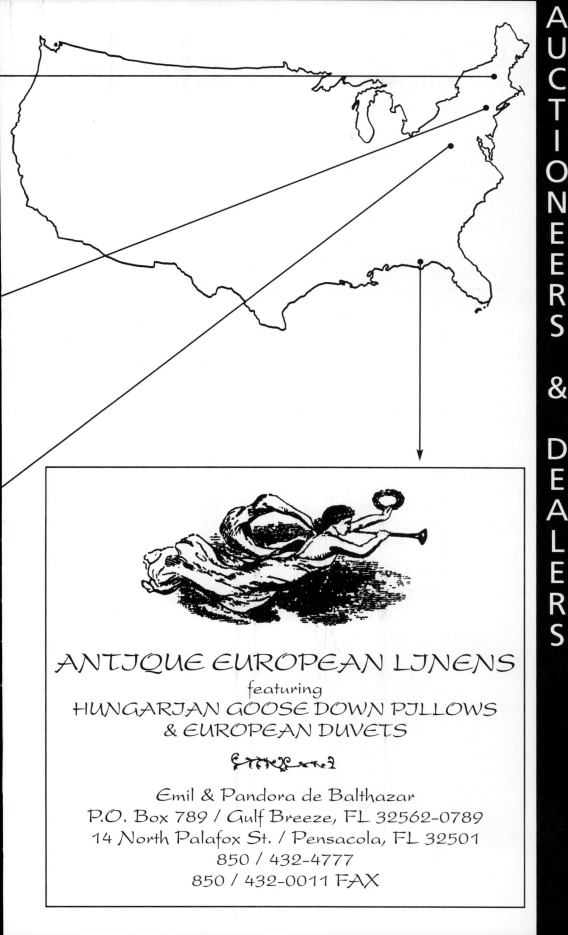

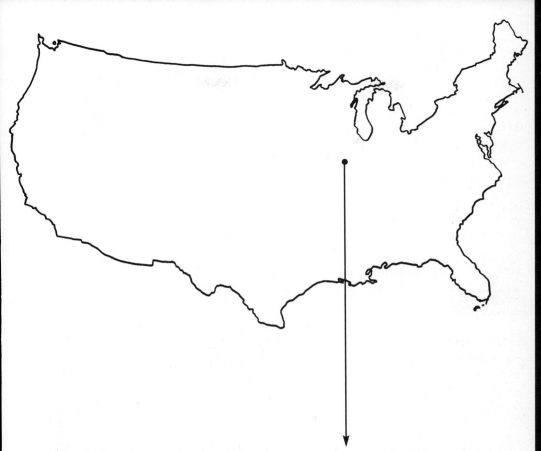

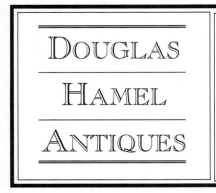

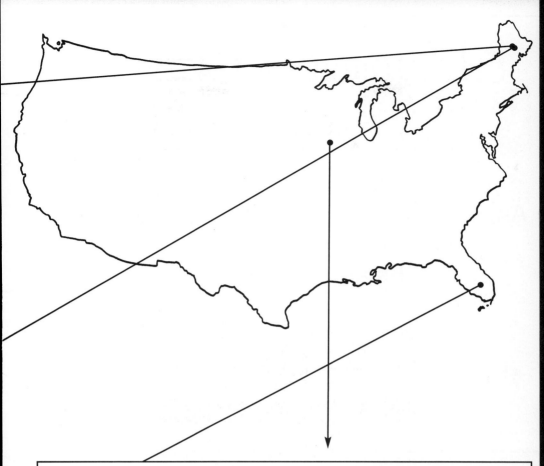

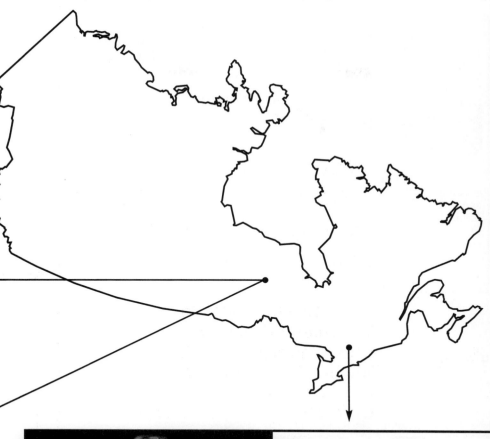

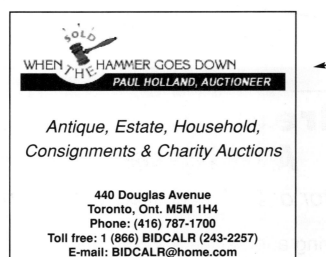

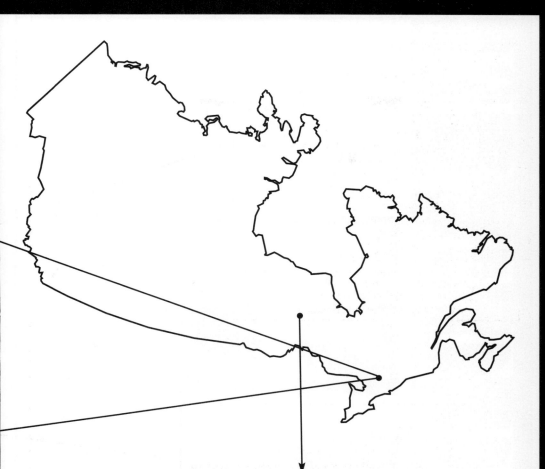

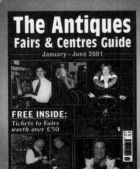

Key to Illustrations

Each illustration and descriptive caption is accompanied by a letter code. By referring to the following list of auctioneers (denoted by *) and dealers (•) the source of any item may be immediately determined. Inclusion in this edition in no way constitutes or implies a contract or binding offer on the part of any of our contributors to supply or sell the goods illustrated, or similar articles, at the prices stated. Advertisers in this year's directory are denoted by †.

If you require a valuation for an item, it is advisable to check whether the dealer or specialist will carry out this service and if there is a charge. Please mention Miller's when making an enquiry. Having found a specialist who will carry out your valuation it is best to send a photograph and description of the item to the specialist together with a stamped addressed envelope for the reply. A valuation by telephone is not possible.

Most dealers are only too happy to help you with your enquiry; however, they are very busy people and consideration of the above points would be welcomed.

KEY TO ILLUSTRATIONS

AB • The Antique Barometer Company, 5 The Lower Mall, 359 Upper Street, Camden Passage, London N1 0PD Tel: 020 7226 4992 sales@antiquebarometer.com www. antiquebarometer.com

AC • AntiqueClocks.com USA

ACO • Angela & Clive Oliver, 68 Watergate Street, Chester CH1 2LA Tel: 01244 312306/335157

AdA • Adams Antiques, Weaver House, 57 Welsh Row, Nantwich, Cheshire CW5 5EW Tel: 01270 625643 Mobile: 07901 855200

AE •† Antique European Linens, PO Box 789, Gulf Breeze, Florida 32562–0789 USA Tel: 001 850 432 4777 pandora@antiqueeuropeanlinens.com

AEF • A & E Foster Buckinghamshire Tel: 01494 562024

AEL • Argyll Etkin Ltd, 1–9 Hills Place, Oxford Circus, London W1R 1AG Tel: 020 7437 7800 argyll.etkin@btconnect.com

AG * Anderson & Garland (Auctioneers), Marlborough House, Marlborough Crescent, Newcastle-upon-Tyne, Tyne & Wear NE1 4EE Tel: 0191 232 6278

AH *† Andrew Hartley, Victoria Hall Salerooms, Little Lane, Ilkley, Yorkshire LS29 8EA Tel: 01943 816363 ahartley.finearts@talk21.com

AHa • Adrian Harrington, 64a Kensington Church Street, London W8 4DB Tel: 020 7937 1465

AL •† Ann Lingard, Ropewalk Antiques, Ropewalk, Rye, East Sussex TN31 7NA Tel: 01797 223486

ALA • Alexander Antiques, Post House, Small Dole, Henfield, West Sussex BN5 9XE Tel: 01273 493121

ALiN • Andrew Lineham Fine Glass, The Mall, Camden Passage, London N1 8ED Tel: 020 7704 0195/ 01243 576241 Mobile: 07767 702722 andrew@andrewlineham.co.uk www.andrewlineham.co.uk

ALS •† Allan Smith Clocks, Amity Cottage, 162 Beechcroft Road, Upper Stratton, Swindon, Wiltshire SN2 7QE Tel: 01793 822977 Mobile: 07778 834342 allansmithclocks@lineone.net www.allan-smith-antique-clocks.co.uk

Alte • Altea Antique Maps & Books, 3rd Floor, 91 Regent Street, London W1R 7TB Tel: 020 7494 9060

AMH •† Amherst Antiques, Monomark House, 27 Old Gloucester Street, London WC1N 3XX Mobile: 07850 350212 amherstantiques@monomark.co.uk

AMP • Acanthus Maps & Prints, 3 Marty's Lane, 17 Hampstead High Street, London NW3 1QW Tel: 0207 433 1238 aart@acanthusmaps.com www.acanthusmaps.com

AMR • Amron Antiques Tel: 01782 566895

ANA * Anthemion Auctions, 2 Llandough Trading Park, Penarth Road, Cardiff, Wales CF11 8RR Tel: 029 2071 2608

ANG •† Ancient & Gothic, Bournemouth, Dorset BH7 6JT Tel: 01202 431721

ANO •† Art Nouveau Originals, Stamford Antiques, Stamford, Lincolnshire PE9 1PX Tel: 01780 762605 anoc@compuserve.com

AnS • The Antique Shop, 30 Henley Street, Stratford-upon-Avon, Warwickshire CV37 6QW Tel: 01789 292485

AnSh • Antique Shop, 136A High Street, Tenterden, Kent TN30 6HT

ANTH • Anthea, Grays Antique Market, South Molton Lane, London W1Y 2LP Tel: 020 7493 7564

AOH • Antiques on High, 85 High Street, Oxford OX1 4BG Tel: 01865 251075

AOT • Annie's Old Things, PO Box 6, Camphill, Queensland 4152, Australia Tel: 0061412353099 annie@fan.net.au

APC • Antique Photographic Company Ltd, Lincolnshire Tel: 01949 842192 alpaco@lineone.net www.thesaurus.co.uk/cook

APO •† Apollo Antiques Ltd, The Saltisford, Birmingham Road, Warwick CV34 4TD Tel: 01926 494746/494666 www.apolloantiques.com

ARB • Arbour Antiques Ltd, Poet's Arbour, Sheep Street, Stratford-upon-Avon, Warwickshire CV37 6EF Tel: 01789 293453

ArM • Arthur Millner, 180 New Bond Street, London W1S 4RL Tel: 020 7499 4484 info@arthurmillner.com www.arthurmillner.com

ART •† Artemis Decorative Arts Ltd, 36 Kensington Church Street, London W8 4BX Tel: 020 7376 0377/ 020 7937 9900 Artemis.w8@btinternet.com

ASA •† A. S. Antiques, 26 Broad Street, Pendleton, Salford, Greater Manchester M6 5BY Tel: 0161 737 5938 Mobile: 07836 368230 as@sternshine.demon.co.uk

ASAA • ASA Antiques, 5–10 Bartlett Street, Bath, Somerset BA1 2QZ Tel: 01225 312781

ASB •† Andrew Spencer Bottomley, The Coach House, Thongs Bridge, Holmfirth, Yorkshire HD7 2TT Tel: 01484 685234 andrewbottomley@compuserve.com

ASH •† Ashburton Marbles, Great Hall, North Street, Ashburton, Devon TQ13 7DU Tel: 01364 653189

AUG • Augustus Decorative Arts Ltd, Box 700, New York, USA NY 10101 Tel: 212 333 7888 elle@portrait-miniatures.com www.portrait-miniatures.com

AW •† Alan Walker, Halfway Manor, Halfway, Nr Newbury, Berkshire RG20 8NR Tel: 01488 657670 Mobile: 07770 728397 www.alanwalker-barometers.com

B&J • Bromlea & Jonkers, 24 Hart Street, Henley-on-Thames, Oxfordshire RG9 2AU Tel: 01491 576427 bromlea.jonkers@bjbooks.co.uk www.bjbooks.co.uk

B&L * Bonhams and Langlois, Westaway Chambers, 39 Don Street, St Helier, Jersey JE2 4TR Tel: 01534 22441

B&R • Bread & Roses, Durham House Antique Centre, Sheep Street, Stow-on-the-Wold, Gloucestershire GL54 1AA Tel: 01926 817342/01451 870404

BaN • Barbara Ann Newman, London House Antiques, 4 Market Square, Westerham, Kent TN16 1AW Tel: 01959 564479 Mobile: 07850 016729

BAO • Bath Antiques Online, Bartlett Street Antiques Centre, Bartlett Street, Bath, Somerset BA1 2QZ Tel: 01225 311061 info@bathantiquesonline.com www.BathAntiquesOnline.com

BAY • George Bayntun, Manvers Street, Bath, Somerset BA1 1JW Tel: 01225 466000 EBayntun@aol.com

BB(L) * Butterfields, 7601 Sunset Boulevard, Los Angeles CA 90046, USA Tel: 00 1 323 850 7500

BB(S) * Butterfields, 220 San Bruno Avenue, San Francisco CA 94103 USA Tel: 00 1 415 861 7500

BBA * Bloomsbury Book Auctions, 3/4 Hardwick Street, Off Rosebery Avenue, London EC1R 4RY Tel: 020 7636 1945

BBo •† Bazaar Boxes, Hertfordshire Tel: 01992 504 454 Mobile: 07970 909 206 bazaarboxes@hotmail.com

BBR * BBR, Elsecar Heritage Centre, Wath Road, Elsecar, Barnsley, Yorkshire S74 8HJ Tel: 01226 745156

BDA • Briar's 20thC Decorative Arts, Yorkshire Tel: 01756 798641

Bea(E) * Bearnes, St Edmund's Court, Okehampton Street, Exeter, Devon EX4 1DU Tel: 01392 422800

BeE • Belle Epoque, 14 Herbert Street, Dublin 2, Republic of Ireland Mobile: 07973 371909

BELL • Bellhouse Antiques, Essex Tel: 01268 710364 bellhouse.antiques@virgin.net

BERA •† Berry Antiques, 3 High Street, Moreton-in-Marsh, Gloucestershire GL56 0AH Tel: 01608 652929 chris@berryantiques.com berryantiques.co.uk

BEV • Beverley, 30 Church Street, Marylebone, London NW8 8EP Tel: 020 7262 1576

BEX •† Daniel Bexfield, 26 Burlington Arcade, London W1V 9AD Tel: 020 7491 1720 antiques@bexfield.co.uk www.bexfield.co.uk

BHa •† Judy & Brian Harden Antiques, PO Box 14, Bourton-on-the-Water, Cheltenham, Gloucestershire GL54 2YR Tel: 01451 810684

BL •† Brian Loomes, Calf Haugh Farm, Pateley Bridge, North Yorkshire HG3 5HW Tel: 01423 711163 www.brianloomes.com

BLA • Blair Antiques, 14 Bonnethill Road, Pitlochry, Perthshire, Scotland PH16 5BS Tel: 01796 472624

BLH * Ambrose, Ambrose House, Old Station Road, Loughton, Essex IG10 4PE Tel: 020 8502 3951

Bns •† Brittons Jewellers, 34 Scotland Road, Nelson, Lancashire BB9 7UU Tel: 01282 697659 info@brittons-watches.co.uk www.brittons-watches.co.uk www.antique-jewelry.co.uk

Bon *† Bonhams & Brooks, Montpelier Street, Knightsbridge, London SW7 1HH Tel: 020 7393 3900

Bon(C) * Bonhams & Brooks, 65–69 Lots Road, Chelsea, London SW10 0RN Tel: 020 7393 3900

Bon(G) * Bonhams & Martel Maides Ltd, Allez Street Auction Rooms, 29 High Street, St Peter Port, Guernsey, Channel Islands GY1 4NY Tel: 01481 713463/722700

Bon(M) * Bonhams & Brooks, St Thomas's Place, Hillgate, Stockport, Greater Manchester SK1 3TZ Tel: 0161 429 8283

Bon(W) * Bonhams & Brooks West Country, Devon Fine Art Auction House, Dowell Street, Honiton, Devon EX14 8LX Tel: 01404 41872

BP •† Barling Porcelain, Essex Tel: 01621 890058 stuart@barling.uk.com www.barling.uk.com

BrH • Bright Helm Antiques & Interiors, 40 Sydney Street, Brighton, East Sussex BN1 4EP Tel: 01273 572059 Mobile: 07973 558051

Bri *† Bristol Auction Rooms, St John's Place, Apsley Road, Clifton, Bristol, Gloucestershire BS8 2ST Tel: 0117 973 7201 www.bristolauctionrooms.co.uk

BrW • Brian Watson Antique Glass, Foxwarren Cottage, High Street, Marsham, Norwich, Norfolk NR10 5QA Tel: 01263 732519 BY APPOINTMENT

BTC • Beatcity, 331 High Street, Rochester, Kent ME1 1DA Tel: 01634 305383

BUR • House of Burleigh Leicestershire Tel: 01664 454570/454114 HousBurl@aol.com

BWA • Bow Well Antiques, 103 West Bow, Edinburgh, Scotland EH1 2JP Tel: 0131 225 3335

BWe *† Biddle and Webb Ltd, Ladywood, Middleway, Birmingham, West Midlands B16 0PP Tel: 0121 455 8042 antiques@biddleandwebb.freeserve.co.uk

Byl • Bygones of Ireland Ltd, Lodge Road, Westport, County Mayo, Republic of Ireland Tel: 00 353 98 26132/25701

C&A •† Campbell & Archard Ltd, Lychgate House, Church Street, Seal, Kent TN15 0AR Tel: 01732 761153 pnarchard@aol.com www.campbellandarchard.co.uk

CAG *† The Canterbury Auction Galleries, 40 Station Road West, Canterbury, Kent CT2 8AN Tel: 01227 763337

CalT • The Calico Teddy USA Tel: 410 366 7011 CalicTeddy@aol.com www.calicoteddy.com

CAT •† Lennox Cato, 1 The Square, Church Street, Edenbridge, Kent TN8 5BD Tel: 01732 865988 Mobile: 07836 233473 cato@lennoxcato.com www.lennoxcato.com

CBO • The Chaucer Bookshop, 6–7 Beer Cart Lane, Canterbury, Kent CT1 2NY Tel: 01227 453912 chaucerbooks@canterbury.dialnet.com www.chaucer-bookshop.co.uk/main.html

CBP *† Comic Book Postal Auctions Ltd, 40–42 Osnaburgh Street, London NW1 3ND Tel: 020 7424 0007 comicbook@compuserve.com www.compalcomics.com

CCB • Colin C. Bowdell, PO Box 65, Grantham, Lincolnshire NG31 6QR Tel: 01476 563206

CDC * Capes Dunn & Co, The Auction Galleries, 38 Charles Street, Off Princess Street, Greater Manchester M1 7DB Tel: 0161 273 6060/1911

CF • Country Furniture, 79 St Leonards Road, Windsor, Berkshire SL4 3BZ Tel: 01488 683986

CGC * Cheffins Grain & Comins, 2 Clifton Road, Cambridge CB2 4BW Tel: 01223 213343

CHA • Chislehurst Antiques, 7 Royal Parade, Chislehurst, Kent BR7 6NR Tel: 020 8467 1530

ChA • No longer trading

CHE • Chelsea Clocks & Antiques, Stand H3–4, Antiquarius Market, 135 Kings Road, London SW3 4PW Tel: 020 7352 8646

CMS * Calcutt Maclean Standen, The Estate Office, Stone Street, Cranbrook, Kent TN17 3HD Tel: 01580 713828

CoA • Country Antiques (Wales), Castle Mill, Kidwelly, Carmarthenshire, Wales SA17 4UU Tel: 01554 890534

COB • Cobwebs, 78–80 Northam Road, Southampton, Hampshire SO14 0PB Tel: 023 8022 7458 www.cobwebs.uk.com

CoCo • Country Collector, 11–12 Birdgate, Pickering, Yorkshire YO18 7AL Tel: 01751 477481

CoD • Clocks of Distinction, Mississauga, Ontario, Canada info@clocksofdistinction.com www.clocksofdistinction.com

CoHA •† Corner House Antiques and Ffoxe Antiques, High Street, Lechlade, Gloucestershire GL7 3AE Tel: 01367 252007

COLL • Collinge Antiques, Old Fyffes Warehouse, Conwy Road, Llandudno Junction, Wales LL31 9LU Tel: 01492 580022 Mobile: 07836 506354

CORO •† Coromandel, London Tel: 020 8543 9115 Mobile: 07932102756

CrF • Crowdfree Antiques, Fairview, The Street, Stanton, Suffolk IP31 2DQ Tel: 0870 444 0791 info@crowdfree.com

CRN • The Crow's Nest, 3 Hope Square, opp. Brewers Quay, Weymouth, Dorset DT4 8TR Tel: 01305 786930

CRU • Mary Cruz Antiques, 5 Broad Street, Bath, Somerset BA1 5LJ Tel: 01225 334174

CS • Christopher Sykes, The Old Parsonage, Woburn, Milton Keynes, Buckinghamshire MK17 9QM Tel: 01525 290259

CTO •† Collector's Corner, PO Box 8, Congleton, Cheshire CW12 4GD Tel: 01260 270429 dave.popcorner@ukonline.co.uk

CWO • Collectors World, Stand G101, G130/143 Alfies Antique Market, 13–25 Church Street, Marylebone, London NW8 8DT Tel: 020 7723 0564 Mobile: 078 60 791588 collectorsworld@btinternet.com www.collectorsworld.net

CYA • Courtyard Antiques, 108A Causewayside, Edinburgh, Scotland EH9 1PU Tel: 0131 662 9008

DA *† Dee, Atkinson & Harrison, The Exchange Saleroom, Driffield, Yorkshire YO25 7LJ Tel: 01377 253151 exchange@dee-atkinson-harrison.co.uk www.dee-atkinson-harrison.co.uk

DAD • Decorative Arts @ Doune, Stand 26, Scottish Antique and Arts Centre, By Doune, Stirling, Scotland FK16 6HD Tel: 01786 461 439 Mobile: 077 78 475 974 gordonfoster@excite.co.uk fionamacsporran@btinternet.com

DaH • Dale House Antiques, High Street, Moreton-in-Marsh, Gloucestershire GL56 0AD Tel: 01608 650763

DAN • Andrew Dando, 4 Wood Street, Queen Square, Bath, Somerset BA1 2JQ Tel: 01225 422702 www.andrewdando.co.uk

DAn • Doll Antiques Tel: 0121 449 0637

DBA •† Douglas Bryan Antiques, The Old Bakery, St Davids Bridge, Cranbrook, Kent TN17 3HN Tel: 01580 713103

DD *† David Duggleby, The Vine Street Salerooms, Scarborough, Yorkshire YO11 1XN Tel: 01723 507111 auctions@davidduggleby.freeserve.co.uk www.davidduggleby.com

DDM * Dickinson Davy & Markham, Wrawby Street, Brigg, Humberside DN20 8JJ Tel: 01652 653666

DE • Decades, 20 Lord Street West, Blackburn, Lancashire BB2 1JX Tel: 01254 693320

DeA • Delphi Antiques, Powerscourt Townhouse Centre, South William Street, Dublin 2, Republic of Ireland Tel: 00 353 1 679 0331

DEC • Decorative Antiques, 47 Church Street, Bishop's Castle, Shropshire SY9 5AD Tel: 01588 638851 enquiries@decorative-antiques.co.uk www.decorative-antiques.co.uk

DeG • Denzil Grant, Suffolk Fine Arts, Drinkstone House, Drinkstone, Bury St Edmunds, Suffolk IP30 9TG Tel: 01449 736576

Del • Delomosne & Son Ltd, Court Close, North Wraxall, Chippenham, Wiltshire SN14 7AD Tel: 01225 891505

DFA •† Delvin Farm Antiques, Gormonston, Co Meath, Republic of Ireland Tel: 00 353 1 841 2285 info@delvinfarmpine.com john@delvinfarmpine.com www.delvinfarmpine.com

DHA • Durham House Antiques Centre, Sheep Street, Stow-on-the-Wold, Gloucestershire GL54 1AA Tel: 01451 870404

DHu • Diana Huntley Antiques, 8 Camden Passage, Islington, London N1 8ED Tel: 020 7226 4605 diana@dianahuntleyantiques.co.uk www.dianehuntleyantiques.co.uk

DIA • Mark Diamond, London Tel: 020 8508 4479

DIC • D. & B. Dickinson, The Antique Shop, 22 & 22a New Bond Street, Bath, Somerset BA1 1BA Tel: 01225 466502

DID • Didier Antiques, 58–60 Kensington Church Street, London W8 4DB Tel: 020 7938 2537 Mobile: 078 36 232634

DLC *† Lloyds International Auction Galleries, 118 Putney Bridge Road, London SW15 2NQ Tel: 020 8788 7777 www.lloyds-auction.co.uk

DLP •† The Dunlop Collection, PO Box 6269, Statesville, NC 28687 USA Tel: (704) 871 2626 or Toll Free Telephone (800) 227 1996

DMa • David March, Abbots Leigh, Bristol, BS8 3QB
Tel: 0117 937 2422

DMC * Diamond Mills & Co, 117 Hamilton Road, Felixstowe, Suffolk IP11 7BL Tel: 01394 282281

DN * Dreweatt Neate, Donnington Priory, Donnington, Newbury, Berkshire RG13 2JE Tel: 01635 553553
fineart@dreweatt-neate.co.uk

DNo • Desmond & Amanda North, The Orchard, 186 Hale Street, East Peckham, Kent TN12 5JB
Tel: 01622 871353

DNW • Dix-Noonan-Webb, 1 Old Bond Street, London W1X 3TD Tel: 020 7499 5022

DOA • Dorchester Antiques, 3 High Street, Dorchester-on-Thames, Oxfordshire OX10 7HH
Tel: 01865 341 373

DOC * Dockree's, Landmark House, 1st Floor, Station Road, Cheadle Hulme, Cheshire SK8 5AT
Tel: 0161 485 1258

DOD * Dodds Property World, Victoria Auction Galleries, 9 Chester Street, Mold, Flintshire CH7 1EB
Tel: 01352 752552

DOL •† Dollectable, 53 Lower Bridge Street, Chester, Cheshire CH1 1RS Tel: 01244 344888/679195

DOR • Dorset Reclamation, Cow Drove, Bere Regis, Wareham, Dorset BH20 7JZ Tel: 01929 472200
info@dorsetrec.u-net.com
www.dorset-reclamation.co.uk

DORO * Dorotheum, Palais Dorotheum, A–1010 Wien, Dorotheergasse 17, 1010 Austria
Tel: 0043 1 515 600

DQ • Dolphin Quay Antique Centre, Queen Street, Emsworth, Hampshire PO10 7BU
Tel: 01243 379994/379994
www.dolphin-quay-antiques.co.uk

Dri • Drivepast Automobilia, Gloucestershire
Tel: 01452 790672

DSG • Delf Stream Gallery, 14 New Street, Sandwich, Kent CT13 9AB Tel: 01304 617684

DuM * Du Mouchelles, 409 East Jefferson, Detroit, Michigan 48226, USA Tel: 001 313 963 6255

DW *† Dominic Winter Book Auctions, The Old School, Maxwell Street, Swindon, Wiltshire SN1 5DR
Tel: 01793 611340 info@dominicwinter.co.uk
www.dominicwinter.co.uk

E *† Ewbank, Burnt Common Auction Room, London Road, Send, Woking, Surrey GU23 7LN
Tel: 01483 223101
www.ewbankauctions.co.uk

EH *† Edgar Horn Fine Art Auctioneers, 46–50 South Street, Eastbourne, East Sussex BN21 4XB
Tel: 01323 410419 www.edgarhorns.com

ELM • Elms Lesters Painting Rooms
tribalelms-lesters.demon.co.uk
www.elms-lesters.demon.co.uk

ELR * ELR Auctions Ltd, The Nichols Building, Shalesmoor, Sheffield, Yorkshire S3 8UJ Tel: 0114 281 6161

EP *† Evans & Partridge, Agriculture House, High Street, Stockbridge, Hampshire SO20 6HF
Tel: 01264 810702

ERC • Zenith Antiques (Elizabeth Coupe), Hemswell Antiques Centre, Caenby Corner Estate, Hemswell Cliff, Gainsborough, Lincolnshire DN21 5TJ
Tel: 01427 668389

ES • Ernest R. Sampson, 33 West End, Redruth, Cornwall TR15 2SA Tel: 01209 212536

ESA • East Street Antiques, 42 East Street, Crewkerne, Somerset TA18 7AG Tel: 01460 78600

ET •† Early Technology, Monkton House, Old Craighall, Musselburgh, Midlothian, Scotland EH21 8SF
Tel: 0131 665 5753
michael.bennett-levy@virgin.net www.earlytech.com

EW • Elaine Whobrey, Bartlett Street Antique Centre, 5–10 Bartlett Street, Bath, Somerset BA12QZ
Tel: 01225 466689

F&C * Finan & Co, The Square, Mere, Wiltshire BA12 6DJ Tel: 01747 861411

FA • Fagins Antiques, The Old Whiteways Cider Factory, Hele, Exeter, Devon EX5 4PW Tel: 01392 882062

Fai • Fair Finds Antiques, Rait Village Antiques Centre, Rait, Perthshire, Scotland PH2 7RT
Tel: 01821 670379

FAN • Fantiques, 30 Hastings Road, Ealing, London W13 8QH Tel: 020 8840 4761 Mobile: 07956 242450

FBG * Frank H. Boos Gallery, 420 Enterprise Court, Bloomfield Hills, Michigan 48302, USA
Tel: 001 248 332 1500

FCL • French Country Living, rue de Remparts & 21 rue de L'Eglise, 06250 Mougins, France
Tel: 00 33 4 93 75 53 03
F.C.L.com@wanadoo.fr

FHF * Frank H. Fellows & Sons, Augusta House, 19 Augusta Street, Hockley, Birmingham, West Midlands B18 6JA Tel: 0121 212 2131

FIN •† M. Finkel & Daughter, 936 Pine Street, Philadelphia, Pennsylvania 19107–6128, USA
Tel: 001 215 627 7797 mailbox@finkelantiques.com
www.finkelantiques.com

FMa • Francesca Martire, Stand F131–137, Alfie's Antique Market, 13–25 Church Street, London NW8 0RH
Tel: 020 7724 4802 Mobile: 07990 523891

G(B) *† Gorringes Auction Galleries, Terminus Road, Bexhill-on-Sea, East Sussex TN39 3LR
Tel: 01424 212994 bexhill@gorringes.co.uk
www.gorringes.co.uk

G(T) * Gorringes, 15 The Pantiles, Tunbridge Wells, Kent TN2 5TD Tel: 01892 619670 www.gorringes.co.uk

G&CC •† Goss & Crested China Centre & Museum, incorporating Milestone Publications, 62 Murray Road, Horndean, Hampshire PO8 9JL
Tel: (023) 9259 7440
info@gosschinaclub.demon.co.uk
www.gosscrestedchina.co.uk

GAA • Gabrian Antiques, Hertfordshire
Tel: 01923 859675 gabrian.antiques@virgin.net

GAK *† Keys, Aylsham Salerooms, Off Palmers Lane, Aylsham, Norfolk NR11 6JA Tel: 01263 733195
www.aylshamsalerooms.co.uk

Gam * Clarke Gammon, The Guildford Auction Rooms, Bedford Road, Guildford, Surrey GU1 4SJ
Tel: 01483 880915

GBr • Geoffrey Breeze Antiques, 6 George Street, Bath, Somerset BA1 2EH Tel: 01225 466499

GH * Gardiner Houlgate, The Bath Auction Rooms, 9 Leafield Way, Corsham, Nr Bath, Somerset SN13 9SW Tel: 01225 812912 gardiner-houlgate.co.uk
www.invaluable.com/gardiner-houlgate

GHC • Great Haul of China, PO Box 233, Sevenoaks, Kent TN13 3ZN

GIL *† Gildings, 64 Roman Way, Market Harborough, Leicestershire LE16 7PQ Tel: 01858 410414
sales@gildings.co.uk

GKe • Gerald Kenyon, 6 Great Strand Street, Dublin 1, Republic of Ireland
Tel: 00 3531 873 0625/873 0488

GLa • Glassdrumman Antiques, 7 Union Square, The Pantiles, Tunbridge Wells, Kent TN4 8HE
Tel: 01892 538615

GLD •† Glade Antiques, PO Box 939, Marlow, Buckinghamshire SL7 1SR Tel: 01628 487255
Mobile: 07771 552 328 sonia@gladeantiques.com
www.gladeantiques.com

Gle * Glendinings & Co, 101 New Bond Street, London W1Y 9LG Tel: 020 7493 2445

GME *† Garry M. Emms & Co Ltd, Great Yarmouth Salerooms, Beevor Road (off South Beach Parade), Great Yarmouth, Norfolk NR30 3PS
Tel: 01493 332668 www.gt-yarmouth-auctions.com

GN •† Gillian Neale Antiques, PO Box 247, Aylesbury, Buckinghamshire HP20 1JZ
Tel: 01296 423754 Mobile: 07860 638700

GRG • Gordon Reece Galleries, Finkle Street, Knaresborough, Yorkshire HG5 8AA
Tel: 01423 866219 www.gordonreecegalleries.com

GRI • Grimes House Antiques, High Street, Moreton-in-Marsh, Gloucestershire GL56 0AT
Tel: 01608 651029 grimes_house@cix.co.uk
grimeshouse.co.uk cranberryglass.co.uk

GS • Ged Selby Antique Glass, Yorkshire
Tel: 01756 799673 by appointment

GTH * Greenslade Taylor Hunt Fine Art, Magdelene House, Church Square, Taunton, Somerset TA1 1SB Tel: 01823 332525

GV •† Garth Vincent, The Old Manor House, Allington, Nr Grantham, Lincolnshire NG32 2DH Tel: 01400 281358
garthvincent@cs.com www.guns.uk.com

GWe • Graham Webb, 59 Ship Street, Brighton, East Sussex BN1 1AE Tel: 01273 321803

GY • Gallery Yacou, 127 Fulham Road, London SW3 6RT Tel: 020 7584 2929

HA • Hallidays, The Old College, Dorchester-on-Thames, Oxfordshire OX10 7HL
Tel: 01865 340028/68 Mobile: 07860 625917

Hal * Halls Fine Art Auctions, Welsh Bridge, Shrewsbury, Shropshire SY3 8LA Tel: 01743 231212

Hal(C) * Halls Fine Art Auctions, Booth Mansion, 30 Watergate Street, Chester, Cheshire CH1 2LA
Tel: 01244 312300/312112

HAld *† Henry Aldridge & Son, Unit 1, Bath Road Business Centre, Devizes, Wiltshire SN10 1XA
Tel: 01380 729199

HALL • Hall's Nostalgia, 389 Chatham Street, Lynn MA 01902, USA Tel: 001 781 595 7757
playball@hallsnostalgia.com www.hallsnostalgia.com

HAM *† Hamptons International, Baverstock House, 93 High Street, Godalming, Surrey GU7 1AL
Tel: 01483 423567 fineart@hamptons-int.com
www.hamptons.co.uk

HARP •† Harpers Jewellers Ltd, 2/6 Minster Gates, York YO1 7HL Tel: 01904 632634
harpers@talk21.com www.vintage-watches.co.uk

HCJ • High Class Junk, 26 The Street, Appledore, Kent TN26 2BX Tel: 01233 758502

HEB • Hebeco, 47 West Street, Dorking, Surrey RH4 1BU Tel: 01306 875396 Mobile: 07710 019790

HEL • Helios Gallery, 292 Westbourne Grove, London W11 2PS Tel: 077 11 955 997 heliosgallery@btinternet.com

Herm * Hermann Historica OHG, Postfach 201009, 80010 Munchen, Germany Tel: 00 49 89 5237296

HHO • Howard Hope, 21 Bridge Road, East Molesey, Surrey KT8 9EU Tel: 020 8941 2472/8398 7130 Mobile: 07885 543267

HIS •† Erna Hiscock & John Shepherd, Chelsea Galleries, 69 Portobello Road, London W11 Tel: 01233 661407 Mobile: 0771 562 7273 erna@ernahiscockantiques.com www.ernahiscockantiques.com

HOA •† Bob Hoare Antiques, Unit Q, Phoenix Place, North Street, Lewes, East Sussex BN7 2DQ Tel: 01273 480557 bob@antiquebob.demon.co.uk www.antiquebob.demon.co.uk

HOB •† Hobday Toys, Middlesex Tel: 01895 636737 wendyhobday@freenet.co.uk

HOK * Hamilton Osborne King, 4 Main Street, Blackrock, Co Dublin, Republic of Ireland Tel: 353 1 288 5011 blackrock@hok.ie www.hok.ie

HOLL *† Holloways (RICS), 49 Parsons Street, Banbury, Oxfordshire OX16 5PF Tel: 01295 817777 enquiries@hollowaysauctioneers.co.uk www.hollowaysauctioneers.co.uk

HON •† Honan's Antiques, Crowe Street, Gort, County Galway, Republic of Ireland Tel: 00 353 91 631407 www.honansantiques.com

HOP • The Antique Garden, Grosvenor Garden Centre, Wrexham Road, Belgrave, Chester, Cheshire CH4 9EB Tel: 01244 629191 info@antique-garden.co.uk

HRQ • Harlequin Antiques, 79–81 Mansfield Road, Daybrook, Nottingham NG5 6BH Tel: 0115 967 4590

HUM • Humbleyard Fine Art, Unit 32 Admiral Vernon Arcade, Portobello Road, London W11 2DY Tel: 01362 637793 Mobile: 07836 349416

HUN • Huntercombe Manor Barn, Henley-on-Thames, Oxon RG9 5RY Tel: 01491 641349

HUNT *† Hunt Auctions, 75 E. Uwchlan Avenue, Suite 130, Exton, Pennsylvania 19341, USA Tel: 001 610 524 0822 info@huntauctions.com www.huntauctions.com

HYD * Hy Duke & Son, Dorchester Fine Art Salerooms, Dorchester, Dorset DT1 1QS Tel: 01305 265080

ICO • Iconastas, 5 Piccadilly Arcade, London W1 Tel: 020 7629 1433 iconastas@compuserve.com

IS •† Ian Sharp Antiques, 23 Front Street, Tynemouth, Tyne & Wear NE30 4DX Tel: 0191 296 0656 iansharp@sharpantiques.demon.co.uk www.sharpantiques.demon.co.uk

IW •† Islwyn Watkins, Offa's Dyke Antique Centre, 4 High Street, Knighton, Powys, Wales LD7 1AT Tel: 01547 520145

JAA * Jackson's Auctioneers & Appraisers, 2229 Lincoln Street, Cedar Falls IA 50613, USA Tel: 00 1 319 277 2256

JACK • Michael Jackson Antiques, The Quiet Woman Antiques Centre, Southcombe, Chipping Norton, Oxfordshire OX7 5QH Tel: 01608 646262 mjcig@cards.fsnet.co.uk www.our-web-site.com/cigarette-cards

JAd * James Adam & Sons, 26 St Stephen's Green, Dublin 2, Republic of Ireland Tel: 00 3531 676 0261

JaG • Japanese Gallery, 23 Camden Passage, London N1 8EA Tel: 020 7226 3347

JAK • Clive & Lynne Jackson, Gloucestershire Tel: 01242 254375 Mobile: 07710 239351

JBB • Jessie's Button Box, Great Western Antique Centre, Bartlett Street, Bath, Somerset BA1 5DY Tel: 0117 929 9065

JBe * John Bellman Auctioneers, New Pound Business Park, Wisborough Green, Billingshurst, West Sussex RH14 0AZ Tel: 01403 700858 jbellman@compuserve.com

JBL • Judi Bland, Tel: 01276 857576

JD * Gorringes inc Julian Dawson, 56 High Street, Lewes, East Sussex BN7 1XE Tel: 01273 472503 www.lewesauctions.com

JE •† Julian Eade, Surrey Tel: 020 8394 1515 Mobile: 07973 542971

JeF •† Jeffrey Formby, Orchard Cottage, East Street, Moreton-in-Marsh, Gloucestershire GL56 0LQ Tel: 01608 650558 www.formby-clocks.co.uk

JEZ • Jezebel, 14 Prince Albert Street, Brighton, East Sussex BN1 1HE Tel: 01273 206091

JH *† Jacobs & Hunt, 26 Lavant Street, Petersfield, Hampshire GU32 3EF Tel: 01730 233933 www.jacobsandhunt.co.uk

JHa • Jeanette Hayhurst Fine Glass, 32a Kensington Church Street, London W8 4HA Tel: 020 7938 1539

JHo •† Jonathan Horne, 66 Kensington Church Street, London W8 4BY Tel: 020 7221 5658 JH@jonathanhorne.co.uk www.jonathanhorne.co.uk

JIL •† Jillings Antique Clocks, Croft House, 17 Church Street, Newent, Gloucestershire GL18 1PU Tel: 01531 822100 Mobile: 07973 830110 clocks@jillings.com www.jillings.com

JJ • Jen Jones, Pontbrendu, LLanybydder, Ceredigion, Wales SA40 9UJ Tel: 01570 480610

JNic * John Nicholson, The Auction Rooms, Longfield, Midhurst Road, Fernhurst, Surrey GU27 3HA Tel: 01428 653727

JOL • Kaizen International Ltd, 88 The High Street, Rochester, Kent ME1 1JT Tel: 01634 814132

JOP • Jonathan Potter Ltd Antique Maps, 125 New Bond Street, London W1S 1DY Tel: 020 7491 3520 jpmaps@attglobal.net

JoV • Joe Vickers, Bartlett Street Antiques Market, Bath, Somerset BA1 2QZ Tel: 01225 466689

JP •† Paull's of Kenilworth, Beehive House, 125 Warwick Road, Old Kenilworth, Warwickshire CV8 1HY Tel: 01926 855253 Mobile: 07831 691254 janicepaull@btinternet.com www.janicepaull-ironstone.com

JPr • Joanna Proops Antique Textiles, 34 Belvedere, Lansdown Hill, Bath, Somerset BA1 5HR Tel: 01225 310795

JRe • John Read, 29 Lark Rise, Martlesham Heath, Ipswich, Suffolk IP5 7SA Tel: 01473 624897

JSM • J & S. Millard Antiques, Assembly Antiques, 5–8 Saville Row, Bath, Somerset BA1 2QP Tel: 01225 469785

JuC • Julia Craig, Bartlett Street Antiques Centre, 5–10 Bartlett Street, Bath, Somerset BA1 2QZ Tel: 01225 448202/310457 Mobile: 07771 786846

JUP • Jupiter Antiques, PO Box 609, Rottingdean, East Sussex BN2 7FW Tel: 01273 302865

JVM • Malchione Antiques & Sporting Collectibles, 110 Bancroft Road, Kennett Square, PA 19348, USA Tel: 610–444–3509

JW • Julian Wood, Exeter Antique Lighting, Cellar 15, The Quay, Exeter, Devon EX2 4AY Tel: 01392 490848

K • Kite, 15 Langton Street, Chelsea, London SW10 0JL Tel: 020 7351 2108 Mobile: 077 11 887120

K&D •† Kembery Antique Clocks, Bartlett Street Antiques Centre, 5 Bartlett Street, Bath, Somerset BA1 2QZ Tel: 0117 956 5281 Mobile: 07850 623237 kembery@kdclocks.co.uk www.kdclocks.co.uk

KB •† Knole Barometers, Bingham House, West Street, Somerton, Somerset TA11 7PS Tel: 01458 241015 Mobile: 07785 364567 dccops@btconnect.com

KID *† George Kidner, The Old School, The Square, Pennington, Lymington, Hampshire SO41 8GN Tel: 01590 670070 www.georgekidner.co.uk

KJ • Katie Jones, 195 Westbourne Grove, London W11 2SB Tel: 020 7243 5600

KOLN * Auction Team Koln, Postfach 50 11 19, 50971 Koln, Germany Tel: 00 49 0221 38 70 49 auction@breker.com

KT * Kidson Trigg, Estate Office, Friars Farm, Sevenhampton, Highworth, Swindon, Wiltshire SN6 7PZ Tel: 01793 861000

L • Lawrence Fine Art Auctioneers, South Street, Crewkerne, Somerset TA18 8AB Tel: 01460 73041

L&E * Locke & England, 18 Guy Street, Leamington Spa, Warwickshire CV32 4RT Tel: 01926 889100 www.auctions-online.com/locke

L&L • Linen & Lace, Shirley Tomlinson, Halifax Antiques Centre, Queens Road/Gibbet Street, Halifax, Yorkshire HX1 4LR Tel: 01422 366657 Mobile: 07711 763454

L&T * Lyon & Turnbull, 33 Broughton Place, Edinburgh, Scotland EH1 3RR Tel: 0131 557 8844

Lan • Lovejo Ann'tiques, PO Box 8289, Tamworth, West Midlands B79 9EE Tel: 01827 373254 Mobile: 07767 881161 joanne@lovejoanntiques.fsnet.co.uk

LAY * David Lay ASVA, Auction House, Alverton, Penzance, Cornwall TR18 4RE Tel: 01736 361414

LBO • Laura Bordignon Antiques, PO Box 6247, Finchingfield CM7 4ER Tel: 01371 811 791 Mobile: 07778 787929 laurabordignon@hotmail.com

LBr • Lynda Brine, Assembly Antique Centre, 5–8 Saville Row, Bath, Somerset BA1 2QP Tel: 01225 448488

LCM * Galeria Louis C. Morton, GLC A7073L IYS, Monte Athos 179, Col. Lomas de Chapultepec, CP11000, Mexico Tel: 52 5520 5005 glmorton@prodigy.net.mx www.lmorton.com

LDC • L & D Collins, London Tel: 020 7584 0712

LEW * Gorringes inc Julian Dawson, 56 High Street, Lewes, East Sussex BN7 1XE Tel: 01273 478221

LF * Lambert & Foster, 102 High Street, Tenterden, Kent TN30 6HT Tel: 01580 763233

LFA *† Law Fine Art, Fir Tree Cottage, Church Lane, Brimpton, Berkshire RG7 4TJ Tel: 0118 971 0353 info@lawfineart.co.uk www.lawfineart.co.uk

LIB • Libra Antiques Tel: 01580 860569

LIN • Peter Linden, Georges Avenue, Blackrock, Dublin, Republic of Ireland Tel: 00 3531 288 5875 lind@indigo.ie www.peterlinden.com

KEY TO ILLUSTRATIONS

LJ   *   Leonard Joel Auctioneers, 333 Malvern Road, South Yarra, Victoria 3141, Australia Tel: 03 9826 4333 decarts@ljoel.com.au or jewellery@ljoel.com.au www.ljoel.com.au

LT   *†   Louis Taylor Auctioneers & Valuers, Britannia House, 10 Town Road, Hanley, Stoke-on-Trent, Staffordshire ST1 2QG Tel: 01782 214111

LW   *†   Lawrences Auctioneers, Norfolk House, 80 High Street, Bletchingley, Surrey RH1 4PA Tel: 01883 743323 www.lawrencesbletchingley.co.uk

M   *   Morphets of Harrogate, 6 Albert Street, Harrogate, Yorkshire HG1 1JL Tel: 01423 530030

Ma   •   Marie Antiques, Stand G136–138, Alfie's Antique Market,13–25 Church Street, London NW8 8DT Tel: 020 7706 3727 marie136@globalnet.co.uk www.marieantiques.co.uk

MAA   •   Mario's Antiques, 23 The Mall, Camden Passage, 359 Upper Street, London N1 0PD Tel: 0207 226 2426 marwan@barazi.sreaming.net www.marios.antiques.com

MAG   •   Magna Gallery, 41 High Street, Oxford OX1 4AP Tel: 01865 245805

Mal(O)   *   Mallams, Bocardo House, 24 St Michael's Street, Oxford OX1 2EB Tel: 01865 241358 oxford@mallams.co.uk

MAR   *   Frank R. Marshall & Co, Marshall House, Church Hill, Knutsford, Cheshire WA16 6DH Tel: 01565 653284

MAr   •   Mint Arcade, 71 The Mint, Rye, East Sussex TN31 7EW Tel: 01797 225952

MARK   •   20th Century Marks, 12 Market Square, Westerham, Kent TN16 1AW Tel: 01959 562221 lambarda@msn.com

MAT   *   Christopher Matthews, 23 Mount Street, Harrogate, Yorkshire HG2 8DQ Tel: 01423 871756

MB   •†   Mostly Boxes, 93 High Street, Eton, Windsor, Berkshire SL4 6AF Tel: 01753 858470

MCA   *†   Mervyn Carey, Twysden Cottage, Benenden, Cranbrook, Kent TN17 4LD Tel: 01580 240283

MD   •   Much Ado About Deco, The Antiques Centre, 59–60 Ely Street, Stratford-upon-Avon, Warwickshire CV37 6LN Tel: 01789 204180

MEA   *†   Mealy's, Chatsworth Street, Castle Comer, Co Kilkenny, Republic of Ireland Tel: 00 353 56 41229 info@mealys.com www.mealys.com

MFB   •   Manor Farm Barn Antiques Tel: 01296 658941 Mobile: 07720 286607 mfbn@btinternet.com btwebworld.com/mfbantiques

MGa   •   Marilyn Garrow, Mobile: 07774 842074 marogarrow@aol.com

MI   •†   Mitofsky, 101 Terenure Road East, Dublin 6, Republic of Ireland Tel: 00 353 1 492 0033 info@mitofskyartdeco.com www.mitofskyartdeco.com

MIN   •   Ministry of Pine, The Ministry, St James Hall, Union Street, Trowbridge, Wiltshire BA14 8RU Tel: 01225 719500 Mobile: 07770 588536 ministryofpine@virgin.net

Mit   *   Mitchells, Fairfield House, Station Road, Cockermouth, Cumbria Tel: 01900 827800

MLa   •†   Marion Langham, London Tel: 020 7730 1002 ladymarion@btinternet.co.uk www.ladymarion.co.uk

MLL   •†   Millers Antiques Ltd, Netherbrook House, 86 Christchurch Road, Ringwood, Hampshire BH24 1DR Tel: 01425 472062 mail@millers-antiques.co.uk www.millers-antiques.co.uk

MLu   •   Michael Lucas Antiques, Admiral Vernon Antiques Arcade, Portobello Road, London W11 Tel: 020 8650 1107 Mobile: 07850 388288

MoS   •   Morgan Stobbs Mobile: 07702 206817 By appointment

MSB   •   Marilynn and Sheila Brass, PO Box 380503, Cambridge MA 02238–0503, USA Tel: 617 491 6064

MTay   •†   Martin Taylor Antiques, 140B Tettenhall Road, Wolverhampton, West Midlands WV6 0BQ Tel: 01902 751166 Mobile: 07836 636524 enquiries@mtaylor-antiques.co.uk www.mtaylor-antiques.co.uk

MUL   *†   Mullock & Madeley, The Old Shippon, Wall-under-Heywood, Church Stretton, Shropshire SY6 7DS Tel: 01694 771771 auctions@mullockmadeley.co.uk www.mullockmadeley.co.uk

NAW   •†   Newark Antiques Warehouse, Old Kelham Road, Newark, Nottinghamshire NG24 1BX Tel: 01636 674869 enquiries@newarkantiques.co.uk

NCA   •   New Century, 69 Kensington Church Street, London W8 4BG Tel: 020 7376 2810/020 7937 2410

NCL   •†   Northern Clocks, Boothsbank Farm, Worsley, Manchester M28 1LL Tel: 0161 790 8414 info@northernclocks.co.uk www.northernclocks.co.uk

NEW   •   Newsum Antiques, 2 High Street, Winchcombe, Gloucestershire GL54 5HT Tel: 01242 603446 Mobile: 07968 196668

NOA   *   New Orleans Auction Galleries, Inc., 801 Magazine Street, AT 510 Julia, New Orleans, Louisiana 70130, USA Tel: 00 1 504 566 1849

NOST   •†   Nostalgia, Hollands Mill, 61 Shaw Heath, Stockport, Cheshire SK3 8BH Tel: 0161 477 7706 www.nostalgiafireplaces.co.uk

NOTT   •   Notts Pine, The Old Redhouse Farm, Stratton-on-the-Fosse, Bath, Somerset BA3 4QE Tel: 01761 419911

NS   •   Nicholas Shaw Antiques, Great Grooms Antiques Centre, Parbrook, Billingshurst, West Sussex RH14 9EU Tel: 01403 786656/01403 785731 Mobile: 07785 643000 silver@nicholas-shaw.com www.nicholas-shaw.com

NSF   *   Neal Sons & Fletcher, 26 Church Street, Woodbridge, Suffolk IP12 1DP Tel: 01394 382263

OCH   •   Gillian Shepherd, Old Corner House Antiques, 6 Poplar Road, Wittersham, Tenterden, Kent TN30 7PG Tel: 01797 270236

OCS   •†   The Old Clock Shop, 63 High Street, West Malling, Kent Tel: 01732 843246 www.theoldclockshop.co.uk

OD   •   Offa's Dyke Antique Centre, 4 High Street, Knighton, Powys, Wales LD7 1AT Tel: 01547 528635/528940

OE   •   Orient Expressions, Assembly Antiques Centre, 5–8 Saville Row, Bath, Somerset BA1 2QP Tel: 01225 313399 Mobile: 0788 1588 314

OFM   •   The Old French Mirror Company, Nightingales, Greys Green, Rotherfield Greys, Henley-on-Thames, Oxon RG9 4QQ Tel: 01491 629913 bridget@debreanski.freeserve.co.uk www.frenchmirrors.co.uk

OIA   •   Oliff's Architectural Antiques, 21 Lower Redland Road, Redland, Bristol BS6 6TB Tel: 0117 923 9232/0117 942 2900 marcus@olliffs.com www.olliffs.com

Oli   *†   Olivers, Olivers Rooms, Burkitts Lane, Sudbury, Suffolk CO10 1HB Tel: 01787 880305

OND   •   Ondines, 14 The Mall, Camden Passage, London N1 Tel: 01865 882465

ONS   *   Onslow's, The Depot, 2 Michael Road, London SW6 2AD Tel: 020 7371 0505 Mobile: 078 31 473 400

OO   •   Pieter Oosthuizen, Unit 4 Bourbon Hanby Antiques Centre, 151 Sydney Street, London SW3 6NT Tel: 020 7460 3078

OPB   •   Olde Port Bookshop, 18 State Street, Newburyport, Massachusetts 01950, USA Tel: 001 978 462 0100 Oldeport@ttlc.net

OTB   •   Old Tackle Box, PO Box 55, Cranbrook, Kent TN17 3ZU Tel: 01580 713979

OT   •   Otter Antiques, 20 High Street, Wallingford, Oxon OX10 0BP Tel: 01491 825544

P   *†   Phillips, 101 New Bond Street, London W1Y 0AS Tel: 020 7629 6602 www.phillips-auctions.com

P(B)   *   Phillips, 1 Old King Street, Bath, Somerset BA1 2JT Tel: 01225 310609

P(Ba)   *   Phillips Bayswater, 10 Salem Road, London W2 4DL Tel: 020 7229 9090

P(E)   *   Phillips, 38–39 Southernhay East, Exeter, Devon EX1 1PE Tel: 01392 439025

P(EA)   *   Phillips, 32 Boss Hall Road, Ipswich, Suffolk IP1 59J Tel: 01473 740494

P(Ed)   *   Phillips Scotland, 65 George Street, Edinburgh, Scotland EH2 2JL Tel: 0131 225 2266

P(L)   *   Phillips Leeds, 17a East Parade, Leeds, Yorkshire LS1 2BH Tel: 0113 2448011

P(NW)   *   Phillips North West, New House, 150 Christleton Road, Chester CH3 5TD Tel: 01244 313936

P(Pr)   *   Phillips Cornwall, Cornubia Hall, Eastcliffe Road, Par, Cornwall PL24 2AQ Tel: 0172 681 4047

P(S)   *   Phillips Fine Art Auctioneers, 49 London Road, Sevenoaks Kent TN13 1AR Tel: 01732 740310

P(Sy)   *   Phillips Sydney, 162 Queen Street, Woollahra, Sydney NSW 2025, Australia Tel: 00 612 9326 1588

P(WM)   *   Phillips, The Old House, Station Road, Knowle, Solihull, West Midlands B93 0HT Tel: 01564 776151

P(Z)   *   Phillips, Kreuzstrasse 54 8008, Zurich, Switzerland Tel: 00 41 1 254 2400

P&T   •   Pine & Things, Portobello Farm, Campden Road, Nr Shipston-on-Stour, Warwickshire CV36 4PY Tel: 01608 663849

PAB   •   Paolo Bonino, Stand SO01, Alfies Antique Market, 13–25 Church Street, London NW8 8DT Tel: 07767 498766/020 7624 2481

PAC   •   The Potteries Antique Centre, 271 Waterloo Road, Cobridge, Stoke on Trent, Staffordshire ST6 3HR Tel: 01782 201455

PAO   •†   P. A. Oxley Antique Clocks, The Old Rectory, Cherhill, Nr Calne, Wiltshire SN11 8UX Tel: 01249 816227 p.a.oxley@btinternet.com www.british-antiqueclocks.com

PCA   •   Patricia Cater, Gloucestershire Tel: 01451 830944 Patriciacareorg@aol.com www.PatriciaCater-OreintalArt.com

PEx   •†   Piano-Export, Bridge Road, Kingswood, Bristol, Gloucestershire BS15 4FW Tel: 0117 956 8300

PF *† Peter Francis, Curiosity Sale Room, 19 King Street, Carmarthen, South Wales SA31 1BH Tel: 01267 233456 Peterfrancis@valuers.fsnet.co.uk www.peterfrancis.co.uk

PFK *† Penrith Farmers' & Kidd's plc, Skirsgill Salerooms, Penrith, Cumbria CA11 0DN Tel: 01768 890781 penrith.farmers@virgin.net

PGA • Paul Gibbs Antiques, 25 Castle Street, Conwy, Gwynedd, Wales LL32 8AY Tel: 01492 593429 teapot@marketsite.co.uk

PHA •† Paul Hopwell, 30 High Street, West Haddon, Northamptonshire NN6 7AP Tel: 01788 510636 hopwellp@aol.com www.antiqueoak.co.uk

PHo • Paul Howard, Bourbon Hanby Antiques Centre, 151 Sydney Street, Chelsea, London SW3 6NT Tel: 020 7352 4113 Mobile: 079 73 507145

PIC • David & Susan Pickles Tel: 01282 707673 Mobile: 07976 236983

PJo • Paul Jones, The Quiet Woman Antiques Centre, Southcombe, Chipping Norton, Oxfordshire OX7 5QH Tel: 01608 646262

PLB • Planet Bazaar, 149 Drummond Street, London NW1 2PB Tel: 0207 387 8326 Mobile: 07956 326301 maureen@planetbazaar.demon.co.uk www.planetbazaar.co.uk

POT • Pot Board Tel: 01267 236623 Gill@potboard.co.uk www.potboard.co.uk

PPC •† Period Piano Company, Park Farm Oast, Hareplain Road, Biddenden, Nr Ashford, Kent TN27 8LJ Tel: 01580 291393 www.periodpiano.com

PrB • Pretty Bizarre, 170 High Street, Deal, Kent CT14 6BQ Tel: 07973 794537

PSA •† Pantiles Spa Antiques, 4, 5, 6 Union House, The Pantiles, Tunbridge Wells, Kent TN4 8HE Tel: 01892 541377 Mobile: 07711 283655 psa.wells@btinternet.com www.antiques-tun-wells-kent.co.uk

PSC • Peter & Sonia Cashman, Bartlett Street Antique Centre, 5–10 Bartlett Street, Bath, Somerset BA1 2QZ Tel: 01225 469497 Mobile: 0780 8609860

PT •† Pieces of Time, (1–7 Davies Mews), 26 South Molton Lane, London W1Y 2LP Tel: 020 7629 2422 info@antique-watch.com www.antique-watch.com

PTh • Patrick Thomas, 62a West Street, Dorking, Surrey RH4 1BS Tel: 01306 743661

PVD •† Puritan Values at the Dome, St Edmunds Business Park, St Edmunds Road, Southwold, Suffolk IP18 6BZ Tel: 01502 722211 Mobile: 07966 371676 sales@puritanvalues.com www.puritanvalues.com

Q&C •† Q&C Militaria, 22 Suffolk Road, Cheltenham, Gloucestershire GL50 2AQ Tel: 01242 519815 Mobile: 07778 613977 john@qc-militaria.freeserve.co.uk www.qcmilitaria.com

RAR * Romsey Auction Rooms CLOSING DOWN IN MARCH 2001

RAV • Ravenwood Antique Tel: 01886 884 456 alan@arthur81.freeserve.co.uk

RAY • Derek & Tina Rayment Antiques, Orchard House, Barton Road, Barton, Nr Farndon, Cheshire SY14 7HT Tel: 01829 270429

RBA • Roger Bradbury Antiques, Church Street, Coltishall, Norfolk NR12 7DJ Tel: 01603 737444

RBB *† Brightwells Ltd, Ryelands Road, Leominster, Herefordshire HR6 8NZ Tel: 01568 611122 fineart@brightwells.com www.brightwells.com

RdeR •† Rogers de Rin, 76 Royal Hospital Road, London SW3 4HN Tel: 020 7352 9007

RdV • Sudbury Antiques, Roger de Ville, Derbyshire Tel: 01889 564311 Mobile: 07798 793857

Recl/ RECL • Minchinhampton Architectural Salvage Co, Cirencester Road, Chalford, Stroud, Gloucestershire GL6 8PE Tel: 01285 760886 masco@catbrain.com www.catbrain.com

RED • Red Lion Antiques, New Street, Petworth, West Sussex GU28 0AS Tel: 01798 344485

REEL • The Reel Poster Gallery, 72 Westbourne Grove, London W2 5SH Tel: 020 7727 4488

REI •† Reindeer Antiques Ltd, 43 Watling Street, Potterspury, Nr Towcester, Northamptonshire NN12 7QD Tel: 01908 542407 www.reindeerantiques.co.uk

ReJ • Regal Jewellery, 372 Sheffield Road, Chesterfield, Derbyshire S41 8LE Tel: 01246 233972 info@regaljewellry.com

REN • Paul & Karen Rennie, 13 Rugby Street, London WC1N 3QT Tel: 020 7405 0220

RES • Resners

RFA * Rowley Fine Art, The Old Bishop's Palace, Little Downham, Ely, Cambridgeshire CB6 2TD Tel: 01353 699177 mail@rowleyfineart.com www.rowleyfineart.com

RGa • Richard Gardner Antiques, Swanhouse Market Square, Petworth, West Sussex GU28 0AN Tel: 01798 343411

RKa • Richardson & Kailas London Tel: 020 7371 0491 By appointment

RL • Roger Lamb Antiques, The Square, Stow-on-the Wold, Gloucestershire GL54 1AB Tel: 01451 831 371

RM * RM Auctions, Inc, One Classic Car Drive, Ontario NOP 1AO, Canada Tel: 00 519 352 4575

RMC •† Romsey Medal Centre, 5 Bell Street, Romsey, Hampshire SO51 8GY Tel: 01794 324488 post@romseymedals.co.uk www.romseymedals.co.uk

ROSc *† R. O. Schmitt Fine Art, Box 1941, Salem, New Hampshire 03079, USA Tel: 603 893 5915 bob@roschmittfinearts.com www.antiqueclockauction.com

RPh •† Robert Phelps Ltd, 133–135 St Margaret's Road, East Twickenham, Middlesex TW1 1RG Tel: 020 8892 1778/7129 antiques@phelps.co.uk www.phelps.co.uk

RPI *† Raymond P. Inman, The Auction Galleries, 35 & 40 Temple Street, Brighton, East Sussex BN1 3BH Tel: 01273 774777 www.raymondinman.co.uk

RTo *† Rupert Toovey & Co Ltd, Star Road, Partridge Green, West Sussex RH13 8RA Tel: 01403 711744 auctions@rupert-toovey.com www.rupert-toovey.com

RTW •† Richard Twort Somerset Tel: 01934 641900 Mobile: 07711 939789

RUL • Rules Antiques, 62 St Leonards Road, Windsor, Berkshire Tel: 01753 833211/01491 642062

RUSK • Ruskin Decorative Arts, 5 Talbot Court, Stow-on-the-Wold, Cheltenham, Gloucestershire GL54 1DP Tel: 01451 832254

RWA • Ray Walker Antiques, Burton Arcade, 296 Westbourne Grove, London W11 2PS Tel: 020 8464 7981 rw.walker@btinternet.com

RYA •† Robert Young Antiques, 68 Battersea Bridge Road, London SW11 3AG Tel: 020 7228 7847

S * Sotheby's, 34–35 New Bond Street, London W1A 2AA Tel: 020 7293 5000

S(Am) * Sotheby's Amsterdam, De Boelelaan 30, 1083 HJ Amsterdam, Netherlands Tel: 00 31 20 550 22 00

S(G) * Sotheby's, 13 Quai du Mont Blanc, Geneva CH–1201, Switzerland Tel: 00 41 22 908 4800

S(Mon) * Sotheby's Monaco, Le Sporting d'Hiver, Place du Casino 98001, Cedex Monaco Tel: 00 377 93 30 8880

S(NY) * Sotheby's, 1334 York Avenue, New York NY 10021, USA Tel: 00 1 212 606 7000

S(S) * Sotheby's Sussex, Summers Place, Billingshurst, West Sussex RH14 9AD Tel: 01403 833500

S(Z) * Sotheby's Zurich, Gessneralee 1, CH–8021 Zurich, Switzerland Tel: 00 41 1 226 2200

SAA/ SAAC • Scottish Antique and Arts Centre, Carse of Cambus, Doune, Perthshire, Scotland FK16 6HD Tel: 01786 841203

Sam •† Sambourne House Antiques, Minety, Malmesbury, Wiltshire SN16 9RQ Tel: 01666 860288

Sama • Samax, Bartlett Street Antiques Centre, 5–10 Bartlett Street, Bath, Somerset BA1 2QZ Tel: 01225 466689

SAMI • Samiramis Ltd, E18–20 Grays Mews Antique Market, Davies Mews, London W1Y 2DY Tel: 020 7629 1161

SAN • Steven F. Anton Antiques & Collectables, Scottish Antique and Arts Centre, Carse of Cambus, Doune, Perthshire, Scotland FK16 6HD Tel: 01786 841203/01383 860520

SAS *† Special Auction Services, The Coach House, Midgham Park, Reading, Berkshire RG7 5UG Tel: 0118 971 2949 www.invaluable.com/sas/

SCO • Peter Scott, Stand 39, Bartlett Street Antiques Centre, Bath, Somerset BA1 2QZ Tel: 01225 310457/0117 986 8468 Mobile: 07850 639770

SEA •† Mark Seabrook Antiques, 9 West End, West Haddon, Northamptonshire NN6 7AY Tel: 01788 510772 Mobile: 07770 721931

SeH •† Seventh Heaven, Chirk Mill, Chirk, Wrexham, County Borough, Wales LL14 5BU Tel: 01691 777622 www.seventh-heaven.co.uk

SER •† Serendipity, 125 High Street, Deal, Kent CT14 6BQ Tel: 01304 369165/01304 366536 dipityantiques@aol.com

SEY • Mike Seymour, The Directors Cut, The Antiques Centre, Ely Street, Stratford-upon-Avon, Warwickshire CV37 6LN Mobile: 07931 345784 mike@seymour.gsbusiness.co.uk

SHa •† Shapiro & Co, Stand 380, Gray's Antique Market, 58 Davies Street, London W1Y 5LP Tel: 020 7491 2710

SIL • The Silver Shop, Powerscourt Townhouse Centre, St Williams Street, Dublin 2, Republic of Ireland Tel: 00 3531 6794147

SK * Skinner Inc, The Heritage On The Garden, 63 Park Plaza, Boston MA 02116, USA Tel: 001 617 350 5400

SK(B) * Skinner Inc, 357 Main Street, Bolton MA 01740, USA Tel: 00 1 978 779 6241

SLM	*	Sloan's Auctioneers & Appraisers, Miami Gallery, 8861 NW 18th Terrace, Suite 100, Miami, Florida 33172, USA Tel: 00 1 305 592 2575/800 660 4524
SLN	*	Sloan's, C G Sloan & Company Inc., 4920 Wyaconda Road, North Bethesda MD 20852, USA Tel: 00 1 301 468 4911/669 5066 www.sloansauction.com
SMI	•†	Skip & Janie Smithson, Lincolnshire Tel: 01754 810265 Mobile: 07831 399180
SMW	•	Sporting Memorabilia of Warwick, 13 Market Place, Warwick CV34 4FS Tel: 01926 410600 Mobile: 07860 269340 sales@sportantiques.com sportsantiques.com
SO	•†	Sam Orr Antique Clocks, 36 High Street, Hurstpierpoint, Nr Brighton, East Sussex BN6 9RG Tel: 01273 832081 Mobile: 07860 230888 www.samorr.co.uk
Som	•†	Somervale Antiques, 6 Radstock Road, Midsomer Norton, Bath, Somerset BA3 2AJ Tel: 01761 412686 Mobile: 07885 088022 ronthomas@somervaleantiquesglass.co.uk www.somervaleantiquesglass.co.uk
SPA	•	Sporting Antiques, 10 Union Square, The Pantiles, Tunbridge Wells, Kent TN4 8HE RTel: 01892 522661
SPT	•	Sporting Times Gone By Tel: 01903 885656 Mobile: 07976 942059 www.sportingtimes.co.uk
SQA	•	Squirrel Antiques, Scottish Antique and Arts Centre, Carse of Cambus, Doune, Perthshire, Scotland FK16 6HD Tel: 01786 841203
STA	•	Michelina & George Stacpoole, Main Street, Adare, Co Limerick, Republic of Ireland Tel: 00 353 61 396 409
StC	§	St Clere Carlton Ware, PO Box 161, Sevenoaks, Kent TN15 6GA Tel: 01474 853630 stclere@aol.com www.stclere.co.uk
STS	•	Shaw to Shore, Church Street Antiques Centre, Stow-on-the-Wold, Gloucestershire GL54 1BB Tel: 01451 870186
SuA	•	Suffolk House Antiques, High Street, Yoxford, Suffolk IP17 3EP Tel: 01728 668122 Mobile: 07860 521583
SWA	•†	S.W. Antiques, Abbey Showrooms, Newlands, Pershore, Worcestershire WR10 1BP Tel: 01386 555580 sw-antiques@talk21.com www.sw-antiques.co.uk
SWB	•†	Sweetbriar Gallery, Robin Hood Lane, Helsby, Cheshire WA6 9NH Tel: 01928 723851 sweetbr@globalnet.co.uk www.sweetbriar.co.uk
SWG	•	Swan Gallery, High Street, Burford, Oxfordshire OX18 4RE Tel: 01993 822244
SWO	*†	G. E. Sworder & Sons, 14 Cambridge Road, Stansted Mountfitchet, Essex CM24 8BZ Tel: 01279 817778 www.sworder.co.uk
TAM	*	Tamlyn & Son, 56 High Street, Bridgwater, Somerset TA6 3BN Tel: 01278 458241
TED	•†	Teddy Bears of Witney, 99 High Street, Witney, Oxfordshire OX8 6LY Tel: 01993 702616/706616
TEMP	•	Bob Templeman at Scottish Antique and Arts Centre, Carse of Cambus, Doune, Perthshire, Scotland FK16 6HD Tel: 01786 841203
TEN	*	Tennants, The Auction Centre, Harmby Road, Leyburn, Yorkshire DL8 5SG Tel: 01969 623780
TeW	•	Terry West, 2 Taylors Avenue, Cleethorpes, Lincolnshire DN35 0LD Tel: 01472 508729 Mobile: 07808 693287
THOM	•	S & A Thompson Tel: 01306 711970 Mobile: 07770 882746
TIC	•	Tickers, 31 Old Northam Road, Southampton, Hampshire SO14 0NZ Tel: 02380 234431
TLG	•	The Lamp Gallery, Talbot Walk Antiques Centre,The Talbot Hotel, High Street, Ripley, Surrey GU23 6BB Tel: 01483 211724
TMA	*†	Brown & Merry, Tring Market Auctions, The Market Premises, Brook Street, Tring, Hertfordshire HP23 5EF Tel: 01442 826446 sales@tringmarketauctions.co.uk www.tringmarketauctions.co.uk
TO	•	Tombland Antique Centre, Augustine Steward House, 14 Tombland, Norwich, Norfolk Tel: 01603 619129
TOM	•†	Charles Tomlinson Chester Tel: 01244 318395 Charles.Tomlinson@lineone.net charles.tomlinson@btinternet.com www.lineone.net/-charles.tomlinson
TOT	•	Totem, 168 Stoke Newington, Church Street, London 020 7275 0234
TPC	•†	Pine Cellars, 39 Jewry Street, Winchester, Hampshire SO23 8RY Tel: 01962 777546/867014
TRA	•	Tramps, Tuxford Hall, Lincoln Road, Tuxford, Newark, Nottinghamshire NG22 0HR Tel: 01777 872 543 info@trampsuk.com
TREA	*	Treadway Gallery, Inc and John Toomey Gallery, Treadway Gallery, Inc, 2029 Madison Road, Cincinnati, Ohio 45208, USA Tel: 001 513 321 6742
TRL	•	Thomson, Roddick & Medcalf, Coleridge House, Shaddongate, Carlisle, Cumbria CA2 5TU Tel: 01228 528939
TRM	*	Thomson Roddick & Medcalf, 20 Murray Street, Annan, Scotland DG12 6EG Tel: 01461 202575
TT	•	Treasures in Textiles, 53 Russian Drive, Liverpool, Merseyside L13 7BS Tel: 0151 281 6025
TUN	•	Union Square, The Pantiles, Tunbridge Wells, Kent TN4 8HE Tel: 01892 533708 twantique@aol.com www.staffordshirefigures.com
TWAC	•	Talbot Walk Antiques Centre, The Talbot Hotel, High Street, Ripley, Surrey GU23 6BB Tel: 01483 211724
TWD	•	The Watch Department, 49 Beauchamp Place, London SW3 1NY Tel: 020 7589 4005 thewatch.dept@virgin.net www.watchdept.co.uk
TWh	•	Tim Wharton, 24 High Street, Redbourn, Nr St Albans, Hertfordshire AL3 7LL Tel: 01582 794371 Mobile: 07850 622880
TWr	•	Tim Wright Antiques, Richmond Chambers, 147 Bath Street, Glasgow G2 4SQ, Scotland Tel: 0141 221 0364
UNI	•	Unicorn Antique Centre, 2 Romney Enterprise Centre, North Street, New Romney, Kent TN28 8DW Tel: 01797 361940
US	•	Ulla Stafford Tel: 0118 934 3208 Mobile: 07944 815104
VB	•	Variety Box, 16 Chapel Place, Tunbridge Wells, Kent TN1 1YQ Tel: 01892 531868
VBo	•	Vernon Bowden, Bournemouth, Dorset Tel: 01202 763806
VS	*†	T. Vennett-Smith, 11 Nottingham Road, Gotham, Nottinghamshire NG11 0HE Tel: 0115 983 0541 info@vennett-smith.com www.vennett-smith.com
VSP	*	Van Sabben Poster Auctions, PO Box 2065, 1620 EB Hoorn, Netherlands Tel: 31 229 268203 uboersma@sabbenposterauctions.nl www.vsabbenposterauctions.nl
WA	*†	Whyte's Auctioneers, 30 Marlborough Street, Dublin 1, Republic of Ireland Tel: 00 353 1 874 6161 info@whytes.ie www.whytes.ie
Wa	•	Wartski Ltd, 14 Grafton Street, London W1X 4DE Tel: 020 7493 1141 www.wartski.com
WAB	•	Warboys Antiques, St Ives, Cambridgeshire Tel: 01480 463891 john.lambden@virgin.net
WAC	•	Worcester Antiques Centre, Reindeer Court, Mealcheapen Street, Worcester WR1 4DF Tel: 01905 610680
Wai	•	Peter Wain, Glynde Cottage, Longford, Market Drayton, Shropshire TF9 3PW Tel: 01630 638358
WAL	*†	Wallis & Wallis, West Street Auction Galleries, Lewes, East Sussex BN7 2NJ Tel: 01273 480208 auctions@wallisandwallis.co.uk www.wallisandwallis.co.uk
WBB	•†	William Bentley Billiards, Standen Manor Farm, Hungerford, Berkshire RG17 0RB Tel: 01488 681711
WD	*	Weller & Dufty Ltd, 141 Bromsgrove Street, Birmingham, West Midlands B5 6RQ Tel: 0121 692 1414 wellerdufty@freewire.co.uk www.welleranddufty.co.uk
WeA	•	Wenderton Antiques Kent Tel: 01227 720295 By appointment only
WEL	•	Wells Reclamation & Co, Coxley, Nr Wells, Somerset Tel: 01749 677087
WELD	•	J. W. Weldon, 55 Clarendon Street, Dublin 2, Republic of Ireland Tel: 00 353 1 677 1638
WELL	•†	Anthony Welling, Broadway Barn, High Street, Ripley, Surrey GU23 6AQ Tel: 01483 225384
WI	•	David Winstone, Bartlett Street Antique Centre, 5–10 Bartlett Street, Bath, Somerset BA1 2QZ Tel: 01225 466689 Mobile: 07979 506415 winstampok@netscapeonline.co.uk
WiA	•	Witney Antiques, 96–100 Corn Street, Witney, Oxfordshire Tel: 01993 703902
WilP	•	W & H Peacock, 26 Newnham Street, Bedford MK40 3JR Tel: 01234 266366
WIM	•	Wimpole Antiques, Stand 349, Grays Antique Market, 58 Davies Street, London W1Y 2LP Tel: 020 7499 2889
WL	*†	Wintertons Ltd, Lichfield Auction Centre, Wood End Lane, Fradley, Lichfield, Staffordshire WS13 8NF Tel: 01543 263256
WM	*	West Middlesex Auction Rooms, 113–114 High Street, Brentford, Middlesex TW8 8AT Tel: 020 8568 9080
WRe	•	Walcot Reclamations, 108 Walcot Street, Bath, Somerset BA1 5BG Tel: 01225 444404
WSA	•†	West Street Antiques, 63 West Street, Dorking, Surrey RH4 1BS Tel: 01306 883487 weststant@aol.com www.antiquearmsandarmour.com
WW	•	Woolley & Wallis, Salisbury Salerooms, 51–61 Castle Street, Salisbury, Wiltshire SP1 3SU Tel: 01722 424500
WWo	•	Woman's Work Tel: 020 8940 2589 Mobile: 07971 691748
WWW	•	W. W. Warner, The Forge, The Green, Brasted, Kent TN16 1JL Tel: 01959 563698
ZOOM	•†	Zoom, Arch 65, Cambridge Grove, London W6 Tel: 07000 9666 2002 Mobile: 07958 372975 eddiesandham@hotmail.com www.retrozoom.com

Index to Advertisers

Index

Italic page numbers denote colour pages; **bold** numbers refer to information and pointer boxes

INDEX